Capital Tax Acts

2002

Stamp Duties
Capital Acquisitions Tax
Residential Property Tax
Anti-Speculative Property Tax

Butterworths
A Member of the LexisNexis Group

Capital
Tax Acts
2002

Stamp Duties
Capital Acquisitions Tax
Residential Property Tax
Anti-Speculative Property Tax

Editor **Michael Buckley B.A. Dip in Legal Studies**

Butterworths
A Member of the LexisNexis Group

Members of LexisNexis Group worldwide:

Ireland	Butterworth (Ireland) Ltd, 24-26 Upper Ormond Quay, DUBLIN 7
Argentina	Abeledo Perrot, Jurisprudencia Argentina and Depalma, BUENOS AIRES
Australia	Butterworths, a Division of Reed International Books Australia Pty Ltd, CHATSWOOD, New South Wales
Austria	ARD Betriebsdienst and Verlag Orac, VIENNA
Canada	Butterworths Canada Ltd, MARKHAM, Ontario
Chile	Publitecsa and Conosur Ltda, SANTIAGO DE CHILE
Czech Republic	Orac sro, PRAGUE
France	Editions du Juris-Classeur SA, PARIS
Hong Kong	Butterworths Asia (Hong Kong), HONG KONG
Hungary	Hvg Orac, BUDAPEST
India	Butterworths India, NEW DELHI
Italy	Giuffré, MILAN
Malaysia	Malayan Law Journal Sdn Bhd, KUALA LUMPUR
New Zealand	Butterworths of New Zealand, WELLINGTON
Poland	Wydawnictwa Prawnicze PWN, WARSAW
Singapore	Butterworths Asia, SINGAPORE
South Africa	Butterworths Publishers (Pty) Ltd, DURBAN
Switzerland	Stämpfli Verlag AG, BERNE
United Kingdom	Butterworths Tolley, a Division of Reed Elsevier (UK) Ltd, Halsbury House, 35 Chancery Lane, LONDON, WC2A 1EL, and 4 Hill Street, EDINBURGH EH2 3JZ
USA	LexisNexis, DAYTON, Ohio

© Butterworth Ireland Ltd 2002

A CIP Catalogue record for this book is available from the British Library.

This work is intended to be a general guide and cannot be a substitute for professional advice. Neither the authors nor the publisher accept any repsonsibility for loss ocassioned to any person acting or refraining from acting as a result of material contained in this publication.

ISBN for this book

ISBN 1-85475-643-5

9 781854 756435

Typeset by Marie Armah-Kwantreng, Dublin
Printed by Antony Rowe Ltd, Chippenham, Wiltshire
Visit us at our website: http//www.butterworths.ie

HOW TO USE THIS WORK

Tracing legislation

This book sets out consolidated versions of the Stamp Duties Consolidation Act 1999; the Capital Acquisitions Tax Act 1976, the Residential Property Tax Legislation (Finance Act 1983) and the Anti-Speculative Property Tax Legislation (Finance (No 2) Act 2000); together with the relevant non-amending sections of the Finance Acts from 1950 to 2002 inclusive. Each section is annotated in respect of amendments, cross-references, definitions, construction, statutory instruments, statements of practice and former enactments.

The legislation is set out in the following manner:

(*a*) the full text of an amending provision is normally omitted, but effect is given to the amendment in the amended provision,

(*b*) the full text of a repealing provision is normally omitted, but effect is given to the repeal in the repealed provision.

Section and Schedule headings of repealed or amended legislation are retained for the purposes of clarity.

For ease of reference, section and Schedule numbers are conspicuously marked at the top of the page. If the section or Schedule is known, it can be found immediately because the legislation is printed in chronological order. Where only the subject matter is known, it may be traced through the index. The present location of the text of the former enactments may be traced through the destination table.

Standard abbreviations

The following are the standard abbreviations used in Butterworth Ireland Tax publications:

General

s, ss	section (or sections) of an Act
subs, subss	subsection (or subsections) of a section
Sch	Schedule to an Act
para, paras	paragraph (or paragraphs) of a Schedule
subpara, subparas	subparagraph (or subparagraphs) of a Schedule
Pt	Part (of an Act)
Ch	Chapter (or a Part of an Act)
r, reg	regulation (of a statutory instrument)

Statutes

CA	Companies Act
CATA 1976	Capital Acquisitions Act 1976

CGTA 1975	Capital Gains Tax Act 1975
CGTAA 1978	Capital Gains Tax (Amendment) Act 1978
CTA 1976	Corporation Tax Act 1976
FA	Finance Act
F(No 2)A	Finance (No 2) Act
F(MP)A	Finance (Miscellaneous Provisions) Act
IA 1937	Interpretation Act 1937
IRRA 1890	Inland Revenue Regulation Act 1890
ITA 1967	Income Tax Act 1967
PCTA 1927	Provisional Collection of Taxes Act 1927
TD(SC)A 1942	Taxes and Duties (Special Circumstances) Act 1942
VATA 1972	Value Added Tax 1972

Statutory Instruments

ITER	Income Tax (Employments) Regulations
SI 28/1960	Statutory Instrument Number 28 of 1960
IT(CC)R	Income Tax (Construction Contracts) Regulations

Practice

SP	Statement of Practice

Case law

ITR	Irish Tax Reports
IR	Irish Reports
STC	Simon's Tax Cases
TC	Tax Cases
TL	Tax Leaflet
ITC	Irish Tax Cases
ECJ	European Court of Justice

TAXPAYERS CHARTER OF RIGHTS

GET TO KNOW YOUR RIGHTS

In your dealings with the Revenue Commissioners, you are entitled to:

COURTESY AND CONSIDERATION

- to expect that Revenue staff will at all times carry out their duties courteously and considerately.

PRESUMPTION OF HONESTY

- to be presumed to have dealt with your tax affairs honestly unless there is reason to believe to the contrary and subject to the Revenue Commissioners' responsibility for ensuring compliance with the law.

INFORMATION

- to expect that every reasonable effort will be made to give you access to full, accurate and timely information about Revenue law and your entitlements and obligations under it. So that they can do this, Revenue staff are entitled to expect that you will give them all the facts and the full co-operation which they need to deal with your affairs.

IMPARTIALITY

- to have your affairs dealt with in an impartial manner by Revenue staff who seek to collect only the correct amount of tax or duty, no more or no less.

PRIVACY AND CONFIDENTIALITY

- to expect that personal and business information provided by you will be treated in strict confidence and used only for purposes allowed by law.

INDEPENDENT REVIEW

- to object to a charge to tax or duty if you think the law has been applied incorrectly and to ask that your case be reviewed. If the matter cannot be resolved to your satisfaction by Revenue officials you have rights in law to independent review.

COMPLIANCE COSTS

- to expect that the Revenue Commissioners and their staff recognise the need to keep to the minimum necessary the costs you incur in complying with Revenue law, subject to their responsibility to carry out their functions efficiently and economically.

CONSISTENT ADMINISTRATION

- to expect that the Revenue Commissioners will administer the law consistently and apply it firmly to those who try to evade paying their lawful share.

OUR OBJECTIVE

The objective of the Revenue Commissioners is to collect the taxes, duties and other charges placed under our care and management in an efficient way and at the least possible cost to the public. This objective is to be achieved in a manner which:

- fosters the highest degree of public confidence in our integrity, efficiency and fairness, and

- encourages voluntary compliance with Revenue law and deters evasion and avoidance.

CONTENTS

STAMP DUTY (LEGISLATION)

FORGERY ACT 1913

(3 & 4 Geo V c 27)
(Date of passing: 15th August, 1913)

ARRANGEMENT OF SECTIONS

Section

SCHEDULE
ENACTMENTS REPEALED

5 Forgery of seals and die

(1) ....

(4) Forgery of the following dies, if committed with intent to defraud or deceive, shall be felony and punishable with penal servitude for any term not exceeding fourteen years:—

    (*a*)   Any die provided, made, or used by the Revenue Commissioners;

    (*b*)   ....

Cross-references

Penalty for frauds in relation to duties: Stamp Duties Management Act 1891 s 21.

Definitions

"die": s 18, SDCA 1999 s 1.

---

8 Possession of forged documents, seals, and die

(1) ....

(2) Every person shall be guilty of felony and on conviction thereof shall be liable to penal servitude for any term not exceeding fourteen years, who, without lawful authority or excuse, the proof whereof shall lie on the accused, and knowing the same to be forged, has in his custody or possession—

    (*a*)   ...

    (*b*)   any forged stamp or die as defined by the [Part 11 of the Stamp Duties Consolidation Act, 1999];[1]

    (*c*)   ....

Amendments

¹   Substituted by SDCA 1999 s 162 and Sch 4; previously "Stamp Duties Management Act, 1891 (as amended by the Finance Act, 1989)".

Cross-references

Other provisions relating to stamps and dies: SDCA 1999 s 145.

Definitions

"die": s 18, SDCA 1999 s 1; "person": IA 1937 s 11(*c*); "stamp": s 18, SDCA 1999 s 1.

9 Making or having in possession paper or implements for forgery

Every person shall be guilty of felony and on conviction thereof shall be liable to penal servitude for any term not exceeding seven years, who, without lawful authority or excuse, the proof whereof shall lie on the accused :—

(*a*)   Makes, uses, or knowingly has in his custody or possession any paper intended to resemble and pass as—

(i)   ...

(ii)   Revenue paper;

(*b*)   Makes, uses, or knowingly has in his custody or possession, any frame, mould, or instrument for making such paper, or for producing in or on such paper any words, figures, letters, marks, lines, or devices peculiar to and used in or on any such paper;

(*c*)   ...

(*d*)   Uses or knowingly has in his custody or possession any plate, wood, stone, or other material, upon which any such words, figures, letters, marks, lines, or devices have been engraved or in anywise made as aforesaid;

(*e*)   Uses or knowingly has in his custody or possession any paper upon which any such words, figures, letters, marks, lines, or devices have been printed or in anywise made as aforesaid.

Cross-references

SDCA 1999.

Definitions

"material": SDCA 1999 s 1.

10 Purchasing or having in possession certain paper before it has been duly stamped and issued

Every person shall be guilty of a misdemeanour and on conviction thereof shall be liable to imprisonment, with or without hard labour, for any term not exceeding two years, who, without lawful authority or excuse the proof whereof shall lie on the accused, purchases, receives, or knowingly has in his custody or possession—

(*a*)   Any Revenue paper before such paper has been duly stamped, signed, and issued for public use;

(*b*)   Any die peculiarly used in the manufacture of any such paper.

18 Interpretation

(1) In this Act unless the context otherwise requires—

The expression **"die"** includes any plate, type, tool, or implement whatsoever, and also any part of any die plate, type, tool, or implement, and any stamp or impression thereof or any part of such stamp or impression:

The expression **"revenue paper"** means any paper provided by the proper authority for the purpose of being used for stamps, licences, permits, Post Office money orders, or postal orders, or for any purpose whatever connected with the public revenue:

The expression **"seal"** includes any stamp or impression of a seal or any stamp or impression made or apparently intended to resemble the stamp or impression of a seal, as well as the seal itself:

The expression **"stamp"** includes a stamp impressed by means of a die as well as an adhesive stamp:

....

[(1A) Notwithstanding subsection (1) of this section, the expressions "die" and "stamp", when used in this Act in relation to the Revenue Commissioners, have the same meanings, respectively, as are assigned to them by the [Part 11 of the Stamp Duties Consolidation Act, 1999.][1]

(2) References in this Act to any Act in force at the commencement of this Act shall be held to include a reference to that Act as amended, extended, or applied by any other Act.

(3) References in this Act to any Government department shall in relation to any functions performed by that department be held to include references to any other Government department by which the same functions were previously performed.

20 Repeals

The enactments specified in the schedule to this Act are hereby repealed as to England and Ireland to the extent specified in the third column of that schedule.

22 Short title and commencement

This Act may be cited as the Forgery Act, 1913, and shall come into operation on the first day of January one thousand nine hundred and fourteen.

SCHEDULE
ENACTMENTS REPEALED

PART I

Note

This Schedule repealed: Stamp Duties Management Act 1891 s 13(1)-(2); in s 13(8) the words "any forged stamp or" and in s 13(9) the words "any forged die or stamp or"; ss 14-15.

ACQUISITION OF LAND (ASSESSMENT OF COMPENSATION) ACT 1919

(9 & 10 Geo V c 57)
(Date of passing: 19 August 1919)

ARRANGEMENT OF SECTIONS

Section

1 Tribunal for assessing compensation in respect of land compulsorily acquired for public purpose

(1) Where by or under any statute (whether passed before or after the passing of this Act) land is authorised to be acquired compulsorily by any Government Department or any local or public authority, any question of disputed compensation, and, where any part of the land to be acquired is subject to a lease which comprises land not acquired, any question as to the apportionment of the rent payable under the lease, shall be referred to and determined by the arbitration of such one of a panel of official arbitrators to be appointed under this section as may be selected in accordance with rules made by the Reference Committee under this section.

(2) Such number of persons, being persons with special knowledge in the valuation of land, as may be appointed for.....Ireland by the Reference Committee, shall form a panel of persons to act as official arbitrators for the purposes of this Act in... Ireland...

(3) A person appointed to be a member of the panel of official arbitrators shall hold office for such term certain as may be determined by the Minister for Finance before his appointment, and whilst holding office shall not himself engage, or be a partner of any other person who engages, in private practice or business.

(4) There shall be paid out of moneys provided by the Oireachtas to official arbitrators such salaries or remuneration as the Minister for Finance may determine.

(5) The Reference Committee

...

(c)   for Ireland, shall consist of the Chief Justice, ... and the President of the Surveyors' Institution, or (if the President of the Surveyors' Institution thinks fit) a person, being a member of the council of that institution and having special knowledge of valuation of land in Ireland appointed by him to act in his place.

Note

Section 1 amended SA 1891 s 13.

In the matter of The Air Navigation and Transport Act 1936 and others and The Acquisition of Land (Assessment of Compensation) Act 1919 and The Property Values (Arbitrations and Appeals) Act 1960: compensation awarded by arbitrator not to include the capital gains tax liability of the owners of the lands compulsorily acquired.

Definitions

"money": SDCA 1999 s 1; "person": IA 1937 s 11(c); "statute": IA 1937 s 3.

ARBITRATIONS AND SECTIONS

PROVISIONAL COLLECTION OF TAXES ACT 1927

(1927 Number 7)

ARRANGEMENT OF SECTIONS

Section

AN ACT TO GIVE STATUTORY EFFECT FOR A LIMITED PERIOD TO RESOLUTIONS OF THE COMMITTEE ON FINANCE OF DÁIL ÉIREANN IMPOSING, RENEWING, VARYING, OR ABOLISHING TAXATION, AND TO MAKE PROVISION WITH RESPECT TO PAYMENTS, DEDUCTIONS, ASSESSMENTS, CHARGES, AND OTHER THINGS MADE OR DONE ON ACCOUNT OF ANY TEMPORARY TAX IN ANTICIPATION OF THE RENEWAL OF THE TAX BY THE OIREACHTAS. [19TH MARCH, 1927]

1 Definitions

In this Act—

the expression **"Committee on Finance"** means the Committee on Finance of Dáil Éireann when and so long as such Committee is a committee of the whole House;

[the expression **"new tax"** when used in relation to a resolution under this Act means a tax which was not in force immediately before the date on which the resolution is expressed to take effect or, where no such date is expressed, the passing of the resolution by Dáil Éireann;][1]

the expression **"permanent tax"** means a tax which was last imposed without any limit of time being fixed for its duration;

the expression **"temporary tax"** means a tax which was last imposed or renewed for a limited period only;

the expression **"normal expiration"** when used in relation to a temporary tax means the end of the limited period for which the tax was last imposed or renewed;

the word **"tax"** includes duties of customs, duties of excise, income tax, ...[2] ...[3] [and value-added tax][4] [and capital gains tax][5] ...[6] [and corporation tax][7] [and gift tax and inheritance tax][8] [and residential property tax][9] [and stamp duties][10] but no other tax or duty.

Amendments

1   Definition of "new tax" substituted by FA 2002 s 139(*a*) with effect from 25 March 2002.

2   Words "and super-tax" repealed by FA 1974 s 86 and Sch 2 Pt I for 1974-75 and later tax years.

3   Words "and also turnover tax" repealed by VATA 1972 s 41.

4   Inserted by VATA 1972 s 38.

5   Inserted by CGTA 1975 s 50.

6   Words "and wealth tax" deleted by FA 1978 s 38.

7   Inserted by CTA 1976 s 6.

8   Inserted by CATA 1976 s 69.

9   Inserted by FA 1983 s 114(1).

10   Inserted by FA 1986 s 100.

2 Certain resolutions to have statutory effect

Whenever a resolution (in this Act referred to as a resolution under this Act) is passed by [Dáil Éireann][1] resolving—

    (*a*)   that a new tax specified in the resolution be imposed, or

    (*b*)   that a specified permanent tax in force [immediately before the date on which the resolution is expressed to take effect or, where no such date is expressed, the passing of the resolution by Dáil Éireann][2] be increased, reduced, or otherwise varied, or be abolished, or

    (*c*)   that a specified temporary tax in force [immediately before the immediately before the date on which the resolution is expressed to take effect or, where no such date is expressed, the passing of the resolution by Dáil Éireann][2] be renewed (whether at the same or a different rate and whether with or without modification) as from the date of its normal expiration or from an earlier date or be discontinued on a date prior to the date of its normal expiration,

and the resolution contains a declaration that it is expedient in the public interest that the resolution should have statutory effect under the provisions of this Act, the resolution shall, subject to the provisions of this Act, have statutory effect as if contained in an Act of the Oireachtas.

Amendments

1   Substituted by FA 1974 s 85(1)(*a*) with effect from 23 October 1974 (SI 312/1974); previously "the Committee on Finance".

2   Substituted by FA 2002 s 139(*b*) with effect from 25 March 2002; previously "immediately before the end of the previous financial year".

3 Application of general taxing enactments

(1) Whenever a new tax is imposed by a resolution under this Act and such resolution describes the tax as a duty of customs or as a duty of excise or as an income tax ...[1], the enactments which [immediately before the date on which the resolution is expressed to take effect or, where no such date is expressed, the passing of the resolution by Dáil Éireann][2] were in force in relation to customs duties generally, or excise duties generally, or income tax generally, ...[3] (as the case may require) shall, subject to the provisions of this Act, apply to and have full force and effect in respect of such new tax so long as the resolution continues to have statutory effect.

(2) Whenever a permanent tax is increased, reduced, or otherwise varied by a resolution under this Act, all enactments which were in force with respect to that tax [immediately before the immediately before the date on which the resolution is expressed to take effect or, where no such date is expressed, the passing of the resolution by Dáil Éireann][2] shall, so long as the resolution continues to have statutory effect and subject to the provisions of this Act, have full force and effect with respect to the tax as so increased, reduced, or otherwise varied.

(3) Whenever a temporary tax is renewed (whether at the same or a different rate and whether with or without modification) by a resolution under this Act, all enactments which were in force with respect to that tax [immediately before the immediately before the date on which the resolution is expressed to take effect or, where no such date is expressed, the passing of the resolution by Dáil Éireann][2] shall, so long as the resolution continues to have statutory effect and subject to the provisions of this Act, have full force and effect with respect to the tax as renewed by the resolution.

Amendments

[1]   Words "or as a super-tax" repealed by FA 1974 s 86 and Sch 2 Pt 1 for 1974-75 and later tax years.

[2]   Substituted by FA 2002 s 139(*b*) with effect from 25 March 2002; previously "immediately before the end of the previous financial year".

[3]   Words "or super-tax generally" repealed by FA 1974 s 86 and Sch 2 Pt 1 for 1974-75 and later tax years.

4 Duration of statutory effect of resolution

[A resolution under this Act shall cease to have statutory effect upon the happening of whichever of the following events first occurs, that is to say:

   [(*a*)   subject to section 4A of this Act, if a Bill containing provisions to the same effect (with or without modifications) as the resolution is not read a second time by Dáil Éireann—

      (i)   where Dáil Éireann is in recess on any day between the eighty-second and the eighty-fourth day after the resolution is passed by Dáil Éireann, within the next five sitting days of the resumption of Dáil Éireann after that recess,

      (ii)   in any other case, within the next eighty-four days after the resolution is passed by Dáil Éireann,][1]

   (*b*)   if those provisions of the said bill are rejected by Dáil Éireann during the passage of the Bill through the Oireachtas;

   (*c*)   the coming into operation of an Act of the Oireachtas containing provisions to the same effect (with or without modification) as the resolution;

   (*d*)   [subject to section 4A of this Act][2] the expiration of a period of four months from that date on which the resolution is expressed to take effect or, where no such date is expressed, from the passing of the resolution by Dáil Éireann.][3]

Amendments

[1]   Para (*a*) substituted by Appropriation Act 1991 s 2(*a*)(i).

[2]   Inserted by Appropriation Act 1991 s 2(*a*)(ii).

[3]   Section 4 substituted by FA 1974 s 85(1)(*b*) with effect from 23 October 1974 (SI 312/1974).

4A Effect of dissolution of Dáil Éireann

[Where Dáil Éireann, having passed a resolution under this Act, has been dissolved on the date the resolution was so passed or within four months of that date, then the period of dissolution shall be disregarded for the purposes of calculating any period to which paragraph (*a*) or (*d*) of section 4 of this Act relates.][1]

Amendments

[1]   Section originally inserted by Appropriation Act 1991; substituted by FA 1992 s 250.

Definitions

"Dáil Éireann": IA 1937 Sch.

5 Repayment of certain payments and deductions

(1) Whenever a resolution under this Act ceases to have statutory effect by reason of the happening of any event other than the coming into operation of an Act of the Oireachtas containing provisions to the same effect (with or without modification) as the resolution, all moneys paid in pursuance of the resolution shall be repaid or made good and every deduction made in pursuance of the resolution shall be deemed to be an unauthorised deduction.

(2) ...[1].

(3) Whenever an Act of the Oireachtas comes into operation containing provisions to the same effect with modifications as a resolution under this Act and such resolution ceases by virtue of such coming into operation to have statutory effect, all moneys paid in pursuance of such resolution which would not be payable under such Act shall be repaid or made good and every deduction made in pursuance of such resolution which would not be authorised by such Act shall be deemed to be an unauthorised deduction.

Amendments

[1]   Subs (2) repealed by FA 1974 s 85(1)(*c*) with effect from 23 October 1974 (SI 312/1974).

6 Certain payments and deductions deemed to be legal

(1) Any payment or deduction on account of a temporary tax to which this section applies made within two months after the expiration of such tax in respect of a period or event occurring after such expiration shall, if such payment or deduction would have been a legal payment or deduction if the tax had not expired, be deemed to be a legal payment or deduction subject to the conditions that—

(*a*)   if a resolution under this Act renewing the tax (with or without modification) is not passed by [Dáil Éireann][1] within two months after the expiration of the tax, the amount of such payment or deduction shall be repaid or made good on the expiration of such two months, and

(*b*)   if (such resolution having been so passed) an Act of the Oireachtas renewing the tax (with or without modification) does not come into operation when or before such resolution ceases to have statutory effect, the amount of such payment or deduction shall be repaid or made good on such cesser, and

(*c*)   if (such Act having been so passed) the tax is renewed by such Act with such modifications that the whole or some portion of such payment or deduction is not a legal payment or deduction under such Act, the whole or such portion (as the case may be) of such payment or deduction shall be repaid or made good on the coming into operation of such Act.

(2) This section applies only to a temporary tax which was last imposed or renewed for a limited period not exceeding eighteen months and was in force immediately before the end of the financial year next preceding the financial year in which the payment or deduction under this section is made.

Amendments

1   Substituted by FA 1974 s 85(1)(*d*) with effect from 23 October 1974 (SI 312/1974); previously "the Committee on Finance".

7 Repeal

The Provisional Collection of Taxes Act, 1913, is hereby repealed.

8 Short title

This Act may be cited as the Provisional Collection of Taxes Act, 1927.

INTERPRETATION ACT 1937

(1937 Number 38)
(Date of passing: 8 December 1937)

ARRANGEMENT OF SECTIONS

SCHEDULE
INTERPRETATION OF PARTICULAR EXPRESSIONS AND WORDS

PART I
PRELIMINARY AND GENERAL

1 Short title

This Act may be cited as the Interpretation Act, 1937.

2 Commencement

This Act shall come into operation immediately after the coming into operation of the Constitution of Ireland lately enacted by the People.

3 Definitions

In this Act—

the word **"statute"** includes (in addition to Acts of the Oireachtas) Acts of the Oireachtas of Saorstát Éireann, Acts of the Parliament of the former United Kingdom of Great Britain and Ireland, and Acts of a Parliament sitting in Ireland at any time before the coming into force of the Union with Ireland Act, 1800;

the word **"instrument"** means an order, regulation, rule, bye-law, warrant, licence, certificate, or other like document;

the expression **"statutory instrument"** means an instrument made, issued, or granted under a power or authority conferred by statute;

references to instruments made wholly or partly under an Act of the Oireachtas shall be construed as referring to instruments made, issued, or granted under a power or authority conferred by an Act of the Oireachtas or conferred by the joint operation of an Act of the Oireachtas and some other statute.

4 Application to certain Acts of the Oireachtas of Saorstát Éireann

Save as is otherwise expressly provided by this Act, every provision of this Act which relates to Acts of the Oireachtas shall apply and have effect in relation to this Act and every other Act of the Oireachtas of Saorstát Éireann (whether passed before or after this Act) which is expressed to come into operation immediately after the coming into operation of the Constitution, and accordingly this Act and every such other Act shall, for the purpose of such application but no further or otherwise, be deemed to be an Act of the Oireachtas and (save as is otherwise expressly provided by this Act) the expression **"Act of the Oireachtas"** shall in this Act be construed and have effect as including this Act and every such other Act of the Oireachtas of Saorstát Éireann.

5 Non-application of the Interpretation Act, 1923

(1) The Interpretation Act, 1923 (No 46 of 1923), shall not apply to any Act of the Oireachtas or to any instrument made wholly or partly under any such Act.

(2) The foregoing subsection of this section shall not preclude or prejudice the application to this Act and to other Acts of the Oireachtas of Saorstát Éireann which are expressed to come into operation immediately after the coming into operation of the

Constitution of so much of the Interpretation Act, 1923 (No 46 of 1923), as concerns events happening or things to be done in relation to an Act before it comes into operation.

Definition

"instrument": s 3; "Act of the Oireachtas": s 4.

PART II
FORM, CITATION, AND OPERATION OF ACTS OF THE OIREACHTAS

6 Form of Acts of the Oireachtas

(1) Every Act of the Oireachtas shall be a public document and shall be judicially noticed.

(2) Every Act of the Oireachtas shall be divided into sections numbered consecutively and any such section may be sub-divided in such manner and to such extent as is convenient.

(3) The sections of an Act of the Oireachtas may, where convenient, be grouped in Parts, Chapters, or other divisions numbered consecutively.

Definition

Act of the Oireachtas: s 4.

7 Citation of Acts of the Oireachtas

(1) Every Act of the Oireachtas may be cited in any other Act of the Oireachtas or in any instrument or other document either by the short title of the Act so cited or by the calendar year in which the Act so cited was passed and the consecutive number of such Act in such year.

(2) Any enactment contained in an Act of the Oireachtas may be cited in any other Act of the Oireachtas or in any instrument or other document by reference to the Part, section, subsection, or other sub-division of the first-mentioned Act which contains the enactment so cited.

Definition

"Act of the Oireachtas": s 4.

8 Date of passing of Acts of the Oireachtas

(1) The date of the passing of every Act of the Oireachtas shall be the date of the day on which the Bill for such Act is signed by the President.

(2) Immediately after the passing of every Act of the Oireachtas the Clerk of Dáil Éireann shall endorse on such Act, immediately after the title thereof, the date of the passing of such Act, and such date shall be taken to be part of such Act.

(3) Every enactment contained in an Act of the Oireachtas shall, unless the contrary intention is expressed in such Act, be deemed to be in operation as from the end of the day before the date of the passing of such Act.

(4) This section shall not apply to this Act or to any other Act of the Oireachtas of Saorstát Éireann which is expressed to come into operation immediately after the coming into operation of the Constitution, and accordingly the expression **"Act of the Oireachtas"** shall not in this section include any such Act of the Oireachtas of Saorstát Éireann.

Definition

"Act of the Oireachtas": s 4.

9 Commencement of Acts and instruments

(1) Where an Act of the Oireachtas, or a portion of any such Act, or an instrument made wholly or partly under any such Act, or a portion of any such instrument is expressed to come into operation on a particular day (whether such day is before or after the date of the passing of such Act or the making of such instrument and whether such day is named in such Act or instrument or is to be fixed or ascertained in any particular manner), such Act, portion of an Act, instrument, or portion of an instrument shall come into operation at the end of the day before such particular day.

(2) Every instrument made wholly or partly under an Act of the Oireachtas shall, unless the contrary intention is expressed in such instrument, be deemed to be in operation as from the end of the day before the day on which the instrument is made.

Definition

"instrument": s 3; "Act of the Oireachtas": s 4.

10 Exercise of statutory powers before commencement of the Act

(1) Where an Act of the Oireachtas or any particular enactment contained in any such Act is expressed to come into operation on a day subsequent to the date of the passing of such Act, the following provisions shall have effect, that is to say:—

    (*a*)   if the day on which such Act or such enactment (as the case may be) comes into operation is to be fixed or ascertained in any particular manner, the instrument, act, or thing whereby such day is fixed or ascertained may, subject to any restrictions imposed by such Act, be made or done at any time after the passing of such Act;

    (*b*)   if such Act confers a power to make or do, for the purposes of such Act or such enactment (as the case may be), any instrument, act, or thing the making or doing of which is necessary or expedient to enable such Act or enactment to have full force and effect immediately upon its coming into operation, such power may, subject to any restrictions imposed by such Act, be exercised at any time after the passing of such Act.

(2) In the application of this section to an Act of the Oireachtas of Saorstát Éireann which is expressed to come into operation immediately after the coming into operation of the Constitution, nothing in this section shall operate to enable any instrument, act, or thing to be made or done under or in relation to any such Act before the coming into operation of the Constitution.

Definition

"instrument": s 3; "Act of the Oireachtas": s 4.

PART III
MEANING AND CONSTRUCTION OF PARTICULAR WORDS AND EXPRESSIONS

11 Certain general rules of construction

The following provisions shall apply and have effect in relation to the construction of every Act of the Oireachtas and of every instrument made wholly or partly under any such Act, that is to say:—

(*a*) *Singular and plural.* Every word importing the singular shall, unless the contrary intention appears, be construed as if it also imported the plural, and every word importing the plural shall, unless the contrary intention appears, be construed as if it also imported the singular;

(*b*) *Masculine and feminine.* Every word importing the masculine gender shall, unless the contrary intention appears, be construed as if it also imported the feminine gender;

(*c*) *Person.* The word **"person"** shall, unless the contrary intention appears, be construed as importing a body corporate (whether a corporation aggregate or a corporation sole) and an unincorporated body of persons as well as an individual;

(*d*) *Time.* Every word or expression relating to time and every reference to a point of time shall, unless the contrary intention appears, be construed as relating or referring to Greenwich mean time, but subject to the provisions of any enactment whereunder the time in Ireland differs from Greenwich mean time during a specified period;

(*e*) *Distance.* Every word or expression relating to the distance between two points and every reference to the distance from or to a point shall, unless the contrary intention appears, be construed as relating or referring to such distance measured in a straight line on a horizontal plane;

(*f*) *Citations.* Every description of or citation from any statute, instrument, or other document shall, unless the contrary intention appears, be construed as including the word, subsection, section, or other portion mentioned or referred to as forming the beginning or as forming the end of the portion comprised in the description or citation or as being the point from which or to which such portion extends;

(*g*) *Marginal notes.* No marginal note placed at the side of any section or provision to indicate the subject, contents, or effect of such section or provision and no heading or cross-line placed at the head or beginning of a Part, section or provision or a group of sections or provisions to indicate the subject, contents, or effect of such Part, section, provision, or group shall be taken to be part of the Act or instrument or be considered or judicially noticed in relation to the construction or interpretation of the Act or instrument or any portion thereof;

17

(*h*) *Periods of time.* Where a period of time is expressed to begin on or be reckoned from a particular day, that day shall, unless the contrary intention appears, be deemed to be included in such period, and, where a period of time is expressed to end on or be reckoned to a particular day, that day shall, unless the contrary intention appears, be deemed to be included in such period;

(*i*) *Offences by corporations.* References to a person in relation to an offence (whether punishable on indictment or on summary conviction) shall, unless the contrary intention appears, be construed as including references to a body corporate.

Cross-references

Para (*b*): as regards legislation passed after 22 December 1993, every word importing the feminine gender, unless the contrary intention appears, also imports the masculine gender: Interpretation (Amendment) Act 1993.

Case law

Words in a charging provision, in the absence of a definition, to be interpreted according to normal usage: *De Brún v Kiernan* [1982] ILRM 13.

Interpretation, misclassification of goods under customs tariff, negligence of Revenue Commissioners, legitimate expectation: *Carbery Milk Products Ltd v Minister for Agriculture,* HC, 23 April 1993, IV ITR 492

Definition

"person": s 11(*c*); "instrument": s 3; "Act of the Oireachtas": s 4.

12 Interpretation of the expressions and words in the Schedule

In every Act of the Oireachtas and every instrument made wholly or partly under any such Act, every word and every expression to which a particular meaning, construction, or effect is assigned in the Schedule to this Act shall, unless the contrary intention appears, have the meaning, construction, or effect so assigned to it.

Case law

Words in a charging provision, in the absence of a definition, to be interpreted according to normal usage: *De Brún v Kiernan* [1982] ILRM 13, III ITR 19.

Definition

"instrument": s 3; "Act of the Oireachtas": s 4.

13 Construction of certain statutory instruments

Every expression and every word used in an instrument made wholly or partly under an Act of the Oireachtas shall, unless the contrary intention appears, have in such instrument the same meaning as it has in the Act or Acts under which such instrument is made.

Definition

"instrument": s 3; "Act of the Oireachtas": s 4.

14 Offences under two or more laws

Where any act, whether of commission or omission, constitutes an offence under two or more statutes or under a statute and at common law, the offender shall, unless the contrary intention appears, be liable to be prosecuted and punished under either or any of those statutes or at common law, but shall not be liable to be punished twice for the same offence.

Definition

"statute": s 3.

PART IV
STATUTORY POWERS AND DUTIES

15 Construction and exercise of statutory powers

(1) Every power conferred by an Act of the Oireachtas or by an instrument made wholly or partly under any such Act may, unless the contrary intention appears in such Act or instrument, be exercised from time to time as occasion requires.

(2) Every power conferred by an Act of the Oireachtas or by an instrument made wholly or partly under any such Act on the holder of an office as such shall, unless the contrary intention appears in such Act or instrument, be deemed to be conferred on and may accordingly be exercised by the holder for the time being of such office.

(3) Every power conferred by an Act of the Oireachtas to make any regulations, rules, or bye-laws shall, unless the contrary intention appears in such Act, be construed as including a power, exercisable in the like manner and subject to the like consent and conditions (if any), to revoke or amend any regulations, rules, or bye-laws made under such power and (where requisite) to make other regulations, rules, or bye-laws in lieu of those so revoked.

Definition

"instrument": s 3; "Act of the Oireachtas": s 4.

---

16 Construction and performance of statutory duties

(1) Every duty imposed by an Act of the Oireachtas or by an instrument made wholly or partly under any such Act shall, unless the contrary intention appears in such Act or instrument, be performed from time to time as occasion requires.

(2) Every duty imposed by an Act of the Oireachtas or by an instrument made wholly or partly under any such Act on the holder of an office as such shall, unless the contrary intention appears in such Act or instrument, be deemed to be imposed on and shall accordingly be performed by the holder for the time being of such office.

Definition

"instrument": s 3; "Act of the Oireachtas": s 4.

---

17 Rules of Court

Whenever an Act of the Oireachtas confers any new jurisdiction on a court of justice or extends or varies an existing jurisdiction of a court of justice, the authority having for the time being power to make rules or orders regulating the practice and procedure of such court shall have, and may at any time exercise, power to make rules or orders for regulating the practice and procedure of such court in the exercise of the jurisdiction so conferred, extended, or varied.

Definition
"Act of the Oireachtas": s 4.

18 Service by post

Where an Act of the Oireachtas or an instrument made wholly or partly under any such Act authorises or requires a document to be served by post, whether the word "serve" or any of the words "give", "deliver", or "send", or any other word is used, then, unless the contrary intention appears, the service of such document may be effected by properly addressing, prepaying (where requisite), and posting a letter containing such document, and in such case the service of such document shall, unless the contrary is proved, be deemed to have been effected at the time at which such letter would be delivered in the ordinary course of post.

Definition
"instrument": s 3; "Act of the Oireachtas": s 4.

PART V
EFFECT OF REPEALS AND REVOCATIONS

19 Date of operation of repeals and revocations

(1) Where an Act of the Oireachtas repeals the whole or a portion of a previous statute and substitutes other provisions for the statute or portion of a statute so repealed, the statute or portion of a statute so repealed shall, unless the contrary is expressly provided in the repealing Act, continue in force until the said substituted provisions come into operation.

(2) Where an instrument made wholly or partly under an Act of the Oireachtas revokes the whole or a portion of a previous statutory instrument (whether made wholly or partly under such Act or under another statute) and substitutes other provisions for the instrument or portion of an instrument so revoked, the instrument or portion of an instrument so revoked shall, unless the contrary is expressly provided in the revoking instrument, continue in force until the said substituted provisions come into operation.

Definition
"statute", "instrument", "statutory instrument": s 3; "Act of the Oireachtas": s 4.

20 Construction of references to repealed statutes and revoked instruments

(1) Whenever any statute or portion of a statute is repealed and re-enacted, with or without modification, by an Act of the Oireachtas, references in any other statute or in any statutory instrument to the statute or portion of a statute so repealed and re-enacted shall, unless the contrary intention appears, be construed as references to the portion of such Act of the Oireachtas containing such re-enactment.

(2) Whenever a statutory instrument or a portion of a statutory instrument is revoked and re-enacted, with or without modification, by an instrument made wholly or partly under an Act of the Oireachtas, references in any other statutory instrument to the statutory instrument or portion of a statutory instrument so revoked and re-enacted shall,

unless the contrary intention appears, be construed as references to the said instrument containing such re-enactment.

Definition

"statute", "instrument", "statutory instrument": s 3; "Act of the Oireachtas": s 4.

21 Operation of repeals, cessers, and terminations of statutes

(1) Where an Act of the Oireachtas repeals the whole or a portion of a previous statute, then, unless the contrary intention appears, such repeal shall not—

    (*a*)   revive anything not in force or not existing immediately before such repeal takes effect, or

    (*b*)   affect the previous operation of the statute or portion of a statue so repealed or anything duly done or suffered thereunder, or

    (*c*)   affect any right, privilege, obligation, or liability acquired, accrued, or incurred under the statute or portion of a statue so repealed, or

    (*d*)   affect any penalty, forfeiture, or punishment incurred in respect of any offence against or contravention of the statute or portion of a statute so repealed which was committed before such repeal, or

    (*e*)   prejudice or affect any legal proceedings, civil or criminal, pending at the time of such repeal of any such right, privilege, obligation, liability, offence, or contravention as aforesaid.

(2) Where an Act of the Oireachtas repeals the whole or a portion of a previous statute, then, unless the contrary intention appears, any legal proceedings, civil or criminal, in respect of any right, privilege, obligation, or liability acquired, accrued, or incurred under or any offence against or contravention of the statute or portion of a statute so repealed may be instituted, continued or enforced, and any penalty, forfeiture, or punishment in respect of any such offence or contravention may be imposed and carried out as if such statute or portion of a statute had not been repealed.

(3) Where an Act of the Oireachtas or a portion of any such Act ceases by any means or for any reason (other than repeal by a subsequent Act of the Oireachtas) to be in force, the preceding subsections of this section shall apply and have effect in relation to such Act or portion of an Act as if such cesser were caused by a repeal effected by an Act of the Oireachtas, and accordingly, for the purposes of such application, every reference in either of the said preceding subsections to a repeal shall be construed as a reference to a cesser by any means or for any reason (other than such repeal) to be in force.

Definition

"statute": s 3; "Act of the Oireachtas": s 4.

22 Operation of revocations, cessers and terminations of statutory instruments

(1) Where an instrument made wholly or partly under an Act of the Oireachtas revokes the whole or a portion of a previous statutory instrument, then, unless the contrary intention appears, such revocation shall not—

(*a*) revive anything not in force or not existing immediately before such revocation takes effect, or

(*b*) affect the previous operation of the statutory instrument or portion of a statutory instrument so revoked or anything duly done or suffered thereunder, or

(*c*) affect any right, privilege, obligation, or liability acquired, accrued, or incurred under the statutory instrument or portion of a statutory instrument so revoked, or

(*d*) affect any penalty, forfeiture, or punishment incurred in respect of any offence against or contravention of the statutory instrument or portion of a statutory instrument so revoked which was committed before such revocation, or

(*e*) prejudice or affect any legal proceedings, civil or criminal, pending at the time of such revocation in respect of any such right, privilege, obligation, liability, offence, or contravention as aforesaid.

(2) Where an instrument made wholly or partly under an Act of the Oireachtas revokes the whole or a portion of a previous statutory instrument, then, unless the contrary intention appears, any legal proceedings, civil or criminal, in respect of any right, privilege, obligation, or liability acquired, accrued, or incurred under or any offence against or contravention of the statutory instrument or portion of the statutory instrument so revoked may be instituted, continued, or enforced and any penalty, forfeiture, or punishment in respect of any such offence or contravention may be imposed and carried out as if such statutory instrument or portion of a statutory instrument had not been revoked.

(3) Where an instrument made wholly or partly under an Act of the Oireachtas or a portion of an instrument so made ceases by any means or for any reason (other than revocation by a subsequent such instrument) to be in force, the preceding subsections of this section shall apply and have effect in relation to such instrument or portion of an instrument as if such cesser were caused by a revocation effected by a subsequent such instrument, and accordingly, for the purposes of such application, every reference in either of the said preceding subsections to a revocation shall be construed as a reference to a cesser by any means or for any reason (other than such revocation) to be in force.

Definition

"instrument", "statutory instrument": s 3; "Act of the Oireachtas": s 4.

SCHEDULE
INTERPRETATION OF PARTICULAR EXPRESSIONS AND WORDS

1. The word "affidavit", in the case of persons for the time being allowed by law to declare instead of swearing, includes declaration.

2. The expression **"the Bank of Ireland"** means either, as the context requires, the Governor and Company of the Bank of Ireland or the bank of the said Governor and Company.

3. The expression **"British statute"** means an Act of the Parliament of the late United Kingdom of Great Britain and Ireland.

4. The expression **"the Circuit Court"**, means the Circuit Court of Justice as established and for the time being maintained by law.

5. The word **"commencement"**, when used in relation to a statute or a statutory instrument or a portion of a statute or statutory instrument, means the time at which such statute, statutory instrument, or portion of a statute or statutory instrument comes into operation.

6. The expression **"consular officer"** means a person in the Civil Service of Ireland who is a consul-general, a consul, or a vice-consul.

7. The expression **"the Constitution"** means the Constitution of Ireland enacted by the people on the 1st day of July, 1937.

8. The expression **"Dáil Éireann"** means the House of the Oireachtas to which that name is given by section 1 of Article 15 of the Constitution.

9. The expression **"the District Court"** means the District Court of Justice as established and for the time being maintained by law.

10. ...[1].

11. The expression **"the Government"** means the Government mentioned in Article 28 of the Constitution.

12. The expression **"Great Britain"** does not include the Channel Islands or the Isle of Man.

13. The expression **"the High Court"** means the High Court of Justice established and for the time being maintained by law in pursuance of Article 34 of the Constitution.

14. The word **"land"** includes messuages, tenements, and hereditaments, houses and buildings, of any tenure.

15. The expression **"the Lands Clauses Acts"** means the Lands Clauses Consolidation Act, 1845, the Lands Clauses Consolidation Acts Amendment Act, 1860, the Railways Act (Ireland), 1851, the Railways Act (Ireland), 1860, the Railways Act (Ireland), 1864, the Railways Traverse Act, the Acquisition of Land (Assessment of Compensation) Act, 1919, and every statute for the time being in force amending those Acts or any of them.

16. ...[1].

17. The word **"midnight"** means, in relation to any particular day, the point of time at which such day ends.

18. The expression [**"Minister of the Government"**][2] means a member of the Government having charge of a Department of State.

19. The word **"month"** means a calendar month.

20. The word **"oath"**, in the case of persons for the time being allowed by law to affirm instead of swearing, includes affirmation.

21. The expression **"the Oireachtas"** means the National Parliament provided for by Article 15 of the Constitution.

22. The expression **"ordnance map"** means a map made under the powers conferred by the Survey (Ireland) Acts, 1825 to 1870, and the statutes for the time being in force amending those Acts or any of them.

23. The expression **"the President"** means the President of Ireland and includes any commission or other body or authority for the time being lawfully exercising the powers and performing the duties of the President.

24. The expression **"pre-union Irish statute"** means an Act passed by a Parliament sitting in Ireland at any time before the coming into force of the Union with Ireland Act, 1800.

25. The expression **"rateable valuation"** means the valuation under the Valuation Acts of the property in relation to which the expression is used.

26. The expression **"rules of court"** means rules made by the authority for the time being having power to make rules regulating the practice and procedure of the court in relation to which the expression is used.

27. The expression **"Saorstát Éireann statute"** means an Act of the Oireachtas of Saorstát Éireann.

28. The expression **"Seanad Éireann"** means the House of the Oireachtas to which that name is given by section 1 of Article 15 of the Constitution.

29. The expression **"statutory declaration"** means a declaration made by virtue of the Statutory Declarations Act, 1835.

30. The expression **"the Supreme Court"** means the Supreme Court of Justice as established and for the time being maintained by law in pursuance of Article 34 of the Constitution.

31. The word **"swear"**, in the case of persons for the time being allowed by law to affirm or declare instead of swearing, includes affirm and declare.

32. The word **"town"** means the area comprised in a town (not being an urban district) in which the Towns Improvement (Ireland) Act, 1854, is in operation.

33. The expression **"Valuation Acts"** means the Act for the time being in force relating to the valuation of rateable property.

34. The word **"week"**, when used without qualification, means the period between midnight on any Saturday and midnight on the next following Saturday.

35. The word **"week-day"** means a day which is not a Sunday.

36. The word **"writing"** includes printing, type-writing, lithography, photography, and other modes of representing or reproducing words in visible form, and cognate words shall be construed accordingly.

37. The word **"year"**, when used without qualification, means a period of twelve months beginning on the 1st day of the month of January in any year.

Amendments

[1]   Repealed by Exchequer and Local Financial Years Act 1974 s 2 except in relation to before 1 January 1975.

[2]   Substituted by the Ministers and Secretaries (Amendment) (No 2) Act 1977.

Definition

"person": s 11(*c*).

ADOPTION ACT 1952

(1952 Number 25)
(Date of passing: 13 December 1952)

ARRANGEMENT OF SECTIONS

Section

27   Succession duty, legacy duty, customs duty and stamp duty on land

27 Succession duty, legacy duty, customs duty and stamp duty on land

For the purposes of—

(*a*)   ...

(*b*)   the stamp duties chargeable on conveyances or transfers of land,

(*c*)   ...

an adopted person shall be considered as the child of the adopter or adopters born to him, her or them in lawful wedlock and not to be the child of any other person.

Cross-references

Relief in case of foreign adoptions: FA 1972 s 45 (as amended by FA 1992 s 214).
Foreign adoption: Adoption Act 1991 s 1.

Definitions

"person": IA 1937 s 11(*c*); "stamp": SDCA 1999 s 1.

PROPERTY VALUES (ARBITRATIONS AND APPEALS) ACT 1960

(1960 Number 45)
(Date of passing: 21 December 1960)

ARRANGEMENT OF SECTIONS

1 Interpretation

In this Act—

"the Act of 1910" means the Finance (1909-10) Act, 1910;

"the Act of 1919" means the Acquisition of Land (Assessment of Compensation) Act, 1919;

"the Act of 1945" means the Arterial Drainage Act, 1945;

"the Reference Committee" means the Reference Committee established by section 1 of the Act, of 1919 as amended by the Acquisition of Land (Reference Committee) Act, 1925.

2 Property arbitrators

(1) The Reference Committee may appoint one or more persons having special knowledge of the valuation of land or having such other qualifications as the Reference Committee considers suitable to be an arbitrator or arbitrators for the purposes of Part I of the Act, of 1910, the Act of 1919 and the Act of 1945 and a person so appointed shall be known, and is referred to in this Act, as a property arbitrator.

(2) A property arbitrator shall hold office on such terms and conditions, other than those provided for under subsection (3) of this section, as the Reference Committee may from time to time determine with the approval of the Minister for Finance.

(3) A property arbitrator shall be paid out of moneys provided by the Oireachtas, such remuneration and allowances for expenses as the Minister for Finance may from time to time determine.

(4) Where, immediately before the date of the passing of this Act, a person holds office as a member of the panel of official arbitrators under the Act of 1919 and is in receipt of

an annual salary in respect of such office, that person shall be deemed to have been appointed under this section on such date to be a property arbitrator for the purposes of Part I of the Act of 1910, the Act of 1919 and the Act of 1945 and to hold office on terms and conditions (including terms and conditions relating to remuneration and allowances for expenses) not less favourable than those on which he held office as a member of the panel aforesaid.

Definitions

"money": SDCA 1999 s 1; "person": IA 1937 s 11(c).

3 Arbitrators for the purposes of section 33 of Act of 1910

(1) An appeal under section 33 of the Act of 1910 shall be referred to a property arbitrator who shall be nominated by the Reference Committee for the purposes of such reference in accordance with rules made by the Reference Committee under this section and, accordingly—

    (a)   so much of subsection (2) of the said section 33 as provides for the reference of an appeal thereunder to such one of a panel of referees appointed under Part I of the Act of 1910 as may be selected in manner provided by rules under the said section 33 shall cease to have effect, and

    (b)   references in the said section 33 to a referee selected under that section shall be construed as references to a property arbitrator nominated under this section and the reference in the said section 33 to the Reference Committee established under that section shall be construed as a reference to the Reference Committee.

(2) Where, in an appeal under the said section 33, the value of any minerals is relevant to the determination of the property arbitrator, the appellant and the Revenue Commissioners may each, in addition to the persons, if any, nominated under subsection (3) of the said section 33, nominate one person having experience in the valuation of minerals to consult the property arbitrator and, in determining the appeal, the property arbitrator shall consult any person nominated under this subsection.

Definitions

"person": IA 1937 s 11(c).

4 Amendment of section 1 of Act of 1919

The arbitration referred to in subsection (1) of section 1 of the Act of 1919 shall, in relation to the reference and determination under that subsection of any question, be the arbitration of a property arbitrator nominated for the purposes of such reference and determination by the Reference Committee in accordance with rules made by the Reference Committee under this section and, accordingly—

    (a)   so much of the said subsection (1) as provided for the reference of questions to and their determination by such one of a panel of official arbitrators to be appointed under the said section 1 as may be selected as therein provided shall cease to have effect, and (*b*) reference in the Act of 1919 to an official arbitrator shall be construed as references to a property arbitrator nominated under this section.

5 Arbitrators for the purposes of Act of 1945

The arbitrator for any purpose for which an arbitrator is required under the Act of 1945 shall be a property arbitrator who shall be nominated for that purpose by the Reference Committee and, accordingly, references in the Act of 1945 to an arbitrator nominated or appointed by the Reference Committee from the Panel of Drainage Arbitrators shall be construed as references to a property arbitrator nominated by the Reference Committee under this section.

6 Provisions in relation to arbitrations and appeals before the passing of this Act

(1) This Act, other than this section, shall not have effect in respect of—

(*a*) any appeal under section 33 of the Act of 1910 in relation to which a referee has been selected under that section before the date of the passing of this Act,

(*b*) any question in relation to which an official arbitrator has been selected under the Act of 1919 before the date of the passing of this Act, or

(*c*) any dispute, claim, objection or matter in relation to which an arbitrator has been nominated or appointed under the Act of 1945 before the date of the passing of this Act.

(2) For the purposes of the validity of—

(*a*) any decision of a referee under section 33 of the Act of 1910 in relation to an appeal referred to him under that section before the date of the passing of this Act,

(*b*) the reference of the appeal to the referee, and

(*c*) the selection of the referee for the determination of the appeal,

the referee shall be deemed to have been selected in accordance with the provisions of that section from a panel of referees appointed under Part I of the Act of 1910 and consisting of at least two persons.

(3) For the purposes of the validity of—

(*a*) any decision or award of an official arbitrator under the Act of 1919 in relation to a question referred to arbitration under that Act before the date of the passing of this Act,

(*b*) the reference of the question to the official arbitrator, and

(*c*) the selection of the official arbitrator for the determination of the question,

the official arbitrator shall be deemed to have been selected in accordance with the provisions of that Act from a panel of official arbitrators appointed under that Act and consisting of at least two persons.

Definitions

"person": IA 1937 s 11(*c*).

---

7 Repeals

Each enactment mentioned in the second column of the Schedule to this Act is hereby repealed to the extent mentioned in the third column of that Schedule opposite the mention of that enactment.

SCHEDULE
Enactments repealed

Note

This Schedule repealed Finance (1909-10) Act 1910 s 33(5) words "and with respect to the mode in which the referee to whom any references is to be made is to be selected," and from "The Reference Committee for England" to end of subsection; s 34; Courts of Justice Act, 1924 s 20.

STOCK TRANSFER ACT 1963

(1963 Number 34)
(Date of passing: 24 December 1963)

ARRANGEMENT OF SECTIONS

Section

1 Interpretation

In this Act—

"registered securities" means securities the holders of which are entered in a register;

"securities" includes shares, stock, debentures, debenture stock, loan stock and bonds;

....

Definitions
"stock": SDCA 1999 s 1.

4 Prohibition of circulation of blank transfers

(1) Where a transfer in blank relating to registered securities has been delivered, pursuant to a sale of those securities, to or to the order of the purchaser or any person acting on his behalf, any person who in the State parts with possession of that transfer, or who removes it or causes or permits it to be removed from the State, before it has been duly completed shall, as well as being liable for the stamp duty chargeable in respect of that transfer, be liable to [a penalty of £500][1], and the penalty shall be recoverable in the same manner as if it were part of the duty.

(2) For the purposes of this section "transfer in blank" means a transfer in which the name of the transferee has not been inserted, and a transfer shall be treated as duly completed if, and only if, the name of the transferee is inserted therein, being the name of—

    (*a*) the purchaser of the securities under the sale;

    (*b*) a person entitled to a charge upon the securities for money lent to that purchaser;

    (*c*) a nominee holding as a bare trustee for that purchaser or for any such person as is mentioned in paragraph (*b*) of this subsection; or

    (*d*) a person acting as the agent of that purchaser for the purposes of the sale.

(3) The foregoing provisions of this section shall apply in relation to a transfer delivered by way of or pursuant to a voluntary disposition inter vivos, being a transfer to which [section 30 of the Stamp Duties Consolidation Act, 1999],[2] applies, as they apply in relation to a transfer delivered pursuant to a sale, and as if for any reference to the

31

purchaser there were substituted a reference to the person (in this section referred to as the donee) to whom the disposition is made.

(4) References in this section to the purchaser or donee of any registered securities include references to any person to whom the rights of the purchaser or donee are transmitted by operation of law: and in relation to a transfer chargeable with duty in accordance with [subsection (1) or (2) of section 46 of the Stamp Duties Consolidation Act, 1999],[3] references in this section to the purchaser and a sale shall be construed as references to the sub-purchaser and a sub-sale.

Amendments

[1]   Substituted by FA 1991 s 107 with effect from 1 November 1991.

[2]   Substituted by SDCA 1999 s 162 and Sch 4; previously "section 74 of the Finance (1909-10) Act, 1910".

[3]   Substituted by SDCA 1999 s 162 and Sch 4; previously "subsection (4) or subsection (5) of section 58 of the Stamp Act, 1891".

Definitions

"money": SDCA 1999 s 1; "person": IA 1937 s 11(*c*).

7 Short title and commencement

(1) This Act may be cited as the Stock Transfer Act, 1963.

(2) This Act shall come into operation on such day as the Minister appoints by order.

REGISTRATION OF TITLE ACT 1964

(1964 Number 16)

ARRANGEMENT OF SECTIONS

Section

104   Stamp duties

104 Stamp duties

Before registering a purchaser as first registered owner of land and before registering any disposition of registered land, it shall be the duty of the Registrar to ascertain that all such stamp duties have been satisfied as would be payable if the land had been conveyed by an unregistered disposition to the purchaser or the disposition to be registered had been an unregistered disposition.

Cross-references

Penalty for registering instrument not duly stamped: SDCA 1999 s 141.

Definitions

"stamp": SDCA 1999 s 1.

HOUSING ACT 1966

(1966 Number 21)
(Date of passing: 12 July 1966)

ARRANGEMENT OF SECTIONS

PART I

PART VI

Note

By the Housing Act 1966 (Commencement) Order 1966 (SI 277/1966) all parts of this Act, except ss 88, 90 and 115 came into operation on 31 December 1966.

FIRST SCHEDULE
Repeals

PART I

6 Repeals

(1) The enactments mentioned in the First Schedule to this Act are hereby repealed to the extent specified in the third column of that Schedule.

(2) Notwithstanding subsection (1) of this section, grants under any enactment repealed by that subsection may be made in respect of works commenced before the repeal of the enactment.

....

PART VI

50 Remission of stamp duties on certain agreements, etc

No stamp duty shall be payable on any agreement, deed, or other instrument relating to a letting of a dwelling mentioned in subsection (3) of subsection 58 of this Act on a tenancy for a month or a less period than a month.

Definitions

"instrument", "stamp": SDCA 1999 s 122(1)

51 Amendment of section 12 of Finance Act, 1895

Amendment

1   Section 51 repealed by FA 1997 s 197 and Sch 6 with effect from 25 March 1999.

---

58 Management and control of certain dwellings and of any ancillary amenities, works or services provided in connection therewith

(1) Subject to the following provisions of this section and to such regulations as may be made by the Minister for the purposes of this section, the management and control of any dwelling, building or other land of which a housing authority are the owner and of any works or services, provided by the authority under this Act, shall be vested in and exercised by the authority.

....

(3) Subject to the said regulations, a housing authority may as respects a dwelling provided under this Act of which they are the owner charge such rent or other payment for the tenancy or occupation thereof as they may determine from time to time and as respects any buildings or other land or works or services provided under this Act the authority may make such charge, whether by way of rent or otherwise, as they shall think fit.

FIRST SCHEDULE
Repeals

Note

This Schedule repealed the following; Public Works Loans Act 1881 s 11; Labourers (Ireland) Act 1883; Labourers (Ireland) Act 1885; Labourers (Ireland) Act 1886; Housing of the Working Classes Act 1890 ss 2-87, ss 59-92; s 88 the words "or county council" and "in pursuance of Part I. or Part II. of this Act"; ss 99 to 103; and all the Schedules except the Second Schedule; Purchase of Land (Ireland) Act 1891 s 38; Labourers (Ireland) Act 1891; Labourers (Ireland) Act 1892; Housing of the Working Classes Act 1893; Housing of the Working Classes Ireland) Act 1896; Labourers (Ireland) Act 1896; Small Dwellings Acquisition Act 1899; Irish Land Act 1903 Part IV s 100(4); Labourers (Ireland) Act 1906; Local Registration of Title (Ireland) Amendment Act 1908; Housing of the Working Classes (Ireland) Act 1908; Irish Land Act 1909 ss 10,11; Labourers (Ireland) Act 1911; Labourers (Ireland) Act 1914; Housing (No. 2) Act 1914; Housing (No. 2) (Amendment) Act 1914; Local Government (Emergency Provisions) Act 1916 s 13(4); Labourers (Ireland) Act 1918; Housing (Ireland) Act 1919 The whole Act except ss 31, 35, 36 and the Sch 3; Labourers (Ireland) Act 1919; Housing (Additional Powers) Act 1919; Public Works Loans Act 1920 ss 2,5; Housing Act 1921; Housing (Building Facilities) Act 1924; Housing (Building Facilities) (Amendment) Act 1924; Housing Act 1925; Housing Act 1928; Housing Act 1929; Housing (Miscellaneous Provisions) Act 1931; Housing (Financial and Miscellaneous Provisions) Act 1932; Housing (Financial and Miscellaneous Provisions) Act 1934; Labourers Act 1936 ss 4, 5, 9, 10, 12, 18; 24(5)(e); Housing and Labourers Act 1937 Part II and Schedule; Housing (Amendment) Act 1939; Housing (Amendment) Act 1940; County Management Act 1940 Sch 2 Paragraph 11; Housing (Amendment) Act 1941; Housing (Amendment) Act 1942; Housing (Amendment) Act 1944; Housing (Amendment) Act 1946; Housing (Amendment) Act 1948; Housing (Amendment) Act 1949; Housing (Amendment) Act 1950; Housing (Amendment) Act 1952; Housing (Amendment) Act 1954; Housing (Amendment) Act 1956; Small Dwellings Acquisition Act 1957; Housing (Amendment) Act 1958; Housing (Amendment) Act 1960; Housing (Loans and Grants) Act 1962.

TAXES CONSOLIDATION ACT 1997

(1997 Number 39)

ARRANGEMENT OF SECTIONS

INTERPRETATION AND BASIC CHARGING PROVISIONS

PART 1
INTERPRETATION

PART 26
LIFE ASSURANCE COMPANIES

CHAPTER 1
General Provisions

PART 33
ANTI-AVOIDANCE

CHAPTER 2
Miscellaneous

MANAGEMENT PROVISIONS

PART 37
ADMINISTRATION

PART 38
RETURNS OF INCOME AND GAINS, OTHER OBLIGATIONS AND RETURNS, AND REVENUE POWERS

CHAPTER 4
Revenue powers

SCHEDULE 31

INTERPRETATION AND BASIC CHARGING PROVISIONS

PART 1

INTERPRETATION

7 Application to certain taxing statutes of Age of Majority Act, 1985

(1) Notwithstanding subsection (4) of section 2 of the Age of Majority Act, 1985 (in this section referred to as **"the Act of 1985"**), subsections (2) and (3) of that section shall,

subject to subsection (2), apply for the purposes of the Income Tax Acts and any other statutory provision (within the meaning of the Act of 1985) dealing with the imposition, repeal, remission, alteration or regulation of any tax or other duty under the care and management of the Revenue Commissioners, and accordingly section 2(4)(*b*)(vii) of the Act of 1985 shall cease to apply.

(2) Nothing in subsection (1) shall affect a claimant's entitlement to [relief][1] under section 462 or 465.

Amendments

[1]   Substituted by FA 2000 s 14 and Sch 1 para 2; previously "a deduction".

Cross-references

This section to be construed together with the Customs Acts, in so far as relating to customs, and with the statutes which relate to excise duty, in so far as relating to that duty: s 1104(2).

This section to be construed together with the Value Added Tax Acts 1972-1997, in so far as relating to value added tax: s 1104(3).

This section to be construed together with the Stamp Duties Consolidation Act 1999 and the enactments amending or extending that Act, in so far as relating to stamp duties: s 1104(4).

This section to be construed together with the Capital Acquisitions Tax Act 1976, and the enactments amending or extending that Act, in so far as relating to capital acquisitions tax: s 1104(5).

This section to be construed together with FA 1983 Pt VI and the enactments amending or extending that Part, in so far as relating to residential property tax: s 1104(6).

Definition

Income Tax Acts: s 1(2).

Former enactment

FA 1986 s 112(1)-(2).

8 Construction of certain taxing statutes in accordance with Status of Children Act, 1987

(1) In this section, **"the Acts"** means—

   (*a*)   the Tax Acts,

   (*b*)   the Capital Gains Tax Acts,

   (*c*)   the Capital Acquisitions Tax Act, 1976, and the enactments amending or extending that Act, and

   (*d*)   the statutes relating to stamp duty,

and any instruments made thereunder.

(2) Notwithstanding any provision of the Acts or the dates on which they were passed, in deducing any relationship between persons for the purposes of the Acts, the Acts shall be construed in accordance with section 3 of the Status of Children Act, 1987.

Definition

person: IA 1937 s 11(*c*); Tax Acts: s 1(2); Capital Gains Tax Acts: s 1(2).

Former enactment

FA 1988 s 74(1)-(2).

PART 15
PERSONAL ALLOWANCES AND RELIEFS AND CERTAIN OTHER INCOME TAX AND CORPORATION TAX RELIEFS

CHAPTER 3
Corporation Tax Reliefs

487 Corporation tax: credit for

(1) (*a*)   In this section—

"accounting profit" means the amount of profit, after taxation and before extraordinary items—

(i)   shown in the profit and loss account—

(I)   in the case of a company resident in the State, which is required under section 148 of the Companies Act, 1963, to be laid before the annual general meeting of the company, or which would be so shown but for subsection (4) of section 149 of that Act, and

(II)   in the case of a company not resident in the State and carrying on a trade in the State through a branch or agency, of that branch or agency and which is certified by the auditor appointed under section 160 of the Companies Act, 1963, or under the law of the state in which the company is incorporated and which corresponds to that section, as presenting a true and fair view of the profit or loss attributable to that branch or agency,

(ii)   reduced by the amount of such profit as is attributable to—

(I)   dividends received from companies resident in the State which are members of the group of which that company is a member,

(II)   gains on disposal of capital assets,

(III)   relevant trading operations within the meaning of section 446,

(IV)   trading operations carried on outside of the State and in respect of which the company is chargeable to corporation tax in the State and to tax on income in another state, and

(V)   dividends received from companies not resident in the State,

and

(iii)   increased—

(I)   as respects income from sources specified in subparagraphs (III), (IV) and (V) of paragraph (ii), by an amount determined by the formula—

$$\frac{100 \times T}{R}$$

where—

    T   is the corporation tax chargeable in respect of that income computed in accordance with the provisions of the Corporation Tax Acts and after allowing relief under Parts 14 and 35, and

    R   is the rate of corporation tax for the accounting period concerned and to which section 21 relates, but where part of the accounting period falls in one financial year and the other part falls in the financial year succeeding the first-mentioned financial year, R shall be determined by applying the formula specified in section 78(3)(*b*), and

  (II) by the amount of stamp duty charged under section 64 of the Finance Act, 1989, section 108 of the Finance Act, 1990, section 200 of the Finance Act, 1992, or section 142 of the Finance Act, 1995, and under [section 126 of the Stamp Duties Consolidation Act, 1999],[1] as has been taken into account in computing that amount of profit, after taxation and before extraordinary items;

"adjusted group base tax", in relation to a relevant period, means—

  (i) an amount determined by the formula—

$$\frac{T \times P}{B}$$

where—

    T is the group base tax,

    P is the group profit of the relevant period, and

    B is the group base profit,

    or

  (ii) if it is greater, the group advance corporation tax of the relevant period;

"advance corporation tax", in relation to a relevant period, means the aggregate of the amounts of advance corporation tax paid or treated as paid by a company, and not repaid, under Chapter 8 of Part 6, in respect of distributions made in accounting periods falling wholly or partly within the relevant period and, where an accounting period falls partly within a relevant period, the aggregate shall include a part of the advance corporation tax so paid proportionate to the part of the accounting period falling within the relevant period;

"base profit", in relation to a company, means 50 per cent of the aggregate of the amounts of accounting profit of a company for accounting periods falling wholly or partly in the period beginning on the 1st day of April, 1989, and ending on the 31st day of March, 1991, and, where an accounting period falls partly within that period, the aggregate shall include a part of the accounting profit of the accounting period proportionate to the part of the accounting period falling within that period;

"base tax" means 50 per cent of the aggregate of the corporation tax chargeable on a company, exclusive of the corporation tax on the part of the company's profits attributable to chargeable gains and before the set-off of advance corporation tax under Chapter 8 of Part 6, for accounting periods falling wholly or partly in the period beginning on the 1st day of April, 1989, and ending on the 31st day of March, 1991, and, where an accounting period falls partly within that period, the aggregate shall include a part of the corporation tax so chargeable for the accounting period proportionate to the part of the accounting period falling within that period;

"group advance corporation tax", in relation to a relevant period, means the aggregate of the amounts of advance corporation tax in relation to the relevant period of companies which throughout the relevant period are members of the group;

"group base profit" means the aggregate of the amounts of base profit of companies which throughout the relevant period are members of the group;

"group base tax" means the aggregate of the amounts of base tax of companies which throughout the relevant period are members of the group, but where the amount of the group base tax is an amount which is—

(i)   greater than 43 per cent, or

(ii) lower than 10 per cent,

of the group base profit, computed in accordance with this section but without regard to subparagraphs (III), (IV) and (V) of paragraph (ii), or subparagraph (I) of paragraph (iii), of the definition of **"accounting profit"**, the group base tax shall be deemed to be an amount equal to 25 per cent of the group base profit as so computed;

"group profit", in relation to a relevant period, means the aggregate of the amounts of profit of the relevant period of companies which throughout that period are members of the group;

"group tax liability", in relation to a relevant period, means the aggregate of the amounts of tax liability of the relevant period of companies which throughout that period are members of the group;

"levy payment" means the aggregate of the amounts charged in the year 1992 or in any later year under section 200 of the Finance Act, 1992, or section 142 of the Finance Act, 1995, and which have been paid, on or before the date by which the amounts are payable, by companies which are members of a group;

"profit", in relation to a relevant period, means the aggregate of the accounting profit, computed on the same basis as that on which the base profit of the company is computed, of a company for accounting periods falling wholly or partly within the relevant period and, where an accounting period falls partly within a relevant period, the aggregate shall include a part of the accounting profit of the accounting period proportionate to the part of the accounting period falling within that relevant period;

"**relevant period**", in relation to a levy payment, means a period beginning on the 1st day of April preceding the date on or before which the levy payment is to be made and ending on the 31st day of March next after that date;

"**tax liability**", in relation to a relevant period, means the aggregate of the corporation tax which apart from this section would be chargeable on a company, exclusive of the corporation tax on the part of the company's profits attributable to chargeable gains and before the set-off of advance corporation tax under Chapter 8 of Part 6, for accounting periods falling wholly or partly within the relevant period and, where an accounting period falls partly within that period, the aggregate shall include a part of the corporation tax so chargeable for the accounting period proportionate to the part of the accounting period falling within that period.

(*b*) For the purposes of this section—

    (i) 2 companies shall be deemed to be members of a group if one company is a 75 per cent subsidiary of the other company or both companies are 75 per cent subsidiaries of a third company; but—

        (I) in determining whether one company is a 75 per cent subsidiary of another company, the other company shall be treated as not being the owner of—

            (A) any share capital which it owns directly in a company if a profit on a sale of the shares would be treated as a trading receipt of its trade, or

            (B) any share capital which it owns indirectly, and which is owned directly by a company for which a profit on a sale of the shares would be a trading receipt,

        and

        (II) a company which is an assurance company within the meaning of section 706 shall not be a member of a group,

    (ii) sections 412 to 418 shall apply for the purposes of this paragraph as they apply for the purposes of Chapter 5 of Part 12,

    (iii) a company and all its 75 per cent subsidiaries shall form a group and, where that company is a member of a group as being itself a 75 per cent subsidiary, that group shall comprise all its 75 per cent subsidiaries and the first-mentioned group shall be deemed not to be a group; but a company which is not a member of a group shall be treated as if it were a member of a group which consists of that company, and accordingly references to group advance corporation tax, group base profit, group base tax, group profit and group tax liability shall be construed as if they were respectively references to advance corporation tax, base profit, base tax, profit and tax liability of that company,

    (iv) the part of a company's profits attributable to chargeable gains for an accounting period shall be taken to be the amount brought into the company's profits for that period for the purposes of corporation tax in respect of chargeable gains before any deduction for charges on income, expenses of management or other amounts which can be deducted from or set against or treated as reducing profits of more than one description,

(v) the income or profit attributable to any trading operations or dividends shall be such amount of the income or profit as appears to the inspector or on appeal to the Appeal Commissioners to be just and reasonable, and

(vi) corporation tax chargeable in respect of any income shall be the corporation tax which would not have been chargeable but for that income.

(2) Where for a relevant period in relation to a levy payment the group tax liability exceeds the adjusted group base tax of that relevant period, all or part of the levy payment, not being greater than the excess of the group tax liability over the adjusted group base tax, may be set against the group tax liability of the relevant period in accordance with this section.

(3) (*a*) In this subsection, **"appropriate inspector"** has the same meaning as in section 950.

(*b*) Where under subsection (2) an amount of levy payment may be set against the group tax liability of a relevant period, so much (in this paragraph referred to as **"the apportionable part"**) of the amount as bears to that amount the same proportion as the tax liability of the relevant period of a company which is a member of the group bears to the group tax liability of the relevant period shall be apportioned to the company, and the companies which are members of the group may, by giving notice in writing to the appropriate inspector within a period of 9 months after the end of the relevant period, elect to have the apportionable part apportioned in such manner as is specified in the notice.

(4) Where an amount is apportioned to a company under subsection (3), that amount shall be set against the tax liability of the relevant period of the company and, to the extent that an amount is so set off, it shall be treated for the purposes of the Corporation Tax Acts as if it were a payment of corporation tax made on the day on which that corporation tax is to be paid; but an amount or part of an amount which is to be treated as if it were a payment of corporation tax may not be repaid to a company by virtue of a claim to relief under the Corporation Tax Acts or for any other reason.

(5) Where under subsection (4) an amount is to be set against the tax liability of a relevant period of a company and the tax liability of the relevant period consists of the aggregate of corporation tax chargeable for more accounting periods than one, the amount shall be set against the corporation tax of each of those accounting periods in the proportion which the corporation tax of the accounting period or the part of the accounting period, as the case may be, and which is included in the tax liability of the relevant period bears to the tax liability of the relevant period.

(6) Where—

(*a*) the end of an accounting period (in this subsection referred to as **"the first-mentioned accounting period"**) of a company which is a member of a group does not coincide with the end of the relevant period, (*b*) the tax liability of—

    (i) one or more accounting periods of the company ending after the end of the first-mentioned accounting period, or

    (ii) one or more accounting periods of any other member of the group ending after the end of the first-mentioned accounting period,

is to be taken into account in determining the amount of the levy payment which may be set off under this section against the corporation tax of—

    (I) the first-mentioned accounting period, or one or more accounting periods ending before the end of that period, of the company, or

    (II) one or more accounting periods of any other member of the group ending on or before the end of the first-mentioned accounting period,

and

(*c*) on the specified return date (within the meaning of section 950) it is not possible—

    (i) for the first-mentioned accounting period, or any other accounting period ending before the end of that period, of the company, or

    (ii) for one or more accounting periods of any other member of the group ending on or before the end of the first-mentioned accounting period,

to determine the amount of the levy payment which may be so set off,

then, the amount of levy payment which may be set off under this section against the corporation tax of an accounting period shall be taken to be the amount which would have been so set off if a period of 12 months ending on the last day of the most recent accounting period of the parent company (being a member of the group which is not a subsidiary of any other member of the group) which ends in the relevant period were the relevant period; but, where a part only of that period of 12 months falls after the 31st day of March, 1992, the amount to be set off under this subsection shall be reduced to an amount proportionate to the part of that period of 12 months falling after that day.

(7) (*a*) A company shall deliver, as soon as they become available, such particulars as are required to determine the amount of levy payment which apart from subsection (6) is to be set off against the corporation tax of an accounting period.

(*b*) Where an amount of levy payment has been set off against corporation tax of an accounting period under subsection (6) and the company delivers such particulars as are required to be delivered in accordance with paragraph (*a*), the inspector shall adjust any computation or assessment by reference to the difference between these amounts and any amount of corporation tax overpaid shall be repaid and any amount of corporation tax underpaid shall be paid.

(8) (*a*) An amount of tax to be repaid under subsection (7) shall be repaid with interest in all respects as if it were a repayment of preliminary tax under section 953(7).

(*b*) Interest shall not be charged under section 1080 on any amount of tax underpaid under this subsection unless the amount is not paid within one month of the date on which the amount of the underpayment is notified to the chargeable person by the inspector, and the amount of tax so unpaid shall not be treated as part of the tax payable for the chargeable period for the purposes of section 958(4)(*b*).

Amendments

¹   Substituted by SDCA 1999 s 162 and Sch 4; previously "section 94 of the Finance Act, 1986".

Definitions

Appeal Commissioners: s 2(1); branch or agency: s 4(1); charges on income: ss 4(1), 243(1); company: ss 4(1), 5(1); Corporation Tax Acts: s 1(2); month: IA 1937 Sch; person: IA 1937 s 11(*c*); profits: s 4(1); shares: s 5(1); trade: ss 3(1), 4(1), 5(1); writing: IA 1937 Sch.

Former enactments

FA 1992 s 45; FA 1995 s 56; FA 1997 s 146(1) and Sch 9 Pt I para 16(1).

PART 26
LIFE ASSURANCE COMPANIES

Cross-references

UK double taxation agreement: s 832(4)(*c*).

CHAPTER 1
General Provisions

707 Management expenses

(1) Subject to sections 709 and 710, section 83 shall apply for computing the profits of a company carrying on life business, whether mutual or proprietary (and not charged to corporation tax in respect of it under Case I of Schedule D), whether or not the company is resident in the State, as that section applies in relation to an investment company, except that—

    (*a*)   there shall be deducted from the amount treated as expenses of management for any accounting period—

        (i)   any repayment or refund receivable in the period of the whole or part of a sum disbursed by the company for that period or any earlier period as expenses of management, including commissions (in whatever manner described),

       (ii)   reinsurance commissions earned by the company in the period, and

      (iii)   the amount of any fines or fees receivable in the period or profits arising from reversions in the period,

        and in calculating profits arising from reversions the company may set off against those profits any losses arising from reversions in any previous accounting period during which any enactment granting this relief was in operation in so far as they have not already been so set off, and

   [(*b*)   no deduction shall be made under section 83(2)(*b*) other than in respect of the amount of any income (other than receipts from premiums) which, if the profits of the company were chargeable to corporation tax under Case I of Schedule D, would be taken into account in computing those profits and any such deduction from the amount treated as expenses of management under that

46

section shall not be regarded as reducing acquisition expenses within the meaning of section 708.]¹

(2) (*a*) Where the life assurance business of an assurance company includes more than one of the following classes of business—

    (i)   pension business,

    (ii) general annuity business,

    (iii) special investment business, and

    (iv) life assurance business (excluding such pension business, general annuity business and special investment business),

then, for the purposes of the Corporation Tax Acts, the business of each such class shall be treated as though it were a separate business, and subsection (1) shall apply separately to each such class of business as if it were the only business of the company.

(*b*) Any amount of an excess referred to in section 83(3) which is carried forward from an accounting period ending before the 27th day of May, 1986, may for the purposes of section 83(2) be deducted in computing the profits of the company for a later accounting period in respect of such of the classes of business referred to in paragraph (*a*) as the company may elect; but any amount so deducted in computing the profits from one of those classes of business shall not be deducted in computing the profits of the company from another of those classes of business.

(3) ...²

(4) Relief under subsection (1) shall not be given to any such company in so far as it would, if given in addition to all other reliefs to which the company is entitled, reduce the corporation tax borne by the company on the income and gains of its life business for any accounting period to less than would have been paid if the company had been charged to tax at the rate specified in section 21(1) in respect of that business under Case I of Schedule D and, where relief has been withheld in respect of any accounting period by virtue of this subsection, the excess to be carried forward by virtue of section 83(3) shall be increased accordingly.

(5) (*a*) For the purposes of subsection (4)—

    ...³

    (iii) relief for the management expenses, if any, attributable to the life business, other than special investment business, of a company shall be withheld before any relief for management expenses attributable to the special investment business of the company is withheld, and

    (iv) sections 709(2), 710 and 714 shall, and section 396(5)(*b*) shall not, apply for the purposes of computing the profits of the life assurance business or the industrial assurance business, as the case may be, which would have been charged to tax under Case I of Schedule D.

(*b*) The reference in section 551(2) to computing income or profits or gains or losses shall not be taken as applying to a computation of a company's income for the purposes of subsection (4).

Amendments

[1]   Subs (1)(*b*) substituted by FA 1999 s 86(1) for income accruing for accounting periods commencing on or after 1 January 1999.

[2]   Subs (3) repealed by FA 1999 s 197 and Sch 6 with effect from 25 March 1999.

[3]   Subs (5)(*a*)(i)-(ii) repealed by FA 2000 s 69(2) and Sch 2 Part 2 with effect from 6 April 1999 in the case of income tax and as respects accounting periods commencing on or after that date in the case of corporation tax.

Cross-references

Approved pension schemes, exemptions and reliefs, subs (4): s 774(6)(*b*).

Business entertainment expenses: s 840(2)(*b*).

Capital gains tax, exclusion of sums chargeable to income tax: s 551(2).

Cars, limit on renewals allowance: s 375(*c*); restriction of deduction in respect of running expenses: s 376(1) (qualifying expenditure).

Chargeable gains of life business, subs (2)(*a*)(iii)-(iv): s 711(3).

Costs of establishing profit sharing schemes: s 518(1).

Employee share ownership trusts: s 519(2).

Foreign life assurance funds: s 718(5)(*a*).

Group relief, losses that may be surrendered: s 420(5).

Life assurance companies, acquisition expenses: s 708(4)(*b*), (6).

Life assurance companies, annuity business, separate charge on profits: s 715(2)(*b*).

Life assurance companies, computation of profits: s 714.

Life assurance companies, management expenses deduction, subs (2): s 706(4)(*b*).

Overseas life assurance companies, management expenses: s 728.

Profit sharing schemes, payments to trustees: s 517(1)(*b*).

Profits of life business: s 710(2)(*a*)(iv), (4), (5)(*b*).

Redundancy payments, deduction: s 109(3).

Restrictive covenants, management expense deduction: s 127(5).

Special investment policies, subs (4): s 723(6).

Transactions in certificates of deposit: s 814(6).

UK double taxation agreement: s 832(4)(*a*).

Definition

company: s 4(1); distribution: ss 4(1), 436, 437; profits: s 4(1); tax credit: ss 2(1), 136.

Former enactment

CTA 1976 s 33(1)-(2); FA 1986 s 59(*a*); FA 1992 s 44(*a*); FA 1993 s 11(*a*) and (*b*).

PART 33
ANTI-AVOIDANCE

CHAPTER 2
Miscellaneous

811 Transactions to avoid liability to tax

(1) (*a*)   In this section—

    "the Acts" means—

      (i)   the Tax Acts,

      (ii)   the Capital Gains Tax Acts,

      (iii)   the Value-Added Tax Act, 1972, and the enactments amending or extending that Act,

      (iv)   the Capital Acquisitions Tax Act, 1976, and the enactments amending or extending that Act,

(v) Part VI of the Finance Act, 1983, and the enactments amending or extending that Part, and

(vi) the statutes relating to stamp duty,

and any instruments made thereunder;

"business" means any trade, profession or vocation;

"notice of opinion" means a notice given by the Revenue Commissioners under subsection (6);

"tax" means any tax, duty, levy or charge which in accordance with the Acts is placed under the care and management of the Revenue Commissioners and any interest, penalty or other amount payable pursuant to the Acts;

"tax advantage" means—

(i) a reduction, avoidance or deferral of any charge or assessment to tax, including any potential or prospective charge or assessment, or

(ii) a refund of or a payment of an amount of tax, or an increase in an amount of tax, refundable or otherwise payable to a person, including any potential or prospective amount so refundable or payable,

arising out of or by reason of a transaction, including a transaction where another transaction would not have been undertaken or arranged to achieve the results, or any part of the results, achieved or intended to be achieved by the transaction;

"tax avoidance transaction" has the meaning assigned to it by subsection (2);

"tax consequences", in relation to a tax avoidance transaction, means such adjustments and acts as may be made and done by the Revenue Commissioners pursuant to subsection (5) in order to withdraw or deny the tax advantage resulting from the tax avoidance transaction;

"transaction" means—

(i) any transaction, action, course of action, course of conduct, scheme, plan or proposal,

(ii) any agreement, arrangement, understanding, promise or undertaking, whether express or implied and whether or not enforceable or intended to be enforceable by legal proceedings, and

(iii) any series of or combination of the circumstances referred to in paragraphs (i) and (ii),

whether entered into or arranged by one person or by 2 or more persons—

(I) whether acting in concert or not,

(II) whether or not entered into or arranged wholly or partly outside the State, or

(III) whether or not entered into or arranged as part of a larger transaction or in conjunction with any other transaction or transactions.

(b) In subsections (2) and (3), for the purposes of the hearing or rehearing under subsection (8) of an appeal made under subsection (7) or for the purposes of the determination of a question of law arising on the statement of a case for the opinion of the High Court, the references to the Revenue Commissioners shall, subject to any necessary modifications, be construed as references to the Appeal Commissioners or to a judge of the Circuit Court or, to the extent necessary, to a judge of the High Court, as appropriate.

(2) For the purposes of this section and subject to subsection (3), a transaction shall be a **"tax avoidance transaction"** if having regard to any one or more of the following—

(a) the results of the transaction,

(b) its use as a means of achieving those results, and

(c) any other means by which the results or any part of the results could have been achieved,

the Revenue Commissioners form the opinion that—

(i) the transaction gives rise to, or but for this section would give rise to, a tax advantage, and

(ii) the transaction was not undertaken or arranged primarily for purposes other than to give rise to a tax advantage,

and references in this section to the Revenue Commissioners forming an opinion that a transaction is a tax avoidance transaction shall be construed as references to the Revenue Commissioners forming an opinion with regard to the transaction in accordance with this subsection.

(3) (a) Without prejudice to the generality of subsection (2), in forming an opinion in accordance with that subsection and subsection (4) as to whether or not a transaction is a tax avoidance transaction, the Revenue Commissioners shall not regard the transaction as being a tax avoidance transaction if they are satisfied that—

(i) notwithstanding that the purpose or purposes of the transaction could have been achieved by some other transaction which would have given rise to a greater amount of tax being payable by the person, the transaction—

(I) was undertaken or arranged by a person with a view, directly or indirectly, to the realisation of profits in the course of the business activities of a business carried on by the person, and

(II) was not undertaken or arranged primarily to give rise to a tax advantage,

or

(ii) the transaction was undertaken or arranged for the purpose of obtaining the benefit of any relief, allowance or other abatement provided by any provision of the Acts and that the transaction would not result directly or indirectly in a misuse of the provision or an abuse of the provision having regard to the purposes for which it was provided.

(*b*) In forming an opinion referred to in paragraph (*a*) in relation to any transaction, the Revenue Commissioners shall have regard to—

    (i) the form of that transaction,

    (ii) the substance of that transaction,

    (iii) the substance of any other transaction or transactions which that transaction may reasonably be regarded as being directly or indirectly related to or connected with, and

    (iv) the final outcome and result of that transaction and any combination of those other transactions which are so related or connected.

(4) Subject to this section, the Revenue Commissioners as respects any transaction may at any time—

(*a*) form the opinion that the transaction is a tax avoidance transaction,

(*b*) calculate the tax advantage which they consider arises, or which but for this section would arise, from the transaction,

(*c*) determine the tax consequences which they consider would arise in respect of the transaction if their opinion were to become final and conclusive in accordance with subsection (5)(*e*), and

(*d*) calculate the amount of any relief from double taxation which they would propose to give to any person in accordance with subsection (5)(*c*).

(5) (*a*) Where the opinion of the Revenue Commissioners that a transaction is a tax avoidance transaction becomes final and conclusive, they may, notwithstanding any other provision of the Acts, make all such adjustments and do all such acts as are just and reasonable (in so far as those adjustments and acts have been specified or described in a notice of opinion given under subsection (6) and subject to the manner in which any appeal made under subsection (7) against any matter specified or described in the notice of opinion has been finally determined, including any adjustments and acts not so specified or described in the notice of opinion but which form part of a final determination of any such appeal) in order that the tax advantage resulting from a tax avoidance transaction shall be withdrawn from or denied to any person concerned.

(*b*) Subject to but without prejudice to the generality of paragraph (*a*), the Revenue Commissioners may—

    (i) allow or disallow in whole or in part any deduction or other amount which is relevant in computing tax payable, or any part of such deduction or other amount,

    (ii) allocate or deny to any person any deduction, loss, abatement, relief, allowance, exemption, income or other amount, or any part thereof, or

    (iii) recharacterize for tax purposes the nature of any payment or other amount.

(*c*) Where the Revenue Commissioners make any adjustment or do any act for the purposes of paragraph (*a*), they shall afford relief from any double taxation which they consider would but for this paragraph arise by virtue of any adjustment made or act done by them pursuant to paragraphs (*a*) and (*b*).

(*d*) Notwithstanding any other provision of the Acts, where—

    (i) pursuant to subsection (4)(*c*), the Revenue Commissioners determine the tax consequences which they consider would arise in respect of a transaction if their opinion that the transaction is a tax avoidance transaction were to become final and conclusive, and

    (ii) pursuant to that determination, they specify or describe in a notice of opinion any adjustment or act which they consider would be, or be part of, those tax consequences,

then, in so far as any right of appeal lay under subsection (7) against any such adjustment or act so specified or described, no right or further right of appeal shall lie under the Acts against that adjustment or act when it is made or done in accordance with this subsection, or against any adjustment or act so made or done that is not so specified or described in the notice of opinion but which forms part of the final determination of any appeal made under subsection (7) against any matter specified or described in the notice of opinion.

(*e*) For the purposes of this subsection, an opinion of the Revenue Commissioners that a transaction is a tax avoidance transaction shall be final and conclusive—

    (i) if within the time limited no appeal is made under subsection (7) against any matter or matters specified or described in a notice or notices of opinion given pursuant to that opinion, or

    (ii) as and when all appeals made under subsection (7) against any such matter or matters have been finally determined and none of the appeals has been so determined by an order directing that the opinion of the Revenue Commissioners to the effect that the transaction is a tax avoidance transaction is void.

(6) (*a*) Where pursuant to subsections (2) and (4) the Revenue Commissioners form the opinion that a transaction is a tax avoidance transaction, they shall immediately on forming such an opinion give notice in writing of the opinion to any person from whom a tax advantage would be withdrawn or to whom a tax advantage would be denied or to whom relief from double taxation would be given if the opinion became final and conclusive, and the notice shall specify or describe—

    (i) the transaction which in the opinion of the Revenue Commissioners is a tax avoidance transaction,

    (ii) the tax advantage or part of the tax advantage, calculated by the Revenue Commissioners which would be withdrawn from or denied to the person to whom the notice is given,

    (iii) the tax consequences of the transaction determined by the Revenue Commissioners in so far as they would refer to the person, and

(iv) the amount of any relief from double taxation calculated by the Revenue Commissioners which they would propose to give to the person in accordance with subsection (5)(*c*).

(*b*) Section 869 shall, with any necessary modifications, apply for the purposes of a notice given under this subsection or subsection (10) as if it were a notice given under the Income Tax Acts.

(7) Any person aggrieved by an opinion formed or, in so far as it refers to the person, a calculation or determination made by the Revenue Commissioners pursuant to subsection (4) may, by notice in writing given to the Revenue Commissioners within 30 days of the date of the notice of opinion, appeal to the Appeal Commissioners on the grounds and, notwithstanding any other provision of the Acts, only on the grounds that, having regard to all of the circumstances, including any fact or matter which was not known to the Revenue Commissioners when they formed their opinion or made their calculation or determination, and to this section—

(*a*) the transaction specified or described in the notice of opinion is not a tax avoidance transaction,

(*b*) the amount of the tax advantage or the part of the tax advantage, specified or described in the notice of opinion which would be withdrawn from or denied to the person is incorrect,

(*c*) the tax consequences specified or described in the notice of opinion, or such part of those consequences as shall be specified or described by the appellant in the notice of appeal, would not be just and reasonable in order to withdraw or to deny the tax advantage or part of the tax advantage specified or described in the notice of opinion, or

(*d*) the amount of relief from double taxation which the Revenue Commissioners propose to give to the person is insufficient or incorrect.

(8) The Appeal Commissioners shall hear and determine an appeal made to them under subsection (7) as if it were an appeal against an assessment to income tax and, subject to subsection (9), the provisions of the Income Tax Acts relating to the rehearing of an appeal and to the statement of a case for the opinion of the High Court on a point of law shall apply accordingly with any necessary modifications; but on the hearing or rehearing of the appeal—

(*a*) it shall not be lawful to enquire into any grounds of appeal other than those specified in subsection (7), and

(*b*) at the request of the appellants, 2 or more appeals made by 2 or more persons pursuant to the same opinion, calculation or determination formed or made by the Revenue Commissioners pursuant to subsection (4) may be heard or reheard together.

(9) (*a*) On the hearing of an appeal made under subsection (7), the Appeal Commissioners shall have regard to all matters to which the Revenue Commissioners may or are required to have regard under this section, and—

    (i) in relation to an appeal made on the grounds referred to in subsection (7)(*a*), the Appeal Commissioners shall determine the appeal, in so far as it is made on those grounds, by ordering, if they or a majority of them—

        (I) consider that the transaction specified or described in the notice of opinion or any part of that transaction is a tax avoidance transaction, that the opinion or the opinion in so far as it relates to that part is to stand,

        (II) consider that, subject to such amendment or addition thereto as the Appeal Commissioners or the majority of them deem necessary and as they shall specify or describe, the transaction, or any part of it, specified or described in the notice of opinion, is a tax avoidance transaction, that the transaction or that part of it be so amended or added to and that, subject to the amendment or addition, the opinion or the opinion in so far as it relates to that part is to stand, or

        (III) do not so consider as referred to in clause (I) or (II), that the opinion is void,

    (ii) in relation to an appeal made on the grounds referred to in subsection (7)(*b*), they shall determine the appeal, in so far as it is made on those grounds, by ordering that the amount of the tax advantage or the part of the tax advantage specified or described in the notice of opinion be increased or reduced by such amount as they shall direct or that it shall stand,

    (iii) in relation to an appeal made on the grounds referred to in subsection (7)(*c*), they shall determine the appeal, in so far as it is made on those grounds, by ordering that the tax consequences specified or described in the notice of opinion shall be altered or added to in such manner as they shall direct or that they shall stand, or

    (iv) in relation to an appeal made on the grounds referred to in subsection (7)(*d*), they shall determine the appeal, in so far as it is made on those grounds, by ordering that the amount of the relief from double taxation specified or described in the notice of opinion shall be increased or reduced by such amount as they shall direct or that it shall stand.

  (*b*) This subsection shall, subject to any necessary modifications, apply to the rehearing of an appeal by a judge of the Circuit Court and, to the extent necessary, to the determination by the High Court of any question or questions of law arising on the statement of a case for the opinion of the High Court.

(10) The Revenue Commissioners may at any time amend, add to or withdraw any matter specified or described in a notice of opinion by giving notice (in this subsection referred to as **"the notice of amendment"**) in writing of the amendment, addition or withdrawal to each and every person affected thereby, in so far as the person is so affected, and subsections (1) to (9) shall apply in all respects as if the notice of amendment were a notice of opinion and any matter specified or described in the notice of amendment were specified or described in a notice of opinion; but no such amendment, addition or withdrawal may be made so as to set aside or alter any matter

which has become final and conclusive on the determination of an appeal made with regard to that matter under subsection (7).

(11) Where pursuant to subsections (2) and (4) the Revenue Commissioners form the opinion that a transaction is a tax avoidance transaction and pursuant to that opinion notices are to be given under subsection (6) to 2 or more persons, any obligation on the Revenue Commissioners to maintain secrecy or any other restriction on the disclosure of information by the Revenue Commissioners shall not apply with respect to the giving of those notices or to the performance of any acts or the discharge of any functions authorised by this section to be performed or discharged by them or to the performance of any act or the discharge of any functions, including any act or function in relation to an appeal made under subsection (7), which is directly or indirectly related to the acts or functions so authorised.

(12) The Revenue Commissioners may nominate any of their officers to perform any acts and discharge any functions, including the forming of an opinion, authorised by this section to be performed or discharged by the Revenue Commissioners, and references in this section to the Revenue Commissioners shall with any necessary modifications be construed as including references to an officer so nominated.

(13) This section shall apply as respects any transaction where the whole or any part of the transaction is undertaken or arranged on or after the 25th day of January, 1989, and as respects any transaction undertaken or arranged wholly before that date in so far as it gives rise to, or would but for this section give rise to—

(a) a reduction, avoidance or deferral of any charge or assessment to tax, or part thereof, where the charge or assessment arises by virtue of any other transaction carried out wholly on or after a date, or

(b) a refund or a payment of an amount, or of an increase in an amount, of tax, or part thereof, refundable or otherwise payable to a person where that amount or increase in the amount would otherwise become first so refundable or otherwise payable to the person on a date,

which could not fall earlier than the 25th day of January, 1989.

Cross-references

Meaning of "the Acts" applied: Asset Covered Securities Act 2001 s 81(2).

Shipping tonnage tax, requirement not to enter into tax avoidance arrangements, meaning of "tax advantage" applied: s 697F(2)(a).

This section to be construed together with the Value Added Tax Acts 1972-1997, in so far as relating to value added tax: s 1104(3).

This section to be construed together with the Stamp Act 1891 and the enactments amending or extending that Act, in so far as relating to stamp duties: s 1104(4).

This section to be construed together with the Capital Acquisitions Tax Act 1976, and the enactments amending or extending that Act, in so far as relating to capital acquisitions tax: s 1104(5).

This section to be construed together with FA 1983 Pt VI and the enactments amending or extending that Part, in so far as relating to residential property tax: s 1104(6).

Case law

Bona fide commercial motives: *Marwood Homes Ltd v IRC*, [1996] STI 51.

Expenditure on plant funded by non-recourse borrowings allowable: *Airspace Investments Ltd v Moore*, HC, Lynch J, 15 April 1994. Contrast *Ensign Tankers (Leasing) Ltd v Stokes*, [1992] STC 226.

Meaning of "tax advantage": *IRC v Universities Superannuation Scheme*, [1997] STC 1.

Definitions

Appeal Commissioners: ss 2(1), 5(1); Circuit Court: IA 1937 Sch; High Court: IA 1937 Sch; person: IA 1937 s 11(*c*); profession: ss 2(1), 5(1); profits: s 4(1); statute: s 2(1), IA 1937 s 3; Tax Acts: s 1(2); trade: s 3(1); writing: IA 1937 Sch.

Former enactments

FA 1989 s 86.

PART 37
ADMINISTRATION

858 Evidence of authorisation

(1) In this section, except where the context otherwise requires—

"the Acts" means—

(*a*) (i) the Customs Acts,

(ii) the statutes relating to the duties of excise and to the management of those duties,

(iii) the Tax Acts,

(iv) the Capital Gains Tax Acts,

(v) the Value-Added Tax Act, 1972, and the enactments amending or extending that Act,

(vi) the Capital Acquisitions Tax Act, 1976, and the enactments amending or extending that Act,

(vii) the statutes relating to stamp duty and to the management of that duty,

and any instruments made thereunder or under any other enactment and relating to tax, and

(*b*) the European Communities (Intrastat) Regulations, 1993 (S.I. No. 136 of 1993);

"authorised officer" means an officer of the Revenue Commissioners who is authorised, nominated or appointed under any provision of the Acts to exercise or perform any functions under any of the specified provisions, and **"authorised"** and **"authorisation"** shall be construed accordingly;

"functions" includes powers and duties;

"identity card", in relation to an authorised officer, means a card which is issued to the officer by the Revenue Commissioners and which contains—

(*a*) a statement to the effect that the officer—

(i) is an officer of the Revenue Commissioners, and

(ii) is an authorised officer for the purposes of the specified provisions,

(*b*) a photograph and signature of the officer,

(*c*) a hologram showing the logo of the Office of the Revenue Commissioners,

(*d*) the facsimile signature of a Revenue Commissioner, and (*e*) particulars of the specified provisions under which the officer is authorised;

"specified provisions", in relation to an authorised officer, means either or both the provisions of the Acts under which the authorised officer—

(*a*) is authorised and which are specified on his or her identity card, and

(*b*) exercises or performs functions under the Customs Acts or any statutes relating to the duties of excise and to the management of those duties;

"tax" means any tax, duty, levy or charge under the care and management of the Revenue Commissioners.

(2) Where, in the exercise or performance of any functions under any of the specified provisions in relation to him or her, an authorised officer is requested to produce or show his or her authorisation for the purposes of that provision, the production by the authorised officer of his or her identity card—

(*a*) shall be taken as evidence of authorisation under that provision, and

(*b*) shall satisfy any obligation under that provision which requires the authorised officer to produce such authorisation on request.

(3) This section shall come into operation on such day as the Minister for Finance may appoint by order.

Cross-references

This section to be construed together with the Customs Acts, in so far as relating to customs: s 1104(2).

This section to be construed together with the Value Added Tax Acts 1972-1997, in so far as relating to value added tax: s 1104(3).

This section to be construed together with the Stamp Duties Consolidation Act 1999 and the enactments amending or extending that Act, in so far as relating to stamp duties: s 1104(4).

This section to be construed together with the Capital Acquisitions Tax Act 1976, and the enactments amending or extending that Act, in so far as relating to capital acquisitions tax: s 1104(5).

Former enactment

FA 1997 s 159.

---

859 Anonymity of authorised officers in relation to certain matters

(1) In this section—

"authorised officer" means an officer of the Revenue Commissioners nominated by them to be a member of the staff of the body;

"the body" has the meaning assigned to it by section 58;

"proceedings" includes any hearing before the Appeal Commissioners (within the meaning of the Revenue Acts);

"the Revenue Acts" means—

(*a*) the Customs Acts,

(*b*) the statutes relating to the duties of excise and to the management of those duties,

(*c*) the Tax Acts,

(*d*) the Capital Gains Tax Acts,

(e) the Value-Added Tax Act, 1972, and the enactments amending or extending that Act,

(f) the Capital Acquisitions Tax Act, 1976, and the enactments amending or extending that Act,

(g) the statutes relating to stamp duty and the management of that duty,

(h) Chapter IV of Part II of the Finance Act, 1992, and

(i) Part VI of the Finance Act, 1983,

and any instruments made thereunder or under any other enactment and relating to tax;

"tax" means any tax, duty, levy or charge under the care and management of the Revenue Commissioners.

(2) Notwithstanding any requirement made by or under any enactment or any other requirement in administrative and operational procedures, including internal procedures, all reasonable care shall be taken to ensure that the identity of an authorised officer shall not be revealed.

(3) In particular and without prejudice to the generality of subsection (2):

(a) where, for the purposes of exercising or performing his or her powers or duties under the Revenue Acts in pursuance of the functions of the body, an authorised officer may apart from this section be required to produce or show any written authority or warrant of appointment under those Acts or otherwise to identify himself or herself, the authorised officer shall—

(i) not be required to produce or show any such authority or warrant of appointment or to so identify himself or herself, for the purposes of exercising or performing his or her powers or duties under those Acts, and

(ii) be accompanied by a member of the Garda Síochána who shall, on request by a person affected, identify himself or herself as a member of the Garda Síochána and shall state that he or she is accompanied by an authorised officer;

(b) where, in pursuance of the functions of the body, an authorised officer exercises or performs in writing any of his or her powers or duties under the Revenue Acts or any provision of any other enactment, whenever passed, which relates to Revenue, such exercise or performance of his or her powers or duties shall be done in the name of the body and not in the name of the individual authorised officer involved, notwithstanding any provision to the contrary in any of those enactments;

(c) in any proceedings arising out of the exercise or performance, in pursuance of the functions of the body, of powers or duties by an authorised officer, any documents relating to such proceedings shall not reveal the identity of any authorised officer, notwithstanding any requirements to the contrary in any provision, and in any proceedings the identity of such officer other than as an authorised officer shall not be revealed other than to the judge or the Appeal Commissioner, as the case may be, hearing the case;

(*d*) where, in pursuance of the functions of the body, an authorised officer is required, in any proceedings, to give evidence and the judge or the Appeal Commissioner, as the case may be, is satisfied that there are reasonable grounds in the public interest to direct that evidence to be given by such authorised officer should be given in the hearing and not in the sight of any person, he or she may so direct.

Cross-references

This section to be construed together with the Customs Acts, in so far as relating to customs: s 1104(2).

This section to be construed together with the Value Added Tax Acts 1972-1997, in so far as relating to value added tax: s 1104(3).

This section to be construed together with the Stamp Duties Consolidation Act 1999 and the enactments amending or extending that Act, in so far as relating to stamp duties: s 1104(4).

This section to be construed together with the Capital Acquisitions Tax Act 1976, and the enactments amending or extending that Act, in so far as relating to capital acquisitions tax: s 1104(5).

This section to be construed together with FA 1983 Pt VI and the enactments amending or extending that Part, in so far as relating to residential property tax: s 1104(6).

Former enactment

FA 1993 s 19A; DCITPA 1996 s 12; CABA 1996 s 23.

872 Use of information relating to other taxes and duties

(1) Any information acquired, whether before or after the passing of this Act, in connection with any tax or duty under the care and management of the Revenue Commissioners may be used by them for any purpose connected with any other tax or duty under their care and management.

…

Cross-references

Subs (1) to be construed together with the Customs Acts, in so far as relating to customs: s 1104(2).

Subs (1) to be construed together with the Value Added Tax Acts 1972-1997, in so far as relating to value added tax: s 1104(3).

Subs (1) to be construed together with the Stamp Duties Consolidation Act 1999 and the enactments amending or extending that Act, in so far as relating to stamp duties: s 1104(4).

Subs (1) to be construed together with the Capital Acquisitions Tax Act 1976, and the enactments amending or extending that Act, in so far as relating to capital acquisitions tax: s 1104(5).

Subs (1) to be construed together with FA 1983 Pt VI and the enactments amending or extending that Part, in so far as relating to residential property tax: s 1104(6).

Former enactment

FA1928 s34(2); FA 1996 s 130.

875 Exemption of appraisements and valuations from stamp duty

Amendments

Section 875 repealed by FA 1999 s 197 and Sch 6 with effect from 25 March 1999.

PART 38
RETURNS OF INCOME AND GAINS, OTHER OBLIGATIONS AND RETURNS, AND REVENUE POWERS

CHAPTER 4
Revenue powers

905 Inspection of documents and records

(1) In this section—

"authorised officer" means an officer of the Revenue Commissioners authorised by them in writing to exercise the powers conferred by this section;

"property" means any asset relating to a tax liability;

[**"records"** means any document or any other written or printed material in any form, and includes any information stored, maintained or preserved by means of any mechanical or electronic device, whether or not stored, maintained or preserved in a legible form—

    (i)   which relates to a business carried on by a person, or

    (ii)   which a person is obliged by any provision relating to tax to keep, retain, issue or produce for inspection or which may be inspected under any provision relating to tax;][1]

"tax" means any tax, duty, levy or charge under the care and management of the Revenue Commissioners;

"tax liability" means any existing liability to tax or further liability to tax which may be established by an authorised officer following the exercise or performance of his or her powers or duties under this section.

(2) (*a*)   An authorised officer may at all reasonable times enter any premises or place where the authorised officer has reason to believe that—

    (i)   any trade, profession or other activity, the profits or gains of which are chargeable to tax, is or has been carried on,

    (ii)   anything is or has been done in connection with any trade, profession or other activity the profits or gains of which are chargeable to tax,

    (iii)   any records relating to—

        (I)   any trade, profession, other source of profits or gains or chargeable gains,

        (II)   any tax liability, or

        (III)   any repayments of tax in regard to any person,

      are or may be kept, or

    (iv)   any property is or has been located,

and the authorised officer may—

(A) require any person who is on those premises or in that place, other than a person who is there to purchase goods or to receive a service, to produce any records or property,

(B) if the authorised officer has reason to believe that any of the records or property which he or she has required to be produced to him or her under this subsection have not been produced, search on those premises or in that place for those records or property,

(C) examine any records or property and take copies of or extracts from any records,

(D) remove any records and retain them for a reasonable time for the purposes of their further examination or for the purposes of any legal proceedings instituted by an officer of the Revenue Commissioners or for the purposes of any criminal proceedings, and

(E) examine property listed in any records.

(*b*) An authorised officer may in the exercise or performance of his or her powers or duties under this section require any person whom he or she has reason to believe—

(i) is or was carrying on any trade, profession or other activity the profits or gains of which are chargeable to tax,

(ii) is or was liable to any tax, or

(iii) has information relating to any tax liability,

to give the authorised officer all reasonable assistance, including providing information and explanations or furnishing documents and making available for inspection property as required by the authorised officer in relation to any tax liability or any repayment of tax in regard to any person.

(*c*) Nothing in this subsection shall be construed as requiring any person carrying on a profession, or any person employed by any person carrying on a profession, to produce to an authorised officer any documents relating to a client, other than such documents—

(i) as pertain to the payment of fees to the person carrying on the profession or to other financial transactions of the person carrying on the profession,

(ii) as are otherwise material to the tax liability of the person carrying on the profession, or

(iii) as are already required to be provided following a request issued under [section 128 of the Stamp Duties Consolidation Act, 1999],[2]

and in particular that person shall not be required to disclose any information or professional advice of a confidential nature given to a client.

...[3]

(*e*) An authorised officer shall not, without the consent of the occupier, enter any premises, or that portion of any premises, which is occupied wholly and exclusively as a private residence, except on production by such officer of a warrant issued by a Judge of the District Court expressly authorising the authorised officer to so enter.

(*f*) A Judge of the District Court may issue a warrant under paragraph (*e*) if satisfied by information on oath that it is proper to do so for the purposes of this section.

[(2A)(*a*) In this subsection **"the Acts"** has the meaning assigned to it by section 1078(1).

(*b*) Without prejudice to any power conferred by subsection (2), if a Judge of the District Court is satisfied by information on oath that there are reasonable grounds for suspecting—

  (i) that a person may have failed or may fail to comply with any provision of the Acts,

  (ii) that any such failure is likely to have led or to lead to serious prejudice to the proper assessment or collection of tax (having regard to the amount of any tax liability that arises or might arise from such failure), and

  (iii) that records, which are material to the proper assessment or collection of tax are likely to be kept or concealed at any premises or place,

the Judge may issue a search warrant.

(*c*) A search warrant issued under this subsection shall be expressed and shall operate to authorise an authorised officer accompanied by such other named officers of the Revenue Commissioners and such other named persons as the authorised officer considers necessary, at any time or times within one month of the date of issue of the warrant, to enter (if need be by force) the premises or other place named or specified in the warrant, to search such premises or other place, to examine anything found there, to inspect any records found there and, if there are reasonable grounds for suspecting that any records found there are material to the proper assessment or collection of tax, or that the records may be required for the purpose of any legal proceedings instituted by an officer of the Revenue Commissioners or for the purpose of any criminal proceedings, remove such records and retain them for so long as they are reasonably required for the purpose aforesaid.][4]

(3) A person who does not comply with any requirement of an authorised officer in the exercise or performance of the authorised officer's powers or duties under this section shall be liable to a penalty of [€1,265][5].

(4) An authorised officer when exercising or performing his or her powers or duties under this section shall on request show his or her authorisation for the purposes of this section.

Amendments

[1] Defintion of "records" substituted by FA 2002 s 132(*d*) with effect from 1 January 2002.

[2] Substituted by SDCA 1999 s 162 and Sch 4 with effect from 15 December 1999; previously "section 16 of the Stamp Act, 1891".

[3] Subs (2)(*d*) deleted by FA 1999 s 207(*f*)(i) with effect from 25 March 1999.

4   Subs (2A) inserted by FA 1999 s 207(*f*)(ii) with effect from 25 March 1999.

5   Substituted by FA 2001 s 240(1) and (2)(*k*) and Sch 5 Pt 1 as respects any act or omission which takes place or begins on or after 1 January 2002; previously "£1,000".

Cross-references

Authorised officers and Garda Síochána: s 906.

This section to be construed together with the Customs Acts, in so far as relating to customs: s 1104(2).

This section to be construed together with the Value Added Tax Acts 1972-1997, in so far as relating to value added tax: s 1104(3).

This section to be construed together with the Stamp Duties Consolidation Act 1999 and the enactments amending or extending that Act, in so far as relating to stamp duties: s 1104(4).

This section to be construed together with the Capital Acquisitions Tax Act 1976, and the enactments amending or extending that Act, in so far as relating to capital acquisitions tax: s 1104(5).

This section to be construed together with FA 1983 Pt VI and the enactments amending or extending that Part, in so far as relating to residential property tax: s 1104(6).

Revenue information

Information leaflet IT32 - Revenue Audit - Guide for Small Businesses

Code of Practice for Revenue Auditors (Nov. 1998)

Statement of practice

Revenue powers: SP GEN/1/94, May 1994.

Case law

Held was a clear implication that the time and place for such inspection set by the taxpayer had to be reasonable: *Johnson v IRC*, [1996] STI 270.

Definition

inspector: ss 2(1), 5(1), 852; person: IA 1937 s 11(*c*); profession: ss 2(1), 5(1); trade: ss 3(1), 4(1), 5(1).

Former enactment

FA 1976 s 34; FA 1992 s 232.

906 Authorised officers and Garda Síochána

Where an authorised officer (within the meaning of section 903, 904 or 905, as the case may be) in accordance with section 903, 904 or 905 enters any premises or place, the authorised officer may be accompanied by a member or members of the Garda Síochána, and any such member may arrest without warrant any person who obstructs or interferes with the authorised officer in the exercise or performance of his or her powers or duties under any of those sections.

Cross-references

This section to be construed together with the Customs Acts, in so far as relating to customs: s 1104(2).

This section to be construed together with the Value Added Tax Acts 1972-1997, in so far as relating to value added tax: s 1104(3).

This section to be construed together with the Stamp Duties Consolidation Act 1999 and the enactments amending or extending that Act, in so far as relating to stamp duties: s 1104(4).

This section to be construed together with the Capital Acquisitions Tax Act 1976, and the enactments amending or extending that Act, in so far as relating to capital acquisitions tax: s 1104(5).

This section to be construed together with FA 1983 Pt VI and the enactments amending or extending that Part, in so far as relating to residential property tax: s 1104(6).

Former enactment

FA 1992 s 236.

906A Information to be furnished by financial institutions

[(1) In this section and in sections 907 and 908—

"the Acts" has the meaning assigned to it by section 1078(1);

"authorised officer" means an officer of the Revenue Commissioners authorised by them in writing to exercise the powers conferred by this section, or, as the case may be, section 907 or 908;

"books, records or other documents" includes—

    (*a*)   any records used in the business of a financial institution, or used in the transfer department of a financial institution acting as registrar of securities, whether—

        (i)   comprised in bound volume, loose-leaf binders or other loose-leaf filing system, loose-leaf ledger sheets, pages, folios or cards, or

        (ii)   kept on microfilm, magnetic tape or in any non-legible form (by the use of electronics or otherwise) which is capable of being reproduced in a legible form,

    (*b*)   every electronic or other automatic means, if any, by which any such thing in non-legible form is so capable of being reproduced,

    (*c*)   documents in manuscript, documents which are typed, printed, stencilled or created by any other mechanical or partly mechanical process in use from time to time and documents which are produced by any photographic or photostatic process, and

    (*d*)   correspondence and records of other communications between a financial institution and its customers;

"connected person" has the same meaning as in section 10; but an individual (other than in the capacity as a trustee of a settlement) shall be connected with another individual only if that other individual is the spouse of or a minor child of the first-mentioned individual;

"deposit" and **"interest"** have, respectively, the meaning assigned to them by section 256(1);

[**"financial institution"** means—

    (*a*)   a person who holds or has held a licence under section 9 of the Central Bank Act, 1971,

    (*b*)   a person referred to in section 7(4) of the Central Bank Act, 1971, or

    (*c*)   a credit institution (within the meaning of the European Communities (Licensing and Supervision of Credit Institutions) Regulations, 1992 (SI No 395 of 1992)) which has been authorised by the Central Bank of Ireland to carry on business of a credit institution in accordance with the provisions of the supervisory enactments (within the meaning of those Regulations);][1]

"liability" in relation to a person means any liability in relation to tax to which the person is or may be, or may have been, subject, or the amount of such liability;

"tax" means any tax, duty, levy or charge under the care and management of the Revenue Commissioners.

(2) Notwithstanding any obligation as to secrecy or other restriction upon disclosure of information imposed by or under statute or otherwise, and subject to this section, an authorised officer may, for the purpose of enquiring into a liability in relation to a person (in this section referred to as the **"taxpayer"**), serve on a financial institution a notice in writing requiring the financial institution, within such period as may be specified in the notice, not being less than 30 days from the date of the service of the notice, to do either or both of the following, namely—

(a) to make available for inspection by the authorised officer such books, records or other documents as are in the financial institution's power, possession or procurement and as contain, or may (in the authorised officer's opinion formed on reasonable grounds) contain, information relevant to a liability in relation to the taxpayer,

(b) to furnish to the authorised officer, in writing or otherwise, such information, explanations and particulars as the authorised officer may reasonably require, being information, explanations and particulars that are relevant to any such liability,

and which are specified in the notice.

(3) Where, in compliance with the requirements of a notice under subsection (2), a financial institution makes available for inspection by an authorised officer, books, records or other documents, it shall afford the authorised officer reasonable assistance, including information, explanations and particulars, in relation to the use of all the electronic or other automatic means, if any, by which the books, records or other documents, in so far as they are in a non-legible form, are capable of being reproduced in a legible form and any data equipment or any associated apparatus or material.

(4) An authorised officer shall not serve a notice on a financial institution under subsection (2) without the consent in writing of a Revenue Commissioner and without having reasonable grounds to believe that the financial institution is likely to have information relevant to a liability in relation to the taxpayer.

(5) Without prejudice to the generality of subsection (2), the books, records or other documents which a financial institution may be required by notice under that subsection to deliver or to make available and the information, explanations and particulars which it may likewise be required to furnish, may include books, records or other documents and information, explanations and particulars relating to a person who is connected with the taxpayer.

(6) The persons who may be treated as a taxpayer for the purposes of this section include a company which has been dissolved and an individual who has died.

(7) A notice served under subsection (2) shall name the taxpayer in relation to whose liability the authorised officer is enquiring.

(8) Where an authorised officer serves a notice under subsection (2), a copy of such notice shall be given by the authorised officer to the taxpayer concerned.

(9) Where, in compliance with a notice served under subsection (2), a financial institution makes books, records or other documents available for inspection by an

authorised officer, the authorised officer may make extracts from or copies of all or any part of the books, records or other documents.

(10) A financial institution which fails or refuses to comply with a notice issued under subsection (2) or which fails or refuses to afford reasonable assistance to an authorised officer as required under subsection (3), shall be liable to a penalty of [€19,045][2] and, if the failure or refusal to comply with such notice continues after the expiry of the period specified in the notice served under subsection (2), a further penalty of [€2,535][3] for each day on which the failure or refusal continues.][4]

Amendments

[1]   Definition of "financial institution" substituted by FA 2000 s 68(*c*) with effect from 6 April 2000.

[2]   Substituted by FA 2001 s 240(1) and (2)(*k*) and Sch 5 Pt 1 as respects any act or omission which takes place or begins on or after 1 January 2002; previously "£15,000".

[3]   Substituted by FA 2001 s 240(1) and (2)(*k*) and Sch 5 Pt 1 as respects any act or omission which takes place or begins on or after 1 January 2002; previously "£2,000".

[4]   Section 906A inserted by FA 1999 s 207(*g*) with effect from 25 March 1999.

910 Power to obtain information from Minister of the Government

[(1) For the purposes of the assessment, charge, collection and recovery of any tax or duty placed under their care and management, the Revenue Commissioners may, by notice in writing, request any Minister of the Government or any body established by or under statute to provide them with such information in the possession of that Minister or body in relation to payments for any purposes made by that Minister or by that body, whether on that Minister's or that body's own behalf or on behalf of any other person, to such persons or classes of persons as the Revenue Commissioners may specify in the notice and a Minister of the Government or body of whom or of which such a request is made shall provide such information as may be so specified.][1]

(2) The Revenue Commissioners may nominate any of their officers to perform any acts and discharge any functions authorised by this section to be performed or discharged by the Revenue Commissioners.

Amendments

[1]   Subs (1) substituted by FA 1999 s 208 with effect from 25 March 1999.

Cross-references

This section to be construed together with the Customs Acts, in so far as relating to customs: s 1104(2).

This section to be construed together with the Value Added Tax Acts 1972-1997, in so far as relating to value added tax: s 1104(3).

This section to be construed together with the Stamp Act 1891 and the enactments amending or extending that Act, in so far as relating to stamp duties: s 1104(4).

This section to be construed together with the Capital Acquisitions Tax Act 1976, and the enactments amending or extending that Act, in so far as relating to capital acquisitions tax: s 1104(5).

This section to be construed together with FA 1983 Pt VI and the enactments amending or extending that Part, in so far as relating to residential property tax: s 1104(6).

Definitions

person: IA 1937 s 11(*c*); tax: s 3(1).

Former enactment

FA 1995 s 175.

PART 42
COLLECTION AND RECOVERY

CHAPTER 1
Income Tax

969 Duration of imprisonment for non-payment of income tax

Amendments

Section 969 repealed by FA 1999 s 197 and Sch 6 with effect from 25 March 1999.

CHAPTER 5
Miscellaneous provisions

1002 Deduction from payments due to defaulters of amounts due in relation to tax

(1) (*a*) In this section, except where the context otherwise requires—

"the Acts" means—

(i) the Customs Acts,

(ii) the statutes relating to the duties of excise and to the management of those duties,

(iii) the Tax Acts,

(iv) the Capital Gains Tax Acts,

(v) the Value-Added Tax Act, 1972, and the enactments amending or extending that Act,

(vi) the Capital Acquisitions Tax Act, 1976, and the enactments amending or extending that Act, and

(vii) the [Stamp Duties Consolidation Act, 1999],[1] and the enactments amending or extending that Act,

and any instruments made thereunder;

"additional debt", in relation to a relevant person who has received a notice of attachment in respect of a taxpayer, means any amount which, at any time after the time of the receipt by the relevant person of the notice of attachment but before the end of the relevant period in relation to the notice, would be a debt due by the relevant person to the taxpayer if a notice of attachment were received by the relevant person at that time;

"debt", in relation to a notice of attachment given to a relevant person in respect of a taxpayer and in relation to that relevant person and taxpayer, means, subject to paragraphs (*b*) to (*e*), the amount or aggregate amount of any money which, at the time the notice of attachment is received by the relevant person, is due by the relevant person (whether on that person's own account or as an agent or trustee) to the taxpayer, irrespective of whether the taxpayer has applied for the payment (to the taxpayer or any other person) or for the withdrawal of all or part of the money;

"deposit" means a sum of money paid to a financial institution on terms under which it will be repaid with or without interest and either on demand or at a time or in circumstances agreed by or on behalf of the person making the payment and the financial institution to which it is made;

"emoluments" means anything assessable to income tax under Schedule E;

"financial institution" means a holder of a licence issued under section 9 of the Central Bank Act, 1971, or a person referred to in section 7(4) of that Act, and includes a branch of a financial institution which records deposits in its books as liabilities of the branch;

"further return" means a return made by a relevant person under subsection (4);

"interest on unpaid tax", in relation to a specified amount specified in a notice of attachment, means interest that has accrued to the date on which the notice of attachment is given under any provision of the Acts providing for the charging of interest in respect of the unpaid tax, including interest on an undercharge of tax which is attributable to fraud or neglect, specified in the notice of attachment;

"notice of attachment" means a notice under subsection (2);

"notice of revocation" means a notice under subsection (10);

"penalty" means a monetary penalty imposed on a taxpayer under a provision of the Acts;

"relevant period", in relation to a notice of attachment, means, as respects the relevant person to whom the notice of attachment is given, the period commencing at the time at which the notice is received by the relevant person and ending on the earliest of—

(i)   the date on which the relevant person completes the payment to the Revenue Commissioners out of the debt, or the aggregate of the debt and any additional debt, due by the relevant person to the taxpayer named in the notice, of an amount equal to the specified amount in relation to the taxpayer,

(ii)   the date on which the relevant person receives a notice of revocation of the notice of attachment, and

(iii)   where the relevant person or the taxpayer named in the notice—

    (I)   is declared bankrupt, the date the relevant person or the taxpayer is so declared, or

    (II)   is a company which commences to be wound up, the relevant date within the meaning of section 285 of the Companies Act, 1963, in relation to the winding up;

"relevant person", in relation to a taxpayer, means a person whom the Revenue Commissioners have reason to believe may have, at the time a notice of attachment is received by such person in respect of a taxpayer, a debt due to the taxpayer;

"return" means a return made by a relevant person under subsection (2)(*a*)(iii);

"specified amount" has the meaning assigned to it by subsection (2)(*a*)(ii);

"tax" means any tax, duty, levy or charge which in accordance with any provision of the Acts is placed under the care and management of the Revenue Commissioners;

"taxpayer" means a person who is liable to pay, remit or account for tax to the Revenue Commissioners under the Acts.

(*b*)   Where a relevant person is a financial institution, any amount or aggregate amount of money, including interest on that money, which at the time the notice of attachment is received by the relevant person is a deposit held by the relevant person—

    (i)   to the credit of the taxpayer for the taxpayer's sole benefit, or

    (ii)   to the credit of the taxpayer and any other person or persons for their joint benefit,

shall be regarded as a debt due by the relevant person to the taxpayer at that time.

(*c*)   Any amount of money due by the relevant person to the taxpayer as emoluments under a contract of service shall not be regarded as a debt due to the taxpayer.

(*d*)   Where there is a dispute as to an amount of money which is due by the relevant person to the taxpayer, the amount in dispute shall be disregarded for the purposes of determining the amount of the debt.

(*e*)   In the case referred to in paragraph (*b*), a deposit held by a relevant person which is a financial institution to the credit of the taxpayer and any other person or persons (in this paragraph referred to as **"the other party or parties"**) for their joint benefit shall be deemed (unless evidence to the contrary is produced to the satisfaction of the relevant person within 10 days of the giving of the notices specified in subsection (2)(*e*)) to be held to the benefit of the taxpayer and the other party or parties to the deposit equally, and accordingly only the portion of the deposit so deemed shall be regarded as a debt due by the relevant person to the taxpayer at the time the notice of attachment is received by the relevant person and, where such evidence is produced within the specified time, only so much of the deposit as is shown to be held to the benefit of the taxpayer shall be regarded as a debt due by the relevant person to the taxpayer at that time.

(2) (*a*)   Subject to subsection (3), where a taxpayer has made default whether before or after the passing of this Act in paying, remitting or accounting for any tax, interest on unpaid tax, or penalty to the Revenue Commissioners, the Revenue Commissioners may, if the taxpayer has not made good the default, give to a relevant person in relation to the taxpayer a notice in writing (in this section referred to as **"the notice of attachment"**) in which is entered—

    (i)   the taxpayer's name and address,

(ii) (I) the amount or aggregate amount, or

(II) in a case where more than one notice of attachment is given to a relevant person or relevant persons in respect of a taxpayer, a portion of the amount or aggregate amount,

of the taxes, interest on unpaid taxes and penalties in respect of which the taxpayer is in default at the time of the giving of the notice or notices of attachment (the amount, aggregate amount, or portion of the amount or aggregate amount, as the case may be, being referred to in this section as **"the specified amount"**), and

(iii) a direction to the relevant person—

(I) subject to paragraphs (*b*) and (*c*), to deliver to the Revenue Commissioners, within the period of 10 days from the time at which the notice of attachment is received by the relevant person, a return in writing specifying whether or not any debt is due by the relevant person to the taxpayer at the time the notice is received by the relevant person and, if any debt is so due, specifying the amount of the debt, and

(II) if the amount of any debt is so specified, to pay to the Revenue Commissioners within the period referred to in clause (I) a sum equal to the amount of the debt so specified.

(*b*) Where the amount of the debt due by the relevant person to the taxpayer is equal to or greater than the specified amount in relation to the taxpayer, the amount of the debt specified in the return shall be an amount equal to the specified amount.

(*c*) Where the relevant person is a financial institution and the debt due by the relevant person to the taxpayer is part of a deposit held to the credit of the taxpayer and any other person or persons to their joint benefit, the return shall be made within a period of 10 days from—

(i) the expiry of the period specified in the notices to be given under paragraph (*e*), or

(ii) the production of the evidence referred to in paragraph (*e*)(II).

(*d*) A relevant person to whom a notice of attachment has been given shall comply with the direction in the notice.

(*e*) Where a relevant person which is a financial institution is given a notice of attachment and the debt due by the relevant person to the taxpayer is part of a deposit held by the relevant person to the credit of the taxpayer and any other person or persons (in this paragraph referred to as **"the other party or parties"**) for their joint benefit, the relevant person shall on receipt of the notice of attachment give to the taxpayer and the other party or parties to the deposit a notice in writing in which is entered—

(i) the taxpayer's name and address,

(ii) the name and address of the person to whom a notice under this paragraph is given,

    (iii)   the name and address of the relevant person, and

    (iv)   the specified amount,

and which states that—

    (I)   a notice of attachment under this section has been received in respect of the taxpayer,

    (II)   under this section a deposit is deemed (unless evidence to the contrary is produced to the satisfaction of the relevant person within 10 days of the giving of the notice under this paragraph) to be held to the benefit of the taxpayer and the other party or parties to the deposit equally, and

    (III)   unless such evidence is produced within the period specified in the notice given under this paragraph—

        (A)   a sum equal to the amount of the deposit so deemed to be held to the benefit of the taxpayer (and accordingly regarded as a debt due to the taxpayer by the relevant person) shall be paid to the Revenue Commissioners, where that amount is equal to or less than the specified amount, and

        (B)   where the amount of the deposit so deemed to be held to the benefit of the taxpayer (and accordingly regarded as a debt due to the taxpayer by the relevant person) is greater than the specified amount, a sum equal to the specified amount shall be paid to the Revenue Commissioners.

(3) An amount in respect of tax, interest on unpaid tax or a penalty, as respects which a taxpayer is in default as specified in subsection (2), shall not be entered in a notice of attachment unless—

    (*a*)   a period of [14 days]² has expired from the date on which such default commenced, and

    (*b*)   the Revenue Commissioners have given the taxpayer a notice in writing (whether or not the document containing the notice also contains other information being communicated by the Revenue Commissioners to the taxpayer), not later than 7 days before the date of the receipt by the relevant person or relevant persons concerned of a notice of attachment, stating that if the amount is not paid it may be specified in a notice or notices of attachment and recovered under this section from a relevant person or relevant persons in relation to the taxpayer.

(4) If, when a relevant person receives a notice of attachment, the amount of the debt due by the relevant person to the taxpayer named in the notice is less than the specified amount in relation to the taxpayer or no debt is so due and, at any time after the receipt of the notice and before the end of the relevant period in relation to the notice, an additional debt becomes due by the relevant person to the taxpayer, the relevant person shall within 10 days of that time—

    (*a*)   if the aggregate of the amount of any debt so due and the additional debt so due is equal to or less than the specified amount in relation to the taxpayer—

       (i)   deliver a further return to the Revenue Commissioners specifying the additional debt, and

      (ii)   pay to the Revenue Commissioners the amount of the additional debt,

and so on for each subsequent occasion during the relevant period in relation to the notice of attachment on which an additional debt becomes due by the relevant person to the taxpayer until—

      (I)   the aggregate amount of the debt and the additional debt or debts so due equals the specified amount in relation to the taxpayer, or

     (II)   paragraph (*b*) applies in relation to an additional debt, and

  (*b*)   if the aggregate amount of any debt and the additional debt or debts so due to the taxpayer is greater than the specified amount in relation to the taxpayer—

      (i)   deliver a further return to the Revenue Commissioners specifying such portion of the latest additional debt as when added to the aggregate of the debt and any earlier additional debts is equal to the specified amount in relation to the taxpayer, and

      (ii)   pay to the Revenue Commissioners that portion of the additional debt.

(5) Where a relevant person delivers, either fraudulently or negligently, an incorrect return or further return that purports to be a return or further return made in accordance with this section, the relevant person shall be deemed to be guilty of an offence under section 1078.

(6) (*a*)   Where a notice of attachment has been given to a relevant person in respect of a taxpayer, the relevant person shall not, during the relevant period in relation to the notice, make any disbursements out of the debt, or out of any additional debt, due by the relevant person to the taxpayer except to the extent that any such disbursement—

      (i)   will not reduce the debt or the aggregate of the debt and any additional debts so due to an amount that is less than the specified amount in relation to the taxpayer, or

      (ii)   is made pursuant to an order of a court.

  (*b*)   For the purposes of this section, a disbursement made by a relevant person contrary to paragraph (*a*) shall be deemed not to reduce the amount of the debt or any additional debts due by the relevant person to the taxpayer.

(7) (*a*)   Sections 1052 and 1054 shall apply to a failure by a relevant person to deliver a return required by a notice of attachment within the time specified in the notice or to deliver a further return within the time specified in subsection (4) as they apply to a failure to deliver a return referred to in section 1052.

  (*b*)   A certificate signed by an officer of the Revenue Commissioners which certifies that he or she has examined the relevant records and that it appears from those records that during a specified period a specified return was not received from a relevant person shall be evidence until the contrary is proved that the relevant person did not deliver the return during that period.

(*c*) A certificate certifying as provided by paragraph (*b*) and purporting to be signed by an officer of the Revenue Commissioners may be tendered in evidence without proof and shall be deemed until the contrary is proved to have been so signed.

(8) Where a relevant person to whom a notice of attachment in respect of a taxpayer has been given—

(*a*) delivers the return required to be delivered by that notice but fails to pay to the Revenue Commissioners within the time specified in the notice the amount specified in the return or any part of that amount, or

(*b*) delivers a further return under subsection (4) but fails to pay to the Revenue Commissioners within the time specified in that subsection the amount specified in the further return or any part of that amount,

the amount specified in the return or further return or the part of that amount, as the case may be, which the relevant person has failed to pay to the Revenue Commissioners may, if the notice of attachment has not been revoked by a notice of revocation, be sued for and recovered by action or other appropriate proceedings at the suit of an officer of the Revenue Commissioners in any court of competent jurisdiction.

(9) Nothing in this section shall be construed as rendering any failure by a relevant person to make a return or further return required by this section, or to pay to the Revenue Commissioners the amount or amounts required by this section to be paid by the relevant person, liable to be treated as a failure to which section 1078 applies.

(10)(*a*) A notice of attachment given to a relevant person in respect of a taxpayer may be revoked by the Revenue Commissioners at any time by notice in writing given to the relevant person and shall be revoked forthwith if the taxpayer has paid the specified amount to the Revenue Commissioners.

(*b*) Where in pursuance of this section a relevant person pays any amount to the Revenue Commissioners out of a debt or an additional debt due by the relevant person to the taxpayer and, at the time of the receipt by the Revenue Commissioners of that amount, the taxpayer has paid to the Revenue Commissioners the amount or aggregate amount of the taxes, interest on unpaid taxes and penalties in respect of which the taxpayer is in default at the time of the giving of the notice or notices of attachment, the first-mentioned amount shall be refunded by the Revenue Commissioners forthwith to the taxpayer.

(11) Where a notice of attachment or a notice of revocation is given to a relevant person in relation to a taxpayer, a copy of such notice shall be given by the Revenue Commissioners to the taxpayer forthwith.

(12)(*a*) Where in pursuance of this section any amount is paid to the Revenue Commissioners by a relevant person, the relevant person shall forthwith give the taxpayer concerned a notice in writing specifying the payment, its amount and the reason for which it was made.

(*b*)   On the receipt by the Revenue Commissioners of an amount paid in pursuance of this section, the Revenue Commissioners shall forthwith notify the taxpayer and the relevant person in writing of such receipt.

(13) Where in pursuance of this section a relevant person pays to the Revenue Commissioners the whole or part of the amount of a debt or an additional debt due by the relevant person to a taxpayer, or any portion of such an amount, the taxpayer shall allow such payment and the relevant person shall be acquitted and discharged of the amount of the payment as if it had been paid to the taxpayer.

(14) Where in pursuance of this section a relevant person is prohibited from making any disbursement out of a debt or an additional debt due to a taxpayer, no action shall lie against the relevant person in any court by reason of a failure to make any such disbursement.

(15) Any obligation on the Revenue Commissioners to maintain secrecy or any other restriction on the disclosure of information by the Revenue Commissioners shall not apply in relation to information contained in a notice of attachment.

(16) A notice of attachment in respect of a taxpayer shall not be given to a relevant person at a time when the relevant person or the taxpayer is an undischarged bankrupt or a company being wound up.

(17) The Revenue Commissioners may nominate any of their officers to perform any acts and discharge any functions authorised by this section to be performed or discharged by the Revenue Commissioners.

Amendments

1   Substituted by SDCA 1999 s 162 and Sch 4 with effect from 15 December 1999; previously "Stamp Act, 1891".

2   Substituted by FA 2001 s 238 with effect from 6 April 2001; previously "one month".

Cross-references

Taxes (Offset of Repayments) Regulations 2001, SI No 399 of 2001, reg 2(1) (interpretation - "liability of enforcement" para (*c*)).

This section to be construed together with the Customs Acts, in so far as relating to customs: s 1104(2).

This section to be construed together with the Value Added Tax Acts 1972-1997, in so far as relating to value added tax: s 1104(3).

This section to be construed together with the Stamp Act 1891 and the enactments amending or extending that Act, in so far as relating to stamp duties: s 1104(4).

This section to be construed together with the Capital Acquisitions Tax Act 1976, and the enactments amending or extending that Act, in so far as relating to capital acquisitions tax: s 1104(5).

Penalty, subss (2)(*a*)(iii)(I), (*c*), (4)(*a*)(i), (*b*)(i): Sch 29 column 1.

Definitions

company: ss 4(1), 5(1); person: IA 1937 s 11(*c*); Tax Acts: s 1(2); writing: IA 1937 Sch.

Former enactments

FA 1988 s 73(1)(*b*)-(16) and (18); FA 1992 s 241(*a*)-(*d*).

1006A Offset between taxes

[(1) In this section—

"Acts" means—

(*a*)   the Tax Acts,

(*b*)   the Capital Gains Tax Acts,

(*c*)   the Value-Added Tax Act, 1972, and the enactments amending or extending that Act,

(*d*)   the statutes relating to the duties of excise and to the management of those duties,

(*e*)   the Capital Acquisitions Tax Act, 1976, and the enactments amending or extending that Act,

(*f*)   the Stamp Duties Consolidation Act, 1999,

(*g*)   Part VI of the Finance Act, 1983, and the enactments amending or extending that Part,

(*h*)   Chapter IV of Part II of the Finance Act, 1992,

and any instrument made thereunder;

["**claim**" means a claim that gives rise to either or both a repayment of tax and a payment of interest payable in respect of such a repayment under any of the Acts and includes part of such a claim;][1]

["**liability**" means any tax due or estimated to be due under the Acts for any period or in respect of any event, as may be appropriate in the circumstances, and includes any interest due under the Acts in respect of that tax;][2]

"**overpayment**" means a payment or remittance under the Acts (including part of such a payment or remittance) which is in excess of the amount of the liability against which it is [credited;][3]

["**tax**" means any tax, duty, levy or other charge under any of the Acts.][4]

[(2) Notwithstanding any other provision of the Acts, where the Revenue Commissioners are satisfied that a person has not complied with the obligations imposed on the person by the Acts, in relation to either or both—

(*a*)   the payment of a liability required to be paid, and

(*b*)   the delivery of returns required to be made,

they may, in a case where a repayment is due to the person in respect of a claim or overpayment—

(i)   where paragraph (*a*) applies, or where paragraphs (*a*) and (*b*) apply, instead of making the repayment set the amount of the claim or overpayment against any liability due under the Acts, and

(ii)   where paragraph (*b*) only applies, withhold making the repayment until such time as the returns required to be delivered have been delivered.

(2A) Where the Revenue Commissioners have set or withheld a repayment by virtue of subsection (2), they shall give notice in writing to that effect to the person concerned and, where subsection (2)(ii) applies, interest shall not be payable under any provision of the Acts from the date of such notice in respect of any repayment so withheld.][5]

(3) The Revenue Commissioners shall make regulations for the purpose of giving effect to this section and, without prejudice to the generality of the foregoing, such regulations shall provide for the order of priority of liabilities due under the Acts against which any claim or overpayment is to be set in accordance with subsection (2).

(4) Every regulation made under this section shall be laid before Dáil Éireann as soon as may be after it is made and, if a resolution annulling the regulation is passed by Dáil Éireann within the next 21 days on which Dáil Éireann has sat after the regulation is laid before it, the regulation shall be annulled accordingly, but without prejudice to the validity of anything previously done thereunder.

[(5) Any act to be performed or function to be discharged (other than the making of regulations) by the Revenue Commissioners which is authorised by this section may be performed or discharged by any of their officers acting under their authority.][6][7]

Amendments

[1]   Definition of "claim" substituted by FA 2002 s 125(*a*)(i)(I) with effect from 25 March 2002.

[2]   Definition of "liability" substituted by FA 2002 s 125(*a*)(i)(II) with effect from 25 March 2002.

[3]   Substituted by FA 2002 s 125(*a*)(i)(III) with effect from 25 March 2002; previously "credited.".

[4]   Definition of "tax" substituted by FA 2002 s 125(*a*)(i)(IV) with effect from 25 March 2002.

[5]   Subs (2) substituted and subs (2A) inserted by FA 2001 s 239(*b*) with effect from 6 April 2001.

[6]   Subs (5) inserted by FA 2002 s 125(*a*)(ii) with effect from 25 March 2002.

[7]   Section 1006A inserted by FA 2000 s 164 with effect from 23 March 2000.

Cross-references

Relief on retirement for certain income of certain sportsperson: s 480A(2).

Regulations

Taxes (Offset of Repayments) Regulations 2001, SI No 399 of 2001.

Tax Briefing

TB45 Oct 2001 pp 10-11 - Offset of Repayment Regulations.

Definitions

Dáil Éireann: IA 1937 Sch; person: IA 1937 s 11(*c*); writing: IA 1937 Sch.

PART 47
PENALTIES, REVENUE OFFENCES, INTEREST ON OVERDUE TAX AND OTHER SANCTIONS

CHAPTER 4
Revenue offences

1078 Revenue offences

(1) In this Part—

"the Acts" means—

    (*a*) the Customs Acts,

    (*b*) the statutes relating to the duties of excise and to the management of those duties,

    (*c*) the Tax Acts,

    (*d*) the Capital Gains Tax Acts,

    (*e*) the Value-Added Tax Act, 1972, and the enactments amending or extending that Act,

    (*f*) the Capital Acquisitions Tax Act, 1976, and the enactments amending or extending that Act,

    (*g*) the statutes relating to stamp duty and to the management of that duty, and (*h*)   Part VI of the Finance Act, 1983,

and any instruments made thereunder and any instruments made under any other enactment and relating to tax;

"authorised officer" means an officer of the Revenue Commissioners authorised by them in writing to exercise any of the powers conferred by the Acts;

"tax" means any tax, duty, levy or charge under the care and management of the Revenue Commissioners.

(2) A person shall, without prejudice to any other penalty to which the person may be liable, be guilty of an offence under this section if the person—

(*a*)   knowingly or wilfully delivers any incorrect return, statement or accounts or knowingly or wilfully furnishes any incorrect information in connection with any tax,

(*b*)   knowingly aids, abets, assists, incites or induces another person to make or deliver knowingly or wilfully any incorrect return, statement or accounts in connection with any tax,

(*c*)   claims or obtains relief or exemption from, or repayment of, any tax, being a relief, exemption or repayment to which, to the person's knowledge, the person is not entitled,

(*d*)   knowingly or wilfully issues or produces any incorrect invoice, receipt, instrument or other document in connection with any tax,

[(*dd*)   (i)   fails to make any deduction of dividend withholding tax (within the meaning of Chapter 8A of Part 6) required to be made by the person under section 172B(1),

(ii)   fails, having made that deduction, to pay the sum deducted to the Collector-General within the time specified in that behalf in section 172K(2),

(iii)   fails to make any reduction required to be made by the person under section 172B(2),

(iv)   fails, having made that reduction, to pay to the Collector-General the amount referred to in section 172B(2)(*d*), which amount is treated under that section as if it were a deduction of dividend withholding tax (within the meaning of Chapter 8A of Part 6), within the time specified in that behalf in section 172K(2), or

(v)   fails to pay to the Collector-General, within the time specified in that behalf in section 172K(2), an amount referred to in section 172B(3)(*a*) which is required to be paid by the person to the Collector-General and which is treated under that section as if it were a deduction of dividend withholding tax (within the meaning of Chapter 8A of Part 6),][1]

(*e*)   (i)   fails to make any deduction required to be made by the person under section 257(1),

(ii)   fails, having made the deduction, to pay the sum deducted to the Collector-General within the time specified in that behalf in section 258(3), or

(iii)   fails to pay to the Collector-General an amount on account of appropriate tax (within the meaning of Chapter 4 of Part 8) within the time specified in that behalf in section 258(4),

(f) (i) fails to make any deduction required to be made by the person under section 734(5), or

    (ii) fails, having made the deduction, to pay the sum deducted to the Collector-General within the time specified in paragraph 1(3) of Schedule 18,

(g) [fails without reasonable excuse]² to comply with any provision of the Acts requiring—

    (i) the furnishing of a return of income, profits or gains, or of sources of income, profits or gains, for the purposes of any tax,

    (ii) the furnishing of any other return, certificate, notification, particulars, or any statement or evidence, for the purposes of any tax,

    (iii) the keeping or retention of books, records, accounts or other documents for the purposes of any tax, or

    (iv) the production of books, records, accounts or other documents, when so requested, for the purposes of any tax,

(h) knowingly or wilfully, and within the time limits specified for their retention, destroys, defaces or conceals from an authorised officer—

    (i) any documents, or

    (ii) any other written or printed material in any form, including any information stored, maintained or preserved by means of any mechanical or electronic device, whether or not stored, maintained or preserved in a legible form, which a person is obliged by any provision of the Acts to keep, to issue or to produce for inspection,

[(hh) knowingly or wilfully falsifies, conceals, destroys or otherwise disposes of, or causes or permits the falsification, concealment, destruction or disposal of, any books, records or other document—

    (i) which the person has been given the opportunity to deliver, or as the case may be, to make available in accordance with section 900(3), or

    (ii) which the person has been required to deliver or, as the case may be, to make available in accordance with a notice served under section 900, 902, 906A or 907, or an order made under section 901, 902A or 908.]³

(i) fails to remit any income tax payable pursuant to Chapter 4 of Part 42, and the regulations under that Chapter, or value-added tax within the time specified in that behalf in relation to income tax or value-added tax, as the case may be, by the Acts, or

(j) obstructs or interferes with any officer of the Revenue Commissioners, or any other person, in the exercise or performance of powers or duties under the Acts for the purposes of any tax.

(3) A person convicted of an offence under this section shall be liable—

(a) on summary conviction to a fine of [€1,900]⁴ which may be mitigated to not less than one fourth part of such fine or, at the discretion of the court, to imprisonment for a term not exceeding 12 months or to both the fine and the imprisonment, or

(b) on conviction on indictment, to a fine not exceeding [€126,970][5] or, at the discretion of the court, to imprisonment for a term not exceeding 5 years or to both the fine and the imprisonment.

[(3A) Where a person has been convicted of an offence referred to in subparagraph (i), (ii) or (iv) of subsection (2)(g), then, if an application is made, or caused to be made to the court in that regard, the court may make an order requiring the person concerned to comply with any provision of the Acts relating to the requirements specified in the said subparagraph (i), (ii) or (iv), as the case may be.][6]

[(3B) A person shall, without prejudice to any other penalty to which the person may be liable, be guilty of an offence under this section if the person fails or refuses to comply with an order referred to in subsection (3A).][7]

(4) Section 13 of the Criminal Procedure Act, 1967, shall apply in relation to an offence under this section as if, in place of the penalties specified in subsection (3) of that section, there were specified in that subsection the penalties provided for by subsection (3)(a), and the reference in subsection (2)(a) of section 13 of the Criminal Procedure Act, 1967, to the penalties provided for in subsection (3) of that section shall be construed and apply accordingly.

(5) Where an offence under this section is committed by a body corporate and the offence is shown to have been committed with the consent or connivance of any person who, when the offence was committed, was a director, manager, secretary or other officer of the body corporate, or a member of the committee of management or other controlling authority of the body corporate, that person shall also be deemed to be guilty of the offence and may be proceeded against and punished accordingly.

(6) In any proceedings under this section, a return or statement delivered to an inspector or other officer of the Revenue Commissioners under any provision of the Acts and purporting to be signed by any person shall be deemed until the contrary is proved to have been so delivered and to have been signed by that person.

(7) Notwithstanding any other enactment, proceedings in respect of an offence under this section may be instituted within 10 years from the date of the commission of the offence or incurring of the penalty, as the case may be.

(8) Section 1 of the Probation of Offenders Act, 1907, shall not apply in relation to offences under this section.

(9) Sections 987(4) and 1052(4), subsections (3) and (7) of section 1053, and sections 1068 and 1069 and sections 26(6) and 27(7) of the Value-Added Tax Act, 1972, shall, with any necessary modifications, apply for the purposes of this section as they apply for the purposes of those sections, including, in the case of such of those sections as are applied by the Capital Gains Tax Acts, the Corporation Tax Acts, or Part VI of the Finance Act, 1983, the purposes of those sections as so applied.

Amendments

1.   Subs (2)(*dd*) inserted by FA 1999 s 27(*b*) with effect from 6 April 1999.

2.   Substituted by FA 2002 s 133(*a*) with effect from 25 March 2002; previously "knowingly or wilfully fails".

3.   Subs (2)(*hh*) inserted by FA 1999 s 211(*a*) with effect from 25 March 1999.

[4]   Substituted by FA 2001 s 233(2)(*a*) with effect from 1 January 2002; previously "£1,500".

[5]   Substituted by FA 2001 s 240(1) and (2)(*k*) and Sch 5 Pt 1 as respects any act or omission which takes place or begins on or after 1 January 2002; previously "£100,000".

[6]   Subs (3A) inserted by FA 1999 s 211(*c*) with effect from 25 March 1999.

[7]   Subs (3B) inserted by FA 2002 s 133(*b*) with effect from 25 March 2002.

Cross-references

Application to High Court: information from third party, meaning of "the Acts" applied: s 902A(1).

Company law, subs (1): Companies Act 1990 s 21(1)(*a*)(i)(V).

Deduction from payments due to defaulters: s 1002(5), (9).

Information to be furnished by financial institutions, meaning of "the Acts" applied: s 906A(1).

Information to be furnished by third party: request of an authorised officer: s 902(11).

Inspection of documents and records, meaning of "the Acts" applied: s 905(2A)(*a*).

Penalty for false statement made to obtain allowance, subss (4), (6)-(8): s 1056(4).

Revenue offence: power to obtain information from financial institutions, meaning of "offence" applied: s 908A(1); subs (1): s 908A(1) ("the Acts").

This section to be construed together with the Customs Acts, in so far as relating to customs: s 1104(2).

This section to be construed together with the Value Added Tax Acts 1972-1997, in so far as relating to value added tax: s 1104(3).

This section to be construed together with the Stamp Act 1891 and the enactments amending or extending that Act, in so far as relating to stamp duties: s 1104(4).

This section to be construed together with the Capital Acquisitions Tax Act 1976, and the enactments amending or extending that Act, in so far as relating to capital acquisitions tax: s 1104(5).

This section to be construed together with FA 1983 Pt VI and the enactments amending or extending that Part, in so far as relating to residential property tax: s 1104(6).

Case law

Meaning of "criminal matter": *Director of Public Prosecutions v Seamus Boyle*, ITR Vol IV, p 395.

Subs (2)(*e*): District Justice not entitled to conclude, on basis of Revenue certificate, that taxpayer had "knowingly and wilfully" failed to submit return of income; taxpayer not present at District Court hearing and was entitled to defend himself: *O'Callaghan v Clifford and others*, ITR Vol IV, p 478.

Tax Briefing

TB36 June 1999 pp 3-4 - Revenue's Prosecution Policy.

TB38 Dec 1999 pp 10-11 - Criminal Proceedings.

Definitions

Collector-General: ss 2(1), 851; inspector: ss 2(1), 5(1), 852; month: IA 1937 Sch; person: IA 1937 s 11(*c*); profits: s 4(1); statute: s 2(1), IA 1937 s 3; Tax Acts: s 1(2).

Former enactments

FA 1983 s 94; FA 1986 s 40(2); FA 1989 s 18 and Sch 1 para 3(2); FA 1992 s 243; FA 1996 s 132(1)-(2) and Sch 5 Pt I para 13(2) and Pt II.

1079 Duties of relevant person in relation to certain revenue offences

(1) In this section—

"the Acts" means—

    (*a*)   the Customs Acts,

    (*b*)   the statutes relating to the duties of excise and to the management of those duties,

    (*c*)   the Tax Acts,

    (*d*)   the Capital Gains Tax Acts,

    (*e*)   the Value-Added Tax Act, 1972, and the enactments amending or extending that Act,

    (*f*)   the Capital Acquisitions Tax Act, 1976, and the enactments amending or extending that Act,

(g)   the statutes relating to stamp duty and to the management of that duty,

and any instruments made thereunder and any instruments made under any other enactment and relating to tax;

"appropriate officer" means any officer nominated by the Revenue Commissioners to be an appropriate officer for the purposes of this section;

"company" means any body corporate;

"relevant person", in relation to a company and subject to subsection (2), means a person who—

(a)   (i)   is an auditor to the company appointed in accordance with section 160 of the Companies Act, 1963 (as amended by the Companies Act, 1990), or

(ii)   in the case of an industrial and provident society or a friendly society, is a public auditor to the society for the purposes of the Industrial and Provident Societies Acts, 1893 to 1978, and the Friendly Societies Acts, 1896 to 1977,

or

(b)   with a view to reward, assists or advises the company in the preparation or delivery of any information, declaration, return, records, accounts or other document which he or she knows will be or is likely to be used for any purpose of tax;

"relevant offence" means an offence committed by a company which consists of the company—

(a)   knowingly or wilfully delivering any incorrect return, statement or accounts or knowingly or wilfully furnishing or causing to be furnished any incorrect information in connection with any tax,

(b)   knowingly or wilfully claiming or obtaining relief or exemption from, or repayment of, any tax, being a relief, exemption or repayment to which there is no entitlement,

(c)   knowingly or wilfully issuing or producing any incorrect invoice, receipt, instrument or other document in connection with any tax, or

(d)   knowingly or wilfully failing to comply with any provision of the Acts requiring the furnishing of a return of income, profits or gains, or of sources of income, profits or gains, for the purposes of any tax, but an offence under this paragraph committed by a company shall not be a relevant offence if the company has made a return of income, profits or gains to the Revenue Commissioners in respect of an accounting period falling wholly or partly in the period of 3 years preceding the accounting period in respect of which the offence was committed;

"tax" means any tax, duty, levy or charge under the care and management of the Revenue Commissioners.

(2) For the purposes of paragraph (b) of the definition of **"relevant person"**, a person who but for this subsection would be treated as a relevant person in relation to a company shall not be so treated if the person assists or advises the company solely in the person's capacity as an employee of the company, and a person shall be treated as assisting or advising the company in that capacity where the person's income from

assisting or advising the company consists solely of emoluments to which Chapter 4 of Part 42 applies.

(3) If, having regard solely to information obtained in the course of examining the accounts of a company, or in the course of assisting or advising a company in the preparation or delivery of any information, declaration, return, records, accounts or other document for the purposes of tax, as the case may be, a person who is a relevant person in relation to the company becomes aware that the company has committed, or is in the course of committing, one or more relevant offences, the person shall, if the offence or offences are material—

   (*a*)   communicate particulars of the offence or offences in writing to the company without undue delay and request the company to—

      (i)   take such action as is necessary for the purposes of rectifying the matter, or

      (ii)   notify an appropriate officer of the offence or offences,

      not later than 6 months after the time of communication, and

   (*b*)   (i)   unless it is established to the person's satisfaction that the necessary action has been taken or notification made, as the case may be, under paragraph (*a*), cease to act as the auditor to the company or to assist or advise the company in such preparation or delivery as is specified in paragraph (*b*) of the definition of **"relevant person"**, and

      (ii)   shall not so act, assist or advise before a time which is the earlier of—

         (I)   3 years after the time at which the particulars were communicated under paragraph (*a*), and

         (II)   the time at which it is established to the person's satisfaction that the necessary action has been taken or notification made, as the case may be, under paragraph (*a*).

(4) Nothing in paragraph (*b*) of subsection (3) shall prevent a person from assisting or advising a company in preparing for, or conducting, legal proceedings, either civil or criminal, which are extant or pending at a time which is 6 months after the time of communication under paragraph (*a*) of that subsection.

(5) Where a person, being in relation to a company a relevant person within the meaning of paragraph (*a*) of the definition of **"relevant person"**, ceases under this section to act as auditor to the company, then, the person shall deliver—

   (*a*)   a notice in writing to the company stating that he or she is so resigning, and

   (*b*)   a copy of the notice to an appropriate officer not later than 14 days after he or she has delivered the notice to the company.

(6) A person shall be guilty of an offence under this section if the person—

   (*a*)   fails to comply with subsection (3) or (5), or

   (*b*)   knowingly or wilfully makes a communication under subsection (3) which is incorrect.

(7) Where a relevant person is convicted of an offence under this section, the person shall be liable—

(*a*) on summary conviction, to a fine of [€1,265][1] which may be mitigated to not less than one-fourth part of such fine, or

(*b*) on conviction on indictment, to a fine not exceeding [€6,345][2] or, at the discretion of the court, to imprisonment for a term not exceeding 2 years or to both the fine and the imprisonment.

(8) Section 13 of the Criminal Procedure Act, 1967, shall apply in relation to this section as if, in place of the penalties specified in subsection (3) of that section, there were specified in that subsection the penalties provided for by subsection (7)(*a*), and the reference in subsection (2)(*a*) of section 13 of the Criminal Procedure Act, 1967, to the penalties provided for in subsection (3) of that section shall be construed and apply accordingly.

(9) Notwithstanding any other enactment, proceedings in respect of this section may be instituted within 6 years from the time at which a person is required under subsection (3) to communicate particulars of an offence or offences in writing to a company.

(10) It shall be a good defence in a prosecution for an offence under subsection (6)(*a*) in relation to a failure to comply with subsection (3) for an accused (being a person who is a relevant person in relation to a company) to show that he or she was in the ordinary scope of professional engagement assisting or advising the company in preparing for legal proceedings and would not have become aware that one or more relevant offences had been committed by the company if he or she had not been so assisting or advising.

(11) Where a person who is a relevant person takes any action required by subsection (3) or (5), no duty to which the person may be subject shall be regarded as having been contravened and no liability or action shall lie against the person in any court for having taken such action.

(12) The Revenue Commissioners may nominate an officer to be an appropriate officer for the purposes of this section, and the name of an officer so nominated and the address to which copies of notices under subsection (3) or (5) shall be delivered shall be published in Iris Oifigiúil.

(13) This section shall apply as respects a relevant offence committed by a company in respect of tax which is—

(*a*) assessable by reference to accounting periods, for any accounting period beginning after the 30th day of June, 1995,

(*b*) assessable by reference to years of assessment, for the year 1995-96 and subsequent years of assessment,

(*c*) payable by reference to a taxable period, for a taxable period beginning after the 30th day of June, 1995,

(*d*) chargeable on gifts or inheritances taken on or after the 30th day of June, 1995,

(*e*) chargeable on instruments executed on or after the 30th day of June, 1995, or

(*f*) payable in any other case, on or after the 30th day of June, 1995.

Amendments

[1] Substituted by FA 2001 s 240(1) and (2)(*k*) and Sch 5 Pt 1 as respects any act or omission which takes place or begins on or after 1 January 2002; previously "£1,000".

[2] Substituted by FA 2001 s 240(1) and (2)(*k*) and Sch 5 Pt 1 as respects any act or omission which takes place or begins on or after 1 January 2002; previously "£5,000".

Cross-references

This section to be construed together with the Customs Acts, in so far as relating to customs: s 1104(2).

This section to be construed together with the Value Added Tax Acts 1972-1997, in so far as relating to value added tax: s 1104(3).

This section to be construed together with the Stamp Act 1891 and the enactments amending or extending that Act, in so far as relating to stamp duties: s 1104(4).

This section to be construed together with the Capital Acquisitions Tax Act 1976, and the enactments amending or extending that Act, in so far as relating to capital acquisitions tax: s 1104(5).

Definitions

month: IA 1937 Sch; person: IA 1937 s 11(c); writing: IA 1937 Sch; year: IA 1937 Sch; year of assessment: ss 2(1), 5(1).

Former enactment

FA 1995 s 172.

CHAPTER 6
Other sanctions

1086 Publication of names of tax defaulters

(1) In this section—

"the Acts" means—

    (*a*)   the Tax Acts,

    (*b*)   the Capital Gains Tax Acts,

    (*c*)   the Value-Added Tax Act, 1972, and the enactments amending or extending that Act,

    (*d*)   the Capital Acquisitions Tax Act, 1976, and the enactments amending or extending that Act,

    [(*e*)   the Stamp Duties Consolidation Act, 1999, and the enactments amending or extending that Act]¹

    (*f*)   Part VI of the Finance Act, 1983,

    [(*g*)   the Customs Acts,

    (*h*)   the statutes relating to the duties of excise and to the management of those duties,]²

and any instruments made thereunder;

["**tax**" means any tax, duty, levy or charge under the care and management of the Revenue Commissioners.]³

(2) The Revenue Commissioners shall, as respects each relevant period (being the period beginning on the 1st day of January, 1997, and ending on the 30th day of June, 1997, and each subsequent period of 3 months beginning with the period ending on the 30th day of September, 1997), compile a list of the names and addresses and the occupations or descriptions of every person—

    (*a*)   on whom a fine or other penalty was imposed by a court under any of the Acts during that relevant period,

    (*b*)   on whom a fine or other penalty was otherwise imposed by a court during that relevant period in respect of an act or omission by the person in relation to [tax,]⁴

(c) in whose case the Revenue Commissioners, pursuant to an agreement made with the person in that relevant period, refrained from initiating proceedings for the recovery of any fine or penalty of the kind mentioned in paragraphs (a) and (b) and, in place of initiating such proceedings, accepted or undertook to accept a specified sum of money in settlement of any claim by the Revenue Commissioners in respect of any specified liability of the person under any of the Acts for—

    (i) payment of any tax,

    [(ii) except in the case of tax due by virtue of paragraphs (g) and (h) of the definition of "the Acts", payment of interest on that tax, and

    (iii) a fine or other monetary penalty in respect of that tax including penalties in respect of the failure to deliver any return, statement, declaration, list or other document in connection with the tax, or][5]

[(d) in whose case the Revenue Commissioners, having initiated proceedings for the recovery of any fine or penalty of the kind mentioned in paragraphs (a) and (b), and whether or not a fine or penalty of the kind mentioned in those paragraphs has been imposed by a court, accepted or undertook to accept, in that relevant period, a specified sum of money in settlement of any claim by the Revenue Commissioners in respect of any specified liability of the person under any of the Acts for—

    (i) payment of any tax,

    [(ii) except in the case of tax due by virtue of paragraphs (g) and (h) of the definition of "the Acts", payment of interest on that tax, and

    (iii) a fine or other monetary penalty in respect of that tax including penalties in respect of the failure to deliver any return, statement, declaration, list or other document in connection with the tax.][6]][7]

[(2A) For the purposes of subsection (2), the reference to a specified sum in paragraphs (c) and (d) of that subsection includes a reference to a sum which is the full amount of the claim by the Revenue Commissioners in respect of the specified liability referred to in those paragraphs.][8]

(3) Notwithstanding any obligation as to secrecy imposed on them by the Acts or the Official Secrets Act, 1963—

    (a) the Revenue Commissioners shall, before the expiration of 3 months from the end of each relevant period, cause each such list referred to in subsection (2) in relation to that period to be published in Iris Oifigiúil, and

    [(b) the Revenue Commissioners may, at any time after each such list referred to in subsection (2) has been published as provided for in paragraph (a), cause any such list to be publicised or reproduced, or both, in whole or in part, in such manner, form or format as they consider appropriate.][9]

(4) [Paragraph (c) and (d)][10] of subsection (2) shall not apply in relation to a person in whose case—

    (a) the Revenue Commissioners are satisfied that, before any investigation or inquiry had been commenced by them or by any of their officers into any matter occasioning a liability referred to in [those paragraphs][11] of the person, the person had voluntarily furnished to them complete information in relation to and full particulars of that matter,

(b)　section 72 of the Finance Act, 1988, or section 3 of the Waiver of Certain Tax, Interest and Penalties Act, 1993, [applied,][12]

(c)　the specified sum referred to in [paragraph (c) or (d), as the case may be,][13] of subsection (2) does not exceed [€12,700, or][14]

[(d)　the amount of fine or other penalty included in the specified sum referred to in paragraph (c) or (d), as the case may be, of subsection (2) does not exceed 15 per cent of the amount of tax included in that specified sum.][15]

(5) Any list referred to in subsection (2) shall specify in respect of each person named in the list such particulars as the Revenue Commissioners think fit—

(a)　of the matter occasioning the fine or penalty of the kind referred to in subsection (2) imposed on the person or, as the case may be, the liability of that kind to which the person was subject, and

(b)　of any interest, fine or other monetary penalty, and of any other penalty or sanction, to which that person was liable, or which was imposed on that person by a court, and which was occasioned by the matter referred to in paragraph (a).

[(5A) Without prejudice to the generality of paragraph (a) of subsection (5), such particulars as are referred to in that paragraph may include—

(a)　in a case to which paragraph (a) or (b) of subsection (2) applies, a description, in such summary form as the Revenue Commissioners may think fit, of the act, omission or offence (which may also include the circumstances in which the act or omission arose or the offence was committed) in respect of which the fine or penalty referred to in those paragraphs was imposed, and

(b)　in a case to which paragraph (c) or (d) of subsection (2) applies, a description, in such summary form as the Revenue Commissioners may think fit, of the matter occasioning the specified liability (which may also include the circumstances in which that liability arose) in respect of which the Revenue Commissioners accepted, or undertook to accept, a settlement, in accordance with those paragraphs.][16]

Amendments

1　Definition of "the Acts" para (e) substituted by FA 2002 s 126(1)(a)(i)(I) as respects fines or other penalties, as are referred to in s 1086(2)(a) and (b), which are imposed by a court, and as respects specified sums, as are referred to in s 1086(2)(c) and (d), which the Revenue Commissioners accepted, or undertook to accept, in settlement of a specified liability, on or after 25 March 2002.

2　Definition of "the Acts" paras (g) and (h) inserted by FA 2002 s 126(1)(a)(i)(II) as respects fines or other penalties, as are referred to in s 1086(2)(a) and (b), which are imposed by a court, and as respects specified sums, as are referred to in s 1086(2)(c) and (d), which the Revenue Commissioners accepted, or undertook to accept, in settlement of a specified liability, on or after 25 March 2002.

3　Definition of "tax" substituted by FA 2002 s 126(1)(a)(ii) as respects fines or other penalties, as are referred to in s 1086(2)(a) and (b), which are imposed by a court, and as respects specified sums, as are referred to in s 1086(2)(c) and (d), which the Revenue Commissioners accepted, or undertook to accept, in settlement of a specified liability, on or after 25 March 2002.

4　Substituted by FA 2000 s 162(1)(a)(i) as respects fines or other penalties, as are referred to in s 1086(2)(a)-(b), which are imposed by a court, and as respects specified sums, as are referred to in s 1086(2)(c)-(d), which the Revenue Commissioners accepted, or undertook to accept, in settlement of a specified liability, on or after 23 March 2000; previously "tax, or".

5   Subs (2)(*c*)(ii)-(iii) substituted by FA 2002 s 126(1)(*b*)(i) as respects fines or other penalties, as are referred to in s 1086(2)(*a*) and (*b*), which are imposed by a court, and as respects specified sums, as are referred to in s 1086(2)(*c*) and (*d*), which the Revenue Commissioners accepted, or undertook to accept, in settlement of a specified liability, on or after 25 March 2002.

6   Subs (2)(*d*)(ii)-(iii) substituted by FA 2002 s 126(1)(*b*)(ii) as respects fines or other penalties, as are referred to in s 1086(2)(*a*) and (*b*), which are imposed by a court, and as respects specified sums, as are referred to in s 1086(2)(*c*) and (*d*), which the Revenue Commissioners accepted, or undertook to accept, in settlement of a specified liability, on or after 25 March 2002.

7   Subs (2)(*d*) inserted by FA 2000 s 162(1)(*a*)(ii) as respects fines or other penalties, as are referred to in s 1086(2)(*a*)-(*b*), which are imposed by a court, and as respects specified sums, as are referred to in s 1086(2)(*c*)-(*d*), which the Revenue Commissioners accepted, or undertook to accept, in settlement of a specified liability, on or after 23 March 2000.

8   Subs (2A) inserted by FA 2000 s 162(1)(*b*) as respects fines or other penalties, as are referred to in s 1086(2)(*a*)-(*b*), which are imposed by a court, and as respects specified sums, as are referred to in s 1086(2)(*c*)-(*d*), which the Revenue Commissioners accepted, or undertook to accept, in settlement of a specified liability, on or after 23 March 2000.

9   Subs (3)(*b*) substituted by FA 2002 s 126(1)(*c*) as respects fines or other penalties, as are referred to in s 1086(2)(*a*) and (*b*), which are imposed by a court, and as respects specified sums, as are referred to in s 1086(2)(*c*) and (*d*), which the Revenue Commissioners accepted, or undertook to accept, in settlement of a specified liability, on or after 25 March 2002.

10   Substituted by FA 2000 s 162(1)(*c*)(i) as respects fines or other penalties, as are referred to in s 1086(2)(*a*)-(*b*), which are imposed by a court, and as respects specified sums, as are referred to in s 1086(2)(*c*)-(*d*), which the Revenue Commissioners accepted, or undertook to accept, in settlement of a specified liability, on or after 23 March 2000; previously "Paragraph (c)".

11   Substituted by FA 2002 s 126(1)(*d*)(i) as respects fines or other penalties, as are referred to in s 1086(2)(*a*) and (*b*), which are imposed by a court, and as respects specified sums, as are referred to in s 1086(2)(*c*) and (*d*), which the Revenue Commissioners accepted, or undertook to accept, in settlement of a specified liability, on or after 25 March 2002; previously "that paragraph".

12   Substituted by FA 2002 s 126(1)(*d*)(ii) as respects fines or other penalties, as are referred to in s 1086(2)(*a*) and (*b*), which are imposed by a court, and as respects specified sums, as are referred to in s 1086(2)(*c*) and (*d*), which the Revenue Commissioners accepted, or undertook to accept, in settlement of a specified liability, on or after 25 March 2002; previously "applied, or".

13   Substituted by FA 2000 s 162(1)(*c*)(ii) as respects fines or other penalties, as are referred to in s 1086(2)(*a*)-(*b*), which are imposed by a court, and as respects specified sums, as are referred to in s 1086(2)(*c*)-(*d*), which the Revenue Commissioners accepted, or undertook to accept, in settlement of a specified liability, on or after 23 March 2000; previously "paragraph (c)".

14   Substituted by FA 2002 s 126(1)(*d*)(iii) as respects fines or other penalties, as are referred to in s 1086(2)(*a*) and (*b*), which are imposed by a court, and as respects specified sums, as are referred to in s 1086(2)(*c*) and (*d*), which the Revenue Commissioners accepted, or undertook to accept, in settlement of a specified liability, on or after 25 March 2002; previously "€12,700, or".

15   Subs (4)(*d*) inserted by FA 2002 s 126(1)(*d*)(iv) as respects fines or other penalties, as are referred to in s 1086(2)(*a*) and (*b*), which are imposed by a court, and as respects specified sums, as are referred to in s 1086(2)(*c*) and (*d*), which the Revenue Commissioners accepted, or undertook to accept, in settlement of a specified liability, on or after 25 March 2002.

16   Subs (5A) inserted by FA 2000 s 162(1)(*d*) as respects fines or other penalties, as are referred to in s 1086(2)(*a*)-(*b*), which are imposed by a court, and as respects specified sums, as are referred to in s 1086(2)(*c*)-(*d*), which the Revenue Commissioners accepted, or undertook to accept, in settlement of a specified liability, on or after 23 March 2000.

Cross-references

This section to be construed together with the Value Added Tax Acts 1972-1997, in so far as relating to value added tax: s 1104(3).

This section to be construed together with the Stamp Act 1891 and the enactments amending or extending that Act, in so far as relating to stamp duties: s 1104(4).

This section to be construed together with the Capital Acquisitions Tax Act 1976, and the enactments amending or extending that Act, in so far as relating to capital acquisitions tax: s 1104(5).

This section to be construed together with FA 1983 Pt VI and the enactments amending or extending that Part, in so far as relating to residential property tax: s 1104(6).

Definitions

statute: s 2(1), IA 1937 s 3; Tax Acts: s 1(2).

Former enactments

FA 1983 s 23; FA 1992 s 240; WCTIPA 1993 s 3(7); FA 1997 s 158.

PART 48
MISCELLANEOUS AND SUPPLEMENTAL

1089 Status of interest on certain unpaid taxes and duties

(1) Interest payable under —

    (*a*)   [section 14 and subsections (3) and (4) of section 117 of the Stamp Duties Consolidation Act, 1999],[1]

    (*b*)   section 21 of the Value-Added Tax Act, 1972, or

    (*c*)   section 531(9) or 991,

shall be payable without any deduction of income tax and shall not be allowed in computing any income, profits or losses for any of the purposes of the Income Tax Acts.

(2) Interest payable under section 18 of the Wealth Tax Act, 1975, or section 41 of the Capital Acquisitions Tax Act, 1976, shall not be allowed in computing any income, profits or losses for any of the purposes of the Tax Acts.

Amendments

[1]   Substituted by SDCA 1999 s 162 and Sch 4; previously "section 15 of the Stamp Act, 1891 and subsections (2) and (3) of section 69 of the Finance Act, 1973".

Definitions

company: ss 4(1), 5(1); Income Tax Acts: s 1(2); Tax Acts: s 1(2).

Former enactments

FA 1973 s 35; FA 1975 s 27; FA 1976 s 29.

1093 Disclosure of information to Ombudsman

Any obligation to maintain secrecy or other restriction on the disclosure or production of information (including documents) obtained by or furnished to the Revenue Commissioners, or any person on their behalf, for taxation purposes, shall not apply to the disclosure or production of information (including documents) to the Ombudsman for the purposes of an examination or investigation by the Ombudsman under the Ombudsman Act, 1980, of any action (within the meaning of that Act) taken by or on behalf of the Revenue Commissioners, being such an action taken in the performance of administrative functions in respect of any tax or duty under the care and management of the Revenue Commissioners.

Cross-references

This section to be construed together with the Customs Acts, in so far as relating to customs: s 1104(2).

This section to be construed together with the Value Added Tax Acts 1972-1997, in so far as relating to value added tax: s 1104(3).

This section to be construed together with the Stamp Act 1891 and the enactments amending or extending that Act, in so far as relating to stamp duties: s 1104(4).

This section to be construed together with the Capital Acquisitions Tax Act 1976, and the enactments amending or extending that Act, in so far as relating to capital acquisitions tax: s 1104(5).

This section to be construed together with FA 1983 Pt VI and the enactments amending or extending that Part, in so far as relating to residential property tax: s 1104(6).

Definition

person: IA 1937 s 11(*c*).

Former enactment

FA 1981 s 52.

PART 49
COMMENCEMENT, REPEALS, TRANSITIONAL PROVISIONS, ETC

1100 Consequential amendments to other enactments

Schedule 31, which provides for amendments to other enactments consequential on the passing of this Act, shall apply for the purposes of this Act.

1104 Short title and construction

(1) This Act may be cited as the Taxes Consolidation Act, 1997.

...

(4) Sections 7, 8, 811, 858, 859, 872(1), 875, 905, 906, 910, 1002, 1078, 1079, 1086 and 1093 (in so far as relating to stamp duties) shall be construed together with the Stamp Act, 1891, and the enactments amending or extending that Act.

...

SCHEDULE 31
Consequential amendments

[Section 1100]

In the enactments specified in Column (1) of the following Table for the words set out or referred to in Column (2) there shall be substituted the words set out in the corresponding entry in Column (3).

Enactment amended (1)	Words to be replaced (2)	Words to be substituted (3)
... The Capital Acquisitions Tax Act, 1976: section 16(2), in the definition of "private company"	section 95 of the Corporation Tax Act, 1976	section 431 of the Taxes Consolidation Act, 1997

Enactment amended	Words to be replaced	Words to be substituted
(1)	(2)	(3)
	subsection (1)	subsection (3)
	subsection (4)	subsection (6)
section 52(1), in the definition of "Appeal Commissioners"	section 156 of the Income Tax Act, 1967	section 850 of the Taxes Consolidation Act, 1997
section 58(2)(*b*)	section 142 of the Income Tax Act, 1967	section 466 of the Taxes Consolidation Act, 1997
section 63(9)	sections 128(4), 507, 508, 510, 511, 512, 517 and 518 of the Income Tax Act, 1967	sections 987(4), 1061, 1062, 1063, 1064, 1065, 1066 and 1068 of the Taxes Consolidation Act, 1997
Second Schedule, Part I, paragraph 9, in the definition of "investment income"	section 2 of the Income Tax Act, 1967	section 3 of the Taxes Consolidation Act, 1997
The Finance Act, 1984, section 108(1)(*b*)(ii)	subsection (9) of section 235 of the Income Tax Act, 1967	subsection (1) of section 783 of the Taxes Consolidation Act, 1997
	section 235A	section 785
...		
The Finance Act, 1990:		
...		
section 129(1)	subsection (9) of section 235 of the Income Tax Act, 1967	subsection (1) of section 783 of the Taxes Consolidation Act, 1997
The Finance Act, 1991:		
...		
section 129(1), in the definition of "the Collector"	section 162 of the Income Tax Act, 1967	section 851 of the Taxes Consolidation Act, 1997
section 129(3)	Section 187 of the Income Tax Act, 1967	Section 928(1) and 964(2) of the Taxes Consolidation Act, 1997
...		

STAMP DUTIES CONSOLIDATION ACT 1999

(1999 Number 31)

ARRANGEMENT OF SECTIONS

PART 1
INTERPRETATION

PART 5
PROVISIONS APPLICABLE TO PARTICULAR INSTRUMENTS

CHAPTER 1
Bills of Exchange and Promissory Notes

CHAPTER 2
Conveyances on Sale

CHAPTER 3
Conveyances on any occasion except sale or mortgage

CHAPTER 4
Leases

PART 8
COMPANIES CAPITAL DUTY

PART 9
LEVIES

PART 10
ENFORCEMENT

PART 11
MANAGEMENT PROVISIONS

CHAPTER 1
Interpretation, Application and Care and Management

CHAPTER 2
Mode of recovering money received for duty

CHAPTER 3
Offences

CHAPTER 4
Sale of stamps

CHAPTER 5
Allowance for spoiled or misused stamps

CHAPTER 6
Miscellaneous

PART 12
REPEALS, ETC

SCHEDULE 1
STAMP DUTIES ON INSTRUMENTS

SCHEDULE 2
QUALIFICATIONS FOR APPLYING FOR RELIEF FROM STAMP DUTY IN RESPECT OF TRANSFERS TO YOUNG TRAINED FARMERS

SCHEDULE 3
ENACTMENTS REPEALED OR REVOKED

SCHEDULE 4
CONSEQUENTIAL AMENDMENTS

AN ACT TO CONSOLIDATE CERTAIN ENACTMENTS RELATING TO STAMP DUTIES AND THE MANAGEMENT OF THOSE DUTIES. [15th DECEMBER, 1999]

PART I
INTERPRETATION

1 Interpretation

(1) In this Act, unless the context otherwise requires—

"accountable person" means—

   (*a*)   the person referred to in column (2) of the Table to this definition in respect of the corresponding instruments set out in column (1) of that Table by reference to the appropriate heading in Schedule 1,

   (*b*)   in the case of an instrument which operates, or is deemed to operate, as a voluntary disposition inter vivos under section 30 or 54, the parties to such instrument,

   (*c*)   in the case of any other instrument, the parties to that instrument,

   (*d*)   notwithstanding paragraphs (*a*), (*b*) and (*c*), in the case of any person who would be an accountable person if alive, the accountable person shall be the personal representative of such person:

TABLE

Instrument Heading specified in Schedule 1	Accountable person
(1)	(2)
CONVEYANCE or TRANSFER on sale of any stocks or marketable securities.	The purchaser or transferee.
CONVEYANCE or TRANSFER on sale of any property other than stocks or marketable securities or a policy of insurance or a policy of life insurance.	The purchaser or transferee.
DUPLICATE or COUNTERPART of any instrument chargeable with any duty.	Any of the persons specified in this column, as appropriate.
LEASE.	The lessee.
MORTGAGE, BOND, DEBENTURE, COVENANT (except a marketable security) which is a security for the payment or repayment of money which is a charge or incumbrance on property situated in the State other than shares in stocks or funds of the Government or the Oireachtas.	The mortgagee or obligee; in the case of a transfer, the transferee.

"**bill of exchange**" includes draft, order, cheque, and letter of credit, and any document or writing (except a bank note) entitling or purporting to entitle any person, whether named in the bill or not, to payment by any other person of, or to draw on any other person for, any sum of money;

"**Commissioners**" means Revenue Commissioners;

"**conveyance on sale**" includes every instrument, and every decree or order (including a decree or order for, or having the effect of an order for, foreclosure) of any court or of any commissioners, whereby any property, or any estate or interest in any property, on the sale or compulsory acquisition of that property or that estate or that interest is transferred to or vested in a purchaser, or any other person on such purchaser's behalf or by such purchaser's direction;

"**die**" includes any plate, type, tool, implement, apparatus, appliance, device, process and any other means, used by or under the direction of the Commissioners for expressing or denoting any duty, or rate of duty or the fact that any duty or rate of duty or penalty has been paid or that an instrument is duly stamped or is not chargeable with any duty or for denoting any fee, and also any part or combination of any such plate, type, tool, implement, apparatus, appliance, device, process and any such other means;

"**equitable mortgage**" means an agreement or memorandum, under hand only, relating to the deposit of any title deeds or instruments constituting or being evidence of the title to any property (other than stock or marketable security), or creating a charge on such property;

"**executed**" and "**execution**", in relation to instruments not under seal, mean signed and signature;

"forge" includes counterfeit and **"forged"** shall be construed accordingly;

"impressed" includes any method of applying, producing or indicating a stamp on instruments or material by means of a die;

"instrument" includes every written document;

"marketable security" means a security of such a description as to be capable of being sold in any stock market in the State;

"material" includes every sort of material on which words or figures can be expressed;

"Minister" means the Minister for Finance;

"money" includes all sums expressed in the currency of the State or in any foreign currency;

"mortgage" means a security by means of mortgage for the payment of any definite and certain sum of money advanced or lent at the time, or previously due and owing, or forborne to be paid, being payable, or for the repayment of money to be thereafter lent, advanced, or paid, or which may become due on an account current, together with any sum already advanced or due, or without, as the case may be, and includes—

(*a*) further charge, and heritable bond, disposition, assignation, or tack in security, of or affecting any lands, estate, or property, real or personal, heritable or movable,

(*b*) any conveyance of any lands, estate, or property in trust to be sold or otherwise converted into money, intended only as a security, and redeemable before the sale or other disposal of the lands, estate or property, either by express stipulation or otherwise, except where the conveyance is made for the benefit of creditors generally, or for the benefit of creditors specified who accept the provision made for payment of their debts, in full satisfaction of those debts, or who exceed 5 in number,

(*c*) any defeazance, letter of reversion, declaration, or other deed or writing for defeating or making redeemable or explaining or qualifying any conveyance, transfer, disposition or assignation of any lands, estate, or property, apparently absolute, but intended only as a security,

(*d*) any agreement (other than an agreement chargeable with duty as an equitable mortgage), contract, or bond accompanied with a deposit of title deeds for making a mortgage, or any other security or conveyance already referred to of any lands, estate, or property comprised in the title deeds, or for pledging or charging the same as a security, and

(*e*) any deed operating as a mortgage of any stock or marketable security:

"policy of insurance" includes every writing whereby any contract of insurance is made or agreed to be made, or is evidenced, and **"insurance"** includes assurance;

"policy of life insurance" means a policy of insurance on any life or lives or on any event or contingency relating to or depending on any life or lives except a policy of insurance for any payment agreed to be made on the death of any person only from accident or violence or otherwise than from a natural cause;

"promissory note" includes any document or writing (except a bank note) containing a promise to pay any sum of money;

"residential property", in relation to a sale or lease, means—

> (a) a building or part of a building which, at the date of the instrument of conveyance or lease—
>
> > (i)   was used or was suitable for use as a dwelling,
> >
> > (ii) was in the course of being constructed or adapted for use as a dwelling, or
> >
> > (iii) had been constructed or adapted for use as a dwelling and had not since such construction or adaptation been adapted for any other use,
>
> and
>
> (b) the curtilage of the residential property up to an area (exclusive of the site of the residential property) of one acre;

but where—

> (I) in the year ending on the 31st day of December immediately prior to the date of that instrument of conveyance or lease—
>
> > (A) a rate was made by a rating authority as regards any hereditament to which section 3 of the Local Government (Financial Provisions) Act, 1978, did not apply,
> >
> > (B) a rate was made by a rating authority, and an allowance made under that section of that Act, as regards any hereditament which was at the time the rate was made a mixed hereditament, secondary school or community hall (each within the meaning assigned by section 1 of the Local Government (Financial Provisions) Act, 1978), or
> >
> > (C) a hereditament was described as exempt, or partially exempt, from rating in the valuation lists (being the valuation lists referred to in the Valuation Acts),
>
> then the whole or an appropriate part of that hereditament as is referable to ordinary use other than as a dwelling at the date of that instrument of conveyance or lease or, where appropriate, when last ordinarily used, shall not be residential property, in relation to that sale or lease,
>
> or
>
> (II) the area of the curtilage (exclusive of the site of the residential property) exceeds one acre, then the part which shall be residential property shall be taken to be the part which, if the remainder were separately occupied, would be the most suitable for occupation and enjoyment with the residential property;

"stamp" means—

> (a) any stamp, image, type, mark, seal, impression, imprint or perforation impressed by means of a die,
>
> (b) any receipt in whatever form issued by or under the direction of the Commissioners, or
>
> (c) an adhesive stamp issued by or under the direction of the Commissioners,

for denoting any duty or fee;

"stamped", in relation to instruments and material, applies as well to instruments and material impressed with stamps by means of a die as to instruments and material having adhesive stamps affixed to them;

"stock" includes any share in any stocks or funds transferable at the Bank of England or at the Bank of Ireland and any share in the stocks or funds of any foreign state or government, or in the capital stock or funded debt of any county council, corporation, company, or society in the State, or of any foreign corporation, company, or society;

"stock certificate to bearer" includes every stock certificate to bearer issued under any Act authorising the creation of debenture stock, county stock, corporation stock, municipal stock, or funded debt, by whatever name known.

(2) References in this Act to any enactment shall, except where the context otherwise requires, be construed as references to that enactment as amended or extended by any subsequent enactment.

(3) In this Act a reference to a Part, Chapter, section or Schedule is to a Part, Chapter or section of, or Schedule to, this Act, unless it is indicated that reference to some other enactment is intended.

(4) In this Act a reference to a subsection, paragraph, subparagraph, clause or subclause is to the subsection, paragraph, subparagraph, clause or subclause of the provision (including a Schedule) in which the reference occurs, unless it is indicated that reference to some other provision is intended.

Notes

Exemptions and reliefs:
Aircraft: Sch 1.
Amalgamations: s 80.
Associated companies: s 79.
Charities: s 82.
Conveyance on sale other than of marketable securities and certain policies of insurance for a consideration not exceeding £5,000 with the appropriate finance certificate: Sch 1.
Exploration leases and licences: s 104.
Financial instruments: s 90; foreign immovable property: s 98.
Foreign marketable securities: s 88.
Government stock: s 89.
Industrial and provident societies: s 93.
Loan capital: s 85.
National Treasury Management Agency: s 108.
New houses: s 91.
Oireachtas funds — payment/duty from: s 111.
Reconstructions: s 80.
Relatives: Sch 1 Heading of "Conveyance" para (15) relating to property other than shares (half the normal rate applies).
Renunciation of a renounceable letter of allotment in a quoted company: s 63.
Shared ownership leases: s 53.
Ships: Sch 1.
Spouses: s 96.
Stock of Semi-State bodies: s 86.
Trained young farmers, conveyance to: s 81.
Temple Bar Properties, acquisitions by: s 160.
Units in certain collective investment undertakings: s 88.
Woodlands: s 95.
Consideration may be:
Stock or debt: s 41; produce or goods in the case of a lease: s 51; but does not include VAT: s 48.

Note

Policy of Life Insurance

Group policies are charged to duty on the total value of the benefits assured and a member may withdraw from the scheme and be replaced by another without further charge to duty provided the member withdrawing takes no benefit and the overall value of benefits does not increase.

Cross-references

Cancellation of stamp and provisions relating to unstamped bills: s 25.

Charge and exemptions: Sch 1 BILL OF EXCHANGE Heading.

Definition of "cheque": Bills of Exchange Act 1882.

Definition of bills of exchange, not as broad: Bills of Exchange Act 1882 s 3.

General direction as to cancellation of adhesive stamps: s 10.

One bill only of a set need be stamped: s 24.

Prohibition on stamping by impressed stamp after execution: s 23.

Stamping of foreign bills: s 27.

Bills charged on local note to be stamped as promissory notes: s 26.

Meaning of "negotiates": Bills of Exchange Act 1882 s 31(1).

Notes purporting to be foreign notes: s 22.

Promissory note, definition not as broad as s 1: Bills of Exchange Act 1882 s 83.

PROMISSORY NOTE head and exemptions: Sch 1.

Instruments chargeable as conveyances:

Anti-avoidance: conveyances subject to agreements for lease, lease in contemplation of sale: s 34.

Certain contracts: s 31.

Contracts for leasehold interests: s 36.

Conveyance in consideration of debts: s 41.

Conveyance in consideration of stocks, marketable securities and shares: s 40.

Conveyance in contemplation of sale: s 33.

Conveyances of property at an undervalue: s 302.

Court orders: s 49.

Decree or order for foreclosure: s 39

Documents evidencing the surrender or merger of leasehold interests: s 67.

Gifts inter vivos: s 30

Renunciations of renounceable letters of allotment: s 63.

Sale of annuity or right not before in existence: s 32.

Rates of duty on mortgages: Sch 1 Mortgage head of charge.

Exemption from stamp duty for certain certificates of indebtedness of the Minister for Finance: s 112.

Mortgage given to a company by a subsidiary: s 83.

Assignment of policy to be stamped before payment of sum assured: s 130.

Composition: s 5.

Duty on policies: POLICY OF INSURANCE and POLICY OF LIFE INSURANCE Heads of charge in Sch 1.

Levy on insurance premiums: s 125.

Location of risk for insurance purposes: s 61.

Meaning of policy of life insurance: s 1.

Short-term life insurance policies: s 60.

Transfer on sale of insurance policies: Head of charge in Sch 1.

Meaning of stock certificate to bearer: s 64.

Recovery of fines: s 121.

Share warrant and stock certificate to bearer, Head of charge in Sch 1.

Uncertificated securities (CREST system), definition of "accountable person" applied: s 71.

UK legislation

Stamp Act 1891 s 54.

Case law

A document although containing a promise to pay a sum of money which was not given or accepted as a promissory note is not chargeable as one: *Yeo v Dawe* (1885) 33 WR 739.

"... 'containing a promise to pay' must mean that that is the substance of the document, the whole contents; it cannot mean containing a promise to pay forming one of a number of stipulations' as per Lindley, L.J., in *Mortgage Insurance Corporation v IRC* (1888) 21 QBD 352, CA followed in *Wirth v Weigel Leygonie & Co Ltd,* [1939]3 All ER 712.

The sum to be paid must be certain: *Henderson v Dawson* (1895) 22 R. Ct. of Sess 895.

The promise to pay must not be merely incidental to the main purpose of the instrument. *Thomson v Ball* (1894) 22 R. Ct. of Sess 16.

For distinction between a promissory note and an assignment of debt: *Buck v Robson* (1878) 3 QBD 686.

"conveyance on sale"

A lease may be a conveyance for certain purposes: *Littlewoods Mail Order Stores Ltd v IRC* [1962]2 All ER 279.

A document worded as a receipt for purchase money may in certain circumstances operate as a conveyance on sale: *Fleetwood-Hesketh v IRC* [1936]1 KB 351.

Declaration of trust: *Chesterfield Brewery Co v IRC* (1899) 2 QB 7.

Agreement creating an option to purchase land may be stamped as a conveyance on sale: *George Wimpey & Co Ltd v IRC* [1975]2 All ER 45.

Dissolution of a partnership may constitute a conveyance: *Christie v IRC* (1866) LR 2 Ex 46.

Contract for sale of land where vendor agrees to hold as nominee for purchase, a conveyance: *Peter Bone Ltd v IRC*, Ch D, 27 July 1995.

Deed of release of option (in a series of transactions): *Cherry Court v Revenue Commisssioners*, HC, McCracken J, 23 May 1995, V ITR 180.

"instrument"

Includes documents of every nature whether under seal or hand: *National Telephone Co v IRC* [1900] AC 1.

It includes an order of the court which is executed when it is drawn up passed and entered: *Sun Alliance Insurance Ltd v IRC* [1972] Ch 133.

An instrument attracts duty as a conveyance on sale if it is intended by the parties to implement an agreement for sale between them: *Oughtred v IRC* [1960] AC 206.

Stamp duty chargeable at ad valorem rates where instrument transfers legal interest but beneficial interest has already transferred *Cohen and Moore v IRC* (1933 2 KB 126).

"property"

A declaration of trust by a vendor in favour of a purchaser is a conveyance or transfer on sale: *Chesterfield Brewery Co v IRC* [1899]2 QB 7; *West Syndicate v IRC* [1989]1 QB 226, at p 240.

Property is that which belongs to a person exclusive of others and which can be the subject of bargain and sale to another: *Potter v IRC* 1854 10 Exch 147.

The benefit of a contract is property: *Western Abyssinian Syndicate v IRC* (1935) 46 TC 407.

Goodwill is property: *West London Syndicate v IRC* (1898) 2 QB 507.

"Know-how" is not property: *Phipps v Boardman* (1967) 2 AC 46, there is no property right in "know-how" that can be transferred: *Musker v English Electric Co Ltd* (1964) TC Vol 41 p 556.

Patents, copyright and trademarks are forms of property: *Brooke & Co Ltd v IRC* [1895]2 QB 536.

The benefit of contract is property: *Drages Ltd v IRC* (1927) 6 ATC 727.

A licence to sell intoxicating liquor is inalienable and must attach to the premises: *Macklin and McDonald v Gracen and Co Ltd and others* [1982] ILRM 182.

"upon the sale thereof"

A sale will exist provided there is in existence at the date of the sale a contract for sale: *Ridge Nominees Ltd v IRC* [1962] Ch 376,

It will also exist if the conveyance or transfer brings the sale into existence: *Escoigne Properties Ltd v IRC* [1958] AC 549.

Although sale implies a price in money, ss 6 and 55 provides for valuing the consideration for a sale where it consists of stock or securities, this converts such a transfer into a sale for stamp duty purposes: *John Foster & Sons v IRC* (1894) 1 QB 516.

"is transferred to or vested in"

The property must be transferred to or vest in the purchaser or someone on his behalf: *Jopling v IRC* [1940]2 KB 282.

It need not be the property actually sold: *Att Gen v Brown* (1849) 3 Ex 662.

It is not sufficient that the property conveyed has come to represent the property sold: *Henty & Constable (Brewers) Ltd v IRC* [1961] 3 All ER 1146.

The vendor may not be the person who does the vesting: *Att Gen v Brown* (1849) 3 Ex 662.

The consideration for the sale need not be paid to the vendor: *M'Innes v IRC* (1934) SC 424; or be provided by the purchaser: *Central & District Properties Ltd v IRC* [1966]1 WLR 1015.

General

A conveyance containing a covenant to reside with the transferor and "to care for, support, clothe, keep and maintain in a fit and proper manner during her lifetime" is a conveyance for valuable consideration and is not a voluntary disposition: *Colreavy v Colreavy and Keenan* [1939] IR 71.

"The court is entitled to look at the reality of what has been due. Just because the parties put a particular label on a transaction the court is not obliged to accept that label blindly..." *Waterford Glass (Group Services) Ltd v Revenue Commissioners*, HC 21 June 1989, [1990] IR 334.

Paras (*a*)-(*c*) of definition of "mortgage" do not extend the introductory words of the section or add cases not covered by the words: *City of London Brewery Co v IRC* [1899] 1 QB 121.

An assignment of an assurance policy as security for a debt is a mortgage: *Caldwell v Dawson* (1850) 5 Ex 1.

A security for contingent future payments is within the definition: *Canning (Lord) v Roper* (1852) 1 E & B 164.

Stamp duty is not charged on interest even if it is in arrear unless it is capitalised and made part of the principal sum: *Prudential Mutual Assurance Investment and Loan Association v Curzon* (1852) 8 Ex 97.

Endowment policy is a policy of life assurance: *Prudential Assurance Co v IRC* [1904] 2 KB 658.

A policy providing for the return of premiums paid to the assured on reaching 65 years or in the event of his death before then not a life policy: *General Accident Assurance Corporation Ltd v Commrs* (1908) 8 F(Court Sess) 477.

Endorsements and other variations to insurance policies may constitute new policies subject to duty in respect of the difference of the sums originally assured and the revised sums: *Prudential Assurance Company Ltd v IRC* [1935] 1 KB 101; [1934] 3 All ER 515.

The order for payment of a sum of money must be for payment of a definite sum: *Jones v Simpson* (1823) 2 B & C 318.

The definition of "bill of exchange" is wide enough to include a promissory note but an instrument which is a promissory note is chargeable as such and not as a bill of exchange: *Dettinger v Cohn* (1908) KB 582.

"Executed" in the context of the doctrine of escrow: *Terrapin International Ltd v IRC* [1976]2 All ER 461.

In relation to leases: *Alan Estates Ltd v WG Stores Ltd* (1980) 254 Estates Gazette 989.

"Marketable security": *Texas Land and Cattle Co v IRC* (1888) 16 R 69, see also *Speyer Bros v IRC* [1907]1 KB 246 and *Brown Shipley & Co v IRC* [1895] 2 QB 598.

Narrative

Irish Stamp Duty Law, Chapter 4, Chapter 9.

Definitions

"person" IA 1937 s 11(*c*).

Former enactment

SDMA 1891 s 27 (part); SA 1891 ss 32, 33(1), 54, 86, 91, 98(1), 108, 122(1); FA 1898 s 6 (part); FA 1989 s 67(*a*)-(*c*); FA 1996 ss 115, 118; FA 1997 ss 115, 118; FA 1998 s 125 and Sch 8.

PART 2
CHARGING AND STAMPING OF INSTRUMENTS

2 Charging of, liability for, and recovery of stamp duty

(1) Any instrument which—

    (*a*) is specified in Schedule 1, and

    (*b*) is executed in the State or, wherever executed, relates to any property situated in the State or any matter or thing done or to be done in the State,

shall be chargeable with stamp duty.

(2) The stamp duties to be charged for the benefit of the Central Fund on the several instruments specified in Schedule 1 shall be the several duties specified in that Schedule, which duties shall be subject to the exemptions contained in this Act and in any other enactment for the time being in force.

(3) (*a*) Any instrument chargeable with stamp duty shall, unless it is written on duly stamped material, be duly stamped with the proper stamp duty before the expiration of 30 days after it is first executed, unless the opinion of the Commissioners with respect to the amount of duty with which the instrument is chargeable, has, before such expiration, been required under this Act.

(b) If the opinion of the Commissioners with respect to any instrument chargeable with stamp duty has been required within 30 days after its first execution, the instrument shall be stamped in accordance with the assessment of the Commissioners within 14 days after notice of the assessment.

(4) Where any instrument chargeable with stamp duty is not stamped or is insufficiently stamped—

(a) the accountable person shall be liable, and

(b) where there is more than one such accountable person they shall be liable jointly and severally,

for the payment of the stamp duty or, where the instrument is insufficiently stamped, the additional stamp duty and such duty, additional duty and any penalty relating to any such duty shall be deemed to be a debt due by the accountable person to the Minister for the benefit of the Central Fund and shall be payable to the Commissioners and may (without prejudice to any other mode of recovery of the duty, additional duty and any penalty relating to such duty) be sued for and recovered by action, or other appropriate proceedings, at the suit of the Attorney General or the Minister or the Commissioners in any court of competent jurisdiction, notwithstanding anything to the contrary contained in the Inland Revenue Regulation Act, 1890.

Note

In addition to the duties in Sch 1 other legislation provides for duties as follows:
Companies capital duty: s 114-120.
Levy on insurance premiums:s 125.
Duty on charge cards and credit cards: s 124.
Duty on cash cards: s 123.
Duty on gifts (voluntary dispositions) s 30.
Prior to 1 November, 1991 there were no provisions comparable to ss (4) and (5) above. For this reason stamp duty had characteristics of a "voluntary" tax. Notwithstanding the changes in FA 1991 instruments executed prior to 1 November 1991 retain those characteristics.

Cross-references

Alternative to stamping instruments individually: s 50. See also Composition Agreements and Statement of Practice SP SD 3/90.
Common exemptions include: spouses: s 96; reconstructions and amalgamations of companies s 80; financial instruments: s 90; woodlands: s 95; charities: s 82; foreign immovable property: s 98; foreign quoted securities: s 88; and general exemptions in Sch 1.
Instrument may be liable to more than one charge: s 20.
"opinion of the Commissioners": s 14.
Penalties for late stamping: s 15.
Uncertificated securities, CREST system: s 71.

Case law

The onus is on the person claiming it to show that an exemption applies: *Yewens v Noakes* (1880) 50 LJ QB 132.
Stamp duty is *prima facie* a tax on instruments: *Royal Liver Friendly Society v IRC* (1870) LR 5 Ex 78.
An instrument must be stamped for its leading and principal object, objectively determined: *Limmer Asphalt Paving Co. Ltd v IRC* (1872) LR 7 Ex. 211.
The court is entitled to look at the reality of the transaction in respect of which an instrument is executed and at the legal effect and the legal rights of the parties resulting from the transaction; the Revenue stamp what a document is and not what it purports to be: *Waterford Glass (Group Services) Limited v The Revenue Commissioners* [1990] IR 334, IV ITR 187.
The court is entitled to read a document as a whole and to ascertain the purpose and intention of the parties therefrom but not to rewrite the document so as to render it liable to a tax which its form and purpose has not attracted: *Viek Investments Ltd. v The Revenue Commissioners*, IV ITR 367.

A doubt in a stamp duty provision is to be construed in favour of the taxpayer: *O'Sullivan v The Revenue Commissioners* (1994) I IR 46.

Revenue interpretation

Meaning of "relates to any property situated in the State on any matter or thing done or to be done in the State (See Revenue's Notes for Guidance on SDCA 1999 s 2(1)).

Definitions

"accountable person", "Commissioners", "executed", "instrument", "material": s 122(1); "person" IA 1937 s 11(*c*); "stamp", "stamped": s 122(1).

Former enactment

SA 1891 s 1(1)-(4); FA 1991 s 94; FA 1999 s 186(*a*), (*b*).

3 Variation of certain rates of duty by order

(1) Subject to this section, the Minister may—

    (*a*) by order vary the rate of duty chargeable on any instrument specified in Schedule 1 or may exempt such instrument from duty, and

    (*b*) make such order in respect of any particular class of instrument,

but no order shall be made under this section for the purpose of increasing any of the rates of duty.

(2) No order shall be made under this section for the purpose of varying the duty on any instrument or class of instrument where

    (*a*) such instrument or class of instrument relates to—

        (i) any immovable property situated in the State or any rights or interest in such property,

        (ii) any stock or share of a company having a register in the State, or

        (iii) any risk situated in the State in relation to the heading "INSURANCE" in Schedule 1,

      or

    (*b*) such instrument or class of instrument is a bill of exchange or a promissory note.

(3) Notwithstanding anything to the contrary contained in subsection (2), the Minister may make an order in respect of an instrument which is executed for the purposes of debt factoring.

(4) The Minister may by order amend or revoke an order under this section, including an order under this subsection.

(5) An order under this section shall be laid before Dail Eireann as soon as may be after it has been made and, if a resolution annulling the order is passed by Dail Eirearnn within the next 21 days on which Dail Eireann has sat after the order is laid before it, the order shall be annulled accordingly, but without prejudice to the validity of anything previously done under that order.

(6) Every order under this section shall have statutory effect on the making of that order and, subject to subsection (5), unless the order either is confirmed by Act of the Oireachtas passed not later than the end of the year following that in which the order is made, or, is an order merely revoking wholly an order previously made under that

subsection, the order shall cease to have statutory effect at the expiration of that period but without prejudice to the validity of anything previously done under that order.

Cross-references

Stamp Duty (Variation) Order 1991 (SI 277/1991).

Definitions

"instrument": s 1; IA 1937 s 3; "property": CATA 1976 s 2(1); "share": CATA 1976 s 2(1); "stock": s 5.

Former enactment

FA 1991 s 95.

4 How duties are to be paid

All stamp duties for the time being chargeable by law on any instruments are to be paid and denoted according to this Act and except where express provision is made to the contrary are to be denoted by impressed stamps only.

Cross-references

Composition for stamp duty: SDCA 1999 s 5.

Duty may be denoted by adhesive stamp in some cases: SDCA 1999 s 25.

Uncertificated securities (CREST system) this section does not apply: SDCA 1999 s 71(*e*).

Definitions

"impressed", "instrument", "stamp": SDCA 1999 s 1

Statement of Practice

SP 50/3/90 - Agreement as to the Payments of Stamp Duty on Instruments (Composition Agreements).

Former enactment

SA 1891 s 2.

5 Agreement as to payment of stamp duty on instruments

(1) Where in the opinion of the Commissioners it is inexpedient or impractical for any person carrying on a business and who—

    (*a*) in the course of that business, is a party to instruments liable to stamp duty under Schedule 1, or

    (*b*) acts as agent for any such party,

to pay stamp duty in respect of each such instrument, then the Commissioners may enter into an agreement with that person for the delivery to them of accounts for specified periods giving such particulars as may be required of such instruments.

(2) The agreement shall be in such form and shall contain such terms and conditions as the Commissioners consider proper.

(3) Where an agreement has been entered into under this section between the Commissioners and any person, and any instrument to which the agreement relates—

    (*a*) is issued during the period the agreement is in force, and

    (*b*) contains a statement that the appropriate stamp duty has been or will be paid to the Commissioners in accordance with this section,

then that instrument shall not be chargeable with any stamp duty but in lieu of such stamp duty, and by means of composition, there shall be charged, in respect of the instruments to which the agreement relates which were issued during each period of account under that agreement a stamp duty of an amount equal to the aggregate of the amounts of stamp duty which, but for this section, would have been chargeable on each of the instruments concerned, and the stamp duty chargeable under this subsection (by means of such composition) shall be paid by the person to the Commissioners on the delivery of the account.

(4) Where a person makes default in delivering any account required by any agreement under this section or in paying the duty payable on the delivery of any such account, the person shall be liable to a penalty not exceeding [€125][1] for every day during which the default continues and shall also be liable to pay, in addition to the duty, interest on the duty (which shall be recoverable in the same manner as if it were part of the duty) at the rate of [0.0322 per cent for each day or part of a day][2] from the date when the default begins.

Amendments

[1]   Substituted by FA 2001 s 240 and Sch 5 Pt 6 with effect from 1 January 2002; previously "£100".

[2]   Substituted by FA 2002 s 129(6)(*a*) with effect from 1 September 2002 in respect of an amount due to be paid or remitted, whether before, on, or after that date; previously "1 per cent for each month or part of a month".

Statement of practice

Agreement as to Payments of Stamp Duty on Instruments (Composition Agreements): SP-SD/3/90.

Definitions

"instrument": s 1; IA 1937 s 3; "person": IA 1937 s 11(*c*); "stamp": s 1.

Former enactment

FA 1990 s 113(1)-(4); FA 1998 s 124(1).

6 How instruments are to be written and stamped

(1) Every instrument—

     (*a*)   written on stamped material shall be written in such manner, and

     (*b*)   partly or wholly written before being stamped shall be so stamped,

so as to have the stamp appear on the face of the instrument, and to prevent it being used for or applied to any other instrument written on the same piece of material.

(2) If more than one instrument is written on the same piece of material, every one of the instruments shall be separately and distinctly stamped with the duty with which it is chargeable.

Cross-references

Several distinct matters in one instrument to be charged separately: SDCA 1999 s 7.

Uncertificated securities (CREST system) this section does not apply: SDCA 1999 s 71(*e*).

Case law

A memorandum endorsed on a life assurance policy was held to constitute a separate policy requiring a separate stamp: *Prudential Assurance Co Ltd v IRC* [1935] 1 KB 101.

Definitions

"instrument", "material", "stamp", "stamped": s 1.

Former enactment

SA 1891 s 3.

7 Instruments to be separately charged with duty in certain cases

Except where express provision to the contrary is made by this or any other Act—

(*a*) an instrument containing or relating to several distinct matters shall be separately and distinctly charged, as if it were a separate instrument, with duty in respect of each of the matters;

(*b*) an instrument made for any consideration in respect of which it is chargeable with ad valorem duty, and also for any further or other valuable consideration or considerations, shall be separately and distinctly charged, as if it were a separate instrument, with duty in respect of each of the considerations;

(*c*) without prejudice to the generality of paragraphs (*a*) and (*b*), where the consideration (other than rent) for the sale or lease of any property is partly attributable to residential property and partly attributable to property which is not residential property the instrument of conveyance or transfer or lease shall be chargeable to ad valorem stamp duty on the basis that it is a separate conveyance or transfer or lease of residential property to the extent that that consideration is attributable to residential property and also a separate conveyance or transfer or lease of property which is not residential property to the extent that that consideration is attributable to property which is not residential property.

Note

Re application of section 4 to certain leases see Revenue Act 1909 (9 Edw. VII, c. 43), s 8.

Cross-references

"... express provision to the contrary is made"

covenant for improvement in a conveyance on sale: s 43;

covenant for improvement in a lease: s 52(1);

equity of redemption in a mortgage: s 57(4);

further security in a transfer of mortgage: s 57(3);

penal rent reserved by a lease: s 52(1);

security for periodic payments in conveyance: s 42(3);

several instruments effecting one transaction: s 45(4);

but is specifically not made in provisions relating to certain financial instruments: SDCA 1999 s 90(4) and in respect of consideration in the form of certain covenants in leases.

Case law

An instrument executed twice and having two distinct operations one as a lease and one as a conveyance on sale: *Brightman v IRC* (1868), 18 LT 412.

An order of the Charity Commissioners appointing new trustees of charity and vesting the property in the new trustees was held liable to two stamps, one as an "appointment of new trustees" and one as a "conveyance": *Hadgett v IRC* (1877), 3 Ex D 46.

A surrender of lease and grant of new lease held not liable to two charges : *Doe Phillips v Phillips* (1840), 11 Ad & El 796).

Instrument executed by several persons in pursuance of a common object, only one stamp is required: *Baker v Jardine* (1784) 13 East 235 (assignment of prize money of several seamen payable out of one fund; *Wills v Bridge* (1849), 4 Exch 193 (conveyance by several shareholders jointly)).

An instrument is to be stamped for its leading and principal object and that stamp covers everything accessory to that object: *Wills v Bridge* (1849), 4 Exch 193.

To determine if an object is an accessory or a principal object the test is to see if it would stand on its own feet: *General Accident Assurance Corp v IRC* (1906) 8 F(Ct of Sess) 477 at p 482.

An alteration of substance in an executed and stamped instrument requires stamping as a new instrument: *London & Brighton Railway v Fairclough* (1841) 2 M& G 674.

Where the alteration arises by reason of the terms of the instrument itself further stamping of the instrument is not required: *Baker v Merckel* (1960) 1 QB 657.

Where an instrument although relating to only one matter is chargeable under more than one head of charge the Revenue are entitled to charge the higher duty: *Speyer Bros v IRC* [1908]AC 92, *Anderson v IRC* [1939]1 KB 341.

An instrument chargeable under a specific head is not in general charged with a larger duty under a more general head. Duty should be charged by reference to the particular description which, in the ordinary use of legal language appears to fit the instrument in question best: *North of Scotland Bank v IRC* [1931] AC 149.

Subs 4(6): "the consideration in respect whereof it is chargeable with ad valorem duty" is the consideration ascertainable at the time of execution of the instrument, though not necessarily appearing therein: *Underground Electric Rly Co of London Ltd v IRC* [1906]AC 21.

Definitions

"instrument": s 1.

Former enactment

SA 1891 s 4; F(No 2)A 1998 s 58.

---

8 Facts and circumstances affecting duty to be set forth in instruments, etc

(1) Except as provided for in this section, all the facts and circumstances affecting the liability of any instrument to duty, or the amount of the duty with which any instrument is chargeable, are to be fully and truly set forth in the instrument.

(2) Where it is not practicable to set out all the facts and circumstances, to which subsection (1) refers, in an instrument, additional facts and circumstances which—

    (*a*)   affect the liability of such instrument to duty,

    (*b*)   affect the amount of the duty with which such instrument is chargeable, or

    (*c*)   may be required from time to time by the Commissioners,

are to be fully and truly set forth in a statement which shall be delivered to the Commissioners together with such instrument and the form of any such statement may from time to time be prescribed by the Commissioners.

(3) Any person who—

    (*a*)   fraudulently or negligently executes any instrument, or

    (*b*)   being employed or concerned in or about the preparation of any instrument, fraudulently or negligently prepares any such instrument,

in which all the facts and circumstances affecting the liability of such instrument to duty, or the amount of the duty with which such instrument is chargeable, are not fully and truly set forth in the instrument or in any statement to which subsection (2) relates, shall incur a penalty of

    (i)   [€1,265][1], and

    (ii) the amount, or in the case of fraud, twice the amount, of the difference between—

        (I)   the amount of duty payable in respect of the instrument based on the facts and circumstances set forth and delivered, and

        (II) the amount of duty which would have been the amount so payable if the instrument and any accompanying statement had fully and truly set forth all the facts and circumstances referred to in subsections (1) and (2).

(4) Where any instrument was executed neither fraudulently nor negligently by a person and it comes to such person's notice, or it would have come to such person's notice, if such person had taken reasonable care, that such instrument or any statement to which

subsection (2) relates does not fully and truly set forth all those facts and circumstances then, unless the Commissioners are informed of the error without unreasonable delay, such matter shall be treated, for the purposes of subsection (3), as having been negligently done by such person.

(5) Where an instrument operates, or is deemed to operate, as a voluntary disposition inter vivos under section 30 or 54 such fact shall be brought to the attention of the Commissioners in the statement delivered under subsection (2) and such statement shall contain a statement of the value of the property, or in the case of a lease the minimum amount or value referred to in section 54, and where the requirements of this subsection are not complied with any person who executes such instrument shall for the purposes of subsection (3) be presumed, until the contrary is proven, to have acted negligently.

(6) Where such person as may be liable to a penalty under subsection (3) is in doubt as to the application of law to, or the treatment for tax purposes of, any matter to be contained in an instrument, or in a statement to which subsection (2) relates, to be delivered by such person to the Commissioners, such person may deliver the instrument and, where applicable, the statement to the best of such person's belief as to the application of law to, or the treatment for the purposes of stamp duty of, that matter but such person shall draw the attention in writing of the Commissioners to the matter in question in the instrument or statement, as appropriate, by specifying the doubt and, if such person so does, he or she shall be treated as making a full and true disclosure with regard to that matter.

(7) Subsection (6) shall not apply where the Commissioners are not satisfied that the doubt specified under that subsection was genuine and are of the opinion that the person who specified the doubt was acting with a view to the evasion or avoidance of tax and in such a case the person shall be deemed not to have made a full and true disclosure with respect to the matter in question.

Amendments

1 Substituted by FA 2001 s 240 and Sch 5 Pt 6 with effect from 1 January 2002; previously "£1,000".

Note

The concept of "fraudulently or negligently" appears in TCA 1997 s 1053. TCA 1997 s 1078 refers to "knowingly or wilfully". See Revenue Notes for Guidance on SDCA 1999 s 8(4) as to what constitutes "negligence".

Penalties are the price of late payment (s 14) and are enforceable in the same way as duty (s 2).

Uncertificated securities (CREST system) this section does not apply: SDCA 1999 s 71(*e*).

Cross-reference

Negligence in respect of "residential consideration": SDCA 1999 s 16.

Case law

Purchase price for all property passing must be included in the consideration: *Eastbourne Corporation v AG*, [1904] AC 155.

Definitions

"Commissioners", "executed", "instrument": s 1; "person" IA 1937 s 11(*c*); "stamp": s 1.

Former enactment

SA 1891 s 5; FA 1991 s 97; FA 1999 s 156(*a*), (*b*).

9 Mode of calculating ad valorem duty in certain cases

Where an instrument is chargeable with ad valorem duty in respect of money in any currency other than the currency of the State, such duty shall be calculated on the value of that money in the currency of the State according to the rate of exchange current at the date of execution of such instrument.

Definitions

"instrument", "money", "stamp": s 1(1).

Former enactment

FA 1933 s 40; FA 1999 s 193.

---

10 Adhesive stamps

(1) Any stamp duties on instruments which are permitted by law to be denoted by adhesive stamps shall, if denoted by adhesive stamps, be denoted by adhesive stamps issued by the Commissioners.

(2) An instrument, the duty on which is required or permitted by law to be denoted by an adhesive stamp, shall not be deemed duly stamped with an adhesive stamp, unless the person required by law to cancel the adhesive stamp cancels the same by writing on or across the stamp his or her name or initials, or the name or initials of his or her firm, together with the true date of his or her so writing, or otherwise effectively cancels the stamp and renders the same incapable of being used for any other instrument or unless it is otherwise proved that the stamp appearing on the instrument was affixed to the instrument at the proper time.

(3) Where 2 or more adhesive stamps are used to denote the stamp duty on an instrument, each or every stamp shall be cancelled in the manner set out in subsection (2).

(4) Every person who, being required by law to cancel an adhesive stamp, neglects or refuses duly and effectually to do so in the manner set out in subsection (2), shall incur a penalty of [€630][1].

(5) If any person—

(a) fraudulently removes or causes to be removed from any instrument any adhesive stamp, or affixes to any other instrument any adhesive stamp which has been so removed, with intent that the stamp may be used again, or

(b) sells or offers for sale, or utters, any adhesive stamp which has been so removed, or utters any instrument, having any adhesive stamp on it which has to such person's knowledge been removed in the manner specified in paragraph (a),

such person shall, without prejudice to any other fine or penalty to which that person may be liable, be guilty of an offence and section 1078 (which relates to revenue offences) of the Taxes Consolidation Act, 1997, shall for the purposes of such offence be construed in all respects as if such offence were an offence under subsection (2) of that section.

Amendments

¹   Substituted by FA 2001 s 240 and Sch 5 Pt 6 with effect from 1 January 2002; previously "£500".

Note

The only duties to which this section refers are those imposed on promissory notes and bills of exchange.

Cross-references

Heading: Bill of Exchange in Sch 1.
Meaning of "bill of exchange" and "promissory note": s 1.
Stamping of bills and notes: s 25; Revenue offences: TCA 1997 s 1078.

Definitions

"Commissioners", "instrument", "stamp", "stamped": s 1; "person": IA 1937 s 11(*c*).

Remarks

See Destimation Table under SA 1891 ss 7, 8, 9.

Former enactment

SA 1891 ss 7, 8, 9(1); FA 1984 s 101; FA 1991 s 106; FA 1998 s 125 and Sch 8; FA 1999 ss 157, 158.

11 Denoting stamps

Where the duty with which an instrument is chargeable depends in any manner on the duty paid on another instrument, the payment of the last-mentioned duty shall, on application to the Commissioners and production of both the instruments, be denoted on the first-mentioned instrument in such manner as the Commissioners think fit.

Note

The denoting stamps are:
Collateral security: para (2) of MORTGAGE head in Sch 1.
Duplicate or counterpart: s 13 and Sch 1.
Instruments requiring adjudication to be impressed with a denoting stamp: s 20(4)-(5).
Uncertificated securities (CREST system) this section does not apply: s 71(*e*).

Definitions

"Commissioners", "instrument", "stamp": s 1.

Former enactment

SA 1891 s 11.

12 Particulars delivered stamps

(1) In this section **"fee simple"**, **"interest"**, **"land"** and **"lease"** have the same meanings, respectively, as in section 41 of the Finance (1909-10) Act, 1910, and references to a **"transferee"** or a "lessee" include the personal representatives of any transferee or lessee.

(2) It shall be the duty of the transferee or lessee, on the occasion of any transfer of the fee simple of any land or of any interest in land or on the grant of any lease of any land for a term exceeding 14 years (whether the transfer or lease is on sale or operates as a voluntary disposition inter vivos), to present to the Commissioners such particulars in relation to such class or category of transfer or lease as they may prescribe by regulations and, without prejudice to the generality of the foregoing, the regulations may make provision in relation to all or any of the following matters:

    (*a*)   the form in which the particulars are to be delivered;
    (*b*)   the time limits within which the particulars are to be delivered;
    (*c*)   the manner in which the land is to be described or classified;
    (*d*)   the furnishing of tax reference numbers of the parties to the instrument.

(3) Notwithstanding anything in section 20 or 127, any transfer or lease to which regulations made pursuant to subsection (2) apply shall not, other than in criminal proceedings or in civil proceedings by the Commissioners to recover stamp duty, be given in evidence, or be available for any purpose unless it is stamped with a stamp denoting that all particulars prescribed by the Commissioners have been delivered.

(4) If the transferee or lessee fails to comply with this provision, such person shall be guilty of an offence and section 1078 (which relates to revenue offences) of the Taxes Consolidation Act, 1997, shall for the purposes of such offence be construed in all respects as if such offence were an offence under subsection (2) of that section.

Notes

The Revenue Commissioners are empowered to make regulations specifying the particulars to be included in relation to sales or leases (including voluntary dispositions inter vivos) of land or buildings. Regulations were made with effect from 1 September 1995 - Stamp Duty (Particulars to be Delivered) Regulations 1995 (SI 144/1995).

Revenue offences: TCA 1997 s 1078.

Definitions

"land": IA 1937 Sch; "person": IA 1937 s 11(*c*); "Commissioners", "stamped": s 1.

Former enactment

FA 1994 s 107(1)-(3), (6); FA 1995 s 149(*a*)-(*b*); FA 1999 s 167(*a*)-(*b*).

13 Duplicates and counterparts

The duplicate or counterpart of an instrument chargeable with duty (except the counterpart of an instrument chargeable as a lease, such counterpart not being executed by or on behalf of any lessor or grantor,) shall not be deemed duly stamped unless—

     (*a*)   it is stamped as an original instrument, or

     (*b*)   it appears by some stamp impressed on it that the full and proper duty has been paid on the original instrument of which it is the duplicate or counterpart.

Cross-references

Duplicate and counterpart stamps are denoting stamps for the purposes of s 153.

Heading DUPLICATE or COUNTERPART in Sch 1.

Definitions

"executed", "impressed", "instrument", "stamp", "stamped": s 1.

Former enactment

SA 1891 s 72.

14 Penalty on stamping instruments after execution

(1) Except where express provision is in this Act made, any instrument which is unstamped or insufficiently stamped may be stamped after the expiration of the time for stamping provided for in subsection (3) of section 2, on payment of the unpaid duty and on payment of a [penalty of €25][1] and also by means of further penalty, where the unpaid duty [exceeds €30][2], of interest on such duty, at the rate of [0.0322 per cent for each day or part of a day][3] from the day on which that instrument was first executed to the day of payment of the unpaid duty.

(2) Where—

    (*a*) any instrument referred to in column (1) of the Table to the definition of "accountable person" in section 1, or

    (*b*) any instrument which operates, or is deemed to operate, as a voluntary disposition inter vivos,

has not been or is not duly stamped in conformity with subsection (3) of section 2, the accountable person shall, in addition to the penalties provided for in subsection (1), be liable to pay an amount by means of further penalty as follows:

    (i) an amount equivalent to 10 per cent of the unpaid duty on the instrument, where such instrument is stamped not later than 6 months after the day on which such instrument was first executed;

    (ii) an amount equivalent to 20 per cent of the unpaid duty on the instrument, where such instrument is stamped more than 6 months but not later than 12 months after the day on which such instrument was first executed:

    (iii) an amount equivalent to 30 per cent of the unpaid duty on the instrument, where such instrument is stamped more than 12 months after the day on which such instrument was first executed.

(3) Subject to any other express provision in this Act in relation to any particular instrument, the Commissioners may, if they think fit, remit any penalty payable on stamping.

(4) The payment of any penalty payable on stamping shall be denoted on the instrument by a particular stamp.

(5) Any penalty payable by operation of this section shall be chargeable and recoverable in the same manner as if it were part of the duty on the instrument to which it relates.

Amendments

1   Substituted by FA 2001 s 240 and Sch 5 Pt 6 with effect from 1 January 2002; previously "penalty of £20".

2   Substituted by FA 2001 s 240 and Sch 5 Pt 6 with effect from 1 January 2002; previously "exceeds £20".

3   Substituted by FA 2002 s 129(6)(*b*) with effect from 1 September 2002 in respect of an amount due to be paid or remitted, whether before, on, or after that date; previously "1 per cent per month or part of a month".

Cross-references

Stamping of foreign bills of exchange: s 27.

Uncertificated securities (CREST system) subs (4) does not apply: FA 1996 s 104(*d*).

Case law

The Interpretation Act 1937 s 19(1) provides that where a statute repeals the whole or portion of a previous statute and substitutes other provisions for the statute or portion of the statute so repealed the statute or portion of a statute so repealed shall (unless the contrary is expressly provided in the repealing Act) continue in force until the said substituted provisions come into operation. This was applied by Supreme Court in determining that the penalties pertaining under this section (s 15) continued to apply between the date of passing of FA 1991 (29 May 1991) and 1 November 1991 (the date of the coming into effect of the provision): *O'Leary v Revenue Commissioners,* IV ITR 357.

Note

The date of first execution is taken in practice as the date when the instrument first becomes effective rather than, as is more accurately the case, the date one of the parties signs the instrument. See: *Beesly v Hallwood Estates* [1961] Ch 105.

For the operation of the Revenue Commissioners' power of mitigation of penalties see the *Law Society Gazette,* April 1993 (Vol 87 No 3).

Revenue practices

Penalties are rounded down (see Revenue Notes for Guidance on SDCA 1999 s 14(1)).

44 days may elapse before penalties incurred (see Revenue Notes for Guidance on s 14(1), (2) and (3)).

Definitions

"accountable person", "Commissioners", "executed", "execution", "instrument": s 1; "person" IA 1937 s 11(*c*); "stamp", "stamped": s 1.

Former enactment

SA 1891 s 15(1)-(5); FA 1991 s 100, FA 1998 s 124.

15 Surcharges for undervaluation in case of voluntary dispositions inter vivos

(1) Where an instrument operates or is deemed to operate as a voluntary disposition inter vivos by operation of section 30 or 54 and the statement of value of such property, or in the case of a lease the minimum amount or value referred to in section 54, provided to the Commissioners under subsection (5) of section 8 (in this section referred to as the **"submitted value"**) is less than the value of the property as agreed with, or ascertained by, the Commissioners, subject to the right of appeal under section 21, (in this section referred to as the **"ascertained value"**) then, as a penalty, the duty chargeable on the conveyance or transfer, or lease, shall be increased by an amount (in this section referred to as the **"surcharge"**) calculated according to the following provisions:

    (*a*)   subject to subsection (2), where the submitted value is less than the ascertained value by an amount which is greater than 15 per cent of the ascertained value but not greater than 30 per cent of the ascertained value, a surcharge equal to 25 per cent of the total duty chargeable on the instrument;

    (*b*)   where the submitted value is less than the ascertained value by an amount which is greater than 30 per cent of the ascertained value but not greater than 50 per cent of the ascertained value, a surcharge equal to 50 per cent of the total duty chargeable on the instrument;

    (*c*)   where the submitted value is less than the ascertained value by an amount which is greater than 50 per cent of the ascertained value, a surcharge equal to the total duty chargeable on the instrument.

(2) No surcharge shall be chargeable under paragraph (*a*) of subsection (1) where the difference between the submitted value and the ascertained value is less than [€6,350][1].

(3) Where a statement of value, or in the case of a lease the minimum amount or value referred to in section 54, is not provided in accordance with subsection (5) of section 8, then the liability of an instrument to a surcharge under this section may be ascertained by the Commissioners by the substitution of the consideration, other than rent in the case of lease, stated in the instrument for the submitted value.

(4) Any surcharge payable by operation of this section shall be chargeable and recoverable in the same manner as if it were part of the duty on the instrument to which it relates.

Amendments

[1]   Substituted by FA 2001 s 240 and Sch 5 Pt 6 with effect from 1 January 2002; previously "£5,000".

Definitions

"Commissioners", "executed": s 1; "instrument": s 1, IA 1937 s 3; "stamp": s 1.

Former enactment

FA 1991 s 103(1)-(3); FA 1994 s 103(1)(*a*)-(*c*) and (2); FA 1999 s 175(i).

16 Surcharges to apply when apportionment is not just and reasonable

(1) In this section **"residential consideration"** means—

    (*a*) in the case of a sale to which section 45(2)(*a*) refers, or a lease to which section 52(5)(*a*) refers, the amount or value of the consideration for the sale or lease which is deemed to be attributable to residential property, and

    (*b*) in the case of a sale to which section 45(2)(*b*) refers, or a lease to which section 52(5)(*b*) refers, the amount or value of the aggregate consideration (within the meaning of section 45(2) or 52(5), respectively) which is deemed to be attributable to residential property.

(2) Where—

    (*a*) in relation to any sale, section 45(2) refers, an estimate (in this section referred to as the **"vendor's estimate"** or as the **"purchaser's estimate"**, as the case may be) of the residential consideration shall be made by the vendor and by the purchaser, and

    (*b*) in relation to any lease, section 52(5) refers, an estimate (in this section referred to as the **"lessor's estimate"** or as the **"lessee's estimate"**, as the case may be) of the residential consideration shall be made by the lessor and by the lessee,

and those estimates together with the amount or value of the aggregate consideration (within the meaning of section 45(2) or 52(5), as appropriate) shall be brought to the attention of the Commissioners in the statement delivered under section 8(2) and that statement shall be signed by the vendor or lessor and by the purchaser or lessee, as appropriate, and where the requirements of this subsection are not complied with any person who executes the instrument whereby that sale or lease is effected shall for the purposes of section 8(3) be presumed, until the contrary is proven, to have acted negligently.

(3) Where the purchaser's or lessee's estimate (in this subsection referred to as the **"submitted value"**) is less than or greater than the residential value agreed with, or ascertained by, the Commissioners, subject to the right of appeal under section 21, (in this subsection referred to as the **"ascertained value"**) then, as a penalty, the duty chargeable on the instrument, shall, where an assessment of duty based on the ascertained value would result in a greater amount than an assessment based on the submitted value, be increased by an amount (in this subsection referred to as the **"surcharge"**) calculated according to the following provisions:

    (*a*) where the submitted value is less than or greater than the ascertained value by an amount which is greater than 10 per cent of the ascertained value but not greater than 30 per cent of the ascertained value, a surcharge equal to 50 per cent of the difference between the duty chargeable by reference to the ascertained value and the duty chargeable by reference to the submitted value;

    (*b*) where the submitted value is less than or greater than the ascertained value by an amount which is greater than 30 per cent of the ascertained value, a surcharge equal to the difference between the duty chargeable by reference to the ascertained value and the duty chargeable by reference to the submitted value.

(4) (*a*) Notwithstanding any other provision to the contrary in this Act, the purchaser or lessee, as the case may be, shall, subject to paragraph (*b*), be entitled to recover from the vendor or lessor one-half of that surcharge.

    (*b*) Where the estimate of the vendor or lessor, as the case may be, is less than or greater than the submitted value, the amount which the purchaser or lessee shall be entitled to recover from the vendor or lessor shall not exceed one-half of what the surcharge would be if the submitted value were equal to the vendor's or lessor's estimate.

(5) Any surcharge payable by operation of this section shall be chargeable and recoverable in the same manner as if it were part of the duty on the instrument to which it relates.

Notes

To arrive at a just and reasonable apportionment between the commercial and the residential parts of a property, the vendor and the purchaser of the property should make independent calculations of the value apportionable to the residential part.

A stamp duty surcharge of 50% of the undercharge applies where a property is undervalued by 10%-30%.

A stamp duty surcharge of 100% of the undercharge applies where a property is undervalued by more than 30%.

The purchaser may recover up to half of the surcharge from the vendor.

Former enactment

FA 1997 s 121; F(No 2)A 1998 s 13; FA 1999 s 145(*a*)-(*d*).

17 Furnishing of an incorrect certificate

The furnishing of an incorrect certificate for the purpose of Schedule 1 shall be deemed to constitute the delivery of an incorrect statement for the purposes of section 1078 of the Taxes Consolidation Act, 1997.

Notes

The furnishing of an incorrect stamp duty certificate is a Revenue offence - with a potential fine of up to £10,000 and/or five years' imprisonment.

Former enactment

FA 1997 s 122.

PART 3
VALUATION

18 Mode of valuing property

For the purposes of sections 30 and 33(1), the value of property conveyed or transferred by an instrument chargeable with duty in accordance with either of those sections shall be determined without regard to—

    (*a*) any power (whether or not contained in the instrument) on the exercise of which the property, or any part of or any interest in, the property, may be revested in the person from whom it was conveyed or transferred or in any person on his or her behalf,

(b)   any annuity or other periodic payment reserved out of the property or any part of it, or any life or other interest so reserved, being an interest which is subject to forfeiture, or

(c)   any right of residence, support, maintenance, or other right of a similar nature which the property is subject to or charged with, except where such rights are reserved in favour of the transferor or the spouse of the transferor and in any such case regard shall be had to such rights only to the extent that their value does not exceed 10 per cent of the unencumbered value of the property,

but if on a claim made to the Commissioners not later than 6 years after the making or execution of the instrument it is shown to their satisfaction that any such power as is mentioned in paragraph (a) has been exercised in relation to the property and the property or any property representing it has been reconveyed or retransferred in the whole or in part in consequence of that exercise, the Commissioners shall repay the stamp duty paid by virtue of this section, in a case where the whole of such property has been so reconveyed or retransferred, so far as it exceeds the stamp duty which would have been payable apart from this section and, in any other case, so far as it exceeds the stamp duty which would have been payable if the instrument had operated to convey or transfer only such property as is not so reconveyed or retransferred.

Case law

William Cory and Son Ltd v IRC [1965] 1 All ER 917, and *Stanyforth v IRC* [1930] AC 339.

Former enactment

FA 1978 s 34(5); FA 1993 s 105.

19 Valuation of property chargeable with stamp duty

The Commissioners shall ascertain the value of property the subject of an instrument chargeable with stamp duty in the same manner, subject to any necessary modification, as is provided for in section 15 of the Capital Acquisitions Tax Act, 1976.

Definitions

"Commissioners": s 1; "executed": s 1; "instrument": s 1; IA 1937 s 3; "stamp": s 1.

Former enactment

FA 1991 s 105(1).; FA 1994 s 104.

PART 4
ADJUDICATION AND APPEALS

20 Assessment of duty by the Commissioners

(1) Subject to such regulations as the Commissioners may think fit to make, the Commissioners may be required by any person to express their opinion, or may express their opinion, with reference to any executed instrument on the following questions:

(a)   whether it is chargeable with any duty;

(b)   with what amount of duty it is chargeable.

(2) Where an instrument which is chargeable with stamp duty has not been delivered to the Commissioners for assessment of duty or impressing of stamps, the Commissioners shall make an assessment of such amount of stamp duty as, to the best of their

knowledge, information (including information received from a member of the Garda Siochana) and belief, ought to be charged, levied and paid on the instrument; and the accountable person shall be liable for the payment of the stamp duty so assessed unless, on delivery of the instrument to them, the Commissioners make another assessment to be substituted for such assessment.

(3) The Commissioners may require to be furnished with a copy of the instrument, together with such evidence as they may deem necessary, in order to show to their satisfaction whether all the facts and circumstances affecting the liability of the instrument to duty, or the amount of the duty chargeable on the instrument, are fully and truly set forth in the instrument.

(4) If the Commissioners are of opinion that the instrument is not chargeable with any duty, it may be stamped with a particular stamp denoting that it is not chargeable with any duty.

(5) If the Commissioners are of opinion that the instrument is chargeable with duty, they shall assess the duty with which it is in their opinion chargeable, and when the instrument is stamped in accordance with the assessment it may be stamped with a particular stamp denoting that it is duly stamped.

(6) Every instrument stamped with the particular stamp denoting either that it is not chargeable with any duty, or is duly stamped, shall be admissible in evidence, and available for all purposes notwithstanding any objection relating to duty.

(7) An instrument on which the duty has been assessed by the Commissioners shall not, if it is unstamped or insufficiently stamped, be stamped otherwise than in accordance with the assessment.

(8) Nothing in this section shall—

    (*a*)   extend to any instrument chargeable with ad valorem duty, and made as a security for money or stock without limit, or

    (*b*)   authorise the stamping after its execution of any instrument which by law cannot be stamped after execution.

(9) A statutory declaration made for the purpose of this section shall not be used against any person making the same in any proceeding, except in an inquiry as to the duty with which the instrument to which it relates is chargeable.

(10) If at any time it appears that for any reason an assessment is incorrect the Commissioners shall make such other assessment as they consider appropriate, which assessment shall be substituted for the first-mentioned assessment.

(11) If at any time it appears, in respect of an instrument which has been stamped in accordance with an assessment, that for any reason the assessment was an underassessment the Commissioners shall make such additional assessment as they consider appropriate.

Cross-references

Appeals: s 21.
Adjudication is obligatory as follows:
Capital duty exemptions: s 120.

Conveyance in contemplation of sale: s 33.

Farmers (young), transfers of interest in land to: s 81.

Mortgage between associated companies: s 83.

Reconstructions and amalgamations of companies: s 80.

Transfer to a charity:s 82.

Transfers and leases, particulars to be delivered: s 12.

Uncertificated securities (CREST system) this section does not apply: s 71(*e*).

Voluntary disposition with right of revocation: s 33.

Voluntary dispositions and deemed voluntary dispositions: s 30.

Case law

Where any person obliged to register a stampable instrument requires the instrument to be adjudicated it must then be adjudicate: *R v Registrar of Joint Stock Companies* (1882) 21 QB 131.

Narrative

Irish Stamp Duty Law, Chapters 13, 14.

Definitions

"accountable person", "Commissioners", "executed", "execution", "money", "instrument": s 1; "person" IA 1937 s 11(*c*); "stamp", "stamped", "stock": s 1.

Former enactment

SA 1891 s 12; FA 1991 s 98(*a*)-(*d*); Criminal Assets Bureau Act 1996 s 6(*d*); Disclosure of Certain Information for Taxation and Other Purposes Act 1996 s 7(*a*); FA 1999 s 187.

21 Right of appeal of persons dissatisfied with assessment

(1) In this section—

"Appeal Commissioners" has the meaning assigned to it by section 850 of the Taxes Consolidation Act, 1997:

"appellant" means a person who appeals to the Appeal Commissioners under subsection (2).

(2) Any person who is dissatisfied with the assessment of the Commissioners and who is an accountable person in relation to such assessment may, on payment of duty in conformity with the assessment, appeal to the Appeal Commissioners against the assessment and the appeal shall be heard and determined by the Appeal Commissioners whose determination shall be final and conclusive unless the appeal is required to be reheard by a judge of the Circuit Court or a case is required to be stated in relation to it for the opinion of the High Court on a point of law.

(3) A person who intends to appeal under this section against an assessment shall, within 30 days after the date of the assessment, give notice in writing to the Commissioners of such intention.

(4) Subject to this section, Chapter 1 of Part 40 (Appeals) of the Taxes Consolidation Act, 1997, shall, with any necessary modifications, apply as they apply for the purpose of income tax.

(5) Notwithstanding subsection (2)—

    (*a*) any person dissatisfied with any decision of the Commissioners as to the value of any land for the purpose of an assessment under this Act may appeal against such decision in the manner prescribed by section 33 (as amended by the Property Values (Arbitrations and Appeals) Act, 1960) of the Finance (1909-

10) Act, 1910, and so much of Part I of that Act as relates to appeals shall apply to an appeal under this subsection;

(*b*) an appeal shall not lie under subsection (2) on any question relating to the value of any land.

(6) The particulars of any transfer or lease which are presented to or obtained by the Commissioners under section 12 shall, in any appeal under this section, be received as prima facie evidence of all matters and things stated in such particulars.

Cross-references

Uncertificated securities (CREST system) this section does not apply: s 7(*e*).

Note

Up to 23 May 1994 there was no general right of appeal to the Appeal Commissioners and the Circuit Court. From that date (FA 1994 s 109) there is such a right but in respect of instruments executed from that date only. As regards instruments executed before 23 May 1994: appeals against valuations of stocks and shares (to the Property Arbitrator) were governed by FA 1972 s 36; appeals against valuations made for the purposes of companies capital duty were governed by FA 1973 s 74.

Case law

Court's decision on an appeal is an order, not a judgment: *Onslow v Commissioners for Inland Revenue* (1890) 25 QBD 465.

Oral evidence was admitted to supplement the case stated in: *Speyer Bros v IRC* [1906]1 KB 318.

Stamp duty based on substance of transaction: *Viek Investments v Revenue Commissioners*, (decision in *Waterford Glass* case applied) IV ITR 369.

Premises purchased by the Society not exempt from stamp duty under Building Society Act 1976 s 91(*e*): *Irish Nationwide Building Society v Revenue Commissioners*, IV ITR 296.

Definitions

"Commissioners", "instrument": s 122(1); "person" IA 1937 s 11(*c*).

Narrative

Irish Stamp Duty Law, Ch 14.

Former enactment

SA 1891 s 13; FA 1994 s 109(1), TCA 1997 s 1100 and Sch 31; FA 1999 s 173(*a*)-(*b*).

PART 5
PROVISIONS APPLICABLE TO PARTICULAR INSTRUMENTS

CHAPTER 1
Bills of Exchange and Promissory Notes

22 Bills and notes purporting to be drawn outside the State

A bill of exchange or promissory note which purports to be drawn or made outside the State shall, for the purpose of the stamp duty on such bill of exchange or promissory note, be deemed to have been so drawn or made, although it may in fact have been drawn or made in the State.

Cross-references

Notes promising the payment of sum of money is a deemed promissory note for that sum of money: s 28.

Definitions

"bill of exchange"; "promissory note"; "stamp": s 1.

Former enactment

SA 1891 s 36; FA 1961 s 39 and Sch 3.

23 Restriction on stamping after execution

No bill of exchange or promissory note shall be stamped with an impressed stamp after its execution.

Definitions

"bill of exchange"; "execution", "impressed", "material"; "promissory note"; "stamp", "stamped": s 1.

Former enactment

SA 1891 s 37(2); FA 1961 s 39 and Sch 3.

24 One bill only of a set need be stamped

(1) When a bill of exchange is drawn in a set according to the custom of merchants, and one of the set is duly stamped, the other or others of the set shall, unless issued or in some manner negotiated apart from the stamped bill, be exempt from duty.

(2) On proof of the loss or destruction of a duly stamped bill of exchange forming one of a set, any other bill of the set which has not been issued or in any manner negotiated apart from the lost or destroyed bill may, although unstamped, be admitted in evidence to prove the contents of the lost or destroyed bill.

Definitions

"bill of exchange", "stamped": s 1.

Former enactment

SA 1891 s 39.

25 Denotion of duty by adhesive stamps

(1) The duty on a bill of exchange or a promissory note may be denoted by an adhesive stamp which shall be cancelled by the person by whom the bill or note is signed before such person delivers it out of his or her hands, custody or power.

(2) Every person who issues, endorses, transfers, negotiates, presents for payment, or pays any bill of exchange or promissory note liable to duty and not being duly stamped shall incur a penalty of [€630][1], and the person who takes or receives from any other person any such bill or note either in payment or as a security, or by purchase or other-wise, shall not be entitled to recover on such bill or note, or to make the same available for any purpose.

(3) Notwithstanding subsection (2), if any bill of exchange is presented for payment unstamped, the person to whom it is presented may affix to it an adhesive stamp of the amount of duty chargeable under this Act in respect of that bill, and cancel the same, as if he or she had been the drawer of that bill, and may, having affixed the stamp and cancelled it, pay the sum in that bill mentioned, and charge the duty in account against the person by whom that bill was drawn, or deduct the duty from that sum, and that bill shall, so far as respects the duty, be deemed valid and available.

(4) The affixing of an adhesive stamp to a bill of exchange in accordance with subsection (3) shall not relieve any person from any penalty incurred by such person in relation to such bill.

Amendments

¹   Substituted by FA 2001 s 240 and Sch 5 Pt 6 with effect from 1 January 2002; previously "£500".

Note

Section 41(7) repealed SA 1891 ss 35, 38 with effect from 1 February 1971; FA 1961 s 31 with effect from 15 February 1971.

Definitions

"person": IA 1937 s 11(c); "stamp": s 1.

Former enactment

FA 1970 s 41(2)-(3); FA 1999 s 165.

26 Certain bills issued by local authorities to be chargeable as promissory notes

Where under the power conferred by any Act any county council or municipal corporation issue bills repayable not later than 12 months from their date, those bills shall, notwithstanding that by the same or any other Act they are charged or secured on any property, fund, or rate, and that the statutory charge is referred to in the bills, be treated for the purpose of this Act, and any Act amending this Act, as promissory notes and not as marketable securities.

Former enactment

FA 1897 s 8

27 Stamping of certain foreign bills of exchange

Notwithstanding any enactment to the contrary, a bill of exchange which is presented for acceptance or is accepted or payable outside the State shall not be invalid in the State by reason only that it is not stamped in accordance with the law for the time being in force in the State in relation to stamp duties, and sections 14(1) and 127 shall apply to every such bill of exchange which is unstamped or insufficiently or not properly stamped as if it were an instrument which may legally be stamped after it has been executed within the meaning of sections 14(1) and 127.

Former enactment

FA 1936 s 25.

28 Notes promising the payment of sum of money out of a particular fund, etc

A note promising the payment of any sum of money out of any particular fund which may or may not be available, or on any condition or contingency which may or may not be performed or happen, shall be deemed a promissory note for that sum of money.

Cross-references

Bills charged on local note to be stamped as promissory notes: s 26.
Meaning of "negotiates": Bills of Exchange Act 1882 s 31(1).
Notes purporting to be foreign notes: s 22.
Promissory note, definition not as broad as s 1: Bills of Exchange Act 1882 s 83.
PROMISSORY NOTE head and exemptions: Sch 1.

Case law

A document although containing a promise to pay a sum of money which was not given or accepted as a promissory note is not chargeable as one: *Yeo v Dawe* (1885) 33 WR 739.
"... 'containing a promise to pay' must mean that that is the substance of the document, the whole contents; it cannot mean containing a promise to pay forming one of a number of stipulations' as per Lindley, L.J., in

Mortgage Insurance Corporation v IRC (1888) 21 QBD 352, CA followed in *Wirth v Weigel Leygonie & Co Ltd*, [1939]3 All ER 712.

The sum to be paid must be certain: *Henderson v Dawson* (1895) 22 R. Ct. of Sess 895.

The promise to pay must not be merely incidental to the main purpose of the instrument.

Thomson v Ball (1894) 22 R. Ct. of Sess 16.

For distinction between a promissory note and an assignment of debt: *Buck v Robson* (1878) 3 QBD 686.

Former enactment

SA 1891 s 33(2).

CHAPTER 2

Conveyances on Sale

29 Conveyance on sale combined with building agreement for dwellinghouse or apartment

(1) (*a*)　In this section—

"**building**" includes any improvement of any land, and any alteration to the character of any land, preliminary to the erection on that land of a dwellinghouse or apartment;

"**land**" includes any interest in any land but does not include the result of any act of building.

(*b*)　For the purposes of this section, references to the repayment of stamp duty to a person who paid it include reference to any other person who satisfies the Commissioners that he or she is entitled to recover moneys owing to the person.

(2) Notwithstanding section 43, where, in connection with, or as part of any arrangement involving, a sale of any land, a dwellinghouse or apartment has been built, or is in the course of being built, or is to be built, on that land, any instrument whereby such sale is effected shall be chargeable to stamp duty under the heading "CONVEYANCE or TRANSFER on sale of any property other than stocks or marketable securities or a policy of insurance or a policy of life insurance" in Schedule 1, as if the property concerned were residential property on an amount equal to the aggregate of—

(*a*)　any consideration paid in respect of the sale of that land, and

(*b*)　any consideration paid, or to be paid, in respect of the building of the dwellinghouse or apartment on that land.

(3) Without prejudice to the generality of subsection (2), a dwellinghouse or apartment shall be regarded as having been built or being in the course of being built or to be built in connection with, or as part of any arrangement involving, a sale of any land where building has commenced prior to the execution of any instrument effecting the sale.

(4) (*a*)　Where in the case of any instrument of sale to which this section applies, the aggregate consideration to which subsection (2) relates cannot, in the opinion of the Commissioners, be ascertained at the date on which the instrument is presented for stamping, then the instrument shall be chargeable to stamp duty as if the amount of the aggregate consideration which is chargeable under subsection (2) was equal to 10 times the unencumbered open market value of the land at the date of the instrument of sale or to such lower multiple, not

     being less than 5, of the open market value of the land as the Commissioners consider appropriate having regard to the relevant information available to them.

(*b*)   Where it is shown to the satisfaction of the Commissioners that the amount of the stamp duty paid under this subsection exceeded the stamp duty with which the instrument would have been charged under subsection (2) had the aggregate consideration paid or to be paid in respect of the dwellinghouse or apartment been ascertainable at the date of stamping of the instrument, then the amount of such excess stamp duty shall, on an application to the Commissioners within 3 years after the date of stamping of the instrument, be repaid to the person or persons by whom the stamp duty was paid and such repayment shall bear simple interest at the rate of [0.0161 per cent, or such other rate (if any) as stands prescribed by the Minister by regulations, for each day or part of a day]¹ or part of a month from the date of payment of the excess duty up until the date of such repayment and income tax shall not be deductible on payment of interest under this subsection and such interest shall not be reckoned in computing income for the purposes of the Tax Acts.

(5) For the purpose of determining whether this section shall apply to any instrument, the Commissioners may require the delivery to them, in such form as they may specify, of a statement or a statutory declaration by—

(*a*)   any person directly or indirectly concerned with the sale of the land or with the building of a dwellinghouse or apartment on the land, and

(*b*)   any solicitor acting on behalf of any person to whom paragraph (*a*) relates,

of any facts which the Commissioners consider relevant in making any such determination.

(6) Any instrument to which the heading "CONVEYANCE or TRANSFER on sale of any property other than stocks or marketable securities or a policy of insurance or a policy of life insurance" in Schedule 1 applies shall contain a statement, in such form as the Commissioners may specify, certifying whether or not this section is applicable to such instrument, and the furnishing of an incorrect certificate shall be deemed to constitute the delivery of an incorrect statement for the purposes of section 1078 of the Taxes Consolidation Act, 1997.

(7) Where stamp duty has been charged on any instrument by reference to this section and, within 2 years after the date of stamping of the instrument, building has not commenced, then this section shall be deemed not to have applied to the instrument and, accordingly, the Commissioners shall, on application to them within 3 years after the date of stamping of the instrument by the person or persons by whom the stamp duty was paid, repay to such person or persons the amount of the stamp duty paid by such person or persons which, but for the other provisions of this section, would not have been chargeable and such repayment shall bear simple interest at the rate of [0.0161 per cent, or such other rate (if any) as stands prescribed by the Minister by regulations, for each day or part of a day]¹ from the date of payment of the excess duty up until the date of such repayment and income tax shall not be deductible on payment of interest under this subsection and such interest shall not be reckoned in computing income for the purposes of the Tax Acts.

(8) Every regulation made under this section shall be laid before Dail Eireann as soon as may be after it is made and, if a resolution annulling the regulation is passed by Dail Eireann within the next 21 days on which Dail Eireann has sat after the regulation is laid before it, the regulation shall be annulled accordingly, but without prejudice to the validity of anything previously done under that regulation.

Amendments

¹ Substituted by FA 2002 s 129(6)(c) with effect from 1 September 2002 in respect of an amount due to be paid or remitted, whether before, on, or after that date; previously "0.5 per cent, or such other rate (if any) as stands prescribed by the Minister by regulations, for each month or part of a month".

Cross -references

Exemption for houses under 125m² in floor area: s 91.
New dwelling-house or apartment with no floor area certificate, amount chargeable to duty:s 92.
Procedure to apply where consideration cannot be ascertained. This provision does not apply where s 3(*a*) applies: ss 44 and 55.
Subs (2) does not apply where house or apartment was occupied prior to the sale agreement: s 92.

Definitions

"execution": s 1; "instrument": s 1, IA 1937 s 3; "marketable security", "stamp", "stock": s 1.

Former enactment

FA 1990 s 112(1)-(8)(part); TCA 1997 s 100 and Sch 31; FA 1998 s 124(3); F(No 2)A 1998 s 12(*a*) and (*b*).

30 Voluntary dispositions inter vivos chargeable a conveyances or transfers on sale

(1) Any conveyance or transfer operating as a voluntary disposition inter vivos shall be chargeable with the same stamp duty as if it were a conveyance or transfer on sale, with the substitution in each case of the value of the property conveyed or transferred for the amount or value of the consideration for the sale.

(2) Notwithstanding subsection (1), this section shall not apply to a conveyance or transfer operating as a voluntary disposition of property to a body of persons incorporated by a special Act, if that body is by its Act precluded from dividing any profit among its members and the property conveyed is to be held for the purposes of an open space or for the purposes of its preservation for the benefit of the nation.

(3) Notwithstanding anything in section 20, the Commissioners may be required to express their opinion under that section on any conveyance or transfer operating as a voluntary disposition inter vivos, and no such conveyance or transfer shall, notwithstanding section 127, be given in evidence, except in criminal proceedings or in civil proceedings by the Commissioners to recover stamp duty, or be available for any purpose unless it is stamped in accordance with subsection (4) or subsection (5) of section 20.

(4) Any conveyance or transfer (not being a disposition made in favour of a purchaser or incumbrancer or other person in good faith and for valuable consideration) shall, for the purposes of this section, be deemed to be a conveyance or transfer operating as a voluntary disposition inter vivos, and the consideration for any conveyance or transfer shall not for this purpose be deemed to be valuable consideration where marriage is the consideration, or part of the consideration, or where the Commissioners are of opinion that by reason of the inadequacy of the sum paid as consideration or other circumstances the conveyance or transfer confers a substantial benefit on the person to whom the property is conveyed or transferred.

(5) Subsections (1) to (4) shall not apply in relation to conveyances or transfers coming within any of the following classes (whether the circumstances by virtue of which the conveyance or transfer comes within any such class are or are not stated in the conveyance or transfer), that is, a conveyance or transfer—

(*a*) made for nominal consideration for the purpose of securing the repayment of an advance or loan,

(*b*) made for effectuating the appointment of a new trustee or the retirement of a trustee (whether the trust is expressed or implied),

(*c*) under which no beneficial interest passes in the property conveyed or transferred,

(*d*) made to a beneficiary by a trustee or other person in a fiduciary capacity under any trust whether expressed or implied, or

(*e*) which is a disentailing assurance not limiting any new estate other than an estate in fee simple in the person disentailing the property.

Cross-references

Conveyances in contemplation of sale: s 33.

Exemption of certain transfers from stamp duty following the dissolution of a marriage: s 97.

Leases which are deemed voluntary dispositions: s 54.

Meaning of "conveyance": s 1.

Presumption of negligence if the application of this section not brought to the attention of Revenue Commissioners: s 8.

spouse exemption on transfers: s 96.

Sub sales: s 46).

Subss (1)-(5) do not apply: transfer for nominal consideration for securing a loan; transfer for effecting charge of trustee; transfer passing no beneficial interest; transfer to a beneficiary of a trust, a transfer which is a disentailing assurance: FA 1943 s 14.

Surcharges for under statement of valuations: s 15.

Uncertificated securities (CREST system), subs (2): s 71.

Value of property where rights are reserved out of the property or it is subject to a power of reversion to the transferor: s 18.

Voluntary dispositions between relatives: Sch 1 CONVEYANCE Head para (15).

Case law

The section applies to voluntary settlements *Baker v IRC* [1923] 1 KB 323.

A conveyance containing a covenant to reside with the transferor and "to care for, support, clothe, keep and maintain (her) in a fit and proper manner during her lifetime" is a conveyance for valuable consideration not a voluntary disposition: *Colreavy v Colreavy and Keenan* [1939] IR 71.

Definitions

"Accountable person": s 1; "Commissioners": s 1; "execution"; "instrument": s 1, IA 1937 s 3; "person": IA 1937 s 11(*c*); "stamp": s 1.

Former enactment

F(1909-10)A 1910 s 74(1), (2), (5) and (6); FA 1943 s 14, FA 1988 s 92(1); FA 1999 s 180.

---

31 Certain contracts to be chargeable as conveyances on sale

(1) Any contract or agreement—

(*a*) for the sale of any equitable estate or interest in any property, or

(*b*) for the sale of any estate or interest in any property except lands, tenements, hereditaments, or heritages, or property locally situated outside the State, or goods, wares or merchandise, or stock or marketable securities (being stock or marketable securities other than any share warrant issued in accordance with section 88 of the Companies Act, 1963), or any ship or vessel or aircraft, or part interest, share, or property of or in any ship or vessel or aircraft,

shall be charged with the same ad valorem duty, to be paid by the purchaser, as if it were an actual conveyance on sale of the estate, interest, or property contracted or agreed to be sold.

(2) Where the purchaser has paid the ad valorem duty in accordance with subsection (1) and before having obtained a conveyance or transfer of the property enters into a contract or agreement for the sale of the same, the contract or agreement shall be charged, if the consideration for that sale is in excess of the consideration for the original sale, with the ad valorem duty payable in respect of such excess consideration, but shall not otherwise be chargeable with duty.

(3) Where duty has been duly paid in conformity with subsections (1) and (2), the conveyance or transfer made to the purchaser or sub-purchaser, or any other person on his or her behalf or by his or her direction, shall not be chargeable with any duty, and the Commissioners, on application, either shall denote the payment of the ad valorem duty on the conveyance or transfer, or shall transfer the ad valorem duty to the conveyance or transfer on production of the contract or agreement, or contracts or agreements, duly stamped.

(4) The ad valorem duty paid on any contract or agreement to which this section applies shall be returned by the Commissioners in case the contract or agreement be afterwards rescinded or annulled, or for any other reason be not substantially performed or carried into effect, so as to operate as or be followed by a conveyance or transfer.

Cross-references

Exemption for a range of financial services instruments which would otherwise come within this section: s 90.
Subsales of land: s 46.
UK legislation
Stamp Act 1891 s 59.
Stamp Act 1891 First Schedule
Heading Bill of Exchange or Promissory Note

Case law

An agreement for the sale of a legal interest in land, with an option enabling the purchaser to take a declaration of trust in lieu thereof, is not an agreement for the sale of an equitable interest: *West London Syndicate v IRC* [1895]1 QB 227, [1898]2 QB 507, CA. See also *Peter Bone Ltd v IRC*, Ch D , 27 July 1995.
A receipt for monies received for a reversionary interest under a will held to be an agreement for sale of an equitable interest *Fleetwood v IRC* (1936) 1 KB 351.
Contract for sale of an option to purchase a property at a price is not an agreement for the sale of an equitable interest: *Muller & Co's Margarine Ltd v IRC* [1900]1 QB 310, CA.
The words of exception in subs (1) refer only to "the sale of any estate or interest in any property ...": *Farmer & Co v IRC* [1898]2 QB 141.
Goodwill is property capable of being sold separately from other property: *West London Syndicate v IRC* [1898]2 QB 507.
Goodwill is situated where a trade mark in respect of the product to which the goodwill attaches is registered: *Benjamin Brooke Co v IRC* [1896]2 QB 536.
Tenants' fixtures are neither an interest in land nor goods: *Lee v Gaskell* (1876) 1 QBD 700.
Cash in a deposit account is a chose in action and does not fall under the exception: *Foley v Hill* (1848) 2 HL Cas 28. By Revenue concession, this does not apply to cash in a current account.
Where apportionment is required as a result of the operation of s 59 it must reflect the true value of the properties: *West London Syndicate v IRC* [1898]2 QB 507, also, to be an agreement for the sale of an equitable interest the instrument must infer an obligation on the vendor to grant such an interest and the purchaser must be obliged to accept it.

An agreement to hold property on trust in consideration of money or marketable securities comes within the section as an agreement for sale of an equitable interest: *Chesterfield Brewery Co v IRC* [1899]2 QB 7.

It may be necessary to separate the goods from the benefit of a hire purchase debt if they are sold with the benefit of the right to receive the debt: *Drages Ltd v IRC* (1927) 6 ATC 727.

The interest of a pledgee in goods pledged to him is "goods" and therefore excepted property: *Arthur Riley Ltd v IRC* (1931) 46 TC 402.

A contract of agreement between parties at arm's length may be a voluntary disposition and in such a case duty under section 59 could be assessed on the basis of a voluntary disposition: *Lap Shun Textiles Industrial Co Ltd v Collector of Stamp Revenue* [1976] STC 83.

Only tangible property capable of having a local situation and accordingly the expression "property of locally situate outside the State" was held not to include a half share of a patent in New South Wales: *Smelting Co of Australia v IRC* (1897) 1 QB 175.

Narrative

Irish Stamp Duty Law, Chapter 5.

Definitions

"Commissioners", "impressed", "marketable security": s 1; "person" IA 1937 s 11(*c*); "stamped", "stock": s 1.

Former enactment

SA 1891 s 59(1)-(3), (6), (7).; 1909 s 12 and Sch; FA 1970 ss 46(1)(*c*), 60 and Sch 12; FA 1971 s 43(1)(*a*); FA 1998 s 119; FA 1999 s 197 and Sch 6.

32 As to sale of an annuity or right not before in existence

Where on the sale of any annuity or other right not previously in existence such annuity or other right is not created by actual grant or conveyance, but is only secured by bond, warrant of attorney, covenant, contract, or otherwise, the bond or other instrument, or some one of such instruments, if there be more than one, is to be charged with the same duty as an actual grant or conveyance, and is for the purposes of this Act to be deemed an instrument of conveyance on sale.

Cross-references

Security for payment of an annuity by way of repayment of a loan: s 57(2).

Security for an annuity except upon the original creation thereof: para (1) BOND, COVENANT etc head of charge in Sch 1.

Case law

Section 32 applies to the grant of a perpetual annuity in consideration of a sum of money: *Mersey Docks and Harbour Board v IRC* (1897) 1 QB 786.

Instrument securing an annuity agreed to be paid in consideration of the transfer of property is not given upon the sale of an annuity: *Blandy v Herbert* (1829) 9 B&C 396.

Limitations to the application of the section considered in *Great Northern Railway Co v IRC* [1901]1 IK 415 — the right must take its origin from the transaction of sale itself and must be one the sale of which is capable of being completed by grant or conveyance.

The annuity or right must be created in circumstances constituting a sale for stamp duty purposes i.e. consideration in cash, shares or liabilities: *Faber v IRC* (1936) 155 LT 228.

Definitions

"conveyance on sale"; "instrument": s 1.

Former enactment

SA 1891 s 60.

33 Conveyance or transfer in contemplation of sale

(1) Subject to this section, any instrument whereby property is conveyed or transferred to any person in contemplation of a sale of that property shall be treated for the purposes of this Act as a conveyance or transfer on sale of that property for a consideration equal to the value of that property.

(2) If on a claim made to the Commissioners not later than 6 years after the making or execution of an instrument chargeable with duty in accordance with subsection (1), it is shown to their satisfaction—

(*a*) that the sale in contemplation of which the instrument was made or executed has not taken place and the property has been reconveyed or retransferred to the person from whom it was conveyed or transferred or to a person to whom his or her rights have been transmitted on death or bankruptcy, or

(*b*) that the sale has taken place for a consideration which is less than the value in respect of which duty was paid on the instrument by virtue of this section,

the Commissioners shall repay the duty paid by virtue of this section, in a case falling under paragraph (*a*), so far as it exceeds the stamp duty which would have been payable apart from this section and, in a case falling under paragraph (*b*), so far as it exceeds the stamp duty which would have been payable if the instrument had been stamped in accordance with subsection (1) in respect of a value equal to the consideration in question.

(3) In a case to which subsection (2)(*b*) relates, duty shall not be repayable if it appears to the Commissioners that the circumstances are such that a conveyance or transfer on the sale in question would have been chargeable with duty under section 30 by virtue of subsection (4) of that section.

(4) No instrument chargeable with duty in accordance with subsection (1) shall be deemed to be duly stamped unless the Commissioners have been required to express their opinion on the instrument under section 20 and have expressed their opinion on the instrument in accordance with that section.

(5) This section shall apply whether or not an instrument conveys or transfers other property in addition to the property in contemplation of the sale of which it is made or executed, but this section shall not affect the stamp duty chargeable on the instrument in respect of that other property.

Case law

William Cory and Son Ltd v IRC [1965] 1 All ER 917, and *Stanyforth v IRC* [1930] AC 339.

Former enactment

FA 1978 s 34(1)-(4).

34 Agreements in connection with, or in contemplation of, sale

Where, in connection with, or in contemplation of, a sale of property, the vendor enters into—

(*a*) an agreement for the grant of a lease of the property for a term exceeding 35 years, or

(*b*) an agreement (other than a contract for the sale of the property) under which the vendor grants any other rights in relation to the property,

any conveyance or transfer, subject to the agreement, of the property by the vendor shall be charged to stamp duty as a conveyance or transfer on sale of the property for a consideration equal to the value of the property and the value shall be determined without regard to the agreement.

Note

This section was preceded with effect from 11 June 1985 by a statutory instrument (SI 277/85) in similar terms.

Cross-references

Agreement for a lease for a term exceeding 35 years to be charged as a lease: s 50.
Valuation of property: s 19.

Definitions

"conveyance": s 1; "executed", "instrument": s 1, IA 1937 s 3; "property": CATA 1976 s 2(1); "stamp": s 1.

Former enactment

FA 1986 s 96(1).

---

35 Deeds of enlargement

(1) A declaration by deed under section 65(2) of the Conveyancing Act, 1881, to the effect that, from and after the execution of the deed, a term subsisting in land shall be enlarged, shall, where the term was created by an instrument executed within 6 years of the date of the execution of the deed, be charged to stamp duty as a conveyance or transfer on sale of that land for a consideration equal to the value of the land and that value shall be determined without regard to that term or any part of that term.

(2) Section 82 shall not apply to a deed which is chargeable to stamp duty under subsection (1).

Note

This section was preceded with effect from 11 June 1985 by a statutory instrument (SI 277/85) in similar terms.

Cross-references

Agreement for a lease for a term exceeding 35 years to be charged as a lease: s 50.
Valuation of property: s 19.

Definitions

"conveyance": s 1; "executed", "instrument": s 1, IA 1937 s 3; "property": CATA 1976 s 2(1); "stamp": s 1.

Former enactment

FA 1986 s 96(2)-(3).

---

36 Certain contracts for sale of leasehold interests to be chargeable as conveyances on sale

(1) For the purposes of this section **"transfer"**, other than the last-mentioned reference in paragraph (ii) of subsection (2), means a transfer which would but for this section be chargeable with stamp duty.

(2) A contract or agreement for the sale of any leasehold interest in any immovable property shall, if—

    (*a*) the purchaser enters into possession of the property before having obtained a transfer, duly stamped, of such interest, and

    (*b*) a transfer of such interest made in pursuance of the contract or agreement is not duly stamped within the period of 9 months from the first execution of the contract or agreement or such longer period as the Commissioners may specify in writing, being a period which they consider reasonable in all the circumstances of the case, be charged with the same ad valorem stamp duty, to be paid by the purchaser, as if it were an actual transfer on sale of the leasehold interest contracted or agreed to be sold, and where the ad valorem stamp duty charged on the contract or agreement has been duly paid in conformity with this section—

   (i)   the transfer of that leasehold interest made in pursuance of the contract or agreement shall not be chargeable with any duty,

   (ii)   the Commissioners, on application, either shall denote the payment of that duty on the transfer, or shall transfer it to the transfer on production of the contract or agreement duly stamped, and

   (iii)   that duty shall be returned where it is shown to the satisfaction of the Commissioners that the contract or agreement has been rescinded or annulled.

Former enactment

FA 1978 s 31(1)-(1A); FA 1999 s 181.

37 Exchanges

Any instrument effecting a conveyance or transfer of any immovable property in exchange for any other property, wherever situated, whether movable or immovable and with or without the payment of any consideration, shall be chargeable in respect of such conveyance or transfer under the heading "CONVEYANCE or TRANSFER on sale of any property other than stocks or marketable securities or a policy of insurance or a policy of life insurance" in Schedule 1, with the substitution of the value of immovable property situated in the State thereby conveyed or transferred for the amount or value of the consideration for the sale.

Note

Relief under s 38 continues to apply to partitions or severances of immovable property.

Former enactment

FA 1993 s 104(2).

38 Partitions or divisions

(1) Where on the partition or division of any real or heritable property any consideration exceeding in amount or value [€130][1] is paid or given, or agreed to be paid or given, for equality, the principal or only instrument whereby the partition or division is effected shall be charged with the same ad valorem duty as a conveyance on sale for the consideration, and with that duty only.

(2) Where, in a case to which subsection (1) applies, there are several instruments for completing the title of either party, the principal instrument is to be ascertained, and the other instruments are to be charged with duty in the manner provided for in this Act in the case of several instruments of conveyance.

Amendments

[1]   Substituted by FA 2001 s 240 and Sch 5 Pt 6 with effect from 1 January 2002; previously "£500".

Note

In view of the provision in FA 1993 s 104(4) that s 38 shall not apply to any exchange to which s 104 applies, s 38 in effect applies almost entirely only to partitions of property.

Cross-references

Exchanges: FA 1953 s 12 repealed by FA 1993 s 104 in respect of instruments executed on or after 18 June 1993. EXCHANGE head of charge in Sch 1.

Principal instrument, how to be ascertained: s 47.

Case law

Distinction between exchange and conveyance on sale: *Portman Trustees v IRC* [1956] 35 ATC 349.

Duty under this head applies exclusively to the case of an exchange of any real or heritable property or the partition or division of such property: *IRC v Littlewoods Mail Order Stores Ltd* [1962] 2 All ER 279.

Deed of exchange delivered or escrow takes effect when the conditions of escrow are satisfied: *Terrapin International Ltd v IRC* [1976] 2 All ER 461.

Exchange of shares for shares held to constitute a sale for stamp duty purposes: *Coats (J & P) v IRC* [1897] 1 AB 779; [1897] 2 QB 423.

Partition is not a sale: *Henniker v Henniker* (1852) 1 E & B 54.

This section applies only to immovable property and does not apply to partitions of any other property even where equity money is paid: *MacLeod v IRC* (1885) 12 R(Ct of Sess) 1045.

See also cases listed at LEASE Heading in Sch 1.

Definitions

"instrument": s 1.

Former enactment

SA 1891 s 73.

---

39 Decree or order for foreclosure, etc, and stamp duty

(1) In relation to a conveyance on sale, ad valorem stamp duty on a decree or order for, or having the effect of an order for foreclosure, shall not exceed the duty on a sum equal to the value of the property to which the decree or order relates, and where the decree or order states that value that statement shall be conclusive for the purpose of determining the amount of the duty.

(2) Where ad valorem stamp duty is paid on a decree or order for, or having the effect of an order for, foreclosure, any conveyance following on such decree or order shall be exempt from the ad valorem stamp duty.

Former enactment

FA 1898 s 6(part).

---

40 Calculation of ad valorem duty on stock and securities

(1) Where the consideration, or any part of the consideration, for a conveyance on sale consists of any stock or marketable security, the conveyance shall be charged with ad valorem duty in respect of the value of that stock or security.

(2) Where the consideration, or any part of the consideration, for a conveyance on sale consists of any security not being a marketable security, the conveyance is to be charged with ad valorem duty in respect of the amount due on the day of the date of the conveyance for principal and interest on that security.

Cross-references

Valuation of property: s 19.

Case law

Assessments under s 40 upheld by the court: *Great Western Ry Co v IRC* [1894] 1 QB 507; *Coats (J & P) v IRC* [1897] 2 AB 423, CA; *Chesterfield Brewery Co v IRC* [1899] 2 QB 7; *Foster (John) & Sons v IRC* [1894] 1 QB 516.

Principles to be applied in valuing shares for stamp duty: *Hatrick v IRC*; *Public Trustee v IRC*, [1963] NZLR 641.

The value of the consideration in the case where shares are the consideration may be arrived at by valuing the property conveyed or transferred: *Carlyon Estate v IRC* (1937) 16 ATC 339.

Where the section refers to the "value" of consideration shares it is their actual not their nominal value which is intended: *Crane Fruehauf Ltd v IRC* [1975] 1 All ER 429 at p 434.

Definitions

"conveyance on sale"; "stock": s 1.

Former enactment

SA 1891 s 55.

41 How conveyance in consideration of debt, etc, to be charged

Where any property is conveyed to any person in consideration, wholly or in part, of any debt due to such person, or subject either certainly or contingently to the payment or transfer of any money or stock, whether being or constituting a charge or incumbrance on the property or not, the debt, money, or stock shall be deemed the whole or part, as the case may be, of the consideration in respect of which the conveyance is chargeable with ad valorem duty.

Cross-references

In the case of foreclosure decrees duty shall be charged on a sum which does not exceed the value of the property: s 39.

Conveyance or transfer on sale: s 31.

Case law

Mortgage debt, subject to the payment of which the property was sold, held to form part of the consideration for sale even if the sale takes place as part of a family arrangement: *IRC v City of Glasgow Bank Liquidators* (1881), 8 R (Ct of Sess) 389; *Bristol (Marquess) v IRC* [1901] 2 KB 336.

Conveyance to an equitable mortgagee in pursuance of an order for foreclosure liable to ad valorem duty: *Huntington v IRC* [1896] 1 QB 422.

Liabilities, certain or contingent, subject to which the property is conveyed form the whole or part, of the consideration *Furness Ry Co v IRC* (1864) 33 LJ Ex 173.

Where a creditor takes over the property of his debtor in consideration of the release of his debt, the transaction is a sale and chargeable under the section even if the debt may have been regarded as a bad debt: *IRC v North British Railway Co* (1901) 4 (Ct of Sess) 27.

Where a business is transferred, and the transferee agrees to pay the business debts of the vendor the amount of the face value of these debts will be added to the consideration: *E. Gomme Ltd v IRC* [1964] 1 WLR 1348 at 1356.

Where the transaction is one of sale it does not matter whether or not the purchaser is personally liable for the debt: *IRC v City of Glasgow Bank Liquidation* (1881) 8 R (Ct of Sess) 389.

Definitions

"money": s 1; "person" IA 1937 s 11(*c*); "stock": s 1.

Former enactment

SA 1891 s 57.

42 Charging of consideration consisting of periodical payments

(1) Where the consideration, or any part of the consideration, for a conveyance on sale consists of money payable periodically for a definite period not exceeding 20 years, so that the total amount to be paid can be previously ascertained, the conveyance shall be charged in respect of that consideration with ad valorem duty on such total amount.

(2) Where the consideration, or any part of the consideration, for a conveyance on sale consists of money payable periodically for a definite period exceeding 20 years, the

conveyance shall be charged in respect of that consideration with ad valorem duty on the total amount which will or may, according to the terms of sale, be payable during the period of 20 years next after the day of the date of the instrument.

(3) Notwithstanding subsections (1) and (2), a conveyance on sale chargeable with ad valorem duty in respect of any periodical payments which contains a provision for securing the payments shall not be charged with any duty in respect of such provision, and any separate instrument made in such case for securing the payments shall not be charged with any higher duty than [€12.50][1].

Amendments

[1]   Substituted by FA 2001 s 240 and Sch 5 Pt 6 with effect from 1 January 2002; previously "£10".

Cross-references

Interaction with sub-sale provisions: s 46.
Procedure to apply where consideration cannot be ascertained: 44.

Case law

Periodical payments which are inherently incidental to the property sold do not form part of the consideration unlike periodical payments which are new stipulations forming part of the bargain for sale: *Swayne v IRC* [1900] 1 QB 172.

Covenant to pay balance of purchase money by instalments chargeable: *Limmer Asphalt Paving Co v IRC* (1872) LR 7 Exch 211.

Interest on the purchase price is not included in the amount on which duty is payable: *Hotung v Collector of Stamp Revenue* [1965] AC 766 at p 775.

For money to be payable periodically for a period a payment must fall to be made between the payment which marked the beginning of the period and the payment which marked the end: *Blendett v IRC* and *Quietlece v IRC* both [1984] STC 95

Subs (4): the exemption is excluded where the separate instrument securing the payments comes into existence before the conveyance on sale which it secures: *Western United Investment Co Ltd v IRC* [1958] 1 All ER 257; [1958] Ch. 392.

Money payable within 20 years only in the event of a breach of contract is not included: *Western United Investments C v IRC* [1958] 1 All ER 257; [1958] Ch. 392.

A period of a number of years liable to earlier determination on a contingency is not an indefinite period: *Earl Mount Edgcumbe v IRC* [1911] 2 KB 24.

Definitions

"conveyance on sale"; "instrument", "money": s 1.

Former enactment

SA 1891 s 56; FA 1992 s 204(*b*); FA 1998 s 125 and Sch 8.

43 Further consideration in respect of substantial improvements not chargeable

A conveyance on sale made for any consideration in respect of which it is chargeable with ad valorem duty and in further consideration of a covenant—

(*a*)   by the purchaser to make, or of the purchaser's having previously made, any substantial improvement of or addition to the property conveyed to such purchaser, or

(*b*)   relating to the subject matter of the conveyance,

shall not be chargeable with any duty in respect of such further consideration.

Note

Purchase of a site for building together with the entering into a building contract: ss 29, 53.

Cross-references

Meaning of "conveyance on sale": s 1.

Former enactment
FA 1900 s 10.

44 Procedure to apply where consideration, etc, cannot be ascertained

(1) Where the consideration for a sale cannot be ascertained at the date of execution of a conveyance and such consideration would, if ascertainable, be chargeable with ad valorem duty in respect of such sale, then stamp duty shall be charged on such sale based on the amount or value of the consideration that could be obtained from a purchaser paying full consideration for such sale.

(2) This section shall not apply to any instrument in relation to which subsection (4)(*a*) of section 29 applies.

Definitions
"instrument": s 1, IA 1937 s 3; "stamp": s 1.
Former enactment
FA 1991 s 104(part); FA 1992 s 213.

45 Directions as to apportionment of consideration

(1) Where property contracted to be sold for one consideration for the whole of it is conveyed to the purchaser in separate parts or parcels by different instruments, then the consideration shall be apportioned in such manner, as the parties think fit, so that a distinct consideration for each separate part or parcel is set forth in the conveyance relating to such separate part or parcel, and such conveyance shall be charged with ad valorem duty in respect of such distinct consideration.

(2) Where—

    (*a*) any property which consists partly of an interest in residential property is sold to any person and the sale (in this subsection referred to as "the first-mentioned sale") does not form part of a larger transaction or of a series of transactions, or

    (*b*) the sale to any person of property consisting in whole or in part of such an interest forms part of a larger transaction or of a series of transactions,

then the consideration attributable to the first-mentioned sale and the aggregate consideration (other than rent) attributable to that larger transaction or series of transactions, as the case may be, shall be apportioned, on such basis as is just and reasonable, as between that interest in residential property and the other property or part concerned, and that aggregate consideration shall likewise be apportioned as between each other such interest (if any) comprised in that larger transaction or series of transactions and the other property or parts concerned, and notwithstanding the amount or value of the consideration set forth in any instrument

    (i) the consideration so apportioned to that interest shall be deemed to be the amount or the value of the consideration for the sale which is attributable to that interest and the consideration so apportioned to the aggregate of all such interests comprised in that larger transaction or series of transactions shall be deemed to be the amount or value of that aggregate consideration which is attributable to residential property, and

(ii) the consideration so apportioned to the other property or part or parts concerned shall be deemed to be the amount or value of the consideration for the sale, or of that aggregate consideration, as the case may be, which is attributable to property which is not residential property.

(3) Where property contracted to be purchased for one consideration for the whole of it by 2 or more persons jointly, or by any person for such person and others, or wholly for others, is conveyed in parts or parcels by separate instruments to the persons by or for whom the same was purchased for distinct parts of the consideration, then the conveyance of each separate part or parcel shall be charged with ad valorem duty in respect of the distinct part of the consideration specified in the conveyance.

(4) Where there are several instruments of conveyance for completing the purchaser's title to property sold, the principal instrument of conveyance only shall be charged with ad valorem duty, and the other instruments shall be respectively charged with such other duty as they may be liable to, but the last-mentioned duty shall not exceed the ad valorem duty payable in respect of the principal instrument.

Cross-reference

Parties may determine which of several instruments is the principal one: s 47.

Periodic payments: s 42.

Sub-sales of property such as goodwill and benefit of contract: s 31(2).

Surcharges (subs (1A)): s 16.

Voluntary dispositions: s 30.

Spouses exemption: s 96.

Case law

Where property which is contracted to be bought for one consideration is conveyed by the purchaser in various parts some to himself and some to sub-purchasers the conveyance to himself will attract a duty on a proportionate part of the consideration originally contracted for: *Maples v IRC* [1914] 3 KB 303.

Section 45 prevents the charging of duty on both of the conveyances — from the vendor to the sub-purchaser and from the purchaser to the sub-purchaser: *Escoigne Properties Ltd v IRC* [1958] AC 549.

Definitions

"Conveyance on sale"; "instrument": s 1; "person" IA 1937 s 11(*c*); "stamp"; "stamped": s 1.

Former enactment

SA 1891 s 58(1)-(3); FA 1997 ss 116, 119; F(No 2)A 1998 s 9.

46 Directions as to sub-sales

(1) Where—

    (*a*) a person having contracted for the purchase of any property, but not having obtained a conveyance of that property, contracts to sell the same to any other person, and

    (*b*) the property is in consequence conveyed immediately to the sub-purchaser,

then the conveyance shall be charged with ad valorem duty in respect of the consideration moving from the sub-purchaser.

(2) Where—

    (*a*) a person having contracted for the purchase of any property but not having obtained a conveyance contracts to sell the whole, or any part or parts of that property, to any other person or persons, and (*b*)   the property is in consequence conveyed by the original seller to different persons in parts or parcels,

then the conveyance of each part or parcel shall be charged with ad valorem duty in respect only of the consideration moving from the sub-purchaser of such part or parcel, without regard to the amount or value of the original consideration.

(3) Where—

(*a*)   a sub-purchaser takes an actual conveyance of the interest of the person immediately selling to such sub-purchaser, which is chargeable with ad valorem duty in respect of the consideration moving from such sub-purchaser, and

(*b*)   such conveyance is duly stamped accordingly,

then any conveyance to be afterwards made to such sub-purchaser of the same property by the original seller shall be chargeable only with such other duty as it may be liable to, but the last-mentioned duty shall not exceed the ad valorem duty.

(4) (*a*)   In paragraph (*b*) **"the original seller"** means, in relation to a case to which subsection (1) applies, the person from whom the property is conveyed to the sub-purchaser and, in relation to a case to which subsection (2) or (3) applies, the original seller referred to in subsection (2) or (3), as the case may be.

(*b*)   The consideration moving from the sub-purchaser shall, in a case to which subsection (1), (2) or (3) applies, be ascertained without regard to the value of any covenant, power, condition or arrangement relating to the subject matter of the conveyance which was not in the contract for sale entered into by the original seller and also without regard to any consideration the duty on which or on any part of which would be charged in accordance with subsection (2) of section 42.

(5) Paragraph (15) of the heading "CONVEYANCE or TRANSFER on sale of any property other than stocks or marketable securities or a policy of insurance or a policy of life insurance" in Schedule 1 shall not apply to determine the stamp duty to be charged on any conveyance referred to in subsection (1), (2) or (3).

(6) A conveyance in respect of which subsection (4) applies shall be deemed to be a conveyance operating as a voluntary disposition inter vivos for the purposes of section 30.

Cross-reference

Parties may determine which of several instruments is the principal one: s 47.
Periodic payments: s 42.
Sub-sales of property such as goodwill and benefit of contract: s 31(2).
Surcharges (subs (1A)): s 16.
Voluntary dispositions: s 30.
Spouses exemption: s 96.

Case law

Relief applies only where there is nothing done other than a signing of a contract and the property is not altered *Fitch Lovell Ltd v IRC* [1962] 3 All ER 685.
Where property which is contracted to be bought for one consideration is conveyed by the purchaser in various parts some to himself and some to sub-purchasers the conveyance to himself will attract a duty on a proportionate part of the consideration originally contracted for *Maples v IRC* [1914] 3 KB 303.

Section 46 prevents the charging of duty on both of the conveyances — from the vendor to the sub-purchaser and from the purchaser to the sub-purchaser: *Escoigne Properties Ltd v IRC* [1958] AC 549.

Definitions

"Conveyance on sale"; "instrument": s 1; "person" IA 1937 s 11(*c*); "stamp"; "stamped": s 1.

Former enactment

SA 1891 s 58(4)-(9); FA 1981 s 47; FA 1997 s 197 and Sch 6; FA 1999 s 189.

47 Principal instrument, how to be ascertained

The parties may determine for themselves which of several instruments is to be deemed the principal instrument, and may pay the ad valorem duty on the principal instrument accordingly.

Definitions

"instrument": s 1.

Former enactment

SA 1891 s 61(2); FA 1970 s 60 and Sch 2.

48 Stamp duty and value-added tax

The consideration chargeable under the heading "CONVEYANCE or TRANSFER on sale of any property other than stocks or marketable securities or a policy of insurance or a policy of life insurance" in Schedule 1 shall exclude any value-added tax chargeable under section 2 of the Value-Added Tax Act, 1972, on such sale.

Notes

Property transfers on or after 11 April 1994 are chargeable to stamp duty on the VAT-exclusive value of the consideration. Deeds executed prior to 11 April 1994, with a charge to stamp duty based on the VAT-exclusive value of the consideration, are deemed to have been executed correctly.

Definitions

"instrument", "stamped", "Commissioners", "marketable securities", "marketable securities": s 1.

Former enactment

FA 1994 s 108(1) (part).

CHAPTER 3
Conveyances on any occasion except sale or mortgage

49 Certain transfers, etc, not sales or mortgages, deemed to be conveyances

Every instrument, and every decree or order of any court or of any commissioners, whereby any property on any occasion, except a sale or mortgage, is transferred to or vested in any person, shall be charged with duty as a conveyance or transfer of property.

Case law

An assent in writing under the hand but not the seal of an executor, to a devisee of real estate by his testator not chargeable: *Kemp v IRC* [1905] 1 KB 581.

Definitions

"Commissioners", "instrument": s 1; "person" IA 1937 s 11(*c*).

Former enactment

SA 1891 s 62; FA 1999 s 197 and Sch 6.

CHAPTER 4
Leases

50 Agreements for not more than 35 years charged as leases

An agreement for a lease or with respect to the letting of any lands, tenements, or heritable subjects for any term not exceeding 35 years, or for any indefinite term, shall be charged with the same duty as if it were an actual lease made for the term and consideration mentioned in the agreement.

Cross-references

Agreement for a lease exceeding 35 year term made in contemplation of sale: s 34.

Duty payable under s 50 — LEASE heading in Sch 1.

Increases in rent: s 52(4).

Lessee the accountable person: s 1.

Penal rent not to be charged with duty: s 52.

Procedure to apply where average annual rent or consideration other than rent for a lease cannot be ascertained: ss 44, 55.

Produce as consideration for a lease: s 51.

Case law

An agreement for a lease is as good as a lease: *Walsh v Lonsdale* (1882) 21 Ch. 9.

Narrative

Irish Stamp Duty Law, Chapter 6.

Definitions

"stamped": s 1.

Former enactment

SA 1891 s 75(1); FA 1970 s 60 and Sch 2.

51 Leases how to be charged in respect of produce, etc

(1) Where the consideration, or any part of the consideration, for which a lease is granted or agreed to be granted consists of any produce or other goods, the value of the produce or goods shall be deemed a consideration in respect of which the lease or agreement is chargeable with ad valorem duty.

(2) Where it is stipulated that the value of the produce or goods is to amount at least to, or is not to exceed, a given sum, or where the lessee is specially charged with, or has the option of paying after any permanent rate of conversion, the value of the produce or goods shall, for the purpose of assessing the ad valorem duty, be estimated at the given sum, or according to the permanent rate.

(3) If a lease or agreement for a lease made either wholly or partially for any consideration to which subsection (1) relates—

    (*a*)   contains a statement of the value of such consideration, and

    (*b*)   is stamped in accordance with the statement,

it shall, in respect of the subject matter of the statement, be deemed duly stamped, unless or until it is otherwise shown that the statement is incorrect, and that the lease or agreement is in fact not duly stamped.

Cross-references

Agreement for leases: s 50.

Definitions

"stamped": s 1.

Former enactment

SA 1891 s 76.

52 Charging of duty on leases, etc

(1) A lease, or agreement for a lease, or with respect to any letting, shall not be charged with any duty in respect of any penal rent, or increased rent in the nature of a penal rent, thereby reserved or agreed to be reserved or made payable, or by reason of being made in consideration of the surrender or abandonment of any existing lease, or agreement, of or relating to the same subject matter.

(2) A lease made for any consideration in respect of which it is chargeable with ad valorem duty, and in further consideration either of a covenant by the lessee to make, or of such lessee having previously made, any substantial improvement of or addition to the property demised to such lessee, or of any covenant relating to the matter of the lease, shall not be charged with any duty in respect of such further consideration.

(3) Subsection (2) shall not apply as respects any further consideration in the lease consisting of a covenant which if it were contained in a separate deed would be chargeable with ad valorem stamp duty and, accordingly, the lease shall in any such case be charged with duty in respect of any such further consideration under section 7

(4) An instrument whereby the rent reserved by any other instrument chargeable with duty and duly stamped as a lease is increased shall not be charged with duty otherwise than as a lease in consideration of the additional rent thereby made payable.

(5) Where—

    (*a*) any property which consists partly of an interest in residential property is leased to any person and that lease (in this subsection referred to as **"the first-mentioned lease"**) does not form part of a larger transaction or of a series of transactions, or

    (*b*) the lease to any person of property consisting in whole or in part of such an interest forms part of a larger transaction or of a series of transactions,

then the consideration (other than rent) attributable to the first-mentioned lease and the aggregate consideration (other than rent) attributable to that larger transaction or series of transactions, as the case may be, shall be apportioned, on such basis as is just and reasonable, as between that interest in residential property and the other property or part concerned, and that aggregate consideration shall likewise be apportioned as between each other such interest (if any) comprised in that larger transaction or series of transactions and the other property or parts concerned, and notwithstanding the amount or value of the consideration set forth in any instrument—

    (i) the consideration so apportioned to that interest shall be deemed to be the amount or the value of the consideration for the lease which is attributable to that interest and the consideration so apportioned to the aggregate of all such interests comprised in that larger transaction or series of transactions shall be deemed to be the amount or value of that aggregate consideration which is attributable to residential property, and

(ii) the consideration so apportioned to the other property or part or parts concerned shall be deemed to be the amount or value of the consideration for the lease, or of that aggregate consideration, as the case may be, which is attributable to property which is not residential property.

Case law

Penal rent: *Pollitt v Forest* (1848) 11 QB 969.

Liability on instrument increasing rent reserved by lease: *Gable Construction Ltd v IRC* [1968] 2 All ER 968. See also *Jenkin R Lewis & Son Ltd v Kerman* [1970] 3 WLR 673.

Definitions

"stamped": s 1.

Former enactment

SA 1891 s 77(1), (2), (5), (6); RA 1909 s 8; RA 1909 s 8; FA 1998 s 125 & Sch 8, FA 1997 ss 116 and 120; F(No 2)A 1998 s 10; FA 1999 s 190.

53 Lease combined with building agreement for dwellinghouse or apartment

(1) (*a*) In this section—

"building" includes any improvement of any land, and any alteration to the character of any land, preliminary to the erection on that land of a dwellinghouse or apartment;

"land" includes any interest in any land but does not include the result of any act of building.

(*b*) For the purposes of this section, references to the repayment of stamp duty to a person who paid it include reference to any other person who satisfies the Commissioners that such person is entitled to recover moneys owing to the person.

(2) Notwithstanding subsection (2) of section 52, where, in connection with, or as part of any arrangement involving, a lease of any land, a dwellinghouse or apartment has been built, or is in the course of being built, or is to be built, on that land, any instrument whereby such lease is effected shall be chargeable to stamp duty under subparagraph (*a*) of paragraph (3) of the heading "LEASE" in Schedule 1, as if the property concerned were residential property on an amount equal to the aggregate of—

(*a*) any consideration (other than rent) paid in respect of the lease of that land, and

(*b*) any consideration paid, or to be paid, in respect of the building of the dwellinghouse or apartment on that land.

(3) Without prejudice to the generality of subsection (2), a dwellinghouse or apartment shall be regarded as having been built or being in the course of being built or to be built in connection with, or as part of any arrangement involving, a lease of any land where building has commenced prior to the execution of any instrument effecting the lease.

(4) (*a*) Where in the case of any instrument of lease to which this section applies, the aggregate consideration to which subsection (2) relates cannot, in the opinion of the Commissioners, be ascertained at the date on which the instrument is presented for stamping, then the instrument shall be chargeable to stamp duty

as if the amount of the aggregate consideration which is chargeable under subsection (2) was equal to 10 times the unencumbered open market value of the land at the date of the instrument of lease or to such lower multiple, not being less than 5, of the open market value of the land as the Commissioners consider appropriate having regard to the relevant information available to them.

(b) Where it is shown to the satisfaction of the Commissioners that the amount of the stamp duty paid under this subsection exceeded the stamp duty with which the instrument would have been charged under subsection (2) had the aggregate consideration paid or to be paid in respect of the dwellinghouse or apartment been ascertainable at the date of stamping of the instrument, then the amount of such excess stamp duty shall, on an application to the Commissioners within 3 years after the date of stamping of the instrument, be repaid to the person or persons by whom the stamp duty was paid and such repayment shall bear simple interest at the rate of [0.0161 per cent, or such other rate (if any) as stands prescribed by the Minister by regulations, for each day or part of a day][1] from the date of payment of the excess duty up until the date of such repayment and income tax shall not be deductible on payment of interest under this subsection and such interest shall not be reckoned in computing income for the purposes of the Tax Acts.

(5) For the purpose of determining whether this section shall apply to any instrument, the Commissioners may require the delivery to them, in such form as they may specify, of a statement or a statutory declaration by—

(a) any person directly or indirectly concerned with the lease of the land or with the building of a dwellinghouse or apartment on the land, and

(b) any solicitor acting on behalf of any person to whom paragraph (a) relates,

of any facts which the Commissioners consider relevant in making any such determination.

(6) Any instrument to which the heading "LEASE" in Schedule 1 applies shall contain a statement, in such form as the Commissioners may specify, certifying whether or not this section is applicable to such instrument, and the furnishing of an incorrect certificate shall be deemed to constitute the delivery of an incorrect statement for the purposes of section 1078 of the Taxes Consolidation Act, 1997.

(7) Where stamp duty has been charged on any instrument by reference to this section and, within 2 years after the date of stamping of the instrument, building has not commenced, then this section shall be deemed not to have applied to the instrument and, accordingly, the Commissioners shall, on application to them within 3 years after the date of stamping of the instrument by the person or persons by whom the stamp duty was paid, repay to such person or persons the amount of the stamp duty paid by such person or persons which, but for the other provisions of this section, would not have been chargeable and such repayment shall bear simple interest at the rate of [0.0161 per cent, or such other rate (if any) as stands prescribed by the Minister by regulations, for each day or part of a day][1] from the date of payment of the excess duty up until the date of such repayment and income tax shall not be deductible on payment of interest under

this subsection and such interest shall not be reckoned in computing income for the purposes of the Tax Acts.

(8) Every regulation made under this section shall be laid before Dail Eireann as soon as may be after it is made and, if a resolution annulling the regulation is passed by Dail Eireann within the next 21 days on which Dail Eireann has sat after the regulation is laid before it, the regulation shall be annulled accordingly, but without prejudice to the validity of anything previously done under that regulation.

Amendments

1   Substituted by FA 2002 s 129(6)(c) with effect from 1 September 2002 in respect of an amount due to be paid or remitted, whether before, on, or after that date; previously "0.5 per cent, or such other rate (if any) as stands prescribed by the Minister by regulations, for each month or part of a month".

Cross -references

Exemption for houses under 125m^2 in floor area: ss 91 and 93.
New dwelling-house or apartment with no floor area certificate, amount chargeable to duty:s 92.
Procedure to apply where consideration cannot be ascertained. This provision does not apply where s 3(a) applies: ss 44 and 55.
Subs (2) does not apply where house or apartment was occupied prior to the sale agreement: s 92.

Definitions

"execution": s 1; "instrument": s 1, IA 1937 s 3; "marketable security", "stamp", "stock": s 1.

Former enactment

FA 1990 s 112(1)-(8) (part).

54 Leases deemed to operate as voluntary dispositions inter vivos

(1) Any lease, not being executed in good faith and for valuable consideration, shall, for the purposes of this section, be deemed to be a lease operating as a voluntary disposition inter vivos, and the consideration for any lease shall not, for this purpose, be deemed to be valuable consideration where the Commissioners are of opinion that, by reason of the inadequacy of consideration or other circumstances, the lease confers a substantial benefit on the lessee.

(2) Where by operation of this section any lease is deemed to operate as a voluntary disposition inter vivos the reference to consideration (other than rent) in the heading "LEASE" in Schedule 1 shall be construed in relation to duty chargeable on such lease as a reference to the minimum amount or value that would be necessary in order that the lease, any rent under the lease remaining unchanged, would not be a lease operating as a voluntary disposition inter vivos.

(3) Subsection (3) of section 30 shall, with any necessary modifications, apply to a lease operating as a voluntary disposition inter vivos in the same manner as to a conveyance or transfer operating as a voluntary disposition inter vivos.

Note

There is no relief for leases among related parties similar to that which applies in the case of conveyances between relatives.

Cross-references

Similar provisions relating to conveyances: s 30.
Presumption of negligence for the purpose of imposing liability under s 8 in circumstances where the fact that an instrument falling under this section is not brought to the attention of the Revenue Commissioners: s 8.
Surcharges for understatement of valuation: s 15.

Definitions

"executed"; "stamp": s 1.

Former enactment

FA 1949 s 24; FA 1991 s 102.

55 Procedure to apply where consideration, etc, cannot be ascertained

(1) Where the average annual rent or consideration other than rent for a lease cannot be ascertained at the date of execution of a lease and such consideration or rent would, if ascertainable, be chargeable with ad valorem duty in respect of such lease, then stamp duty shall be charged on such lease based on the amount or value of the consideration or rent that could be obtained from a tenant paying full consideration or rent for such lease.

(2) Where, in the case of a lease to which subsection (1) would apply but for the fact that both the rent and the consideration other than rent payable cannot be ascertained, then stamp duty shall be charged on such lease based on the amount or value of the consideration other than rent that could be obtained from a tenant paying full consideration for such lease if the rent reserved in the lease was a nil amount.

(3) This section shall not apply to any instrument in relation to which subsection (4)(*a*) of section 53 applies.

Definitions

"instrument": s 1, IA 1937 s 3; "stamp": s 1.

Former enactment

FA 1991 s 104 (part).

56 Stamp duty and value-added tax

The consideration or rent chargeable under the heading "LEASE" in Schedule 1 shall exclude any value-added tax chargeable under section 2 of the Value-Added Tax Act, 1972, on such lease.

Notes

Property transfers on or after 11 April 1994 are chargeable to stamp duty on the VAT-exclusive value of the consideration. Deeds executed prior to 11 April 1994, with a charge to stamp duty based on the VAT-exclusive value of the consideration, are deemed to have been executed correctly.

Definitions

"instrument", "stamped", "Commissioners", "marketable securities", "marketable securities": s 1.

Former enactment

FA 1994 s 108(1) (part).

CHAPTER 5
Mortgages, etc

57 Charging of duty on mortgages, etc

(1) A security for the transfer or retransfer of any stock shall be charged with the same duty as a similar security for a sum of money equal in amount to the value of the stock, and a transfer, assignment, disposition, or assignation of any such security shall be charged with the same duty as an instrument of the same description relating to a sum of money equal in amount to the value of the stock.

(2) A security for the payment of any rentcharge, annuity, or periodical payments, by means of repayment, or in satisfaction or discharge of any loan, advance, or payment intended to be so repaid, satisfied, or discharged, shall be charged with the same duty as a similar security for the payment of the sum of money so lent, advanced, or paid.

(3) A transfer of a duly stamped security, and a security by means of further charge for money or stock, added to money or stock previously secured by a duly stamped instrument, shall not be charged with any duty by reason of its containing any further or additional security for the money or stock transferred or previously secured, or the interest or dividends of that money or stock, or any new covenant, proviso, power, stipulation, or agreement in relation to that security, or any further assurance of the property comprised in the transferred or previous security.

(4) An instrument chargeable with ad valorem duty as a mortgage shall not be charged with any further duty by reason of the equity of redemption in the mortgaged property being thereby conveyed or limited in any other manner than to a purchaser, or in trust for, or according to the direction of, a purchaser.

Definitions

"instrument", "money", "stamped", "stock": s 1.

Former enactment

SA 1891 s 87(1)-(3), (6); FA 1970 s 60 and Sch 2; FA 1998 s 125 and Sch 8.

---

58 Security for future advances, how to be charged

(1) A security for the payment or repayment of money to be lent, advanced, or paid, or which may become due on an account current, either with or without money previously due, shall be charged, where the total amount secured or to be ultimately recoverable is in any way limited, with the same duty as a security for the amount so limited.

(2) Where such total amount is unlimited, the security shall—

    (*a*) if unstamped, or if stamped with ad valorem duty to cover an amount not exceeding [€254,000]¹, be available only for [€254,000]¹, and

    (*b*) if stamped with ad valorem duty to cover an amount exceeding £20,000, be available for such amount only,

but where any advance or loan is made in excess of £20,000 or such greater amount as may be covered by that duty, the security shall, for the purpose of stamp duty, be deemed to be a new and separate instrument, executed on the day on which the advance or loan is made.

(3) Notwithstanding subsections (1) and (2), no money to be advanced for the insurance of any property comprised in the security against damage by fire, or for keeping up any policy of life insurance comprised in the security, or for effecting in lieu of the policy of life insurance comprised in the security any new policy, or for the renewal of any grant or lease of any property comprised in the security on the dropping of any life on which the property is held, shall be reckoned as forming part of the amount in respect of which the security is chargeable with ad valorem duty.

Amendments

1   Substituted by FA 2001 s 202(1)(*b*) in relation to instruments executed on or after 1 January 2002; previously "£20,000".

Cross-references

Definition of mortgage: s 51.

Rates of duty on mortgage: Mortgage heading in Sch 1.

Stamp Duty on mortgages and further advances: SP SD 3/92.

Case law

Duty is payable upon the limit of an amount secured however contingent that amount: *International Power and Paper Co of Newfoundland v IRC* (1933) 12 ATC 413.

A mortgage for an unlimited sum need be stamped to cover only that amount in respect of which the mortgagee would look to the mortgage as security *Re Waterhouse's Policy* [1937]2 All ER 91.

Definitions

"executed", "instrument", "money", "stamped": s 1.

Former enactment

SA 1891 s 88; FA 1973; FA 1991 s 92.

CHAPTER 6
Policies of Insurance

59 Penalty for policy of insurance not duly stamped

(1) Every person who—

    (*a*)   receives, or takes credit for, any premium or consideration for any insurance, and does not, within one month after receiving, or taking credit for, the premium or consideration, make out and execute a duly stamped policy of insurance, or

    (*b*)   makes, executes, or delivers out, or pays or allows in account, or agrees to pay or allow in account, any money on or in respect of any policy which is not duly stamped,

shall incur a penalty of [€630][1].

(2) Subsection (1) shall not apply in relation to an insurance or a policy effecting an insurance if the insurance is such that a policy effecting it is exempt from all stamp duties.

Amendments

1   Substituted by FA 2001 s 240 and Sch 5 Pt 6 with effect from 1 January 2002; previously "£500".

Cross-references

Assignment of policy to be stamped before payment of sum assured: s 130.

Composition: s 5.

Duty on policies: POLICY OF INSURANCE and POLICY OF LIFE INSURANCE Heads of charge in Sch 1.

Levy on insurance premiums: s 125.

Location of risk for insurance purposes: s 61.

Meaning of policy of life insurance: s 1.

Short-term life insurance policies: s 60.

Transfer on sale of insurance policies: Head of charge in Sch 1.

Definitions

"person" IA 1937 s 11(*c*).

Former enactment

SA 1891 s 100; FA 1959 s 75(4); FA 1959 s 75(4); FA 1991 s 106; FA 1999 s 161.

60 Short-term life insurance policies

Amendments

[1] Repealed by FA 2001 s 203 in relation to instruments executed and policies of life insurance varied on or after 11 January 2001.

Former enactment

FA 1970 s 43(1)-(2).

61 Location of insurance risk for stamp duty purposes

(1) In paragraph (*d*) of subsection (2) **"branch"** means an agency or branch of a policyholder or any permanent presence of a policyholder in the State even if that presence does not take the form of an agency or branch but consists merely of an office managed by the policyholder's own staff or by a person who is independent but has permanent authority to act for the policyholder in the same way as an agency.

(2) For the purpose of charging stamp duty, the risk to which a policy of insurance or a policy of life insurance relates shall be deemed to be located in the State—

(*a*) where the insurance relates either to buildings or to buildings and their contents, in so far as the contents are covered by the same insurance policy, if the property is situated in the State;

(*b*) where the insurance relates to vehicles of any kind, if such vehicles are registered in the State;

(*c*) in the case of policies of a duration of 4 months or less covering travel or holiday risks, if the policyholder took out the policy in the State:

(*d*) in any other case, if the policyholder has his or her habitual residence in the State, or where the policyholder is a legal person other than an individual, if the policyholder's head office or branch to which the policy relates is situated in the State.

Note

For the meaning of "establishment" see text of European Communities (Non-Life Insurance) (Amendment) (No 2) Regulations 1991 (SI No 142 of 1991).

Cross-references

Stamp Duty (Variation) Order 1991 para 4(*g*) (SI No 277 of 1991) effective from 1 November 1991.

Definitions

"stamp": s 1.

Former enactment

FA 1992 s 208; FA 1999 s 196(*a*)-(*b*).

62 Limitation of stamp duty on certain instruments relating to 2 or more distinct matters

An instrument shall not be charged with duty exceeding [€1][1] by reason only that it contains or relates to 2 or more distinct matters each falling within the heading

"POLICY OF INSURANCE other than Life Insurance where the risk to which the policy relates is located in the State" in Schedule 1.

Amendments

1   Substituted by FA 2001 s 240 and Sch 5 Pt 6 with effect from 1 January 2002; previously "£1".

Former enactment

FA 1982 s 94(4)(*b*)(ii).

CHAPTER 7
Releases or Renunciations of any property, or of any right or interest in any property

63 Letters of renunciation

(1) In this section—

"share" includes stock;

"unquoted company" means a company none of whose shares, stocks or debentures are listed in the official list of a recognised stock exchange or dealt in on an unlisted securities market recognised by such a stock exchange.

(2) Any instrument which releases or renounces or has the effect of releasing or renouncing a right under a letter of allotment, or under any other document having the effect of a letter of allotment, to any share in an unquoted company shall be chargeable to stamp duty as if it were a release or renunciation of property consisting of stocks or marketable securities by reference to the heading "RELEASE or RENUNCIATION of any property, or of any right or interest in any property" in Schedule 1 and that schedule shall be construed accordingly.

Note

This section does not apply to releases or renunciation of allotments of shares in companies if any of the shares, stocks or debentures are listed in the official list of a recognised stock exchange or dealt in on an unlisted securities market recognised by such a stock exchange.

Definitions

"executed", "marketable security", "stamp", "stock": s 1.

Former enactment

FA 1986 s 95(1)-(2); FA 1999 s 197 and Sch 6.

CHAPTER 8
Share Warrants and Stock Certificates to Bearer, etc

64 Instruments passing by delivery in pursuance of usage

For the purposes of this Chapter, an instrument used for the purpose of assigning, transferring, or in any manner negotiating the right to any share or stock shall, if delivery of such share or stock is by usage treated as sufficient for the purpose of a sale on the market, whether that delivery constitutes a legal assignment, transfer, or negotiation or not, be deemed an instrument to bearer and the delivery of such share or stock an assignment, transfer, or negotiation.

Definitions

"instrument": s 1; IA 1937 s 3; "marketable security", "stock": s 1.

Former enactment

FA 1899 s 6; FA 1999 s 197 and Sch 6.

65 Penalty for issuing share warrant not duly stamped

If a share warrant which is chargeable to stamp duty, or any instrument to bearer having a like effect as such a share warrant, is issued without being duly stamped, the company issuing the same, and also every person who, at the time when it is issued, is the managing director or secretary or other principal officer of the company, shall incur a penalty of [€630][1].

Amendments

[1]   Substituted by FA 2001 s 240 and Sch 5 Pt 6 with effect from 1 January 2002; previously "£500".

Cross-references

Meaning of stock certificate to bearer: s 1.

Provision as to instruments passing by delivery in pursuance of usage: s 64.

Share warrant and stock certificate to bearer, Head of charge in Sch 1.

"stock or marketable securities" does not include share warrant in the case of sale of certain contracts: s 3(1).

Definitions

"person" IA 1937 s 11(*c*); "stamped": s 1.

Former enactment

SA 1891 s 107; FA 1899 s 5(2) (part); FA 1991 s 106; FA 1999 s 162(*c*), (*b*).

66 Penalty for issuing stock certificate not duly stamped, etc

(1) Where the holder of a stock certificate to bearer, or any instrument to bearer having a like effect as such stock certificate to bearer, has been entered on the register of the local authority, or company or body of persons, as the case may be, as the owner of the share of stock described in the certificate, the certificate shall be forthwith cancelled so as to be incapable of being re-issued to any person.

(2) Every person by whom a stock certificate to bearer which is chargeable to stamp duty, or any instrument to bearer having a like effect as such stock certificate to bearer, is issued without being duly stamped shall incur a penalty of [€630][1].

Amendments

[1]   Substituted by FA 2001 s 240 and Sch 5 Pt 6 with effect from 1 January 2002; previously "£500".

Cross-references

Provision as to instruments passing by delivery in pursuance of usage: s 64.

SHARE WARRANT AND STOCK CERTIFICATE TO BEARER, head of charge in Sch 1.

Definitions

"person" IA 1937 s 11(*c*); "stamped", "stock": s 1; "stock certificate to bearer": s 1.

Former enactment

SA 1891 s 109; FA 1899 s 5(2) (part), FA 1991 s 106; FA 1999 s 163(*a*), (*b*).

CHAPTER 9
Surrenders of any property, or of any right or interest in any property

67 Surrender and merger of leasehold interests

An instrument bearing witness to, or acknowledging—

    (*a*) the surrender, by parol or otherwise, of a leasehold interest in immovable property, or

    (*b*) the merger of such an interest in a superior interest,

shall be charged to the same stamp duty as if it were a surrender of that leasehold interest.

Former enactment

FA 1986 s 99(2).

PART 6
SPECIAL PROVISIONS RELATING TO UNCERTIFICATED SECURITIES

68 Interpretation (Part 6)

(1) In this Part—

"certificated securities" means securities other than uncertificated securities;

" market maker" means a person who—

    (*a*) holds himself or herself out at all normal times in compliance with the rules of the Irish Stock Exchange Limited, or the London Stock Exchange Limited, as willing to buy and sell securities at a price specified by him or her, and

    (*b*) is recognised as doing so by the Irish Stock Exchange Limited or the London Stock Exchange Limited;

"member firm" means a member firm of the Irish Stock Exchange Limited, or of the London Stock Exchange Limited, which is not acting in the ordinary course of business as a market maker in securities of the kind concerned;

"relevant period" means any period of 6 months ending on the 30th day of September or the 31st day of March;

"securities" means any stocks or marketable securities;

"uncertificated securities" means any securities, title to which is, by virtue of the Companies Act, 1990 (Uncertificated Securities) Regulations, 1996 (SI No 68 of 1996), transferable by means of a relevant system.

(2) In this Part, **"generate"**, **"instruction"**, **"operator"**, **"operator instruction"**, **"relevant system"** and **"system-member"** have the same meanings, respectively, as in the Companies Act, 1990 (Uncertificated Securities) Regulations, 1996.

(3) In this Part, references to title to securities include any legal or equitable interest in securities.

Notes

The Companies Act, 1990 (Uncertified Securities) Regulations, 1996 ("the Regulations") allow title to shares to be transferred and evidenced electronically without the need for a Stock Transfer Form.

In order to ensure that there is no loss of revenue due to the changeover from the paper-based system (TALISMAN) to the electronic settlement system provided by CREST, a type of transaction fee based on the electronic transfer of shares is due to replace the previously document-based system for stamp duty.

It will still be possible for smaller investors to hold on to paper certificates if they choose to, but it is believed that the cost of settling a paper transaction within CREST would be twice that of an electronic one (however, the overall cost of settlement is expected to fall).

Under the new electronic system it will be necessary to actually be a CREST member or a sponsored member in order to have your name placed on the company register as the holder of the shares.

FA 1996 Pt IV Ch I (ss 101 to 119) made minimal alterations to the stamp duty legislation as its object is to give effect to the anticipated changeover to uncertified securities so as to ensure that they will come within the duty.

Definitions

"Commissioners": s 1; "person": IA 1937 s 11(c); "marketable security"; "stock": s 1.

Former enactment

FA 1996 s 101(1).

69 Operator-instruction deemed to be an instrument of conveyance or transfer

(1) Where a transfer of title to securities through a relevant system is effected by an operator-instruction, that operator-instruction shall, for all purposes of this Act, be deemed to be an executed instrument of conveyance or transfer of such securities and the date of execution shall be taken to be the date the operator-instruction is generated.

(2) Where an operator-instruction is generated in connection with the transfer through a relevant system of an equitable interest in securities, that transfer shall be deemed for the purposes of subsection (1) to have been effected by that operator-instruction.

(3) Where no operator-instruction is generated in connection with the transfer through a relevant system of an equitable interest in securities, that transfer shall, for the purposes of this Part, be deemed to have been effected by an operator-instruction generated on the date of the transfer.

Notes

This section deems the operator-instruction to be an instrument of conveyance or transfer thereby bringing it within the stamp duty charging provisions contained in s 2. The date of execution of the instrument shall be taken to be the date the operator-instruction is generated.

Definitions

"executed": s 1.

Former enactment

FA 1996 s 102.

70 Rate of duty

(1) Where an operator-instruction is, by virtue of section 69, chargeable with stamp duty under or by reference to the heading "CONVEYANCE or TRANSFER on sale of any stocks or marketable securities" in Schedule 1, the rate at which the duty is charged under that heading shall be the rate of 1 per cent of the consideration for the sale to which that operator-instruction gives effect.

(2) Notwithstanding subsection (1)—

    (*a*) where the transfer operates as a voluntary disposition inter vivos, the reference in subsection (1) to the amount or value of the consideration for the sale shall, in relation to the duty so chargeable, be construed as a reference to the value of the securities transferred,

    (*b*) where the calculation results in an amount which is not a multiple of one penny, the amount so calculated shall be rounded to the nearest penny, and any half of a penny [cent][1] shall be rounded up to the next whole penny [cent][1].

Amendments

[1]   Substituted by FA 2001 s 240 and Sch 5 Pt 6 with effect from 1 January 2002; previously "penny".

Notes

This section provides that the rate of stamp duty applicable to electronically transferred shares shall be 1% of the consideration for the sale. This replaces the current rate of £1 per £100 (or part of £100) and will facilitate the calculation of duty by CREST.

Definitions

"marketable security"; "stamp"; "stock": s 1.

Former enactment

FA 1996 s 103.

71 Application and adaptation of other Parts of this Act

In relation to a charge for stamp duty arising by virtue of section 69—

    (*a*) the definition of "accountable person" in subsection (1) of section 1 shall be construed as if the reference, in the Table to that definition, to the purchaser or transferee were a reference to the transferee,

    (*b*) notwithstanding section 2(3), the operator-instruction which is charged to stamp duty by virtue of section 69 shall not be required to be stamped and, accordingly—

        (i) any duty so charged shall be due and payable and shall be paid to the Commissioners on the date on which that operator-instruction is generated, and

        (ii) that operator-instruction shall for the purposes of section 2(4) and notwithstanding section 30(3) be deemed to be duly stamped with the proper stamp duty when such duty and any penalty relating to such duty has been paid to the Commissioners,

    (*c*) notwithstanding paragraph (*b*), where an agreement referred to in section 72 is in force between the Commissioners and an operator, any duty paid in respect of that operator-instruction in accordance with such agreement shall be deemed to have been paid to the Commissioners on the date on which it became due and payable,

    (*d*) subject to paragraph (*e*), section 14 shall apply with the modification that the penalties imposed for not duly stamping the operator-instruction, which is charged to stamp duty by virtue of section 69 within a particular period of the date of first execution, shall be imposed for non-payment of the stamp duty within that period, and with any other necessary modifications,

    (*e*) sections 4, 6, 8, 11, 14 (4), 20, 127 and 129(1) shall not apply, (*f*) (i) if at any time it appears that for any reason no duty, or insufficient duty, has been paid to the Commissioners, they shall make an assessment of such amount of duty or additional duty as, to the best of their knowledge, information and belief, ought to be charged, levied and paid and the accountable person shall be liable for the payment of the duty so assessed,

    (ii) if at any time it appears that for any reason an assessment is incorrect, the Commissioners shall make such other assessment as they consider appropriate, which assessment shall be substituted for the first-mentioned assessment,

    (iii) section 21 shall apply to an assessment under this paragraph as if it were an assessment mentioned in that section,

(*g*) any reliefs or exemptions from stamp duty which are conditional on an instrument being stamped in accordance with section 20 with a particular stamp denoting either that it is not chargeable with any duty or that it is duly stamped shall apply notwithstanding such condition not having been complied with.

Notes

This section makes the necessary alterations in order for stamp duty to apply to uncertificated shares.

    (*a*) the transferee is made accountable for the duty;

    (*b*) the duty is due and payable on the date the operator-instruction is generated and it can be recovered as a debt due to the Minister for Finance in any court of competent jurisdiction;

    (*c*) the same penalties for late payment of stamp duty will apply to electronic transfers as apply to paper ones;

    (*d*) this sets out the sections which will not apply to uncertificated securities;

    (*e*) the Revenue Commissioners may make an assessment of any duty due on an electronic transfer and the appeal procedures contained in s 21 will apply to such assessment;

    (*f*) any reliefs or exemptions which require an adjudication by the Revenue Commissioners will apply despite the fact that the operation-instruction is not itself adjudicated.

Definitions

"accountable person"; "Commissioners"; "stamp": s 1.

Former enactment

FA 1996 s 104.

72 Collection and payment of duty

The Commissioners may enter into an agreement with an operator, in such form and on such terms and conditions as they think fit, in relation to the collection of stamp duty and the payment of such duty to the Commissioners.

Notes

This section permits the Revenue Commissioners to enter into an Agreement with an operator (CRESTCO is expected to be approved as the operator in Ireland) whereby the operator will collect the stamp duty which is due and then pass it on to the Revenue Commissioners.

Definitions

"Commissioners"; "stamp": s 1.

Former enactment

FA 1996 s 105.

73 Exemptions

(1) Section 69 shall not apply—

    (*a*)   to the extent that it would give rise to a charge to stamp duty under the heading "CONVEYANCE or TRANSFER of any kind not already described in this Schedule" in Schedule 1,

    (*b*)   in respect of a transfer of title to securities to a purchaser in completion of a contract for sale to the extent to which the interest transferred has, following that transfer, been retransferred in completion of a separate contract for sale made by that purchaser prior to that transfer to that purchaser provided that both contracts were due for completion on the same day and are in fact completed within 25 days after the making of whichever of those contracts was earlier in priority.

(2) Stamp duty shall not be chargeable under or by reference to any heading in Schedule 1 other than the heading "CONVEYANCE or TRANSFER on sale of any stocks or marketable securities" on an instrument effecting a transfer of securities if the transferee is a system-member and the instrument is in a form which will, in accordance with the rules of the system, enable certificated securities to be converted into uncertificated securities so that title to them may become transferable by means of the relevant system.

Notes

This section provides that certain transfers are to be exempt from stamp duty.

    (1)(*a*)Due to the increase in share transfers that is envisaged under the new system, transactions which transfer legal title only will be exempt from the £10 fixed duty so as not to disadvantage purchasers (as they would otherwise be subject to 1% plus £10 for each transfer).

    (*b*)This ensures that any transfer made through CREST will continue to benefit from the stamp duty sub-sale provisions and that where shares are sold prior to their actual acquisition, but are in fact acquired prior to the completion of the sale, then the acquisition of the shares will benefit from the stamp duty exemption.

    (2) In order to encourage people to convert their shares from paper to electronic form, the depositing of shares into the CREST system will not attract stamp duty so long as only the legal ownership is being transferred.

    (3) Allows market makers to purchase shares without incurring any stamp duty liability.

Cross-references

Spouses exemption, s 96.

Definitions

"instrument": s 1; "person": IA 1937 s 11(*c*); "stamp": s 1.

Former enactment

FA 1996 s 106(1)-(2); FA 1997 s 197 and Sch 6.

74 Exemption for market makers

Stamp duty shall not be chargeable on any instrument of transfer whereby any securities are on the sale of such securities transferred to a market maker acting in the ordinary course of business as a market maker in securities of the kind concerned or to a person acting as nominee of such market maker.

Former enactment

FA 1996 s 106(3).

75 Relief for member firms

(1) Stamp duty shall not be chargeable on any instrument of transfer whereby any securities are on the sale of such securities transferred to a member firm acting on its own behalf in the ordinary course of that member firm's business or to a nominee of such member firm.

(2) Notwithstanding subsection (1)—

(*a*) if and to the extent that the member firm does not transfer the securities referred to in subsection (1) to a bona fide purchaser before the expiration of the period of one month from the date of transfer, in this section referred to as "the specified period", the member firm shall pay to the Commissioners within 14 days after the expiration of the specified period the amount of ad valorem duty which would have been chargeable on the transfer if this section had not been enacted;

(*b*) the member firm may, in relation to any such sale with a completion date not later than 30 days from the date of the contract for sale and prior to the date of the contract, elect to have such completion date treated as the date of the second-mentioned transfer referred to in paragraph (*a*) and, in that event, that completion date shall be deemed, for the purposes of paragraph (*a*), to be the date of that second-mentioned transfer.

(3) If any member firm fails to pay any sum due to the Commissioners under subsection (2), that sum, together with interest on that sum at the rate of [0.0322 per cent for each day or part of a day][1] from the first day after the expiration of the specified period to the date of payment of that sum and, by means of further penalty, a sum equal to 1 per cent of the duty for each day the duty remains unpaid, shall be recoverable from the member firm as a debt due to the Minister for the benefit of the Central Fund.

(4) Where subsection (1) applies in relation to a transfer of securities to a member firm, the member firm shall within 30 days of the end of the relevant period within which the transfer is made deliver to the Commissioners a statement in writing or in such other manner as the Commissioners may agree to in writing—

(*a*) showing in respect of each such transfer—

(i) full details in relation to the type, nominal value, description and amount of the securities comprised in the transfer;

(ii) what part (if any) of the securities comprised in the transfer has been transferred by the member firm to a bona fide purchaser within the specified period and what part of the securities has not been so transferred;

(iii) the date of the transfer and, if any part of the securities has been transferred to a bona fide purchaser within the specified period, the date on which that part was so transferred;

(iv) the amount of stamp duty (if any) payable by virtue of subsection (2) and the date of payment;

(*b*) certifying in respect of each such transfer that—

(i) the member firm was acting on its own behalf in the ordinary course of its business, and

(ii)   any securities transferred in respect of which the stamp duty has not been paid were transferred on sale to a bona fide purchaser within the period of one month after the date of the transfer,

and shall produce such further evidence by means of statutory declaration or otherwise in relation to the matters set out in paragraphs (*a*) and (*b*) as the Commissioners require.

(5) A member firm which fails to deliver a statement within the period specified in subsection (4) shall be liable to a penalty of [€1,265][2].

Amendments

[1]   Substituted by FA 2002 s 129(6)(*b*) with effect from 1 September 2002 in respect of an amount due to be paid or remitted, whether before, on, or after that date; previously "1 per cent per month or part of a month".

[2]   Substituted by FA 2001 s 240 and Sch 5 Pt 6 with effect from 1 January 2002; previously "£1,000".

Notes

This section extends the relief provided by FA 1920 s 42 for purchases of shares by member firms by removing the liability to stamp duty in the case of Irish or UK member firms in situations where the shares are sold on within one month of purchase.

Cross references

UK legislation

FA 1986 s 89.

Definitions

"Commissioners"; "instrument"; "stamp": SA 1891 s 122(1); "writing": IA 1937 Sch.

Former enactment

FA 1996 s 107(1)-(4); FA 1998 ss 123, 124(1); FA 1999 s 169.

76 Obligations of system-members

(1) Where an instruction is entered or is caused to be entered in a relevant system by a system-member, and the effect of that instruction is that no stamp duty is calculated by the relevant system, that system-member shall retain evidence in legible written form, or readily convertible into such a form, for a period of [6 years][1] from the date of such instruction, in sufficient detail to establish that the related operator-instruction is not chargeable with stamp duty, and the system-member shall make any such evidence available to the Commissioners on request.

(2) A system-member who fails to comply with subsection (1) shall be liable to a penalty of [€1,265][2].

(3) Where a system-member fraudulently or negligently enters or causes to be entered an incorrect instruction in a relevant system and such incorrect instruction gives rise to an underpayment of stamp duty, or results in a claim for exemption from duty to which there is no entitlement, that system-member shall incur a penalty of [€1,265][2] together with the amount, or twice the amount in the case of fraud, of the difference between the duty so paid (if any) and the duty which would have been payable if the instruction had been entered correctly.

(4) A system-member shall be deemed to have acted negligently for the purposes of subsection (3) if it comes to the system-member's notice, or it would have come to the system-member's notice if the system-member had taken reasonable care, that an incorrect instruction has resulted in an underpayment of stamp duty, unless the system-

member notifies the Commissioners accordingly, in writing, without unreasonable delay.

(5) An incorrect instruction to which subsection (3) applies shall be deemed to be the production of an incorrect document for the purposes of section 1078(2)(*d*) of the Taxes Consolidation Act, 1997.

Amendments

1   Substituted by FA 2002 s 112(1) with effect from 25 March 2002; previously "3 years".
2   Substituted by FA 2001 s 240 and Sch 5 Pt 6 with effect from 1 January 2002; previously "£1,000".

Notes

This section places certain obligations on system-members, which will apply if the stamp duty is underpaid as a result of fraud or neglect.

Definitions

"accountable person"; "Commissioners"; "stamp": s 1; "year": IA 1937 Sch.

Former enactment

FA 1996 s 108; FA 1999 s 170(*a*)-(*b*).

77 Overpayment of duty

(1) Where on a claim it is proved to the satisfaction of the Commissioners that there has been an overpayment of duty in relation to a charge to duty by virtue of section 69, the overpayment shall be repaid.

(2) A claim under this section shall—

    (*a*)   be made within a period of 6 years beginning on the date on which the payment was made,

    (*b*)   set out the grounds on which the repayment is claimed,

    (*c*)   contain a computation of the amount of the repayment claimed,

    (*d*)   if so required by the Commissioners, be supported by such documentation as may be necessary to prove the entitlement to a repayment of the amount claimed, and

    (*e*)   if the claim arises by virtue of the operation of section 73(1)(*b*)—

        (i)   it shall be made on a form prescribed by the Commissioners, and

        (ii)   it shall not be made to the Commissioners before the 21st day of the month following the month in which the overpayment of duty arose.

(3) Where the claimant is not resident in the State and has no branch or agency in the State the Commissioners may require the claimant, as a condition for obtaining a repayment, to appoint and maintain a tax representative in the State who shall be personally liable to the Commissioners for any loss of duty arising out of an incorrect claim.

(4) A person shall not be a tax representative under this section unless that person—

    (*a*)   has a business establishment in the State, and

    (*b*)   is approved by the Commissioners.

Notes

This section sets out a system by which the Revenue Commissioners can refund duty in cases where it has been overpaid.

Definitions

"Commissioners": s 1; "year": IA 1937 Sch.

Former enactment

FA 1996 s 109.

78 Regulations

(1) The Commissioners may make such regulations as seem to them to be necessary for the purpose of giving effect to this Part and of enabling them to discharge their functions in relation to administration, assessment, collection, recovery and repayment under this Part.

(2) Every regulation made under this section shall be laid before Dail Eireann as soon as may be after it is made and, if a resolution annulling the regulation is passed by Dail Eireann within the next 21 days on which Dail Eireann has sat after the regulation is laid before it, the regulation shall be annulled accordingly, but without prejudice to the validity of anything previously done under the regulation.

Notes

This section provides that the Revenue Commissioners can make the regulations necessary to give effect to their duties in respect of the administration, assessment, collection, recovery and repayment of stamp duty which is paid under this Chapter.

Definitions

"Commissioners": s 1.

Former enactment

FA 1996 s 110.

PART 7
EXEMPTIONS AND RELIEFS FROM STAMP DUTY

CHAPTER 1
Instruments which must be presented to the Commissioners for adjudication in order to obtain exemption or relief

79 Conveyances and transfers of property between certain bodies corporate

(1) Stamp duty shall not be chargeable under or by reference to the following headings in Schedule 1—

    (*a*) "CONVEYANCE or TRANSFER on sale of any stocks or marketable securities",

    (*b*) "CONVEYANCE or TRANSFER on sale of a policy of insurance or a policy of life insurance where the risk to which the policy relates is located in the State", or

    (*c*) "CONVEYANCE or TRANSFER on sale of any property other than stocks or marketable securities or a policy of insurance or a policy of life insurance",

on any instrument to which this section applies.

(2) Subsection (1) shall not apply to an instrument unless it has, in accordance with section 20, been stamped with a particular stamp denoting that it is not chargeable with any duty or that it is duly stamped.

(3) This section applies to any instrument as respects which it is shown to the satisfaction of the Commissioners that the effect of the instrument was to convey or transfer a beneficial interest in property from one body corporate to another, and that at the time of the execution of the instrument the bodies in question were associated, that is, one was the beneficial owner of not less than 90 per cent of the issued share capital of the other, or a third such body was the beneficial owner of not less than 90 per cent of the issued share capital of each and that this ownership was ownership either directly or through another body corporate or other bodies corporate, or partly directly and partly through another body corporate or other bodies corporate, and subsections (5) to (10) of section 9 of the Taxes Consolidation Act, 1997, shall apply for the purposes of this section as if—

[(a)   references to company were references to body corporate,

(b)   references to companies were references to bodies corporate, and

(c)   references to ordinary share capital were references to issued share capital.][1]

(4) Notwithstanding that at the time of execution of any instrument the bodies corporate between which the beneficial interest in the property was conveyed or transferred were associated within the meaning of subsection (3), they shall not be treated as having been so associated unless, additionally, at that time—

(a)   one such body was beneficially entitled to not less than 90 per cent of any profits available for distribution to the shareholders of the other such body or a third such body was beneficially entitled to not less than 90 per cent of any profits available for distribution to the shareholders of each, and

(b)   one such body would be beneficially entitled to not less than 90 per cent of any assets of the other such body available for distribution to its shareholders on a winding-up or a third such body would be beneficially entitled to not less than 90 per cent of any assets available for distribution to the shareholders of each on a winding-up,

and, for the purposes of this section—

(i)   the percentage to which one body corporate is beneficially entitled of any profits available for distribution to the shareholders of another body corporate, and

(ii)   the percentage to which one body corporate would be beneficially entitled of any assets of another body corporate on a winding-up,

means the percentage to which the first body corporate is, or would be, so entitled either directly or through another body corporate or other bodies corporate or partly directly and partly through another body corporate or other bodies corporate.

(5) This section shall not apply to an instrument unless it is also shown to the satisfaction of the Commissioners that the instrument was not executed in pursuance of or in connection with an arrangement under which—

(a)   the consideration, or any part of the consideration, for the conveyance or transfer was to be provided or received, directly or indirectly by a person, other than a body corporate which at the time of the execution of the instrument was associated within the meaning of [subsections (3) and (4)][2] with either the transferor or the transferee (being, respectively, the body from whom and the body to whom the beneficial interest was conveyed or transferred),

(b)   that interest was previously conveyed or transferred, directly or indirectly, by such a person, or

(c)   the transferor and the transferee were to cease to be associated within the meaning of subsections (3) and (4),

and, without prejudice to the generality of paragraph (a), an arrangement shall be treated as within that paragraph if it is one under which the transferor or the transferee, or a body corporate associated with either as there mentioned, was to be enabled to provide any of the consideration, or was to part with any of it, by or in consequence of the carrying out of a transaction or transactions involving, or any of them involving, a payment or other disposition by a person other than a body corporate so associated.

(6) (a)   The Commissioners may, for the purposes of this section, require the delivery to them of a statutory declaration in such form as they may direct made, as they may direct, by a responsible officer of a body corporate or by a solicitor of the Courts of Justice or by both and of such further evidence (if any) as they may require.

(b)   The powers conferred on the Commissioners by paragraph (a) shall be in addition to and not in substitution for the powers conferred on them by section 20.

(7) If—

(a)   where any claim for exemption from duty under this section has been allowed, it is subsequently found that any declaration or other evidence furnished in support of the claim was untrue in any material particular, or

(b)   the transferor and transferee cease to be associated within the meaning of [subsections (3) and (4)][3] within a period of 2 years from the date of the conveyance or transfer,

then the exemption shall cease to be applicable and stamp duty shall be chargeable in respect of the conveyance or transfer as if subsection (1) had not been enacted together with interest on the duty, by means of penalty, at the rate of [0.0322 per cent for each day or part of a day][4] to the day on which the duty is paid, in a case to which paragraph (a) applies, from the date of the conveyance or transfer or, in a case to which paragraph (b) applies, from the date the transferor and transferee ceased to be so associated.

(8) For the purposes of subsection (4)—

(a)   the percentage to which one body is beneficially entitled of any profits available for distribution to shareholders of another company has, subject to any necessary modifications, the meaning assigned to it by section 414 of the Taxes Consolidation Act, 1997, and

(b)   the percentage to which one body is beneficially entitled of any assets of another body available for distribution on a winding-up has, subject to any necessary modifications, the meaning assigned to it by section 415 of the Taxes Consolidation Act, 1997.

Amendments

1   Subs (3)(*a*)-(*c*) substituted by FA 2002 s 138 and Sch 6 para 4 with effect on or after 15 December 1999.
2   Substituted by FA 2001 s 204(1)(*a*) with effect from 6 March 2001.
3   Substituted by FA 2001 s 204(1)(*b*) with effect from 15 February 2001.
4   Substituted by FA 2002 s 129(6)(*b*) with effect from 1 September 2002 in respect of an amount due to be paid or remitted, whether before, on, or after that date; previously "1 per cent per month or part of a month".

Note

This section provides relief under the "CONVEYANCE or TRANSFER on SALE ..." heads of charge only. Duties payable under other heads e.g. lease duty are not affected.

Cross-references

Reconstructions and amalgamations of companies: s 80.

Case law

The relief is intended to apply to inter company transfers where the association between the companies is so close that there is in effect little or no change in control of the assets transferred: *Escoigne Properties Ltd v IRC* [1958] AC 549.

If a company cannot deal with property as it wishes it cannot be regarded as the beneficial owner of it: *Baytrust Holdings Ltd v IRC* [1971] 3 All ER 76.

"Beneficial interest was previously conveyed or transferred": wide construction on words: *IRC v Angus* (1889) 23 QBD 579.

A company ceases to be the beneficial owner of its property on liquidation: *Ayerst v C & K Construction Ltd* [1975] 2 All ER 537.

"Issued share capital" refers to the nominal value rather than the actual value of the share capital: *Canada Safeway Ltd v IRC* [1972] 1 All ER 666.

"Arrangement" (s 53) means a scheme with a number of steps taken in order to bring about a result: *IRC v Payne* (1940) 23 TC 610 at 626.

There need not be a prior contractual relationship to carry out the steps nor need the steps be determined at the outset of the arrangement: *Crossland v Hawkins* [1961] 2 All ER 812 and *Shop and Store Developments Ltd v IRC* [1967] 1 All ER 42.

The 90% shareholding association must subsist before the transfer: it is not sufficient that the transfer itself creates it: *Holmleigh (Holdings) Ltd v IRC* (1958) 46 TC 435.

If consideration is left unpaid and payment is guaranteed by an unassociated company that company will be considered to have provided the consideration for the purposes of ss (3)(*a*): unless the consideration is borrowing and the terms for repayment do not themselves conflict with the relief provisions: *Curzon Offices Ltd v IRC* [1944] 1 All ER 163.

Narrative

Irish Stamp Duty Law, Chapter 8.

Definitions

"conveyance on sale", "executed", "execution", "instrument", "marketable security", "material": s 1; "person": IA 1937 s 11(*c*); "stamp", "stamped", "stock": s 1.

Former enactment

FA 1952 s 19; FA 1980 s 85(1); FA 1990 s 116(*a*), (*b*); FA 1995 s 143(*a*)-(*c*), TCA 1997 s 1100 and Sch 31; FA 1999 s 182(*a*),(*b*).

80 Reconstructions or amalgamations of companies

(1) (*a*)   In this section, unless the context otherwise requires, "shares" includes stock and references to the undertaking of a target company include references to a part of the undertaking of a target company;

(*b*)   In this section references to "acquiring company" are references only to a company with limited liability.

(2) Where it is shown to the satisfaction of the Commissioners that there exists a scheme for the bona fide reconstruction of any company or companies or the amalgamation of

any companies and that, in connection with the scheme, there exist the following conditions, that is—

(*a*)   a company with limited liability is to be registered, or a company has been established by Act of the Oireachtas, or the nominal share capital of a company has been increased;

(*b*)   the company (in this section referred to as the "acquiring company") is to be registered or has been established or has increased its capital with a view to the acquisition of either—

(i)   the undertaking of a particular existing company (in this section referred to as the "target company"), or

(ii)   not less than 90 per cent of the issued share capital of a target company;

(*c*)   the consideration for the acquisition (except such part of that consideration as consists in the transfer to or discharge by the acquiring company of liabilities of the target company) consists as to not less than 90 per cent of that consideration—

(i)   where an undertaking is to be acquired, in the issue of shares in the acquiring company to the target company or to holders of shares in the target company, or

(ii)   where shares are to be acquired, in the issue of shares in the acquiring company to the holders of shares in the target company in exchange for the shares held by them in the target company,

then, subject to this section, stamp duty under the following headings in Schedule 1—

(I)   "CONVEYANCE or TRANSFER on sale of any stocks or marketable securities",

(II)   "CONVEYANCE or TRANSFER on sale of a policy of insurance or a policy of life insurance where the risk to which the policy relates is located in the State", or

(III)   "CONVEYANCE or TRANSFER on sale of any property other than stocks or marketable securities or a policy of insurance or a policy of life insurance",

shall not be chargeable on any instrument made for the purposes of or in connection with the transfer of the undertaking or shares, or on any instrument made for the purposes of or in connection with the assignment to the acquiring company of any debts, secured or unsecured, of the target company.

(3) (*a*)   This section shall not apply to an instrument unless it has, in accordance with section 20, been stamped with a particular stamp denoting either that it is not chargeable with any duty or that it is duly stamped.

(*b*)   In the case of an instrument made for the purposes of or in connection with a transfer to a company within the meaning of the Companies Act, 1963, subsection (2) shall not apply unless the instrument is either—

(i)   executed within a period of 12 months from the date of the registration of the acquiring company or the date of the resolution for the increase of the nominal share capital of the acquiring company, as the case may be, or

(ii) made for the purpose of effecting a conveyance or transfer in pursuance of an agreement which has been filed, or particulars of which have been filed, with the registrar of companies within that period of 12 months.

(4) This section shall not apply unless the scheme of reconstruction or amalgamation is effected for bona fide commercial reasons and does not form part of a scheme or arrangement of which the main purpose, or one of the main purposes, is avoidance of liability to stamp duty, income tax, corporation tax, capital gains tax or capital acquisitions tax.

(5) For the purposes of a claim for exemption under subsection (2), a company which has, in connection with a scheme of reconstruction or amalgamation, issued any unissued share capital shall be treated as if it had increased its nominal share capital.

(6) A company shall not be deemed to be a target company within the meaning of this section unless it is provided by the memorandum of association of, or Act establishing, the acquiring company that one of the objects for which the company is formed is the acquisition of the undertaking of, or shares in, the target company, or unless it appears from the resolution, Act or other authority for the increase of the capital of the acquiring company that the increase is authorised for the purpose of acquiring the undertaking of, or shares in, the target company.

(7) (*a*) Where a claim is made for exemption under this section, the Commissioners may require the delivery to them of a statutory declaration in such form as they may direct, made by a solicitor of the Courts of Justice, and of such further evidence (if any) as they may require.

(*b*) The powers conferred on the Commissioners by paragraph (*a*) shall be in addition to and not in substitution for the powers conferred on them by section 20.

(8) If—

(*a*) in respect of any claim for exemption from duty under this section which has been allowed, it is subsequently found that any declaration or other evidence furnished in support of the claim was untrue in any material particular, or that the conditions specified in subsection (2) are not fulfilled in the reconstruction or amalgamation as actually carried out,

(*b*) in respect of shares in the acquiring company which have been issued to the target company in consideration of the acquisition, the target company within a period of 2 years from the date, as the case may be, of the registration or establishment, or of the authority for the increase of the capital, of the acquiring company ceases, otherwise than in consequence of reconstruction, amalgamation or liquidation, to be the beneficial owner of the shares so issued to it, or

(*c*) in respect of any such exemption which has been allowed in connection with the acquisition by the acquiring company of shares in the target company, the acquiring company within a period of 2 years from the date of its registration or establishment or of the authority for the increase of its capital, as the case may be, ceases, otherwise than in consequence of reconstruction, amalgamation or liquidation, to be the beneficial owner of the shares so acquired, then the exemption shall cease to be applicable and stamp duty shall be chargeable in respect of the conveyance or transfer as if subsection (2) had not been enacted together with interest on the duty, by means of penalty, at the rate of [0.0322 per cent for each day or part of a day][1] to the day on which the duty is paid, in a case to which paragraph (*a*) applies, from the date of the conveyance or transfer or, in a case to which paragraph (*b*) applies, from the date the target company ceased to be the beneficial owner of the shares so issued to it or, in a case to which paragraph (*c*) applies, from the date the acquiring company ceased to be the beneficial owner of the shares so acquired.

(9) If in the case of any scheme of reconstruction or amalgamation the Commissioners are satisfied that at the proper time for making a claim for exemption from duty under subsection (2) there were in existence all the necessary conditions for such exemption other than the condition that not less than 90 per cent of the issued share capital of the target company would be acquired by the acquiring company, the Commissioners may—

(*a*) if it is proved to their satisfaction that not less than 90 per cent of the issued capital of the target company has under the scheme been acquired within a period of 6 months from—

(i) the last day of the period of one month after the first allotment of shares made for the purposes of the acquisition, or

(ii) the date on which an invitation was issued to the shareholders of the target company to accept shares in the acquiring company,

whichever first occurs,

and

(*b*) on production of the instruments on which the duty paid has been impressed,

repay such an amount of duty as would have been remitted if that condition had been originally fulfilled.

(10) This section shall apply notwithstanding—

(*a*) that the acquiring company referred to in this section is incorporated in another Member State of the European Union, or

(*b*) that the target company referred to in this section is incorporated outside the State,

but only where such acquiring company or target company incorporated outside the State corresponds, under the law of the place where it is incorporated, to an acquiring company or target company, as the case may be, within the meaning of this section and subject to any necessary modifications for the purpose of so corresponding, all the other provisions of this section are met.

Amendments

1 Substituted by FA 2002 s 129(6)(*b*) with effect from 1 September 2002 in respect of an amount due to be paid or remitted, whether before, on, or after that date; previously "1 per cent per month or part of a month".

Former enactment

FA 1965 s 31(1)-(3), (5)-(8); FA 1965 s 31(1)-(3), (5)-(8); FA 1994 s 144(1)(*b*); FA 1995 s 144(2); FA 1996 s 116; FA 1999 ss 183(*a*)-(*b*), 197 and Sch 6.

81 Young trained farmers

(1) In this section and Schedule 2—

"an interest in land" means an interest which is not subject to any power (whether or not contained in the instrument) on the exercise of which the land, or any part of or any interest in the land, may be revested in the person from whom it was conveyed or transferred or in any person on behalf of such person;

"land" means agricultural land and includes such farm buildings, farm houses and mansion houses (together with the lands occupied with such farm buildings, farm houses and mansion houses) as are of a character appropriate to the land;

"young trained farmer" means a person in respect of whom it is shown to the satisfaction of the Commissioners—

    (*a*) that such person had not attained the age of 35 years on the date on which the instrument, as respect which relief is being claimed under this section, was executed, and

    (*b*) (i) that such person is the holder of a qualification set out in Schedule 2 and, in the case of a qualification set out in subparagraph (*c*), (*d*), (*e*), (*f*) or (*g*) of paragraph 3 or paragraph 4 of that Schedule, is also the holder of a certificate issued by Teagasc certifying that such person has satisfactorily attended a course of training in farm management, the aggregate duration of which exceeded 80 hours, or

        (ii) (I) that such person has satisfactorily attended full-time a course at a third-level institution in any discipline for a period of not less than 2 years' duration, and

           (II) is the holder of a certificate issued by Teagasc certifying satisfactory attendance at a course of training in either or both agriculture and horticulture, the aggregate duration of which exceeded 180 hours,

or

        (iii) if born before 1 January 1968 that such person is the holder of a certificate issued by Teagasc certifying that such person—

           (I) has had farming as the principal occupation for a period of not less than 3 years, and

           (II) has satisfactorily attended a course of training in either or both agriculture and horticulture, the aggregate duration of which exceeded 180 hours,

and notwithstanding paragraphs (*a*) and (*b*), where Teagasc certifies that any other qualification corresponds to a qualification which is set out in Schedule 2, the Commissioners shall, for the purposes of this section, treat that other qualification as if it were the corresponding qualification so set out.

[(2) No stamp duty shall be chargeable under or by reference to the heading "CONVEYANCE or TRANSFER on sale of any property other than stocks or marketable securities or a policy of insurance or a policy of life insurance" in Schedule 1 on any instrument to which this section applies.][1]

(3) This section applies to any instrument which operates as a conveyance or transfer (whether on sale or as a voluntary disposition inter vivos) of an interest in land to a young trained farmer where—

(*a*) the instrument contains a certificate that this section applies,

(*b*) a declaration made in writing by the young trained farmer, or each of them if there is more than one, is furnished to the Commissioners when the instrument is presented for stamping, confirming, to the satisfaction of the Commissioners, that it is the intention of such person, or each such person, for a period of not less than 5 years from the date of execution of the instrument to—

     (i) spend not less than 50 per cent of that person's normal working time farming the land, and

     (ii) retain ownership of the land,

and

(*c*) the identifying reference number, known as the Revenue and Social Insurance (RSI) Number, of the young trained farmer, or each of them if there is more than one, is furnished to the Commissioners when the instrument is presented for stamping.

(4) Notwithstanding subsection (3), this section shall apply where the property is conveyed or transferred into joint ownership where all the joint owners are young trained farmers or where any of the joint owners is a spouse of another joint owner who is a young trained farmer.

(5) Where this section would have applied to the instrument, except for the fact that a person to whom the land is being conveyed or transferred is not a young trained farmer on the date when the instrument was executed, by reason of not being the holder of one of the qualifications, or an equivalent qualification, specified in Schedule 2 or, in the case of the requirement in paragraph (*b*)(ii)(I) of the definition of "young trained farmer" in subsection (1), not having attended full-time for the required 2 years' duration, but that such person had completed on that date at least one academic year of the prescribed course leading to an award of such qualification, or the course prescribed in paragraph (*b*)(ii)(I) of that definition, then—

(*a*) if such person becomes a holder of such qualification, or satisfactorily attends such course full-time for a period of 2 years, within a period of 3 years from the date of execution of the instrument, the Commissioners shall, on production of the stamped instrument to them within 6 months after the date when such person became the holder of such qualification, or completed the required 2 years' attendance on such course, and on furnishing satisfactory evidence of compliance with this subsection, the declaration and the Revenue and Social Insurance (RSI) Number, as provided for in subsection (3), cancel and refund, without payment of interest on the duty, such duty as would not have been chargeable had this section applied to the instrument when it was first presented for stamping, and

(*b*) the period of 5 years provided for in subsection (3) in relation to the declaration to be made by such person, as it applies to normal working time, shall be reduced by the period of time that elapsed between the date of the instrument and the date on which such person became the holder of such qualification or completed the required 2 years' attendance on such course.

[(6) Subsection (2) shall not apply to an instrument unless it has, in accordance with section 20, been stamped with a particular stamp denoting that it is not chargeable with any duty or that it is duly stamped.][2]

[(7) (*a*)   If and to the extent that any person to whom land was conveyed or transferred by any instrument in respect of which relief from duty under this section was allowed

    (i)   disposes of such land, or part of such land, within a period of 5 years from the date of execution of the instrument, and

    (ii)   does not replace such land with other land within a period of one year from the date of such disposal, then such person or, where there is more than one such person, each such person, jointly and severally, shall become liable to pay to the Commissioners a penalty equal to the amount of the duty which would have been charged

in the first instance if the land disposed of had been conveyed or transferred by an instrument to which this section had not applied, together with interest on that amount as may so become payable charged at a rate of [0.0322 per cent for each day or part of a day][3] from the date of disposal of the land to the date the penalty is remitted.

(*b*)   Where any claim for relief from duty under this section has been allowed and it is subsequently found that a declaration made, or a certificate contained in the instrument, in accordance with subsection (3)

    (i)   was untrue in any material particular which would have resulted in the relief afforded by this section not being granted, and

    (ii)   was made, or was included, knowing same to be untrue or in reckless disregard as to whether it was true or not,

then any person who made such a declaration, or where a false certificate has been included, the person or persons to whom the land is conveyed or transferred by the instrument, jointly and severally, shall be liable to pay to the Commissioners as a penalty an amount equal to 125 per cent of the duty which would have been charged on the instrument in the first instance had all the facts been truthfully declared and certified, together with interest on that amount as may so become payable charged at a rate of [0.0322 per cent for each day or part of a day][3] from the date when the instrument was executed to the date the penalty is remitted.][4]

(8) Notwithstanding subsection (7)—

(*a*)   where relief under this section was allowed in respect of any instrument, a disposal by a young trained farmer of part of the land to a spouse for the purpose of creating a joint tenancy in the land, or where the instrument conveyed or transferred the land to joint owners, a disposal by one joint owner to another of any part of the land, shall not be regarded as a disposal to which subsection (7) applies, but on such disposal, such part of the land shall be treated for the purposes of subsection (7) as if it had been conveyed or transferred immediately to the spouse or other joint owner by the instrument in respect of which relief from duty under this section was allowed in the first instance;

(b) a person shall not be liable to more than one penalty under paragraph (b) of subsection (7);

(c) a person shall not be liable to a penalty under paragraph (a) of subsection (7) if and to the extent that such person has paid a penalty under paragraph (b) of subsection (7), and

(d) a person shall not be liable to a penalty under paragraph (b) of subsection (7), if and to the extent that such person has paid a penalty under paragraph (a) of subsection (7).

(9) This section shall apply as respects instruments executed on or before [31 December 2002].[5]

Amendments

[1]   Subs (2) substituted by FA 2000 s 126(1)(a) in relation to instruments executed on or after 1 January 2000.

[2]   Subs (6) substituted by FA 2000 s 126(1)(b) in relation to instruments executed on or after 1 January 2000.

[3]   Substituted by FA 2002 s 129(6)(b) with effect from 1 September 2002 in respect of an amount due to be paid or remitted, whether before, on, or after that date; previously "1 per cent per month or part of a month".

[4]   Subs (7) substituted by FA 2000 s 126(1)(c) in relation to instruments executed on or after 1 January 2000.

[5]   Substituted by FA 2000 s 126(1)(d) in relation to instruments executed on or after 1 January 2000; previously "31 December 1999".

Notes

Stamp duty on a transfer of farming land to a trained farmer (who is under 35 years of age) will be reduced by two thirds of the amount that would normally apply. The relief only applies to deeds executed between 7 December 1994 and 31 December 1996.

It is proposed by the Budget of 1 December 1999 to extend the relief on transfers of land to young farmers, which was due to expire on 31 December, to 31 December 2002.

The transfer deed must contain a clause stating that the provisions of this section apply, and the young farmer must provide his (RSI) Revenue and Social Insurance Number and sign a declaration that he will continue to own the farm land and spend at least half of his time working on the land.

A farmer who is in college but is not fully trained (because he has not completed his course of studies) may obtain the relief provided he completes the course within three years of the date of the transfer deed.

If the young farmer disposes of the farm within five years of the date of transfer any relief already given is withdrawn, and interest will apply to any underpaid duty at 1% per month from the date of the original transfer.

Definitions

"Commissioners"; "conveyance on sale"; "marketable securities"; "policy of life insurance"; "stocks": s 1; "writing": IA 1937 Sch.

Former enactment

FA 1994 s 112; FA 1997 s 126; FA 1998 s 124(1); FA 1999 s 168(a)-(c).

82 Charities

(1) Stamp duty shall not be chargeable on any conveyance, transfer or lease of land made, or agreed to be made, for charitable purposes in the State or Northern Ireland to a body of persons established for charitable purposes only or to the trustees of a trust so established.

(2) Subsection (1) shall not apply to a conveyance, transfer or lease unless that conveyance, transfer or lease has, in accordance with section 20, been stamped with a particular stamp denoting that it is not chargeable with stamp duty.

Cross-references

Stamp duty on agreements for lease and certain other agreements: s 35.

Former enactment

FA 1979 s 50.

83 Instruments given by means of security to company by subsidiary

(1) The whole amount of duty payable under or by reference to the heading "MORTGAGE,BOND, DEBENTURE, COVENANT (except a marketable security) which is a security for the payment or repayment of money which is a charge or incumbrance on property situated in the State other than shares in stocks or funds of the Government or the Oireachtas" in Schedule 1 on any instrument given by means of security to a company by a subsidiary of that company shall not exceed [€12.50][1].

(2) For the purposes of this section a company is a subsidiary of another company only if not less than 90 per cent of its issued share capital is in the beneficial ownership of the other company.

(3) An instrument to which this section applies and which is stamped with an amount of duty less than the amount which, but for this section, would be chargeable shall not be deemed to be duly stamped unless the Commissioners have expressed their opinion on that instrument in accordance with section 20 and the instrument is stamped with a particular stamp denoting that it is duly stamped.

Amendments

[1]   Substituted by FA 2001 s 240 and Sch 5 Pt 6 with effect from 1 January 2002; previously "£10".

Note

Unlike the relief for transfers between associated companies the shares in the subsidiary company must be directly and beneficially owned by the parent company.

Cross-references

Denoting stamp: s 11.
Transfers of property between associated companies: s 79.
Relief for reconstruction and amalgamation of companies: s 80.

Definitions

"instrument"; "mortgage"; "stamp"; "stamped": s 1.

Former enactment

FA 1961 s 30; FA 1992 s 204.

83A Transfer of site to child

[(1) In this section—

"site", in relation to an instrument of conveyance, transfer or lease, includes any interest in land but does not include the site of a building which at the date of that instrument—

(a)   was used or was suitable for use as a dwelling or for another or other purposes, or

(b)   was in the course of being constructed or adapted for use as a dwelling or for another or other purposes.

(2) Stamp duty shall not be chargeable on any conveyance, transfer or lease of a site to which this section applies.

(3) This section applies to any instrument which operates as a conveyance, transfer or lease of a site and which contains a statement, in such form as the Commissioners may specify, certifying—

    (*a*)   that the person becoming entitled to the entire beneficial interest in the site is a child of the person or of each of the persons immediately theretofore entitled to the entire beneficial interest in the site,

    (*b*)   that at the date of the instrument the value of that site does not exceed [€254,000][1] and that the transaction thereby effected does not form part of a larger transaction or of a series of transactions whereby property with a value in excess of [€254,000][1] is conveyed, transferred or leased to that child,

    (*c*)   that the purpose of the conveyance, transfer or lease is to enable that child to construct a dwellinghouse on that site which will be occupied by that child as his or her only or main residence, and

    (*d*)   that the transaction thereby effected is the first and only conveyance, transfer or lease of a site for the benefit of that child from either or both of the parents of that child which contains the certificate specified in this section.

(4) Subsection (2) shall not apply to an instrument unless it has, in accordance with section 20, been stamped with a particular stamp denoting that it is not chargeable with any duty or that it is duly stamped.

(5) The furnishing of an incorrect statement within the meaning of subsection (3) shall be deemed to constitute the delivery of an incorrect statement for the purposes of section 1078 of the Taxes Consolidation Act, 1997.][2]

Amendments

[1]   Substituted by FA 2001 s 206(2) in relation to instruments executed on or after 1 January 2002; previously "£200,000".

[2]   Section 83A inserted by FA 2001 s 206(1) in relation to instruments executed on or after 6 December 2000.

CHAPTER 2
Other instruments

84 Repayment of stamp duty on certain transfers of shares

(1) In this section **"approved scheme"**, **"participant"**, **"the release date"** and **"shares"** have the same meanings, respectively, as in section 509 of the Taxes Consolidation Act, 1997.

(2) Where, in relation to an instrument, it is shown to the satisfaction of the Commissioners that the instrument gives effect, on or after the release date, to the transfer of shares by, or on behalf of, a person who is, or had become, entitled to those shares as a participant in an approved scheme, the Commissioners shall repay such an amount of the stamp duty as was paid, by reference to the heading "CONVEYANCE or TRANSFER on sale of any stocks or marketable securities" in Schedule 1, on the instrument in respect of those shares.

Definitions
"instrument": s 1; IA 1937 s 3; "marketable security": s 1; "person": IA 1937 s 11(*c*); "stock": s 1.
Former enactment
FA 1986 s 98(1)(*b*), (2).

85 Certain loan capital and securities

(1) In this section **"loan capital"** means any debenture stock, bonds or funded debt, by whatever name known, or any capital raised which is borrowed or has the character of borrowed money, whether in the form of stock or in any other form.

(2) Stamp duty shall not be chargeable on—

    (*a*) the issue, whether in bearer form or otherwise, of—

        (i) any Government loan within the meaning assigned by section 134(10) of the Finance Act, 1990, or

        (ii) any other loan capital but where the instrument is chargeable to stamp duty under the heading "MORTGAGE, BOND, DEBENTURE, COVENANT (except a marketable security) which is a security for the payment or repayment of money which is a charge or incumbrance on property situated in the State other than shares in stocks or funds of the Government or the Oireachtas" in Schedule 1 the instrument shall be chargeable with that duty;

    (*b*) the transfer of loan capital of a company or other body corporate which—

        (i) does not carry a right of conversion into stocks or marketable securities (other than loan capital) of a company having a register in the State or into loan capital having such a right,

        (ii) does not carry rights of the same kind as shares in the capital of a company, including rights such as voting rights, a share in the profits or a share in the surplus on liquidation,

        (iii) is redeemable within 30 years of the date of issue and not thereafter,

        (iv) is issued for a price which is not less than 90 per cent of its nominal value, and

        (v) does not carry a right to a sum in respect of repayment or interest which is related to certain movements in an index or indices specified in any instrument or other document relating to the loan capital,

    and

    (*c*) the issue or transfer of securities issued by a qualifying company within the meaning of section 110 of the Taxes Consolidation Act, 1997, where the money raised by such securities is used in the course of its business.

Former enactment

FA 1993 s 106; FA 1994 s 106(*a*)-(*c*); TCA 1997 s 1100 and Sch 31; FA 1999 s 143.

86 Certain loan stock

Stamp duty shall not be chargeable on transfers of any loan stock—

    (*a*) of a company registered or established in the State or a Board established by or under an Act of the Oireachtas or the Oireachtas of Sáorstat Eireann the payment of the interest on which is guaranteed by the Minister, or

    (*b*) of the Electricity Supply Board, Radio Telefis Eireann, [ICC Bank public limited company],[1] ...,[2] [or Bord Gáis Éireann][3] to which paragraph (*a*) does not apply.

Amendments

¹   Substituted by FA 2000 s 127(1)(*a*) in relation to transfers of loan stock executed on or after 10 February 2000; previously "Industrial Credit Corporation p.l.c.".

²   Deleted by FA 2000 s 127(1)(*b*) in relation to transfers of loan stock executed where the loan stock was issued on or after 10 February 2000; previously "Bord Telecome Éireann".

²   Substituted by FA 2001 s 207(1) as respects instruments executed on or after 15 February 2001; previously "Bord Gáis Éireann or Irish Telecommunications Investments plc".

Former enactment

FA 1970 s 44(1)-(2); FA 1989 s 71; FA 1999 s 217.

87 Stock borrowing

(1) In this section—

"collateral stock", in relation to a stock borrowing, means stock which is transferred to the lender by means of security for the performance of the undertaking referred to in paragraph (*b*) of the definition of "stock borrowing";

"equivalent stock" means stock of an identical type, nominal value, description and amount as was so obtained from the lender or where, since the date of the stock borrowing, such stock has been paid or has been converted, subdivided, consolidated, redeemed, made the subject of a takeover, call on partly paid stock, capitalisation issue, rights issue, distribution or other similar event, then "equivalent stock" means—

    (*a*)   in the case of conversion, subdivision or consolidation, the stock into which the borrowed stock has been converted, subdivided or consolidated,

    (*b*)   in the case of redemption, a sum of money equivalent to the proceeds of the redemption,

    (*c*)   in the case of takeover, a sum of money or stock, being the consideration or alternative consideration which the lender has directed the stock borrower to accept,

    (*d*)   in the case of a call on partly paid stock, the paid-up stock but only where the lender shall have paid to the stock borrower the sum due,

    (*e*)   in the case of a capitalisation issue, the borrowed stock together with the stock allotted by means of a bonus on that borrowed stock,

    (*f*)   in the case of a rights issue, the borrowed stock together with the stock allotted on that borrowed stock, which the lender has directed the borrower to take up but only where the lender shall have paid to the stock borrower all and any sum due in respect of the stock allotted,

    (*g*)   in the event that a distribution is made in respect of the borrowed stock in the form of stock or a certificate which may at a future date be exchanged for stock or where an option is exercised to take a distribution in the form of stock or a certificate which may at a future date be exchanged for stock, the borrowed stock together with stock or a certificate equivalent to those allotted, and

    (*h*)   in the case of any event similar to any of the foregoing, the borrowed stock together with or replaced by a sum of money or stock equivalent to that received in respect of such borrowed stock resulting from such events;

...¹

...²

["**Stock borrowing**" means a transaction in which a person other than an individual (in this section referred to as the "stock borrower")—

(*a*) obtains stock from another person other than an individual (in this section referred to as the "lender"), and

(*b*) gives an undertaking to provide to the lender, not later than 6 months after the date on which the said stock borrower obtained the stock referred to in paragraph (*a*), equivalent stock;][3]

"**stock return**", in relation to a stock borrowing, means a transaction or transactions in which, in respect of such stock borrowing, the undertaking referred to in paragraph (*b*) of the definition of "stock borrowing" is carried out within the period referred to in that paragraph.

(2) Stamp duty shall not be chargeable—

(*a*) on a stock borrowing or on a stock return, or

(*b*) on the transfer of collateral stock to the lender.

(3) If and to the extent that the stock borrower does not return or cause to be returned to the lender before the expiration of the period of [6 months][4] from the date of the stock borrowing equivalent stock the stock borrower shall pay to the Commissioners within 14 days after the expiration of that period the amount of ad valorem duty which would have been chargeable on the stock so obtained if this section had not been enacted and if any stock borrower fails to duly pay any sum which that borrower is liable to pay under this subsection, that sum, together with interest on that sum at the rate of [0.0322 per cent for each day or part of a day][4] from the first day after the expiration of that period of [6 months][5] to the date of payment of that sum and, by means of further penalty, a sum equal to 1 per cent of the duty for each day the duty remains unpaid, shall be recoverable from the stock borrower as a debt due to the Minister for the benefit of the Central Fund.

(4) Every stock borrower shall maintain [, for a period of 3 years from the date of the stock borrowing,][6] separate records of each stock borrowing and any stock return made in respect of that stock borrowing and such records shall include, in respect of each stock borrowing, the following:

(*a*) ...[7]

(*b*) the name and address of the lender;

(*c*) the type, nominal value, description and amount of stock borrowed from the lender;

(*d*) the date on which the stock was transferred from the lender to the stock borrower;

(*e*) the date on which equivalent stock should be returned to the lender;

(*f*) the type, nominal value, description and amount of the stock returned to the lender and the date of the stock return;

(*g*) where paragraph (*a*), (*b*), (*c*), (*d*), (*e*), (*f*), (*g*) or (*h*) of the definition of "equivalent stock" in subsection (1) applies, full details of that equivalent stock.

Amendments

[1]   Definition of "stock" deleted by FA 2000 s 128(1)(*a*)(i) in relation to stock borrowing transactions entered into on or after 6 April 1999.

2   Definition of "stock borrower" deleted by FA 2000 s 128(1)(*a*)(i) in relation to stock borrowing
    transactions entered into on or after 6 April 1999.
3   Definition of "stock borrowing" substituted by FA 2000 s 128(1)(*a*)(ii) in relation to stock borrowing
    transactions entered into on or after 6 April 1999.
4   Substituted by FA 2002 s 129(6)(*b*) with effect from 1 September 2002 in respect of an amount due to be
    paid or remitted, whether before, on, or after that date; previously "1 per cent per month or part of a month".
5   Substituted by FA 2000 s 128(1)(*b*) in relation to stock borrowing transactions entered into on or after 6
    April 1999; previously "3 months".
6   Inserted by FA 2000 s 128(1)(*c*)(i) in relation to stock borrowing transactions entered into on or after 10
    February 2000.
7   Subs (4)(*a*) deleted by FA 128(1)(*c*)(ii) in relation to stock borrowing transactions entered into on or after
    10 February 2000.

Former enactment

FA 1995 s 150; FA 1996 s 111(*a*)-(*b*); FA 1998 s 124(1); FA 1999 s 144.

87A Stock repo

[(1) In this section—

"equivalent stock" has the meaning assigned to it by section 87 subject to references—

    (*a*) to "obtained from the lender" being read as "transferred to the repo buyer",

    (*b*) to "stock borrowing" being read as "stock transfer".

    (*c*) to "lender" being read as "repo seller",

    (*d*) to "stock borrower" being read as "repo buyer",

    (*e*) to "borrowed stock" being read as "stock transferred", and

    (*f*) to "borrower" being read as "repo buyer";

"repurchase agreement" means an agreement between a person other than an individual (in this section referred to as the "repo seller") and another person other than an individual (in this section referred to as the "repo buyer") whereby the repo seller agrees to sell stock to the repo buyer on terms that the repo seller will repurchase, and the repo buyer will resell, equivalent stock not later than 6 months after the date of the stock transfer;

"stock return" means a transaction or transactions whereby a repo buyer conveys equivalent stock to a repo seller in pursuance of a repurchase agreement and within the 6 month time limit referred to in the repurchase agreement:

"stock transfer" means a transaction whereby a repo seller conveys stock to a repo buyer in pursuance of a repurchase agreement.

(2) Stamp duty shall not be chargeable on a stock transfer or on a stock return.

(3) If and to the extent that the repo seller does not repurchase or cause to be repurchased from the repo buyer before the expiration of the period of 6 months from the date of the stock transfer equivalent stock the repo buyer shall pay to the Revenue Commissioners within 14 days after the expiration of that period the amount of ad valorem duty which would have been chargeable on the stock so transferred if this section had not been enacted.

(4) If any repo buyer fails to duly pay any sum which that repo buyer is liable to pay under subsection (3), that sum, together with—

(*a*) interest on that sum at the rate of [0.0322 per cent for each day or part of a day]¹ from the first day after the expiration of the period of 6 months referred to in subsection (3) to the date of payment of that sum, and

(*b*) by means of further penalty, a sum equal to 1 per cent of the duty for each day the duty remains unpaid,

shall be recoverable from the repo buyer as a debt due to the Minister for Finance for the benefit of the Central Fund.

(5) Every repo buyer shall maintain, for a period of 3 years from the date of the stock transfer, separate records of each stock transfer and any stock return made in respect of that stock transfer and such records shall include, in respect of each stock transfer, the following:

(*a*) the name and address of the repo seller;

(*b*) the type, nominal value, description and amount of the stock transferred by the repo seller;

(*c*) the date on which the stock was transferred to the repo buyer;

(*d*) the date on which equivalent stock should be repurchased by the repo seller;

(*e*) the type, nominal value, description and amount of the stock returned by the repo buyer to the repo seller and the date of such return;

(*f*) where paragraph (*a*), (*b*), (*c*), (*d*), (*e*), (*f*), (*g*) or (*h*) of the definition of "equivalent stock" applies, full details of that equivalent stock.]²

Amendments

¹ Substituted by FA 2002 s 129(6)(*b*) with effect from 1 September 2002 in respect of an amount due to be paid or remitted, whether before, on, or after that date; previously "1 per cent per month or part of a month".

² Section 87A inserted by FA 2000 s 129(1), subs (1) and (2) are effective for stock transfers and stock returns executed on or after 6 April 1999, subs (3), (4) and (5) are effect for stock transfers and stock returns executed on or after 10 February 2000.

88 Certain stocks and marketable securities

(1) (*a*) In subparagraph (ii) of paragraph (*b*)—

"collective investment scheme" means a scheme which is an arrangement made for the purpose, or having the effect, solely or mainly, of providing facilities for the participation by the public or other investors, as beneficiaries, in profits or income arising from the acquisition, holding, management or disposal of securities or any other property;

"units" includes shares and any other instruments granting an entitlement to shares in the investments or income of, or receive a distribution from, a collective investment scheme.

(*b*) Subject to subsection (2), stamp duty shall not be chargeable on any conveyance or transfer of—

(i) units in a collective investment undertaking within the meaning of section 734 of the Taxes Consolidation Act, 1997,

(ii) units in a collective investment scheme which is incorporated or otherwise formed under the law of a territory outside the State,

(iii) units of a unit trust to which subsection (6) of section 731 of the Taxes Consolidation Act, 1997, relates, or

(iv) stocks or marketable securities of a company which is not registered in the State.

(2) Paragraph (*b*) of subsection (1) shall not apply where the conveyance or transfer of units (being units within the meaning of subparagraph (ii) of paragraph (*b*) of subsection(1)) or stocks or marketable securities (being stocks or marketable securities within the meaning of subparagraph (iv) of paragraph (*b*) of subsection (1)), as the case may be, relates to—

(*a*) any immovable property situated in the State or any right over or interest in such property, or

(*b*) any stocks or marketable securities of a company, other than a company which is a collective investment undertaking within the meaning of section 734 of the Taxes Consolidation Act, 1997, which is registered in the State.

Former enactment

FA 1992 s 206; FA 1994 s 105(*a*)-(*d*); TCA 1997 s 1100 and Sch 31.

Cross-references

Subs (1)(*b*)(iii)-(iv) replace the provisions of the Stamp Duty (Variation) Order 1991 (SI 277/1991) para 4(*i*) and 4(*n*) which became effective on 1 November 1991.

Foreign government securities, exemption: s 89.

Definitions

"marketable security", "stamp", "stock": s 1.

88A Reorganisation of undertakings for collective investment

[Stamp duty shall not be chargeable on any conveyance or transfer of assets in respect of which no chargeable gain accrues by virtue of section 739A (inserted by the Finance Act, 2000) of the Taxes Consolidation Act, 1997.][1]

Amendments

[1] Section 88A inserted by FA 2000 s 130 in respect of a conveyance or transfer executed on or after 23 March 2000.

89 Foreign Government securities

Stamp duty shall not be chargeable on any conveyance or transfer of stocks or other securities of the government of any territory outside the State.

Note

Stamp duty is not to be charged on transfers of foreign government securities.

Definitions

"stamp"; "stock": s 1.

Former enactment

FA 1994 s 111.

90 Certain financial services instruments

(1) In this section—

"American depositary receipt" means an instrument—

(*a*) which acknowledges—

(i) that a depositary or a nominee acting on such depositary's behalf, holds stocks or marketable securities, and

(ii) that the holder of the instrument has rights in or in relation to such stocks or marketable securities including the right to receive such stocks or marketable securities from the depositary or such depositary's nominee,

and

(b) which—

(i) is dealt in on a recognised stock exchange which is situated in the United States of America or Canada, or

(ii) represents stocks or marketable securities which are so dealt in;

"commodities" means tangible assets (other than currency, securities, debts or other assets of a financial nature) which are dealt in on a recognised commodity exchange;

"debt factoring agreement" means an agreement for the sale, or a transfer on sale, of a debt or part of a debt where such sale occurs in the ordinary course of the business of the vendor or the purchaser;

"depositary" means a person who holds stocks or marketable securities in trust for or on behalf of holders of depositary receipts and who maintains a register of ownership of such depositary receipts;

"financial futures agreement" means a forward agreement which is for the time being dealt in on a recognised futures exchange or a recognised stock exchange;

"forward agreement" means—

(a) an agreement under which a party to the agreement agrees—

(i) to buy or sell commodities, currency, stocks or marketable securities, or

(ii) to pay or receive a sum of money, whether or not such money is actually paid or received,

at a specified date or within a specified or determinable period of time and pursuant to which the price or currency exchange rate concerned or, in the case of a sum of money, the interest (if any) payable, or expressed to be payable, on such sum of money is determined or determinable at the time of the execution of the agreement, or

(b) an agreement conferring the right to receive certain payments and imposing the liability to make certain payments, the receipt and making of the payments being dependent on and related to certain movements in a specified stock exchange index or specified stock exchange indices;

"option agreement" means an agreement under which a right is conferred on a party to the agreement to do, at the party's discretion, either or both of the following, that is—

(a) to buy from or sell to or buy from and sell to another party to the agreement—

(i) specified stocks, marketable securities, commodities or currency,

(ii) an agreement conferring the right to receive certain payments and imposing the liability to make certain payments, the receipt and making of the payments being dependent on and related to certain movements in a specified stock exchange index or specified stock exchange indices, on or before a specified date at a price that is determined or determinable at the time of the execution of the agreement,

(b) to borrow money from or lend money to another party to the agreement for or within a specified period in consideration of the payment of interest by the party by whom the money is borrowed or to whom it is lent to the other party concerned at a rate that is determined or determinable at the time of the execution of the agreement;

"swap agreement" means an agreement under which the parties to the agreement exchange payments or repayments of money in respect of which such parties have obligations or rights and which are denominated in a specified currency or are subject to the payment of a specified rate of interest or relate to the price of specified commodities, stocks or marketable securities, for payments or repayments of the same kind which are denominated in another specified currency or are subject to the payment of a specified different rate of interest or relate to the price of other specified commodities, stocks or marketable securities.

(2) Stamp duty shall not be chargeable on any of the following instruments:

(a) a debt factoring agreement;
(b) a swap agreement;
(c) a forward agreement:
(d) a financial futures agreement;
(e) an option agreement;
(f) a combination of any 2 or more of the instruments specified in paragraphs (a) to (e);
(g) a transfer of, or an agreement to transfer—

    (i) any instrument specified in paragraphs (a) to (e), or a combination of any 2 or more such instruments,
   (ii) a lease, other than a lease to which any heading in Schedule 1 applies, or
 (iii) an American depositary receipt.

(3) Subsection (2) shall not apply if the instrument, other than an instrument which is a transfer of, or an agreement to transfer, an American depositary receipt relates to—

(a) immovable property situated in the State or any right over or interest in such property, or
(b) the stocks or marketable securities of a company, other than a company which is a collective investment undertaking within the meaning of section 734 of the Taxes Consolidation Act, 1997, which is registered in the State.

(4) Notwithstanding that, in respect of any particular provision it contains, an instrument is exempt from stamp duty under this section, if the instrument is liable to stamp duty in respect of any other provision it contains under any heading in Schedule 1, the instrument shall be chargeable with the latter stamp duty.

Cross-references

This section replaces the provisions of paragraph 4(a)-(g) and (i) of the Stamp Duty (Variation) Order 1991 ("the Order") (SI 277/1991) which became effective on 1 November 1991 with the exception of para 4(h) of the Order which is re-enacted in s 98. The exemptions for transfers of certain leases and of American depositary receipts (s 90(g)(ii)-(iii), supra) were introduced by this section.

Definitions

"execution"; "marketable security"; "money"; "stamp"; "stock": s 1.

Former enactment

FA 1992 s 207; FA 1996 s 115(*a*), (*b*); FA 1997 s 125(*a*), (*b*); FA 1999 s 142(1)(*a*)-(*c*).

91 New dwellinghouses and apartments with floor area certificate

(1) Subject to subsection (2), an instrument giving effect to the purchase of a dwellinghouse or apartment on the erection of that dwellinghouse or apartment shall be exempt from all stamp duties.

(2) (*a*) In this subsection, **"floor area certificate"** means a certificate issued by the Minister for the Environment and Local Government certifying that that Minister is satisfied, on the basis of the information available to that Minister at the time of so certifying, that the total floor area of that dwellinghouse or apartment measured in the manner referred to in section 4(2)(*b*) of the Housing (Miscellaneous Provisions) Act, 1979, does not or will not exceed the maximum total floor area standing specified in regulations under that section 4(2)(*b*) and is not or will not be less than the minimum total floor area standing so specified.

   (*b*) Subsection (1) shall have effect in relation to an instrument only if the instrument contains a statement, in such form as the Commissioners may specify, certifying that—

   (i) the instrument gives effect to the purchase of a dwellinghouse or apartment on the erection of that dwellinghouse or apartment,

   (ii) until the expiration of the period of 5 years commencing on the date of the execution of the instrument or the subsequent sale (other than a sale the contract for which, if it were a written conveyance, would not, apart from section 82, be charged with full ad valorem duty or a sale to a company under the control of the vendor or of any person entitled to a beneficial interest in the dwellinghouse or apartment immediately prior to the sale or to a company which would, in relation to a notional gift of shares in that company taken, immediately prior to the sale, by any person so entitled, be under the control of the donee or successor within the meaning of section 16 of the Capital Acquisitions Tax Act, 1976, irrespective of the shares the subject matter of the notional gift) of the dwellinghouse or apartment concerned, whichever event first occurs, that dwellinghouse or apartment will be occupied as the only or principal place of residence of the purchaser, or if there be more than one purchaser, of any one or more of the purchasers or of some other person in right of the purchaser or, if there be more than one purchaser, of some other person in right of any one or more of the purchasers and that [no person—

   (I) other than a person who, while in such occupation, derives rent or payment in the nature of rent in consideration for the provision, on or after 6 April 2001, of furnished residential accommodation in part of the dwellinghouse or apartment concerned, or

   (II) other than by virtue of a title prior to that of the purchaser, will derive any rent or payment in the nature of rent for the use of that dwellinghouse or apartment, or of any part of it, during that period, and][1]

(iii) on the date of execution of the instrument there exists a valid floor area certificate in respect of that dwellinghouse or apartment.

(c) Where, in relation to an instrument which is exempted from stamp duty by virtue of subsection (1) and at any time during the period referred to in paragraph (b)(ii), [some person, other than a person referred to in clause (I) or (II) of subsection (2)(b)(ii)],[2] derives any rent or payment in the nature of rent for the use of the dwellinghouse or apartment concerned, or of any part of it, the purchaser, or where there be more than one purchaser, each such purchaser, shall—

   (i) jointly and severally become liable to pay to the Commissioners a penalty equal to the amount of the duty which would have been charged in the first instance if the dwellinghouse or apartment had been conveyed or transferred or leased by an instrument to which this section had not applied together with interest on that amount charged at a rate of [0.0322 per cent for each day or part of a day][3] from the date when the rent or payment is first received to the date the penalty is remitted, and

   (ii) the person who receives the rent or payment shall, within 6 months after the date of the payment, notify the payment to the Commissioners on a form provided, or approved of, by them for the purposes of this section, unless that person is already aware that the Commissioners have already received such a notification from another source.

(d) The furnishing of an incorrect statement within the meaning of paragraph (b) shall be deemed to constitute the delivery of an incorrect statement for the purposes of section 1078 of the Taxes Consolidation Act, 1997.

Amendments

[1] Substituted by FA 2001 s 208(1)(a)(i) with effect in relation to instruments executed on or after 6 December2000; previously "no person, other than by virtue of a title prior to that of the purchaser, will derive any rent or payment in the nature of rent for the use of that dwellinghouse or apartment, or of any part of it, during that period, and".

[2] Substituted by FA 2001 s 208(1)(a)(ii) with effect in relation to instruments executed on or after 6 December2000; previously "some person, other than by virtue of a title prior to that of the purchaser".

[3] Substituted by FA 2002 s 129(6)(b) with effect from 1 September 2002 in respect of an amount due to be paid or remitted, whether before, on, or after that date; previously "1 per cent per month or part of a month".

Note

Subs (2)(b): the maximum floor area allowed within this relief is 125m2.

Cross-references

Relief for other new houses: ss 24, 53.

Relief for conveyance etc of house by or to a housing authority: Housing (Miscellaneous Provisions) Act 1992 s 8.

Case law

"upon erection" means within a reasonable time after erection. What is reasonable depends on the circumstances: *Dunne v The Revenue Commissioners*, HC, December 1977 [1982] ILRM 438. See also Tax Briefing 22 June 1996.

Revenue Information

Leaflets SD4: Stamp duty - conveyances and leases of residential property (May 1998); SD7: Stamp duty - Certificates required in deeds (December 1999); SD9A Stamp duty - Conveyance and leases of residential property (August 2000); SD 10; Stamp duty - Revenue Certificates required in deeds (May 2001).

Definitions

"instrument"; "regulations", "stamp": s 1.

Former enactment

FA 1969 s 49(1), (2B); FA 1976 s 48; FA 1996 s 113(1); TCA 1997 s 1100; FA 1998 s 125 and Sch 8; F(No 2)A 1998 s 11(*a*)-(*c*); FA 1999 ss 164(*a*)-(*c*), 197 and Sch 6.

92 New dwellinghouses and apartments with no floor area certificate

(1) (*a*)   Where, in relation to an instrument to which this subsection applies—

(i)   the instrument is one to which section 29 applies, that section shall apply to that instrument as if—

(I)   the following subsection were substituted for subsection (2) of that section:

"(2) Notwithstanding section 43, where, in connection with, or as part of any arrangement involving, a sale of any land, a dwellinghouse or apartment has been built, or is in the course of being built, or is to be built, on that land, any instrument whereby such sale is effected shall be chargeable to stamp duty under the heading "CONVEYANCE or TRANSFER on sale of any property other than stocks or marketable securities or a policy of insurance or a policy of life insurance" in Schedule 1, as if the property concerned were residential property on an amount which is the greater of—

(*a*)   any consideration paid in respect of the sale of that land, and

(*b*)   25 per cent of the aggregate of the consideration at paragraph (*a*) and the consideration paid, or to be paid, in respect of the building of the dwellinghouse or apartment on that land.";

(II)   the following paragraphs were inserted into subsection (3) of that section:

"(*b*)   This subsection does not apply where the dwellinghouse or apartment concerned was occupied by any person, other than in connection with the building of that dwellinghouse or apartment, at any time prior to the agreement for sale of the land.

(*c*)   The amount on which stamp duty is chargeable by virtue of this section shall be deemed to be the amount or value of the consideration for the sale in respect of which that duty is chargeable.";

and

(III)   "such aggregate consideration" were substituted for "the aggregate consideration which is chargeable under subsection (2)" in paragraph (*a*) of subsection (4) of that section;

(ii)   the instrument is one to which section 53 applies, that section shall apply to that instrument as if—

(I)   the following subsection were substituted for subsection (2) of that section:

"(2) Notwithstanding subsection (2) of section 52, where, in connection with, or as part of any arrangement involving, a lease of any land, a dwellinghouse or apartment has been built, or is in the course of being built, or is to be built, on that land, any instrument whereby such lease is effected shall be chargeable to stamp duty under subparagraph (*a*) of paragraph (3) of the heading "LEASE" in Schedule 1, as if the property concerned were residential property on an amount which is the greater of—

(*a*) any consideration (other than rent) paid in respect of the lease of that land, and

(*b*) 25 per cent of the aggregate of the consideration at paragraph (*a*) and the consideration paid, or to be paid, in respect of the building of the dwellinghouse or apartment on that land.":

(II) the following paragraphs were inserted into subsection (3) of that section:

"(*b*) This subsection does not apply where the dwellinghouse or apartment concerned was occupied by any person, other than in connection with the building of that dwellinghouse or apartment, at any time prior to the agreement for lease of the land.

(*c*) The amount on which stamp duty is chargeable by virtue of this section shall be deemed to be the amount or value of the consideration for the lease in respect of which that duty is chargeable.";

and

(III) "such aggregate consideration" were substituted for "the aggregate consideration which is chargeable under subsection (2)" in paragraph (*a*) of subsection (4) of that section;

and

(iii) the instrument gives effect to the purchase of a dwellinghouse or apartment on the erection of that dwellinghouse or apartment and sections 29, 53 and 91 do not apply, the consideration (other than rent) for the sale shall for the purposes of ad valorem duty be treated as being reduced by 75 per cent.

(*b*) This subsection applies to an instrument which contains a statement, in such form as the Commissioners may specify, certifying that—

(i) the instrument—

(I) is one to which section 29 or 53, applies, or

(II) gives effect to the purchase of a dwellinghouse or apartment on the erection of that dwellinghouse or apartment and that sections 29, 53 and 91 do not apply,

and

(ii) until the expiration of the period of 5 years commencing on the date of the execution of the instrument or the subsequent sale (other than a sale the contract for which, if it were a written conveyance, would not, apart from section 82, be charged with full ad valorem duty or a sale to a company under the control of the vendor or of any person entitled to a beneficial interest in the dwellinghouse or apartment immediately prior to the sale or to a company which would, in relation to a notional gift of shares in that company taken, immediately prior to the sale, by any person so entitled, be under the control of the donee or successor within the meaning of section 16 of the Capital Acquisitions Tax Act, 1976, irrespective of the shares the subject matter of the notional gift) of the dwellinghouse or apartment concerned, whichever event first occurs, that dwellinghouse or apartment will be occupied as the only or principal place of residence of the purchaser, or if there be more than one purchaser, of any one or more of the purchasers or of some other person in right of the purchaser or, if there be more than one purchaser, of some other person in right of any one or more of the purchasers and that [no person—

(I)   other than a person who, while in such occupation, derives rent or payment in the nature of rent in consideration for the provision, on or after 6 April 2001, of furnished residential accommodation in part of the dwellinghouse or apartment concerned, or

(II)   other than by virtue of a title prior to that of the purchaser,

will derive any rent or payment in the nature of rent for the use of that dwellinghouse or apartment, or of any part of it, during that period.][1]

(2) Where subsection (1) applies to an instrument and at any time during the period referred to in paragraph (*b*)(ii) of that subsection, [some person, other than a person referred to in clause (I) or (II) of subsection (1)(*b*)(ii)],[2] derives any rent or payment in the nature of rent for the use of the dwellinghouse or apartment concerned, or of any part of it, the purchaser, or where there be more than one purchaser, each such purchaser, shall—

(*a*)   jointly and severally become liable to pay to the Commissioners a penalty equal to the difference between the amount of the duty which would have been charged in the first instance if the dwellinghouse or apartment had been conveyed or transferred or leased by an instrument to which subsection (1) had not applied and the amount of duty which was actually charged together with interest on that amount charged at a rate of [0.0322 per cent for each day or part of a day][3] from the date when the rent or payment is first received to the date the penalty is remitted, and

(*b*)   the person who receives the rent or payment shall, within 6 months after the date of the payment, notify the payment to the Commissioners on a form provided, or approved of, by them for the purposes of this section, unless that person is already aware that the Commissioners have already received such a notification from another source.

Amendments

1   Substituted by FA 2001 s 208(1)(*b*)(i) with effect in relation to instruments executed on or after 6 December 2000; previously "no person, other than by virtue of a title prior to that of the purchaser, will derive any

rent or payment in the nature of rent for the use of that dwellinghouse or apartment, or any part of it, during that period.".

2 Substituted by FA 2001 s 208(1)(*b*)(ii) with effect in relation to instruments executed on or after 6 December 2000; previously "some person, other than by virtue of a title prior to that of the purchaser".

3 Substituted by FA 2002 s 129(6)(*b*) with effect from 1 September 2002 in respect of an amount due to be paid or remitted, whether before, on, or after that date; previously "1 per cent per month or part of a month".

Notes

The rate of stamp duty on transfers or leases of large new houses is determined by the consideration for the transfer or lease (not by the greater of (*a*) the consideration for the site or (*b*) 25% of the combined consideration for the site plus building contract).

The stamp duty exemption for new houses does not apply to second-hand houses.

Former enactment

F(No 2)A 1998 s 14; FA 1997 ss 123, 124; F(No 2)A 1998 s 14; FA 1999 s 171.

Revenue information

Leaflets SD4: Stamp duty - conveyances and leases of residential property (May 1998); SD7: Stamp duty - Certificates required in deeds (December 1999) and SD9A: Stamp duty - conveyances and leases of residential property (August 2000); SD10: Stamp duty - Revenue certificates required in deeds (May 2001).

92A Residential property owner occupier relief

[(1) The amount of stamp duty chargeable under or by reference to paragraphs (1) to (6) of the Heading "CONVEYANCE or TRANSFER on sale of any property other than stocks or marketable securities or a policy of insurance or a policy of life insurance" or clauses (i) to (vi) of paragraph (3)(*a*) of the Heading "LEASE", as the case may be, in Schedule 1 on any instrument to which this section applies shall be reduced, where paragraph (1) or clause (i) applies, to nil, and where—

(*a*) paragraph (2) or clause (ii) applies, to an amount equal to three-ninths,
(*b*) paragraph (3) or clause (iii) applies, to an amount equal to four-ninths,
(*c*) paragraph (4) or clause (iv) applies, to an amount equal to five-ninths,
(*d*) paragraph (5) or clause (v) applies, to an amount equal to six-ninths,
(*e*) paragraph (6) or clause (vi) applies, to an amount equal to seven and one half-ninths,

of the amount which would otherwise have been chargeable but where the amount so obtained is a fraction of [€1][1] that amount shall be rounded [down to the nearest €][2].

(2) This section shall apply to—

(*a*) any instrument to which section 92 applies, or
(*b*) any instrument, other than one to which section 92 applies, which contains a statement, in such form as the Commissioners may specify, certifying that—

(i) the instrument gives effect to the purchase of a dwellinghouse or apartment, and

(ii) until the expiration of the period of 5 years commencing on the (late of the execution of the instrument or the subsequent sale (other than a sale the contract for which, if it were a written conveyance, would not, apart from section 82, be charged with full ad valorem duty or a sale to a company under the control of the vendor or of any person entitled to a beneficial interest in the dwellinghouse or apartment immediately prior to the sale or to a company which would, in relation to a notional gift of shares in that company taken, immediately prior to the sale, by any person so entitled, be under the control of the donee or successor within the meaning of section 16 of the Capital Acquisitions Tax Act, 1976, irrespective of the shares the subject matter of the notional gift) of the dwellinghouse or apartment concerned, whichever event first occurs, that dwellinghouse or apartment will be occupied as the only or principal place of residence of the purchaser, or if there be more than one purchaser, of any one or more of the purchasers or of some other person in right of the purchaser or, if there be more than one purchaser, of some other person in right of any one or more of the purchasers and that [no person—

(I) other than a person who, while in such occupation, derives rent or payment in the nature of rent in consideration for the provision, on or after 6 April 2001, of furnished residential accommodation in part of the dwellinghouse or apartment concerned, or

(II) other than by virtue of a title prior to that of the purchaser,

will derive any rent or payment in the nature of rent for the use of that dwellinghouse or apartment, or of any part of it, during that period.]³

(3) Where subsection (1) applies to an instrument and at any time during the period referred to in section 92(1)(*b*)(ii) or in subsection (2)(*b*)(ii) of this section, [some person, other than a person referred to in clause (I) or (II) of subsection (2)(*b*)(ii)],⁴ derives any rent or payment in the nature of rent for the use of the dwellinghouse or apartment concerned, or of any part of it, the purchaser, or where there be more than one purchaser, each such purchaser, shall—

(*a*) jointly and severally become liable to pay to the Commissioners a penalty equal to the difference between the amount of the duty which would have been charged in the first instance if the dwellinghouse or apartment had been conveyed or transferred or leased by an instrument to which subsection (1) had not applied and the amount of duty which was actually charged together with interest on that amount charged at a rate of [0.0322 per cent for each day or part of a day]⁵ from the date when the rent or payment is first received to the date the penalty is remitted, and

(*b*) the person who receives the rent or payment shall, within 6 months after the date of the payment, notify the payment to the Commissioners on a form provided, or approved of, by them for the purposes of this section, unless that person is already aware that the Commissioners have already received such a notification from another source.

(4) Where the instrument is one to which this section and section 92 applies—

(*a*) the reference in subsection (3) to the amount of duty which would have been charged in the first instance shall be construed as a reference to the duty which would have been charged had the relief under section 92 continued to apply, and

(*b*) the reference to the amount of duty which was actually charged in subsection (2)(*a*) of section 92 shall be construed as a reference to the duty which would have been charged had the relief under this section been denied, and the penalty referred to in subsection (3) shall be in addition to any penalty payable under section 92.

(5) Notwithstanding subsection (2), subsection (1) shall not apply unless the consideration for the sale or lease concerned which is attributable to residential property is wholly attributable to residential property which would otherwise qualify for relief under this section or where the sale or lease concerned forms part of a larger transaction or of a series of transactions unless the aggregate consideration for that larger transaction or series of transactions which is attributable to residential property is wholly attributable to residential property which would otherwise qualify for relief under this section.

(6) Notwithstanding subsection (2), this section shall not apply to an instrument to which section 92B applies.]⁶

[(7) Notwithstanding subsection (2), subsection (3) shall not apply to an instrument to which subsection (1) applied and which was executed before 6 December 2001 to the extent that any rent or payment in the nature of rent is derived on or after 6 December 2001, for the use of the dwellinghouse or apartment or any part of the dwellinghouse or apartment.

(8) This section shall not apply to an instrument executed on or after 6 December 2001.]⁷

Amendments

1 Substituted by FA 2001 s 240 and Sch 5 Pt 6 with effect from 1 January 2002; previously "£1".
2 Substituted by FA 2001 s 240 and Sch 5 Pt 6 with effect from 1 January 2002; previously "up to the nearest £".
3 Substituted by FA 2001 s 208(1)(c)(i) in effect in relation to instruments executed on or after 6 December 2000; previously "no person, other than by virtue of a title prior to that of the purchaser, will derive any rent or payment in the nature of rent for the use of that dwellinghouse or apartment, or any part of it, during that period.".
4 Substituted by FA 2001 s 208(1)(c)(ii) in effect in relation to instruments executed on or after 6 December 2000; previously "some person, other than by virtue of a title prior to that of the purchaser".
5 Substituted by FA 2002 s 129(6)(b) with effect from 1 September 2002 in respect of an amount due to be paid or remitted, whether before, on, or after that date; previously "1 per cent per month or part of a month".
6 Section 92A inserted by F(No2)A 2000 s 4 with effect for instruments executed on or after 15 June 2000. However, where an instrument executed on or before 31 January 2001 would increase the duty chargeable on the instrument and the instrument contains a statement certifying that the instrument was executed solely in pursuance of a contract which was evidenced in writing before 15 June 2000 the section does not apply.
7 Subs (7)-(8) inserted by FA 2002 s 113(1)(a) with effect on and from 6 December 2001.

Revenue information

Leaflets SD9A: Stamp duty - conveyances and leases of residential property (August 2000); SD10: Stamp duty - Revenue certificates required in deeds.

92B Residential property first time purchase relief

[(1) In this section **"first time purchaser"** means—

   (a) a person, or
   (b) as respects instruments executed on or after 27 June 2000, a person, being an individual,

who, at the time, of the execution of the instrument to which this section applies, has not, either individually or jointly with any other person or persons, previously purchased (other than the purchase of a leasehold interest by way of grant or assignment for any term not exceeding one year), previously built—

(i) directly or indirectly on his or her own behalf, or

(ii) as respects instruments executed on or after 27 June 2000, in a fiduciary capacity,

another dwellinghouse or apartment or a part of another dwellinghouse or apartment and for the purposes of this definition—

(I) any dwellinghouse or apartment taken under a conveyance or transfer operating as a voluntary disposition within the meaning of section 30 of the Principal Act shall be deemed to have been taken by way of purchase where that conveyance or transfer was executed on or after 22 June 2000, and

(II) any part of a dwellinghouse or apartment taken under a conveyance or transfer operating as a voluntary disposition within the meaning of section 20 of the Principal Act shall be deemed to have been taken by way of purchase where that conveyance or transfer was executed on or after 27 June 2000.

[(2) The amount of stamp duty chargeable under or by reference to paragraphs (2) to (5) of the Heading "CONVEYANCE or TRANSFER on sale of any property other than stocks or marketable securities or a policy of insurance or a policy of life insurance" or clauses (ii) to (v) of paragraph (3)(*a*) of the Heading "LEASE", as the case may be, in Schedule 1 on any instrument to which this section applies shall be reduced, where paragraph (2) or clause (ii) applies, to nil, and where—

(*a*) paragraph (3) or clause (iii) applies, to an amount equal to three-fourths,

(*b*) paragraph (4) or clause (iv) applies, to an amount equal to three and three quarter-fifths,

(*c*) paragraph (5) or clause (v) applies, to an amount equal to four and one half-sixths,

of the amount which would otherwise have been chargeable but where the amount so obtained is a fraction of €1 that amount shall be rounded down to the nearest €.][1]

(3) This section shall apply to—

(*a*) any instrument to which section 92 applies and which contains a statement, in such form as the Commissioners may specify, certifying that the purchaser, or where there is more than one purchaser, each and every one of the purchasers, is a first time purchaser, or

(*b*) any instrument, other than one to which section 92 applies, which contains a statement, in such form as the Commissioners may specify, certifying that the purchaser, or where there is more than one purchaser, each and every one of the purchasers, is a first time purchaser, and that—

(i) the instrument gives effect to the purchase of a dwellinghouse or apartment, and

(ii) until the expiration of the period of 5 years commencing on the date of the execution of the instrument or the subsequent sale (other than a sale the contract for which, if it were a written conveyance, would not, apart from section 82, be charged with full ad valorem duty or a sale to a company under the control of the vendor or of any person entitled to a beneficial interest in the dwellinghouse or apartment immediately prior to the sale or to a company which would, in relation to a notional gift of shares in that company taken, immediately prior to the sale, by any person so entitled, be under the control of the donee or successor within the meaning of section 16 of the Capital Acquisitions Tax Act, 1976, irrespective of the shares the subject matter of the notional gift) of the dwellinghouse or apartment concerned, whichever event first occurs, that dwellinghouse or apartment will be occupied as the only or principal place of residence of the purchaser, or if there be more than one purchaser, of any one or more of the purchasers or of some other person in right of the purchaser or, if there be more than one purchaser, of some other person in right of any one or more of the purchasers and that [no person—

    (I)   other than a person who, while in such occupation, derives rent or payment in the nature of rent in consideration for the provision, on or after 6 April 2001, of furnished residential accommodation in part of the dwellinghouse or apartment concerned, or

    (II) other than by virtue of a title prior to that of the purchaser,

will derive any rent or payment in the nature of rent for the use of that dwellinghouse or apartment, or of any part of it, during that period.]²

(4) Where subsection (2) applies to an instrument and at any time during the period referred to in section 92(1)(*b*)(ii) or in subsection (3)(*b*)(ii) of this section, [some person, other than a person referred to in clause (I) or (II) of subsection (3)(*b*)(ii)],³ derives any rent or payment in the nature of rent for the use of the dwellinghouse or apartment concerned, or of any part of it, the purchaser, or where there be more than one purchaser, each such purchaser, shall—

    (*a*) jointly and severally become liable to pay to the Commissioners a penalty equal to the difference between the amount of the duty which would have been charged in the first instance if the dwellinghouse or apartment had been conveyed or transferred or leased by an instrument to which subsection (2) had not applied and the amount of duty which was actually charged together with interest on that amount charged at a rate of [0.0322 per cent for each day or part of a day]⁴ from the date when the rent or payment is first received to the date the penalty is remitted, and

    (*b*) the person who receives the rent or payment shall, within 6 months after the date of the payment, notify the payment to the Commissioners on a form provided, or approved of, by them for the purposes of this section, unless that person is already aware that the Commissioners have already received such a notification from another source.

(5) Where the instrument is one to which this section and section 92 applies—

    (*a*) the reference in subsection (4) to the amount of duty which would have been charged in the first instance shall be construed as a reference to the duty which would have been charged had the relief under section 92 continued to apply, and (*b*)   the reference to the amount of duty which was actually charged in subsection (2)(*a*) of section 92 shall be construed as a reference to the duty which would have been charged had the relief under this section been denied,

and the penalty referred to in subsection (4) shall be in addition to any penalty payable under section 92.

(6) Notwithstanding subsection (3), subsection (2) shall not apply to an instrument which gives effect to a sale or lease of more than one unit of residential property or where the sale or lease concerned forms part of a larger transaction or of a series of transactions comprising more than one unit of residential property.

(7) Notwithstanding subsection (1), a trustee of a trust to which section 189A of the Taxes Consolidation Act, 1997, applies shall be deemed to be a first time purchaser for the purposes of the definition in subsection (1), in respect of a conveyance or transfer including a conveyance or transfer operating as a voluntary disposition within the meaning of section 30 of the Principal Act, to that trustee of that trust, of a dwellinghouse or apartment or a part of a dwellinghouse or apartment, subject to—

(*a*)   where there is only one beneficiary of that trust, this subsection applying to one such conveyance or transfer only, being the first such conveyance or transfer executed on or after the date of the establishment of that trust, and

(*b*)   where there is more than one beneficiary of that trust, this subsection applying to as many conveyances or transfers, executed on or after the date of the establishment of that trust, as there are beneficiaries of that trust for whose benefit any such conveyance or transfer is made.

(8) (*a*)   Notwithstanding subsection (1), a spouse, to a marriage the subject of a decree of judicial [separation, a decree of divorce, a decree of nullity or a deed of separation],[5] shall be deemed to be a first time purchaser for the purposes of the definition in subsection (1), in respect of a conveyance or transfer including a conveyance or transfer operating as a voluntary disposition within the meaning of section 30 of the Principal Act, to that spouse after the granting of [that decree or the execution of that deed of separation by both spouses to that marriage],[6] of a dwellinghouse or apartment or a part of a dwellinghouse or apartment but only in respect of the first such conveyance or transfer, provided at the date of execution of the instrument giving effect to such conveyance or transfer—

(i)   that spouse is not beneficially entitled to an interest in the dwellinghouse or apartment or that part of the dwellinghouse or apartment referred to in [subparagraph (ii)],[7] and

(ii)   that the other spouse to that marriage continues to occupy, since the date of [the decree or the date of the execution of the deed of separation by both spouses to that marriage],[8] as his or her only or main residence, the dwellinghouse or apartment most recently acquired prior to the date of the decree or that part of the dwellinghouse or apartment most recently acquired prior to the date of [the decree or the date of the execution of the deed of separation by both spouses to that marriage][8] which was the only or main residence of both spouses at some time prior to the date of the decree.

(*b*) In this subsection—

"decree of divorce" means a divorce under section 5 of the Family Law (Divorce) Act, 1996, or any decree to like effect that was granted under the law of a country or jurisdiction other than the State and is recognised in the State;

"decree of judicial separation" means a decree under section 3 of the Judicial Separation and Family Law Reform Act, 1989, or any decree to like effect that was granted under the law of a country or jurisdiction other than the State and is recognised in the ["the State;][9]

["**decree of nullity"** means a decree granted by the High Court declaring a marriage to be null and void or any decree to like effect that was granted under the law of a country or judisdiction other than the State and is recognised in the State.][10][11]

Amendments

[1]   Subs (2) substituted by FA 2002 s 113(1)(*b*) in relation to instruments executed on or after 6 December 2001 subject to substituting, in subsection (2) of section 92B (inserted by subsection (1)), "£1" for "€1" and "up to the nearest £" for "down to the nearest €" for instruments executed on or after 6 December 2001 and before 1 January 2002.

[2]   Substituted by FA 2001 s 208(1)(*d*)(i) in effect in relation to instruments executed on or after 6 December 2000; previously "no person, other than by virtue of a title prior to that of the purchaser, will derive any rent or payment in the nature of rent for the use of that dwellinghouse or apartment, or any part of it, during that period.".

[3]   Substituted by FA 2002 s 129(6)(*b*) with effect from 1 September 2002 in respect of an amount due to be paid or remitted, whether before, on, or after that date; previously "1 per cent per month or part of a month".

[4]   Substituted by FA 2001 s 208(1)(*d*)(ii) in effect in relation to instruments executed on or after 6 December 2000; previously "some person, other than by virtue of a title prior to that of the purchaser".

[5]   Substituted by FA 2001 s 208(1)(*d*)(iii)(I) in effect in relation to instruments executed on or after 15 June 2000; previously "separation or a decree of divorce".

[6]   Substituted by FA 2001 s 208(1)(*d*)(iii)(II) in effect in relation to instruments executed on or after 15 June 2000; previously "that decree".

[7]   Substituted by FA 2001 s 208(1)(*d*)(iv) in effect in relation to instruments executed on or after 15 February 2000; previously "paragraph (*b*)".

[8]   Substituted by FA 2001 s 208(1)(*d*)(v) in effect in relation to instruments executed on or after 15 June 2000; previously "the decree".

[9]   Substituted by FA 2001 s 208(1)(*d*)(vi) in effect in relation to instruments executed on or after 15 June 2000; previously "the State.".

[10] Definition of "decree of nullity" inserted by FA 2001 s 208(1)(*d*)(vi) in effect in relation to instruments executed on or after 15 June 2000.

[11] Section 92B inserted by F(No2)A 2000 s 4 with effect for instruments executed on or after 15 June 2000. However, where an instrument executed on or before 31 January 2001 would increase the duty chargeable on the instrument and the instrument contains a statement certifying that the instrument was executed solely in pursuance of a contract which was evidenced in writing before 15 June 2000 the section does not apply.

92C Residential property investor relief

Amendments

[1]   Deleted by FA 2002 s 113(1)(*c*) in relation to instruments executed on or after 6 December 2001.

Revenue information

Leaflet SD10: Stamp duty - Revenue certificates required in deeds (May 2001).

---

93 Houses acquired from industrial and provident societies

Stamp duty shall not be chargeable on a conveyance, transfer or lease of a house by a society registered under the Industrial and Provident Societies Acts, 1893 to 1978, and made, in accordance with a scheme for the provision of houses for its members, to a member or to such member and the spouse of the member.

Former enactment

FA 1969 s 49(3).

93A Approved voluntary body

[(1) Stamp duty shall not be chargeable on any conveyance, transfer or lease of land to a voluntary body, approved by the Minister for the Environment and Local Government under section 6 of the Housing (Miscellaneous Provisions) Act, 1992, for the purposes of the Housing Acts, 1966 to 1998.]

Amendments

1   Section 93A inserted by FA 2001 s 210 with effect in relation to instruments executed on or after 15 February 2001.

94 Purchase of land from Land Commission

(1) In this section **"qualified person"** has the same meaning as in section 5 of the Land Act, 1965, and **"advance"** means an advance under that section.

(2) Stamp duty shall not be chargeable on an instrument giving effect to the purchase of land by a qualified person, being an instrument either—

    (*a*) which contains a charge on the land in favour of the Irish Land Commission for repayment of an advance, or

    (*b*) on which there is endorsed an order made by the Irish Land Commission charging the land with an advance.

Definitions

"instrument": s 1, IA 1937 s 3; "person": IA 1937 s 11(*c*).

Former enactment

FA 1967 s 20.

95 Commercial woodlands

(1) In this section **"trees"** means woodlands managed on a commercial basis and with a view to the realisation of profits.

(2) This section applies to an instrument, being a conveyance or transfer on sale of land, or a lease of land, where the instrument contains a certificate to the effect that trees are growing on a substantial part of such land.

(3) Stamp duty shall not be chargeable on any instrument to which this section applies, in respect of such part of the consideration for the sale or lease as represents the value of trees growing on the land.

Definitions

"conveyance": s 1; "instrument": s 1, IA 1937 s 3; "stamp": s 1.

Former enactment

FA 1990 s 120.

96 Transfers between spouses

(1) Subject to subsection (2), stamp duty shall not be chargeable on any instrument, other than a conveyance or transfer referred to in subsection (1), (2), (3) or (4) of section 46 or subsection (1)(*b*) of section 73 whereby any property is transferred by a spouse or spouses of a marriage to either spouse or to both spouses of that marriage.

(2) Subsection (1) shall not apply to an instrument whereby any property or any part of, or beneficial interest in, any property is transferred to a person other than a spouse referred to in that subsection.

(3) Section 30(3) shall not apply to an instrument to which subsection (1) applies.

Notes

FA 1992 s 212 in effect affirmed that this provision applies only where no person other than the spouses is a part to the instruments.

Definitions

"instrument": s 1, IA 1937 s 3; "stamp": s 1.

Former enactment

FA 1990 s 114; FA 1999 s 141(1).

97 Certain transfers following the dissolution of a marriage

(1) Subject to subsection (2), stamp duty shall not be chargeable on an instrument by which property is transferred pursuant to an order to which this subsection applies by either or both of the spouses who were parties to the marriage concerned to either or both of them.

(2) (*a*) Subsection (1) applies—

  (i) to a relief order, within the meaning of section 23 of the Family Law Act, 1995, made following the dissolution of a marriage, ...[1]

  (ii) to an order under Part III of the Family Law (Divorce) Act, [1996, or][2]

  [(iii) to an order or other determination to like effect, which is analogous to an order referred to in subparagraph (i) or (ii), of a court under the law of another territory made under or in consequence of the dissolution of a marriage, being a dissolution that is entitled to be recognised as valid in the State.][3]

  (*b*) Subsection (1) does not apply in relation to an instrument referred to in that subsection by which any part of or beneficial interest in the property concerned is transferred to a person other than the spouses concerned.

(3) Section 30(3) shall not apply to a transfer to which subsection (1) applies.

Amendments

1 Deleted by FA 2000 s 131(1)(*a*) as respects an order or other determination to like effect where the order or the determination is made on or after 10 February 2000; previously "or".

2 Substituted by FA 2000 s 131(1)(*b*) as respects an order or other determination to like effect where the order or the determination is made on or after 10 February 2000; previously "1996".

3 Subs (2)(*a*)(iii) inserted by FA 2000 s 131(1)(*c*) as respects an order or other determination to like effect where the order or the determination is made on or after 10 February 2000.

Notes

Stamp duty does not apply to a property transfer, ordered by a court, between separated or divorced marriage partners.

Former enactment

FA 1997 s 127(1)-(3).

98 Foreign immovable property

(1) Stamp duty shall not be chargeable on any instrument which is a conveyance, transfer, assignment, lease or licence of any immovable property situated outside the State.

(2) Subsection (1) shall not apply if the instrument relates to—

    (*a*)   any immovable property situated in the State, or any right over or interest in such property, or

    (*b*)   any stocks or marketable securities of a company having a register in the State.

Cross-references

Stamp Duty (Variation) Order 1991 para 4(*h*) (SI 277/1991) effective from 1 November 1991.

Definitions

"instrument": s 1, IA 1937 s 3; "marketable security"; "stamp"; "stock": s 1.

Former enactment

FA 1992 s 209.

99 Dublin Docklands Development Authority

[(1) In this section "wholly-owned subsidiary" has the meaning assigned to it by section 9 of the Taxes Consolidation Act, 1997 (as amended by the Finance Act, 2001).

(2) Stamp Duty shall not be chargeable on any instrument under which any land, easement, way-leave, water right or any right over or in respect of the land or water is acquired by the Dublin Docklands Development Authority or any of its wholly-owned subsidiaries.]

Amendments

1 Section 99 substituted by FA 2001 s 205.

Notes

Stamp duty does not apply to purchases of land made by the Dublin Docklands Development Authority.

Former enactment

FA 1997 s 128(1).

100 Temple Bar Properties Limited

(1) Stamp duty shall not be chargeable on any instrument under which any land, or any interest in land, easement, way-leave, water right or any other right is acquired in the Temple Bar area, that is, "the area" as described in the First Schedule in the Temple Bar Area Renewal and Development Act, 1991, by Temple Bar Properties Limited, or any subsidiary of Temple Bar Properties Limited.

(2) For the purposes of subsection (1), a company shall be deemed to be a subsidiary of Temple Bar Properties Limited if—

    (*a*)   Temple Bar Properties Limited—

        (i)   is a member of the company and controls the composition of at least half of the company's board of directors,

        (ii)   holds at least half in nominal value of the company's equity share capital, or

        (iii)   holds at least half in nominal value of the company's shares carrying voting rights (other than voting rights which arise only in specified circumstances),

    or

(*b*) the company is a subsidiary of any company which is a subsidiary of Temple Bar Properties Limited.

Definitions

Former enactment

FA 1992 s 216(1)-(3).
"instrument": s 1; IA 1937 s 3; "stamp": s 1.

101 Community and international trade marks

(1) In this section **"Community trade mark"** and **"international trade mark"** have the same meanings, respectively, as in section 56 and section 58 of the Trade Marks Act, 1996.

(2) Stamp duty shall not be chargeable on an instrument relating to a Community trade mark or an international trade mark, or an application for any such mark, by reason only of the fact that such a mark has legal effect in the State.

Definitions

"instrument"; "stamp": s 1.

Former enactment

FA 1996 s 118.

102 The Alfred Beit Foundation

Stamp duty shall not be chargeable or payable on any conveyance, transfer or letting made by Alfred Lane Beit and Clementine Mabel Beit, or either of them, to The Alfred Beit Foundation, which was incorporated under the Companies Act, 1963, on 23 March 1976.

Former enactment

FA 1977 s 48.

103 Shared ownership leases

(1) In this section—

"appropriate person" means any one of the following, namely—

(a) a person who holds a licence granted by the Central Bank of Ireland under section 9 of the Central Bank Act, 1971, or under section 10 of the Trustee Savings Banks Act, 1989,

(b) where there are subsisting regulations under section 4 of the ACC Bank Act, 1992, for the supervision by the Central Bank of Ireland of the ACC Bank public limited company, that bank,

(c) where there are subsisting regulations under section 3 of the ICC Bank Act, 1992, for the supervision by the Central Bank of Ireland of the ICC Bank public limited company, that bank,

(d) a building society which has been incorporated under the Building Societies Act, 1989, or which is deemed by virtue of section 124(2) of that Act to be so incorporated,

(e) the holder of an authorisation for the purposes of the European Communities (Non-Life Insurance) Regulations, 1976 (SI No 115 of 1976), as amended by the European Communities (Non-Life Insurance) (Amendment) Regulations, 1991 (SI No 142 of 1991),

(f) the holder of an authorisation granted under the European Communities (Life Assurance) Regulations, 1984 (SI No 57 of 1984),

(g) a body approved of by the Minister for the Environment and Local Government for the purposes of section 6 of the Housing (Miscellaneous Provisions) Act, 1992,

(h) the National Building Agency Limited,

(i) a company within the meaning of section 2 of the Companies Act, 1963, which the Minister for the Environment and Local Government has certified to the satisfaction of the Commissioners to be a company incorporated with the principal object of providing assistance on a non-profit making basis with a view to enabling persons to acquire housing for themselves,

(j) a society registered under the Industrial and Provident Societies Acts, 1893 to 1978, in respect of which the Minister for the Environment and Local Government has certified to the satisfaction of the Commissioners to be a society established with the principal object of providing assistance on a non-profit making basis with a view to enabling persons to acquire housing for themselves;

"shared ownership lease" has the same meaning as in section 2 of the Housing (Miscellaneous Provisions) Act, 1992.

(2) Subject to subsection (3), stamp duty shall not be chargeable—

(a) a shared ownership lease, or

(b) an instrument whereby the lessee of a shared ownership lease exercises the right referred to in section 2(1)(c) of the Housing (Miscellaneous Provisions) Act, 1992,

other than such a lease or instrument where such lease was granted on the erection of a house which at that time exceeded the maximum floor area then standing specified in regulations made under section 4(2)(*b*) of the Housing (Miscellaneous Provisions) Act, 1979.

(3) Subsection (2) shall apply where the shared ownership lease concerned has been granted by an appropriate person.

Cross-references

Other exemptions and reliefs relating to housing: ss 91, 93 (exemption for new houses up to 125m₂ in floor area); ss 29, 53 (relief for larger new houses)

Former enactment

FA 1993 s 101(1), (2)(*b*) and (3); FA 1997 s 197 and Sch 6.

104 Licences and leases granted under Petroleum and Other Minerals Development Act, 1960, etc

Stamp duty shall not be chargeable on—

    (*a*)   a licence granted under section 8, 9 or 19 of the Petroleum and Other Minerals Development Act, 1960,

    (*b*)   a lease granted under section 13 of that Act, or

    (*c*)   an instrument for the sale, assignment or transfer of any such licence or lease or any right or interest in any such licence or lease.

Definitions

"instrument": s 1; IA 1937 s 3; "stamp": s 1.

Former enactment

FA 1991 s 93.

105 Securitisation agreements

(1) In this section **"designated body"** and **"housing authority"** have the same meanings, respectively, as in section 1(1) of the Securitisation (Proceeds of Certain Mortgages) Act, 1995.

(2) Stamp duty shall not be chargeable on—

    (*a*)   the transfer, sale, or assignment of mortgages by a housing authority to a designated body, or

    (*b*)   the transfer of securities issued by a designated body.

Definitions

"stamp": s 1.

Former enactment

FA 1996 s 117(1)-(2).

106 Housing Finance Agency

Stamp duty shall not be chargeable on any agreement or other instrument made for the purposes of, or in connection with, securing the advancement of moneys to housing authorities (within the meaning of the Housing Act, 1966) by the Housing Finance Agency plc.

Definitions

"executed": s 1; "instrument": s 1,s IA 1937 s 3; "money"; "stamp": s 1.

Former enactment

FA 1989 s 66(1)-(2).

106A Certain policies of insurance

[(1) Stamp duty shall not be chargeable on any conveyance, transfer or lease of land to the National Building Agency Limited for the purposes of the Housing Acts, 1966 to 1998.]

Amendments

1   Section 106A inserted by FA 2001 s 211 with effect in relation to instruments executed on or after 26 January 2001.

107 Certain mortgages of stock

(1) Every instrument under hand only (not being a promissory note or bill of exchange) given on the occasion of the deposit of any share warrant or stock certificate to bearer, or foreign share certificate, or any security for money transferable by delivery, by means of security for any loan, shall not be chargeable with duty.

(2) Every instrument under hand only (not being a promissory note or bill of exchange) making redeemable or qualifying a duly stamped transfer or a transfer which is not chargeable to duty, intended as a security, of any registered stock or marketable security, shall not be chargeable with duty.

Definitions

"bill of exchange"; "instrument"; "money"; "promissory note"; "stamped"; "stock": s 122(1).

Former enactment

SA 1891 s 23(1)-(2); FA 1970 s 46(1)(*b*), FA 1998 s 125 and Sch 8; FA 1999 s 177.

108 National Treasury Management Agency, etc

Stamp duty shall not be chargeable on any instrument executed by or on behalf of—

(*a*)   the National Treasury Management Agency, or

(*b*)   the Minister in relation to a function exercised by the Minister which is capable of being delegated to that Agency under section 5 of the National Treasury Management Agency Act, 1990,

or on any disposition of such an instrument or of any right or interest created by such an instrument.

Cross-references

Stamp Duty (Variation) Order 1991 para 4(*p*) (SI 277/1991) effective from 1 November 1991.

Definitions

"disposition": CATA 1976 s 2(1); "executed": s 1; "instrument": s 1, IA 1937 s 3; "stamp": s 1.

Former enactment

FA 1992 s 210.

109 Certain instruments made in anticipation of a formal insurance policy

Stamp duty shall not be chargeable on—

(a) cover notes, slips and other instruments usually made in anticipation of the issue of a formal policy, not being instruments relating to life insurance,

(b) instruments embodying alterations of the terms or conditions of any policy of insurance other than life insurance,

and an instrument exempted by virtue of paragraph (a) shall not be taken for the purposes of this Act to be a policy of insurance.

Former enactment

FA 1982 s 94(4)(b)(i).

110 Certain health insurance contracts

Stamp duty shall not be chargeable on a health insurance contract (being a health insurance contract within the meaning of section 2 of the Health Insurance Act, 1994).

Notes

Health insurance policies are exempt from the fixed stamp duty of £1.

Former enactment

FA 1997 s 129(1).

110A Certain policies of insurance

[(1) This section shall apply to a policy of insurance, being insurance of a class specified in Part A of Annex I to the European Communities (Life Assurance) Framework Regulations, 1994 (SI No 360 of 1994), which—

(a) provides for periodic payments to an individual in the event of loss or diminution of income in consequence of ill health, or

(b) provides for the payment of an amount or amounts to an individual in consequence of ill health, disability, accident or hospitalisation.

(2) Stamp duty shall not be chargeable under or by reference to the Heading "POLICY OF INSURANCE other than Life Insurance where the risk to which the policy relates is located in the State." in Schedule 1 on any policy of insurance to which this section applies.]

Amendments

[1] Section 110A inserted by FA 2001 s 212 with effect in relation to instruments executed on or after 1 January 2001.

111 Oireachtas funds

Stamp duty shall not be chargeable on any instrument where the amount of such duty chargeable on the instrument, but for this section, would be payable solely out of moneys provided by the Oireachtas.

Definitions

"executed": s 1; "instrument": s 1, IA 1937 s 3; "stamp", "stamped": s 1.

Former enactment

FA 1958 s 59.

---

112 Certificates of indebtedness, etc

(1) In this section **"certificate of indebtedness"** means a document, whether sealed with the official seal of the Minister or signed by the Minister or by one of his or her officers authorised in that behalf by the Minister, whereby the Minister or any such officer so authorised certifies (either expressly or impliedly) the amount of the indebtedness of the State or of a public fund of the State in respect of moneys or securities or both moneys and securities borrowed from a particular person by the Minister in exercise of a power conferred on him or her by statute.

(2) Neither a certificate of indebtedness nor any agreement, receipt, bill of exchange, promissory note, mortgage, bond, covenant, or other instrument embodied or contained in a certificate of indebtedness and relating to the transaction to which such certificate relates shall be liable to any stamp duty.

Definitions

"bill of exchange", "instrument","mortgage": s 1; "person": IA 1937 s 11(*c*); "promissory note", "stamp": s 1; "statute": IA 1937 s 3.

Former enactment

FA 1943 s 15; FA 1997 s 197 and Sch 6.

---

113 Miscellaneous instruments

Stamp duty shall not be chargeable on any of the following instruments:

- (*a*) instruments transferring shares in—
    - (i) stocks or funds of the Government or Oireachtas,
    - (ii) any stock or other form of security to which section 39 of the Taxes Consolidation Act, 1997, applies,
    - (iii) any stock or other form of security to which section 40 of the Taxes Consolidation Act, 1997, applies,
    - (iv) stocks or funds of the Government or Parliament of the late United Kingdom of Great Britain and Ireland which are registered in the books of the Bank of Ireland in Dublin;
- (*b*) instruments for the sale, transfer, or other disposition, either absolutely or by means of mortgage, or otherwise, of any ship or vessel or aircraft, or any part, interest, share, or property of or in any ship or vessel or aircraft;
- (*c*) testaments and testamentary instruments;
- (*d*) bonds given to sheriffs or other persons on the replevy of any goods or chattels, and assignments of such bonds;
- (*e*) instruments made by, to, or with the Commissioners of Public Works in Ireland.

Former enactment

SA 1891 Sch 1.

PART 8
COMPANIES CAPITAL DUTY

114 Interpretation (Part 8)

(1) In this Part, except where the context otherwise requires—

"capital company" means one of the following, namely—

(a) a company incorporated with limited liability, or a limited partnership formed under the law of the State or a company or partnership which is incorporated or formed in any other Member State and which, under the law of that State, corresponds to any such company or partnership,

(b) any other company, firm, association or legal person the shares in whose capital or assets can be dealt in on a stock exchange,

(c) any other company, firm, association or legal person operating for profit whose members have the right to dispose of their shares to third parties without prior authorisation and are responsible for the debts of the company, firm, association or legal person only to the extent of their shares;

"Member State" means a Member State of the European Community;

"registrar" means the registrar of companies within the meaning of the Companies Act, 1963;

"stamp duty" means the stamp duty imposed by section 116;

"statement" means the statement required to be delivered under section 117(1);

"third country" means a State which is not a Member State;

"transaction" means a transaction to which section 116(1) applies.

(2) In this Part, except where the context otherwise requires, reference to stamp duty paid means stamp duty paid to the Commissioners.

Note

"operative date": this section became operative on 4 August 1973.
Private unlimited companies and partnerships which are not limited partnerships within the Limited Partnership Act 1907 are not capital companies.

Cross-references

EC Directives relating to companies capital duty: see end of Stamp Duty Part of this book.

Case law

National courts are required to interpret national law which was introduced in order to implement a Directive in the light of the wording and the purpose of the Directive in order to achieve the result referred to in the third paragraph of Article 189 of the EEC Treaty: *Johnston v Chief Constable of the RUC* [1986] ECR at 1690, *Von Colson and Kamann v Land Nordrahein - Westfalen* [1984] ECR 1891.
An unincorporated body of persons comes within Article 3(2) of the Directive (corresponding to paragraph 3 above) but it is for the national legislature to determine whether or not it is to be regarded as a capital company for the purposes of charging capital duty: *Amro AAndelen Fonds v Inspecteur der Registratie en Successie* [1987] ECR 4453.

Definitions

"Stamp": s 1.

Former enactment

FA 1973 s 67.

---

115 Restriction of application (Part 8)

This Part shall not apply to—

(*a*) any undertaking for collective investment in transferable securities (UCITS) to which Council Directive 85/611/EEC of 20 December, 1985 (OJ No L375, 31/12/85), and any Directive amending that Council Directive, relates,

(*b*) any investment company to which Part XIII of the Companies Act, 1990, relates, or

(*c*) any investment limited partnership within the meaning of section 3 of the Investment Limited Partnerships Act, 1994.

Former enactment

FA 1973 ss 67A, 67B, 67C; FA 1990 s 115; FA 1991 s 110; FA 1995 s 145.

116 Charge of stamp duty

(1) This section applies to the following transactions:

(*a*) the formation of a capital company;

(*b*) the conversion into a capital company of a company, firm, association or legal person which is not a capital company;

(*c*) an increase in the capital of a capital company by the contribution of assets of any kind other than an increase in capital through capitalisation of profits or of reserves, whether temporary or permanent reserves, but including the conversion of loan stock of a capital company into share capital;

(*d*) an increase in the assets of a capital company by the contribution of assets of any kind in consideration, not of shares in the capital or assets of the company, but of rights of the same kind as those of members of the company such as voting rights, a share in the profits or a share in the surplus on liquidation;

(*e*) the transfer from a third country to the State of the effective centre of management of a capital company whose registered office is in a third country;

(*f*) the transfer from a third country to the State of the registered office of a capital company whose effective centre of management is in a third country:

(*g*) the transfer from a Member State to the State of the effective centre of management of a capital company which is not considered to be a capital company in the other Member State;

(*h*) the transfer from a Member State to the State of the registered office of a capital company whose effective centre of management is in a third country and which is not considered to be a capital company in the Member State from which the registered office is being transferred.

(2) Stamp duty shall be charged on the statement required to be delivered under this Part where, at the date of a transaction, or as a result of the transaction—

(*a*) the effective centre of management of the capital company is in the State, or

(*b*) if the effective centre of management of the capital company is in a third country, the registered office of the capital company is in the State,

and the provisions of this Act shall, subject to the provisions of this Part, apply in relation to this duty as if it were imposed by section 2.

Cross-references

Issue of shares by a company in place of shares redeemed: Companies Act 1963 s 64 as amended by FA 1990 s 119.

Narrative

Irish Stamp Duty Law, Chapter 7.

Definitions

"person": IA 1937 s 11(*c*).

Former enactment

FA 1973 s 68.

117 Statement to be charged with stamp duty

(1) Where any transaction takes place, a statement of the assets, liabilities and expenses referred to in section 118 shall be delivered to the registrar—

(*a*) in the case of the formation of a capital company which is to be incorporated under the Companies Act, 1963, or formed under the Limited Partnerships Act, 1907, before the incorporation or registration of that capital company or partnership, and

(*b*) in any other case, within 30 days after the date of the transaction,

and the statement shall be charged with stamp duty at the rate of 1 per cent of the amount determined in accordance with section 118 but where the calculation results in an amount which is not a multiple of [€1][1] the amount so calculated shall be rounded [down to the nearest €][2].

(2) Notwithstanding subsection (1), in the case referred to in paragraph (*a*) of subsection (1)—

(*a*) the statement shall be charged with stamp duty of not less than [€1][3];

(*b*) if there is difficulty in ascertaining the exact amount in respect of which stamp duty is chargeable, the statement shall be charged in the first instance with stamp duty at the rate specified in subsection (1) in respect of such amount as the Commissioners consider appropriate and, if afterwards—

(i) it is established that too little duty has been paid, the additional duty shall be payable and be treated as duty in arrear, and

(ii) it is established that too much duty has been paid, the excess shall be repaid by the Commissioners with interest at the rate of [0.0161 per cent per day or part of a day][5].

(3) Simple interest shall be payable by means of penalty on so much of the stamp duty charged on the statement required to be delivered under subsection (1)(*b*) as remains unpaid after the expiration of one month from the date of the transaction which gave rise to the charge for duty, and such interest shall be payable at the rate of 1 per cent for each month or part of a month for which duty so remains unpaid and it shall be chargeable and recoverable in the same manner as if it were part of the duty.

(4) Interest on the additional duty payable under subsection (2)(*b*)(i) shall be charged at the rate of [0.0322 per cent for each day or part of a day][6] from the date of the transaction which gave rise to the charge for duty until the date of payment of the duty.

(5) The registrar shall not incorporate a capital company which is to be incorporated under the Companies Act, 1963, or register a capital company which is to be formed under the Limited Partnerships Act, 1907, until the statement referred to in subsection (1) in relation to the company is duly stamped or in the case of a capital company specified in section 120 the statement has, in accordance with the provisions of section 20, been stamped with a particular stamp denoting that it is not chargeable with stamp duty.

Amendments

1   Substituted by FA 2001 s 240 and Sch 5 Pt 6 with effect from 1 January 2002; previously "£1".
2   Substituted by FA 2001 s 240 and Sch 5 Pt 6 with effect from 1 January 2002; previously "up to the nearest £".
3   Substituted by FA 2001 s 240 and Sch 5 Pt 6 with effect from 1 January 2002; previously "£1".
4   Substituted by FA 2002 s 129(6)(*a*) with effect from 1 September 2002 in respect of an amount due to be paid or remitted, whether before, on, or after that date; previously "1 per cent for each month or part of a month".
5   Substituted by FA 2002 s 129(6)(*d*) with effect from 1 September 2002 in respect of an amount due to be paid or remitted, whether before, on, or after that date; previously "6 per cent per annum".
6   Substituted by FA 2002 s 129(6)(*b*) with effect from 1 September 2002 in respect of an amount due to be paid or remitted, whether before, on, or after that date; previously "1 per cent per month or part of a month".

Former enactment
FA 1973 s 69; FA 1979 s 53; FA 1998 s 124(1)-(2); FA 1999 ss 194(*a*)-(*c*), 197 and Sch 6.

---

118 Amount on which stamp duty chargeable

(1) Stamp duty shall be charged—

    (*a*) in the case of a transaction specified in paragraph (*a*), (*c*) or (*d*) of section 116(1), in respect of the amount of the actual value, at the date of the transaction, of the assets of any kind contributed or to be contributed in connection with the transaction by the members of the capital company concerned after the deduction of the liabilities attaching to such assets and assumed by the capital company and of the expenses incurred by the capital company in connection with such contribution;

    (*b*) in the case of a transaction specified in paragraph (*b*), (*e*), (*f*), (*g*) or (*h*) of section 116(1), in respect of the amount of the actual value, at the date of the transaction, of the assets of any kind of the capital company concerned after the deduction of its liabilities on that date and of the expenses incurred by the company in connection with the transaction.

(2) Notwithstanding subsection (1)—

    (*a*) the amount in respect of which stamp duty is charged shall not be less than the nominal value of the shares (if any) in the company concerned allotted to the members of the capital company in connection with the transaction or belonging to the members of the capital company immediately after the transaction;

    (*b*) in arriving at the amount of the actual value in respect of which the duty is charged, there shall be excluded the amount of any assets referred to in subsection (1) contributed in connection with the transaction by a member with unlimited liability or the share of such a member in the assets of the company.

119 Reconstructions or amalgamations of capital companies

(1) If, in the case of a transaction, a capital company or a capital company which is in the process of being formed (in this section referred to as the "acquiring company") acquires either—

   (*a*) the undertaking or part of the undertaking of another capital company (in this section referred to as the "target company"), or

   (*b*) share capital of another capital company to an extent that, after that transaction, but not necessarily as a result of that transaction, the acquiring company owns at least 75 per cent of the issued share capital of that other company (in this section referred to as the "target company"),

then, subject to this section, stamp duty on the statement delivered in accordance with section 117(1) shall be charged at the rate of zero per cent (in this section referred to as the "reduced rate").

(2) Notwithstanding subsection (1), where the percentage referred to in paragraph (*b*) of subsection (1) is reached by means of 2 or more transactions, the reduced rate shall apply only to the transaction whereby this percentage is achieved and to any transaction subsequent to the achievement and retention of that percentage.

(3) Subsection (1) of this section shall apply only where the consideration for the acquisition (except such part of the consideration as consists of the transfer to or discharge by the acquiring company of liabilities of the target company) consists—

   (*a*) where the undertaking or part of the undertaking of the target company is acquired, of the issue of shares in the acquiring company to the target company or to holders of shares in the target company, or

   (*b*) where shares of the target company are acquired, of the issue of shares in the acquiring company to the holders of shares in the target company in exchange for shares held by them in the target company,

with or without a payment in cash, but where there is a payment in cash that payment shall not exceed 10 per cent of the nominal value of the shares in the acquiring company which are comprised in the consideration.

(4) The statement, which by virtue of this section is charged at the reduced rate, shall become chargeable with stamp duty at the rate specified in section 117 if the acquiring company does not retain, for a period of 5 years from the date of the transaction in respect of which stamp duty at the reduced rate was charged, at least 75 per cent of the issued share capital of the target company and all the shares which it held following that transaction, including the shares acquired whether by means of a transaction or otherwise before that transaction and held at the time of the transaction.

(5) Notwithstanding subsection (4), the reduced rate shall continue to apply if the transfer, as a result of which the shares in question were not held for a period of 5 years, was either—

(a) a transfer forming part of a transaction which would of itself qualify for the reduced rate pursuant to subsection (1), or

(b) a transfer in the course of the liquidation of the acquiring company.

(6) Where, by reason of subsection (4), stamp duty becomes chargeable at the rate specified in section 117 when the acquiring company concerned within a period of 5 years from the date of any transaction in respect of which stamp duty was charged at the reduced rate—

(a) ceases to retain at least 75 per cent of the issued share capital of the target company concerned, or

(b) disposes of any of the shares of the target company which it held after the transaction to which the reduced rate was applied,

then the statement which was delivered to the registrar pursuant to section 117(1) in relation to the transaction in respect of which stamp duty was charged at the reduced rate shall be charged with stamp duty at the rate which would have been charged in the first instance if subsection (1) had not applied to the transaction and the statement thus charged shall have applied to it this Part except that, for the purposes of subsections (3) and (4) of section 117, the date of the transaction shall be the date on which the event specified in paragraph (a) or (b), as the case may be, occurred.

(7) This section shall apply only where the effective centre of management or the registered office of the target company concerned is in a Member State.

(8) For the purposes of this section, a company, partnership, firm, association or legal person that is considered to be a capital company in another Member State shall be deemed to be a target company notwithstanding that it is not considered to be a capital company.

Cross-references

Stamp duty relief in the case of the reconstruction and amalgamation of companies: s 80.

Case law

Many of the cases listed under s 80 are relevant to this section also.

Narrative

Irish Stamp Duty Law, Chapter 8.

Definitions

"stamp": s 1.

Former enactment

FA 1973 s 72; FA 1979 s 52.

120 Exemption for certain companies

Stamp duty shall not be charged in the case of a transaction that is effected by—

(a) a capital company which is formed for the purpose of and carries on exclusively the business of supplying a public service such as public transport or port facilities, or supplying water, gas or electricity, and not less than 50 per cent of the issued capital of which is owned by the State or a local authority, or

(*b*)   a capital company whose objects are exclusively cultural, charitable or educational.

Definitions

"stamp", "stamped": s 1.

Former enactment

FA 1973 s 73; FA 1997 s 197 and Sch 6.

120A Relief in respect of certain payments of stamp duty

[The statement required to be delivered pursuant to this Part in respect of a transaction specified in section 116(1)(*c*) shall, in any case where, within the period of 4 years immediately before the date of the transaction and on or after 4 August 1973, there has been a reduction in the issued capital of the capital company concerned as a result of losses sustained by the company, be charged at the rate of zero per cent in respect of so much of the amount determined in accordance with section 118 as corresponds to the reduction in issued capital or to so much of the reduction in issued capital to which the rate of zero per cent had not been applied in respect of an earlier transaction occurring since the reduction in capital.][1]

Amendments

[1]   Section 120A inserted by FA 2000 s 132 in relation to transactions executed on or after 15 December 1999.

121 Appeals in certain cases

A person who is dissatisfied with a decision of the Commissioners under this Part on the amount of the actual value of any assets referred to in section 118 may—

(*a*)   in the case of land, appeal against the decision in the manner prescribed by section 33 of the Finance (1909-10) Act, 1910, and so much of Part I of that Act as relates to appeals shall, with any necessary modifications, apply to an appeal under this section as if the appeal were an appeal under that section,

(*b*)   in the case of assets other than land, appeal against the decision to the Appeal Commissioners (within the meaning of section 850 of the Taxes Consolidation Act, 1997) and the provisions of Chapter 1 of Part 40 (Appeals) of the Taxes Consolidation Act, 1997, shall, with any necessary modifications, apply as they apply for the purpose of income tax.

Definitions

"person": IA 1937 s 11(*c*); "stock": s 1.

Former enactment

FA 1973 s 74; FA 1994 s 109(3); FA 1999 s 174.

122 Recovery of stamp duty and furnishing of information

(1) Stamp duty and the interest on such duty shall be recoverable from the capital company concerned and, in any case where the capital company is not a body corporate, shall be recoverable from the members of the capital company jointly and severally.

(2) All statements used for the purpose of this Part shall be in such form and contain such particulars as may be required by the Commissioners and every person accountable for stamp duty shall, if so required by the Commissioners, verify such particulars and deliver to them such evidence as they may require relating to any transaction or to any company concerned in any such transaction.

Definitions

"person": IA 1937 s 11(*c*); "stamp": s 1.

Former enactment

FA 1973 s 75.

PART 9
LEVIES

123 Cash cards

(1) In this section—

"accounting period" has the same meaning as it has for the purposes of section 27 of the Taxes Consolidation Act, 1997;

"bank" means one of the following, namely—

    (*a*) a person who holds a licence granted by the Central Bank of Ireland under section 9 of the Central Bank Act, 1971, or under section 10 of the Trustee Savings Banks Act, 1989,

    (*b*) where there are subsisting regulations under section 4 of the ACC Bank Act, 1992, for the supervision by the Central Bank of Ireland of the ACC Bank public limited company, that bank,

    (*c*) where there are subsisting regulations under section 3 of the ICC Bank Act, 1992, for the supervision by the Central Bank of Ireland of the ICC Bank public limited company, that bank;

"building society" means a building society which stands incorporated, or deemed by section 124(2) of the Building Societies Act, 1989, to be incorporated, under that Act and includes a company registered under section 106 of that Act;

"card account" means an account maintained by a promoter to which amounts of cash obtained by a person by means of a cash card are charged;

" cash card" means a card issued by a promoter to a person having an address in the State by means of which cash may be obtained in the State by the person from an automated teller machine;

"due date", in relation to any year, means the date of the end of the accounting period ending in that year;

"promoter" means a bank or a building society.

(2) A promoter shall, in each year, within one month of the due date, deliver to the Commissioners a statement in writing showing the number of cash cards issued at any time by the promoter and which are valid at any time during the accounting period ending in that year.

(3) Notwithstanding subsection (2)—

    (*a*) if the cash card is not used at any time during any accounting period referred to in subsection (2),

    (*b*) if the cash card is issued in respect of a card account—

        (i) which is a deposit account, and

        (ii) the average of the daily positive balances in the account does not exceed [€12.70][1] in any accounting period referred to in subsection (2), or

    (*c*) if the cash card is a replacement for a cash card which is already included in the relevant statement,

then it shall not be included in the statement relating to such period.

(4) There shall be charged on every statement delivered in pursuance of subsection (2) a stamp duty at the rate of [€6.25][2] in respect of each card included in the number of cards shown in the statement.

(5) The duty charged by subsection (4) on a statement delivered by a promoter pursuant to subsection (2) shall be paid by the promoter on delivery of the statement.

(6) There shall be furnished to the Commissioners by a promoter such particulars as the Commissioners may deem necessary in relation to any statement required by this section to be delivered by the promoter.

(7) In the case of failure by a promoter to deliver any statement required by subsection (2) within the time provided for in that subsection or of failure to pay the duty chargeable on any such statement on the delivery of the statement, the promoter shall be liable to pay, by means of penalty, in addition to the duty, interest on the duty at the rate of [0.0322 per cent for each day or part of a day][3] from the date to which the statement relates (in this subsection referred to as the "due date") to the date on which the duty is paid and also, by means of further penalty, a sum of [€380][4] for each day the duty remains unpaid after the expiration of one month from the due date and each penalty shall be recoverable in the same manner as if the penalty were part of the duty.

(8) The delivery of any statement required by subsection (2) may be enforced by the Commissioners under section 47 of the Succession Duty Act, 1853, in all respects as if such statement were such account as is mentioned in that section and the failure to deliver such statement were such default as is mentioned in that section.

(9) A promoter shall be entitled to charge to the card account the amount of stamp duty payable in respect of the cash card by virtue of this section and may apply the terms and conditions governing that account to interest on that amount.

(10) An account, charge card, company charge card or supplementary card within the meaning, in each case, assigned to it by section 124 and which attracts the payment of the stamp duty payable by virtue of that section shall not attract the payment of the stamp duty payable by virtue of this section.

(11) Where a promoter changes its accounting period and, as a result, stamp duty under this section would not be chargeable or payable in a year (in this section referred to as "the relevant year"), then the following provisions shall apply:

(a) duty shall be chargeable and payable in the relevant year as if the accounting period had not been changed,

(b) duty shall also be chargeable and payable within one month of the date of the end of the accounting period ending in the relevant year, and

(c) the duty chargeable and payable by virtue of paragraph (b) shall, subject to subsection (3), be chargeable and payable in respect of cash cards issued at any time by the promoter and which are valid at any time during the period from the due date as determined by paragraph (a) to the due date as determined by paragraph (b).

Amendments

1   Substituted by FA 2001 s 240 and Sch 5 Pt 6 with effect from 1 January 2002; previously "£1".

2   Substituted by FA 2001 s 240 and Sch 5 Pt 6 with effect from 1 January 2002; previously "£10".

3   Substituted by FA 2002 s 129(6)(b) with effect from 1 September 2002 in respect of an amount due to be paid or remitted, whether before, on, or after that date; previously "1 per cent per month or part of a month".

4   Substituted by FA 2001 s 240 and Sch 5 Pt 6 with effect from 1 January 2002; previously "£300".

Definitions

"Commissioners": s 1; "person": IA 1937 s 11(c); "stamp": s 1.

Narrative

Irish Stamp Duty Law, Ch 10.

Former enactment

FA 1992 s 203.; FA 1993 s 10(a), (b); FA 1996 s 114; FA 1998 ss 122(a)-(b), 124.

124 Credit cards and charge cards

(1) (a)   In this subsection—

"account" means an account maintained by a bank to which amounts in respect of goods, services or cash obtained by an individual by means of a credit card are charged;

"credit card" means a card issued by a bank to an individual having an address in the State by means of which goods, services and cash may be obtained by the individual and amounts in respect of the goods, services and cash may be charged to the account.

(b)   A bank shall, in each year, within 3 months of the 1st day of April in that year, deliver to the Commissioners a statement in writing showing the number of accounts maintained by the bank on that 1st day of April.

(c)   There shall be charged on every statement delivered in pursuance of paragraph (b) a stamp duty at the rate of [€19][1] in respect of each account included in the number of accounts shown in the statement.

(2) (a)   In this subsection—

"account" means an account maintained by a promoter to which amounts in respect of goods, services or cash obtained by an individual by means of a charge card are charged;

"charge card" means a card (other than a card known as "an in-house card") issued by a person (in this section referred to as "a promoter") to an individual having an address in the State by means of which goods, services or cash may be obtained by the individual and amounts in respect of the goods, services or cash may be charged to the account;

"company charge card" means—

(i) a charge card issued by a promoter to a person (other than an individual) having an address in the State which, if it were issued to an individual, would be regarded as a charge card, or

(ii) a charge card issued by a promoter to an employee, nominee or agent of such a person in such person's capacity as such employee, nominee or agent;

"quarter" means a period of 3 months ending on the 31st day of March, the 30th day of June, the 30th day of September or the 31st day of December;

"supplementary card" means a company charge card which is issued by a promoter to a person (other than an individual) and is additional to another company charge card issued by the promoter to that person.

(*b*) A promoter shall, in each year, within 2 months of the end of each quarter, deliver to the Commissioners a statement in writing showing the number of charge cards, company charge cards and supplementary cards issued or renewed by the promoter during that quarter.

(*c*) There shall be charged on every statement delivered in pursuance of paragraph (*b*) a stamp duty at the rate of [€9.50][2] for each period of 6 months or part of 6 months for which each charge card, company charge card and supplementary card shown in the statement as having been issued or renewed is expressed to be valid.

(*d*) (i) A promoter may, within 3 months of the 1st day of April, in any year, with the consent of the Commissioners, deliver to them a statement in writing showing the number of charge cards, company charge cards and supplementary cards issued or renewed by the promoter and expressed to be valid for a period that includes the 1st day of April in that year.

(ii) There shall be charged on every statement delivered in accordance with subparagraph (1), and paid on the delivery of the statement, a stamp duty at the rate of [€19][3] in respect of each charge card, company charge card and supplementary card included in the number of cards shown in the statement.

(iii) Notwithstanding paragraph (*b*), where a promoter delivers a statement in accordance with this paragraph, paragraph (*b*) shall not apply in relation to the promoter in respect of the quarters occurring in the year in which the statement is delivered.

(3) There shall be furnished to the Commissioners by a bank or a promoter, as the case may be, such particulars as the Commissioners may deem necessary in relation to any statement required by this section to be delivered by the bank or promoter.

(4) (*a*) The duty charged by subsection (1)(*c*) on a statement delivered by a bank pursuant to subsection (1)(*b*) shall be paid by the bank on delivery of the statement.

(b) The duty charged by subsection (2)(c) on a statement delivered by a promoter pursuant to subsection (2)(b) shall be paid by the promoter on delivery of the statement.

(5) (a) In this subsection **"due date"** means—

    (i) in relation to a statement required to be delivered pursuant to subsection (1)(b), the 1st day of April in the year in which the statement is required by that subsection to be delivered to the Commissioners, and

    (ii) in relation to a statement required to be delivered pursuant to subsection (2)(b), the end of the quarter within 2 months of which the statement is required by that subsection to be delivered to the Commissioners.

(b) In the case of failure by a bank or promoter, as the case may be, to deliver any statement required by subsection (1) or (2) within the time specified in those subsections or of failure to pay the duty chargeable on any such statement on the delivery of that statement, the bank or promoter, as the case may be, shall be liable to pay, by means of penalty, in addition to the duty, interest on the duty at the rate of [0.0322 per cent for each day or part of a day][4] from the due date until the day on which the duty is paid and also, by means of further penalty, a sum of [€380][5] for each day the duty remains unpaid after the expiration of 3 months from the due date and each penalty shall be recoverable in the same manner as if the penalty were part of the duty.

(6) The delivery of any statement required by subsection (1) or (2) may be enforced by the Commissioners under section 47 of the Succession Duty Act, 1853, in all respects as if such statement were such account as is mentioned in that section and the failure to deliver such statement were such default as is mentioned in that section.

(7) A bank or a promoter, as the case may be, shall be entitled to charge to the relevant account the amount of the stamp duty payable under this section by reference to that account or by reference to the charge card, company charge card or supplementary card to which the account relates and may apply the terms and conditions governing that account to interest on that amount.

Amendments

[1]   Substituted by FA 2001 s 240 and Sch 5 Pt 6 with effect from 1 January 2002; previously "£15".

[2]   Substituted by FA 2001 s 240 and Sch 5 Pt 6 with effect from 1 January 2002; previously "£7.50".

[3]   Substituted by FA 2001 s 240 and Sch 5 Pt 6 with effect from 1 January 2002; previously "£15".

[4]   Substituted by FA 2002 s 129(6)(b) with effect from 1 September 2002 in respect of an amount due to be paid or remitted, whether before, on, or after that date; previously "1 per cent per month or part of a month".

[5]   Substituted by FA 2001 s 240 and Sch 5 Pt 6 with effect from 1 January 2002; previously "£300".

Former enactment

F(No 2)A 1981 s 17; FA 1983 s 91; FA 1992 s 202; FA 1998 s 124(1).

125 Certain premiums of insurance

(1) In this section—

"assessable amount", in relation to a quarter, means the gross amount received by an insurer by means of premiums (including, in the case of an insurer who is a leading insurer (within the meaning of the European Communities (Co-insurance) Regulations, 1983 (SI No 65 of 1983)), the amount received by means of overall premiums (within the above meaning)) in that quarter in respect of policies of insurance to the extent that the risks to which those policies relate are located in the State (being risks deemed to be located in the State by virtue of section 61), but without having regard to an excluded amount;

"excluded amount" means—

(a) an amount received in the course or by means of reinsurance;

(b) a premium received in respect of business in the following classes of the Annex to First Council Directive 73/239/EEC of 24 July 1973 (OJ No L228, 16/8/ 1973), namely, 4, 5, 6, 7, 11 and 12, in classes 1 and 10 in so far as they relate to the insurance of passengers in marine and aviation vehicles and carriers liability insurance, respectively, and in class 14 in so far as it relates to export credit;

(c) a premium received in respect of business in classes I, II, III, IV, V, VI, VII, VIII and IX of the Annex to First Council Directive 79/267/EEC of 5 March 1979 (OJ No L63, 13/3/1979);

(d) a premium received in respect of health insurance business (being health insurance business within the meaning of section 2 of the Health Insurance Act, 1994);

"insurer" means a person who is the holder of an assurance licence under the Insurance Act, 1936, or is the holder of an authorisation within the meaning of the European Communities (Non-Life Insurance) Framework Regulations, 1994 (SI No 359 of 1994), or who carries on the business of insurance in compliance with the Assurance Companies Act, 1909;

"premium" has the same meaning as in the Insurance Act, 1936;

"quarter" means a period of 3 months ending on the 31st day of March, the 30th day of June, the 30th day of September or the 31st day of December.

(2) An insurer shall, in each year, within 30 days from the end of each quarter, deliver to the Commissioners a statement in writing showing the assessable amount for that insurer in respect of that quarter.

(3) There shall be charged on every statement delivered in pursuance of subsection (2) a stamp duty of an amount equal to 2 per cent of the assessable amount shown in the statement.

(4) The duty charged by subsection (3) on a statement delivered by an insurer pursuant to subsection (2) shall be paid by the insurer on delivery of the statement.

(5) There shall be furnished to the Commissioners by an insurer such particulars as the Commissioners may deem necessary in relation to any statement required by this section to be delivered by the insurer.

(6) In the case of failure by an insurer to deliver any statement required by subsection (2) within the time specified in that subsection or of failure by an insurer to pay any duty chargeable on any such statement on the delivery of that statement, the insurer shall be liable to pay, by means of penalty and in addition to the duty, interest on the duty at the

rate of [0.0322 per cent for each day or part of a day][1] from the expiration of the quarter to which the statement relates until the day on which the duty is paid.

(7) The delivery of any statement required by subsection (2) may be enforced by the Commissioners under section 47 of the Succession Duty Act, 1853, in all respects as if such statement were such account as is mentioned in that section and the failure to deliver such statement were such default as is mentioned in that section.

Amendments

[1]   Substituted by FA 2002 s 129(6)(*b*) with effect from 1 September 2002 in respect of an amount due to be paid or remitted, whether before, on, or after that date; previously "1 per cent per month or part of a month".

Note

For the definition per Council Directives 73/239/EEC and 79/267/EEC see text of Directives in European Legislation Council Directives.

Cross-references

Location of risk for insurance purposes: s 61.
Meaning of policy of insurance: s 1.
Meaning of policy of life insurance: s 1.
Other levies: s 126 (Levy on certain statement of interest).
Stamp duty on insurance policies: Heads of charge in Sch 1.

Narrative

Irish Stamp Duty Law, Ch 10.

Former enactment

FA 1982 s 92(1)-(7); FA 1983 s 93(1)(*a*)(*b*); FA 1993 s 103; FA 1995 s 146(*a*), (*b*); FA 1998 ss 121, 124; FA 1999 s 195(*a*)(*b*).

126 Certain statements of interest

(1) (*a*)   In this section—

"**corporation tax**" means the corporation tax charged by the Taxes Consolidation Act, 1997;

"**Corporation Tax Acts**" has the same meaning as in section 1 of the Taxes Consolidation Act, 1997;

"**relevant interest**" means any interest or other distribution which—

(i)   is received by a company (in this section referred to as "the lender") which is within the charge to corporation tax,

(ii)   is payable out of the assets of another company (in this subsection referred to as "the borrower") which is resident in the State for the purposes of corporation tax, in respect of a security of the borrower which is a security falling within subparagraph (ii), (iii) (I) or (v) of section 130(2)(*d*) of the Taxes Consolidation Act, 1997, and

(iii)   is a distribution for the purposes of the Corporation Tax Acts;

"**relevant period**" means any period of 6 months ending on the 31st day of January or the 31st day of July.

(*b*)   For the purposes of this section, any amount which, in a relevant period, is debited to a borrower's account with a lender in respect of relevant interest shall be treated as an amount received by the lender in that relevant period.

(2) A lender shall, within 30 days from the end of each relevant period, deliver to the Commissioners a statement in writing showing the amount of the relevant interest for that lender in respect of that relevant period.

(3) There shall be charged on every statement delivered in pursuance of subsection (2) a stamp duty of an amount equal to 12 per cent of the amount of the relevant interest shown in the statement.

(4) Notwithstanding subsection (3), in a case where the amount of the relevant interest received by a lender in respect of a security referred to in subsection (1) is an amount which is less than what would have been received by that lender had the security yielded simple interest at the rate of 6 per cent per annum throughout the period for which the relevant interest was payable, the stamp duty charged on the statement on the amount of the relevant interest for that security shall be an amount equal to 8 per cent of the amount received.

(5) The duty charged by subsection (3) on a statement delivered by a lender pursuant to subsection (2) shall be paid by the lender on delivery of the statement.

(6) There shall be furnished to the Commissioners by a lender such particulars as the Commissioners may deem necessary in relation to any statement required by this section to be delivered by a lender.

(7) In the case of failure by a lender to deliver any statement required by subsection (2) within the time specified in that subsection or of failure by a lender to pay any duty chargeable on any such statement on the delivery of such statement, the lender shall be liable to pay, by means of penalty, in addition to the duty, interest on the duty at the rate of 2.5 per cent for each month or part of a month from the expiration of the relevant period to which the statement relates until the date on which the duty is paid.

(8) The delivery of any statement required by subsection (2) may be enforced by the Commissioners under section 47 of the Succession Duty Act, 1853, in all respects as if such statement were such account as is mentioned in that section and the failure to deliver such statement were such default as is mentioned in that section.

(9) The stamp duty charged by this section shall not be allowed as a deduction for the purposes of the computation of any tax or duty under the care and management of the Commissioners payable by the lender.

Former enactment

FA 1986 s 94(1) to (8); TCA 1997 s 1100 and Sch 31.

PART 10
ENFORCEMENT

127 Terms on which instruments not duly stamped may be received in evidence

(1) On the production of an instrument chargeable with any duty as evidence in any court of civil judicature in any part of the State, or before any arbitrator or referee, notice shall be taken by the judge, arbitrator, or referee of any omission or insufficiency of the stamp on the instrument, and if the instrument is one which may legally be stamped after execution, it may, on payment to the officer of the court whose duty it is to read the

instrument, or to the arbitrator or referee, of the amount of the unpaid duty, and the penalty payable on stamping the same, be received in evidence, saving all just exceptions on other grounds.

(2) The officer, or arbitrator, or referee receiving the duty and penalty shall give a receipt for the same, and make an entry in a book kept for that purpose of the payment and of the amount of the payment, and shall communicate to the Commissioners the name or title of the proceeding in which, and of the party from whom, the officer, or arbitrator, or referee, as the case may be, received the duty and penalty, and the date and description of the instrument, and shall pay over to such person as the Commissioners may appoint the money received by such officer, arbitrator or referee, as the case may be, for the duty and penalty.

(3) On production to the Commissioners of any instrument in respect of which any duty or penalty has been paid, together with the receipt, the payment of the duty and penalty shall be denoted on the instrument.

(4) Except as provided for in this section, an instrument executed in any part of the State, or relating, wherever executed, to any property situated, or to any matter or thing done or to be done, in any part of the State, shall not, except in criminal proceedings or in civil proceedings by the Commissioners to recover stamp duty, be given in evidence, or be available for any purpose, unless it is not chargeable with duty or it is duly stamped in accordance with the law in force at the time when it was first executed.

Cross-references

A condition of sale framed with a view of precluding an objection to stamping is void: s 131
Transfers and leases, particulars to be delivered: s 12.
Uncertificated securities (CREST system) this section does not apply: s 71(*e*).

Case law

An unstamped document cannot be admitted in evidence: *Sun Alliance Insurance Ltd v IRC* [1972] Ch 133.
Judges have duty to see originals of documents to be stamped, and that duty cannot be avoided, even by consent of both parties: *Bowker v Williamson* (1889), 5 TLR 382; *Nixon v Albion Marine Insurance Co* (1867), LR 2 Exch 338.
Ruling of a judge that a document is sufficiently stamped or does not require a stamp is final: *Blewitt v Tritton* [1892] 2 QB 327.
Insufficiency of stamping will not affect the validity of the transaction or the instrument giving effect to it: *Marx v Estates & General Investment Ltd* [1976]1 WLR 380.
An incomplete instrument may be produced in evidence unstamped although it would require to be stamped if complete: *Sinclair v IRC* (1942) 24 TC 432.
An instrument delivered as an escrow is complete only on fulfilment of the condition subject to which it was delivered: *Byrne v Revenue Commissioners* (1935) IR 664 and *Terrapin International Ltd v IRC* [1976] 1 WLR 665.
An instrument requiring stamping cannot, if unstamped, be used to prove collateral matters:
Hamilton Finance Ltd v Coverley Westray Welbaum and Tosetti Ltd [1969] 1 Lloyds Rep 53 — but it can be used to refresh memory: *Birchell v Bullough* [1896] 1 QB 325.
A court will accept a stamped copy of a lost instrument: *Nally v Nally* [1953] IR 19.
Except in Revenue cases, it is unprofessional for counsel to object that an instrument is not properly stamped unless the lack of stamping goes to the validity of the instrument: *Wirth v Weigel Leygonie & Co Ltd* [1939] 3 All ER 712. This may no longer be applicable in this jurisdiction. See *Allied Irish Banks plc v James Bolger & Joan Bolger*, V ITR 1 and *Joseph Kenny v Revenue Commissioners and Laurence J Goodman and Gemon Ltd*, HC, 24 June 1996, V ITR 362.
Presumption of proper stamping in the case of a lost instrument: *Henty & Constable (Brewers) Ltd v IRC* (1961) 3 All ER 1146.
The expression "relating" is far-reaching and is not confined to the operative part of the instrument: *IRC v Maple & Co (Paris) Ltd* [1908] AC 22.

The words "criminal proceedings" include proceedings before justices for recovery of a penalty: *R v Lee* (1882) 9 QBD 394.

It has been held that a rent tribunal may not refuse to look at a document on the ground of absence of or insufficiency of stamp: *R v Fulham, Hammersmith and Kennington Rent Tribunal, ex p Zerek* [1951] 2 KB 1.

If an original instrument is unstamped no secondary evidence of it can be admitted: *Mattock v Saville Perfumery Ltd* (1958) 108 LJ 81.

The reference in s 14(4) to the time when the instrument was "first executed" was taken in practice to mean the time when it first becomes effective as an instrument. *Beesly v Hallwood Estates Ltd* [1961] Ch 105.

A transfer on sale which appears to be sufficiently stamped by reference to the consideration stated therein but not by reference to the actual consideration is not "duly stamped" within the meaning of s 14(4): *Lap Shun Textiles Industrial Co Ltd v Collector of Taxes* [1976] 1 All ER 833.

Events of default are to be ignored when considering the liability of an instrument to duty: *Gilchrist v Herbert* (1872) 26 LT 381.

Patents (assignment of), whether unstamped assignment rendered fresh assignment void: *Re Brown & Root McDermott Fabricators Ltd* [1996] STC 483.

Unstamped declaration of trust executed abroad inadmissible: *Parin v Hatfield v IRC* [1996] STC 333.

Definitions

"Commissioners", "executed", "execution", "instrument", "money": s 1; "person" IA 1937 s 11(*c*); "stamp", "stamped": s 1.

Former enactment

SA 1891 s 14; FA 1991 s 99; FA 1999 ss 188, 197 and Sch 6.

128 Rolls, books, etc, to be open to inspection

(1) In this section **"document"** includes—

    (*a*) any instrument, roll, book or record,

    (*b*) any record of an entry in a document, and

    (*c*) any information stored, maintained or preserved by means of any mechanical or electronic device, whether or not stored, maintained or preserved in a legible form.

(2) Subject to subsection (3), any person who is a party to any instrument, or who has in his or her custody or under his or her control any document, the inspection of which may tend to secure any duty, or to prove or lead to the discovery of any fraud, negligence, or omission in relation to any duty shall, within 14 days of a request by means of a notice in writing from the Commissioners—

    (*a*) provide such information as the Commissioners deem necessary, and

    (*b*) permit any person authorised by the Commissioners, to inspect any such document and to take such notes, extracts, prints, printouts and copies as such person may deem necessary,

and in case of refusal to so provide or permit by the first-mentioned person, that refusal shall be deemed to constitute a failure by that person to comply with subparagraph (iv) of paragraph (*g*) of subsection (2) of section 1078 of the Taxes Consolidation Act, 1997, and if the refusal continues after conviction such person shall be guilty of a further offence on every day on which the refusal continues and for each such offence such person shall be liable to a fine not exceeding [€125][1].

(3) It shall be a good defence in a prosecution for an offence under subsection (2) for the accused to show that the accused is required or entitled by law to refuse the request of the Commissioners.

Amendments

¹   Substituted by FA 2001 s 240 and Sch 5 Pt 6 with effect from 1 January 2002; previously "£100".

Cross-references

Revenue offences: TCA 1997 s 1078.

Definitions

"Commissioners", "instrument": s 1; "person" IA 1937 s 11(*c*).

Former enactment

SA 1891 s 16; FA 1991 s 101; FA 1999 s 159.

129 Penalty for enrolling, etc, instrument not duly stamped, etc

(1) If any person whose office it is to enrol, register, or enter in or on any rolls, books, or records any instrument chargeable with duty, enrols, registers, or enters any such instrument not being duly stamped, such person shall incur a penalty of [€630]¹.

(2) A bill of sale which is chargeable to stamp duty shall not be registered under any Act for the time being in force relating to the registration of bills of sale unless the original, duly stamped, is produced to the proper officer.

Amendments

¹   Substituted by FA 2001 s 240 and Sch 5 Pt 6 with effect from 1 January 2002; previously "£500".

Cross-references

Duty of a registrar with respect to stamp duty: Registration of Title Act 1964 s 104.
Uncertificated securities (CREST system) this section does not apply: 71(*e*).

Case law

A person should apply to the Revenue Commissioners for adjudication on an instrument which a company secretary has refused to enrol or register on the grounds that in his opinion it is incorrectly stamped. In determining whether an instrument is duly stamped the officer concerned is entitled to go beyond what appears to be on the face of the document: *R v Registrar of Joint Stock Companies* (1888) 21 QBD 131; *Maynard v Consolidated Kent Collieries* [1903]2 KB 121.
There is authority [obiter]that the registration of a transfer of shares while inadequately stamped is not effective as a legal transfer of the shares under the name of the transferee: *Re Indo-China Steam Navigation Co* (1917) Ch 100.
This dicta was disapproved by the Privy Council in a later case: *Lap Shun Textiles Industrial Co Ltd v Collector of Stamp Revenue* [1976] 1 All ER 833.

Definitions

"instrument": s 1; "person" IA 1937 s 11(*c*); "stamped": s 1.

Former enactment

SA 1891 ss 17, 41; FA 1991 s 106, FA 1999 ss 160 and 178.

130 Assignment of policy of life insurance to be stamped before payment of money assured

(1) No assignment of a policy of life insurance which is chargeable to stamp duty shall confer on the assignee named in that assignment, the assignee's executors, administrators, or assigns, any right to sue for the moneys assured or secured by the policy, or to give a valid discharge for the moneys, or any part of the moneys, unless the assignment is duly stamped, and no payment shall be made to any person claiming under any such assignment unless the same is duly stamped.

(2) If any payment is made in contravention of this section, the stamp duty not paid on the assignment, together with the penalty payable on stamping the same, shall be a debt

due to the Minister for the benefit of the Central Fund from the person by whom the payment is made and shall be payable to the Commissioners and may (without prejudice to any other mode of recovery of the duty or of the penalty payable on stamping) be sued for and recovered by action, or other appropriate proceeding, at the suit of the Attorney General in any court of competent jurisdiction.

Cross-references

Assignment by way of security or further security is chargeable under the MORTGAGE, BOND head of charge in Sch 1.

Assignment by way of sale is chargeable under the CONVEYANCE ON SALE OF A POLICY OF INSURANCE Head of charge in Sch 1.

Case law

An insurer may refuse to pay out the sum assured if the assignment of the policy is unstamped: *Re Waterhouse's Policy* [1937] Ch 415.

Definitions

"money": s 1; "person" IA 1937 s 11(*c*); "policy of insurance", policy of "life insurance", "stamp", "stamped": s 1.

Former enactment

SA 1891 s 118; FA 1924 s 38(1); FA 1999 s 179.

131 Conditions and agreements as to stamp duty void

Every condition of sale framed with the view of precluding objection or requisition on the ground of absence or insufficiency of stamp on any instrument and every contract, arrangement, or under-taking for assuming the liability on account of absence or insufficiency of stamp on any such instrument or indemnifying against such liability, absence, or insufficiency, shall be void.

Cross-references

Obligation to pay duty imposed on the "accountable person": s 1.

Case law

A purchaser is entitled to have every deed necessary to prove the vendor's title to the property duly stamped: *Whiting to Loomes* (1881) 17 Ch D 1.

Stipulation in a contract that any unstamped or insufficiently stamped instrument shall not be stamped at once but that the vendor will undertake to pay the penalty if it ever becomes necessary to stamp it seems not be enforceable: *Abbot v Stratton* (1856) 3 Jo & Lat 603 [s 117 reverses that part of the decision as to penalties only].

Definitions

"accountable person" , "executed", "instrument", "stamp": s 1.

Former enactment

SA 1891 s 117.

132 Application of section 962 of Taxes Consolidation Act, 1997

Section 962 of the Taxes Consolidation Act, 1997, shall, subject to any necessary modifications, apply to stamp duty in the same manner as it applies to income tax and where that section 962 is exercised with regard to stamp duty it shall be exercised as if stamp duty was a tax to be collected and levied by the Collector-General.

Definitions

"executed": s 1; "instrument": s 1; IA 1937 s 3; "stamp": s 1.

Former enactment

FA 1991 s 108(1); TCA 1997 s 1100 and Sch 31.

133 Application of certain provisions relating to penalties under Taxes Consolidation Act, 1997

Sections 987(4), 1061, 1062, 1063, 1064, 1065, 1066 and 1068 of the Taxes Consolidation Act, 1997, shall, with any necessary modifications, apply to a fine or penalty under—

(*a*) this Act, or

(*b*) any other enactment providing for fines or penalties in relation to stamp duty,

as if the fine or penalty were a penalty under the Income Tax Acts, and section 22 of the Inland Revenue Regulation Act, 1890, shall not apply in a case to which any of those sections of the Taxes Consolidation Act, 1997, apply by virtue of this section.

Definitions

"executed": s 1; "instrument": s 1, IA 1937 s 3; "stamp": s 1.

Former enactment

FA 1991 s 109(1); FA 1991 s 109(1); TCA 1997 s 1100 and Sch 31; FA 1999 s 166.

134 Evidence in proceedings for recovery of stamp duty, etc

(1) In any proceedings in the Circuit Court or the District Court for or in relation to the recovery of stamp duty, additional stamp duty or penalty relating to such duty, an affidavit duly made by an officer of the Commissioners deposing to any of the following matters—

(*a*) that the assessment of duty was duly made,

(*b*) that the assessment has become final and conclusive,

(*c*) that the duty or any specified part of the duty is due and outstanding,

(*d*) that demand for the payment of the duty has been duly made, shall be evidence until the contrary is proved of the matters so deposed to.

(2) Where the averments in the affidavit are not disputed by the defendant or respondent, it shall not be necessary for the officer by whom such affidavit was made to attend or give oral evidence at the hearing of the proceedings nor shall it be necessary to produce or put in evidence at the hearing any register, file, book of assessment or other record relating to the duty.

(3) Where any averment in the affidavit is disputed by the defendant or respondent, the judge shall, on such terms as to costs as he or she thinks just, give a reasonable opportunity by adjournment of the hearing or otherwise for the officer by whom the affidavit was made to attend and give oral evidence in the proceedings and for any register, file, book of assessment or other record relating to the duty to be produced and put in evidence in the proceedings.

Cross-references

Evidence of extrinsic circumstances may be admitted by a court in interpreting a document if it is relevant to explain the circumstances under which the document was executed and to establish the interest of the parties, The *Revenue Commissioners v Moroney*, Supreme Court, January 1971 [1972] IR 374 V ITR 589.

Former enactment

SA 1891 s 1(5); FA 1926 s 39; FA 1991 s 94.

PART 11
MANAGEMENT PROVISIONS

CHAPTER 1
Interpretation, Application and Care and Management

135 Interpretation (Part 11)

In this Part—

"duty" means any stamp duty for the time being chargeable by law;

"office of the Commissioners" means an office of the Commissioners where stamps are provided;

"officer" means officer of the Commissioners;

"stamp" is a stamp provided or to be provided by a Government Department.

Cross-references

SDCA 1999 s 1, definition of stamp.
Forgery Act 1913 s 18, definition of stamp.

Former enactment

SDMA 1891 s 27 (part); Par 16(1) IR(Adap)O 1923.

---

136 Application (Part 11)

This Part shall apply to all duties and to all fees which are for the time being directed to be collected or received by means of stamps.

Notes

Powers and duties in relation to postage and insurance stamps no longer exercised by the Revenue Commissioners. Relevant provisions contained in FA 1911, 1918 and 1928, in various Insurance Acts and in Orders made pursuant to those Acts.

Former enactment

SDMA 1891 s 1(part).

---

137 Stamp duties under care and management of the Commissioners

All duties for the time being chargeable by law as stamp duties shall be under the care and management of the Commissioners.

Notes

Powers and duties in relation to postage and insurance stamps no longer exercised by the Revenue Commissioners. Relevant provisions contained in FA 1911, 1918 and 1928, in various Insurance Acts and in Orders made pursuant to those Acts.

Former enactment

SDMA 1891 s 1 (part).

CHAPTER 2
Mode of recovering money received for duty

138 Moneys received for duty and not appropriated to be recoverable in High Court

(1) Every person who, having received any sum of money as or for any duty, or any fee collected by means of a stamp, does not apply the money to the due payment of the duty or fee, and improperly withholds or detains the same, shall be accountable for the amount of the duty or fee, and the same shall be a debt from such person to the Minister for the benefit of the Central Fund and shall be payable to the Commissioners and may (without prejudice to any other mode of recovery of the sum of money) be sued for and recovered by action, or other appropriate proceeding, at the suit of the Attorney General in any court of competent jurisdiction.

(2) The Commissioners may sue out of the High Court a writ of summons commanding any such person to deliver an account of every sum of money so received by such person, and withheld or detained, and to pay the money to them, together with the costs of the proceedings, or to show cause to the contrary.

(3) If cause is shown the court shall make such order as to the court seems just.

Case law

Solicitor held accountable under s 2: *Lord Advocate v Gordon* (1901) 8 SLT 439.

Remarks

See Destination Table.

Former enactment

SDMA 1891 s 2; FA 1924 s 38(1).

CHAPTER 3
Offences

139 Certain offences in relation to dies and stamps provided by the Commissioners to be offences

Every person who does, or causes or procures to be done, or knowingly aids, abets, or assists in doing, any of the acts following, that is—

(a) fraudulently prints or makes an impression on any material from a genuine die;

(b) fraudulently cuts, tears, or in any way removes from any material any stamp, with intent that any use should be made of such stamp or of any part of such stamp;

(c) fraudulently mutilates any stamp, with intent that any use should be made of any part of such stamp;

(d) fraudulently fixes or places on any material or on any stamp, any stamp or part of a stamp which, whether fraudulently or not, has been cut, torn, or in any way removed from any other material, or out of or from any other stamp;

(e) fraudulently erases or otherwise either really or apparently removes from any stamped material any name, sum, date, or other matter or thing written on the stamped material, with the intent that any use should be made of the stamp on such material:

(f) knowingly sells or exposes for sale or utters or uses any stamp which has been fraudulently printed or impressed from a genuine die;

(g) knowingly, and without lawful excuse (the proof of which shall lie on the person accused) has in such person's possession any stamp which has been fraudulently printed or impressed from a genuine die, or any stamp or part of a stamp which has been fraudulently cut, torn, or otherwise removed from any material, or any stamp which has been fraudulently mutilated, or any stamped material out of which any name, sum, date, or other matter or thing has been fraudulently erased or otherwise either really or apparently removed,

shall be guilty of an offence and section 1078 (which relates to revenue offences) of the Taxes Consolidation Act, 1997, shall for the purposes of such offence be construed in all respects as if such offence were an offence under subsection (2) of that section.

Remarks

See Destination Table for repeals.

Former enactment

SDMA 1891 s 13(3)-(9); Forgery Act 1913 s 20 and Sch 3; FA 1999 s 152.

140 Proceedings for detection of forged dies, etc

On information given before a judge of the District Court on oath that there is just cause to suspect any person of being guilty of any of the offences specified in section 139, such judge may, by a warrant under his or her hand, cause every house, room, shop, building, or place belonging to or occupied by the suspected person, or where such person is suspected of being or having been in any way engaged or concerned in the commission of any such offence, or of secreting any machinery, implements, or utensils applicable to the commission of any such offence, to be searched, and if on such search any of those several matters and things are found, the same may be seized and carried away, and shall afterwards be delivered over to the Commissioners.

Cross-references

Definition of "die", Forgery Act 1913 s 18.
Extention to paper used for Excise licences, Revenue Act 1898 s 12.

Former enactment

SDMA 1891 s 16.

141 Proceedings for detection of stamps stolen or obtained fraudulently

(1) Any judge of the District Court having jurisdiction in the place where any stamps are known or supposed to be concealed or deposited, may, on reasonable suspicion that the same have been stolen or fraudulently obtained, issue a warrant for the seizure of the stamps, and for apprehending and bringing before such judge or any other judge of the District Court within the same jurisdiction the person in whose possession or custody the stamps may be found, to be dealt with according to law.

(2) If the person does not satisfactorily account for the possession of the stamps or it does not appear that the same were purchased by such person at an office of the Commissioners, or from some person duly appointed to sell and distribute stamps or duly licensed to deal in stamps, the stamps shall be forfeited, and shall be delivered over to the Commissioners.

(3) Notwithstanding subsections (1) and (2), if at any time within 6 months after the delivery of the stamps under subsection (2) any person makes out to the satisfaction of the Commissioners that any stamps so forfeited were stolen or otherwise fraudulently obtained from such person, and that the same were purchased by such person at an office of the Commissioners, or from some person duly appointed to sell and distribute stamps, or duly licensed to deal in stamps, such stamps may be delivered up to such person.

Former enactment

SDMA 1891 s 17.

142 Licensed person in possession of forged stamps to be presumed guilty until contrary is shown

(1) If any forged stamps are found in the possession of any person appointed to sell and distribute stamps, or being or having been licensed to deal in stamps, that person shall be deemed and taken, unless the contrary is satisfactorily proved, to have had the same in his or her possession knowing them to be forged, and with intent to sell, use, or utter them, and shall be liable to the punishment imposed by law on a person selling, using, uttering, or having in possession forged stamps knowing the same to be forged.

(2) If the Commissioners have cause to suspect any such person of having in such person's possession any forged stamps, they may by warrant under their hands authorise any person to enter between the hours of 9 a.m. and 7 p.m. into any house, room, shop, or building of or belonging to the suspected person, and if on demand of admittance, and notice of the warrant, the door of the house, room, shop, or building, or any inner door of such house, room, shop, or building is not opened, the authorised person may break open the same and search for and seize any stamps that may be found in the house, room, shop or building or in the custody or possession of the suspected person.

(3) All members of the Garda Siochana are required, on request by any person authorised pursuant to subsection (2), to aid and assist in the execution of the warrant.

(4) Any person who—

   (*a*)   refuses to permit any such search or seizure to be made in accordance with subsection (2), or

   (*b*)   assaults, opposes, molests, or obstructs any person so authorised in the due execution of the powers conferred by this section or any person acting to aid or assist a person so authorised,

and any member of the Garda Siochana who on a request under subsection (3) refuses or neglects to aid and assist any person so authorised in the due execution of such person's powers shall incur a penalty of [€1,265][1].

Amendments

[1]   Substituted by FA 2001 s 240 and Sch 5 Pt 6 with effect from 1 January 2002; previously "£1,000".

Former enactment

SDMA 1891 s 18; FA 1999 s 153.

143 Mode of proceeding when stamps are seized

Where stamps are seized under a warrant, the person authorised by the warrant shall, if required, give to the person in whose custody or possession the stamps are found an acknowledgement of the number, particulars, and amount of the stamps, and permit the stamps to be marked before the removal of those stamps.

Former enactment

SDMA 1891 s 19.

144 Defacement of adhesive stamps

(1) Every person who by any writing in any manner defaces any adhesive stamp before it is used shall incur a penalty of [€630][1].

(2) Notwithstanding subsection (1), any person may with the express sanction of the Commissioners, and in conformity with the conditions which they may prescribe, write on or otherwise appropriate an adhesive stamp before it is used for the purpose of identification of such stamp.

Amendments

[1]   Substituted by FA 2001 s 240 and Sch 5 Pt 6 with effect from 1 January 2002; previously "£500".

Former enactment

SDMA 1891 s 20; FA 1991 s 106; FA 1999 s 154.

145 Penalty for frauds in relation to duties

Any person who practises or is concerned in any fraudulent act, contrivance, or device, not specially provided for by law, with intent to defraud the State of any duty shall be guilty of an offence and section 1078 (which relates to revenue offences) of the Taxes Consolidation Act, 1997, shall for the purposes of such offence be construed in all respects as if such offence were an offence under subsection (2) of that section.

Cross-references

Definition of "die", "paper", "seal" and "stamp": Forgery Act 1913 s 18.
Forfeiture of used stamps: Revenue Act 1898 s 11.
Penalty for forgery of die: Forgery Act 1913 s 5.
Penalty for possession of forged die: Forgery Act 1913 s 8.
Penalty for possession of paper or implements for forging: Forgery Act 1913 s 9.
Penalty for possession of unstamped Revenue paper: Forgery Act 1913 s 10.

Former enactment

SDMA 1891 s 21; FA 1999 s 155.

CHAPTER 4
Sale of stamps

146 Power to grant licences to deal in stamps

(1) The Commissioners may, in their discretion, grant a licence to any person to deal in stamps at any place to be named in the licence.

(2) The licence shall specify the full name and place of abode of the person to whom the same is granted, and a description of every house, shop, or place, in or at which such person is authorised to deal in stamps.

(3) Every person to whom a licence is granted shall give security in the sum of [€1,265][1] in such manner and form as the Commissioners shall prescribe, and, if by bond, the bond shall be exempt from stamp duty.

(4) One licence and one bond only shall be required for any number of persons in partnership, and the licence may at any time be revoked by the Commissioners.

(5) Every person licensed to deal in stamps shall cause to be visibly and legibly painted and shall keep so painted in letters of not less than one inch in length on some conspicuous place on the outside of the front of every house, shop, or place in or at which such person is licensed to deal in stamps, such person's full name, together with the words "Licensed to sell stamps", and for every neglect or omission so to do shall incur a penalty of [€1,265][2].

Amendments

[1] Substituted by FA 2001 s 240 and Sch 5 Pt 6 with effect from 1 January 2002; previously "£1,000".
[2] Substituted by FA 2001 s 240 and Sch 5 Pt 6 with effect from 1 January 2002; previously "£1,000".

Former enactment

SDMA 1891 s 3; FA 1999 s 149(*a*), (*b*).

147 Penalty for unauthorised dealing in stamps, etc

(1) If any person who is not duly appointed to sell and distribute stamps deals in any manner in stamps, without being licensed so to do, or at any house, shop, or place not specified in such person's licence such person shall be guilty of an offence and section 1078 (which relates to revenue offences) of the Taxes Consolidation Act, 1997, shall for the purposes of such offence be construed in all respects as if such offence were an offence under subsection (2) of that section.

(2) If any person who is not duly appointed to sell and distribute stamps, or duly licensed to deal in stamps, has, or puts on such person's premises either in the inside or on the outside of the premises, or on any board or any material exposed to public view, and whether the same be affixed to such person's premises or not, any letters importing or intending to import that such person deals in stamps, or is licensed so to do, such person shall incur a penalty of [€1,265][1].

Amendments

[1] Substituted by FA 2001 s 240 and Sch 5 Pt 6 with effect from 1 January 2002; previously "£1,000".

Former enactment

SDMA 1891 s 4; FA 1999 s 150(*a*), (*b*).

148 Provisions as to determination of a licence

(1) If the licence of any person to deal in stamps expires or is revoked, or if any person licensed to deal in stamps dies or becomes bankrupt, and any such person at the expiration or revocation of his or her licence, or at the time of his or her death or bankruptcy, has in his or her possession any stamps, such person, or such person's

executor or administrator, or the receiver or trustee or official assignee under such person's bankruptcy, may, within 6 months after the expiration or revocation of the licence, or after the death or bankruptcy, as the case may be, bring or send the stamps to an office of the Commissioners.

(2) The Commissioners may in any such case pay to the person bringing or sending stamps the amount of the duty on the stamps, deducting from such amount the proper discount, if proof to their satisfaction is furnished that the same were actually in the possession of the person, whose licence has expired or been revoked, or so dying or becoming bankrupt, for the purpose of sale, at the time of the expiration or revocation of the licence, or of his or her death or bankruptcy, and that the stamps were purchased or procured by that person at an office of the Commissioners, or from some person duly appointed to sell and distribute stamps, or duly licensed to deal in stamps.

Former enactment

SDMA 1891 s 5.

149 Penalty for hawking stamps

(1) If any person, whether licensed to deal in stamps or not, hawks or carries about for sale or exchange, any stamps, the following shall apply:

- (*a*) such person shall, in addition to any other fine or penalty to which he or she may be liable, be guilty of an offence and section 1078 (which relates to revenue offences) of the Taxes Consolidation Act, 1997, shall for the purposes of such offence be construed in all respects as if such offence were an offence under subsection (2) of that section;
- (*b*) all stamps which are found in the possession of the offender shall be forfeited, and shall be delivered to the Commissioners, to be disposed of as they think fit.

(2) Any person may arrest a person found committing an offence under this section, and take that person before a judge of the District Court having jurisdiction where the offence is committed, who shall hear and determine the matter.

Former enactment

SDMA 1891 s 6; FA 1999 s 151 (*a*), (*b*).

150 Discount

On the sale of stamps such discount shall be allowed to the purchasers of the stamps as the Minister directs.

Remarks

See Destination Table.

Former enactment

SDMA 1891 s 8.

CHAPTER 5
Allowance for spoiled or misused stamps

151 Allowance for spoiled stamps

(1) Subject to such regulations as the Commissioners may think proper to make, and to the production of such evidence by statutory declaration or otherwise as the Commissioners may require, allowance shall be made by the Commissioners for stamps in any of the following cases:

(a) the stamp on any material inadvertently and undesignedly spoiled, obliterated, or by any means rendered unfit for the purpose intended, before the material bears the signature of any person or any instrument written on the material is executed by any party;

(b) any adhesive stamp which has been inadvertently and undesignedly spoiled or rendered unfit for use and has not in the opinion of the Commissioners been affixed to any material;

(c) any adhesive stamp representing a fee capable of being collected by means of such stamp which has been affixed to material where a certificate from the proper officer is produced to the effect that the stamp should be allowed;

(d) the stamp on any bill of exchange signed by or on behalf of the drawer which has not been accepted or made use of in any manner or delivered out of such drawer's hands for any purpose other than by means of tender for acceptance;

(e) the stamp on any promissory note signed by or on behalf of the maker which has not been made use of in any manner or delivered out of such maker's hands;

(f) the stamp on any bill of exchange or promissory note which from any omission or error has been spoiled or rendered useless, although the same, being a bill of exchange, may have been accepted or endorsed, or, being a promissory note, may have been delivered to the payee, where another completed and duly stamped bill of exchange or promissory note is produced identical in every particular, except in the correction of the error or omission, with the spoiled bill or note;

(g) the stamp used for any of the following instruments, that is—

  (i) an instrument executed by any party to the instrument, but afterwards found to be absolutely void from the beginning,

  (ii) an instrument executed by any party to the instrument, but afterwards found unfit, by reason of any error or mistake in the instrument, for the purpose originally intended,

  (iii) an instrument executed by any party to the instrument which has not been made use of for any purpose, and which by reason of the inability or refusal of some necessary party to sign the same or to complete the transaction according to the instrument, is incomplete and insufficient for the purpose for which it was intended,

  (iv) an instrument executed by any party to the instrument, which by reason of the refusal of any person to act under the same, or for want of enrolment or registration within the time required by law, fails of the intended purpose or becomes void, or

(v)   an instrument executed by any party to the instrument which is inadvertently and undesignedly spoiled, and in lieu of which another instrument made between the same parties and for the same purpose is executed and duly stamped, or which becomes useless in consequence of the transaction intended to be effected by the instrument being effected by some other instrument duly stamped.

(2) Notwithstanding subsection (1), allowance shall not be made by the Commissioners for spoiled stamps unless—

(a)   the application for relief is made within 6 years after the stamp has been spoiled or become useless or in the case of an executed instrument after the date of the instrument, or, if it is not dated, within 6 years after the execution of the instrument by the person by whom it was first or alone executed or within such further time as the Commissioners may prescribe in the case of any instrument sent outside the State for execution or when from unavoidable circumstances any instrument for which another has been substituted cannot be produced within that period,

(b)   in the case of an executed instrument no legal proceeding has been commenced in which the instrument could or would have been given or offered in evidence, and that the instrument is given up to be cancelled,

(c)   in the case of an executed instrument the instrument has not achieved the purpose for which it was intended being the purpose of registering title to the property being conveyed or transferred by that instrument.

Remarks

See Destination Table: SDMA 1891 s 9(*a*)(proviso)(*c*), unnecessary.

Former enactment

SDMA 1891 s 9; FA 1976 s 47; FA 1999 s 184.

152 Allowance for misused stamps

When any person has inadvertently used for an instrument liable to duty a stamp of greater value than was necessary, or has inadvertently used a stamp for an instrument not liable to any duty, the Commissioners may, on application made within 6 years after the date of the instrument, or, if it is not dated, within 6 years after the execution of the instrument by the person by whom it was first or alone executed, and on the instrument, if liable to duty, being stamped with the proper duty, cancel and allow as spoiled the stamp so misused.

Case law

The courts are not empowered to extend the statutory periods within which a refund is to be claimed: *Byrne v The Revenue Commissioners* [1935] IR 664.

Former enactment

SDMA 1891 s 10.

153 Allowance, how to be made

In any case in which allowance is made for spoiled or misused stamps the Commissioners may give in lieu of the allowance other stamps of the same denomination and value, or if required, and they think proper, stamps of any other denomination to the same amount in value, or in their discretion, the same value in money, deducting from the value of the stamps the discount allowed on the purchase of stamps of the like description.

Case law

Common law right to recover tax plus interest paid in mistake of law: *O'Rourke v The Revenue Commissioners* HC 18 December 1996, V ITR 321.

Former enactment

SDMA 1891 s 11.

154 Stamps not wanted may be repurchased by the Commissioners

When any person is possessed of a stamp which has not been spoiled or rendered unfit or useless for the purpose intended, but for which such person has no immediate use, the Commissioners may, if they think fit, repay to such person the value of the stamp in money, deducting the proper discount, on such person's delivering up the stamp to be cancelled, and proving to their satisfaction that it was purchased by such person at an office of the Commissioners, or from some person duly appointed to sell and distribute stamps or duly licensed to deal in stamps, within the period of 6 years next preceding the application and with a bona fide intention to use it.

Former enactment

SDMA 1891 s 12; RA 1898 s 13; FA 1976 s 47(1).

155 Allowance for lost instruments

(1) Where an instrument which was executed and duly stamped has been accidentally lost (in this section referred to as the "lost instrument") the Commissioners may—

    (*a*) on application made by the person by whom it was first or alone executed,

    (*b*) on the giving of an undertaking by that person to deliver up the lost instrument to them to be cancelled if it is subsequently found, and

    (*c*) on satisfactory proof of the payment of the duty,

give other stamps of the same value in money but the stamps so given shall only be used for the purpose of stamping another instrument made between the same persons and for the same purpose.

(2) For the purposes of this section the Commissioners may require the delivery to them, in such form as they may specify, of a statutory declaration by any person who was concerned with the delivery of the lost instrument to them for stamping.

Former enactment

SDMA 1891 s 12A as inserted by FA 1999 s 185.

CHAPTER 6
Miscellaneous

156 Discontinuance of dies

(1) Whenever the Commissioners determine to discontinue the use of any die, and provide a new die to be used in lieu of the discontinued die, and give public notice of their determination in the Iris Oifigiuil, then from and after any day to be stated in the

notice (such day not being within one month after the same is so published) the new die shall be the only lawful die for denoting the duty chargeable in any case in which the discontinued die would have been used and every instrument first executed by any person, or bearing date after the day so stated, and stamped with the discontinued die, shall be deemed to be not duly stamped.

(2) Whenever the Commissioners give public notice in the Iris Oifigiuil that the use of any die has been discontinued, then, whether a new die has been provided or not, from and after any day to be stated in the notice (that day not being within one month after the notice is so published), that die shall not be a lawful die for denoting the payment of duty, and every instrument first executed by any person, or bearing date, after the day so stated in the notice, and stamped with duty denoted by the discontinued die, shall be deemed to be not duly stamped.

(3) (*a*)   If any instrument stamped with a discontinued die, and first executed after the day so stated at any place outside the State, is brought to the Commissioners within 14 days after it has been received in the State, then on proof of the facts to the satisfaction of the Commissioners the stamp on that instrument shall be cancelled, and the instrument shall be stamped with the same amount of duty by means of a lawful die without the payment of any penalty.

(*b*)   All persons having in their possession any material stamped with the discontinued die, and which by reason of the providing of such new die has been rendered useless, may at any time within 6 months after the day stated in the notice send the same to an office of the Commissioners, and the Commissioners may on receipt of that material cause the stamp on such material to be cancelled, and the same material, or, if the Commissioners think fit, any other material, to be stamped with a lawful die in lieu of and to an equal amount with the stamp so cancelled.

Cross-references

Notice in Iris Oifigiúil; Revenue Act 1898 s 10.

Remarks

See Destination Table.

Former enactment

SDMA 1891 s 22; RA 1898 s 10(1)-(2); RA 1898 s 10(1), (2).

157 Declarations, affidavits and oaths, how to be made

Any statutory declaration, affidavit or oath to be made in pursuance of or for the purposes of this or any other Act for the time being in force relating to duties may be made before any of the Commissioners, or any officer or person authorised by them in that behalf, or before any commissioner for oaths or any peace commissioner or notary public in any part of the State, or at any place outside the State, before any person duly authorised to administer oaths there.

Cross-references

This section applies to affidavits and oaths, RA 1898 s 7(6).

Remarks

See Destination Table under SDMA 1891 s 24.

Former enactment

SDMA 1891 s 24; RA 1898 s 7(6).

158 Mode of granting licences

Any licence or certificate to be granted by the Commissioners under this Part or any other Act for the time being in force relating to duties may be granted by such officer or person, as the Commissioners may authorise in that behalf.

Former enactment

SDMA 1891 s 25.

159 Recovery of penalties, etc

(1) Any penalty imposed by this Part or any forfeiture incurred in connection with duty shall be deemed to be a debt due to the Minister for the benefit of the Central Fund and shall be payable to the Commissioners and may (without prejudice to any other mode of recovery) be sued for and recovered by action, or other appropriate proceedings, at the suit of the Attorney General or the Minister or the Commissioners in any court of competent jurisdiction, notwithstanding anything to the contrary contained in the Inland Revenue Regulation Act, 1890.

(2) The provisions of section 134 shall apply in any proceedings in the Circuit Court or the District Court for or in relation to the recovery of a penalty referred to in subsection (1).

Former enactment

SDMA 1891 s 26; FA 1999 s 172.

PART 12
REPEALS, ETC

160 Repeals

(1) Subject to subsection (2), each enactment mentioned in column (2) of Schedule 3 (which in this Act are collectively referred to as "the repealed enactments") is hereby repealed or revoked to the extent specified opposite that mentioned in column (3) of that Schedule.

(2) This Act shall not apply in relation to stamp duty on—

    (*a*)   instruments specified in Schedule 1 which were executed before the date of the passing of this Act,

    (*b*)   transactions, within the meaning of section 116, taking place before the date of the passing of this Act,

    (*c*)   statements, within the meaning of sections 123(2), 124(1)(*b*), 124(2)(*b*), 124(2)(*d*)(i), 125(2) and 126(2), which would fall to be delivered under the repealed enactments before the date of the passing of this Act,

and the repealed enactments shall continue to apply in relation to stamp duty on the—

    (i)   instruments mentioned in paragraph (*a*),

    (ii) transactions mentioned in paragraph (*b*), and

    (iii) statements mentioned in paragraph (*c*),

to the same extent that they would have applied if this Act had not been enacted.

(3) Notwithstanding subsection (1), any provision of the repealed enactments which imposes a fine, forfeiture, penalty or punishment for any act or omission shall, in relation to any act or omission which took place or began before the date of the passing of this Act, continue to apply in substitution for the provision of this Act to which it corresponds.

(4) Anything done under or in connection with the provisions of the repealed enactments which correspond to the provisions of this Act shall be deemed to have been done under or in connection with the provisions of this Act to which those provisions of the repealed enactments correspond; but nothing in this subsection shall affect the operation of subsections (3) and (4) of section 163.

161 Saving for enactments not repealed

This Act (other than subsections (2) to (4) of section 163) shall apply subject to so much of any Act as contains provisions relating to or affecting stamp duties as—

(a) is not repealed by this Act, and

(b) would have operated in relation to stamp duties if this Act had not been substituted for the repealed enactments.

162 Consequential amendments to other enactments

Schedule 4, which provides for amendments to other enactments consequential on the passing of this Act, shall apply for the purposes of this Act.

163 Continuity and construction of certain references to old and new law

(1) The Commissioners shall have all the jurisdictions, powers and duties in relation to stamp duties and fees collected by means of stamps under this Act which they had before the passing of this Act.

(2) The continuity of the operation of the law relating to stamp duties and fees collected by means of stamps shall not be affected by the substitution of this Act for the repealed enactments.

(3) Any reference, whether express or implied, in any enactment or document (including this Act and any Act amended by this Act) —

(a) to any provision of this Act, or

(b) to things done or to be done under or for the purposes of any provisions of this Act,

shall, if and in so far as the nature of the reference permits, be construed as including, in relation to the times, years or periods, circumstances or purposes in relation to which the corresponding provision in the repealed enactments applied or had applied, a reference to, or, as the case may be, to things done or to be done under or for the purposes of, that corresponding provision.

(4) Any reference, whether express or implied, in any enactment or document (including the repealed enactments and enactments passed and documents made after the passing of this Act) —

(a) to any provision of the repealed enactments, or

(b) to things done or to be done under or for the purposes of any provisions of the repealed enactments, shall, if and in so far as the nature of the reference permits, be construed as including, in relation to the times, years or periods, circumstances or purposes in relation to which the corresponding provision of this Act applies, a reference to, or, as the case may be, to things done or to be done under or for the purposes of, that corresponding provision.

164 Short title

This Act may be cited as the Stamp Duties Consolidation Act, 1999.

SCHEDULE 1
STAMP DUTIES ON INSTRUMENTS

[Section 2]

Heading	Duty
AGREEMENT or CONTRACT, accompanied with a deposit.	
See MORTGAGE, etc.	
AGREEMENT for a Lease, or for any letting.	
See LEASE.	
AGREEMENT for sale of property.	
See CONVEYANCE or TRANSFER on sale.	
ANNUITY.	
Conveyance in consideration of.	
See CONVEYANCE or TRANSFER on sale.	
Purchase of.	
See CONVEYANCE or TRANSFER on sale.	
Creation of, by way of security.	
See MORTGAGE, etc.	
ASSIGNMENT.	
By way of security, or of any security.	
See MORTGAGE, etc.	
On a sale or otherwise.	
See CONVEYANCE or TRANSFER.	
ASSURANCE.	
See POLICY.	
BILL OF EXCHANGE or PROMISSORY NOTE.	
Where drawn on an account in the State	[€0.08][1]
In any other case:	
where drawn or made in the State	[€0.08][1].

Exemptions

(1) Draft or order drawn by any banker in the State on any other banker in the State, not payable to bearer or to order, and used solely for the purpose of settling or clearing any account between such bankers.

(2) Letter written by a banker in the State to any other banker in the State, directing the payment of any sum of money, the same not being payable to bearer or to order, and such letter not being sent or delivered to the person to whom payment is to be made or to any person on such person's behalf.

(3) Letter of credit granted in the State, authorising drafts to be drawn out of the State payable in the State.

(4) Draft or order drawn by the Accountant of the Courts of Justice.

(5) Coupon or warrant for interest attached to and issued with any security, or with an agreement or memorandum for the renewal or extension of time for payment of a security.

(6) Coupon for interest on a marketable security being one of a set of coupons whether issued with the security or subsequently issued in a sheet.

(7) Bill drawn on any form supplied by the Commissioners for the purpose of remitting amounts of tax in accordance with Regulation 31(1) of the Income Tax (Employments) Regulations, 1960 (SI No 28 of 1960).

(8) Bill drawn on any form supplied by the Commissioners for the purpose of remitting amounts of turnover tax, wholesale tax, or value-added tax.

(9) Bill drawn on any form supplied by the Commissioners for the purpose of remitting amounts of tax in accordance with Regulation 10 of the Income Tax (Construction Contracts) Regulations, 1971 (SI No 1 of 1971).

(10) Direct debits and standing orders.

(11) Bill drawn on an account outside the State.

(12) Bill drawn on or on behalf of the Minister by which payment in respect of prize bonds is effected.

BILL OF SALE.

Absolute.

See CONVEYANCE or TRANSFER on sale.

By way of security.

See MORTGAGE, etc.

BOND in relation to any annuity on the original creation and sale of that annuity.

See CONVEYANCE or TRANSFER on sale.

BOND, accompanied with a deposit of title deeds, for making a mortgage or other security on any estate or property comprised in the mortgage or other security.

See MORTGAGE, etc.

BOND, DECLARATION, or other DEED or WRITING for making redeemable any disposition apparently absolute, but intended only as a security.

See MORTGAGE, etc.

CHEQUE.

See BILL OF EXCHANGE.

CONTRACT.

See AGREEMENT.

CONVEYANCE or TRANSFER on sale of any stocks or marketable securities

1 per cent of the consideration but where the calculation results in an amount which is not a multiple of [€1]² the amount so calculated shall be rounded [down to the nearest €]³.

Exemption

Foreign loan security issued by or on behalf of a company or body of persons corporate or unincorporate formed or established in the State. For the purposes of this exemption a "foreign loan security" means a security issued outside the State in respect of a loan which is expressed in a currency other than the currency of the State and is neither offered for subscription in the State nor offered for subscription with a view to an offer for sale in the State of securities in respect of the loan.

CONVEYANCE or TRANSFER on sale of a policy of insurance or a policy of life insurance where the risk to which the policy relates is located in the State

0. 1 per cent of the consideration but where the calculation results in an amount which is not a multiple of [€1]² the amount so calculated shall be rounded [down to the nearest €]³.

CONVEYANCE or TRANSFER on sale of any property other than stocks or marketable securities or a policy of insurance or a policy of life insurance.

[(1) Where the amount or value of the consideration for the sale which is attributable to residential property, or would be so attributable if the contents of residential property were considered to be residential property, does not exceed [€127,000]⁴and the instrument contains a statement certifying that the consideration for the sale is, as the case may be

   (*a*) wholly attributable to residential property, or

   (*b*) partly attributable to residential property,

and that the transaction effected by that instrument does not form part of a larger transaction or of a series of transactions in respect of which the amount or value, or the aggregate amount or value, of the consideration which is attributable to residential property, or which would be so attributable if the contents of residential property were considered to be residential property, [exceeds €127,000: for the consideration which is attributable to residential property

Exempt]⁵

(2) Where paragraph (1) does not apply and the amount or value of the consideration for the sale which is attributable to residential property, or would be so attributable if the contents of residential property were considered to be residential property, does not exceed [€190,500][6] and the instrument contains a statement certifying that the consideration for the sale is, as the case may be

    (*a*) wholly attributable to residential property, or

    (*b*) partly attributable to residential property,

and that the transaction effected by that instrument does not form part of a larger transaction or of a series of transactions in respect of which the amount or value, or the aggregate amount or value, of the consideration which is attributable to residential property, or which would be so attributable if the contents of residential property were considered to be residential property, exceeds [€190,500][6]

[3 per cent][7] of the consideration which is attributable to residential property but where the calculation results in an amount which is not a multiple of [€1][2] the amount so calculated shall be rounded [down to the nearest €][3].

(3) Where paragraphs (1) and (2) do not apply and the amount or value of the consideration for the sale which is attributable to residential property, or would be so attributable if the contents of residential property were considered to be residential property, does not exceed [€254,000][8] and the instrument contains a statement certifying that the consideration for the sale is, as the case may be

    (*a*) wholly attributable to residential property, or

    (*b*) partly attributable to residential property,

and that the transaction effected by that instrument does not form part of a larger transaction or of a series of transactions in respect of which the amount or value, or the aggregate amount or value, of the consideration which is attributable to residential property, or which would be so attributable if the contents of residential property were considered to be residential property, exceeds [€254,000][8]

[4 per cent][9] of the consideration which is attributable to residential property but where the calculation results in an amount which is not a multiple of [€1][2] the amount so calculated shall be rounded [down to the nearest €][3].

(4) Where paragraphs (1) to (3) do not apply and the amount or value of the consideration for the sale which is attributable to residential property, or would be so attributable if the contents of residential property were considered to be residential property, does not exceed [€317,500][10] and the instrument contains a statement certifying that the consideration for the sale is, as the case may be

   (*a*) wholly attributable to residential property, or

   (*b*) partly attributable to residential property,

and that the transaction effected by that instrument does riot form part of a larger transaction or of a series of transactions in respect of which the amount or value, or the aggregate amount or value, of the consideration which is attributable to residential property, or which would be so attributable if the contents of residential property were considered to be residential property, exceeds [€317,500][10]

[5 per cent][11] of the consideration which is attributable to residential property but where the calculation results in an amount which is not a multiple of [€1][2] the amount so calculated shall be rounded [down to the nearest €][3].

(5) Where paragraphs (1) to (4) do not apply and the amount or value of the consideration for the sale which is attributable to residential property, or would be so attributable if the contents of residential property were considered to be residential property, does not exceed [€381,000][12] and the instrument contains a statement certifying that the consideration for the sale is, as the case may be

   (*a*) wholly attributable to residential property, or

   (*b*) partly attributable to residential property,

and that the transaction effected by that instrument does not form part of a larger transaction or of a series of transactions in respect of which the amount or value, or the aggregate amount or value, of the consideration which is attributable to residential property, or which residential property, or which would be so attributable if the contents of residential property were considered to be residential property, exceeds [€381,000][12]

[6 per cent][13] of the consideration which is attributable to residential property but where the calculation results in an amount which is not a multiple of [€1][2] the amount so calculated shall be rounded [down to the nearest €][3].

(6) Where paragraphs (1) to (5) do not apply and the amount or value of the consideration for the sale which is attributable to residential property, or would be so attributable if the contents of residential property were considered to be residential property, does not exceed [€635,000][14] and the instrument contains a statement certifying that the consideration for the sale is, as the case may be

(*a*) wholly attributable to residential property, or

(*b*) partly attributable to residential property,

and that the transaction effected by that instrument does not form part of a larger transaction or of a series of transactions in respect of which the amount or value, or the aggregate amount or value, of the consideration which is attributable to residential property, or which would be so attributable if the contents of residential property were considered to be residential property, exceeds [€635,000][14]

[7.5 per cent][15] of the consideration which is attributable to residential property but where the calculation results in an amount which is not a multiple of [€1][2] the amount so calculated shall be rounded [down to the nearest €][3].

(6A) Where paragraphs (1) to (6) do not apply and the amount or value of the consideration for the sale is wholly or partly attributable to residential property

9 per cent of the consideration which is attributable to residential property but where the calculation results in an amount which is not a multiple of [€1][2] the amount so calculated shall be rounded [down to the nearest €][3].][16]

(7) Where the amount or value of the consideration for the sale which is attributable to property which is not residential property does not exceed [€6,350][17] and the instrument contains a statement certifying that the consideration for the sale is, as the case may be

(*a*) wholly attributable to property which is not residential property, or

(*b*) partly attributable to residential property,

and that the transaction effected by that instrument does not form part of a larger transaction or of a series of transactions in respect of which the amount or value, or the aggregate amount or value, of the consideration which is attributable to property which is not residential property exceeds [€6,350][17]:

for the consideration which is attributable to property which is not residential property	Exempt.

(8) Where paragraph (7) does not apply and the amount or value of the consideration for the sale which is attributable to property which is not residential property does not exceed [€12,700][18] and the instrument contains a statement certifying that the consideration for the sale is, as the case may be

    (*a*) wholly attributable to property which is not residential property, or

    (*b*) partly attributable to residential property,

and that the transaction effected by that instrument does not form part of a larger transaction or of a series of transactions in respect of which the amount or value, or the aggregate amount or value, of the consideration which is attributable to property which is not residential property exceeds [€12,700][18]	1 per cent of the consideration which is attributable to property which is not residential property but where the calculation results in an amount which is not a multiple of [€1][2] the amount so calculated shall be rounded [down to the nearest €][3].

(9) Where paragraphs (7) and (8) do not apply and the amount or value of the consideration for the sale which is attributable to property which is not residential property does not exceed [€19,050][19] and the instrument contains a statement certifying that the consideration for the sale is, as the case may be

    (*a*) wholly attributable to property which is not residential property, or

    (*b*) partly attributable to residential property,

and that the transaction effected by that instrument does not form part of a larger transaction or of a series of transactions in respect of which the amount or value, or the aggregate amount or value, of the consideration which is attributable to property which is not residential property exceeds [€19,050][19]	2 per cent of the consideration which is attributable to property which is not residential property but where the calculation results in an amount which is not a multiple of [€1][2] the amount so calculated shall be rounded [down to the nearest €][3].

(10) Where paragraphs (7) to (9) do not apply and the amount or value of the consideration for the sale which is attributable to property which is not residential property does not exceed [€31,750][20] and the instrument contains a statement certifying that the consideration for the sale is, as the case may be

   (*a*) wholly attributable to property which is not residential property, or

   (*b*) partly attributable to residential property,

and that the transaction effected by that instrument does not form part of a larger transaction or of a series of transactions in respect of which the amount or value, or the aggregate amount or value, of the consideration which is attributable to property which is not residential property exceeds [€31,750][20]

3 per cent of the consideration which is attributable to property which is not residential property but where the calculation results in an amount which is not a multiple of [€1][2] the amount so calculated shall be rounded [down to the nearest €][3].

(11) Where paragraphs (7) to (10) do not apply and the amount or value of the consideration for the sale which is attributable to property which is not residential property does not exceed [€63,500][21] and the instrument contains a statement certifying that the consideration for the sale is, as the case may be

   (*a*) wholly attributable to property which is not residential property, or

   (*b*) partly attributable to residential property,

and that the transaction effected by that instrument does not form part of a larger transaction or of a series of transactions in respect of which the amount or value, or the aggregate amount or value, of the consideration which is attributable to property which is not residential property exceeds [€63,500][21]

4 per cent of the consideration which is attributable to property which is not residential property but where the calculation results in an amount which is not a multiple of [€1][2] the amount so calculated shall be rounded [down to the nearest €][3].

(12) Where paragraphs (7) to (11) do not apply and the amount or value of the consideration for the sale which is attributable to property which is not residential property does not exceed [€76,200][22] and the instrument contains a statement certifying that the consideration for the sale is, as the case may be

   (*a*) wholly attributable to property which is not residential property, or

   (*b*) partly attributable to residential property,

and that the transaction effected by that instrument does not form part of a larger transaction or of a series of transactions in respect of which the amount or value, or the aggregate amount or value, of the consideration which is attributable to property which is not residential property exceeds [€76,200][22]

5 per cent of the consideration which is attributable to property which is not residential property but where the calculation results in an amount which is not a multiple of [€1][2] the amount so calculated shall be rounded [down to the nearest €][3].

(13) Where paragraphs (7) to (12) do not apply and the instrument contains a statement certifying that the consideration for the sale is, as the case may be

   (*a*) wholly attributable to property which is not residential property, or

   (*b*) partly attributable to residential property

6 per cent of the consideration which is attributable to property which is not residential property but where the calculation results in an amount which is not a multiple of [€1][2] the amount so calculated shall be rounded [down to the nearest €][3].

(14) Where paragraphs (7) to (13) do not apply and the amount or value of the consideration for the sale is wholly or partly attributable to property which is not residential property

9 per cnt of the consideration which is attributable to property which is not residential property but where the calculation results in an amount which is not a multiple of [€1]² the amount so calculated shall be rounded [down to the nearest €]³.

[(15) Where in the case of a conveyance or transfer on sale or in the case of a conveyance or transfer operating as a voluntary disposition inter vivos the instrument contains a certificate by the party to whom the property is being conveyed or transferred to the effect that the person becoming entitled to the entire beneficial interest in the property (or, where more than one person becomes entitled to a beneficial interest in the property, each of them) is related to the person or each of the persons immediately theretofore entitled to the entire beneficial interest in the property in one or other of the following ways, that is, as a lineal descendant, parent, grandparent, step-parent, husband or wife, brother or sister of a parent or brother or sister, or lineal descendant of a parent, husband or wife or brother or sister

a duty of an amount equal to one-half of the ad valorem stamp duty which, but for the provisions of this paragraph, would be chargeable under this heading but where the calculation results in an amount which is not a multiple of [€1]² the amount so calculated shall be rounded [down to the nearest €]³.]²³

CONVEYANCE or TRANSFER by way of security of any property, or of any security.

   See MORTGAGE, etc.

CONVEYANCE or TRANSFER of any kind not already described in this Schedule.

   where such instrument relates to

(a) immovable property situated in the State, or any right over or interest in such property, or

(b) the stocks or marketable securities of a company having a register in the State.

[€12.50]²⁴

Exemption.

Instrument which contains a statement certifying that the instrument is a conveyance or transfer on any occasion, not being a sale or mortgage.

COUNTERPART.

    See DUPLICATE.

COVENANT for securing the payment or repayment of money, or the transfer or retransfer of stock.

    See MORTGAGE, etc.

COVENANT in relation to any annuity on the original creation and sale of that annuity.

    See CONVEYANCE or TRANSFER on sale.

DEFEAZANCE. Instrument of defeazance of any conveyance, transfer or disposition, apparently absolute, but intended only as a security for money or stock.

    See MORTGAGE, etc.

DEPOSIT of title deeds.

    See MORTGAGE, etc.

DRAFT for money.

    See BILL OF EXCHANGE.

DUPLICATE or COUNTERPART of any instrument chargeable with any duty.

Where such duty does not amount to [€12.50][25]	The same duty as the original instrument.
In any other case	[€12.50][25].

EQUITABLE MORTGAGE.

    See MORTGAGE, etc.

EXCHANGE - instruments effecting.

In the case specified in section 37, see that section.

In any other case	[€12.50][26].

Exemption

Instrument which contains a statement certifying that the instrument is an instrument effecting an exchange which is not an exchange which is specified in section 37.

FURTHER CHARGE or FURTHER SECURITY.

    See MORTGAGE, etc.

INSURANCE.

    See POLICY.

LEASE.

(1) For any indefinite term or any term not exceeding 35 years of any dwellinghouse, part of a dwellinghouse, or apartment at a rent not exceeding [€19,050][27] per annum	Exempt.
(2) For any definite term less than a year of any lands, tenements or heritable subjects	The same duty as a lease for a year at the rent reserved for the definite term.

(3) For any other definite term or for any indefinite term of any lands, tenements, or heritable subjects

[(*a*) where the consideration, or any part of the consideration (other than rent), moving either to the lessor or to any other person, consists of any money, stock or security, and

    (i) the amount or value of such consideration which is attributable to residential property, or would be so attributable if the contents of residential property were considered to be residential property, does not exceed [€127,000][28] and the lease contains a statement certifying that the consideration (other than rent) for the lease is, as the case may be

        (I) wholly attributable to residential property, or

        (II) partly attributable to residential property,

and that the transaction effected by that instrument does not form part of a larger transaction or of a series of transactions in respect of which the amount or value, or the aggregate amount or value, of the consideration (other than rent) which is attributable to residential property, or which would be so attributable if the contents of residential property were considered to be residential property, [exceeds €127,000: for the consideration which is attributable to residential property

                                          Exempt.][29]

    (ii) the amount or value of such consideration which is attributable to residential property, or would be so attributable if the contents of residential property were considered to be residential property, does not exceed [€190,500][30] and the lease contains a statement certifying that the consideration (other than rent) for the lease is, as the case may be

        (I) wholly attributable to residential property, or

        (II) partly attributable to residential property,

and that the transaction effected by that instrument does not form part of a larger transaction or of a series of transactions in respect of which the amount or value, or the aggregate amount or value, of the consideration (other than rent) which is attributable to residential property, or which would be so attributable if the contents of residential property were considered to be residential property, exceeds [€190,500][30] and clause (i) does not apply

[3 per cent][31] of the consideration which is attributable to residential property but where the calculation results in an amount which is not a multiple of [€1][2] the amount so calculated shall be rounded [down to the nearest €][3].

(iii) the amount or value of such consideration which is attributable to residential property. or would be so attributable if the contents of residential property were considered to be residential property, does riot exceed [€254,000][32] and the lease contains a statement certifying that the consideration (other than rent) for the lease is, as the case may be

   (I) wholly attributable to residential property, or

   (II) partly attributable to residential property,

and that the transaction effected by that instrument does not form part of a larger transaction or of a series of transactions in respect of which the amount or value, or the aggregate amount or value, of the consideration (other than rent) which is attributable to residential property, or which would be so attributable if the contents of residential property were considered to be residential property, exceeds [€254,000][32] and clauses (i) and (ii) do not apply

[4 per cent][33] of the consideration which is attributable to residential property but where the calculation results in an amount which is not a multiple of [€1][2] the amount so calculated shall be rounded [down to the nearest €][3].

(iv) the amount or value of such consideration which is attributable to residential property, or would be so attributable if the contents of residential property were considered to be residential property, does not exceed [€317,500][34] and the lease contains a statement certifying that the consideration (other than rent) for the lease is, as the case may be

   (I) wholly attributable to residential property, or

   (II) partly attributable to residential property,

and that the transaction effected by that instrument does not form part of a larger transaction or of a series of transactions in respect of which the amount or value, or the aggregate amount or value, of the consideration (other than rent) which is attributable to residential property, or which would be so attributable if the contents of residential property were considered to be residential property, exceeds [€317,500][34] and clauses (i) to (iii) do not apply

[5 per cent][35] of the consideration which is attributable to residential property but where the calculation results in an amount which is not a multiple of [€1][2] the amount so calculated shall be rounded [down to the nearest €][3].

(v) the amount or value of such consideration which is attributable to residential property, or would be so attributable if the contents of residential property were considered to be residential property, does not exceed [€381,000][36] and the lease contains a statement certifying that the consideration (other than rent) for the lease is, as the case may be

    (I) wholly attributable to residential property, or

    (II) partly attributable to residential property,

and that the transaction effected by that instrument does not form part of a larger transaction or of a series of transactions in respect of which the amount or value, or the aggregate amount or value, of the consideration (other than rent) which is attributable to residential property, or which would be so attributable if the contents of residential property were considered to be residential property, exceeds [€381,000][36] and clauses (i) to (iv) do not apply

[6 per cent][37] of the consideration which is attributable to residential property but where the calculation results in an amount which is not a multiple of [€1][2] the amount so calculated shall be rounded [down to the nearest €][3].

(vi) the amount or value of such consideration which is attributable to residential property, or would be so attributable if the contents of residential property were considered to be residential property, does not exceed [€635,000][38] and the lease contains a statement certifying that the consideration (other than rent) for the lease is, as the case may be

    (I) wholly attributable to residential property, or

    (II) partly attributable to residential property,

and that the transaction effected by that instrument does not form part of a larger transaction or of a series of transactions in respect of which the amount or value, or the aggregate amount or value, of the consideration (other than rent) which is attributable to residential property, or which would be so attributable if the contents of residential property were considered to be residential property, exceeds [€635,000][38] and clauses (i) to (v) do not apply	[7.5 per cent][39] of the consideration which is attributable to residential property but where the calculation results in an amount which is not a multiple of [€1][2] the amount so calculated shall be rounded [down to the nearest €][3].
(vii) the amount or value of such consideration is wholly or partly attributable to residential property and clauses (i) to (vi) do not apply	9 per cent of the consideration which is attributable to residential property but where the calculation results in an amount which is not a multiple of [€1][2] the amount so calculated shall be rounded [down to the nearest €][3].][40]

(*b*) where the consideration, or any part of the consideration (other than rent), moving either to the lessor or to any other person, consists of any money, stock or security, and

    (i) the amount or value of such consideration which is attributable to property which is not residential property does not exceed [€6,350][41] and the lease contains a statement certifying that the consideration for the lease is, as the case may be

        (I) wholly attributable to property which is not residential property, or

        (II) partly attributable to residential property,

    and that the transaction effected by that instrument does not form part of a larger transaction or of a series of transactions, in respect of which the amount or value, or the aggregate amount or value, of the consideration (other than rent) which is attributable to property which is not residential property exceeds [€6,350][41]:

for the consideration which is attributable to property which is not residential property

Exempt.

(ii) the amount or value of such consideration which is attributable to property which is not residential property does not exceed [€12,700]⁴² and the lease contains a statement certifying that the consideration for the lease is, as the case may be

    (I) wholly attributable to property which is not residential property, or

    (II) partly attributable to residential property,

and that the transaction effected by that instrument does not form part of a larger transaction or of a series of transactions in respect of which the amount or value, or the aggregate amount or value, of the consideration (other than rent) which is attributable to property which is not residential property exceeds [€12,700]⁴² and clause (i) does not apply

1 per cent of the consideration which is attributable to property which is not residential property but where the calculation results in an amount which is not a multiple of [€1]² the amount so calculated shall be rounded [down to the nearest €]³.

(iii) the amount or value of such consideration which is attributable to property which is not residential property does not exceed [€19,050]⁴³ and the lease contains a statement certifying that the consideration for the lease is, as the case may be

    (I) wholly attributable to property which is not residential property, or

    (II) partly attributable to residential property,

and that the transaction effected by that instrument does not form part of a larger transaction or of a series of transactions in respect of which the amount or value, or the aggregate amount or value, of the consideration (other than rent) which is attributable to property which is not residential property exceeds [€19,050]⁴³ and clauses (i) and (ii) do not apply

2 per cent of the consideration which is attributable to property which is not residential property but where the calculation results in an amount which is not a multiple of [€1]² the amount so calculated shall be rounded [down to the nearest €]³.

(iv) the amount or value of such consideration which is attributable to property which is not residential property does not exceed [€31,750]⁴⁴ and the lease contains a statement certifying that the consideration for the lease is, as the case may be

  (I) wholly attributable to property which is not residential property, or

  (II) partly attributable to residential property,

and that the transaction effected by that instrument does not form part of a larger transaction or of a series of transactions in respect of which the amount or value, or the aggregate amount or value, of the consideration (other than rent) which is attributable to property which is not residential property exceeds [€31,750]⁴⁴ and clauses (i) to (iii) do not apply

3 per cent of the consideration which is attributable to property which is not residential property but where the calculation results in an amount which is not a multiple of [€1]² the amount so calculated shall be rounded [down to the nearest €]³.

(v) the amount or value of such consideration which is attributable to property which is not residential property does not exceed [€63,500]⁴⁵ and the lease contains a statement certifying that the consideration for the lease is, as the case may be

  (I) wholly attributable to property which is not residential property, or

  (II) partly attributable to residential property,

and that the transaction effected by that instrument does not form part of a larger transaction or of a series of transactions in respect of which the amount or value, or the aggregate amount or value, of the consideration (other than rent) which is attributable to property which is not residential property exceeds [€63,500][45] and clauses (i) to (iv) do not apply

4 per cent of the consideration which is attributable to property which is not residential property but where the calculation results in an amount which is not a multiple of [€1][2] the amount so calculated shall be rounded [down to the nearest €][3].

(vi) the amount or value of such consideration which is attributable to property which is not residential property does not exceed [€76,200][46] and the lease contains a statement certifying that the consideration for the lease is, as the case may be

(I) wholly attributable to proper which is not residential property, or

(II) partly attributable to residential property,

and that the transaction effected by that instrument does not form part of a larger transaction or of a series of transactions in respect of which the amount or value, or the aggregate amount or value, of the consideration (other than rent) which is attributable to property which is not residential property exceeds [€76,200][46] and clauses (i) to (v) do not apply

5 per cent of the consideration which is attributable to property which is not residential property but where the calculation results in an amount which is not a multiple of [€1][2] the amount so calculated shall be rounded [down to the nearest €][3].

(vii) the instrument contains a statement certifying that the consideration for the lease is, as the case may be

(I) wholly attributable to property which is not residential property, or

(II) partly attributable to residential property,

and clauses (i) to (vi) do not apply

6 per cent of the consideration which is attributable to property which is not residential property but where the calculation results in an amount which is not a multiple of [€1]² the amount so calculated shall be rounded [down to the nearest €]³.

(viii) the amount or value of such consideration is wholly or partly attributable to property which is not residential property and clauses (i) to (vii) do not apply

9 per cent of the consideration which is attributable to property which is not residential property but where the calculation results in an amount which is not a multiple of [€1]² the amount so calculated shall be rounded [down to the nearest €]³.

(c) where the consideration or any part of the consideration is any rent, in respect of such consideration, whether reserved as a yearly rent or otherwise:

(i) if the term does not exceed 35 years or is indefinite

1 per cent of the average annual rent but where the calculation results in an amount which is not a multiple of [€1]² the amount so calculated shall be rounded [down to the nearest €]³.

(ii) if the term exceeds 35 years but does not exceed 100 years

	6 per cent of the average annual rent but where the calculation results in an amount which is not a multiple of [€1]^2 the amount so calculated shall be rounded [down to the nearest €]^3.
(iii) if the term exceeds 100 years	12 per cent of the average annual rent but where the calculation results in an amount which is not a multiple of [€1]^2 the amount so calculated shall be rounded [down to the nearest €]^3.
(4) Lease made subsequently to, and in conformity with, an agreement duly stamped under the provisions of section 50	[€12.50]^{47}
(5) Of any other kind not already described under this heading which relates to immovable property situated in the State or to any right over or interest in such property	[€12.50]^{47}

LETTER OF CREDIT.

See BILL OF EXCHANGE.

MORTGAGE, BOND, DEBENTURE, COVENANT (except a marketable security) which is a security for the payment or repayment of money which is a charge or incumbrance on property situated in the State other than shares in stocks or funds of the Government or the Oireachtas.

(1) Being the only or principal or primary security (other than an equitable mortgage):	
where the amount secured does not exceed [€254,000]^{48}	Exempt.
where the amount secured exceeds [€254,000]^{48}	0. 1 percent of the amount secured and where the calculation results in an amount which is not a multiple of [€1]^2 the amount so calculated shall be rounded [down to the nearest €]^3 but in no case shall the duty so charged exceed [€630]^{49}.

(2) Being a collateral, or auxiliary, or additional, or substituted security (other than an equitable mortgage), or by way of further assurance for the above-mentioned purpose where the principal or primary security is not chargeable to duty or is duly stamped:

where the amount secured does not exceed [€254,000][48]

Exempt.

where the amount secured exceeds [€254,000][48]

[€12.50][38].

(3) Being an equitable mortgage:

where the amount secured does not exceed [€254,000][48]

Exempt

where the amount secured exceeds [€254,000][48]

0.05 per cent of the amount secured and where the calculation results in an amount which is not a multiple of [€1][2] the amount so calculated shall be rounded [down to the nearest €][3] but in no case shall the duty so charged exceed [€630][49].

(4) Transfer, assignment or disposition of any such mortgage, bond, debenture, or covenant (except a marketable security) or of any money or stock secured by any such instrument or by any judgement:

where the amount secured does not exceed [€254,000][48]

Exempt.

where the amount secured exceeds [€254,000][48]

0.05 per cent of the amount transferred, assigned, or disposed, exclusive of interest which is not in arrear and where the calculation results in an amount which is not a multiple of [€1][2] the amount so calculated shall be rounded [down to the nearest €][3] but in no case shall the duty so charged exceed [€630][49].

where any further money is added to the money already secured

The same duty as a principal security for such further money.

MORTGAGE OF STOCK or MARKETABLE SECURITY.

By deed. See MORTGAGE, etc.

ORDER for the payment of money.

See BILL OF EXCHANGE.

PARTITION or DIVISION instruments effecting.

In the case specified in section 38, see that section.

...[50]

POLICY OF INSURANCE other than Life Insurance where the risk
to which the policy relates is located in the State.

Where there is one premium only and the amount of that premium [€1][52].
equals or exceeds [€20][51] or, where there is more than one premium
and the total amount payable in respect of that premium in any
period of 12 months equals or exceeds [€20][51]

PROMISSORY NOTE.

See BILL OF EXCHANGE.

RELEASE or RENUNCIATION of any property, or of any right or
interest in any property.

On a sale.

See CONVEYANCE or TRANSFER on sale.

In any other case   [€12.50][53].

Exemption

Instrument which contains a statement certifying that the instrument is
a release or renunciation of property, or of a right or interest in property,
which is not a release or renunciation on a sale.

SHARE WARRANT issued under the provisions of the Companies
Act, 1963, and STOCK CERTIFICATE to bearer, and any instrument to
bearer issued by or on behalf of any company or body of persons
formed or established in the State and having a like effect as such a
share warrant or such a stock certificate to bearer, expressed in the
currency of the State

A duty of an amount
equal to 3 times the
amount of the ad
valorem stamp duty
which would be
chargeable on a deed
transferring the share
or shares or stock
specified in the
warrant or certificate
or instrument having a
like effect as such a
warrant or certificate
if the consideration for
the transfer were the
nominal value of such
share or shares or
stock.

SURRENDER of any property, or of any right or interest in any
property.

On a sale.

See CONVEYANCE or TRANSFER.

In any other case   [€12.50][54].

Exemption

Instrument which contains a statement certifying that the instrument is
a surrender of property, or of a right or interest in property, not being a
surrender on a sale.

TRANSFER.

See CONVEYANCE or TRANSFER.

Amendments

[1]   Substituted by FA 2001 s 240 and Sch 5 Pt 6 with effect from 1 January 2002; previously "7p".

[2]   Substituted by FA 2001 s 240 and Sch 5 Pt 6 with effect from 1 January 2002; previously "£1".

[3]   Substituted by FA 2001 s 240 and Sch 5 Pt 6 with effect from 1 January 2002; previously "up to the nearest
         £".

[4]   Substituted by FA 2001 s 240 and Sch 5 Pt 6 with effect from 1 January 2002; previously "£100,000".

[5]   Substituted by FA 2002 s 114(1)(*a*)(i) with effect for instruments executed on or after 6 December 2001
         subject to substituting "£100,000" for "€127,000", for instruments executed on or after 6 December 2001
         and before 1 January 2002.

[6]   Substituted by FA 2001 s 240 and Sch 5 Pt 6 with effect from 1 January 2002; previously "£150,000".

[7]   Substituted by FA 2002 s 114(1)(*a*)(ii) with effect for instruments executed on or after 6 December 2001;
         previously "9 per cent".

[8]   Substituted by FA 2001 s 240 and Sch 5 Pt 6 with effect from 1 January 2002; previously "£200,000".

[9]   Substituted by FA 2002 s 114(1)(*a*)(iii) with effect for instruments executed on or after 6 December 2001;
         previously "9 per cent".

[10]   Substituted by FA 2001 s 240 and Sch 5 Pt 6 with effect from 1 January 2002; previously "£250,000".

[11]   Substituted by FA 2002 s 114(1)(*a*)(iv) with effect for instruments executed on or after 6 December 2001;
         previously "9 per cent".

[12]   Substituted by FA 2001 s 240 and Sch 5 Pt 6 with effect from 1 January 2002; previously "£300,000".

[13]   Substituted by FA 2002 s 114(1)(*a*)(v) with effect for instruments executed on or after 6 December 2001;
         previously "9 per cent".

[14]   Substituted by FA 2001 s 240 and Sch 5 Pt 6 with effect from 1 January 2002; previously "£500,000".

[15]   Substituted by FA 2002 s 114(1)(*a*)(vi) with effect for instruments executed on or after 6 December 2001;
         previously "9 per cent".

[16]   Heading "CONVEYANCE or TRANSFER on sale of any property other than stocks or marketable
         securities or a policy of insurance or a policy of life insurance" paras (1) to (6) substituted by F(No2)A
         2000 s 3(*a*) and Sch Pt 1 with effect for instruments executed on or after 15 June 2000. However, where an
         instrument executed on or before 31 January 2001 would increase the duty chargeable on the instrument
         and the instrument contains a statement certifying that the instrument was executed solely in pursuance of

         a contract which was evidenced in writing before 15 June 2000 the substitution does not apply; previously:

         (1) Where the amount or value of the consideration for the sale
         which is attributable to residential property, or would be so
         attributable if the contents of residential property were considered
         to be residential property, does not exceed £60,000 and the
         instrument contains a statement certifying that the consideration
         for the sale is, as the case may be—

         (*a*)   wholly attributable to residential property, or

         (*b*)   partly attributable to residential property,

         and that the transaction effected by that instrument does not form
         part of a larger transaction or of a series of transactions in respect
         of which the amount or value, or the aggregate amount or value, of
         the consideration which is attributable to residential property, or
         which would be so attributable if the contents of residential
         property were considered to be residential property, exceeds
         £60,000:

for the consideration which is attributable to residential property   Exempt.

(2) Where paragraph (1) does not apply and the amount or value of the consideration for the sale which is attributable to residential property, or would be so attributable if the contents of residential property were considered to be residential property, does not exceed £100,000 and the instrument contains a statement certifying that the consideration for the sale is, as the case may be—

(*a*)   wholly attributable to residential property, or

(*b*)   partly attributable to residential property,

and that the transaction effected by that instrument does not form part of a larger transaction or of a series of transactions in respect of which the amount or value, or the aggregate amount or value, of the consideration which is attributable to residential property, or which would be so attributable if the contents of residential property were considered to be residential property, exceeds £100,000

3 per cent of the consideration which is attributable to residential property but where the calculation results in an amount which is not a multiple of £1 the amount so calculated shall be rounded up to the nearest £.

(3) Where paragraphs (1) and (2) do not apply and the amount or value of the consideration for the sale which is attributable to residential property, or would be so attributable if the contents of residential property were considered to be residential property, does not exceed £170,000 and the instrument contains a statement certifying that the consideration for the sale is, as the case may be—

(*a*)   wholly attributable to residential property, or

(*b*)   partly attributable to residential property,

and that the transaction effected by that instrument does not form part of a larger transaction or of a series of transactions in respect of which the amount or value, or the aggregate amount or value, of the consideration which is attributable to residential property, or which would be so attributable if the contents of residential property were considered to be residential property, exceeds £170,000

4 per cent of the consideration which is attributable to residential property but where the calculation results in an amount which is not a multiple of £1 the amount so calculated shall be rounded up to the nearest £.

(4) Where paragraphs (1) to (3) do not apply and the amount or value of the consideration for the sale which is attributable to residential property, or would be so attributable if the contents of residential property were considered to be residential property, does not exceed £250,000 and the instrument contains a statement certifying that the consideration for the sale is, as the case may be—

(*a*)   wholly attributable to residential property, or

(*b*)   partly attributable to residential property,

and that the transaction effected by that instrument does not form part of a larger transaction or of a series of transactions in respect of which the amount or value, or the aggregate amount or value, of the consideration which is attributable to residential property, or which would be so attributable if the contents of residential property were considered to be residential property, exceeds £250,000

5 per cent of the consideration which is attributable to residential property but where the calculation results in an amount which is not a multiple of £1 the amount so calculated shall be rounded up to the nearest £.

(5) Where paragraphs (1) to (4) do not apply and the amount or value of the consideration for the sale which is attributable to residential property, or would be so attributable if the contents of residential property were considered to be residential property, does not exceed £500,000 and the instrument contains a statement certifying that the consideration for the sale is, as the case may be—

(a) wholly attributable to residential property, or

(b) partly attributable to residential property,

and that the transaction effected by that instrument does not form part of a larger transaction or of a series of transactions in respect of which the amount or value, or the aggregate amount or value, of the consideration which is attributable to residential property, or which would be so attributable if the contents of residential property were considered to be residential property, exceeds £500,000

7 per cent of the consideration which is attributable to residential property but where the calculation results in an amount which is not a multiple of £1 the amount so calculated shall be rounded up to the nearest £.

(6) Where paragraphs (1) to (5) do not apply and the amount or value of the consideration for the sale is wholly or partly attributable to residential property

9 per cent of the consideration which is attributable to residential property but where the calculation results in an amount which is not a multiple of £1 the amount so calculated shall be rounded up to the nearest £.

17   Substituted by FA 2001 s 240 and Sch 5 Pt 6 with effect from 1 January 2002; previously "£5,000".

18   Substituted by FA 2001 s 240 and Sch 5 Pt 6 with effect from 1 January 2002; previously "£10,000".

19   Substituted by FA 2001 s 240 and Sch 5 Pt 6 with effect from 1 January 2002; previously "£15,000".

20   Substituted by FA 2001 s 240 and Sch 5 Pt 6 with effect from 1 January 2002; previously "£25,000".

21   Substituted by FA 2001 s 240 and Sch 5 Pt 6 with effect from 1 January 2002; previously "£50,000".

22   Substituted by FA 2001 s 240 and Sch 5 Pt 6 with effect from 1 January 2002; previously "£60,000".

23   Para (15) substituted by FA 2000 s 133(1)(a) in relation to instruments executed on or after 10 February 2000.

24   Substituted by FA 2001 s 240 and Sch 5 Pt 6 with effect from 1 January 2002; previously "£10".

25   Substituted by FA 2001 s 240 and Sch 5 Pt 6 with effect from 1 January 2002; previously "£10".

26   Substituted by FA 2001 s 240 and Sch 5 Pt 6 with effect from 1 January 2002; previously "£10".

27 Substituted by FA 2001 s 240 and Sch 5 Pt 6 with effect from 1 January 2002; previously "£15,000" (FA 2000 s 133(1)(*b*)).

28 Substituted by FA 2001 s 240 and Sch 5 Pt 6 with effect from 1 January 2002; previously "£100,000".

29 Substituted by FA 2002 s 114(1)(*b*)(i) with effect for instruments executed on or after 6 December 2001 subject to substituting "£100,000" for "€127,000", for instruments executed on or after 6 December 2001 and before 1 January 2002.

30 Substituted by FA 2001 s 240 and Sch 5 Pt 6 with effect from 1 January 2002; previously "£150,000".

31 Substituted by FA 2002 s 114(1)(*b*)(ii) with effect for instruments executed on or after 6 December 2001; previously "9 per cent".

32 Substituted by FA 2001 s 240 and Sch 5 Pt 6 with effect from 1 January 2002; previously "£200,000".

31 Substituted by FA 2002 s 114(1)(*b*)(ii) with effect for instruments executed on or after 6 December 2001; previously "9 per cent".

32 Substituted by FA 2001 s 240 and Sch 5 Pt 6 with effect from 1 January 2002; previously "£250,000".

33 Substituted by FA 2002 s 114(1)(*b*)(iii) with effect for instruments executed on or after 6 December 2001; previously "9 per cent".

34 Substituted by FA 2001 s 240 and Sch 5 Pt 6 with effect from 1 January 2002; previously "£300,000".

33 Substituted by FA 2002 s 114(1)(*b*)(iv) with effect for instruments executed on or after 6 December 2001; previously "9 per cent".

34 Substituted by FA 2001 s 240 and Sch 5 Pt 6 with effect from 1 January 2002; previously "£500,000".

35 Substituted by FA 2002 s 114(1)(*b*)(v) with effect for instruments executed on or after 6 December 2001; previously "9 per cent".

36 Heading of "Lease" para (3)(*a*) substituted by F(No2)A 2000 s 3(*b*) and Sch Pt 2 with effect for instruments executed on or after 15 June 2000, however, where an instrument executed on or before 31 January 2001 would increase the duty chargeable on the instrument and the instrument contains a statement certifying that the instrument was executed solely in pursuance of a contract which was evidenced in writing before 15 June 2000 the substitution does not apply; previously:

(*a*) where the consideration, or any part of the consideration (other than rent), moving either to the lessor or to any other person, consists of any money, stock or security, and—

 (i) the amount or value of such consideration which is attributable to residential property, or would be so attributable if the contents of residential property were considered to be residential property, does not exceed £60,000 and the lease contains a statement certifying that the consideration (other than rent) for the lease is, as the case may be—

  (I) wholly attributable to residential property, or

  (II) partly attributable to residential property,

 and that the transaction effected by that instrument does not form part of a larger transaction or of a series of transactions, in respect of which the amount or value, or the aggregate amount or value, of the consideration (other than rent) which is attributable to residential property, or which would be so attributable if the contents of residential property were considered to be residential property, exceeds £60,000:

 for the consideration which is attributable to residential property

 (ii) the amount or value of such consideration which is attributable to residential property, or would be so attributable if the contents of residential property were considered to be residential property, does not exceed £100,000 and the lease contains a statement certifying that the consideration (other than rent) for the lease is, as the case may be—

  (I) wholly attributable to residential property, or

(II) partly attributable to residential property,

and that the transaction effected by that instrument does not form part of a larger transaction or of a series of transactions in respect of which the amount or value, or the aggregate amount or value, of the consideration (other than rent) which is attributable to residential property, or which would be so attributable if the contents of residential property were considered to be residential property, exceeds £100,000 and clause (i) does not apply

3 per cent of the consideration which is attributable to residential property but where the calculation results in an amount which is not a multiple of £ 1 the amount so calculated shall be rounded up to the nearest £.

(iii) the amount or value of such consideration which is attributable to residential property, or would be so attributable if the contents of residential property were considered to be residential property, does not exceed £170,000 and the lease contains a statement certifying that the consideration (other than rent) for the lease is, as the case may be—

(I) wholly attributable to residential property, or

(II) partly attributable to residential property,

and that the transaction effected by that instrument does not form part of a larger transaction or of a series of transactions in respect of which the amount or value, or the aggregate amount or value, of the consideration (other than rent) which is attributable to residential property, or which would be so attributable if the contents of residential property were considered to be residential property, exceeds £170,000 and clauses (i) and (ii) do not apply

4 per cent of the consideration which is attributable to residential property but where the calculation results in an amount which is not a multiple of £1 the amount so calculated shall be rounded up to the nearest £.

(iv) the amount or value of such consideration which is attributable to residential property, or would be so attributable if the contents of residential property were considered to be residential property, does not exceed £250,000 and the lease contains a statement certifying that the consideration (other than rent) for the lease is, as the case may be—

(I) wholly attributable to residential property, or

(II) partly attributable to residential property,

and that the transaction effected by that instrument does not form part of a larger transaction or of a series of transactions in respect of which the amount or value, or the aggregate amount or value, of the consideration (other than rent) which is attributable to residential property, or which would be so attributable if the contents of residential property were considered to be residential property, exceeds £250,000 and clauses (i) to (iii) do not apply

5 per cent of the consideration which is attributable to residential property but where the calculation results in an amount which is not a multiple of £1 the amount so calculated shall be rounded up to the nearest £.

(v) the amount or value of such consideration which is attributable to residential property, or would be so attributable if the contents of residential property were considered to be residential property, does not exceed £500,000 and the lease contains a statement certifying that the consideration (other than rent) for the lease is, as the case may be—

(I) wholly attributable to residential property, or

(II) partly attributable to residential property,

and that the transaction effected by that instrument does not form part of a larger transaction or of a series of transactions in respect of which the amount or value, or the aggregate amount or value, of the consideration (other than rent) which is attributable to residential property, or which would be so attributable if the contents of residential property were considered to be residential property, exceeds £500,000 and clauses (i) to (iv) do not apply

7 per cent of the consideration which is attributable to residential property but where the calculation results in an amount which is not a multiple of £1 the amount so calculated shall be rounded up to the nearest £.

(vi) the amount or value of such consideration is wholly or partly attributable to residential property and clauses (i) to (v) do not apply

9 per cent of the consideration which is attributable to residential property but where the calculation results in an amount which is not a multiple of £1 the amount so calculated shall be rounded up to the nearest £.

---

[40] Substituted by FA 2002 s 114(1)(*b*)(vi) with effect for instruments executed on or after 6 December 2001; previously "9 per cent".

[41] Substituted by FA 2001 s 240 and Sch 5 Pt 6 with effect from 1 January 2002; previously "£5,000".

[42] Substituted by FA 2001 s 240 and Sch 5 Pt 6 with effect from 1 January 2002; previously "£10,000".

[43] Substituted by FA 2001 s 240 and Sch 5 Pt 6 with effect from 1 January 2002; previously "£15,000".

[44] Substituted by FA 2001 s 240 and Sch 5 Pt 6 with effect from 1 January 2002; previously "£25,000".

[45] Substituted by FA 2001 s 240 and Sch 5 Pt 6 with effect from 1 January 2002; previously "£50,000".

[46] Substituted by FA 2001 s 240 and Sch 5 Pt 6 with effect from 1 January 2002; previously "£60,000".

[47] Substituted by FA 2001 s 240 and Sch 5 Pt 6 with effect from 1 January 2002; previously "£10".

[48] Substituted by FA 2001 s 213(1)(*b*) with effect in relation to instruments executed on or after 1 January 2002; previously "£20,000" (FA 2001 s 213(1)(*a*)).

[49] Substituted by FA 2001 s 240 and Sch 5 Pt 6 with effect from 1 January 2002; previously "£500".

[50] Heading "POLICY OF LIFE INSURANCE made for a period exceeding 2 years where the risk to which the policy relates is located in the State" deleted by FA 2001 s 213(1)(*c*) with effect in relation to instruments executed on or after 1 January 2001.

[51] Substituted by FA 2001 s 240 and Sch 5 Pt 6 with effect from 1 January 2002; previously "£15".

[52] Substituted by FA 2001 s 240 and Sch 5 Pt 6 with effect from 1 January 2002; previously "£1".

[53] Substituted by FA 2001 s 240 and Sch 5 Pt 6 with effect from 1 January 2002; previously "£10".

[54] Substituted by FA 2001 s 240 and Sch 5 Pt 6 with effect from 1 January 2002; previously "£10".

Notes

FA 2002 ss 113 and 114 give effect to the re-alignment of the investor stamp duty rates for transfers of new and second-hand residential property with those for owner-occupiers (other than first-time buyers) purchasing second-hand residential property. The change is effective for transfers executed on or after 6 December 2001.

Cross-references

SDCA 1999 ss 92A and 92B.

Former enactment

SA 1891 Sch 1; FA 1899 s 5(1).

SCHEDULE 2

QUALIFICATIONS FOR APPLYING FOR RELIEF FROM STAMP DUTY IN RESPECT OF TRANSFERS TO YOUNG TRAINED FARMERS

1. Qualifications awarded by Teagasc:

   (*a*) Certificate in Farming;

   (*b*) Diploma in Commercial Horticulture;

   (*c*) Diploma in Amenity Horticulture;

   (*d*) Diploma in Pig Production;

   (*e*) Diploma in Poultry Production.

2. Qualifications awarded by the Farm Apprenticeship Board:

   (*a*) Certificate in Farm Management;

   (*b*) Certificate in Farm Husbandry;

   (*c*) Trainee Farmer Certificate.

3. Qualifications awarded by a third-level institution:

   (*a*) Degree in Agricultural Science awarded by the National University of Ireland through University College Dublin, National University of Ireland, Dublin;

   (*b*) Degree in Horticultural Science awarded by the National University of Ireland through University College Dublin, National University of Ireland, Dublin;

   (*c*) Degree in Veterinary Science awarded by the National University of Ireland through University College Dublin, National University of Ireland, Dublin:

   (*d*) Degree in Rural Science awarded by the National University of Ireland through University College Cork-National University of Ireland, Cork or by the University of Limerick;

   (*e*) Diploma in Rural Science awarded by the National University of Ireland through University College Cork-National University of Ireland, Cork;

    (*f*) Degree in Dairy Science awarded by the National University of Ireland through University College Cork - National University of Ireland, Cork;

    (*g*) Diploma in Dairy Science awarded by the National University of Ireland through University College-Cork National University of Ireland, Cork.

4.Certificates awarded by the National Council for Educational Awards:

    (*a*) National Certificate in Agricultural Science studied through Kildalton Agricultural College and Waterford Institute of Technology;

    (*b*) National Certificate in Business Studies (Agri-business) studied through the Franciscan Brothers Agricultural College, Mountbellew, and Galway-Mayo Institute of Technology.

Former enactment

FA 1994 s 112, Sch 6.

SCHEDULE 3
ENACTMENTS REPEALED OR REVOKED

[Section 160]

PART 1
ACTS REPEALED

Session and Chapter or Year and Number	Short Title	Extent of Repeal
(1)	(2)	(3)
54 & 55 Vict., c.38.	Stamp Duties Management Act, 1891.	The whole Act, in so far as it is unrepealed.
54 & 55 Vict., c.39.	Stamp Act, 1891.	The whole Act, in so far as it is unrepealed.
57 & 58 Vict., c.30.	Finance Act, 1894.	Section 39.
58 Vict., c. 16.	Finance Act, 1895.	Section 16 and the Schedule.
60 & 61 Vict., c.24.	Finance Act, 1897.	Section 8.
61 & 62 Vict., c.10.	Finance Act, 1898.	Sections 5 and 6.
61 & 62 Vict., c.46.	Revenue Act, 1898.	Sections 7, 10 and 13.
62 & 63 Vict., c.9.	Finance Act, 1899.	Sections 5, 6 and 14.
63 Vict., c. 7.	Finance Act, 1900.	Section 10.
3 Edw. 7, c.46.	Revenue Act, 1903.	Section 9.
9 Edw. 7, c.43.	Revenue Act, 1909.	Sections 7 and 8.
10 Edw. 7, c.8.	Finance (1909-10) Act, 1910.	Sections 4 and 74.
10 & 11 Geo. 5, c. 18.	Finance Act, 1920.	Sections 37 and 43.
12 & 13 Geo. 5, c. 17.	Finance Act, 1922.	Sections 46 and 47.

No 27 of 1924.	Finance Act, 1924.	Section 38, in so far as it relates to stamp duties.
No 35 of 1926.	Finance Act, 1926.	Section 39, in so far as it relates to stamp duties.
No 5 of 1929.	Finance (Customs and Stamp Duties) Act, 1929.	Section 5.
No 32 of 1929.	Finance Act, 1929.	Section 36.
No 31 of 1931.	Finance Act, 1931.	Section 32.
No 20 of 1932.	Finance Act, 1932.	Section 50.
No 15 of 1933.	Finance Act, 1933.	Sections 40, 41 and 43.
No 31 of 1934.	Finance Act, 1934.	Section 34.
No 7 of 1935.	Finance (Miscellaneous Provisions) Act, 1935.	Section 6 and Part II of the Schedule.
No 31 of 1936.	Finance Act, 1936.	Section 25.
No 14 of 1942.	Finance Act, 1942.	Section 21.
No 16 of 1943.	Finance Act, 1943.	Sections 14 to 16.
No 13 of 1949.	Finance Act, 1949.	Section 24.
No 14 of 1952.	Finance Act, 1952.	Section 19.
No 22 of 1954.	Finance Act, 1954.	Section 23.
No 36 of 1954.	Solicitors Act, 1954.	Section 72.
No 13 of 1955.	Finance Act, 1955.	Section 16.
No 25 of 1958.	Finance Act, 1958.	Sections 59 and 60.
No 18 of 1959.	Finance Act, 1959.	Sections 75(4) and 76.
No 19 of 1960.	Finance Act, 1960.	Section 36.
No 23 of 1961.	Finance Act, 1961.	Sections 29 and 30.
No 15 of 1962.	Finance Act, 1962.	Sections 17 and 18.
No 23 of 1963.	Finance Act, 1963.	Sections 40, 41 and 43.
No 22 of 1965.	Finance Act, 1965.	Section 31.
No 17 of 1967.	Finance Act, 1967.	Section 20.
No 21 of 1969.	Finance Act, 1969.	Sections 49 and 50.
No 14 of 1970.	Finance Act, 1970.	Sections 40 to 47 and the First Schedule.
No 23 of 1971.	Finance Act, 1971.	Sections 43 and 44.
No 19 of 1972.	Finance Act, 1972.	Section 35.
No 22 of 1972.	Value-Added Tax Act, 1972.	Section 38(4).

No 19 of 1973.	Finance Act, 1973.	Sections 62 to 75 and section 92(6).
No 27 of 1974.	Finance Act, 1974.	Sections 81 to 83.
No 6 of 1975.	Finance Act, 1975.	Sections 48 and 49 and the Fourth Schedule.
No 16 of 1976.	Finance Act, 1976.	Sections 47 and 48.
No 18 of 1977.	Finance Act, 1977.	Sections 47 and 48.
No 21 of 1978.	Finance Act, 1978.	Sections 31 to 35.
No 11 of 1979.	Finance Act, 1979.	Sections 50 to 53 and section 56.
No 14 of 1980.	Finance Act, 1980.	Sections 85 to 87.
No 16 of 1981.	Finance Act, 1981.	Sections 47 to 50.
No 28 of 1981.	Finance (No 2) Act, 1981.	Sections 16 and 17.
No 14 of 1982.	Finance Act, 1982.	Sections 91 to 96 and the Fourth Schedule.
No 15 of 1983.	Finance Act, 1983.	Sections 90 to 93.
No 24 of 1983.	Postal and Telecommunications Services Act, 1983.	Section 5(4)(*c*).
No 9 of 1984.	Finance Act, 1984.	Sections 97 to 103.
No 10 of 1985.	Finance Act, 1985.	Sections 55 to 57.
No 13 of 1986.	Finance Act, 1986.	Sections 92 to 99 and section 101.
No 10 of 1987.	Finance Act, 1987.	Sections 48 and 49.
No 12 of 1988.	Finance Act, 1988.	Sections 64 and 65.
No 10 of 1989.	Finance Act, 1989.	Sections 64, 66, 67, 68, 71 and 72.
No 10 of 1990.	Finance Act, 1990.	Sections 108 to 116, sections 118 and 120 and the Ninth Schedule.
No 13 of 1991.	Finance Act, 1991.	Sections 88 to 106, sections 108 to 111 and the Fifth Schedule.
No 9 of 1992.	Finance Act, 1992.	Sections 199 to 211, section 213, sections 215 to 217 and the Seventh Schedule.

No 28 of 1992.	Finance (No 2) Act, 1992.	Section 28.
No 13 of 1993.	Finance Act, 1993.	Sections 100 to 106.
No 13 of 1994.	Finance Act, 1994.	Sections 102 to 109, sections 111, 112 and 161(4) and the Sixth Schedule.
No 8 of 1995.	Finance Act, 1995.	Sections 142 to 150.
No 9 of 1996.	Finance Act, 1996.	Sections 101 to 111, sections 113 to 119 and the Fourth Schedule.
No 25 of 1996.	Disclosure of Certain Information for Taxation and Other Purposes Act, 1996.	Section 7.
No 31 of 1996.	Criminal Assets Bureau Act, 1996.	Section 24(3).
No 22 of 1997.	Finance Act, 1997.	Sections 115 to 130 and the Eighth Schedule.
No 3 of 1998.	Finance Act, 1998.	Sections 118 to 125 and Schedule 8.
No 15 of 1998.	Finance (No 2) Act, 1998.	Sections 5 to 14 and the Schedule.
No 2 of 1999.	Finance Act, 1999.	Sections 140 to 197 and Schedules 5 and 6.

PART 2
Statutory Instrument Revoked

Year and Number	Citation	Extent of Revocation
No 4 of 1923.	Inland Revenue (Adaptation of Taxing Acts) Order, 1923.	Paragraphs 16 and 17.

SCHEDULE 4
CONSEQUENTIAL AMENDMENTS

[Section 162]

In the enactments specified in column (1) of the following Table for the words set out or referred to in column (2) there shall be substituted the words set out in the corresponding entry in column (3).

Enactment amended (1)	Words to be replaced (2)	Words to be substituted (3)
Forgery Act, 1913: section 8(2)(*b*)	Stamp Duties Management Act, 1891 (as amended by the Finance Act, 1989)	Part 11 of the Stamp Duties Consolidation Act, 1999
section 18(1A)	Stamp Duties Management Act, 1891 (as amended by the Finance Act, 1989)	Part 11 of the Stamp Duties Consolidation Act, 1999
Electricity (Supply) Act, 1927, section 95	section fifty-nine of the Stamp Act, 1891	section 31 of the Stamp Duties Consolidation Act, 1999
Statute of Limitations, 1957, section 60	Stamp Act, 1891	Stamp Duties Consolidation Act, 1999
Companies Act, 1963: section 58(2)	Stamp Act, 1891	Stamp Duties Consolidation Act, 1999
section 58(2)	section 12	section 20
Stock Transfer Act, 1963: section 4(3)	section 74 of the Finance (1909-10) Act, 1910	section 30 of the Stamp Duties Consolidation Act, 1999
section 4(4)	subsection (4) or (5) of section 58 of the Stamp Act, 1891	subsection (1) or (2) of section 46 of the Stamp Duties Consolidation Act, 1999
Finance Act, 1980, section 78(6)	Stamp Duties Management Act, 1891	Part 11 of the Stamp Duties Consolidation Act, 1999
Housing Finance Agency Act, 1981, section 16	section 44 of the Finance Act, 1970	section 86 of the Stamp Duties Consolidation Act, 1999
	said section 44	that section 86

Postal and Telecommunications Services Act, 1983: section 5 (4) (*b*)	Stamp Act, 1891	Stamp Duties Consolidation Act, 1999
section 69(2)	sections 4, 6, 13 and 16 to 20 of the Stamp Duties Management Act, 1891	sections 139 to 144 and 147 and 149 of the Stamp Duties Consolidation Act, 1999
section 69(3)	section 16 or 17 of the Stamp Duties Management Act, 1891	section 140 or 141 of the Stamp Duties Consolidation Act, 1999
section 69(5)	section 9 of the Stamp Act, 1891	section 10(5) of the Stamp Duties Consolidation Act, 1999
section 69(8)	section 18(2) of the Stamp Duties Management Act, 1891	section 142(2) of the Stamp Duties Consolidation Act, 1999
Finance Act, 1989: section 48(1)	Stamp Duties Management Act, 1891	Part 11 of the Stamp Duties Consolidation Act, 1999
section 48(3)	Stamp Duties Management Act, 1891	Part 11 of the Stamp Duties Consolidation Act, 1999
Building Societies Act, 1989, section 118(2)	sections 67 to 75 of the Finance Act, 1973	Part 8 of the Stamp Duties Consolidation Act, 1999
Trustee Savings Banks Act, 1989, section 64	sections 67 to 75 of the Finance Act, 1973	Part 8 of the Stamp Duties Consolidation Act, 1999
Companies Act, 1990, section 208, para (*c*)	section 68 of the Finance Act, 1973	section 116 of the Stamp Duties Consolidation Act, 1999
	section 69 of the Finance Act, 1973	section 117 of the Stamp Duties Consolidation Act, 1999
Solicitors (Amendment) Act, 1994, section 72(1)	section 24 of the Stamp Duties Management Act, 1891	section 157 of the Stamp Duties Consolidation Act, 1999

Stamp Duty (Particulars to be Delivered) Regulations, 1995 (SI No 144 of 1995)	section 107 of the Finance Act, 1994 (No 13 of 1994)	section 12 of the Stamp Duties Consolidation Act, 1999
Taxes Consolidation Act, 1997:		
section 487(1)(*a*) in paragraph (iii)(II) of the definition of "accounting profit"	section 94 of the Finance Act, 1986	section 126 of the Stamp Duties Consolidation Act, 1999
section 905(2)(*c*)(iii)	section 16 of the Stamp Act, 1891	section 128 of the Stamp Duties Consolidation Act, 1999
section 1002(1)(*a*), in the definition of "the Acts"	Stamp Act, 1891	Stamp Duties Consolidation Act, 1999
section 1089(1)	section 15 of the Stamp Act, 1891, and subsections (2) and (3) of section 69 of the Finance Act, 1973	section 14 and subsections (3) and (4) of section 117 of the Stamp Duties Consolidation Act, 1999

FINANCE ACT 2000

(2000 Number 3)
(Date passed: 23 March 2000)

ARRANGEMENT OF SECTIONS

PART 4
STAMP DUTIES

AN ACT TO CHARGE AND IMPOSE CERTAIN DUTIES OF CUSTOMS AND INLAND REVENUE (INCLUDING EXCISE), TO AMEND THE LAW RELATING TO CUSTOMS AND INLAND REVENUE (INCLUDING EXCISE) AND TO MAKE FURTHER PROVISIONS IN CONNECTION WITH FINANCE.
[23rd MARCH 2000]

PART 4
STAMP DUTIES

125 Interpretation (Part 4)

In this Part **"Principal Act"** means the Stamp Duties Consolidation Act, 1999.

126 Amendment of section 81 (relief from stamp duty in respect of transfers to young trained farmers) of Principal Act

Notes

Subs (1)(*a*) substituted SDCA 1999 s 81(2) in relation to instruments executed on or after 1 January 2000.
Subs (1)(*b*) substituted SDCA 1999 s 81(6) in relation to instruments executed on or after 1 January 2000.
Subs (1)(*c*) substituted SCCA 1999 s 81(7) in relation to instruments executed on or after 1 January 2000.
Subs (1)(*d*) substituted "31 December 2002" for "31 December 1999" in SDCA 1999 s 81(9) in relation to instruments executed on or after 1 January 2000.

127 Amendment of section 86 (exemption from stamp duty in respect of certain loan stock) of Principal Act

Notes

Subs (1)(*a*) substituted "ICC Bank public limited company" for "Industrial Credit Corporation p.l.c." in SDCA 1999 s 86(*b*) in relation to transfers of loan stock executed on or after 10 February 2000.
Subs (1)(*b*) deleted "Bord Telecom Éireann" from SDCA 1999 s 86(*b*) in relation to transfers of loan stock executed where the loan stock was issued on or after 10 February 2000.

128 Amendment of section 87 (stock borrowing) of Principal Act

Notes

Subs (1)(*a*)(i) deleted SDCA 1999 s 87(1)(definitions of "stock" and "stock borrower") in relation to stock borrowing transactions entered into on or after 6 April 1999.
Subs (1)(*a*)(ii) substituted SDCA 1999 s 87(1)(definition of "stock borrowing") in relation to stock borrowing transactions entered into on or after 6 April 1999.
Subs (1)(*b*) substituted "6 months" for "3 months" in both places where it occurs in SDCA 1999 s 87(3) in relation to stock borrowing transactions entered into on or after 6 April 1999.
Subs (1)(*c*)(i) inserted ", for a period of 3 years from the date of the stock borrowing," in SDCA 1999 s 87(4) in relation to stock borrowing transactions entered into on or after 10 February 2000.
Subs (1)(*c*)(ii) deleted SDCA 1999 s 87(4)(*a*) in relation to stock borrowing transactions entered into on or after 10 February 2000.

129 Stock repo

Notes

Section 129 inserted SDCA 1999 s 87A to apply in relation to SDCA 1999 s 87A(1)-(2) to a stock transfer and a stock return in respect of such stock transfer each of which are executed on or after 6 April 1999, and in relation to SDCA 1999 s 87A(3)-(5) to a stock transfer and a stock return in respect of such stock transfer each of which are executed on or after 10 February 2000.

130 Reorganisation of undertakings for collective investment

Notes

Section 130 inserted SDCA 1999 s 88A in respect of a conveyance or transfer executed on or after 23 March 2000.

131 Amendment of section 97 (certain transfers following the dissolution of a marriage) of Principal Act

Notes

Subs (1)(*a*) deleted "or" from SDCA 1999 s 97(2)(*a*)(i) as respects an order or other determination to like effect where the order or the determination is made on or after 10 February 2000.

Subs (1)(*b*) substituted "1996, or" for "1996" in SDCA 1999 s 97(2)(*a*)(ii) as respects an order or other determination to like effect where the order or the determination is made on or after 10 February 2000.
Subs (1)(*c*) inserted SDCA 1999 s 97(2)(*a*)(iii) as respects an order or other determination to like effect where the order or the determination is made on or after 10 February 2000

132 Relief in respect of certain payments of stamp duty

Notes

Section 132 inserted SDCA 1999 s 120A in relation to transactions executed on or after 15 December 1999.

133 Amendment of Schedule 1 to Principal Act

Notes

Subs (1)(*a*) substituted SDCA 1999 Sch 1 Heading of "CONVEYANCE or TRANSFER on sale of any property other than stocks or marketable securities or a policy of insurance or a policy of life insurance" para (15) in relation to instruments executed on or after 10 February 2000.
Subs (1)(*b*) substituted "£15,000" for "£6,000" in SDCA 1999 Sch 1 Heading of "LEASE" para 1 in relation to instruments executed on or after 1 December 1999.

PART 7
MISCELLANEOUS

154 Interpretation (Part 7)

In this Part **"Principal Act"** means the Taxes Consolidation Act, 1997.

162 Amendment of section 1086 (publication of names of tax defaulters) of Principal Act

Notes

Subs (1)(*a*)(i) substituted "tax," for "tax, or" in TCA 1997 s 1086(2)(*b*) and "tax, or" for "tax." in TCA 1997 s 1086(2)(*c*)(iii) as respects fines or other penalties, as are referred to in s 1086(2)(*a*)-(*b*), which are imposed by a court, and as respects specified sums, as are referred to in s 1086(2)(*c*)-(*d*), which the Revenue Commissioners accepted, or undertook to accept, in settlement of a specified liability, on or after 23 March 2000.
Subs (1)(*a*)(ii) inserted TCA 1997 s 1086(2)(*d*) as respects fines or other penalties, as are referred to in s 1086(2)(*a*)-(*b*), which are imposed by a court, and as respects specified sums, as are referred to in s 1086(2)(*c*)-(*d*), which the Revenue Commissioners accepted, or undertook to accept, in settlement of a specified liability, on or after 23 March 2000.
Subs (1)(*b*) inserted TCA 1997 s 1086(2A) as respects fines or other penalties, as are referred to in s 1086(2)(*a*)-(*b*), which are imposed by a court, and as respects specified sums, as are referred to in s 1086(2)(*c*)-(*d*), which the Revenue Commissioners accepted, or undertook to accept, in settlement of a specified liability, on or after 23 March 2000.
Subs (1)(*c*)(i) substituted "Paragraph (*c*) and (*d*)" for "Paragraph (*c*)" in TCA 1997 s 1086(4) as respects fines or other penalties, as are referred to in s 1086(2)(*a*)-(*b*), which are imposed by a court, and as respects specified sums, as are referred to in s 1086(2)(*c*)-(*d*), which the Revenue Commissioners accepted, or undertook to accept, in settlement of a specified liability, on or after 23 March 2000.
Subs (1)(*c*)(ii) substituted "paragraph (*c*) or (*d*), as the case may be," for "paragraph (*c*)" in TCA 1997 s 1086(4)(*c*) as respects fines or other penalties, as are referred to in s 1086(2)(*a*)-(*b*), which are imposed by a court, and as respects specified sums, as are referred to in s 1086(2)(*c*)-(*d*), which the Revenue Commissioners accepted, or undertook to accept, in settlement of a specified liability, on or after 23 March 2000.
Subs (1)(*d*) inserted TCA 1997 s 1086(5A) as respects fines or other penalties, as are referred to in s 1086(2)(*a*)-(*b*), which are imposed by a court, and as respects specified sums, as are referred to in s 1086(2)(*c*)-(*d*), which the Revenue Commissioners accepted, or undertook to accept, in settlement of a specified liability, on or after 23 March 2000.

165 Care and management of taxes and duties

All taxes and duties imposed by this Act are by virtue of this section placed under the care and management of the Revenue Commissioners.

166 Short title, construction and commencement

(1) This Act may be cited as the Finance Act, 2000.

...

(5) Part 4 shall be construed together with the Stamp Duties Consolidation Act, 1999.

...

(8) Part 7 (so far as relating to income tax) shall be construed together with the Income Tax Acts and (so far as relating to corporation tax) shall be construed together with the Corporation Tax Acts and (so far as relating to capital gains tax) shall be construed together with the Capital Gains Tax Acts and (so far as relating to customs) shall be construed with the Customs Acts and (so far as relating to duties of excise) shall be construed together with the statutes which relate to duties of excise and the management of those duties and (so far as relating to value-added tax) shall be construed together with the Value-Added Tax Acts, 1972 to 2000, and (so far as relating to stamp duty) shall be construed together with the Stamp Duties Consolidation Act, 1999, and (so far as relating to residential property tax) shall be construed together with Part VI of the Finance Act, 1983, and the enactments amending or extending that Part and (so far as relating to gift tax or inheritance tax) shall be construed together with the Capital Acquisitions Tax Act, 1976, and the enactments amending or extending that Act.

...

(11) Any reference in this Act to any other enactment shall, except so far as the context otherwise requires, be construed as a reference to that enactment as amended by or under any other enactment including this Act.

(12) In this Act, a reference to a Part, section or Schedule is to a Part or section of, or Schedule to, this Act, unless it is indicated that reference to some other enactment is intended.

(13) In this Act, a reference to a subsection, paragraph, subparagraph, clause or subclause is to the subsection, paragraph, subparagraph, clause or subclause of the provision (including a Schedule) in which the reference occurs, unless it is indicated that reference to some other provision is intended.

FINANCE (No 2) ACT 2000

(2000 Number 19)
(Date passed: 5 July 2000)

ARRANGEMENT OF SECTIONS

PART 1
STAMP DUTIES

Section

PART 3
MISCELLANEOUS

SCHEDULE
STAMP DUTY ON INSTRUMENTS

AN ACT TO CHARGE AND IMPOSE CERTAIN DUTIES OF INLAND REVENUE, TO AMEND THE LAW RELATING TO INLAND REVENUE AND TO MAKE FURTHER PROVISIONS IN CONNECTION WITH FINANCE

PART 1
STAMP DUTIES

1 Interpretation (Part 1)

In this Part—

"Principal Act" means the Stamp Duties Consolidation Act, 1999;

"Commissioners" means the Revenue Commissioners;

"Schedule l" means Schedule 1 to the Principal Act.

2 Commencement (Part 1)

(1) Subject to subsection (2) and except where otherwise expressly provided, this Part shall have effect as respects instruments executed on or after 15 June 2000.

(2) Subsection (1) shall not apply as respects any instrument executed on or before [31 July 2001],[1] where—

  (*a*) the effect of the application of subsection (1) would be to increase the duty otherwise chargeable on the instrument, and

275

(b)   the instrument contains a statement in such form as the Commissioners may specify, certifying that the instrument was executed solely in pursuance of a contract which was evidenced in writing prior to 15 June 2000.

(3) The furnishing of an incorrect certificate for the purposes of subsection (2) shall be deemed to constitute the delivery of an incorrect statement for the purposes of section 1078 of the Taxes Consolidation Act, 1997.

Amendments

1   Substituted by FA 2001 s 214; previously "31 January 2001".

3 Amendment of Schedule 1 to Principal Act

Notes

Para (a) and Sch Pt 1 substituted SDCA 1999 Sch 1 Heading "CONVEYANCE or TRANSFER on sale of any property other than stocks or marketable securities or a policy of insurance or a policy of life insurance" paras (1)-(6).
Para (b) and Sch Pt 2 substituted SDCA 1999 Sch 1 Heading "Lease" para (3)(a).

4 Amendment of Chapter 2 of Part 7 of Principal Act

Notes

Section 4 inserted SDCA 1999 ss 92A and 92B.

PART 3
MISCELLANEOUS

28 Care and management of taxes and duties

All taxes and duties imposed by this Act are by virtue of this section placed under the care and management of the Revenue Commissioners.

29 Short title and construction

(1) This Act may be cited as the Finance (No 2) Act, 2000.

(2) Part 1 shall be construed together with the Stamp Duties Consolidation Act, 1999, and the enactments amending or extending that Act.

(3) Any reference in this Act to any other enactment shall, except so far as the context otherwise requires, be construed as a reference to that enactment as amended by or under any other enactment including this Act.

(4) In this Act, a reference to a Part, section or Schedule is to a Part or section of, or Schedule to, this Act, unless it is indicated that reference to some other enactment is intended.

(5) In this Act, a reference to a subsection or paragraph is to the subsection or paragraph of the provision in which the reference occurs, unless it is indicated that reference to some other provision is intended.

SCHEDULE
STAMP DUTY ON INSTRUMENTS

[Section 3]
PART 1

CONVEYANCE OR TRANSFER ON SALE OF ANY PROPERTY OTHER THAN STOCKS OR MARKETABLE SECURITIES OR A POLICY OF INSURANCE OR A POLICY OF LIFE INSURANCE

Notes

Section 3(*a*) and Sch Pt 1 substituted SDCA 1999 Sch 1 Heading "CONVEYANCE or TRANSFER on sale of any property other than stocks or marketable securities or a policy of insurance or a policy of life insurance" paras (1)-(6) with effect for instruments executed on or after 15 June 2000. However, where an instrument executed on or before 31 January 2001 would increase the duty chargeable on the instrument and the instrument contains a statement certifying that the instrument was executed solely in pursuance of a contract which was evidenced in writing before 15 June 2000 the substitution does not apply.

PART 2
LEASE

Notes

Section 3(*b*) and Sch Pt 2 substituted SDCA 1999 Sch 1 Heading "Lease" para (3)(*a*) with effect for instruments executed on or after 15 June 2000. However, where an instrument executed on or before 31 January 2001 would increase the duty chargeable on the instrument and the instrument contains a statement certifying that the instrument was executed solely in pursuance of a contract which was evidenced in writing before 15 June 2000 the substitution does not apply.

FINANCE ACT 2001

(2001 Number 7)
(Date passed: 30 March 2001)

ARRANGEMENT OF SECTIONS

PART 5
STAMP DUTIES

Section

PART 8
MISCELLANEOUS

SCHEDULE 5
AMENDMENT OF ENACTMENTS CONSEQUENT ON CHANGEOVER TO EURO

AN ACT TO PROVIDE FOR THE IMPOSITION, REPEAL, REMISSION, ALTERATION AND REGULATION OF TAXATION, OF STAMP DUTIES AND OF DUTIES RELATING TO EXCISE AND OTHERWISE TO MAKE FURTHER

PROVISION IN CONNECTION WITH FINANCE INCLUDING THE
REGULATION OF CUSTOMS. [30TH MARCH 2001]

PART 5
STAMP DUTIES

201 Interpretation (Part 5)

In this Part **"Principal Act"** means the Stamp Duties Consolidation Act, 1999.

202 Amendment of section 58 (security for future advances, how to be charged) of Principal Act

Notes

Subs (1)(*a*) substituted "£200,000" for "£20,000" in SDCA 1999 s 58(2) in each place where it occurs in relation to instruments executed on or after 26 January 2001
Subs (1)(*b*) substituted "€254,000" for "£200,000" in SDCA 1999 s 58(2) in relation to instruments executed on or after 1 January 2002.

203 Repeal of section 60 (short-term life insurance policies) of Principal Act

Notes

This section repealed SDCA 1999 s 60 in relation to instruments executed and policies of life insurance varied on or after 1 January 2001.

204 Amendment of section 79 (conveyances and transfers of property between certain bodies corporate) of Principal Act

Notes

Subs (1)(*a*) substituted "subsections (3) and (4)" for "subsection (3)" in SDCA 1999 s 79(7)(*b*) in relation to instruments executed on or after 15 February 2001.
Subs (1)(*b*) substituted "subsections (3) and (4)" for "subsection (3)" in SDCA 1999 s 77(5)(*a*) in relation to instruments executed on or after 6 March 2001.

205 Dublin Docklands Development Authority

Notes

This section substituted SDCA 1999 s 99.

206 Transfer of site to child

Notes

Subs (1) inserted SDCA 1999 s 83A in relation to instruments executed on or after 6 December 2000.
Subs (2) substituted "€254,000" for "£200,000" in SDCA 1999 s 83A(3)(*b*) for instruments executed on or after 1 January 2002.

207 Amendment of section 86 (certain loan stock) of Principal Act

Notes

Subs (1) substituted "or Bord Gáis Éireann" for "Bord Gáis Éireann or Irish Telecommunications Investments p.l.c." in SDCA 1999 s 86(*b*) in relation to instruments executed on or after 15 February 2001 but only in relation to loan stock issued on or after 15 February 2001.

208 Rent-a-room, etc

Notes

Subs (1)(*a*)(i) substituted "no person—

    (I)   other than a person who, while in such occupation, derives rent or payment in the nature of rent in consideration for the provision, on or after 6 April 2001, of furnished residential accommodation in part of the dwellinghouse or apartment concerned, or

    (II)   other than by virtue of a title prior to that of the purchaser,

will derive any rent or payment in the nature of rent for the use of that dwellinghouse or apartment, or of any part of it, during that period, and"

for "no person, other than by virtue of a title prior to that of the purchaser, will derive any rent or payment in the nature of rent for the use of that dwellinghouse or apartment, or of any part of it, during that period, and" in SDCA 1999 s 91(2)(*b*)(ii) in relation to instruments executed on or after 6 December 2000.

Subs (1)(*a*)(ii) substituted "some person, other than a person referred to in clause (I) or (II) of subsection (2)(*b*)(ii)" for "some person, other than by virtue of a title prior to that of the purchaser" in SDCA 1999 s 91(2)(*c*) in relation to instruments executed on or after 6 December 2000.

Subs (1)(*b*)(i) substituted "no person—

    (I)   other than a person who, while in such occupation, derives rent or payment in the nature of rent in consideration for the provision, on or after 6 April 2001, of furnished residential accommodation in part of the dwellinghouse or apartment concerned, or

    (II)   other than by virtue of a title prior to that of the purchaser,

will derive any rent or payment in the nature of rent for the use of that dwellinghouse or apartment, or of any part of it, during that period."

for "no person, other than by virtue of a title prior to that of the purchaser, will derive any rent or payment in the nature of rent for the use of that dwellinghouse or apartment, or any part of it, during that period." in SDCA 1999 s 92(1)(*b*)(ii) in relation to instruments executed on or after 6 December 2000.

Subs (1)(*b*)(ii) substituted "some person, other than a person referred to in clause (I) or (II) of subsection (1)(*b*)(ii)" for "some person, other than by virtue of a title prior to that of the purchaser" in SDCA 1999 s 92(2) in relation to instruments executed on or after 6 December 2000.

Subs (1)(*c*)(i) substituted "no person—

    (I)   other than a person who, while in such occupation, derives rent or payment in the nature of rent in consideration for the provision, on or after 6 April 2001, of furnished residential accommodation in part of the dwellinghouse or apartment concerned, or

    (II)   other than by virtue of a title prior to that of the purchaser,

will derive any rent or payment in the nature of rent for the use of that dwellinghouse or apartment, or of any part of it, during that period."

for "no person, other than by virtue of a title prior to that of the purchaser, will derive any rent or payment in the nature of rent for the use of that dwellinghouse or apartment, or any part of it, during that period." in SDCA 1999 s 92A(2)(b)(ii) in relation to instruments executed on or after 6 December 2000.

Subs (1)(*c*)(ii) substituted "some person, other than a person referred to in clause (I) or (II) of subsection (2)(*b*)(ii)" for "some person, other than by virtue of a title prior to that of the purchaser" in SDCA 1999 s 92A(3) in relation to instruments executed on or after 6 December 2000.

Subs (1)(*d*)(i) substituted "no person—

    (I)   other than a person who, while in such occupation, derives rent or payment in the nature of rent in consideration for the provision, on or after 6 April 2001, of furnished residential accommodation in part of the dwellinghouse or apartment concerned, or

    (II)   other than by virtue of a title prior to that of the purchaser,

will derive any rent or payment in the nature of rent for the use of that dwellinghouse or apartment, or of any part of it, during that period."

for "no person, other than by virtue of a title prior to that of the purchaser, will derive any rent or payment in the nature of rent for the use of that dwellinghouse or apartment, or any part of it, during that period." in SDCA 1999 s 92B(3)(*b*)(ii) in relation to instruments executed on or after 6 December 2000.

Subs (1)(*d*)(ii) substituted "some person, other than a person referred to in clause (I) or (II) of subsection (3)(*b*)(ii)" for "some person, other than by virtue of a title prior to that of the purchaser" in SDCA 1999 s 92B(4) in relation to instruments executed on or after 6 December 2000.

Subs (1)(*d*)(iii)(I) substituted "separation, a decree of divorce, a decree of nullity or a deed of separation" for "separation or a decree of divorce" in SDCA 1999 s 92B(8)(*a*) in relation to instruments executed on or after 15 June 2000.

Subs (1)(*d*)(iii)(II) substituted "that decree or the execution of that deed of separation by both spouses to that marriage" for "that decree" in SDA 1999 s 92B(8)(*a*) in relation to instruments executed on or after 15 June 2000.

Subs (1)(*d*)(iv) substituted "subparagraph (ii)" for "paragraph (*b*)" in SDCA 1999 s 92B(8)(*a*)(i) in relation to instruments executed on or after 14 February 2001.

Subs (1)(*d*)(v) substituted "the decree or the date of the execution of the deed of separation by both spouses to that marriage" for "the decree" in SDCA 1999 s 92B(8)(*a*)(ii) in relation to instruments executed on or after 15 June 2000.

Subs (1)(*d*)(vi) substituted "the State;" for "the State." in definition of "decree of judicial separation" and inserted definition of "decree of nullity"in SDCA 1999 s 92B(8)(*b*) in relation to instruments executed on or after 15 June 2000.

209 Amendment of Chapter 2 of Part 7 of Principal Act

Notes

Subs (1) inserted SDCA 1999 s 92C as respects instruments executed on or after 27 February 2001.

Subs (2) substituted "down to nearest €" for "up to the nearest £" in SDCA 1999 s 92C(1) as respects instruments executed on or after 1 January 2002.

210 Approved voluntary body

Notes

This section inserted SDCA 1999 s 93A in relation to instruments executed on or after 15 February 2001.

211 National Building Agency Limited

Notes

This section inserted SDCA 1999 s 106A in relation to instruments executed on or after 26 January 2001.

212 Certain policies of insurance

Notes

This section inserted SDCA 1999 s 110A in relation to instruments executed on or after 1 January 2001.

213 Amendment of Schedule 1 to Principal Act

Notes

Subs (1)(*a*) substituted "£200,000" for "£20,000" in SDCA 1999 Sch 1 Heading "MORTGAGE, BOND, DEBENTURE, COVENANT (except a marketable security) which is a security for the payment or repayment of money which is a charge or incumbrance on property situated in the State other than shares in stocks or funds of the Government or the Oireachtas." in relation to instruments executed on or after 26 January 2001.

Subs (1)(*b*) substituted "€254,000" for "£200,000" where it occurs in SDCA 1999 Sch 1 in relation to instruments executed on or after 1 January 2002.

Subs (1)(*c*) deleted SDCA 1999 Sch 1 Heading "POLICY OF LIFE INSURANCE made for a period exceeding 2 years where the risk to which the policy relates is located in the State." in relation to instruments executed and policies of life insurance varied on or after 1 January 2001.

214 Amendment of section 2 (commencement (Part 1)) of Finance (No 2) Act, 2000

Notes

This section substituted "31 July 2001" for "31 January 2001" in F(No 2)A 2000 s 2(2).

PART 8
MISCELLANEOUS

231 Interpretation (Part 8)

In this Part **"Principal Act"** means the Taxes Consolidation Act, 1997.

233 Amendment of section 1078 (revenue offences) of Principal Act

Notes

Subs (1) substituted "£1,500" for "£1,000" in TCA 1997 s 1078(3)(*a*) with effect from 6 April 2001.
Subs (2)(*a*) substituted "€1,900" for "£1,500" in TCA 1997 s 1078(3)(*a*) with effect from 1 January 2002.

238 Amendment of section 1002 (deduction from payments due to defaulters of amounts due in relation to tax) of Principal Act

Notes

This section substituted "14 days" for "one month" in TCA 1997 s 1002(3)(*a*).

239 Amendment of section 1006A (offset between taxes) of Principal Act

Notes

Para (*a*) inserted ", and includes any interest due under the Acts in relation to such tax, duty, levy or other charge" in TCA 1997 s 1006A(1) definition of "liability" with effect from 6 April 2001.
Para (*b*) substituted TCA 1997 s 1006A(2) with effect from 6 April 2001.

240 Amendment of enactments consequent on changeover to Euro

(1) (*a*) Subject to subsection (2), in each provision specified in column (1) of Schedule 5 for the words or amount set out in column (2) of that Schedule at that entry there shall be substituted the words or amount set out at the corresponding entry in column (3) of that Schedule.

(*b*) Where words are or an amount is mentioned more than once in a provision specified in column (1) of Schedule 5, then the substitution provided for by paragraph (*a*) shall apply as respects those words or that amount to each mention of those words or that amount in that provision.

(2) Subsection (1) shall apply—

(*a*) to the extent that the amendments relate to income tax and related matters, other than the amendments relating to such matters referred to in subparagraphs (ii), (iii), (iv), (v) and (vi) of paragraph (*m*), as respects the year of assessment 2002 and subsequent years of assessment,

(*b*) to the extent that the amendments relate to capital gains tax and related matters, other than the amendments relating to such matters referred to in paragraph (*m*)(vii),as respects the year of assessment 2002 and subsequent years of assessment, (*c*) to the extent that the amendments relate to corporation tax and related matters, other than the amendments relating to such matters referred to in subparagraphs (i), (iii) and (iv) of paragraph (*l*), for accounting periods ending on or after 1 January 2002,

...

(*i*) to the extent that section 1086 of the Taxes Consolidation Act, 1997 is amended, as respects specified sums such as are referred to in paragraphs (*c*) and (*d*) of section 1086(2) of that Act which the Revenue Commissioners accept or undertake to accept on or after 1 January 2002,

...

(*k*) to the extent that the enactment amended imposes any fine, forfeiture, penalty or punishment for any act or omission, as respects any act or omission which takes place or begins on or after 1 January 2002,

...

241 Care and management of taxes and duties

All the taxes and duties imposed by this Act are placed under the care and management of the Revenue Commissioners.

242 Short title, construction and commencement

(1) This Act may be cited as the Finance Act, 2001.

(2) Part 1 (so far as relating to income tax) shall be construed together with the Income Tax Acts and (so far as relating to corporation tax) shall be construed together with the Corporation Tax Acts and (so far as relating to capital gains tax) shall be construed together with the Capital Gains Tax Acts.

...

(5) Part 5 shall be construed together with the Stamp Duties Consolidation Act, 1999.

...

(11) Any reference in this Act to any other enactment shall, except so far as the context otherwise requires, be construed as a reference to that enactment as amended by or under any other enactment including this Act.

(12) In this Act, a reference to a Part, section or Schedule is to a Part or section of, or Schedule to, this Act, unless it is indicated that reference to some other enactment is intended.

(13) In this Act, a reference to a subsection, paragraph, subparagraph, clause or subclause is to the subsection, paragraph, subparagraph, clause or subclause of the provision (including a Schedule) in which the reference occurs, unless it is indicated that reference to some other provision is intended.

SCHEDULE 5
AMENDMENT OF ENACTMENTS CONSEQUENT ON CHANGEOVER TO EURO

[Section 240]

PART 6
STAMP DUTIES AND RELATED MATTERS

Notes

Sch 5 Pt 6 amended Stamp Duties Consolidation Act, 1999 with effect from 1 January 2002 as follows:
s 5(4): "£100" substituted by "€125"; s 8(3): "£1,000" substituted by "€1,265"; s 10(4): "£500" substituted by "€630"; s 14(1): "penalty of £20" substituted by "penalty of €25"; s 14(1) : "exceeds £20" substituted by "exceeds €30"; s 15 (2): "£5,000" substituted by "€6,350"; s 25(2): "£500" substituted by "€630"; s 38(1): "£100" substituted by "€130"; s 42(3): "£10" substituted by "€12.50"; s 59(1): "£500" substituted by "€630"; s 62: "£1" substituted by "€1"; s 65: "£500" substituted by "€630"; s 66(2): "£500" substituted by "€630"; s 70(2)(*b*): "penny " substituted by "cent"; s 75(5): "£1,000" substituted by "€1,265"; s 76(2): "£1,000" substituted by "€1,265"; s 76(3): "£1,000" substituted by "€1,265"; s 83(1): "£10" substituted by "€12.50"; s 92A(1): "£1" substituted by "€1"; s 92A(1) : "up to the nearest £" substituted by "down to the nearest €"; s 92B(2): "£1" substituted by "€1"; s 92B(2) : "up to the nearest £" substituted by "down to the nearest €"; s 117(1): "£1" substituted by "€1"; s 117(1): "up to the nearest £" substituted by "down to the nearest €"; s 117(2)(*a*): "£1" substituted by "€1"; s 123(3)(*b*)(ii): "£10" substituted by "€12.70"; s 123(4): "£5" substituted by "€6.25"; s 123(7): "£300" substituted by "€380"; s 124(1)(*c*): "£15" substituted by "€19"; s 124(2)(*c*): "£7.50" substituted by "€9.50"; s 124(2)(*d*)(ii): "£15" substituted by "€19"; s 124(5)(*b*): "£300" substituted by "€380"; s 128(2): "£100" substituted by "€125"; s 129(1): "£500" substituted by "€630"; s 142(4): "£1,000" substituted by "€1,265"; s 144(1): "£500" substituted by "€630"; s 146(3): "£1,000" substituted by "€1,265"; s 146(5): "£1,000" substituted by "€1,265"; s 147(2): "£1,000" substituted by "€1,265"; Heading "BILL OF EXCHANGE or PROMISSORY NOTE.", in Schedule 1: "7p" substituted by "€0.08"; Heading "CONVEYANCE or TRANSFER on sale of any stocks or marketable securities.", in Schedule 1: "£1" substituted by "€1"; Heading "CONVEYANCE or TRANSFER on sale of any stocks or marketable securities.", in Schedule 1: "up to the nearest £" substituted by "down to the nearest €"; Heading "CONVEYANCE or TRANSFER on sale of a policy of insurance or a policy of life insurance where the risk to which the policy relates is located in the State.", in Schedule 1: "£1" substituted by "€1"; Heading "CONVEYANCE or TRANSFER on sale of a policy of insurance or a policy of life insurance where the risk to which the policy relates is located in the State.", in Schedule 1: "up to the nearest £" substituted by "down to the nearest €"; Heading "CONVEYANCE or TRANSFER on sale of any property other than stocks or marketable securities or a policy of insurance or a policy of life insurance.: para (1): "£100,000" substituted by "€127,000"; para (1): "£1" substituted by "€1"; para (1): "up to the nearest £" substituted by "down to the nearest €"; para (2): "£150,000" substituted by "€190,500"; para (2): "£1" substituted by "€1"; para (2): "up to the nearest £" substituted by "down to the nearest €"; para (3): "£200,000" substituted by "€254,000"; para (3): "£1" substituted by "€1"; para (3): "up to the nearest £" substituted by "down to the nearest €"; para (4): "£250,000" substituted by "€317,500"; para (4): "£1" substituted by "€1"; para (4): "up to the nearest £" substituted by "down to the nearest €"; para (5): "£300,000" substituted by "€381,000"; para (5): "£1" substituted by "€1"; para (5): "up to the nearest £" substituted by "down to the nearest €"; para (6): "£500,000" substituted by "€635,000"; para (6): "£1" substituted by "€1"; para (6): "up to the nearest £" substituted by "down to the nearest €"; para (6A): "£1" substituted by "€1"; para (6A): "up to the nearest £" substituted by "down to the nearest €"; para (7): "£5,000" substituted by "€6,350"; para (8): "£10,000" substituted by "€12,700"; para (8): "£1" substituted by "€1"; para (8): "up to the nearest £" substituted by "down to the nearest €"; para (9): "£15,000" substituted by "€19,050"; para (9): "£1" substituted by "€1"; para (9): "up to the nearest £" substituted by "down to the nearest €"; para (10): "£25,000" substituted by "€31,750"; para (10): "£1" substituted by "€1"; para (10): "up to the nearest £" substituted by "down to the nearest €"; para (11): "£50,000" substituted by "€63,500"; para (11): "£1" substituted by "€1"; para (11): "up to the nearest £" substituted by "down to the nearest €"; para (12): "£60,000" substituted by "€76,200"; para (12): "£1" substituted by "€1"; para (12): "up to the nearest £" substituted by "down to the nearest €"; para (13): "£1" substituted by "€1"; para (13): "up to the nearest £" substituted by "down to the nearest €"; para (14): "£1" substituted by "€1"; para (14): "up to the nearest £" substituted by "down to the nearest €"; para (15): "£1" substituted by "€1"; para (15): "up to the nearest £" substituted by "down to the nearest €"; Heading "CONVEYANCE or TRANSFER of any kind not already described in this Schedule.", in Schedule 1: "£10"

substituted by "€12.50"; Heading "DUPLICATE or COUNTERPART of any instrument chargeable with any duty.", in Schedule 1: "£10" substituted by "€12.50"; Heading "EXCHANGE — instruments effecting.", in Schedule 1: "£10" substituted by "€12.50"; Heading "LEASE.": para (1): "£15,000" substituted by "€19,050"; para (3)(*a*)(i): "£100,000" substituted by "€127,000"; para (3)(*a*)(i): "£1" substituted by "€1"; para (3)(*a*)(i): "up to the nearest £" substituted by "down to the nearest €"; para (3)(*a*)(ii): "£150,000" substituted by "€190,500"; para (3)(*a*)(ii): "£1" substituted by "€1"; para (3)(*a*)(ii): "up to the nearest £" substituted by "down to the nearest €"; para (3)(*a*)(iii): "£200,000" substituted by "€254,000"; para (3)(*a*)(iii): "£1" substituted by "€1"; para (3)(*a*)(iii): "up to the nearest £" substituted by "down to the nearest €"; para (3)(*a*)(iv): "£250,000" substituted by "€317,500"; para (3)(*a*)(iv): "£1" substituted by "€1"; para (3)(*a*)(iv): "up to the nearest £" substituted by "down to the nearest €"; para (3)(*a*)(v): "£300,000" substituted by "€381,000"; para (3)(*a*)(v): "£1" substituted by "€1"; para (3)(*a*)(v): "up to the nearest £" substituted by "down to the nearest €"; para (3)(*a*)(vi): "£500,000" substituted by "€635,000"; para (3)(*a*)(vi): "£1" substituted by "€1"; para (3)(*a*)(vi): "up to the nearest £" substituted by "down to the nearest €"; para (3)(*a*)(vii): "£1" substituted by "€1"; para (3)(*a*)(vii): "up to the nearest £" substituted by "down to the nearest €"; para (3)(*b*)(i): "£5,000" substituted by "€6,350"; para (3)(*b*)(ii): "£10,000" substituted by "€12,700"; para (3)(*b*)(ii): "£1" substituted by "€1"; para (3)(*b*)(ii): "up to the nearest £" substituted by "down to the nearest €"; para (3)(*b*)(iii): "£15,000" substituted by "€19,050"; para (3)(*b*)(iii): "£1" substituted by "€1"; para (3)(*b*)(iii): "up to the nearest £" substituted by "down to the nearest €"; para (3)(*b*)(iv): "£25,000" substituted by "€31,750"; para (3)(*b*)(iv): "£1" substituted by "€1"; para (3)(*b*)(iv): "up to the nearest £" substituted by "down to the nearest €"; para (3)(*b*)(v): "£50,000" substituted by "€63,500"; para (3)(*b*)(v): "£1" substituted by "€1"; para (3)(*b*)(v): "up to the nearest £" substituted by "down to the nearest €"; para (3)(*b*)(vi): "£60,000" substituted by "€76,200"; para (3)(*b*)(vi): "£1" substituted by "€1"; para (3)(*b*)(vi): "up to the nearest £" substituted by "down to the nearest €"; para (3)(*b*)(vii): "£1" substituted by "€1"; para (3)(*b*)(vii): "up to the nearest £" substituted by "down to the nearest €"; para (3)(*b*)(viii): "£1" substituted by "€1"; para (3)(*b*)(viii): "up to the nearest £" substituted by "down to the nearest €"; para (3)(*c*)(i): "£1" substituted by "€1"; para (3)(*c*)(i): "up to the nearest £" substituted by "down to the nearest €"; para (3)(*c*)(ii): "£1" substituted by "€1"; para (3)(*c*)(ii): "up to the nearest £" substituted by "down to the nearest €"; para (3)(*c*)(iii): "£1" substituted by "€1"; para (3)(*c*)(iii): "up to the nearest £" substituted by "down to the nearest €"; para (4): "£10" substituted by "€12.50"; para (5): "£10" substituted by "€12.50"; Heading "MORTGAGE, BOND, DEBENTURE, COVENANT (except a marketable security) which is a security for the payment or repayment of money which is a charge or incumbrance on property situated in the State other than shares in stocks or funds of the Government or the Oireachtas.": para (1): "£1" substituted by "€1"; para (1): "up to the nearest £" substituted by "down to the nearest €"; para (1): "£500" substituted by "€630"; para (2): "£10" substituted by "€12.50"; para (3): "£1" substituted by "€1"; para (3): "up to the nearest £" substituted by "down to the nearest €"; para (3): "£500" substituted by "€630"; para (4): "£1" substituted by "€1"; para (4): "up to the nearest £" substituted by "down to the nearest €"; para (4): "£500" substituted by "€630"; Heading "POLICY OF INSURANCE other than Life Insurance where the risk to which the policy relates is located in the State.", in Schedule 1: "£15" substituted by "€20"; Heading "POLICY OF INSURANCE other than Life Insurance where the risk to which the policy relates is located in the State.", in Schedule 1: "£1" substituted by "€1"; Heading "RELEASE or RENUNCIATION of any property, or of any right or interest in any property.", in Schedule 1: "£10" substituted by "€12.50"; Heading "SURRENDER of any property, or of any right or interest in any property.", in Schedule 1: "£10" substituted by "€12.50".

FINANCE ACT 2002

(2002 Number 5)
(Date of passing: 25 March 2002)

ARRANGEMENT OF SECTIONS

PART 4
STAMP DUTIES

PART 6
MISCELLANEOUS

SCHEDULE 6
MISCELLANEOUS TECHNICAL AMENDMENTS IN RELATION TO TAX

An Act to provide for the imposition, repeal, remission, alteration and regulation of taxation of stamp duties and of duties relating to excise and otherwise to make further provision in connection with finance including the regulation of customs [*25th March 2002*]

PART 4
STAMP DUTIES

111 Interpretation (Part 4)

In this Part "Principal Act" means the Stamp Duties Consolidation Act 1999.

112 Amendment of section 76 (obligations of system-members) of Principal Act

---

Notes

Section 112 substituted "6 years" for "3 years" in SDCA 1999 s 76 in relation to instructions entered or caused to be entered in a relevant system by a system-member on or after 25 March 2002.

---

113 Amendment of Chapter 2 of Part 7 of Principal Act

Notes

Subs (1)(*a*) inserted in SDCA 1999 s 92A(7)-(8) with effect on and from 6 December 2001.

Subs (1)(*b*) substituted SDCA 1999 s 92B(2) in relation to instruments executed on or after 6 December 2001 subject to substituting, in subsection (2) of section 92B (inserted by subsection (1)), "£1" for "€1" and "up to the nearest £" for "down to the nearest €" for instruments executed on or after 6 December 2001 and before 1 January 2002.

Subs (1)(*c*) deleted SDCA 1999 s 92C in relation to instruments executed on or after 6 December 2001.

114 Amendment of Schedule 1 to Principal Act

Notes

Subs (1)(*a*)(i) substituted "exceeds €127,000: for the consideration which is attributable to residential property .... Exempt." for "exceeds €127,000 ... 9 per cent of the consideration which is attributable to residential property but where the calculation results in an amount which is not a multiple of €1 the amount so calculated shall be rounded down to the nearest €." in SDCA 1999 Sch 1 Heading "CONVEYANCE or TRANSFER on sale of any property other than stocks or marketable securities or a policy of insurance or a policy of life insurance" para (1) with effect for instruments executed on or after 6 December 2001 subject to substituting "£100,000" for "€127,000", for instruments executed on or after 6 December 2001 and before 1 January 2002.

Subs (1)(*a*)(ii) substituted "3 per cent" for "9 per cent" in SDCA 1999 Sch 1 Heading "CONVEYANCE or TRANSFER on sale of any property other than stocks or marketable securities or a policy of insurance or a policy of life insurance" para (2) with effect for instruments executed on or after 6 December 2001.

Subs (1)(*a*)(iii) substituted "4 per cent" for "9 per cent" in SDCA 1999 Sch 1 Heading "CONVEYANCE or TRANSFER on sale of any property other than stocks or marketable securities or a policy of insurance or a policy of life insurance" para (3) with effect for instruments executed on or after 6 December 2001.

Subs (1)(*a*)(iv) substituted "5 per cent" for "9 per cent" in SDCA 1999 Sch 1 Heading "CONVEYANCE or TRANSFER on sale of any property other than stocks or marketable securities or a policy of insurance or a policy of life insurance" para (4) with effect for instruments executed on or after 6 December 2001.

Subs (1)(*a*)(v) substituted "6 per cent" for "9 per cent" in SDCA 1999 Sch 1 Heading "CONVEYANCE or TRANSFER on sale of any property other than stocks or marketable securities or a policy of insurance or a policy of life insurance" para (5) with effect for instruments executed on or after 6 December 2001.

Subs (1)(*a*)(vi) substituted "7.5 per cent" for "9 per cent" in SDCA 1999 Sch 1 Heading "CONVEYANCE or TRANSFER on sale of any property other than stocks or marketable securities or a policy of insurance or a policy of life insurance" para (6) with effect for instruments executed on or after 6 December 2001.

Subs (1)(*b*)(i) substituted "exceeds €127,000: for the consideration which is attributable to residential property ... Exempt." for "exceeds €127,000 ... 9 per cent of the consideration which is attributable to residential property but where the calculation results in an amount which is not a multiple of €1 the amount so calculated shall be rounded down to the nearest €." in SDCA 1999 Sch 1 Heading "LEASE" para (3)(*a*)(i) with effect for instruments executed on or after 6 December 2001 subject to substituting "£100,000" for "€127,000", for instruments executed on or after 6 December 2001 and before 1 January 2002.

Subs (1)(*b*)(ii) substituted "3 per cent" for "9 per cent" in SDCA 1999 Sch 1 Heading "LEASE" para (3)(*a*)(ii) with effect for instruments executed on or after 6 December 2001.

Subs (1)(*b*)(iii) substituted "4 per cent" for "9 per cent" in SDCA 1999 Sch 1 Heading "LEASE" para (3)(*a*)(iii) with effect for instruments executed on or after 6 December 2001.

Subs (1)(*b*)(iv) substituted "5 per cent" for "9 per cent" in SDCA 1999 Sch 1 Heading "LEASE" para (3)(*a*)(iv) with effect for instruments executed on or after 6 December 2001.

Subs (1)(*b*)(v) substituted "6 per cent" for "9 per cent" in SDCA 1999 Sch 1 Heading "LEASE" para (3)(*a*)(v) with effect for instruments executed on or after 6 December 2001.

Subs (1)(*b*)(vi) substituted "7.5 per cent" for "9 per cent" in SDCA 1999 Sch 1 Heading "LEASE" para (3)(*a*)(vi) with effect for instruments executed on or after 6 December 2001.

PART 6
MISCELLANEOUS

123 Interpretation (Part 6)

In this Part "Principal Act" means the Taxes Consolidation Act 1997.

125 Amendment of Chapter 5 (miscellaneous provisions) of Part 42 of Principal Act

Notes

Para (*a*)(i)(I) substituted TCA 1997 s 1006A(1) definition of "claim" with effect from 25 March 2002.

Para (*a*)(i)(II) substituted TCA 1997 s 1006A(1) definition of "liability" with effect from 25 March 2002.

Para (*a*)(i)(III) substituted "credited;" for "credited." In TCA 1997 s 1006A(1) definition of "overpayment" with effect from 25 March 2002.

Para (*a*)(i)(IV) inserted TCA 1997 s 1006A(1) definition of "tax" with effect from 25 March 2002.

Para (*a*)(ii) inserted TCA 1997 s 1006A(5) with effect from 25 March 2002.

Para (*b*) inserted TCA 1997 s 1006B(5) with effect from 25 March 2002.

126 Amendment of section 1086 (publication of names of tax defaulters) of Principal Act

Notes

Subs (1)(*a*)(i)(I) substituted TCA 1997 s 1086(1) definition of "the Acts" para (*e*) as respects fines or other penalties, as are referred to in TCA 1997 s 1086(2)(*a*)-(*b*), which are imposed by a court, and as respects specified sums, as are referred to in TCA 1997 s 1086(2)(*c*)-(*d*), which the Revenue Commissioners accepted, or undertook to accept, in settlement of a specified liability, on or after 25 March 2002.

Subs (1)(*a*)(i)(II) inserted TCA 1997 s 1086(1) definition of "the Acts" paras (*g*)-(*h*) as respects fines or other penalties, as are referred to in TCA 1997 s 1086(2)(*a*)-(*b*), which are imposed by a court, and as respects specified sums, as are referred to in TCA 1997 s 1086(2)(*c*)-(*d*), which the Revenue Commissioners accepted, or undertook to accept, in settlement of a specified liability, on or after 25 March 2002.

Subs (1)(*a*)(ii) substituted TCA 1997 s 1086(1) definition of "tax" as respects fines or other penalties, as are referred to in TCA 1997 s 1086(2)(*a*)-(*b*), which are imposed by a court, and as respects specified sums, as are referred to in TCA 1997 s 1086(2)(*c*)-(*d*), which the Revenue Commissioners accepted, or undertook to accept, in settlement of a specified liability, on or after 25 March 2002.

Subs (1)(*b*)(i) substituted TCA 1997 s 1086(2)(*c*)(ii)-(iii) as respects fines or other penalties, as are referred to in TCA 1997 s 1086(2)(*a*)-(*b*), which are imposed by a court, and as respects specified sums, as are referred to in TCA 1997 s 1086(2)(*c*)-(*d*), which the Revenue Commissioners accepted, or undertook to accept, in settlement of a specified liability, on or after 25 March 2002.

Subs (1)(*b*)(ii) substituted TCA 1997 s 1086(2)(*d*)(ii)-(iii) as respects fines or other penalties, as are referred to in TCA 1997 s 1086(2)(*a*)-(*b*), which are imposed by a court, and as respects specified sums, as are referred to in TCA 1997 s 1086(2)(*c*)-(*d*), which the Revenue Commissioners accepted, or undertook to accept, in settlement of a specified liability, on or after 25 March 2002.

Subs (1)(*c*) substituted TCA 1997 s 1086(3)(*b*) as respects fines or other penalties, as are referred to in TCA 1997 s 1086(2)(*a*)-(*b*), which are imposed by a court, and as respects specified sums, as are referred to in TCA 1997 s 1086(2)(*c*)-(*d*), which the Revenue Commissioners accepted, or undertook to accept, in settlement of a specified liability, on or after 25 March 2002.

Subs (1)(*d*)(i) substituted "those paragraphs" for "that paragraph" in TCA 1997 s 1086(4)(*a*) as respects fines or other penalties, as are referred to in TCA 1997 s 1086(2)(*a*)-(*b*), which are imposed by a court, and as respects specified sums, as are referred to in TCA 1997 s 1086(2)(*c*)-(*d*), which the Revenue Commissioners accepted, or undertook to accept, in settlement of a specified liability, on or after 25 March 2002.

Subs (1)(*d*)(ii) substituted "applied," for "applied, or" in TCA 1997 s 1086(4)(*b*) as respects fines or other penalties, as are referred to in TCA 1997 s 1086(2)(*a*)-(*b*), which are imposed by a court, and as respects specified sums, as are referred to in TCA 1997 s 1086(2)(*c*)-(*d*), which the Revenue Commissioners accepted, or undertook to accept, in settlement of a specified liability, on or after 25 March 2002.

Subs (1)(*d*)(iii) substituted "€12,700, or" for "€12,700." in TCA 1997 s 1086(4)(*c*) as respects fines or other penalties, as are referred to in TCA 1997 s 1086(2)(*a*)-(*b*), which are imposed by a court, and as respects

specified sums, as are referred to in TCA 1997 s 1086(2)(*c*)-(*d*), which the Revenue Commissioners accepted, or undertook to accept, in settlement of a specified liability, on or after 25 March 2002.

Subs (1)(*d*)(iv) inserted TCA 1997 s 1086(4)(*d*) as respects fines or other penalties, as are referred to in TCA 1997 s 1086(2)(*a*)-(*b*), which are imposed by a court, and as respects specified sums, as are referred to in TCA 1997 s 1086(2)(*c*)-(*d*), which the Revenue Commissioners accepted, or undertook to accept, in settlement of a specified liability, on or after 25 March 2002.

129 Interest on unpaid and overpaid tax

Notes

Subs (6)(*a*) substituted "0.0322 per cent for each day or part of a day" for "1 per cent for each month or part of a month" in SDCA 1999 ss 5(4) and 117(3) with effect from 1 September 2002 in respect of interest chargeable or payable as regards an amount due to be paid or remitted or to be repaid or retained, whether before, on, or after that date.

Subs (6)(*b*) substituted "0.0322 per cent for each day or part of a day" for "1 per cent per month or part of a month" in SDCA 1999 ss 14(1), 75(3), 79(7), 80(8), 81(7)(*a*)-(*b*), 87(3), 87A(4)(*a*), 91(2)(*c*)(i), 92(2)(*a*), 92A(3)(*a*), 92B(4)(*a*), 117(4), 123(7), 124(5)(*b*) and 125(6) with effect from 1 September 2002 in respect of interest chargeable or payable as regards an amount due to be paid or remitted or to be repaid or retained, whether before, on, or after that date.

Subs (6)(*c*) substituted "0.0161 per cent, or such other rate (if any) as stands prescribed by the Minister by regulations, for each day or part of a day" for "0.5 per cent, or such other rate (if any) as stands prescribed by the Minister by regulations, for each month or part of a month" in SDCA 1999 ss 29(4)(*b*) and (7), 53(4)(*b*) and (7) with effect from 1 September 2002 in respect of interest chargeable or payable as regards an amount due to be paid or remitted or to be repaid or retained, whether before, on, or after that date.

Subs (6)(*d*) substituted "0.0161 per cent per day or part of a day" for "6 per cent per annum" in SDCA 1999 s 117(2)(*b*)(ii) with effect from 1 September 2002 in respect of interest chargeable or payable as regards an amount due to be paid or remitted or to be repaid or retained, whether before, on, or after that date.

133 Amendment of section 1078 (revenue offences) of Principal Act

Notes

Para (*a*) substituted "fails without reasonable excuse" for "knowingly or wilfully fails" in TCA 1997 s 1078(2)(*g*) with effect from 25 March 2002.

Para (*b*) inserted TCA 1997 s 1078(3B) with effect from 25 March 2002.

138 Miscellaneous technical amendments in relation to tax

The enactments specified in Schedule 6 are amended to the extent and in the manner specified in that Schedule.

139 Amendment of Provisional Collection of Taxes Act 1927

Notes

Para (*a*) substituted Provisional Collection of Taxes 1927 s 1 definition of "new tax" with effect from 25 March 2002.

Para (*b*) substituted "immediately before the date on which the resolution is expressed to take effect or, where no such date is expressed, the passing of the resolution by Dáil Éireann" for "immediately before the end of the previous financial year" in Provisional Collection of Taxes 1927 ss 2-3 with effect from 25 March 2002.

140 Care and management of taxes and duties

All taxes and duties imposed by this Act are placed under the care and management of the Revenue Commissioners.

141 Short title, construction and commencement

(1) This Act may be cited as the Finance Act 2002.

...

(5) Part 4 shall be construed together with the Stamp Duties Consolidation Act 1999 and the enactments amending or extending that Act.

(6) Part 5 (so far as relating to capital acquisitions tax) shall be construed together with the Capital Acquisitions Tax Act 1976 and the enactments amending or extending that Act.

...

(10) Any reference in this Act to any other enactment shall, except so far as the context otherwise requires, be construed as a reference to that enactment as amended by or under any other enactment including this Act.

(11) In this Act, a reference to a Part, section or Schedule is to a Part or section of, or Schedule to, this Act, unless it is indicated that reference to some other enactment is intended.

(12) In this Act, a reference to a subsection, paragraph, subparagraph, clause or subclause is to the subsection, paragraph, subparagraph, clause or subclause of the provision (including a Schedule) in which the reference occurs, unless it is indicated that reference to some other provision is intended.

SCHEDULE 6
MISCELLANEOUS TECHNICAL AMENDMENTS IN RELATION TO TAX

Notes

Para 4 and s 138 substituted SDCA 1999 s 79(3)(*a*)-(*b*) with effect on or after 15 December 1999.

STAMP DUTY (REGULATIONS)

FINANCE ACT 1920 LAND REGULATIONS

Made by the Revenue Commissioners under section 4 of the Finance (1909-10) Act, 1910, as amended by the Finance Act, 1920

Presentation of instruments

Production of instruments in evidence

(1) Having regard to the provisions of Part I of the Finance (1909-10) Act, 1910, as amended by the Finance Act, 1920, it is necessary that, on the occasion of any transfer on sale of the fee simple of any land or of any interest in land, or on the grant of any lease of any land, for a term exceeding fourteen years, the transferor or lessor shall present to the Revenue Commissioners the instrument by means of which the transfer or the lease is agreed or agreed to be effected, or reasonable particulars thereof. The land in question is only such as is situate within the State.

(2) Under the arrangements made by the Commissioners the instrument or the required particulars thereof, may be presented at ... the following Stamp Offices at which the stamp mentioned in section 4, sub-section 3, of the Finance (1909-10) Act, 1910, as amended by the Finance Act, 1920, will be impressed:

Dublin Castle, Dublin

Cork, The Office of the Collector of Customs and Excise.

The forms referred to in these Regulations may be obtained at ... the above-mentioned offices, ... and at or through any Money Order Office authorised to transact Inland Revenue business.

(3) If the instrument itself be presented the presentation should take place, if possible, after execution by the transferor or lessor. The instrument must be accompanied either by a copy, or by an abstract such (but containing the further particulars required) as is presented with an instrument lodged for adjudication under section 12 of the Stamp Act, 1891. The abstract should set out fully, for purposes of identification, the description of the property sold or leased, and if the instrument contains or refers to a plan, a copy of such plan should be furnished. A full statement should be made, in so far as they affect the consideration, of any easements or reservations affecting the land, of any covenant restricting its use, and of any agreement or obligation to repair, or to pay outgoings. Any covenant or undertaking or liability to discharge any incumbrance, and any covenant or undertaking to erect buildings or to expend any sums upon the property, should be set out in sufficient abstract. The official form of application for a "Particulars Delivered" stamp, duly filled up and signed, should also be lodged. The official form of abstract can be used if desired.

(4) The instrument, the abstract and the form of application, when presented, will be retained by the proper officer of the Commissioners for examination, a ticket being given by way of receipt, to the person presenting them.

(5) Assuming that the various documents or papers so presented are found on examination to contain the particulars necessary, the instrument will be impressed with the "Particulars Delivered" stamp, and will be returned on presentation of the ticket after the expiration of the time mentioned therein.

(6) Where an instrument is so stamped it will be deemed to be duly stamped so far as respects, the provisions of Part I of the Finance (1909-10) Act, 1910, as amended by the Finance Act, 1920. Unless so stamped the instrument cannot, except in criminal proceedings, be given in evidence, or be made available for any purpose whatever.

(7) The Act, (section 4, sub-section 7) provides that where any agreement for a transfer, or agreement for a lease, is stamped with the special stamp provided, it will not be necessary to stamp in a similar manner any conveyance, assignment, or lease made subsequently to and in conformity with the agreement. But, if desired, a corresponding stamp will be impressed on the conveyance, assignment, or lease on presentation of both instruments .... Similarly a duplicate of any instrument which has been stamped in accordance with the above section will be impressed with a corresponding stamp on both documents being produced at the Office for the purpose.

If, however, an agreement for a transfer is intended to be followed shortly by an actual conveyance, the Commissioners will not require the agreement, or particulars thereof, to be presented under these Regulations, but will accept the presentation in due course of the actual conveyance, or particulars thereof, as a compliance with the provisions of the Act. But an agreement for a lease, or particulars thereof, should be presented without waiting for the actual lease.

(8) The fact that an instrument has been presented under these Regulations, and stamped with the "Particulars Delivered" stamp, will not in any way affect the liability of the instrument to the ordinary Stamp Duty imposed by the Stamp Act, 1891, or any amending Act. It will be necessary therefore that the instrument, if not drawn on material duly stamped, be presented within thirty days of execution, to be impressed with the proper ordinary Stamp Duty (Stamp Act, 1891, section 15). Should, however, the transferor or lessor desire to have this duty impressed at the same time as the "Particulars Delivered" stamp, so as to avoid the necessity for a second presentation of the instrument, he should pay the amount of the duty when presenting the instrument, abstract &c. ...

(9) In the case of instruments lodged at the Head Office in Dublin Castle, Dublin, for adjudication under section 12 of the Stamp Act, 1891, the application for the "Particulars Delivered" stamp may be made at the same time, the application form being accompanied by a separate copy or abstract of the instrument, any abstract to contain a full statement as regards easements, covenants, &c. The "Particulars Delivered" stamp will then be impressed when the instrument is stamped with the adjudication stamp.

Presentation of particulars

(10) If the instrument itself be not presented by the transferor or lessor, reasonable particulars thereof, in the form of the various documents mentioned in paragraph 3, must be furnished by him. Such particulars can be lodged at ... the offices mentioned in paragraph 2, and a receipt will be given therefor. The transferor or lessor should at the same time lodge the form of application duly filled up.

(11) The presentation of such particulars, in lieu of the instrument itself, will free the transferor or lessor from liability to the fine imposed by section 4, sub-section 2, of the Finance (1909-10) Act, 1910, as amended. But the instrument will not be "duly stamped" until it bears, in addition to the ordinary Stamp Duty to which it is liable, the special stamp mentioned in paragraph 5. Provided, however, the necessary particulars, as

above, have been furnished by the transferor or lessor, the appropriate stamp will be impressed at any future date, if the instrument and the receipt for the particulars are lodged for the requisite length of time at the Head Office, Dublin Castle.

Presentation at other offices

(12) Where it is not possible or convenient to present the instrument or the required particulars at one of the offices mentioned in paragraph 2, it will be open to the transferor or lessor to lodge the various documents (including the form of application) at ... any Money Order Office authorised to transact Inland Revenue business, with a request that they may be forwarded to the Head Office, in the same way as documents requiring to be stamped with the ordinary Stamp Duties may now be lodged. In such cases the examination of the documents will be made at the Head Office only, and in due course the conveyance or lease or agreement, stamped as required by Part I of the Finance (1909-10) Act, 1910, as amended by the Finance Act, 1920, will be returned to the ... Post Office for delivery to the transferor or lessor on personal application for it.

Correspondence

(13) Should occasion arise for correspondence in connection with the presentation of an instrument or the delivery of particulars, the letter should be addressed to the Secretary, Revenue Commissioners, Dublin Castle, the envelope being marked in the left-hand corner "Particulars Delivered".

(14) ....

IRELAND

[(15) Paragraphs (1) to (12) of these Regulations shall not apply to conveyances or leases of houses by a housing authority, within the meaning of the Housing Act, 1966 (No 21 of 1966), under section 90 of that Act, and it shall not be necessary to present such conveyances or leases to the Commissioners or to furnish them with reasonable particulars thereof.][1]

With this exception paragraphs 1 to 12 of the above Regulations shall apply in Ireland to all conveyances on sale and leases exceeding 14 years.

Amendments

[1]   Substituted by SI 181/1977 with effect from 4 July 1977.

AMENDMENT
Particulars delivered

Order made by Commissioners on 13th May, 1921

The Board have decided to dispense with the presentation of particulars (Forms A and B) of all Leases for a term not exceeding 30 years, and Assignments of Leases, when the unexpired term does not exceed 30 years. On and after 18th May, 1921, the Particulars Delivered stamp required under the provisions of section 4(2) of the Finance (1909-10) Act, 1910, may be impressed, without question, on all such instruments.

In future it will not be necessary to furnish a plan of the property, except in the case of vacant building plots, or where the particulars given in paragraph 5 of the Particulars Delivered Form B, or in the copy or abstract, are insufficient for identification purposes and cannot be supplemented in any other way.

Order made by the Revenue Commissioners on 11th August, 1970

The Revenue Commissioners have decided to dispense with the presentation of particulars (Forms A and B) in all cases of sales or leases of houses by a housing authority under the provisions of Section 90, Housing Act, 1966, and it shall no longer be necessary to present the transfer orders effecting such sales or leases to the Commissioners or to furnish them with "reasonable particulars" thereof.

PROPERTY VALUES (ARBITRATIONS AND APPEALS) RULES 1961

1961 No 91

We, the Reference Committee, in exercise of the powers conferred on us by section 33 of the Finance (1909-10) Act, 1910, the Acquisition of Land (Assessment of Compensation) Act, 1919, and sections 3 and 4 of the Property Values (Arbitrations and Appeals) Act, 1960 (No 45 of 1960), hereby make the following Rules, with the approval of the Minister for Finance in so far as they are made under the said section 33:

1. These Rules may be cited as the Property Values (Arbitrations and Appeals) Rules, 1961.

2. The Interpretation Act, 1937 (No 38 of 1937), applies to these Rules.

3. (1) In these Rules—

"the Act of 1910" means the Finance (1909-10) Act, 1910;

"the Act of 1919" means the Acquisition of Land (Assessment of Compensation) Act, 1919;

"question" means a question referred to in section 1 of the Act of 1919;

"the Reference Committee" means the Reference Committee established by section 1 of the Act of 1919, as amended by the Acquisition of Land (Reference Committee) Act, 1925 (No 22 of 1925);

"the Rules of 1911" means the Land Values (Referee) (Ireland) Rules, 1911;

"the Rules of 1920" means the Acquisition of Land (Assessment of Compensation) Rules, 1920.

(2) These Rules shall, in so far as they amend the Rules of 1911, be construed as one with the Rules of 1911 and shall, in so far as they amend the Rules of 1920, be construed as one with the Rules of 1920.

4. (1) An appeal under section 33 of the Act of 1910 to a property arbitrator may be made by sending to the Reference Committee and to the Revenue Commissioners within the period provided for by the Rules of 1911 or in a form to the like effect specifying the matter to which the appeal relates and giving particulars of the grounds of the appeal.

(2) The Revenue Commissioners shall cause printed copies of the forms of notices of appeal set out in Schedule to the Rules of 1911 to be furnished free of charge on application by any person to the Revenue Commissioners or to any person authorised by the Revenue Commissioners to furnish the forms.

5. Whenever the Reference Committee receives, pursuant to Rule 4 of these Rules, a notice of appeal in writing, it shall, as soon as may be, nominate a property arbitrator for the purpose of the reference and determination of the appeal to which the notice relates, and shall, as soon as it has nominated the property arbitrator, inform the Revenue Commissioners and the appellant of his name and address.

6. In the Rules of 1911—

    (*a*)   references to the Reference Committee for Ireland constituted under section 33 of the Act of 1910, shall be construed as references to the Reference Committee,

    (*b*)   references to a referee and the reference in Rule 8 to the referee selected shall be construed as references to a property arbitrator nominated under these Rules, and

    (*c*)   Rules 3, 7, 11 and 14 shall be revoked.

7. (1) Where a question has arisen, any party to or affected by, the acquisition in relation to which the question has arisen—

    (*a*)   may, at any time after expiration of fourteen days from the date on which notice to treat was served in relation to the acquisition, send to the Reference Committee an application in writing for the nomination of a property arbitrator for the purposes of the reference and determination of the question, and

    (*b*)   shall, if he sends the application specified in paragraph (*a*) of this Rule, as soon as may be after such sending, send a copy thereof to every other party to, or affected by, the acquisition aforesaid.

(2) An application under this Rule shall be in writing and shall specify the parties to, or affected by the acquisition, the land to be acquired, the nature of the question to which the application relates, the statutory provisions under which the question arises and, if compensation is claimed, the interest in respect of which it is claimed.

8. Whenever the Reference Committee receives, pursuant to Rule 7 of these Rules, a valid application in writing for the appointment of a property arbitrator, it shall, as soon as may be, nominate a property arbitrator for the purpose of the reference and determination of the question to which the notice relates, and shall, as soon as it has nominated the property arbitrator, inform the parties to, or affected by, the acquisition in relation to which the question has arisen of his name and address.

9. In the Rules of 1920—

    (*a*)   the definition of "arbitrator" in Rule 2 shall be deleted,

    (*b*)   "nomination" shall be substituted for "appointment" in each place where it occurs and "nominated" shall be substituted for "appointed" in each place where it occurs,

    (*c*)   references to an official arbitrator shall be construed as references to a property arbitrator nominated under these Rules, and

    (*d*)   Rules 3, 4, 6 and 9 and the Schedule shall be revoked.

10. The Reference Committee may, in the case of the death or incapacity of a property arbitrator nominated for the purposes of the reference and determination of an appeal under section 33 of the Act of 1910 or a question, or if it is shown to the Reference Committee that it is expedient so to do, in any other case, at any time before the determination of the appeal or question, as the case may be, revoke the nomination of the property arbitrator and nominate another property arbitrator for the purposes of the reference and determination of the appeal or question, as the case may be, and the

Reference Committee shall as soon as it has nominated the other property arbitrator, inform—

(*a*) in the case of an appeal, the Revenue Commissioners and the appellant, and

(*b*) in the case of a question, every party to, or affected by, the acquisition to which the question relates,

of the name and address of the other property arbitrator.

11. Any notice or other document required or authorised by the Rules of 1911, the Rules of 1920 or these Rules to be sent to the Reference Committee or any other person shall be deemed to be duly sent by post—

(*a*) in the case of the Reference Committee, to the Secretary of the Reference Committee, Four Courts, Dublin, and

(*b*) in the case of any other person, to his usual address.

12. These Rules shall not have effect in respect of—

(*a*) any appeal under section 33 of the Act of 1910 in relation to which a referee has been selected under the Rules of 1911 before the 21st day of December, 1960 or

(*b*) any question in relation to which an official arbitrator has been selected under the Rules of 1920 before the 21st day of December, 1960.

EUROPEAN COMMUNITIES (NON-LIFE INSURANCE) (AMENDMENT) (NO 2) REGULATIONS 1991

1991 No 142

1. (1) These Regulations may be cited as the European Communities (Non-Life Insurance) (Amendment) (No 2) Regulations, 1991, and shall come into operation on the 17th June, 1991.

(2) These Regulations shall be construed as one with the Principal Regulations, as amended.

...

4. (1) Article 291) of the Principal Regulations is hereby amended by the addition of the following definitions—

"the first Directive" means EEC Council Directive 72/239/EEC [OJ No L 228, 16.8.1973, p 3];

"the second Directive" means EEC Council Directive 88/357/EEC [OJ No L 172, 4.7.1988, p 1];

"undertaking", except where the context otherwise requires, means—

(i) 'for the purposes of carrying on non-life insurance in the State from an establishment in the State:

the holder of an authorisation under Article 6 or Article 23 of the first Directive;

(ii) for the purposes of carrying on non-life insurance by way of services into the State from an establishment in another Member State:

the holder of an authorisation under Article 6 of the first Directive;

"establishment" means the head office, agency or branch of an undertaking subject to Article 3 of the second Directive;

"Member State where the risk is situated" means:

(i) the Member State in which the property is situated, where the insurance relates either to buildings or to buildings and their contents, in so far as the contents are covered by the same insurance policy,

(ii) the Member State of registration, where the insurance relates to vehicles of any type,

(iii) the Member State where the policyholder took out the policy in the case of policies of a duration of four months or less covering travel or holiday risks, whatever the class concerned,

(iv) the Member State where the policyholder has his habitual residence or, if the policyholder is a legal person, the Member State where the latter's establishment, to which the contract relates, is situated, in all cases not explicitly covered by the foregoing subparagraphs;

"Member State of establishment" means the Member State in which the establishment covering the risk is situated;

"Member State of provision of services" means the Member State in which the risk is situated when it is covered by an establishment situated in another Member State;

"large risks" has the meaning assigned to it by Article 3A of the Principal Regulations, inserted by Article 5 of these Regulations.

(2) Article 2 of the Principal Regulations is hereby amended by the substitution, for subarticle (2) , of the following:

> "(2) In these Regulations any word or phrase to which a meaning is assigned by the first Directive or by the second Directive has that meaning."

...

STAMP DUTY (PARTICULARS TO BE DELIVERED) REGULATIONS 1995

1995 No 144

The Revenue Commissioners, in exercise of the powers conferred on them by section 107 (as amended by section 149 of the Finance Act, 1995 (No 8 of 1995)) of the Finance Act, 1994 (No 13 of 1994), hereby make the following regulations:

1. These Regulations may be cited as the Stamp Duty (Particulars to be Delivered) Regulations, 1995.

2. These Regulations shall have effect in relation to any instrument executed on or after the 1st day of September, 1995.

3. In these Regulations "particulars to be delivered" means the particulars to be delivered for the purposes of [section 12 of the Stamp Duties Consolidation Act, 1999].[1]

4. Subject to Regulation 5, these Regulations shall apply to—

(*a*) any conveyance or other transfer on sale of the fee simple of any land or interest in land;

(*b*) any conveyance or other transfer operating as a voluntary disposition *inter vivos* for the fee simple of any land or interest in land;

(*c*) the grant of any lease of any land for a term exceeding 30 years;

(*d*) the assignment of any lease of any land where the unexpired term of that lease exceeds 30 years.

5. These Regulations shall not apply to—

(*a*) any transaction creating a joint tenancy between spouses to which section 14 of the Family Home Protection Act, 1976 (No 27 of 1976), relates and it shall not be necessary to present the instrument concerned to the Revenue Commissioners or to furnish them with particulars thereof, or

(*b*) conveyances, transfers or leases of houses, buildings or land by or to a housing authority to which section 8 of the Housing (Miscellaneous Provisions) Act, 1992 (No 18 of 1992), relates and it shall not be necessary to present such conveyance, transfer or lease to the Revenue Commissioners or to furnish them with particulars thereof.

6. (1) The particulars to be delivered shall contain the information required in the form (in this Regulation referred to as **"the first-mentioned form"**) which is set out in the Schedule to these Regulations and shall—

(*a*) be in the first-mentioned form, or

(*b*) where the printed document containing those particulars has been produced with computer assistance in a form other than the first-mentioned form, be in such order and layout as approximates to the first-mentioned form as the Revenue Commissioners may agree to, and any such form, duly completed and signed together with a copy thereof, shall be presented and lodged along with the instruments concerned at one of the offices of the Revenue Commissioners specified in Regulation 7 of these Regulations before the expiration of 30 days after that instrument is first executed.

(2) In the first-mentioned form the reference to **"Tax No"** means—

    (i) in the case of an individual who has a number known as the Revenue and Social Insurance (RSI) number, such number;

    (ii) in the case of any other person, the reference number stated on any return form or notice of assessment issued to that person by an inspector of taxes.

(3) For convenience of reference there are set out in the Schedule to these Regulations, after the first-mentioned form, notes for the completion of that form.

7. The particulars to be delivered shall be presented at either of the following offices of the Revenue Commissioners at which the stamp known as "Particulars Delivered" is impressed:

    (*a*) The Stamp Duty Office, Capital Taxes Division, Stamping Building, Dublin Castle, Dublin 2;

    (*b*) The Stamp Duty Office, Customs and Excise, Government Buildings, Sullivans Quay, Cork.

8. If a form duly presented and lodged for the purposes of these Regulations is found on examination to contain the particulars necessary, the instrument to which that form relates shall be impressed with the stamp known as "Particulars Delivered" and that instrument shall be returned to the person who presented it.

Amendments

[1]   Substituted by SDCA 1999 s 162 and Sch 4; previously "section 107 of the Finance Act, 1994 (No 13 of 1994)".

Notes on Completion of Form ST.21

This form should be completed in duplicate and submitted by the transferee or lessee or solicitor for the transferee or lessee.
[A word-processed facsimile may be used provided it contains all of the details requested in broadly
the same order and layout.]

DATE

Complete the date in numerals. For example, 1 October, 1995 would be written as: **1/10/95**.
Date of related contract/agreement need only be completed if one exists.
In the case of a lease (or an assignment of a lease) enter the date on which the term of the (original) lease commenced/will commence.

CLASS OF INSTRUMENT

Enter term of the lease and rent review period (where appropriate) in numerals.

DETAILS OF TRANSFEROR/
LESSOR AND TRANSFEREE/
LESSEE

If there are more than two parties to the instrument, the information required should be provided on a separate sheet to be attached to this form.

TAX (REFERENCE) NUMBER

The following information should be furnished:
In the case of an individual his or her Revenue and Social Insurance (RSI) number;
In any other case (eg a company, partnership, trust) the reference number stated on any return form or notice of assessment issued to the person concerned by an Inspector of Taxes.
If a Tax Number is not included for one or more of the parties named in sections C or D, complete the appropriate part of the declaration in section G or H. Where a tax number is not included a substantive reason for its omission must be furnished (it will not be acceptable simply to state that a number is not available.

LOCATION AND DESCRIPTION
OF PROPERTY

Insert the townland and county if the property is a rural one.
If urban, insert street (including number), town and county.
Insert Folio No. if the property is registered.
Insert Land Area only where an area in excess of 1 acre is being transferred or leased. Location map/plan should be provided.

CONSIDERATION

In the case of the ***transfer of the fee simple*** of any land or any interest in land, whether on sale or as a voluntary disposition, the amount of the consideration (including any liabilities assumed) is to be inserted.
In the case of the ***grant of any lease*** of any land the amount of the annual rent payable at the commencement of the term of the lease and the amount of any premium are to be inserted.
In the case of an ***assignment of the lease*** the amount of the annual rent payable at the date of commencement of the assignment and any premium are to be inserted.
The box marked "Voluntary Disposition" should be ticked if there is ***no consideration or if the consideration is less than the open market value*** of the property

STAMP DUTY (EUROPEAN LEGISLATION)

COUNCIL DIRECTIVE

of 17 July 1969

69/335/EEC

(OJ 1969 L249/25)

concerning indirect taxes on the raising of capital amended by council directive of 9 april 1973 (73/79) and modified by adaptation council decision of 1 january 1973 (oj 1973, l2, 1.1.1973 p 1)

THE COUNCIL OF THE EUROPEAN COMMUNITIES

Having regard to the Treaty establishing the European Economic Community, in particular Articles 99 and 100 thereof;

Having regard to the proposal from the Commission;

Having regard to the Opinion of the European Parliament [OJ No 119 3 July, 1965, p 2057/65];

Having regard to the Opinion of the Economic and Social Committee [OJ No 134, 23 July 1965, p 2227/65];

Whereas the objective of the Treaty is to create an economic union whose characteristics are similar to those of a domestic market and whereas one of the essential conditions for achieving this is the promotion of the free movement of capital;

Whereas the indirect taxes on the raising of capital, in force in the Member States at the present time, namely the duty chargeable on contributions of capital to companies and firms and the stamp duty on securities, give rise to discrimination, double taxation and disparities which interfere with the free movement of capital and which, consequently, must be eliminated by harmonisation;

Whereas the harmonisation of such taxes on the raising of capital must be arranged in such a way as to minimise the budgetary repercussions for Member States;

Whereas the charging of stamp duty by a Member State on securities from other Member States introduced into or issued within its territory is contrary to the concept of a common market whose characteristics are those of a domestic market; whereas, in addition, it has become evident that the retention of stamp duty on the issue of securities in respect of internal loans and on the introduction or issue on the market of a Member State of foreign securities is both undesirable from the economic point of view and inconsistent with current developments in the tax laws of the Member States in this field;

Whereas, in these circumstances, it is advisable to abolish the stamp duty on securities, regardless of the origin of such securities, and regardless of whether they represent a company's own capital or its loan capital;

Whereas it is inherent in the concept of a common market whose characteristics are those of a domestic market that duty on the raising of capital within the common market by a company or firm should be charged only once and that the level of this duty should be the same in all Member States so as not to interfere with the movement of capital;

Whereas, therefore, this duty should be harmonised, with regard both to its structures and to its rates;

Whereas the retention of other indirect taxes with the same characteristics as the capital duty or the stamp duty on securities might frustrate the purpose of the measures provided for in this Directive and those taxes should therefore be abolished;

HAS ADOPTED THIS DIRECTIVE:

Article 1

Member States shall charge on contributions of capital to capital companies a duty harmonised in accordance with the provisions of Articles 2 to 9 and hereinafter called **"capital duty"**.

Case law

Capital duty could be levied on a waiver by a parent company in whole or in part of a claim against its subsidiary on the grounds that it both lead to an increase in the assets of the company and the value of the shares of the company. *Delkakabel BV v Staatssecretaris Financien* [1993] 1 CMLR 116.

A Member State was not entitled to charge capital duty solely on the basis of an increase in the nominal capital which did not contribute to the economic strengthening of the company. Ministeriet for Skatter OG Afgifter Mod Investeringsforeningen Dansk Sparinvest, Judgment of the Court 2 February 1988.

Article 2

1. Transactions subject to capital duty shall only be taxable in the Member State in whose territory the effective centre of management of a capital company is situated at the time when such transactions take place.

2. When the effective centre of management of a capital company is situated in a third country and its registered office is situated in a Member State, transactions subject to capital duty shall be taxable in the Member State where the registered office is situate.

3. When the registered office and the effective centre of management of a capital company are situated in a third country, the supplying of fixed or working capital to a branch situated in a Member State may be taxed in the member State in whose territory the branch is situated.

Article 3

[**1.** For the purposes of this Directive, the expression **"capital company"** means:

(*a*) companies under Belgian, Danish, German, French, [Hellenic,] Irish, Italian, Luxembourg, Netherlands [Portuguese,] [Spanish,] and United Kingdom law, known respectively as:

— société anonyme/naamloze vennootschap, aktieselskab, aktiengesellschaft, société anonyme, companies incorporated with limited liability, società per azione, société anonyme, naamloze vennoorschap, companies incorporated with limited liability, [Ανωυνμος 'Εταιρεια';] [sociedad anonima; sociedade anonima;]

— société commandite par actions/commanditaire vennootschap op sandelen, kommandit-aktieselskab, Kommanditgesellschaft auf Aktien, société en commandite par actions, società in accommandita per azione, société en commandite par actions, commanditaire veennootschap op sandelen; [Κατα μετοχας ετερορυθμος εταιρεια;] [sociedad commandetaria por acciones; sociedada em comandita por accoes;]

— société de personnes à responsabilité limitée/personenvennootschap met beperkte ansprakelijkheid, Gesellschaft mit beschrankter Haftung, société a responsabilité limitée, società a responsabilità limitata, société à responsabilité limitée.] [Εταιρεια περιωρισμενης ευθυωης] [sociedad de responsabilidad limitada sociedade por quotas].]

(*b*) any company, firm, association or legal person the shares in whose capital or assets can be dealt in on a stock exchange;

(*c*) any company, firm, association or legal person operating for profit, whose members have the right to dispose of their shares to third parties without prior authorisation and are only responsible for the debts of the company, firm, association or legal person to the extent of their shares.

2. For the purposes of the application of this Directive, any other company, firm, association or legal person operating for profits shall be deemed to be a capital company. However a Member State shall have the right not to consider it as such for the purpose of charging capital duty.

Case law

In *Amro Aandelen Fonds v Inspecteur der Registratie En Successie*, [1987] ECR 4453, the court ruled that the object of article 3(2) was to prevent the choice of a particular legal form leading to a different fiscal treatment of activities which in substance and economically were the same. Accordingly it rules that a grouping of persons which did not have legal personality and whose members provided capital for a separate fund with a view to making profits was to be deemed to be a capital company. However the court ruled that this article gave a discretion to Member States to determine whether or not such a grouping was to be regarded as a "capital company" for the purposes of charging capital duty.

Article 4

1. The following transactions shall be subject to capital duty:

(*a*) the formation of a capital company;

(*b*) the conversion into a capital company of a company, firm, association or legal person which is not a capital company;

(*c*) an increase in the capital of a capital company by contribution of assets of any kind;

(*d*) an increase in the assets of a capital company by contribution of assets of any kind, in consideration, not of shares in the capital or assets of the company, but of rights of the same kind as those of members, such as voting rights, a share in the profits or a share in the surplus upon liquidation;

(*e*) the transfer from a third company to a Member State of the effective centre of management of a company, firm, association or legal person, whose registered office is in a third country and which is considered in that Member State, for the purposes of charging capital duty, as a capital company;

(*f*) the transfer from a third country to a Member State of the registered office of a company, firm, association or legal person, whose effective centre of management is in a third country and which is considered in that Member State, for the purposes of charging capital duty, as a capital company;

(*g*) the transfer from a Member State to another Member State of the effective centre of management of a company, firm, association or legal person which is considered in the latter Member State, for the purposes of charging capital duty, as a capital company, but is not so considered in the other Member State;

(*h*) the transfer from a Member State to another Member State of the registered office of a company, firm, association or legal person, whose effective centre of management is in a third country and which is considered in the latter Member State, for the purposes of charging capital duty, as a capital company, but is not so considered in the other Member State.

[2. The following transactions may, to the extent that they were taxed at the rate of 1% as at 1 July 1984, continue to be subject to capital duty:][1]

(*a*) an increase in the capital of a capital company by capitalisation of profits or of permanent or temporary reserves;

(*b*) an increase in the assets of a capital company through the provision of services by a member which do not entail an increase in the company's capital, but which do result in variation in the rights in the company or which may increase the value of the company's shares;

(*c*) a loan taken up by a capital company, if the creditor is entailed to a share in the profits of the company;

(*d*) a loan taken up by a capital company with a member or a member's spouse or child, or a loan taken up with a third party, if it is guaranteed by a member, on condition that such loans have the same function as an increase in the company's capital.

[However, the Hellenic Republic shall determine which of the transactions listed above it will be subject to capital duty.][2]

3. Formation, within the meaning of paragraph 1(*a*), shall not include any alteration of the constituent instrument or regulations of a capital company and in particular:

(*a*) the conversion of a capital company into a different type of capital company;

(*b*) the transfer from a Member State to another Member State of the effective centre of management or of the registered office of a company, firm, association or legal person which is considered in both Member States, for the purposes of charging capital duty, as a capital company;

(*c*) a change in the objects of a capital company;

(*d*) the extension of the period of existence of a capital company.

Amendments

1   Substituted by Council Directive 85/303/EEC of 10 June 1985, art 1 with effect from 1 January 1986.

2   Inserted by Council Directive 85/303/EEC of 10 June 1985, art 1 with effect from 1 January 1986.

Case law

The granting of a interest free loan which allowed a company to have capital available without having to bear its cost and which resulted in a saving in interest was an increase in the assets of a company within the meaning of article 4(2)(b) of this Directive as it allowed a company to avoid expenditure which it would otherwise have to bear. *Trave Schiffahrts-GmbH and Co KG v Finanzamt Kiel-Nord* [1992] 3 CMLR 777. See also *A/S Richard Frederiksen and Co v Skatteministeriet*, [1997] STC 264, ECJ 287/94.

The absorption of a company's losses by a shareholder, pursuant to a profit and loss transfer agreement concluded before those losses determined did not increase the assets of that company for the purposes of article 4(2)(b) and was not therefore a chargeable transaction. *Waldrich Siegen Werkzeugnaschinen GmbH v Finanzamt Hagen* ECJ 38/88. See also *Commerz-Credit AG v Finamzamt Saarbruecken* ECJ 50/91.

Article 5

1. The duty shall be charged:

(a)   in the case of formation of a capital company or of an increase in its capital or assets, as referred to in Article 4(1)(a), (c) and (d): on the actual value of assets of any kind contributed or to be contributed by the members, after the deduction of liabilities assumed and of expenses borne by the company as a result of each contribution. Member States may postpone the charging of capital duty until the contributions have been effected;

(b)   in the case of conversion into a capital company or of the transfer of the effective centre of management or of the registered office of a capital company, as referred to in Article 4(1)(b), (e), (f), (g) and (h): on the actual value of the assets of any kind belonging to the company at the time of the conversion or transfer, after the deduction of liabilities and expenses for which the company is responsible at that time;

(c)   in the case of an increase in the capital by capitalisation of profits reserves, or provisions, as referred to in Article 4(2)(a): on the nominal amount of such increase;

(d)   in the case of an increase in the assets, as referred to in Article 4(2)(b): on the actual value of the services provided, after deduction of the liabilities assumed and the expenses borne by the company as a result of the provision of such services;

(e)   in the case of loans referred to in Article (2)(c) and (d): on the nominal amount of the loan taken up.

[**2.** In the cases referred to in paragraph 1(a) and (b), Member States may base the amount on which to charge capital duty on the actual value of the shares in the company allotted or belonging to each member. This does not apply, to those cases in which contributions are made only in cash. The amount on which duty is charged shall in no circumstances be less than the nominal amount of the shares in the company allotted or belonging to each member.][1]

315

3. The amount on which the duty is charged in the case of an increase in capital shall not include:

> the amount of the assets belonging to the capital company which are allocated to the increase in capital and which have already been subjected to capital duty;

> the amount of the loans taken up by the capital company which are converted into shares in the company and which have already been subjected to capital duty.

Amendments

[1]   Para (2) substituted by Council Directive 74/553/EEC of 7 November 1974, art 1.

Article 6

1. Each Member State may exclude from the basis of assessment, as determined in accordance with Article 5, the amount of the capital contributed by a member with unlimited liability for the obligations of a capital company as well as one share of such a member in the company's assets.

2. Where a member State exercises the power provided for in paragraph 1 the following shall be subject to capital duty:

> the transfer of the effective centre of management of a capital company to another Member State which does not exercise that power;

> the transfer of the registered office of a capital company whose effective centre of management is in a third country to another Member State which does not exercise that power;

> any transaction as a result of which the liability of a member is limited to his share in the company's capital, in particular when the limitation of liability results from the conversion of a capital company into a different type of capital company.

Capital duty shall be charged in all such cases on the value of the share the company's assets belonging to members with unlimited liability for the company's obligations.

[Article 7

1. Member States shall exempt from capital duty transactions, other than those referred to in Article 9, which were, as at 1 July 1984, exempted or taxed at a rate of 0,50% or less.

The exemption shall be subject to the conditions which were applicable, on that date, for the grant of the exemption or, as the case may be, for imposition at a rate of 0,50% or less.

The Hellenic Republic shall determine which transactions it shall exempt from capital duty.

2. Member States may either exempt from capital duty all transactions other than those referred to in paragraph 1 or charge duty on them at a single rate not exceeding 1%.

3. In the case of an increase in a company's capital in accordance with Article 4(1)(*c*), following a reduction in the company's capital as a result of losses sustained, that part of the increase which corresponds to the reduction in capital may be exempted, provided this increase occurs within four years of the reduction in capital.]¹

Amendments

¹   Art (7) substituted by Council Directive 85/303/EEC of 10 June 1985 with effect from 1 January 1985.

Case law

Proportional duty on contribution by one company of its assets to another company, in return for shares, held incompatible with Art 7(1): *Societé Bautiaa v directeur Des Services Fiscaux des Landes*, ECJ 197/94, 252/94.

Article 8

[Subject to Article 7(1), Member States may exempt from capital duty the transactions referred to in Article 4(1) and (2) concerning:]¹

> capital companies which supply public services, such as public transport undertakings, port authorities or undertakings supplying water, gas or electricity, in cases where the State or regional or local authorities own at least half of the company's capital;

> capital companies which, in accordance with their regulations and in fact, pursue exclusively and directly cultural, charitable, relief or educational objectives.

Amendments

¹   Substituted by Council Directive 85/303/EEC of 10 June 1985 with effect from 1 January 1986.

Article 9

Certain types of transactions or of capital companies may be the subject of exemptions, reductions or increases in rates in order to achieve fairness in taxation, or for social considerations, or to enable a Member State to deal with special situations. The Member State which proposed to take such a measure shall refer the matter to the Commission in good time, having regard to the application of Article 102 of the Treaty.

Article 10

Apart from capital duty, Member States shall not charge, with regard to companies, firms, associations or legal persons operating for profits, any taxes whatsoever:

(*a*)   in respect of the transactions referred to in Article 4;

(*b*)   in respect of contributions, loans or the provision of services, occurring as part of the transactions referred to in Article 4;

(*c*)   in respect of registration or any other formality required before the commencement of business to which a company, firm, association or legal person operating for profit may be subject by reason of its legal form.

Article 11

Member States shall not subject to any form of taxation whatsoever:

(*a*) the creation, issue, admission to quotation on a stock exchange, making available on the market or dealing in stocks, shares or other securities of the same type, or of the certificates representing such securities, by whomsoever issued;

(*b*) loans, including government bonds, raised by the issue of debentures or other negotiable securities, by whomsoever issued, or any formalities relating thereto, or the creation, issue, admission to quotation on a stock exchange, making available on the market or dealing in such debentures or other negotiable securities.

Case law

Article 10 and 11 of the Directive mean that it is not possible for Member States to subject "capital companies" to taxes or duties other than capital duty and the duties mentioned in Article 12. *Spa Maxi DI Ufficio del Registro de Bolzana, ECJ 15/88.*

Article 12

1. Notwithstanding Articles 10 and 11, Member States may charge:

(*a*) duties on the transfer of securities, whether charged at a flat rate or not;

(*b*) transfer duties, including land registration taxes, on the transfer, to a company, firm, association or legal person operating for profit, of businesses or immovable property situated within their territory;

(*c*) transfer duties on assets of any kind transferred to a company, firm, association or legal person operating for profit, in so far as such property is transferred for a consideration other than shares in the company;

(*d*) duties on the creation, registration or discharge of mortgages or other charges on land or other property;

(*e*) duties paid by way of fees or dues;

(*f*) value added tax.

2. The duties and taxes referred to in paragraph 1(*b*), (*c*), (*d*) and (*e*) shall be the same, whether the effective centre of management or the registered office of the company, firm, association or legal person operating for profit is situated within the territory of the Member State charging the duties or taxes or not; nor may these duties and taxes exceed those which are applicable to like transactions in the Member State charging them.

Article 13

Member States shall bring into force by 1 January 1972 such provisions by way of law, regulation or administrative action as may be necessary to comply with the provisions of this Directive and shall forthwith inform the Commission thereof.

Article 14

Member States shall ensure that the texts of the main provisions of internal law which subsequently adopt in the field covered by this Directive are forwarded to the Commission.

Article 15

This Directive is addressed to the Member States.

FIRST COUNCIL DIRECTIVE

of 24 July 1973

73/239/EEC

(OJ 1973 L228)

on the coodination of laws, regulations and administrative provisions relating to the taking up and pursuit of the business of direct insurance other than life insurance (73/ 239/eec)

THE COUNCIL OF THE EUROPEAN COMMUNITIES

Having regard to the Treaty establishing the European Economic Community, in particular Article 57(1) thereof;

Having regard to the General Programme [OJ No 2, 15.1.1962, p 36/62] for the abolition of restrictions on freedom of establishment, and in particular Title IV C thereof;

Having regard to the proposal from the Commission;

Having regard to the Opinion of the European Parliament [OJ No C 27, 28.3.1968, p 15];

Having regard to the Opinion of the Economic and Social Committee [OJ No 158, 18.7.1967, p 1];

Whereas by virtue of the General Programme the removal of restrictions on the establishment of agencies and branches is, in the case of the direct insurance business, dependent on the coordination of the conditions for the taking-up and pursuit of this business; whereas such coordination should be effected in the first place in respect of direct insurance other than life assurance;

Whereas a classification of risks in the different classes of insurance is necessary in order to determine, in particular, the activites subject to a compulsory authorisation and the amount of the minium guarantee fund fixed for the class of insurance concerned;

Wherease is it desirable to exclude from the application of this Directive mutual associations which, by virtue of their legal status, fulfil appropriate conditions as to security and financial guarantees; whereas it is further desirable to exclude certain institutions in several Member States whose business covers a very limited sector only and is restricted by law to a specified territory or to specified persons;

Whereas the various laws contain different rules as to the simultaneous undertaking of health insurance, credit and suretyship insurance and insurance in respect of recourse against third parties and legal defence, whether with one or with other classes of insurance; whereas continuance of this divergence after the abolition of restrictions on the right of establishment in classes other than life assurance would mean that obstacles to establishment would continue to exist; whereas a solution to this problem must be provided in subsequent coordination to be effected within a relatively short period of time;

Whereas it is necessary to extend supervision in each Member State to all the classes of insurance to which this Directive applies; whereas such supervision is not possible unless the undertaking of such classes of insurance is subject to an official authorisation; whereas provision must be made for a right to apply to the courts should an authorisation be refused or withdrawn.

Whereas it is desirable to bring the classes of insurance known as transport classes bearing Nos 4, 5, 6, 7 and 12 in Paragraph A of the Annex, and the credit insurance classes bearing Nos 14 and 15 in paragraph A of the Annex, under more flexible rules in view of the continual fluctuations in conditions affecting goods and credit;

Whereas the search for a common method of calculating technical reserves is at present the subject of studies at Community level; whereas it therefore appears to be desirable to reserve the attainment of coordination in this matter, as well as questions relating to the determination of categories of investments and the valuation of assets, for subsequent directives;

Whereas it is necessary that insurance undertakings should possess, over and above technical reserves of sufficient amount to meet their underwriting liabilities, a supplementary reserve, to be known as the solvency margin, and represented by free assets, in order to provide against business fluctuations; whereas in order to ensure that the requirements imposed for such purposes are determined according to objective criteria, whereby undertakings of the same size are placed on an equal footing as regards competition, it is desirable to provide that such margin shall be related to the overall volume of business of the undertaking and be determined by reference to two indices of security, one based on premiums and the other on claims;

Whereas is it desirable to require a minimum guarantee fund related to the size of the risk in the classes undertaken, in order to ensure that undertakings possess adequate resources when they are set up and that in the subsequent course of business the solvency margin shall in no event fall below a minimum of security;

Whereas it is necessary to make provision for the case where the financial condition of the undertaking becomes such that it is difficult for it to meet its underwriting liabilities;

Whereas the coordination rules concerning the taking-up and pursuit of the business or direct insuance within the Community should, in principle, apply to all undertakings entering the market and, consequently, also to agencies and branches where the head office of the undertaking is situated outside the Community; whereas it is, nevertheless, desirable as regards the methods of supervision to make special provision with respect to such agencies or branches in view of the fact that the assets of the undertakings to which they belong are situated outside the Community'

Whereas it is, however, desirable to permit the relaxation of such special conditions, while observing the principle that such agencies and branches should not obtain more favourable treatment than undertakings within the Community;

Whereas certain transitional provisions are required in order, in particular, to permit small and medium-sized undertakings already in existence to adapt themselves to the requirements which must be imposed by the Member States in pursuance of this Directive, subject to the application of Article 53 of the Treaty;

Whereas it is important to guarantee the uniform application of coordinated rules and to provide, in this respect, for close collaboration between the Commission and the Member States in this field;

HAS ADOPTED THIS DIRECTIVE:

...

ANNEX

A. Classification of risks according to classes of insurance

1. Accident (including industrial injury and occupational diseases):	- fixed pecuniary benefits,
	- benefits in the nature of indemnity,
	- combination of the two,
	- injury to passengers.
2. Sickness:	- fixed pecuniary benefits,
	- benefits in the nature of indemnity,
	- combination of the two.
3. Land vehicles (other than railway rolling stock)	All damage to or loss of:
	- land motor vehicles,
	- land vehicles other than motor vehicles.
4. Railway rolling stock	All damage to or loss of railway rolling stock.
5. Aircraft	All damage to or loss of aircraft.
6. Ships (sea, lake and river and canal vessels)	All damage to or loss or:
	- river and canal vessels,
	- lake vessels,
	- sea vessels.
7. Goods in transit (including merchandise, baggage, and all other goods)	All damage to or loss of goods in transit or baggage, irrespective of the form of transport.
8. Fire and natural forces	All damage to or loss of property (other than property included in classes 3, 4, 5, 6 and 7) due to fire:
	- explosion,
	- storm,
	- natural forces other than storm,
	- nuclear energy,
	- land subsidence.

9. Other damage to property — All damage to or loss of property (other than property included in classes 3, 4, 5, 6 and 7) due to hail or frost, and any event such as theft, other than those mentioned under 8.

10. Motor vehicle liability — All liability arising out of the use of motor vehicles operating on the land (including carrier's liability).

11. Aircraft liability — All liability arising out of the use or aircraft (including carrier's liability)

12. Liability for ships (sea, lake and river and canal vessels) — All liability arising out of the use of ships, vessels or boats on the sea, lakes, rivers or canals (including carrier's liability).

13. General liability — All liability other than those forms mentioned under Nos 10, 11 and 12.

- insolvency (general),
- instalment credit,

14. Credit (contd)
- mortgages,
- agricultural credit.

15. Suretyship
- suretyship (direct),
- suretyship (indirect).

16. Miscellaneous financial loss
- employment risks,
- insufficiency of income (general),
- bad weather,
- loss of benefits,
- continuing general expenses,
- unforeseen trading expenses,
- loss of market value,
- loss of rent or revenue,
- indirect trading losses other than those mentioned above,
- other financial loss (non-trading),
- other forms of financial loss.

17. Legal expenses — Legal expenses and costs of litigation.

The risks included in a class may not be included in any other class except in the cases referred to in point C.

B. Description of authorisations granted for more than one class of insurance.

Where authorisation simultaneously covers:

(a) Classes Nos 1 and 2, it shall be named "Accident and Health Insurance";

(b) Classes Nos 1 (fourth indent), 3, 7, 10, it shall be named "Motor Insurance";

(c) Classes Nos 1 (fourth indent), 4, 6, 7 and 12, it shall be named "Marine and Transport Insurance";

(d) Classes Nos 1 (fourth indent), 5, 7 and 11, it shall be named "Aviation Insurance";

(e) Classes Nos 8 and 9, it shall be named "Insurance against Fire and other Damage to Property";

(f) Classes Nos 10, 11, 12 and 13, it shall be named "Liability Insurance";

(g) Classes Nos 14 and 15, it shall be named "Credit and Suretyship Insurance";

(h) All classes, it shall be named at the choice of the Member State in question, which shall notify the other member States and the Commission of its choice.

C. Ancillary risks

Any undertaking obtaining an authorisation for a principal risk belonging to one class or a group of classes may also insure risks included in another class without an authorisation being necessary for them if they:

- are connected with the principal risk,

- concern the object which is covered against the principal risk, and

- are covered by the contract insuring the principal risk.

However, the risks included in classes 14 and 15 in point A of this Annex may not be regarded as risks ancillary to other classes.

COUNCIL DIRECTIVE

of 5 March 1979

79/267/EEC

(OJ 1979 L063)

on the coodination of laws, regulations and administrative provisions relating to the taking up and pursuit of the business of direct life insurance (79/267/eec)

THE COUNCIL OF THE EUROPEAN COMMUNITIES

Having regard to the Treaty establishing the European Economic Community, in particular Articles 49 and 57 thereof;

Having regard to the proposal from the Commission [OJ No C 35, 28.3.1974, p 9];

Having regard to the Opinion of the European Parliament [OJ No C 140, 13.11.1974, p 44];

Having regard to the Opinion of the Economic and Social Committee [OJ No C 109, 19.9.1974, p 1];

Whereas, in order to facilitate the taking up and pursuit of the business of life assurance, it is essential to eliminate certain divergences which exist between national supervisory legislation; whereas, in order to achieve this objective and at the same time ensure adequate protection for policy-holders and beneficiaries in all Member States, the provisions relating to the Financial guarantees required of life assurance undertakings should be coordinated;

Whereas a classification by class of insurance is necessary in order to determine, in particular, the activities subject to compulsory authorisation;

Whereas certain mutual associations, which, by virtue of their legal status, fulfil requirements as to security and other specific financial guarantees should be excluded from the scope of this Directive; whereas certain organisations whose activity covers only a very restricted sector and is limited by their articles of association should also be excluded;

Whereas the Member States have different regulations and practices as to the simultaneous carrying on of life assurance and non-life insurance; whereas newly formed undertakings should no loger be authorised to carry on these two activities simultaneously; whereas Member States should be allowed to continue to do so provided that separate management is adopted for each of their activities, in order that the respective interests of life policy-holders and non-life policy-holders are safeguarded and the minimum financial obligations in respect of one of the activites are not borne by the other activity; whereas, when one of the undertakings wishes to establish itself in a subsidiary for that purpose, which may be eligible on a transitional basis for certain facilities; whereas, Member States should be given the option of requiring those existing undertakings established in their territory which carry on life assurance and non-life insurance simultaneously to put an end to this practice; whereas, moreover, specialised undertakings should be subject to special supervision where a non-life undertaking belongs to the same financial group as a life undertaking;

Whereas life assurance is subject to official authorisation and supervision in each Member State; whereas the conditions for the granting or withdrawal of such authorisation should be defined; whereas provision must be made for the right to apply to the courts should an authorisation be refused or withdrawn;

Whereas, as regards technical reserves, including mathematical reserves, the same rules may be adopted as in the case of non-life insurance, namely, they must be localized in the country where activites are carried on and the rules of that country are to govern the methods of calculation, the determination of investment categories and the valuation of assets; whereas, although it is desirable that these various subjects should be coordinated, this is not essential for the purposes of this Directive and may be carried out subsequently;

Where it is necessary that, over and above technical reserves, including mathematical reserves, of sufficient amount to meet their underwriting liabilities, insurance undertakings should possess a supplementary reserve, known as the insolvency margin, represented by free assets and, with the agreement of the supervisory authority, by other implicit assets, in order to provide against business fluctuations, whereas, in order to ensure that the requirements imposed for such purposes are determined according to objective criteria whereby undertakings of the same size will be placed on an equal footing as regards competition, it is desirable to provide that this margin shall be related to all the commitments of the undertaking and to the nature and gravity of the risks presented by the various activities falling within the scope of the Directive; whereas this margin should therefore vary according to whether the risks are of investment, death or management only; whereas it should accordingly be determined in terms of mathematical reserves and capital at risk underwritten by an undertaking, of premiums or contributions received, of reserves only or of the assets of tontines;

Whereas it is necessary to require a guarantee fund, the amount and composition of which are such as to provide an assurance that the undertakings possess adequate resources when they are set up and that in the subsequent course of business the solvency margin in no event falls below a minimum of security; whereas the whole or a specified part of this guarantee fund must consist of explicit asset items;

Whereas it is necessary to provide for measures in cases where the financial position of the undertaking becomes such that is is difficult for it to meet its underwriting liabilities;

Whereas the coordinated rules concerning the pursuit of the business of direct insurance within the Community should, in principle, apply to all undertakings operating on the market and, consequently, also to agencies and branches where the head office of the undertaking is situated outside the Community; whereas it is, nevertheless, desirable as regards the methods of supervision to lay down special provisions with respect to such agencies or branches in view of the fact that the assets of the undertakings to which they belong are situated outside the Community;

Whereas it is, however, desirable to permit the relaxation of such special conditions, while observing the principle that such agencies and branches should not obtain more favourable treatment than undertakings within the Community;

Whereas certain transitional provisions are required in order, in particular, to permit small and medium-sized undertakings already in existence to adapt themselves to the requirements which must be imposed by the Member States in pursuance of this Directive, subject to the application of Article 53 of the Treaty;

Whereas Article 52 of the EEC Treaty has been directly applicable since the end of the transitional period; whereas since that time there has accordingly been no need for the adoption of Directives abolishing restrictions on the freedom of establishment; whereas, however, the provisions concerning proof of good repute and no previous bankruptcy contained in Council Directive 73/240/EEC of 24 July 1973, abolishing restrictions on freedom of establishment in the business of direct insurance other than life assurance [OJ No L 229, 16.9.1973, p 20] do not strictly speaking constitute restrictions and are also required in life assurance; whereas they should accordingly be included in this coordination Directive;

Whereas it is important to guarantee the uniform application of coordinated rules and to provide, in this respect, for close collaboration between the Commission and the Member States in this field;

HAS ADOPTED THIS DIRECTIVE:

TITLE I
GENERAL PROVISIONS

Article 1

This Directive concerns the taking up and pursuit of the self-employed activity of direct insurance carried on by undertakings which are established in a Member State or wish to become established there in the form of the activities defined below:

1. The following kinds of insurance where they are on a contractual basis:

(*a*) life assurance, that is to say, the class of insurance which comprises, in particular, assurance on survival to a stipulated age only, assurance on death only, assurance on survival to a stipulated age or on earlier death, life assurance with return of premiums, marriage assurance, birth assurance;

(*b*) annuities;

(*c*) supplementary insurance carried on by life assurance undertakings, that is to say, in particular, insurance against personal injury including incapacity for employment, insurance against death resulting from an accident and insurance against disability resulting from an accident or sickness, where these various kinds of insurance are underwritten in addition to life assurance;

(*d*) the type of insurance existing in Ireland and the United Kingdom known as permanent health insurance not subject to cancellation.

2. The following operations, where they are on a contractual basis, in so far as they are subject to supervision by the administrative authorities responsible for the supervision of private insurance and are authorised in the country concerned:

(*a*) tontines whereby associations of subscribers are set up with a view to jointly capitalising their contributions and subsequently distributing the assets thus accumulated among the survivors or among the beneficiaries of the deceased;

(*b*) capital redemption operations based on actuarial calculation whereby, in return for single or periodic payments agreed in advance, commitments of specified duration and amount are undertaken;

(*c*) management of group pension funds, ie operations consisting, for the undertaking concerned, in managing the investments, and in particualr the assets representing the reserves of bodies that effect payments on death or survival or in the event of discontinuance or curtailment of activity;

(*d*) the operations referred to in (*c*) where they are accompanied by insurance covering either conservation of capital or payment of a minimum interest;

(*e*) the operations carried out by insurance companies such as those referred to in Chapter 1, Title 4 of Book IV of the French "Code des Assurances".

3. Operations relating to the length of human life which are prescribed by or provided for in social insurance legislation, when they are effected or managed at their own risk by assurance undertakings in accordance with the laws of a Member State.

ANNEX
Classes of Insurance

I. The assurance referred to in Article 1(1)(*a*), (*b*) and (*c*) excluding those referred to in II and III.

II. Marriage assurance, birth insurance.

III. The assurance referred to in Article 1(1)(*a*) and (*b*), which are linked to investment funds.

IV. Permanent health insurance, referred to in Article 1(1)(*d*).

V. Tontines, referred to in Article 1(2)(*a*).

VI. Capital redemption operations, referred to in Article 1(2)(*b*).

VII. Management of group pension funds, referred to in Article 1(2)(*c*) and (*d*).

VIII. The operations referred to in Article 1(2)(*e*).

IX. The operations referred to in Article 1(3).

STAMP DUTY (EXEMPTIONS MISCELLANEOUS ACTS)

Broadcasting Authority Act 1960 s 32
Building Societies Act 1989 s 118
Canals Act 1986 s 2
Central Bank Act 1971 ss 42 and 48
Charitable Loan Societies (Ireland) Act 1843 s 26
Common Law Procedure Amendment Act (Ireland) 1856 s 36
Companies Act 1990 s 208
Companies Act 1963 ss 64, 65 and 95
Congested Districts Board (Ireland) Act 1899 s 3
Diplomatic Relations and Immunities Act 1967 Articles 23, 28, 34 and 49
Diseases of Animals Act 1966 s 6
Electricity (Supply) Act, 1927 s 95
Erne Drainage and Development Act 1950 s 12
Export Promotion Act 1959 s 6
Family Home Protection Act 1976 s 12
Family Law (Miscellaneous Provisions) Act 1997 s 6
Fire Services Act 1981 s 17
Fisheries Act 1980 s 62
Forestry Act 1946 ss 19, 20, 21 and 26
Foyle Fisheries Act 1952 s 9
Friendly Societies Act 1896 s 33
Glebe Loans (Ireland) Act 1879 s 8
Grass Meal (Production) Act 1953 s 4(2)
Great Northern Railway Act 1958 s 4
Harbours Act 1996 s 98
Higher Education Authority Act 1971 s 18
Hospitals Federation and Amalgamation Act 1961 s 19
Housing (Miscellaneous Provisions) Act 1992 s 8
Housing Finance Agency Act 1981 s 16
Industrial Development Act 1986 s 17

Industrial Development Act 1995 s 9
Irish Film Board Act 1980 s 33
Irish Land Act 1903 s 50
Irish Land Act 1909 s 10
Irish News Agency Act 1949 s 4(3)
Land Act 1931 s 2
Land Act 1950 ss 27, 28 and 30
Land Act 1965 s 5
Landed Property Improvement (Ireland) Act 1847 s 59
Marine Institute Act 1991 s 20
Merchant Shipping Act 1894 ss 108, 196, 309, 320, 342, 395, 563 and 721
National College of Art and Design Act 1971 s 29
National Film Studios of Ireland Limited Act 1980 s 17
National Stud Act 1945 s 5(3) and (4)
Postal and Telecommunications Services Act 1983 ss 43, 68 and 106
Railways Act 1924 s 9
Sea Fisheries Act 1952 s 30
Social Welfare (Consolidation) Act 1981 s 302
State Property Act, 1954 s 6
Statute of Limitations 1957 s 60
Succession Act 1965 s 52
The Institute of Civil Engineers of Ireland (Charter Amendment) Act 1969 s 11
Transport Act 1944 s 58(3) and (4)
Transport Act 1950 ss 26, 27, 38, 39, 40, 42 and 67
Trustee Savings Banks Act 1989 s 64
Údarás na Gaeltachta Act 1979 s 25
Wildlife Act 1976 s 14 and 55

TABLE OF CASES

TABLE OF STATUTORY REFERENCES
(STAMP DUTIES)

DESTINATION TABLE

This table may be used to trace the present location of older legislation as re-enacted in the Stamp Duties Consolidation Act, 1999.

Former Enactment   *Destination in SDCA 1999*

Stamp Duties Management Act 1891

s 1 ....ss 136, 137

2 .... FA 1924 s 38(1) provides for new recovery provisions ...s 138
consequent on the establishment of
Saorstát Éireann.

In SDMA 1891 s 2(2) the words "England or"
and ", or of the Court of Session sitting as
the Court of Exchequer in Scotland, as the
case may require," repealed by FA 1999
s 197 and Sch 6.

The functions of the High Court existing on
the foundation of the Saorstát Éireann were
transferred to the High Court established
under CJA 1924 s 17. The Constitution of
Ireland Art 58 provides for the continuity of
the High Court established under the 1924
Act until such time as a High Court was
established under the Constitution of Ireland
Art 34. This happened in 1961. The High
Court established by C(EC)A 1961 s 2
exercises the same jurisdiction as was
exercised by the High Court established
under the 1924 Act - C(SP)A 1961 s 8 refers.

3 ....s 146

4 ....s 147

5 ....s 148

6 ....s 149

7 .... Repealed by PTSA 1983 s 7 and Sch 3 Pt 1.

8 .... The words "Minister for Finance" substituted..................s 150
for the words "Treasury" by RCO No 2 of
1923 para 17.

9 .... In para (a) the word "abroad" replaced by the words ....s 151
"outside the State".

para (c) to proviso to s 9 unnecessary
(obsolete).

10 ....s 152

11 ....s 153

12 ....s 154

12A .... (s 12A inserted by FA 1999 s 185)....................................s 155

13 (1), (2) ...... Repealed by FYA 1913 s 20 and Sch.

Stamp Duties Management Act 1891 (contd)

s 13 (3)-(9)........In SDMA 1891 s 13(8) the words "any forged stamp or" s 139
and in SDMA 1891 s 13(9) the words "any
forged die or stamp or" repealed by FYA
1913 s 20 and Sch.

14 ....Repealed by FYA 1913 s 20 and Sch.

15 ....Repealed by FYA 1913 s 20 and Sch.

16 .... s 140

17 .... s 141

18 .... s 142

19 .... s 143

20 .... s 144

21 .... s 145

22 ....The words "Iris Oifigiúil" substituted for the words .... s 156(1), (3)
"the London, Edinburgh and Dublin
Gazettes" by IR(Adap)O 1923 para 16(2).

The words "Saorstát Éireann" substituted for
the words "United Kingdom" by IR(Adap)O
1923 para 9(1) and the words "Ireland"
substituted for the words "Saorstát Éireann"
by C(CP)A 1937 s 2(1). "Ireland" is referred
to as the "State".

23 ....Repealed by FA 1999 s 197 and Sch 6.

24 ....The words "Saorstát Éireann" substituted for the .... s 157
words "United Kingdom" by IR(Adap)O
1923 para 9(1) and the word "Ireland"
substituted for the words "Saorstát Éireann"
by C(CP)A 1937 s 2(1). "Ireland" is referred
to as the "State". Powers of district justices in
relation to administering oaths and taking
declarations transferred to peace
commissioners by CJA 1924 s 88(3).

25 .... s 158

26 .... s 159

27 ....(definition of "impressed" inserted by FA 1989 s 67.)...... ss 1, 135
Definitions of "chief office", "head offices"
and "justice" unnecessary (duplication).
In the definition of "Commissioners"
"Revenue Commissioners" substituted for
"Commissioners of Inland Revenue" by RCO
No 2 of 1923 para 11. FA 1934 s 35
confirmed that all the jurisdictions, powers
and duties which were vested in, exercisable
by, or incumbent on the Commissioners of
Inland Revenue in relation to stamp duties
became and were, on 21 February, 1923,
vested in, exercisable by, or incumbent on the
Revenue Commissioners.

In the definition of "justice" "district justice"
substituted for "justice of the peace" by AE
1922 s 6.

Stamp Duties Management Act 1891 (contd)

s 28 .... s 28 to "Provided that" repealed by SLRA 1908 s 1 and Sch.
            Unnecessary (transitional)

29 .... Repealed by SLRA 1908 s 1 and Sch.

30 .... Unnecessary (short title).

Sch .... Repealed by SLRA 1908 s 1 and Sch.

Stamp Act 1891

Part I

s 1 (1)-(4) ....s 2

(5) ....s 134

2 ....s 4

3 ....s 6

4 .... (s 4(c) inserted by F(No 2)A 1998 s 8) ....s 7

5 ....s 8

6 .... Repealed by FA 1998 s 125 and Sch 8.

7 .... The words "of an amount not exceeding 7p" ....s 10(1)
            and "not appropriated by any word or words
            on the face of them to any particular
            description of instrument" repealed by FA
            1998 s 125 and Sch 8.

8 .... In s 8(1) the words ", or for any postal purpose," ....s 10(2)-(4)
            repealed by FA 1998 s 125 and Sch 8.

9 (1) .... In s 9(1)(a) the words "or used for any postal ....s 10(5)
            purpose" repealed by FA 1998 s 125 and Sch
            8.

(2) .... Repealed by RA 1898 s 7(4).

10 .... Repealed by FA 1998 s 125 and Sch 8.

11 ....s 11

12 ....s 20

13 ....s 21

14 .... In SA 1891 s 14(1) and (4) the words "Saorstát ....s 127
            Éireann" substituted for the words "United
            Kingdom" by IR(Adap)O 1923 para 9(1) and
            the word "Ireland" substituted for the words
            "Saorstát Éireann" by C(CP)A 1937 s 2(1).
            "Ireland" is referred to as the "State".
            In s 14(1) the words "and of further sum of
            one pound," repealed by FA 1999 s 197 and
            Sch 6.

15 (1)-(5) ....s 14

(6) .... Unnecessary (commencement).

16 ....s 128

17 ....s 129(1)

Part II

s 18 .... Repealed by FA 1970 s 60 and Sch 2.

19 .... Repealed by FA 1970 s 60 and Sch 2.

20 .... Repealed by FA 1970 s 60 and Sch 2.

21 .... Repealed by FA 1970 s 60 and Sch 2.

22 .... Repealed by FA 1970 s 60 and Sch 2.

Stamp Act 1891 (contd)

s 23 (1), (2) .... The words "or colonial" in s 23(1) omitted .... s 107
as they do not apply to the State.

    (3) .... Repealed by FA 1998 s 125 and Sch 8.

24 .... Repealed by FA 1970 s 60 and Sch 2.

25 .... Repealed by FA 1970 s 60 and Sch 2.

26 .... Unnecessary (does not apply to the State).

27 .... Repealed by FA 1970 s 60 and Sch 2.

28 .... Repealed by FA 1970 s 60 and Sch 2.

29 .... Repealed by CA 1927 s 3 and Sch 1.

30 .... Repealed by CA 1927 s 3 and Sch 1.

31 .... Repealed by CA 1927 s 3 and Sch 1.

32 .... The words from "; and the expression 'bill .... s 1
of exchange payable on demand' includes -
"to end of section repealed by FA 1998 s 125
and Sch 8.

33 (1) .... s 1

    (2) .... s 28

34 .... Repealed by FA 1961 s 39 and Sch 3 Pt III

35 .... Repealed by FA 1970 s 41(7)

36 .... The words "determining the mode in which" .... s 22
and the words "is to be denoted" repealed by
FA 1961 s 39 and Sch 3 Pt III.
The words "Saorstát Éireann" substituted for
the words "United Kingdom" by IR(Adap)O
1923 para 9(1) and the word "Ireland"
substituted for the words "Saorstát Éireann"
by C(CP)A 1937 s 2(1). "Ireland" is referred
to as the "State".
The word "abroad" replaced by the words
"outside the State".

37 (1) .... Repealed by FA 1961 s 39 and Sch 3.

    (2) .... The words "Except as aforesaid" repealed by .... s 23
FA 1961 s 39 and Sch 3 Pt III.

38 .... Repealed by FA 1970 s 41(7).

39 .... s 24

40 .... Repealed by FA 1963 s 104 and Sch 6 Pt IV.

41 .... s 129(2)

42 .... Repealed by FA 1970 s 60 and Sch 2.

43 .... Repealed by FA 1955 s 19 and Sch 3.

44 .... Repealed by SOLA 1954 s 7 and Sch 1.

45 .... Repealed by FA 1955 s 19 and Sch 3.

46 .... Repealed by FA 1996 s 119 and Sch 4.

47 .... Repealed by FA 1955 s 19 and Sch 3.

48 .... Repealed by FA 1955 s 19 and Sch 3.

49 .... Repealed by FA 1970 s 60 and Sch 2.

50 .... Repealed by FA 1970 s 60 and Sch 2.

51 .... Repealed by FA 1970 s 60 and Sch 2.

52 .... Repealed by F(1909-10)A 1910 s 96 and Sch 6.

Stamp Act 1891 (contd)

s 53 .... Repealed by F(1909-10)A 1910 s 96 and Sch 6.

54 .... s 1

55 .... s 40

56 .... The words "or in perpetuity, or for any indefinite .... s 42
period not terminable with life" in SA 1891 s
56(2), (3) repealed by FA 1998 s 125 and Sch
8.

57 .... s 41

58 (1)-(3) .... (s 58(1A) as inserted by FA 1997 s 119 .... s 45
substituted by F(No 2)A 1998 s 9).

(4)-(9) .... (s 58(7)-(9) inserted by FA 1981 s 47.) .... s 46
In s 58(7) the words "or (3)" repealed by FA
1999 s 197 and Sch 6.

59 (1) .... The words "Saorstát Éireann" substituted for .... s 31(1)
the words "United Kingdom" by IR(Adap)O
1923 para 9(1) and the word "Ireland"
substituted for the words "Saorstát Éireann"
by C(CP)A 1937 s 2(1). "Ireland" is referred
to as the "State".
The words "made in England or Ireland under
seal, or under hand only, or made in Scotland,
with or without any clause of registration"
repealed by RA 1909 s 12 and Sch.

(2), (3) .... In s 59(2) the words "except (where appropriate) .... s 31(2), (3)
with the fixed duty of £10" repealed by FA
1999 s 197 and Sch 6.

(4) .... Repealed by FA 1970 s 60 and Sch 2.

(5) .... Repealed by FA 1999 s 197 and Sch 6.

(6) .... s 31(4)

(7) .... (s 59(7) inserted by FA 1998 s 119) .... s 31(1)

60 .... s 32

61 (1) .... Repealed by FA 1970 s 60 and Sch 2.

(2) .... The words "In any other case" repealed by .... s 47
FA 1970 s 60 and Sch 2.

62 .... The proviso repealed by FA 1999 s 197 and Sch 6 .... s 49

63 .... Repealed by FA 1970 s 60 and Sch 2.

64 .... Repealed by FA 1954 s 29 and Sch 3.

65 .... Repealed by FA 1970 s 60 and Sch 2.

66 .... Repealed by FA 1970 s 60 and Sch 2.

67 .... Repealed by FA 1970 s 60 and Sch 2.

68 .... Repealed by FA 1970 s 60 and Sch 2.

69 .... Repealed by FA 1905 s 8 and Sch.

70 .... Repealed by FA 1905 s 8 and Sch.

71 .... Repealed by FA 1905 s 8 and Sch.

72 .... s 13

73 .... The words "in any such case" unnecessary. .... s 38

74 .... Unnecessary (does not apply to the State).

Former Enactment	*Destination in SDCA 1999*

Stamp Act 1891 (contd)

s 75 (1)..............The words "or tack" wherever they occur.......................s 50
omitte as they do not apply to the State.

(2)..............Repealed by FA 1970 s 60 and Sch 2.

76 ....The words " or tack" wherever they occur ....s 51
and "tack," omitted as they do not apply to the
State.

77 (1)..............The words " or tack" wherever they occur ....s 52(1)
and "tack," omitted as they do not apply to the
State.

(2)...s 52(2)

(3), (4).......Repealed by FA 1998 s 125 and Sch 8.

(5)..............The words " or tack" wherever they occur ....s 52(4)
omitted as they do not apply to the State.

(6)..............(s 77(6) as inserted by FA 1997 s 120 ....s 52(5)
substituted by F(No 2)A 1998 s 10

78 ....Repealed by FA 19991 s 91.

79 ....Repealed by FA 1964 s 33 and Sch 5 Pt IV.

80 ....Repealed by FA 1964 s 33 and Sch 5 Pt IV.

81 ....Repealed by FA 1917 s 30(2).

82 ....Repealed by FA 1970 s 60 and Sch 2.

83 ....Repealed by FA 1998 s 125 and Sch 8.

84 ....Repealed by FA 1998 s 125 and Sch 8.

85 ....Repealed by CIRA 1893 s 4(2).

86 (1)..............The words "Conditional surrender by way of ....s 1
mortgage" in s 86(1)(a) repealed by FA 1970
s 60 and Sch 2. The words "wadset," in s
86(1)(a) and (e), "and eik to a reversion" in s
86(1)(a) and "back bond" and "or tack" in s
86(1)(d) and s 86(1)(b) and (f) omitted as they
do not apply to the State.

(2)...s 1

87 (1)..............The words ", and a reconveyance, release, ...s 57(1)
discharge, surrender, re-surrender, warrant to
vacate, or renunciation of any such security,"
repealed by FA 1998 s 125 and Sch 8.

(2), (3)..s 57(2), (3)

(4), (5).......Repealed by FA 1970 s 60 and Sch 2.

(6)...s 57(4)

88 ....s 58

89 ....Repealed by FA 1970 s 60 and Sch 2.

90 ....Repealed by FA 1964 s 33 and Sch 5 Pt IV.

91 ....s 1

92 ....Repealed by FA 1959 s 80 and Sch 4 Pt II.

93 ....Repealed by FA 1959 s 80 and Sch 4 Pt II.

94 ....Repealed by FA 1959 s 80 and Sch 4 Pt II.

95 ....Repealed by FA 1959 s 80 and Sch 4 Pt II.

96 ....Repealed by FA 1959 s 80 and Sch 4 Pt II.

97 ....Repealed by FA 1959 s 80 and Sch 4 Pt II.

Stamp Act 1891 (contd)

s 98 (1) .... The words from "against accident; and" to .... s 1
                 "a policy of insurance" and from "or as
                 compensation" to the end of that subsection
                 repeald by FA 1959 s 80 and Sch 4 Pt II.

   (2) .... Repealed by FA 1959 s 80 and Sch 4 Pt II.

99 .... Repealed by FA 1970 s 60 and Sch 2.

100(1) .... The words "other than a sea insurance" .... s 59(1)
                 repealed by FA 1959 s 80 and Sch 4 Pt II.

   (2) .... The words "other than a policy of sea insurance" .... s 59(1)
                 repealed by FA 1959 s 80 and Sch 4 Pt II.

101 .... Repealed by FA 1996 s 119 and Sch 4.

102 .... Repealed by FA 1970 s 60 and Sch 2.

103 .... Repealed by FA 1970 s 60 and Sch 2

104 .... Repealed by FA 1999 s 197 and Sch 6.

105 .... Repealed by FA 1999 s 197 and Sch 6.

106 .... Repealed by FA 1999 s 197 and Sch 6.

107 .... s 65

108 .... Reference to "Local Autorities Loans Act, ... s 1
                 1875" omitted as that Act does not apply to
                 the State.

109 .... s 66

110 .... Repealed by FA 1996 s 119 and Sch 4.

111 .... Repealed by FA 1970 s 60 and Sch 2.

Part III

s 112 .... Repealed by FA 1973 s 96 and Sch 11.

113 .... Repealed by FA 1973 s 96 and Sch 11.

114 .... Unnecessary (does not apply to the State).

115 .... Repealed by FA 1998 s 125 and Sch 8.

116 .... Repealed by FA 1970 s 60 and Sch 2.

117 .... s 131

118 .... FA 1924 s 38(1) provides for new recovery .... s 130
                 provisions consequent on the establishment
                 of Saorstát Éireann.

119 .... Unnecessary (does not apply to the State).

120 .... Repealed by FA 1970 s 60 and Sch 2.

121 .... Repealed by FA 1999 s 197 and Sch 6.

122(1) .... (definition of "accountable person" inserted by .... s 1
                 FA 1991 s 96, definition of "die" inserted by
                 FA 1989 s 68 and definition of "residential
                 property" inserted by FA 1997 s 118.
                 In the Table to the definition of "accountable
                 person" the words "BOND, COVENANT or
                 INSTRUMENT of any kind whatsoever." in
                 column (1) and the words "The obligee,
                 covenantee, or other person taking the
                 security," in column (2) repealed by FA 1996
                 s 119 and Sch 4 and the words
                 "SETTLEMENT" in column (1) and the
                 words "The settlor" in column (2) repealed by
                 FA 1999 s 197 and Sch 6.

351

Stamp Act 1891 (contd)

s 122(contd)   The words "or colonial" in the definitions of "money" and "stock" and the definition of "steward" in SA 1891 s 122(1) omitted as they do not apply to the State.

In the definition of "money" "British" replaced by "currency of the State".

In the definitions of "marketable security" and "stock" the words "Saorstát Éireann" substitued for the words "United Kingdom" by IR(Adap)O 1923 para 9(1) and the word "Ireland" substituted for the words "Saorstát Éireann" by C(CP)A 1937 s 2: "Ireland" is referred to as the "State".

In the definition of "stock" the words "India promissory notes," repealed by FA 1999 s 197 and Sch 6.

Definitions of "Commissioners", "die", "executed", "execution", "impressed", "instrument", "material", "stamp" and "stamped" unnecessary (duplication).

(2) .... Unnecessary (does not apply to the State).

123 .... Repealed by SLRA 1908 s 1 and Sch.

124 .... Unneccessary (commencement).

125 .... Unneccessary (short title).

First Sch .... First Sch as substituted by FA 1970 s 40(1) .... Sch 1, s 113
was substituted by FA 1999 s 176 and Sch 5.

Second Sch .... Repealed by FA 1998 s 125 and Sch 8.

Third Sch .... Repealed by SLRA 1908 s 1 and Sch.

Customs and Inland Revenue Act 1893

s 3   .... Repealed by F(1909-10)A 1910 s 96 and Sch 6.

4   .... Repealed by SLRA 1908 s 1 and Sch.

Finance Act 1894

s 39   .... Unnecessary (extension of SA 1891 s 114).

40   .... Repealed by FA 1999 s 197 and Sch 6.

Finance Act 1895

s 9   .... Repealed by FA 1970 s 60 and Sch 2.

10   .... Repealed by SLRA 1908 s 1 and Sch.

11   .... Repealed by FA 1917 s 30(2).

12   .... Repealed by FA 1998 s 125 and Sch 8.

13   .... Repealed by FA 1959 s 80 and Sch 4 Pt II.

14   .... Repealed by FA 1970 s 60 and Sch 2.

15   .... Repealed by SLRA 1908 s 1 and Sch.

16   .... Unnecessary (does not apply to the State).

Finance Act 1896

s 12   .... Repealed by FA 1973 s 96 and Sch 11.

13   .... Repealed by FA 1959 s 80 and Sch 4 Pt II.

Finance Act 1897

s 8   .... s 26

Former Enactment   *Destination in SDCA 1999*

Finance Act 1902

    s 9 ....Repealed by FA 1999 s 197 and Sch 6.

Revenue Act 1903

    s 5 ....Repealed by FA 1973 s 96 and Sch 11.

    6 ....Repealed by FA 1905 s 8 and Sch.

    7 ....Repealed by FA 1970 s 60 and Sch 2.

    8 ....Repealed by FA 1959 s 80 and Sch 4 Pt II.

    9 ....Unnecessary (obsolete).

Finance Act 1905

    s 5 ....Repealed by FA 1970 s 60 and Sch 2.

Revenue Act 1906

    s 9 ....Repealed by FA 1970 s 60 and Sch 2.

Finance Act 1907

    s 6 ....Repealed by FA 1970 s 60 and Sch 2.

    7 ....Repealed by FA 1999 s 197 and Sch 6.

    8 ....Repealed by FA 1959 s 80 and Sch 4 Pt II.

    9 ....Repealed by FA 1964 s 33 and Sch 5 Pt IV.

    10 ....Repealed by FA 1973 s 96 and Sch 11.

    11 ....Repealed by FA 1970 s 60 and Sch 2.

Finance Act 1908

    s 5 ....Repealed by FA 1970 s 60 and Sch 2.

Revenue Act 1909

    s 7 ....Unnecessary (cesser of limitation of SA 1891 s 59 in respect of certain contracts).

    8 ....Limitation of application of SA 1891 s 77(2)...................s 52(3)

    9 ....Repealed by FA 1964 s 33 and Sch 5 Pt IV.

    10 ....Repealed by FA 1961 s 39 and Sch 3 Pt III.

Finance (1909-10) Act 1910

    s 4 ....Ceased by FA 1994 s 107(5) for instruments executed before 1 September 1995.

    73 ....Repealed by FA 1970 s 60 and Sch 2.

    74 (1), (2).......The words "the Revenue Commissioners" ....s 30(1)-(3) substituted for the words "the Commissioners" by RCO No 2 of 1923 para 11.

    (3).............Repealed by FA 1991 s 103(5).

    (4).............Repealed by FA 1999 s 197 and Sch 6.

    (5)...s 30(4)

    (6)...s 30(5)

    75 ....Repealed by FA 1970 s 60 and Sch 2.

    76 ....Repealed by FA 1970 s 60 and Sch 2.

    77 ....Repealed by FA 1970 s 60 and Sch 2.

    78 ....Repealed by FA 1970 s 60 and Sch 2.

    79 ....Repealed by FA 1970 s 60 and Sch 2.

Former Enactment   *Destination in SDCA 1999*

Revenue Act 1911

   s 15 .... Repealed by FA 1970 s 60 and Sch 2.

Finance Act 1911

   s 13 .... Repealed by FA 1970 s 60 and Sch 2.

Finance Act 1917

   s 30 .... Repealed by FA 1970 s 60 and Sch 2.

Finance Act 1918

   s 36 .... Repealed by FA 1961 s 39 and Sch 3 Pt III.

Finance Act 1920

   s 34 .... Repealed by FA 1970 s 60 and Sch 2.
     35 .... Repealed by FA 1964 s 33 and Sch 5 Pt IV.
     36 .... Repealed by FA 1970 s 60 and Sch 2.
     37 (1) .... Unnecessary (extension fo SA 1891 s 114).
      (2), (3) ...... Unnecessary (obsolete).
     38 .... Repealed by FA 1970 s 60 and Sch 2.
     39 .... Repealed by FA 1996 s 119 and Sch 4.
     40 .... Repealed by FA 1970 s 60 and Sch 2.
     41 .... Repealed by FA 1959 s 80 and Sch 4 Pt II.
     42 .... Repealed by FA 1996 s 107(5).
     43 .... Unnecessary (intepretation and commencement).
     46 .... Unnecessary (extension of 1891 s 114).
     47 .... Unnecessary (obsolete).

Inland Revenue (Adaptation of Taxing Acts) Order 1923

   para 16(1) .... Amendment of SDMA 1891.
       (2) .... Amendment of SDMA 1891 s 22.
      17 .... Unnecessary (redundant).

Finance Act 1923

   s 19 .... Repealed by FA 1999 s 197 and Sch 6.

Finance Act 1924

   s 38 (1) .... s 38(1) provided that all stamp duties and also ....ss 130, 138
               every fine, penalty or forfeiture incurred in
               connection with any stamp duties would be a
               debt due to the Minister for Finance, for the
               benefit of the Central Fund of Saorstát
               Éireann. It also set out how stamp duties, etc,
               were to be recovered. C(CP)A 1937 s 7(3)
               provides that all moneys owed to any
               Minister for the benefit of the Cental Fund of
               Saorstát Éireann immediately before th
               coming into operation of the Constitution of
               Ireland shall be payable and recoverable, in
               the same manner as set out in FA 1924
               s 38(1), for the benefit of the Central Fund of
               Ireland which was established by that
               Constitution.
               Constitution of Ireland Art 59 provided for
               the continuance of the Attorney General of
               Saorstát Éireann.
      (2) .... Repealed by FA 1999 s 197 and Sch 6.

Former Enactment   *Destination in SDCA 1999*

Finance Act 1925

s 46 ....Repealed by FA 1933 s 46.

47 ....Repealed by FA 1998 s 125 and Sch 8.

48 ....Repealed by FA 1999 s 197 and Sch 6.

Finance Act 1926

s 37 ....Repealed by FA 1996 s 119 and Sch 4.

38 ....Repealed by FA 1970 s 60 and Sch 2.

39 ....s 134

Finance (Customs and Stamp Duties) Act 1929

s 5 ....Ceased by FA 1990 s 118.

Finance Act 1929

s 35 ....Repealed by FA 1970 s 60 and Sch 2.

36 ....Amendment of F(CSD)A 1929 s 5(1).

Finance Act 1930

s 15 ....Repealed by FA 1996 s 119 and Sch 4.

16 ....Repealed by FA 1999 s 197 and Sch 6.

Finance Act 1931

s 31 ....Repealed by FA 1970 s 60 and Sch 2.

32 ....Amendment of FA 1920 s 39(1).

Finance Act 1932

s 49 ....Repealed by CBA 1942 s 4 and Sch 1 Pt II.

50 ....Unnecessary (obsolete).

Finance Act 1933

s 40 ....The word "Ireland" substituted for the words ....s 9
"Saorstát Éireann" by C(CP)A 1937 s 2(1).
"Ireland" is referred to as the "State".

41 ....Unnecessary (obsolete).

42 ....Repealed by FA 1970 s 60 and Sch 2.

43 ....Unnecessary (obsolete).

Finance Act 1934

s 34 ....Amendment of F(CSD)A 1929 s 5(1).

Finance (Miscellaneous Provisions) Act 1935

s 6(3) ....Cesser of certain exemptions from stamp duty.

Finance Act 1935

s 35 ....Repealed by FA 1996 s 107(5).

36 ....Repealed by FA 1953 s 13(2).

Finance Act 1936

s 25 ....The word "Ireland" substituted for the words ....s 27
"Saorstát Éireann" by C(CP)A 1937 s 2(1).
"Ireland" is referred to as the "State".

Finance Act 1937

s 15 ....Repealed by CBA 1942 s 4 and Sch 1 Pt II.

Former Enactment   *Destination in SDCA 1999*

Finance Act 1941

  s 47 .... Repealed by FA 1996 s 119 and Sch 4.

  48 .... Repealed by FA 1996 s 119 and Sch 4.

Finance Act 1942

  s 21 .... Unnecessary (obsolete).

Finance Act 1943

  s 14 .... Substitution of F(1909-10)A 1910 s 74(6).

  15 .... The words ", and no certificate of indebtedness ....s 112
                        and no such instrument as aforesaid
                        embodied or contained in a certificate of
                        indebtedness shall be prevented from being
                        given in evidence or being made available for
                        any purpose merely by reason of the fact that
                        no stamp duty had been paid in respect
                        thereof" repealed by FA 1999 s 197 and Sch
                        6.

  16   Unnecessary (construction and obsolete).

Finance Act 1947

  s 18 .... Repealed by FA 1970 s 60 and Sch 2.

  19 .... Repealed by FA 1996 s 119 and Sch 4.

Finance (No 2) Act 1947

  s 13 .... Repealed by FA 1970 s 60 and Sch 2.

Finance Act 1948

  s 11 .... Repealed by FA 1999 s 197 and Sch 6.

  12 .... Repealed by FA 1970 s 60 and Sch 2.

Finance Act 1949

  s 24 .... The words "shall be deemed never to have ....s 54
                        applied   or   had   effect"   unnecessary
                        (redundant)

  25 .... Repealed by FA 1970 s 60 and Sch 2.

  26 .... Repealed by FA 1965 s 66 and Sch 3 Pt VIII.

  27 .... Repealed by FA 1970 s 60 and Sch 2.

Finance Act 1950

  s 16 .... Repealed by FA 1969 s 49(6).

  17 .... Repealed by FA 1970 s 60 and Sch 2.

  18 .... Repealed by FA 1970 s 60 and Sch 2.

  19 .... Repealed by FA 1990 s 113(5)(a)(i).

Finance Act 1951

  s 17 .... Repealed by FA 1970 s 60 and Sch 2.

  18 .... Repealed by FA 1970 s 60 and Sch 2.

  19 .... Repealed by FA 1970 s 60 and Sch 2.

  20 .... Repealed by FA 1970 s 60 and Sch 2.

Finance Act 1952

  s 18 .... Repealed by FA 1965 s 66 and Sch 3 Pt VIII.

  19 .... (s 19(2A) inserted by FA 1990 s 116). ....s 79

  20 .... Repealed by FA 1970 s 60 and Sch 2.

Former Enactment	*Destination in SDCA 1999*

Finance Act 1952 (contd)

21 ....Repealed by FA 1970 s 60 and Sch 2.

22 ....Repealed by FA 1965 s 66 and Sch 3 Pt VIII.

Finance Act 1953

s 12 ....Repealed by FA 1993 s 104(5).

13 ....Repealed by FA 1970 s 60 and Sch 2.

14 ....Repealed by FA 1970 s 60 and Sch 2.

Finance Act 1954

s 23 ....Unnecessary (obsolete).

24 ....Repealed by FA 1970 s 60 and Sch 2.

25 ....Repealed by FA 1970 s 60 and Sch 2.

26 ....Repealed by FA 1970 s 60 and Sch 2.

27 ....Repealed by FA 1970 s 60 and Sch 2.

Solicitors Act 1954

s 72 ....Unnecessary (obsolete).

Finance Act 1955

s 16 ....Unnecessary (obsolete).

17 ....Repealed by FA 1999 s 197 and Sch 6.

Finance Act 1956

s 29 ....Repealed by FA 1970 s 60 and Sch 2.

30 ....Repealed by FA 1961 s 39 and Sch 3 Pt II.

31 ....Repealed by FA 1961 s 39 and Sch 3 Pt II.

Finance (Miscellaneous Provisions) Act 1956

s 24 ....Repealed by FA 1999 s 197 and Sch 6.

Finance Act 1957

s 24 ....Repealed by FA 1970 s 60 and Sch 2.

Finance Act 1958

s 57 ....Repealed by FA 1990 s 113(5)(a)(ii).

58 ....Repealed by FA 1970 s 60 and Sch 2.

59 .... s 111

60 ....Unnecessary (obsolete).

Finance Act 1959

s 75 (1)-(3),

(4)(c) ....Repealed by FA 1970 s 60 and Sch 2.

(4)..............para (a) and (b) unnecessary .... s 59(2)
(cesser of certain provisions).

76 ....Amendment of FA 1952 s 19.

Finance Act 1960

s 35 ....Repealed by FA 1970 s 60 and Sch 2.

36 ....Unnecessary (obsolete).

37 ....Repealed by FA 1970 s 60 and Sch 2.

Former Enactment   *Destination in SDCA 1999*

Finance Act 1961

s 29 .... Unnecessary (obsolete).

  30 ....s 83

  31 .... Repealed by FA 1970 s 41(7).

  32 .... Repealed by FA 1996 s 107(5).

  33 .... Repealed by FA 1965 s 66 and Sch 3 Pt VIII.

  34 .... Repealed by FA 1965 s 66 and Sch 3 Pt VIII.

  35 .... Repealed by FA 1965 s 66 and Sch 3 Pt VIII.

Finance Act 1962

s 15 .... Repealed by FA 1965 s 66 and Sch 3 Pt VIII.

  16 .... Repealed by FA 1965 s 66 and Sch 3 Pt VIII.

  17 .... Unnecessary (obsolete).

  18 .... Amendment of FA 1961 s 32(2).

Finance Act 1963

s 40 .... Unnecessary (obsolete).

  41 .... Amendment of SA 1891 First Sch.

  42 .... Repealed by FA 1965 s 66 and Sch 3 Pt VIII.

  43 .... Extension of FA 1950 s 19.

  44 .... Repealed by FA 1970 s 60 and Sch 2.

  45 .... Repealed by FA 1964 s 33 and Sch 5 Pt III.

Finance Act 1964

s 23 .... Repealed by FA 1999 s 197 and Sch 6.

  24 .... Repealed by FA 1990 s 113(5)(a)(iii).

Finance Act 1965

s 31(1)-(3)......... (s 31(1A) inserted by FA 1995 s 144(1)(a).) ....s 80(2)-(6)
                    s 31(1)(A) repealed by FA 1973 s 96 and Sch
                    11.
                    The words ", nor shall any such duty be
                    chargeable under section 12 of the Finance
                    Act, 1895 on a copy of any Act of the
                    Oireachtas, or on any instrument vesting, or
                    relating to the vesting of, the undertaking or
                    shares in the transferee company" in s
                    31(1)(B) repealed by FA 1999 s 197 and Sch
                    6.
                    s 31(1)(proviso)(c) unnecessary (redundant).

  (4)............. Repealed by FA 1973 s 96 and Sch 11.

  (5)..s 80(7)

  (6)..s 80(8)

  (7)..s 80(9)

  (7A), (8) ... (s 31(7A) inserted by FA 1995 s 144(1)(b).) ....s 80(1).

Finance Act 1966

s 20 .... Repealed by FA 1998 s 125 and Sch 8.

Finance Act 1967

s 20 ....s 94.

Former Enactment	*Destination in SDCA 1999*

Finance (Miscellaneous Provisions) Act 1968

s 10 ....Repealed by FA 1970 s 60 and Sch 2.

11 ....Repealed by FA 1996 s 119 and Sch 4.

12 ....Repealed by FA 1999 s 197 and Sch 6.

Finance Act 1969

s 47 ....Repealed by FA 1970 s 60 and Sch 2.

48 ....Repealed by FA 1970 s 60 and Sch 2.

49 (1)...s 91(1)

(2), (2A)....Repealed by FA 1998 s 125 and Sch 8.
(s 49(2A) inserted by FA 1981 s 48.)

(2B)...........(s 49(2B) as inserted by FA 1984 s 100 ....s 91(2)
was substituted by FA 1996 s 113(1).
The words "Notwithstanding subsections (2)
and (2A) of this section," and the words
"(apart from the said subsections (2) and
(2A))" repealed by FA 1998 s 125 and Sch 8.

(3).............The words "a conveyance, transfer or lease of ....s 93
a house by a local authority under the
provisions of the Housing Act, 1966, or of
"repealed by FA 1999 s 197 and Sch 6.

(4), (5).......Repealed by FA 1999 s 197 and Sch 6.

(6).............Unnecessary (repeals).

(7).............Unnecessary (commencement).

50 ....Ceased by FA 1978 s 35.

Finance Act 1970

s 40 (1).............Substitution of SA 1891 First Sch.

(2).............Unnecessary (commencement).

41 (1).............Unnecessary (duplication).

(2), (3) ....s 25

(4).............Unnecessary (obsolete).

(5).............Unnecessary (commencment).

(6).............Unnecessary (cesser of duty on certain
bills of exchange).

(7).............Unnecessary (repeals).

42 (1).............Amendment of FA 1899 s 8(2).

(2).............Amendment of FA 1907 s 10(1)

(3).............Unnecessary (commencement).

43 (1), (2) ....s 60

(3).............Unnecessary (commencement).

44 (1), (2) ....s 86

(3).............Unnecessary (cesser of composition agreement
under SA 1891 s 115).

(4).............Unnecessary (commencement).

45 ....Amendment of FA 1969 s 50.

46 (1)(a) ....Amendment of SA 1891 s 7.

(b).........Amendment of SA 1891 s 23(1) and (2).

(c).........Amendment of SA 1891 s 59(2).

(d).........Amendment of SA 1891 s 59(5).

Former Enactment   *Destination in SDCA 1999*
Finance (No 2) Act 1981

s 16 .... Unnecessary (spent).

17 .... (s 17(2)(d) inserted by FA 1983 s 91.).............................s 124

Finance Act 1982

s 91 .... Unnecessary (spent).

92 (1)-(7) .... (s 92(1) definition of "excluded amount" ....s 125
                  para (d) inserted by FA 1995 s 146 and
                  s 92(8) inserted by FA 1984 s 98.)

(8)............. Repealed by FA 1998 s 121(2).

93 .... Unnecessary (spent).

94 (1)............. Unnecessary (definition).

(2)............. Amendment of SA 1891 s 56, 59, 62 and 106
               and First Sch, FA 1902 s 9, FA 1920 s 42 and
               FA 1961 s 30.

(3),(4)(a),(5)Amendment of SA 1891 First Sch.

(4)(b)(i)..s 109

(4)(b)(ii) ....s 62

(6)............. Unnecessary (commencement).

95 (1)............. Amendment of FA 1970 s 41.

(2), (3) ...... Unnecessary (revocation and commencement).

96 (1)............. Substitution of FA 1952 s 19(1).

(2), (3) ...... Unnecessary (revocation and commencement).

Finance Act 1983

s 90 .... Unnecessary (spent).

91 .... Insertion of F(No 2)A 1981 s 17(2)(d).

92 (1)............. Substitution of F(1909-10)A 1910 s 74(5).

(2)............. Unnecessary (commencement).

93 (1)............. Amendment of FA 1982 s 92.

(2)............. Unnecessary (commencement).

Finance Act 1984

s 97 .... Unnecessary (spent).

98 .... Insertion of FA 1982 s 92(8).

99 .... Amendment of FA 1982 s 93(5).

100(1)............. Insertion of FA 1969 s 49(2B).

(2), (3) ...... Unnecessary (revocation and commencement).

101(1)............. Substitution of SA 1891 s 7.

(2)............. Amendment of FA 1970 s 41.

(3)............. Unnecessary (commencement).

102 .... Amendment of F(No 2)A 1981 s 17(1) and (2).

103 .... Unnecessary (revocation).

Finance Act 1985

s 55 .... Unnecessary (spent).

56 .... Unnecessary (revocation, cesser of FA 1980 s 86 and definition).

57 .... Amendment of FA 1982 s 93(5).

Former Enactment	*Destination in SDCA 1999*

Finance Act 1991 (contd)

s 106(1) ....Amendment of SA 1891 ss 8(3), 9, 17, 83, 100, 107, 109(2), SDMA 1891 ss 20, 21, F(1909-10)A 1910 s 4(2) and FA 1970 s 41(3).

   (2)............Unnecessary (commencement).

107 ....Amendment of Stock Transfer Act 1963 s 4(1).

108(1) ....s 132

   (2)............Unnecessary (commencement).

109(1) ....s 133

   (2)............Unnecessary (commencement).

110................Insertion of FA 1973 s 67B.

111................Amendment of FA 1982 s 92(8)

Finance Act 1992

s 199................Unnecessary (definitions).

200................Unnecessary (spent).

201................Unnecessary (transitional).

202................Amendment of F(No 2)A 1981 s 17(1) and (2).

203................(s 203(10) inserted by FA 1993 s 102.)............s 123
          Definition of "date of publication" unnecessary (commencement).

204(a)............Amendment of SA 1891 First Sch.

  (b)............Amendment of SA 1891 ss 56, 59, 62 and 106.

  (c)............Amendment of FA 1902 s 9.

  (d)............Amendment of FA 1920 s 42.

  (e)............Amendment of FA 1961 s 30.

205(1)-(9) ....Amendment of SA 1891 First Sch.

  (10)...........Repealed by FA 1999 s 197 and Sch 6.

206...s 88

207...s 90

208................(s 208(2) inserted by FA 1999 s 196.)............s 61

209................The words "Notwithstanding the provisions of ....s 98
          section 1 of the Act of 1891 and the provisions of the First Schedule," unnecessary (superfluous).

210...s 108

211................Unnecessary (revocation).

212................Repealed by FA 1999 s 141(2).

213................Substitution of FA 1991 s 104.

214................Amendment of FA 1972 s 45(1).

215................Unnecessary (repeals and commencement).

216(1)-(3) ....s 100

  (4)............Unnecessary (repeal).

  (5)............Unnecessary (commencement).

217................Amendment of FA 1970 s 44.

Finance (No 2) Act 1992

s 28 ....Unnecessary (provison for cesser of certain levies).

| *Former Enactment* | *Destination in SDCA 1999* |

Finance Act 1993

s 100 .... Substitution of FA 1990 s 112(1)(a) and (b) and
 amendment of FA 1990 s 112(3)(a).

101(1),(2)(b),(3) .... s 103

(2)(a) .... Repealed by FA 1999 s 197 and Sch 6.

(4) .... Unnecessary (commencement).

102(a) .... Substitution of FA 1992 s 203(1) definition of "bank".

(b) .... Insertion of FA 1992 s 203(10).

103(1) .... Amendment of FA 1982 s 92(3).

(2) .... Unnecessary (commencement).

104(1) .... Unnecessary (definition).

(2) .... Amendment of FA 1953 s 12 in so far as s 12 .... s 37
 covers "exchanges".

(3) .... Amendment of SA 1891 First Sch.

(4) .... Non-application of SA 1891 s 73 to exchanges.

(5) .... Unnecessary (repeal).

105 .... Substitution of FA 1978 s 34(5)(b).

106 .... s 85.

Finance Act 1994

s 102 .... Unnecessary (definitions).

103(1) .... Amendment of FA 1991 s 103(1).

(2), (3) ...... Unnecessary (repeal and commencement).

104(1) .... Amendment of FA 1991 s 105(1).

(2) .... Unnecessary (commencement).

105 .... Amendment of FA 1992 s 206.

106 .... Amendment of FA 1993 s 106.

107(1)-(3) .... s 12(2)-(4)

(4), (5) ...... Unnecessary (commencement and cesser of
 F(1909-10)A 1910 s 4).

(6) .... s 12(1)

108(1) .... ss 48, 56

(2) .... Unnecessary (relates to instruments stamped
 prior to 11 April, 1994).

109(1) .... Substitution of SA 1891 s 13.

(2) .... Repealed by FA 1999 s 197 and Sch 6.

(3) .... Unnecessary (repeals).

(4) .... Unnecessary (commencement).

110 .... Repealed by FA 1999 s 197 and Sch 6.

111 .... s 89

112 .... s 81

161(4) .... Amendment of SA 1891 First Sch.

Sixth Sch. .... Sch 2

Finance Act 1995

s 142 .... Unnecessary (spent).

143(1) .... Amendment of FA 1952 s 19.

(2) .... Unnecessary (commencement).

Former Enactment	*Destination in SDCA 1999*

Criminal Assets Bureau Act 1996

s 24(3) .... Unnecessary (deletion of SA 1891 s 12(6)(d) as inserted by Disclosure of Certain Information for Taxation and Other Purposes Act 1996 s 7).

Finance Act 1997

s 115 .... Definitions of "the Act of 1891", "the Act of .... s 1 1978", "the Commissioners" and "the First Schedule" unnecessary (interpretation and duplication).

116 .... Unnecessary (commencement).

117 .... Amendment of SA 1891 First Sch.

118 .... Insertion of SA 1891 s 122(1) definition of .... s 1 "residential property".

119 .... Insertion of SA 1891 s 58(1A).

120 .... Insertion of SA 1891 s 77(6).

121 .... FA 1997 s 121(1)(a)-(d) unnecessary (duplication)........... s 16

122 .... s 17

123 .... s 92(1)(a)(i)(II), (ii)(II)

124 .... Declaratory words unnecessary. .... s 92(1)(a)(i)(II), (ii)(II)

125 .... Amendment of FA 1992 s 207(1), (2).

126 .... Amendment of FA 1994 s 112(7).

127(1)-(3)... s 97

(4) .... Unnecessary (repeals).

128(1)... s 99

(2), (3) ...... Unnecessary (commencement and repeal).

129(1)... s 110

(2) .... Unnecessary (commencement).

130 .... Unnecessary (repeal and commencement).

Taxes Consolidation Act 1997

Sch 31 .... Amendment of SA 1891 ss 13(1) and (4), FA 1952 s 19(2), FA 1969 s 49(2B)(c), FA 1986 s 94(1)(a), FA 1990 s 112(5), FA 1991 ss 108(1) and 109(1), FA 1992 ss 206(a), (aa) and (c)(ii) and 207(2), FA 1993 s 106(2)(b) and FA 1996 s 108(4).

Finance Act 1998

s 118 .... Amendment of SA 1891 s 54.

119(1)............. Insertion of SA 1891 s 59(7).

(2) .... Unnecessary (commencement).

120 .... Amendment of SA 1891 First Sch.

121(1)............. Amendment of FA 1982 s 92(1).

(2) .... Unnecessary (repeal).

122 .... Amendment of FA 1992 s 203(2).

123(1)............. Amendment of FA 1996 s 107.

(2) .... Unnecessary (commencement).

Former Enactment	*Destination in SDCA 1999*

Finance Act 1999 (contd)

s 164 .... Amendment of FA 1969 s 49(2B).

165 .... Amendment of FA 1970 s 41(3).

166 .... Amendment of FA 1991 s 109(1).

167 .... Amendment of FA 1994 s 107(2) and (3).

168 .... Amendment of FA 1994 s 112(6).

169 .... Amendment of FA 1996 s 107(4).

170 .... Amendment of FA 1996 s 108(2) and (3).

171 .... Amendment of F(No 2)A 1998 s 14(2).

172 .... Amendment of SDMA 1891 s 26.

173 .... Amendment of SA 1891 s 13.

174 .... Amendment of FA 1973 s 74.

175 .... Amendment of FA 1991 s 103(1).

176 .... Amendment of SA 1891 First Sch.

177 .... Amendment of SA 1891 s 23(2).

178 .... Amendment of SA 1891 s 41.

179 .... Amendment of SA 1891 s 118(1).

180 .... Amendment of F(1909-10)A 1910 s 74(2).

181 .... Amendment of FA 1978 s 31.

182 .... Amendment of FA 1952 s 19.

183 .... Amendment of FA 1965 s 31(1) and (6).

184 .... Amendment of SDMA 1891 s 9.

185 .... Insertion of SDMA 1891 s 12A.

186 .... Amendment of SA 1891 s 1(3) and (4).

187 .... Amendment of SA 1891 s 12(2).

188 .... Amendment of SA 1891 s 14(4).

189 .... Amendment of SA 1891 s 58(8).

190 .... Amendment of SA 1891 s 77(6).

191 .... Amendment of SA 1891 s 122(1).

192 .... Amendment of FA 1899 s 5(1).

193 .... Amendment of FA 1933 s 40.

194 .... Amendment of FA 1973 s 69.

195 .... Amendment of FA 1982 s 92(1) and (6).

196 .... Amendment of FA 1992 s 208.

197 .... Unnecessary (repeals).

INDEX (STAMP DUTIES)

LEGISLATION (CAPITAL ACQUISITIONS TAX)

FINANCE (1909-10) ACT 1910

(10 Edw VII c 8)
(Date of passing: 29 April 1910)

ARRANGEMENT OF SECTIONS

PART I

PART I

33 Appeals to referees

(1) Except as expressly provided in this Part of this Act, any person aggrieved may appeal within such time and in such manner as may be provided by rules made under this section against the first or any subsequent determination by the Commissioners of the total value or site value of any land; or against the amount of any assessment of duty under this Part of this Act; or against a refusal of the Commissioners to make any allowance or to make the allowance claimed, where the Commissioners have power to make such an allowance under this Part of the Act or against any apportionment of the value of land or of duty or any assessment or apportionment of the consideration on any transfer or lease made by the Commissioners under this Part of this Act; or against the determination of any other matter which the Commissioners are to determine or may determine under this Part of this Act:

Provided that

    (*a*) an appeal shall not lie against a provisional valuation made by the Commissioners of the total or site value of any land except on the part of a person who has made an objection to the provisional valuation in accordance with this Act; and

    (*b*) the original total value and the original site value and the site value as ascertained under any subsequent valuation shall be questioned only by means of an appeal against the determination by the Commissioners of that value where there is an appeal under this Act, and shall not be questioned in any case on an appeal against an assessment of duty.

(2) An appeal under this section shall be referred to such one of the panel of referees appointed under this Part of this Act as may be selected in manner provided by rules under this section, and the decision of the referee to whom the matter is so referred shall be given in the form provided by rules under this section and shall, subject to appeal to the Court under this section, be final.

(3) The referee shall determine any matter referred to him in a consultation with the Commissioners and the appellant, or any persons nominated by the Commissioners and the appellant respectively for this purpose, and may, if he thinks fit, order that any expenses incurred by the appellant be paid by the Commissioners, and that any such

expenses incurred by the Commissioners be paid by the appellant. Any order of the referee as to expenses may be made a rule of the High Court.

(4) Any person aggrieved by the decision of the referee may appeal against the decision to the High Court within the time and in the manner and on the conditions directed by Rules of Court (including conditions enabling the Court to require the payment of or the giving of security for any duty claimed); and subsections two, three, and four of section ten of the Finance Act, 1894, shall apply with reference to any such appeal:

Provided that where the total or site value as alleged by the Commissioners of the property in respect of which the dispute arises does not exceed five hundred pounds, the appeal under this section may be to the Circuit Court for the county or place in which the appellant resides or the property is situate, and this section shall for the purpose of the appeal apply as if such Circuit Court were the High Court, and in every such case any party shall have a right of appeal to the Supreme Court.

(5) Provision shall be made by rules under this section with respect to the time within which and the manner in which an appeal may be made to a referee under this section, ...1 and with respect to the form in which any decision of a referee is to be given, and with respect to any other matter for which it appears necessary or expedient to provide in order to carry this section into effect:

Those rules shall be made by the Reference Committee, subject to the approval of the Minister for Finance.

...1.

Amendments

1　Deleted by Property Values (Arbitrations and Appeals) Act, 1960 s 7 and Sch.

Cross-references

Appeals against valuations of property other than stocks and securities: FA 1923 s 19.
Appeals against valuations of stocks and securities: FA 1972 s 36.
Appeals in the case of companies capital duty: FA 1973 s 74.
Particulars to be evidence in certain appeals: FA 1925 s 48.
Subs (4): see also Courts of Justice Acts regarding jurisdictional limits of the courts.

Definitions

"Commissioners": SA 1891 s 122(1); CATA 1976 s 2(1); "person": IA 1937 s 11(c); "property": CATA 1976 s 2(1).

PROVISIONAL COLLECTION OF TAXES ACT 1927

(1927 Number 7)

ARRANGEMENT OF SECTIONS

Section

   1   Definitions

AN ACT TO GIVE STATUTORY EFFECT FOR A LIMITED PERIOD TO
RESOLUTIONS OF THE COMMITTEE ON FINANCE OF DÁIL ÉIREANN
IMPOSING, RENEWING, VARYING, OR ABOLISHING TAXATION, AND TO
MAKE PROVISION WITH RESPECT TO PAYMENTS, DEDUCTIONS,
ASSESSMENTS, CHARGES, AND OTHER THINGS MADE OR DONE ON
ACCOUNT OF ANY TEMPORARY TAX IN ANTICIPATION OF THE
RENEWAL OF THE TAX BY THE OIREACHTAS. [19TH MARCH, 1927]

In this Act—

the expression **"Committee on Finance"** means the Committee on Finance of Dáil
Éireann when and so long as such Committee is a committee of the whole House;

[the expression **"new tax"** when used in relation to a resolution under this Act means a
tax which was not in force immediately before the date on which the resolution is
expressed to take effect or, where no such date is expressed, the passing of the resolution
by Dáil Éireann;][1]

the expression **"permanent tax"** means a tax which was last imposed without any limit
of time being fixed for its duration;

the expression **"temporary tax"** means a tax which was last imposed or renewed for a
limited period only;

the expression **"normal expiration"** when used in relation to a temporary tax means the
end of the limited period for which the tax was last imposed or renewed;

the word **"tax"** includes duties of customs, duties of excise, income tax, ...[2] ...[3] [and
value-added tax][4] [and capital gains tax][5] ...[6] [and corporation tax][7] [and gift tax and
inheritance tax][8] [and residential property tax][9] [and stamp duties][10] but no other tax or
duty.

Amendments

[1]   Definition of "new tax" substituted by FA 2002 s 139(*a*) with effect from 25 March 2002.

[2]   Words "and super-tax" repealed by FA 1974 s 86 and Sch 2 Pt I for 1974-75 and later tax years.

[3]   Words "and also turnover tax" repealed by VATA 1972 s 41.

[4]   Inserted by VATA 1972 s 38.

[5]   Inserted by CGTA 1975 s 50.

[6]   Words "and wealth tax" deleted by FA 1978 s 38.

[7]   Inserted by CTA 1976 s 6.

[8]   Inserted by CATA 1976 s 69.

[9]   Inserted by FA 1983 s 114(1).

[10]   Inserted by FA 1986 s 100.

FINANCE ACT 1950

(1950 Number 18)
(Date of passing: 5 July 1950)

10 Confirmation of Convention set forth in First Schedule

(1) The convention set forth in the First Schedule to this Act and concluded on the 13th day of September, 1949, between the Government and the Government of the United States of America (in this section referred to as the Convention) is hereby confirmed and shall have the force of law.

(2) Subsection (4) of section 7 of the Finance Act, 1894 (which provides for relief in respect of duty payable in a foreign country) shall not have effect in relation to estate tax chargeable under the laws of the United States of America to which the provisions of the Convention apply.

FIRST SCHEDULE

CONVENTION BETWEEN THE GOVERNMENT OF IRELAND AND THE GOVERNMENT OF THE UNITED STATES OF AMERICA FOR THE AVOIDANCE OF DOUBLE TAXATION AND THE PREVENTION OF FISCAL EVASION WITH RESPECT TO TAXES ON THE ESTATES OF DECEASED PERSONS

The Government of Ireland and the Government of the United States of America,

Desiring to conclude a Convention for the avoidance of double taxation and the prevention of fiscal evasion with respect to taxes on estates of deceased persons,

Have appointed for that purpose as their Plenipotentiaries:

The Government of Ireland:

Patrick McGilligan, Minister for Finance;

Sean MacBride, Minister for External Affairs;

and

The Government of the United States of America:

George A Garrett, Envoy Extraordinary and Minister Plenipotentiary of the United States of America at Dublin;

Who, having exhibited their respective full powers, found in good and due form, have agreed as follows:—

Article I

(1) The taxes which are the subject of the present Convention are:

    (*a*)   In the United States of America, the Federal estate tax, and

    (*b*)   In Ireland, the estate duty imposed in that territory.

(2) The present Convention shall also apply to any other taxes of a substantially similar character imposed by either Contracting Party subsequently to the date of signature of the present Convention.

Article II

(1) In the present Convention, unless the context otherwise requires:

(*a*)   The term **"United States"** means the United States of America, and when used in a geographical sense means the States, the Territories of Alaska and of Hawaii, and the District of Columbia.

(*b*)   The term **"Ireland"** means the Republic of Ireland.

(*c*)   The term **"territory"** when used in relation to one or the other Contracting Party means the United States or Ireland, as the context requires.

(*d*)   The term **"tax"** means the estate duty imposed in Ireland or the United States Federal estate tax, as the context requires.

(2) In the application of the provisions of the present Convention by one of the Contracting Parties, any term not otherwise defined shall, unless the context otherwise requires, have the meaning which it has under the laws of that Contracting Party relating to the taxes which are the subject of the present Convention.

Article III

(1) For the purposes of the present Convention, the question whether a decedent was domiciled in any part of the territory of one of the Contracting Parties at the time of his death shall be determined in accordance with the law in force in that territory.

(2) Where a person dies domiciled in any part of the territory of one Contracting Party, the situs of any rights or interests, legal or equitable, in or over any of the following classes of property which for the purposes of tax form part of the estate of such person or pass on his death, shall, for the purposes of the imposition of tax and for the purposes of the credit to be allowed under Article V, be determined exclusively in accordance with the following rules, but in cases not within such rules the situs of any such rights or interests shall be determined for those purposes in accordance with the law relating to tax in force in the territory of the other Contracting Party:

(*a*)   Immovable property shall be deemed to be situated at the place where such property is located;

(*b*)   Tangible movable property (other than such property for which specific provision is hereinafter made) and bank or currency notes, other forms of currency recognised as legal tender in the place of issue, negotiable bills of exchange and negotiable promissory notes, shall be deemed to be situated at the place where such property, notes, currency or documents are located at the time of death, or, if in transitu, at the place of destination;

(*c*)   Debts, secured or unsecured, other than the forms of indebtedness for which specific provision is made herein, shall be deemed to be situate at the place where the decedent was domiciled at the time of death;

(*d*) Shares or stock in a corporation other than a municipal or governmental corporation (including shares or stock held by a nominee where the beneficial ownership is evidenced by scrip certificates or otherwise) shall be deemed to be situated at the place in or under the law of which such corporation was created or organised; but, if such corporation was created or organised under the laws of the United Kingdom of Great Britain and Northern Ireland or under the laws of Northern Ireland, and if the shares or stock of such corporation when registered on a branch register of such corporation kept in Ireland are deemed under the laws of the United Kingdom or of Northern Ireland and of Ireland to be assets situated in Ireland, such shares or stock shall be deemed to be assets situated in Ireland;

(*e*) Moneys payable under a policy of assurance or insurance on the life of the decedent shall be deemed to be situated at the place where the decedent was domiciled at the time of death;

(*f*) Ships and aircraft and shares thereof shall be deemed to be situated at the place of registration or documentation of the ship or aircraft;

(*g*) Goodwill as a trade, business or professional asset shall be deemed to be situated at the place where the trade, business or profession to which it pertains is carried on;

(*h*) Patents, trade-marks and designs shall be deemed to be situated at the place where they are registered;

(*i*) Copyright, franchises, and rights or licences to use any copyrighted material, patent, trademark or design shall be deemed to be situated at the place where the rights arising therefrom are exercisable;

(*j*) Rights or causes of action ex delicto surviving for the benefit of an estate of a decedent shall be deemed to be situated at the place where such rights or causes of action arose;

(*k*) Judgment debts shall be deemed to be situated at the place where the judgment is recorded;

provided that if, apart from this paragraph, tax would be imposed by one Contracting Party on any property which is situated in its territory, this paragraph shall not apply to such property unless, by reason of its application or otherwise, tax is imposed or would but for some specific exemption be imposed thereon by the other Contracting Party.

Article IV

(1) In determining the amount on which tax is to be computed, permitted deductions shall be allowed in accordance with the law in force in the territory in which the tax is imposed.

(2) Where tax is imposed by one Contracting Party on the death of a person who at the time of his death was not domiciled in any part of the territory of that Contracting Party but was domiciled in some part of the territory of the other Contracting Party, no account shall be taken in determining the amount or rate of such tax of property situated

outside the former territory: provided that this paragraph shall not apply as respects tax imposed—

(*a*) In the United States in the case of a United States citizen dying domiciled in any part of Ireland; or

(*b*) In Ireland in the case of property passing under a disposition governed by the law of Ireland.

Article V

(1) Where one Contracting Party imposes tax by reason of a decedent's being domiciled in some part of its territory or being its national, that party shall allow against so much of its tax (as otherwise computed) as is attributable to property situated in the territory of the other Contracting Party, a credit (not exceeding the amount of the tax so attributable) equal to so much of the tax imposed in the territory of such other Party as is attributable to such property; but this paragraph shall not apply as respects any such property as is mentioned in paragraph (2) of this Article.

(2) Where each Contracting Party imposes tax by reason of a decedent's being domiciled in some part of its territory, each Party shall allow against so much of its tax (as otherwise computed) as is attributable to property which is situated, or is deemed under paragraph (2) of Article III to be situated,

(*a*)   in the territory of both Parties, or

(*b*)   outside both territories,

a credit which bears the same proportion to the amount of its tax so attributable or to the amount of the other party's tax attributable to the same property, whichever is the less, as the former amount bears to the sum of both amounts.

(3) Where Ireland imposes duty on property passing under a disposition governed by its law, that Party shall allow a credit similar to that provided by paragraph (1) of this Article.

(4) For the purposes of this Article, the amount of tax of a Contracting Party attributable to any property shall be ascertained after taking into account any credit, allowance or relief, or any remission or reduction of tax, otherwise than in respect of tax payable in the territory of the other Contracting Party; and if, in respect of property situated outside the territories of both parties, a Contracting Party allows against its tax a credit for tax payable in the country where the property is situated, that credit shall be taken into account in ascertaining, for the purposes of paragraph (2) of this Article, the amount of the tax of that Party attributable to the property.

Article VI

(1) Any claim for a credit or for a refund of tax founded on the provisions of the present Convention shall be made within six years from the date of the death of the decedent in respect of whose estate the claim is made, or, in the case of a reversionary interest where payment of tax is deferred until on or after the date on which the interest falls into possession, within six years from that date.

(2) Any such refund shall be made without payment of interest on the amount so refunded, save to the extent to which interest was paid on the amount so refunded when the tax was paid.

Article VII

(1) The taxation authorities of the Contracting Parties shall exchange such information (being information available under the respective taxation laws of the Contracting Parties) as is necessary for carrying out the provisions of the present Convention or for the prevention of fraud or the administration of statutory provisions against legal avoidance in relation to the taxes which are the subject of the present Convention. Any information so exchanged shall be treated as secret and shall not be disclosed to any person other than those concerned with the assessment and collection of the taxes which are the subject of the present Convention. No information shall be exchanged which would disclose any trade secret or trade process.

(2) As used in this Article, the Term **"taxation authorities"** means, in the case of the United States, the Commissioner of Internal Revenue. or his authorised representative; in the case or Ireland, the Revenue Commissioners or their authorised representative.

Article VIII

(1) The present Convention shall be ratified and the instruments of ratification shall be exchanged at Washington, District of Columbia, as soon as possible.

(2) The present Convention shall come into force on the date1 of exchange of ratifications and shall be effective only as to

> (*a*)   the estates of persons dying on or after such date; and

> (*b*)   the estate of any person dying before such date and after the last day of the calendar year immediately preceding such date whose personal representative elects, in such manner as may be prescribed, that the provisions of the present Convention shall be applied to such estate.

Article IX

(1) The present Convention shall remain in force for not less than three years after the date of its coming into force.

(2) If not less than six months before the expiration of such period of three years, neither of the Contracting Parties shall have given to the other Contracting Party, through diplomatic channels, written notice of its intention to terminate the present Convention, the Convention shall remain in force after such period of three years until either of the Contracting Parties shall have given written notice of such intention, in which event the present Convention shall not be effective as to the estates of persons dying on or after the date (not being earlier than the sixtieth day after the date of such notice) specified in such notice, or, if no date is specified, on or after the sixtieth day after the date of such notice.

IN WITNESS WHEREOF the above-named Plenipotentiaries have signed the present Convention and have affixed thereto their seals.

Done at Dublin, in duplicate, this 13th day of September, 1949.

For the Government of Ireland:

(Signed)   PATRICK McGILLIGAN

                      SEAN MacBRIDE

For the Government of the United States of America:

(Signed)   GEORGE A GARRETT

Note

[1]   The Convention came into force on 20 December 1951 and is applied to inheritance tax and probate tax.

FINANCE ACT 1951

(1951 Number 15)
(Date of passing: 11 July 1951)

PART III
DEATH DUTIES

12 Operation of certain exemptions

(1) In this section "exemption to which this section applies" means—

(*a*) an exemption from taxation by virtue of a condition for such exemption under section 47 of the Finance (No 2) Act, 1915, or that section as amended, adapted or amended and adapted,

(*b*) an exemption from taxation under section 63 of the Finance Act, 1916, or that section as amended, adapted or amended and adapted,

(*c*) an exemption from taxation by virtue of a condition for such exemption under subsection (1) of section 21 of the Finance Act, 1923 (No 21 of 1923), or that subsection as adapted,

or

(*d*) an exemption from taxation under subsection (1) of section 37 of the Finance Act, 1929 (No 32 of 1929), or that subsection as adapted.

FINANCE ACT 1954

(1954 Number 22)
(Date of passing: 13 July 1954)

ARRANGEMENT OF SECTIONS

PART IV
DEATH DUTIES

PART VI

PART IV
DEATH DUTIES

22 Discharge of death duties by transfer of securities

(1) In this section—

"the Minister" means the Minister for Finance;

"the Account" means such account as is prescribed pursuant to subsection (4) of this section.

(2) This section applies to the following securities:

    (*a*) the 4 1/2% National Loan, 1973/78;

    (*b*) any security which—

        (i) after the passing of this Act is created and issued by the Minister on terms that, subject to specified conditions, it will be accepted in payment of any death duty, and

        (ii) is charged on the Central Fund.

(3) For the purposes of this section—

    (*a*) the value at the date of transfer of any security transferred to the Account shall be the nominal face value with the addition of any interest accrued due at the date of the transfer but then remaining unpaid, after deducting any interest which may be receivable by the transferor after that date, and

    (*b*) interest on any such security shall be deemed to accrue from day to day.

(4) A person from whom any sum is due on account of any death duty may, subject to the relevant regulations under this section, pay the sum or any part thereof by means of a transfer, to such account of the Minister as is prescribed by the regulations, of so much of any security to which this section applies as is equal in value at the date of the transfer

to the sum or part, and the transfer shall be accepted by the Revenue Commissioners as a cash payment to them of the sum or part.

(5) The Minister may make regulations prescribing the conditions under which any security to which this section applies shall be accepted in payment of any death duty.

(6) Securities transferred to the Account may be held therein or sold, cancelled or otherwise dealt with as the Minister directs.

(7) The Minister shall pay out of the Account to the Revenue Commissioners the values at the dates of transfer of all securities transferred to the Account.

(8) Sums paid by way of interest on or redemption of securities held in the Account and sums derived from sales of or other dealings with such securities shall be paid into the Account.

(9) Sums paid into the Account shall be applied in or towards meeting payments which the Minister is required by this section to make to the Revenue Commissioners out of the Account, and any balance shall, as and when the Minister directs, be paid into the Exchequer in repayment of moneys advanced to the Account from the Central Fund or the growing produce thereof, and, if the balance is in excess of the sum required for repaying moneys advanced from the Central Fund or the growing produce thereof, the excess amount shall be disposed of for the benefit of the exchequer in such manner as the Minister directs.

(10) There shall be issued out of the Central Fund or the growing produce thereof to the Account such sums as may be required to meet any payments under this section by the Minister to the Revenue Commissioners out of the Account which are not met under subsection (9) of this section, and so much of the sums issued as is not authorised by this section to be met by borrowing by the Minister shall be charged on the Central Fund and the growing produce thereof.

(11) For the purpose of providing, wholly or partly, for so much of the issues authorised by this section to be made out of the Central Fund or the growing produce thereof as is equal to the price at which the relevant security was issued for public subscription, the Minister may borrow from any person any sum or sums, and for the purpose of such borrowing he may create and issue securities bearing such rates of interest and subject to such conditions as to repayment, redemption or any other matter as he thinks fit, and he shall pay any moneys so borrowed into the Exchequer.

(12) The principal of and interest on any securities issued under subsection (11) of this section and the expenses incurred in connection with the issue of such securities shall be charged on and payable out of the Central Fund or the growing produce thereof.

(13)(*a*) Where stock of the 4 1/2 per cent National Loan, 1973/78, has been accepted by the Revenue Commissioners in payment of death duties pursuant to the Prospectus of that Loan and has been transferred to them before the passing of this Act, the stock shall be deemed to have been a cash payment to them of a sum equal to the value of the stock at the date of the transfer, such value being the nominal face value of the stock with the addition of any interest accrued due (on the basis of interest accruing from day to day) at the date of the transfer but then remaining unpaid, after deducting any interest which may be receivable by the transferor after that date.

(*b*) As soon as may be after the passing of this Act, the Revenue Commissioners shall, as respects any stock so transferred and held by them, transfer the stock to such account as is prescribed by the regulations under this section relating to the 4 1/2 per cent National Loan, 1973/78, and shall pay into that account any interest which has been paid to them on the stock, but the payment to be made under subsection (7) of this section is relation to the stock shall be the value referred to in paragraph (*a*) of this subsection.

PART VI

29 Repeals

Each enactment specified in column (2) of the Third Schedule to this Act is hereby repealed to the extent specified in column (3) of the said Schedule as on and from the date mentioned in column (4) of the said Schedule.

30 Care and management of taxes and duties

All taxes and duties imposed by this Act are hereby placed under the care and management of the Revenue Commissioners.

31 Short title, construction and commencement

(1) This Act may be cited as the Finance Act, 1954.

....

(4) Part V of this Act shall be construed together with the Stamp Act, 1891, and the enactments amending or extending that Act.

Note

Regulations were made by SI 15/1954 which are applied to inheritance tax only.

---

SUCCESSION ACT 1965

(1965 Number 27)

ARRANGEMENT OF SECTIONS

Sections

72A   Distribution of disclaimed estate

72A Distribution of disclaimed estate

[Where the estate, or part of the estate, as to which a person dies intestate is disclaimed after the passing of the Family Law (Miscellaneous Provisions) Act, 1997 (otherwise than under section 73 of this Act), the estate or part, as the case may be, shall be distributed in accordance with this Part—

(*a*)   as if the person disclaiming had died immediately before the death of the intestate, and

(*b*)   if that person is not the spouse or a direct lineal ancestor of the intestate, as if that person had died without leaving issue.][1]

Amendments

[1]   Section 72A inserted by Family Law (Miscellaneous) Act 1997 s 6.

CAPITAL ACQUISITIONS TAX ACT 1976

(1976 Number 8)
(Date of passing: 31 March 1976)

ARRANGEMENT OF SECTIONS

PART I
PRELIMINARY

PART II
GIFT TAX

PART III
INHERITANCE TAX

PART IV
VALUE OF PROPERTY FOR TAX

PART V
PROVISIONS RELATING TO GIFTS AND INHERITANCES

PART X
MISCELLANEOUS

FIRST SCHEDULE
Valuation of limited interests

SECOND SCHEDULE
Computation of tax

AN ACT TO CHARGE AND IMPOSE ON CERTAIN GIFTS AND
INHERITANCES DUTIES OF INLAND REVENUE TO BE KNOWN AS GIFT
TAX AND INHERITANCE TAX, TO AMEND THE LAW RELATING TO
INLAND REVENUE AND TO MAKE FURTHER PROVISIONS IN
CONNECTION WITH FINANCE [31ST MARCH, 1976]

PART I
PRELIMINARY

1 Short title

This Act may be cited as the Capital Acquisitions Tax Act, 1976.

2 Interpretation

(1) In this Act, unless the context otherwise requires—

"absolute interest", in relation to property, includes the interest of a person who has a general power of appointment over the property;

"accountable person" means a person who is accountable for the payment of tax by virtue of section 35;

"benefit" includes any estate, interest, income or right;

[**"child"** includes—

(a)   a stepchild;

(b)   a child adopted—

      (i)   under the Adoption Acts, l952 to 1991; or

      (ii)   under a foreign adoption which by virtue of section 2, 3, 4 or 5 of the Adoption Act, 1991, is deemed to have been effected by a valid adoption order within the meaning of section 1 of that Act;][1]

"Commissioners" means the Revenue Commissioners;

"date of the disposition" means—

(a)   in the case of a will, the date of the testator's death;

(b)   in the case of an intestacy or a partial intestacy, the date of death of the intestate;

(c)   in the case of a benefit under Part IX or section 56 of the Succession Act, 1965, the date of death of the relevant testator or other deceased person, and correspondingly in the case of an analogous benefit under the law of another territory;

(d)   in the case of a disposition which consists of the failure to exercise a right or a power, the date of the latest time when the disponer could have exercised the right or the power if he were *sui juris* and not under any physical disability; and

(e)   in any other case, the date on which the act (or where more than one act is involved, the last act) of the disponer was done by which he provided or bound himself to provide the property comprised in the disposition;

"date of the gift" means the date of the happening of the event upon which the donee, or any person in right of the donee or on his behalf, becomes beneficially entitled in possession to the benefit, and a reference to the time when a gift is taken shall be construed as a reference to the date of the gift;

"date of the inheritance" means—

(a)   in the case where the successor or any person in right of the successor or on his behalf becomes entitled in possession to the benefit on the happening of any such event as is referred to in section 3(2), the date of the event;

(b)   in the case of a gift which becomes an inheritance by reason of its being taken under a disposition where the date of the disposition is within two years prior to the death of the disponer, the date which would have been the date of the gift if the entitlement were a gift; and

(c) in any other case, the date of the latest death which had to occur for the successor, or any person in right of the successor or on his behalf, to become beneficially entitled in possession to the benefit,

and a reference to the time when an inheritance is taken shall be construed as a reference to the date of the inheritance;

"discretionary trust" means any trust whereby, or by virtue or in consequence of which, property is held on trust [to accumulate the income or part of the income of the property, or any trust whereby, or by virtue or in consequence of which, property (other than property to which for the time being a person is beneficially entitled for an interest in possession) is held on trust][2] to apply, or with a power to apply, the income or capital or part of the income or capital of the property for the benefit of any person or persons or of any one or more of a number or of a class of persons whether at the discretion of trustees or any other person and notwithstanding that there may be a power to accumulate all or any part of the income;

"disponer", in relation to a disposition, means the person who, for the purpose of the disposition, directly or indirectly provided the property comprised in the disposition, and in any case where more than one person provided the property each shall be deemed to be the disponer to the extent that he so provided the property; and for the purposes of this definition—

(a) the testator shall be the disponer in the case of a disposition referred to in paragraph (k) of the definition of "disposition";

(b) the intestate shall be the disponer in the case of a disposition referred to in paragraph (l) of that definition;

(c) the deceased person referred to in paragraph (m) of that definition shall be the disponer in the case of a disposition referred to in that paragraph; and

(d) a person who has made with any other person a reciprocal arrangement by which that other person provided property comprised in the disposition shall be deemed to have provided that property;

"disposition" includes—

(a) any act or omission by a person as a result of which the value of his estate immediately after such act or omission is less than it would be but for such act or omission;

(b) any trust, covenant, agreement or arrangement, whether made by a single operation or by associated operations;

(c) the creation of a debt or other right enforceable against the disponer personally or against any estate or interest he may have in property;

(d) the payment of money;

(e) the allotment of shares in a company;

(f) the grant or the creation of any benefit;

(*g*)   the grant or the creation of any lease, mortgage, charge, licence, option, power, partnership or joint tenancy or other estate or interest in or over any property;

(*h*)   the release, forfeiture, surrender or abandonment of any debt or benefit, or the failure to exercise a right; and, for the purpose of this paragraph, a debt or benefit shall be deemed to have been released when it has become unenforceable by action through lapse of time (save to the extent that it is recovered subsequent to its becoming so unenforceable);

(*i*)   the exercise of a general power of appointment in favour of any person other than the holder of the power;

(*j*)   a *donatio mortis causa*;

(*k*)   a will or other testamentary disposition;

(*l*)   an intestacy, whether total or partial;

(*m*)   the payment of a share as a legal right under Part IX of the Succession Act, 1965, to a deceased person's spouse, or the making of provision for a widow or child of a deceased person under section 56 or section 117 of the Succession Act, 1965, or an analogous share or provision paid or made on the death of a deceased person to or for the benefit of any person under the law of another territory; and

(*n*)   a resolution passed by a company which is deemed by subsection (3) to be a disposition;

"donee" means a person who takes a gift;

"entitled in possession" means having a present right to the enjoyment of property as opposed to having a future such right, and without prejudice to the generality of the foregoing a person shall also, for the purposes of this Act, be deemed to be entitled in possession to an interest or share in a partnership, joint tenancy or estate of a deceased person, in which he is a partner, joint tenant or beneficiary, as the case may be, but he shall not be deemed to be entitled in possession to an interest in expectancy until an event happens whereby this interest ceases to be an interest in expectancy;

"general power of appointment" includes every power, right, or authority whether exercisable only by will or otherwise which would enable the holder thereof to appoint or dispose of property to whomsoever he thinks fit or to obtain such power, right or authority, but exclusive of any power exercisable solely in a fiduciary capacity under a disposition not made by himself, or exercisable by a tenant for life under the Settled Land Act, 1882, or as mortgagee;

"gift" means a gift which a person is by this Act deemed to take;

"inheritance" means an inheritance which a person is by this Act deemed to take;

"interest in expectancy" includes an estate in remainder or reversion and every other future interest, whether vested or contingent, but does not include a reversion expectant on the determination of a lease;

"limited interest" means—

    (*a*)   an interest (other than a leasehold interest) for the duration of a life or lives or for a period certain; or

    (*b*)   any other interest which is not an absolute interest;

"local authority" has the meaning assigned to it by section 2(2) of the Local Government Act, 1941, and includes a body established under the Local Government Services (Corporate Bodies) Act, 1971;

"market value", in relation to property, means the market value thereof ascertained in accordance with sections 15,16 and 17;

"minor child" means a child who has not attained the age of [18][3] years;

"personal property" means any property other than real property;

"personal representative" means the executor or administrator for the time being of a deceased person and includes any person who takes possession of or intermeddles with the property of a deceased person and also includes any person having, in relation to the deceased person, under the law of another country, any functions corresponding to the functions, for administration purposes under the law of the State, of an executor or administrator;

"property" includes rights and interests of any description;

"real property" means real and chattel real property;

"regulations" means regulations made under section 71;

"relative" means a relative within the meaning of subsection (4);

"return" means such a return as is referred to in section 36;

"share", in relation to a company, includes any interest whatsoever in the company which is analogous to a share in the company, and "shareholder" shall be construed accordingly;

"special power of appointment" means a power of appointment which is not a general power of appointment;

"successor" means a person who takes an inheritance;

"tax" means any tax chargeable under this Act;

"valuation date" has the meaning assigned to it by section 21.

[**"year of assessment"** has the meaning assigned to it by section 1 of the Income Tax Act, 1967.][4]

(2) For the purpose of the definition of **"general power of appointment"** contained in subsection (1), a person shall be deemed to have a general power of appointment—

    (*a*)   notwithstanding that he is not *sui juris* or is under a physical disability;

    (*b*)   over money which he has a general power to charge on property; and

    (*c*)   over property of which he is tenant in tail in possession.

(3) For the purpose of the definition of **"disposition"** contained in subsection (1), the passing by a company of a resolution which, by the extinguishment or alteration of the rights attaching to any share of the company, results, directly or indirectly, in the estate of any shareholder of the company being increased in value at the expense of the estate of any other shareholder, shall be deemed to be a disposition made by that other shareholder if he could have prevented the passing of the resolution by voting against it or otherwise; and in this subsection, **"share"** includes a debenture and loan stock and **"shareholder"** includes a debenture holder and a holder of loan stock.

(4) For the purposes of this Act, the following persons and no other person shall be relatives of another person, that is to say—

(*a*)   the spouse of that other person;

(*b*)   the father, mother, and any child, uncle or aunt of that other person;

(*c*)   any child (other than that other person), and any child of a child, of any person who is by virtue of paragraph (*a*) or (*b*) a relative of that other person; and

(*d*)   the spouse of a person who is by virtue of paragraph (*b*) or (*c*) a relative of that other person;

(*e*)   the grandparent of that other person.

(5) For the purposes of this Act—

(*a*)   the relationship between a child, adopted in the manner referred to in paragraph (*b*) of the definition of **"child"** contained in subsection (1), and any other person, or between other persons, that would exist if such child had been born to the adoptor or adoptors in lawful wedlock, shall be deemed to exist between such child and that other person or between those other persons, and the relationship of any such child and any person that existed prior to his being so adopted shall be deemed to have ceased; and

(*b*)   an illegitimate child who has not been—

(i)   legitimated; or

(ii)   adopted under—

(I)   the Adoption Acts, 1952 to 1974; or

(II)   an adoption law other than the Adoption Acts, 1952 to 1974, having the effect referred to in paragraph (*b*)(ii) of the definition of **"child"** contained in subsection (1),

shall be the child of his mother.

[(5A) For the purposes of this Act—

(*a*)   a reference to a person being resident in the State on a particular date shall be construed as a reference to that person being resident in the State in the year of assessment in which that date falls (but, for those purposes, the provisions of Part 34 of the Taxes Consolidation Act, 1997, relating to residence of individuals shall not be construed as requiring a year of assessment to have elapsed before a determination of whether or not a person is resident in the State on a date falling in that year may be made), and (*b*) a reference to a person being ordinarily resident in the State on a particular date shall be construed as a reference to that person being ordinarily resident in the State in the year of assessment in which that date falls.][5]

(6) In this Act, references to any enactment shall, unless the context otherwise requires, be construed as references to that enactment as amended or extended by any subsequent enactment.

(7) In this Act, a reference to a section or Schedule is a reference to a section of or Schedule to this Act unless it is indicated that reference to some other enactment is intended.

(8) In this Act, a reference to a subsection, paragraph or sub-paragraph is to the subsection, paragraph or subparagraph of the provision (including a Schedule) in which the reference occurs, unless is indicated that reference to some other provision is intended.

Amendments

[1] Definition of "child" substituted by FA 1992 s 223(1) as regards gifts or inheritances taken on or after 30 May 1991.

[2] Definition of "discretionary trust" extended by FA 1984 s 105.

[3] Substituted by FA 1986 s 112(3) for gifts or inheritances taken after 5 April 1986; previously "21".

[4] Definition of "year of assessment" inserted by FA 1995 s 157.

[5] Subs (5A) inserted by FA 2000 s 137 for gifts or inheritances taken on or after 1 December 1999.

Cross-references

Disposition, disponer: dispositions involving powers of appointment: s 27.

Free of tax: where a gift or inheritance is taken "free of tax", the benefit taken is deemed to include the amount of tax chargeable: FA 1982 s 98.

Gifts or inheritances taken after 13 January 1988 the relationship between persons is to be construed by reference to the Status of Children Act 1987 s 3.

Relative, definition extended in respect of private companies to include a private company under the control (defined) of the donee or successor: s 16(3).

Share, definition extended in respect of private companies, to include debentures and loan stock: s 16(2).

Case law

Meaning of "child": the word "issue" means the issue or descendants of a marriage, and for intestacy purposes, adopted children are not children of a marriage: *In the matter of John Stamp deceased, Patrick Stamp v Noel Redmond and others,* IV ITR 415; see also *OB v S* [1984] IR 329, [1985] ILRM 86.

The nature of a discretionary trust; the discretion of trustees to appoint the trust funds to beneficiaries is absolute: *In the matter of the Trustee Act 1891 s 36 and others,* HC, 24 July 1991.

Revenue practice

See CAT Work Manual (revised July 2001), Pt 10 para 11.

Narrative

Capital Acquisitions Tax, Chapters 1, 2.

Definitions

"person": IA 1937 s 11(*c*).

3 Meaning of "on a death"

(1) In this Act, **"on a death"**, in relation to a person becoming beneficially entitled in possession, means—

(*a*) on the death of a person or at a time ascertainable only by reference to the death of a person;

(*b*)   under a disposition where the date of the disposition is the date of the death of the disponer;

(*c*)   under a disposition where the date of the disposition is on or after the 1st day of April, 1975, and within two years prior to the death of the disponer; or

(*d*)   on the happening, after the cesser of an intervening life interest, of any such event as is referred to in subsection (2).

(2) The events referred to in subsection (1)(*d*) are any of the following—

(*a*)   the determination or failure of any charge, estate, interest or trust;

(*b*)   the exercise of a special power of appointment;

(*c*)   in the case where a benefit was given under a disposition in such terms that the amount or value of the benefit could only be ascertained from time to time by the actual payment or application of property for the purpose of giving effect to the benefit, the making of any payment or the application of the property; or

(*d*)   any other event which, under a disposition, affects the right to property, or to the enjoyment thereof.

Definitions

"benefit", "special power of appointment": s 2(1); "person": IA 1937 s 11(*c*); "property": s 2(1).

PART II
GIFT TAX

4 Charge of gift tax

A capital acquisitions tax, to be called gift tax and to be computed as hereinafter provided, shall, subject to this Act and the regulations thereunder, be charged, levied and paid upon the taxable value of every taxable gift taken by a donee, where the date of the gift is on or after the 28th day of February, 1974.

Cross-references

Date of gift: s 2(1).
Taxable gift: s 6.
Taxable value: s 18.

Narrative

Capital Acquisitions Tax, Chapter 4.

Definitions

"donee": s 2(1); "gift": s 2(1).

5 Gift deemed to be taken

(1) For the purposes of this Act, where, under or in consequence of any disposition, a person becomes beneficially entitled in possession, otherwise than on a death, to any benefit (whether or not the person becoming so entitled already has any interest in the property in which he takes such benefit), otherwise than for full consideration in money or money's worth paid by him,[1] he shall be deemed to take a gift.

(2) A gift shall be deemed—

    (*a*) to consist of the whole or the appropriate part, as the case may be, of the property in which the donee takes a benefit, or on which the benefit is charged or secured or on which the donee is entitled to have it charged or secured; and

    (*b*) if the benefit is an annuity or other periodic payment which is not charged on or secured by any property and which the donee is not entitled to have so charged or secured, to consist of such sum as would, if invested on the date of the gift in the security of the Government which was issued last before that date for subscription in the State and is redeemable not less than 10 years after the date of issue, yield, on the basis of the current yield on the security, an annual income equivalent to the annual value of the annuity or of the other periodic payment receivable by the donee.

(3) For the purposes of section 6(1)(*c*), the sum referred to in subsection (2)(*b*) shall be deemed not to be situate in the State at the date of the gift.

(4) Where a person makes a disposition under which a relative of the person becomes beneficially entitled in possession to any benefit, the creation or disposition in favour of the person of an annuity or other interest limited to cease on the death, or at a time ascertainable only by reference to the death, of the person, shall not be treated for the purposes of this section as consideration for the grant of such benefit or of any part thereof.

(5) For the purposes of this Act, **"appropriate part"**, in relation to property referred to in subsection (2), means that part of the entire property in which the benefit subsists, or on which the benefit is charged or secured, or on which the donee is entitled to have it so charged or secured, which bears the same proportion to the entire property as the gross annual value of the benefit bears to the gross annual value of the entire property, and the gift shall be deemed to consist of the appropriate part of each and every item of property comprised in the entire property.

(6) (*a*) Where ...[2] a contract or agreement was entered into, under or as a consequence of which a person acquired the right, otherwise than for full consideration in money or money's worth, to have a benefit transferred to him, or to another in his right or on his behalf, and an act or acts is or are done, on or after that date, in pursuance of, or in performance or satisfaction, whether in whole or in part, of such contract or agreement, then the gift or inheritance, as the case may be, taken by or in right or on behalf of that person, shall be deemed to have been taken, not when the right was acquired as aforesaid, but either—

        (i) when the benefit was transferred to him or to another in his right or on his behalf; or

        (ii) when he or another in his right or on his behalf became beneficially entitled in possession to the benefit,

    whichever is the later.

  (*b*) In this subsection, a reference to a contract or agreement does not include a reference to a contract or agreement—

        (i) which is a complete grant, transfer, assignment or conveyance; or

        (ii) which was enforceable by action ...[3] .

Amendments

1   Subs (1): Private company shares taken on or after 24 February 1993: words in italics are regarded as deleted: FA 1993 s 121(1). FA 1994 s 147 substantially restored the pre-1993 position by providing that FA 1993 s 121(1) will apply only where the consideration could not reasonably (taking into account the disponer's position prior to the disposition) be regarded as representing full consideration to the disponer for having made such a disposition.

2   Deleted by FA 1982 s 99 as regards gifts or inheritances taken on or after 2 June 1982; previously ", before the 28th day of February, 1974,".

3   Deleted by FA 1982 s 99 as regards gifts or inheritances taken on or after 2 June 1982; previously "prior to the 28th day of February, 1974".

Cross-references

Person becoming beneficially entitled in possession, otherwise than for full consideration, under terms of a discretionary trust (other than such a trust created by will, by disposition dated within two years prior to death of disponer, or by disposition inter vivos coming into operation on a death), is deemed to take a gift: s 22.

Probate tax, exemption for dwelling house of dependent child or dependent relative, meaning of "appropriate part" (subs (5)) applied: FA 1993 s 112(*d*).

Successor taking a house (or part of a house) from a deceased brother or sister (inheritances taken on or after 30 January 1991), meaning of "appropriate part" (subs (5)) applied: FA 1991 s 117.

Narrative

Capital Acquisitions Tax, Chapter 4.

Definitions

"benefit", "disposition", "donee", "entitled in possession": s 2(1); "gift", "inheritance": s 2(1); "on a death": s 3; "person": IA 1937 s 11(*c*); "property", "relative": s 2(1).

6 Taxable gift

[(1) In this Act **"taxable gift"** means—

     (*a*)   in the case of a gift, other than a gift taken under a discretionary trust, where the disponer is resident or ordinarily resident in the State at the date of the disposition under which the donee takes the gift, the whole of the gift;

     (*b*)   in the case of a gift taken under a discretionary trust where the disponer is resident or ordinarily resident in the State at the date of the disposition under which the donee takes the gift or at the date of the gift or was (in the case of a gift taken after the death of the disponer) so resident or ordinarily resident at the date of that death, the whole of the gift;

     (*c*)   in the case where the donee is resident or ordinarily resident in the State at the date of the gift, the whole of the gift; and

     (*d*)   in any other case, so much of the property of which the gift consists as is situate in the State at the date of the gift.]¹

(2) For the purposes of [subsection (1)(*d*)]², a right to the proceeds of sale of property shall be deemed to be situate in the State to the extent that such property is unsold and situate in the State.

[(3) For the purposes of subsection (1), a person who is not domiciled in the State on a particular date shall be treated as not resident and not ordinarily resident in the State on that date unless—

(a) that date occurs on or after 1 December 2004,

(b) that person has been resident in the State for the 5 consecutive years of assessment immediately preceding the year of assessment in which that date falls, and

(c) that person is either resident or ordinarily resident in the State on that date.

(4) (a) In this subsection—

"**company**" means a private company within the meaning assigned to it by section 16(2);

"**company controlled by the donee**" has the same meaning as is assigned to "company controlled by the donee or successor" by section 16 (3);

"**share**" has the meaning assigned to it by section 16(2).

(b) For the purposes of subsection (1)(d), a proportion of the market value of any share in a private company incorporated outside the State which (after the taking of the gift) is a company controlled by the donee shall be deemed to be a sum situate in the State and shall be the amount determined by the following formula—

$$A \times \frac{B}{C}$$

where

A is the market value of that share at the date of the gift ascertained under section 16,

B is the market value of all property in the beneficial ownership of that company which is situate in the State at the date of the gift, and

C is the total market value of all property in the beneficial ownership of that company at the date of the gift.

(c) Paragraph (b) shall not apply in a case where the disponer was domiciled outside the State at all times up to and including the date of the gift or, in the case of a gift taken after the death of the disponer, up to and including the date of that death or where the share in question is actually situate in the State at the date of the gift.][3]

Amendments

[1] Subs (1) substituted by FA 2000 s 138(1)(a) for gifts taken on or after 1 December 1999, provided the date of the disposition under which the gift is taken is after 1 December 1999.

[2] Substituted by FA 2002 s 138 and Sch 6 para 2(a) in relation to gifts taken on or after 1 December 1999; previously "subsection (1)(c)".

[3] Subs (3) substituted and subs (4) inserted by FA 2000 s 138(1)(b) for gifts taken on or after 1 December 1999, provided the date of the disposition under which the gift is taken is after 1 December 1999.

Definitions

"date of the gift", "discretionary trust", "disponer", "donee", "gift", "property": s 2(1).

7 Liability to gift tax in respect of gift taken by joint tenants

The liability to gift tax in respect of a gift taken by persons as joint tenants shall be the same in all respects as if they took the gift as tenants in common in equal shares.

Narrative

Capital Acquisitions Tax, Chapter 14.

Definitions

"gift": s 2(1).

8 Disponer in certain connected dispositions

(1) Where a donee takes a gift under a disposition made by a disponer (in this section referred to as the original disponer) and, within the period commencing three years before and ending three years after the date of that gift, the donee makes a disposition under which a second donee takes a gift and whether or not the second donee makes a disposition within the same period under which a third donee takes a gift, and so on, each donee shall be deemed to take a gift from the original disponer (and not from the immediate disponer under whose disposition the gift was taken); and a gift so deemed to be taken shall be deemed to be an inheritance (and not a gift) taken by the donee, as successor, from the original disponer if—

(*a*) the original disponer dies within two years after the date of the disposition made by him; and

(*b*) the date of the disposition was on or after the 1st day of April, 1975.

(2) This section shall not apply in the case of any disposition (in this subsection referred to as the first-mentioned disposition) in so far as no other disposition, which was connected in the manner described in subsection (1) with such first-mentioned disposition, was made with a view to enabling or facilitating the making of the first-mentioned disposition or the recoupment in any manner of the cost thereof.

Definitions

"disponer", "dispositions, "donee", "gift", "inheritance", "successor": s 2(1).

9 Aggregable gifts

Amendments

This section does not apply as regards gifts taken on or after 26 March 1984: FA 1984 s 110(2). Prior to its repeal it read:

Any gift taken by a donee on or after the 28th day of February, 1969, and before the 28th day of February, 1974, so far as it is a taxable gift, shall for the purpose of computing tax—

(*a*) on any taxable gift taken by that donee from the same disponer on or after the 28th day of February, 1974; and

(*b*) on any taxable inheritance taken by that donee, as successor, from the same disponer on or after the 1st day of April, 1975,

be aggregated with the latter taxable gift or taxable inheritance in accordance with the provisions of the Second Schedule.

PART III
INHERITANCE TAX

10 Charge of inheritance tax

A capital acquisitions tax, to be called inheritance tax and to be computed as hereinafter provided, shall. subject to this Act and the regulations thereunder, be charged, levied and paid upon the taxable value of every taxable inheritance taken by a successor, where the date of the inheritance is on or after the 1st day of April, 1975.

Narrative
Capital Acquisitions Tax, Chapter 4.
Definitions
"date of the inheritance", "inheritance", "regulations": s 2(1); "taxable inheritance": s 12; "taxable value": s 18.

11 Inheritance deemed to be taken

(1) For the purposes of this Act, where, under or in consequence of any disposition, a person becomes beneficially entitled in possession on a death to any benefit (whether or not the person becoming so entitled already has any interest in the property in which he takes such benefit), *otherwise than for full consideration in money or money's worth paid by him*,[1] he shall be deemed to take an inheritance.

(2) The provisions of subsections (2), (4), and (5) of section 5 shall apply, with any necessary modifications, in relation to an inheritance as they apply in relation to a gift.

(3) For the purposes of section 12(1)(*b*) the sum referred to in section 5(2)(*b*) shall be deemed not to be situate in the State at the date of the inheritance.

Amendments

[1] Subs (1): Private company shares taken on or after 24 February 1993: words in italics are regarded as deleted: FA 1993 s 121(1). FA 1994 s 148 substantially restored the pre-1993 position by providing that FA 1993 s 121(1) will apply only where the consideration could not reasonably (taking into account the disponer's position prior to the disposition) be regarded as representing full consideration to the disponer for having made such a disposition.

Cross-references
Person becoming beneficially entitled in possession, otherwise than for full consideration, under terms of a discretionary trust (created by will, by disposition dated within two years prior to death of disponer, or by disposition inter vivos coming into operation on a death), is deemed to take an inheritance: s 22.
Definitions
"benefit", "disposition", "entitled in possession", "gift", "inheritance": s 2(1); "on a death": s 3; "person": IA 1937 s 11(*c*); "property": s 2(1).

12 Taxable inheritance

[(1) In this Act, **"taxable inheritance"** means—

    (*a*) the case where the disponer is resident or ordinarily resident in the State at the date of the disposition under which the successor takes the inheritance, the whole of the inheritance;

    (*b*) in the case where the successor (not being a successor in relation to a charge for tax arising by virtue of section 106 of the Finance Act, 1984, section 103 of the Finance Act, 1986, or section 110 of the Finance Act, 1993) is resident or ordinarily resident in the State at the date of the inheritance, the whole of the inheritance; and

(c) in any case, other than a case referred to in paragraph (a) or (b), where at the date of the inheritance

    (i) the whole of the property—

        (I) which was to be appropriated to the inheritance; or

        (II) out of which property was to be appropriated to the inheritance, was situate in the State, the whole of the inheritance;

    (ii) a part or proportion of the property—

        (I) which was to be appropriated to the inheritance; or

        (II) out of which property was to be appropriated to the inheritance,

    was situate in the State, that part or proportion of the inheritance.][1]

(2) For the purposes of [subsection (1)(c)][2]—

(a) "property which was to be appropriated to the inheritance" and "property out of which property was to be appropriated to the inheritance" shall not include any property which was not applicable to satisfy the inheritance; and

(b) a right to the proceeds of sale of property shall be deemed to be situate in the State to the extent that such property is unsold and situate in the State.

[(3) For the purposes of subsection (1), a person who is not domiciled in the State on a particular date shall be treated as not resident and not ordinarily resident in the State on that date unless—

(a) that date occurs on or after 1 December 2004,

(b) that person has been resident in the State for the 5 consecutive years of assessment immediately preceding the year of assessment in which that date falls, and

(c) that person is either resident or ordinarily resident in the State on that date.

(4) (a) In this subsection—

"**company**" means a private company within the meaning of section 16(2);

"**company controlled by the successor**" has the same meaning as is assigned to "company controlled by the donee or successor" by section 16(3);

"**share**" has the meaning assigned to it by section 16(2).

(b) For the purposes of subsection (1)(b), a proportion of the market value of any share in a private company incorporated outside the State which (after the taking of the inheritance) is a company controlled by the successor shall be deemed to be a sum situate in the State and shall be the amount determined by the following formula—

$$A \times \frac{B}{C}$$

where

A is the market value of that share at the date of the inheritance ascertained under section 16,

B is the market value of all property in the beneficial ownership of that company which is situate in the State at the date of the inheritance, and

C is the total market value of all property in the beneficial ownership of that company at the date of the inheritance.

(*c*) Paragraph (*b*) shall not apply in a case where the disponer was not domiciled in the State at the date of the disposition under which the successor takes the inheritance or where the share in question is actually situate in the State at the date of the inheritance.][3]

Amendments

[1] Subs (1) substituted by FA 2000 s 139(1)(*a*) for inheritances taken on or after 1 December 1999 provided the date of the disposition under which the inheritance is taken is after 1 December 1999.

[2] Substituted by FA 2000 s 139(1)(*b*) for inheritances taken on or after 1 December 1999 provided the date of the disposition under which the inheritance is taken is after 1 December 1999; previously "subsection (1)(*b*)".

[3] Subss (3)-(4) inserted by FA 2000 s 139(1)(*c*) for inheritances taken on or after 1 December 1999 provided the date of the disposition under which the inheritance is taken is after 1 December 1999.

Definitions

"date of the inheritance", "disponer", "inheritance", "property", "successor": s 2(1).

---

13 Disclaimer

(1) If—

(*a*) (i) a benefit under a will or an intestacy; or

(ii) an entitlement to an interest in settled property, is disclaimed;

(*b*) a claim—

(i) under a purported will in respect of which a grant of representation (within the meaning of the Succession Act, 1965) was not issued; or

(ii) under an alleged intestacy where a will exists in respect of which such a grant was issued,

is waived; or

(*c*) a right under Part IX of the Succession Act, 1965, or any analogous right under the law of another territory, is renounced, disclaimed, elected against or lapses,

any liability to tax in respect of such benefit, entitlement, claim or right shall cease as if such benefit, entitlement, claim or right, as the case may be, had not existed.

(2) Notwithstanding anything contained in this Act—

(*a*) a disclaimer of a benefit under a will or intestacy or of an entitlement to an interest in settled property;

(b)   the waiver of a claim—

    (i)   under a purported will in respect of which a grant of representation (within the meaning of the Succession Act, 1965) was not issued; or

    (ii)   under an alleged intestacy where a will exists in respect of which such a grant issued; or

(c)   (i)   the renunciation or disclaimer of;

    (ii)   the election against; or

    (iii)   the lapse of,

a right under Part IX of the Succession Act, 1965, or any analogous right under the law of another territory,

shall not be a disposition for the purposes of this Act.

(3) Subsection (1) shall not have effect to the extent of the amount of any consideration in money or money's worth received for the disclaimer, renunciation, election or lapse or for the waiver of a claim; and the receipt of such consideration shall he deemed to be a gift or an inheritance, as the case may be, in respect of which no consideration was paid by the donee or successor and which was derived from the disponer who provided the property in relation to which the benefit, entitlement, claim or right referred to in subsection (1), arose.

Note

A disclaimer of an intestate share may have resulted in the State succeeding as "ultimate successor": Irish Tax Review Vol 6 p 76.

Family Law (Miscellaneous Provisions) Act 1997 which was signed by the President on 5 May 1997 amends this statutorily by allowing disclaimers of intestate shares.

Revenue practice

See CAT Work Manual (revised July 2001), Pt 10 para 6.

Definitions

"disponer", "donee", "gift", "inheritance", "property": s 2(1); "benefit": s 2().

14 Surviving joint tenant deemed to take an inheritance, etc

(1) On the death of one of several persons who are beneficially and absolutely entitled in possession as joint tenants, the surviving joint tenant or surviving joint tenants shall be deemed to take an inheritance of the share of the deceased joint tenant, as successor or successors from the deceased joint tenant as disponer.

(2) The liability to inheritance tax in respect of an inheritance taken by persons as joint tenants shall be the same in all respects as if they took the inheritance as tenants in common in equal shares.

Narrative

Capital Acquisitions Tax, Chapter 14.

Definitions

"disponer", "entitled in possession", "inheritance", "share": s 2(1).

PART IV
VALUE OF PROPERTY FOR TAX

15 Market value of property

(1) Subject to the provisions of this Act, the market value of any property for the purposes of this Act shall be estimated to be the price which, in the opinion of the Commissioners, such property would fetch if sold in the open market on the date on which the property is to be valued in such manner and subject to such conditions as might reasonably be calculated to obtain for the vendor the best price for the property.

(2) In estimating the market value of any property, the Commissioners shall not make any reduction in the estimate on account of the estimate being made on the assumption that the whole property is to be placed on the market at one and the same time.

(3) The market value of any property shall be ascertained by the Commissioners in such manner and by such means as they think fit, and they may authorise a person to inspect any property and report to them the value thereof for the purposes of this Act, and the person having the custody or possession of that property shall permit the person so authorised to inspect it at such reasonable times as the Commissioners consider necessary.

(4) Where the Commissioners require a valuation to be made by a person named by them, the costs of such valuation shall be defrayed by the Commissioners.

(5) Subject to the provisions of this Act, in estimating the price which unquoted shares or securities might be expected to fetch if sold in the open market, it shall be assumed that in that market there is available to any prospective purchaser of the shares or securities all the information which a prudent prospective purchaser might reasonably require if he were proposing to purchase them from a willing vendor by private treaty and at arm's length.

(6) In subsection (5), **"unquoted shares or securities"** means shares or securities which are not dealt in on a stock exchange.

Narrative

Capital Acquisitions Tax, Chapter 6.

Case law

Avoidance scheme, whether s 17 (repealed) subject to s 15: *Revenue Commissioners v Henry Young*, HC, Keane J, 23 February 1996, SC, Murphy J, 31 July 1997, V ITR 294.

Definitions

"Commissioners", "market value": s 2(1); "person": IA 1937 s 11(*c*); "property": s 2(1).

---

16 Market value of certain shares in private trading companies

[(1)(*a*) The market value of each share in a private company which (after the taking of the gift or of the inheritance) is, on the date of the gift or on the date of the inheritance, a company controlled by the donee or successor, shall be ascertained by the Commissioners, for the purposes of tax, as if, on the date on which the market value is to be ascertained, it formed an apportioned part of the market value of a group of shares in that company, such apportionment, as between shares of a particular class, to be by reference to nominal amount, and, as between different classes of shares, to have due regard to the rights attaching to each of the different classes.

(b) For the purpose of ascertaining the market value of a share in a private company in the manner described in paragraph (a), the benefit to any private company (in this paragraph referred to as "the first-mentioned company") by virtue of its ownership of an interest in shares in another private company (in this paragraph referred to as "the second-mentioned company"), shall, where each of the companies so connected is a company which (after the taking of the gift or of the inheritance) is, on the date of the gift or on the date of the inheritance, a company controlled by the donee or successor, be deemed to be—

    (i) such benefit as would be appropriate to the ownership of that interest if the second-mentioned company were under the control of the first-mentioned company in the same manner as (on the date on which the market value is to be ascertained) the second-mentioned company is under the control of the following, that is to say, the first-mentioned company, the donee or successor, the relatives of the donee or successor, nominees of the donee or successor, nominees of relatives of the donee or successor, and the trustees of a settlement whose objects include the donee or successor or relatives of the donee or successor, or

    (ii) the actual benefit appropriate to the ownership of that interest,

    whichever is the greater.][1]

(2) In this section—

["group of shares", in relation to a private company, means the aggregate of the shares in the company of the donee or successor, the relatives of the donee or successor, nominees of the donee or successor, nominees of relatives of the donee or successor, and the trustees of a settlement whose objects include the donee or successor or relatives of the donee or successor;][2]

"nominee" includes a person who may be required to exercise his voting power on the directions of, or who holds shares directly or indirectly on behalf of, another person;

["private company" means a body corporate (wherever incorporated) which—

    (a) is under the control of not more than five persons, and

    (b) is not a company which would fall within [section 431 of the Taxes Consolidation Act, 1997],[3] if the words "private company" were substituted for the words "close company" in [subsection (3)][4] of that section, and if the words "if beneficially held by a company which is not a private company" were substituted for the words of paragraph (a) of [subsection (6)][5] of that section.][6]

...[7].

["share", in relation to a private company and in addition to the interpretation of "share" in section 2(1), includes every debenture, or loan stock, issued otherwise than as part of a transaction which is wholly and exclusively a *bona fide* commercial transaction.][8]

(3) In this section, a reference to a company controlled by the donee or successor is a reference to a company that is under the control of any one or more of the following, that is to say, the donee or successor, the relatives of the donee or successor, nominees of the donee or successor, nominees of relatives of the donee or successor, and the trustees of a settlement whose objects include the donee or successor or relatives of the donee or successor; and for the purposes of this section, a company which is so controlled by the donee or successor shall be regarded as being itself a relative of the donee or successor.

(4) For the purposes of this section—

   (*a*) a company shall be deemed to be under the control of not more than five persons if any five or fewer persons together exercise, or are able to exercise, or are entitled to acquire, control whether direct or indirect, of the company; and for this purpose—

      (i) persons who are relatives of any other person together with that other person;

      (ii) persons who are nominees of any other person together with that other person;

      (iii) persons in partnership; and

      (iv) persons interested in any shares or obligations of the company which are subject to any trust or are part of the estate of a deceased person,

      shall respectively be treated as a single person; and

   (*b*) a person shall be deemed to have control of a company at any time if—

      (i) he then had control of the powers of voting on all questions, or on any particular question, affecting the company as a whole, which, if exercised, would have yielded a majority of the votes capable of being exercised thereon, or could then have obtained such control by an exercise at that time of a power exercisable by him or at his direction or with his consent;

      (ii) he then had the capacity, or could then by an exercise of a power exercisable by him or at his direction or with his consent obtain the capacity, to exercise or to control the exercise of any of the following powers, that is to say—

         (I) the powers of a board of directors of the company;

         (II) powers of a governing director of the company;

         (III) power to nominate a majority of the directors of the company or a governing director thereof;

         (IV) the power to veto the appointment of a director of the company, or

         (V) powers of a like nature;

      (iii) he then had a right to receive, or the receipt of, more than one-half of the total amount of the dividends of the company, whether declared or not, and for the purposes of this subparagraph, "dividend" shall be deemed to include interest on any debentures of the company; or

(iv) he then had an interest in the shares of the company of an aggregate nominal value representing one-half or more of the aggregate nominal value of the shares of the company.

Amendments

1 Subs (1)(*a*) substituted by FA 1993 s 125(1)(*a*) as regards gifts or inheritances taken on or after 24 February 1993.

2 Definition of "group of shares" inserted by FA 1993 s 125(1)(*b*)(i) as regards gifts or inheritances taken on or after 24 February 1993.

3 Substituted by TCA 1997 s 1100 and Sch 31; previously "section 95 of the Corporation Tax Act, 1976".

4 Substituted by TCA 1997 s 1100 and Sch 31; previously "subsection (1)".

5 Substituted by TCA 1997 s 1100 and Sch 31; previously "subsection (4)".

6 Definition of "private company" substituted by FA 1996 s 121 as respects gifts and inheritances taken on or after 28 March 1996.

7 Definition of "private trading company" deleted by FA 1993 s 125(1)(*b*)(ii) as regards gifts or inheritances taken on or after 24 February 1993.

Previously: **"private trading company"** means a private company which is not a private non-trading company within the meaning of section 17."

8 Definition of "share" inserted by FA 1993 s 125(1)(*b*)(iii) as regards gifts or inheritances taken on or after 24 February 1993.

Cross-references

Discretionary trust once off charge, company controlled by successor: FA 1984 s 107(*a*).

Discretionary trust annual charge, company controlled by successor: FA 1986 s 104(*a*).

Anti-avoidance, transfer of rights attaching to particular shares in a private company to other shareholders in the same company without any transfer of shares being involved, value of the transferred rights is to be regarded as a gift, or inheritance (as appropriate) in the hands of the beneficial recipient; meaning of private company applied: FA 1989 s 90.

Probate tax, company controlled by successor: FA 1993 s 111(*a*).

Business property relief applies to shares in private companies controlled within this meaning if the company is wholly or mainly a trading company.

Narrative

Capital Acquisitions Tax, Chapter 6.

Definitions

"benefit", "Commissioners", "date of the gift", "date of the inheritance", "donee", "gift", "inheritance", "market value": s 2(1); "person": IA 1937 s 11(*c*); "relative", "share", "successor": s 2(1).

17 Market value of certain shares in private non-trading companies

Amendments

Section 17 repealed by FA 1993 s 134 as regards gifts or inheritances from 24 February 1993. Previously:

(1) The market value of each share in a private non-trading company which (after the taking of the gift or of the inheritance) is, on the date of the gift or on the date of the inheritance, a company controlled by the donee or the successor, shall for the purposes of this Act, be such sum as would have been payable in respect of the share to the owner thereof if the company had been voluntarily wound up and all the assets realised on the date at which the share is to be valued.

(2) In this section—

"investment income", in relation to a private company, means income which, if the company were an individual, would not be earned income within the meaning of section 2 of the Income Tax Act, 1967;

"private company" and **"company controlled by the donee or the successor"** have the meanings assigned to them by section 16;

"private non-trading company" means a private company—

(*a*) whose income (if any) in the twelve months preceding the date at which a share therein is to be valued consisted wholly or mainly of investment income; and (*b*) whose property, on the date referred to in paragraph (*a*), consisted wholly or mainly of property from which investment income is derived.

(3) Where the assets of such a private non-trading company as is referred to in subsection (1) include a share in another such private non-trading company (hereinafter referred to as the latter company), the market value of such share shall be ascertained on the basis that the latter company is voluntarily wound up and its assets realised on the date on which the share is to be value

(4) In determining the market value of the share referred to in subsection (1) or (3), no allowance shall be made for the costs of winding up any company or of realising its assets.

(5) In ascertaining, for the purposes of subsection (1) or (3), the amount which the assets of a company would realise, the assets shall be deemed to realise the amount of their market value as at the date at which the share referred to in subsection (1) or (3) is to be valued.

Case law

Avoidance scheme, whether s 17 subject to s 15: *Revenue Commissioners v Henry Young*, unreported, HC, Keane J, 23 February 1996.

18 Taxable value of a taxable gift or taxable inheritance

(1) In this section, **"incumbrance-free value"**, in relation to a taxable gift or a taxable inheritance, means the market value at the valuation date of the property of which the taxable gift or taxable inheritance consists at that date, after deducting any liabilities, costs and expenses that are properly payable out of the taxable gift or taxable inheritance.

(2) Subject to the provisions of this section (but save as provided in section 19), the taxable value of a taxable gift or a taxable inheritance (where the interest taken by the donee or successor is not a limited interest) shall be ascertained by deducting from the incumbrance-free value thereof the market value of any *bona fide* consideration in money or money's worth, paid by the donee or successor for the gift or inheritance, including—

    (*a*) any liability of the disponer which the donee or successor undertakes to discharge as his own personal liability; and

    (*b*) any other liability to which the gift or inheritance is subject under the terms of the disposition under which it is taken,

and the amount so ascertained shall be the taxable value:

Provided that no deduction shall be made under this subsection in respect of any liability which falls to be deducted in ascertaining the incumbrance-free value.

(3) Where a liability (other than a liability within the meaning of subsection (9)) for which a deduction may be made under the provisions of subsection (1) or (2) falls to be discharged after the time at which it falls to be taken into account as a deduction under either of those subsections, it shall be valued for the purpose of making such a deduction at its current market value at the time at which it falls to be so taken into account.

(4) The taxable value of a taxable gift or a taxable inheritance, where the interest taken by the donee or the successor is a limited interest, shall be ascertained as follows—

    (*a*) the value of the limited interest in a capital sum equal to the incumbrance-free value shall be ascertained in accordance with the Rules contained in the First Schedule; and

(b) from the value ascertained in accordance with paragraph (a) a deduction shall be made in respect of the market value of any *bona fide* consideration in money or money's worth paid by the donee or the successor for the gift or the inheritance and the amount remaining after such deduction shall be the taxable value:

Provided that no deduction shall be made under this paragraph in respect of any liability which falls to be deducted in ascertaining the incumbrance-free value.

(5) A deduction shall not be made under the provisions of this section—

(a) in respect of any liability the payment of which is contingent on the happening of some future event:

Provided that if the event on the happening of which the liability is contingent happens and the liability is paid, then, on a claim for relief being made to the Commissioners and subject to the other provisions of this section, a deduction shall be made in respect of the liability and such adjustment of tax as is appropriate shall be made; and such adjustment shall be made on the basis that the donee or successor had taken an interest in possession in the amount which falls to be deducted for the liability, for a period certain which was equal to the actual duration of the postponement of the payment of the liability;

(b) in respect of any liability, costs or expenses in so far as the donee or successor has a right of reimbursement from any source, unless such reimbursement cannot be obtained;

(c) in respect of any liability created by the donee or successor or any person claiming in right of the donee or successor or on his behalf;

(d) in respect of tax, interest or penalties chargeable under this Act in respect of the gift or inheritance, or of the costs, expenses or interest incurred in raising or paying the same;

(e) in respect of any liability in so far as such liability is an incumbrance on, or was created or incurred in acquiring, any property which is comprised in any gift or inheritance and which is exempt from tax under any provision of this Act or otherwise;

(f) in the case of any gift or inheritance referred to into in [section 6(1)(d) or 12(1)(c)]¹ in respect of—

(i) any liability, costs or expenses due to a person resident outside the State (save in so far as such liability is required by contract to be paid in the State or is charged on the property which is situate in the State and which is comprised in the gift or inheritance); or

(ii) any liability, costs or expenses in so far as the same are charged on or secured by property which is comprised in the gift or inheritance and which is not situate in the State,

save to the extent that all the property situate outside the State and comprised in the gift or inheritance is insufficient for the payment of the liability, costs or expenses;

(g)   for any tax in respect of which a credit is allowed under the provisions of section 66 or 67.

(6) In the case of a gift or inheritance referred to in subsection (5)(*f*), any deduction to be made under subsection (2) or (4)(*b*) shall be restricted to the proportion to the consideration which bears the same proportion to the whole of the consideration as the taxable gift or taxable inheritance bears to the whole of the gift or the whole of the inheritance.

(7) A deduction shall not be made under the provisions of this section—

(a)   more than once for the same liability, costs, expenses or consideration, in respect of all gifts and inheritances taken by the donee or successor from the disponer; or

(b)   for any liability, costs, expenses or consideration, a proportion of which falls to be allowed under the provisions of section 19(2)(ii) or (iii) in respect of a gift or inheritance taken by the donee or successor from the disponer.

(8) Where a taxable gift or a taxable inheritance is subject to a liability within the meaning of subsection (9), the deduction to be made in respect thereof under this section shall be an amount equal to the market value of the whole or the appropriate part, as the case may be, of the property, within the meaning of section 5(5).

(9) For the purpose of subsection (8), **"liability"**, in relation to a taxable gift or a taxable inheritance, means a liability which deprives the donee or successor, whether permanently or temporarily, of the use, enjoyment or income in whole or in part of the property, or of any part of the property, of which the taxable gift or taxable inheritance consists.

(10) Where—

(a)   *bona fide* consideration in money or money's worth has been paid by a person for the granting to him, by a disposition, of an interest in expectancy in property; and

(b)   at the coming into possession of the interest in expectancy, that person takes a gift or an inheritance of that property under that disposition,

the deduction to be made under subsection (2) or (4)(*b*) for consideration paid by that person shall be a sum equal to the same proportion of the taxable value of the taxable gift or taxable inheritance (as if no deduction had been made for such consideration) as the amount of the consideration so paid bore to the market value of the interest in expectancy at the date of the payment of the consideration.

(11) Any deduction, under the provisions of this section, in respect of a liability which is an incumbrance on any property shall so far as possible be made against that property.

Amendments

1   Substituted by FA 2001 s 216 with effect in relation to gifts and inheritances taken under a disposition on or after 1 December 1999; previously "section 6(1)(*c*) or section 12(1)(*b*)".

Cross-references

Probate tax: application of this section: FA 1993 s 111(*g*); (subs (4)(*a*)), exemption for dwelling house of dependent child or dependent relative: FA 1993 s 112(*d*).

Capital gains tax payable on the same event (subs (2)(*a*)) as gives rise to the claim for gift tax or inheritance tax cannot be regarded as a liability within the meaning of this section: FA 1985 s 63.

Revenue practice

See CAT Work Manual (revised July 2001), Pt 10 paras 3 and 4.

Narrative

Capital Acquisitions Tax, Chapter 5.

Definitions

"disponer", "donee", "gift", "inheritance", "interest in expectancy, "limited interest": s 2(1); "taxable gift": s 6; "successor": s 2(1); "taxable inheritance": s 12; "valuation date", "market value": s 2(1); "person": IA 1937 s 11(*c*); "property": s 2(1).

19 Value of agricultural property

(1) In this section—

["**agricultural property**" means agricultural land, pasture and woodland situate in the State and crops, trees and underwood growing on such land and also includes such farm buildings, farm houses and mansion houses (together with the lands occupied therewith) as are of a character appropriate to the property, and farm machinery, livestock and bloodstock thereon;][1]

["**agricultural value**" means the market value of agricultural property reduced by **90 per cent** of that value;][2]

["**farmer**" in relation to a donee or successor, means an individual who is domiciled in the State and in respect of whom not less than 80 per cent of the market value of the property to which the individual is beneficially entitled in possession is represented by the market value of property in the State which consists of agricultural property, and, for the purposes of this definition—

(*a*) no deduction shall be made from the market value of property for any debts or encumbrances, and

(*b*) an individual shall be deemed to be beneficially entitled in possession to—

(i) an interest in expectancy, notwithstanding the definition of "entitled in possession" in section 2, and

(ii) property which is subject to a discretionary trust under or in consequence of a disposition made by the individual where the individual is an object of the trust.][3]

(2) Save as provided in subsection (7), in so far as any gift or inheritance consists of agricultural property—

(*a*) at the date of the gift or at the date of the inheritance; and

(*b*) at the valuation date,

and is taken by a donee or successor who is, on the valuation date and after taking the gift or inheritance, a farmer, the provisions of section 18 (other than subsection 7(*b*) thereof) shall apply in relation to agricultural property as they apply in relation to other property subject to the following modifications—

(i) in subsection (1) of that section, the reference to market value shall be construed as a reference to agricultural value;

(ii) where a deduction is to be made for any liability, costs or expenses in accordance with subsection (1) of that section only a proportion of such liability, costs or expenses shall be deducted and that proportion shall be the proportion that the agricultural value of the agricultural property bears to the market value of that property; and

(iii) where a deduction is to be made for any consideration under subsection (2) or (4)(*b*) of that section, only a proportion of such consideration shall be deducted and that proportion shall be the proportion that the agricultural value of the agricultural property bears to the market value of that property.

(3) Where a taxable gift or a taxable inheritance is taken by a donee or successor subject to the condition that the whole or part thereof will be invested in agricultural property and such condition is complied with within two years after the date of the gift or the date of the inheritance, then the gift or inheritance shall be deemed, for the purposes of this section, to have consisted—

(*a*) at the date of the gift or at the date of the inheritance; and

(*b*) at the valuation date,

of agricultural property to the extent to which the gift or inheritance is subject to such condition and has been so invested.

...⁴

(5) [(*a*) The agricultural value shall cease to be applicable to agricultural property, other than crops, trees or underwood, if and to the extent that such property, or any agricultural property which directly or indirectly replaces such property

(i) is sold or compulsorily acquired within the period of 6 years after the date of the gift or the date of the inheritance; and

(ii) is not replaced, within a year of the sale [or within [6 years]⁵ of the compulsory acquisition],⁶ by other agricultural property,

and tax shall be chargeable in respect of the gift or inheritance as if the property were not agricultural property:

Provided that this paragraph shall not have effect where the donee or successor dies before the property is sold or compulsorily acquired.]⁷

(*b*) If an arrangement is made, in the administration of property subject to a disposition, for the appropriation of property in or towards the satisfaction of a benefit under the disposition, such arrangement shall be deemed not to be a sale or a compulsory acquisition for the purposes of paragraph (*a*).

[(*c*) The agricultural value in relation to a gift or inheritance referred to in subsection (2) shall cease to be applicable to agricultural property, other than crops, trees or underwood, if the donee or successor is not resident in the State for any of the three years of assessment immediately following the year of assessment in which the valuation date falls.]⁸

(6) For the purposes of subsection (2), if, in the administration of property subject to a disposition, property is appropriated in or towards the satisfaction of a benefit in respect

of which a person is deemed to take a gift or an inheritance under the disposition, the property so appropriated, if it was subject to the disposition at the date of the gift or at the date of the inheritance, shall be deemed to have been comprised in that gift or inheritance at the date of the gift or at the date of the inheritance.

(7) The provisions of subsection (2) shall have effect in relation to agricultural property which consists of trees or underwood as if the words "and is taken by a donee or successor who is, on the valuation date and after taking the gift or inheritance, a farmer," were omitted therefrom.

(8) In this section, other than in subsection (4), any reference to a donee or successor shall include a reference to the transferee referred to in section 23(1).

Amendments

[1]   Definition of "agricultural property" substituted by FA 1994 s 141(1)(*a*) in relation to gifts or inheritances taken on or after 11 April 1994.

[2]   Definition of "agricultural value" substituted by FA 1997 s 134(1)(*a*) in relation to gifts or inheritances taken on or after 23 January 1997.

[3]   Definition of "farmer" substituted by FA 2000 s 140(1)(*a*) for gifts or inheritances taken on or after 10 February 2000.

[4]   Subs (4) deleted by FA 1996 s 122(1)(*b*) in relation to gifts or inheritances taken on or after 23 January 1996.

[5]   Substituted by FA 2002 s 116(1) in relation to compulsory acquisitions made on or after 25 March 2002; previously "4 years".

[6]   Substituted by FA 2001 s 217 in relation to compulsory acquisitions made on or after 6 December 2000; previously "or compulsory acquisition".

[7]   Subs (5)(*a*) substituted by FA 2000 s 140(1)(*b*) where the sale or compulsory acquisition which causes the agricultural value to cease to be applicable occurs on or after 10 February 2000.

[8]   Subs (5)(*c*) inserted by FA 1995 s 158(*d*) in relation to gifts and inheritances taken on or after from 2 June 1995.

Cross-references

Business relief, agricultural property, meaning applied: FA 1994 s 124(1).

Inheritances taken on or after 30 January 1991: if a successor takes a house (or part of a house) from a deceased brother or sister, and the successor had resided with the deceased in that house for at least five years prior to the date of the inheritance, the market value of the house for inheritance tax purposes is reduced by 50% or £50,000 (increased to 60% or £60,000: FA 1994 s 144 and to £80,000 by FA 1997 s 138) whichever is the lesser. The relief does not apply to a house that is included as part of agricultural property that qualifies for agricultural relief (s 19 above).

Instalment payments (subss (2), (5)): FA 1995 s 164(2)(*a*).

Probate tax, this section does not apply: FA 1993 s 111(*f*).

Revenue practice

See CAT Work Manual (revised July 2001), Pt 10 para 16.

Narrative

Capital Acquisitions Tax, Chapter 9.

Definitions

"benefit", "date of the gift", "date of the inheritances", "disponer", "disposition", "donee", "gift", "inheritance", "valuation date", "market value": s 2(1); "person": IA 1937 s 11(*c*); "property", "real property", "taxable gift", "taxable inheritance", "year of assessment": s 2(1).

Revenue information

Leaflet CAT5 - Agricultural relief: 2000 Finance Act.

---

20 Contingencies affecting gifts or inheritances

Where, under a disposition, a person becomes beneficially entitled in possession to any benefit and, under the terms of the disposition, the entitlement, or any part thereof, may cease upon the happening of a contingency (other than the revocation of the entitlement upon the exercise by the disponer of such a power as is referred to in section 30), the taxable value of any taxable gift or taxable inheritance taken by that person on becoming so entitled to that benefit shall be ascertained as if no part of the entitlement were so to cease; but, in the event and to the extent that the entitlement so ceases, the tax payable by that person shall, to that extent, be adjusted (if, by so doing, a lesser amount of tax would be payable by him) on the basis that he had taken an interest in possession for a period certain which was equal to the actual duration of his beneficial entitlement in possession:

Provided that nothing in this section shall prejudice any charge for tax on the taking by such person of a substituted gift or inheritance on the happening of such a contingency.

Cross-reference

Probate tax, where entitlement within the meaning of this section ceases because of an enlargement of that interest, exemption (not to be reduced) for dwelling house of dependent child or dependent relative: FA 1993 s 112(*d*).

Narrative

Capital Acquisitions Tax, Chapter 16.

Definitions

"benefit", "disponer", "disposition", "entitled in possession", "gift", "inheritance": s 2(1); "person": IA 1937 s 11(*c*); "taxable gift", "taxable inheritance", "taxable value": s 2(1).

21 Valuation date for tax purposes

(1) Subject to the provisions of subsection (7), the valuation date of a taxable gift shall be the date of the gift.

(2) The valuation date of a taxable inheritance shall be the date of death of the deceased person on whose death the inheritance is taken if the successor or any person in right of the successor or on his behalf takes the inheritance—

    (*a*) as a donatio mortis causa; or

    (*b*) by reason of the failure to exercise a power of revocation.

(3) If a gift becomes an inheritance by reason of its being taken under a disposition where the date of the disposition is within two years prior to the death of the disponer, the valuation date thereof shall be determined as if it were a gift.

(4) The valuation date of a taxable inheritance, other than a taxable inheritance referred to in subsection (2) or (3), shall be the earliest date of the following—

    (*a*) the earliest date on which a personal representative or trustee or the successor or any other person is entitled to retain the subject matter of the inheritance for the benefit of the successor or of any person in right of the successor or on his behalf;

    (*b*) the date on which the subject matter of the inheritance is so retained; or

(c) the date of delivery, payment or other satisfaction or discharge of the subject matter of the inheritance to the successor or for his benefit or to or for the benefit of any person in right of the successor or on his behalf.

(5) If any part of a taxable inheritance referred to in subsection (4) may be retained, or is retained, delivered, paid or otherwise satisfied, whether by way of part payment, advancement, payment on account or in any manner whatsoever, before any other part or parts of such inheritance, the appropriate valuation date for each part of the inheritance shall be determined in accordance with that subsection as if each such part respectively were a separate inheritance.

(6) The Commissioners may give to an accountable person a notice in writing of the date determined by them to be the valuation date in respect of the whole or any part of an inheritance, and, subject to any decision on appeal pursuant to subsection (9), the date so determined shall be deemed to be the valuation date.

(7) If a taxable inheritance referred to in subsection (4) or (5) is disposed of, ceases or comes to an end before the valuation date referred to in those subsections in such circumstances as to give rise to a taxable gift, the valuation date in respect of such taxable gift shall be the same date as the valuation date of the taxable inheritance.

(8) Notwithstanding anything contained in this section, the Commissioners may, in case of doubt, with the agreement in writing of the accountable person or his agent, determine the valuation date of the whole or any part of any taxable inheritance and the valuation date so determined shall be substituted for the valuation date which would otherwise be applicable by virtue of this section.

(9) An appeal shall lie against any determination made by the Commissioners under subsection (6) and the provisions of section 52 shall apply, with any necessary modifications, in relation to an appeal under this subsection as they apply in relation to an appeal against an assessment of tax.

Cross-references

Discretionary trust once off charge, this section applies but valuation date of the taxable inheritance is the date of the inheritance, or the valuation date as ascertained by s 21 above, whichever is the later: FA 1984 s 107(b). Discretionary trust annual charge, this section does not apply: FA 1986 s 104(g). Probate tax, this section does not apply: FA 1993 s 111(f).

Narrative

Capital Acquisitions Tax, Chapter 9.

Definitions

"accountable person", "benefit", "Commissioners", "date of the disposition", "disponer", "disposition", "donee", "gift": "inheritance", "valuation date": s 2(1); "person": IA 1937 s 11(c); "personal representative", "taxable gift", "taxable inheritance", "successor": s 2(1).

PART V
PROVISIONS RELATING TO GIFTS AND INHERITANCES

22 Discretionary trusts

Where a person becomes beneficially entitled in possession to any benefit—

(a) under a discretionary trust, other than a discretionary trust referred to in paragraph (b), otherwise than for full consideration in money or money's worth paid by him, he shall be deemed to have taken a gift;

(*b*)   under a discretionary trust created—

> (i)   by will at any time;
>
> (ii)   by a disposition, where the date of the disposition is on or after the 1st day of April, 1975, and within two years prior to the death of the disposer; or
>
> (iii)   by a disposition *inter vivos* and limited to come into operation on a death occurring before or after the passing of this Act,
>
> otherwise than for full consideration in money or money's worth paid by him, he shall be deemed to have taken an inheritance.

Cross-references

Gift deemed to be taken: s 5.

Inheritance deemed to be taken: s 11.

As to the disposer: s 7.

Narrative

Capital Acquisitions Tax, Chapter 17.

Definitions

"benefit", "date of the disposition", "discretionary trust", "disponer", "disposition", "gift", "inheritance": s 2(1); "person": IA 1937 s 11(*c*).

23 Dealings with future interests

(1) Where a benefit, to which a person (in this section referred to as the remainderman) is entitled under a disposition, devolves, or is disposed of, either in whole or in part, before it has become an interest in possession so that, at the time when the benefit comes into possession, it is taken, either in whole or in part, by a person (in this section referred to as the transferee) other than the remainderman to whom it was limited by the disposition, then tax shall be payable, in respect of a gift or inheritance, as the case may be, of the remainderman in all respects as if, at that time, the remainderman had become beneficially entitled in possession to the full extent of the benefit limited to him under the disposition, and the transferee shall be the person primarily accountable for the payment of tax to the extent that the benefit is taken by him.

(2) The provisions of subsection (1) shall not prejudice any charge for tax in respect of any gift or inheritance affecting the same property or any part of it under any other disposition.

(3) In subsection (1), **"benefit"** includes the benefit of the cesser of a liability referred to in section 28.

Cross-references

Allowance for prior tax on the same event: s 34A.

Narrative

Capital Acquisitions Tax, Chapter 16.

Definitions

"accountable person": s 35; "benefit", "disposition", "gift", "entitled in possession", "inheritance": s 2(1); "person": IA 1937 s 11(*c*); "property": s 2(1).

24 Release of limited interests, etc

(1) Where an interest in property, which is limited by the disposition creating it to cease on an event, has come to an end (whether by another disposition, the taking of successive interests into one ownership, or by any means whatever other than the happening of another event on which the interest was limited by the first-mentioned disposition to cease) before the happening of such event, tax shall be payable under the first-mentioned disposition in all respects as if the event on which the interest was limited to cease under that disposition had happened immediately before the coming to an end of the interest.

(2) The provisions of subsection (1) shall not prejudice any charge for tax in respect of any gift or inheritance affecting the same property or any part of it under any disposition other than that first mentioned in subsection (1).

(3) Notwithstanding anything contained in subsection (2), if—

    (*a*)   an interest in property which was limited to cease on an event was limited to the disponer by the disposition creating that interest; and

    (*b*)   on the coming to an end of that interest, the provisions of subsection (1) have effect in relation to a gift or inheritance which was taken by a donee or successor under that disposition and which consists of the property in which that interest subsisted, then—

a further gift or inheritance taken by the same donee or successor under another disposition made by the same disponer (being the disposition by which that interest has come to an end) shall not be a taxable gift or a taxable inheritance in so far as it consists of the whole or any part of the same property.

(4) In this section, **"event"** includes—

    (*a*)   a death; and

    (*b*)   the expiration of a specified period.

Cross-references

Allowance for prior tax on the same event: s 34A.

Narrative

Capital Acquisitions Tax, Chapter 16.

Definitions

"disponer", "disposition", "donee", "gift", "inheritance", "property", "successor", "taxable gift", "taxable inheritance": s 2(1).

---

25 Settlement of an interest not in possession

(1) Where any donee or successor takes a gift or an inheritance under a disposition made by himself then, if at the date of such disposition he was entitled to the property comprised in the disposition, either expectantly on the happening of an event, or subject to a liability within the meaning of section 18(9), and such event happens or such liability ceases during the continuance of the disposition, tax shall be charged on the taxable value of the taxable gift or taxable inheritance which he would have taken on the

happening of such event, or on the cesser of such liability, if no such disposition had been made.

(2) The provisions of subsection (1) shall not prejudice any charge for tax in respect of any gift or inheritance affecting the same property or any part of it under the said disposition.

(3) In this section, **"event,"** has the same meaning as it has in section 24.

Cross-references

Allowance for prior tax on the same event: s 34A.

Narrative

Capital Acquisitions Tax, Chapter 16.

Definitions

"date of the disposition", "disposition", "donee", "gift", "inheritance", "property", "successor", "taxable gift", "taxable inheritance", "taxable value": s 2(1).

26 Enlargement of interests

(1) Where a person, having a limited interest in possession in property (in this section referred to as the first-mentioned interest), takes a further interest (in this section referred to as the second-mentioned interest) in the same property, as a taxable gift or a taxable inheritance, in consequence of which he becomes the absolute owner of the property, the taxable value of the taxable gift or taxable inheritance of the second-mentioned interest at the valuation date shall be reduced by the value at that date of the first-mentioned interest, taking such value to be the value, ascertained in accordance with the Rules contained in the First Schedule, of a limited interest which—

(*a*)   is a limited interest in a capital sum equal to the value of the property;

(*b*)   commences on that date; and

(*c*)   is to continue for the unexpired balance of the term of the first-mentioned interest.

(2) For the purposes of subsection (1)(*a*), **"value"** means such amount as would be the incumbrance-free value, within the meaning of section 18(1), if the limited interest were taken, at the date referred to in subsection (1), as a taxable gift or taxable inheritance.

(3) The provisions of this section shall not have effect where the second-mentioned interest is taken under the disposition under which the first mentioned interest was created.

Narrative

Capital Acquisitions Tax, Chapter 16.

Definitions

"disposition", "gift", "incumbrance free value": s 18(1); "inheritance", "limited interest", "valuation date": s 2(1); "person": IA 1937 s 11(*c*); "property", "taxable gift", "taxable inheritance", "taxable value": s 2(1).

27 Dispositions involving powers of appointment

(1) Where, by virtue of or in consequence of the exercise of, or the failure to exercise, or the release of, a general power of appointment by any person having such a power, a person becomes beneficially entitled in possession to any benefit, then, for the purposes

of this Act, the disposition shall be the exercise of, or the failure to exercise, or the release of, the power and not the disposition under which the power was created, and the person exercising, or failing to exercise, or releasing, the power shall be the disponer.

(2) Where, by virtue of or in consequence of the exercise of, or the failure to exercise, or the release of, a special power of appointment by any person having such a power, a person becomes beneficially entitled in possession to any benefit, then, for the purposes of this Act, the disposition shall be the disposition under which the power was created and the person who created the power shall be the disponer.

Narrative

Capital Acquisitions Tax, Chapter 4.

Definitions

"benefit", "disponer", "disposition", "entitled in possession", "general power of appointment": s 2(1); "person": IA 1937 s 11(c); "special power of appointment", "general power of appointment": s 2(1).

28 Cesser of liabilities

(1) The benefit of the cesser of—

    (a)   a liability within the meaning of section 18(9); or

    (b)   any liability similar to that referred to in paragraph (a) to which the taking of a benefit which was a gift or inheritance was subject,

shall be deemed to be a gift or an inheritance, as the case may be, which shall be deemed—

    (i)   to the extent that the liability is charged on or secured by any property at the time of its cesser, to consist of the whole or the appropriate part, as the case may be, of that property; and

    (ii)   to the extent that the liability is not charged on or secured by any property at the time of its cesser, to consist of such sum as would, under the provisions of section 5(2)(b), be the sum the annual income of which would be equal to the annual value of the liability.

(2) In this section, **"appropriate part"** has the meaning assigned to it by section 5(5).

(3) For the purposes of sections 6(1)(c) and 12(1)(b), the sum referred to in subparagraph (ii) of subsection (1) shall be deemed not to be situate in the State at the date of the gift or at the date of the inheritance.

Narrative

Capital Acquisitions Tax, Chapter 5.

Definitions

"benefit", "date of the gift", "date of the inheritance", "gift", "inheritance", "property": s 2(1).

29 Disposition enlarging value of property

(1) In this section, **"property"** does not include any property to which a donee or successor became beneficially entitled in possession prior to the 28th day of February, 1969.

(2) Where the taking by any person of a beneficial interest in any property (hereinafter in this section referred to as additional property) under any disposition made by a disponer has the effect of increasing the value of any other property (hereinafter in this section referred to as original property) to which that person is beneficially entitled in possession, and which had been derived from the same disponer, the following provisions shall have effect—

(*a*) the increase in value so effected shall be deemed to be a gift or an inheritance, as the case may be, arising under that disposition and taken by that person, as donee or successor, from that disponer, at the time he took the beneficial interest in the additional property;

(*b*) the original property shall be treated as having been increased in value if the market value of that property at the time referred to in paragraph (*a*) would be greater if it was sold as part of an aggregate of the original property and the additional property rather than as a single item of property, and the increase in value for the purposes of this section shall be the amount by which the market value of the original property if sold at that time as part of such aggregate would be greater than the amount of the market value of that property if sold at that time as a single item of property;

(*c*) the additional property shall, for the purpose of determining its market value, be deemed to be part of an aggregate of the original property and the additional property; and

(*d*) the market value of any property which is to be valued as part of an aggregate of property shall be ascertained as being so much of the market value of such aggregate as may reasonably be ascribed to that part.

(3) For the purpose of this section, the donee or successor shall be deemed to be beneficially entitled in possession to any property notwithstanding that within five years prior to such a disposition as is referred to in subsection (2) he has divested himself of such property, or any part thereof, otherwise than for full consideration in money or money's worth or has disposed of it to a company of which he is, at any time within that period of five years, deemed to have control within the meaning of section 16(4)(*b*).

(4) In subsection (3), **"company"** means a private company within the meaning of section 16(2).

Narrative

Capital Acquisitions Tax, Chapter 20.

Definitions

"disponer", "disposition", "donee", "entitled in possession", "gift", "inheritance", "market value": s 2(1); "person": IA 1937 s 11(*c*); "property", "successor": s 2(1).

---

30 Gift subject to power of revocation

Where, under any disposition, a person becomes beneficially entitled in possession to any benefit and, under the terms of the disposition, the disponer has reserved to himself the power to revoke the benefit, such person shall, for the purposes of this Act, be deemed not to be beneficially entitled in possession to the benefit unless and until the power of revocation is released by the disponer, or otherwise ceases to be exercisable.

Note

Becoming "entitled in possession" to the benefit determines the date of the gift or inheritance.

Narrative

Capital Acquisitions Tax, Chapter 20.

Definitions

"benefit", "disponer", "disposition", "entitled in possession": s 2(1); "person": IA 1937 s 11(*c*).

---

31 Free use of property, free loans, etc

(1) A person shall be deemed to take a gift in each relevant period during the whole or part of which he is allowed to have the use, occupation or enjoyment of any property (to which property he is not beneficially entitled in possession) otherwise than for full consideration in money or money's worth.

(2) In subsections (1) and (4), **"relevant period"**, in relation to any use, occupation or enjoyment of property, means the period from the 28th day of February, 1974, to the 31st day of December, 1974, and thereafter the period of twelve months ending on the 31st day of December in each year.

(3) A gift referred to in subsection (1) shall be deemed to consist of a sum equal to the difference between the amount of any consideration in money or money's worth, given by the person referred to in subsection (1) for such use, occupation or enjoyment, and the best price obtainable in the open market for such use, occupation or enjoyment.

(4) A gift referred to in subsection (1) shall be treated as being taken at the end of the relevant period or, if earlier, immediately prior to the time when the use, occupation or enjoyment referred to in subsection (1) comes to an end.

(5) In any case where the use, occupation or enjoyment of property is allowed to a person, not being beneficially entitled in possession to that property, under a disposition—

    (*a*)   made by will;

    (*b*)   where the date of the disposition is on or after the 1st day of April, 1975, and within two years prior to the death of the disponer: or

    (*c*)   which is a disposition *inter vivos* and the use, occupation or enjoyment is had by that person after the cesser of another person's life interest,

subsections (1), (3) and (4) shall have effect in relation to that property as if a reference to an inheritance were substituted for the reference to a gift wherever it occurs in those subsections, and for the purpose of this subsection **"relevant period"** in subsections (1) and (4), in relation to the use, occupation or enjoyment of property, means the period of nine months ending on the 31st day of December, 1975, and thereafter the period of twelve months ending on the 31st day of December in any year.

(6) For the purposes of [sections 6(1)(*d*) and 12(1)(*c*)]¹, the sum referred to in subsection (3) shall be deemed not to be situate in the State at the date of the gift or at the date of the inheritance.

Amendments

¹   Substituted by FA 2002 s 138 and Sch 6 para 2(*b*) in relation to gifts or inheritances taken on or after 1 December 1999; previously "sections 6(1)(*c*) and 12(1)(*b*)".

Cross-references

Discretionary trust once off charge, no double charge: FA 1984 s 108.

Narrative

Capital Acquisitions Tax, Chapter 20.

Definitions

"date of the disposition", "date of the gift", "date of the inheritance", "disponer", "disposition", "entitled in possession", "gift", "inheritance": s 2(1); "person": IA 1937 s 11(*c*); "property": s 2(1).

32 When interest in assurance policy becomes interest in possession

(1) For the purposes of this Act. an interest in a policy of assurance upon human life shall be deemed to become an interest in possession when and only when, either—

    (*a*)   the policy matures; or

    (*b*)   prior to the maturing of the policy, the policy is surrendered to the insurer for a consideration in money or money's worth:

Provided that if, during the currency of the policy, the insurer makes a payment of money or money's worth, in full or partial discharge of the policy, the interest shall be deemed to have come into possession to the extent of such payment.

(2) This section shall have effect in relation to a contract for a deferred annuity, and for the purposes of this section such a contract shall be deemed to mature on the date when the first instalment of the annuity falls due.

Cross-references

Discretionary trust once off charge, interest in policy of assurance on human life does not become property in possession until it matures or is surrendered: FA 1984 s 106(3).

33 Provisions to apply where section 98 of Succession Act, 1965, has effect

(1) If, on the death of a testator and by virtue of the provisions of section 98 of the Succession Act, 1965, or otherwise a disposition takes effect as if a person, who had predeceased the testator, had survived the testator, the benefit taken by the estate of that person shall not be deemed to be an inheritance.

(2) Where a person survives a testator, and—

    (*a*)   such person becomes beneficially entitled, under a disposition made by a person who predeceased the testator, to any benefit in relation to any property devised or bequeathed by the testator; and

    (*b*)   section 33 of the Wills Act, 1837, or section 98 of the Succession Act, 1965, or any analogous provision of the law of another territory has effect in relation to the devise or bequest,

such person shall be deemed for the purposes of inheritance tax to derive the benefit from the testator, as disponer.

Narrative

Capital Acquisitions Tax, Chapter 4.

Definitions

"benefit", "disponer", "disposition", "inheritance": s 2(1); "person": IA 1937 s 11(c); "property": s 2(1).

34 Disposition by or to a company

[(1) For the purposes of this Act—

    (*a*)   consideration paid by, or a disposition made by, a company shall be deemed to be consideration, or a disposition (as the case may be) paid or made, and

    (*b*)   consideration, or a gift, or an inheritance taken by a company shall be deemed to be consideration, or a gift or an inheritance (as the case may be) taken,

by the beneficial owners of the shares in the company and the beneficial owners of the entitlements under any liability incurred by the company (otherwise than for the purposes of the business of the company, wholly and exclusively) in the same proportions as the specified amounts relating to their respective beneficial interests in the shares and entitlements bear to each other.

(2) In this section—

"company" means a private company within the meaning of section 16(2);

"market value" means—

    (*a*)   in the case of a person's beneficial interest in shares and entitlements, the market value of that interest on the date of the payment, disposition, gift or inheritance, as the case may be, ascertained by reference to the market value on that date of the shares and entitlements in which the interest subsists, and

    (*b*)   in the case of a share in which a beneficial interest subsists, the market value of that share ascertained in the manner described in section 16 as if, on the date on which the market value is to be ascertained, it formed an apportioned part of the market value of a group of shares consisting of all the shares in the company issued and outstanding at that date;

"share" has the same meaning as it has in section 16 (as amended by the Finance Act, 1993);

"specified amount", in relation to a person's beneficial interest in shares and entitlements, means—

    (*a*)   in the case of consideration paid, or a disposition made, by the company, a nil amount or, if greater, the amount by which the market value of the beneficial interest was decreased as a result of the payment of the consideration or the making of the disposition, and

    (*b*)   in the case of consideration, or a gift, or an inheritance taken by the company, a nil amount or, if greater, the amount by which the market value of the beneficial interest was increased as a result of the taking of the consideration, gift or inheritance.][1]

(3) For the purposes of subsection (1) all acts, omissions and receipts of the company shall be deemed to be those of the beneficial owners of the shares and entitlements, referred to in subsection (1), in the company, in the proportions mentioned in that subsection.

(4) Where the beneficial owner of any shares in a company or of any entitlement of the kind referred to in subsection (1), is itself a company, the beneficial owners of the shares and entitlements, referred to in subsection (1), in the latter company, shall be deemed to be the beneficial owners of the latter company's shares and entitlements in the former company, in the proportions in which they are the beneficial owners of the shares and entitlements in the latter company.

(5) So far as the shares and entitlements referred to in subsection (1) are held in trust and have no ascertainable beneficial owners, consideration paid, or a disposition made, by the company shall be deemed to be paid or made by the disponer who made the disposition under which the shares and entitlements are so held in trust.

Amendments

[1]   Subss (1)-(2) substituted by FA 1993 s 129 where the date of the payment, gift or disposition is on or after
       24 February 1993.

Narrative

Capital Acquisitions Tax, Chapter 20.

Definitions

"disponer", "gift", "inheritance": s 2(1).

34A Allowance for prior tax on the same event

[Where tax is charged more than once in respect of the same property on the same event, the net tax payable which is earlier in priority shall not be deducted in ascertaining the taxable value for the purposes of the tax which is later in priority, but shall be deducted from the tax which is later in priority as a credit against the same, up to the net amount of the same.][1]

Amendments

[1]   Section 34A inserted by FA 1985 s 62 and deemed always to have had effect.

Narrative

Capital Acquisitions Tax, Chapter 8.

Definitions

"disposition", "gift", inheritance", "property": s 2(1).

PART VI
RETURNS AND ASSESSMENTS

35 Accountable persons

(1) The person primarily accountable for the payment of tax shall be—

    (*a*)   save as provided in paragraph (*b*), the donee or successor, as the case may be; and

    (*b*)   in the case referred to in section 23(1), the transferee referred to in that subsection, to the extent referred to in that subsection.

(2) Subject to subsections (3) and (4), the following persons shall also be accountable for the payment of any amount of the tax for which the persons referred to in subsection (1) are made primarily accountable—

    (*a*)   in the case of a gift—

        (i)   the disponer; and

        (ii)   every trustee, guardian, committee, personal representative, agent or other person in whose care any property comprised in the gift or the income therefrom is placed at the date of the gift or at any time thereafter and every person in whom the property is vested after that date, other than a *bona fide* purchaser or mortgagee for full consideration in money or money's worth, or a person deriving title from or under such a purchaser or mortgagee;

    (*b*)   in the case of an inheritance, every trustee, guardian, committee, personal representative, agent or other person in whose care any property comprised in the inheritance or the income therefrom is placed at the date of the inheritance or at any time thereafter and every person in whom the property is vested after that date, other than a *bona fide* purchaser or mortgagee for full consideration in money or money's worth, or a person deriving title from or under such a purchaser or mortgagee:

Provided that the disponer as such shall not be so accountable in the case where the date of the disposition was prior to the 28th day of February, 1974.

(3) No person referred to in subsection (2)(*a*)(ii) or (*b*) shall (unless he is a person who is also primarily accountable under subsection (1)) be liable for tax chargeable on any gift or inheritance to an amount in excess of—

    (*a*)   the market value of so much of the property of which the gift or inheritance consists; and

    (*b*)   so much of the income from such property,

which has been received by him, or which, but for his own neglect or default, would have been received by him or to which he is beneficially entitled in possession.

(4) A person who acts solely in the capacity of an agent shall not be liable for tax chargeable on a gift or inheritance to an amount in excess of the market value of so much of the property of which the gift or inheritance consists and of the income from such property which he held, or which came into his possession, at any time after the serving on him of the notice referred to in subsection (5).

(5) The Commissioners may serve on any person who acts solely in the capacity of agent in relation to any property comprised in a gift or an inheritance a notice in writing informing him of his liability under this section.

(6) The tax shall be recoverable from any one or more of—

    (*a*)   the accountable persons; and

    (*b*)   the personal representatives of any accountable persons who are dead,

on whom the Commissioners have served notice in writing of the assessment of tax in exercise of the power conferred on them by section 39:

Provided that the liability of a personal representative under this subsection shall not exceed the amount for which the accountable person, of whom he is the personal representative, was liable.

(7) Any person referred to in subsection (2)(*a*) or (*b*) or in subsection (6)(*b*) who is authorised or required to pay, and pays, any tax in respect of any property comprised in a gift or in an inheritance may recover the amount paid by him in respect of tax from the person primarily accountable therefor [unless—

(*a*) the latter person is the donee or successor referred to in paragraph (*a*) of subsection (1) and the interest taken by him is a limited interest, or

(*b*) in the case referred to in paragraph (*b*) of the said subsection (1), the latter person is the transferee and the interest taken by the remainderman is a limited interest][1].

(8) A person—

(*a*) who is primarily accountable for the payment of tax; or

(*b*) referred to in subsection (2)(*a*) or (*b*) or in subsection (6)(*b*) who is authorised or required to pay tax,

in respect of any property shall, for the purpose of paying the tax, or raising the amount of the tax when already paid, have power, whether the property is or is not vested in him, to raise the amount of such tax and any interest and expenses properly paid or incurred by him in respect thereof, by the sale or mortgage of, or a terminable charge on, that property or any part thereof.

(9) If a person, who is primarily accountable for the payment of tax in respect of a gift or inheritance (in this subsection and in subsection (11) referred to as the first gift or inheritance) derived from a disponer, has not paid the tax on the first gift or inheritance, the Commissioners may serve a notice in writing in accordance with subsection (11) on any person who is, by virtue of paragraph (*a*)(ii) or (*b*) of subsection (2), accountable for the payment of tax on any other gift or inheritance (referred to in subsections (10) and (11) as the second gift or inheritance) taken by the same donee or successor from the same disponer, and the person on whom the notice is served shall thereupon become accountable for the payment of tax in respect of the first gift or inheritance.

(10) The provisions of subsections (3), (4), (5), (6), (7) and (8) shall apply in relation to a person made accountable under subsection (9) as they apply in relation to a person referred to in paragraph (*a*)(ii) or (*b*) of subsection (2) and, for the purposes of this subsection—

(*a*) references in subsections (3) and (4) to the property of which the gift or inheritance consists; and

(*b*) the second and third references to property in subsection (8), shall be construed as references to the property of which the second gift or inheritance consists, in so far as the last-mentioned property had not been duly paid out at the date of the service of the notice under subsection (9).

(11) A notice under subsection (9) shall refer expressly to the first and the second gift or inheritance, and shall inform the person on whom it is served of his accountability in respect of the first gift or inheritance.

(12) Every public officer having in his custody any rolls, books, records, papers, documents, or proceedings, the inspection whereof may tend to secure the tax, or to prove or lead to the discovery of any fraud or omission in relation to the tax, shall at all reasonable times permit any person thereto authorised by the Commissioners to inspect the rolls, books, records, papers, documents and proceedings, and to take notes and extracts as he may deem necessary.

Amendments

[1]   Additional words inserted in subs (7) by FA 1980 s 84 as respects a gift taken on or after the 28 February 1974 or an inheritance taken on or after 1 April 1975.

Narrative

Capital Acquisitions Tax, Chapter 21.

Cross-references

Discretionary trust once off charge: objects of the trust are secondarily accountable (subs (2)): FA 1984 s 107(*d*); subs (1) does not apply: FA 1984 s 107(*g*).

Discretionary trust annual charge: objects of the trust are secondarily accountable (subs (2)): FA 1986 s 104(*d*); subs (1) does not apply: FA 1986 s 104(*g*).

Probate tax: subs (1) does not apply: FA 1993 s 111(*f*); personal representative is primarily accountable: FA 1993 s 111(*c*); beneficiaries are secondarily accountable (subs (2)): FA 1993 s 111(*d*).

Gift treated as an inheritance due to the death of a disponer within two years after the date of gift, subs (2)(*a*)(i) extended by: FA 1989 s 81.

Self-assessment, as regards dispositions dated on or after 1 May 1989, disponer is a secondarily accountable person in the case of an inheritance taken before the date of death of the disponer, and subss (3) and (9) above do not apply to such a disponer: FA 1989 s 81.

Definitions

"accountable person", "Commissioners", "date of the disposition", "date of the gift", "date of the inheritance", "disponer", "disposition", "donee", "gift", "inheritance", "market value": s 2(1); "person": IA 1937 s 11(*c*); "personal representative", "property", "successor": s 2(1).

36 Delivery of returns

[(1) In this section—

    (*a*)   notwithstanding anything contained in sections 6 and 12—

        (i)   a reference to a taxable gift is a reference to a taxable gift taken on or after the 28th day of February, 1974;

       (ii)   a reference to a taxable inheritance is a reference to a taxable inheritance taken on or after the 1st day of April, 1975; and

     [(iii)   a reference, other than in subparagraph (i) or subsection (13) or (14), to a gift or a taxable gift includes a reference to an inheritance or a taxable inheritance, as the case may be; and][1]

    (*b*)   a reference to a donee includes a reference to a successor.

(2) Any person who is primarily accountable for the payment of tax by virtue of section 35(1), or by virtue of paragraph (*c*) of section 107 of the Finance Act, 1984, shall, within **four months** after the relevant date referred to in subsection (5)—

(*a*) deliver to the Commissioners a full and true return of—

    (i) every gift in respect of which he is so primarily accountable;

    (ii) all the property comprised in such gift on the valuation date;

    (iii) an estimate of the market value of such property on the valuation date; and

    (iv) such particulars as may be relevant to the assessment of tax in respect of such gift;

(*b*) notwithstanding the provisions of section 39, make on that return an assessment of such amount of tax as, to the best of his knowledge, information and belief, ought to be charged, levied and paid on that valuation date; and

(*c*) duly pay the amount of such tax.

(3) The provisions of subsection (2)(*c*) shall be complied with—

(*a*) where the tax due and payable in respect of any part of the gift is being paid by instalments under the provisions of section 43, by the due payment of—

    (i) an amount which includes any instalment of tax which has fallen due prior to or on the date of the assessment of the tax referred to in subsection (2)(*b*); and

    (ii) any further instalments of such tax on the due dates in accordance with that section;

(*b*) where the tax due and payable is inheritance tax which is being wholly or partly paid by the transfer of securities to the Minister for Finance under the provisions of section 45, by—

    (i) delivering to the Commissioners with the return an application to pay all or part of the tax by such transfer;

    (ii) completing the transfer of the securities to the Minister for Finance within such time, not being less than 30 days, as may be specified by the Commissioners by notice in writing; and

    (iii) duly paying the excess, if any, of the amount of tax referred to in subsection (2)(*b*), or in paragraph (*a*)(i), over the nominal face value of the securities tendered in payment of the tax in accordance with the provisions of subparagraph (i).

[(4) Subsection (2) applies to a charge for tax arising by reason of the provisions of section 106 of the Finance Act, 1984, and to any other gift where—

(*a*) the aggregate of the taxable values of all taxable gifts taken by the donee on or after [5 December 1991][2], which have the same group threshold (as defined in the Second Schedule) as that other gift, exceeds an amount which is 80 per cent of the threshold amount (as defined in the Second Schedule) which applies in the computation of tax on that aggregate; or

(*b*) the donee or, in a case to which section 23(1) applies, the transferee (within the meaning of, and to the extent provided for by, that section) is required by notice in writing by the Commissioners to deliver a return, and for the purposes of this subsection, a reference to a gift includes a reference to a part of a gift or to a part of a taxable gift, as the case may be.]³

(5) For the purposes of this section, the relevant date shall be—

    (a) the valuation date or the 1st day of September, 1989, whichever is the later; or

    (b) where the donee or, in a case to which section 23(1) applies, the transferee (within the meaning of, and to the extent provided for by, that section) is required by notice in writing by the Commissioners to deliver a return, the date of the notice.

(6) Any person who is accountable for the payment of tax by virtue of subsection (2) or (9) of section 35 shall, if he is required by notice in writing by the Commissioners to do so, comply with the provisions of paragraphs (a), (b) and (c) of subsections (2) of this section (as if he were a person primarily accountable for the payment of tax by virtue of section 35(1)) within such time, not being less than 30 days, as may be specified in the notice.

(7) (a) Any accountable person shall, if he is so required by the Commissioners by notice in writing, deliver and verify to the Commissioners within such time, not being less than 30 days, as may be specified in the notice—

        (i) a statement (where appropriate, on a form provided, or approved of, by them) of such particulars relating to any property; and

        (ii) such evidence as they require,

    as may, in their opinion, be relevant to the assessment of tax in respect of the gift.

    (b) The Commissioners may authorise a person to inspect—

        (i) any property comprised in a gift; or

        (ii) any books, records, accounts or other documents, in whatever form they are stored, maintained or preserved, relating to any property as may in their opinion be relevant to the assessment of tax in respect of a gift,

    and the person having the custody or possession of that property, or of those books, records, accounts or documents, shall permit the person so authorised to make that inspection at such reasonable times as the Commissioners consider necessary.

(8) The Commissioners may by notice in writing require any accountable person to—

    (a) deliver to them within such time, not being less than 30 days, as may be specified in the notice, an additional return, if it appears to the Commissioners that a return made by that accountable person is defective in a material respect by reason of anything contained in or omitted from it.

    (b) notwithstanding the provisions of section 39, make on that additional return an assessment of such amended amount of tax as, to the best of his knowledge, information and belief, ought to be charged, levied and paid on the relevant gift; and

(c) duly pay the outstanding tax, if any, for which he is accountable in respect of that gift;

and

   (i) the requirements of subparagraphs (ii), (iii) and (iv) of subsection (2)(*a*) shall apply to such additional return required by virtue of paragraph (*a*); and

   (ii) the provisions of subsection (3) shall, with any necessary modifications; apply to any payment required by virtue of paragraph (*c*).

(9) Where any accountable person who has delivered a return or an additional return is aware or becomes aware at any time that the return or additional return is defective in a material respect by reason of anything contained in or omitted from it, he shall, without application from the Commissioners and within three months of so becoming aware—

(*a*) deliver to them an additional return;

(*b*) notwithstanding the provisions of section 39, make on that additional return an assessment of such amended amount of tax as, to the best of his knowledge, information and belief, ought to be charged, levied and paid on the relevant gift; and

(*c*) duly pay the outstanding tax, if any, for which he is accountable in respect of that gift;

and

   (i) the requirements of subparagraphs (ii), (iii) and (iv) of subsection (2)(*a*) shall apply to such additional return required by virtue of paragraph (*a*); and

   (ii) the provisions of subsection (3) shall, with any necessary modifications, apply to any payment required by virtue of paragraph (*c*).

(10) Any amount of tax payable by an accountable person in respect of an assessment of tax made by him on a return delivered by him (other than an amount of that tax payable by the transfer of securities to the Minister for Finance under the provisions of section 45) shall accompany the return and be paid to the Accountant-General of the Commissioners.

(11) Any assessment or payment of tax made under the provisions of this section shall include interest upon tax payable in accordance with the provisions of section 41.][4]

[(12) The Commissioners may by notice in writing require any person to deliver to them within such time, not being less than 30 days, as may be specified in the notice, a full and true return showing details of every taxable gift (including the property comprised therein) taken by that person during the period specified in the notice or, as the case may be, indicating that that person has taken no taxable gift during that period.

(13) As respects a taxable gift to which this subsection applies, any accountable person who is a disponer shall within 4 months of the valuation date deliver to the Commissioners a full and true return—

(*a*) of all the property comprised in such gift on the valuation date,

(*b*) of an estimate of the market value of such property on the valuation date, and

(c) of such particulars as may be relevant to the assessment of tax in respect of the gift.

(14) Subsection (13) applies to a taxable gift taken on or after the 11th day of February, 1999, in the case where—

[(a) the taxable value of the taxable gift exceeds an amount which is 80 per cent of the group threshold (as defined in the Second Schedule) which applies in relation to that gift for the purposes of the computation of the tax on that gift.][5]

(b) the taxable value of the taxable gift taken by the donee from the disponer increases the total taxable value of all taxable gifts and taxable inheritances taken on or after [5 December 1991][6], by the donee from the disponer from an amount less than or equal to the amount specified in paragraph (a) to an amount which exceeds the amount so specified, or

(c) the total taxable value of all taxable gifts and taxable inheritances taken on or after [5 December 1991][6], by the donee from the disponer exceeds the amount specified in paragraph (a) and the donee takes a further taxable gift from the disponer.

(15) Where, on or after the 11th day of February, 1999, under or in consequence of any disposition made by a person who is living and domiciled in the State at the date of the disposition, property becomes subject to a discretionary trust, the disponer shall within 4 months of the date of the disposition deliver to the Commissioners a full and true return of—

(a) the terms of the discretionary trust,

(b) the names and addresses of the trustees and objects of the discretionary trust, and

(c) an estimate of the market value at the date of the disposition of the property becoming subject to the discretionary trust.][7]

Amendments

[1]   Subs (1)(a)(iii) substituted by FA 1999 s 200(a).
[2]   Substituted by FA 2002 s 117(1)(a) for gifts or inheritances taken on or after 1 December 2001; previously "2 December 1988".
[3]   Subs (4) substituted by FA 2000 s 141(1)(a) for gifts or inheritances taken on or after 1 December 1999.
[4]   The entire section was substituted by FA 1989 s 74 as regards valuation dates on or after 1 September 1989.
[5]   Subs (14)(a) substituted by FA 2000 s 141(1)(b) for gifts or inheritances taken on or after 1 December 1999.
[6]   Substituted by FA 2002 s 117(1)(b) for gifts or inheritances taken on or after 1 December 2001; previously "the 2nd day of December, 1988".
[7]   Subss (12)-(15) inserted by FA 1999 s 200(c).

Cross-references

Discretionary trust annual charge, subss (2)-(5) inclusive do not apply: FA 1986 s 104(g).
Revenue may make assessments: FA 1989 s 75.
Probate tax
For "four months" (subs (2)), read "nine months" and regard references to the primarily accountable person as references to the personal representative: FA 1993 s 111(e);
subs (4) does not apply: FA 1993 s 111(f);
regard reference in subs (6) to a primarily accountable person as a reference to the personal representative: FA 1993 s 111(j);
self-assessment by persons applying for probate or letters of administration: FA 1993 s 116(1); subs (3)(b) applies: FA 1993 s 116(2).

Statement of practice

Revenue powers: SP GEN 1/94

Narrative

Capital Acquisitions Tax, Chapter 21.

Definitions

"accountable person": ss 2(1), 35; "additional return", "Commissioners", "disponer", "donee", "gift", "inheritance": s 2(1); "material": SA 1891 s 122(1); "market value": s 2(1); "person": IA 1937 s 11(c); "property", "return", "taxable gift", "taxable inheritance", "taxable value", "successor", "valuation date": s 2(1).

37 Signing of returns, etc

(1) A return or an additional return required to be delivered under this Act shall be signed by the accountable person who delivers the return or the additional return and shall include a declaration by the person signing it that the return or additional return is, to the best of his knowledge, information and belief, correct and complete.

(2) The Commissioners may require a return or an additional return to be made on oath.

(3) The Commissioners may, if they so think fit, accept a return or an additional return under this Act that has not been signed in accordance with this section and such return or additional return shall be deemed to be duly delivered to the Commissioners under this Act.

[(4) (*a*)   A return or additional return delivered under this Act shall—

  (i)   be made on a form provided, or approved of, by the Commissioners, or

  (ii)   except in a case to which subsection (2) relates but in a case where subsection (3) applies, be in a form approved of by the Commissioners and delivered by any electronic, photographic or other process approved of by them and in circumstances where the use of such process has been agreed by them and subject to such conditions as they may impose.

  (*b*)   An affidavit, additional affidavit, account or additional account, delivered under this Act, shall be made on a form provided, or approved of, by the Commissioners.][1]

(5) Any oath or affidavit to be made for the purposes of this Act may be made—

  (*a*)   before the Commissioners;

  (*b*)   before any officer or person authorised by the Commissioners in that behalf;

  (*c*)   before any Commissioner for Oaths or any Peace Commissioner or Notary Public in the State; or

  (*d*)   at any place outside the State, before any person duly authorised to administer oaths there.

Amendments

[1]   Subs (4) substituted by FA 1989 s 82.

Case law

On the practice of Revenue acceptance of late returns where estimated assessments have been made see *Bairead v McDonald*, IV ITR 475.

Narrative

Capital Acquisitions Tax, Chapter 21.

Definitions

"accountable person": ss 2(1); 35; "additional return", "Commissioners": s 2(1); "person": IA 1937 s 11(*c*); "return": s 2(1).

38 Affidavits and accounts

(1) In this section, **"Inland Revenue affidavit"** has the meaning assigned to it by section 22(1)(*n*) of the Finance Act, 1894.

(2) The Inland Revenue affidavit required for an application for probate or letters of administration shall extend to the verification of a statement of the following particulars—

(*a*) details of all property in respect of which the grant of probate or administration is required and, in the case of a deceased person who died domiciled in the State, details of all property, wheresoever situate, the beneficial ownership of which, on his death, is affected—

(i) by his will;

(ii) by the rules for distribution on intestacy; or

(iii) by Part IX or section 56 of the Succession Act, 1965;

(*b*) details of any property which was the subject matter of a disposition *inter vivos* made by the deceased person where the date of the disposition was within two years prior to his death or of a *donatio mortis causa*;

(*c*) details of the inheritances arising under the will or intestacy of the deceased person or under Part IX or section 56 of the Succession Act, 1965, or under the analogous law of another territory, together with a copy of any such will;

(*d*) particulars of the inheritances (including the property comprised therein) other than those referred to in paragraphs (*b*) and (*c*), arising on the death of the deceased person;

(*e*) the name and address of each person who takes an inheritance on the death of the deceased person and his relationship to the disponer; and

(*f*) such other particulars as the Commissioners may require for the purposes of this Act.

(3) Where the interest of the deceased person was a limited interest and that person died on or after the 1st day of April, 1975, the trustee of the property in which the limited interest subsisted shall deliver an account which shall contain the following particulars—

(*a*) details of each inheritance arising on the death of the deceased person under the disposition under which the limited interest of the deceased person arose, including the name and address of each person taking such inheritance and his relationship to the disponer; and

(*b*) such other particulars as the Commissioners may require for the purposes of this Act.

(4) If at any time it shall appear that any material error or omission was made in an affidavit or account referred to in this section, the persons liable to deliver an affidavit or account shall be liable to deliver an additional affidavit or an additional account, correcting the error or omission.

Narrative

Capital Acquisitions Tax, Chapter 21.

Definitions

"Commissioners", "disponer", "disposition", "inheritance", "limited interest": s 2(1); "person": IA 1937 s 11(*c*); "property": s 2(1).

39 Assessment of tax

(1) Assessments of tax under this Act shall be made by the Commissioners.

(2) If at any time it appears that for any reason an assessment was incorrect, the Commissioners may make a correcting assessment, which shall be substituted for the first-mentioned assessment.

(3) If at any time it appears that for any reason too little tax was assessed, the Commissioners may make an additional assessment.

(4) The Commissioners may serve notice in writing of the assessment of tax on any accountable person or, at the request of an accountable person, on his agent, or on the personal representative of an accountable person if that person is dead.

(5) Where the place of residence of the accountable person or of his personal representative is not known to the Commissioners they may publish in the *Iris Oifigiúil* a notice of the making of the assessment with such particulars thereof as they shall think proper and on the publication of the notice in the *Iris Oifigiúil* the accountable person or his personal representative, as the case may be, shall be deemed to have been served with the notice of the assessment on the date of such publication.

(6) Any assessment, correcting assessment or additional assessment under this section may be made by the Commissioners from any return or additional return delivered under the provisions of section 36 or from any other information in the possession of the Commissioners or from any one or more of these sources.

[(7) The Commissioners, in making any assessment, correcting assessment or additional assessment, otherwise than from a return or an additional return which is satisfactory to them, shall make an assessment of such amount of tax as, to the best of their knowledge, information (including information received from a member of the Garda Síochána) and belief, ought to be charged, levied and paid.][1]

...[2]

Amendments

[1]   Subs (7) substituted by Disclosure of Certain Information for Taxation and Other Purposes Act 1996 s 8.

[2]   Proviso deleted by Criminal Assets Bureau Act 1996 s 24(4).

Cross-references

Revenue may make assessments: FA 1989 s 75.

Narrative

Capital Acquisitions Tax, Chapter 21.

Statement of practice

Revenue powers: SP GEN 1/94
Appeal Commissioners Determinations, 25 AC 2000.

Definitions

"accountable person": ss 2(1), 35; "additional return", "Commissioners": s 2(1); "person": IA 1937 s 11(*c*);
"personal representative", "return": s 2(1).

40 Computation of tax

The amount of tax payable shall be computed in accordance with the provisions of the
Second Schedule.

Cross-references

Discretionary trust once off charge, this section does not apply: FA 1984 s 107(*g*).
Discretionary trust annual charge, this section does not apply: FA 1986 s 104(*g*).
Probate tax, this section does not apply: FA 1993 s 111(*f*).

PART VII
PAYMENT AND RECOVERY OF TAX

41 Payment of tax and interest on tax

(1) Tax shall be due and payable on the valuation date.

(2) Simple interest at the rate of [**1 per cent**][1] per month or part of a month, without
deduction of income tax, shall be payable upon the tax from the valuation date to the
date of payment of the tax and shall be chargeable and recoverable in the same manner
as if it were part of the tax.

[(2A) Notwithstanding the provisions of subsection (2), interest shall not be payable
upon the tax—

    (*a*) to the extent to which section 19(5)(*a*) applies, for the duration of the period
from the valuation date to the date the agricultural value ceases to be
applicable,

    (*b*) to the extent to which [subsection (3) or (4) of section 55][2] applies, for the
duration of the period from the valuation date to the date the exemption ceases
to apply,

    (*c*) to the extent to which section 135(2) of the Finance Act, 1994, applies, for the
duration of the period from the valuation date to the date the reduction which
would otherwise fall to be made under section 126 of that Act ceases to be
applicable,

    (*d*) to the extent to which section 166(6) of the Finance Act, 1995, applies, for the
duration of the period from the valuation date to the date the exemption ceases
[to apply,][3]

  [(*e*) to the extent to which subsection (5) or (6) of section 59C applies, for the
duration of the period from the valuation date to the date the exemption ceases
to apply.][4]][5]

[(3) Notwithstanding the provisions of subsection (2), interest shall not be payable on tax which is paid within three months of the valuation date, and where tax and interest, if any, thereon is paid within thirty days of the date of assessment thereof, interest shall not run on that tax for the period of thirty days from the date of the assessment or any part of that period:

Provided that, in relation to an assessment of tax made by an accountable person on a return delivered by him, interest shall not be payable on tax which is paid within four months of the valuation date.][6]

(4) A payment on account of tax shall be applied—

    (*a*)   if there is interest due on tax at the date of the payment, to the discharge, so far as may be, of the interest so due; and

    (*b*)   if there is any balance of that payment remaining, to the discharge of so much tax as is equal to that balance.

(5) Subject to the provisions of subsections (2), (3) and (4), payments on account may be made at any time, and when a payment on account is made, interest shall not be chargeable in respect of any period subsequent to the date of such payment on so much of the payment on account as is to be applied in discharge of the tax.

(6) In the case of a gift which becomes an inheritance by reason of its being taken under a disposition where the date of the disposition is within two years prior to the death of the disponer, the provisions of this section shall have effect as if the references to the valuation date in subsections (1), (2) and (3) were references to the date of death of the disponer.

(7) In the case of a gift or inheritance taken prior to the date of the passing of this Act, the provisions of this section shall have effect as if the references to the valuation date in subsections (1), (2) and (3) were references to the date of the passing of this Act, or to the valuation date, whichever is the later.

(8) Where the value of a limited interest falls to be ascertained in accordance with rule 8 of the First Schedule as if it were a series of absolute interests, this section shall have effect, in relation to each of those absolute interests, as if the references to the valuation date in subsections (1), (2) and (3) were references to the date of the taking of that absolute interest.

(9) All sums due under the provisions of this Act shall be paid to the Accountant-General of the Commissioners.

Amendments

1   Substituted by FA 1998 s 133(4)(*a*) with effect from 27 March 1998 for any month or part of a month, in respect of an amount paid or remitted or an amount due to be repaid or retained, before on or after that date; previously "1.25 per cent" (FA 1978 s 43).

2   Substituted by FA 2002 s 118(1)(*a*) where the event which causes the exemption to cease to be applicable occurs on or after 11 February 1999; previously "section 55(4)".

3   Substituted by FA 2002 s 118(1)(*b*) where the event which caused the exemption to cease to be applicable occurs on or after 1 December 1999; previously "to apply.".

4   Subs (2A)(*e*) inserted by FA 2002 s 118(1)(*c*) where the event which causes the exemption to cease to be applicable occurs on or after 1 December 1999.

⁵   Subs (2A) inserted by FA 1999 s 202 still has effect where the event which causes the exemption or reduction to cease to apply occurs on or after 11 February 1999.

⁶   Subs (3) substituted by FA 1989 s 76(1).

Cross-references

Agricultural or business property, payment of tax by instalments: FA 1995 s 164(2)(*b*).

Attachment of debts of tax defaulters, Revenue power: FA 1988 s 73.

Discretionary trust once off charge, this section applies but the references to the valuation date in subss (1),(2) and (3) are to be construed as references to 23 May 1984 (date of passing of FA 1984) or the valuation date, whichever is the later: FA 1984 s 107(*f*).

Discretionary trust annual charge, this section applies but the references to the valuation date in subss (1),(2) and (3) are to be construed as references to 27 May 1986 (date of passing of FA 1986) or the valuation date, whichever is the later: FA 1986 s 104(*f*).

Income tax collection provisions applied by: FA 1991 s 129.

Poundage and sheriff fees etc: FA 1988 s 71.

Probate tax, subs s (1) to (3) do not apply: FA 1993 s 111(*f*).

Self-assessment, payment by accountable person to be treated as payment on account: FA 1989 s 76; surcharge for undervaluation of property, interest also applies to surcharge as if it were tax: FA 1989 s 79(2).

Statement of practice

Revenue powers: SP GEN 1/94

Narrative

Capital Acquisitions Tax, Chapter 23.

Definitions

"absolute interest", "accountable person", "Commissioners", "date of the disposition", "disponer", "disposition", "gift", "inheritance", "limited interest", "return", "valuation date": s 2(1).

42 Set-off of gift tax paid in respect of an inheritance

Where an amount has been paid in respect of gift tax (or interest thereon) on a gift which, by reason of the death of the disponer within two years after the date of the disposition under which the gift was taken, becomes an inheritance in respect of which inheritance tax is payable, the amount so paid shall be treated as a payment on account of the inheritance tax.

Narrative

Capital Acquisitions Tax, Chapter 23.

Definitions

"date of the disposition", "disponer", "disposition", "gift", "inheritance": s 2(1).

43 Payment of tax by instalments

(1) Subject to the payment of interest in accordance with section 41 and save as hereinafter provided, the tax due and payable in respect of a taxable gift or a taxable inheritance may, at the option of the person delivering the return or additional return, be paid by five equal yearly instalments, the first of which shall be due at the expiration of twelve months from the date on which the tax became due and payable and the interest on the unpaid tax shall be added to each instalment and shall be paid at the same time as such instalment.

(2) An instalment not due may be paid at any time before it falls due.

(3) In any case where and to the extent that the property of which the taxable gift or taxable inheritance consists is sold or compulsorily acquired, all unpaid instalments shall, unless the interest of the donee or successor is a limited interest, be paid on

completion of the sale or compulsory acquisition and, if not so paid, shall be tax in arrear.

(4) This section shall not apply in any case where and to the extent to which a taxable gift or a taxable inheritance consists of personal property in which the donee, or the successor, or the transferee referred to in section 23(1), as the case may be, takes an absolute interest.

(5) In any case where the interest taken by a donee or a successor is an interest limited to cease on his death, and his death occurs before all the instalments of the tax in respect of the taxable gift or taxable inheritance would have fallen due if such tax were being paid by instalments, any instalment of such tax which would not have fallen due prior to the date of the death of that donee or successor shall cease to be payable, and the payment, if made, of any such last-mentioned instalment shall be treated as an overpayment of tax for the purposes of section 46.

Cross-references

Agricultural or business property, payment of tax by instalments: FA 1995 s 164(2)(*a*).
Discretionary trust annual charge, this section does not apply: FA 1986 s 104(*g*).
Probate tax, this section does not apply: FA 1993 s 111(*f*).

Narrative

Capital Acquisitions Tax, Chapter 23.

Definitions

"absolute interest", "additional return", "donee", "gift", "inheritance", "limited interest": s 2(1); "person": IA 1937 s 11(*c*); "personal property", "property", "return", "taxable gift", "taxable inheritance", "successor": s 2(1).

44 Postponement, remission and compounding of tax

(1) Where the Commissioners are satisfied that tax leviable in respect of any gift or inheritance cannot without excessive hardship be raised at once, they may allow payment to be postponed for such period, to such extent and on such terms (including the waiver of interest) as they think fit.

(2) If, after the expiration of the relevant period immediately following the date on which any tax became due and payable, the tax or any part thereof remains unpaid, the Commissioners may, if they think fit, remit the payment of any interest accruing after such expiration on the unpaid tax; and in this subsection, **"relevant period"** means the period at the end of which the interest on an amount payable in respect of tax would, at the rate from time to time chargeable during that period in respect of interest on tax, equal the amount of such tax.

(3) If, after the expiration of twenty years from the date on which any tax became due and payable, the tax or any part thereof remains unpaid, the Commissioners may, if they think fit, remit the payment of such tax or any part thereof and all or any interest thereon.

(4) Where, in the opinion of the Commissioners, the complication of circumstances affecting a gift or inheritance or the value thereof or the assessment or recovery of tax thereon are such as to justify them in doing so, they may compound the tax payable on the gift or inheritance upon such terms as they shall think fit, and may give a discharge

to the person or persons accountable for the tax upon payment of the tax according to such composition.

Narrative
Capital Acquisitions Tax, Chapter 23.
Definitions
"accountable person", "Commissioners", "gift", "inheritance": s 2(1); "person": IA 1937 s 11(*c*).

45 Payment of inheritance tax by transfer of securities

The provisions of section 22 of the Finance Act, 1954, (which relates to the payment of death duties by the transfer of securities to the Minister for Finance) and the regulations made thereunder shall apply, with any necessary modifications, to the payment of inheritance tax by the transfer of securities to the Minister for Finance, as they apply to the payment of death duties by the transfer of securities to the Minister for Finance.

Cross-references
Discretionary trust once off charge, this section does not apply: FA 1984 s 107(*g*).
Discretionary trust annual charge, this section does not apply: FA 1986 s 104(*g*).
Regulations made under SI 15/1954 which are now applied to inheritance tax.
Narrative
Capital Acquisitions Tax, Chapter 23.
Definitions
"inheritance", "regulations": s 2(1).

46 Overpayment of tax

(1) Where, on application to the Commissioners for relief under this section, it is proved to their satisfaction that an amount has been paid in excess of the liability for tax or for interest on tax, they shall give relief by way of repayment of the excess or otherwise as is reasonable and just; and any such repayment shall carry simple interest (not exceeding the amount of such excess), [at the rate of **[0.5 per cent]**[1], or such other rate (if any) as stands prescribed by the Minister for Finance by regulations, for each month or part of a month from the date on which the payment was made, and income tax shall not be deductible on payment of interest under this section and such interest shall not be reckoned in computing income for the purposes of the Taxes Acts.][2]

[(2) Every regulation made under this section shall be laid before Dáil Éireann as soon as may be after it is made and, if a resolution annulling the regulation is passed by Dáil Éireann within the next twenty-one days on which Dáil Éireann has sat after the regulation is laid before it, the regulation shall be annulled accordingly, but without prejudice to the validity of anything previously done thereunder.][3]

Amendments
[1]   Substituted by FA 1998 s 133(4)(*b*) with effect from 27 March 1998 for any month or part of a month, in respect of an amount paid or remitted or an amount due to be repaid or retained, before on or after that date; previously "0.6" (Payment of Interest on Overpaid Tax Regulations 1990 (SI 176/1990)); previously the rate was 1 per cent per month.

2   Substituted by FA 1986 s 109(1)(*a*) in relation to interest payable under this section for any month or part of a month from 27 May 1986.

3   Subs (2) inserted by FA 1986 s 109(1)(*b*) in relation to interest payable under this section for any month or part of a month from 27 May 1986.

Cross-references

Discretionary trust once off charge, increase to 6%, no repayment of interest: FA 1994 s 143(4).

Double aggregation, relief from, no repayment of interest on tax paid prior to 30 May 1985 (date of passing of FA 1985): FA 1985 s 61(2).

Marriage settlements made before 1 April 1975, no repayment of interest: FA 1981 s 46.

Definitions

"Commissioners": s 2(1).

47 Tax to be a charge

(1) Tax due and payable in respect of a taxable gift or a taxable inheritance shall, subject to the provisions of this section, be and remain a charge on the property (other than money or negotiable instruments) of which the taxable gift or taxable inheritance consists at the valuation date and the tax shall have priority over all charges and interests created by the donee or successor or any person claiming in right of the donee or successor or on his behalf:

Provided that where any settled property comprised in any taxable gift or taxable inheritance shall be subject to any power of sale, exchange, or partition, exercisable with the consent of the donee or successor, or by the donee or successor with the consent of another person, the donee or successor shall not be precluded by the charge of tax on his taxable gift or taxable inheritance from consenting to the exercise of such power, or exercising any power with proper consent, as the case may be; and where any such power is exercised, the tax shall be charged upon the property acquired, in substitution for charging it on the property previously comprised in the gift or inheritance, and upon all moneys arising from the exercise of any such power, and upon all investments of such moneys.

(2) Property comprised in a taxable gift or taxable inheritance shall not, as against a bona fide purchaser or mortgagee for full consideration in money or money's worth, or a person deriving title from or under such a purchaser or mortgagee, remain charged with or liable to the payment of tax after the expiration of twelve years from the date of the gift or the date of the inheritance.

(3) Tax shall not be a charge on property under subsection (1) as against a bona *fide* purchaser or mortgagee of such property for full consideration in money or money's worth without notice, or a person deriving title from or under such a purchaser or mortgagee.

Cross-references

Probate tax, in relation to persons dying after 17 June 1993, surviving spouse becoming beneficially entitled in possession to limited interest created by will of deceased, tax borne by property in which limited interest subsists does not become abated to nil, but becomes due and payable on the cesser of the limited interest: FA 1993 s 115A(1)(proviso)(*b*).

As to the application to limited interests, see s 35(7).

Narrative

Capital Acquisitions Tax, Chapter 24.

Definitions

"date of the gift", "date of the inheritance", "donee", "gift", "inheritance", "valuation date": s 2(1); "person": IA 1937 s 11(*c*); "property", "taxable gift", "taxable inheritance", "successor": s 2(1).

48 Receipts and certificates

(1) When any amount in respect of tax is paid, the Commissioners shall give a receipt for the payment.

(2) The Commissioners shall, on application to them by a person who has paid the tax in respect of any property comprised in any taxable gift or taxable inheritance, give to the person a certificate, in such form as they think fit, of the amount of the tax paid by him in respect of that property.

[(3) The Commissioners shall, on application to them by a person who is an accountable person in respect of any of the property of which a taxable gift or taxable inheritance consists, if they are satisfied that the tax charged on the property in respect of the taxable gift or taxable inheritance has been or will be paid, or that there is no tax so charged, give a certificate to the person, in such form as they think fit, to that effect.

(3A) Where a person who is an accountable person in respect of the property of which a taxable gift or taxable inheritance consists has—

    (*a*)   delivered to the Commissioners, a full and true return of all the property comprised in the gift or inheritance on the valuation date and such particulars as may be relevant to the assessment of tax in respect of the gift or inheritance,

    (*b*)   made on that return an assessment of such amount of tax as, to the best of that person's knowledge, information and belief, ought to be charged, levied and paid, and

    (*c*)   duly paid the amount of such tax (if any),

the Commissioners may give a certificate to the person, in such form as they think fit, to the effect that the tax charged on the. property in respect of the taxable gift or taxable inheritance has been paid or that there is no tax so charged.

(4) A certificate referred to in subsection (3) or (3A) shall discharge the property from liability for tax (if any) in respect of the gift or inheritance, to the extent specified in the certificate, but shall not discharge the property from tax in case of fraud or failure to disclose material facts and, in any case, shall not affect the tax payable in respect of any other property or the extent to which tax is recoverable from any accountable person or from the personal representatives of any accountable person:

Provided that a certificate purporting to be a discharge of the whole tax payable in respect of any property included in the certificate in respect of a gift or inheritance shall exonerate from liability for such tax a bona fide purchaser or mortgagee for full consideration in money or money's worth without notice of such fraud or failure and a person deriving title from or under such a purchaser or mortgagee.

(5) Subject to the provisions of subsection (6), where tax is chargeable on the taxable value of a taxable gift or taxable inheritance and

(*a*) application is made to the Commissioners by any person (in this section referred to as "the applicant")—

    (i) who is a person accountable, but not primarily accountable, for the payment of the whole or part of the tax, or

    (ii) who is the personal representative of any person referred to in subparagraph (i),

    and

(*b*) the applicant—

    (i) delivers to the Commissioners a full and true return of all the property comprised in the gift or inheritance and such particulars as may be relevant to the assessment of tax in respect of the gift or inheritance, and

    (ii) makes on that return an assessment of such amount of tax as, to the best of that person's knowledge, information and belief, ought to be charged, levied and paid,

the Commissioners may, upon payment of the tax assessed by the applicant, give a certificate to the applicant which shall discharge the applicant from any other claim for tax in respect of the gift or inheritance.][1]

[(6) A certificate by the Commissioners under subsection (5) shall not discharge the applicant in the case of fraud or failure to disclose material facts within his own knowledge and shall not affect any further tax that may be payable by the applicant if any further property is afterwards shown to have been comprised in the taxable gift or taxable inheritance to which the certificate relates and in respect of which further property the applicant is liable for the tax.][2]

...[3]

Amendments

[1]   Subss (3)-(5) substituted by FA 2000 s 142(*a*).

[2]   Subs (6) inserted by FA 1984 s 113 as respects gifts or inheritances taken on or after 2 June 1982.

[3]   Subs (7) deleted by FA 2000 s 142(*b*).

Narrative

Capital Acquisitions Tax, Chapter 23.

Definitions

"accountable person": s 2(1); 35; "Commissioners", "gift", "inheritance": s 2(1); "person": IA 1937 s 11(*c*); "personal representative", "property", "taxable gift", "taxable inheritance", "taxable value", "valuation date": s 2(1).

49 Recovery of tax and penalties

(1) Any sum due and payable in respect of tax or interest thereon and any penalty incurred in connection with tax or interest thereon shall be deemed to be a debt due by the accountable person or, if he is dead, by his personal representative, to the Minister for Finance for the benefit of the Central Fund and shall be payable to the Commissioners and may (without prejudice to any other mode of recovery thereof) be sued for and recovered by action, or other appropriate proceeding, at the suit of the Attorney General or the Minister for Finance or the Commissioners in any court of

competent jurisdiction, notwithstanding anything to the contrary contained in the Inland Revenue Regulation Act, 1890.

(2) Any person who, having received any sum of money as or for any tax, interest, or penalty under this Act, does not apply the money to the due payment of the tax, interest or penalty, and improperly withholds or detains the same, shall be accountable for the payment of the tax, interest or penalty to the extent of the amount so received by him and the same shall be a debt due by him to the Minister for Finance for the benefit of the Central Fund and shall be recoverable in like manner as a debt under subsection (1).

(3) If any accountable person is liable under section 36 to deliver to the Commissioners a return or an additional return and makes default in so doing, the Attorney General or the Minister for Finance or the Commissioners may sue by action or other appropriate proceeding in the Circuit Court for an order directing the person so making default to deliver such return or additional return or to show cause to the contrary; and the Circuit Court may by order direct such accountable person to deliver such return or additional return within such time as may be specified in the order.

(4) Whenever property is subject to a charge by virtue of section 47, the Attorney-General or the Minister for Finance or the Commissioners may sue by action or other appropriate proceeding in any court of competent jurisdiction for, and the court may make, an order directing the owner of the property to pay the tax with which the property is charged.

Statement of practice

Revenue powers: SP GEN 1/94.

Narrative

Capital Acquisitions Tax, Chapters 22, 23.

Definitions

"accountable person": ss 2(1); 35; "additional return", "Commissioners": s 2(1); "person": IA 1937 s 11(*c*); "personal representative", "property", "return": s 2(1).

---

50 Evidence in proceedings for recovery of tax

The provisions of section 39 of the Finance Act, 1926, shall apply in any proceedings in the Circuit Court or the District Court for or in relation to the recovery of the tax.

PART VIII
APPEALS

51 Appeals regarding value of real property

If a person is aggrieved by the decision of the Commissioners as to the market value of any real property, he may appeal against the decision in the manner prescribed by section 33 of the Finance (1909-10) Act, 1910, and the provisions as to appeals under that section of that Act shall apply accordingly with any necessary modifications.

[(2) The particulars of any transfer or lease which are presented to or obtained by the Commissioners under section 107 of the Finance Act, 1994, shall, in any appeal under this section, be received as prima facie evidence of all matters and things stated in such particulars.][1]

Amendments
[1]   Subs (2) inserted by FA 1999 s 203.
Narrative
Capital Acquisitions Tax, Chapter 22.
Definitions
"Commissioners", "market value": s 2(1); "person": IA 1937 s 11(*c*); "property", "real property": s 2(1).

52 Appeals in other cases

(1) In this section—

"Appeal Commissioners" has the meaning assigned to it by [section 850 of the Taxes Consolidation Act, 1997];[1]

"appellant" means a person who appeals to the Appeal Commissioners under subsection (2) of this section.

(2) Subject to the other provisions of this Act, a person who is called upon by the Commissioners to pay an assessment of tax in respect of any property and who is aggrieved by the assessment may, in accordance with the provisions of this section, appeal to the Appeal Commissioners against the assessment and the appeal shall be heard and determined by the Appeal Commissioners whose determination shall be final and conclusive unless the appeal is required to be reheard by a judge of the Circuit Court or a case is required to be stated in relation to it for the opinion of the High Court on a point of law.

(3) An appeal shall not lie under this section in relation to the market value of real property.

(4) A person who intends to appeal under this section against an assessment shall, within 30 days after the date of the assessment, give notice in writing to the Commissioners of his intention to appeal against the assessment.

(5) (*a*)   Subject to the provisions of this section, the provisions of the Income Tax Acts relating to—

    (i)   the appointment of times and places for the hearing of appeals;

    (ii)   the giving of notice to each person who has given notice of appeal of the time and place appointed for the hearing of his appeal;

    (iii)   the determination of an appeal by agreement between the appellant and an officer appointed by the Commissioners in that behalf;

    (iv)   the determination of an appeal by the appellant giving notice of his intention not to proceed with the appeal;

    (v)   the hearing and determination of an appeal by the Appeal Commissioners, including the hearing and determination of an appeal by one Appeal Commissioner;

    [(*va*)   the publication of reports of determinations of the Appeal Commissioners;][2]

(vi) the determination of an appeal through the neglect or refusal of a person who has given notice of appeal to attend before the Appeal Commissioners at the time and place appointed;

(vii) the extension of the time for giving notice of appeal and the readmission of appeals by the Appeal Commissioners and the provisions which apply where action by way of court proceedings has been taken;

(viii) the rehearing of an appeal by a judge of the Circuit Court and the statement of a case for the opinion of the High Court on a point of law;

(ix) the payment of tax in accordance with the determination of the Appeal Commissioners notwithstanding that an appeal is required to be reheard by a judge of the Circuit Court or that a case for the opinion of the High Court on a point of law has been required to be stated or is pending;

(x) the procedures for appeal,

[(xi) the refusal of an application for an appeal hearing,]³

shall, with any necessary modifications, apply to an appeal under this section as if the appeal were an appeal against an assessment to income tax.

(b) The Commissioners shall, subject to their giving notice in writing in that behalf to the appellant within ten days after the determination of an appeal by the Appeal Commissioners, have the same right as the appellant to have the appeal reheard by a judge of the Circuit Court.

(c) The rehearing of an appeal under this section by a judge of the Circuit Court shall be by a judge of the Circuit Court in whose circuit the appellant or one of the appellants resides or (in the case of a body corporate) has its principal place of business:

Provided that—

(i) in any case where no appellant is resident in or (in the case of a body corporate) has a place of business in the State; or

(ii) in any case where there is a doubt or a dispute as to the circuit,

the appeal shall be reheard by a judge of the Circuit Court assigned to the Dublin Circuit.

(6) (a) Where a notice or other document which is required or authorised to be served by this section falls to be served on a body corporate, such notice shall be served on the secretary or other officer of the body corporate.

(b) Any notice or other document which is required or authorised by this section to be served by the Commissioners or by an appellant may be served by post and in the case of a notice or other document addressed to the Commissioners, shall be sent to the Secretaries, Revenue Commissioners, Dublin Castle, Dublin 2.

(c) Any notice or other document which is required or authorised to be served by the Commissioners on an appellant under this section may be sent to the solicitor, accountant or other agent of the appellant and a notice thus served shall be deemed to have been served on the appellant unless the appellant proves to the satisfaction of the Appeal Commissioners, or the Circuit Court, as the case may be, that he had, before the notice or other document was served, withdrawn the authority of such solicitor, accountant or other agent to act on his behalf.

[(7) *Prima facie* evidence of any notice given under this section by the Commissioners or by an officer of the Commissioners may be given in any proceedings by the production of a document purporting—

    (a) to be a copy of the notice, or

    (b) if the details specified in the notice are contained in an electronic, photographic or other record maintained by the Commissioners, to reproduce those details in so far as they relate to the said notice,

and it shall not be necessary to prove the official position of the person by whom the notice purports to be given or, if it is signed, the signature, or that the person signing and giving it was authorised to do so.]⁴

(8) (a) The Commissioners may serve notice in writing, referring expressly to this subsection, on any person whom they have reason to believe to be accountable for the payment of tax, of any decision they have made which is relevant to such tax.

    (b) Any person who is informed of a decision in accordance with paragraph (a) may appeal to the Appeal Commissioners against the decision.

    (c) The Appeal Commissioners shall hear and determine an appeal to them under this subsection as if it were an appeal to them against an assessment to tax, and the provisions of this section relating to an appeal or to the rehearing of an appeal or to the statement of a case for the opinion of the High Court on a point of law shall, with any necessary modifications, apply accordingly.

Amendments

¹   Substituted by TCA 1997 s 1100 and Sch 31; previously "section 156 of the Income Tax Act, 1967".

²   Subs (5)(va) inserted by FA 1998 s 134(3)(b) with effect from 27 March 1998.

³   Subs (5)(a)(xi) inserted by FA 1995 s 159.

⁴   Subs (7) substituted by FA 2002 s 119 in relation to evidence of any notice given by the Commissioners or by an officer of the Commissioners in any proceedings on or after 25 March 2002.

Cross-references

Self-assessment, surcharge for undervaluation of property, this section applied by: FA 1989 s 79(4).

Note

The right of the Commissioners (subs (5)(b)) to have an appeal heard in the Circuit Court is in addition to the provisions of the Income Tax Acts relating to appeals.

Case law

While it is normal practice that each side bears its own costs in appeals before the Appeal Commissioners and the Circuit Court it was held in *Revenue Commissioners v Arida Ltd*, IV ITR 401, that a Circuit Court judge has jurisdiction to afford costs to the successful party. This is the standard practice in High Court revenue appeals. It is understood the decision in the Arida case is under appeal to the Supreme Court.

Revenue Material

Form CAT6 Capital Acquisitions Tax Review and Appeal Procedures

Narrative

Capital Acquisitions Tax, Chapter 22.

Definitions

"Commissioners", "market value": s 2(1); "person": IA 1937 s 11(c); "property", "real property": s 2(1).

52A Conditions before appeal may be made

[No appeal shall lie under section 51 or 52 until such time as the person aggrieved by the decision or assessment (as the case may be) complies with section 36(2) in respect of the gift or inheritance in relation to which the decision or assessment is made, as if there were no time-limit for complying with section 36(2) and that person were a person primarily accountable for the payment of tax by virtue of section 35(1) and required by notice in writing by the Commissioners to deliver a return.][1]

Amendments

[1]   Section 52A inserted by FA 1998 s 129 in relation to gifts or inheritances taken on or after 12 February 1998.

PART IX
EXEMPTIONS

53 Exemption of small gifts

(1) The first [€1,270][1] of the total taxable value of all taxable gifts taken by a donee from any one disponer in any relevant period shall be exempt from tax and shall not be taken into account in computing tax.

(2) In the case of a gift which becomes an inheritance by reason of its being taken under a disposition where the date of the disposition is within two years prior to the death of the disponer, the same relief shall be granted in respect thereof under subsection (1) as if it were a gift.

(3) ...[2]

(4) In this section, **"relevant period"** means the period commencing on the 28th day of February, 1969, and ending on the 31st day of December, 1969, and thereafter the period of twelve months ending on the 31st day of December in each year.

Amendments

[1]   Substituted by FA 2001 s 240 and Sch 5 Part 5 with effect from 1 January 2002; previously "£1,000" FA 1999 s 204 as regards relevant periods ending after 31 December 1998; previously "£500" for gifts taken on or after 31 December 1978; for gifts prior to 31 December 1978 the exemption is £250.

[3]   Subs (3) (which dealt with aggregation of gifts taken between 28 February 1969 and 27 February 1974 with later gifts or inheritances taken on or after 31 March 1976: s 9) deleted by FA 1984 s 110(2) as regards gifts or inheritances taken on or after 26 March 1984.

Narrative

Capital Acquisitions Tax, Chapter 11.

Definitions

"date of the disposition"; "disponer", "disposition", "donee", "gift", "inheritance", "taxable gift", "taxable value": s 2(1).

54 Provisions relating to charities, etc

[(1) Where any person takes a benefit for public or charitable purposes that person shall be deemed—

    (*a*) for the purposes of sections 5(1) and 11(1), to have taken that benefit beneficially, and

    (*b*) for the purposes of the Second Schedule, to have taken a gift or an inheritance accordingly to which the group threshold of [€19,050][1] applies.][2]

[(2) A gift or an inheritance which is taken for public or charitable purposes shall be exempt from tax and shall not be taken into account in computing tax, to the extent that the Commissioners are satisfied that it has been, or will be, applied to purposes which, in accordance with the law of the State, are public or charitable.][3]

(3) Save as provided in section 56(4), a gift or inheritance which a person takes on becoming entitled to any benefit on the application to public or charitable purposes of property (including moneys provided by the Oireachtas or a local authority) held for such purposes shall be exempt from tax and shall not be taken into account in computing tax.

Amendments

[1]   Substituted by FA 2001 s 240 and Sch 5 Part 5 with effect from 1 January 2002; previously "£15,000".

[2]   Subs (1) substituted by FA 2000 s 143 for gifts or inheritances taken on or after 1 December 1999.

[3]   Subs (2) substituted by FA 1987 s 50 as regards gifts or inheritances taken on or after 9 July 1987.

Narrative

Capital Acquisitions Tax, Chapter 11.

Definitions

"benefit": s 2(1); "class threshold": Sch 2; "Commissioners", "donee", "gift", "inheritance", "local authority": 2(1); "person": IA 1937 s 11(*c*); "property": s 2(1).

55 Exemption of certain objects

(1) This section applies to the following objects, that is to say, any pictures, prints, books, manuscripts, works of art, jewellery, scientific collections or other things not held for the purposes of trading—

    (*a*) which, on a claim being made to the Commissioners, appear to them to be of national, scientific, historic or artistic interest;

    (*b*) which are kept permanently in the State except for such temporary absences outside the State as are approved by the Commissioners; and

    (*c*) in respect of which reasonable facilities for viewing are allowed to members of the public or to recognised bodies or to associations of persons.

(2) (*a*) Any object to which this section applies and which, at the date of the gift or at the date of inheritance, and at the valuation date, is comprised in a gift or an inheritance taken by a person shall be exempt from tax in relation to that gift or inheritance, and the value thereof shall not be taken into account in computing tax on any gift or inheritance taken by that person ...[1] unless the exemption ceases to apply under the provisions of subsection (3) or (4).

(*b*) The provisions of section 19(6) shall apply, for the purposes of this subsection, as they apply in relation to agricultural property.

[(3) If an object exempted from tax by virtue of subsection (2) is sold within 6 years after the valuation date, and before the death of the donee or successor, the exemption referred to in subsection (2) shall cease to apply to such object:

Provided that, if the sale of such object is a sale by private treaty to the National Gallery of Ireland, the National Museum of Science and Art or any other similar national institution, any university in the State or any constituent college thereof, a local authority or the Friends of the National Collections of Ireland, the exemption referred to in subsection (2) shall continue to apply.][2]

[(4) The exemption referred to in subsection (2) shall cease to apply to an object, if at any time after the valuation date and—

(*a*) before the sale of the object,

(*b*) before the death of the donee or successor, and

(*c*) before such object again forms part of the property comprised in a gift or an inheritance (other than an inheritance arising by virtue of section 103 of the Finance Act, 1986) in respect of which gift or inheritance an absolute interest is taken by a person other than the spouse of that donee or successor, there has been a breach of any condition specified in paragraph (*b*) or (*c*) of subsection (1).][3]

[(5) Any work of art normally kept outside the State which is comprised in an inheritance which is charged to tax by virtue of section 12(1)(*c*) shall be exempt from tax and shall not be taken into account in computing tax, to the extent that the Commissioners are satisfied that it was brought into the State solely for public exhibition, cleaning or restoration.][4]

Amendments

[1]   Deleted by FA 1984 s 110(4) as regards gifts or inheritances taken on or after 26 March 1984.

[2]   Subs (3) substituted by FA 1995 s 160(1)(*a*) in relation to gifts or inheritances taken on or after 12 April 1995.

[3]   Subs (4) substituted by FA 2000 s 144 for gifts or inheritances taken on or after 10 February 2000.

[4]   Subs (5) inserted by FA 2001 s 218 in relation to inheritances taken on or after 26 January 2001.

Cross-references

Heritage property of companies, "relevant heritage property" means objects to which this section applies: FA 1995 s 166(1); breach of conditions specified in subs (1)(*b*) or (*c*): FA 1995 s 166(6)(*b*).

Houses or gardens of national, scientific or historic interest, extension of this section: FA 1978 s 39 and FA 1997 s 137.

Probate tax, discretionary trust inheritance deemed to be taken after, unless exempted (subss (3)-(4) above): FA 1993 s 110(2); references in subs (4) to the successor to be construed as a reference to the person who would be the successor if Probate Tax legislation had not been enacted: FA 1993 s 111(*k*).

Statutory instrument

Capital Acquisitions Tax (Heritage Houses and Gardens) Regulations 1987 (SI 28/1987) now replaced by FA 1997 s 157 with effect from 1 February 1987.

Narrative

Capital Acquisitions Tax, Chapter 11.

Definitions

"Commissioners", "date of the gift", "date of the inheritance", "disponer", "donee", "gift", "inheritance", "local authority", "property", "successor", "tax" "valuation date": 2(1); "person",: IA 1937 s 11(*c*); "year": IA 1937 Sch.

56 Payments relating to retirement, etc

(1) Subject to the provisions of subsection (2), any payment to an employee or former employee by, or out of funds provided by, his employer or any other person, *bona fide* by way of retirement benefit, redundancy payment or pension shall not be a gift or an inheritance.

(2) Subsection (1) shall not have effect in relation to a payment referred to in that subsection, and any such payment shall be deemed to be a gift or an inheritance where—

    (*a*)   (i)   the employee is a relative of the employer or other disponer; or

          (ii)   the employer is a private company within the meaning of section 16(2), and of which private company the employee is deemed to have control within the meaning of that section;

    (*b*)   the payment is not made under a scheme (relating to superannuation, retirement or redundancy) approved by the Commissioners under the Income Tax Acts; and

    (*c*)   the Commissioners decide that in the circumstances of the case the payment is excessive.

(3) The Commissioners shall serve on an accountable person a notice in writing of their decision referred to in subsection (2) and the accountable person concerned may appeal against such decision and section 52 shall apply with any necessary modifications in relation to such appeal as it applies in relation to an appeal against an assessment of tax.

(4) Any benefit taken by a person other than the person in respect of whose service the benefit arises, under the provisions of any superannuation fund, or under any superannuation scheme, established solely or mainly for persons employed in a profession, trade, undertaking or employment, and their dependants, shall (whether or not any person had a right enforceable at law to the benefit) be deemed to be a gift or an inheritance, as the case may be, derived under a disposition made by the person in respect of whose service the benefit arises and not by any other person.

(5) In this section—

"superannuation scheme" includes any arrangement in connection with employment for the provision of a benefit on or in connection with the retirement or death of an employee;

"employment" includes employment as a director of a body corporate and cognate words shall be construed accordingly.

Narrative

Capital Acquisitions Tax, Chapter 11.

Definitions

"accountable person": ss 2(1); 35; "benefit", "Commissioners", "disponer", "gift", "inheritance": s 2(1); "person": IA 1937 s 11(*c*); "relative": s 2(1).

57 Exemption of certain securities

(1) In this section—

"security" means any security, stock, share, debenture, debenture stock, certificate of charge or other form of security issued, whether before or after the passing of this Act, and which by virtue of any enactment or by virtue of the exercise of any power conferred by any enactment is exempt from taxation when in the beneficial ownership of a person neither domiciled nor ordinarily resident in the State;

[**"unit trust scheme"** means an authorised unit trust scheme within the meaning of the Unit Trusts Act, 1990, whose deed expressing the trusts of the scheme restricts the property subject to those trusts to securities.]¹

[(2) Securities, or units (within the meaning of the [Unit Trusts Act, 1990]²,) of a unit trust scheme, comprised in a gift or an inheritance taken on or after the 14th day of April, 1978, shall be exempt from tax (and shall not be taken into account in computing tax on any gift or inheritance taken by the donee or successor ...³) if, but only if, it is shown to the satisfaction of the Commissioners that—

[(*a*) the securities or units were comprised in the disposition continuously for a period of six years immediately before the date of the gift or the date of the inheritance, and any period immediately before the date of the disposition during which the securities or units were continuously in the beneficial ownership of the disponer shall be deemed, for the purpose of this paragraph, to be a period or part of a period immediately before the date of the gift or the date of the inheritance during which they were continuously comprised in the disposition;]⁴

(*b*) the securities or units were comprised in the gift or inheritance—

(i)   at the date of the gift or the date of the inheritance; and

(ii) at the valuation date;

and

(*c*) the donee or successor is at the date of the gift or the date of the inheritance neither domiciled nor ordinarily resident in the State,

and the provisions of section 19(6) shall apply, for the purposes of this subsection, as they apply in relation to agricultural property.

(3) Subsection (2)(*a*) shall not apply in a case where the disponer was neither domiciled nor ordinarily resident in the State at the date of the [disposition]⁵.]⁶

Amendments

¹   Definition of "unit trust scheme" substituted by FA 1991 s 121(1)(*a*) as regards gifts or inheritances taken on or after 26 December 1990.

²   Substituted by FA 1991 s 121(1)(*a*) as regards gifts or inheritances taken on or after 26 December 1990.

3   Words "from the same disponer" deleted by FA 1984 s 110(5) as regards gifts or inheritances taken on or after 26 March 1984.

4   Subs (2)(*a*) substituted by FA 2001 s 219 in relation to securities or units comprised in a gift or an inheritance where the date of the gift or inheritance is on or after 15 February 2001 or the securities or units come into the beneficial ownership of the disponer on or after 15 February 2001 or become subject to the disposition on or after that date without having been previously in the beneficial ownership of the disponer.

5   Substituted by FA 1997 s 135 in relation to securities or units comprised in a gift or inheritance where the date of the gift or the date of the inheritance is on or after 26 March 1997 and the securities or units come into the beneficial ownership of the disponer on or after 26 March 1997, or become subject to the disposition on or after that date without having been previously in the beneficial ownership of the disponer.

6   Subss (2)-(3) substituted by FA 1978 s 40.

Cross-references

Discretionary trust once off charge, this section does not apply: FA 1984 s 107(*g*).

Discretionary trust annual charge, this section does not apply: FA 1986 s 104(*g*).

Probate tax, subs (2)(*a*) does not apply, and subs (2)(*c*) is to be construed as if the reference to the donee or successor were a reference to the deceased: FA 1993 s 111(*i*).

Narrative

Capital Acquisitions Tax, Chapter 11.

Definitions

"Commissioners", "date of the disposition", "date of the gift", "date of the inheritance", "disponer", "disposition", "donee", "gift", "inheritance", "valuation date": s 2(1); "person": IA 1937 s 11(*c*); "property", "share", "successor": s 2(1).

---

58 Exemption of certain receipts

(1) The following shall not be gifts or inheritances—

   (*a*) the receipt by a person of any sum *bona fide* by way of compensation or damages for any wrong or injury suffered by him in his person, property, reputation or means of livelihood;

   (*b*) the receipt by a person of any sum *bona fide* by way of compensation or damages for any wrong or injury resulting in the death of any other person;

   (*c*) the receipt by a person of any sum *bona fide* by way of winnings from betting (including pool betting) or from any lottery, sweepstake or game with prizes;

   (*d*) any benefit arising out of—

      (i)   the payment to the Official Assignee in Bankruptcy of money which has been provided by, or which represents property provided by, friends of a bankrupt; or

      (ii) a remission or abatement of debts by the creditors of a bankrupt,

      to enable the bankrupt to fulfil an offer of composition after bankruptcy in accordance with the provisions of section 149 of the Irish Bankrupt and Insolvent Act, 1857; and

   (*e*) any benefit arising out of—

      (i)   the payment to the Official Assignee in Bankruptcy of money which has been provided by, or which represents property provided by, friends of an arranging debtor; or

      (ii) a remission or abatement of debts by the creditors of an arranging debtor, to enable the debtor to carry out the terms of a proposal made by him under section 345 of the Irish Bankrupt and Insolvent Act, 1857, which has been accepted by his creditors and approved and confirmed by the High Court.

(2) Notwithstanding anything contained in this Act, the receipt in the lifetime of the disponer of money or money's worth—

    (*a*) by—

        (i) the spouse or child of the disponer; or

        (ii) a person in relation to whom the disponer stands *in loco parentis*,

        for support, maintenance or education; or

    (*b*) by a person who is in relation to the disponer a dependent relative under [section 466 of the Taxes Consolidation Act, 1997],[1] for support or maintenance,

shall not be a gift or an inheritance, where the provision of such support, maintenance or education, or such support or maintenance—

        (i) is such as would be part of the normal expenditure of a person in the circumstances of the disponer; and

        (ii) is reasonable having regard to the financial circumstances of the disponer.

[(3) (*a*) The receipt by an incapacitated individual of the whole or any part of trust funds which are held on a qualifying trust, or of the income therefrom, shall not be a gift or an inheritance.

    (*b*) In this subsection "incapacitated individual", "trust funds" and "qualifying trust" have the meanings assigned to them, respectively, by section 189A (inserted by the Finance Act, 1999) of the Taxes Consolidation Act, 1997.

    (*c*) This subsection shall apply in relation to gifts or inheritances taken on or after the 6th day of April, 1997.][2]

[(4) The receipt by a minor child of the disponer of money or money's worth for support, maintenance or education, at a time when the disponer and the other parent of that minor child are dead, shall not be a gift or an inheritance where the provision of such support, maintenance or education—

    (*a*) is such as would be part of the normal expenditure of a person in the circumstances of the disponer immediately prior to the death of the disponer; and

    (*b*) is reasonable having regard to the financial circumstances of the disponer immediately prior to the death of the disponer.][3]

Amendments

[1]   Substituted by TCA 1997 s 1100 and Sch 31; previously "section 142 of the Income Tax Act, 1967".

[2]   Subs (3) inserted by FA 1999 s 205.

[3]   Subs (4) inserted by FA 2000 s 152 for gifts or inheritances taken on or after 23 March 2000.

Narrative

Capital Acquisitions Tax, Chapter 11.

Definitions
"benefit", "child", "disponer", "gift", "inheritance": s 2(1); "person": IA 193 s 11(*c*); "property": s 2(1).

59 Exemption where disposition was made by the donee or successor

(1) Tax shall not be chargeable upon a gift or an inheritance taken by the donee or successor under a disposition made by himself.

(2) Where, at the date of the gift, two companies are associated in the manner described in subsection (3), a gift taken by one of them under a disposition made by the other shall be deemed to be a gift to which subsection (1) applies.

(3) For the purposes of subsection (2), two companies shall be regarded as associated if

(*a*)   one company would be beneficially entitled to not less than 90 per cent. of any assets of the other company available for distribution to the owners of its shares and entitlements of the kind referred to in section 34(1) on a winding up; or

(*b*)   a third company would be beneficially entitled to not less than 90 per cent. of any assets of each of them available as in paragraph (*a*).

(4) In this section, **"company"** means a body corporate (wherever incorporated), other than a private company within the meaning of section 16(2).

Narrative
Capital Acquisitions Tax, Chapter 11.
Definitions
"disposition", "donee", "gift", "inheritance", "share", "successor": s 2(1).

59A Exemption relating to qualifying expenses of incapacitated persons

[(1) A gift or inheritance which is taken exclusively for the purpose of discharging qualifying expenses of an individual who is permanently incapacitated by reason of physical or mental infirmity shall, to the extent that the Commissioners are satisfied that it has been or will be applied to such purpose, be exempt from tax and shall not be taken into account in computing tax.

(2) In this section "qualifying expenses" means expenses relating to medical care including the cost of maintenance in connection with such medical care.]¹

Amendments
¹   Section 59A inserted by FA 1996 s 123(1) in relation to gifts or inheritances taken on or after 28 March 1996.
Cross-references
Discretionary trust once off charge FA 1984 s 108 (physical, mental or legal incapacity).
Discretionary trust annual charge FA 1986 s 105 (physical, mental or legal incapacity).
Definitions
"gift", "inheritance": s 2(1).

59B Exemption relating to retirement benefits

[(1) The whole or any part of a retirement fund which is comprised in an inheritance which is taken upon the death of a disponer dying on or after the date of the passing of the Finance Act, 1999, shall be exempt from tax in relation to that inheritance and in relation to a charge for tax arising on that death by virtue of section 110 of the Finance Act, 1993, and the value thereof shall not be taken into account in computing tax, where—

(a) the disposition under which the inheritance is taken is the will or intestacy of the disponer, and

(b) the successor is a child of the disponer and had attained 21 years of age at the date of that disposition.

(2) In this section "retirement fund", in relation to an inheritance taken on the death of a disponer, means an approved retirement fund or an approved minimum retirement fund, within the meaning of section 784A or 784C of the Taxes Consolidation Act, 1997, being a fund which is wholly comprised of all or any of the following, that is to say—

(a) property which represents in whole or in part the accrued rights of the disponer, or of a predeceased spouse of the disponer, under an annuity contract or retirement benefits scheme approved by the Revenue Commissioners for the purposes of Chapter 1 or Chapter 2 of Part 30 of that Act,

(b) any accumulations of income thereof, or

(c) property which represents in whole or in part those accumulations.][1]

Amendments

[1]   Section 59B inserted by FA 1999 s 206.

59C Exemption relating to certain dwellings

[(1) In this section—

"dwelling-house" means—

(a) a building or part (including an appropriate part within the meaning of subsection (5) of section 5) of a building which was used or was suitable for use as a dwelling, and

(b) the curtilage of the dwelling-house up to an area (exclusive of the site of the dwelling-house) of one acre but if the area of the curtilage (exclusive of the site of the dwelling-house) exceeds one acre then the part which comes within this definition is the part which, if the remainder were separately occupied, would be the most suitable for occupation and enjoyment with the dwelling-house;

"relevant period", in relation to a dwelling-house comprised in a gift or inheritance, means the period of 6 years commencing on the date of the gift or the date of the inheritance.

[(1A) In this section any reference to a donee or successor shall be construed as including a reference to the transferee referred to in section 23(1).][1]

(2) Subject to subsections (3), (4), (5) and (6), a dwellinghouse comprised in a gift or inheritance which is taken by a donee or successor who—

(*a*)   has continuously occupied as his or her only or main residence

　　(i)   that dwelling-house throughout the period of 3 years immediately preceding the date of the gift or the date of the inheritance, or

　　(ii)   where that dwelling-house has directly or indirectly replaced other property, that dwelling-house and that other property for periods which together comprised at least 3 years falling within the period of 4 years immediately preceding the date of the gift or the date of the inheritance,

(*b*)   is not, at the date of the gift or at the date of the inheritance, beneficially entitled to any other dwellinghouse or to any interest in any other dwelling-house, and

(*c*)   continues to occupy that dwelling-house as his or her only or main residence throughout the relevant period,

shall be exempt from tax in relation to that gift or inheritance, and the value thereof shall not be taken into account in computing tax on any gift or inheritance taken by that person unless the exemption ceases to apply under subsection (5) or (6).

(3) The condition in paragraph (*c*) of subsection (2) shall not apply where the donee or successor has attained the age of 55 years at the date of the gift or at the date of the inheritance.

(4) For the purpose of paragraph (*c*) of subsection (2), the donee or successor shall be deemed to occupy the dwellinghouse concerned as his or her only or main residence throughout any period of absence during which he or she worked in an employment or office all the duties of which were performed outside the State.

(5) If a dwelling-house exempted from tax by virtue of subsection (2) is sold or disposed of, either in whole or in part, within the relevant period, and before the death of the donee or successor (not being a donee or successor who had attained the age of 55 years at the date of the gift or inheritance), the exemption referred to in that subsection shall cease to apply to such dwelling-house unless the sale or disposal occurs in consequence of the donee or successor requiring long-term medical care in a hospital, nursing home or convalescent home.

(6) The exemption referred to in subsection (2) shall cease to apply to a dwelling-house, if at any time during the relevant period and

(*a*)   before the dwelling-house is sold or disposed of, and

(*b*)   before the death of the donee or successor,

the condition specified in paragraph (*c*) of subsection (2) has not been complied with unless that non-compliance occurs in consequence of the donee or successor requiring long-term medical care in a hospital, nursing home or convalescent home, or in consequence of any condition imposed by the employer of the donee or successor requiring the donee or successor to reside elsewhere.

(7) Where a dwelling-house exempted from tax by virtue of subsection (2) (hereafter in this section referred to as the "first-mentioned dwelling-house") is replaced within the relevant period by another dwelling-house, the condition specified in paragraph (*c*) of

subsection (2) shall be treated as satisfied if the donee or successor has occupied as his or her only or main residence the first-mentioned dwelling-house, that other dwellinghouse and any dwelling-house which has within the relevant period directly or indirectly replaced that other dwelling-house for periods which together comprised at least 6 years falling within the period of 7 years commencing on the date of the gift or the date of the inheritance.

(8) Any period of absence which would satisfy the condition specified in paragraph (*c*) of subsection (2) in relation to the first-mentioned dwelling-house shall, if it occurs in relation to any dwelling-house which has directly or indirectly replaced that dwelling-house, likewise satisfy the said condition as it has effect by virtue of subsection (7).

(9) Subsection (5) shall not apply to a case falling within subsection (7), but the extent of the exemption under this section in such a case shall, where the donee or successor had not attained the age of 55 years at the date of the gift or at the date of the inheritance, not exceed what it would have been had the replacement of one dwelling- house by another referred to in subsection (7), or any one or more of such replacements, taken place immediately prior to that date.]²

Amendments

¹   Subs (1A) inserted by FA 2001 s 220 in relation to a gift or inheritance taken on or after 1 December 1999.

²   Section 59C inserted by FA 2000 s 151 for gifts or inheritances taken on or after 1 December 1999.

Notes

See article entitled "Exemption from CAT for certain dwelling houses" by Ann Williams in Irish Tax Review, Vol 14 No 1.

Revenue information

Leaflet CAT 10 - Gift/Inheritance Tax Exemption for Dwelling-house.

59D Gifts and inheritances taken by foster children

[(1) In this section—

"the appropriate period" means periods which together comprised at least 5 years falling within the 18 years immediately following the birth of the donee or successor.

(2) Where, on a claim being made to them in that behalf in relation to a gift or inheritance taken on or after 6 December 2000, the Commissioners are, subject to subsection (3), satisfied—

    (*a*)   where the inheritance is taken by a successor on the date of death of the disponer, that the successor had, prior to the date of the inheritance, been placed in the foster care of the disponer under the Child Care (Placement of Children in Foster Care) Regulations, 1995 (SI No 260 of 1995), or the Child Care (Placement of Children with Relatives) Regulations, 1995 (SI No 261 of 1995), or

    (*b*)   that throughout the appropriate period the donee or successor

        (i)   has resided with the disponer, and

        (ii)   was under the care of and maintained by the disponer at the disponer's own expense, then, subject to subsection (3), for the purpose of computing the tax payable on that gift or inheritance, that donee or successor shall be deemed to bear to that disponer the relationship of a child.

(3) Relief under subsection (2) shall not apply where the claim for such relief is based on the uncorroborated testimony of one witness.][1]

Amendments

[1]   Section 59D inserted by FA 2001 s 221.

59E Gifts and inheritances taken by adopted children from natural parent

[Where, on a claim being made to them in that behalf in relation to a gift or inheritance taken on or after the date of the passing of the Finance Act, 2001, the Commissioners are satisfied that—

(*a*)   the donee or successor had at the date of the gift or the date of the inheritance been adopted in the manner referred to in paragraph (*b*) of the definition of "child" contained in section 2(1), and

(*b*)   the disponer is the natural mother or the natural father of the donee or successor,

then, notwithstanding section 2(5)(a), for the purpose of computing the tax payable on that gift or inheritance, that donee or successor shall be deemed to bear to that disponer the relationship of a child.][1]

Amendments

[1]   Section 59E inserted by FA 2001 s 222.

PART X
MISCELLANEOUS

60 Certificates for probate

(1) Where an Inland Revenue affidavit has been delivered to the Commissioners and they are satisfied—

(*a*)   that an adequate payment on account of inheritance tax in respect of the property passing under the deceased person's will or intestacy or Part IX or section 56 of the Succession Act, 1965, has been made; or

(*b*)   that the payment of inheritance tax in respect of such property may be deferred for the time being,

they shall certify in writing—

(i)   that the Inland Revenue affidavit was delivered to them; and

(ii)   (I)   that a payment referred to in paragraph (*a*) has been made; or

(II)   that the payment referred to in paragraph (*b*) has been deferred for the time being, as the case may be.

(2) In this section **"Inland Revenue affidavit"** has the meaning referred to in section 38(1).

(3) If, in the opinion of the Commissioners, the payment of inheritance tax in respect of the property passing under the deceased person's will or intestacy or Part IX or section 56 of the Succession Act, 1965, cannot be deferred for the time being without serious risk of such tax not being recovered, they may refuse to issue the certificate referred to in subsection (1) until the tax has been paid, or until such payment as is referred to in paragraph (*a*) of that subsection has been made.

(4) The certificate required by section 30 of the Customs and Inland Revenue Act, 1881, to be made by the proper officer of the court, shall not be made until a certificate of the Commissioners issued under subsection (1) has been produced to such officer and shall (instead of showing that the affidavit, if liable to stamp duty, has been duly stamped) show that the Commissioners have issued a certificate under subsection (1) and shall state the substance of the certificate so issued by the Commissioners.

(5) The form of certificate required to be given by the proper officer of the court under section 30 of the Customs and Inland Revenue Act, 1881, may be prescribed by rule of court in such manner as may be necessary for giving effect to this Act.

(6) This section shall apply only where the deceased person dies on or after the 1st day of April, 1975.

Cross-references

Probate tax, this section applies, but Commissioners may refuse to issue certificate where

(*a*) tax is being paid by transfer of securities (until such security as they think fit has been give),

(*b*) tax is being paid by instalments, or

(*c*) until all the tax has been paid, together with any related interest: FA 1993 s 111(*h*).

Narrative

Capital Acquisitions Tax, Chapter 21.

Definitions

"Commissioners", "inheritance": s 2(1); "person": IA 1937 s 11(*c*); "property": s 2(1).

---

61 Payment of money standing in names of two or more persons

(1) Where, either before or after the passing of this Act, a sum of money exceeding [€31,750][1] is lodged or deposited (otherwise than on a current account) in the State with a banker, in the joint names of two or more persons, and one of such persons (in this section referred to as the deceased) dies on or after the 1st day of April, 1975, the banker shall not pay such money or any part thereof to the survivor or all or any of the survivors of such persons, or to any other person, unless or until there is furnished to such banker a certificate by the Commissioners certifying that there is no outstanding claim for inheritance tax in connection with the death of the deceased in respect of such money or any part thereof or a consent in writing by the Commissioners to such payment pending the ascertainment and payment of such tax.

(2) Notwithstanding anything contained in this Act, tax chargeable on the death of the deceased shall be deemed for the purposes of this section to become due on the day of the death of the deceased.

(3) A banker who, after the passing of this Act, pays money in contravention of this section shall be liable to a penalty of [€1,265][2].

(4) Where a penalty is demanded of a banker under this section, the onus of proving that such certificate or such consent as is mentioned in this section was furnished to such banker before he paid such money shall lie on such banker.

(5) Where a penalty is demanded of a banker under this section, it shall be a good defence to prove that, at the time when such banker paid such money, he had reasonable ground for believing that none of the persons in whose joint names such money was lodged or deposited with him was dead.

(6) Section 33 of the Finance Act, 1935, shall not have effect in any case where the death of a person, referred to in that section as the deceased, occurs on or after the 1st day of April, 1975.

(7) In this section—

"banker" means a person who carries on banking business in the State and includes a friendly society, an industrial and provident society, a building society, the Post Office Savings Bank, a trustee savings bank, ...[3] the Agricultural Credit Corporation Limited and any person with whom money is lodged or deposited;

"pay" includes transfer in the books of a banker and any dealings whatsoever with any moneys which were lodged or deposited in the name of a person who died after the time of the lodgment or deposit and any other person or persons;

"current account" means an account which is customarily operated upon by means of a cheque or banker's order;

"banking business" has the meaning assigned to it by section 2 of the Central Bank Act, 1971;

references to moneys lodged or deposited include references to shares of a building society, friendly society or industrial and provident society.

[(8) This section shall not apply or have effect where the sum of money referred to in subsection (1) is lodged or deposited in the joint names of two persons, one of whom dies on or after the 30th day of January, 1985, and is at the time of his death the spouse of the other person.][4]

Amendments

[1] Substituted by FA 2001 s 223(*b*) as respects a death occurring on or after 1 January 2002; previously "£5,000".
[2] Substituted by FA 2001 s 240 and Sch 5 Part 5 with effect from 1 January 2002; previously "£1,000".
[3] Deleted by ICC Bank Act 2000 Sch with effect from 12 February 2001.
[4] Subs (8) inserted by FA 1986 s 110.

Cross-references

Subs (1): restriction not applicable to deposit accounts in joint names of husband and wife for deaths occurring after 29 January 1985: FA 1986 s 110.

Narrative

Capital Acquisitions Tax, Chapter 14.

Definitions

"Commissioners", "inheritance": s 2(1); "person": IA 1937 s 11(*c*).

62 Court to provide for payment of tax

Where any suit is pending in any court for the administration of any property chargeable with tax under this Act, such court shall provide, out of any such property which may be in the possession or control of the court, for the payment to the Commissioners of any of the tax or the interest thereon which remains unpaid.

Narrative

Capital Acquisitions Tax, Chapter 24.

Definitions

"Commissioners", "property": s 2(1).

---

63 Penalties

[(1) (a) Any person who contravenes or fails to comply with any requirement or provision under section 36 shall be liable to a penalty of [€2,535][1].

   (b) Where the contravention or failure referred to in paragraph (a) continues after judgment has been given by the court before which proceedings for the penalty have been commenced, the person concerned shall be liable to a further penalty of [€30][2] for each day on which the contravention or failure so continues.][3]

(2) Where, under, or for the purposes of, any of the provisions of this Act, a person is authorised to inspect any property for the purpose of reporting to the Commissioners the market value thereof and the person having custody or possession of that property prevents such inspection or obstructs the person so authorised in the performance of his functions in relation to the inspection, the person so having custody or possession shall be liable to a penalty of [€1,265][4].

(3) Where an accountable person fraudulently or negligently—

   (a) delivers any incorrect return or additional return;

   (b) makes or furnishes any incorrect statement, declaration, evidence or valuation in connection with any property comprised in any disposition;

   (c) makes or furnishes any incorrect statement, declaration, evidence or valuation in connection with any claim for any allowance, deduction, exemption or relief; or

   (d) makes or furnishes any incorrect statement, declaration, evidence or valuation in connection with any other matter,

on the basis of which the amount of tax assessable in respect of a taxable gift or taxable inheritance would be less than it would have been if the correct return, additional return, statement, declaration, evidence or valuation had been delivered, made or furnished, he shall be liable to a penalty of—

   (i) [€6,345][5]; and

   (ii) the amount, or in the case of fraud, twice the amount, of the difference specified in subsection (5).

(4) Where any such return, additional return, statement, declaration, evidence or valuation as is mentioned in subsection (3) was delivered, made or furnished neither fraudulently nor negligently by a person and it comes to his notice that it was incorrect,

then, unless the error is remedied without unreasonable delay, such matter shall be treated, for the purposes of this section, as having been negligently done by him.

(5) The difference referred to in subsection (3) is the difference between—

   (*a*) the amount of tax payable in respect of the taxable gift or taxable inheritance to which the return, additional return, statement, declaration, evidence or valuation relates; and

   (*b*) the amount which would have been the amount so payable if the return, additional return, statement, declaration, evidence or valuation as made or submitted had been correct.

(6) For the purpose of subsection (3), where anything referred to in that subsection is delivered, made or furnished on behalf of a person, it shall be deemed to have been delivered, made or furnished by that person unless he proves that it was done without his knowledge or consent.

(7) Any person who assists in or induces the delivery, making or furnishing for any purposes of the tax of any return, additional return, statement, declaration, evidence or valuation which he knows to be incorrect shall be liable to a penalty of [€1,265][6].

(8) The provisions of this section shall not affect any criminal proceedings.

(9) Subject to the provisions of this section, [sections 987(4), 1061, 1062, 1063, 1064, 1065, 1066 and 1068 of the Taxes Consolidation Act, 1997],[7] shall, with any necessary modifications, apply to a penalty under this Act as if the penalty were a penalty under the Income Tax Acts.

Amendments

[1]   Substituted by FA 2001 s 240 and Sch 5 Part 5 with effect from 1 January 2002; previously "£2,000".

[2]   Substituted by FA 2001 s 240 and Sch 5 Part 5 with effect from 1 January 2002; previously "£25".

[3]   Subs (1) substituted by FA 1989 s 77(*a*).

[4]   Substituted by FA 2001 s 240 and Sch 5 Part 5 with effect from 1 January 2002; previously "£1,000".

[5]   Substituted by FA 2001 s 240 and Sch 5 Part 5 with effect from 1 January 2002; previously "£5,000".

[6]   Substituted by FA 2001 s 240 and Sch 5 Part 5 with effect from 1 January 2002; previously "£1,000".

[7]   Substituted by TCA 1997 s 1100 and Sch 31; previously "sections 128(4), 507, 508, 510, 511, 512, 517 and 518 of the Income Tax Act, 1967".

Cross-references

Probate tax, this section applies, but
(*a*) in subs (1)(*a*), substitute "£400" for "£2,000";
(*b*) in subs (1)(*b*), substitute "£5" for "£25";
(*c*) in subss (2) and (7), substitute "£200" for "£1,000";
(*d*) in subs (3), substitute "£1,000" for "£5,000";
(FA 1993 s 111(*l*)).

Narrative

Capital Acquisitions Tax, Chapter 22.

Definitions

"accountable person": ss 2(1); 35; "additional return", "Commissioners", "disposition", "gift", "inheritance", "market value": s 2(1); "person": IA 1937 s 11(*c*); "property", "return", "taxable gift", "taxable inheritance": s 2(1).

---

64 Liability to tax in respect of certain sales and mortgages

(1) In this section—

"death duties" has the meaning assigned to it by section 30 of the Finance Act, 1971; and

"purchaser or mortgagee" includes a person deriving title from or under a purchaser or mortgagee in the case of such a sale or mortgage as is referred to in this section.

(2) Where an interest in expectancy has, prior to the 1st day of April, 1975, been *bona fide* sold or mortgaged for full consideration in money or money's worth, and that interest comes into possession on a death occurring on or after that date, the following provisions shall have effect, that is to say—

(a)   the purchaser or mortgagee shall not be liable in respect of inheritance tax on the inheritance referred to in paragraph (b) for an amount greater than that referred to in paragraph (c);

(b)   the inheritance referred to in paragraph (a) is the inheritance of property in which the interest so sold or mortgaged subsists and which arises in respect of the interest of the remainderman referred to in section 23 so coming into possession;

(c)   the amount referred to in paragraph (a) shall be the amount that would then have been payable by the purchaser or mortgagee in respect of death duties on the property in which the interest subsists as property passing under the same disposition as that under which the said inheritance is taken, if the property, on so coming into possession, had been chargeable to death duties—

(i)   under the law in force; and

(ii)   at the rate or rates having effect,

at the date of the sale or mortgage;

(d)   where such an interest is so mortgaged, any amount of inheritance tax payable in respect of the inheritance referred to in paragraph (b), and from the payment of which the mortgagee is relieved under this section, shall, notwithstanding the priority referred to in section 47(1), rank, in relation to property charged with such tax under that section, as a charge subsequent to the mortgage;

(e)   any person, other than the purchaser or mortgagee, who is accountable for the payment of so much of the inheritance tax as is not the liability of the purchaser or mortgagee by virtue of the relief given by this section, shall not be liable for the payment of any amount in respect thereof in excess of the amount which is available to him for such payment by reason of there being, at the time when the interest comes into possession, other property, or an equity of redemption, or both, subject to the same trusts, under the disposition referred to in paragraph (c), as the property in which the interest in expectancy subsists; and

(f)   nothing in section 35(7) or (8) or section 47(1) shall be construed as derogating from the relief given by this section to a purchaser or mortgagee.

Narrative

Capital Acquisitions Tax, Chapter 24.

Definitions

"accountable person", "disposition", "inheritance", "interest in expectancy: s 2(1); "person": IA 1937 s 11(*c*); "property": s 2(1).

65 References in deeds and wills, etc. to death duties

In so far as a provision in a document refers (in whatever terms) to any death duty to arise on any death occurring on or after the 1st day of April, 1975, it shall have effect, as far as maybe, as if the reference included a reference to inheritance tax—

(*a*) if that document was executed prior to the passing of this Act, and the reference is to legacy duty and succession duty or either of them;

(*b*) if that document was so executed, and the reference is to estate duty, and it may reasonably be inferred from all the circumstances (including any similarity of the incidence of inheritance tax to that of estate duty) that the inclusion of the reference to inheritance tax would be just; and

(*c*) whether the document was executed prior to or after the passing of this Act, if the reference is to death duties, without referring to any particular death duty.

Narrative

Capital Acquisitions Tax, Chapter 24.

Definitions

"inheritance": s 2(1).

66 Arrangements for relief from double taxation

(1) If the Government by order declare that arrangements specified in the order have been made with the government of any territory outside the State in relation to affording relief from double taxation in respect of gift tax or inheritance tax payable under the laws of the State and any tax imposed under the laws of that Territory which is of a similar character or is chargeable by reference to death or to gifts *inter vivos* and that it is expedient that those arrangements should have the force of law, the arrangements shall, notwithstanding anything in any enactment, have the force of law.

(2) Any arrangements to which the force of law is given under this section may include provision for relief from tax charged before the making of the arrangements and provisions as to property which is not itself subject to double tax, and the provisions of this section shall have effect accordingly.

(3) For the purposes of subsection (1), arrangements made with the head of a foreign state shall be regarded as made with the government thereof.

(4) Where any arrangements have the force of law by virtue of this section, the obligation as to secrecy imposed by any enactment shall not prevent the Commissioners from disclosing to any authorised officer of the government with which the arrangements are made such information as is required to be disclosed under the arrangements.

(5) (*a*) Any order made under this section may be revoked by a subsequent order and any such revoking order may contain such transitional provisions as appear to the Government to be necessary or expedient.

   (*b*) Where a order is proposed to be made under this section, a draft thereof shall be laid before Dáil Éireann and the order shall not be made until a resolution approving of the draft has been passed by Dáil Éireann.

Cross-references

Only two such negotiated agreements apply: FA 1950 to USA (by concession to probate tax and inheritance tax only); and the UK Convention 1997 (to inheritance tax).

Narrative

Capital Acquisitions Tax, Chapter 13.

Definitions

"Commissioners", "gift", "inheritance", "property": s 2(1).

---

67 Other relief from double taxation

(1) (*a*) In this section—

   "foreign tax" means any tax which is chargeable under the laws of any territory outside the State and is of a character similar to estate duty, gift tax or inheritance tax;

   "event" means—

   (i) a death; or

   (ii) any other event,

   by reference to which the date of the gift or the date of the inheritance is determined.

   (*b*) For the purposes of this section, a reference to property situate in a territory outside the State is a reference to property situate in that territory at the date of the gift or the date of the inheritance, as the case may be, or to property representing such property.

(2) Where the Commissioners are satisfied that a taxable gift or taxable inheritance, taken under a disposition by a donee or successor on the happening of any event, is reduced by the payment of foreign tax which is chargeable in connection with the same event under the same disposition in respect of property which is situate in the territory outside the State in which that foreign tax is chargeable, they shall allow a credit in respect of that foreign tax against the gift tax or inheritance tax payable by that donee or successor on that taxable gift or taxable inheritance; but such credit shall not exceed—

   (*a*) the amount of the gift tax or inheritance tax payable in respect of the same property by reason of such property being comprised in any taxable gift or taxable inheritance taken under that disposition on the happening of that event; or

   (*b*) the amount of that foreign tax,

whichever is the lesser.

(3) The provisions of this section shall be subject to any arrangement to which the force of law is given under section 66, and, if any such arrangement provides for the allowance of the amount of a tax payable in a territory outside the State as a credit against gift tax or inheritance tax, the provisions of the arrangement shall apply in relation to the tax payable in that territory in lieu of the provisions of subsection (2).

(4) ...[1]

(5) Where the foreign tax in respect of property comprised in a taxable gift or a taxable inheritance taken under a disposition on the happening of an event is, under the terms of the disposition, directed to be paid out of a taxable gift or a taxable inheritance (taken under that disposition on the happening of the same event) other than the taxable gift or taxable inheritance out of which it would be payable in the absence of such a direction, then, for the purposes of subsection (2), the taxable gift or taxable inheritance out of which the foreign tax would be payable in the absence of such a direction, and no other taxable gift or taxable inheritance, shall be treated as reduced by the payment of the foreign tax.

Amendments

[1]   Subs (4) deleted by FA 1977 s 54(3) and Sch 2 Part IV as regards gifts or inheritances taken on or after 1 June 1977.

Narrative

Capital Acquisitions Tax, Chapter 13.

Definitions

"Commissioners", "date of the gift", "date of the inheritance", "disposition", "donee", "gift", "inheritance", "property", "taxable gift", "taxable inheritance", "successor": s 2(1).

68 Tax, in relation to certain legislation

(1) Inheritance tax shall not be a duty or a death duty for the purposes of section 9 of the Succession Act, 1965, but it shall be a death duty for the purposes of—

    (*a*)   section 34(3) of that Act;

    (*b*)   the definition of pecuniary legacy in section 3(1) of that Act; and

    (*c*)   paragraph 8 of Part II of the First Schedule to that Act.

(2) Section 72 of the Registration of Title Act, 1964, shall apply as if gift tax and inheritance tax were therein mentioned as well as estate duty and succession duty.

Narrative

Capital Acquisitions Tax, Chapter 24.

Definitions

"gift", "inheritance": s 2(1).

69 Extension of certain Acts

(1) Section 1 of the Provisional Collection of Taxes Act, 1927, is hereby amended by the insertion of "and gift tax and inheritance tax" before "but no other tax or duty".

(2) Section 39 of the Inland Revenue Regulation Act, 1890, is hereby amended by the insertion of "gift tax and inheritance tax," before "stamp duties".

Narrative
Capital Acquisitions Tax, Chapter 24.
Definitions
"gift", "inheritance": s 2(1).

70 Delivery, service and evidence of notices and forms, etc

(1) Any notice which under this Act is authorised or required to be given by the Commissioners may be served by post.

(2) A notice or form which is to be served on a person may be either delivered to him or left at his usual or last known place of abode.

[(3) *Prima facie* evidence of any notice given under this Act by the Commissioners or by an officer of the Commissioners may be given in any proceedings by the production of a document purporting—

    (*a*) to be a copy of that notice, or

    (*b*) if the details specified in that notice are contained in an electronic, photographic or other record maintained by the Commissioners, to reproduce those details in so far as they relate to that notice,

and it shall not be necessary to prove the official position of the person by whom the notice purports to be given or, if it is signed, the signature, or that the person signing and giving it was authorised to do so.]¹

(4) In any case where a time limit is specified by or under this Act, other than Part VIII hereof, for the doing of any act required by or under this Act, other than Part VIII hereof, to be done by any person other than the Commissioners, the Commissioners may, in their discretion, extend such time limit.

Amendments

¹   Subs (3) substituted by FA 2002 s 120(1) in relation to evidence of any notice given by the Commissioners or by an officer of the Commissioners in any proceedings on or after 25 March 2002.

Narrative
Capital Acquisitions Tax, Chapter 24.
Definitions
"Commissioners": s 2(1); "person": IA 1937 s 11(*c*).

71 Regulations

(1) The Commissioners shall make such regulations as seem to them to be necessary for the purpose of giving effect to this Act and of enabling them to discharge their functions thereunder.

(2) Every regulation made under this section shall be laid before Dáil Éireann as soon as may be after it is made and, if a resolution annulling the regulation is passed by Dáil Éireann within the next twenty-one days on which Dáil Éireann has sat after the regulation is laid before it, the regulation shall be annulled accordingly, but without prejudice to the validity of anything previously done thereunder.

Narrative
Capital Acquisitions Tax, Chapter 24.

Definitions

"Commissioners", "regulations": s 2(1).

72 Care and management

(1) Tax is hereby placed under the care and management of the Commissioners.

(2) Subject to the direction and control of the Commissioners, any power. function or duty conferred or imposed on the Commissioners by this Act may be exercised or performed on their behalf by an officer of the Commissioners.

Narrative

Capital Acquisitions Tax, Chapter 24.

Definitions

"Commissioners": s 2(1).

FIRST SCHEDULE
Valuation of limited interests

PART I
RULES RELATING TO THE VALUATION OF LIMITED INTERESTS UTILISING TABLES A AND B IN PARTS II AND III OF THIS SCHEDULE

1. The value of an interest for a single life in a capital sum shall be that sum multiplied by the factor, contained in column 3 or 4 respectively of Table A, which is appropriate to the age and sex of the person in respect of the duration of whose life the interest is to be valued.

2. The value of an interest in a capital sum for the joint continuance of two lives shall be the value of an interest in that sum for the older life, ascertained in accordance with rule 1, multiplied by the joint factor in column 2 of Table A which is appropriate to the younger life.

3. The value of an interest in a capital sum for the joint continuance of three or more lives shall be the value of an interest in that sum for the joint continuance of the two oldest of those lives, ascertained in accordance with rule 2, multiplied by the joint factor of the youngest of those lives.

4. The value of an interest in a capital sum for the longer of two lives shall be ascertained by deducting from the total of the values of an interest in that sum for each of those lives, ascertained in accordance with rule 1, the value of an interest in the capital sum for the joint continuance of the same two lives. ascertained in accordance with rule 2.

5. Where an interest is given for the longest of more than two lives, it shall be valued, in accordance with rule 4, as if it were for the longer of the two youngest of those lives.

6. The value of an interest in a capital sum for a period certain shall be the aggregate of—

483

(*a*) the value of the capital sum, multiplied by the factor in Table B which is appropriate to the number of whole years in that period (or zero if that period is less than a whole year); and

(*b*) where the period is not an integral number of years, a fraction (of which the numerator is the number of days in excess of the number of whole years, if any, in that period and the denominator is 365) of the difference between—

(i)   the value of an interest in the capital sum for one year longer than the number of whole years, if any, in the period; and

(ii) the value ascertained under the provisions of paragraph (*a*) (or zero, where so provided in the said paragraph).

7. In the case of a limited interest where the interest is for a life or lives, but is guaranteed for a period certain, the value shall be the higher of—

(*a*) the value of an interest for such life or lives, ascertained in accordance with the appropriate rule in this part of this Schedule; and

(*b*) the value of an interest for the period certain, ascertained in accordance with rule 6.

8. The value of a limited interest for which the other rules in this Part of this Schedule provide no method of valuing shall be ascertained as if the interest taken were a series of absolute interests in the property applied in satisfaction of the interest from time to time, taken as separate gifts or inheritances as the case may be.

Narrative

Capital Acquisitions Tax, Chapter 5.

Definitions

"absolute interest", "gift", "inheritance", "limited interest": s 2(1); "person": IA 1937 s 11(*c*); "property": s 2(1).

PART II

TABLE A

1	2	3	4
Years of age	Joint Factor	Value of an interest in a capital of [€1][1] for a male life aged as in column 1	Value of an interest in a capital of [€1][1] for a female life aged as in column 1
0	.99	.9519	.9624
1	.99	.9767	.9817
2	.99	.9767	.9819
3	.99	.9762	.9817
4	.99	.9753	.9811
5	.99	.9742	.9805
6	.99	.9730	.9797
7	.99	.9717	.9787

1	2	3	4
Years of age	Joint Factor	Value of an interest in a capital of [€1][1] for a male life aged as in column 1	Value of an interest in a capital of [€1][1] for a female life aged as in column 1
8	.99	.9703	.9777
9	.99	.9688	.9765
10	.99	.9671	.9753
11	.98	.9653	.9740
12	.98	.9634	.9726
13	.98	.9614	.9710
14	.98	.9592	.9693
15	.98	.9569	.9676
16	.98	.9546	.9657
17	.98	.9522	.9638
18	.98	.9497	.9617
19	.98	.9471	.9596
20	.97	.9444	.9572
21	.97	.9416	.9547
22	.97	.9387	.9521
23	.97	.9356	.9493
24	.97	.9323	.9464
25	.97	.9288	.9432
26	.97	.9250	9399
27	.97	.9209	.9364
28	.97	.9165	.9328
29	.97	.9119	.9289
30	.96	.9068	.9248
31	.96	.9015	.9205
32	.96	.8958	.9159
33	.96	.8899	.9111
34	.96	.8836	.9059
35	.96	.8770	.9005
36	.96	.8699	.8947
37	.96	.8626	.8886
38	.95	.8549	.8821
39	.95	.8469	.8753
40	.95	.8384	.8683
41	.95	.8296	.8610

1	2	3	4
Years of age	Joint Factor	Value of an interest in a capital of [€1][1] for a male life aged as in column 1	Value of an interest in a capital of [€1][1] for a female life aged as in column 1
42	.95	.8204	.8534
43	.95	.8107	.8454
44	.94	.8005	.8370
45	.94	.7897	.8283
46	.94	.7783	.8192
47	.94	.7663	.8096
48	.93	.7541	.7997
49	.93	.7415	.7896
50	.92	.7287	.7791
51	.91	.7156	.7683
52	.90	.7024	.7572
53	.89	.6887	.7456
54	.89	.6745	.7335
55	.88	.6598	.7206
56	.88	.6445	.7069
57	.88	.6288	.6926
58	.87	.6129	.6778
59	.86	.5969	.6628
60	.86	.5809	.6475
61	.86	.5650	.6320
62	.86	.5492	.6162
63	.85	.5332	.6000
64	.85	.5171	.5830
65	.85	.5007	.5650
66	.85	.4841	.5462
67	.84	.4673	.5266
68	.84	.4506	.5070
69	.84	.4339	.4873
70	.83	.4173	.4679
71	.83	.4009	.4488
72	.82	.3846	.4301
73	.82	.3683	.4114
74	.81	.3519	.3928
75	.80	.3352	.3743

1	2	3	4
Years of age	Joint Factor	Value of an interest in a capital of [€1][1] for a male life aged as in column 1	Value of an interest in a capital of [€1][1] for a female life aged as in column 1
76	.79	.3181	.3559
77	.78	.3009	.3377
78	.76	.2838	.3198
79	.74	.2671	.3023
80	.72	.2509	.2855
81	.71	.2353	.2693
82	.70	.2203	.2538
83	.69	.2057	.2387
84	.68	.1916	.2242
85	.67	.1783	.2104
86	.66	.1657	.1973
87	.65	.1537	.1849
88	.64	.1423	.1730
89	.62	.1315	.1616
90	.60	.1212	.1509
91	.58	.1116	.1407
92	.56	.1025	.1310
93	.54	.0939	.1218
94	.52	.0858	.1132
95	.50	.0781	.1050
96	.49	.0710	.0972
97	.48	.0642	.0898
98	.47	.0578	.0828
99	.45	.0517	.0762
100 or over	.43	.0458	.0698

Amendments

[1]   Substituted by FA 2001 s 240 and Sch 5 Part 5 with effect from 1 January 2002; previously "£1".

PART III
TABLE B

(Column 2 shows the value of an interest in a capital of [€1][1] for the number of years shown in column 1).

1 Number of years	2 Value	3 Number of years	4 Value
1	.0654	26	.8263
2	.1265	27	.8375
3	.1836	28	.8480
4	.2370	29	.8578
5	.2869	30	.8669
6	.3335	31	.8754
7	.3770	32	.8834
8	.4177	33	.8908
9	.4557	34	.8978
10	.4913	35	.9043
11	.5245	36	.9100
12	.5555	37	.9165
13	.5845	38	.9230
14	.6116	39	.9295
15	.6369	40	.9360
16	.6605	41	.9425
17	.6826	42	.9490
18	.7032	43	.9555
19	.7225	44	.9620
20	.7405	45	.9685
21	.7574	46	.9750
22	.7731	47	.9815
23	.7878	48	.9880
24	.8015	49	.9945
25	.8144	50 and over	1.0000

Amendments

[1]   Substituted by FA 2001 s 240 and Sch 5 Part 5 with effect from 1 January 2002; previously "£1".

SECOND SCHEDULE
Computation of tax

PART I
PRELIMINARY

[**1.** In this Schedule—

"group threshold", in relation to a taxable gift or a taxable inheritance taken on a particular day, means—

(*a*) [€381,000][1], where—

    (i)   the donee or successor is on that day the child, or minor child of a deceased child, of the disponer, or

    (ii) the successor is on that day a parent of the disponer and—

        (I)   the interest taken is not a limited interest, and

        (II) the inheritance is taken on the death of the disponer;

(*b*) [€38,100][2], where the donee or successor is on that day, a lineal ancestor, a lineal descendant (other than a child, or a minor child of a deceased child), a brother, a sister, or a child of a brother or of a sister of the disponer:

(*c*) [€19,050][3], where the donee or successor (who is not a spouse of the disponer) does not, on that day, stand to the disponer in a relationship referred to in subparagraph (*a*) or (*b*);

"the consumer price index number", in relation to a year, means the All Items Consumer Price Index Number for that year as compiled by the Central Statistics Office and expressed on the basis that the consumer price index number at mid-November 1996 is 100;

"Table" means the Table contained in Part 11 of this Schedule;

"threshold amount" in relation to the computation of tax on any aggregate of taxable values under paragraph 3, means the group threshold that applies in relation to all of the taxable gifts and taxable inheritances included in that aggregate but, in computing under this Schedule the tax chargeable on a taxable gift or taxable inheritance taken after 31 December 2000, that group threshold shall, for the purposes of this definition, be multiplied by the figure, rounded to the nearest third decimal place, determined by dividing by 104.8 the consumer price index number for the year immediately preceding the year in which that taxable gift or taxable inheritance is taken.

2. In the Table **"Value"** means the appropriate aggregate referred to in paragraph 3.

3. The tax chargeable on the taxable value of a taxable gift or a taxable inheritance (hereafter in this Schedule referred to as the first-mentioned gift or inheritance) taken by a donee or successor shall be of an amount equal to the amount by which the tax computed on aggregate A exceeds the tax computed on aggregate B, where

(*a*) aggregate A is the aggregate of the following:

    (i)   the taxable value of the first-mentioned gift or inheritance, and

(ii)   the taxable value of each and every taxable gift and taxable inheritance taken previously by the said donee or successor on or after [5 December 1991][4], which has the same group threshold as the first-mentioned gift or inheritance,

(b)   aggregate B is the aggregate of the taxable values of all such taxable gifts and taxable inheritances so previously taken which have the same group threshold as the first-mentioned gift or inheritance, and

(c)   the tax on an aggregate is computed at the rate or rates of tax applicable under the Table to that aggregate:

Provided that—

(i)   in a case where no such taxable gift or taxable inheritance was so previously taken, the amount of the tax computed on aggregate B shall be deemed to be nil, and

(ii)   the amount of an aggregate that comprises only a single taxable value shall be equal to that value.

4. In the Table any rate of tax shown in the second column is that applicable to such portion of the value (within the meaning of paragraph 2) as is shown in the first column.

5. For the purposes of this Schedule, all gifts and inheritances which have the same group threshold and which are taken by a donee or successor on the same day shall count as one, and to ascertain the amount of tax payable on one such gift or inheritance of several so taken on the same day, the amount of tax computed under this Schedule as being payable on the total of such gifts and inheritances so taken on that day shall be apportioned rateably, according to the taxable values of the several taxable gifts and taxable inheritances so taken on that day.][5]

8. Where any donee or successor is, at the date of the gift or at the date of the inheritance, the surviving spouse of a deceased person who, at the time of his death, was of nearer relationship than such donee or successor to the disponer, then such donee or successor shall, in the computation of the tax payable on such taxable gift or taxable inheritance, be deemed to bear to the disponer the relationship of that deceased person.

[**9.** (1) In this paragraph—

[**"company"** means a private company which, for the relevant period—

(a)   is a private company controlled by the disponer and of which the disponer is a director, and

(b)   is not a private non-trading company;][6]

...[7]

"control", in relation to a company, shall be construed in accordance with section 16(4)(b);

[**"investment income"**, in relation to a private company, means income which, if the company were an individual, would not be earned income within the meaning of [section 3 of the Taxes Consolidation Act, 1997];[8]][9]

"nominee" has the same meaning as it has in section 16(2);

[**"private company"** has the meaning assigned to it by section 16(2);

"private company controlled by the disponer" means a private company that is under the control of any one or more of the following, that is to say—

(a)   the disponer,

(b)   nominees of the disponer,

(c)   the trustees of a settlement made by the disponer;

"private non-trading company" means a private company—

(a)   whose income (if any) in the twelve months preceding the date at which a share therein is to be valued consisted wholly or mainly of investment income; and

(b)   whose property, on the date referred to in paragraph (a), consisted wholly or mainly of property from which investment income is derived;][10]

[**"relevant period"** means—

(a)   the period of five years ending on the date of the disposition; or

(b)   where, at the date of the disposition,

(i)   an interest in possession in—

(I)   the property referred to in subparagraph (2)(a), or

(II)   the shares referred to in subparagraph (2)(b),

as the case may be, is limited to the disponer under the disposition, and

(ii)   such property is not, or such shares are not, property consisting of the appropriate part of property, within the meaning of section 5(5), on which is charged or secured an annuity or other annual right limited to cease on the death of the disponer,

the period of five years ending on the coming to an end of that interest,

subject, in relation to work, to the exclusion of reasonable periods of annual or sick leave from that period of five years.

(2) For the purpose of computing the tax payable on a gift or inheritance, the donee or successor shall be deemed to bear to the disponer the relationship of a child in any case where the donee or successor is a child of a brother, or a child of a sister, of the disponer and either—

(a)   the donee or successor has worked substantially on a full-time basis for the disponer for the relevant period in carrying on, or in assisting in carrying on, the trade, business or profession of the disponer, and the gift or inheritance consists of property which was used in connection with that business, trade or profession; or

(b)   the donee or successor has worked substantially on a full-time basis for a company for the relevant period in carrying on, or in assisting in carrying on, the trade, business or profession of the company, and the gift or inheritance consists of shares in that company.

(3) Without prejudice to the generality of subparagraph (2), a donee or successor shall not be deemed to be working substantially on a full-time basis for a disponer or a company unless—

    (*a*) where the gift or inheritance consists of property which was used in connection with the business, trade or profession of the disponer, the donee or successor works—

        (i) more than 24 hours a week for the disponer, at a place where that business, trade or profession, is carried on; or

        (ii) more than 15 hours a week for the disponer, at a place where that business, trade or profession is carried on, and such business , trade or profession is carried on exclusively by the disponer, any spouse of the disponer, and the donee or successor;

    or

    (*b*) where the gift or inheritance consists of shares in the company, the donee or successor works—

        (i) more than 24 hours a week for the company, at a place where the business, trade or profession of the company is carried on; or

        (ii) more than 15 hours a week for the company, at a place where the business, trade or profession of the company is carried on, and such business, trade or profession is carried on exclusively by the disponer, any spouse of the disponer, and the donee or successor.

(4) The provisions of this paragraph shall not apply to a gift or inheritance taken by a donee or successor under a discretionary trust.][11]

[**10.** (*a*)In the paragraph **"specified disposition"** means a disposition—

        (i) the date of which is a date prior to the 1st day of April, 1975,

        (ii) in relation to which the disponer is a grandparent of the donee or successor, and

        (iii) in which the marriage of the parents of the donee or successor was, at the date of the disposition, expressed to be the consideration.

    (*b*) Where, on the cesser of a limited interest to which a parent of the donee or successor was entitled in possession, the donee or successor takes a gift or an inheritance under a specified disposition, then, for the purpose of computing the tax payable on the gift or inheritance, the donee or successor shall be deemed to bear to the disponer the relationship of a child.][12]

[**11.** For the purposes of this Schedule, a reference to a gift or an inheritance, or to a taxable gift or a taxable inheritance, includes a reference to a part of a gift or an inheritance, or to a part of a taxable gift or a taxable inheritance, as the case may be.][13]

Amendments

[1]   Substituted by FA 2001 s 240 and Sch 5 Part 5 with effect from 1 January 2002; previously "£300,000".

[2]   Substituted by FA 2001 s 240 and Sch 5 Part 5 with effect from 1 January 2002; previously "£30,000".

[3]   Substituted by FA 2001 s 240 and Sch 5 Part 5 with effect from 1 January 2002; previously "£15,000".

4 Substituted by FA 2002 s 121(1) in relation to gifts or inheritances taken on or after 5 December 2001; previously "2 December 1988".

5 Paras 1-5 substituted for paras 1-7 by FA 2000 s 145(1)(a) for gifts or inheritances taken on or after 1 December 1999.

6 Para 9, definition of "company" substituted by FA 1993 s 130(a) as regards gifts or inheritances taken on or after 24 February 1993.

7 Para 9, definition of "company controlled by the disponer" deleted by FA 1993 s 130(b) as regards gifts or inheritances taken on or after 24 February 1993. Previously

> **"company controlled by the disponer"** means a company that is under the control of any one or more of the following, that is to say—
>
> (*a*) the disponer,
>
> (*b*) nominees of the disponer,
>
> (*c*) the trustees of a settlement made by the disponer;

8 Substituted by TCA 1997 s 1100 and Sch 31; previously "section 2 of the Income Tax Act, 1967".

9 Para 9, definition of "investment income" inserted by FA 1993 s 130(c) as regards gifts or inheritances taken on or after 25 February 1993.

10 Para 9, definitions of "private company", "private company controlled by the disponer" and "private non-trading company" inserted by FA 1993 s 130(d) as regards gifts or inheritances taken on or after 24 February 1993.

11 Para 9, definition of "relevant period" substituted by FA 1989 s 83 as regards gifts or inheritances taken on or after 1 May 1989.

12 Para 10 inserted by FA 1981 s 46(1).

13 Para 11 inserted by FA 1982 s 102(1)(a)(ii) in relation to gifts or inheritances taken on or after 2 June 1982.

Cross-references

Gifts or inheritances taken prior to 1 January 1990, the class thresholds of £150,000, £20,000 and £10,000 (FA 1984 s 111) applied. Thereafter, these thresholds are to be indexed to take account of the effects of inflation, in line with the consumer price index: FA 1990 s 128.

Inheritances taken on or after 2 June 1982, by a parent from his or her child, the £150,000 class threshold (as indexed) applies: FA 1991 s 116.

Discretionary trust once off charge, this schedule does not apply: FA 1984 s 107(*g*).

Discretionary trust annual charge, this schedule does not apply: FA 1986 s 104(*g*).

Double aggregation, relief from, para 7 does not apply: FA 1985 s 61(2).

No interest on refunds of tax arising by virtue of para 10: FA 1981 s 46(2).

Case law

Whether niece worked substantially full time on farm (para 9(2)): *AE v Revenue Commissioners*, Vol V ITR 686.

Statement of practice

Indexation: SP CAT 2/90, 1/91, 1/93, 1/94, 1/96, 1/97, 1/98, 1/99.

Indexation factors

In respect of taxable gifts/inheritances taken in the following years, the index factors to be used are:

1 The Indexed class thresholds since 1994 are:

1990	1.04	} To be
1991	1.076	} applied to
1992	1.109	} the
1993	1.145	} threshold
1994		} amount
(prior to 11 April)	1.160	
1994		} To be
(on or after 11 April)	1.160	} applied to
1995	1.188	} the class
1996	1.217	} threshold
1997	1.237	} To be
1998	1.256	} applied to

1999	1.286	} the class
2000	-	} threshold
2001	1.056	} To be applied to the group threshold
2002	1.108	} To be applied to the group threshold

Indexed class threshold

Class	Relationship for example	1994	1995	1996	1997	1998	1999	2000	2001	2002
A	son/daughter parent*	£174,000	£178,200	£182,550	£185,550	£188,400	£192,900	£300,000	£316,800	€422,148
B	for example niece/ nephew/ brother/sister/ grandchildren	£23,200	£23,760	£24,340	£24,740	£25,120	£25,720	£30,000	£31,680	€42,215
C	for example stranger/ cousins	£11,600	£11,880	£12,170	£12,370	£12,560	£12,860	£15,000	£15,840	€21,108

* In the case of a gift or an inheritance other than an absolute inheritance a parent falls into Class B.

Narrative

Capital Acquisitions Tax, Chapter 8.
Paras 8-10: *Capital Acquisitions Tax*, Chapter 12.

Definitions

"child", "date of the disposition", "date of the gift", "date of the inheritance", "disponer", "disposition", "donee", "gift", "inheritance", "limited interest, "minor child": s 2(1); "person": IA 1937 s 11(c); "property", "taxable gift", "taxable inheritance", "taxable value", "share", "successor": s 2(1).

[PART II]

TABLE

Portion of Value	Rate of tax Per cent
The threshold amount	Nil
The balance	20][1]

Amendments

[1]   Current table of rates substituted by FA 2000 s 145(1)(b) for gifts or inheritances taken on or after 1 December 1999; previously:

"Portion of Value	Rate of tax Per cent
The threshold amount	Nil
The next £10,000	20
The next £30,000	30
The balance	40"

(FA 1994 s 142(1) in relation to gifts and inheritances taken on or after 11 April 1994.)
Previously:

"Portion of Value	Rate of tax

					Per cent
The threshold amount					Nil
The next £10,000	..	..	..		20
The next £40,000	..	..	..		30
The next £50,000	..	..	..		35
The balance	..	..	..		40"

(FA 1991 s 115 as regards gifts or inheritances taken on or after 30 January 1991.)

Previously:

"[Portion of Value

	Rate of tax
	Per cent
The threshold amount	Nil
The next £10,000	20
The next £40,000	30
The next £50,000	35
The next £50,000	40
The next £50,000	45
The balance	55][1]

[1] Substituted by FA 1984 s 111 as regards gifts or inheritances taken on or after 26 March 1984."

Previously.

"[TABLE I

Applicable where the donee or successor is the spouse, child, or minor child of a deceased child, of the disponer

Portion of Value		Rate of tax
Lower limit	Upper limit	Per cent
£		£
0	150,000	Nil
150,000	200,000	25
200,000	250,000	30.
250,000	300,000	35
300,000	350,000	40
350,000	400,000	45
400,000		50

TABLE II

Applicable where the donee or successor is a lineal ancestor or lineal descendant (other than a child, or a minor child of a deceased child) of the disponer

Portion of Value		Rate of tax
Lower limit	Upper limit	Per cent
£	£	£
0	30,000	Nil
30,000	33,000	5
33,000	38,000	7
38,000	48,000	10
48,000	58,000	13
58,000	68,000	16
68,000	78,000	19
78,000	88,000	22
88,000	103,000	25
103,000	118,000	28
118,000	133,000	31

133,000	148,000	34
148,000	163,000	37
163,000	178,000	40
178,000	193,000	43
193,000	208,000	46
208,000	223,000	49
223,000		50

TABLE III

Applicable where the donee or successor is a brother or a sister, or a child or a brother or of a sister, of the disponer

Portion of Value		Rate of tax
Lower limit	Upper limit	Per cent
£	£	£
0	20,000	Nil
20,000	23,000	10
23,000	28,000	12
28,000	38,000	15
38,000	48,000	19
48,000	58,000	23
58,000	68,000	27
68,000	78,000	31
78,000	93,000	35
93,000	108,000	40
108,000	123,000	45
123,000		50

TABLE IV

Applicable where the donee or successor does not stand to the disponer in a relationship referred to in Table I, II or III of this Part of the Schedule.

Portion of Value		Rate of tax
Lower limit	Upper limit	Per cent
£	£	£
0	10,000	Nil
10,000	13,000	20
13,000	18,000	22
18,000	28,000	25
28,000	38,000	30
38,000	48,000	35
48,000	58,000	40
58,000	68,000	45
68,000	83,000	50
83,000	98,000	55
98,000		60][1]

[1]   Substituted by FA 1978 Sch 3."

Previously.

"[TABLE I

Applicable where the donee or successor is the spouse, child, or minor child of a deceased child, of the disponer

Portion of Value		Rate of tax
Lower limit	Upper limit	Per cent

£	£	£
0	150,000	Nil
150,000	200,000	25
200,000	250,000	30
250,000	300,000	35
300,000	350,000	40
350,000	400,000	45
400,000		50

TABLE II

Applicable where the donee or successor is a lineal ancestor or lineal descendant (other than a child, or a minor child of a deceased child) of the disponer.

Portion of Value		Rate of tax
Lower limit	Upper limit	Per cent
£	£	£
0	15,000	Nil
15,000	18,000	5
18,000	23,000	7
23,000	33,000	10
33,000	43,000	13
43,000	53,000	16
53,000	63,000	19
63,000	73,000	22
73,000	88,000	25
88,000	103,000	28
103,000	118,000	31
118,000	133,000	34
133,000	148,000	37
148,000	163,000	40
163,000	178,000	43
178,000	193,000	46
193,000	208,000	49
208,000		50

TABLE III

Applicable where the donee or successor is a brother or a sister, or a child or a brother or of a sister, of the disponer.

Portion of Value		Rate of tax
Lower limit	Upper limit	Per cent
£	£	£
0	10,000	Nil
10,000	13,000	10
13,000	18,000	12
18,000	28,000	15
28,000	38,000	19
38,000	48,000	23
48,000	58,000	27
58,000	68,000	31
68,000	83,000	35
83,000	98,000	40

98,000	113,000	45
113,000		50

TABLE IV

Applicable where the donee or successor does not stand to the disposer in a relationship referred to in Table I, II or III of this Part of the Schedule.

Portion of Value		Rate of tax
Lower limit	Upper limit	Per cent
£	£	£
0	5,000	Nil
5,000	8,000	20
8,000	13,000	22
13,000	23,000	25
23,000	33,000	30
33,000	43,000	35
43,000	53,000	40
53,000	63,000	45
63,000	78,000	50
78,000	93,000	55
93,000		60]"

Statement of practice

Gifts and inheritances taken on or after 26 March 1984: Computation of tax, aggregation and indexation: SP CAT 2/90; SP CAT 1/91.

FINANCE ACT 1976

(1976 Number 16)
(Date of passing: 27 May 1976)

ARRANGEMENT OF SECTIONS

PART I

INCOME TAX, SUR-TAX, CORPORATION PROFITS TAX, CORPORATION TAX AND CAPITAL GAINS TAX

CHAPTER VI
Section

PART VI

MISCELLANEOUS

PART I
CHAPTER VI

29 Interest on unpaid wealth tax and capital acquisitions tax

Interest payable under section 18 of the Wealth Tax Act, 1975, or section 41 of the Capital Acquisitions Tax Act, 1976, shall not be allowed in computing any income, profits or losses for any of the purposes of the Tax Acts or of any of the enactments relating to corporation profits tax.

Definition

"the Tax Acts": CTA 1976 s 155(2).

---

34 Inspection of documents and records

[(1) In this section—

"authorised officer" means an officer of the Revenue Commissioners authorised by them in writing to exercise the powers conferred by this section;

"property" means any asset relating to a tax liability;

"records" means any document, or any other written or printed material in any form including any information stored, maintained or preserved by means of any mechanical or electronic device, whether or not stored, maintained or preserved in a legible form, which a person is obliged by any provision relating to tax to keep, to retain, to issue, to produce for inspection or which may be inspected under any provision relating to tax;

"tax" means any tax, duty, levy or charge under the care and management of the Revenue Commissioners;

"tax liability" means any existing liability to tax or further liability to tax which may be established by an authorised officer following the exercise or performance of his powers or duties under this section.

(2) (*a*) An authorised officer may at all reasonable times enter any premises or place where he has reason to believe that—

    (i) any trade or profession or other activity, the profits or gains of which are chargeable to tax, is or has been carried on,

    (ii) anything is or has been done in connection with any trade, profession or other activity the profits or gains of which are chargeable to tax,

    (iii) any records relating to—

        (I) any trade, profession, other source of profits or gains or chargeable gains,

        (II) any tax liability, or

        (III) any repayments of tax in regard to any person are or may be kept,

      or

    (iv) any property is or has been located,

  and may

    (A) require any person who is on those premises or in that place, other than a person who is there to purchase goods or to receive a service, to produce any records or property,

    (B) if he has reason to believe that any of the records or property which he has required to be produced to him under the provisions of this subsection have not been produced, search on those premises or in that place for those records or property,

    (C) examine any records or property and take copies of or extracts from any records,

    (D) remove any records and retain them for a reasonable time for the purposes of their further examination or for the purposes of any legal proceedings instituted by an officer of the Revenue Commissioners, or for the purposes of any criminal proceedings, and

    (E) examine property listed in any records.

(*b*) An authorised officer, may in the exercise or performance of his powers or duties under this section, require any person, whom he has reason to believe—

    (i) is or was carrying on any trade, profession or other activity the profits or gains of which are chargeable to tax,

    (ii) is or was liable to any tax, or

    (iii) has information relating to any tax liability,

to give the authorised officer all reasonable assistance including providing information and explanations or furnishing documents and making available for inspection property as required by the authorised officer in relation to any tax liability or any repayment of tax in regard to any person.

(*c*) Nothing in this subsection shall be construed as requiring any person carrying on a profession, or any person employed by any person carrying on a profession, to produce to an authorised officer any documents relating to a client, other than such documents—

   (i) as pertain to the payment of fees to the person carrying on the profession or to other financial transactions of the person carrying on the profession,

   (ii) as are otherwise material to the tax liability of the person carrying on the profession, or

   (iii) as are already required to be provided following a request issued under the provisions of section 16 (inserted by section 101 of the Finance Act, 1991) of the Stamp Act, 1891,

and, in particular, he shall not be required to disclose any information or professional advice of a confidential nature given to a client.

(*d*) This subsection shall not apply to any premises or place where a banking business, within the meaning of the Central Bank Act, 1971, is carried on or to any person, or an employee of any person, carrying on such a business.

(*e*) (i) An authorised officer shall not, without the consent of the occupier, enter any premises, or that portion of any premises, which is occupied wholly and exclusively as a private residence, except on production by such officer of a warrant issued by a Judge of the District Court expressly authorising the authorised officer to so enter.

   (ii) A judge of the District Court may issue a warrant under subparagraph (i), if satisfied by information on oath that it is proper for him to do so for the purposes of this section.

(3) A person who does not comply with any requirement of an authorised officer in the exercise or performance of his powers or duties under this section shall be liable to a penalty of £1,000.

(4) An authorised officer, when exercising or performing his powers or duties under this section, shall on request show his authorisation for the purposes of this section.][1]

Amendments

[1]   Substituted by FA 1992 s 232.

Cross-references

Subs (2): tax defaulters, publication of names: FA 1983 s 23; Revenue offences, penalties: FA 1983 s 93.

PART VI
MISCELLANEOUS

81 Repeals

(1) The enactment mentioned in column (2) of Part I of the Fifth Schedule to this Act is hereby repealed to the extent specified in column (3) of that Schedule.

(2) The enactment mentioned in column (2) of Part II of the Fifth Schedule to this Act is hereby repealed to the extent specified in column (3) of that Schedule.

(3) (*a*) Subsection (1) of this section shall be deemed to have come into operation on the 6th day of April, 1976.

    (*b*) Subsection (2) of this section shall be deemed to have come into operation on the 1st day of March, 1976.

82 Care and management of taxes and duties

All taxes and duties (except the excise duties on mechanically propelled vehicles) imposed by this Act are hereby placed under the care and management of the Revenue Commissioners.

83 Short title, construction and commencement

(1) This Act may be cited as the Finance Act, 1976.

...

(4) Part III of this Act shall be construed together with the Stamp Act 1891 and the enactments amending or extending that Act.

...

(7) Any reference in this Act to any other enactment shall, except so far as the context otherwise requires, be construed as a reference to that enactment as amended by or under any other enactment including this Act.

FINANCE ACT 1978

(1978 Number 21)
(Date of passing: 5 July 1978)

ARRANGEMENT OF SECTIONS

PART VI
CAPITAL ACQUISITIONS TAX

39 Extension of section 55 (exemption of certain objects) of Capital Acquisitions Tax Act, 1976

(1) Section 55 of the Capital Acquisitions Tax Act, 1976, shall apply, as it applies to the objects specified therein, to a house or garden that is situated in the State and is not held for the purpose of trading and—

    (*a*)   which, on a claim being made to the Commissioners, appears to them to be of national, scientific, historic or artistic interest,

    (*b*)   in respect of which reasonable facilities for viewing were allowed to members of the public from the date of the passing of this Act to the date of the gift or the date of the inheritance, or during the three years immediately before the date of the gift or the date of the inheritance, and

    (*c*)   in respect of which reasonable facilities for viewing are allowed to members of the public,

with the modification that the reference in subsection (4) of that section to subsection (1)(*b*) or (*c*) of that section shall be construed as a reference to paragraph (*c*) of this subsection and with any other necessary modifications.

[(1A) Without prejudice to the generality of subsection (1), the provision of facilities for the viewing by members of the public of a house or garden shall not be regarded as reasonable in relation to any year, which is the year 1997 or any subsequent year and which is taken into account for the purposes of paragraphs (*b*) and (*c*) of subsection (1), unless—

503

(a) Bord Fáilte Éireann (hereinafter in this section referred to as **"the Board"**) has, as regards the year 1997, on or before the 1st day of July, 1997, and, as regards any subsequent year, on or before the 1st day of January in that year, been provided with particulars of—

   (i) the name, if any, and address of the house or garden, and

   (ii) the days and times during the year when access to the house or garden is afforded to the public and the price, if any, payable for such access, and

(b) in the opinion of the Commissioners—

   (i) subject to such temporary closure necessary for the purpose of the repair, maintenance or restoration of the house or garden as is reasonable, access to the house or garden is afforded for not less than 60 days (including not less than 40 days during the period commencing on the 1st day of May and ending on the 30th day of September [of which not less than 10 of the days during that period shall fall on a Saturday or a Sunday or both])[1] in that year;

   (ii) on each day on which access to the house or garden is afforded, the access is afforded in a reasonable manner and at reasonable times for a period, or periods in the aggregate, of not less than four hours;

   (iii) access to the whole or to a substantial part of the house or garden is afforded at the same time; and

   (iv) the price, if any, paid by members of the public in return for that access is reasonable in amount and does not operate to preclude members of the public from seeking access to the house or garden.][2]

(2) This section shall apply where the date of the gift or the date of the inheritance is on or after the date of passing of this Act.

Amendments

[1]   Inserted by FA 2000 s 146 for gifts and inheritances taken on or after 10 February 2000.

[2]   Subs (1A) inserted by FA 1997 s 137(1) in relation to gifts or inheritances taken on or after 1 February 1987.

The Capital Acquitions Tax (Houses and Gardens) Regulations 1987 (SI No 28 of 1987) are revoked with effect from 1 January 1997 and substituted by FA 1997 s 137 with effect from 1 February 1987.

Definitions

"Commissioners": SA 1891 s 122(1); CATA 1976 s 2(1); "date of the gift", "date of the inheritance", "inheritance", "gift": CATA 1976 s 2(1).

Cross-references

Heritage property of companies, "relevant heritage property" means objects to which this section applies: FA 1995 s 166(1); breach of conditions specified in subs (1)(c): FA 1995 s 166(6)(b).

Note

This section, by extending CATA 1976 s 55, granted exemption from gift or inheritance tax where the gift or inheritance consists of a house or garden of national, scientific, historic or artistic interest.

Narrative

Capital Acquisitions Tax, Chapter 11.

40 Amendment of section 57 (exemption of certain securities) of Capital Acquisitions Tax Act, 1976

Note

This section amended CATA 1976 s 57(2)-(3) and is incorporated in that section.

It provides that after 14 April 1978, securities issued by the State or semi State bodies etc with a condition that they are to be exempt from capital taxation when held by a person who is not resident or domiciled in the State, will only qualify for relief in the hands of a donee or successor (who is thus non resident and non domiciled) if the disponer has held the securities for at least three years before the date of the disposition under which the gift or inheritance is taken. A similar restriction applies to units in a unit trust scheme (within the Unit Trusts Acts 1972) if the underlying investments of the scheme consist of such State or semi State securities. Previously, the requirement was that the donee or successor retain the security for one year. There were no requirements on the disponer.

41 Alteration of rates of tax

Note

This section, by substituting CATA 1976 Sch 2 Part II, provided new rates of tax.

42 Amendment of section 36 (delivery or returns) of Capital Acquisitions Tax Act, 1976

Note

This section, by substituting CATA 1976 s 36(3) with effect from 31 March 1976, imposed an obligation to furnish the necessary gift or inheritance tax return where a gift or inheritance (or the combined value of all aggregable gifts and/or inheritances) exceeded 80% of the lowest applicable taxable value. CATA 1976 s 36(3) was subsequently repealed by FA 1982 s 101.

43 Amendment of section 41 (payment of tax and interest on tax) of Capital Acquisitions Tax Act, 1976

Note

This section, by substituting "1.25 per cent." for "one and one-half per cent." in CATA 1976 s 41(2), provided that after 4 July 1978, the rate of interest on unpaid capital acquisitions tax is 1.25% per month or part of a month, instead of the earlier 1.5%.

44 Amendment of section 53 (exemption of small gifts) of Capital Acquisitions Tax Act, 1976

Note

This section by substituting "£500" for "£250" in CATA 1976 s 53(1) for relevant periods ending on or after 31 December 1978, provided an increased annual small gifts exemption.

PART VII
MISCELLANEOUS

54 Short title, construction and commencement

(1) This Act may be cited as the Finance Act, 1978.

....

(3) Part III of this Act shall be construed together with the Stamp Act, 1891, and the enactments amending or extending that Act.

....

(7) Part V of this Act shall be construed together with the Capital Acquisitions Tax Act, 1976, and the enactments amending or extending that Act.

....

THIRD SCHEDULE
Rates of capital acquisitions tax

Note

This Schedule substituted Capital Acquisitions Act, 1976, Sch 2 Part II.

FINANCE ACT 1980

(1980 Number 14)
(Date of passing: 25 June 1980)

ARRANGEMENT OF SECTIONS

PART IV
CAPITAL ACQUISITIONS TAX

PART VI
MISCELLANEOUS

PART IV
CAPITAL ACQUISITIONS TAX

83 Amendment of section 19 of Capital Acquisitions Tax Act, 1976

Note

This section, by amending CATA 1976 s 19, increased the maximum deduction allowable in computing the "agricultural value" of property to £150,000 (from £100,000) as respects a gift or inheritance taken on or after 1 April 1980. The limit was subsequently increased to £200,000 by FA 1982 s 100.

84 Amendment of section 35 of Capital Acquisitions Tax Act, 1976

Note

CATA 1976 s 35(7) provided that a secondarily accountable person could recover any tax he had paid from a primarily accountable person. This section, by extending CATA 1976 s 35(7), restricts that right of recovery to primarily accountable persons who have taken an absolute interest in a benefit.

PART VI
MISCELLANEOUS

95 Care and management of taxes and duties

All taxes and duties imposed by this Act are hereby placed under the care and management of the Revenue Commissioners.

96 Short title, construction and commencement

(1) This Act may be cited as the Finance Act, 1980.

...

(8) Any reference in this Act to any other enactment shall, except so far as the context otherwise requires, be construed as a reference to that enactment as amended by or under any other enactment including this Act.

FINANCE ACT 1981

(1981 Number 16)
(Date of passing: 28 May 1981)

ARRANGEMENT OF SECTIONS

PART IV
CAPITAL ACQUISITIONS TAX

PART IV
CAPITAL ACQUISITIONS TAX

46 Relief in respect of certain marriage settlements

(1)...

(2) Notwithstanding the provisions of section 46 of the Capital Acquisitions Tax Act, 1976, interest shall not be payable on any repayment of tax which arises by virtue of this section where such tax was paid prior to the date of the passing of this Act.

Amendments

Subs (1) inserted CATA 1976 Sch 2 Pt 1 para 10. As regards certain marriage settlements drawn up before 1 April 1975, after the cesser of a limited interest by a parent of a donee or successor, the person taking the benefit is a grandchild of the disponer of the settlement. In such circumstances, the grandchild will be regarded as a child of the disponer, for capital acquisitions tax purposes.

PART VI
MISCELLANEOUS

52 Disclosure of information to the Ombudsman

Any obligation to maintain secrecy or other restriction upon the disclosure or production of information (including documents) obtained by or furnished to the Revenue Commissioners, or any person on their behalf, for taxation purposes, shall not apply to the disclosure or production of information (including documents) to the Ombudsman for the purposes of an examination or investigation by the Ombudsman, under the Ombudsman Act, 1980, of any action (within the meaning of the Ombudsman Act, 1980) taken by or on behalf of the Revenue Commissioners, being such an action taken in the performance of administrative functions in respect of any tax or duty under the care and management of the Revenue Commissioners.

53 Care and management of taxes and duties

All taxes and duties imposed by this Act are hereby placed under the care and management of the Revenue Commissioners.

54 Short title, construction and commencement

(1) This Act may be cited as the Finance Act, 1981.

...

(5) Part IV of this Act shall be construed together with the Capital Acquisitions Tax Act, 1976, and the enactments amending or extending that Act.

...

(8) Any reference in this Act to any other enactment shall, except so far as the context otherwise requires, be construed as a reference to that enactment as amended by or under any other enactment including this Act.

FINANCE ACT 1982

(1982 Number 14)
(Date of passing: 17 July 1982)

ARRANGEMENT OF SECTIONS

PART V
CAPITAL ACQUISITIONS TAX

PART VI
MISCELLANEOUS

PART V
CAPITAL ACQUISITIONS TAX

97 Interpretation

In this Part **"the Principal Act"** means the Capital Acquisitions Tax Act, 1976.

98 Exemption of certain benefits

Where a gift or an inheritance is taken, by direction of the disponer, free of tax on or after the date of the passing of this Act, the benefit taken shall be deemed to include the amount of tax chargeable on such gift or inheritance but not the amount of tax chargeable on such tax.

Notes

CATA 1976 s 65 provides that a reference in a deed or will to a benefit free of death duties is to be construed as a benefit free of inheritance tax. There is no exemption available for the tax included in the tax free benefit taken by a successor. This section simplifies the position for benefits taken on or after 17 July 1982 by providing that tax (A) is first calculated on the taxable value of the aggregated sums in the normal way; the liability figure (B) is added to the earlier aggregated figure (B). The revised gross figure (A + B) is charged to tax. The problem in determining the ultimate value of tax-free benefits persists where a successor takes a share of the *residue* of an estate together with a further benefit on a tax-free basis or on unequal share of residue on a tax free basis.

Narrative

Capital Acquisitions Tax, Chapter 24.

Definitions

"benefit", "disponer", "gift", "inheritance": CATA 1976 s 2(1).

---

99 Amendment of section 5 (gift deemed to be taken) of Principal Act

---

Note

This section deleted ", before the 28th day of February, 1974," and "prior to the 28th day of February, 1974" from CATA 1976 s 5(6) with effect from 2 June 1982. CATA 1976 s 5(6) still provides, for later periods, that a future right to a gift (under a contract) that cannot be transferred or taken into possession until the contract is completed is to be taxable at the time transfer is made or the possession is taken.

100 Amendment of section 19 (value of agricultural property) of Principal Act

Note

This section, by amending CATA 1976 s 19, increased the maximum deduction allowable in computing the "agricultural value" of property to £200,000 (from £150,000) as respects a gift or inheritance taken on or after 1 April 1982. The limit was previously increased to £150,000 by FA 1980 s 83.

101 Amendment of section 36 (delivery of returns) of Principal Act

Note

This section, by substituting CATA 1976 s 36(3) with effect from 2 June 1982, repeals the effect of FA 1978 s 42 which had previously replaced CATA 1976 s 36(3). The revised wording was required because of the new aggregation procedures to be introduced by s 102 below.

The revised wording provides that a gift or inheritance tax return must be furnished where a taxable gift or inheritance, aggregated as necessary with any other taxable gifts or inheritances received from the same disponer, exceeds 80% of the value at which tax becomes chargeable.

102 Amendment of Second Schedule to Principal Act

Note

This section by substituting CATA 1976 Sch 2 paras 3, 4, 7 and inserting "or disponers" after "disponer" in CATA 1976 Sch 2 Pt I para 1 and Pt II, provides a new structure for computing tax.

Under CATA 1976 as enacted, aggregation of taxable gifts (taken on or after 28 February 1969) and taxable inheritances (taken on or after 1 April 1975) only applied to gifts or inheritances taken from the same disponer.

The new computation method, effective for gifts or inheritances taken on or after 2 June 1982, provides for aggregation of benefits taken from the same Table of Charge in CATA 1976 Sch 2.

Taxable gifts or inheritances taken before 2 June 1982 are not to be aggregated.

PART VI
MISCELLANEOUS

104 Care and management of taxes and duties

All taxes and duties imposed by this Act are hereby placed under the care and management of the Revenue Commissioners.

105 Short title, construction and commencement

(1) This Act may be cited as the Finance Act, 1982.

....

(5) Part IV of this Act shall be construed together with the Capital Acquisitions Tax Act, 1976, and the enactments amending or extending that Act.

(6) Part V of this Act shall construed together with the Capital Acquisitions Tax Act, 1976, and the enactments amending or extending that Act.

....

FINANCE ACT 1983

(1983 Number 15)
(Date of passing: 8 June 1983)

ARRANGEMENT OF SECTIONS

PART V
REVENUE OFFENCES

PART VII
MISCELLANEOUS

PART V
REVENUE OFFENCES

94 Revenue offences

(1) In this Part —

"the Acts" means —

(a)   the Customs Acts,

(b)   the statutes relating to the duties of excise and to the management of those duties,

(c)   the Tax Acts,

(d)   the Capital Gains Tax Acts,

(e)   the Value-Added Tax Act, 1972, and the enactments amending or extending that Act,

(f)   the Capital Acquisitions Tax Act, 1976, and the enactments amending or extending that Act,

(g)   the statutes relating to stamp duty and to the management of that duty, and

(h)   Part VI,

and any instruments made thereunder and any instruments made under any other enactment and relating to tax;

[**"an authorised officer"** means an officer of the Revenue Commissioners authorised by them in writing to exercise any of the powers conferred by the Acts;][1]

"tax" means any tax, duty, levy or charge under the care and management of the Revenue Commissioners.

(2) A person shall, without prejudice to any other penalty to which he may be liable, be guilty of an offence under this section if, after the date of the passing of this Act, he —

513

(a) knowingly or wilfully delivers any incorrect return, statement or accounts or knowingly or wilfully furnishes any incorrect information in connection with any tax,

(b) knowingly aids, abets, assists, incites or induces another person to make or deliver knowingly or wilfully any incorrect return, statement or accounts in connection with any tax,

(c) claims or obtains relief or exemption from, or repayment of, any tax, being a relief, exemption or repayment to which, to his knowledge, he is not entitled,

(d) knowingly or wilfully issues or produces any incorrect invoice, receipt, instrument or other document in connection with any tax,

[(dd) (i) fails to make any deduction required to be made by him under section 32(1) of the Finance Act, 1986,

(ii) fails, having made the deduction, to pay the sum deducted to the Collector-General within the time specified in that behalf in section 33(3) of that Act, or

(iii) fails to pay to the Collector-General an amount on account of appropriate tax (within the meaning of Chapter IV of Part I of that Act) within the time specified in that behalf in section 33(4) of that Act,]²

[(ddd) (i) fails to make any deduction required to be made by him under section 18(5) of the Finance Act, 1989, or

(ii) fails, having made the deduction, to pay the sum deducted to the Collector-General within the time specified in paragraph 1(3) of the First Schedule to that Act]²,

(e) knowingly or wilfully fails to comply with any provision of the Acts requiring—

(i) the furnishing of a return of income, profits or gains, or of sources of income, profits or gains, for the purposes of any tax,

(ii) the furnishing of any other return, certificate, notification, particulars, or any statement or evidence, for the purposes of any tax,

(iii) the keeping or retention of books, records, accounts or other documents for the purposes of any tax, or

(iv) the production of books, records, accounts or other documents, when so requested, for the purposes of any tax,

[(ee) knowingly or wilfully, and within the time limits specified for their retention, destroys, defaces, or conceals from an authorised officer—

(i) any documents, or

(ii) any other written or printed material in any form, including any information stored, maintained or preserved by means of any mechanical or electronic device, whether or not stored, maintained or preserved in a legible form, which a person is obliged by any provision of the Acts to keep, to issue or to produce for inspection,]⁴

(f) fails to remit any income tax payable pursuant to Chapter IV of Part V of the Income Tax Act, 1967, and the regulations thereunder, or section 7 of the Finance Act, 1968, and the said regulations, or value-added tax within the time specified in that behalf in relation to income tax or value-added tax, as the case may be, by the Acts, or

(g) obstructs or interferes with any officer of the Revenue Commissioners, or any other person, in the exercise or performance of powers or duties under the Acts for the purposes of any tax.

(3) A person guilty of an offence under this section shall be liable —

[(a) on summary conviction to a fine of £1,000 which may be mitigated to not less than one fourth part thereof or, at the discretion of the court, to imprisonment for a term not exceeding 12 months or to both the fine and the imprisonment, or][5]

(b) on conviction on indictment, to a fine not exceeding £10,000 or, at the discretion of the court, to imprisonment for a term not exceeding 5 years or to both the fine and the imprisonment.

(4) Section 13 of the Criminal Procedure Act, 1967, shall apply in relation to an offence under this section as if, in lieu of the penalties specified in subsection (3) of the said section 13, there were specified therein the penalties provided for by subsection (3) (a) of this section, and the reference in subsection (2)(a) of the said section 13 to the penalties provided for in the said subsection (3) shall be construed and have effect accordingly.

(5) Where an offence under this section is committed by a body corporate and the offence is shown to have been committed with the consent or connivance of any person who, when the offence was committed, was a director, manager, secretary or other officer of the body corporate, or a member of the committee of management or other controlling authority of the body corporate, that person shall also be deemed to be guilty of the offence and may be proceeded against and punished accordingly.

(6) In any proceedings under this section, a return or statement delivered to an inspector or other officer of the Revenue Commissioners under any provision of the Acts and purporting to be signed by any person shall be deemed, until the contrary is proved, to have been so delivered, and to have been signed, by that person.

(7) Notwithstanding the provisions of any other enactment, proceedings in respect of an offence under this section may be instituted within 10 years from the date of the commission of the offence or incurring of the penalty (as the case may be).

(8) Section 1 of the Probation of Offenders Act, 1907, shall not apply in relation to offences under this section.

(9) The provisions of section 128(4), 500(4), 501(3), 502(3), 506 and 507 of the Income Tax Act, 1967, and sections 26(6) and 27(7) of the Value-Added Tax Act, 1972, shall, with any necessary modifications, apply for the purposes of this section as they apply for the purposes of those provisions, including, in the case of such of those provisions as were applied by the Capital Gains Tax Act, 1975, the Corporation Tax Act, 1976, or Part VI, the purposes of those provisions as so applied.

Amendments

[1]   Definition inserted by FA 1992 s 243(a)(i).

[2]   Subs (2)(dd) inserted by FA 1986 s 40(2).

3   Subs (2)(*ddd*) inserted by FA 1989 Sch 1 para 3(2).

4   Subs (2)(*ee*) inserted by FA 1996s 132(1) and Sch 5 Pt I para 13.

5   Subs (3)(*a*) substituted by FA 1992 s 243(*b*).

Cross-references

Stamp duty, incorrect certificates: FA 1969 s 49(2B); FA 1997 s 122.

Case law

Meaning of "criminal matter": *Director of Public Prosecutions v Seamus Boyle*, HC, 6 May 1992, IV ITR 395. Subs (2)(*e*): District Justice not entitled to conclude, on basis of Revenue certificate, that taxpayer had "knowingly and wilfully" failed to submit return of income; taxpayer not present at District Court hearing and was entitled to defend himself: *O'Callaghan v Clifford and others,* SC, 1 April 1993.

Narrative

Capital Acquisitions Tax, Chapter 22.

Definition

"inspector": CGTA 1975 s 2(1), ITA 1967 ss 1(1), 161; "month": IA 1937 Sch; "profits": CTA 1976 s 1(5)(*c*); "statute": IA 1937 s 3, ITA 1967 s 1(1); "the Tax Acts": CTA 1976 s 155(2).

PART VII
MISCELLANEOUS

121 Care and management of taxes and duties

All taxes and duties imposed by this Act (apart from income levy collectible by health boards) are hereby placed under the care and management of the Revenue Commissioners.

122 Short title, construction and commencement

(1) This Act may be cited as the Finance Act, 1983.

...

(5) Part IV and (so far as relating to stamp duty) Parts I and V shall be construed together with that statutes which relate to stamp duty and to the management of that duty.

...

(8) Any reference in this Act to any other enactment shall, except so far as the context otherwise requires, be construed as a reference to that enactment as amended by or under any other enactment including this Act.

(9) In this Act, a reference to a Part, section or schedule is to a Part or section of, or schedule to, this Act, unless it is indicated that reference to some other enactment is intended.

(10) In this Act, a reference to a subsection, paragraph or subparagraph is to the subsection, paragraph or subparagraph of the provision (including a schedule) in which the reference occurs, unless it is indicated that reference to some other provision is intended.

FINANCE ACT 1984

(1984 Number 9)
(Date of passing: 23 May 1984)

ARRANGEMENT OF SECTIONS

PART V
CAPITAL ACQUISITIONS TAX

CHAPTER I
Discretionary trusts

CHAPTER II
Revised computation

CHAPTER III
Certificate of discharge

PART VI
MISCELLANEOUS

PART V
CAPITAL ACQUISITIONS TAX

CHAPTER I
Discretionary trusts

104 Interpretation (Part V)

In this Part—

"the Principal Act" means the Capital Acquisitions Tax Act, 1976;

"object", in relation to a discretionary trust, means a person for whose benefit the income or capital, or any part of the income or capital, of the trust property is applied, or may be applied;

"principal objects", in relation to a discretionary trust, means such objects, if any, of the trust for the time being as are—

    (*a*)   the spouse of the disponer,

    (*b*)   the children of the disponer, or

    (*c*)   the children of a child of the disponer where such child predeceased the disponer.

Note

This Chapter (ss 104 to 109) imposes a once off 3% charge on the chargeable value of discretionary trusts in existence on or after 25 January 1984. Exempt (see s 108) are:

    (*a*)   Trusts where any of the principal objects of the trust (spouse of disponer, child of disponer, or child of a deceased child of the disponer) are under 21 years of age. A liability arises once this condition ceases to be satisfied.

    (*b*)   Trusts created for public or charitable purposes in the State or Northern Ireland.

    (*c*)   Revenue-approved pension scheme trusts.

    (*d*)   Trusts operative for the purposes of a units scheme within the meaning of the Unit Trust Act 1972.

    (*e*)   Trusts which came into existence to assist one or more incapacitated individuals.

    (*f*)   Trusts where the proceeds are used for the upkeep of an approved stately home or garden (see FA 1978 s 39).

Cross-references

Discretionary trust annual charge, object, principal objects, meaning applied: FA 1986 s 102.

Heritage property of companies, relevant business property: FA 1995 s 166(4).

Probate tax, discretionary trust inheritance deemed to be taken after, unless exempted (CATA 1976 s 55(3)- (4)): FA 1993 s 110(2).

Case law

The discretion of trustees under a discretionary trust to appoint the trust funds to beneficiaries is absolute, *In the matter of the Trustee Act 1893 s 36 and others*, HC, 24 July 1991.

Narrative

Capital Acquisitions Tax, Chapter 17.

Definitions

"benefit", "child", "discretionary trust", "disponer": CATA 1976 s 2(1); "person": IA 1937 s 11(*c*); "property": CATA 1976 s 2(1).

---

105 Amendment of section 2 (interpretation) of Principal Act

Note

This section extended CATA 1976 s 2(1) definition of "discretionary trust". The additional wording provides that a trust where the income is accumulated (other than in respect of a property where a person is beneficially entitled in possession) is a discretionary trust for capital acquisitions tax purposes. The earlier definition only applied to trusts where the trustees had power to accumulate.

---

106 Acquisitions by discretionary trusts

(1) Where, on or after the 25th day of January, 1984, under or in consequence of any disposition, property becomes subject to a discretionary trust (which expression has in this Part the meaning assigned to it by the Principal Act as amended by section 105) ...¹, the trust shall be deemed, on—

(a) the date on which that property becomes or became subject to the discretionary trust;

(b) the date of death of the disponer; or

(c) where there are principal objects of the trust, the date on which there ceases to be a principal object of the trust who is under the age of [21 years][2],

whichever date is the latest, to become or to have become beneficially entitled in possession to an absolute interest in so much, if any, of that property or of property representing that property and of accumulations of income thereof or of property representing those accumulations as remains subject to the discretionary trust on that latest date, and to take or to have taken an inheritance accordingly as if the trust, and the trustees as such for the time being of the trust, were together a person for the purposes of the Principal Act, and that latest date shall be the date of the inheritance.

(2) Property which, under or in consequence of any disposition, was subject to a discretionary trust on the 25th day of January, 1984, shall, for the purposes of subsection (1), be deemed to have become subject to the trust on that date.

[(2A) Property which, under or in consequence of any disposition, is subject to a discretionary trust on the 31st day of January, 1993, shall, for the purposes of subsection (1), be deemed to become subject to the trust on that date.][3]

(3) For the purposes of this section—

(a) an interest in expectancy shall not be property until an event happens whereby the interest ceases to be an interest in expectancy or is represented by property which is not an interest in expectancy;

(b) an interest in a policy of assurance upon human life shall not be property until, and then only to the extent that, the interest becomes an interest in possession under the provisions of section 32 of the Principal Act or is represented by property which is not an interest in expectancy.

(4) Where, apart from this subsection, property or property representing such property would be chargeable under this section with tax more than once under the same disposition, such property shall be so chargeable with tax once only, that is to say, on the earliest occasion on which such property becomes so chargeable with tax.

Amendments

[1] Deleted by FA 1985 s 64.

[2] Substituted by FA 1992 s 224(1)(a) as regards any property which becomes subject to a discretionary trust on or after 31 January 1993; previously "25 years".

[3] Subs (2A) inserted by FA 1992 s 224(1)(b).

Cross-references

Business relief, applies to gifts or inheritances taken on or after 11 April 1994, but not inheritances taken by virtue of subs (1) above: FA 1994 s 125.

Computation: s 109.

Discretionary trust annual charge, no double charge in same year: FA 1986 s 103(4).

Exemptions: s 108.

Increase to 6%, a relevant inheritance is an inheritance which on or after 11 April 1994 is deemed to be taken by virtue of subs (1): FA 1994 s 143(1).

Narrative

Capital Acquisitions Tax, Chapter 17.

Definitions

"absolute interest", "date of the inheritance", "discretionary trust", "disponer", "disposition", "entitled in possession", "inheritance", "interest in expectancy": CATA 1976 s 2(1); "money": SA 1891 s 122(1); "property": CATA 1976 s 2(1).

107 Application of Principal Act

In relation to a charge for tax arising by reason of the provisions of section 106—

[(a) a reference in section 16 of the Principal Act to a company controlled by the successor and the definition in that section of "group of shares" shall be construed as if (for the purpose of that reference) the list of persons contained in subsection (3) of that section and (for the purpose of that definition) the list of persons contained in that definition included the following, that is to say, the trustees of the discretionary trust, the living objects of the discretionary trust, the relatives of those objects, nominees of those trustees or of those objects or of the relatives of those objects, and the trustees of a settlement whose objects include the living objects of the discretionary trust or relatives of those living objects;][1]

(b) section 21 of the Principal Act shall apply, with the modification that the valuation date of the taxable inheritance shall be—

   (i) the date of the inheritance, or

  (ii) the valuation date ascertained in accordance with that section,

whichever is the later, and with any other necessary modifications;

(c) a person who is a trustee of the discretionary trust concerned for the time being at the date of the inheritance or at any date subsequent thereto shall be a person primarily accountable for the payment of the tax;

(d) an object of the discretionary trust concerned to whom or for whose benefit any of the property subject to the trust is applied or appointed shall also be accountable for the payment of tax the charge in respect of which has arisen prior to the date of the application or appointment of the property to him or for his benefit, and the Principal Act shall have effect, in its application to that charge for tax, as if that object of the discretionary trust were a person referred to in section 35(2) of the Principal Act;

(e) ...[2]

(f) the provisions of section 41 of the Principal Act shall have effect, in the application of the Principal Act to any such charge for tax as aforesaid arising before the date of the passing of this Act, as if the references to the valuation date in subsections (1), (2) and (3) of that section were references to the date of the passing of this Act, or to the valuation date, whichever is the later;

and

[(g) section 35(1), 40, 45 and 57 of, and the Second Schedule to, the Principal Act shall not apply.][3]

Amendments

[1] Para (a) substituted by FA 1993 s 131 as regards an inheritance taken on or after 24 February 1993; previously:

(a) a reference in section 16 of the Principal Act to a company controlled by the successor shall be construed as including a reference to a company that is under the control of any one or more of the following, that is to say, the trustees of the discretionary trust, the living objects of the discretionary trust, the relatives of those objects, and nominees of those trustees or of those objects or of the relatives of those objects;"

²   Para (*e*) deleted by FA 1989 s 78(*a*).

³   Para (*g*) substituted by FA 1989 s 78(*b*).

Narrative

Capital Acquisitions Tax, Chapter 17.

Definitions

"accountable person", "benefit": CATA 1976 s 2(1); "Commissioners": SA 1891 s 122(1); CATA 1976 s 2(1); "date of inheritance", "discretionary trust", "inheritance", "nominee": CATA 1976 s 2(1); "person": IA 1937 s 11(*c*); "property", "relative", "return", "taxable inheritance", "valuation date": CATA 1976 s 2(1).

108 Exemptions

[(1)] Section 106 shall not apply or have effect in relation to a discretionary trust which is shown to the satisfaction of the Commissioners to have been created exclusively—

(*a*)   for public or charitable purposes in the State or Northern Ireland;

(*b*)   for the purposes of—

    (i)   any scheme for the provision of superannuation benefits on retirement established by or under any enactment or by or under an instrument made under any enactment, or

    (ii)   any sponsored superannuation scheme within the meaning of [subsection (1) of section 783 of the Taxes Consolidation Act, 1997],¹ or a trust scheme or part of a trust scheme approved by the Commissioners under that section or [section 785]² of that Act;

(*c*)   for the purposes of a registered unit trust scheme within the meaning of the Unit Trusts Act, 1972;

(*d*)   (i)   for the benefit of one or more named individuals, and

    (ii)   for the reason that such individual, or all such individuals, is or are, because of age or improvidence, or of physical, mental or legal incapacity, incapable of managing his or their affairs; or

(*e*)   for the purpose of providing for the upkeep of a house or garden referred to in section 39 of the Finance Act, 1978.

[(2) Section 106 shall not apply or have effect—

(*a*)   in relation to a discretionary trust in respect of the property subject to or becoming subject to the trust which, on the termination of the trust, is comprised in a gift or an inheritance taken by the State; or

(*b*)   in respect of an inheritance which, apart from this subsection, would be deemed, by the combined effect of section 31 of the Principal Act and section 106, to be taken by a discretionary trust.]³

Amendments

¹   Substituted by TCA 1997 s 1100 and Sch 31; previously "subsection (9) of section 235 of the Income Tax Act, 1967".

²   Substituted by TCA 1997 s 1100 and Sch 31; previously "section 235A".

³   Subs (2) added by FA 1985 s 65.

Cross-references

Anti-avoidance, with effect from 5 April 1990 the exemption from the once off and the annual charges on discretionary trusts (imposed by FA 1984 Pt V Ch I and FA 1986 Pt V Ch I respectively) for pension schemes (within ITA 1967 s 235(9)) where the scheme includes arrangements that do not relate to the employment does not apply: FA 1990 s 129.

Narrative

Capital Acquisitions Tax, Chapter 17.

Definitions

"benefit": CATA 1976 s 2(1); "Commissioners": SA 1891 s 122(1); CATA 1976 s 2(1); "discretionary trust", "gift", "inheritance": CATA 1976 s 2(1); "instrument": IA 1937 s 3; SA 1891 s 122(1); "property": CATA 1976 s 2(1).

109 Computation of tax

The tax chargeable on the taxable value of a taxable inheritance which is charged to tax by reason of the provisions of section 106 shall be computed at the rate of [**six per cent**][1] of such taxable value.

Amendments

[1]   Substituted by FA 1994 s 143(2); previously "three per cent". For circumstances in which the 3% rate continues to apply, see FA 1994 s 143(2)(proviso).

Narrative

Capital Acquisitions Tax, Chapter 17.

Definitions

"inheritance", "taxable inheritance", "taxable value": CATA 1976 s 2(1).

CHAPTER II
Revised computation

110 Amendment of certain sections of Principal Act

Note

As regards gifts or inheritances taken on or after 26 March 1984:

CATA 1976 s 36(3) provided that a return is required where the aggregate value of gifts or inheritances exceed 80% of the taxable value. Subs (1), by substituting a new CATA 1976 s 36(3) for s 36(3)-(4), provides that such a return is required where the aggregate value of gifts or inheritances (irrespective of class thresholds) exceeds 80% of the sum on which liability arises (the threshold amount).

CATA 1976 s 9 was concerned with the aggregation of gifts taken between 28 February 1969 and 27 February 1974 with later gifts or inheritances taken on or after 31 March 1976. Subs (2) deleted CATA 1976 ss 9 with effect from 26 March 1984. There is a consequential deletion of the original wording in CATA 1976 s 53(3); subs (2) also extended the scope of the annual small gifts exemption to the taxable value of aggregated gifts within CATA 1976 s 9.

CATA 1976 s 54 provides relief for gifts or inheritances to charitable bodies. Subs (3) substituted CATA 1976 s 54(1) to provide that such bodies were to be entitled to the minimum threshold of £10,000 (see s 111) as regards gifts or inheritances not applied in the State. FA 1987 s 50 subsequently introduced exemption for gifts or inheritances taken by such bodies but applied outside the State.

Subs (4) deleted "from the same disponer" from CATA 1976 s 55(2)(a); these words are no longer required with the introduction of aggregation from all classes.

Subs (5) deleted "from the same disponer" from CATA 1976 s 57(2); these words are no longer required with the introduction of aggregation from all classes.

111 Amendment of Second Schedule to Principal Act

Note

Under CATA 1976 Sch 2 (as enacted), aggregation of taxable gifts (taken on or after 28 February 1969) and taxable inheritances (taken on or after 1 April 1975) only applied to gifts or inheritances taken from the same disponer.

FA 1982 s 102 provided a new computation method, effective for gifts or inheritances taken on or after 2 June 1982, with aggregation of benefits taken from the same class of disponer (Table of Charge in CATA 1976 Sch 2). Taxable gifts or inheritances taken before 2 June 1982 are not to be aggregated.

This section by substituting CATA 1976 Sch 2 paras 1-5, 7 and Tables I to IV as regards taxable gifts or inheritances taken on or after 26 March 1984, provides a new structure for computing tax:

Gifts or inheritances taken on or after 26 March 1984 are to be aggregated with earlier gifts or inheritances taken on or after 2 June 1982, irrespective of the disponer involved.

Tax is chargeable (by reference to a single Table of rates) on the excess over the threshold amount of the taxable value of the sum of the current and any aggregated taxable gift or inheritance. A tax credit is allowed for any tax that arose on any aggregated amount included in the gross sum chargeable.

The taxable value of a taxable gift or inheritance is the amount remaining after deducting from the value of the gift or inheritance, any costs expenses or charges applicable, and, subsequently, the amount of any consideration given.

The threshold amount is calculated as follows:

(a) Each taxable value of a taxable gift or inheritance included in any aggregate has a class threshold of £150,000, £20,000 or £10,000. These figures apply up to 31 December 1989: indexation relief by reference to annual inflation figures is available thereafter (FA 1990 s 128).

(b) A revised class threshold must be computed for each taxable gift or inheritance taken on or after 2 June 1982. This is the lower of:

(i) The class threshold figure at (a) which applies to the current gift or inheritance being charged, or

(ii) the total of the taxable values of the gifts or inheritances (including aggregations) taken in possession on or after 2 June 1982 within that class threshold.

If the revised class threshold determined is less than the lowest class threshold of any of the gifts or inheritances included, current or aggregated, in the taxable value of the sum chargeable, a relieving proviso ensures that this lowest class threshold is to be the revised class threshold applicable.

112 Application of Chapter II

This Chapter shall have effect in relation to gifts and inheritances taken on or after the 26th day of March, 1984.

Definitions

"gift", "inheritance": CATA 1976 s 2(1).

113 Extension of section 48 (receipts and certificates) of Principal Act

Note

This section inserted CATA 1976 s 48(5)-(7).

The need for these additional subsections arose following the introduction of aggregation of benefits taken from the same class, on or after 2 June 1982.

Persons who are not primarily liable for payment of tax may not be aware of aggregable taxable gifts or inheritances taken by a donee or successor. Such persons may obtain a certificate of discharge from capital acquisitions tax after two years from the date of the taxable gift or inheritance, provided that full returns of property (within the knowledge of the appropriate personal representative, trustee or other person concerned) have been submitted to the Revenue and the tax paid.

PART VI
MISCELLANEOUS

115 Care and management of taxes and duties

All taxes and duties imposed by this Act are hereby placed under the care and management of the Revenue Commissioners.

116 Short title, construction and commencement

(1) This Act may be cited as the Finance Act, 1984.

...

(5) Part IV shall be construed together with the Stamp Act, 1891, and the enactments amending or extending that Act.

...

...

(9) Any reference in this Act to any other enactment shall, except so far as the context otherwise requires, be construed as a reference to that enactment as amended by or under any other enactment including this Act.

(10) In this Act, a reference to a Part, section or Schedule is to a Part or section of, or Schedule to, this Act, unless it is indicated that reference to some other enactment is intended.

(11) In this Act, a reference to a subsection, paragraph or subparagraph is to the subsection, paragraph or subparagraph of the provision (including a Schedule) in which the reference occurs, unless it is indicated that reference to some other provision is intended.

FINANCE ACT 1985

(1985 Number 10)
(Date of passing: 30 May 1985)

ARRANGEMENT OF SECTIONS

PART V
CAPITAL ACQUISITIONS TAX

PART V
CAPITAL ACQUISITIONS TAX

58 Interpretation (Part V)

In this Part **"the Principal Act"** means the Capital Acquisitions Tax Act, 1976.

59 Exemption for spouses

(1) Notwithstanding the provisions of the Principal Act, an inheritance taken by a successor, who is at the date of the inheritance the spouse of the disponer, shall be exempt from tax and shall not be taken into account in computing tax.

(2) This section shall have effect in relation to an inheritance taken on or after the 30th day of January, 1985.

Notes

This section introduced complete exemption from capital acquisitions tax on property inherited by a surviving spouse from the dead spouse. A similar exemption applies to gifts (taken on or after 31 January 1990) between spouses; FA 1990 s 127.

Revenue practice

See CAT Work Manual (revised July 2001), Pt 10 para 13.

Narrative

Capital Acquisitions Tax, Chapter 11.

Definitions

"disponer", "inheritance", "successor": CATA 1976 s 2(1).

---

60 Relief in respect of certain policies of insurance

(1) In this section—

"qualifying insurance policy" means a policy of insurance—

    (*a*) which is in a form approved by the Commissioners for the purposes of this section;

    (*b*) in respect of which annual premiums are paid by the insured during his life; and

    (*c*) which is expressly effected under this section for the purpose of paying relevant tax;

"relevant tax" means inheritance tax payable in respect of an inheritance (excluding, in the computation of such tax, an interest in a qualifying insurance policy) taken under a disposition made by the insured, where the inheritance is taken on or after the date of death of the insured and not later than one year after that death.

[(1A) In this section **"insured"** means an individual or, in relation to a qualifying insurance policy where—

    (*a*) the insured is an individual and the spouse of that individual at the date the policy is effected;

    (*b*) annual premiums are paid by either or both of them during their joint lives, and the survivor of them during the life of such survivor; and

    (*c*) the proceeds of the policy are payable on the death of such survivor, or on the simultaneous deaths of both such spouses,

means—

       (i) where the proceeds of the policy are so payable on the death of such survivor, that survivor, and the proceeds of the policy shall be deemed to have been provided by such survivor, as disponer; or

      (ii) where the proceeds of the policy are so payable on the simultaneous deaths of both such spouses, each of the spouses, and each such spouse shall be deemed to have provided the proceeds of the policy—

          (I) to the extent that such proceeds are applied in paying the relevant tax of the insured who is that spouse, and

        (II) where the proceeds of the policy are not applied in paying relevant tax, to the extent that the proceeds not so applied are comprised in an inheritance taken under a disposition made by that spouse.]

(2) (*a*) An interest in a qualifying insurance policy which is comprised in an inheritance taken under a disposition made by the insured shall, to the extent that the proceeds thereof are applied in paying relevant tax, be exempt from tax in relation to that inheritance and shall not be taken into account in computing tax.

    (*b*) An interest in qualifying insurance policy which is comprised in an inheritance taken under a disposition made by the insured shall, to the extent that the proceeds thereof are not applied in paying relevant tax, and notwithstanding the provisions of the Principal Act, be deemed to be taken on a day immediately after—

(i)   the date of the death of the insured; or

(ii)   the latest date (if any) on which an inheritance is taken in respect of which that relevant tax is payable,

whichever is the later.

(3) Section 143 of the Income Tax Act, 1967, is hereby amended by the substitution, in subsection (5), of the following paragraphs for paragraph (*b*)-

"(*b*)   be given in respect of premiums or payments payable during the period of deferment in respect of a policy of deferred assurance; or

(*c*)   be given for the year 1985-86 and subsequent years of assessment in respect of premiums payable in respect of a qualifying insurance policy within the meaning of section 60 of the Finance Act, 1985:"

Amendments

¹   Subs (1A) inserted by FA 1989 s 84.

Notes

The proceeds of life assurance policies, taken out expressly to pay inheritance tax due by the successors of the disponer are exempt from capital acquisitions tax, provided the inheritance is taken on or after the death of the insured and not later than one year after the death. The policy proceeds are also excluded from aggregation with any other taxable gifts or inheritances, to the extent that they are used to pay inheritance tax due by the successor.

The annual premium is not allowable as a deduction for income tax purposes.

The original relief applied to policies effected by individuals. The relief was extended (subs (1A)) to apply to joint policies effected by spouses to cover inheritance tax payable by the successors of the survivor of either spouse.

The relief was further extended (FA 1990 s 130) to cover succession of property on the survivor's death (cesser of a life interest) or where an inheritance from the predeceased spouse is only taken in the event of the insured not surviving his or her partner for up to 31 days. In such circumstances the policy proceeds may be used to pay tax due by the successors of the predeceased spouse.

The relief was further extended (FA 1991 s 118) to provide that proceeds of a qualifying policy in the sole name of a life tenant, taking under a deceased spouse's will may be used to pay inheritance tax arising on the cesser of the life interest. FA 1996 s 124 removed the requirement that the proceeds be taken under a deceased spouse's will.

Narrative

Capital Acquisitions Tax, Chapter 18.

Statement of practice

[FA 1985] Section 60 policies: SP CAT 3/90, 2/91

[FA 1991] Section 119 policies: SP CAT 2/91

Definitions

"Commissioners": SA 1891 s 122(1); CATA 1976 s 2(1);"disponer", "disposition", "inheritance": CATA 1976 s 2(1).

61 Relief from double aggregation

(1) Property in respect of which tax is chargeable more than once on the same event shall not be included more than once in relation to that event in any aggregate referred to in the Second Schedule to the Principal Act.

(2) Paragraph 7 of Part I of the said Second Schedule shall not have effect in ascertaining the tax payable in respect of property which is chargeable to tax as being taken more than once on the same day.

(3) This section shall have effect in relation to gifts and inheritances taken on or after the 2nd day of June, 1982.

(4) Notwithstanding the provisions of section 46 of the Principal Act, interest shall not be payable on any repayment of tax which arises by virtue of this section where such tax was paid prior to the date of the passing of this Act.

Note

As regards gifts or inheritances taken on or after 2 June 1982, the same property, if chargeable to either gift tax or inheritance tax more than once on the same event, is not to be included more than once on one person for capital acquisitions tax charging purposes. This relief would apply for example on the release by a life tenant of his or her interest in favour of the remainderman under the original governing disposition.

Narrative

Capital Acquisitions Tax, Chapter 8.

Definitions

"gift", "inheritance", "property": CATA 1976 s 2(1).

62 Allowance for prior tax on the same event

Narrative

Capital Acquisitions Tax, Chapter 8.

Note

This section, which inserted CATA 1976 s 34A, like the preceding section, relates to property passing from trusts. If tax is paid more than once on the same event (for example, where a benefit in expectancy has been transferred at a earlier time before it came into possession) the net tax arising which is earlier in priority is not to be *deducted* in arriving at the taxable value of the later gift or inheritance but is to be allowed as a *credit* against any liability arising on the later benefit.

63 Allowance for capital gains tax on the same event

(1) Where gift tax or inheritance tax is charged in respect of property on an event happening on or after the 30th day of January, 1985, and the same event constitutes for capital gains tax purposes a disposal of an asset (being the same property or any part of the same property), the capital gains tax, if any, chargeable on the disposal shall not be deducted in ascertaining the taxable value for the purposes of the gift tax or inheritance tax but, in so far as it has been paid, shall be deducted from the net gift tax or inheritance tax as a credit against the same.

[Provided that, in relation to each asset, or to a part of each asset, so disposed of, the amount deducted shall be the lesser of—

    (*a*) an amount equal to the amount of the capital gains tax attributable to such asset, or to the part of such asset, or

    (*b*) an amount equal to the amount of gift tax or inheritance tax attributable to the property which is that asset, or that part of that asset.]

(2) For the purposes of any computation of the amount of capital gains tax to be deducted under this section, any necessary apportionments shall be made of any reliefs or expenditure and the method of apportionment adopted shall be such method as appears to the Commissioners, or on appeal to the Appeal Commissioners, to be just and reasonable.

Amendments

¹   Subs (1)(proviso) substituted by FA 1988 s 66 where gift or inheritance tax is charged in respect of property
      on an event happening on or after 6 April 1988; previously:

      "(1) In computing in accordance with the provisions of the Second Schedule to the Principal Act the tax
      chargeable on the taxable value of a taxable gift or a taxable inheritance taken by a donee or successor on
      or after the 1st day of January, 1990, the threshold amount in relation to the computation of tax on any
      relevant aggregate of taxable values under the provisions of paragraph 3 of Part I of that Schedule (inserted
      by section 111 of the Finance Act, 1984) shall be adjusted by multiplying each such threshold amount by
      the figure, rounded to the nearest third decimal place, determined by dividing by 133.5 the consumer price
      index number for the year immediately preceding the year in which that taxable gift or taxable inheritance
      is taken:

      Provided that, where the tax so computed on the taxable value of that taxable gift or that taxable inheritance
      is a minus amount, that tax shall be nil."

Narrative

Capital Acquisitions Tax, Chapter 8.

Note

Where after 29 January 1985, a capital acquisitions tax charge and a capital gains tax charge arise on the same
event in relation to the same property, no deduction is given for the capital gains tax liability in computing the
taxable value of the gift or inheritance. The liability is allowed by way of credit against the capital acquisitions
tax due. For events happening on or after 6 April 1988 the relief is confined to the lesser of the capital gains tax
charge and the gift or inheritance tax charge.

Definitions

"Commissioners": SA 1891 s 122(1); CATA 1976 s 2(1); "gift", "inheritance", "property", "taxable value":
CATA 1976 s 2(1).

64 Amendment of section 106 (acquisitions by discretionary trusts) of Finance Act, 1984

Note

This section, by deleting "otherwise than for full consideration in money or money's worth paid by he trustees
of the trust from FA 1984 s 106(1), removes any doubt that the 3% once off discretionary trust charge applies
not only to property originally settled in the discretionary trust but also to any substituted property comprised
in the settlement.

65 Amendment of section 108 (exemptions) of Finance Act, 1984

Note

With effect from 26 January 1984, this section, by inserting FA 1984 s 108(2), extends exemption from the 3%
once off discretionary trust charge to

(*a*) property comprised in a gift or inheritance taken by the State, and

(*b*) an inheritance taken by a discretionary trust that represents free use of property or a non-interest bearing
       loan.

PART VI
MISCELLANEOUS

70 Care and management of taxes and duties

All taxes and duties ... imposed by this Act are hereby placed under the care and
management of the Revenue Commissioners.

71 Short title, construction and commencement

(1) This Act may be cited as the Finance Act, 1985.

...

(5) Part IV shall be construed together with the Stamp Act, 1891, and the enactments amending or extending that Act.

(6) Part V shall be construed together with the Capital Acquisitions Tax Act, 1976, and the enactments amending or extending that Act and (so far as relating to income tax) shall be construed together with the Income Tax Acts and (so far as relating to capital gains tax) shall be construed together with the Capital Gains Tax Acts.

...

(9) Any reference in this Act to any other enactment shall, except so far as the context otherwise requires, be construed as a reference to that enactment as amended by or under any other enactment including this Act.

(10) In this Act, a reference to a Part, section or Schedule is to a Part or section of, or Schedule to, this Act, unless it is indicated that reference to some other enactment is intended.

(11) In this Act, a reference to a subsection, paragraph or subparagraph is to the subsection, paragraph or subparagraph of the provision (including a Schedule) in which the reference occurs, unless it is indicated that reference to some other provision is intended.

FINANCE ACT 1986

(1986 Number 13)
(Date of passing: 27 May 1986)

ARRANGEMENT OF SECTIONS

PART V
CAPITAL ACQUISITIONS TAX

CHAPTER I
Discretionary trusts

PART V
CAPITAL ACQUISITIONS TAX

CHAPTER I
Discretionary trusts

102 Interpretation (Part V)

In this Part—

"the Principal Act" means the Capital Acquisitions Tax Act, 1976;

"chargeable date", in relation to any year, means the 5th day of April in that year;

"chargeable discretionary trust" means a discretionary trust in relation to which—

(*a*)   the disponer is dead, and

(*b*)   none of the principal objects of the trust, if any, is under the age of [21]¹ years;

"object" and **"principal objects"**, in relation to a discretionary trust, have the meanings respectively assigned to them by section 104 of the Finance Act, 1984.

Amendments

¹   Substituted by FA 1992 s 225 as regards any chargeable date occurring on or after 5 April 1994; previously "25". See also s 106(1).

Notes

Chapter I imposes a 1% annual charge on the value of property held under discretionary trusts in existence on or after 25 January 1984 (discretionary trusts that are subject to the 3% once off charge introduced by FA 1984 Pt V (ss 104-109)). The valuation date for the charge is 5 April each year. Discretionary trusts that are exempt (FA 1984 s 108) from the 3% once off charge are also exempt from the 1% annual charge.

The once off 6% charge and the 1% annual charge cannot both be imposed in the same 12 month (s 103(4)).

The trustees are primarily accountable for the tax (s 104(*c*)) and they must lodge returns and pay the tax on a self-assessment basis within three months of the valuation date.

Real property and certain unquoted shares, may, by agreement with the Revenue Commissioners, retain the same valuation for a three year period.

Narrative

Capital Acquisitions Tax, Chapter 17.

Definitions

"discretionary trust", "disponer": CATA 1976 s 2(1).

---

103 Annual acquisitions by discretionary trusts

(1) Where, in any year commencing with the year 1986, under or in consequence of any disposition, property is subject to a chargeable discretionary trust on the chargeable date, the trust shall be deemed on each such date to become beneficially entitled in possession to an absolute interest in the property, and to take on each such date an inheritance accordingly as if the trust, and the trustees as such for the time being of the trust, were together a person for the purposes of the Principal Act, and each such chargeable date shall be the date of such inheritance.

(2) (*a*)   Where—

    (i)   under or in consequence of any disposition, property was subject to a discretionary trust prior to a chargeable date,

    (ii)   that property is not on that chargeable date subject to that discretionary trust (being on that date a chargeable discretionary trust) because such property is on that date property to which for the time being a person is beneficially entitled for an interest in possession, and

    (iii)   on the chargeable date that property is property which is limited to become subject again to that chargeable discretionary trust, or will do so by the exercise of a power of revocation,

that property shall be deemed to be subject to that chargeable discretionary trust on that chargeable date if that interest in possession is an interest which is revocable or which is limited to cease on an event other than—

    (I)   the death of that person, or

    (II)   the expiration of a specified period, where that interest is taken by that person under a power of appointment contained in that disposition and is, at the time of the appointment thereof, an interest for a period certain of five years or more.

(*b*) In this subsection, **"property"** includes property representing such property.

(3) For the purposes of this section—

(*a*) an interest in expectancy shall not be property until an event happens whereby the interest ceases to be an interest in expectancy or is represented by property which is not an interest in expectancy;

(*b*) an interest in a policy of assurance upon human life shall not be property until, and then only to the extent that, the interest becomes an interest in possession under the provisions of section 32 of the Principal Act or is represented by property which is not an interest in expectancy.

(4) This section shall not apply or have effect in relation to property which is subject to a chargeable discretionary trust on a chargeable date if that property or property representing that property is subject to a charge for tax arising under or in consequence of the same disposition by reason of the provisions of section 106 of the Finance Act, 1984, on that same date or within the year prior to that date.

Cross-references

Agricultural or business property, payment of tax by instalments does not apply: FA 1995 s 164(4).

Business relief, applies to gifts or inheritances taken on or after 11 April 1994, but not inheritances taken by virtue of subs (1) above: FA 1994 s 125.

Computation of tax: s 106.

Exemptions (s 105): FA 1984 s 108.

Values may be agreed for several years: s 107.

Narrative

Capital Acquisitions Tax, Chapter 17.

Definitions

"absolute interest": CATA 1976 s 2(1); "discretionary trust": CATA 1976 s 2(1); "disposition": CATA 1976 s 2(1); "entitled in possession": CATA 1976 s 2(1); "inheritance": CATA 1976 s 2(1); "interest in expectancy": CATA 1976 s 2(1); "person": IA 1937 s 11(*c*); "property": CATA 1976 s 2(1).

104 Application of Principal Act

In relation to a charge for tax arising by reason of the provisions of section 103—

[(*a*) a reference in section 16 of the Principal Act to a company controlled by the successor and the definition in that section of 'group of shares' shall be construed as if (for the purpose of that reference) the list of persons contained in subsection (3) of that section and (for the purpose of that definition) the list of persons contained in that definition included the following, that is to say, the trustees of the discretionary trust, the living objects of the discretionary trust, the relatives of those objects, nominees of those trustees or of those objects or of the relatives of those objects, and the trustees of a settlement whose objects include the living objects of the discretionary trust or relatives of those living objects;][1]

(*b*) (i) subject to the provisions of subparagraph (ii), the valuation date of the taxable inheritance shall be the relevant chargeable date;

(ii) where—

    (I) a charge for tax arises on a particular date by reason of the provisions of section 106 of the Finance Act, 1984, giving rise to a taxable inheritance (in this subparagraph called the first taxable inheritance),

    (II) on a later date, a charge for tax arises under or in consequence of the same disposition by reason of the provisions of section 103 giving rise to a taxable inheritance (in this subparagraph called the second taxable inheritance) comprising the same property or property representing that property, and

    (III) the valuation date of the first taxable inheritance is a date after the chargeable date of the second taxable inheritance,

the valuation date of the second taxable inheritance shall be the same date as the valuation date of the first taxable inheritance;

(c) a person who is a trustee of the discretionary trust concerned for the time being at the date of the inheritance or at any date subsequent thereto shall be a person primarily accountable for the payment of the tax;

(d) an object of the discretionary trust concerned to whom or for whose benefit any of the property subject to the trust is applied or appointed shall also be accountable for the payment of tax the charge in respect of which has arisen prior to the date of the application or appointment of the property to him or for his benefit, and the Principal Act shall have effect, in its application to that charge for tax, as if that object of the discretionary trust were a person referred to in section 35(2) of the Principal Act;

(e) any person who is primarily accountable for the payment of tax by virtue of paragraph (c) shall, within three months after the valuation date or the date of the passing of this Act, whichever is the later—

(i) deliver to the Commissioners a full and true return—

    (I) of every inheritance in respect of which he is so primarily accountable;

    (II) of all the property comprised in such inheritance; and

    (III) of an estimate of the market value of such property;

(ii) notwithstanding the provisions of the Principal Act, make an assessment of such amount of tax as, to the best of his knowledge, information and belief, ought to be charged, levied and paid on that valuation date; and

(iii) pay the amount of such tax to the Accountant-General of the Commissioners;

(f) the provisions of section 41 of the Principal Act shall have effect, in the application of the Principal Act to any such charge for tax as aforesaid arising before the date of the passing of this Act, as if the references to the valuation date in subsections (1), (2) and (3) of that section were references to the date of the passing of this Act, or to the valuation date, whichever it the later;

and

(g) section 21, subsection (1) of section 35, subsections (2), (3), (4) and (5) of section 36 and sections 40, 43, 45 and 57 of, and the Second Schedule to, the Principal Act shall not apply.

Amendments

¹ Para (*a*) substituted by FA 1993 s 132 in relation to an inheritance taken on or after 24 February 1993; previously:

"(*a*) a reference in section 16 of the Principal Act to a company controlled by the successor shall be construed as including a reference to a company that is under the control of any one or more of the following, that is to say, the trustees of the discretionary trust, the living objects of the discretionary trust, the relatives of those objects, the nominees of those trustees or of those objects or of the relatives of those objects;"

Cross-references

Penalty: s 108.

Narrative

Capital Acquisitions Tax, Chapter 17.

Definitions

"accountable person", "benefit": CATA 1976 s 2(1); "Commissioners": SA 1891 s 122(1); CATA 1976 s 2(1); "discretionary trust", "disposition", "inheritance", "market value": CATA 1976 s 2(1); "person": IA 1937 s 11(*c*); "property", "relative", "taxable value", "successor", "valuation date": CATA 1976 s 2(1).

105 Exemptions

Section 103 shall not apply or have effect in relation to a discretionary trust referred to in section 108 of the Finance Act, 1984, or in respect of the property or the inheritance referred to in section 65 of the Finance Act, 1985.

Narrative

Capital Acquisitions Tax, Chapter 17.

Definitions

"discretionary trust", "inheritance", "property": CATA 1976 s 2(1).

106 Computation of tax

The tax chargeable on the taxable value of a taxable inheritance which is charged to tax by reason of the provisions of section 103 shall be computed at the rate of **one per cent** of such taxable value.

Narrative

Capital Acquisitions Tax, Chapter 17.

Definitions

"inheritance", taxable inheritance", taxable value": CATA 1976 s 2(1).

107 Values agreed

(1) Where—

- (*a*) under or in consequence of any disposition, a charge for tax arises by reason of the provisions of section 103 on a chargeable date (in this section called the first chargeable date),
- (*b*) an accountable person has furnished all the information necessary to enable the Commissioners to ascertain the market value of—
  - (i) real property, or
  - (ii) shares which are not dealt in on a stock exchange,

comprised in the taxable inheritance so taken on the valuation date of that taxable inheritance,

(*c*)   pursuant to an application in writing to the Commissioners on that behalf, the market value of such property on that valuation date is agreed on between that person and the Commissioners,

(*d*)   under or in consequence of the same disposition, a charge for tax arises by reason of the provisions of section 103 on either or both of the two chargeable dates in the years next following the year in which the first chargeable date occurs (in this section called the subsequent chargeable dates), and

(*e*)   the same property at subparagraph (i) or (ii) of paragraph (*b*) is comprised in the taxable inheritances so taken on the subsequent chargeable dates,

the value so agreed on shall be treated for the purposes of this Part as the market value of such property on that valuation date and on the valuation dates of the taxable inheritances so taken on the subsequent chargeable dates.

(2) Notwithstanding the provisions of subsection (1), the market value so agreed shall not be binding—

(*a*)   in any case where there is failure to disclose material facts in relation to any part of the property comprised in the taxable inheritances taken on the first chargeable date or on the subsequent chargeable dates, or

(*b*)   where, at any time after the first chargeable date and before the third of those chargeable dates—

(i)   in the case of real property, there is any alteration in the tenure under which the property is held or let, or

(ii)   in the case of shares, there is any alteration in the capital or the ownership of the capital of the company concerned or of the rights of the shareholders *inter se*, or

(*c*)   where, at any time after the first chargeable date and before the third of those chargeable dates—

(i)   in the case of real property, there is any change whatever, whether affecting that or any other property, which would materially increase or decrease the market value over and above any increase or decrease which might normally be expected if such a change had not occurred, or

(ii)   in the case of shares, there has been any material change in the assets of the company or in their market value over and above any such change which might normally be expected,

and in such cases the market value of the real property, or of the shares, may be ascertained again by the Commissioners for each of the relevant valuation dates:

Provided that, in the case of any change referred to in paragraph (*c*), the market value may be ascertained again by the Commissioners only at the request of the person primarily accountable for the payment of the tax arising by reason of the provisions of section 103 on that relevant valuation date.

(3) Any agreement made under this section shall be binding only on the persons who as such are accountable for the payment of the tax arising by reason of the provisions of section 103 on the first chargeable date and on the subsequent chargeable dates.

Narrative

Capital Acquisitions Tax, Chapter 17.

Definitions

"accountable person": SA 1891 s 122(1); CATA 1976 s 2(1); "Commissioners": SA 1891 s 122(1); CATA 1976 s 2(1); "disposition", "inheritance", "market value": CATA 1976 s 2(1); "material": SA 1891 s 122(1); "person": IA 1937 s 11(*c*); "property", "real property", "return", "share", "taxable inheritances": CATA 1976 s 2(1); "stock": SA 1891 s 122(1); "valuation date": CATA 1976 s 2(1).

108 Penalty

Any person who contravenes or fails to comply with any requirement under paragraph (*e*) of section 104 shall be liable to a penalty of—

    (*a*) [€1,265][1], or

    (*b*) twice the amount of tax payable in respect of the taxable inheritance to which the return relates,

whichever is the lesser.

Amendments

[1]   Substituted by FA 2001 s 240 and Sch 5 Part 5 with effect from 1 January 2002; previously "£1,000".

Narrative

Capital Acquisitions Tax, Chapter 17.

Definitions

"inheritance": CATA 1976 s 2(1);"person": IA 1937 s 11(*c*); "return", "taxable inheritance": CATA 1976 s 2(1).

CHAPTER II
General

109 Amendment of section 46 (overpayment of tax) of Principal Act

Note

CATA 1976 s 46 (as enacted) allowed for repayment of overpaid tax with additional interest at the interest rate prevailing for overdue tax. With effect from 27 May 1986, this section, by amending CATA 1976 s 4(1) and inserting s 46(2), reduces the interest rate on overpaid tax to 1% per month or part thereof (or such other rate as the Minister for Finance prescribes by regulations), and exempts such interest from the charge to income tax.

110 Amendment of section 61 (payment of money standing in names of two or more persons) of Principal Act

Note

This section, by inserting CATA 1976 s 61(8), enables financial institutions, on or after 30 May 1985 to pay the proceeds of joint deposit accounts held in the joint names of husband and wife to the surviving spouse. See also FA 1985 s 59 (exemption for spouses). The general restrictions imposed on financial institutions (CATA 1976 s 61) do not apply to current accounts.

PART VI
MISCELLANEOUS

112 Application of Age of Majority Act, 1985

(1) Notwithstanding the provisions of subsection (4) of section 2 of the Age of Majority Act, 1985, subsections (2) and (3) of the said section 2 shall, subject to subsection (2), apply and have effect for the purposes of the Income Tax Acts and any other statutory provision (within the meaning of the said Act) dealing with the imposition, repeal, remission, alteration or regulation of any tax or other duty under the care and management of the Revenue Commissioners and accordingly subparagraph (vii) of paragraph (*b*) of the said subsection (4) shall cease to have effect.

(2) Nothing in subsection (1) shall affect a claimant's entitlement to a deduction under section 138A (inserted by the Finance Act, 1985) or section 141 (inserted by this Act) of the Income Tax Act, 1967.

(3) This section shall be deemed to have come into force and shall take effect as on and from the 6th day of April, 1986, and so far as it relates to gift tax or inheritance tax shall have effect in relation to gifts and inheritances taken on or after that date.

Notes

This section, overriding a restriction contained in the Age of Majority Act 1985 s 2(4), provides that with effect from 6 April 1986, as regards all taxes and duties managed by the Revenue Commissioners, the age of majority is reduced to 18 years from 21 years.

Narrative

Capital Acquisitions Tax, Chapter 8.

Definition

"Income Tax Acts": ITA 1967 s 3.

113 Use of electronic data processing

(1) In this section —

"the Acts" means—

    (*a*) the Tax Acts,
    (*b*) the Capital Gains Tax Acts,
  [(*c*) the Value-Added Tax Act, 1972,]¹
    (*d*) the Capital Acquisitions Tax Act, 1976, and the enactments amending or extending that Act, and
    (*e*) Part VI of the Finance Act, 1983,

and any instruments made thereunder;

"records" means documents which a person is obliged by any provision of the Acts to keep, to issue or to produce for inspection, and any other written or printed material;

"tax" means income tax, corporation tax, capital gains tax, value-added tax or residential property tax, as the case may be.

(2) Subject to the agreement of the Revenue Commissioners, records may be stored, maintained, transmitted, reproduced or communicated, as the case may be, by any electronic, photographic or other process approved of by the Revenue Commissioners,

and in circumstances where the use of such process has been agreed by them and subject to such conditions as they may impose.

(3) Where, in pursuance of subsection (2), records are preserved by electronic, photographic or other process, a statement contained in a document produced by any such process shall, subject to the rules of court, be admissible in evidence in any proceedings, whether civil or criminal, to the same extent as the records themselves.

(4) Notwithstanding anything in the Tax Acts, duplicates of assessments need not be made, transmitted or delivered.

(5) The entering by an inspector or other authorised officer of details of an assessment and the tax charged therein in an electronic, photographic or other record from which the Collector-General may extract such details by electronic, photographic or other process shall constitute transmission of such details by the inspector or other authorised officer to the Collector-General.

(6) In any proceedings in the Circuit Court, the District Court or the High Court for or in relation to the recovery of any tax, a certificate signed by the Collector-General or other authorised officer certifying that, before the institution of proceedings, a stated sum of tax as so transmitted became due and payable by the defendant —

    (*a*) (i)   under an assessment which had become final and conclusive,

          (ii) under the provisions of section 429(4) (inserted by the Finance Act, 1971) of the Income Tax Act, 1967, or

         (iii) under the provisions relating to the specified amount of tax within the meaning of section 30 of the Finance Act, 1976,

    and

    (*b*) that demand for the payment of the tax has been duly made,

shall be prima facie evidence, until the contrary has been proved, of those facts and a certificate certifying as aforesaid and purporting to be signed by the Collector-General or other authorised officer may be tendered in evidence without proof and shall be deemed, until the contrary is proved, to have been signed by the Collector-General or other authorised officer.

Amendments

¹   Substituted by FA 1993 s 99; previously "(*c*) section 24 of the Value-Added Tax Act, 1972,".

Cross-references

Subs (6), self-assessment, preliminary tax notice: FA 1988 s 12(6).

Definition

"the Circuit Court": IA 1937 Sch; "District Court": IA 1937 Sch; "the High Court": IA 1937 Sch; "person": IA 1937 s 11(*c*); "rules of court": IA 1937 Sch; "the Tax Acts": CTA 1976 s 155(2).

117 Care and management of taxes and duties

All taxes and duties... imposed by this Act are hereby placed under the care and management of the Revenue Commissioners.

118 Short title, construction and commencement

(1) This Act may be cited as the Finance Act, 1986.

...

(5) Part IV shall be construed together with the Stamp Act, 1891, and the enactments amending or extending that Act and (so far as relating to corporation tax) shall be construed together with the Corporation Tax Acts.

(6) Part V shall be construed together with the Capital Acquisitions Tax Act, 1976, and the enactments amending or extending that Act.

...

(10) Any reference in this Act to any other enactment shall, except so far as the context otherwise requires, be construed as a reference to that enactment as amended by or under any other enactment including this Act.

(11) In this Act, a reference to a Part, section or Schedule is to a Part or section of, or Schedule to, this Act, unless it is indicated that reference to some other enactment is intended.

(12) In this Act, a reference to a subsection, paragraph or subparagraph is to the subsection, paragraph or subparagraph of the provision (including a Schedule) in which the reference occurs, unless it is indicated that reference to some other provision is intended.

FINANCE ACT 1987

(1987 Number 10)
(Date of passing: 9 July 1987)

ARRANGEMENT OF SECTIONS

PART V
CAPITAL ACQUISITIONS TAX

PART VI
MISCELLANEOUS

PART V
CAPITAL ACQUISITIONS TAX

50 Amendment of section 54 (provisions relating to charities etc) of Capital Acquisitions Tax Act, 1976

Note

This section, by substituting CATA 1976 s 54(2) with effect from 9 July 1987, provides that gifts or inheritances taken by charities will be exempt from capital acquisitions tax, provided the gift or inheritance is applied for public or charitable purposes. Gifts or inheritances taken by charities prior to 9 July 1987 were required to be applied charitable etc purposes *in the State* in order to qualify for exemption.

PART VI
MISCELLANEOUS

54 Care and management of taxes and duties

All taxes and duties imposed by this Act are hereby placed under the care and management of the Revenue Commissioners.

55 Short title, construction and commencement

(1) This Act may be cited as the Finance Act, 1987.

...

(5) Part IV shall be construed together with the Stamp Act, 1891, and the enactments amending or extending that Act.

(6) Part V shall be construed together with the Capital Acquisitions Tax Act, 1976, and the enactments amending or extending that Act.

...

(9) Any reference in this Act to any other enactment shall, except so far as the context otherwise requires, be construed as a reference to that enactment as amended by or under any other enactment including this Act.

(10) In this Act, a reference to a Part, section or Schedule is to a Part or section of, or Schedule to, this Act, unless it is indicated that reference to some other enactment is intended.

(11) In this Act, a reference to a subsection, paragraph or subparagraph is to the subsection, paragraph or subparagraph of the provision (including a Schedule) in which the reference occurs, unless it is indicated that reference to some other provision is intended.

FINANCE ACT 1988

(1988 Number 12)
(Date of passing: 25 May 1988)

ARRANGEMENT OF SECTIONS

PART V
CAPITAL ACQUISITIONS TAX

66 Amendment of section 63 (allowance for capital gains tax on the same event) of Finance Act, 1985

(1) ...

(2) This section shall apply where gift tax or inheritance tax is charged in respect of property or an event happening on or after 6th day of April 1988.

Note

Where after 29 January 1985, a capital acquisitions tax charge and a capital gains tax charge arise on the same event in relation to the same property, no deduction is given for the capital gains tax liability in computing the taxable value of the gift or inheritance. The liability is allowed by way of credit against the capital acquisitions tax due. For events happening on or after 6 April 1988 the relief is confined to the lesser of the capital gains tax charge and the inheritance tax charge.

PART VI
MISCELLANEOUS

71 Poundage and certain other fees

(1) (*a*)   In this section —

"**the Acts**" means —

(*a*)   the Tax Acts,

(*b*)   the Capital Gains Tax Acts,

(c)   the Value-Added Tax Act, 1972, and the enactments amending or extending that Act,

(d)   the Capital Acquisitions Tax Act, 1976, and the enactments amending or extending that Act, and

(e)   Part VI of the Finance Act, 1983, and the enactments amending or extending that Part,

and any instruments made thereunder;

"certificate" means a certificate issued under section 485 of the Income Tax Act, 1967;

"county registrar" means a person appointed to be a county registrar under section 35 of the Court Officers Act, 1926;

"defaulter" means a person specified or certified in an execution order or certificate upon whom a relevant amount specified or certified in the order or certificate is leviable;

"execution order" has the same meaning as in the Enforcement of Court Orders Act, 1926;

"fees" means the fees known as poundage fees payable under section 14(1) of the Enforcement of Court Orders Act, 1926, and orders made thereunder for services in or about the execution of an execution order directing or authorising the execution of an order of a court by the seizure and sale of a person's property or, as may be appropriate, the fees, corresponding to the fees aforesaid, payable under section 485 of the Income Tax Act, 1967, for the execution of a certificate;

"interest on unpaid tax" means interest that has accrued under any provision of the Acts providing for the charging of interest in respect of unpaid tax including interest on an undercharge of tax which is attributable to fraud or neglect;

"relevant amount" means an amount of tax or interest on unpaid tax;

"tax" means any tax, duty, levy or charge which, in accordance with any provision of the Acts, is placed under the care and management of the Revenue Commissioners.

(b)   References, as respects an execution order, to a relevant amount include references to any amount of costs specified in the order.

(2) (a)   Where —

(i)   an execution order or certificate specifying or certifying a defaulter and relating to a relevant amount is lodged, whether before or after the passing of this Act, with the appropriate sheriff or county registrar for execution,

(ii)   the sheriff or, as the case may be, the county registrar gives notice to the defaulter of the lodgment or of his intention to execute the execution order or certificate by seizure of the property of the defaulter to which it relates, or demands payment by the defaulter of the relevant amount, and

(iii) the whole or part of the relevant amount is paid to the sheriff or, as the case may be, the county registrar or to the Collector-General, after the giving of the notice or the making of the demand, aforesaid,

then, for the purpose of the liability of the defaulter for the payment of fees and of the exercise of any rights or powers in relation to the collection of fees for the time being vested by law in sheriffs and county registrars —

(I) the sheriff or, as the case may be, the county registrar shall be deemed to have entered, in the execution of the execution order or certificate, into possession of the property aforesaid, and

(II) the payment mentioned in subparagraph (iii) shall be deemed to have been levied, in the execution of the execution order or certificate, by the sheriff or, as the case may be, the county registrar,

and fees shall be payable by the defaulter to such sheriff or, as the case may be, country registrar accordingly in respect of the payment mentioned in subparagraph (iii),

(b) Paragraph (*a*) shall, with any necessary modifications, apply also in a case which such a notice or demand as is mentioned in subparagraph (ii) of that paragraph was given or made before the passing of this Act if the fees concerned were paid to the sheriff or county registrar concerned before such passing.

Notes

Where tax owed by a defaulter is being collected by a sheriff or county registrar, the defaulter must also pay the sheriff's costs known as "poundage" (in addition to any tax or interest owing).

Definition

"person": IA 1937 s 11(*c*); "the Tax Acts": CTA 1976 s 155(2).

73 Deduction from payments due to defaulters of amounts due in relation to tax

(1) (*a*) This section shall apply and have effect as on and from the 1st day of October, 1988.

(*b*) In this section, except where the context otherwise requires —

["**the Acts**" means—

(i) the Customs Acts,

(ii) the statutes relating to the duties of excise and to the management of those duties,

(iii) the Tax Acts,

(iv) the Capital Gains Tax Acts,

(v) the Value-Added Tax Act, 1972, and the enactments amending or extending that Act,

(vi) the Capital Acquisitions Tax Act, 1976, and the enactments amending or extending that Act, and

(vii) the Stamp Act, 1891, and the enactments amending or extending that Act,

and any instrument made thereunder;]'

"**additional debt**" means, in relation to a relevant person who has received a notice of attachment in respect of a taxpayer, any amount which, at any time after the time of the receipt by the relevant person of the notice of attachment but before the end of the relevant period in relation to the notice, would be a debt due by him to the taxpayer if a notice of attachment were received by him at that time;

"debt" means, in relation to a notice of attachment given to a relevant person in respect of a taxpayer and in relation to the said relevant person and taxpayer, the amount or aggregate amount of any money which, at the time the notice of attachment is received by the relevant person, is due by the relevant person (whether on his own account, or as an agent or trustee) to the taxpayer, irrespective of whether the taxpayer has applied for the payment (to himself or any other person) or for the withdrawal of all or part of the money:

Provided that—

[(i) where a relevant person is a financial institution, any amount or aggregate amount of money, including interest thereon, which at that time is a deposit held by the relevant person—

    (I) to the credit of the taxpayer for his sole benefit, or

    (II) to the credit of the taxpayer and any other person or persons for their joint benefit,

shall be regarded as a debt due by the relevant person to the taxpayer at that time,][2]

(ii) any amount of money due by the relevant person to the taxpayer as emoluments under a contract of service shall not be so regarded, and

(iii) where there is a dispute as to an amount of money which is due by the relevant person to the taxpayer, the amount in dispute shall be disregarded for the purposes of determining the amount of the debt;

[Provided also that, in the case of paragraph (i) of the preceding proviso, a deposit held by a relevant person which is a financial institution to the credit of the taxpayer and any other person or persons (hereafter referred to in this proviso as "the other party or parties") for their joint benefit shall be deemed (unless evidence to the contrary is produced to the satisfaction of the relevant person within 10 days of the giving of the notices specified in paragraph (*c*) of subsection (2)) to be held to the benefit of the taxpayer and the other party or parties to the deposit equally and, accordingly, only the portion thereof so deemed shall be regarded as a debt due by the relevant person to the taxpayer at that time and where such evidence is produced within the specified time only so much of the deposit as is shown to be held to the benefit of the taxpayer shall be regarded as a debt due by the relevant person to the taxpayer at that time;][3]

"deposit" means a sum of money paid to a financial institution on terms under which it will be repaid with or without interest and either on demand or at a time or in circumstances agreed by or on behalf of the person making the payment and the person to whom it is made;

"emoluments" means anything assessable to income tax under Schedule E;

"**financial institution**" means a holder of a licence issued under section 9 of the Central Bank Act, 1971, or a person referred to in section 7(4) of that Act and includes a branch of a financial institution that records deposits in its books as liabilities of the branch;

"**further return**" means a return made by a relevant person under subsection (4);

["**interest on unpaid tax**", in relation to a specified amount specified in a notice of attachment, means interest, that has accrued to the date on which the notice of attachment is given, under any provision of the Acts providing for the charging of interest in respect of the unpaid tax, including interest on an undercharge of tax which is attributable to fraud or neglect, specified in the notice of attachment;]⁴

"**notice of attachment**" means a notice under subsection (2);

"**notice of revocation**" means a notice under subsection (10);

"**penalty**" means a monetary penalty imposed on a taxpayer under a provision of the Acts;

"**relevant period**", in relation to a notice of attachment, means, as respects the relevant person to whom the notice of attachment is given, the period commencing at the time at which the notice is received by the relevant person and ending on —

(i)   the date on which he completes the payment to the Revenue Commissioners out of the debt, or the aggregate of the debt and any additional debt, due by him to the taxpayer named in the notice, of an amount equal to the specified amount in relation to the taxpayer,

(ii)   the date on which he receives a notice of revocation of the notice of attachment, or

(iii)   where he or the taxpayer named in the notice is —

(I)   declared bankrupt, the date he or the taxpayer is so declared, or

(II)   a company which commences to be wound up, the "**relevant date**" within the meaning of section 285 of the Companies Act, 1963, in relation to the winding up,

whichever is the earliest;

"**relevant person**" means, in relation to a taxpayer, a person in respect of whom the Revenue Commissioners have reason to believe that he may have, at the time a notice of attachment is received by him in respect of a taxpayer, a debt due to the taxpayer;

"**return**" means a return made by a relevant person under subsection (2)(*a*)(iii);

"**specified amount**" has the meaning assigned to it by subsection (2)(*a*)(ii);

"**tax**" means any tax, duty, levy or charge which, in accordance with any provision of the Acts, is placed under the care and management of the Revenue Commissioners;

"taxpayer" means a person who is liable to pay, remit or account for tax to the Revenue Commissioners under the Acts.

(2) (*a*) Subject to subsection (3), where a taxpayer has made default, whether before or after the passing of this Act, in paying, remitting, or accounting for, any tax, interest on unpaid tax, or penalty to the Revenue Commissioners, the Revenue Commissioners may, if the taxpayer has not made good the default, give to a relevant person in relation to the taxpayer a notice in writing (in this section referred to as **"the notice of attachment"**) in which is entered —

    (i) the taxpayer's name and address,

    [(ii) (I) the amount or aggregate amount, or

         (II) in a case where more than one notice of attachment is given to a relevant person or relevant persons in respect of a taxpayer, a portion of the amount or aggregate amount,

of the taxes, interest on unpaid taxes and penalties in respect of which the taxpayer is in default at the time of the giving of the notice or notices of attachment (the said amount, aggregate amount, or portion of the amount or aggregate amount, as the case may be, being referred to in this section as **"the specified amount"**),]⁵

    (iii) a direction to the relevant person —

         (I) to deliver to the Revenue Commissioners, within the period of 10 days from the time at which the notice of attachment is received by him, a return in writing specifying whether or not any debt is due by him to the taxpayer at the time the notice is received by him, and if any debt is so due, specifying the amount of the debt:

Provided that where the amount of the debt due by the relevant person to the taxpayer is equal to or greater than the specified amount in relation to the taxpayer, the amount of the debt specified in the return shall be an amount equal to the specified amount,

[Provided also that where the relevant person is a financial institution and the debt due by the relevant person to the taxpayer is part of a deposit held to the credit of the taxpayer and any other person or persons to their joint benefit the said return shall be made within a period of 10 days from—

         (A) the expiry of the period specified in the notices to be given under paragraph (*c*), or

         (B) the production of the evidence referred to in paragraph (*c*) (II),]⁶

      and

         (II) if the amount of any debt is so specified to pay to the Revenue Commissioners within the period aforesaid a sum equal to the amount of the debt so specified.

    (*b*) A relevant person to whom a notice of attachment has been given shall comply with the direction in the notice.

[(*c*) Where a relevant person which is a financial institution is given a notice of attachment and the debt due by the relevant person to the taxpayer is part of a deposit held by the relevant person to the credit of the taxpayer and any other person or persons (hereafter in this paragraph referred to as **"the other party or parties"**) for their joint benefit, the relevant person shall, on receipt of the notice of attachment, give to the taxpayer and the other party or parties to the deposit a notice in writing in which is entered—

   (i)   the taxpayer's name and address,

   (ii)   the name and address of the person to whom a notice under this paragraph is given,

   (iii)   the name and address of the relevant person, and

   (iv)   the specified amount,

and which states that—

     (I)   a notice of attachment under this section has been received in respect of the taxpayer,

     (II)   under this section, a deposit is deemed (unless evidence to the contrary is produced to the satisfaction of the relevant person within 10 days of the giving of the notice under this paragraph) to be held to the benefit of the taxpayer and the other party or parties to the deposit equally, and

     (III)   unless such evidence is produced within the period specified in the notice given under this paragraph, a sum equal to the amount of the deposit so deemed to be held to the benefit of the taxpayer, and, accordingly, regarded as a debt due to the taxpayer by the relevant person, shall be paid to the Revenue Commissioners where that amount is equal to or less than the specified amount and where that amount is greater than the specified amount an amount equal to the specified amount shall be paid to the Revenue Commissioners.][7]

(3) An amount in respect of tax, interest on unpaid tax or a penalty, as respects which a taxpayer is in default as specified in subsection (2), shall not be entered in a notice of attachment unless —

   (*a*)   a period of one month has expired from the date on which such default commenced, and

   [(*b*)   the Revenue Commissioners have given the taxpayer a notice in writing (whether or not the document containing the notice also contains other information being communicated by the Revenue Commissioners to the taxpayer), not later than 7 days before the date of the receipt by the relevant person or relevant persons concerned of a notice of attachment, stating that, if the amount is not paid, it may be specified in a notice or notices of attachment and recovered under this section from a relevant person or relevant persons in relation to the taxpayer.][8]

(4) If, when a relevant person receives a notice of attachment, the amount of the debt due by him to the taxpayer named in the notice is less than the specified amount in relation to the taxpayer or no debt is so due and, at any time thereafter before the end of the

relevant period in relation to the notice, an additional debt becomes due by the relevant person to the taxpayer, the relevant person shall, within 10 days of that time —

(a) if the aggregate of the amount of any debt so due and the additional debt so due is equal to or less than the specified amount in relation to the taxpayer —

    (i) deliver a further return to the Revenue Commissioners specifying the additional debt, and

    (ii) pay to the Revenue Commissioners the amount of the additional debt,

and so on for each subsequent occasion during the relevant period in relation to the notice of attachment on which an additional debt becomes due by the relevant person to the taxpayer until the aggregate amount of the debt and the additional debt or debts so due equals the specified amount in relation to the taxpayer or the provisions of paragraph (b) apply in relation to an additional debt, and

(b) if the aggregate amount of any debt and the additional debt or debts so due to the taxpayer is greater than the specified amount in relation to the taxpayer —

    (i) deliver a further return to the Revenue Commissioners specifying such portion of the latest additional debt as when added to the aggregate of the debt and any earlier additional debts is equal to the specified amount in relation to the taxpayer, and

    (ii) pay to the Revenue Commissioners the said portion of the additional debt.

(5) Where a relevant person delivers, either fraudulently or negligently, an incorrect return or further return that purports to be a return or further return made in accordance with this section, he shall be deemed to be guilty of an offence under section 94 of the Finance Act, 1983.

(6) (a) Where a notice of attachment has been given to a relevant person in respect of a taxpayer, the relevant person shall not, during the relevant period in relation to the notice, make any disbursements out of the debt, or any additional debt, due by him to the taxpayer save to the extent that any such disbursement —

    (i) will not reduce the debt or the aggregate of the debt and any additional debts so due to an amount that is less than the specified amount in relation to the taxpayer, or

    (ii) is made pursuant to an order of a court.

(b) For the purposes of this section, a disbursement made by a relevant person contrary to paragraph (a) shall be deemed not to reduce the amount of the debt or any additional debts due by him to the taxpayer.

(7) (a) Sections 500 and 503 of the Income Tax Act, 1967, shall apply to a failure by a relevant person to deliver a return required by a notice of attachment within the time specified in the notice or to deliver a further return within the time specified in subsection (4) as they apply to a failure to deliver a return referred to in the said section 500 and Schedule 15 to the said Act is hereby amended by the insertion in Column 1 of "Finance Act, 1988, paragraph (a)(iii)(I) of subsection (2) and paragraphs (a)(i) and (b)(i) of subsection (4) of section 73".

(b) A certificate signed by an officer of the Revenue Commissioners which certifies that he has examined the relevant records and that it appears from them that, during a specified period, a specified return was not received from a relevant person shall be evidence until the contrary is proved that the relevant person did not deliver the return during that period and a certificate certifying as provided by this paragraph and purporting to be signed by an officer of the Revenue Commissioners may be tendered in evidence without proof and shall be deemed until the contrary is proved to have been so signed.

(8) Where a relevant person to whom a notice of attachment in respect of a taxpayer has been given —

(*a*) delivers the return required to be delivered by the said notice but fails to pay to the Revenue Commissioners, within the time specified in the notice, the amount specified in the return or any part of that amount, or

(*b*) delivers a further return under subsection (4) but fails to pay to the Revenue Commissioners, within the time specified in the said subsection (4), the amount specified in the further return or any part of that amount,

the amount specified in the return or further return, or the part of that amount, as the case may be, which he has failed to pay to the Revenue Commissioners may, if the notice of attachment has not been revoked by a notice of revocation, be sued for and recovered by action, or other appropriate proceedings, at the suit of an officer of the Revenue Commissioners in any court of competent jurisdiction.

(9) Nothing in this section shall be construed as rendering any failure by a relevant person to make a return or further return required by this section, or pay to the Revenue Commissioners the amount or amounts required by this section to be paid by him, liable to be treated as a failure to which section 94 of the Finance Act, 1983, applies.

(10)(*a*) A notice of attachment given to a relevant person in respect of a taxpayer may be revoked by the Revenue Commissioners, at any time, by notice in writing given to the relevant person and shall be revoked forthwith if the taxpayer has paid the specified amount to the Revenue Commissioners.

(*b*) Where, in pursuance of this section, a relevant person pays any amount to the Revenue Commissioners out of a debt or an additional debt due by him to the taxpayer and, at the time of the receipt by the Revenue Commissioners of the said amount, the taxpayer has paid the [amount or aggregate amount of the taxes, interest on unpaid taxes and penalties in respect of which the taxpayer is in default at the time of the giving of the notice or notices of attachment][9] to the Revenue Commissioners, the first-mentioned amount shall be refunded by the Revenue Commissioners forthwith to the taxpayer.

(11) If a notice of attachment or a notice of revocation is given to a relevant person in relation to a taxpayer a copy thereof shall be given by the Revenue Commissioners to the taxpayer forthwith.

(12)(*a*) If, in pursuance of this section, any amount is paid to the Revenue Commissioners by a relevant person, the relevant person shall forthwith give the taxpayer concerned a notice in writing specifying the payment, its amount and the reason for which it was made.

(*b*) On the receipt by the Revenue Commissioners of an amount paid in pursuance of this section, the Revenue Commissioners shall forthwith notify the taxpayer and the relevant person in writing of such receipt.

(13) If, in pursuance of this section, a relevant person pays to the Revenue Commissioners the whole or part of the amount of a debt, or an additional debt, due by him to a taxpayer, or any portion of such an amount, the taxpayer shall allow such payment and the relevant person shall be acquitted and discharged of the amount of the payment as if it had been paid to the taxpayer.

(14) If, in pursuance of this section, a relevant person is prohibited from making any disbursement out of a debt, or an additional debt, due to a taxpayer, no action shall lie against the relevant person in any court by reason of a failure to make any such disbursement.

(15) Any obligation on the Revenue Commissioners to maintain secrecy or any other restriction upon the disclosure of information by the Revenue Commissioners shall not apply in relation to information contained in a notice of attachment.

(16) A notice of attachment in respect of a taxpayer shall not be given to a relevant person at a time when the relevant person or the taxpayer is an undischarged bankrupt or a company being wound up.

(17)...[10].

(18) The Revenue Commissioners may nominate any of their officers to perform any acts and discharge any functions authorised by this section to be performed or discharged by the Revenue Commissioners.

Amendments

[1]   Definition of "the Acts" substituted by FA 1992 s 241(*a*)(i).

[2]   Substituted by FA 1992 s 241(*a*)(ii).

[3]   Proviso inserted by FA 1992 s 241(*a*)(iii).

[4]   Definition of "interest on unpaid tax" substituted by FA 1992 s 241(*a*)(iv).

[5]   Substituted by FA 1992 s 241(*b*)(i).

[6]   Proviso inserted by FA 1992 s 241(*b*)(ii).

[7]   Subs (2)(*c*) inserted by FA 1992 s 241(*b*)(iii).

[8]   Subs (3)(*b*) substituted by FA 1992 s 241(*c*).

[9]   Substituted by FA 1992 s 241(*d*); previously "specified amount".

[10] Subs (17) deleted by FA 1992 s 241(*e*).

Notes

The power of attachment allows the Revenue Commissioners to collect tax by instructing a person who owes money to a tax defaulter (for example an insurance company) to pay that debt directly to the Revenue Commissioners. The power is similar to a garnishee order (Rules of the Superior Courts 1986 Order 43).

Narrative

Capital Acquisitions Tax, Chapter 22.

Cross-references

Tax (incentive) amnesty, relevant tax does not include tax that before 25 May 1993 was included in a notice of attachment and not revoked: WCTIPA 1993 s 2(2)(proviso).

74 Construction of certain Acts in accordance with Status of Children Act, 1987

(1) In this section **"the Acts"** means —

(i)   the Tax Acts,

(ii) the Capital Gains Tax Acts,

(iii) the Capital Acquisitions Tax Act, 1976, and the enactments amending or extending that Act, and

(iv) the statutes relating to stamp duty,

and any instruments made thereunder.

(2) Notwithstanding any provision of the Acts or the dates on which they were passed, in deducing any relationship between persons for the purposes of the Acts, the Acts shall be construed in accordance with section 3 of the Status of Children Act, 1987.

(3) This section shall have effect —

(i)   in relation to the Tax Acts, as respects the year 1987-88 and subsequent years of assessment or accounting periods ending on or after the 14th day of January, 1988, as the case may be,

(ii) in relation to the Capital Gains Tax Acts, as respects disposals made on or after the 14th day of January, 1988,

(iii) in relation to the Capital Acquisitions Tax Act, 1976, as respects gifts and inheritances taken on or after the 14th day of January, 1988, and

(iv) in relation to the statutes relating to stamp duties, as respects any instrument executed on or after the 14th day of January, 1988.

Notes

On or after 14 January 1988, the effect of the Status of Children Act 1987 s 3 (which abolished the concept of illegitimacy) is to be recognised in all statutes, irrespective of the date on which they were passed. This means that for capital acquisitions tax purposes, as regards gifts or inheritance taken on or after 14 January 1988, children formerly regarded as illegitimate qualify for the £150,000 threshold (as indexed: FA 1990 s 128).

Narrative

Capital Acquisitions Tax, Chapter 2.

Definition

"person": IA 1937 s 11(*c*); "the Tax Acts": CTA 1976 s 155(2).

---

76 Care and management of taxes and duties

All taxes and duties imposed by this Act are hereby placed under the care and management of the Revenue Commissioners.

77 Short title, construction and commencement

(1) This Act may be cited as the Finance Act, 1988.

...

...

(6) Part V shall be construed together with the Capital Acquisitions Tax Act, 1976, and the enactments amending or extending that Act and (so far as relating to capital gains tax) shall be construed together with the Capital Gains Tax Acts.

...

...

(10) Any reference in this Act to any other enactment shall, except so far as the context otherwise requires, be construed as a reference to that enactment as amended by or under any other enactment including this Act.

(11) In this Act, a reference to a Part, section or Schedule is to a Part or section of, or Schedule to, this Act, unless it is indicated that reference to some other enactment is intended.

(12) In this Act, a reference to a subsection, paragraph or subparagraph is to the subsection, paragraph or subparagraph of the provision (including a Schedule) in which the reference occurs, unless it is indicated that reference to some other provision is intended.

FINANCE ACT 1989

(1989 Number 10)
(Date of passing: 24 May 1989)

ARRANGEMENT OF SECTIONS

PART V
CAPITAL ACQUISITIONS TAX

CHAPTER I

PART V
CAPITAL ACQUISITIONS TAX

73 Interpretation (Part V)

In this Part **"the Principal Act"** means the Capital Acquisitions Tax Act, 1976

CHAPTER II
Arrangements with regard to returns and assessments

74 Delivery of returns

Note

A limited measure of self-assessment was introduced for the 1% annual discretionary tax charge imposed by FA 1986 Pt V Ch I.

555

This section, by substituting CATA 1976 s 36 introduced full self-assessment for capital acquisitions tax. Previously the person primarily accountable for the tax was obliged to furnish a return of chargeable property within three months of the valuation date. The new CATA 1976 s 36 widens the scope of self-assessment to cover all gifts and inheritances and also the once off 6% discretionary trust charge, for valuation dates on or after 1 September 1989.

The primarily accountable person must furnish the return of chargeable property within four months of the valuation date, together with a computation of the tax arising, and a remittance for any tax due and/or an application for payment by instalments and/or an application to pay tax by transfer of government securities (CATA 1976 s 45). Instalment arrangements are not granted for personal property taken absolutely.

The self-assessment return must be submitted once the taxable value of a gift or inheritance exceeds 80% of the sum on which a tax liability would arise.

The Revenue Commissioners are empowered, as before, to require any accountable person to deliver a return or an additional return.

75 Application of section 39 (assessment of tax) of Principal Act

Nothing in section 36 of the Principal Act shall preclude the Commissioners from making an assessment of tax, a correcting assessment of tax, or an additional assessment of tax, under the provisions of section 39 of that Act.

Notes

This section preserves the rights of the Revenue Commissioners despite the introduction of self-assessment, to make assessments of capital acquisitions tax owed.

Definitions

"Commissioners": SA 1891 s 122(1); CATA 1976 s 2(1).

76 Amendment of section 41 (payment of tax and interest on tax) of Principal Act

(1) ...

(2) A payment by an accountable person of tax shall be treated as a payment on account of tax for the purposes of section 41 of the Principal Act, notwithstanding that the payment may be conditional or that the assessment of tax is incorrect.

Note

Subs (1) substituted CATA 1976 s 41(3). Interest on overdue tax is not to be charged in a self-assessment case if the tax is paid within four months of the valuation date. Otherwise interest accrues at the monthly rate applicable.

Definitions

"accountable person": SA 1891 s 122(1); CATA 1976 s 2(1).

77 Amendment of section 63 (penalties) of Principal Act

Note

Para (*a*) substituted CATA 1976 s 63(1); para (*b*) substituted "£1,000" for "£500" in CATA 1976 s 63(2); para (*c*) substituted "£5,000" for "£1,000" in CATA 1976 s 63(3); para (*d*) substituted "£1,000" for "£250" in CATA 1976 s 63(7).

The section increases the penalties for

    (*a*) failure to comply with the new self-assessment procedures;

    (*b*) obstruction of authorised personnel on official inspections;

    (*c*) the fraudulent or negligent delivery of a return;

    (*d*) The furnishing of any incorrect return, statement, declaration, evidence or valuation.

78 Amendment of section 107 (application of Principal Act) of Finance Act, 1984

Note

Section 78(*a*) deleted FA 1984 s 107(*e*) and substituted FA 1984 s 107(*g*). These changes are consequential upon the 3% once off discretionary trust charge being brought within the self-assessment system.

---

79 Surcharge for undervaluation of property

(1) Where—

- (*a*) an accountable person delivers a return, and
- (*b*) the estimate of the market value of any asset comprised in a gift or inheritance and included in that return, when expressed as a percentage of the ascertained value of that asset, is within any of the percentages specified in column (1) of the Table to this section,

then the amount of tax attributable to the property which is that asset shall be increased by a sum (hereafter in this section referred to as the **"surcharge"**) equal to the corresponding percentage, set out in column (2) of that Table opposite the relevant percentage in the said column (1), of that amount of tax.

(2) Interest shall be payable under the provisions of section 41 of the Principal Act upon any surcharge as if the surcharge were tax, and the surcharge and any interest thereon shall be chargeable and recoverable as if the surcharge and that interest were part of the tax.

(3) Any person aggrieved by the imposition on him of a surcharge under this section in respect of any asset may, within 30 days of the notification to him of the amount of such surcharge, appeal to the Appeal Commissioners against the imposition of such surcharge on the grounds, and only on the grounds, that, having regard to all the circumstances, there were sufficient grounds on which he might reasonably have based his estimate of the market value of the asset.

(4) The Appeal Commissioners shall hear and determine an appeal to them under subsection (3) as if it were an appeal to them against an assessment to tax, and the provisions of section 52 of the Principal Act relating to an appeal or to the rehearing of an appeal or to the statement of a case for the opinion of the High Court on a point of law shall, with any necessary modifications, apply accordingly.

(5) In this section **"ascertained value"** means the market value subject to the right of appeal under section 51 or section 52 of the Principal Act.

Estimate of the market value of the asset in the return, expressed as a percentage of the ascertained value of that asset	Surcharge
(1)	(2)
Equal to or greater than 0 per cent but less than 40 per cent	30 per cent
Equal to or greater than 40 per cent but less than 50 per cent	20 per cent
Equal to or greater than 50 per cent but less than 67 per cent	10 per cent

Notes

This section is intended to discourage, by means of a surcharge, the understating of the values of assets included in self-assessment returns. If only 40% of the true value of an asset is shown on the return the surcharge can be as high as 30%. Interest is also payable on the surcharge as if it were tax. The imposition of a surcharge may be appealed to the Appeal Commissioners, and there is a consequent further right of Appeal to the Circuit Court and the High Court.

Narrative

Capital Acquisitions Tax, Chapters 6, 19.

Definitions

"accountable person": SA 1891 s 122(1); CATA 1976 s 2(1); "gift", "inheritance", "market value", "property", "return": CATA 1976 s 2(1).

CHAPTER III
Miscellaneous

80 Amendment of section 2 (interpretation) of Principal Act

Note

As regards gifts or inheritances taken on or after 26 July 1988:

Para (*a*) amended CATA 1976 s 2(1) definition of "child"; the net effect is that children adopted under adoptions made under the Adoption Act 1988 are recognised as children for capital acquisitions tax purposes. Such children therefore qualify for the £150,000 (as indexed) class threshold. CATA 1976 s 2(1) already applies to children adopted under the provisions of earlier adoption legislation.

Para (*b*) made a corresponding adjustment to CATA 1976 s 2(5).

81 Extension of section 35 (accountable persons) of Principal Act

(1) In the case of an inheritance taken on or before the date of death of the disponer, the disponer shall also be a person accountable for the payment of any amount of the tax for which the persons referred to in section 35(1) of the Principal Act are made primarily accountable and subject to subsection (2), the Principal Act shall have effect as if such disponer were a person referred to in section 35(2)(*b*) of that Act:

Provided that the disponer as such shall not be so accountable in the case where the date of the disposition was prior to the 1st day of May, 1989.

(2) The provisions of subsections (3) and (9) of section 35 of the Principal Act shall not apply to a disponer who is accountable for the payment of tax under subsection (1).

Notes

Prior to the enactment of this section, a disponer was an accountable person for payment of gift tax, but not where a gift became an inheritance due to the death of the disponer within two years of the date of the gift. This section provides that, as regards gifts made on or after 1 May 1989, such a disponer is an accountable person for the payment of tax.

Definitions

"accountable person": SA 1891 s 122(1); CATA 1976 s 2(1); "date of disposition", "disponer", "disposition", "inheritance": CATA 1976 s 2(1); "person": IA 1937 s 11(*c*).

82 Amendment of section 37 (signing of returns, etc) of Principal Act

Note

This section, by substituting CATA 1976 s 37(4), provides for the acceptance of returns, affidavits etc in a form approved by the Revenue Commissioners, including electronic, photographic or other processes.

83 Amendment of Second Schedule to Principal Act

Note

This section substituted CATA 1976 Sch 2 Part I para 9 (the "favourite nephew relief") as regards gifts or inheritances taken on or after 1 May 1989.

The nephew (or niece) must, as before, have worked substantially on a full time basis in the business for five years.

The donee or successor must now also meet the "qualifying work period" requirement (24 hours weekly) unless the business operations are carried out exclusively by the disponer, any spouse of the disponer and the donee or successor. In such circumstances, the weekly work period is reduced to 15 hours.

The relief has been extended to include bequests taken on the cesser of a limited interest where all the of the necessary conditions are met. The favourable treatment does not apply to a gift or an inheritance taken from a discretionary trust.

84 Amendment of section 60 (relief in respect of certain policies of insurance) of Finance Act, 1985

Note

The proceeds of life assurance policies, taken out expressly to pay inheritance tax due by the successors of the disponer are exempt from capital acquisitions tax, provided the inheritance is taken on or after the death of the insured and not later than one year after the death. The policy proceeds are also excluded from aggregation with any other taxable gifts or inheritances, to the extent that they are used to pay inheritance tax due by the successor.

The annual premium is not allowable as an income tax allowance for income tax years to 1990-91 (life assurance relief was abolished for 1991-92 and later tax years).

The original relief applied to policies effected by individuals. This section, by inserting FA 1985 s 60(1A), extended the relief to apply to joint policies effected by spouses to cover inheritance tax payable by the successors of the survivor of either spouse.

The relief was further extended (FA 1990 s 130) to cover succession of property on the survivor's death (cesser of a life interest) or where an inheritance from the predeceased spouse is only taken in the event of the insured not surviving his or her partner for up to 31 days. In such circumstances the policy proceeds may be used to pay tax due by the successors of the predeceased spouse.

The relief was further extended (FA 1991 s 118) to provide that proceeds of a qualifying policy in the sole name of a life tenant, taking under a deceased spouse's will may be used to pay inheritance tax arising on the cesser of the life interest.

85 Exemption of specified collective investment undertakings

[(1) In this section—

"investment undertaking" has the meaning assigned to it by section 739B of the Taxes Consolidation Act, 1997;

"specified collective investment undertaking" has the meaning assigned to it by section 734 of the Taxes Consolidation Act, 1997;

"unit", in relation to an investment undertaking, has the meaning assigned to it by section 739B of the Taxes Consolidation Act, 1997;

"unit", in relation to a specified collective investment undertaking, has the meaning assigned to it by section 734 of the Taxes Consolidation Act, 1997.

(2) Where any unit of an investment undertaking or of a specified collective investment undertaking is comprised in a gift or an inheritance, then such unit—

   (*a*)   shall be exempt from tax, and

(b)   shall not be taken into account in computing tax on any gift or inheritance taken by the donee or successor,

if, but only if, it is shown to the satisfaction of the Commissioners that—

(i)   the unit is comprised in the gift or inheritance—

(I)   at the date of the gift or at the date of the inheritance, and

(II)   at the valuation date,

(ii)   at the date of the disposition, the disponer is neither domiciled nor ordinarily resident in the State, and

(iii)   at the date of the gift or at the date of the inheritance, the donee or successor is neither domiciled nor ordinarily resident in the State.][1]

(3) This section shall have effect as respects gifts and inheritances taken on or after the date of the passing of this Act.

Notes

Under the FA 1989 s 85 dispositions comprising the transfer of an in interest in a collective investment undertaking (of a unit trust nature) are exempt from capital acquisitions tax if the qualifying disposition is governed by foreign law and the donee or successor is not regarded as either domiciled or ordinarily resident in the State at the date of the disposition or in the date of the gift or inheritance.

Amendments

[1]   Subss (1)-(2) substituted by FA 2001 s 224(1) with effect from 1 April 2000 for units of an investment undertaking comprised in a gift or an inheritance where the date of the gift or the date of the inheritance is on or after 1 April 2000 and from 15 February 2001 for units of a specified collective investment undertaking comprised in a gift or an inheritance where the date of the gift or the date of the inheritance is on or after 15 February 2001 and the units come into the beneficial ownership of the disponer on or after 15 February 2001, or become subject to the disposition on or after that date without having been previously in the beneficial ownership of the disponer.

In relation to any unit of an investment undertaking comprised in a gift or an inheritance, s 85(2)(ii), shall, notwithstanding that the disponer was domiciled or ordinarily resident in the State at the date of the disposition, be treated as satisfied where the proper law of the disposition was not the law of the State at the date of the disposition, and the unit came into the beneficial ownership of the disponer or became subject to the disposition prior to 15 February 2001.

Definitions

"Commissioners", "date of the disposition", "date of the gift", "date of the inheritance", "disponer", "disposition", "donee", "gift", "inheritance", "valuation date", "successor": CATA 1976 s 2(1)

PART VI

ANTI-AVOIDANCE

86 Transactions to avoid liability to tax

(1) (a)   In this section —

"the Acts" means —

(i)   the Tax Acts,

(ii)   the Capital Gains Tax Acts,

(iii)   the Value-Added Tax Act, 1972, and the enactments amending or extending that Act,

(iv)   the Capital Acquisitions Tax Act, 1976, and the enactments amending or extending that Act,

    (v)   Part VI of the Finance Act, 1983, and the enactments amending or extending that Part, and

    (vi)   the statutes relating to stamp duty,

and any instrument made thereunder;

"business" means any trade, profession or vocation;

"notice of opinion" means a notice given by the Revenue Commissioners under the provisions of subsection (6);

"tax" means any tax, duty, levy or charge which, in accordance with the provisions of the Acts, is placed under the care and management of the Revenue Commissioners and any interest, penalty or other amount payable pursuant to those provisions;

"tax advantage" means —

    (i)   a reduction, avoidance or deferral of any charge or assessment to tax, including any potential or prospective charge or assessment, or

    (ii)   a refund of or a payment of an amount of tax, or an increase in an amount of tax, refundable or otherwise payable to a person, including any potential or prospective amount so refundable or payable,

arising out of, or by reason of, a transaction, including a transaction where another transaction would not have been undertaken or arranged to achieve the results, or any part of the results, achieved or intended to be achieved by the transaction;

"tax avoidance transaction" has the meaning assigned to it by subsection (2);

"tax consequences" means, in relation to a tax avoidance transaction, such adjustments and acts as may be made and done by the Revenue Commissioners pursuant to subsection (5) in order to withdraw or deny the tax advantage resulting from the tax avoidance transaction;

"transaction" means —

    (i)   any transaction, action, course of action, course of conduct, scheme, plan or proposal and

    (ii)   any agreement, arrangement, understanding, promise or undertaking, whether express or implied and whether or not enforceable or intended to be enforceable by legal proceedings, and

    (iii) any series of or combination of the circumstances referred to in paragraphs (i) and (ii),

whether entered into or arranged by one person or by two or more persons —

        (I)   whether acting in concert or not, or

        (II)   whether or not entered into or arranged wholly or partly outside the State, or

        (III)   whether or not entered into or arranged as part of a larger transaction or in conjunction with any other transaction or transactions.

  (b)   In subsections (2) and (3), for the purposes of the hearing or rehearing under subsection (8) of an appeal made under subsection (7) or for the purposes of the determination of a question of law arising on the statement of a case for the opinion of the High Court, the references to the Revenue Commissioners shall, subject to any necessary modifications, be construed as references to the Appeal Commissioners or to a judge of the Circuit Court or, to the extent necessary, to a judge of the High Court, as appropriate.

(2) For the purposes of this section and subject to subsection (3), a transaction is a "**tax avoidance transaction**" if, having regard to any one or more of the following, that is to say —

(*a*) the results of the transaction,

(*b*) its use as a means of achieving those results, and

(*c*) any other means by which the results or any part of the results could have been achieved,

the Revenue Commissioners form the opinion that—

(i) it gives rise to, or but for this section, would give rise to, a tax advantage, and

(ii) the transaction was not undertaken or arranged primarily for purposes other than to give rise to a tax advantage,

and references in this section to the Revenue Commissioners forming an opinion that a transaction is a tax avoidance transaction shall be construed as references to them forming an opinion with regard to the transaction in accordance with the provisions of this subsection.

(3) Without prejudice to the generality of the provisions of subsection (2), in forming an opinion in accordance with that subsection and subsection (4), as to whether or not a transaction is a tax avoidance transaction, the Revenue Commissioners shall not regard the transaction as being a tax avoidance transaction if they are satisfied that —

(*a*) notwithstanding that the purpose or purposes of the transaction could have been achieved by some other transaction which would have given rise to a greater amount of tax being payable by the person, the transaction —

(i) was undertaken or arranged by a person with a view, directly or indirectly, to the realisation of profits in the course of the business activities of a business carried on by the person, and

(ii) was not undertaken or arranged primarily to give rise to a tax advantage,

or

(*b*) the transaction was undertaken or arranged for the purpose of obtaining the benefit of any relief, allowance or other abatement provided by any provision of the Acts and that transaction would not result directly or indirectly in a misuse of the provision or an abuse of the provision having regard to the purposes for which it was provided:

Provided that, in forming an opinion as aforesaid in relation to any transaction, the Revenue Commissioners shall have regard to —

(I) the form of that transaction,

(II) the substance of that transaction,

    (III)   the substance of any other transaction or transactions which that transaction may reasonably be regarded as being directly or indirectly related to or connected with, and

    (IV)   the final outcome and result of that transaction and any combination of those other transactions which are so related or connected.

(4) Subject to the provisions of this section, the Revenue Commissioners, as respects any transaction, may, at any time —

    (*a*)   form the opinion that the transaction is a tax avoidance transaction,

    (*b*)   calculate the tax advantage which they consider arises, or which, but for this section, would arise, from the transaction,

    (*c*)   determine the tax consequences which they consider would arise in respect of the transaction if their opinion were to become final and conclusive in accordance with subsection (5)(*e*), and

    (*d*)   calculate the amount of any relief from double taxation which they would propose to give to any person in accordance with the provisions of subsection (5)(*c*).

(5) (*a*)   Where the opinion of the Revenue Commissioners that a transaction is a tax avoidance transaction becomes final and conclusive they may, notwithstanding any other provision of the Acts, make all such adjustment and do all such acts as are just and reasonable (in so far as those adjustments and acts have been specified or described in a notice of opinion given under subsection (6) and subject to the manner in which any appeal made under subsection (7) against any matter specified or described in the notice of opinion has been finally determined, including any adjustments and acts not so specified or described in the notice of opinion but which form part of a final determination of any appeal as aforesaid) in order that the tax advantage resulting from a tax avoidance transaction shall be withdrawn from or denied to any person concerned.

  (*b*)   Subject to, but without prejudice, to the generality of paragraph (*a*), the Revenue Commissioners may —

    (i)   allow or disallow, in whole or in part, any deduction or other amount which is relevant in computing tax payable, or any part thereof,

    (ii)   allocate or deny to any person any deduction, loss, abatement, relief, allowance, exemption, income or other amount, or any part thereof, or

    (iii)   recharacterize for tax purposes the nature of any payment or other amount.

  (*c*)   Where the Revenue Commissioners make any adjustment or do any act for the purposes of paragraph (*a*), they shall afford relief from any double taxation which they consider would, but for this paragraph, arise by virtue of any adjustment made or act done by them pursuant to the foregoing provisions of this subsection.

  (*d*)   Notwithstanding any other provision of the Acts, where —

    (i)   pursuant to subsection (4)(*c*), the Revenue Commissioners determine the tax consequences which they consider would arise in respect of a transaction if their opinion, that the transaction is a tax avoidance transaction, were to become final and conclusive, and

(ii) pursuant to that determination, they specify or describe in a notice of opinion any adjustment or act which they consider would be, or be part of, the said tax consequences,

then, in so far as any right of appeal lay under subsection (7) against any such adjustment or act so specified or described, no right or further right of appeal shall lie under the Acts against that adjustment or act when it is made or done in accordance with the provisions of this subsection or against any adjustment or act so made or done that is not so specified or described in the notice of opinion but which forms part of the final determination of any appeal made under the said subsection (7) against any matter specified or described in the notice of opinion.

(e) For the purposes of this subsection an opinion of the Revenue Commissioners that a transaction is a tax avoidance transaction shall be final and conclusive—

(i) if, within the time limited, no appeal is made under subsection (7) against any matter or matters specified or described in a notice or notices of opinion given pursuant to that opinion, or

(ii) as and when all appeals made under the said subsection (7) against any such matter or matters have been finally determined and none of the appeals has been so determined by an order directing that the opinion of the Revenue Commissioners to the effect that the transaction is a tax avoidance transaction is void.

(6) (a) Where, pursuant to subsections (2) and (4), the Revenue Commissioners form the opinion that a transaction is a tax avoidance transaction, they shall immediately thereupon give notice in writing of the opinion to any person from whom a tax advantage would be withdrawn or to whom a tax advantage would be denied or to whom relief from double taxation would be given, if the opinion became final, and conclusive, and the notice shall specify or describe—

(i) the transaction which in the opinion of the Revenue Commissioners is a tax avoidance transaction,

(ii) the tax advantage, or part thereof, calculated by the Revenue Commissioners which would be withdrawn from or denied to the person to whom the notice is given,

(iii) the tax consequences of the transaction determined by the Revenue Commissioners, in so far as they would refer to the person, and

(iv) the amount of any relief from double taxation calculated by the Revenue Commissioners which they would propose to give to the person in accordance with subsection (5)(c).

(b) Section 542 of the Income Tax Act, 1967, shall, with any necessary modifications, apply for the purposes of a notice given under this subsection, or subsection (10), as if it were a notice given under that Act.

(7) Any person aggrieved by an opinion formed or, in so far as it refers to the person, a calculation or determination made by the Revenue Commissioners pursuant to subsection (4) may, by notice in writing given to the Revenue Commissioners within 30 days of the date of the notice of opinion, appeal to the Appeal Commissioners on the

grounds and, notwithstanding any other provision of the Acts, only on the grounds that, having regard to all of the circumstances, including any fact or matter which was not known to the Revenue Commissioners when they formed their opinion or made their calculation or determination, and to the provisions of this section —

(*a*) the transaction specified or described in the notice of opinion is not a tax avoidance transaction, or

(*b*) the amount of the tax advantage, or the part thereof, specified or described in the notice of opinion which would be withdrawn from or denied to the person is incorrect, or

(*c*) the tax consequences specified or described in the notice of opinion, or such part thereof as shall be specified or described by the appellant in the notice of appeal, would not be just and reasonable in order to withdraw or to deny the tax advantage, or part thereof, specified or described in the notice of opinion, or

(*d*) the amount of relief from double taxation which the Revenue Commissioners propose to give to the person is insufficient or incorrect.

(8) The Appeal Commissioners shall hear and determine an appeal made to them under subsection (7) as if it were an appeal against an assessment to income tax and, subject to subsection (9), all the provisions of the Income Tax Act, 1967, relating to the rehearing of an appeal and the statement of a case for the opinion of the High Court on a point of law shall apply accordingly with any necessary modifications:

Provided that on the hearing or rehearing of the appeal —

(*a*) it shall not be lawful to go into any grounds of appeal other than those specified in subsection (7), and

(*b*) at the request of the appellants, two or more appeals made by two or more persons pursuant to the same opinion, calculation or determination formed or made by the Revenue Commissioners pursuant to subsection (4) may be heard or reheard together.

(9) (*a*) On the hearing of an appeal made under subsection (7) the Appeal Commissioners shall have regard to all matters to which the Revenue Commissioners may or are required to have regard under the provisions of this section and —

(i)   in relation to an appeal made on the grounds referred to in paragraph (*a*) of subsection (7), they shall determine the appeal, in so far as it is made on those grounds, by ordering, if they, or a majority of them —

(I)   consider that the transaction specified or described in the notice of opinion, or any part of that transaction, is a tax avoidance transaction, that the opinion, or the opinion in so far as it relates to that part, is to stand good, or

(II) consider that, subject to such amendment or addition thereto as the Appeal Commissioners, or the said majority of them, deem necessary and as they shall specify or describe the transaction, or any part of it, specified or described in the notice of opinion, is a tax avoidance transaction, that the transaction, or that part of it, be so amended or added to and that, subject to the amendment or addition, the opinion, or the opinion in so far as it relates to that part, is to stand good, or

(III)   do not so consider as referred to in clause (I) or (II), that the opinion is void,

or

(ii)   in relation to an appeal made on the grounds referred to in paragraph (*b*) of subsection (7), they shall determine the appeal, in so far as it is made on those grounds, by ordering that the amount of the tax advantage, or the part thereof, specified or described in the notice of opinion be increased or reduced by such amount as they shall direct or that it shall stand good,

or

(iii)   in relation to an appeal made on the grounds referred to in paragraph (*c*) of subsection (7), they shall determine the appeal, in so far as it is made on those grounds, by ordering that the tax consequences specified or described in the notice of opinion shall be altered or added to in such manner as they shall direct or that they shall stand good,

or

(iv)   in relation to an appeal made on the grounds referred to in paragraph (*d*) of subsection (7), they shall determine the appeal, in so far as it is made on those grounds, by ordering that the amount of the relief from double taxation specified or described in the notice of opinion shall be increased or reduced by such amount as they shall direct or that it shall stand good.

(*b*)   The provisions of this subsection shall, subject to any necessary modifications, apply to the rehearing of an appeal by a judge of the Circuit Court and, to the extent necessary, to the determination by the High Court of any question or questions of law arising on the statement of a case for the opinion of the High Court.

(10) The Revenue Commissioners may, at any time, amend, add to or withdraw any matter specified or described in a notice of opinion by giving notice (hereafter in this subsection referred to as the **"notice of amendment"**) in writing of the amendment, addition or withdrawal to each and every person affected thereby, in so far as the person is so affected, and the foregoing provisions of this section shall apply in all respects as if the notice of amendment were a notice of opinion and any matter specified or described in the notice of amendment were specified or described in a notice of opinion:

Provided that no such amendment, addition or withdrawal may be made so as to set aside or alter any matter which has become final and conclusive on the determination of an appeal made with regard to that matter under subsection (7).

(11) Where pursuant to subsections (2) and (4), the Revenue Commissioners form the opinion that a transaction is a tax avoidance transaction and, pursuant to that opinion, notices are to be given under subsection (6) to two or more persons, any obligation on the Revenue Commissioners to maintain secrecy or any other restriction upon the disclosure of information by the Revenue Commissioners shall not apply with respect to the giving of the notices as aforesaid or to the performance of any acts or the discharge of any functions authorised by this section to be performed or discharged by them or to the performance of any act or the discharge of any functions, including any act or

function in relation to an appeal made under subsection (7), which is directly or indirectly related to the acts or functions so authorised.

(12) The Revenue Commissioners may nominate any of their officers to perform any acts and discharge any functions, including the forming of an opinion, authorised by this section to be performed or discharged by the Revenue Commissioners and references in this section to the Revenue Commissioners shall, with any necessary modifications, be construed as including references to an officer so nominated.

(13) This section shall apply as respects any transaction where the whole or any part of the transaction is undertaken or arranged on or after the 25th day of January, 1989, and as respects any transaction undertaken or arranged wholly before that date in so far as it gives rise to, or would, but for this section, give rise to —

(a) a reduction, avoidance or deferral of any charge or assessment to tax, or part thereof, where the charge or assessment arises by virtue of any other transaction carried out wholly on or after a date, or

(b) a refund or a payment of an amount, or of an increase in an amount, of tax, or part thereof, refundable or otherwise payable to a person where that amount, or increase in the amount, would otherwise become first so refundable or otherwise payable to the person on a date,

which could not fall earlier than the said 25th day of January, 1989, as the case may be.

Notes

This section was introduced following the judgment of the Supreme Court in *McGrath and others v MacDermott* [1988] ILRM 647, where it was held that it is the function of the legislature to positively provide for the bringing of a transaction within the charge the tax. Artificial transactions (for example that create paper losses) that are carried out purely for tax purposes, with little or no commercial reality may be disregarded by the Revenue Commissioners in computing a person's tax liability if the Revenue Commissioners are of the opinion that a "tax advantage" has arisen. There is a right of appeal to the Appeal Commissioners against such a Revenue opinion.

Narrative

Capital Acquisitions Tax, Chapter 20.

Case law

Tax avoidance issues arose in *O'Grady v Laragan Quarries Ltd*, IV ITR 269; *Dilleen v Kearns*, IV ITR 547; *Airspace Investments Ltd v M Moore*, V ITR 3.
Bona fide commercial motives: *Marwood Homes v IRC*, [1996] STI 52.
Meaning of "tax advantage": *IRC v Universities Superannuation Scheme*, [1997] STC 1.

90 Arrangements reducing value of company shares

(1) In this section—

"arrangement" includes—

(a) any act or omission by a person or by the trustees of a disposition;
(b) any act or omission by any person having an interest in shares in a company;
(c) the passing by any company of a resolution; or
(d) any combination of acts, omissions or resolutions referred to in paragraphs (a), (b) and (c);

"company" means a private company within the meaning assigned by section 16(2) of the Principal Act;

"company controlled by a donee or successor" has the same meaning as is assigned to **"company controlled by the donee or the successor"** by section 16 of the Principal Act;

"event" includes—

    (*a*)   a death; and

    (*b*)   the expiration of a specified period;

"the Principal Act" means the Capital Acquisitions Tax Act, 1976;

"related shares" means the shares in a company, the market value of which shares is increased by any arrangement;

"related trust" has the meaning assigned to it by subsections (2) and (4);

"specified amount" means an amount equal to the difference between—

    (*a*)   the market value of shares in a company immediately before an arrangement is made, and ascertained under the provisions of section 16 ...¹ of the Principal Act as if each share were a share in a company controlled by a donee or successor; and

    (*b*)   the market value of those shares, or of property representing those shares, immediately after the arrangement is made, and ascertained under the provisions of section 15 of the Principal Act,

and such specified amount shall be deemed to be situate where the company is incorporated.

(2) Where—

    (*a*)   a person has an absolute interest in possession in shares in a company; and

    (*b*)   any arrangement results in the market value of those shares, or of property representing those shares, immediately after that arrangement is made, being less than it would be but for that arrangement,

then, tax shall be payable in all respects as if a specified amount which relates to that arrangement were a benefit taken, immediately after that arrangement is made, from that person, as disponer, by—

    (i)   the beneficial owners of the related shares in that company; and

    (ii)   so far as the related shares in that company are held in trust (in this section referred to as the "related trust") and have no ascertainable beneficial owners, by the disponer in relation to that related trust as if, immediately after that arrangement is made, that disponer was the absolute beneficial owner of those related shares,

in the same proportions as the market value of the related shares, which are beneficially owned by them or are deemed to be so beneficially owned, is increased by that arrangement.

(3) Where—

    (*a*)   an interest in property is limited by the disposition creating it to cease on an event;

(b) immediately before the making of an arrangement to which paragraph (c) relates, the property includes shares in a company; and

(c) the arrangement results in the market value of those shares, or of property representing those shares, immediately after that arrangement is made, being less than it would be but for that arrangement,

then, tax shall be payable under that disposition in all respects—

(i) where the interest in property is an interest in possession, as if such property included a specified amount which relates to that arrangement;

(ii) where the interest in property is not an interest in possession, as if it were an interest in possession and such property included a specified amount which relates to that arrangement; and

(iii) as if the event on which the interest was limited to cease under that disposition had happened, to the extent of the specified amount, immediately before that arrangement is made.

(4) Where—

(a) shares in a company are, immediately before the making of an arrangement to which paragraph (b) relates, subject to a discretionary trust under or in consequence of any disposition; and

(b) the arrangement results in those shares, or property representing those shares, remaining subject to that discretionary trust but, immediately after that arrangement is made, the market value of those shares, or of property representing those shares, is less than it would be but for that arrangement,

then, tax shall be payable under that disposition in all respects as if a specified amount, which relates to that arrangement, were a benefit taken immediately after that arrangement is made—

(i) by the beneficial owners of the related shares in that company; and

(ii) so far as the related shares in that company are held in trust (in this section referred to as the "related trust") and have no ascertainable beneficial owners, by the disponer in relation to that related trust as if, immediately after that arrangement is made, that disponer was the absolute beneficial owner of those related shares,

in the same proportions as the market value of the related shares, which are beneficially owned by them or are deemed to be so beneficially owned, is increased by that arrangement.

(5) The provisions of subsections (2), (3) and (4) shall not prejudice any charge for tax in respect of any gift or inheritance taken under any disposition or after the making of an arrangement referred to in those subsections and comprising shares in a company, or property representing such shares.

(6) Where shares in a company, which are held in trust under a disposition made by any disponer, are related shares by reason of any arrangement referred to in this section, any gift or inheritance taken under the disposition on or after the arrangement is made and comprising those related shares, or property representing those related shares, shall be deemed to be taken from that disponer.

(7) In relation to the tax due and payable in respect of any gift or inheritance taken under the provisions of paragraph (ii) of subsection (2) or paragraph (ii) of subsection (4), and notwithstanding the provisions of the Principal Act—

(a) the disponer in relation to the related trust shall not be a person primarily accountable for the payment of such tax; and

(b) a person who is a trustee of the related trust concerned for the time being at the date of the gift or at the date of the inheritance, or at any date subsequent thereto, shall be so primarily accountable.

(8) A person who is accountable for the payment of tax in respect of any specified amount, or part of a specified amount, taken as a gift or an inheritance under this section shall, for the purpose of paying the tax, or raising the amount of the tax when already paid, have power, whether the related shares are or are not vested in him, to raise the amount of such tax and any interest and expenses properly paid or incurred by him in respect thereof, by the sale or mortgage of, or a terminable charge on, the related shares in the relevant company.

(9) Tax due and payable in respect of a taxable gift or a taxable inheritance taken under this section shall be and remain a charge on the related shares in the relevant company.

(10) Where related shares are subject to a discretionary trust immediately after an arrangement is made in accordance with the provisions of this section, the amount by which the market value of such shares is increased by such arrangement shall be property for the purposes of a charge for tax arising by reason of the provisions of section 106 of the Finance Act, 1984.

(11) This section shall apply only as respects a gift or an inheritance taken as a result of an arrangement which is made on or after the 25th day of January, 1989.

[(12) Where, immediately after and as a result of an arrangement, shares in a company have been redeemed, the redeemed shares shall, for the purpose of the references to property representing shares in subsection (1) and subsection (2), (3) or (4), except a reference in relation to which the redeemed shares are actually represented by property, be deemed, immediately after the arrangement, to be represented by property, and the market value of the property so deemed to represent the redeemed shares shall be deemed to be nil.]²

Amendments

¹   Words "or 17" deleted by FA 1993 s 126(1)(*a*) with effect from 24 February 1993.

²   Subs (12) inserted by FA 1993 s 126(1)(*b*) in relation to an arrangement made on or after 6 May 1993.

Notes

This anti-avoidance section deals with the transfer of rights attaching to particular shares in a private company to other shareholders in the same company without any transfer of shares being involved. The value of the transferrred rights is to be regarded as a gift, or inheritance (as appropriate) in the hands of the beneficial recipient.

Narrative

Capital Acquisitions Tax, Chapter 20.

PART VII
MISCELLANEOUS

99 Care and management of taxes and duties

All taxes and duties (except the excise duty on driving licences) imposed by this Act are hereby placed under the care and management of the Revenue Commissioners.

100 Short title, construction and commencement

(1) This Act may be cited as the Finance Act, 1989.

...

...

(6) Part V and (so far as relating to gift tax or inheritance tax) Part VII shall be construed together with the Capital Acquisitions Tax Act, 1976, and the enactments amending or extending that Act.

...

(11) Any reference in this Act to any other enactment shall, except so far as the context otherwise requires, be construed as a reference to that enactment as amended by or under any other enactment including this Act.

(12) In this Act, a reference to a Part, section or Schedule is to a Part or section of, or Schedule to, this Act, unless it is indicated that reference to some other enactment is intended.

(13) In this Act, a reference to a subsection, paragraph or subparagraph is to the subsection, paragraph or subparagraph of the provision (including a Schedule) in which the reference occurs, unless it is indicated that reference to some other provision is intended.

FINANCE ACT 1990

(1990 Number 10)
(Date of passing: 30 May 1990)

ARRANGEMENT OF SECTIONS

PART VI
CAPITAL ACQUISITIONS TAX

PART VI
CAPITAL ACQUISITIONS TAX

126 Interpretation (Part VI)

In this Part **"the Principal Act"** means the Capital Acquisitions Tax Act, 1976.

127 Exemption for spouses (gifts)

(1) Notwithstanding the provisions of the Principal Act, a gift taken by a donee, who is at the date of the gift the spouse of the disponer, shall be exempt from tax and shall not be taken into account in computing tax.

(2) This section shall have effect in relation to a gift taken on or after the 31st day of January, 1990.

Notes

FA 1985 s 59 introduced complete exemption from capital acquisitions tax on property inherited by a surviving spouse from the dead spouse. This section provides a similar exemption for gifts (taken on or after 31 January 1990) between spouses.

Narrative

Capital Acquisitions Tax, Chapter 12.

Definitions

"disponer", "donee", "gift": CATA 1976 s 2(1).

---

128 Amendment of Second Schedule to Principal Act

Amendments

Repealed by FA 2000 s 153 for gifts or inheritances taken on or after 1 December 1999.

---

129 Application of section 108 (exemptions) of Finance Act, 1984

(1) For the purposes of section 108(*b*)(ii) of the Finance Act, 1984, a sponsored superannuation scheme within the meaning of [subsection (1) of section 783 of the Taxes Consolidation Act, 1997],[1] shall not include a scheme or arrangement which relates to matters other than service in particular offices or employments.

(2) This section shall have effect in relation to a charge for tax which, apart from section 108(*b*)(ii) of the Finance Act, 1984, arises on or after the 5th day of April, 1990, under the provisions of section 106 of the said Act of 1984 or of section 103 of Finance Act, 1986.

Amendments

[1]   Substituted by TCA 1997 s 1100 and Sch 31; previously "subsection (9) of section 235 of the Income Tax Act, 1967".

Notes

This is an anti-avoidance measure. It withdraws from 5 April 1990 the exemption from the once off and the annual charges on discretionary trusts (imposed by FA 1984 Pt V Ch I and FA 1986 Pt V Ch I respectively) for pension schemes (within ITA 1967 s 235(9)) where the scheme includes arrangements that do not relate to the employment.

130 Application of section 60 (relief in respect of certain policies of insurance) of Finance Act, 1985

For the purposes of section 60 of the Finance Act, 1985, "relevant tax" shall be deemed to include inheritance tax payable in respect of an inheritance taken under a disposition made by the spouse of the insured—

(*a*)   where the inheritance is taken on the date of death of the insured, or

(*b*)   where the inheritance is taken only in the event of the insured not surviving the spouse by a period of up to 31 days,

and the relevant qualifying insurance policy is—

(i)   a policy of insurance within the meaning of paragraphs (*a*), (*b*) and (*c*) of subsection (1A) of that section (inserted by section 84 of the Finance Act, 1989), or

(ii)   a policy of insurance where the insured is an individual and the proceeds of the policy are payable only on the contingency of the insured surviving that spouse.

Notes

The proceeds of life assurance policies, taken out expressly to pay inheritance tax due by the successors of the disponer are exempt from capital acquisitions tax, provided the inheritance is taken on or after the death of the insured and not later than one year after the death. The policy proceeds are also excluded from aggregation with any other taxable gifts or inheritances, to the extent that they are used to pay inheritance tax due by the successor.

The annual premium is not allowable as an income tax allowance for income tax years to 1990-91 (life assurance relief was abolished for 1991-92 and later tax years).

The original relief applied to policies effected by individuals. The relief was extended to apply to joint policies effected by spouses to cover inheritance tax payable by the successors of the survivor of either spouse.

This section further extended the relief to cover succession of property on the survivor's death (cesser of a life interest) or where an inheritance from the predeceased spouse is only taken in the event of the insured not surviving his or her partner for up to 31 days. In such circumstances the policy proceeds may be used to pay tax due by the successors of the predeceased spouse.

The relief was further extended (FA 1991 s 118) to provide that proceeds of a qualifying policy in the sole name of a life tenant, taking under a deceased spouse's will may be used to pay inheritance tax arising on the cesser of the life interest.

Definitions

"disposition": CATA 1976 s 2(1);"inheritance": CATA 1976 s 2(1).

PART VII
MISCELLANEOUS

139 Care and management of taxes and duties

All taxes and duties imposed by this Act are hereby placed under the care and management of the Revenue Commissioners.

140 Short title, construction and commencement

(1) This Act may be cited as the Finance Act, 1990.

...

...

(6) Part V shall be construed together with Part VI of the Finance Act, 1983.

(7) Part VI shall be construed together with the Capital Acquisitions Tax Act, 1976, and the enactments amending or extending that Act.

...

(10) Any reference in this Act to any other enactment shall, except so far as the context otherwise requires, be construed as a reference to that enactment as amended by or under any other enactment including this Act.

(11) In this Act, a reference to a Part, section or Schedule is to a Part or section of, or Schedule to, this Act, unless it is indicated that reference to some other enactment is intended.

(12) In this Act, a reference to a subsection, paragraph, subparagraph, clause or subclause is to the subsection, paragraph, subparagraph, clause or subclause of the provision (including a Schedule) in which the reference occurs, unless it is indicated that reference to some other provision is intended.

FINANCE ACT 1991

(1991 Number 13)
(Date of passing: 29 May 1991)

ARRANGEMENT OF SECTIONS

PART VI
CAPITAL ACQUISITIONS TAX AND DEATH DUTIES

PART VII
MISCELLANEOUS

PART VI
CAPITAL ACQUISITIONS TAX AND DEATH DUTIES

PART VI
CAPITAL ACQUISITIONS TAX AND DEATH DUTIES

113 Interpretation (Part VI)

In this Part **"the Principal Act"** means the Capital Acquisitions Tax Act, 1976.

114 Amendment of section 19 (value of agricultural property) of Principal Act

---

Note

For gifts or inheritances taken on or after 30 January 1991, this section increased to 55% (from 50%) the deduction available to qualifying farmers from the agricultural value of farm property.

For gifts or inheritances taken on or after 30 May 1991, the section increased the percentage value of total assets the must consist of agricultural assets to 80% (from 75%).

---

115 Amendment of Second Schedule to the Principal Act

Note

This section, by substituting CATA 1976 Sch 2 Part II provided a new table of rates for gifts or inheritances taken on or after 30 May 1991.

---

116 Inheritances taken by parents

Amendments

Repealed by FA 2000 s 153 for gifts or inheritances taken on or after 1 December 1999.

117 Reduction in estimated market value of certain dwellings

Amendments

Repealed by FA 2000 s 153 for gifts or inheritances taken on or after 1 December 1999.

118 Application of section 60 (relief in respect of certain policies of insurance) of Finance Act, 1985

For the purposes of section 60 of the Finance Act, 1985, **"relevant tax"** shall be deemed to include inheritance tax payable in respect of an inheritance taken ...[1] on the date of death of the insured.

Amendments

[1]   Words "under a disposition made by the spouse of the insured where the inheritance is taken" deleted by FA 1996 s 124 as regards inheritances taken on or after 28 March 1996.

Notes

The proceeds of life assurance policies, taken out expressly to pay inheritance tax due by the successors of the disponer are exempt from capital acquisitions tax, provided the inheritance is taken on or after the death of the insured and not later than one year after the death. The policy proceeds are also excluded from aggregation with any other taxable gifts or inheritances, to the extent that they are used to pay inheritance tax due by the successor.

The annual premium is not allowable as an income tax allowance for income tax years to 1990-91 (life assurance relief was abolished for 1991-92 and later tax years).

The original relief applied to policies effected by individuals. The relief was extended (subs (1A)) to apply to joint policies effected by spouses to cover inheritance tax payable by the successors of the survivor of either spouse.

The relief was further extended (FA 1990 s 130) to cover succession of property on the survivor's death (cesser of a life interest) or where an inheritance from the predeceased spouse is only taken in the event of the insured not surviving his or her partner for up to 31 days. In such circumstances the policy proceeds may be used to pay tax due by the successors of the predeceased spouse.

This section further extended the relief to provide that proceeds of a qualifying policy in the sole name of a life tenant, taking under a deceased spouse's will may be used to pay inheritance tax arising on the cesser of the life interest.

Definitions

"disposition", "inheritance", "insured": CATA 1976 s 2(1).

119 Relief in respect of certain policies of insurance relating to tax payable on gifts

(1) In this section—

"appointed date" means—

- (a)   a date occurring not earlier than 8 years after the date on which a relevant insurance policy is effected, or
- (b)   a date on which the proceeds of a relevant insurance policy become payable either on the critical illness or the death of the insured, or one of the insured in a case to which paragraph (b) of the definition of "insured" relates, being a date prior to the date to which paragraph (a) of this definition relates;

"insured" means—

- (*a*) where the insured is an individual, that individual, or
- (*b*) where the insured is an individual and the spouse of that individual at the date the policy is effected, that individual and the spouse of that individual, jointly or separately, or the survivor of them, as the case may be;

"relevant insurance policy" means a policy of insurance—

- (*a*) which is in a form approved by the Commissioners for the purposes of this section,
- (*b*) in respect of which annual premiums are paid by the insured,
- (*c*) the proceeds of which are payable on the appointed date, and
- (*d*) which is expressly effected under this section for the purpose of paying relevant tax;

"relevant tax" means gift tax or inheritance tax, payable in connection with an *inter vivos* disposition made by the insured within one year after the appointed date, excluding gift tax or inheritance tax payable on an appointment out of an *inter vivos* discretionary trust set up by the insured.

(2) The proceeds of a relevant insurance policy shall, to the extent that such proceeds are used to pay relevant tax, be exempt from tax and shall not be taken into account in computing such tax.

(3) Subject to the provisions of section 54 of the Principal Act and section 127 of the Finance Act, 1990, where the insured makes an *inter vivos* disposition of the proceeds, or any part of the proceeds, of a relevant insurance policy other than in paying relevant tax, such proceeds shall not be exempt from tax.

(4) A relevant insurance policy shall be a qualifying insurance policy for the purposes of section 60 of the Finance Act, 1985, where the proceeds of such relevant insurance policy become payable on the death of the insured or one of the insured in a case to which paragraph (*b*) of the definition of "insured" relates:

Provided that such relevant insurance policy would have been a qualifying insurance policy if it had been expressly effected under that section.

(5) A qualifying insurance policy for the purposes of section 60 of the Finance Act, 1985, shall be a relevant insurance policy where the proceeds of such qualifying insurance policy are used to pay relevant tax arising under an *inter vivos* disposition made by the insured within one year after the appointed date.

(6) Section 143 of the Income Tax Act, 1967 (as amended by section 60 of the Finance Act, 1985) is hereby amended by the addition to subsection (5) of the following paragraph after paragraph (*c*):

"(*d*) be given for the year 1991-92 and subsequent years of assessment in respect of premiums payable in respect of a relevant insurance policy within the meaning of section 119 of the Finance Act, 1991."

Note

FA 1985 s 60 provides that the proceeds of life assurance policies, taken out expressly to pay inheritance tax due by the successors of the disponer are exempt from capital acquisitions tax, provided the inheritance is taken on or after the death of the insured and not later than one year after the death.

This section extends a similar relief to insurance policies taken out for payment of gift tax on inter vivos dispositions. A qualifying policy must conform to the corresponding principles applicable for inheritance tax policies set out in FA 1985 s 60, and must also be payable on "an appointed date" which is more than eight years from the date the policy is effected. This minimum time requirement is not necessary where the insurer or his spouse dies or becomes critically ill.

A qualifying FA 1985 s 60 policy that has prematurely come to an end (for example due to early surrender or encashment or payment otherwise than on the death of the insured) may come within the relief if it meets the "appointed date" requirement.

The relief does not apply to tax liabilities arising on appointments of property from an inter vivos discretionary trust set up by the insured.

Statement of practice

[FA 1985] Section 60 policies: SP CAT 3/90, 2/91
[FA 1991] Section 119 policies: SP CAT 2/91

Narrative

Capital Acquisitions Tax, Chapter 18.

Definitions

"Commissioners": SA 1891 s 122(1); CATA 1976 s 2(1); "discretionary trust", "disposition", "gift", "inheritance": CATA 1976 s 2(1).

120 Capital acquisitions tax, waiver in respect of certain interest payable, etc

(1) In this section **"donee"** includes a successor and a reference to a gift or a taxable gift includes a reference to an inheritance or a taxable inheritance, as the case may be, and a reference to gift tax includes a reference to inheritance tax.

(2) Where in respect of a gift taken on or before the 30th day of January, 1991—

    (*a*)   gift tax is due and payable by a donee on any date on or before the 30th day of September, 1991, and

    (*b*)   in the period beginning on the 30th day of January, 1991, and ending on the 30th day of September, 1991, a return is delivered and gift tax is assessed in respect of the gift in accordance with the provisions of section 36 (inserted by section 74 of the Finance Act, 1989) of the Principal Act or section 104 of the Finance Act, 1986, and

    (*c*)   such gift tax is paid on or before the 30th day of September, 1991,

interest payable on such gift tax up to the 30th day of April, 1991, shall be waived and penalties, if incurred, shall not be collected.

(3) For the purposes of subsection (2) where—

    (*a*)   gift tax assessed on a taxable gift is being paid by instalments, or

    (*b*)   a payment on account of gift tax has been made,

sums paid in discharge of earlier instalments or as a payment on account of tax shall, notwithstanding the provisions of subsection (4) of section 41 of the Principal Act, be applied or reapplied towards the discharge of tax in the first instance:

Provided that where the sum so paid is in excess of the sum to be so applied or reapplied, the excess shall not be repaid.

(4) This section shall not apply in relation to a gift—

> (*a*) where gift tax is due and payable by the donee concerned in respect of any other gift taken by him, unless such gift tax is paid on or before the 30th day of September 1991,
>
> (*b*) where any capital gains tax is due and payable in respect of a disposal of the property comprised in the gift concerned, unless such capital gains tax and penalties (together with all interest due in respect of that tax) is paid at the same time or prior to the date of payment of the gift tax on that gift.

(5) Where additional gift tax becomes due and payable as a result of a revaluation of property included in a self assessed return, which was delivered on or after the 30th day of January, 1991, interest payable on such additional gift tax shall not be waived.

(6) (*a*) A fine or other penalty imposed by a court in connection with a gift shall not be waived.

> (*b*) Interest on gift tax, which has been ordered to be paid by a court, shall not be waived.

Notes

Interest on capital acquisitions tax arrears due up to 30 April 1991 was waived if the arrears were paid by 30 September 1991.

Definitions

"donee", "gift", "inheritance", "property", "return", "taxable gift", "tax on inheritance", "successor": CATA 1976 s 2(1).

121 Amendment of section 57 (exemption of certain securities) of Capital Acquisitions Tax Act, 1976

Note

This section substituted CATA 1976 s 57(1) definition of "unit trust scheme" and in s 57(2) the words "Units Trusts Act, 1990" for "Unit Trusts Act, 1972" with effect from 26 December 1990.

122 Death duties, waiver in respect of certain interest payable, etc

(1) Where outstanding death duties are paid on or before the 30th day of September, 1991, interest payable on such duties up to the 30th day of April, 1991, shall be waived and penalties, if incurred, shall not be collected.

(2) This section shall not apply to any penalty imposed by a court or to interest on death duties, the payment of which has been ordered by a court.

(3) In this section **"death duties"** has the meaning assigned to it by section 13(3) of the Finance Act, 1894.

Note

This section granted an amnesty for death duties arising before 1 April 1976, on the same basis as the capital acquisitions amnesty introduced by s 120.

PART VII
MISCELLANEOUS

125 Repeals

Each enactment specified in column (2) of the Fourth Schedule is hereby repealed to the extent specified in column (3) of that Schedule.

129 Application of certain income tax provisions in relation to the collection and recovery of capital acquisitions tax etc

(1) In this section—

"the Collector" means the Collector-General appointed under [section 851 of the Taxes Consolidation Act, 1997];[1]

"the Commissioners" means the Revenue Commissioners;

"functions" includes powers and duties;

"the Principal Act" means the Capital Acquisitions Tax Act, 1976;

"tax" means any tax chargeable under the provisions of the Principal Act.

(2) Notwithstanding anything in the Principal Act, all sums due under the provisions of that Act shall be paid to the Collector or to such person as may be nominated under the provisions of this section.

(3) [Section 928(1) and 964(2) of the Taxes Consolidation Act, 1997],[2] shall, with any necessary modifications, apply in relation to an assessment of tax, a correcting assessment of tax, or an additional assessment of tax as it applies in relation to assessments to income tax.

(4) The Collector shall collect and levy the tax from time to time charged in all assessments, correcting assessments and additional assessments of which particulars have been transmitted to him under subsection (3).

(5) All the provisions of the Income Tax Acts relating to the collection and recovery of income tax shall, subject to any necessary modifications, apply in relation to tax as they apply in relation to income tax chargeable under Schedule D.

(6) (*a*)   The Revenue Commissioners may nominate persons to exercise on behalf of the Collector any or all of the functions conferred upon him by this section and, accordingly, those functions, as well as being exercisable by the Collector, shall also be exercisable on his behalf by persons so nominated.

   (*b*)   A person shall not be nominated under this subsection unless he is an officer or employee of the Commissioners.

(7) This section shall apply and have effect as on and from the 1st day of October, 1991.

Amendments

[1]   Substituted by TCA 1997 s 1100 and Sch 31; previously "section 162 of the Income Tax Act, 1967".

[2]   Substituted by TCA 1997 s 1100 and Sch 31; previously "Section 187 of the Income Tax Act, 1967".

Narrative

Capital Acquisitions Tax, Chapter 22.

---

131 Care and management of taxes and duties

All taxes ... imposed by this Act are hereby placed under the care and management of the Revenue Commissioners.

132 Short title, construction and commencement

(1) This Act may be cited as the Finance Act, 1991.

...

(5) ...

(6) ...

(7) Part VI (other than section 122) and sections 129 and 130 (so far as relating to gift tax or inheritance tax) shall be construed together with the Capital Acquisitions Tax Act, 1976, and the enactments amending or extending that Act.

...

(10) Any reference in this Act to any other enactment shall, except so far as the context otherwise requires, be construed as a reference to that enactment as amended by or under any other enactment including this Act.

(11) In this Act, a reference to a Part, section or Schedule is to a Part or section of, or Schedule to, this Act, unless it is indicated that reference to some other enactment is intended.

(12) In this Act, a reference to a subsection, paragraph or subparagraph is to the subsection, paragraph or subparagraph of the provision (including a Schedule) in which the reference occurs, unless it is indicated that reference to some other provision is intended.

FINANCE ACT 1992

(1992 Number 9)
(Date of passing: 28 May 1992)

ARRANGEMENT OF SECTIONS

PART VI
CAPITAL ACQUISITIONS TAX

222 Interpretation (Part VI)

In this Part **"the Principal Act"** means the Capital Acquisitions Tax Act, 1976.

223 Amendment of section 2 (interpretation) of Principal Act

Note

This section substituted CATA 1976 s 2 with effect from 30 May 1991. A child adopted abroad who is covered by the provisions of the Adoption Act 1991 is to be treated as a child of the adopters for capital acquisitions tax purposes. This means such a child will qualify for the £150,000 class threshold (as indexed).

224 Amendment of section 106 (acquisitions by discretionary trusts) of Finance Act, 1984

Note

The age of the youngest beneficiary (spouse, child or grandchild) applicable for an exclusion of the 3% charge on discretionary trusts (FA 1984 Pt V) following the death of the disponer has been reduced from 25 years to 21 years, for trusts created after 30 January 1993.

225 Amendment of section 102 (interpretation (Part V)) of Finance Act, 1986

Note

The age of the youngest beneficiary (spouse, child or grandchild) applicable for an exclusion of the 1% annual charge on discretionary trusts (FA 1986 Pt V) following the death of the disponer has been reduced from 25 years to 21 years.

PART VII
ANTI-AVOIDANCE AND ANTI-EVASION

232 Inspection of documents and records

Note

This section substituted FA 1976 s 34.

237 Inspection of computer documents and records

(1) In this section—

"the Acts" means—

 (*a*) the Customs Acts,

 (*b*) the statutes relating to the duties of excise and to the management of those duties,

 (*c*) the Tax Acts,

 (*d*) the Capital Gains Tax Acts,

 (*e*) the Value-Added Tax Act, 1972, and the enactments amending or extending that Act,

 (*f*) the Capital Acquisitions Tax Act, 1976, and the enactments amending or extending that Act, and

 (*g*) Part VI of the Finance Act, 1983,

and any instruments made thereunder;

"data" means information in a form in which it can be processed;

"data equipment" means any electronic, photographic, magnetic, optical or other equipment for processing data;

"processing" means performing automatically logical or arithmetical operations on data, or the storing, maintenance, transmission, reproduction or communication of data;

"records" means documents which a person is obliged by any provision of the Acts to keep, to issue or to produce for inspection, and any other written or printed material;

"software" means any sequence of instructions used in conjunction with data equipment for the purpose of processing data or controlling the operation of the data equipment.

(2) Any provision under the Acts which—

 (*a*) requires a person to keep, retain, issue or produce any records or cause any records to be kept, retained, issued or produced, or (*b*) permits an officer of the Revenue Commissioners—

   (i)   to inspect any records,
   (ii) to enter premises and search for any records, or
   (iii) to take extracts from or copies of or remove any records,

shall, where the records are processed by data equipment, apply to the data equipment together with any associated software, data, apparatus or material as it applies to the records.

(3) An officer of the Revenue Commissioners may, in the exercise or performance of his powers or duties, require—

(*a*) the person by or on whose behalf the data equipment is or has been used, or
(*b*) any person having charge of, or otherwise concerned with the operation of, the data equipment or any associated apparatus or material,

to afford him all reasonable assistance in relation thereto.

PART VIII
MISCELLANEOUS

248 Amendment of certain provisions of Tax Acts, etc, relating to penalties

Where, after the passing of this Act (but with respect to any year of assessment, or, as the case may be, accounting period, whether ending before or ending after such passing), an act or omission occurs in respect of which a person would, but for this section, have incurred, the penalty or penalties provided for in any provision of the Tax Acts or Part VI of the Finance Act, 1983, specified in column (2) of the Table to this section at any reference number, the person shall, in lieu of the penalty or penalties so provided for be liable to a penalty specified in column (3) of the said Table at that reference number and that provision shall be construed and have effect accordingly.

TABLE

Reference number	Provision of the Tax Acts, etc	Penalty
(1)	(2)	(3)
		£
1	Section 128(1A) of the Income Tax Act, 1967	750
2	Section 173 (6) of the Income Tax Act, 1967	1,200
3	Section 426(3) of the Income Tax Act, 1967	750
4	Section 500(1) of the Income Tax Act, 1967	750
5	Section 500(2) of the Income Tax Act, 1967	1,200
6	Section 31(5) of the Finance Act, 1979	1,000
7	Section 45(8) of the Finance Act, 1980	1,200
8	Section 112(1)(*a*) of the Finance Act, 1983	1,200
9	Section 112(3) of the Finance Act, 1983	2,500

Definition
"the Tax Acts": CTA 1976 s 155(2).

250 Amendment of Provisional Collection of Taxes Act, 1927

Notes
This section substituted PCTA 1927 s 4A.

253 Care and management of taxes and duties

All taxes and duties (except the excise duties on mechanically propelled vehicles imposed by section 163) imposed by this Act are hereby placed under the care and management of the Revenue Commissioners.

254 Short title, construction and commencement

(1) This Act may be cited as the Finance Act, 1992.

...

...

...

(7) Part VI shall be construed together with the Capital Acquisitions Tax Act, 1976, and the enactments amending or extending that Act.

...

(12) Any reference in this Act to any other enactment shall, except so far as the context otherwise requires, be construed as a reference to that enactment as amended by or under any other enactment including this Act.

(13) In this Act, a reference to a Part, section or Schedule is to a Part or section of, or Schedule to, this Act, unless it is indicated that reference to some other enactment is intended.

(14) In this Act, a reference to a subsection, paragraph or sub-paragraph is to the subsection, paragraph or subparagraph of the provision (including a Schedule) in which the reference occurs, unless it is indicated that reference to some other provision is intended.

FINANCE ACT 1993

(1993 Number 13)
(Date of passing: 17 June 1993)

ARRANGEMENT OF SECTIONS

PART VI
CAPITAL ACQUISITIONS TAX

CHAPTER II
Miscellaneous amendments, etc

PART VII
MISCELLANEOUS

PART VI
CAPITAL ACQUISITIONS TAX

CHAPTER I
Taxation of assets passing on inheritance (Probate Tax)

109 Interpretation (Chapter I)

Amendments

Section 109 repealed by FA 2001 s 225(1) with effect in relation to probate tax first due and payable on or from 6 December 2000; previously:

"(1) In this Chapter, except where the context otherwise requires—

'the Act of 1965' means the Succession Act, 1965;

['agricultural property' has the same meaning as it has in section 19 (as amended by the Finance Act, 1994) of the Principal Act but excluding farm machinery, livestock and bloodstock;][1]

['agricultural value' means the market value of agricultural property reduced by 30 per cent. of that value;][1]

'the consumer price index number' means the All Items Consumer Price Index Number for a year as compiled by the Central Statistics Office and expressed on the basis that the consumer price index number at [mid-November, 1996],[2] is 100;

'the deceased', in relation to the disposition referred to in section 110(1), means the disponer;

'**dependent child**', in relation to the deceased, means a child who at the time of the deceased's death—

(a) was living and had not attained the age of 18 years, or

(b) was receiving full-time education or instruction at any university, college, school or other educational establishment and was under the age of 21 years or, if over the age of 21 years, was receiving such full-time education or instruction continuously since before attaining the age of 21 years;

'**dependent relative**', in relation to the deceased, has the meaning assigned to it by [subsection (11) of section 604 of the Taxes Consolidation Act, 1997];[3]

'**the dwelling-house**' means—

(a) a dwelling-house, or part of a dwelling-house, which was occupied by the deceased as his only or principal place of residence, at the date of his death,

(b) the curtilage of the dwelling-house which the deceased had for his own use and enjoyment with that dwelling-house up to an area (exclusive of the site of the dwelling-house) of one acre, and

(c) furniture and household effects being the normal contents of the dwelling-house:

Provided that—

(i) in the case of a dwelling-house, part of which was used mainly for the purpose of a trade, business, profession or vocation or was let, this definition shall not apply to the part so used or let, and

(ii) in a case where more than one dwelling-house is included in the estate of the deceased, and more than one such dwelling-house is used equally as a place of residence this definition shall apply only to one dwelling-house so used;

'**the estate of the deceased**' means the real and personal estate of the deceased as defined by section 10(4) of the Act of 1965;

'**the net market value of the dwelling-house**' means the market value of the dwelling- house at the date of death of the deceased or, if less, that market value less the market value at that date of any sum which is charged or secured on the dwelling-house by the will, or other testamentary disposition, of the deceased and which is comprised in the share of an object of the relevant trust in the estate of the deceased, other than the share of a person whose place of normal residence was at that date the dwelling-house and who was on that date a dependent child or dependent relative of the deceased;

'**object**', in relation to a relevant trust, means a person entitled to a share in the estate of the deceased (otherwise than as a creditor);

'**occupied**', in relation to a dwelling-house or part of a dwelling-house, means having the use thereof, whether actually used or not;

'**the Principal Act**' means the Capital Acquisitions Tax Act, 1976;

['**relevant threshold**' means—

(a) £40,000, where the death of the deceased occurred on or before 31 December 2000, and

(b) in any other case, £40,000 multiplied by the figure, rounded up to the nearest third decimal place, determined by dividing by 104.8 the consumer price index number for the year immediately preceding the year in which the death of the deceased occurred;][4]

'**relevant trust**' means—

(a) any trust under which, by virtue of the provisions of section 10(3) of the Act of 1965, the executors of a deceased person hold the estate of the deceased as trustees for the persons by law entitled thereto, or

(b) any trust of which, by virtue of section 10(3), the President of the High Court is deemed to be a trustee;

'**share**', in relation to the estate of the deceased, includes any share or interest, whether arising—

(a) under a will or other testamentary disposition, or

(b) on intestacy, or

(c) as a legal right under section 111 of the Act of 1965, or

(d) as the subject of an order under section 117 (as amended by the Status of Children Act, 1987) of the Act of 1965, or

(e) in accordance with the law of another country,

and includes also the right to the entire of the estate of the deceased.

(2) A reference in this Act or in any Act of the Oireachtas passed after the passing of this Act to probate tax shall, unless the contrary intention appears, be construed as a reference to the tax chargeable on the taxable value of a taxable inheritance which is charged to tax by virtue of section 110.

Amendments

¹ Definitions of 'agricultural property' and 'agricultural value' inserted by FA 1994 s 137(1) in relation to persons dying after 17 June 1993.

² Substituted by FA 2000 s 147(1)(*a*) for persons dying on or after 1 December 1999; previously 'mid- November 1989'.

³ Substituted by TCA 1997 s 1100 and Sch 31; previously 'subsection (9A)(*a*) (inserted by the Finance Act, 1979) of section 25 of the Capital Gains Tax Act, 1975'.

⁴ Definition of 'relevant threshold' substituted by FA 2000 s 147(1)(*b*) for persons dying on or after 1 December 1999.".

Note

In relation to probate tax, the index factors and the exemption thresholds are as follows:

Year	Index factor	Exemption threshold (£)
1993	-	10,000
1994	1.015	10,150
1995	1.039	10,390
1996	1.065	10,650
1997	1.082	10,820
1998	1.098	10,980
1999	1.125	11,250
2000¹	-	40,000

¹ The exemption threshold is increased to £40,000 effective from 1 December 1999.

110 Acquisitions by relevant trusts

Amendments

Section 110 repealed by FA 2001 s 225(1) with effect in relation to probate tax first due and payable on or from 6 December 2000; previously:

"(1) Where, under or in consequence of any disposition, property becomes subject to a relevant trust on the death of a person dying after the date of the passing of this Act (in this section referred to as **'the disponer'**), the trust shall be deemed on the date of death of the disponer to become beneficially entitled in possession to an absolute interest in that property and to take an inheritance accordingly as if the trust, and the trustees as such for the time being of the trust, were together a person for the purposes of the Principal Act, and that date shall be the date of the inheritance.

(2) The provisions of subsection (1) shall not prejudice any charge for tax in respect of any inheritance affecting the same property or any part of it taken under the disposition referred to in subsection (1)—

(*a*)   by an object of the relevant trust referred to in subsection (1), or

(*b*)   by a discretionary trust by virtue of section 106(1) of the Finance Act, 1984,

and any such inheritance shall, except for the purposes of subsections (3) and (4) of section 55 of the Principal Act, be deemed to be taken after the inheritance referred to in subsection (1).

(3) Where, under the provisions of section 13 of the Act of 1965, the estate of a deceased person vests on the date of death of the deceased in the President of the High Court, then, for the purpose of subsection (1), the President of the High Court shall be deemed to hold that estate as a trustee in trust for the persons by law entitled thereto, and the estate of the deceased shall be deemed to be property which became subject to that trust on that date.

(4) The provisions of sections 10 and 13 of the Act of 1965, shall, for the purposes of subsection (1), be deemed to apply irrespective of the domicile of the deceased or the locality of the estate of the deceased.".

111 Application of Principal Act

Amendments

Section 111 repealed by FA 2001 s 225(1) with effect in relation to probate tax first due and payable on or from 6 December 2000; previously:

"In relation to a charge for tax arising by virtue of section 110—

(a)   the valuation date of the taxable inheritance shall be the date of the inheritance;

(b)   a reference in section 16 of the Principal Act (as amended by the Finance Act, 1993) to a company controlled by the successor and the definition in that section of 'group of shares' shall be construed as if (for the purpose of that reference) the list of persons contained in subsection (3) of that section and (for the purpose of that definition) the list of persons contained in that definition included the following persons, that is to say, the trustees of the relevant trust, the relatives of the deceased, the nominees of those trustees or of those relatives, and the trustees of a settlement whose objects include the relatives of the deceased;

(c)   a person who is a personal representative of the deceased shall be a person primarily accountable for the payment of the tax;

(d)   every person entitled for an interest in possession to a share in the estate of the deceased, and every person to whom or for whose benefit any of the property subject to the relevant trust is applied or appointed, shall also be accountable for the payment of the tax and the Principal Act shall have effect, in its application to that charge for tax, as if each of those persons were a person referred to in section 35(2) of the Principal Act;

(e)   where the total taxable value referred to in paragraph (a) of the proviso to section 113 exceeds the relevant threshold, section 36(2) of the Principal Act (inserted by the Finance Act, 1989) shall have effect, in the application of the Principal Act to any such charge for tax as aforesaid, as if—

   (i)   the reference in that subsection to four months were construed as a reference to nine months, and

   (ii)   the reference in that subsection to a person primarily accountable for the payment of tax were construed as including a reference to a person primarily accountable by virtue of paragraph (c) of this section;

(f)   sections 19, 21, 35(1), 36 (4) and 40, subsections (1) to (3) of section 41, and section 43 of, and the Second Schedule to, the Principal Act shall not apply;

(g)   section 18 of the Principal Act shall have effect, in the application of the Principal Act to any such charge for tax as aforesaid, as if—

   (i)   liabilities, costs or expenses incurred after the death of the deceased, other than reasonable funeral expenses, were not an allowable deduction,

   (ii)   any *bona fide* consideration paid prior to the death of the deceased by an object of the relevant trust, in return for a share in the estate of the deceased, were consideration paid by the relevant trust on the date on which it was paid by the object, ...[1]

[(iia) in so far as the inheritance consists of agricultural property, the reference to market value in subsection (1) of the said section 18 were a reference to agricultural value, and][2]

   (iii) where the property which is exempt from such tax is the dwelling-house, or a part thereof, the restriction on the deduction of any liability referred to in subsection (5)(e) of the said section 18 did not apply;

[Provided that nothing in this subparagraph shall have effect so as to reduce the tax which would but for this subparagraph be borne by property which at the date of death of the deceased represented the share in the estate of the deceased of a person who was not on that date a dependent child or a dependent relative of the deceased;][3]

(h)   section 60 of the Principal Act shall apply with the modification that, notwithstanding subsection (3) of that section, the Commissioners may refuse to issue the certificate referred to in subsection (1) of that section—

   (i)   in a case where the tax is being wholly or partly paid by the transfer of securities to the Minister for Finance under the provisions of section 45 of the Principal Act, until such security as they think fit has been given for the completion of the transfer of the securities to the Minister for Finance, or

      (ii)   in a case where payment of such tax has been postponed under the provisions of section 44(1) of the Principal Act, or under section 118, until such tax as has not been so postponed has been paid together with the interest, if any, thereon, or

      (iii)   in any other case, until the tax has been paid together with the interest, if any, thereon;

  (*i*)   subsection (2)(*a*) of section 57 of the Principal Act (inserted by the Finance Act, 1978) shall not apply and subsection (2)(*c*) of that section shall be construed as if the reference therein to the donee or successor were a reference to the deceased;

  (*j*)   subsection (6) of section 36 of the Principal Act (inserted by the Finance Act, 1989) shall have effect, in the application of the Principal Act to any such charge for tax as aforesaid, as if the reference in that subsection to a person primarily accountable for the payment of tax by virtue of section 35(1) were a reference to a person primarily accountable by virtue of paragraph (*c*) of this section;

  (*k*)   section 55 of the Principal Act shall be construed as if the reference in subsection (4) of that section to the successor were a reference to the person who would be the successor for the purpose of that subsection if this Chapter had not been enacted; and

  (*l*)   section 63 of the Principal Act (as amended by the Finance Act, 1989) shall have effect, in the application of the Principal Act to any such charge for tax as aforesaid, as if—

      (i)   £1,000 [€1,265][4] were substituted for £5,000 [€6,345][5] in subsection (3) of that section,

      (ii)   £400 [€505][5] were substituted for £2,000 [€2,535][6] in subsection (1)(*a*) of that section,

      (iii) £200 [€250][7] were substituted for £1,000 [€1,265}[8] in subsections (2) and (7) of that section, and

      (iv) £5 [€6][9] were substituted for £25 [€30][10] in subsection (1)(*b*) of that section.

Amendments

[1]   Deleted by FA 1994 s 138(1)(*a*) with effect in relation to persons dying after 17 June 1993.

[2]   Para (*g*)(ii*a*) inserted by FA 1994 s 138(1)(*a*) in relation to persons dying after 17 June 1993.

[3]   Para (*g*)(iii)(proviso) inserted by FA 1994 s 139(1)(*b*).

[4]   Substituted by FA 2001 s 240 and Sch 5 Part 5 with effect from 1 January 2002; previously '£1,000'.

[5]   Substituted by FA 2001 s 240 and Sch 5 Part 5 with effect from 1 January 2002; previously '£5,000'.

[6]   Substituted by FA 2001 s 240 and Sch 5 Part 5 with effect from 1 January 2002; previously '£2,000'.

[7]   Substituted by FA 2001 s 240 and Sch 5 Part 5 with effect from 1 January 2002; previously '£200'.

[8]   Substituted by FA 2001 s 240 and Sch 5 Part 5 with effect from 1 January 2002; previously '£1,000'.

[9]   Substituted by FA 2001 s 240 and Sch 5 Part 5 with effect from 1 January 2002; previously '£5'.

[10]   Substituted by FA 2001 s 240 and Sch 5 Part 5 with effect from 1 January 2002; previously '£25'.".

112 Exemptions

Amendments

Section 112 repealed by FA 2001 s 225(1) with effect in relation to probate tax first due and payable on or from 6 December 2000; previously:

"The following property shall be exempt from tax (and shall not be taken into account in computing tax) in relation to a charge for tax arising by virtue of section 110—

  (*a*)   any right to receive any benefit—

      (i)   under—

         (A)   any sponsored superannuation scheme within the meaning of [section 783(1) of the Taxes Consolidation Act, 1997],[1] but excluding any scheme or arrangement which relates to matters other than service in particular offices or employments, or

         (B)   a trust scheme or part of a trust scheme approved under the said [section 784 or section 785][2] of the said Act;

or

   (ii)   under any scheme for the provision of superannuation benefits on retirement established by or under any enactment; or

   (iii) under a contract approved by the Commissioners for the purposes of granting relief for the purposes of [section 787 of the Taxes Consolidation Act, 1997],[3] in respect of the premiums payable in respect thereof;

(b)   property given by the will of the deceased for public or charitable purposes to the extent that the Commissioners are satisfied that it has been, or will be, applied to purposes which, in accordance with the law of the State, are public or charitable;

(c)   ...[4]

[(d)   the dwelling-house comprised in an inheritance which, on the date of death of the deceased, is taken under the will or other testamentary disposition or under the intestacy of the deceased, by a person who was on that date a dependent child of the deceased or a dependent relative of the deceased and whose place of normal residence was on that date the dwelling-house:

Provided that–

   (i)   the total income from all sources of that dependent child or that dependent relative, for income tax purposes, in the year of assessment ending on the 5th day of April next before that date, did not exceed the 'specified amount' referred to in [subsection (1) of section 466 of the Taxes Consolidation Act, 1997],[5]

   (ii)   the amount of the exemption shall (subject, with any necessary modifications, to the provisions of section 18 (4)(a) of the Principal Act in the case of a limited interest, and to the provisions of section 20 of that Act in the case of a contingency) be the whole or, as the case may be, the appropriate part (within the meaning of section 5 (5) of the Principal Act) of the net market value of the dwelling-house, and

   (iii) the amount of the exemption shall not be reduced by virtue of the provisions of section 20 of the Principal Act where an entitlement ceasing within the meaning of that section ceases because of an enlargement of that entitlement.][6]

Amendments

[1]   Substituted by TCA 1997 s 1100 and Sch 31; previously 'section 235(9) of the Income Tax Act, 1967'.

[2]   Substituted by TCA 1997 s 1100 and Sch 31; previously 'section 235 or section 235A'.

[3]   Substituted by TCA 1997 s 1100 and Sch 31; previously 'section 236 of the Income Tax Act, 1967'.

[4]   Para (c) deleted by FA 1994 s 139(1)(a) in relation to persons dying on or after 23 May 1994.

[5]   Substituted by TCA 1997 s 1100 and Sch 31; previously 'subsection (1A) of section 142 of the Income Tax Act, 1967'.

[6]   Para (d) substituted by FA 1994 s 139(1)(b) in relation to persons dying on or after 23 May 1994.".

113 Computation of tax

Amendments

Section 113 repealed by FA 2001 s 225(1) with effect in relation to probate tax first due and payable on or from 6 December 2000; previously:

"The tax chargeable on the taxable value of a taxable inheritance which is charged to tax by virtue of section 110 shall be computed at the rate of **two per cent** of such taxable value:

Provided that—

(a)   where the total taxable value on which tax is chargeable by virtue of section 110 on the death of the deceased does not exceed the relevant threshold, that tax shall be nil, and

(b)   where that total taxable value exceeds the relevant threshold, that tax shall not exceed the amount by which that total taxable value exceeds the relevant threshold.".

114 Relief in respect of quick succession

Amendments

Section 114 repealed by FA 2001 s 225(1) with effect in relation to probate tax first due and payable on or from 6 December 2000; previously:

"Where by virtue of section 110 tax is payable in respect of any property on the death of one party to a marriage, then a charge to tax shall not arise by virtue of that section in respect of that property, or in respect of any property representing that property, on the death of the other party to the marriage within—

(*a*)   one year after the death of the first-mentioned party, or

(*b*)   5 years after the death of the first-mentioned party, if that other party is survived by a dependent child of that other party.".

115 Incidence

Amendments

Section 115 repealed by FA 2001 s 225(1) with effect in relation to probate tax first due and payable on or from 6 December 2000; previously:

"In relation to a charge for tax arising by virtue of section 110, property which, at the date of death of the deceased, represents any share in the estate of the deceased, shall, save to the extent that it is exempt from or not chargeable to such tax, bear its due proportion of such tax, and any dispute as to the proportion of tax to be borne by any such property, or by property representing any such property, may be determined upon application by any person interested in manner directed by rules of court, either by the High Court, or, where the amount in dispute is less than £15,000, by the Circuit Court in whose circuit the person recovering the same resides, or the property in respect of which the tax is paid is situate.".

115A Abatement and postponement of tax

Amendments

Section 115A repealed by FA 2001 s 225(1) with effect in relation to probate tax first due and payable on or from 6 December 2000; previously:

"[(1) Where the spouse of a deceased survives the deceased, probate tax chargeable by virtue of section 110 which is borne by property which, at the date of death of the deceased, represents the share of that spouse in the estate of the deceased, shall be abated to a nil amount:

Provided that–

(*a*)   where the same property represents more than one person's share in the estate of the deceased and that spouse's interest in that property at that date is not a limited interest to which paragraph (*b*) relates, only a proportion of the probate tax borne by that property shall be abated to a nil amount and that proportion shall be the proportion which the value of that interest at that date bears to the total value of the property at that date, and for this purpose the value of that interest at that date shall not include the value of any interest in expectancy created by the will or other testamentary disposition of the deceased;

(*b*)   where a limited interest to which that spouse became beneficially entitled in possession on that date was created by the will or other testamentary disposition of the deceased, probate tax borne by the property in which that limited interest subsisted on that date shall not be abated to a nil amount, but, notwithstanding section 117(*a*), that tax shall not become due and payable until the date of the cesser of that limited interest and every person who (on the cesser of that limited interest) takes an inheritance which consists of all or part of the property in which that limited interest subsisted immediately prior to that cesser (hereinafter in this proviso referred to as 'the said property') and every trustee or other person in whose care the said property or the income therefrom is placed at the date of that cesser and every person in whom the said property is vested after that date, other than a bona fide purchaser or mortgagee for full consideration in money or money's worth, or a person deriving title from or under such a purchaser or mortgagee shall, notwithstanding any other provision to the contrary, be the only persons accountable for the payment of that tax and that tax shall be a charge on the said property in all respects as if the date of the inheritance in respect of which that tax is chargeable were the date of such cesser and the said property were property of which, for the purpose of section 47 of the Principal Act, that inheritance consisted at that date;

(c) if consideration in money or money's worth is paid to that spouse on the coming to an end of the limited interest referred to in paragraph (b) of this proviso before the event on which that interest was limited to cease, an appropriate proportion of the probate tax borne by the said property shall be abated to a nil amount and that proportion shall be the proportion which the value of that consideration bears to the value of the said property at the date of the cesser.

(2) Where the spouse of a deceased survives the deceased, probate tax chargeable by virtue of section 110 which is borne by the dwelling-house, or by any part thereof, shall, notwithstanding subsection (1) and section 117(a), not become due and payable until the date of death of that spouse and, notwithstanding any provision to the contrary, the only persons who shall be accountable for that tax shall be the following, that is to say–

(a) any person who takes an inheritance under the will or other testamentary disposition of the deceased which consists in whole or in part of the dwelling- house, or part thereof, or which consists of property which represents that dwelling-house or part; and

(b) any trustee in whom the property comprised in any such inheritance is vested at the date of death of that spouse or at any time thereafter and any other person in whom the property comprised in any such inheritance becomes vested for a beneficial interest in possession at any time thereafter, other than a bona fide purchaser or mortgagee for full consideration in money or money's worth, or a person deriving title from or under such a purchaser or mortgagee.

(3) Where the date upon which tax becomes due and payable is postponed by virtue of subsection (1)(b) or subsection (2), then, notwithstanding paragraph (b) of section 117, interest upon that tax shall not be payable in respect of the period commencing on the valuation date and ending 9 months after the date on which that tax actually becomes due and payable.]¹

Amendments

¹   Section 115A inserted by FA 1994 s 140 in relation to persons dying after 17 June 1993.".

116 Payment of tax

Amendments

Section 116 repealed by FA 2001 s 225(1) with effect in relation to probate tax first due and payable on or from 6 December 2000; previously:

"(1) The person applying for probate or letters of administration of the estate of the deceased shall—

(a) notwithstanding the provisions of section 36 (inserted by the Finance Act, 1989) or section 39 of the Principal Act, make, on a form provided by the Commissioners, an assessment of the tax arising on the death of the deceased by virtue of section 110, and that assessment shall include the interest, if any, payable on the tax in accordance with paragraph (b) of section 117, and shall be of such amount as to the best of the said person's knowledge, information and belief, ought to be charged, levied and paid, and the form on which the assessment is made shall accompany the Inland Revenue Affidavit which is required to be delivered to the Commissioners, and

(b) on delivering the Inland Revenue Affidavit to the Commissioners, duly pay the amount of such tax and interest,

and the Inland Revenue Affidavit and the form on which the assessment is made shall together, for the purpose of section 36(2) of the Principal Act, be deemed, in relation to the tax arising by virtue of section 110, to be a return delivered by a person primarily accountable.

(2) The provisions of section 36(3)(b) of the Principal Act (inserted by the Finance Act, 1989) shall, with any necessary modifications, apply to any payment required by virtue of this section.".

117 Interest on tax

Amendments

Section 117 repealed by FA 2001 s 225(1) with effect in relation to probate tax first due and payable on or from 6 December 2000; previously:

"In relation to a charge for tax arising by virtue of section 110—

(a)　the tax shall be due and payable on the valuation date;

(b)　simple interest to the date of payment of the tax shall, from the first day after the expiration of the period of 9 months commencing on the valuation date, be payable upon the tax at the rate of [one per cent]¹ per month or part of a month, without deduction of Income Tax, and shall be chargeable and recoverable in the same manner as if it were part of the tax;

(c)　notwithstanding the provisions of paragraph (a), where, during the said period of 9 months, a payment is made on foot of the tax, the tax due at the time of the payment shall be discounted by an amount appropriate to the payment, such discount being calculated on tax at a rate per cent equal to [one per cent]² multiplied by the number of months in the period from the date of payment to the date of the expiration of the said period of 9 months, and for this purpose a month shall include a part of a month:

Provided that insofar as the payment is repaid by the Commissioners in accordance with the provisions of section 46 of the Principal Act, no discount shall be appropriate to the payment;

(d)　notwithstanding the provisions of paragraph (b), the interest payable upon the tax shall not exceed the amount of the tax.

Amendments

¹　Substituted by FA 1998 s 127(a) in relation to probate tax due before, on or after 27 March 1998 where the period in respect of which interest is to be charged, or a discount falls to be made, commences on or after that date; previously 'one and one-quarter per cent'.

²　Substituted by FA 1998 s 127(b) in relation to probate tax due before, on or after 27 March 1998 where the period in respect of which interest is to be charged, or a discount falls to be made, commences on or after that date; previously 'one and one-quarter per cent'.".

118 Postponement of tax

Amendments

Section 118 repealed by FA 2001 s 225(1) with effect in relation to probate tax first due and payable on or from 6 December 2000; previously:

"Where the Commissioners are satisfied that there are insufficient liquid assets comprised in the estate of the deceased to meet any tax arising by virtue of section 110, they may allow payment to be postponed for such period, to such extent and on such terms as they think fit."

119 Application of section 85 of Finance Act, 1989, and section 133 of Finance Act, 1993

Amendments

Section 119 repealed by FA 2001 s 225(1) with effect in relation to probate tax first due and payable on or from 6 December 2000; previously:

"In relation to a charge for tax arising by virtue of section 110, section 85(2)(b)(iii) of the Finance Act, 1989 and section 133(2)(b)(iii) shall not apply.".

CHAPTER II
Miscellaneous amendments, etc

120 Interpretation (Chapter II)

In this Chapter "**the Principal Act**" means the Capital Acquisitions Tax Act, 1976.

121 Amendment of section 5 (gift deemed to be taken) of Principal Act

(1) Where, on or after the 24th day of February, 1993, a person becomes beneficially entitled in possession to a benefit, and the property in which the benefit is taken consists wholly or partly of shares in a private company, section 5 of the Principal Act shall have effect as if "otherwise than for full consideration in money or money's worth paid by him" were deleted in subsection (1) thereof.

(2) In subsection (1) the expression "**shares in a private company**" shall be construed by reference to the meanings that "**share**" (as amended by this Act) and "**private company**" have, respectively, in section 16 of the Principal Act.

Notes

In deciding whether a gift arises on the transfer of shares in a private company, the value of the transferred shares is to be computed in accordance with CATA 1976 s 16 as amended by the new s 125 (below).

This section will apply only where the consideration could not reasonably (taking into account the disponer's position prior to the disposition) be regarded as representing full consideration to the disponer for having made such a disposition: FA 1994 s 147.

Definitions

"benefit", "entitled in possession", "property", "share": CATA 1976 s 2(1).

122 Amendment of section 6 (taxable gift) of Principal Act

Note

This section substituted CATA 1976 s 6(1) as regards gifts taken on or after 17 June 1993. Gifts of foreign assets taken from a person who is not domiciled in the State, under a disposition governed by Irish law are not subject to capital acquisitions tax.

123 Amendment of section 11 (inheritance deemed to be taken) of Principal Act

(1) Where, on or after the 24th day of February, 1993, a person becomes beneficially entitled in possession to a benefit, and the property in which the benefit is taken consists wholly or partly of shares in a private company, section 11 of the Principal Act shall have effect as if "otherwise than for full consideration in money or money's worth paid by him" were deleted in subsection (1) thereof.

(2) In subsection (1) the expression "**shares in a private company**" shall be construed by reference to the meanings that "share" (as amended by this Act) and "**private company**" have, respectively, in section 16 of the Principal Act.

Notes

Inheritances of foreign assets taken on or after 17 June 1993 from a person who is not domiciled in the State, under a disposition governed by Irish law are not subject to capital acquisitions tax.

This section will apply only where the consideration could not reasonably (taking into account the disponer's position prior to the disposition) be regarded as representing full consideration to the disponer for having made such a disposition: FA 1994 s 148.

Definitions

"benefit", "entitled in possession", "property", "share": CATA 1976 s 2(1).

124 Amendment of section 12 (taxable inheritance) of Principal Act

Note

This section substituted CATA 1976 s 12(1)(*a*) for inheritances taken on or after 17 June 1993.

125 Amendment of section 16 (market value of certain shares) of Principal Act

Note

This section amended CATA 1976 s 16 for gifts of inheritances taken on or after 24 February 1993 as follows: subs (1)(*a*) substituted CATA 1976 s 16(1); subs (1)(*b*)(i) inserted CATA 1976 s 16(2) definition of "group of shares"; subs (1)(*b*)(ii) deleted CATA 1976 s 16(2) definition of "private trading company"; subs (1)(*b*)(iii) inserted CATA 1976 s 16(2) definition of "share".

The method of valuing shares in private trading companies now applies to private non-trading companies. Shares in such companies are valued at market value, not on a winding up basis.

126 Amendment of section 90 (arrangements reducing value of company shares) of Finance Act, 1989

(1) ...

(2) This section shall apply where—

(*a*) as respects subsection (1)(*a*), the time referred to in paragraph (*a*) of the definition of "specified amount" is on or after the 24th day of February, 1993, and

(*b*) as respects subsection (1)(*b*), the arrangement to which the said subsection relates is made on or after the 6th day of May, 1993.

Note

Subs (1)(*a*) deleted in FA 1989 s 90(1)(*a*) definition of "specified amount" the words "or 17", subs (1)(*b*) inserted FA 1989 s 90(12).

FA 1989 s 90 deals with the transfer of rights attaching to particular shares in a private company to other shareholders in the same company without any transfer of shares being involved. The value of the transferred rights is to be regarded as a gift, or inheritance (as appropriate) in the hands of the beneficial recipient.

This section amended FA 1989 s 90 to take account of the repeal of CATA 1976 s 17 by s 134 below. FA 1989 s 90 now also applies to benefits conferred by the redemption of shares in a private company where no consideration is paid for that redemption.

127 Construction of certain references in section 16 of Principal Act for purposes of "specified amount" in section 90 of Finance Act, 1989

(1) For the purpose of paragraph (*a*) of the definition of **"specified amount"** in subsection (1) of section 90 of the Finance Act, 1989, section 16 of the Principal Act shall have effect as if—

(*a*) the references therein to the donee or successor were references to the person who, for the purposes of section 90 of the Finance Act, 1989, is the disponer of the specified amount,

(*b*) the references therein to the time at which a company is controlled were references to the time referred to in the said paragraph, and (*c*)   the shares referred to in the said paragraph were, at the time referred to therein, the absolute property of the aforesaid disponer.

(2) This section shall apply where the time referred to in paragraph (*a*) of the definition of **"specified amount"** in subsection (1) of section 90 of the Finance Act, 1989, is on or after the 6th day of May, 1993.

Notes

This section interprets references in CATA 1976 s 16 (share valuation) for the purposes of (FA 1989 s 90 anti-avoidance).

Definitions

"absolute property", "donee", "disponer", "person", "successor", "share": CATA 976 s 2(1).

128 Amendment of section 19 (value of agricultural property) of Principal Act

Note

Gifts of agricultural assets taken on or after 17 June 1993 qualify for agricultural relief of up to £250,000 (previously £200,000), and 55% (previously 75%) of the qualifying farmer's assets must consist of agricultural assets.

129 Amendment of section 34 (disposition by or to a company) of Principal Act

Note

This section substituted CATA 1976 s 34(1)-(2). Gifts or inheritances taken on or after 24 February 1993 by (or provided by) private companies are to be valued on a market value basis not on a winding up basis.

130 Amendment of Second Schedule (computation of tax) to Principal Act

Note

This section amended CATA 1976 Sch 2 para 9 with effect for gifts or inheritances taken on or after 24 February 1993 as follows: para (*a*) substituted the definition of "company"; para (*b*) deleted the definition of "company controlled by the disponer"; para (*c*) inserted the definition of "investment income"; para (*d*) inserted the definitions of "private company" and "private company controlled by the disponer" and "private non-trading company".

These definitions would otherwise have been removed from CATA 1976 by ss 125 to 134.

131 Amendment of section 107 (application of Principal Act) of Finance Act, 1984

Note

This section substituted FA 1984 s 107(*a*) as regards inheritances taken on or after 24 February 1993. The once off discretionary trust charge is amended to take account of the new method of valuing shares in private companies.

132 Amendment of section 104 (application of Principal Act) of Finance Act, 1986

Note

This section substituted FA 1986 s 104(*a*) as regards inheritances taken on or after 24 February 1993. The annual discretionary trust charge is amended to take account of the new method of valuing shares in private companies.

133 Exemption of certain policies of assurance

[(1) In this section—

"assurance company" has the meaning assigned to it by section 706 of the Taxes Consolidation Act 1997;

"new policy" means a contract entered into by an assurance company which is a policy of assurance on the life of any person issued on or after 1 January 2001;

"old policy" means a contract entered into by an assurance company in the course of carrying on a foreign life assurance business within the meaning of section 451 of the Taxes Consolidation Act 1997 and issued on or after 1 December 1992 and before 1 January 2001.][1]

(2) Where any interest in a [new policy or in an old policy][2] is comprised in a gift or an inheritance, then any such interest—

(*a*) shall be exempt from tax, and

(*b*) shall not be taken into account in computing tax on any gift or inheritance taken by a donee or successor,

if, but only if, it is shown to the satisfaction of the Commissioners that—

(i) such interest is comprised in the gift or inheritance at the date of the gift or at the date of the inheritance;

[(ii) at the date of the disposition, the disposer is neither domiciled nor ordinarily resident in the State;][3]

and

(iii) at the date of the gift or at the date of the inheritance, the donee or successor is neither domiciled nor ordinarily resident in the State.

[(3) Where—

(*a*) an interest in a new policy or in an old policy, as the case may be, which is comprised in a gift or inheritance came into the beneficial ownership of the disposer or became subject to the disposition prior to 15 February 2001, and

(*b*) the conditions at subparagraphs (i) and (iii) of subsection (2) are complied with, then that subsection shall apply to that interest in a new policy or in an old policy, as the case may be, if, at the date of the disposition, the proper law of the disposition was not the law of the State.][4]

Amendments

1 Subs (1) substituted by FA 2002 s 122(*a*).

2 Substituted by FA 2002 s 122(*b*); previously "policy".

3 Subs (2)(*b*)(ii) substituted by FA 2001 s 226(1) with effect from 15 February 2001 in relation to a policy comprised in a gift or an inheritance where the date of the gift or inheritance is on or after 15 February 2001 and the policy comes into the beneficial ownership of the disposer on or after 15 February 2001, or becomes subject to the disposition on or after that date without having been previously in the beneficial ownership of the disposer.

4 Subs (3) substituted by FA 2002 s 122(*c*).

Notes

Certain life assurance policies issued to foreign non residents by companies located in the International Financial Services Centre are exempt from gift tax and inheritance tax. Life policies issued by domestic companies on or after 1 January 2001 are also exempt from gift tax and inheritance tax.

Narrative

Capital Acquisitions Tax, Chapters 11, 18.

Definitions

"Commissioners", "date of the disposition", "date of the gift", "date of the inheritance", "donee", "disponer", "disposition", "gift", "inheritance", "successor": CATA 1976 s 2(1).

134 Repeal, etc (Chapter II)

Note

This section repealed CATA 1976 s 17 as regards gifts or inheritances taken on or after 24 February 1993.

PART VII
MISCELLANEOUS

142 Care and management of taxes and duties

All taxes and duties imposed by this Act are hereby placed under the care and management of the Revenue Commissioners.

143 Short title, construction and commencement

(1) This Act may be cited as the Finance Act, 1993.

...

(7) Part VI shall be construed together with the Capital Acquisitions Tax Act, 1976, and the enactments amending or extending that Act.

...

(10) Any reference in this Act to any other enactment shall, except so far as the context otherwise requires, be construed as a reference to that enactment as amended by or under any other enactment including this Act.

(11) In this Act, a reference to a Part, section or Schedule is to a Part or section of, or Schedule to, this Act, unless it is indicated that reference to some other enactment is intended.

(12) In this Act, a reference to a subsection, paragraph, subparagraph or clause is to the subsection, paragraph, subparagraph or clause of the provision (including a Schedule) in which the reference occurs, unless it is indicated that reference to some other provision is intended.

FINANCE ACT 1994

(1994 Number 13)
(Date of passing: 23 May 1994)

ARRANGEMENT OF SECTIONS

PART VI
CAPITAL ACQUISITIONS TAX

CHAPTER I
Business relief

CHAPTER II
Miscellaneous

AN ACT TO CHARGE AND IMPOSE CERTAIN DUTIES OF CUSTOMS AND INLAND REVENUE (INCLUDING EXCISE), TO AMEND THE LAW RELATING TO CUSTOMS AND INLAND REVENUE (INCLUDING EXCISE) AND TO MAKE FURTHER PROVISIONS IN CONNECTION WITH FINANCE

PART VI
CAPITAL ACQUISITIONS TAX

CHAPTER I
Business relief

124 Interpretation (Chapter I)

(1) In this Chapter–

"agricultural property" has the meaning assigned to it by section 19 of the Principal Act (as amended by the Finance Act, 1994);

"associated company" has the meaning assigned to it by section 16(1)(*b*) of the Companies (Amendment) Act, 1986;

"business" includes a business carried on in the exercise of a profession or vocation, but does not include a business carried on otherwise than for gain;

"excepted asset" shall be construed in accordance with section 134;

"full-time working officer or employee", in relation to one or more companies, means any officer or employee who devotes substantially the whole of his time to the service of that company, or those companies taken together, in a managerial or technical capacity;

"holding company" and **"subsidiary"** have the meanings assigned to them, respectively, by section 155 of the Companies Act, 1963;

"the Principal Act" means the Capital Acquisitions Tax Act, 1976;

"quoted", in relation to any shares or securities, means quoted on a recognised stock exchange and "unquoted", in relation to any shares or securities, means not so quoted;

"relevant business property" shall be construed in accordance with section 127.

(2) In this Chapter a reference to a gift shall be construed as a reference to a taxable gift and a reference to an inheritance shall be construed as a reference to a taxable inheritance.

(3) For the purposes of this Chapter a company and all its subsidiaries and any associated company of that company or of any of those subsidiaries and any subsidiary of such an associated company are members of a group.

[(4) In this Chapter any reference to a donee or successor shall be construed as including a reference to the transferee referred to in section 23 (1) of the Principal Act.][1]

Amendments

[1]   Subs (4) inserted by FA 2001 s 124 in relation to gifts or inheritances taken on or after 11 April 1994.

Revenue practice

See CAT Work Manual, Pt 11C regarding "business".

Narrative

Capital Acquisitions Tax, Chapter 10.

Definitions

"gift": CATA 1976 s 2(1); "inheritance": CATA 1976 s 2(1).

125 Application (Chapter I)

The provisions of this Chapter shall have effect in relation to gifts and inheritances taken on or after the 11th day of April, 1994, but those provisions shall not have effect in relation to an inheritance taken by a relevant trust by virtue of section 110(1) of the Finance Act, 1993, or to an inheritance taken by a discretionary trust by virtue of section 106(1) of the Finance Act, 1984, or section 103(1) of the Finance Act, 1986.

Notes

Business relief does not apply to Probate Tax or Discretionary Trust Tax.

Narrative

Capital Acquisitions Tax, Chapter 10.

Definitions

"gift": CATA 1976 s 2(1); "discretionary trust": CATA 1976 s 2(1); "inheritance": CATA 1976 s 2(1); "relevant trust": FA 1993 s 109(1).

126 Business relief

[Where the whole or part of the taxable value of any taxable gift or taxable inheritance is attributable to the value of any relevant business property, the whole or that part of the taxable value shall, subject to the other provisions of this Chapter, be treated as being reduced by [**90 per cent**][1].][2]

Amendments

[1]   Substituted by FA 1997 s 139 in relation to gifts or inheritances taken on or after 23 January 1997; previously "75 per cent" (FA 1996 s 125(1)); previously "50 per cent".

[2]   Section 126 substituted by FA 1995 s 161 in relation to gifts or inheritances taken on or after 8 February 1995.

Notes

For gifts and inheritances of relevant business property taken on or after 11 April 1994 and before 8 February 1995, the relief is given by reducing the taxable value of such relevant business property by 50% of the first £250,000 of that taxable value and by 25% of the balance. A Revenue booklet (form CA4) explains the relief in more detail.

Cross-references

Instalment payments: FA 1995 s 164(2)(*a*).

Narrative

Capital Acquisitions Tax, Chapter 10.

Definitions

"donee": CATA 1976 s 2(1); "gifts": CATA 1976 s 2(1); "inheritance": CATA 1976 s 2(1); "property": CATA 1976 s 2(1); "successor": CATA 1976 s 2(1).

127 Relevant business property

(1) In this Chapter and subject to the following provisions of this section and to sections 128, 130 and 134(3) **"relevant business property"** means, in relation to a gift or inheritance, any one or more of the following, that is to say:

(*a*)   property consisting of a business or interest in a business;

(*b*)   unquoted shares in or securities of a company [whether incorporated in the State or otherwise][1] to which paragraph (*c*) does not relate, and which on the valuation date (either by themselves alone or together with other shares or securities in that company in the absolute beneficial ownership of the donee or successor on that date) give control of powers of voting on all questions affecting the company as a whole which if exercised would yield more than **25 per cent** of the votes capable of being exercised thereon;

[(*c*)   unquoted shares in or securities of a company [whether incorporated in the State or otherwise][1] which is, on the valuation date (after the taking of the gift or inheritance), a company controlled by the donee or successor within the meaning of section 16 of the Principal Act;][2]

(*d*)   unquoted shares in or securities of a company [whether incorporated in the State or otherwise][1] which do not fall within paragraph (*b*) or (*c*) and which on the valuation date (either by themselves alone or together with other shares or securities in that company in the absolute beneficial ownership of the donee or successor on that date) have an aggregate nominal value which represents **10 per cent** or more of the aggregate nominal value of the entire share capital and securities of the company;

Provided that the donee or successor has been a fulltime working officer or employee of the company, or if that company is a member of a group, of one or more companies which are members of the group, throughout the period of 5 years ending on the date of the gift or inheritance;

(*e*) ...[3] any land or building, machinery or plant which, immediately before the gift or inheritance was used wholly or mainly for the purposes of a business carried on by a company of which the disponer then had control or by a partnership of which the disponer then was a partner and for the purposes of this paragraph a person shall be deemed to have control of a company at any time if he then had control of powers of voting on all questions affecting the company as a whole which if exercised would have yielded a majority of the votes capable of being exercised thereon;

(*f*) quoted shares in or securities of a company which, but for the fact that they are quoted, would be shares or securities to which paragraph (*b*), (*c*) or (*d*) would relate:

Provided that such shares or securities, or other shares in or securities of the same company which are represented by those shares or securities, were in the beneficial ownership of the disponer immediately prior to the disposition and were unquoted at the date of the commencement of that beneficial ownership or at the date of the passing of this Act, whichever is the later date.

(2) Where a company has shares or securities of any class giving powers of voting limited to either or both–

(*a*) the question of winding-up the company, and

(*b*) any question primarily affecting shares or securities of that class,

the reference in subsection (1) to all questions affecting the company as a whole shall have effect as a reference to all such questions except any in relation to which those powers are capable of being exercised.

...[4]

(4) A business or interest in a business, or shares in or securities of a company, shall not be relevant business property if the business or, as the case may be, the business carried on by the company consists wholly or mainly of one or more of the following, that is to say, dealing in currencies, securities, stocks or shares, land or buildings, or making or holding investments.

(5) Subsection (4) shall not apply to shares in or securities of a company if the business of the company consists wholly or mainly in being a holding company of one or more companies whose business does not fall within that subsection.

[(6) Any land, building, machinery or plant used wholly or mainly for the purposes of a business carried on as mentioned in subsection (1)(*e*) shall not be relevant business property in relation to a gift or inheritance, unless the disponer's interest in the business is, or shares in or securities of the company carrying on the business immediately before the gift or inheritance are, relevant business property in relation to the gift or inheritance or in relation to a simultaneous gift or inheritance taken by the same donee or successor.

(7) The references to a disponer in subsections (1)(*e*) and (6) shall include a reference to a person in whom the land, building, machinery or plant concerned is vested for a beneficial interest in possession immediately before the gift or inheritance.

(8) Where shares or securities are vested in the trustees of a settlement, any powers of voting which they give to the trustees of the settlement shall, for the purposes of subsection (1)(*e*), be deemed to be given to the person beneficially entitled in possession to the shares or securities except in a case where no individual is so entitled.][5]

Amendments

[1]   Substituted by FA 2001 s 228(1)(*a*) in relation to gifts or inheritances taken on or after 15 February 2001; previously "incorporated in the State".

[2]   Subs (1)(*c*) substituted by FA 1996 s 126(1) in relation to gifts or inheritances taken on or after 28 March 1996.

[3]   Deleted by FA 2001 s 228(1)(*b*) in relation to gifts or inheritances taken on or after 15 February 2001; previously "in so far as situated in the State,".

[4]   Subs (3) deleted by FA 2001 s 228(1)(*c*) in relation to gifts or inheritances taken on or after 15 February 2001.

[5]   Subss (6)-(8) substituted (for subs (6)) by FA 1997 s 140 in relation to gifts or inheritances taken on or after 26 March 1997.

Notes

The following kinds of property will qualify for business relief

(*a*) a business or an interest in a business,

(*b*) unquoted company shares where the beneficiary hold at least 25% of the voting rights,

or at least 10% of the issued share capital (provided he has either worked in the company full time for five years prior to the date of the gift or inheritance, or he can, together with his relatives, control the company),

(*c*) land, buildings or capital equipment owned by the disponer but used by a company controlled by the disponer (provided in the case of a company, the property in question is transferred at the same time as the shares),

(*d*) quoted company shares which were unquoted when the disponer acquired them.

Dealing in land, securities, currencies, investments etc is excluded from the relief.

Cross-references

Relevant business property (subss (1)(*e*), (4)), exclusion of value of agricultural property, excepted assets and excluded property: s 134(2)(proviso), (3), (7)(*b*).

Withdrawal of relief (subs (1)(*d*), (*e*), (*f*)) : s 135.

Revenue practice

See CAT Work Manual (revised July 2001), Pt 11C regarding the "wholly or mainly" test and the meaning of "dealing" and "investment" in s 127(4).

Narrative

Capital Acquisitions Tax, Chapter 10.

Definitions

"business": s 124; "date of the gift": CATA 1976 s 2(1); "date of the inheritance": CATA 1976 s 2(1); "disponer": CATA 1976 s 2(1); "disposition": CATA 1976 s 2(1); "donee": CATA 1976 s 2(1); "gift": CATA 1976 s 2(1); "inheritance": CATA 1976 s 2(1); "land": IA 1937 Sch; "person": IA 1937 s 11(*c*); "property": CATA 1976 s 2(1); "relevant business property": s 124; "share": CATA 1976 s 2(1); "successor": CATA 1976 s 2(1); "valuation date": CATA 1976 s 2(1).

128 Minimum period of ownership

In relation to a gift or an inheritance, property shall not be relevant business property unless it was comprised in the disposition continuously–

(*a*) in the case of an inheritance, which is taken on the date of death of the disponer, for a period of two years immediately prior to the date of the inheritance, or

(*b*) in any other case, for a period of five years immediately prior to the date of the gift or inheritance,

and any period immediately before the date of the disposition during which the property was continuously in the beneficial ownership of the disponer, or of the spouse of the disponer, shall be deemed, for the purposes of this Chapter, to be a period or part of a period immediately before the date of the gift or inheritance during which it was continuously comprised in the disposition.

Notes

Before disposing of the business property, the disponer must have owned it for at least five years prior to the transfer, or, in the case of an inheritance taken on the death of the disponer, for at least two years prior to the transfer. Property given from trust arrangements will qualify for business relief if the property was in the trust (or owned by the disponer or his or her spouse) for the preceding five years. If the disponer himself acquired the business property on the death of another person, he is deemed to own the property, for the purposes of the five (or two) year rule, from the date of death of that disponer.

Cross-references

Agricultural or business property,meaning of relevant business property applied: FA 1995 s 164(4).

Exclusion of value of agricultural property, excepted assets and excluded property: s 134(5).

Replacement property: s 129.

Succession: s 130.

Successive benefits: s 131(1)(*c*).

Withdrawal of relief: s 135(2).

Narrative

Capital Acquisitions Tax, Chapter 10.

Definitions

"date of the gift": CATA 1976 s 2(1); "date of the inheritance": CATA 1976 s 2(1); "disponer": CATA 1976 s 2(1); "disposition": CATA 1976 s 2(1); "gift": CATA 1976 s 2(1); "inheritance": CATA 1976 s 2(1); "on the date": CATA 1976 s 3; "property": CATA 1976 s 2(1); "property": CATA 1976 s 2(1); "relevant business property": s 124.

129 Replacements

(1) Property shall be treated as complying with section 128 if–

(*a*) the property replaced other property and the said property, that other property and any property directly or indirectly replaced by that other property were comprised in the disposition for periods which together comprised–

   (i) in a case referred to at paragraph (*a*) of section 128, at least two years falling within the three years immediately preceding the date of the inheritance. or

   (ii) in a case referred to at paragraph (*b*) of section 128, at least five years falling within the six years immediately preceding the date of the gift or inheritance, and

(*b*) any other property concerned was such that, had the gift or inheritance been taken immediately before it was replaced, it would, apart from section 128, have been relevant business property in relation to the gift or inheritance.

(2) In a case to which subsection (1) relates, relief under this Chapter shall not exceed what it would have been had the replacement or any one or more of the replacements not been made.

(3) For the purposes of subsection (2) changes resulting from the formation, alteration or dissolution of a partnership, or from the acquisition of a business by a company controlled (within the meaning of section 16 of the Principal Act) by the former owner of the business, shall be disregarded.

Notes

Where, within the preceding five year period (or two year period in the case of property taken on the death of the disponer), business property was replaced by other business property, a six year period (or three year period in the case of property taken on the death of the disponer) may apply as the combined ownership period for both sets of property.

Cross-references

Exclusion of value of agricultural property, excepted assets and excluded property (subss (1), (2)): s 134(7)(proviso).

Succession: s 130.

Successive benefits: s 131(2).

Narrative

Capital Acquisitions Tax, Chapter 10.

Definitions

"business": s 124(1); "date of the gift": CATA 1976 s 2(1); "date of the inheritance": CATA 1976 s 2(1); "disposition": CATA 1976 s 2(1); "gift": CATA 1976 s 2(1); "inheritance": CATA 1976 s 2(1); "property": CATA 1976 s 2(1).

130 Succession

For the purposes of sections 128 and 129, where a disponer became beneficially entitled to any property on the death of another person the disponer shall be deemed to have been beneficially entitled to it from the date of that death.

Notes

Before disposing of the business property, the disponer must have owned it for at least five years prior to the transfer, or, in the case of an inheritance taken on the death of the disponer, for at least two years prior to the transfer. If the disponer himself acquired the business property on the death of another person, he is deemed to own the property, for the purposes of the five (or two) year rule, from the date of death of that disponer.

Cross-references

Relevant business property, meaning: s 127(1).

Narrative

Capital Acquisitions Tax, Chapter 10.

Definitions

"disponer": CATA 1976 s 2(1); "on the death": CATA 1976 s 3; "person": IA 1937 s 11(*c*).

131 Successive benefits

(1) Where–

    (*a*)   a gift or inheritance (in this section referred to as **"the earlier benefit"**) was eligible for relief under this Chapter or would have been so eligible if such relief had been capable of being given in respect of gifts and inheritances taken at that time, and (*b*)   the whole or part of the property which, in relation to the earlier benefit was relevant business property became, through the earlier benefit, the property of the person or of the spouse of the person who is the disponer in relation to a subsequent gift or inheritance (in this section referred to as **"the subsequent benefit"**), and

(*c*)   that property, or part, or any property directly or indirectly replacing it, would, apart from section 128, have been relevant business property in relation to the subsequent benefit, and

(*d*)   the subsequent benefit is an inheritance taken on the death of the disponer,

then the property which would have been relevant business property but for section 128 shall be relevant business property notwithstanding that section.

(2) Where the property which, by virtue of subsection (1), is relevant business property replaced the property or part referred to in subsection (1)(*c*), relief under this Chapter shall not exceed what it would have been had the replacement or any one or more of the replacements not been made, and section 129(3) shall apply with the necessary modifications for the purposes of this subsection.

(3) Where, in relation to the earlier benefit, the amount of the taxable value of the gift or inheritance which was attributable to the property or part referred to in subsection (1)(*c*) was part only of its value, a like part only of the value which, apart from this subsection, would fall to be reduced under this Chapter by virtue of this section shall be so reduced.

Notes

Before disposing of the business property, the disponer must have owned it for at least five years prior to the transfer, or, in the case of an inheritance taken on the death of the disponer, for at least two years prior to the transfer. A beneficiary taking from a deceased disponer (who, because of his death, was unable to meet the minimum two year ownership period) may qualify for business relief if that deceased disponer would have qualified for business relief at the time he acquired the business property.

Cross-references

Exclusion of value of agricultural property, excepted assets and excluded property: s 134(3).

Narrative

Capital Acquisitions Tax, Chapter 10.

Definitions

"benefit": CATA 1976 s 2(1); "gift": CATA 1976 s 2(1); "inheritance": CATA 1976 s 2(1); "property": CATA 1976 s 2(1); "relevant business property": s 124.

---

132 Value of business

For the purposes of this Chapter–

(*a*)   the value of a business or of an interest in a business shall be taken to be its net value;

(*b*)   subject to paragraph (*c*), the net value of a business shall be taken to be the market value of the assets used in the business (including goodwill) reduced by the aggregate market value of any liabilities incurred for the purposes of the business;

(*c*)   in ascertaining the net value of an interest in a business, no regard shall be had to assets or liabilities other than those by reference to which the net value of the entire business would fall to be ascertained.

In the case of a sole trader or partnership business, business relief applies to the net asset value of the business. In the case of a company the relief applies to the proportion of the shares that derive their value from the qualifying business activity (dealing in land securities or investments being excluded activities).

Cross-references

Agricultural or business property, payment of tax by instalments, net value (subs (3)): FA 1995 s 164(4).

Narrative

Capital Acquisitions Tax, Chapter 10.

Definitions

"business": s 124; "market value": CATA 1976 s 2(1).

133 Value of certain shares and securities

(1) Where a company is a member of a group and the business of any other company which is a member of the group falls within section 127(4), then, unless that business consists wholly or mainly in the holding of land or buildings wholly or mainly occupied by members of the group whose business does not fall within section 127(4), the value of shares in or securities of the company shall be taken for the purposes of this Chapter to be what it would be if that other company were not a member of the group.

(2) (*a*) In this subsection "shares" include securities and "shares in a company" include other shares in the same company which are represented by those shares.

   (*b*) Where unquoted shares in a company which is a member of a group are comprised in a gift or inheritance and shares in another company which is also a member of the group are quoted on the valuation date, the value of the first-mentioned shares shall be taken, for the purpose of this Chapter, to be what it would be if that other company were not a member of the group, unless those unquoted shares were in the beneficial ownership of the disponer immediately prior to the disposition and those quoted shares were–

      (i) unquoted at some time prior to the gift or inheritance when they were in the beneficial ownership of the disponer or a member of that group, while being a member of such group, or

      (ii) at the date of the passing of this Act,

     whichever is the later date.

Notes

Shares in an Irish holding company that owns one or more qualifying subsidiaries will qualify for relief. The value of shares in non-qualifying subsidiaries or associated companies (for example a subsidiary involved in land or currency dealing) is excluded in calculating the relief applicable to the holding company.

Cross-references

Exclusion of value of agricultural property, excepted assets and excluded property: s 134(2).
Withdrawal of relief (subs (2)(*b*)): s 135(2)(*b*).

Narrative

Capital Acquisitions Tax, Chapter 10.

Definitions

"business": s 124; "disponer": CATA 1976 s 2(1); "disposition": CATA 1976 s 2(1); "gift": CATA 1976 s 2(1); "inheritance": CATA 1976 s 2(1); "land": IA 1937 Sch; "quoted": s 124; "share": CATA 1976 s 2(1); "valuation date": CATA 1976 s 2(1);

134 Exclusion of value of excepted assets

[(1) In determining for the purposes of this Chapter what part of the taxable value of a gift or inheritance is attributable to the value of relevant business property, so much of the last-mentioned value as is attributable to—

(a) any excepted assets within the meaning of subsection (2), or

(b) any excluded property within the meaning of subsection (7),

shall be left out of account.

(2) An asset shall be an excepted asset in relation to any relevant business property if it was not used wholly or mainly for the purposes of the business concerned throughout the whole or the last two years of the relevant period, but where the business concerned is carried on by a company which is a member of a group, the use of an asset for the purposes of a business carried on by another company which at the time of the use and immediately prior to the gift or inheritance was also a member of that group shall be treated as use for the purposes of the business concerned, unless that other company's membership of the group falls to be disregarded under section 133:

Provided that the use of an asset for the purposes of a business to which section 127(4) relates shall not be treated as use for the purposes of the business concerned.]¹

(3) Subsection (2) shall not apply in relation to an asset which is relevant business property by virtue only of section 127(1)(e), and an asset shall not be relevant business property by virtue only of that provision unless either–

(a) it was used in the manner referred to in that provision–

(i) in the case where the disponer's interest in the business or the shares in or securities of the company carrying on the business are comprised in an inheritance taken on the date of death of the disponer, throughout the two years immediately preceding the date of the inheritance, or

(ii) in any other case, throughout the five years immediately preceding the date of the gift or inheritance,

or

(b) it replaced another asset so used and it and the other asset and any asset directly or indirectly replaced by that other asset were so used for periods which together comprised–

(i) in the case referred to at paragraph (a)(i), at least two years falling within the three years immediately preceding the date of the inheritance, or

(ii) in any other case, at least five years falling within the six years immediately preceding the date of the gift or inheritance;

but where section 131 applies paragraphs (a) and (b) shall be deemed to be complied with if the asset, or that asset and the asset or assets replaced by it, was or were so used throughout the period between the earlier and the subsequent benefit mentioned in that section, or throughout the part of that period during which it or they were in the beneficial ownership of the disponer or the disponer's spouse.

(4) Where part but not the whole of any land or building is used exclusively for the purposes of any business and the land or building would, but for this subsection, be an excepted asset, or, as the case may be, prevented by subsection (3) from being relevant business property, the part so used and the remainder shall for the purposes of this section be treated as separate assets, and the value of the part so used shall (if it would otherwise be less) be taken to be such proportion of the value of the whole as may be just.

(5) For the purposes of this section the relevant period, in relation to any asset, shall be the period immediately preceding the gift or inheritance during which the asset or, if the relevant business property is an interest in a business, a corresponding interest in the asset, was comprised in the disposition (within the meaning of section 128) or, if the business concerned is that of a company, was beneficially owned by that company or any other company which immediately before the gift or inheritance was a member of the same group.

(6) For the purposes of this section an asset shall be deemed not to have been used wholly or mainly for the purposes of the business concerned at any time when it was used wholly or mainly for the personal benefit of the disponer or of a relative of the disponer.

[(7) Where, in relation to a gift or an inheritance —

    (*a*) relevant business property consisting of shares in or securities of a company are comprised in the gift or inheritance on the valuation date, and

    (*b*) property consisting of a business, or interest in a business, not falling within section 127(4) (hereinafter in this section referred to as "company business property") is on that date beneficially owned by that company or, where that company is a holding company of one or more companies within the same group, by any company within that group,

that company business property shall, for the purposes of subsection (1), be excluded property in relation to those shares or securities unless it would, apart from section 127(3), have been relevant business property if —

    (i) it had been the subject matter of that gift or inheritance, and

    (ii) it had been comprised in the disposition for the periods during which it was in the beneficial ownership of that first-mentioned company or of any member of that group, while being such a member, or actually comprised in the disposition.

(8) In ascertaining whether or not company business property complies with paragraphs (i) and (ii) of subsection (7), the provisions of section 129 shall, with any necessary modifications, apply to that company business property as to a case to which subsection (1) of section 129 relates.][2]

Amendments

[1]   Subss (1)-(2) substituted by FA 2000 s 148(1)(*a*) for gifts or inheritances taken on or after 10 February 2000.

[2]   Subs (7) substituted and subs (8) inserted by FA 1998 s 128.

Notes

Farming and other assets not used for the business activity are excluded from the relief. Quoted securities are also excluded from the relief unless they were unquoted when acquired by the disponer. Land, buildings or capital equipment personally owned by the disponer but used by a (qualifying) company controlled by him will also qualify for relief, provided such assets were held for the minimum ownership period (s 128) prior to the date of the gift or inheritance.

Cross-references

Relevant business property (subs (3)), meaning: s 127(1).

Relevant business property, payment of tax by instalments, subs (3) does not apply: FA 1995 s 164(1).

Narrative

Capital Acquisitions Tax, Chapter 10.

Definitions

"agricultural property": s 124; "business: s 124; "date of the inheritance": CATA 1976 s 2(1); "disponer": CATA 1976 s 2(1);"gift": CATA 1976 s 2(1); "inheritance": CATA 1976 s 2(1); "property": CATA 1976 s 2(1); "relevant business property": s 124; "shares": CATA 1976 s 2(1);"valuation date": CATA 1976 s 2(1);

135 Withdrawal of relief

[(1) In this section "relevant period", in relation to relevant business property comprised in a gift or inheritance, means the period of 6 years commencing on the date of the gift or inheritance.][1]

(2) The reduction which would fall to be made under section 126 in respect of relevant business property comprised in a gift or inheritance shall cease to be applicable if and to the extent that the property, or any property which directly or indirectly replaces it–

  (*a*)   would not be relevant business property (apart from section 128 and the provisos to paragraphs (*d*) and (*f*) of subsection (1) of section 127 and other than by reason of bankruptcy or a bona fide winding-up on grounds of insolvency) in relation to a notional gift of such property taken by the same donee or successor from the same disponer at any time within the relevant period, unless it would be relevant business property (apart from section 128 and the provisos to paragraphs (*d*) and (*f*) of subsection (1) of section 127) in relation to another such notional gift taken within a year after the first-mentioned notional gift;

  (*b*)   is sold, redeemed or compulsorily acquired within the relevant period and is not replaced, within a year of the sale, redemption or compulsory acquisition, by other property (other than quoted shares or securities or unquoted shares or securities to which section 133(2)(*b*) relates) which would be relevant business property (apart from section 128 and the proviso to section 127(1)(*d*) in relation to a notional gift of that other property taken by the same donee or successor from the same disponer on the date of the replacement,

and tax shall be chargeable in respect of the gift or inheritance as if the property were not relevant business property:

[Provided that—

  (i)   any land, building, machinery or plant which are comprised in the gift or inheritance and which qualify as relevant business property by virtue of section 127(1)(*e*) shall, together with any similar property which has replaced such property, continue to be relevant business property for the purposes of this section for so long as they are used for the purposes of the business concerned,

[(ii)   this section shall not have effect where the donee or successor dies before the event which would otherwise cause the reduction to cease to be applicable.]²]³

Amendments

1   Subs (1) substituted by FA 2000 s 148(1)(*b*)(i) where the event which caused the reduction to cease to be applicable occurs on or after 10 February 2000.

2   Subs (2)(proviso)(ii)-(iii) substituted by FA 2000 s 148(1)(*b*)(ii) where the event which caused the reduction to cease to be applicable occurs on or after 10 February 2000.

3   Subs (2)(proviso) substituted by FA 1996 s 127(1)(*b*) in relation to gifts or inheritances taken on or after 23 January 1996.

Cross-references

Instalment payments: FA 1995 s 164(2)(*a*).

Notes

If, after obtaining business relief, the business is sold, leased, or ceases to qualify for the relief granted, within six years of the valuation date, the relief given may be withdrawn.

Narrative

Capital Acquisitions Tax, Chapter 10.

Definitions

"business": s 124; "donee", "disponer", "successor": CATA 1976 s 2(1); "gift": CATA 1976 s 2(1); "inheritance": CATA 1976 s 2(1); "land": IA 1937 Sch; "property": s 124; "relevant business property": s 124; "the date of the gift": CATA 1976 s 2(1); "the date of the inheritance": CATA 1976 s 2(1); "the valuation date": CATA 1976 s 2(1);

135A Avoidance of double relief

[Where the whole or part of the taxable value of any taxable gift or taxable inheritance is attributable to agricultural property to which subsection (2) of section 19 of the Principal Act applies, such whole or part of the taxable value shall not be reduced under this Chapter.]¹

Amendments

1   Section 135A inserted by FA 2000 s 148(1)(*c*) for gifts or inheritances taken on or after 10 February 2000.

CHAPTER II
Miscellaneous

136 Interpretation (Chapter II)

In this Chapter "**the Principal Act**" means the Capital Acquisitions Tax Act, 1976.

137 Amendment of section 109 (interpretation) of Finance Act. 1993

Amendments

Repealed by FA 2001 s 225(2) with effect in relation to probate tax due and payable on or from 6 December 2000; previously this section inserted in FA 1993 s 109 the definitions of "agricultural property" and "agricultural value" with effect in relation to persons dying after 17 June 1993 but was repealed by FA 2001 s 225(2) with effect in relation to probate tax due and payable on or from 6 December 2000.

138 Amendment of section 111 (application of Principal Act) of Finance Act, 1993

Amendments

This section repealed by FA 2001 s 225(2) with effect in relation to probate tax due and payable on or from 6 December 2000; previously:

Subs (1)(*a*) deleted "and" in para (*g*)(ii) and inserted para (*g*)(ii*a*) in FA 1993 s 111 with effect in respect of persons dying after 17 June 1993;

Subs (1)(*b*) inserted para (*g*)(proviso) in FA 1993 s 111.

With effect from 17 June 1993 (the date of introduction of probate tax) the market value of agricultural land and buildings is reduced by 30%. The part of a mortgage or incumbrance on property that is properly apportionable to an exempt dwelling house must be apportioned to that property. Nevertheless, as regards a dwelling house passing to a dependent child or relative, the part of the mortgage etc apportionable to the dwelling house will be allowed as a deduction against all property passing to those dependants.

139 Amendment of section 112 (exemptions) of Finance Act, 1993

Amendments

Section 139 repealed by FA 2001 s 225(2) with effect in relation to probate tax due and payable on or from 6 December 2000; previously:

In respect of persons dying on or after 23 May 1994:

subs (1)(*a*) deleted FA 1993 s 112(*c*);

subs (1)(*b*) substituted FA 1993 s 112(*d*).

As regards persons dying on or after 23 May 1994, the dwelling house will be exempt from probate tax to the extent that it passes to a surviving spouse or a dependent relative or child, if there is no surviving spouse, and the dwelling house passes to a non-dependant, the probate tax arising does not become payable until nine months after the death of the spouse.

140 Abatement and postponement of tax

Amendments

Section 140 repealed by FA 2001 s 225(2) with effect in relation to probate tax due and payable on or from 6 December 2000; previously: This section inserted FA 1993 s 115A with effect in relation to persons dying after 17 June 1993. That part of a deceased person's estate which is transferred to the deceased person's spouse is exempt from probate tax. If the surviving spouse acquires a life interest in property (without transfer of the property) the resulting tax will not become payable until nine months after the life interest ceases.

141 Amendment of section 19 (value of agricultural property) of Principal Act

Note

In relation to gifts or inheritances taken on or after 11 April 1994:

subs (1)(*a*) substituted the definition of "agricultural property" in CATA 1976 s 19;

subs (1)(*b*) substituted the definition of "agricultural value" in CATA 1976 s 19;

subs (1)(*c*) substituted CATA 1976 s 19(4);

subs (1)(*d*) substituted the definition of "farmer" in CATA 1976 s 19;

subs (1)(*e*) substituted CATA 1976 s 19(5)(*a*).

As regards gifts of agricultural property taken on or after 11 April 1994, the maximum agricultural relief is 80% on the first £300,000 with 30% on the balance (previously 75% relief up to a maximum of £250,000).

As regards inheritances of agricultural property taken on or after 11 April 1994, the maximum agricultural relief is 65% on the first £300,000 with 30% on the balance (previously 55% relief up to a maximum of £200,000).

The £300,000 limit applies to all taxable gifts taken since 28 February 1969, and all taxable inheritances (consisting in whole or in part of agricultural property) since 1 April 1975, by the same beneficiary from the same disponer.

Livestock and farm machinery etc (which previously did not qualify for agricultural relief), qualify for 25% relief as regards gifts and inheritances taken on or after 11 April 1994.

142 Amendment of Second Schedule (computation of tax) to Principal Act

Note

This section amended CATA 1976 Sch 2 Pt II in relation to gifts and inheritances taken on or after 11 April 1994.

The 35% rate of tax is abolished and the 30% rate now applies once the threshold amount has been exceeded by £30,000.

143 Amendment of section 109 (computation of tax) of Finance Act, 1984

(1) In this section–

"earlier relevant inheritance" means a relevant inheritance deemed to be taken on the date of death of the disponer;

"later relevant inheritance" means a relevant inheritance which, after the date of death of the disponer, is deemed to be taken by a discretionary trust by virtue of there ceasing to be a principal object of that trust who is under the age of 21 years;

"relevant inheritance" means an inheritance which, by virtue of section 106(1) of the Finance Act, 1984, is, on or after the 11th day of April, 1994, deemed to be taken by a discretionary trust;

[**"settled relevant inheritance"** means a relevant inheritance taken on the death of a life tenant;][1]

[**"relevant period"** means—

- (*a*) in relation to an earlier relevant inheritance, the period of 5 years commencing on the date of death of the disponer,
- (*b*) in relation to a settled relevant inheritance, the period of 5 years commencing on the date of death of the life tenant concerned, and
- (*c*) in relation to a later relevant inheritance, the period of 5 years commencing on the latest date on which a later relevant inheritance was deemed to be taken from the disponer;][2]

"the appropriate trust", in relation to a relevant inheritance, means the trust by which that inheritance was deemed to be taken.

(2) Section 109 of the Finance Act, 1984, is hereby amended by the substitution of **"six per cent"** for **"three per cent"**:

[Provided that where in the case of each and every earlier relevant inheritance, each and every settled relevant inheritance or each and every later relevant inheritance, as the case may be, taken from one and the same disponer, one or more objects of the appropriate trust became beneficially entitled in possession before the expiration of the relevant period to an absolute interest in the entire of the property of which that inheritance consisted on and at all times after the date of that inheritance (other than property which ceased to be subject to the terms of the appropriate trust by virtue of a sale or exchange of an absolute interest in that property for full consideration in money or money's worth), then, in relation to all such earlier relevant inheritances, all such settled relevant inheritances or all such later relevant inheritances, as the case may be, this section shall cease to apply and tax shall be computed accordingly in accordance with the provisions of the said section 109 as if this section had not been enacted.][3]

(3) Where two or more persons are together beneficially entitled in possession to an absolute interest in property, those persons shall not, by reason only that together they are beneficially so entitled in possession, be regarded for the purposes of subsection (2) as beneficially so entitled in possession.

(4) Notwithstanding the provisions of section 46 of the Principal Act, interest shall not be payable on any repayment of tax which arises by virtue of the provisions of this section.

Amendments

[1]   Definition of "settled relevant inheritance" inserted by FA 2001 s 229(1)(*a*)(i) as respects relevant inheritances taken on or after 26 January 2001.

[2]   Definition of "relevant period" substituted by FA 2001 s 229(1)(*a*)(ii) as respects relevant inheritances taken on or after 26 January 2001.

[3]   Subs (2)(proviso) substituted by FA 2001 s 229(1)(*b*) as respects relevant inheritances taken on or after 26 January 2001.

Note

This section generally increases the once off charge on (new) discretionary trusts from 3% of the trust's assets to 6% of that value. Nevertheless, if the property comprised in trust is absolutely transferred to the beneficiaries within five years of the date of death of the disponer (or, where the trust has principal objects, within five years of the youngest becoming 21 years old) the increase in the charge will be refunded, without interest.

Definitions

"absolute interest": CATA 1976 s 2(1); "date of the inheritance": CATA 1976 s 2(1); "discretionary trust": CATA 1976 s 2(1); "disponer": CATA 1976 s 2(1); "inheritance": CATA 1976 s 2(1)."person": IA 1937 s 11(*c*); "property": s 124; "tax": CATA 1976 s 2(1).

144 Amendment of section 117 (reduction in estimated value of certain dwellings) of Finance Act, 1991

Note

This section substituted "60 per cent." for "50 per cent" and "£60,000" for "£50,000" in FA 1991 s 117(1) in relation to inheritances taken on or after the 11 April 1994.

As regards inheritances taken on or after 11 April 1994, if a successor takes a house (or part of a house) from a deceased brother or sister, and the successor had resided with the deceased in that house for at least five years prior to the date of the inheritance, the market value of the house for inheritance tax purposes is reduced by 60% (previously 50%) or £60,000 (previously £50,000: FA 1991 s 117 as enacted) whichever is the lesser. The relief does not apply to a house that is included as part of agricultural property that qualifies for agricultural relief (CATA 1976 s 19).

145 Amendment of section 128 (amendment of Second Schedule (computation of tax) to Principal Act) of Finance Act, 1990

Note

This section by substituting FA 1990 s 128(1), regularised technical anomalies in relation to the indexation of threshold amounts.

146 Certificate relating to registration of title based on possession

(1) After the passing of this Act a person shall not be registered as owner of property in a register of ownership maintained under the Act of 1964 on foot of an application made to the Registrar on or after the 11th day of April, 1994, which is–

    (*a*) based on possession, and

    (*b*) made under the Rules of 1972, or any other rule made for carrying into effect the objects of the Act of 1964,

unless the applicant produces to the Registrar a certificate issued by the Commissioners to the effect that the Commissioners are satisfied–

        (i) that the property did not become charged with gift tax or inheritance tax during the relevant period, or

        (ii) that any charge for gift tax or inheritance tax to which the property became subject during that period has been discharged, or will (to the extent that it has not been discharged) be discharged within a time considered by the Commissioners to be reasonable.

(2) In the case of an application for registration in relation to which a solicitor's certificate is produced for the purpose of rule 19(3), 19(4) or 35 of the Rules of 1972, the Registrar may accept that the application is not based on possession if the solicitor makes to the Registrar a declaration in writing to that effect.

(3) Where, on application to them by the applicant for registration, the Commissioners are satisfied that they may issue a certificate for the purpose of subsection (1), they shall issue a certificate for that purpose, and the certificate and the application therefor shall be on a form provided by the Commissioners.

(4) A certificate issued by the Commissioners for the purpose of subsection (1) shall be in such terms and subject to such qualifications as the Commissioners think fit, and shall not be a certificate for any other purpose.

[(4A) In subsection (1), the reference to a certificate issued by the Commissioners shall be construed as including a reference to a certificate to which subsection (4B) relates, and the provisions of subsection (1) shall be construed accordingly.

(4B)(*a*) A certificate to which this subsection relates is a certificate by the solicitor for the applicant for registration in which it is certified, on a form provided by the Commissioners, that the solicitor—

        (i) is satisfied—

            (I) in a case where the applicant is a statutory authority within the definition of "statutory authority" contained in section 3(1) of the Act of 1964, that the market value of the relevant property at the time of the application does not exceed [€127,000][1], or

            (II) in any other case, that—

                (A) the area of the relevant property does not exceed five hectares, and

                (B) the market value of the relevant property at the time of the application does not exceed [€19,050][2], and

    (ii)   having investigated the title to the relevant property, has no reason to believe that the relevant particulars, in so far as relating to the relevant property at any time during the relevant period, are particulars which related at that time to significant other real property, that is to say, real property which, if combined with the relevant property for the purposes of subparagraph (i), would cause a limit which applies to the relevant property by virtue of that subparagraph to be exceeded.

  (*b*)   In this subsection—

    "the relevant particulars" means the particulars of title to the relevant property which are required to be produced to the Registrar for the purposes of paragraph 2 of Form 5 of the Schedule of Forms referred to in the definition of "Forms" contained in rule 2(1) of the Rules of 1972;

    "the relevant property" means the property in respect of which the application for registration is being made.

(4C) Notwithstanding the provisions of subsection (4B), a certificate by the solicitor for the applicant for registration shall be a certificate to which subsection (4B) relates if it certifies, on a form provided by the Commissioners, that the solicitor is satisfied that—

  (*a*)   the area of the property in respect of which the application for registration is being made does not exceed 500 square metres,

  (*b*)   the market value of the said property at the time of the application does not exceed [€2,540][3], and

  (*c*)   the application is not part of a series of related applications covering a single piece of property the total area of which exceeds 500 square metres or the market value of which at the time of the application exceeds [€2,540][4].][5]

(5) In this section–

"the Act of 1964" means the Registration of Title Act, 1964;

"the Registrar" means the Registrar of Titles;

"relevant period", in relation to a person's application to be registered as owner of property, means the period commencing on the 28th day of February, 1974, and ending on the date as of which the registration was made:

Provided that–

  (*a*)   where the certificate referred to in subsection (1) is a certificate for a period ending prior to the date of the registration, the period covered by the certificate shall be deemed to be the relevant period if, at the time of the registration, the Registrar had no reason to believe that a death relevant to the application for registration occurred after the expiration of the period covered by the certificate, and

  (*b*)   where the registration of the person (if any) who, at the date of that application, was the registered owner of the property had been made as of a date after the 28th day of February, 1974, the relevant period shall commence on the date as of which that registration was made;

"the Rules of 1972" means the Land Registration Rules, 1972 (SI No 230 of 1972).

Amendments

¹   Substituted by FA 2001 s 240 and Sch 5 Part 5 with effect from 1 January 2002; previously "£100,000".

²   Substituted by FA 2001 s 240 and Sch 5 Part 5 with effect from 1 January 2002; previously "£15,000".

³   Substituted by FA 2001 s 240 and Sch 5 Part 5 with effect from 1 January 2002; previously "£2,000".

⁴   Substituted by FA 2001 s 240 and Sch 5 Part 5 with effect from 1 January 2002; previously "£2,000".

⁵   Subss (4A)-(4C) inserted by FA 1996 s 128.

Notes

With effect from 23 May 1994 (date of passing of FA 1994), a person who applies, on the basis of possession, to be registered as the titleholder to land must produce a capital acquisitions tax (including probate tax) clearance certificate. Without such a certificate, the Land Registry will not be able to entertain the application.

Narrative

Capital Acquisitions Tax, Chapter 2.

Definitions

"Commissioners": CATA 1976 s 2(1); "gift": CATA 1976 s 2(1); "inheritance": CATA 1976 s 2(1); "person": IA 1937 s 11(*c*); "property": s 124; "tax": CATA 1976 s 2(1); "writing": IA 1937 Sch.

---

147 Provision relating to section 5 (gift deemed to be taken) of Principal Act and section 121 of Finance Act, 1993

Without prejudice to the meaning of section 5 of the Principal Act as enacted, that section shall have effect and be deemed always to have had effect as if the provisions of section 121 of the Finance Act, 1993, had not been enacted, except where the consideration referred to in the said section 5, being consideration in relation to a disposition, could not reasonably be regarded (taking into account the disponer's position prior to the disposition) as representing full consideration to the disponer for having made such a disposition.

Notes

As an anti avoidance measure, FA 1993 s 121 provided that, in deciding whether a gift arises on the transfer of shares in a private company, the value of the transferred shares is to based on market value, not on a winding up basis (CATA 1976 s 16 as amended by FA 1993 s 125).

FA 1993 s 121 will apply only where the consideration could not reasonably (taking into account the disponer's position prior to the disposition) be regarded as representing full consideration to the disponer for having made such a disposition.

Definitions

"disponer": CATA 1976 s 2(1); "disposition": CATA 1976 s 2(1); "gift": CATA 1976 s 2(1).

---

148 Provision relating to section 11 (inheritance deemed to be taken) of Principal Act and section 123 of Finance Act, 1993

Without prejudice to the meaning of section 11 of the Principal Act as enacted, that section shall have effect and be deemed always to have had effect as if the provisions of section 123 of the Finance Act, 1993, had not been enacted, except where the consideration referred to in the said section 11, being consideration in relation to a disposition, could not reasonably be regarded (taking into account the disponer's position prior to the disposition) as representing full consideration to the disponer for having made such a disposition.

Notes

As an anti avoidance measure, FA 1993 s 123 provided that, in deciding whether a gift arises on the transfer of shares in a private company, the value of the transferred shares is to based on market value, not on a winding up basis (CATA 1976 s 16 as amended by FA 1993 s 125).

FA 1993 s 123 will apply only where the consideration could not reasonably (taking into account the disponer's position prior to the disposition) be regarded as representing full consideration to the disponer for having made such a disposition.

Definitions

"disponer": CATA 1976 s 2(1); "disposition": CATA 1976 s 2(1); "inheritance": CATA 1976 s 2(1).

PART VII
MISCELLANEOUS

CHAPTER I
Provisions relating to residence of individuals

149 Interpretation (Chapter I)

In this Part–

"the Acts" means–

    (*a*) the Income Tax Acts,

    (*b*) the Corporation Tax Acts,

    (*c*) the Capital Gains Tax Acts, and

    (*d*) the Capital Acquisitions Tax Act, 1976, and the enactments amending or extending that Act,

and any instrument made thereunder;

"authorised officer" means an officer of the Revenue Commissioners authorised by them in writing for the purposes of this Chapter;

"present in the State", in relation to an individual, means the personal presence of the individual in the State;

"tax" means any tax payable in accordance with any provision of the Acts.

Narrative

Irish Income Tax: **Chapter 1**; *Capital Acquisitions Tax*, **Chapter 3**.

Definitions

"tax": ITA 1967 s 1(1); CTA 1976 s 155(3).

---

150 Residence

(1) For the purposes of the Acts, an individual is resident in the State for a year of assessment if the individual is present in the State–

    (*a*) at any one time or several times in the year of assessment for a period in the whole amounting to 183 days or more, or

    (*b*) at any one time or several times–

        (i) in the year of assessment, and

        (ii) in the preceding year of assessment,

for a period (being a period comprising in the aggregate the number of days on which the individual is present in the State in the year of assessment and the number of days on which the individual was present in the State in the preceding year of assessment) in the whole amounting to 280 days or more:

Provided that, notwithstanding paragraph (*b*), where for a year of assessment an individual is present in the State at any one time or several times for a period in the whole amounting to not more than 30 days–

    (*a*) the individual shall not be resident in the State for the year of assessment. and

    (*b*) no account shall be taken of the period for the purposes of the aggregate mentioned in paragraph (*b*).

(2) (*a*) Notwithstanding subsection (1), an individual—

        (i) who is not resident in the State for a year of assessment, and

        (ii) to whom paragraph (*b*) applies,

        may, at any time, elect to be treated as resident in the State for that year and, where an individual so elects, the individual shall, for the purposes of the Acts, be deemed to be resident in the State for that year.

    (*b*) This paragraph applies to an individual who satisfies an authorised officer that the individual is in the State–

        (i) with the intention, and

        (ii) in such circumstances,

        that the individual will be resident in the State for the following year of assessment.

(3) For the purposes of this section, an individual shall be deemed to be present in the State for a day if the individual is present in the State at the end of the day.

Cross-references

Effective date is 1995-96 and later tax years where an individual:

(*a*) was resident for 1991-92 but not resident for 1992-93 and 1993-94;

(*b*) was resident for 1992-93 but not resident for 1993-94;

(*c*) was resident for 1993-94 but not (under the old rules) resident for 1994-95;

(*d*) left the State in 1992-93 or 1993-94 to ordinarily reside elsewhere and did not recommence ordinary residence in the State before 5 April 1994. (FA 1994 s 158(2)).

Narrative

Capital Acquisitions Tax, Chapter 3.

Definitions

"resident": CGTA 1975 s 2(1); "year": IA 1937 Sch; "year of assessment": CGTA 1975 s 2(1), ITA 1967 s 1(1).

---

151 Ordinary residence

(1) For the purposes of the Acts, an individual is ordinarily resident in the State for a year of assessment if the individual has been resident in the State for each of the 3 years of assessment preceding that year.

(2) An individual who is ordinarily resident in the State shall not, for the purposes of the Acts, cease to be ordinarily resident in the State for a year of assessment unless the individual has not been resident in the State in each of the 3 years of assessment preceding that year.

Narrative
Capital Acquisitions Tax, **Chapter 3.**
Definitions
"year": IA 1937 Sch.

152 Application of Part III (Schedule C) and section 52 (Schedule D) of Income Tax Act 1967

(1) Where an individual is not resident but is ordinarily resident in the State, Part III and section 52 of the Income Tax Act, 1967, shall apply and have effect as if the individual were resident in the State:

[Provided that this section shall not apply in respect of(

(*a*) the income of an individual derived from one or more of the following, that is to say, a trade or profession, no part of which is carried on in the State or an office or employment all the duties of which are performed outside the State, and

(*b*) other income of an individual which in any year of assessment does not exceed £3,000.][1]

(2) In determining for the purposes of subsection (1) whether the duties of an office or employment are performed outside the State, any duties performed in the State, the performance of which is merely incidental to the performance of the duties of the office or employment outside the State, shall be treated for the purposes of this section as having been performed outside the State.

Amendments
[1]   Subs (1)(proviso) substituted by FA 1995 s 169(1) as on and from 23 May 1994.
Narrative
Capital Acquisitions Tax, Chapter 3.
Definitions
"profession": ITA 1967 s 1(1); "trade": ITA 1967 s 1(1).

153 Split year residence

(1) For the purposes of a charge to tax on any income, profits or gains from an employment, where, during a year of assessment ("the relevant year")–

(*a*) (i) an individual who has not been resident in the State for the preceding year of assessment, satisfies an authorised officer that the individual is in the State–

(I)   with the intention, and
(II) in such circumstances,

that the individual will be resident in the State for the following year of assessment, or

(ii) an individual who is resident in the State, satisfies an authorised officer that the individual is leaving the State, other than for a temporary purpose,

(I)   with the intention, and
(II) in such circumstances,

that the individual will not be resident in the State for the following year of assessment,

and

(b)   the individual would, but for the provisions of this section, be resident in the State for the relevant year,

subsection (2) shall apply in relation to the individual.

(2) (a)   An individual to whom paragraphs (a)(i) and (b) of subsection (1) apply, shall be deemed to be resident in the State for the relevant year only from the date of his or her arrival in the State.

(b)   An individual to whom paragraphs (a)(ii) and (b) of subsection (1) apply, shall be deemed to be resident in the State for the relevant year only up to and including the date of his or her leaving the State.

(3) Where, by virtue of this section, an individual is resident in the State for part of a year of assessment, all the provisions of the Acts shall apply as if–

(a)   income arising during that part of the year or, in a case to which the provisions of section 76(3) of the Income Tax Act, 1967, apply, amounts received in the State during that part of the year, were income arising or amounts received for a year of assessment in which the individual is resident in the State, and

(b)   income arising or, as the case may be, amounts received in the remaining part of the year, were income arising or amounts received in a year of assessment in which the individual is not resident in the State.

Narrative

Capital Acquisitions Tax, Chapter 3.

Definitions

"profits": CTA 1976 s 1(5)(c); "tax": ITA 1967 s 1(1); CTA 1976 s 155(3); "year of assessment": ITA 1967 s 1(1).

154 Deduction for income earned outside the State

(1) Where for any year of assessment an individual who is resident in the State makes a claim in that behalf to and satisfies an authorised officer that–

(a)   the duties of an office or employment to which this section applies of the individual are performed wholly or partly outside the State, and

(b)   either–

(i)   the number of days in that year which are qualifying days in relation to the office or employment (together with any days which are qualifying days in relation to any other such office or employment of the individual), or

(ii)   the number of such days as aforesaid in a relevant period in relation to that year,

amounts to at least 90 days,

there shall be deducted from the income, profits or gains from the office or employment to be assessed under Schedule D or Schedule E, as may be appropriate, an amount equal to the specified amount.

(2) In this section—

"a qualifying day", in relation to an office or employment of an individual, is a day which is—

    (*a*)   one of at least 14 consecutive days on which the individual is absent from the State for the purposes of the performance of the duties of that office or employment or of those duties and the duties of other offices or employments of the individual outside the State and which (taken as a whole) are substantially devoted to the performance of such duties as aforesaid, and

    (*b*)   one of which the individual concerned is absent from the State at the end of the day:

Provided that no day shall be counted more than once as a qualifying day;

"relevant period", in relation to a year of assessment, means a continuous period of 12 months—

    (*a*)   part only of which is comprised in that year of assessment, and

    (*b*)   no part of which is comprised in another relevant period;

[**"the specified amount"** means an amount determined by the formula—

$$\frac{D \times E}{365}$$

where—

D is the number of qualifying days in the year of assessment concerned, and

E is all the income, profits or gains from an office, employment or pension whether chargeable under Schedule D or Schedule E (including income from offices or employments, the duties of which are performed in the State) of an individual in that year.][1]

(3) This section applies to—

    (*a*)   an office of director of a company which is within the charge to corporation tax or would be within the charge to corporation tax if it were resident in the State and which carries on a trade or profession,

    (*b*)   an employment other than—

        (i)   an employment the emoluments of which are paid out of the revenue of the State, or

        (ii)   an employment with any board, authority or other similar body established by or under statute:

Provided that this section shall not apply in any case where the income from an office or employment—

    (*a*)   is chargeable to tax in accordance with the provisions of section 76(3) of the Income Tax Act, 1967, or

    (*b*)   (i)   is subject to the provisions of Part III of Schedule 6 to the Income Tax Act, 1967, or

     (ii)   would be so subject, if the employment were deemed to be property situated where the employment is exercised, or

    (c) is income to which section 153 applies.

(4) Nothwithstanding anything contained in the Acts, the income, profits or gains from an office or employment shall, for the purposes of this section, be deemed not to include any amounts paid in respect of expenses incurred wholly, exclusively and necessarily in the performance of the duties of the office or employment.

Amendments

¹   Definition of "the specified amount" substituted by FA 1995 s 170(1) as on and from 23 May 1994.

Narrative

Capital Acquisitions Tax, Chapter 3.

Definitions

"month": IA 1937 Sch; "profession": ITA 1967 s 1(1); "profits": CTA 1976 s 1(5)(c "trade": ITA 1967 s 1(1); "year of assessment": ITA 1967 s 1(1).

155 Non-residents

Notes

With effect from 6 April 1994:
para (a) substituted ITA 1967 s 153(2)(c);
para (b) inserted ITA 1967 s 153(3).

Narrative

Capital Acquisitions Tax, Chapter 3.

156 Appeals

(1) An individual who is aggrieved by the decision of an authorised officer on any question arising under those provisions of this Chapter which require an individual to satisfy an authorised officer on such a question may, by notice in writing to that effect given to the authorised officer within two months from the date on which notice of the decision is given to the individual, make an application to have the question heard and determined by the Appeal Commissioners.

(2) Where an application is made under subsection (1), the Appeal Commissioners shall hear and determine the question concerned in like manner as an appeal made to them against an assessment and all the provisions of the Acts relating to such an appeal (including the provisions relating to the rehearing of an appeal and to the statement of a case for the opinion of the High Court on a point of law) shall apply accordingly with any necessary modifications.

Definitions

"Appeal Commissioners": CGTA 1975 s 2(1); ITA 1967 s 1(1), 156; "writing": IA 1937 Sch.

157 Repeals

(1) ...

(2) Where the Revenue Commissioners are satisfied that the repeal of section 76 (4) of the Income Tax Act, 1967, would give rise to hardship in the case of income derived in

the manner mentioned in the said section 76 (4), they may, for the year 1994-95 and for that year of assessment only, grant such relief as in their opinion is just.

Notes

With effect from 6 April 1994 subs (1) repealed ITA 1967 ss 76(4), 199, 206 and FA 1987 s 4.

Cross-references

Effective date is 1995-96 and later tax years where an individual:

(*a*) was resident for 1991-92 but not resident for 1992-93 and 1993-94;

(*b*) was resident for 1992-93 but not resident for 1993-94;

(*c*) was resident for 1993-94 but not (under the old rules) resident for 1994-95;

(*d*) left the State in 1992-93 or 1993-94 to ordinarily reside elsewhere and did not recommence ordinary residence in the State before 5 April 1994. (FA 1994 s 158(2)).

Definitions

"year": IA 1937 Sch; "year of assessment": CGTA 1975 s 2(1), ITA 1967 s 1(1).

158 Commencement (Chapter I)

(1) Subject to subsection (2), this Chapter shall apply as respects the year 1994-95 and subsequent years of assessment.

(2) Where in any case an individual–

    (*a*) was resident in the State for the year of assessment 1991-92 but not resident in the State for the years of assessment 1992-93 and 1993-94, or

    (*b*) was resident in the State for the year of assessment 1992-93 but not resident in the State for the year of assessment 1993-94, or

    (*c*) was resident in the State for the year of assessment 1993-94 and would not, but for section 150, be resident in the State in the year of assessment 1994-95, or

    (*d*) left the State in the years of assessment 1992-93 or 1993-94 for the purpose of commencing a period of ordinary residence outside the State and did not recommence ordinary residence in the State prior to the end of the year of assessment 1993-94,

section 150 and section 157, in so far as it relates to the repeal of section 4 of the Finance Act, 1987, shall apply as respects the year 1995-96 and subsequent years of assessment in that case.

Definitions

"resident": CGTA 1975 s 2(1); "year of assessment": CGTA 1975 s 2(1), ITA 1967 s 1(1).

CHAPTER II
General

165 Care and management of taxes and duties

All taxes and duties imposed by this Act are hereby placed under the care and management of the Revenue Commissioners.

166 Short title, construction and commencement

(1) This Act may be cited as the Finance Act, 1994.

...

(5) Part IV shall be construed together with the Stamp Act, 1891, and the enactments amending or extending that Act.

(6) Part V shall be construed together with Part VI of the Finance Act, 1983, and the enactments amending or extending that Part.

(7) Parts VI and VII (so far as relating to capital acquisitions tax) shall be construed together with the Capital Acquisitions Tax Act, 1976, and the enactments amending or extending that Act.

...

(10) Any reference in this Act to any other enactment shall, except so far as the context otherwise requires, be construed as a reference to that enactment as amended by or under any other enactment including this Act.

(11) In this Act, a reference to a Part, section or Schedule is to a Part or section of, or Schedule to, this Act, unless it is indicated that reference to some other enactment is intended.

(12) In this Act, a reference to a subsection, paragraph, subparagraph, clause or subclause is to the subsection, paragraph, subparagraph, clause or subclause of the provision (including a Schedule) in which the reference occurs, unless it is indicated that reference to some other provision is intended.

FINANCE ACT 1995

(1995 Number 8)
(Date of passing: 2 June 1995)

ARRANGEMENT OF SECTIONS

PART VI
CAPITAL ACQUISITIONS TAX

PART VII
MISCELLANEOUS

CHAPTER II
General

AN ACT TO CHARGE AND IMPOSE CERTAIN DUTIES OF CUSTOMS AND INLAND REVENUE (INCLUDING EXCISE), TO AMEND THE LAW RELATING TO CUSTOMS AND INLAND REVENUE (INCLUDING EXCISE) AND TO MAKE FURTHER PROVISIONS IN CONNECTION WITH FINANCE

PART VI
CAPITAL ACQUISITIONS TAX

156 Interpretation (Part VI)

In this Part "the Principal Act" means the Capital Acquisitions Tax Act, 1976.

157 Amendment of section 2 (interpretation) of Principal Act

Note

This section inserted CATA 1976 s 2(1) definition of "year of assessment".

---

158 Amendment of section 19 (value of agricultural property) of Principal Act

...

(2) Paragraphs (*a*) and (*c*) of subsection (1) shall have effect in relation to gifts or inheritances taken on or after the 8th day of February, 1995, paragraph (*b*) shall have

effect in relation to a gift or inheritance where the valuation date in relation to that gift or inheritance is on or after the 6th day of April, 1994, and paragraph (*d*) shall have effect in relation to gifts and inheritances taken on or after the date of the passing of this Act.

Note

Subs (1)(*a*)(i) substituted "50 per cent." for "75 per cent." in CATA 1976 s 19(1) definition of "agricultural value" para (*a*);

subs (1)(*a*)(ii) substituted "50 per cent." for "70 per cent.", "30 per cent." for "50 per cent." and "£90,000" for "£150,000" in CATA 1976 s 19(1) "definition of "agricultural value" para (*b*);

subs (1)(*a*)(iii) substituted "50 per cent." for "70 per cent.", "15 per cent." for "35 per cent." and "£45,000" for "£105,000" in CATA 1976 s 19 definition of "agricultural value" para (*c*);

subs (1)(*b*) deleted "and ordinarily resident" in CATA 1976 s 19(1) definition of "farmer".

subs (1)(*c*): substituted "30 per cent." for "50 per cent.", "£90,000" for "£150,000" in both places where it occurs, "15 per cent." for "35 per cent." and "£45,000" for "£105,000" in CATA 1976 s 19(4).

subs (1)(*d*) inserted CATA 1976 s 19(5)(*c*).

Definitions

"gift": CATA s 2(1); "inheritance": CATA s 2(1).

159 Amendment of section 52 (appeals in other cases) of Principal Act

Note

This section inserted CATA 1976 s 52(5)(*a*)(xi).

160 Amendment of section 55 (exemption of certain objects) of Principal Act

...

(2) This section shall have effect in relation to gifts or inheritances taken on or after the 12th day of April, 1995.

Note

Subs (1)(*a*) substituted CATA 1976 s 55(3);

subs (1)(*b*) substituted CATA 1976 s 55(4).

Definitions

"gift": CATA s 2(1); "inheritance": CATA s 2(1).

161 Business relief

...

(2) This section shall have effect in relation to gifts or inheritances taken on or after the 8th day of February, 1995.

Note

Subs (1) substituted FA 1994 s 126.

Definitions

"gift": CATA s 2(1); "inheritance": CATA s 2(1).

162 Amendment of section 134 (exclusion of value of excepted assets) of Finance Act, 1994

...

(2) This section shall have effect in relation to gifts or inheritances taken on or after the 12th day of April, 1995.

Note

Subs (1)(*a*) inserted FA 1994 s 134(1)(proviso);
subs (1)(*b*) substituted FA 1994 s 134(2)(proviso).

Definitions

"gift": CATA s 2(1); "inheritance": CATA s 2(1).

163 Amendment of section 135 (withdrawal of relief) of Finance Act, 1994

...

(2) This section shall have effect in relation to gifts or inheritances taken on or after the 12th day of April, 1995.

Note

Subs (1)(*a*) substituted "commencing on the valuation date." for "after the valuation date or the period between the date of the gift or inheritance and the date of a subsequent gift or inheritance consisting of the same property or of property representing that property, whichever is the lesser period." in FA 1994 s 135(1);
subs (1)(*b*) substituted FA 1994 s 135(2)(proviso).

Definitions

"gift": CATA s 2(1); "inheritance": CATA s 2(1).

164 Payment of tax on certain assets by instalments

(1) In this section—

"agricultural property" has the meaning assigned to it by section 19 of the Principal Act (as amended by the Finance Act, 1994);

"relevant business property" has the same meaning as it has in section 127 of the Finance Act, 1994, other than shares in or securities of a company (being shares or securities quoted on a recognised stock exchange) and without regard to sections 128 and 134 (3) of that Act.

(2) Where the whole or part of the tax which is due and payable in respect of a taxable gift or taxable inheritance is attributable to either or both agricultural property and relevant business property—

[(*a*) section 43 of the Principal Act shall apply to that whole or part of the tax notwithstanding subsection (3) or (4) of that section:

Provided that where all or any part of that agricultural property or relevant business property, or any property which directly or indirectly replaces such property, is sold or compulsorily acquired and, by virtue of subsection (5) of section 19 of the Principal Act or section 135 of the Finance Act, 1994, that sale or compulsory acquisition causes the taxable value of such a taxable gift or taxable inheritance to be increased, or would cause such increase if subsection (2) of section 19 of the Principal Act or section 126 of the Finance Act, 1994, applied, all unpaid instalments referable to the property sold or compulsorily acquired shall, unless the interest of the donee or successor is a limited interest, be paid on completion of that sale or compulsory acquisition and, if not so paid, shall be tax in arrear,

and][1]

(*b*) notwithstanding subsection (2) of section 41 of the Principal Act the rate at which interest is payable upon that whole or part of the tax shall be 0.75 per cent., or such other rate (if any) as stands prescribed by the Minister for Finance by regulations, for each month or part of a month instead of at the rate specified in that section and that section shall have effect as regards that whole or part of the tax as if the rate so payable were substituted for the rate specified in that section:

Provided that the rate at which interest is payable upon any overdue instalment of that whole or part of the tax, or upon such part of the tax as would represent any such overdue instalment if that whole or part of the tax were being paid by instalments, shall continue to be at the rate specified in section 41 of the Principal Act.

[(2A) For the purposes of this section reference to an overdue instalment in the proviso to paragraph (*b*) of subsection (2) is a reference to an instalment which is overdue for the purposes of section 43 (as it applies to this section) of the Principal Act or for the purposes of the proviso to paragraph (*a*) of the said subsection (2).][2]

(3) For the purposes of this section the value of a business or of an interest in a business shall be taken to be its net value ascertained in accordance with section 132 of the Finance Act, 1994.

(4) This section shall have effect in relation to gifts and inheritances taken on or after the 8th day of February, 1995, but shall not have effect in relation to an inheritance taken by a relevant trust by virtue of section 110(1) of the Finance Act, 1993, or to an inheritance taken by a discretionary trust by virtue of section 106(1) of the Finance Act, 1984, or section 103(1) of the Finance Act, 1986.

(5) Every regulation made under this section shall be laid before Dáil Éireann as soon as may be after it is made and, if a resolution annulling the regulation is passed by Dáil Éireann within the next twenty-one days on which Dáil Éireann has sat after the regulation is laid before it, the regulation shall be annulled accordingly, but without prejudice to the validity of anything previously done thereunder.

Amendments

1　Subs (2)(*a*) substituted by FA 1996 s 129(1)(*a*) in relation to gifts or inheritances taken on or after 8 February 1995.

2　Subs (2A) inserted by FA 1996 s 129(1)(*b*) in relation to gifts or inheritances taken on or after 8 February 1995.

Definitions

"discretionary trust": CATA s 2(1); "gift": CATA s 2(1); "inheritance": CATA s 2(1); "month": IA 1937 Sch; "share": CATA s 2(1); "tax": CATA s 2(1).

165 Exemption of certain inheritances taken by parents

Notwithstanding the provisions of the Principal Act, an inheritance taken on or after the 12th day of April, 1995, by a person from a disponer shall, where—

(a) that person is a parent of that disponer, and

(b) the date of the inheritance is the date of death of that disponer,

be exempt from tax and shall not be taken into account in computing tax if and only if that disponer took a non-exempt gift or inheritance from either or both of that disponer's parents within the period of 5 years immediately prior to the date of death of that disponer.

Cross references

Inheritances taken by parents: FA 1991 s 116.

Definitions

"disponer": CATA s 2(1); "gift": CATA s 2(1); "inheritance": CATA s 2(1); "person": IA 1937 s 11(c); "year": IA 1937 Sch.

166 Heritage property of companies

(1) In this section—

"relevant heritage property" means any one or more of the following—

(a) objects to which section 55 of the Principal Act applies;

(b) a house or garden referred to in section 39 of the Finance Act, 1978;

"private company" has the meaning assigned to it by section 16 of the Principal Act;

"subsidiary" has the meaning assigned to it by section 155 of the Companies Act, 1963.

(2) Where a gift or inheritance consists in whole or in part—

(a) at the date of the gift or at the date of the inheritance, and

(b) at the valuation date,

of one or more shares in a private company which (after the taking of the gift or inheritance) is, on the date of the gift or on the date of the inheritance, a company controlled by the donee or successor within the meaning of section 16 of the Principal Act, then each such share shall, to the extent that its market value for tax purposes is, at the valuation date, attributable to relevant heritage property, be exempt from tax and the value thereof shall to that extent not be taken into account in computing tax on any gift or inheritance taken by that person unless the exemption ceases to apply under the provisions of subsection (5) or (6):

Provided that that relevant heritage property was in the beneficial ownership of the company on the 12th day of April, 1995, or in the beneficial ownership on that date of another company which was on that date a subsidiary of the first-mentioned company.

(3) The provisions of section 19(6) of the Principal Act shall apply, for the purposes of subsection (2), as they apply in relation to agricultural property.

(4) Where in relation to a gift or inheritance—

    (*a*) a part of a share in a private company is exempt from tax by virtue of subsection (2), and

    (*b*) such share is relevant business property within the meaning of Chapter I of Part VI of the Finance Act, 1994,

then the relevant heritage property to which the market value of such share is partly attributable shall be left out of account in determining for the purposes of that Chapter what part of the taxable value of that gift or inheritance is attributable to such share, but the amount of the reduction (if any) which would but for subsection (2) fall to be made under that Chapter in respect of such share shall not otherwise be restricted notwithstanding subsection (2).

(5) If a share in a private company which is exempted in whole or in part from tax by virtue of subsection (2) is sold within 6 years after the valuation date, and before the death of the donee or successor, the exemption referred to in subsection (2) shall, subject to subsection (7), cease to apply to such share.

(6) Where the whole or part of the market value of a share in a private company which is comprised in a gift or inheritance is on the valuation date attributable to an item of relevant heritage property and—

    (*a*) that item of relevant heritage property is sold within 6 years after the valuation date, and before the death of the donee or successor, or

    (*b*) at any time after the valuation date and—

        (i) before the sale of such share or such item of relevant heritage property,

        (ii) before the death of the donee or successor, and

        (iii) before such share or such item of relevant heritage property forms part of the property comprised in a subsequent gift or inheritance in respect of which gift or inheritance an absolute interest is taken by a person other than the spouse of that donee or successor,

    there has been a breach of any condition specified in subsection (1)(*b*) or (*c*) of section 55 of the Principal Act or in section 39(1)(*c*) of the Finance Act, 1978,

then the exemption referred to in subsection (2) shall, subject to subsection (7), cease to apply to such share to the extent that that market value is attributable to such item of relevant heritage property.

(7) Notwithstanding subsections (5) and (6), the exemption referred to in subsection (2) shall continue to apply if the sale of the share referred to in subsection (5), or the sale of the item of relevant heritage property referred to in subsection (6), is a sale by private treaty to the National Gallery of Ireland, the National Museum of Science and Art or any other similar national institution, any university in the State or any constituent college thereof, a local authority or the Friends of the National Collections of Ireland.

(8) This section shall have effect in relation to gifts and inheritances taken on or after the 12th day of April, 1995.

Definitions
"donee": CATA s 2(1); "gift": CATA s 2(1); "inheritance": CATA s 2(1); "local authority": CATA s 2(1);
"market value": CATA s 2(1); "successor": CATA s 2(1); "tax": CATA s 2(1); "valuation date": CATA s 2(1).

PART VII
MISCELLANEOUS

CHAPTER II
General

172 Duties of a relevant person in relation to certain revenue offences

(1) In this section—

"the Acts" means—

    (*a*) the Customs Acts,

    (*b*) the statutes relating to the duties of excise and to the management of those duties,

    (*c*) the Tax Acts,

    (*d*) the Capital Gains Tax Acts,

    (*e*) the Value-Added Tax Act, 1972, and the enactments amending or extending that Act,

    (*f*) the Capital Acquisitions Tax Act, 1976, and the enactments amending or extending that Act,

    (*g*) the statutes relating to stamp duty and to the management of that duty,

and any instruments made thereunder and any instruments made under any other enactment and relating to tax;

"appropriate officer" means any officer nominated by the Revenue Commissioners to be an appropriate officer for the purposes of this section;

"company" means any body corporate;

"relevant person", in relation to a company, means a person who—

    (*a*) (i) is an auditor to the company appointed in accordance with section 160 of the Companies Act, 1963 (as amended by the Companies Act, 1990), or

        (ii) in the case of an industrial and provident society or a friendly society, is a public auditor to the society for the purposes of the Industrial and Provident Societies Acts, 1893 to 1978, and the Friendly Societies Acts, 1896 to 1977,

    or

    (*b*) with a view to reward assists or advises the company in the preparation or delivery of any information, declaration, return, records, accounts or other document which he or she knows will be, or is likely to be, used for any purpose of tax:

Provided that a person who would, but for this proviso, be treated as a relevant person in relation to a company shall not be so treated if the person assists or advises the company solely in the person's capacity as an employee of the said company, and a person shall be treated as assisting or advising the company in that capacity where the person's income from assisting or advising the company consists solely of emoluments to which Chapter IV of Part V of the Income Tax Act, 1967, applies;

"relevant offence" means an offence committed by a company which consists of the company—

(*a*) knowingly or wilfully delivering any incorrect return, statement or accounts or knowingly or wilfully furnishing or causing to be furnished any incorrect information in connection with any tax,

(*b*) knowingly or wilfully claiming or obtaining relief or exemption from, or repayment of, any tax, being a relief, exemption or repayment to which there is no entitlement,

(*c*) knowingly or wilfully issuing or producing any incorrect invoice, receipt, instrument or other document in connection with any tax,

(*d*) knowingly or wilfully failing to comply with any provision of the Acts requiring the furnishing of a return of income, profits or gains, or of sources of income, profits or gains, for the purposes of any tax:

Provided that an offence under this paragraph committed by a company shall not be a relevant offence if the company has made a return of income, profits or gains to the Revenue Commissioners in respect of an accounting period falling wholly or partly into the period of 3 years immediately preceding the accounting period in respect of which the offence was committed;

"tax" means tax, duty, levy or charge under the care and management of the Revenue Commissioners.

(2) If, having regard solely to information obtained in the course of examining the accounts of a company, or in the course of assisting or advising a company in the preparation or delivery of any information, declaration, return, records, accounts or other document for the purposes of tax, as the case may be, a person who is a relevant person in relation to the company becomes aware that the company has committed, or is in the course of committing, one or more relevant offences, the person shall, if the offence or offences are material—

(*a*) communicate particulars of the offence or offences in writing to the company without undue delay and request the company to—

(i) take such action as is necessary for the purposes of rectifying the matter, or

(ii) notify an appropriate officer of the offence or offences,

not later than 6 months after the time of communication, and

(*b*) (i) unless it is established to the person's satisfaction that the necessary action has been taken or notification made, as the case may be, under paragraph (*a*), cease to act as the auditor to the company or to assist or advise the company in such preparation or delivery as is specified in paragraph (*b*) of the definition of relevant person, and

(ii) shall not so act, assist or advise before a time which is—

(I) 3 years after the time at which the particulars were communicated under paragraph (*a*), or

(II) the time at which it is established to the person's satisfaction that the necessary action has been taken or notification made, as the case may be, under paragraph (*a*),

whichever is the earlier:

Provided that nothing in this paragraph shall prevent a person from assisting or advising a company in preparing for, or conducting, legal proceedings, either civil or criminal, which are extant or pending at a time which is 6 months after the time of communication under paragraph (*a*).

(3) Where a person, being in relation to a company a relevant person within the meaning of paragraph (*a*) of the definition of relevant person, ceases under the provisions of this section to act as auditor to the company, then the person shall deliver—

(*a*) a notice in writing to the company stating that he or she is so resigning, and

(*b*) a copy of the notice to an appropriate officer not later than 14 days after he or she has delivered the notice to the company.

(4) A person shall be guilty of an offence under this section if the person—

(*a*) fails to comply with subsection (2) or (3), or

(*b*) knowingly or wilfully makes a communication under subsection (2) which is incorrect.

(5) Where a relevant person is found guilty of an offence under this section the person shall be liable—

(*a*) on summary conviction to a fine of £1,000 which may be mitigated to not less than one-fourth part thereof, or

(*b*) on conviction on indictment, to a fine not exceeding £5,000 or, at the discretion of the court, to imprisonment for a term not exceeding 2 years or to both the fine and the imprisonment.

(6) Section 13 of the Criminal Procedure Act, 1967, shall apply in relation to this section as if, in lieu of the penalties specified in subsection (3) of the said section 13, there were specified therein the penalties provided for by subsection (5)(*a*) of this section, and the reference in subsection (2)(*a*) of the said section 13 to the penalties provided for in the said subsection (3) shall be construed and have effect accordingly.

(7) Notwithstanding the provisions of any other enactment, proceedings in respect of this section may be instituted within 6 years from the time at which a person is required under subsection (2) to communicate particulars of an offence or offences in writing to a company.

(8) It shall be a good defence in a prosecution for an offence under subsection (4)(*a*) in relation to a failure to comply with subsection (2) for an accused (being a person who is a relevant person in relation to a company) to show that he or she was, in the ordinary scope of professional engagement, assisting or advising the company in preparing for legal proceedings and would not have become aware that one or more relevant offences had been committed by the company if he or she had not been so assisting or advising.

(9) If a person who is a relevant person takes any action required by subsection (2) or (3), no duty to which the person may be subject shall be regarded as contravened and no liability or action shall lie against the person in any court for so doing.

(10) The Revenue Commissioners may nominate an officer to be an appropriate officer for the purposes of this section and the name of an officer so nominated and the address to which copies of notices under subsection (2) or (3) shall be delivered shall be published in the Iris Oifigiúil.

(11) This section shall have effect as respects a relevant offence committed by a company in respect of tax which is—

(*a*) assessable by reference to accounting periods, for any accounting period beginning after the 30th day of June, 1995,

(*b*) assessable by reference to years of assessment, for the year of assessment 1995-96 and subsequent years,

(*c*) payable by reference to a taxable period, for a taxable period beginning after the 30th day of June, 1995,

(*d*) chargeable on gifts or inheritances taken on or after the 30th day of June, 1995,

(*e*) chargeable on instruments executed on or after the 30th day of June, 1995, or

(*f*) payable in any other case, on or after the 30th day of June, 1995.

Narrative

Capital Acquisitions Tax, Chapter 22.

Definitions

"month": IA 1937 Sch; "person": IA 1937 s 11(*c*); "writing": IA 1937 Sch; "year": IA 1937 Sch.

175 Power to obtain information

(1) For the purposes of the assessment, charge, collection and recovery of any tax or duty placed under their care and management, the Revenue Commissioners may, by notice in writing, request any Minister of the Government to provide them with such information in the possession of the Minister in relation to payments for any purposes made by the Minister, whether on his own behalf or on behalf of any other person, to such persons or classes of persons as the Revenue Commissioners may specify in the notice and a Minister so requested shall provide such information as may be specified.

(2) The Revenue Commissioners may nominate any of their officers to perform any acts and discharge any functions authorised by this section to be performed or discharged by the Revenue Commissioners.

Definitions
"person": IA 1937 s 11(*c*).

176 Relief for donations of heritage items

(1) (*a*) In this section—

"**the Acts**" means—

(i) the Tax Acts (other than Chapter IV of Part V of the Income Tax Act, 1967, section 17 of the Finance Act, 1970, and Chapter VII of Part I of the Finance Act, 1983),

(ii) the Capital Gains Tax Acts, and

(iii) the Capital Acquisitions Tax Act, 1976, and the enactments amending or extending that Act,

and any instrument made thereunder;

"**approved body**" means—

(i) the National Archives,

(ii) the National Gallery of Ireland,

(iii) the National Library of Ireland,

(iv) the National Museum of Ireland,

(v) the Irish Museum of Modern Art, or

(vi) in relation to the offer of a gift of a particular item or collection of items, any other such body (being a body owned, or funded wholly or mainly, by the State or by any public or local authority) as may be approved, with the consent of the Minister for Finance, by the Minister for Arts, Culture and the Gaeltacht for the purposes of this section;

"**arrears of tax**" means tax due and payable in accordance with any provision of the Acts (including any interest and penalties payable under any provision of the Acts in relation to such tax)—

(i) in the case of income tax, corporation tax or capital gains tax, in respect of the relevant period, or

(ii) in the case of gift tax or inheritance tax, prior to the commencement of the calendar year in which the relevant gift is made,

which has not been paid at the time a relevant gift is made;

"**current liability**" means—

(i) in the case of income tax or capital gains tax, any liability to such tax arising in the year of assessment in which the relevant gift is made, or

(ii) in the case of corporation tax, any liability to such tax arising in the accounting period in which the relevant gift is made, or

(iii) in the case of gift tax or inheritance tax, any liability to such tax which becomes due and payable in the calendar year in which the relevant gift is made;

"designated officer" means—

(i) the member of the selection committee who represents the appropriate approved body on that committee where the approved body is so represented, or

(ii) in any other case, a person nominated in that behalf by the Minister for Arts, Culture and the Gaeltacht;

"heritage item" has the meaning assigned to it by subsection (2)(*a*);

"market value" has the meaning assigned to it by subsection (3);

"relevant gift" means a gift of a heritage item to an approved body which is made on or after the date of the passing of this Act and in respect of which no consideration whatsoever (other than relief under this section) is received by the person making the gift, either directly or indirectly, from the approved body or otherwise;

"relevant period" means—

(i) in the case of income tax and capital gains tax, any year of assessment preceding the year in which the relevant gift is made, and

(ii) in the case of corporation tax, any accounting period preceding the accounting period in which the relevant gift is made;

"selection committee" means a committee consisting of the Chairperson of the Heritage Council, the Director of the Arts Council, the Director of the National Archives, the Director of the National Gallery of Ireland, the Director of the National Library of Ireland, the Director of the National Museum of Ireland and the Director of the Irish Museum of Modern Art and includes any person duly acting in the capacity of any of the foregoing as a result of the member concerned being unable to fulfil his or her duties for any of the reasons set out in paragraph (*b*)(ii);

"tax" means income tax, corporation tax, capital gains tax, gift tax or inheritance tax, as the case may be, payable in accordance with any provision of the Acts;

"valuation date" means the date on which an application is made, to the selection committee, for a determination under subsection (2)(*a*).

(*b*) (i) The selection committee may act notwithstanding one or more vacancies among its members and may regulate its own procedure.

(ii) If and so long as a member of the selection committee is unable through illness, absence or other cause to fulfil his or her duties, a person nominated in that behalf by the member shall act as the member of the committee in the place of the member.

(2) (*a*) In this section **"heritage item"** means any kind of cultural item including—

(i) any archaeological item, archive, book, estate record, manuscript and painting, and

(ii) any collection of cultural items and any collection thereof in their setting, which, on application to the selection committee in writing in that behalf by a person who owns the item or collection of items (as the case may be), is determined by the selection committee, after consideration of any evidence in relation to the matter which the person submits to the committee and after such consultation (if any) as may seem to the committee to be necessary with such person or body of persons as in the opinion of the committee may be of assistance to them, to be an item or collection of items—

    (I)   which is an outstanding example of the type of item involved, pre-eminent in its class, whose export from the State would constitute a diminution of the accumulated cultural heritage of Ireland, and

    (II)   suitable for acquisition by an approved body.

(*b*) On receipt of an application for a determination under paragraph (*a*) the selection committee shall request the Revenue Commissioners in writing to value the item or collection of items, as the case may be, in accordance with the provisions of subsection (3).

(*c*) The selection committee shall not make a determination under paragraph (*a*) where the market value of the item or collection of items (as the case may be), as determined by the Revenue Commissioners in accordance with subsection (3), at the valuation date—

    (i)   is less than £75,000, or

    (ii)   exceeds an amount (which shall not be less than £75,000) determined by the formula—

$$£[750,000]^1 - M$$

where M is an amount (which may be nil) equal to the market value at the valuation date of the heritage item (if any) or the aggregate of the market values at the respective valuation dates of all the heritage items (if any), as the case may be, in respect of which a determination or determinations, as the case may be, under this subsection has been made by the selection committee in any one calendar year and not revoked in that year.

(*d*) (i) An item or collection of items shall cease to be a heritage item for the purposes of this section if the item or collection of items—

    (I)   is sold or otherwise disposed of to a person other than an approved body, or

    (II)   the owner thereof notifies the selection committee in writing that it is not intended to make a gift thereof to an approved body, or

    (III)   the gift of the item or collection of items is not made to an approved body within the calendar year following the year in which the determination is made under paragraph (*a*).

    (ii) Where the selection committee becomes aware, at any time within the calendar year in which a determination under paragraph (*a*) is made in respect of an item or collection of items, that clause (I) or (II) of subparagraph (i) applies to the item or collection of items the selection committee may revoke its determination with effect from that time.

(3) (*a*) For the purposes of this section, the market value of any item or collection of items (hereafter in this subsection referred to as "the property") shall be estimated to be the price which, in the opinion of the Revenue Commissioners, the property would fetch if sold in the open market on the valuation date in such manner and subject to such conditions as might reasonably be calculated to obtain for the vendor the best price for the property.

(*b*) The market value of the property shall be ascertained by the Revenue Commissioners in such manner and by such means as they think fit, and they may authorise a person to inspect the property and report to them the value thereof for the purposes of this section, and the person having custody or possession of the property shall permit the person so authorised to inspect the property at such reasonable times as the Revenue Commissioners consider necessary.

(*c*) Where the Revenue Commissioners require a valuation to be made by a person authorised by them, the cost of such valuation shall be defrayed by the Revenue Commissioners.

(4) Where a relevant gift is made to an approved body—

(*a*) the designated officer of that body shall give a certificate to the person who made the relevant gift, in such form as the Revenue Commissioners may prescribe, certifying the receipt of that gift and the transfer of the ownership of the heritage item the subject of that gift to the approved body, and

(*b*) the designated officer shall transmit a duplicate of the certificate to the Revenue Commissioners.

(5) Subject to the provisions of this section, where a person has made a relevant gift the person shall, on submission to the Revenue Commissioners of the certificate given to the person in accordance with subsection (4), be treated as having made on the date of such submission a payment on account of tax of an amount equal to the market value of the relevant gift on the valuation date.

(6) A payment on account of tax which is treated as having been made in accordance with the provisions of subsection (5) shall be set, so far as possible, against any liability to tax of the person who is treated as having made such a payment in the following order—

(*a*) firstly, against any arrears of tax due for payment by that person and against an arrear of tax for an earlier period in priority to a later period and, for this purpose, the date on which an arrear of tax became due for payment shall determine whether it is for an earlier or later period, and

(*b*) then, and only then, against any current liability of the person which the person nominates for that purpose,

and such set-off shall accordingly discharge a corresponding amount of that liability.

(7) Where and to the extent that a payment on account of tax has not been set off in accordance with the provisions of subsection (6), the balance remaining shall be set off against any future liability to tax of the person who is treated as having made the payment which that person nominates for that purpose.

(8) Where a person has power to sell any heritage item in order to raise money for the payment of gift tax or inheritance tax, such person shall have power to make a relevant gift of that heritage item in or towards satisfaction of that tax and, except as regards the nature of the consideration and its receipt and application, any such relevant gift shall be subject to the same provisions and shall be treated for all purposes as a sale made in exercise of that power and any conveyances or transfers made or purporting to be made to give effect to such a relevant gift shall have effect accordingly.

(9) A person shall not be entitled to any refund of tax in respect of any payment on account of tax made in accordance with the provisions of this section.

(10) Interest shall not be payable in respect of any overpayment of tax for any period which arises directly or indirectly due to the set-off against any liability for that period of a payment on account of tax made in accordance with the provisions of this section.

(11) Where a person makes a relevant gift and in respect of that gift is treated as having made a payment on account of tax the person concerned shall not be allowed relief under any other provision of the Acts in respect of that gift.

(12)(*a*) The Revenue Commissioners shall, as respects each year (being the calendar year 1995 and subsequent calendar years), compile a list of the names (if any), descriptions and values of the heritage items (if any) in respect of which relief under this section has been given.

(*b*) Notwithstanding any obligation as to secrecy imposed on them by the Acts or the Official Secrets Act, 1963, the Revenue Commissioners shall include in their annual report to the Minister for Finance, commencing with the report for the year 1995, the list (if any) referred to in paragraph (*a*) for the year in respect of which the report is made.

Amendments

[1] Substituted as respects 1996 and subsequent years by FA 1996 s 139.

Narrative

Capital Acquisitions Tax, Chapter 23.

Definitions

"person": IA 1937 s 11(*c*).

178 Care and management of taxes and duties

All taxes and duties (except the excise duties on mechanically propelled vehicles imposed by section 117) imposed by this Act are hereby placed under the care and management of the Revenue Commissioners.

179 Short title, construction and commencement

(1) This Act may be cited as the Finance Act, 1995.

...

(7) Part VI (so far as relating to capital acquisitions tax) shall be construed together with the Capital Acquisitions Tax Act, 1976, and the enactments amending or extending that Act.

...

(11) Any reference in this Act to any other enactment shall, except so far as the context otherwise requires, be construed as a reference to that enactment as amended by or under any other enactment including this Act.

(12) In this Act, a reference to a Part, section or Schedule is to a Part or section of, or Schedule to, this Act, unless it is indicated that reference to some other enactment is intended.

(13) In this Act, a reference to a subsection, paragraph, subparagraph, clause or subclause is to the subsection, paragraph, subparagraph, clause or subclause of the provision (including a Schedule) in which the reference occurs, unless it is indicated that reference to some other provision is intended.

FINANCE ACT 1996

(1996 Number 9)
(Date of passing: 1 May 1996)

ARRANGEMENT OF SECTIONS

PART V
CAPITAL ACQUISITIONS TAX

120 Interpretation (Part V)

In this Part "the Principal Act" means the Capital Acquisitions Tax Act, 1976.

121 Amendment of section 16 (market value of certain shares in private trading companies) of Principal Act

Note

This section substituted the definition of "private company" in CATA 1976 s 16(2) as respects gifts and inheritances taken on or after the 28th day of March, 1996. "Private company" for capital acquisition tax purposes, is now equivalent to a "close company" for corporation tax purposes.

122 Amendment of section 19 (value of agricultural property) of Principal Act

Note

Subs (1) by substituting the definition of "agricultural value" in CATA 1976 s 19(1) in relation to gifts or inheritances taken on or after 23 January 1996, increased agricultural relief to a flat rate of 75%, and extended the clawback period from six to 10 years.

123 Exemption relating to qualifying expenses of incapacitated persons

Note

Subs (1) by inserting CATA 1976 s 59A in relation to gifts or inheritances taken on or after 28 March 1996, exempts gifts or inheritances taken exclusively to discharge medical expenses of a permanently incapacitated person.

124 Amendment of section 118 (application of section 60 (relief in respect of certain policies of Finance Act, 1985) of Finance Act, 1991

Note

Subs (1) by deleting "under a disposition made by the spouse of the insured where the inheritance is taken" from FA 1991 s 118 as regards inheritances taken on or after 28 March 1996, extends the FA 1985 s 60 exemption for life assurance policies where the policy is effected by a life tenant to pay inheritance tax arising on that life tenant's death.

125 Amendment of section 126 (business relief) of Finance Act, 1994

Note

Subs (1) by substituting "75 per cent" for "50 per cent" in FA 1994 s 126 in relation to gifts or inheritances taken on or after 23 January, 1996, increased business relief to a flat rate of 75%.

126 Amendment of section 127 (relevant business property) of Finance Act, 1994

Note

Subs (1) by substituting FA 1994 s 127(1)(c) in relation to gifts or inheritances taken on or after 28 March 1996, amends the definition of relevant business property so that where the beneficiary and his or her relatives control the company the 10% minimum shareholding requirement no longer applies.

127 Amendment of section 135 (withdrawal of relief) of Finance Act, 1994

Note

Subs (1)(a) by substituing "ten years" for "six years" in FA 1994 s 135(1) as regards gifts or inheritances taken on or after 23 January 1996, extends the business relief clawback period from 6 to 10 years.
Subs (1)(b) substituted FA 1994 s 135(2)(proviso) as regards gifts or inheritances taken on or after 23 January 1996.

128 Amendment of section 146 (certificate relating to registration of title based on possession) of Finance Act, 1994

Note

This section by inserting FA 1994 s 146(4A)-(4C), relaxes the capital acquisitions tax clearance certificate requirements by allowing "self-certification" for solicitors who are dealing with applications for registration of title to land based on possession. The property must not be part of a larger property.

129 Amendment of section 164 (payment of tax on certain assets by instalments) of Finance Act, 1995

Note

Subs (1) by substituting FA 1995 s 165(2)(a) and inserting subs (2A) in relation to gifts or inheritances taken on or after 8 February 1995, ensures that the instalment arrangement for business and agricultural property will not be cancelled where the property is sold within the instalment period, provided the proceeds are reinvested in other qualifying property within one year.

PART VII
MISCELLANEOUS

142 Care and management of taxes and duties

All taxes and duties (except the excise duties on mechanically propelled vehicles imposed by section 86) imposed by this Act are hereby placed under the care and management of the Revenue Commissioners.

143 Short title, construction and commencement

(1) This Act may be cited as the Finance Act, 1996.

...

(6) Part V (so far as relating to capital acquisitions tax) shall be construed together with the Capital Acquisitions Tax Act, 1976, and the enactments amending or extending that Act.

(7) Part VII (so far as relating to income tax) shall be construed together with the Income Tax Acts and (so far as relating to corporation tax) shall be construed together with the Corporation Tax Acts and (so far as relating to capital gains tax) shall be construed together with the Capital Gains Tax Acts and (so far as relating to capital acquisitions tax) shall be construed together with the Capital Acquisitions Tax Act, 1976.

...

(11) Any reference in this Act to any other enactment shall, except so far as the context otherwise requires, be construed as a reference to that enactment as amended by or under any other enactment including this Act.

(12) In this Act, a reference to a Part, section or Schedule is to a Part or section of, or Schedule to, this Act, unless it is indicated that reference to some other enactment is intended.

(13) In this Act, a reference to a subsection, paragraph, subparagraph, clause or subclause is to the subsection, paragraph, subparagraph, clause or subclause of the provision (including a Schedule) in which the reference occurs, unless it is indicated that reference to some other provision is intended.

FIFTH SCHEDULE

PART I
PRE-CONSOLIDATION AMENDMENTS

Notes

Para 13(2) inserted FA 1983 s 94(2)(*ee*).

DISCLOSURE OF CERTAIN INFORMATION FOR TAXATION AND OTHER PURPOSES ACT 1996

(1996 Number 25)
(Date of passing: 30 July 1996)

ARRANGEMENT OF SECTIONS

Section

8 Amendment of section 39 (assessment of tax) of Capital Acquisitions Tax Act, 1976

Notes

This section substituted CATA 1976 s 39(7).

CRIMINAL ASSETS BUREAU ACT 1996

(1996 Number 31)
(Date of passing: 11 October 1996)

ARRANGEMENT OF SECTIONS

Section

24 Amendment of certain taxation provisions

Notes

Subs (4) deleted the proviso to CATA 1976 s 39(7) (inserted by the Disclosure of Certain Information for Taxation and Other Purposes Act 1996).

CRIMINAL ASSETS BUREAU ACT 1996

Act No. 31/1996
Date of passing 11 October 1996

ARRANGEMENT OF SECTIONS

Section

24 Amendment of certain taxation provisions

24 Amendment of certain taxation provisions

_____

Notes:

Subs (2) inserted by s. 8(2) of the T.A.) No. 39 1997 (inserted by the Disclosure of Certain Information for Taxation and Other Purposes Act 1996).

FINANCE ACT 1997

(1997 Number 22)
(Date of passing: 10 May 1997)

ARRANGEMENT OF SECTIONS

PART VI
CAPITAL ACQUISITIONS TAX

PART VIII
MISCELLANEOUS

PART VI
CAPITAL ACQUISITIONS TAX

133 Interpretation (Part VI)

In this Part **"the Principal Act"** means the Capital Acquisitions Tax Act, 1976.

134 Amendment of section 19 (value of agricultural property) of Principal Act

Notes

Subss (1)(*a*) and (2) substituted the definition of "agricultural value" in CATA 1976 s 19(1) in relation to gifts or inheritances taken on or after 23 January 1997.

Subss (1)(*b*) and (2) inserted "or section 134 of the Finance Act, 1997," after "Finance Act, 1996," in CATA 1976 s 19(5)(*a*)(proviso)(II) in relation to gifts or inheritances taken on or after 23 January 1997.

For gifts or inheritances taken on or after 23 January 1997, agricultural relief applies at a flat rate of 90%.

If relieved agricultural property is sold within six and 10 years of the valuation date, only the additional relief granted under FA 1996 or FA 1997 is clawed back.

135 Amendment of section 57 (exemption of certain securities) of Principal Act

Notes

This section substituted "disposition" for "disposition, or at the date of the gift or the date of the inheritance" in CATA 1976 s 57(3) in relation to securities or units comprised in a gift or inheritance where the date of the gift or the date of the inheritance is on or after 26 March 1997, and the securities or units come into the beneficial ownership of the disponer on or after that date without having been previously in the beneficial ownership of the disponer.

This is an anti-avoidance provision. Securities beneficially owned by a person who was non-domiciled and non-ordinarily resident for three years before the valuation date are exempt from capital acquisitions tax. For the exemption to apply, two conditions must be satisfied:

(*a*) the beneficiary must be non-domiciled and non-ordinarily resident at the date of the gift or inheritance, and

(*b*) the disponer must be non-domiciled and non-ordinarily resident at the date of the disposition <u>or</u> at the date of the inheritance.

For securities acquired after 26 March 1997, if the disponer was domiciled and ordinarily resident in the State at the date of the disposition, the three year ownership condition applies, irrespective of the disponer's domicile or ordinary residence at the date of the gift or inheritance.

136 Second Schedule (computation of tax) to Principal Act, declaratory provision

(1) ...

(2) Subsection (1) shall not apply to a gift or inheritance in relation to which paragraph 3 of the Second Schedule to the Principal Act was the subject of a determination of the Appeal Commissioners, being a determination made before the 1st day of May, 1997, under section 52 of the Principal Act.

Notes

Subs (1) substituted CATA 1976 Sch 2 para 3.
This is intended to clarify the computation provisions.

137 Amendment of section 39 (extension of section 55 (exemption of certain objects) of Capital Acquisitions Tax Act, 1976) of Finance Act, 1978

Notes

Subss (1) and (3) substituted FA 1978 s 39(1A) in relation to gifts or inheritances taken on or after 1 February 1987.
Subss (2) and (3) revoked the Capital Acquisitions Tax (Heritage Houses and Gardens) Regulations 1987 (SI 28/1987) with effect from 1 January 1997, in relation to gifts or inheritances taken on or after 1 February 1987.
For 1997 and later calendar years, to qualify for exemption from capital acquisitions tax, a heritage house or garden must be open to the public for 60 days per year (including not less than 40 days during the summer months).

138 Amendment of section 117 (reduction of market value of certain dwellings) of Finance Act, 1991

Notes

This section substituted "£80,000" for "£60,000" in FA 1991 s 117(1) in relation to inheritances taken on or after 10 May 1997.
For inheritances taken on or after 10 May 1997, the value of a residence (or part of a residence) inherited by an elderly person from that person's deceased brother or sister is reduced by 60% or £80,000, whichever is the lesser.

139 Amendment of section 126 (business relief) of Finance Act, 1994

Notes

This section substituted "90 per cent" for "75 per cent" in FA 1994 s 126 in relation to gifts or inheritances taken on or after 23 January 1997.
For gifts or inheritances taken on or after 23 January 1997, business relief applies at a flat rate of 90%.

140 Amendment of section 127 (relevant business property) of Finance Act, 1994

Notes

This section substituted FA 1994 s 127(6) in relation to gifts or inheritances taken on or after 26 March 1997.
Business assets used (but not owned by) a company or partnership qualify for business relief - on the termination of a life interest in the assets.

141 Amendment of section 135 (withdrawal of relief) of Finance Act, 1994

Notes

This section substituted "four-ninths" for "one-third" in FA 1994 s 135 in relation to gifts or inheritances taken on or after 23 January 1997.

If relieved business property is sold within six and 10 years of the valuation date, only the additional relief granted under FA 1996 or FA 1997 is clawed back.

142 Exemption of certain transfers from capital acquisitions tax following the dissolution of a marriage

(1) Notwithstanding the provisions of the Principal Act, a gift or inheritance (within the meaning, in each case, of that Act) taken by virtue or in consequence of an order to which this subsection applies by a spouse who was a party to the marriage concerned shall be exempt from any capital acquisitions tax under that Act and shall not be taken into account in computing such a tax.

(2) Subsection (1) applies—

    (*a*)   to a relief order or an order under section 25 of the Family Law Act, 1995, made following the dissolution of a marriage, or

    (*b*)   to a maintenance pending relief order made following the granting of leave under section 23(3) of the Family Law Act, 1995, to a spouse whose marriage has been dissolved,

    (*c*)   to an order referred to in section 41(*a*) of the Family Law Act, 1995, or an order under section 42(1) of that Act made in addition to or instead of an order under section 41(*a*) of that Act, in favour of a spouse whose marriage has been dissolved, ...[1]

    (*d*)   to an order under Part III of the Family Law (Divorce) Act, [1996, and][2]

    [(*e*)   to an order or other determination to like effect, which is analogous to an order referred to in paragraph (*a*), (*b*), (*c*) or (*d*), of a court under the law of another territory made under or in consequence of the dissolution of a marriage, being a dissolution that is entitled to be recognised as valid in the State.][3]

(3) Section 51 of the Family Law Act, 1995, and section 34 of the Family Law (Divorce) Act, 1996, are hereby repealed.

Amendments

[1]   Deleted by FA 2000 s 149(1)(*a*) for an order or other determination to like effect where the order or the determination is made on or after 10 February 2000; previously "and".

[2]   Substituted by FA 2000 s 149(1)(*b*) for an order or other determination to like effect where the order or the determination is made on or after 10 February 2000; previously "1996.".

[3]   Subs (2)(*e*) inserted by FA 2000 s 149(1)(*c*) for an order or other determination to like effect where the order or the determination is made on or after 10 February 2000.

Notes

Capital acquisitions tax does not apply to a property transfer, ordered by a court, between separated or divorced marriage partners.

143 Abatement and postponement of probate tax on certain property

---

Amendments

This section repealed by FA 2001 s 225(2) in relation to probate tax which would but for FA 2001 s 225 first becomes payable on or after 6 December 2000; previously:

(1) Subsection (1) of section 115A of the Finance Act, 1993 (which was inserted by the Finance Act, 1994, and provides for the abatement or postponement of probate tax payable by a surviving spouse)—

    (a)   shall apply to a spouse in whose favour an order has been made—

          (i)   under section 25 of the Family Law Act, 1995, ...[1]

         (ii)   under section 18 of the Family Law (Divorce) Act, [1996, or][2]

      [(iii)   to an order or other determination to like effect, which is analogous to an order referred to in subparagraph (i) or (ii), of a court under the law of another territory made under or in consequence of the dissolution of a marriage, being a dissolution that is entitled to be recognised as valid in the State,][3]

        as it applies to a spouse referred to in the said section 115A, and

    (b)   shall apply to property or an interest in property the subject of such an order as it applies to the share of a spouse referred to in the said section 115A in the estate of a deceased referred to in that section or the interest of such a spouse in property referred to in that section,

with any necessary modifications.

(2) Section 53 of the Family Law Act, 1995, and section 36 of the Family Law (Divorce) Act, 1996, are hereby repealed.

Amendments

    [1]   Deleted by FA 2000 s 150(1)(a) for an order or other determination to like effect where the order or the determination is made on or after 10 February 2000; previously "or".

    [2]   Substituted by FA 2000 s 150(1)(b) for an order or other determination to like effect where the order or the determination is made on or after 10 February 2000; previously "1996,".

    [3]   Subs (1)(a)(iii) inserted by FA 2000 s 150(1)(c) for an order or other determination to like effect where the order or the determination is made on or after 10 February 2000."

Notes

The abatement or postponement of probate tax by a surviving spouse is available to a separated or divorced spouse.

PART VIII
MISCELLANEOUS

165 Care and management of taxes and duties

All taxes and duties imposed by this Act are hereby placed under the care and management of the Revenue Commissioners.

166 Short title, construction and commencement

(1) This Act may be cited as the Finance Act, 1997.

...

(7) Part VI (so far as relating to capital acquisitions tax) shall be construed together with the Capital Acquisitions Tax Act, 1976, and the enactments amending or extending that Act.

(8) Part VIII (so far as relating to income tax) shall be construed together with the Income Tax Acts and (so far as relating to corporation tax) shall be construed together with the Corporation Tax Acts and (so far as relating to capital gains tax) shall be

construed together with the Capital Gains Tax Acts and (so far as relating to value-added tax) shall be construed together with the Value-Added Tax Acts, 1972 to 1996, and (so far as relating to Residential Property Tax) shall be construed together with Part VI of the Finance Act, 1983, and the enactments amending or extending that Act and (so far as relating to capital acquisitions tax) shall be construed together with the Capital Acquisitions Tax Act, 1976, and the enactments amending or extending that Act.

...

(11) Any reference in this Act to any other enactment shall, except so far as the context otherwise requires, be construed as a reference to that enactment as amended by or under any other enactment including this Act.

(12) In this Act, a reference to a Part, section or Schedule is to a Part or section of, or Schedule to, this Act, unless it is indicated that reference to some other enactment is intended.

(13) In this Act, a reference to a subsection, paragraph, subparagraph, clause or subclause is to the subsection, paragraph, subparagraph, clause or subclause of the provision (including a Schedule) in which the reference occurs, unless it is indicated that reference to some other provision is intended.

FAMILY LAW (MISCELLANEOUS PROVISIONS) ACT 1997

(1997 Number 18)
(Date of passing: 18 May 1997)

ARRANGEMENT OF SECTIONS

Section

6   Amendment of Succession Act, 1965

AN ACT TO AMEND THE LAW IN RELATION TO NOTIFICATION OF INTENTION TO MARRY, THE LAW IN RELATION TO BARRING ORDERS, THE LAW IN RELATION TO IRREVOCABLE POWERS OF ATTORNEY AND THE LAW IN RELATION TO THE DISTRIBUTION OF DISCLAIMED ESTATES.

6 Amendment of Succession Act, 1965

Note

Section 6 inserted Succession Act 1965 s 72A.

TAXES CONSOLIDATION ACT 1997

(1997 Number 39)

ARRANGEMENT OF SECTIONS

INTERPRETATION AND BASIC CHARGING PROVISIONS

PART 1
INTERPRETATION

Section

PART 33
ANTI-AVOIDANCE

CHAPTER 2
Miscellaneous

PART 34
PROVISIONS RELATING TO THE RESIDENCE OF INDIVIDUALS

MANAGEMENT PROVISIONS

PART 37
ADMINISTRATION

PART 38
RETURNS OF INCOME AND GAINS, OTHER OBLIGATIONS AND RETURNS, AND REVENUE POWERS

CHAPTER 3
Other obligations and returns

CHAPTER 4
Revenue powers

PART 39
ASSESSMENTS

CHAPTER 1
Income Tax and Corporation Tax

PART 42
COLLECTION AND RECOVERY

CHAPTER 4
Collection and Recovery of Income Tax on Certain Emoluments (PAYE System)

CHAPTER 5
Miscellaneous provisions

PART 47
PENALTIES, REVENUE OFFENCES, INTEREST ON OVERDUE TAX AND OTHER SANCTIONS

CHAPTER 1
Income Tax and Corporation Tax Penalties

SCHEDULE 31
INTERPRETATION AND BASIC CHARGING PROVISIONS

PART 1
INTERPRETATION

7 Application to certain taxing statutes of Age of Majority Act, 1985

(1) Notwithstanding subsection (4) of section 2 of the Age of Majority Act, 1985 (in this section referred to as **"the Act of 1985"**), subsections (2) and (3) of that section shall, subject to subsection (2), apply for the purposes of the Income Tax Acts and any other statutory provision (within the meaning of the Act of 1985) dealing with the imposition, repeal, remission, alteration or regulation of any tax or other duty under the care and management of the Revenue Commissioners, and accordingly section 2(4)(*b*)(vii) of the Act of 1985 shall cease to apply.

(2) Nothing in subsection (1) shall affect a claimant's entitlement to [relief][1] under section 462 or 465.

Amendments

[1]   Substituted by FA 2000 s 14 and Sch 1 para 2; previously "a deduction".

Cross-references

This section to be construed together with the Customs Acts, in so far as relating to customs, and with the statutes which relate to excise duty, in so far as relating to that duty: s 1104(2).

This section to be construed together with the Value Added Tax Acts 1972-1997, in so far as relating to value added tax: s 1104(3).

This section to be construed together with the Stamp Act 1891 and the enactments amending or extending that Act, in so far as relating to stamp duties: s 1104(4).

This section to be construed together with the Capital Acquisitions Tax Act 1976, and the enactments amending or extending that Act, in so far as relating to capital acquisitions tax: s 1104(5).

This section to be construed together with FA 1983 Pt VI and the enactments amending or extending that Part, in so far as relating to residential property tax: s 1104(6).

Definition

Income Tax Acts: s 1(2).

Former enactment

FA 1986 s 112(1)-(2).

8 Construction of certain taxing statutes in accordance with Status of Children Act, 1987

(1) In this section, **"the Acts"** means—

(*a*)   the Tax Acts,

(*b*)   the Capital Gains Tax Acts,

(*c*)   the Capital Acquisitions Tax Act, 1976, and the enactments amending or extending that Act, and

(*d*)   the statutes relating to stamp duty,

and any instruments made thereunder.

(2) Notwithstanding any provision of the Acts or the dates on which they were passed, in deducing any relationship between persons for the purposes of the Acts, the Acts shall be construed in accordance with section 3 of the Status of Children Act, 1987.

Definition

person: IA 1937 s 11(*c*); Tax Acts: s 1(2); Capital Gains Tax Acts: s 1(2).

Former enactment

FA 1988 s 74(1)-(2).

PART 33
ANTI-AVOIDANCE

CHAPTER 2
Miscellaneous

811 Transactions to avoid liability to tax

(1) (*a*)   In this section—

"**the Acts**" means—

(i)   the Tax Acts,

(ii)   the Capital Gains Tax Acts,

(iii)   the Value-Added Tax Act, 1972, and the enactments amending or extending that Act,

(iv) the Capital Acquisitions Tax Act, 1976, and the enactments amending or extending that Act,

(v) Part VI of the Finance Act, 1983, and the enactments amending or extending that Part, and

(vi) the statutes relating to stamp duty,

and any instruments made thereunder;

"business" means any trade, profession or vocation;

"notice of opinion" means a notice given by the Revenue Commissioners under subsection (6);

"tax" means any tax, duty, levy or charge which in accordance with the Acts is placed under the care and management of the Revenue Commissioners and any interest, penalty or other amount payable pursuant to the Acts;

"tax advantage" means—

(i) a reduction, avoidance or deferral of any charge or assessment to tax, including any potential or prospective charge or assessment, or

(ii) a refund of or a payment of an amount of tax, or an increase in an amount of tax, refundable or otherwise payable to a person, including any potential or prospective amount so refundable or payable,

arising out of or by reason of a transaction, including a transaction where another transaction would not have been undertaken or arranged to achieve the results, or any part of the results, achieved or intended to be achieved by the transaction;

"tax avoidance transaction" has the meaning assigned to it by subsection (2);

"tax consequences", in relation to a tax avoidance transaction, means such adjustments and acts as may be made and done by the Revenue Commissioners pursuant to subsection (5) in order to withdraw or deny the tax advantage resulting from the tax avoidance transaction;

"transaction" means—

(i) any transaction, action, course of action, course of conduct, scheme, plan or proposal,

(ii) any agreement, arrangement, understanding, promise or undertaking, whether express or implied and whether or not enforceable or intended to be enforceable by legal proceedings, and

(iii) any series of or combination of the circumstances referred to in paragraphs (i) and (ii),

whether entered into or arranged by one person or by 2 or more persons—

(I) whether acting in concert or not,

(II) whether or not entered into or arranged wholly or partly outside the State, or

        (III)   whether or not entered into or arranged as part of a larger transaction or in conjunction with any other transaction or transactions.

  (b) In subsections (2) and (3), for the purposes of the hearing or rehearing under subsection (8) of an appeal made under subsection (7) or for the purposes of the determination of a question of law arising on the statement of a case for the opinion of the High Court, the references to the Revenue Commissioners shall, subject to any necessary modifications, be construed as references to the Appeal Commissioners or to a judge of the Circuit Court or, to the extent necessary, to a judge of the High Court, as appropriate.

(2) For the purposes of this section and subject to subsection (3), a transaction shall be a **"tax avoidance transaction"** if having regard to any one or more of the following—

  (a) the results of the transaction,

  (b) its use as a means of achieving those results, and

  (c) any other means by which the results or any part of the results could have been achieved,

the Revenue Commissioners form the opinion that—

    (i) the transaction gives rise to, or but for this section would give rise to, a tax advantage, and

    (ii) the transaction was not undertaken or arranged primarily for purposes other than to give rise to a tax advantage,

and references in this section to the Revenue Commissioners forming an opinion that a transaction is a tax avoidance transaction shall be construed as references to the Revenue Commissioners forming an opinion with regard to the transaction in accordance with this subsection.

(3) (a) Without prejudice to the generality of subsection (2), in forming an opinion in accordance with that subsection and subsection (4) as to whether or not a transaction is a tax avoidance transaction, the Revenue Commissioners shall not regard the transaction as being a tax avoidance transaction if they are satisfied that—

    (i) notwithstanding that the purpose or purposes of the transaction could have been achieved by some other transaction which would have given rise to a greater amount of tax being payable by the person, the transaction—

      (I) was undertaken or arranged by a person with a view, directly or indirectly, to the realisation of profits in the course of the business activities of a business carried on by the person, and

      (II) was not undertaken or arranged primarily to give rise to a tax advantage,

    or

    (ii) the transaction was undertaken or arranged for the purpose of obtaining the benefit of any relief, allowance or other abatement provided by any provision of the Acts and that the transaction would not result directly or indirectly in a misuse of the provision or an abuse of the provision having regard to the purposes for which it was provided.

(*b*) In forming an opinion referred to in paragraph (*a*) in relation to any transaction, the Revenue Commissioners shall have regard to—

    (i) the form of that transaction,

    (ii) the substance of that transaction,

    (iii) the substance of any other transaction or transactions which that transaction may reasonably be regarded as being directly or indirectly related to or connected with, and

    (iv) the final outcome and result of that transaction and any combination of those other transactions which are so related or connected.

(4) Subject to this section, the Revenue Commissioners as respects any transaction may at any time—

(*a*) form the opinion that the transaction is a tax avoidance transaction,

(*b*) calculate the tax advantage which they consider arises, or which but for this section would arise, from the transaction,

(*c*) determine the tax consequences which they consider would arise in respect of the transaction if their opinion were to become final and conclusive in accordance with subsection (5)(*e*), and

(*d*) calculate the amount of any relief from double taxation which they would propose to give to any person in accordance with subsection (5)(*c*).

(5) (*a*) Where the opinion of the Revenue Commissioners that a transaction is a tax avoidance transaction becomes final and conclusive, they may, notwithstanding any other provision of the Acts, make all such adjustments and do all such acts as are just and reasonable (in so far as those adjustments and acts have been specified or described in a notice of opinion given under subsection (6) and subject to the manner in which any appeal made under subsection (7) against any matter specified or described in the notice of opinion has been finally determined, including any adjustments and acts not so specified or described in the notice of opinion but which form part of a final determination of any such appeal) in order that the tax advantage resulting from a tax avoidance transaction shall be withdrawn from or denied to any person concerned.

(*b*) Subject to but without prejudice to the generality of paragraph (*a*), the Revenue Commissioners may—

    (i) allow or disallow in whole or in part any deduction or other amount which is relevant in computing tax payable, or any part of such deduction or other amount,

    (ii) allocate or deny to any person any deduction, loss, abatement, relief, allowance, exemption, income or other amount, or any part thereof, or

    (iii) recharacterize for tax purposes the nature of any payment or other amount.

(c)   Where the Revenue Commissioners make any adjustment or do any act for the purposes of paragraph (a), they shall afford relief from any double taxation which they consider would but for this paragraph arise by virtue of any adjustment made or act done by them pursuant to paragraphs (a) and (b).

(d)   Notwithstanding any other provision of the Acts, where—

    (i)   pursuant to subsection (4)(c), the Revenue Commissioners determine the tax consequences which they consider would arise in respect of a transaction if their opinion that the transaction is a tax avoidance transaction were to become final and conclusive, and

    (ii)   pursuant to that determination, they specify or describe in a notice of opinion any adjustment or act which they consider would be, or be part of, those tax consequences,

then, in so far as any right of appeal lay under subsection (7) against any such adjustment or act so specified or described, no right or further right of appeal shall lie under the Acts against that adjustment or act when it is made or done in accordance with this subsection, or against any adjustment or act so made or done that is not so specified or described in the notice of opinion but which forms part of the final determination of any appeal made under subsection (7) against any matter specified or described in the notice of opinion.

(e)   For the purposes of this subsection, an opinion of the Revenue Commissioners that a transaction is a tax avoidance transaction shall be final and conclusive—

    (i)   if within the time limited no appeal is made under subsection (7) against any matter or matters specified or described in a notice or notices of opinion given pursuant to that opinion, or

    (ii)   as and when all appeals made under subsection (7) against any such matter or matters have been finally determined and none of the appeals has been so determined by an order directing that the opinion of the Revenue Commissioners to the effect that the transaction is a tax avoidance transaction is void.

(6) (a)   Where pursuant to subsections (2) and (4) the Revenue Commissioners form the opinion that a transaction is a tax avoidance transaction, they shall immediately on forming such an opinion give notice in writing of the opinion to any person from whom a tax advantage would be withdrawn or to whom a tax advantage would be denied or to whom relief from double taxation would be given if the opinion became final and conclusive, and the notice shall specify or describe—

    (i)   the transaction which in the opinion of the Revenue Commissioners is a tax avoidance transaction,

    (ii)   the tax advantage or part of the tax advantage, calculated by the Revenue Commissioners which would be withdrawn from or denied to the person to whom the notice is given,

    (iii)   the tax consequences of the transaction determined by the Revenue Commissioners in so far as they would refer to the person, and

(iv) the amount of any relief from double taxation calculated by the Revenue Commissioners which they would propose to give to the person in accordance with subsection (5)(*c*).

(*b*) Section 869 shall, with any necessary modifications, apply for the purposes of a notice given under this subsection or subsection (10) as if it were a notice given under the Income Tax Acts.

(7) Any person aggrieved by an opinion formed or, in so far as it refers to the person, a calculation or determination made by the Revenue Commissioners pursuant to subsection (4) may, by notice in writing given to the Revenue Commissioners within 30 days of the date of the notice of opinion, appeal to the Appeal Commissioners on the grounds and, notwithstanding any other provision of the Acts, only on the grounds that, having regard to all of the circumstances, including any fact or matter which was not known to the Revenue Commissioners when they formed their opinion or made their calculation or determination, and to this section—

(*a*) the transaction specified or described in the notice of opinion is not a tax avoidance transaction,

(*b*) the amount of the tax advantage or the part of the tax advantage, specified or described in the notice of opinion which would be withdrawn from or denied to the person is incorrect,

(*c*) the tax consequences specified or described in the notice of opinion, or such part of those consequences as shall be specified or described by the appellant in the notice of appeal, would not be just and reasonable in order to withdraw or to deny the tax advantage or part of the tax advantage specified or described in the notice of opinion, or

(*d*) the amount of relief from double taxation which the Revenue Commissioners propose to give to the person is insufficient or incorrect.

(8) The Appeal Commissioners shall hear and determine an appeal made to them under subsection (7) as if it were an appeal against an assessment to income tax and, subject to subsection (9), the provisions of the Income Tax Acts relating to the rehearing of an appeal and to the statement of a case for the opinion of the High Court on a point of law shall apply accordingly with any necessary modifications; but on the hearing or rehearing of the appeal—

(*a*) it shall not be lawful to enquire into any grounds of appeal other than those specified in subsection (7), and

(*b*) at the request of the appellants, 2 or more appeals made by 2 or more persons pursuant to the same opinion, calculation or determination formed or made by the Revenue Commissioners pursuant to subsection (4) may be heard or reheard together.

(9) (*a*) On the hearing of an appeal made under subsection (7), the Appeal Commissioners shall have regard to all matters to which the Revenue Commissioners may or are required to have regard under this section, and—

    (i) in relation to an appeal made on the grounds referred to in subsection (7)(*a*), the Appeal Commissioners shall determine the appeal, in so far as it is made on those grounds, by ordering, if they or a majority of them—

        (I) consider that the transaction specified or described in the notice of opinion or any part of that transaction is a tax avoidance transaction, that the opinion or the opinion in so far as it relates to that part is to stand,

        (II) consider that, subject to such amendment or addition thereto as the Appeal Commissioners or the majority of them deem necessary and as they shall specify or describe, the transaction, or any part of it, specified or described in the notice of opinion, is a tax avoidance transaction, that the transaction or that part of it be so amended or added to and that, subject to the amendment or addition, the opinion or the opinion in so far as it relates to that part is to stand, or

        (III) do not so consider as referred to in clause (I) or (II), that the opinion is void,

    (ii) in relation to an appeal made on the grounds referred to in subsection (7)(*b*), they shall determine the appeal, in so far as it is made on those grounds, by ordering that the amount of the tax advantage or the part of the tax advantage specified or described in the notice of opinion be increased or reduced by such amount as they shall direct or that it shall stand,

    (iii) in relation to an appeal made on the grounds referred to in subsection (7)(*c*), they shall determine the appeal, in so far as it is made on those grounds, by ordering that the tax consequences specified or described in the notice of opinion shall be altered or added to in such manner as they shall direct or that they shall stand, or

    (iv) in relation to an appeal made on the grounds referred to in subsection (7)(*d*), they shall determine the appeal, in so far as it is made on those grounds, by ordering that the amount of the relief from double taxation specified or described in the notice of opinion shall be increased or reduced by such amount as they shall direct or that it shall stand.

(*b*) This subsection shall, subject to any necessary modifications, apply to the rehearing of an appeal by a judge of the Circuit Court and, to the extent necessary, to the determination by the High Court of any question or questions of law arising on the statement of a case for the opinion of the High Court.

(10) The Revenue Commissioners may at any time amend, add to or withdraw any matter specified or described in a notice of opinion by giving notice (in this subsection referred to as **"the notice of amendment"**) in writing of the amendment, addition or withdrawal to each and every person affected thereby, in so far as the person is so affected, and subsections (1) to (9) shall apply in all respects as if the notice of amendment were a notice of opinion and any matter specified or described in the notice of amendment were specified or described in a notice of opinion; but no such amendment, addition or withdrawal may be made so as to set aside or alter any matter

which has become final and conclusive on the determination of an appeal made with regard to that matter under subsection (7).

(11) Where pursuant to subsections (2) and (4) the Revenue Commissioners form the opinion that a transaction is a tax avoidance transaction and pursuant to that opinion notices are to be given under subsection (6) to 2 or more persons, any obligation on the Revenue Commissioners to maintain secrecy or any other restriction on the disclosure of information by the Revenue Commissioners shall not apply with respect to the giving of those notices or to the performance of any acts or the discharge of any functions authorised by this section to be performed or discharged by them or to the performance of any act or the discharge of any functions, including any act or function in relation to an appeal made under subsection (7), which is directly or indirectly related to the acts or functions so authorised.

(12) The Revenue Commissioners may nominate any of their officers to perform any acts and discharge any functions, including the forming of an opinion, authorised by this section to be performed or discharged by the Revenue Commissioners, and references in this section to the Revenue Commissioners shall with any necessary modifications be construed as including references to an officer so nominated.

(13) This section shall apply as respects any transaction where the whole or any part of the transaction is undertaken or arranged on or after the 25th day of January, 1989, and as respects any transaction undertaken or arranged wholly before that date in so far as it gives rise to, or would but for this section give rise to—

>   (*a*)   a reduction, avoidance or deferral of any charge or assessment to tax, or part thereof, where the charge or assessment arises by virtue of any other transaction carried out wholly on or after a date, or

>   (*b*)   a refund or a payment of an amount, or of an increase in an amount, of tax, or part thereof, refundable or otherwise payable to a person where that amount or increase in the amount would otherwise become first so refundable or otherwise payable to the person on a date,

which could not fall earlier than the 25th day of January, 1989.

Cross-references

Meaning of "the Acts" applied: Asset Covered Securities Act 2001 s 81(2).

Shipping tonnage tax, requirement not to enter into tax avoidance arrangements, meaning of "tax advantage" applied: s 697F(2)(*a*).

This section to be construed together with the Value Added Tax Acts 1972-1997, in so far as relating to value added tax: s 1104(3).

This section to be construed together with the Stamp Act 1891 and the enactments amending or extending that Act, in so far as relating to stamp duties: s 1104(4).

This section to be construed together with the Capital Acquisitions Tax Act 1976, and the enactments amending or extending that Act, in so far as relating to capital acquisitions tax: s 1104(5).

This section to be construed together with FA 1983 Pt VI and the enactments amending or extending that Part, in so far as relating to residential property tax: s 1104(6).

Case law

Bona fide commercial motives: *Marwood Homes Ltd v IRC*, [1996] STI 51.

Expenditure on plant funded by non-recourse borrowings allowable: *Airspace Investments Ltd v Moore*, HC, Lynch J, 15 April 1994. Contrast *Ensign Tankers (Leasing) Ltd v Stokes*, [1992] STC 226.

Meaning of "tax advantage": *IRC v Universities Superannuation Scheme*, [1997] STC 1.

Definitions

Appeal Commissioners: ss 2(1), 5(1); Circuit Court: IA 1937 Sch; High Court: IA 1937 Sch; person: IA 1937 s 11(c); profession: ss 2(1), 5(1); profits: s 4(1); statute: s 2(1), IA 1937 s 3; Tax Acts: s 1(2); trade: s 3(1); writing: IA 1937 Sch.

Former enactments

FA 1989 s 86.

PART 34
PROVISIONS RELATING TO THE RESIDENCE OF INDIVIDUALS

Cross-references

Profits of life business: s 710(3)(b).

---

818 Interpretation (Part 34)

In this Part other than in section 825—

"the Acts" means—

    (a) the Tax Acts,

    (b) the Capital Gains Tax Acts, and

    (c) the Capital Acquisitions Tax Act, 1976, and the enactments amending or extending that Act,

and any instruments made thereunder;

"authorised officer" means an officer of the Revenue Commissioners authorised by them in writing for the purposes of this Part;

"present in the State", in relation to an individual, means the personal presence of the individual in the State;

"tax" means any tax payable in accordance with any provision of the Acts.

Cross-references

Reduction on income tax for certain income earned outside the State, meaning of "authorised officer" applied: s 825A(1).

Seafarer allowance, meaning of "authorised officer" applied: s 472B(1).

Former enactments

FA 1994 s 149.

---

819 Residence

(1) For the purposes of the Acts, an individual shall be resident in the State for a year of assessment if the individual is present in the State—

    (a) at any one time or several times in the year of assessment for a period in the whole amounting to [135 days]¹ or more, or

    (b) at any one time or several times—

        (i) in the year of assessment, and

        (ii) in the preceding year of assessment,

for a period (being a period comprising in the aggregate the number of days on which the individual is present in the State in the year of assessment and the number of days on which the individual was present in the State in the preceding year of assessment) in the aggregate amounting to [244 days]² or more.

(2) Notwithstanding subsection (1)(*b*), where for a year of assessment an individual is present in the State at any one time or several times for a period in the aggregate amounting to not more than [22 days]³—

(*a*) the individual shall not be resident in the State for the year of assessment, and

(*b*) no account shall be taken of the period for the purposes of the aggregate mentioned in subsection (1)(*b*).

(3) (*a*) Notwithstanding subsections (1) and (2), an individual—

(i) who is not resident in the State for a year of assessment, and

(ii) to whom paragraph (*b*) applies,

may at any time elect to be treated as resident in the State for that year and, where an individual so elects, the individual shall for the purposes of the Acts be deemed to be resident in the State for that year.

(*b*) This paragraph shall apply to an individual who satisfies an authorised officer that the individual is in the State—

(i) with the intention, and

(ii) in such circumstances,

that the individual will be resident in the State for the following year of assessment.

(4) For the purposes of this section, an individual shall be deemed to be present in the State for a day if the individual is present in the State at the end of the day.

Amendments

1   Substituted by FA 2001 s 77(2) and Sch 2 para 42(*a*)(i) for 2001; previously "183 days".

2   Substituted by FA 2001 s 77(2) and Sch 2 para 42(*a*)(ii) only as respects 2001 and 2002; previously "280 days".

3   Substituted by FA 2001 s 77(2) and Sch 2 para 42(*b*) for 2001; previously "30 days".

Definitions

resident: s 5(1); year: IA 1937 Sch; year of assessment: ss 2(1), 5(1).

Former enactment

FA 1994 s 150.

820 Ordinary residence

(1) For the purposes of the Acts, an individual shall be ordinarily resident in the State for a year of assessment if the individual has been resident in the State for each of the 3 years of assessment preceding that year.

(2) An individual ordinarily resident in the State shall not for the purposes of the Acts cease to be ordinarily resident in the State for a year of assessment unless the individual

has not been resident in the State in each of the 3 years of assessment preceding that year.

Definitions

resident: s 5(1); year: IA 1937 Sch; year of assessment: ss 2(1), 5(1).

Former enactment

FA 1994 s 151.

821 Application of sections 17 and 18(1) and Chapter 1 of Part 3

(1) Where an individual is not resident but is ordinarily resident in the State, sections 17 and 18(1) and Chapter 1 of Part 3 shall apply as if the individual were resident in the State; but this section shall not apply in respect of—

  (*a*)   the income of an individual derived from one or more of the following—

  (i)   a trade or profession, no part of which is carried on in the State, and

  (ii)   an office or employment, all the duties of which are performed outside the State, and

  (*b*)   other income of an individual which in any year of assessment does not exceed [€3,810][1].

(2) In determining for the purposes of subsection (1) whether the duties of an office or employment are performed outside the State, any duties performed in the State, the performance of which is merely incidental to the performance of the duties of the office or employment outside the State, shall be treated as having been performed outside the State.

Amendments

[1]   Substituted by FA 2001 s 240(1) and (1)(*a*) and Sch 5 Pt 1 for 2002 and later tax years; previously "£3,000" (short tax "year") 2001:£2,000 (FA 2001 s 77(2) and Sch 2 paras 43 and 61(*a*))).

Definitions

profession: s 2(1); resident: s 5(1); trade: s 3(1); year: IA 1937 Sch.

Statement of practice

"Other income" which does not exceed £3,000 means other <u>foreign</u> income: *Tax Briefing 25*, February 1997.

Former enactment

FA 1994 s 152; FA 1995 s 169(1).

822 Split year residence

(1) For the purposes of a charge to tax on any income, profits or gains from an employment, where during a year of assessment (in this section referred to as **"the relevant year"**)—

  (*a*)   (i)   an individual who has not been resident in the State for the preceding year of assessment satisfies an authorised officer that the individual is in the State—

  (I)   with the intention, and

  (II)   in such circumstances,

  that the individual will be resident in the State for the following year of assessment, or

(ii) an individual who is resident in the State satisfies an authorised officer that the individual is leaving the State, other than for a temporary purpose—

   (I) with the intention, and

   (II) in such circumstances,

   that the individual will not be resident in the State for the following year of assessment,

and

(b) the individual would but for this section be resident in the State for the relevant year,

subsection (2) shall apply in relation to the individual.

(2) (a) An individual to whom paragraphs (a)(i) and (b) of subsection (1) apply shall be deemed to be resident in the State for the relevant year only from the date of his or her arrival in the State.

(b) An individual to whom paragraphs (a)(ii) and (b) of subsection (1) apply shall be deemed to be resident in the State for the relevant year only up to and including the date of his or her leaving the State.

(3) Where by virtue of this section an individual is resident in the State for part of a year of assessment, the Acts shall apply as if—

(a) income arising during that part of the year or, in a case to which section 71(3) applies, amounts received in the State during that part of the year were income arising or amounts received for a year of assessment in which the individual is resident in the State, and

(b) income arising or, as the case may be, amounts received in the remaining part of the year were income arising or amounts received in a year of assessment in which the individual is not resident in the State.

Cross references

Deduction for income earned outside the State: s 823(2)(b)(ii).

Definitions

profits: s 4(1); tax: s 3(1); year of assessment: ss 2(1), 5(1).

Former enactment

FA 1994 s 153.

---

823 Deduction for income earned outside the State

(1) In this section—

["qualifying day", in relation to an office or employment of an individual, means a day on or before 31 December 2003 which is one of at least 11 consecutive days throughout the whole of which the individual is absent from the State for the purposes of the performance of the duties of the office or employment or of those duties and the duties of other offices or employments of the individual outside the State and which (taken as a whole) are substantially devoted to the performance of such duties, but no day shall be counted more than once as a qualifying day;][1]

"relevant period", in relation to a year of assessment, means a continuous period of 12 months—

    (*a*) part only of which is comprised in the year of assessment, and

    (*b*) no part of which is comprised in another relevant period;

[**"the specified amount"** in relation to an office or employment means an amount determined by the formula—

$$\frac{D \times E}{[270]^2}$$

$$\frac{D \times E}{[365]^2}$$

where—

    D is the number of qualifying days in relation to the office or employment in the year of assessment concerned, and

    E is all the income, profits or gains from any office, employment or pension whether chargeable under Schedule D or E (including income from offices or employments the duties of which are performed in the State) of an individual in that year after deducting any contribution or qualifying premium in respect of which there is provision for a deduction under section 774(7) or 787 but excluding—

    (*a*) any expense to which 118 applies,

    (*b*) any amount treated as emoluments of an employment under section 121(2)(*b*)(ii) by virtue of a car being made available by reason of the employment,

    (*c*) any sum treated for the purposes of section 112 as a perquisite of an office or employment by virtue of section 122,

    (*d*) any payment to which section 123 applies,

    (*e*) any sum deemed to be profits or gains arising or accruing from an office or employment by virtue of section 127(2), or

    (*f*) any gain to which section 128 applies.][3]

(2) (*a*) Subject to paragraph (*b*), this section shall apply to—

    (i) an office of director of a company which is within the charge to corporation tax, or would be within the charge to corporation tax if it were resident in the State, and which carries on a trade or profession,

    (ii) an employment other than—

        (I) an employment the emoluments of which are paid out of the revenue of the State, or

(II) an employment with any board, authority or other similar body established by or under statute.

(*b*) This section shall not apply in any case where the income from an office or employment—

(i) is chargeable to tax in accordance with section 71(3),

(ii) is subject to section 73, or would be so subject if the employment were deemed to be property situated where the employment is exercised, or

(iii) is income to which section 822 applies.

[(2A)(*a*) In this subsection, "qualifying employment", "qualifying individual" and "sea-going ship" have the same meanings, respectively, as in section 472B.

(*b*) Where in any period of at least [11 consecutive days]⁴ in which a qualifying individual is absent from the State for the purposes of the performance of the duties of a qualifying employment, the sea-going ship on which he or she, in that period, performs those duties—

(i) visits a port in the United Kingdom, and

(ii) also visits a port other than a port in the State or in the United Kingdom,

then subparagraph (ii) of subsection (2)(*b*) shall not apply to the income, profits or gains from the qualifying employment for such period.]⁵

(3) Where for any year of assessment an individual resident in the State makes a claim in that behalf to and satisfies an authorised officer that—

(*a*) the duties of an office or employment to which this section applies of the individual are performed wholly or partly outside the State, and

(*b*) either—

(i) the number of days in that year which are qualifying days in relation to the office or employment (together with any days which are qualifying days in relation to any other such office or employment of the individual), or

(ii) the number of such days referred to in subparagraph (i) in a relevant period in relation to that year,

amounts to at least 90 days [or, in the case where subparagraph (i) applies and the year of assessment concerned is the year of assessment 2001, 67 days]⁶,

there shall be deducted from the income, profits or gains from the office or employment to be assessed under Schedule D or E, as may be appropriate, an amount equal to the specified amount [in relation to that office or employment or the amount of the income, profits or gains [whichever is the lesser; but that amount, or the aggregate of those amounts where there is more than one such office or employment, shall not exceed [€31,750]⁷.]⁸]⁹

(4) Notwithstanding anything in the Acts, the income, profits or gains from an office or employment shall for the purposes of this section be deemed not to include any amounts paid in respect of expenses incurred wholly, exclusively and necessarily in the performance of the duties of the office or employment.

Amendments

1 Definition of "qualifying day" substituted by FA 2001 s 31(1)(*a*)(i) with effect from 26 January 2001.

2 Substituted by FA 2001 s 31(1)(*a*)(ii) for the short tax "year" 2001; previously "365" and reverts to "365" for 2002 and later tax years.

3 Definition of "the specified amount" substituted by FA 1999 s 21(1)(*a*) for 1999-2000 and later tax years and for 1998-99 to the extent that the income, profits or gains to be included in computing the specified amount accrues to an individual on or after 10 March 1999.

4 Substituted by FA 2000 s 47(1)(*b*) with effect from 29 February 2000; previously "14 consecutive days".

5 Subs (2A) inserted by FA 1998 s 14(1)(*c*) with effect from 6 April 1998.

6 Inserted by FA 2001 s 31(1)(*b*)(i) with effect from 6 April 2001.

7 Substituted by FA 2001 s 240(1) and (2)(*a*) and Sch 5 Pt 1 for 2002 and later tax years; previously "£25,000" (short tax "year" 2001: £18,500 (FA 2001 s 31(1)(*b*)(ii))).

8 Substituted by FA 2000 s 47(1)(*c*) with effect for 2000-2001 and later tax years; for 1999-2000, as if the reference to "that amount, or the aggregate of those amounts where there is more than one such office or employment" were a reference to "such portion of that amount, or such portion of the aggregate of those amounts where there is more than one such office or employment, which arises by virtue of income, profits or gains accruing or paid on or after 29 February 2000"; previously "whichever is the lesser".

9 Inserted by FA 1999 s 21(1)(*b*) for 1999-2000 and later tax years and for 1998-99 to the extent that the income, profits or gains to be included in computing the specified amount accrues to an individual on or after 10 March 1999.

Definitions

month: IA 1937 Sch; profession: s 2(1); trade: s 3(1); year of assessment: ss 2(1), 5(1).

Former enactment

FA 1994 s 154; FA 1995 s 170(1).

824 Appeals

(1) An individual aggrieved by a decision of an authorised officer on any question arising under the provisions of this [Part][1] which require an individual to satisfy an authorised officer on such a question may, by notice in writing to that effect given to the authorised officer within 2 months from the date on which notice of the decision is given to the individual, make an application to have the question heard and determined by the Appeal Commissioners.

(2) Where an application is made under subsection (1), the Appeal Commissioners shall hear and determine the question concerned in the like manner as an appeal made to them against an assessment, and the provisions of the Acts relating to such an appeal (including the provisions relating to the rehearing of an appeal and to the statement of a case for the opinion of the High Court on a point of law) shall apply accordingly with any necessary modifications.

Amendments

1 Substituted by FA 2000 s 160; previously "Chapter".

Definitions

Appeal Commissioners: ss 2(1), 850; writing: IA 1937 Sch.

Former enactment

FA 1994 s 156.

825 Residence treatment of donors of gifts to the State

(1) In this section—

"the Acts" means—

    (*a*) the Tax Acts,

    (*b*) the Capital Gains Tax Acts, and

    (*c*) the Capital Acquisitions Tax Act, 1976;

"donor" means an individual who makes a gift to the State;

"gift" means a gift of property to the State which, on acceptance of the gift by the Government pursuant to the State Property Act, 1954, becomes vested pursuant to that Act in a State authority within the meaning of that Act;

"Irish tax" means any tax imposed by the Acts;

"property" includes interests and rights of any description;

"relevant date", in relation to an individual (being a donor or the spouse of a donor), means the date (not being earlier than the 1st day of September, 1974) on which the individual leaves the State for the purpose of residence (other than occasional residence) outside the State;

"tax in that country" means any tax imposed in that country which is identical with or substantially similar to Irish tax;

"visits" means—

    (*a*) in relation to a donor, visits by the donor to the State after the relevant date for the purpose of advising on the management of the property which is the subject of the gift, being visits that are in the aggregate less than [182 days][1] in any year of assessment in which they are made, and

    (*b*) in relation to the spouse of a donor, visits by that spouse when accompanying the donor on visits of the kind referred to in paragraph (*a*).

(2) Where for any year of assessment a person (being a donor or the spouse of a donor) is resident in a country outside the State for the purposes of tax in that country and is chargeable to that tax without any limitation as to chargeability, then, notwithstanding anything to the contrary in the Tax Acts—

    (*a*) as respects the year of assessment in which the relevant date occurs, that person shall not as from the relevant date be regarded as ordinarily resident in the State for the purposes of Irish tax, and

    (*b*) as respects any subsequent year of assessment, in determining whether that person is resident or ordinarily resident in the State for the purposes of Irish tax, visits shall be disregarded.

Amendments

[1]   Substituted by FA 2001 s 77(2) and Sch 2 paras 44 and 61(*a*) for the short tax "year" 2001 ("135 days"); reverts to "182 days" for 2002 and later tax years.

Amendments

[1]   Substituted by FA 2001 s 77(2) and Sch 2 para 44 for 2001; previously "135 days".

Definition

the Government: IA 1937 Sch; person: IA 1937 s 11(*c*); resident: s 5(1); Tax Acts: s 1(2); year of assessment: ss 2(1), 5(1).

Former enactment

FA 1977 s 53.

MANAGEMENT PROVISIONS

PART 37
ADMINISTRATION

850 Appeal Commissioners

(1) The Minister for Finance shall appoint persons to be Appeal Commissioners for the purposes of the Income Tax Acts (in the Tax Acts and the Capital Gains Tax Acts referred to as **"Appeal Commissioners"**) and the persons so appointed shall, by virtue of their appointment and without other qualification, have authority to execute such powers and to perform such duties as are assigned to them by the Income Tax Acts.

(2) Appeal Commissioners shall be allowed such sums in respect of salary and incidental expenses as the Minister for Finance directs.

(3) The Minister for Finance shall cause an account of all appointments of Appeal Commissioners and their salaries to be laid before each House of the Oireachtas within 20 days of their appointment or, in the case of a House not then sitting, within 20 days after the next sitting of that House.

(4) Anything required to be done under the Income Tax Acts by the Appeal Commissioners or any other Commissioners may, except where otherwise expressly provided by those Acts, be done by any 2 or more Commissioners.

Cross-references

Income Tax (Relevant Contracts) Regulations 2000, SI No 71 of 2000, meaning of "Collector-General" applied: ITRCR 2000 reg 2.
Standards in Public Office Act 2001 s 1(1), meaning of "Collector-General" applied.

Definitions

Income Tax Acts: s 1(2); the Oireachtas: IA 1937 Sch; person: IA 1937 s 11(*c*).

Former enactments

ITA 1967 s 156; F(MP)A 1968 s 1(1), s3(2) and Sch Pt II.

851 Collector-General

(1) There shall be a Collector-General, who shall be appointed by the Revenue Commissioners from among their officers and who shall hold such office at their will and pleasure.

(2) The Collector-General shall collect and levy the tax from time to time charged in all assessments to income tax, corporation tax and capital gains tax of which particulars have been transmitted to him or her under section 928.

(3) (*a*) The Revenue Commissioners may nominate persons to exercise on behalf of the Collector-General any or all of the powers and functions conferred on the Collector-General by the Tax Acts and the Capital Gains Tax Acts.

(b) Those powers and functions, as well as being exercisable by the Collector-General, shall also be exercisable on his or her behalf by persons nominated under this subsection.

(c) A person shall not be nominated under this subsection unless he or she is an officer or employee of the Revenue Commissioners.

(4) If and so long as the office of Collector-General is vacant or the holder of that office is unable through illness, absence or other cause to fulfil his or her duties, a person nominated in that behalf by the Revenue Commissioners from among their officers shall act as the Collector-General, and any reference in this or any other Act to the Collector-General shall be construed as including, where appropriate, a reference to a person nominated under this subsection.

(5) The Revenue Commissioners may revoke a nomination under this section.

Cross-references

Collection of capital gains tax: s 976(1).

Income Tax (Employments) (Consolidated) Regulations 2001, SI No 559 of 2001, meaning of "Collector-General" applied: reg 2(1).

Income Tax (Relevant Contracts) Regulations 2000, SI No 71 of 2000, meaning of "Collector-General" applied: ITRCR 2000 reg 2.

Taxes (Offset of Repayments) Regulations 2001, SI No 399 of 2001, meaning of "Collector-General" applied: reg 2(1) (interpretation).

Case law

Subs (2): Collector-General not entitled to take into consideration when dealing with an application for a tax clearance certificate by a company the circumstances of a liquidated company having tax arrears engaged in a similar business and which had common directors and other employees: *Melbarien Enterprises v Revenue Commissioners*, HC 19 April 1985.

Subs (3): An arrangement for allocation of payments between the Collector-General and a company was not affected by the fact that a new managing director was unaware of the arrangement: *Metal Products Ltd, (In receivership) v Hearne*, HC January 1988.

Definitions

person: IA 1937 s 11(c).

Former enactments

ITA 1967 s 162; FA 1974 s 86 Sch 2 Pt I; CGTA 1975 s 51(1) and Sch 4 para 1(3); CTA 1976 s 145(1); FA 1987 s 52; FA 1997 s 157.

858 Evidence of authorisation

(1) In this section, except where the context otherwise requires—

"the Acts" means—

    (a)   (i)   the Customs Acts,

           (ii) the statutes relating to the duties of excise and to the management of those duties,

           (iii) the Tax Acts,

           (iv) the Capital Gains Tax Acts,

           (v) the Value-Added Tax Act, 1972, and the enactments amending or extending that Act,

     (vi) the Capital Acquisitions Tax Act, 1976, and the enactments amending or extending that Act,

    (vii) the statutes relating to stamp duty and to the management of that duty,

       and any instruments made thereunder or under any other enactment and relating to tax, and

  (*b*) the European Communities (Intrastat) Regulations, 1993 (S.I. No. 136 of 1993);

"authorised officer" means an officer of the Revenue Commissioners who is authorised, nominated or appointed under any provision of the Acts to exercise or perform any functions under any of the specified provisions, and **"authorised"** and **"authorisation"** shall be construed accordingly;

"functions" includes powers and duties;

"identity card", in relation to an authorised officer, means a card which is issued to the officer by the Revenue Commissioners and which contains—

  (*a*) a statement to the effect that the officer—

    (i) is an officer of the Revenue Commissioners, and

    (ii) is an authorised officer for the purposes of the specified provisions,

  (*b*) a photograph and signature of the officer,

  (*c*) a hologram showing the logo of the Office of the Revenue Commissioners,

  (*d*) the facsimile signature of a Revenue Commissioner, and

  (*e*) particulars of the specified provisions under which the officer is authorised;

"specified provisions", in relation to an authorised officer, means either or both the provisions of the Acts under which the authorised officer—

  (*a*) is authorised and which are specified on his or her identity card, and

  (*b*) exercises or performs functions under the Customs Acts or any statutes relating to the duties of excise and to the management of those duties;

"tax" means any tax, duty, levy or charge under the care and management of the Revenue Commissioners.

(2) Where, in the exercise or performance of any functions under any of the specified provisions in relation to him or her, an authorised officer is requested to produce or show his or her authorisation for the purposes of that provision, the production by the authorised officer of his or her identity card—

  (*a*) shall be taken as evidence of authorisation under that provision, and

  (*b*) shall satisfy any obligation under that provision which requires the authorised officer to produce such authorisation on request.

(3) This section shall come into operation on such day as the Minister for Finance may appoint by order.

Cross-references

This section to be construed together with the Customs Acts, in so far as relating to customs: s 1104(2).

This section to be construed together with the Value Added Tax Acts 1972-1997, in so far as relating to value added tax: s 1104(3).

This section to be construed together with the Stamp Act 1891 and the enactments amending or extending that Act, in so far as relating to stamp duties: s 1104(4).

This section to be construed together with the Capital Acquisitions Tax Act 1976, and the enactments amending or extending that Act, in so far as relating to capital acquisitions tax: s 1104(5).

Former enactment

FA 1997 s 159.

859 Anonymity of authorised officers in relation to certain matters

(1) In this section—

"authorised officer" means an officer of the Revenue Commissioners nominated by them to be a member of the staff of the body;

"the body" has the meaning assigned to it by section 58;

"proceedings" includes any hearing before the Appeal Commissioners (within the meaning of the Revenue Acts);

"the Revenue Acts" means—

    (*a*)   the Customs Acts,

    (*b*)   the statutes relating to the duties of excise and to the management of those duties,

    (*c*)   the Tax Acts,

    (*d*)   the Capital Gains Tax Acts,

    (*e*)   the Value-Added Tax Act, 1972, and the enactments amending or extending that Act,

    (*f*)   the Capital Acquisitions Tax Act, 1976, and the enactments amending or extending that Act,

    (*g*)   the statutes relating to stamp duty and the management of that duty,

    (*h*)   Chapter IV of Part II of the Finance Act, 1992, and

    (*i*)   Part VI of the Finance Act, 1983,

and any instruments made thereunder or under any other enactment and relating to tax;

"tax" means any tax, duty, levy or charge under the care and management of the Revenue Commissioners.

(2) Notwithstanding any requirement made by or under any enactment or any other requirement in administrative and operational procedures, including internal procedures, all reasonable care shall be taken to ensure that the identity of an authorised officer shall not be revealed.

(3) In particular and without prejudice to the generality of subsection (2):

(*a*) where, for the purposes of exercising or performing his or her powers or duties under the Revenue Acts in pursuance of the functions of the body, an authorised officer may apart from this section be required to produce or show any written authority or warrant of appointment under those Acts or otherwise to identify himself or herself, the authorised officer shall—

    (i) not be required to produce or show any such authority or warrant of appointment or to so identify himself or herself, for the purposes of exercising or performing his or her powers or duties under those Acts, and

    (ii) be accompanied by a member of the Garda Síochána who shall, on request by a person affected, identify himself or herself as a member of the Garda Síochána and shall state that he or she is accompanied by an authorised officer;

(*b*) where, in pursuance of the functions of the body, an authorised officer exercises or performs in writing any of his or her powers or duties under the Revenue Acts or any provision of any other enactment, whenever passed, which relates to Revenue, such exercise or performance of his or her powers or duties shall be done in the name of the body and not in the name of the individual authorised officer involved, notwithstanding any provision to the contrary in any of those enactments;

(*c*) in any proceedings arising out of the exercise or performance, in pursuance of the functions of the body, of powers or duties by an authorised officer, any documents relating to such proceedings shall not reveal the identity of any authorised officer, notwithstanding any requirements to the contrary in any provision, and in any proceedings the identity of such officer other than as an authorised officer shall not be revealed other than to the judge or the Appeal Commissioner, as the case may be, hearing the case;

(*d*) where, in pursuance of the functions of the body, an authorised officer is required, in any proceedings, to give evidence and the judge or the Appeal Commissioner, as the case may be, is satisfied that there are reasonable grounds in the public interest to direct that evidence to be given by such authorised officer should be given in the hearing and not in the sight of any person, he or she may so direct.

Cross-references

This section to be construed together with the Customs Acts, in so far as relating to customs: s 1104(2).

This section to be construed together with the Value Added Tax Acts 1972-1997, in so far as relating to value added tax: s 1104(3).

This section to be construed together with the Stamp Act 1891 and the enactments amending or extending that Act, in so far as relating to stamp duties: s 1104(4).

This section to be construed together with the Capital Acquisitions Tax Act 1976, and the enactments amending or extending that Act, in so far as relating to capital acquisitions tax: s 1104(5).

This section to be construed together with FA 1983 Pt VI and the enactments amending or extending that Part, in so far as relating to residential property tax: s 1104(6).

Former enactment

FA 1993 s 19A; DCITPA 1996 s 12; CABA 1996 s 23.

872 Use of information relating to other taxes and duties

(1) Any information acquired, whether before or after the passing of this Act, in connection with any tax or duty under the care and management of the Revenue Commissioners may be used by them for any purpose connected with any other tax or duty under their care and management.

...

Cross-references

Subs (1) to be construed together with the Customs Acts, in so far as relating to customs: s 1104(2).

Subs (1) to be construed together with the Value Added Tax Acts 1972-1997, in so far as relating to value added tax: s 1104(3).

Subs (1) to be construed together with the Stamp Act 1891 and the enactments amending or extending that Act, in so far as relating to stamp duties: s 1104(4).

Subs (1) to be construed together with the Capital Acquisitions Tax Act 1976, and the enactments amending or extending that Act, in so far as relating to capital acquisitions tax: s 1104(5).

Subs (1) to be construed together with FA 1983 Pt VI and the enactments amending or extending that Part, in so far as relating to residential property tax: s 1104(6).

Former enactment

FA1928 s34(2); FA 1996 s 130.

PART 38
RETURNS OF INCOME AND GAINS, OTHER OBLIGATIONS AND RETURNS, AND REVENUE POWERS

CHAPTER 3
Other obligations and returns

887 Use of electronic data processing

[(1) In this section—

"the Acts" means—

    (*a*) the Tax Acts,

    (*b*) the Capital Gains Tax Acts,

    (*c*) the Value-Added Tax Act, 1972, and the enactments amending or extending that Act,

    (*d*) the Capital Acquisitions Tax Act, 1976, and the enactments amending or extending that Act, and

    (*e*) Part VI of the Finance Act, 1983,

and any instrument made under any of these enactments;

"record" means any document which a person is obliged by the Acts to keep, to issue or to produce for inspection, and any other written or printed material.

(2) For the purposes of the Acts, but subject to section 17 of the Value-Added Tax Act, 1972, a record may be stored, maintained, transmitted, reproduced or communicated, as the case may be, by any electronic, photographic or other process that—

(*a*) provides a reliable assurance as to the integrity of the record from the time when it was first generated in its final form by such electronic, photographic or other process,

(*b*) permits the record to be displayed in intelligible form and produced in an intelligible printed format,

(*c*) permits the record to be readily accessible for subsequent reference in accordance with paragraph (*b*), and

(*d*) conforms to the information technology and procedural requirements drawn up and published by the Revenue Commissioners in accordance with subsection (3).

(3) The Revenue Commissioners shall from time to time draw up and publish in Iris Oifigiúil the information technology and procedural requirements to which any electronic, photographic or other process used by a person for the storage, maintenance, transmission, reproduction and communication of any record shall conform.

(4) The authority conferred on the Revenue Commissioners by this section to draw up and publish requirements shall be construed as including the authority exercisable in a like manner to revoke and replace or to amend any such requirements.

(5) (*a*) Every person who preserves records by any electronic, photographic or other process, when required to do so by a notice in writing from the Revenue Commissioners, shall, within such period as is specified in the notice, not being less than 21 days from the date of service of the notice, supply to the Revenue Commissioners full particulars relating to the process used by that person, including full particulars relating to software (within the meaning of section 912).

(*b*) A person who fails or refuses to comply with a notice served on the person under paragraph (*a*) shall be liable to a penalty of [€1,265].[1]

(6) (*a*) Subject to paragraph (*b*), where records are kept by a person (being a person who is obliged by the Acts to keep such records) by any electronic, photographic or other process which does not conform with the requirements referred to in paragraphs (*a*) to (*d*) of subsection (2), then the person shall be deemed to have failed to comply with that obligation and that person shall be liable to the same penalties as the person would be liable to if the person had failed to comply with any obligation under the Acts in relation to the keeping of records.

(*b*) Paragraph (*a*) shall not apply where the person referred to in that paragraph complies with any obligation under the Acts in relation to the keeping of records other than in accordance with the provisions of subsection (2).

(7) Where records are preserved by any electronic, photographic or other process, information contained in a document produced by any such process shall, subject to the rules of court, be admissible in evidence in any proceedings, whether civil or criminal, to the same extent as the records themselves.

(8) The Revenue Commissioners may nominate any of their officers to discharge any function authorised by this section to be discharged by the Revenue Commissioners.][2]

Amendments

1   Substituted by FA 2001 s 232(3)(*a*)(i) with effect from 1 January 2002; previously "£1,000".

2   Substituted by FA 2001 s 232(1)(*a*) with effect from 15 February 2001 (as a result of FA 2002 s 138 and Sch 6 paras 5(*f*) and 6(*e*)(i)).

Cross-references

Obligation to keep records, subs (2): s 886(3)(*b*).

Power of inspection, PAYE: s 903(1)("records").

This section to be construed together with the Value Added Tax Acts 1972-1997, in so far as relating to value added tax: s 1104(3).

This section to be construed together with the Capital Acquisitions Tax Act 1976, and the enactments amending or extending that Act, in so far as relating to capital acquisitions tax: s 1104(5).

This section to be construed together with FA 1983 Pt VI and the enactments amending or extending that Part, in so far as relating to residential property tax: s 1104(6).

Tax Briefing

TB46 Dec 2001 pp 24-25 - Electronic Storage - Retention of Tax Records in Electronic Format.

Definitions

Capital Gains Tax Acts: s 1(2); person: IA 1937 s 11(*c*); rules of court: IA 1937 Sch; Tax Acts: s 1(2); writing: IA 1937 Sch.

Former enactments

FA 1986 s 113(1)-(3); FA 1993 s 99.

PART 38
RETURNS OF INCOME AND GAINS, OTHER OBLIGATIONS AND RETURNS, AND REVENUE POWERS

CHAPTER 3
Other Obligations and Returns

898 Returns of copies of rates and production of certain valuations

(1) In this section, **"rating authority"** means—

 (*a*)   the corporation of a county or other borough,

 (*b*)   the council of a county, or

 (*c*)   the council of an urban district.

(2) For the purpose of assessing tax chargeable under Schedule D, the secretary, clerk, or person acting as such, to a rating authority shall, when required by notice from an inspector, transmit to the inspector within such time as may be specified in the notice true copies of the last county rate or municipal rate made by the authority for its rating area or any part of that area.

(3) The Revenue Commissioners shall pay to any such person the expenses of making all such copies, not exceeding the rate of [€2][1] for every 100 ratings.

(4) Every person shall, at the request of any inspector or other officer acting in the execution of the Tax Acts, produce as soon as may be to such inspector or officer, as appropriate, any survey, valuation or record on which the rates for any rating area or part of any such area are assessed, made or collected, or any rate or assessment made under any Act relating to the county rate or municipal rate, which is in that person's custody or

possession, and shall permit the inspector or other officer to inspect the same and to take copies of or extracts from any such survey, valuation or record, without any payment.

Amendments

1   Substituted by FA 2001 s 240(1) and (2)(*a*) and Sch 5 Pt 1 for 2002 and later tax years; previously "£1".

Cross-references

Disclosure of information to rating authorities, meaning of "rating authority" applied: s 1092(3).
Penalty: Sch 29 column 2.

Definitions

Tax Acts: s 1(2); inspector: ss 2(1), 5(1), 852; person: IA 1937 s 11(*c*).

Former enactments

FA 1974 s 73(1)-(4); CTA 1976 s 147(1)-(2).

CHAPTER 4
Revenue powers

905 Inspection of documents and records

(1) In this section—

"authorised officer" means an officer of the Revenue Commissioners authorised by them in writing to exercise the powers conferred by this section;

"property" means any asset relating to a tax liability;

[**"records"** means any document or any other written or printed material in any form, and includes any information stored, maintained or preserved by means of any mechanical or electronic device, whether or not stored, maintained or preserved in a legible form—

    (i)   which relates to a business carried on by a person, or

    (ii) which a person is obliged by any provision relating to tax to keep, retain, issue or produce for inspection or which may be inspected under any provision relating to tax;][1]

"tax" means any tax, duty, levy or charge under the care and management of the Revenue Commissioners;

"tax liability" means any existing liability to tax or further liability to tax which may be established by an authorised officer following the exercise or performance of his or her powers or duties under this section.

(2) (*a*) An authorised officer may at all reasonable times enter any premises or place where the authorised officer has reason to believe that—

      (i)   any trade, profession or other activity, the profits or gains of which are chargeable to tax, is or has been carried on,

     (ii) anything is or has been done in connection with any trade, profession or other activity the profits or gains of which are chargeable to tax,

   (iii) any records relating to—

          (I)   any trade, profession, other source of profits or gains or chargeable gains,

(II) any tax liability, or

(III) any repayments of tax in regard to any person,

are or may be kept, or

(iv) any property is or has been located,

and the authorised officer may—

(A) require any person who is on those premises or in that place, other than a person who is there to purchase goods or to receive a service, to produce any records or property,

(B) if the authorised officer has reason to believe that any of the records or property which he or she has required to be produced to him or her under this subsection have not been produced, search on those premises or in that place for those records or property,

(C) examine any records or property and take copies of or extracts from any records,

(D) remove any records and retain them for a reasonable time for the purposes of their further examination or for the purposes of any legal proceedings instituted by an officer of the Revenue Commissioners or for the purposes of any criminal proceedings, and

(E) examine property listed in any records.

(*b*) An authorised officer may in the exercise or performance of his or her powers or duties under this section require any person whom he or she has reason to believe—

(i) is or was carrying on any trade, profession or other activity the profits or gains of which are chargeable to tax,

(ii) is or was liable to any tax, or

(iii) has information relating to any tax liability,

to give the authorised officer all reasonable assistance, including providing information and explanations or furnishing documents and making available for inspection property as required by the authorised officer in relation to any tax liability or any repayment of tax in regard to any person.

(*c*) Nothing in this subsection shall be construed as requiring any person carrying on a profession, or any person employed by any person carrying on a profession, to produce to an authorised officer any documents relating to a client, other than such documents—

(i) as pertain to the payment of fees to the person carrying on the profession or to other financial transactions of the person carrying on the profession,

(ii) as are otherwise material to the tax liability of the person carrying on the profession, or

(iii) as are already required to be provided following a request issued under [section 128 of the Stamp Duties Consolidation Act, 1999],[2] and in particular that person shall not be required to disclose any information or professional advice of a confidential nature given to a client.

...³

(*e*) An authorised officer shall not, without the consent of the occupier, enter any premises, or that portion of any premises, which is occupied wholly and exclusively as a private residence, except on production by such officer of a warrant issued by a Judge of the District Court expressly authorising the authorised officer to so enter.

(*f*) A Judge of the District Court may issue a warrant under paragraph (*e*) if satisfied by information on oath that it is proper to do so for the purposes of this section.

[(2A)(*a*) In this subsection **"the Acts"** has the meaning assigned to it by section 1078(1).

(*b*) Without prejudice to any power conferred by subsection (2), if a Judge of the District Court is satisfied by information on oath that there are reasonable grounds for suspecting—

   (i) that a person may have failed or may fail to comply with any provision of the Acts,

  (ii) that any such failure is likely to have led or to lead to serious prejudice to the proper assessment or collection of tax (having regard to the amount of any tax liability that arises or might arise from such failure), and

 (iii) that records, which are material to the proper assessment or collection of tax are likely to be kept or concealed at any premises or place,

the Judge may issue a search warrant.

(*c*) A search warrant issued under this subsection shall be expressed and shall operate to authorise an authorised officer accompanied by such other named officers of the Revenue Commissioners and such other named persons as the authorised officer considers necessary, at any time or times within one month of the date of issue of the warrant, to enter (if need be by force) the premises or other place named or specified in the warrant, to search such premises or other place, to examine anything found there, to inspect any records found there and, if there are reasonable grounds for suspecting that any records found there are material to the proper assessment or collection of tax, or that the records may be required for the purpose of any legal proceedings instituted by an officer of the Revenue Commissioners or for the purpose of any criminal proceedings, remove such records and retain them for so long as they are reasonably required for the purpose aforesaid.]⁴

(3) A person who does not comply with any requirement of an authorised officer in the exercise or performance of the authorised officer's powers or duties under this section shall be liable to a penalty of [€1,265]⁵.

(4) An authorised officer when exercising or performing his or her powers or duties under this section shall on request show his or her authorisation for the purposes of this section.

1 Defintion of "records" substituted by FA 2002 s 132(*d*) with effect from 1 January 2002.
2 Substituted by SDCA 1999 s 162 and Sch 4 with effect from 15 December 1999; previously "section 16 of the Stamp Act, 1891".
3 Subs (2)(*d*) deleted by FA 1999 s 207(*f*)(i) with effect from 25 March 1999.
4 Subs (2A) inserted by FA 1999 s 207(*f*)(ii) with effect from 25 March 1999.
5 Substituted by FA 2001 s 240(1) and (2)(*k*) and Sch 5 Pt 1 as respects any act or omission which takes place or begins on or after 1 January 2002; previously "£1,000".

Cross-references

Authorised officers and Garda Síochána: s 906.

This section to be construed together with the Customs Acts, in so far as relating to customs: s 1104(2).

This section to be construed together with the Value Added Tax Acts 1972-1997, in so far as relating to value added tax: s 1104(3).

This section to be construed together with the Stamp Act 1891 and the enactments amending or extending that Act, in so far as relating to stamp duties: s 1104(4).

This section to be construed together with the Capital Acquisitions Tax Act 1976, and the enactments amending or extending that Act, in so far as relating to capital acquisitions tax: s 1104(5).

This section to be construed together with FA 1983 Pt VI and the enactments amending or extending that Part, in so far as relating to residential property tax: s 1104(6).

Revenue information

Information leaflet IT32 - Revenue Audit - Guide for Small Businesses
Code of Practice for Revenue Auditors (Nov. 1998)

Statement of practice

Revenue powers: SP GEN/1/94, May 1994.

Case law

Held was a clear implication that the time and place for such inspection set by the taxpayer had to be reasonable: *Johnson v IRC*, [1996] STI 270.

Definition

inspector: ss 2(1), 5(1), 852; person: IA 1937 s 11(*c*); profession: ss 2(1), 5(1); trade: ss 3(1), 4(1), 5(1).

Former enactment

FA 1976 s 34; FA 1992 s 232.

906 Authorised officers and Garda Síochána

Where an authorised officer (within the meaning of section 903, 904 or 905, as the case may be) in accordance with section 903, 904 or 905 enters any premises or place, the authorised officer may be accompanied by a member or members of the Garda Síochána, and any such member may arrest without warrant any person who obstructs or interferes with the authorised officer in the exercise or performance of his or her powers or duties under any of those sections.

Cross-references

This section to be construed together with the Customs Acts, in so far as relating to customs: s 1104(2).

This section to be construed together with the Value Added Tax Acts 1972-1997, in so far as relating to value added tax: s 1104(3).

This section to be construed together with the Stamp Act 1891 and the enactments amending or extending that Act, in so far as relating to stamp duties: s 1104(4).

This section to be construed together with the Capital Acquisitions Tax Act 1976, and the enactments amending or extending that Act, in so far as relating to capital acquisitions tax: s 1104(5).

This section to be construed together with FA 1983 Pt VI and the enactments amending or extending that Part, in so far as relating to residential property tax: s 1104(6).

Former enactment
FA 1992 s 236.

906A Information to be furnished by financial institutions

[(1) In this section and in sections 907 and 908—

"the Acts" has the meaning assigned to it by section 1078(1);

"authorised officer" means an officer of the Revenue Commissioners authorised by them in writing to exercise the powers conferred by this section, or, as the case may be, section 907 or 908;

"books, records or other documents" includes—

(a) any records used in the business of a financial institution, or used in the transfer department of a financial institution acting as registrar of securities, whether—

    (i) comprised in bound volume, loose-leaf binders or other loose-leaf filing system, loose-leaf ledger sheets, pages, folios or cards, or

    (ii) kept on microfilm, magnetic tape or in any non-legible form (by the use of electronics or otherwise) which is capable of being reproduced in a legible form,

(b) every electronic or other automatic means, if any, by which any such thing in non-legible form is so capable of being reproduced,

(c) documents in manuscript, documents which are typed, printed, stencilled or created by any other mechanical or partly mechanical process in use from time to time and documents which are produced by any photographic or photostatic process, and

(d) correspondence and records of other communications between a financial institution and its customers;

"connected person" has the same meaning as in section 10; but an individual (other than in the capacity as a trustee of a settlement) shall be connected with another individual only if that other individual is the spouse of or a minor child of the first-mentioned individual;

"deposit" and **"interest"** have, respectively, the meaning assigned to them by section 256(1);

[**"financial institution"** means—

(a) a person who holds or has held a licence under section 9 of the Central Bank Act, 1971,

(b) a person referred to in section 7(4) of the Central Bank Act, 1971, or

(c) a credit institution (within the meaning of the European Communities (Licensing and Supervision of Credit Institutions) Regulations, 1992 (SI No 395 of 1992)) which has been authorised by the Central Bank of Ireland to carry on business of a credit institution in accordance with the provisions of the supervisory enactments (within the meaning of those Regulations);][1]

"liability" in relation to a person means any liability in relation to tax to which the person is or may be, or may have been, subject, or the amount of such liability;

"tax" means any tax, duty, levy or charge under the care and management of the Revenue Commissioners.

(2) Notwithstanding any obligation as to secrecy or other restriction upon disclosure of information imposed by or under statute or otherwise, and subject to this section, an authorised officer may, for the purpose of enquiring into a liability in relation to a person (in this section referred to as the **"taxpayer"**), serve on a financial institution a notice in writing requiring the financial institution, within such period as may be specified in the notice, not being less than 30 days from the date of the service of the notice, to do either or both of the following, namely—

(*a*) to make available for inspection by the authorised officer such books, records or other documents as are in the financial institution's power, possession or procurement and as contain, or may (in the authorised officer's opinion formed on reasonable grounds) contain, information relevant to a liability in relation to the taxpayer,

(*b*) to furnish to the authorised officer, in writing or otherwise, such information, explanations and particulars as the authorised officer may reasonably require, being information, explanations and particulars that are relevant to any such liability,

and which are specified in the notice.

(3) Where, in compliance with the requirements of a notice under subsection (2), a financial institution makes available for inspection by an authorised officer, books, records or other documents, it shall afford the authorised officer reasonable assistance, including information, explanations and particulars, in relation to the use of all the electronic or other automatic means, if any, by which the books, records or other documents, in so far as they are in a non-legible form, are capable of being reproduced in a legible form and any data equipment or any associated apparatus or material.

(4) An authorised officer shall not serve a notice on a financial institution under subsection (2) without the consent in writing of a Revenue Commissioner and without having reasonable grounds to believe that the financial institution is likely to have information relevant to a liability in relation to the taxpayer.

(5) Without prejudice to the generality of subsection (2), the books, records or other documents which a financial institution may be required by notice under that subsection to deliver or to make available and the information, explanations and particulars which it may likewise be required to furnish, may include books, records or other documents and information, explanations and particulars relating to a person who is connected with the taxpayer.

(6) The persons who may be treated as a taxpayer for the purposes of this section include a company which has been dissolved and an individual who has died.

(7) A notice served under subsection (2) shall name the taxpayer in relation to whose liability the authorised officer is enquiring.

(8) Where an authorised officer serves a notice under subsection (2), a copy of such notice shall be given by the authorised officer to the taxpayer concerned.

(9) Where, in compliance with a notice served under subsection (2), a financial institution makes books, records or other documents available for inspection by an authorised officer, the authorised officer may make extracts from or copies of all or any part of the books, records or other documents.

(10) A financial institution which fails or refuses to comply with a notice issued under subsection (2) or which fails or refuses to afford reasonable assistance to an authorised officer as required under subsection (3), shall be liable to a penalty of [€19,045]² and, if the failure or refusal to comply with such notice continues after the expiry of the period specified in the notice served under subsection (2), a further penalty of [€2,535]³ for each day on which the failure or refusal continues.]⁴

Amendments

¹   Definition of "financial institution" substituted by FA 2000 s 68(*c*) with effect from 6 April 2000.

²   Substituted by FA 2001 s 240(1) and (2)(*k*) and Sch 5 Pt 1 as respects any act or omission which takes place or begins on or after 1 January 2002; previously "£15,000".

³   Substituted by FA 2001 s 240(1) and (2)(*k*) and Sch 5 Pt 1 as respects any act or omission which takes place or begins on or after 1 January 2002; previously "£2,000".

⁴   Section 906A inserted by FA 1999 s 207(*g*) with effect from 25 March 1999.

910 Power to obtain information from Minister of the Government

[(1) For the purposes of the assessment, charge, collection and recovery of any tax or duty placed under their care and management, the Revenue Commissioners may, by notice in writing, request any Minister of the Government or any body established by or under statute to provide them with such information in the possession of that Minister or body in relation to payments for any purposes made by that Minister or by that body, whether on that Minister's or that body's own behalf or on behalf of any other person, to such persons or classes of persons as the Revenue Commissioners may specify in the notice and a Minister of the Government or body of whom or of which such a request is made shall provide such information as may be so specified.]¹

(2) The Revenue Commissioners may nominate any of their officers to perform any acts and discharge any functions authorised by this section to be performed or discharged by the Revenue Commissioners.

Amendments

¹   Subs (1) substituted by FA 1999 s 208 with effect from 25 March 1999.

Cross-references

This section to be construed together with the Customs Acts, in so far as relating to customs: s 1104(2).

This section to be construed together with the Value Added Tax Acts 1972-1997, in so far as relating to value added tax: s 1104(3).

This section to be construed together with the Stamp Act 1891 and the enactments amending or extending that Act, in so far as relating to stamp duties: s 1104(4).

This section to be construed together with the Capital Acquisitions Tax Act 1976, and the enactments amending or extending that Act, in so far as relating to capital acquisitions tax: s 1104(5).

This section to be construed together with FA 1983 Pt VI and the enactments amending or extending that Part, in so far as relating to residential property tax: s 1104(6).

Definitions

person: IA 1937 s 11(*c*); tax: s 3(1).

Former enactment

FA 1995 s 175.

912 Computer documents and records

(1) In this section—

"**the Acts**" means—

- (*a*) the Customs Acts,
- (*b*) the statutes relating to the duties of excise and to the management of those duties,
- (*c*) the Tax Acts,
- (*d*) the Capital Gains Tax Acts,
- (*e*) the Value-Added Tax Act, 1972, and the enactments amending or extending that Act,
- (*f*) the Capital Acquisitions Tax Act, 1976, and the enactments amending or extending that Act, and
- (*g*) Part VI of the Finance Act, 1983,

and any instruments made thereunder;

"**data**" means information in a form in which it can be processed;

"**data equipment**" means any electronic, photographic, magnetic, optical or other equipment for processing data;

"**processing**" means performing automatically logical or arithmetical operations on data, or the storing, maintenance, transmission, reproduction or communication of data;

"**records**" means documents which a person is obliged by any provision of the Acts to keep, issue or produce for inspection, and any other written or printed material;

"**software**" means any sequence of instructions used in conjunction with data equipment for the purpose of processing data or controlling the operation of the data equipment.

(2) Any provision under the Acts which—

- (*a*) requires a person to keep, retain, issue or produce any records or cause any records to be kept, retained, issued or produced, or
- (*b*) permits an officer of the Revenue Commissioners—
  - (i) to inspect any records,
  - (ii) to enter premises and search for any records, or
  - (iii) to take extracts from or copies of or remove any records,

shall, where the records are processed by data equipment, apply to the data equipment together with any associated software, data, apparatus or material as it applies to the records.

(3) An officer of the Revenue Commissioners may in the exercise or performance of his or her powers or duties require—

(a) the person by or on whose behalf the data equipment is or has been used, or

(b) any person having charge of, or otherwise concerned with the operation of, the data equipment or any associated apparatus or material,

to afford him or her all reasonable assistance in relation to the exercise or performance of those powers or duties.

Cross-references

This section to be construed together with the Customs Acts, in so far as relating to customs: s 1104(2).
This section to be construed together with the Value Added Tax Acts 1972-1997, in so far as relating to value added tax: s 1104(3).
This section to be construed together with the Capital Acquisitions Tax Act 1976, and the enactments amending or extending that Act, in so far as relating to capital acquisitions tax: s 1104(5).
This section to be construed together with FA 1983 Pt VI and the enactments amending or extending that Part, in so far as relating to residential property tax: s 1104(6).

Statement of practice

Revenue powers: SP GEN/1/94, May 1994.

Definition

Tax Acts: s 1(2); person: IA 1937 s 11(c).

Former enactment

FA 1992 s 237.

PART 39
ASSESSMENTS

CHAPTER 1
Income Tax and Corporation Tax

928 Transmission to Collector-General of particulars of sums to be collected

(1) After assessments to income tax and corporation tax have been made, the inspectors shall transmit particulars of the sums to be collected to the Collector-General for collection.

(2) The entering by an inspector or other authorised officer of details of an assessment to income tax or corporation tax and of the tax charged in such an assessment in an electronic, photographic or other record from which the Collector-General may extract such details by electronic, photographic or other process shall constitute transmission of such details by the inspector or other authorised officer to the Collector-General.

(3) Subsection (2) shall apply for the purposes of value-added tax as it applies for the purposes of income tax or corporation tax with the substitution of "value-added tax" for "income tax or corporation tax".

Cross-references

Capital gains tax, applied by: s 931(3).

Collection of capital gains tax: s 976(1).

Collector-General: s 851(2).

Corporation tax, subs (1): s 973.

Evidence of electronic transmission of particulars of income tax to be collected in proceedings for recovery of tax, subs (2): s 967.

Generation of estimates by electronic, photographic or other process: s 990A(*b*).

Income Tax (Relevant Contracts) Regulations 2000, SI No 71 of 2000: ITRCR 2000 Reg 15(2).

Self-assessment, notices of preliminary tax, subs (2): s 953(6)(*c*).

Subss (2)-(3) to be construed together with the Value Added Tax Acts 1972-1997, in so far as relating to value added tax: s 1104(3).

Definitions

inspector: ss 2(1), 5(1), 852.

Former enactments

ITA 1967 s 187(1); FA 1974 s 86 and Sch 2 Pt I; CTA 1976 s 147(1)-(2); FA 1986 s 113(5); FA 1996 s 132(2) and Sch 5 Pt II.

PART 42
COLLECTION AND RECOVERY

CHAPTER 4
Collection and Recovery of Income Tax on Certain Emoluments (PAYE System)

987 Penalties for breach of regulations

...

(4) In proceedings for recovery of a penalty under this section—

   (*a*) a certificate signed by an officer of the Revenue Commissioners which certifies that he or she has inspected the relevant records of the Revenue Commissioners and that it appears from them that during a stated period—

      (i) a stated return, statement, notification or certificate was not received from the defendant,

      (ii) stated wages sheets or other records or documents were not produced by the defendant,

      (iii) the defendant did not remit stated tax to the Collector-General, or

      (iv) the defendant did not make a stated deduction or repayment of tax,

      shall be evidence until the contrary is proved that the defendant did not during that period send that return, statement, notification or certificate or did not produce those wages sheets or other records or documents or did not remit that tax to the Collector-General or did not make that deduction or repayment of tax;

   (*b*) a certificate signed by an officer of the Revenue Commissioners which certifies that he or she has inspected the relevant records of the Revenue Commissioners and that it appears from them that a stated return or other document was duly sent to the defendant on a stated day shall be evidence until the contrary is proved that that person received that return or other document in the ordinary course;

(c) a certificate signed by an officer of the Revenue Commissioners which certifies that he or she has inspected the relevant records of the Revenue Commissioners and that it appears from them that during a stated period the defendant was an employer or a person whose name and address were registered in the register kept and maintained under [Regulation 7(4) of the Income Tax (Employments) (Consolidated) Regulations 2001 (SI No 559 of 2001)][1], shall be evidence until the contrary is proved that the defendant was during that period an employer or, as the case may be, a person whose name and address were so registered;

(d) a certificate certifying as provided for in paragraph (a), (b) or (c) and purporting to be signed by an officer of the Revenue Commissioners may be tendered in evidence without proof and shall be deemed until the contrary is proved to have been signed by an officer of the Revenue Commissioners.

Amendments

[1]   Substituted by FA 2002 s 138 and Sch 6 para 3(p)(ii) with effect on and from 1 January 2002; previously "regulation 8(4) of the Income Tax (Employments) Regulations, 1960 (SI No 28 of 1960)".

CHAPTER 5
Miscellaneous provisions

1002 Deduction from payments due to defaulters of amounts due in relation to tax

(1) (a)   In this section, except where the context otherwise requires—

"**the Acts**" means—

(i)   the Customs Acts,

(ii)   the statutes relating to the duties of excise and to the management of those duties,

(iii)   the Tax Acts,

(iv)   the Capital Gains Tax Acts,

(v)   the Value-Added Tax Act, 1972, and the enactments amending or extending that Act,

(vi)   the Capital Acquisitions Tax Act, 1976, and the enactments amending or extending that Act, and

(vii)   the [Stamp Duties Consolidation Act, 1999],[1] and the enactments amending or extending that Act,

and any instruments made thereunder;

"**additional debt**", in relation to a relevant person who has received a notice of attachment in respect of a taxpayer, means any amount which, at any time after the time of the receipt by the relevant person of the notice of attachment but before the end of the relevant period in relation to the notice, would be a debt due by the relevant person to the taxpayer if a notice of attachment were received by the relevant person at that time;

"debt", in relation to a notice of attachment given to a relevant person in respect of a taxpayer and in relation to that relevant person and taxpayer, means, subject to paragraphs (*b*) to (*e*), the amount or aggregate amount of any money which, at the time the notice of attachment is received by the relevant person, is due by the relevant person (whether on that person's own account or as an agent or trustee) to the taxpayer, irrespective of whether the taxpayer has applied for the payment (to the taxpayer or any other person) or for the withdrawal of all or part of the money;

"deposit" means a sum of money paid to a financial institution on terms under which it will be repaid with or without interest and either on demand or at a time or in circumstances agreed by or on behalf of the person making the payment and the financial institution to which it is made;

"emoluments" means anything assessable to income tax under Schedule E;

"financial institution" means a holder of a licence issued under section 9 of the Central Bank Act, 1971, or a person referred to in section 7(4) of that Act, and includes a branch of a financial institution which records deposits in its books as liabilities of the branch;

"further return" means a return made by a relevant person under subsection (4);

"interest on unpaid tax", in relation to a specified amount specified in a notice of attachment, means interest that has accrued to the date on which the notice of attachment is given under any provision of the Acts providing for the charging of interest in respect of the unpaid tax, including interest on an undercharge of tax which is attributable to fraud or neglect, specified in the notice of attachment;

"notice of attachment" means a notice under subsection (2);

"notice of revocation" means a notice under subsection (10);

"penalty" means a monetary penalty imposed on a taxpayer under a provision of the Acts;

"relevant period", in relation to a notice of attachment, means, as respects the relevant person to whom the notice of attachment is given, the period commencing at the time at which the notice is received by the relevant person and ending on the earliest of—

(i) the date on which the relevant person completes the payment to the Revenue Commissioners out of the debt, or the aggregate of the debt and any additional debt, due by the relevant person to the taxpayer named in the notice, of an amount equal to the specified amount in relation to the taxpayer,

(ii) the date on which the relevant person receives a notice of revocation of the notice of attachment, and

(iii) where the relevant person or the taxpayer named in the notice—

(I) is declared bankrupt, the date the relevant person or the taxpayer is so declared, or

(II) is a company which commences to be wound up, the relevant date within the meaning of section 285 of the Companies Act, 1963, in relation to the winding up;

"relevant person", in relation to a taxpayer, means a person whom the Revenue Commissioners have reason to believe may have, at the time a notice of attachment is received by such person in respect of a taxpayer, a debt due to the taxpayer;

"return" means a return made by a relevant person under subsection $(2)(a)$(iii);

"specified amount" has the meaning assigned to it by subsection $(2)(a)$(ii);

"tax" means any tax, duty, levy or charge which in accordance with any provision of the Acts is placed under the care and management of the Revenue Commissioners;

"taxpayer" means a person who is liable to pay, remit or account for tax to the Revenue Commissioners under the Acts.

(b) Where a relevant person is a financial institution, any amount or aggregate amount of money, including interest on that money, which at the time the notice of attachment is received by the relevant person is a deposit held by the relevant person—

    (i) to the credit of the taxpayer for the taxpayer's sole benefit, or

    (ii) to the credit of the taxpayer and any other person or persons for their joint benefit,

shall be regarded as a debt due by the relevant person to the taxpayer at that time.

(c) Any amount of money due by the relevant person to the taxpayer as emoluments under a contract of service shall not be regarded as a debt due to the taxpayer.

(d) Where there is a dispute as to an amount of money which is due by the relevant person to the taxpayer, the amount in dispute shall be disregarded for the purposes of determining the amount of the debt.

(e) In the case referred to in paragraph (b), a deposit held by a relevant person which is a financial institution to the credit of the taxpayer and any other person or persons (in this paragraph referred to as **"the other party or parties"**) for their joint benefit shall be deemed (unless evidence to the contrary is produced to the satisfaction of the relevant person within 10 days of the giving of the notices specified in subsection $(2)(e)$) to be held to the benefit of the taxpayer and the other party or parties to the deposit equally, and accordingly only the portion of the deposit so deemed shall be regarded as a debt due by the relevant person to the taxpayer at the time the notice of attachment is received by the relevant person and, where such evidence is produced within the specified time, only so much of the deposit as is shown to be held to the benefit of the taxpayer shall be regarded as a debt due by the relevant person to the taxpayer at that time.

(2) (*a*) Subject to subsection (3), where a taxpayer has made default whether before or after the passing of this Act in paying, remitting or accounting for any tax, interest on unpaid tax, or penalty to the Revenue Commissioners, the Revenue Commissioners may, if the taxpayer has not made good the default, give to a relevant person in relation to the taxpayer a notice in writing (in this section referred to as **"the notice of attachment"**) in which is entered—

   (i) the taxpayer's name and address,

   (ii) (I) the amount or aggregate amount, or

       (II) in a case where more than one notice of attachment is given to a relevant person or relevant persons in respect of a taxpayer, a portion of the amount or aggregate amount,

       of the taxes, interest on unpaid taxes and penalties in respect of which the taxpayer is in default at the time of the giving of the notice or notices of attachment (the amount, aggregate amount, or portion of the amount or aggregate amount, as the case may be, being referred to in this section as **"the specified amount"**), and

   (iii) a direction to the relevant person—

       (I) subject to paragraphs (*b*) and (*c*), to deliver to the Revenue Commissioners, within the period of 10 days from the time at which the notice of attachment is received by the relevant person, a return in writing specifying whether or not any debt is due by the relevant person to the taxpayer at the time the notice is received by the relevant person and, if any debt is so due, specifying the amount of the debt, and

       (II) if the amount of any debt is so specified, to pay to the Revenue Commissioners within the period referred to in clause (I) a sum equal to the amount of the debt so specified.

   (*b*) Where the amount of the debt due by the relevant person to the taxpayer is equal to or greater than the specified amount in relation to the taxpayer, the amount of the debt specified in the return shall be an amount equal to the specified amount.

   (*c*) Where the relevant person is a financial institution and the debt due by the relevant person to the taxpayer is part of a deposit held to the credit of the taxpayer and any other person or persons to their joint benefit, the return shall be made within a period of 10 days from—

       (i) the expiry of the period specified in the notices to be given under paragraph (*e*), or

       (ii) the production of the evidence referred to in paragraph (*e*)(II).

   (*d*) A relevant person to whom a notice of attachment has been given shall comply with the direction in the notice.

   (*e*) Where a relevant person which is a financial institution is given a notice of attachment and the debt due by the relevant person to the taxpayer is part of a deposit held by the relevant person to the credit of the taxpayer and any other person or persons (in this paragraph referred to as **"the other party or parties"**) for their joint benefit, the relevant person shall on receipt of the notice of attachment give to the taxpayer and the other party or parties to the deposit a notice in writing in which is entered—

(i)   the taxpayer's name and address,

(ii) the name and address of the person to whom a notice under this paragraph is given,

(iii) the name and address of the relevant person, and

(iv) the specified amount,

and which states that—

(I)   a notice of attachment under this section has been received in respect of the taxpayer,

(II) under this section a deposit is deemed (unless evidence to the contrary is produced to the satisfaction of the relevant person within 10 days of the giving of the notice under this paragraph) to be held to the benefit of the taxpayer and the other party or parties to the deposit equally, and

(III) unless such evidence is produced within the period specified in the notice given under this paragraph—

(A)   a sum equal to the amount of the deposit so deemed to be held to the benefit of the taxpayer (and accordingly regarded as a debt due to the taxpayer by the relevant person) shall be paid to the Revenue Commissioners, where that amount is equal to or less than the specified amount, and

(B)   where the amount of the deposit so deemed to be held to the benefit of the taxpayer (and accordingly regarded as a debt due to the taxpayer by the relevant person) is greater than the specified amount, a sum equal to the specified amount shall be paid to the Revenue Commissioners.

(3) An amount in respect of tax, interest on unpaid tax or a penalty, as respects which a taxpayer is in default as specified in subsection (2), shall not be entered in a notice of attachment unless—

(*a*)   a period of [14 days][2] has expired from the date on which such default commenced, and

(*b*)   the Revenue Commissioners have given the taxpayer a notice in writing (whether or not the document containing the notice also contains other information being communicated by the Revenue Commissioners to the taxpayer), not later than 7 days before the date of the receipt by the relevant person or relevant persons concerned of a notice of attachment, stating that if the amount is not paid it may be specified in a notice or notices of attachment and recovered under this section from a relevant person or relevant persons in relation to the taxpayer.

(4) If, when a relevant person receives a notice of attachment, the amount of the debt due by the relevant person to the taxpayer named in the notice is less than the specified amount in relation to the taxpayer or no debt is so due and, at any time after the receipt of the notice and before the end of the relevant period in relation to the notice, an additional debt becomes due by the relevant person to the taxpayer, the relevant person shall within 10 days of that time—

    (*a*) if the aggregate of the amount of any debt so due and the additional debt so due is equal to or less than the specified amount in relation to the taxpayer—

        (i) deliver a further return to the Revenue Commissioners specifying the additional debt, and

        (ii) pay to the Revenue Commissioners the amount of the additional debt,

and so on for each subsequent occasion during the relevant period in relation to the notice of attachment on which an additional debt becomes due by the relevant person to the taxpayer until—

        (I) the aggregate amount of the debt and the additional debt or debts so due equals the specified amount in relation to the taxpayer, or

        (II) paragraph (*b*) applies in relation to an additional debt, and

    (*b*) if the aggregate amount of any debt and the additional debt or debts so due to the taxpayer is greater than the specified amount in relation to the taxpayer—

        (i) deliver a further return to the Revenue Commissioners specifying such portion of the latest additional debt as when added to the aggregate of the debt and any earlier additional debts is equal to the specified amount in relation to the taxpayer, and

        (ii) pay to the Revenue Commissioners that portion of the additional debt.

(5) Where a relevant person delivers, either fraudulently or negligently, an incorrect return or further return that purports to be a return or further return made in accordance with this section, the relevant person shall be deemed to be guilty of an offence under section 1078.

(6) (*a*) Where a notice of attachment has been given to a relevant person in respect of a taxpayer, the relevant person shall not, during the relevant period in relation to the notice, make any disbursements out of the debt, or out of any additional debt, due by the relevant person to the taxpayer except to the extent that any such disbursement—

        (i) will not reduce the debt or the aggregate of the debt and any additional debts so due to an amount that is less than the specified amount in relation to the taxpayer, or

        (ii) is made pursuant to an order of a court.

    (*b*) For the purposes of this section, a disbursement made by a relevant person contrary to paragraph (*a*) shall be deemed not to reduce the amount of the debt or any additional debts due by the relevant person to the taxpayer.

(7) (*a*) Sections 1052 and 1054 shall apply to a failure by a relevant person to deliver a return required by a notice of attachment within the time specified in the notice

or to deliver a further return within the time specified in subsection (4) as they apply to a failure to deliver a return referred to in section 1052.

(b) A certificate signed by an officer of the Revenue Commissioners which certifies that he or she has examined the relevant records and that it appears from those records that during a specified period a specified return was not received from a relevant person shall be evidence until the contrary is proved that the relevant person did not deliver the return during that period.

(c) A certificate certifying as provided by paragraph (b) and purporting to be signed by an officer of the Revenue Commissioners may be tendered in evidence without proof and shall be deemed until the contrary is proved to have been so signed.

(8) Where a relevant person to whom a notice of attachment in respect of a taxpayer has been given—

(a) delivers the return required to be delivered by that notice but fails to pay to the Revenue Commissioners within the time specified in the notice the amount specified in the return or any part of that amount, or

(b) delivers a further return under subsection (4) but fails to pay to the Revenue Commissioners within the time specified in that subsection the amount specified in the further return or any part of that amount,

the amount specified in the return or further return or the part of that amount, as the case may be, which the relevant person has failed to pay to the Revenue Commissioners may, if the notice of attachment has not been revoked by a notice of revocation, be sued for and recovered by action or other appropriate proceedings at the suit of an officer of the Revenue Commissioners in any court of competent jurisdiction.

(9) Nothing in this section shall be construed as rendering any failure by a relevant person to make a return or further return required by this section, or to pay to the Revenue Commissioners the amount or amounts required by this section to be paid by the relevant person, liable to be treated as a failure to which section 1078 applies.

(10)(a) A notice of attachment given to a relevant person in respect of a taxpayer may be revoked by the Revenue Commissioners at any time by notice in writing given to the relevant person and shall be revoked forthwith if the taxpayer has paid the specified amount to the Revenue Commissioners.

(b) Where in pursuance of this section a relevant person pays any amount to the Revenue Commissioners out of a debt or an additional debt due by the relevant person to the taxpayer and, at the time of the receipt by the Revenue Commissioners of that amount, the taxpayer has paid to the Revenue Commissioners the amount or aggregate amount of the taxes, interest on unpaid taxes and penalties in respect of which the taxpayer is in default at the time of the giving of the notice or notices of attachment, the first-mentioned amount shall be refunded by the Revenue Commissioners forthwith to the taxpayer.

(11) Where a notice of attachment or a notice of revocation is given to a relevant person in relation to a taxpayer, a copy of such notice shall be given by the Revenue Commissioners to the taxpayer forthwith.

(12)(*a*) Where in pursuance of this section any amount is paid to the Revenue Commissioners by a relevant person, the relevant person shall forthwith give the taxpayer concerned a notice in writing specifying the payment, its amount and the reason for which it was made.

(*b*) On the receipt by the Revenue Commissioners of an amount paid in pursuance of this section, the Revenue Commissioners shall forthwith notify the taxpayer and the relevant person in writing of such receipt.

(13) Where in pursuance of this section a relevant person pays to the Revenue Commissioners the whole or part of the amount of a debt or an additional debt due by the relevant person to a taxpayer, or any portion of such an amount, the taxpayer shall allow such payment and the relevant person shall be acquitted and discharged of the amount of the payment as if it had been paid to the taxpayer.

(14) Where in pursuance of this section a relevant person is prohibited from making any disbursement out of a debt or an additional debt due to a taxpayer, no action shall lie against the relevant person in any court by reason of a failure to make any such disbursement.

(15) Any obligation on the Revenue Commissioners to maintain secrecy or any other restriction on the disclosure of information by the Revenue Commissioners shall not apply in relation to information contained in a notice of attachment.

(16) A notice of attachment in respect of a taxpayer shall not be given to a relevant person at a time when the relevant person or the taxpayer is an undischarged bankrupt or a company being wound up.

(17) The Revenue Commissioners may nominate any of their officers to perform any acts and discharge any functions authorised by this section to be performed or discharged by the Revenue Commissioners.

Amendments

1   Substituted by SDCA 1999 s 162 and Sch 4 with effect from 15 December 1999; previously "Stamp Act, 1891".

2   Substituted by FA 2001 s 238 with effect from 6 April 2001; previously "one month".

Cross-references

Taxes (Offset of Repayments) Regulations 2001, SI No 399 of 2001, reg 2(1) (interpretation - "liability of enforcement" para (*c*)).

This section to be construed together with the Customs Acts, in so far as relating to customs: s 1104(2).

This section to be construed together with the Value Added Tax Acts 1972-1997, in so far as relating to value added tax: s 1104(3).

This section to be construed together with the Stamp Act 1891 and the enactments amending or extending that Act, in so far as relating to stamp duties: s 1104(4).

This section to be construed together with the Capital Acquisitions Tax Act 1976, and the enactments amending or extending that Act, in so far as relating to capital acquisitions tax: s 1104(5).

Penalty, subss (2)(*a*)(iii)(I), (*c*), (4)a)(i), (*b*)(i): Sch 29 column 1.

Definitions

company: ss 4(1), 5(1); person: IA 1937 s 11(*c*); Tax Acts: s 1(2); writing: IA 1937 Sch.

Former enactments

FA 1988 s 73(1)(*b*)-(16) and (18); FA 1992 s 241(*a*)-(*d*).

1003 Payment of tax by means of donation of heritage items

(1) (*a*) In this section—

"the Acts" means—

(i) the Tax Acts (other than Chapter 8 of Part 6, Chapter 2 of Part 18 and Chapter 4 of this Part),

(ii) the Capital Gains Tax Acts, and

(iii) the Capital Acquisitions Tax Act, 1976, and the enactments amending or extending that Act,

and any instruments made thereunder;

"approved body" means—

(i) the National Archives,

(ii) the National Gallery of Ireland,

(iii) the National Library of Ireland,

(iv) the National Museum of Ireland,

(v) the Irish Museum of Modern Art, or

(vi) in relation to the offer of a gift of a particular item or collection of items, any other such body (being a body owned, or funded wholly or mainly, by the State or by any public or local authority) as may be approved, with the consent of the Minister for Finance, by the Minister for Arts, Heritage, Gaeltacht and the Islands for the purposes of this section;

"arrears of tax" means tax due and payable in accordance with any provision of the Acts (including any interest and penalties payable under any provision of the Acts in relation to such tax)—

(i) in the case of income tax, corporation tax or capital gains tax, in respect of the relevant period, or

(ii) in the case of gift tax or inheritance tax, before the commencement of the calendar year in which the relevant gift is made,

which has not been paid at the time a relevant gift is made;

"current liability" means—

(i) in the case of income tax or capital gains tax, any liability to such tax arising in the year of assessment in which the relevant gift is made,

(ii) in the case of corporation tax, any liability to such tax arising in the accounting period in which the relevant gift is made,

(iii) in the case of gift tax or inheritance tax, any liability to such tax which becomes due and payable in the calendar year in which the relevant gift is made;

"designated officer" means—

(i) the member of the selection committee who represents the appropriate approved body on that committee where the approved body is so represented, or

(ii) in any other case, a person nominated in that behalf by the Minister for Arts, Heritage, Gaeltacht and the Islands;

"heritage item" has the meaning assigned to it by subsection (2)(*a*);

"market value" has the meaning assigned to it by subsection (3);

"relevant gift" means a gift of a heritage item to an approved body in respect of which no consideration whatever (other than relief under this section) is received by the person making the gift, either directly or indirectly, from the approved body or otherwise;

"relevant period" means—

(i) in the case of income tax and capital gains tax, any year of assessment preceding the year in which the relevant gift is made, and

(ii) in the case of corporation tax, any accounting period preceding the accounting period in which the relevant gift is made;

"selection committee" means a committee consisting of—

(i) the Chairperson of the Heritage Council,

(ii) the Director of the Arts Council,

(iii) the Director of the National Archives,

(iv) the Director of the National Gallery of Ireland,

(v) the Director of the National Library of Ireland,

(vi) the Director of the National Museum of Ireland, and

(vii) the Director of the Irish Museum of Modern Art,

and includes any person duly acting in the capacity of any of those persons as a result of the person concerned being unable to fulfil his or her duties for any of the reasons set out in paragraph (*b*)(ii);

"tax" means income tax, corporation tax, capital gains tax, gift tax or inheritance tax, as the case may be, payable in accordance with any provision of the Acts;

"valuation date" means the date on which an application is made to the selection committee for a determination under subsection (2)(*a*).

(*b*) (i) The selection committee may act notwithstanding one or more vacancies among its members and may regulate its own procedure.

(ii) If and so long as a member of the selection committee is unable through illness, absence or other cause to fulfil his or her duties, a person nominated in that behalf by the member shall act as the member of the committee in the place of the member.

(2) (*a*)   In this section, **"heritage item"** means any kind of cultural item, including—

     (i)   any archaeological item, archive, book, estate record, manuscript and painting, and

     (ii)   any collection of cultural items and any collection of such items in their setting,

which, on application to the selection committee in writing in that behalf by a person who owns the item or collection of items, as the case may be, is determined by the selection committee, after consideration of any evidence in relation to the matter which the person submits to the committee and after such consultation (if any) as may seem to the committee to be necessary with such person or body of persons as in the opinion of the committee may be of assistance to them, to be an item or collection of items which is—

     (I)   an outstanding example of the type of item involved, pre-eminent in its class, whose export from the State would constitute a diminution of the accumulated cultural heritage of Ireland [or whose import into the State would constitute a significant enhancement of the accumulated cultural heritage of Ireland][1], and

     (II)   suitable for acquisition by an approved body.

   (*b*)   On receipt of an application for a determination under paragraph (*a*), the selection committee shall request the Revenue Commissioners in writing to value the item or collection of items, as the case may be, in accordance with subsection (3).

   (*c*)   The selection committee shall not make a determination under paragraph (*a*) where the market value of the item or collection of items, as the case may be, as determined by the Revenue Commissioners in accordance with subsection (3), at the valuation date—

     (i)   is less than [€100,000][2], or

     (ii)   exceeds an amount (which shall not be less than [€100,000][2]) determined by the formula—

$$[€6,000,000]^3 - M$$

where M is an amount (which may be nil) equal to the market value at the valuation date of the heritage item (if any) or the aggregate of the market values at the respective valuation dates of all the heritage items (if any), as the case may be, in respect of which a determination or determinations, as the case may be, under this subsection has been made by the selection committee in any one calendar year and not revoked in that year.

   (*d*)   (i)   An item or collection of items shall cease to be a heritage item for the purposes of this section if—

     (I)   the item or collection of items is sold or otherwise disposed of to a person other than an approved body,

(II) the owner of the item or collection of items notifies the selection committee in writing that it is not intended to make a gift of the item or collection of items to an approved body, or

(III) the gift of the item or collection of items is not made to an approved body within the calendar year following the year in which the determination is made under paragraph (*a*).

(ii) Where the selection committee becomes aware, at any time within the calendar year in which a determination under paragraph (*a*) is made in respect of an item or collection of items, that clause (I) or (II) of subparagraph (i) applies to the item or collection of items, the selection committee may revoke its determination with effect from that time.

(3) (*a*) For the purposes of this section, the market value of any item or collection of items (in this subsection referred to as **"the property"**) [shall, subject to paragraph (*d*), be estimated]⁴ to be the price which in the opinion of the Revenue Commissioners the property would fetch if sold in the open market on the valuation date in such manner and subject to such conditions as might reasonably be calculated to obtain for the vendor the best price for the property.

(*b*) The market value of the property shall be ascertained by the Revenue Commissioners in such manner and by such means as they think fit, and they may authorise a person to inspect the property and report to them the value of the property for the purposes of this section, and the person having custody or possession of the property shall permit the person so authorised to inspect the property at such reasonable times as the Revenue Commissioners consider necessary.

(*c*) Where the Revenue Commissioners require a valuation to be made by a person authorised by them, the cost of such valuation shall be defrayed by the Revenue Commissioners.

[(*d*) Where the property is acquired at auction by the person making the gift, the market value of the property shall, for the purposes of this section, be deemed to include the auctioneer's fees in connection with the auction together with—

(i) any amount chargeable under the Value-Added Tax Act, 1972, by the auctioneer to the purchaser of the property in respect of those fees and in respect of which the purchaser is not entitled to any deduction or refund under that Act or any other enactment relating to value-added tax, or

(ii) in the case of an auction in a country other than the State, the amount chargeable to the purchaser of the property in respect of a tax chargeable under the law of that country which corresponds to value-added tax in the State and in relation to which the purchaser is not entitled to any deduction or refund.]⁵

(4) Where a relevant gift is made to an approved body—

(*a*) the designated officer of that body shall give a certificate to the person who made the relevant gift, in such form as the Revenue Commissioners may prescribe, certifying the receipt of that gift and the transfer of the ownership of the heritage item the subject of that gift to the approved body, and

(b) the designated officer shall transmit a duplicate of the certificate to the Revenue Commissioners.

(5) Subject to this section, where a person has made a relevant gift the person shall, on submission to the Revenue Commissioners of the certificate given to the person in accordance with subsection (4), be treated as having made on the date of such submission a payment on account of tax of an amount equal to the market value of the relevant gift on the valuation date.

(6) A payment on account of tax which is treated as having been made in accordance with subsection (5) shall be set in so far as possible against any liability to tax of the person who is treated as having made such a payment in the following order—

(a) firstly, against any arrears of tax due for payment by that person and against an arrear of tax for an earlier period in priority to a later period, and for this purpose the date on which an arrear of tax became due for payment shall determine whether it is for an earlier or later period, and

(b) only then, against any current liability of the person which the person nominates for that purpose,

and such set-off shall accordingly discharge a corresponding amount of that liability.

(7) To the extent that a payment on account of tax has not been set off in accordance with subsection (6), the balance remaining shall be set off against any future liability to tax of the person who is treated as having made the payment which that person nominates for that purpose.

(8) Where a person has power to sell any heritage item in order to raise money for the payment of gift tax or inheritance tax, such person shall have power to make a relevant gift of that heritage item in or towards satisfaction of that tax and, except as regards the nature of the consideration and its receipt and application, any such relevant gift shall be subject to the same provisions and shall be treated for all purposes as a sale made in exercise of that power, and any conveyances or transfers made or purporting to be made to give effect to such a relevant gift shall apply accordingly.

(9) A person shall not be entitled to any refund of tax in respect of any payment on account of tax made in accordance with this section.

(10) Interest shall not be payable in respect of any overpayment of tax for any period which arises directly or indirectly by reason of the set-off against any liability for that period of a payment on account of tax made in accordance with this section.

(11) Where a person makes a relevant gift and in respect of that gift is treated as having made a payment on account of tax, the person concerned shall not be allowed relief under any other provision of the Acts in respect of that gift.

(12)(a) The Revenue Commissioners shall as respects each year compile a list of the titles (if any), descriptions and values of the heritage items (if any) in respect of which relief under this section has been given.

(b) Notwithstanding any obligation as to secrecy imposed on them by the Acts or the Official Secrets Act, 1963, the Revenue Commissioners shall include in their annual report to the Minister for Finance the list (if any) referred to in paragraph (*a*) for the year in respect of which the report is made.

Amendments

1   Inserted by FA 2002 s 124(*a*) with effect from 25 March 2002.

2   Substituted by FA 2002 s 124(*b*)(i) with effect from 25 March 2002; previously "€95,250".

3   Substituted by FA 2002 s 124(*b*)(ii) with effect from 25 March 2002; previously "€3,810,000".

4   Substituted by FA 2002 s 124(*c*) with effect from 25 March 2002; previously "shall be estimated".

5   Subs (3)(*d*) inserted by FA 2002 s 124(*d*) with effect from 25 March 2002.

Revenue information

Information leaflet HET1 - Relief for Donation of Heritage Items.

Tax Briefing

TB20 No 4 of 1995 par1.6 - Relief for Donation of Heritage Items.

Definitions

person: IA 1937 s 11(*c*); tax: s 3(1); Tax Acts: s 1(2); year of assessment: ss 2(1), 5(1).

Former enactments

FA 1995 s 176; FA 1996 s 139.

1006A Offset between taxes

[(1) In this section—

"Acts" means—

    (*a*)   the Tax Acts,

    (*b*)   the Capital Gains Tax Acts,

    (*c*)   the Value-Added Tax Act, 1972, and the enactments amending or extending that Act,

    (*d*)   the statutes relating to the duties of excise and to the management of those duties,

    (*e*)   the Capital Acquisitions Tax Act, 1976, and the enactments amending or extending that Act,

    (*f*)   the Stamp Duties Consolidation Act, 1999,

    (*g*)   Part VI of the Finance Act, 1983, and the enactments amending or extending that Part,

    (*h*)   Chapter IV of Part II of the Finance Act, 1992,

and any instrument made thereunder;

["**claim**" means a claim that gives rise to either or both a repayment of tax and a payment of interest payable in respect of such a repayment under any of the Acts and includes part of such a claim;][1]

["**liability**" means any tax due or estimated to be due under the Acts for any period or in respect of any event, as may be appropriate in the circumstances, and includes any interest due under the Acts in respect of that tax;][2]

"overpayment" means a payment or remittance under the Acts (including part of such a payment or remittance) which is in excess of the amount of the liability against which it is [credited;][3]

[**"tax"** means any tax, duty, levy or other charge under any of the Acts.][4]

[(2) Notwithstanding any other provision of the Acts, where the Revenue Commissioners are satisfied that a person has not complied with the obligations imposed on the person by the Acts, in relation to either or both—

   (*a*)   the payment of a liability required to be paid, and

   (*b*)   the delivery of returns required to be made,

they may, in a case where a repayment is due to the person in respect of a claim or overpayment—

   (i)   where paragraph (*a*) applies, or where paragraphs (*a*) and (*b*) apply, instead of making the repayment set the amount of the claim or overpayment against any liability due under the Acts, and

   (ii)   where paragraph (*b*) only applies, withhold making the repayment until such time as the returns required to be delivered have been delivered.

(2A) Where the Revenue Commissioners have set or withheld a repayment by virtue of subsection (2), they shall give notice in writing to that effect to the person concerned and, where subsection (2)(ii) applies, interest shall not be payable under any provision of the Acts from the date of such notice in respect of any repayment so withheld.][2]

(3) The Revenue Commissioners shall make regulations for the purpose of giving effect to this section and, without prejudice to the generality of the foregoing, such regulations shall provide for the order of priority of liabilities due under the Acts against which any claim or overpayment is to be set in accordance with subsection (2).

(4) Every regulation made under this section shall be laid before Dáil Éireann as soon as may be after it is made and, if a resolution annulling the regulation is passed by Dáil Éireann within the next 21 days on which Dáil Éireann has sat after the regulation is laid before it, the regulation shall be annulled accordingly, but without prejudice to the validity of anything previously done thereunder.][3]

[(5) Any act to be performed or function to be discharged (other than the making of regulations) by the Revenue Commissioners which is authorised by this section may be performed or discharged by any of their officers acting under their authority.][6]][7]

Amendments

[1]   Definition of "claim" substituted by FA 2002 s 125(*a*)(i)(I) with effect from 25 March 2002.
[2]   Definition of "liability" substituted by FA 2002 s 125(*a*)(i)(II) with effect from 25 March 2002.
[3]   Substituted by FA 2002 s 125(*a*)(i)(III) with effect from 25 March 2002; previously "credited.".
[4]   Definition of "tax" substituted by FA 2002 s 125(*a*)(i)(IV) with effect from 25 March 2002.
[5]   Subs (2) substituted and subs (2A) inserted by FA 2001 s 239(*b*) with effect from 6 April 2001.
[6]   Subs (5) inserted by FA 2002 s 125(*a*)(ii) with effect from 25 March 2002.
[7]   Section 1006A inserted by FA 2000 s 164 with effect from 23 March 2000.

Cross-references

Relief on retirement for certain income of certain sportsperson: s 480A(2).

Regulations

Taxes (Offset of Repayments) Regulations 2001, SI No 399 of 2001.

Tax Briefing

TB45 Oct 2001 pp 10-11 - Offset of Repayment Regulations.

Definitions

Dáil Éireann: IA 1937 Sch; person: IA 1937 s 11(*c*); writing: IA 1937 Sch.

PART 47
PENALTIES, REVENUE OFFENCES, INTEREST ON OVERDUE TAX AND OTHER SANCTIONS

CHAPTER 1
Income Tax and Corporation Tax Penalties

1061 Recovery of penalties

(1) Without prejudice to any other mode of recovery of a penalty under the [preceding provisions of this Part, Chapter 4 of Part 38][1] or under section 305, 783, 789 or 886, an officer of the Revenue Commissioners authorised by them for the purposes of this subsection may sue in his or her own name by civil proceedings for the recovery of the penalty in the High Court as a liquidated sum, and section 94 of the Courts of Justice Act, 1924, shall apply accordingly.

(2) Where an officer who has commenced proceedings pursuant to this section, or who has continued the proceedings by virtue of this subsection, dies or otherwise ceases for any reason to be an officer authorised for the purposes of subsection (1)—

    (*a*) the right of such officer to continue the proceedings shall cease and the right to continue them shall vest in such other officer so authorised as may be nominated by the Revenue Commissioners,

    (*b*) where such other officer is nominated under paragraph (*a*), he or she shall be entitled accordingly to be substituted as a party to the proceedings in the place of the first-mentioned officer, and

    (*c*) where an officer is so substituted, he or she shall give notice in writing of the substitution to the defendant.

(3) In proceedings pursuant to this section, a certificate signed by a Revenue Commissioner certifying that—

    (*a*) a person is an officer of the Revenue Commissioners, and

    (*b*) he or she has been authorised by them for the purposes of subsection (1),

shall be evidence of those facts until the contrary is proved.

(4) In proceedings pursuant to this section, a certificate signed by a Revenue Commissioner certifying that—

    (*a*) the plaintiff has ceased to be an officer of the Revenue Commissioners authorised by them for the purposes of subsection (1),

    (*b*) another person is an officer of the Revenue Commissioners,

(c) such other person has been authorised by them for the purposes of subsection (1), and

(d) he or she has been nominated by them in relation to the proceedings for the purposes of subsection (2),

shall be evidence of those facts until the contrary is proved.

(5) In proceedings pursuant to this section, a certificate certifying the facts referred to in subsection (3) or (4) and purporting to be signed by a Revenue Commissioner may be tendered in evidence without proof and shall be deemed until the contrary is proved to have been so signed.

(6) Subject to this section, the rules of the High Court for the time being applicable to civil proceedings shall apply to proceedings pursuant to this section.

Amendments

1 Substituted by FA 2002 s 130(1)(c) with effect from 25 March 2002; previously "preceding provisions of this Part".

Cross-references

Capital gains tax, penalties for failure to make returns etc, and for fraudulently or negligently making incorrect returns, this section applied by: s 1077(1).

Stamp duty, instruments executed on or after 1 November 1991, this section applied by: FA 1991 s 109.

Former enactments

ITA 1967 s 508; FA 1968 s 6(6); CTA 1976 s 147(3)-(4).

1062 Proceedings where penalty recoverable cannot be definitely ascertained

Notwithstanding that the amount of a penalty recoverable under the Tax Acts cannot be definitely ascertained by reason of the fact that the amount of income tax or, as the case may be, corporation tax by reference to which such penalty is to be calculated has not been finally ascertained, proceedings may be instituted for the recovery of such penalty and, if at the hearing of such proceedings the amount of such tax has not then been finally ascertained, the Court may, if it is of the opinion that such penalty is recoverable, adjourn such proceedings and shall not give any judgment or make any order for the payment of such penalty until the amount of such tax has been finally ascertained.

Cross-references

Capital gains tax, penalties for failure to make returns etc, and for fraudulently or negligently making incorrect returns, this section applied by: s 1077(1).

Stamp duty, instruments executed on or after 1 November 1991, this section applied by: FA 1991 s 109.

Former enactments

ITA 1967 s 510; CTA 1976 s 147(3)-(4).

1063 Time limit for recovery of fines and penalties

Proceedings for the recovery of any fine or penalty incurred under the Tax Acts in relation to or in connection with income tax or corporation tax may, subject to section 1060, be begun at any time within 6 years after the date on which such fine or penalty was incurred.

1064 Time for certain summary proceedings

Notwithstanding section 10(4) of the Petty Sessions (Ireland) Act, 1851, summary proceedings under section 889, 987 or 1056 may be instituted within 10 years from the date of the committing of the offence or incurring of the penalty, as the case may be.

1065 Mitigation and application of fines and penalties

(1) (*a*) The Revenue Commissioners may in their discretion mitigate any fine or penalty, or stay or compound any proceedings for the recovery of any fine or penalty, and may also, after judgment, further mitigate the fine or penalty, and may order any person imprisoned for any offence to be discharged before the term of his or her imprisonment has expired.

(*b*) The Minister for Finance may mitigate any such fine or penalty either before or after judgment.

(2) Notwithstanding subsection (1)—

(*a*) where a fine or penalty is mitigated or further mitigated, as the case may be, after judgment, the amount or amounts so mitigated shall, subject to paragraph (*b*), not be greater than 50 per cent of the amount of the fine or penalty, and

(*b*) in relation to an individual, being an individual referred to in section 2(2) of the Waiver of Certain Tax, Interest and Penalties Act, 1993, or a person referred to in section 3(2) of that Act, who—

(i) fails to give a declaration required by section 2(3)(*a*) of that Act, or

(ii) gives a declaration referred to in subparagraph (i) or a declaration under section 3(6)(*b*) of that Act which is false or fails to comply with the requirements of subparagraph (iii) or (iv) of section 2(3)(*a*) of that Act or subparagraph (III) of section 3(6)(*b*) of that Act to the extent that any of those subparagraphs apply to that person,

no mitigation shall be allowed.

(3) Moneys arising from fines, penalties and forfeitures, and all costs, charges and expenses payable in respect of or in relation to such fines, penalties and forfeitures, shall be accounted for and paid to the Revenue Commissioners or as they direct.

Cross-references

Capital gains tax, penalties for failure to make returns etc, and for fraudulently or negligently making incorrect returns, this section applied by: s 1077(1).

Stamp duty, instruments executed on or after 1 November 1991, this section applied by: FA 1991 s 109.

Tax Briefing

TB36 June 1999 pp 6-7 Code of Practice for Revenue Auditors Update - Mitigation of Penalties.

Definitions

person: IA 1937 s 11(*c*).

Former enactments

ITA 1967 s 512; CTA 1976 s 147(3)-(4); WCTIPA 1993 s10.

1066 False evidence: punishment as for perjury

If any person on any examination on oath, or in any affidavit or deposition authorised by the Tax Acts, wilfully and corruptly gives false evidence, or wilfully and corruptly swears any matter or thing which is false or untrue, that person shall on conviction be subject and liable to such punishment as persons convicted of perjury are subject and liable to.

Cross-references

Capital gains tax, penalties for failure to make returns etc, and for fraudulently or negligently making incorrect returns, this section this section applied by: s 1077(1).

Stamp duty, instruments executed on or after 1 November 1991, this section applied by: FA 1991 s 109.

Definitions

affidavit: IA 1937 Sch; oath: IA 1937 Sch; person: IA 1937 s 11(*c*); swear: IA 1937 Sch.

Former enactments

ITA 1967 s 518; CTA 1976 s 147(1)-(2).

CHAPTER 4
Revenue offences

1078 Revenue offences

(1) In this Part—

"the Acts" means—

    (*a*) the Customs Acts,

    (*b*) the statutes relating to the duties of excise and to the management of those duties,

    (*c*) the Tax Acts,

    (*d*) the Capital Gains Tax Acts,

    (*e*) the Value-Added Tax Act, 1972, and the enactments amending or extending that Act,

    (*f*) the Capital Acquisitions Tax Act, 1976, and the enactments amending or extending that Act,

    (*g*) the statutes relating to stamp duty and to the management of that duty, and

    (*h*) Part VI of the Finance Act, 1983,

and any instruments made thereunder and any instruments made under any other enactment and relating to tax;

"authorised officer" means an officer of the Revenue Commissioners authorised by them in writing to exercise any of the powers conferred by the Acts;

"tax" means any tax, duty, levy or charge under the care and management of the Revenue Commissioners.

(2) A person shall, without prejudice to any other penalty to which the person may be liable, be guilty of an offence under this section if the person—

(*a*) knowingly or wilfully delivers any incorrect return, statement or accounts or knowingly or wilfully furnishes any incorrect information in connection with any tax,

(*b*) knowingly aids, abets, assists, incites or induces another person to make or deliver knowingly or wilfully any incorrect return, statement or accounts in connection with any tax,

(*c*) claims or obtains relief or exemption from, or repayment of, any tax, being a relief, exemption or repayment to which, to the person's knowledge, the person is not entitled,

(*d*) knowingly or wilfully issues or produces any incorrect invoice, receipt, instrument or other document in connection with any tax,

[(*dd*)   (i) fails to make any deduction of dividend withholding tax (within the meaning of Chapter 8A of Part 6) required to be made by the person under section 172B(1),

(ii) fails, having made that deduction, to pay the sum deducted to the Collector-General within the time specified in that behalf in section 172K(2),

(iii) fails to make any reduction required to be made by the person under section 172B(2),

(iv) fails, having made that reduction, to pay to the Collector-General the amount referred to in section 172B(2)(*d*), which amount is treated under that section as if it were a deduction of dividend withholding tax (within the meaning of Chapter 8A of Part 6), within the time specified in that behalf in section 172K(2), or

(v) fails to pay to the Collector-General, within the time specified in that behalf in section 172K(2), an amount referred to in section 172B(3)(*a*) which is required to be paid by the person to the Collector-General and which is treated under that section as if it were a deduction of dividend withholding tax (within the meaning of Chapter 8A of Part 6),][1]

(*e*) (i) fails to make any deduction required to be made by the person under section 257(1),

(ii) fails, having made the deduction, to pay the sum deducted to the Collector-General within the time specified in that behalf in section 258(3), or

(iii) fails to pay to the Collector-General an amount on account of appropriate tax (within the meaning of Chapter 4 of Part 8) within the time specified in that behalf in section 258(4),

(*f*) (i) fails to make any deduction required to be made by the person under section 734(5), or

(ii) fails, having made the deduction, to pay the sum deducted to the Collector-General within the time specified in paragraph 1(3) of Schedule 18,

(*g*) [fails without reasonable excuse]² to comply with any provision of the Acts requiring—

(i) the furnishing of a return of income, profits or gains, or of sources of income, profits or gains, for the purposes of any tax,

(ii) the furnishing of any other return, certificate, notification, particulars, or any statement or evidence, for the purposes of any tax,

(iii) the keeping or retention of books, records, accounts or other documents for the purposes of any tax, or

(iv) the production of books, records, accounts or other documents, when so requested, for the purposes of any tax,

(*h*) knowingly or wilfully, and within the time limits specified for their retention, destroys, defaces or conceals from an authorised officer—

(i) any documents, or

(ii) any other written or printed material in any form, including any information stored, maintained or preserved by means of any mechanical or electronic device, whether or not stored, maintained or preserved in a legible form, which a person is obliged by any provision of the Acts to keep, to issue or to produce for inspection,

[(*hh*) knowingly or wilfully falsifies, conceals, destroys or otherwise disposes of, or causes or permits the falsification, concealment, destruction or disposal of, any books, records or other document—

(i) which the person has been given the opportunity to deliver, or as the case may be, to make available in accordance with section 900(3), or

(ii) which the person has been required to deliver or, as the case may be, to make available in accordance with a notice served under section 900, 902, 906A or 907, or an order made under section 901, 902A or 908.]²

(*i*) fails to remit any income tax payable pursuant to Chapter 4 of Part 42, and the regulations under that Chapter, or value-added tax within the time specified in that behalf in relation to income tax or value-added tax, as the case may be, by the Acts, or

(*j*) obstructs or interferes with any officer of the Revenue Commissioners, or any other person, in the exercise or performance of powers or duties under the Acts for the purposes of any tax.

(3) A person convicted of an offence under this section shall be liable—

(*a*) on summary conviction to a fine of [€1,900][4] which may be mitigated to not less than one fourth part of such fine or, at the discretion of the court, to imprisonment for a term not exceeding 12 months or to both the fine and the imprisonment, or

(*b*) on conviction on indictment, to a fine not exceeding [€126,970][5] or, at the discretion of the court, to imprisonment for a term not exceeding 5 years or to both the fine and the imprisonment.

[(3A) Where a person has been convicted of an offence referred to in subparagraph (i), (ii) or (iv) of subsection (2)(*g*), then, if an application is made, or caused to be made to the court in that regard, the court may make an order requiring the person concerned to comply with any provision of the Acts relating to the requirements specified in the said subparagraph (i), (ii) or (iv), as the case may be.][6]

[(3B) A person shall, without prejudice to any other penalty to which the person may be liable, be guilty of an offence under this section if the person fails or refuses to comply with an order referred to in subsection (3A).][7]

(4) Section 13 of the Criminal Procedure Act, 1967, shall apply in relation to an offence under this section as if, in place of the penalties specified in subsection (3) of that section, there were specified in that subsection the penalties provided for by subsection (3)(*a*), and the reference in subsection (2)(*a*) of section 13 of the Criminal Procedure Act, 1967, to the penalties provided for in subsection (3) of that section shall be construed and apply accordingly.

(5) Where an offence under this section is committed by a body corporate and the offence is shown to have been committed with the consent or connivance of any person who, when the offence was committed, was a director, manager, secretary or other officer of the body corporate, or a member of the committee of management or other controlling authority of the body corporate, that person shall also be deemed to be guilty of the offence and may be proceeded against and punished accordingly.

(6) In any proceedings under this section, a return or statement delivered to an inspector or other officer of the Revenue Commissioners under any provision of the Acts and purporting to be signed by any person shall be deemed until the contrary is proved to have been so delivered and to have been signed by that person.

(7) Notwithstanding any other enactment, proceedings in respect of an offence under this section may be instituted within 10 years from the date of the commission of the offence or incurring of the penalty, as the case may be.

(8) Section 1 of the Probation of Offenders Act, 1907, shall not apply in relation to offences under this section.

(9) Sections 987(4) and 1052(4), subsections (3) and (7) of section 1053, and sections 1068 and 1069 and sections 26(6) and 27(7) of the Value-Added Tax Act, 1972, shall, with any necessary modifications, apply for the purposes of this section as they apply for the purposes of those sections, including, in the case of such of those sections as are applied by the Capital Gains Tax Acts, the Corporation Tax Acts, or Part VI of the Finance Act, 1983, the purposes of those sections as so applied.

Amendments

¹   Subs (2)(*dd*) inserted by FA 1999 s 27(*b*) with effect from 6 April 1999.
²   Substituted by FA 2002 s 133(*a*) with effect from 25 March 2002; previously "knowingly or wilfully fails".
³   Subs (2)(*hh*) inserted by FA 1999 s 211(*a*) with effect from 25 March 1999.
⁴   Substituted by FA 2001 s 233(2)(*a*) with effect from 1 January 2002; previously "£1,500".
⁵   Substituted by FA 2001 s 240(1) and (2)(*k*) and Sch 5 Pt 1 as respects any act or omission which takes place or begins on or after 1 January 2002; previously "£100,000".
⁶   Subs (3A) inserted by FA 1999 s 211(*c*) with effect from 25 March 1999.
⁷   Subs (3B) inserted by FA 2002 s 133(*b*) with effect from 25 March 2002.

Cross-references

Application to High Court: information from third party, meaning of "the Acts" applied: s 902A(1).
Company law, subs (1): Companies Act 1990 s 21(1)(*a*)(i)(V).
Deduction from payments due to defaulters: s 1002(5), (9).
Information to be furnished by financial institutions, meaning of "the Acts" applied: s 906A(1).
Information to be furnished by third party: request of an authorised officer: s 902(11).
Inspection of documents and records, meaning of "the Acts" applied: s 905(2A)(*a*).
Penalty for false statement made to obtain allowance, subss (4), (6)-(8): s 1056(4).
Revenue offence: power to obtain information from financial institutions, meaning of "offence" applied: s 908A(1); subs (1): s 908A(1) ("the Acts").
This section to be construed together with the Customs Acts, in so far as relating to customs: s 1104(2).
This section to be construed together with the Value Added Tax Acts 1972-1997, in so far as relating to value added tax: s 1104(3).
This section to be construed together with the Stamp Act 1891 and the enactments amending or extending that Act, in so far as relating to stamp duties: s 1104(4).
This section to be construed together with the Capital Acquisitions Tax Act 1976, and the enactments amending or extending that Act, in so far as relating to capital acquisitions tax: s 1104(5).
This section to be construed together with FA 1983 Pt VI and the enactments amending or extending that Part, in so far as relating to residential property tax: s 1104(6).

Case law

Meaning of "criminal matter": *Director of Public Prosecutions v Seamus Boyle*, ITR Vol IV, p 395.
Subs (2)(*e*): District Justice not entitled to conclude, on basis of Revenue certificate, that taxpayer had "knowingly and wilfully" failed to submit return of income; taxpayer not present at District Court hearing and was entitled to defend himself: *O'Callaghan v Clifford and others*, ITR Vol IV, p 478.

Tax Briefing

TB36 June 1999 pp 3-4 - Revenue's Prosecution Policy.
TB38 Dec 1999 pp 10-11 - Criminal Proceedings.

Definitions

Collector-General: ss 2(1), 851; inspector: ss 2(1), 5(1), 852; month: IA 1937 Sch; person: IA 1937 s 11(*c*); profits: s 4(1); statute: s 2(1), IA 1937 s 3; Tax Acts: s 1(2).

Former enactments

FA 1983 s 94; FA 1986 s 40(2); FA 1989 s 18 and Sch 1 para 3(2); FA 1992 s 243; FA 1996 s 132(1)-(2) and Sch 5 Pt I para 13(2) and Pt II.

1079 Duties of relevant person in relation to certain revenue offences

(1) In this section—

"the Acts" means—

    (*a*)   the Customs Acts,

    (*b*)   the statutes relating to the duties of excise and to the management of those duties,

    (*c*)   the Tax Acts,

    (*d*) the Capital Gains Tax Acts,

    (*e*) the Value-Added Tax Act, 1972, and the enactments amending or extending that Act,

    (*f*) the Capital Acquisitions Tax Act, 1976, and the enactments amending or extending that Act,

    (*g*) the statutes relating to stamp duty and to the management of that duty,

and any instruments made thereunder and any instruments made under any other enactment and relating to tax;

"appropriate officer" means any officer nominated by the Revenue Commissioners to be an appropriate officer for the purposes of this section;

"company" means any body corporate;

"relevant person", in relation to a company and subject to subsection (2), means a person who—

    (*a*) (i) is an auditor to the company appointed in accordance with section 160 of the Companies Act, 1963 (as amended by the Companies Act, 1990), or

          (ii) in the case of an industrial and provident society or a friendly society, is a public auditor to the society for the purposes of the Industrial and Provident Societies Acts, 1893 to 1978, and the Friendly Societies Acts, 1896 to 1977,

      or

    (*b*) with a view to reward, assists or advises the company in the preparation or delivery of any information, declaration, return, records, accounts or other document which he or she knows will be or is likely to be used for any purpose of tax;

"relevant offence" means an offence committed by a company which consists of the company—

    (*a*) knowingly or wilfully delivering any incorrect return, statement or accounts or knowingly or wilfully furnishing or causing to be furnished any incorrect information in connection with any tax,

    (*b*) knowingly or wilfully claiming or obtaining relief or exemption from, or repayment of, any tax, being a relief, exemption or repayment to which there is no entitlement,

    (*c*) knowingly or wilfully issuing or producing any incorrect invoice, receipt, instrument or other document in connection with any tax, or

    (*d*) knowingly or wilfully failing to comply with any provision of the Acts requiring the furnishing of a return of income, profits or gains, or of sources of income, profits or gains, for the purposes of any tax, but an offence under this paragraph committed by a company shall not be a relevant offence if the company has made a return of income, profits or gains to the Revenue Commissioners in respect of an accounting period falling wholly or partly in the period of 3 years preceding the accounting period in respect of which the offence was committed;

"tax" means any tax, duty, levy or charge under the care and management of the Revenue Commissioners.

(2) For the purposes of paragraph (*b*) of the definition of **"relevant person"**, a person who but for this subsection would be treated as a relevant person in relation to a company shall not be so treated if the person assists or advises the company solely in the person's capacity as an employee of the company, and a person shall be treated as assisting or advising the company in that capacity where the person's income from assisting or advising the company consists solely of emoluments to which Chapter 4 of Part 42 applies.

(3) If, having regard solely to information obtained in the course of examining the accounts of a company, or in the course of assisting or advising a company in the preparation or delivery of any information, declaration, return, records, accounts or other document for the purposes of tax, as the case may be, a person who is a relevant person in relation to the company becomes aware that the company has committed, or is in the course of committing, one or more relevant offences, the person shall, if the offence or offences are material—

    (*a*)   communicate particulars of the offence or offences in writing to the company without undue delay and request the company to—

        (i)   take such action as is necessary for the purposes of rectifying the matter, or

        (ii)   notify an appropriate officer of the offence or offences,

         not later than 6 months after the time of communication, and

    (*b*)   (i)   unless it is established to the person's satisfaction that the necessary action has been taken or notification made, as the case may be, under paragraph (*a*), cease to act as the auditor to the company or to assist or advise the company in such preparation or delivery as is specified in paragraph (*b*) of the definition of **"relevant person"**, and

        (ii)   shall not so act, assist or advise before a time which is the earlier of—

            (I)   3 years after the time at which the particulars were communicated under paragraph (*a*), and

            (II)   the time at which it is established to the person's satisfaction that the necessary action has been taken or notification made, as the case may be, under paragraph (*a*).

(4) Nothing in paragraph (*b*) of subsection (3) shall prevent a person from assisting or advising a company in preparing for, or conducting, legal proceedings, either civil or criminal, which are extant or pending at a time which is 6 months after the time of communication under paragraph (*a*) of that subsection.

(5) Where a person, being in relation to a company a relevant person within the meaning of paragraph (*a*) of the definition of **"relevant person"**, ceases under this section to act as auditor to the company, then, the person shall deliver—

    (*a*)   a notice in writing to the company stating that he or she is so resigning, and

    (*b*)   a copy of the notice to an appropriate officer not later than 14 days after he or she has delivered the notice to the company.

(6) A person shall be guilty of an offence under this section if the person—

    (*a*)   fails to comply with subsection (3) or (5), or

    (*b*)   knowingly or wilfully makes a communication under subsection (3) which is incorrect.

(7) Where a relevant person is convicted of an offence under this section, the person shall be liable—

    (*a*)   on summary conviction, to a fine of [€1,265][1] which may be mitigated to not less than one-fourth part of such fine, or

    (*b*)   on conviction on indictment, to a fine not exceeding [€6,345][2] or, at the discretion of the court, to imprisonment for a term not exceeding 2 years or to both the fine and the imprisonment.

(8) Section 13 of the Criminal Procedure Act, 1967, shall apply in relation to this section as if, in place of the penalties specified in subsection (3) of that section, there were specified in that subsection the penalties provided for by subsection (7)(*a*), and the reference in subsection (2)(*a*) of section 13 of the Criminal Procedure Act, 1967, to the penalties provided for in subsection (3) of that section shall be construed and apply accordingly.

(9) Notwithstanding any other enactment, proceedings in respect of this section may be instituted within 6 years from the time at which a person is required under subsection (3) to communicate particulars of an offence or offences in writing to a company.

(10) It shall be a good defence in a prosecution for an offence under subsection (6)(*a*) in relation to a failure to comply with subsection (3) for an accused (being a person who is a relevant person in relation to a company) to show that he or she was in the ordinary scope of professional engagement assisting or advising the company in preparing for legal proceedings and would not have become aware that one or more relevant offences had been committed by the company if he or she had not been so assisting or advising.

(11) Where a person who is a relevant person takes any action required by subsection (3) or (5), no duty to which the person may be subject shall be regarded as having been contravened and no liability or action shall lie against the person in any court for having taken such action.

(12) The Revenue Commissioners may nominate an officer to be an appropriate officer for the purposes of this section, and the name of an officer so nominated and the address to which copies of notices under subsection (3) or (5) shall be delivered shall be published in Iris Oifigiúil.

(13) This section shall apply as respects a relevant offence committed by a company in respect of tax which is—

    (*a*)   assessable by reference to accounting periods, for any accounting period beginning after the 30th day of June, 1995,

    (*b*)   assessable by reference to years of assessment, for the year 1995-96 and subsequent years of assessment,

(c) payable by reference to a taxable period, for a taxable period beginning after the 30th day of June, 1995,

(d) chargeable on gifts or inheritances taken on or after the 30th day of June, 1995,

(e) chargeable on instruments executed on or after the 30th day of June, 1995, or

(f) payable in any other case, on or after the 30th day of June, 1995.

Amendments

1   Substituted by FA 2001 s 240(1) and (2)(*k*) and Sch 5 Pt 1 as respects any act or omission which takes place or begins on or after 1 January 2002; previously "£1,000".

2   Substituted by FA 2001 s 240(1) and (2)(*k*) and Sch 5 Pt 1 as respects any act or omission which takes place or begins on or after 1 January 2002; previously "£5,000".

Cross-references

This section to be construed together with the Customs Acts, in so far as relating to customs: s 1104(2).

This section to be construed together with the Value Added Tax Acts 1972-1997, in so far as relating to value added tax: s 1104(3).

This section to be construed together with the Stamp Act 1891 and the enactments amending or extending that Act, in so far as relating to stamp duties: s 1104(4).

This section to be construed together with the Capital Acquisitions Tax Act 1976, and the enactments amending or extending that Act, in so far as relating to capital acquisitions tax: s 1104(5).

Definitions

month: IA 1937 Sch; person: IA 1937 s 11(*c*); writing: IA 1937 Sch; year: IA 1937 Sch; year of assessment: ss 2(1), 5(1).

Former enactment

FA 1995 s 172.

CHAPTER 6
Other sanctions

1086 Publication of names of tax defaulters

(1) In this section—

"the Acts" means—

    (a) the Tax Acts,

    (b) the Capital Gains Tax Acts,

    (c) the Value-Added Tax Act, 1972, and the enactments amending or extending that Act,

    (d) the Capital Acquisitions Tax Act, 1976, and the enactments amending or extending that Act,

    [(e) the Stamp Duties Consolidation Act, 1999, and the enactments amending or extending that Act]¹

    (f) Part VI of the Finance Act, 1983,

    [(g) the Customs Acts,

    (h) the statutes relating to the duties of excise and to the management of those duties,]²

and any instruments made thereunder;

["**tax**" means any tax, duty, levy or charge under the care and management of the Revenue Commissioners.][3]

(2) The Revenue Commissioners shall, as respects each relevant period (being the period beginning on the 1st day of January, 1997, and ending on the 30th day of June, 1997, and each subsequent period of 3 months beginning with the period ending on the 30th day of September, 1997), compile a list of the names and addresses and the occupations or descriptions of every person—

(a) on whom a fine or other penalty was imposed by a court under any of the Acts during that relevant period,

(b) on whom a fine or other penalty was otherwise imposed by a court during that relevant period in respect of an act or omission by the person in relation to [tax,][4]

(c) in whose case the Revenue Commissioners, pursuant to an agreement made with the person in that relevant period, refrained from initiating proceedings for the recovery of any fine or penalty of the kind mentioned in paragraphs (a) and (b) and, in place of initiating such proceedings, accepted or undertook to accept a specified sum of money in settlement of any claim by the Revenue Commissioners in respect of any specified liability of the person under any of the Acts for—

   (i) payment of any tax,

   [(ii) except in the case of tax due by virtue of paragraphs (g) and (h) of the definition of "the Acts", payment of interest on that tax, and

   (iii) a fine or other monetary penalty in respect of that tax including penalties in respect of the failure to deliver any return, statement, declaration, list or other document in connection with the tax, or][5]

[(d) in whose case the Revenue Commissioners, having initiated proceedings for the recovery of any fine or penalty of the kind mentioned in paragraphs (a) and (b), and whether or not a fine or penalty of the kind mentioned in those paragraphs has been imposed by a court, accepted or undertook to accept, in that relevant period, a specified sum of money in settlement of any claim by the Revenue Commissioners in respect of any specified liability of the person under any of the Acts for—

   (i) payment of any tax,

   [(ii) except in the case of tax due by virtue of paragraphs (g) and (h) of the definition of "the Acts", payment of interest on that tax, and

   (iii) a fine or other monetary penalty in respect of that tax including penalties in respect of the failure to deliver any return, statement, declaration, list or other document in connection with the tax.][6]][7]

[(2A) For the purposes of subsection (2), the reference to a specified sum in paragraphs (c) and (d) of that subsection includes a reference to a sum which is the full amount of the claim by the Revenue Commissioners in respect of the specified liability referred to in those paragraphs.][8]

(3) Notwithstanding any obligation as to secrecy imposed on them by the Acts or the Official Secrets Act, 1963—

(a)   the Revenue Commissioners shall, before the expiration of 3 months from the end of each relevant period, cause each such list referred to in subsection (2) in relation to that period to be published in Iris Oifigiúil, and

[(b)   the Revenue Commissioners may, at any time after each such list referred to in subsection (2) has been published as provided for in paragraph *(a)*, cause any such list to be publicised or reproduced, or both, in whole or in part, in such manner, form or format as they consider appropriate.]⁹

(4) [Paragraph (*c*) and (*d*)]¹⁰ of subsection (2) shall not apply in relation to a person in whose case—

(a)   the Revenue Commissioners are satisfied that, before any investigation or inquiry had been commenced by them or by any of their officers into any matter occasioning a liability referred to in [those paragraphs]¹¹ of the person, the person had voluntarily furnished to them complete information in relation to and full particulars of that matter,

(b)   section 72 of the Finance Act, 1988, or section 3 of the Waiver of Certain Tax, Interest and Penalties Act, 1993, [applied,]¹²

(c)   the specified sum referred to in [paragraph (*c*) or (*d*), as the case may be,]¹³ of subsection (2) does not exceed [€12,700, or]¹⁴

[(d)   the amount of fine or other penalty included in the specified sum referred to in paragraph (*c*) or (*d*), as the case may be, of subsection (2) does not exceed 15 per cent of the amount of tax included in that specified sum.]¹⁵

(5) Any list referred to in subsection (2) shall specify in respect of each person named in the list such particulars as the Revenue Commissioners think fit—

(a)   of the matter occasioning the fine or penalty of the kind referred to in subsection (2) imposed on the person or, as the case may be, the liability of that kind to which the person was subject, and

(b)   of any interest, fine or other monetary penalty, and of any other penalty or sanction, to which that person was liable, or which was imposed on that person by a court, and which was occasioned by the matter referred to in paragraph (*a*).

[(5A) Without prejudice to the generality of paragraph (*a*) of subsection (5), such particulars as are referred to in that paragraph may include—

(a)   in a case to which paragraph (*a*) or (*b*) of subsection (2) applies, a description, in such summary form as the Revenue Commissioners may think fit, of the act, omission or offence (which may also include the circumstances in which the act or omission arose or the offence was committed) in respect of which the fine or penalty referred to in those paragraphs was imposed, and

(b)   in a case to which paragraph (*c*) or (*d*) of subsection (2) applies, a description, in such summary form as the Revenue Commissioners may think fit, of the matter occasioning the specified liability (which may also include the circumstances in which that liability arose) in respect of which the Revenue

Commissioners accepted, or undertook to accept, a settlement, in accordance with those paragraphs.][16]

Amendments

[1] Definition of "the Acts" para (*e*) substituted by FA 2002 s 126(1)(*a*)(i)(I) as respects fines or other penalties, as are referred to in s 1086(2)(*a*) and (*b*), which are imposed by a court, and as respects specified sums, as are referred to in s 1086(2)(*c*) and (*d*), which the Revenue Commissioners accepted, or undertook to accept, in settlement of a specified liability, on or after 25 March 2002.

[2] Definition of "the Acts" paras (*g*) and (*h*) inserted by FA 2002 s 126(1)(*a*)(i)(II) as respects fines or other penalties, as are referred to in s 1086(2)(*a*) and (*b*), which are imposed by a court, and as respects specified sums, as are referred to in s 1086(2)(*c*) and (*d*), which the Revenue Commissioners accepted, or undertook to accept, in settlement of a specified liability, on or after 25 March 2002.

[3] Definition of "tax" substituted by FA 2002 s 126(1)(*a*)(ii) as respects fines or other penalties, as are referred to in s 1086(2)(*a*) and (*b*), which are imposed by a court, and as respects specified sums, as are referred to in s 1086(2)(*c*) and (*d*), which the Revenue Commissioners accepted, or undertook to accept, in settlement of a specified liability, on or after 25 March 2002.

[4] Substituted by FA 2000 s 162(1)(*a*)(i) as respects fines or other penalties, as are referred to in s 1086(2)(*a*)-(*b*), which are imposed by a court, and as respects specified sums, as are referred to in s 1086(2)(*c*)-(*d*), which the Revenue Commissioners accepted, or undertook to accept, in settlement of a specified liability, on or after 23 March 2000; previously "tax, or".

[5] Subs (2)(*c*)(ii)-(iii) substituted by FA 2002 s 126(1)(*b*)(i) as respects fines or other penalties, as are referred to in s 1086(2)(*a*) and (*b*), which are imposed by a court, and as respects specified sums, as are referred to in s 1086(2)(*c*) and (*d*), which the Revenue Commissioners accepted, or undertook to accept, in settlement of a specified liability, on or after 25 March 2002.

[6] Subs (2)(*d*)(ii)-(iii) substituted by FA 2002 s 126(1)(*b*)(ii) as respects fines or other penalties, as are referred to in s 1086(2)(*a*) and (*b*), which are imposed by a court, and as respects specified sums, as are referred to in s 1086(2)(*c*) and (*d*), which the Revenue Commissioners accepted, or undertook to accept, in settlement of a specified liability, on or after 25 March 2002.

[7] Subs (2)(*d*) inserted by FA 2000 s 162(1)(*a*)(ii) as respects fines or other penalties, as are referred to in s 1086(2)(*a*)-(*b*), which are imposed by a court, and as respects specified sums, as are referred to in s 1086(2)(*c*)-(*d*), which the Revenue Commissioners accepted, or undertook to accept, in settlement of a specified liability, on or after 23 March 2000.

[8] Subs (2A) inserted by FA 2000 s 162(1)(*b*) as respects fines or other penalties, as are referred to in s 1086(2)(*a*)-(*b*), which are imposed by a court, and as respects specified sums, as are referred to in s 1086(2)(*c*)-(*d*), which the Revenue Commissioners accepted, or undertook to accept, in settlement of a specified liability, on or after 23 March 2000.

[9] Subs (3)(*b*) substituted by FA 2002 s 126(1)(*c*) as respects fines or other penalties, as are referred to in s 1086(2)(*a*) and (*b*), which are imposed by a court, and as respects specified sums, as are referred to in s 1086(2)(*c*) and (*d*), which the Revenue Commissioners accepted, or undertook to accept, in settlement of a specified liability, on or after 25 March 2002.

[10] Substituted by FA 2000 s 162(1)(*c*)(i) as respects fines or other penalties, as are referred to in s 1086(2)(*a*)-(*b*), which are imposed by a court, and as respects specified sums, as are referred to in s 1086(2)(*c*)-(*d*), which the Revenue Commissioners accepted, or undertook to accept, in settlement of a specified liability, on or after 23 March 2000; previously "Paragraph (c)".

[11] Substituted by FA 2002 s 126(1)(*d*)(i) as respects fines or other penalties, as are referred to in s 1086(2)(*a*) and (*b*), which are imposed by a court, and as respects specified sums, as are referred to in s 1086(2)(*c*) and (*d*), which the Revenue Commissioners accepted, or undertook to accept, in settlement of a specified liability, on or after 25 March 2002; previously "that paragraph".

[12] Substituted by FA 2002 s 126(1)(*d*)(ii) as respects fines or other penalties, as are referred to in s 1086(2)(*a*) and (*b*), which are imposed by a court, and as respects specified sums, as are referred to in s 1086(2)(*c*) and (*d*), which the Revenue Commissioners accepted, or undertook to accept, in settlement of a specified liability, on or after 25 March 2002; previously "applied, or".

[13] Substituted by FA 2000 s 162(1)(*c*)(ii) as respects fines or other penalties, as are referred to in s 1086(2)(*a*)-(*b*), which are imposed by a court, and as respects specified sums, as are referred to in s 1086(2)(*c*)-(*d*), which the Revenue Commissioners accepted, or undertook to accept, in settlement of a specified liability, on or after 23 March 2000; previously "paragraph (c)".

14   Substituted by FA 2002 s 126(1)(*d*)(iii) as respects fines or other penalties, as are referred to in s 1086(2)(*a*) and (*b*), which are imposed by a court, and as respects specified sums, as are referred to in s 1086(2)(*c*) and (*d*), which the Revenue Commissioners accepted, or undertook to accept, in settlement of a specified liability, on or after 25 March 2002; previously "€12,700, or".

15   Subs (4)(*d*) inserted by FA 2002 s 126(1)(*d*)(iv) as respects fines or other penalties, as are referred to in s 1086(2)(*a*) and (*b*), which are imposed by a court, and as respects specified sums, as are referred to in s 1086(2)(*c*) and (*d*), which the Revenue Commissioners accepted, or undertook to accept, in settlement of a specified liability, on or after 25 March 2002.

16   Subs (5A) inserted by FA 2000 s 162(1)(*d*) as respects fines or other penalties, as are referred to in s 1086(2)(*a*)-(*b*), which are imposed by a court, and as respects specified sums, as are referred to in s 1086(2)(*c*)-(*d*), which the Revenue Commissioners accepted, or undertook to accept, in settlement of a specified liability, on or after 23 March 2000.

Cross-references

This section to be construed together with the Value Added Tax Acts 1972-1997, in so far as relating to value added tax: s 1104(3).

This section to be construed together with the Stamp Act 1891 and the enactments amending or extending that Act, in so far as relating to stamp duties: s 1104(4).

This section to be construed together with the Capital Acquisitions Tax Act 1976, and the enactments amending or extending that Act, in so far as relating to capital acquisitions tax: s 1104(5).

This section to be construed together with FA 1983 Pt VI and the enactments amending or extending that Part, in so far as relating to residential property tax: s 1104(6).

Definitions

statute: s 2(1), IA 1937 s 3; Tax Acts: s 1(2).

Former enactments

FA 1983 s 23; FA 1992 s 240; WCTIPA 1993 s 3(7); FA 1997 s 158.

PART 48
MISCELLANEOUS AND SUPPLEMENTAL

1093 Disclosure of information to Ombudsman

Any obligation to maintain secrecy or other restriction on the disclosure or production of information (including documents) obtained by or furnished to the Revenue Commissioners, or any person on their behalf, for taxation purposes, shall not apply to the disclosure or production of information (including documents) to the Ombudsman for the purposes of an examination or investigation by the Ombudsman under the Ombudsman Act, 1980, of any action (within the meaning of that Act) taken by or on behalf of the Revenue Commissioners, being such an action taken in the performance of administrative functions in respect of any tax or duty under the care and management of the Revenue Commissioners.

Cross-references

This section to be construed together with the Customs Acts, in so far as relating to customs: s 1104(2).

This section to be construed together with the Value Added Tax Acts 1972-1997, in so far as relating to value added tax: s 1104(3).

This section to be construed together with the Stamp Act 1891 and the enactments amending or extending that Act, in so far as relating to stamp duties: s 1104(4).

This section to be construed together with the Capital Acquisitions Tax Act 1976, and the enactments amending or extending that Act, in so far as relating to capital acquisitions tax: s 1104(5).

This section to be construed together with FA 1983 Pt VI and the enactments amending or extending that Part, in so far as relating to residential property tax: s 1104(6).

Definition

person: IA 1937 s 11(*c*).

Former enactment
FA 1981 s 52.

PART 49
COMMENCEMENT, REPEALS, TRANSITIONAL PROVISIONS, ETC

1100 Consequential amendments to other enactments

Schedule 31, which provides for amendments to other enactments consequential on the passing of this Act, shall apply for the purposes of this Act.

1104 Short title and construction

(1) This Act may be cited as the Taxes Consolidation Act, 1997.

...

(5) Sections 7, 8, 811, 858, 859, 872(1), 887, 905, 906, 910, 912, 1002, 1003, 1006, 1078, 1079, 1086 and 1093 (in so far as relating to capital acquisitions tax) and Part 34 (in so far as relating to capital acquisitions tax) shall be construed together with the Capital Acquisitions Tax Act, 1976, and the enactments amending or extending that Act.

...

SCHEDULE 31
Consequential amendments

[Section 1100]

In the enactments specified in Column (1) of the following Table for the words set out or referred to in Column (2) there shall be substituted the words set out in the corresponding entry in Column (3)..

Enactment amended (1)	Words to be replaced (2)	Words to be substituted (3)
...		
The Capital Acquisitions Tax Act, 1976:		
section 16(2), in the definition of "private company"	section 95 of the Corporation Tax Act, 1976	section 431 of the Taxes Consolidation Act, 1997
	subsection (1)	subsection (3)
	subsection (4)	subsection (6)
section 52(1), in the definition of "Appeal Commissioners"	section 156 of the Income Tax Act, 1967	section 850 of the Taxes Consolidation Act, 1997
section 58(2)(b)	section 142 of the Income Tax Act, 1967	section 466 of the Taxes Consolidation Act, 1997

Enactment amended	Words to be replaced	Words to be substituted
(1)	(2)	(3)
section 63(9)	sections 128(4), 507, 508, 510, 511, 512, 517 and 518 of the Income Tax Act, 1967	sections 987(4), 1061, 1062, 1063, 1064, 1065, 1066 and 1068 of the Taxes Consolidation Act, 1997
Second Schedule, Part I, paragraph 9, in the definition of "investment income"	section 2 of the Income Tax Act, 1967	section 3 of the Taxes Consolidation Act, 1997
The Finance Act, 1984, section 108(1)(*b*)(ii)	subsection (9) of section 235 of the Income Tax Act, 1967	subsection (1) of section 783 of the Taxes Consolidation Act, 1997
	section 235A	section 785
The Finance Act, 1990:		
...		
section 129(1)	subsection (9) of section 235 of the Income Tax Act, 1967	subsection (1) of section 783 of the Taxes Consolidation Act, 1997
The Finance Act, 1991:		
...		
section 129(1), in the definition of "the Collector"	section 162 of the Income Tax Act, 1967	section 851 of the Taxes Consolidation Act, 1997
section 129(3)	Section 187 of the Income Tax Act, 1967	Section 928(1) and 964(2) of the Taxes Consolidation Act, 1997
...		

FINANCE ACT 1998

(1998 Number 3)
(Date of passing: 27 March 1998)

ARRANGEMENT OF SECTIONS

PART 5
CAPITAL ACQUISITIONS TAX

AN ACT TO CHARGE AND IMPOSE CERTAIN DUTIES OF CUSTOMS AND INLAND REVENUE (INCLUDING EXCISE), TO AMEND THE LAW RELATING TO CUSTOMS AND INLAND REVENUE (INCLUDING EXCISE) AND TO MAKE FURTHER PROVISIONS IN CONNECTION WITH FINANCE.

BE IT ENACTED BY THE OIREACHTAS AS FOLLOWS:

PART 5
CAPITAL ACQUISITIONS TAX

126 Amendment of section 117 (reduction in estimated market value of certain dwellings) of Finance Act, 1991

Notes

This section substituted FA 1991 s 117 in relation to inheritances taken on or after 3 December 1997; previously:

127 Amendment of section 117 (interest on tax) of Finance Act, 1993

Amendments

Section 127 repealed by FA 2001 s 225(2) with effect in relation to probate tax due and payable on or from 6 December 2000; previously:

733

Subs (1)(*a*) substituted "one per cent" for "one and one-quarter per cent" in FA 1993 s 117(*a*) in relation to probate tax due before, on or after March 27 1998 where the period in respect of which interest is to be charged, or a discount falls to be made, commences on or after that date.

Subs (1)(*b*) substituted "one per cent" for "one and one-quarter per cent" in FA 1993 s 117(*b*) in relation to probate tax due before, on or after March 27 1998 where the period in respect of which interest is to be charged, or a discount falls to be made, commences on or after that date.

128 Amendment of section 134 (exclusion of value of excepted assets) of Finance Act, 1994

Notes

This section substituted FA 1994 s 134(7) and is deemed to have always had effect.

129 Conditions before appeal may be made

Notes

This section inserted CATA 1976 s 52A as respects gifts or inheritances taken on or after 12 February 1998.

PART 6
MISCELLANEOUS

131 Interest payments by certain deposit takers

...

Notes

Subs (1)(*a*) substituted CTA 1997 s 256(1)(*a*) definition of "appropriate tax" as and from 6 April 1998.

133 Interest on unpaid or overpaid taxes

...

Notes

Subs (4)(*a*) substituted "1 per cent" for "1.25 per cent" in CATA 1976 s 41(2) for any month or part of, commencing on or after 27 March 1998 in respect of an amount due to be paid or remitted, or repaid or retained before, on or after that date.

Subs (4)(*b*) substituted "0.5 per cent" for "one per cent" in (notwithstanding Payment of Interest on Overpaid Tax Regulations 1990 r 3) in CATA 1976 s 46(1) for any month or part of, commencing on or after 27 March 1998 in respect of an amount due to be paid or remitted, or repaid or retained before, on or after that date.

134 Appeals

...

Notes

Subs (3) inserted CATA 1976 s 52(5)(*a*)(va) as respects appeals determined by the Appeal Commissioners after 27 March 1998.

137 Care and management of taxes and duties

All taxes and duties imposed by this Act are hereby placed under the care and management of the Revenue Commissioners.

138 Short title, construction and commencement

(1) This Act may be cited as the Finance Act, 1998.

...

(6) Part 5 (so far as relating to capital acquisitions tax) shall be construed together with the Capital Acquisitions Tax Act, 1976, and the enactments amending or extending that Act.

(7) Part 6 (so far as relating to income tax) shall be construed together with the Income Tax Acts and (so far as relating to corporation tax) shall be construed together with the Corporation Tax Acts and (so far as relating to capital gains tax) shall be construed together with the Capital Gains Tax Acts and (so far as relating to value-added tax) shall be construed together with the Value-Added Tax Acts, 1972 to 1998, and (so far as relating to residential property tax) shall be construed together with Part VI of the Finance Act, 1983, and the enactments amending or extending that Part and (so far as relating to gift tax or inheritance tax) shall be construed together with the Capital Acquisitions Tax Act, 1976, and the enactments amending or extending that Act and (so far as relating to wealth tax) shall be construed together with the Wealth Tax Act, 1975, and the enactments amending or extending that Act.

...

(10) Any reference in this Act to any other enactment shall, except so far as the context otherwise requires, be construed as a reference to that enactment as amended by or under any other enactment including this Act.

(11) In this Act, a reference to a Part, section or Schedule is to a Part or section of, or Schedule to, this Act, unless it is indicated that reference to some other enactment is intended.

(12) In this Act, a reference to a subsection, paragraph, subparagraph, clause or subclause is to the subsection, paragraph, subparagraph, clause or subclause of the provision (including a Schedule) in which the reference occurs, unless it is indicated that reference to some other provision is intended.

FINANCE ACT 1999

(1999 Number 2)
(Date of passing: 25 March 1999)

PART 1
INCOME TAX, CORPORATION TAX AND CAPITAL GAINS TAX

CHAPTER 3
Dividend Withholding Tax

Section

PART 6
CAPITAL ACQUISITIONS TAX

PART 7
MISCELLANEOUS

AN ACT TO CHARGE AND IMPOSE CERTAIN DUTIES OF CUSTOMS AND INLAND REVENUE (INCLUDING EXCISE), TO AMEND THE LAW RELATING TO CUSTOMS AND INLAND REVENUE (INCLUDING EXCISE) AND TO MAKE FURTHER PROVISIONS IN CONNECTION WITH FINANCE.

BE IT ENACTED BY THE OIREACHTAS AS FOLLOWS:

PART 1
Income Tax, Corporation Tax and Capital Gains Tax

CHAPTER 3
Dividend Withholding Tax

27 Dividend withholding tax

Notes

Para (*b*) inserted TCA 1997 s 1078(2)(*dd*) with effect from 6 April 1999.

PART 6
Capital Acquisitions Tax

199 Interpretation (Part 6)

In this Part "the Principal Act" means the "Capital Acquisitions Tax Act, 1976".

200 Amendment of section 36 (delivery of returns) of Principal Act

---

Notes

Para (*a*) substituted CATA 1976 s 36(1)(*a*)(iii).
Para (*b*) substituted CATA 1976 s 36(4)(*c*)-(*d*).
Para (*c*) inserted CATA 1976 s 36(12)-(15).

---

201 Amendment of Second Schedule (computation of tax) to Principal Act

---

Notes

Subs (1) substituted "2nd day of December, 1988" for "2nd day of June, 1982" in CATA 1976 Sch 2 para 3(*a*)(ii) in relation to gifts or inheritances taken on or after 2 December 1998.

---

202 Amendment of section 41 (payment of tax and interest on tax) of Principal Act

---

Notes

Subs (1) inserted CATA 1976 s 41(2A) where the event which causes the exemption or reduction to cease to apply occurs on or after 11 February 1999.

---

203 Amendment of section 51 (appeals regarding value of real property) of Principal Act

---

Notes

Section 51 inserted CATA 1976 s 51(2).

204 Amendment of section 53 (exemption of small gifts) of Principal Act

---

Notes

Section 204 substituted "£1,000" for "£500" in CATA 1976 s 53(1) in relation to relevant periods ending after the 31st day of December, 1998.

---

205 Amendment of section 58 (exemption of certain receipts) of Principal Act

Notes

Section 205 inserted CATA 1976 s 58(3).

206 Exemption relating to retirement benefits

Notes

Section 206 inserted CATA 1976 s 59B.

PART 7
MISCELLANEOUS

207 Amendment of Chapter 4 (revenue powers) of Part 18 of Taxes Consolidation Act, 1997

Notes

Para (*f*)(i) deleted TCA 1997 s 905(2)(*d*).
Para (*f*)(ii) inserted TCA 1997 s 905(2A).
Para (*g*) inserted TCA 1997 s 906A.

208 Power to obtain information from a Minister of the Government or public body

Notes

Section 208 substituted TCA 1997 s 910(1).

211 Amendment of section 1078 (revenue offences) of Taxes Consolidation Act, 1997

Notes

Para (*a*) inserted TCA 1997 s 1078(2)(*hh*).
Para (*b*) substituted "£10,000" for "£10,000" in TCA 1997 s 1078(3)(*b*).
Para (*c*) inserted TCA 1997 s 1078(3A).

216 Care and management of taxes and duties

All taxes and duties imposed by this Act are hereby placed under the care and management of the Revenue Commissioners.

217 Short title, construction and commencement

(1) This Act may be cited as the Finance Act, 1999.

...

(7) Part 6 (so far as relating to capital acquisitions tax) shall be construed together with the Capital Acquisitions Tax Act, 1976, and the enactments amending or extending that Act.

(8) Part 7 (so far as relating to income tax) shall be construed together with the Income Tax Acts and (so far as relating to corporation tax) shall be construed together with the Corporation Tax Acts and (so far as relating to capital gains tax) shall be construed

together with the Capital Gains Tax Acts and (so far as relating to customs) shall be construed together with the Custom Acts and (so far as relating to duties of excise) shall be construed together with the statutes which relate to duties of excise and the management of those duties and (so far as relating to value-added tax) shall be construed together with the Value-Added Tax Acts, 1972 to 1999, and (so far as relating to stamp duty) shall be construed together with the Stamp Act, 1891, and the enactments amending or extending that Act and (so far as relating to residential property tax) shall be construed together with Part VI of the Finance Act, 1983, and the enactments amending or extending that Part and (so far as relating to gift tax or inheritance tax) shall be construed together with the Capital Acquisitions Tax Act, 1976, and the enactments amending or extending that Act.

...

(11) Any reference in this Act to any other enactment shall, except so far as the context otherwise requires, be construed as a reference to that enactment as amended by or under any other enactment including this Act.

(12) In this Act, a reference to a Part, section or Schedule is to a Part or section of, or Schedule to, this Act, unless it is indicated that reference to some other enactment is intended.

(13) In this Act, a reference to a subsection, paragraph, subparagraph, clause- or subclause is to the subsection, paragraph, subparagraph, clause or subclause of the provision (including a Schedule) in which the reference occurs, unless it is indicated that reference to some other provision is intended.

FINANCE ACT 2000

(2000 Number 3)
(Date passed: 23 March 2000)

ARRANGEMENT OF SECTIONS

PART 6
CAPITAL ACQUISITIONS TAX

PART 7
MISCELLANEOUS

AN ACT TO CHARGE AND IMPOSE CERTAIN DUTIES OF CUSTOMS AND
INLAND REVENUE (INCLUDING EXCISE), TO AMEND THE LAW
RELATING TO CUSTOMS AND INLAND REVENUE (INCLUDING EXCISE)

AND TO MAKE FURTHER PROVISIONS IN CONNECTION WITH FINANCE.
[23rd MARCH 2000]

PART 6
CAPITAL ACQUISITIONS TAX

136 Interpretation (Part 6)

In this Part **"Principal Act"** means the Capital Acquisitions Tax Act, 1976.

137 Amendment of section 2 (interpretation) of Principal Act

Notes

Section 137 inserted CATA 1976 s 2(5A) for gifts or inheritances taken on or after 1 December 1999.

138 Amendment of section 6 (taxable gift) of Principal Act

Notes

Subs (1)(*a*) substituted CATA 1976 s 6(1) for gifts taken on or after 1 December 1999, FA 2000 s 138 does not apply in relation to a gift taken under a disposition where the date of the disposition is before 1 December 1999.
Subs (1)(*b*) substituted CATA 1976 s 6(3) and inserted CATA 1976 s 6(4) for gifts taken on or after 1 December 1999, FA 2000 s 138 does not apply in relation to a gift taken under a disposition where the date of the disposition is before 1 December 1999.

139 Amendment of section 12 (taxable inheritance) of Principal Act

Notes

Subs (1)(*a*) substituted CATA 1976 s 12(1) for inheritances taken on or after 1 December 1999, FA 2000 s 139 does not have effect in relation to an inheritance taken under a disposition where the date of the disposition is before 1 December 1999.
Subs (1)(*b*) substituted "subsection (1)(*c*)" for "subsection (1)(*b*)" in CATA 1976 s 12(2) for inheritances taken on or after 1 December 1999. FA 2000 s 139 does not have effect in relation to an inheritance taken under a disposition where the date of the disposition is before 1 December 1999.
Subs (1)(*c*) inserted CATA 1976 s 12(3)-(4) for inheritances taken on or after 1 December 1999, FA 2000 s 139 does not have effect in relation to an inheritance taken under a disposition where the date of the disposition is before 1 December 1999.

140 Amendment of section 19 (value of agricultural property) of Principal Act

Notes

Subs (1)(*a*) substituted CATA 1976 s 19(1)(definition of "farmer") for gifts or inheritances taken on or after 10 February 2000.
Subs (1)(*b*) substituted CATA 1976 s 19(5)(*a*) where the sale or compulsory acquisition which causes the agricultural value to cease to be applicable occurs on or after 10 February 2000.

141 Amendment of section 36 (delivery of returns) of Principal Act

Notes

Subs (1)(*a*) substituted CATA 1976 s 36(4) for gifts or inheritances taken on or after 1 December 1999.
Subs (1)(*b*) substituted CATA 1976 s 36(14)(*a*) for gifts or inheritances taken on or after 1 December 1999.

142 Amendment of section 48 (receipts and certificates) of Principal Act

Notes

Para (*a*) substituted CATA 1976 s 48(3)-(5).
Para (*b*) deleted CATA 1976 s 48(7).

143 Amendment of section 54 (provisions relating to charities, etc) of Principal Act

Notes

Section 143 substituted CATA 1976 s 54(1) for gifts or inheritances taken on or after 1 December 1999.

144 Amendment of section 55 (exemption of certain objects) of Principal Act

Notes

Section 144 substituted CATA 1976 s 55(4) for gifts or inheritances taken on or after 1 December 1999.

145 Amendment of Second Schedule to Principal Act

Notes

Subs (1)(*a*) substituted CATA 1976 Sch 2 Pt I paras 1-7 for gifts or inheritances taken on or after 1 December 1999.
Subs (1)(*b*) substituted CATA 1976 Sch 2 Pt II Table for gifts or inheritances taken on or after 1 December 1999.

146 Amendment of section 39 (extension of section 55 (exemption of certain objects) of Capital Acquisitions Tax Act, 1976) of Finance Act, 1978

Notes

Section 146 inserted "of which not less than 10 of the days during that period shall fall on a Saturday or a Sunday or both" after "September" in CATA 1976 s 39(1A)(*b*)(i) for gifts and inheritances taken on or after 10 February 2000.

147 Amendment of section 109 (interpretation) of Finance Act, 1993

Amendments

Section 147 repealed by FA 2001 s 225(2) with effect in relation to probate tax due and payable on or from 6 December 2000; previously:
Subs (1)(*a*) substituted "mid-November 1996" for "mid-November, 1989" in FA 1993 s 109 (definition of "the consumer price index number") for persons dying on or after 1 December 1999.
Subs (1)(*b*) substituted FA 1993 s 109 (definition of "relevant threshold") for persons dying on or after 1 December 1999.

148 Amendment of Chapter 1 (business relief) of Part VI of Finance Act, 1994

Notes

Subs (1)(*a*) substituted FA 1994 s 134(1)-(2) for gifts or inheritances taken on or after 10 February 2000.
Subs (1)(*b*)(i) substituted FA 1994 s 135(1) where the event which caused the reduction to cease to be applicable occurs on or after 10 February 2000.
Subs (1)(*b*)(ii) substituted FA 1994 s 135(2)(proviso)(ii)-(iii) where the event which caused the reduction to cease to be applicable occurs on or after 10 February 2000.
Subs (1)(*c*) inserted FA 1994 s 135A for gifts or inheritances taken on or after 10 February 2000.

149 Amendment of section 142 (exemption of certain transfers from capital acquisitions tax following the dissolution of a marriage) of Finance Act, 1997

Notes

Subs (1)(*a*) deleted "and" from FA 1997 s 142(2)(*c*) for an order or other determination to like effect where the order or the determination is made on or after 10 February 2000.

Subs (1)(*b*) substituted "1996" for "1996." in FA 1997 s 142(2)(*d*) for an order or other determination to like effect where the order or the determination is made on or after 10 February 2000

Subs (1)(*c*) inserted FA 1997 s 142(2)(*e*) for an order or other determination to like effect where the order or the determination is made on or after 10 February 2000

150 Amendment of section 143 (abatement and postponement of probate tax on certain property) of Finance Act, 1997

Amendments

Section 150 repealed by FA 2001 s 225(2) with effect in relation to probate tax due and payable on or from 6 December 2000; previously:

Subs (1)(*a*) deleted "or" from FA 1997 s 143(1)(*a*)(i) for an order or other determination to like effect where the order or the determination is made on or after 10 February 2000.

Subs (1)(*b*) substituted "1996, or" for "1996." in FA 1997 s 143(1)(*a*)(ii) for an order or other determination to like effect where the order or the determination is made on or after 10 February 2000.

Subs (1)(*c*) inserted FA 1997 s 143(1)(*a*)(iii) for an order or other determination to like effect where the order or the determination is made on or after 10 February 2000.

151 Exemption relating to certain dwellings

Notes

Section 151 inserted CATA 1976 s 59C for gifts or inheritances taken on or after 1 December 1999.

152 Amendment of section 58 (exemption of certain receipts) of Principal Act

Notes

Section 152 inserted CATA 1976 s 58(4) for gifts or inheritances taken on or after 23 March 2000.

153 Repeals etc

Notes

Section 153 repealed FA 1990 s 128 and FA 1991 ss 1160-117 for gifts or inheritances taken on or after 1 December 1999.

PART 7
MISCELLANEOUS

154 Interpretation (Part 7)

In this Part "Principal Act" means the Taxes Consolidation Act, 1997.

160 Amendment of section 824 (appeals) of Principal Act

Notes

This section substituted "Part" for "Chapter" in TCA 1997 s 824 with effect from 23 March 2000.

161 Amendment of section 1003 (payment of tax by means of donation of heritage items) of Principal Act

Notes

This section substituted "£3,000,000" for "£750,000" in TCA 1997 s 1003(2)(*c*) as respects the calendar year 2000 and subsequent years.

162 Amendment of section 1086 (publication of names of tax defaulters) of Principal Act

Notes

Subs (1)(*a*)(i) substituted "tax," for "tax, or" in TCA 1997 s 1086(2)(*b*) and "tax, or" for "tax." in TCA 1997 s 1086(2)(*c*)(iii) as respects fines or other penalties, as are referred to in s 1086(2)(*a*)-(*b*), which are imposed by a court, and as respects specified sums, as are referred to in s 1086(2)(*c*)-(*d*), which the Revenue Commissioners accepted, or undertook to accept, in settlement of a specified liability, on or after 23 March 2000.

Subs (1)(*a*)(ii) inserted TCA 1997 s 1086(2)(*d*) as respects fines or other penalties, as are referred to in s 1086(2)(*a*)-(*b*), which are imposed by a court, and as respects specified sums, as are referred to in s 1086(2)(*c*)-(*d*), which the Revenue Commissioners accepted, or undertook to accept, in settlement of a specified liability, on or after 23 March 2000.

Subs (1)(*b*) inserted TCA 1997 s 1086(2A) as respects fines or other penalties, as are referred to in s 1086(2)(*a*)-(*b*), which are imposed by a court, and as respects specified sums, as are referred to in s 1086(2)(*c*)-(*d*), which the Revenue Commissioners accepted, or undertook to accept, in settlement of a specified liability, on or after 23 March 2000.

Subs (1)(*c*)(i) substituted "Paragraph (*c*) and (*d*)" for "Paragraph (*c*)" in TCA 1997 s 1086(4) as respects fines or other penalties, as are referred to in s 1086(2)(*a*)-(*b*), which are imposed by a court, and as respects specified sums, as are referred to in s 1086(2)(*c*)-(*d*), which the Revenue Commissioners accepted, or undertook to accept, in settlement of a specified liability, on or after 23 March 2000.

Subs (1)(*c*)(ii) substituted "paragraph (*c*) or (*d*), as the case may be," for "paragraph (*c*)" in TCA 1997 s 1086(4)(*c*) as respects fines or other penalties, as are referred to in s 1086(2)(*a*)-(*b*), which are imposed by a court, and as respects specified sums, as are referred to in s 1086(2)(*c*)-(*d*), which the Revenue Commissioners accepted, or undertook to accept, in settlement of a specified liability, on or after 23 March 2000.

Subs (1)(*d*) inserted TCA 1997 s 1086(5A) as respects fines or other penalties, as are referred to in s 1086(2)(*a*)-(*b*), which are imposed by a court, and as respects specified sums, as are referred to in s 1086(2)(*c*)-(*d*), which the Revenue Commissioners accepted, or undertook to accept, in settlement of a specified liability, on or after 23 March 2000.

165 Care and management of taxes and duties

All taxes and duties imposed by this Act are by virtue of this section placed under the care and management of the Revenue Commissioners.

166 Short title, construction and commencement

(1) This Act may be cited as the Finance Act, 2000.

...

(7) Part 6 (so far as relating to capital acquisitions tax) shall be construed together with the Capital Acquisitions Tax Act, 1976, and the enactments amending or extending that Act.

(8) Part 7 (so far as relating to income tax) shall be construed together with the Income Tax Acts and (so far as relating to corporation tax) shall be construed together with the Corporation Tax Acts and (so far as relating to capital gains tax) shall be construed together with the Capital Gains Tax Acts and (so far as relating to customs) shall be

construed with the Customs Acts and (so far as relating to duties of excise) shall be construed together with the statutes which relate to duties of excise and the management of those duties and (so far as relating to value-added tax) shall be construed together with the Value-Added Tax Acts, 1972 to 2000, and (so far as relating to stamp duty) shall be construed together with the Stamp Duties Consolidation Act, 1999, and (so far as relating to residential property tax) shall be construed together with Part VI of the Finance Act, 1983, and the enactments amending or extending that Part and (so far as relating to gift tax or inheritance tax) shall be construed together with the Capital Acquisitions Tax Act, 1976, and the enactments amending or extending that Act.

...

(11) Any reference in this Act to any other enactment shall, except so far as the context otherwise requires, be construed as a reference to that enactment as amended by or under any other enactment including this Act.

(12) In this Act, a reference to a Part, section or Schedule is to a Part or section of, or Schedule to, this Act, unless it is indicated that reference to some other enactment is intended.

(13) In this Act, a reference to a subsection, paragraph, subparagraph, clause or subclause is to the subsection, paragraph, subparagraph, clause or subclause of the provision (including a Schedule) in which the reference occurs, unless it is indicated that reference to some other provision is intended.

FINANCE ACT 2001

(No 7 of 2001)

ARRANGEMENT OF SECTIONS

PART 6
CAPITAL ACQUISITIONS TAX

PART 8
MISCELLANEOUS

SCHEDULE 5
AMENDMENT OF ENACTMENTS CONSEQUENT ON CHANGEOVER TO EURO

AN ACT TO PROVIDE FOR THE IMPOSITION, REPEAL, REMISSION, ALTERATION AND REGULATION OF TAXATION, OF STAMP DUTIES AND OF DUTIES RELATING TO EXCISE AND OTHERWISE TO MAKE FURTHER PROVISION IN CONNECTION WITH FINANCE INCLUDING THE REGULATION OF CUSTOMS. [30TH MARCH 2001]

PART 6
CAPITAL ACQUISITIONS TAX

215 Interpretation (Part 6)

In this Part **"Principal Act"** means the Capital Acquisitions Tax Act, 1976.

216 Amendment of section 18 (taxable value of a taxable gift or taxable inheritance) of Principal Act

Notes

Subs (1) substituted "section 6(1)(*d*) or 12(1)(*c*)" for "section 6(1)(*c*) or section 12(1)(*b*)" in CATA 1976 s 18(5)(*f*) in relation to gifts or inheritances taken on or after 1 December 1999, but not in relation to gifts or inheritances taken under a disposition where the date of the disposition is before 1 December 1999.

217 Amendment of section 19 (value of agricultural property) of Principal Act

Notes

Subs (1) substituted "or within 4 years of the compulsory acquisition" for "or compulsory acquisition" in CATA 1976 s 19(5)(*a*) in relation to compulsory acquisitions made on or after 6 December 2000.

218 Amendment of section 55 (exemption of certain objects) of Principal Act

Notes

Subs (1) inserted CATA 1976 s 55(5) in relation to inheritances taken on or after 26 January 2001.

219 Amendment of section 57 (exemption of certain securities) of Principal Act

Notes

Subs (1) substituted CATA 1976 s 57(2)(*a*) in relation to securities or units comprised in a gift or an inheritance where the date of the gift or inheritance is on or after 15 February 2001 and the securities or units come into the beneficial ownership of the disponer on or after that date, or become subject to the disposition on or after that date without having been previously in the beneficial ownership of the disponer.

220 Amendment of section 59C (exemption relating to certain dwellings) of Principal Act

Notes

Subs (1) inserted CATA 1976 s 59C(1A) in relation to gift or inheritance taken on or after 1 December 1999.

221 Gifts and inheritances taken by foster children

Notes

This section inserted CATA 1976 s 59D.

222 Gifts and inheritances taken by adopted children from natural parent

Notes

This section inserted CATA 1976 s 59E.

223 Amendment of section 61 (payment of money standing in names of two or more persons) of Principal Act

Notes

Subs (1)(*a*) substituted "£25,000" for "£5,000" in CATA 1976 s 61(1) in relation to persons dying on or after 26 January 2001 and prior to 1 January 2002.

Subs (1)(*b*) substituted "€31,750" for "£5,000" in in CATA 1976 s 61(1) in relation to persons dying on or after 1 January 2002.

224 Amendment of section 85 (exemption of specified collective investment undertakings) of Finance Act, 1989

Notes

Subs (1) substituted FA 1989 s 85(1)-(2) in relation to units of an investment undertaking comprised in a gift or inheritance taken on or after 1 April 2000.

The disponer must have been domiciled or ordinarily resident abroad at the date of the disposition in order to qualify for this exemption, but this does not apply to persons who had already purchased UCITS or units in specified investment undertakings prior to 15 February 2001.

Cross-references

FA 2000 s 58.

225 Abolition of probate tax

(1) Chapter I (which relates to the taxation of assets passing on inheritance) of Part VI of the Finance Act, 1993, is repealed.

(2) Sections 137, 138, 139 and 140 of the Finance Act, 1994, section 143 of the Finance Act, 1997, section 127 of the Finance Act, 1998, and sections 147 and 150 of the Finance Act, 2000, are repealed.

(3) Subsections (1) and (2) shall have effect in relation to probate tax which would but for this section first become due and payable on or after 6 December 2000.

Notes

Subs (1) repealed FA 1993 Part VI Ch I in relation to probate tax which would but for this section first become due and payable on or after 6 December 2000.

Subs (2) repealed FA 1994 ss 137-140; FA 1997 s 143; FA 1998 s 127 and FA 2000 ss 149, 150 in relation to probate tax which would but for this section first become due and payable on or after 6 December 2000.

226 Amendment of section 133 (exemption of certain policies of assurance) of Finance Act, 1993

Notes

Subs (1) substituted FA 1993 s 133(2)(*b*)(ii) in relation to a policy comprised in a gift or an inheritance where the date of the gift or the date of the inheritance is on or after 15 February 2001 and the policy comes into the beneficial ownership of the disponer on or after 15 February 2001, or becomes subject to the disposition on or after that date without having been previously in the beneficial ownership of the disponer.

227 Amendment of section 124 (interpretation (Chapter I)) of Finance Act, 1994

Notes

Subs (1) inserted FA 1994 s 124(4) in relation to gifts or inheritances taken on or after 11 April 1994.

228 Amendment of section 127 (relevant business property) of Finance Act, 1994

Notes

Subs (1)(*a*) substitution of "whether incorporated in the State or otherwise" for "incorporated in the State" in FA 1994 s 127 in relation to gifts or inheritances taken on or after 15 February 2001.

Subs (1)(*b*) deleted from FA 1994 s 127(1)(*e*) in relation to gifts or inheritances taken on or after 15 February 2001.

Subs (1)(*c*) deleted FA 1994 s 127(3) in relation to gifts or inheritances taken on or after 15 February 2001.

229 Amendment of provisions relating to the taxation of discretionary trusts

Notes

Subs (1)(*a*)(i) inserted FA 1994 s 143(1) definition of "settled relevant inheritance" as respects relevant inheritances taken on or after 26 January 2001.

Subs (1)(*a*)(ii) substituted FA 1994 s 143(1) definition of "relevant period" as respects relevant inheritances taken on or after 26 January 2001.

Subs (1)(*b*) substituted FA 1994 s 143(2)(proviso) as respects relevant inheritances taken on or after 26 January 2001.

PART 8

MISCELLANEOUS

231 Interpretation (Part 8)

In this Part **"Principal Act"** means the Taxes Consolidation Act, 1997.

232 Amendment of Chapter 3 (other obligations and returns) of Part 38 of Principal Act

...

(2) (*a*) In this subsection **"chargeable period"** has the same meaning as in section 321(2).

Notes

Subs (1)(*a*) substituted TCA 1997 s 887 [with effect on or after 15 February 2001][1].

Subs (3)(*a*)(i) substituted "€1,265" for "£1,000" in TCA 1997 s 887(5)(*b*) with effect from 1 January 2002.

Amendments

¹   Substituted by subs (2)(*c*) which was substituted by FA 2002 s 138 and Sch 6 para 5(*f*) with effect on and
     from 30 March 2001; previously "as respects any chargeable period (within the meaning of s 321(2))
     commencing on or after 15 February 2001".

233 Amendment of section 1078 (revenue offences) of Principal Act

Notes

Subs (1) substituted "£1,500" for "£1,000" in TCA 1997 s 1078(3)(*a*) with effect from 6 April 2001.

Subs (2)(*a*) substituted "€1,900" for "£1,500" in TCA 1997 s 1078(3)(*a*) with effect from 1 January 2002.

238 Amendment of section 1002 (deduction from payments due to defaulters of amounts due in relation to tax) of Principal Act

Notes

This section substituted "14 days" for "one month" in TCA 1997 s 1002(3)(*a*).

239 Amendment of section 1006A (offset between taxes) of Principal Act

Notes

Para (*a*) inserted ", and includes any interest due under the Acts in relation to such tax, duty, levy or other charge" in TCA 1997 s 1006A(1) definition of "liability" with effect from 6 April 2001.

Para (*b*) substituted TCA 1997 s 1006A(2) with effect from 6 April 2001.

240 Amendment of enactments consequent on changeover to Euro

(1) (*a*)   Subject to subsection (2), in each provision specified in column (1) of
            Schedule 5 for the words or amount set out in column (2) of that Schedule at
            that entry there shall be substituted the words or amount set out at the
            corresponding entry in column (3) of that Schedule.

   (*b*)   Where words are or an amount is mentioned more than once in a provision
            specified in column (1) of Schedule 5, then the substitution provided for by
            paragraph (*a*) shall apply as respects those words or that amount to each
            mention of those words or that amount in that provision.

(2) Subsection (1) shall apply—

   (*a*)   to the extent that the amendments relate to income tax and related matters,
            other than the amendments relating to such matters referred to in
            subparagraphs (ii), (iii), (iv), (v) and (vi) of paragraph (*m*), as respects the year
            of assessment 2002 and subsequent years of assessment,

   (*b*)   to the extent that the amendments relate to capital gains tax and related
            matters, other than the amendments relating to such matters referred to in
            paragraph (*m*)(vii),as respects the year of assessment 2002 and subsequent
            years of assessment,

   (*c*)   to the extent that the amendments relate to corporation tax and related matters,
            other than the amendments relating to such matters referred to in
            subparagraphs (i), (iii) and (iv) of paragraph (*l*), for accounting periods ending
            on or after 1 January 2002,

...

(*i*)　to the extent that section 1086 of the Taxes Consolidation Act, 1997 is amended, as respects specified sums such as are referred to in paragraphs (*c*) and (*d*) of section 1086(2) of that Act which the Revenue Commissioners accept or undertake to accept on or after 1 January 2002,

...

(*k*)　to the extent that the enactment amended imposes any fine, forfeiture, penalty or punishment for any act or omission, as respects any act or omission which takes place or begins on or after 1 January 2002,

242 Care and management of taxes and duties

All the taxes and duties imposed by this Act are placed under the care and management of the Revenue Commissioners.

243 Short title, construction and commencement

(1) This Act may be cited as the Finance Act, 2001.

...

(6) Part 6 (so far as relating to capital acquisitions tax) shall be construed together with the Capital Acquisitions Tax Act, 1976, and the enactments amending or extending that Act.

...

(8) Part 8 (so far as relating to income tax) shall be construed together with the Income Tax Acts and (so far as relating to corporation tax) shall be construed together with the Corporation Tax Acts and (so far as relating to capital gains tax) shall be construed together with the Capital Gains Tax Acts and (so far as relating to value-added tax) shall be construed together with the Value-Added Tax Acts, 1972 to 2001 and (so far as relating to residential property tax) shall be construed together with Part VI of the Finance Act, 1983, and the enactments amending or extending that Part and (so far as relating to gift tax or inheritance tax) shall be construed together with the Capital Acquisitions Tax Act, 1976, and the enactments amending or extending that Act.

...

(11) Any reference in this Act to any other enactment shall, except so far as the context otherwise requires, be construed as a reference to that enactment as amended by or under any other enactment including this Act.

(12) In this Act, a reference to a Part, section or Schedule is to a Part or section of, or Schedule to, this Act, unless it is indicated that reference to some other enactment is intended.

(13) In this Act, a reference to a subsection, paragraph, subparagraph, clause or subclause is to the subsection, paragraph, subparagraph, clause or subclause of the provision (including a Schedule) in which the reference occurs, unless it is indicated that reference to some other provision is intended.

SCHEDULE 5
Amendment of Enactments Consequent on Changeover to Euro

[Section 240]

PART 5
CAPITAL ACQUISITIONS TAX AND RELATED MATTERS

Notes

Sch 5 Part 5 amended the following with effect from 1 January 2002:

Capital Acquisitions Tax Act, 1976:

s 53(1): "£1,000" substituted by " €1,270"; s 54(1)(*b*): "£15,000" substituted by " €19,050"; s 61(3): "£1,000" substituted by " €1,265"; s 63(1)(*a*): "£2,000" substituted by " €2,535"; s 63(1)(*b*): "£25 substituted by " €30"; s 63(2): "£1,000" substituted by " €1,265"; s 63(3)(i): "£5,000" substituted by " €6,345"; s 63(7): "£1,000" substituted by " €1,265"; First Schedule Pt II (Table A): "£1 substituted by " €1"; First Schedule, Pt III (Table B): "£1" substituted by " €1"; Second Schedule Pt I para 1(*a*): "£300,000" substituted by " €381,000"; Second Schedule Pt I para 1(*b*): "£30,000" substituted by " €38,100"; Second Schedule Pt I para 1(*c*): "£15,000" substituted by " €19,050.

Finance Act 1986:

s 108(*a*): "£1,000" substituted by " €1,265.

Finance Act, 1993(No 13 of 1993):

s 111(l)(i): "£1,000" substituted by " €1,265"; s 111(l)(i): "£5,000" substituted by " €6,345"; s 111(l)(ii): "£400" substituted by "€505"; s 111(l)(ii): "£2,000" substituted by " €2,535"; s 111(l)(iii): "£200" substituted by " €250"; s 111(l)(iii): "£1,000" substituted by " €1,265"; s 111(l)(iv): "£5" substituted by " €6"; s 111(l)(iv): "£25 substituted by "€30.

Finance Act, 1994:

s 146(4B)(*a*)(i)(I): "£100,000" substituted by " €127,000"; s 146(4B)(*a*)(i)(II)(B): "£15,000" substituted by " €19,050"; s 146(4C)(*b*): "£2,000" substituted by " €2,540"; s 146(4C)(*c*): "£2,000" substituted by " €2,540.

FINANCE ACT 2002

(2002 Number 5)

ARRANGEMENT OF SECTIONS

PART 5
CAPITAL ACQUISITIONS TAX

PART 6
MISCELLANEOUS

SCHEDULE 6
MISCELLANEOUS TECHNICAL AMENDMENTS IN RELATION TO TAX

An Act to provide for the imposition, repeal, remission, alteration and regulation of taxation of stamp duties and of duties relating to excise and otherwise to make further provision in connection with finance including the regulation of customs

PART 5
CAPITAL ACQUISITIONS TAX

115 Interpretation (Part 5)

In this Part **"Principal Act"** means the Capital Acquisitions Tax Act 1976.

116 Amendment of section 19 (value of agricultural property) of Principal Act

Notes

Section 116 substituted "6 years" for "4 years" in CATA 1976 s 19(5)(*a*)(ii) in relation to compulsory acquisitions made on or after 25 March 2002.

117 Amendment of section 36 (delivery of returns) of Principal Act

Notes

Subs (1)(*a*) substituted "5 December 1991" for "2 December 1988" in CATA 1976 s 36(4)(*a*) in relation to gifts or inheritances taken on or after 5 December 2001.

Subs (1)(*b*) substituted "5 December 1991" for "the 2nd day of December, 1988" in CATA 1976 s 36(14)(*b*)-(*c*) in relation to gifts or inheritances taken on or after 5 December 2001.

118 Amendment of section 41 (payment of tax and interest on tax) of Principal Act

Notes

Subs (1)(*a*) substituted "subsection (3) or (4) of section 55" for "section 55(4)" in CATA 1976 s 41(2A)(*b*) where the event which causes the exemption to cease to be applicable occurs on or after 11 February 1999.

Subs (1)(*b*) substituted "to apply," for "to apply." in CATA 1976 s 41(2A)(*d*).

Subs (1)(*c*) inserted CATA 1976 s 41(2A)(*e*) where the event which causes the exemption to cease to be applicable occurs on or after 1 December 19.

119 Amendment of section 52 (appeals in other cases) of Principal Act

Notes

Section 119 substituted CATA 1976 s 52(7) in relation to evidence of any notice given by the Commissioners or by an officer of the Commissioners in any proceedings on or after 25 March 2002.

120 Amendment of section 70 (delivery, service and evidence of notices and forms, etc) of Principal Act

Notes

Subs (1) substituted CATA 1976 s 70(3) in relation to evidence of any notice given by the Commissioners or by an officer of the Commissioners in any proceedings on or after 25 March 2002.

121 Amendment of Second Schedule (computation of tax) to Principal Act

Notes

Section 121 substituted "5 December 1991" for "2 December 1988" in CATA 1976 Sch 2 para 3(*a*)(ii) in relation to gifts or inheritances taken on or after 5 December 2001.

122 Amendment of section 133 (exemption of certain policies of assurance) of Finance Act 1993

Notes

Para (*a*) substituted FA 1993 s 133(1).

Para (*b*) substituted "new policy or in an old policy" for "policy" in FA 1993 s 133(2).

Para (*c*) substituted FA 1993 s 133(3).

PART 6
MISCELLANEOUS

123 Interpretation (Part 6)

In this Part "Principal Act" means the Taxes Consolidation Act 1997.

125 Amendment of Chapter 5 (miscellaneous provisions) of Part 42 of Principal Act

---

Notes

Para (*a*)(i)(I) substituted TCA 1997 s 1006A(1) definition of "claim" with effect from 25 March 2002.

Para (*a*)(i)(II) substituted TCA 1997 s 1006A(1) definition of "liability" with effect from 25 March 2002.

Para (*a*)(i)(III) substituted "credited;" for "credited." In TCA 1997 s 1006A(1) definition of "overpayment" with effect from 25 March 2002.

Para (*a*)(i)(IV) inserted TCA 1997 s 1006A(1) definition of "tax" with effect from 25 March 2002.

Para (*a*)(ii) inserted TCA 1997 s 1006A(5) with effect from 25 March 2002.

Para (*b*) inserted TCA 1997 s 1006B(5) with effect from 25 March 2002.

---

126 Amendment of section 1086 (publication of names of tax defaulters) of Principal Act

---

Notes

Subs (1)(*a*)(i)(I) substituted TCA 1997 s 1086(1) definition of "the Acts" para (*e*) as respects fines or other penalties, as are referred to in TCA 1997 s 1086(2)(*a*)-(*b*), which are imposed by a court, and as respects specified sums, as are referred to in TCA 1997 s 1086(2)(*c*)-(*d*), which the Revenue Commissioners accepted, or undertook to accept, in settlement of a specified liability, on or after 25 March 2002.

Subs (1)(*a*)(i)(II) inserted TCA 1997 s 1086(1) definition of "the Acts" paras (*g*)-(*h*) as respects fines or other penalties, as are referred to in TCA 1997 s 1086(2)(*a*)-(*b*), which are imposed by a court, and as respects specified sums, as are referred to in TCA 1997 s 1086(2)(*c*)-(*d*), which the Revenue Commissioners accepted, or undertook to accept, in settlement of a specified liability, on or after 25 March 2002.

Subs (1)(*a*)(ii) substituted TCA 1997 s 1086(1) definition of "tax" as respects fines or other penalties, as are referred to in TCA 1997 s 1086(2)(*a*)-(*b*), which are imposed by a court, and as respects specified sums, as are referred to in TCA 1997 s 1086(2)(*c*)-(*d*), which the Revenue Commissioners accepted, or undertook to accept, in settlement of a specified liability, on or after 25 March 2002.

Subs (1)(*b*)(i) substituted TCA 1997 s 1086(2)(*c*)(ii)-(iii) as respects fines or other penalties, as are referred to in TCA 1997 s 1086(2)(*a*)-(*b*), which are imposed by a court, and as respects specified sums, as are referred to in TCA 1997 s 1086(2)(*c*)-(*d*), which the Revenue Commissioners accepted, or undertook to accept, in settlement of a specified liability, on or after 25 March 2002.

Subs (1)(*b*)(ii) substituted TCA 1997 s 1086(2)(*d*)(ii)-(iii) as respects fines or other penalties, as are referred to in TCA 1997 s 1086(2)(*a*)-(*b*), which are imposed by a court, and as respects specified sums, as are referred to in TCA 1997 s 1086(2)(*c*)-(*d*), which the Revenue Commissioners accepted, or undertook to accept, in settlement of a specified liability, on or after 25 March 2002.

Subs (1)(*c*) substituted TCA 1997 s 1086(3)(*b*) as respects fines or other penalties, as are referred to in TCA 1997 s 1086(2)(*a*)-(*b*), which are imposed by a court, and as respects specified sums, as are referred to in TCA 1997 s 1086(2)(*c*)-(*d*), which the Revenue Commissioners accepted, or undertook to accept, in settlement of a specified liability, on or after 25 March 2002.

Subs (1)(*d*)(i) substituted "those paragraphs" for "that paragraph" in TCA 1997 s 1086(4)(*a*) as respects fines or other penalties, as are referred to in TCA 1997 s 1086(2)(*a*)-(*b*), which are imposed by a court, and as respects specified sums, as are referred to in TCA 1997 s 1086(2)(*c*)-(*d*), which the Revenue Commissioners accepted, or undertook to accept, in settlement of a specified liability, on or after 25 March 2002.

Subs (1)(*d*)(ii) substituted "applied," for "applied, or" in TCA 1997 s 1086(4)(*b*) as respects fines or other penalties, as are referred to in TCA 1997 s 1086(2)(*a*)-(*b*), which are imposed by a court, and as respects specified sums, as are referred to in TCA 1997 s 1086(2)(*c*)-(*d*), which the Revenue Commissioners accepted, or undertook to accept, in settlement of a specified liability, on or after 25 March 2002.

Subs (1)(*d*)(iii) substituted "€12,700, or" for "€12,700."in TCA 1997 s 1086(4)(*c* as respects fines or other penalties, as are referred to in TCA 1997 s 1086(2)(*a*)-(*b*), which are imposed by a court, and as respects

specified sums, as are referred to in TCA 1997 s 1086(2)(*c*)-(*d*), which the Revenue Commissioners accepted, or undertook to accept, in settlement of a specified liability, on or after 25 March 2002.

Subs (1)(*d*)(iv) inserted TCA 1997 s 1086(4)(*d*) as respects fines or other penalties, as are referred to in TCA 1997 s 1086(2)(*a*)-(*b*), which are imposed by a court, and as respects specified sums, as are referred to in TCA 1997 s 1086(2)(*c*)-(*d*), which the Revenue Commissioners accepted, or undertook to accept, in settlement of a specified liability, on or after 25 March 2002.

129 Interest on unpaid and overpaid tax

Notes

Subs (3)(*a*) substituted "0.0322 per cent per day or part of a day" for "1 per cent per month or part of a month" in CATA 1976 s 41(2) with effect from 1 September 2002 in respect of interest chargeable or payable as regards an amount due to be paid or remitted or to be repaid or retained, whether before, on, or after that date.

Subs (3)(*b*) substituted "0.0161 per cent, or such other rate (if any) as stands prescribed by the Minister for Finance by regulations, for each day or part of a day" for "0.5 per cent, or such other rate (if any) as stands prescribed by the Minister for Finance by regulations, for each month or part of a month" in CATA 1976 s 46(1) with effect from 1 September 2002 in respect of interest chargeable or payable as regards an amount due to be paid or remitted or to be repaid or retained, whether before, on, or after that date.

132 Amendment of Chapter 4 (revenue powers) of Part 38 of Principal Act

Notes

Para (*d*) inserted TCA 1997 s 905(1) definition of "records" with effect from 25 March 2002.

133 Amendment of section 1078 (revenue offences) of Principal Act

Notes

Para (*a*) substituted "fails without reasonable excuse" for "knowingly or wilfully fails" in TCA 1997 s 1078(2)(*g*) with effect from 25 March 2002.

Para (*b*) inserted TCA 1997 s 1078(3B) with effect from 25 March 2002.

138 Miscellaneous technical amendments in relation to tax

The enactments specified in Schedule 6 are amended to the extent and in the manner specified in that Schedule.

139 Amendment of Provisional Collection of Taxes Act 1927

Notes

Para (*a*) substituted Provisional Collection of Taxes 1927 s 1 definition of "new tax" with effect from 25 March 2002.

Para (*b*) substituted "immediately before the date on which the resolution is expressed to take effect or, where no such date is expressed, the passing of the resolution by Dáil Éireann" for "immediately before the end of the previous financial year" in Provisional Collection of Taxes 1927 ss 2-3 with effect from 25 March 2002.

140 Care and management of taxes and duties

All taxes and duties imposed by this Act are placed under the care and management of the Revenue Commissioners.

141 Short title, construction and commencement

(1) This Act may be cited as the Finance Act 2002.

...

(6) Part 5 (so far as relating to capital acquisitions tax) shall be construed together with the Capital Acquisitions Tax Act 1976 and the enactments amending or extending that Act.

(7) Part 6 (so far as relating to income tax) shall be construed together with the Income Tax Acts and (so far as relating to corporation tax) shall be construed together with the Corporation Tax Acts and (so far as relating to capital gains tax) shall be construed together with the Capital Gains Tax Acts and (so far as relating to value-added tax) shall be construed together with the Value-Added Tax Acts 1972 to 2002 and (so far as relating to residential property tax) shall be construed together with Part VI of the Finance Act 1983, and the enactments amending or extending that Part and (so far as relating to gift tax or inheritance tax) shall be construed together with the Capital Acquisitions Tax Act 1976, and the enactments amending or extending that Act.

...

(10) Any reference in this Act to any other enactment shall, except so far as the context otherwise requires, be construed as a reference to that enactment as amended by or under any other enactment including this Act.

(11) In this Act, a reference to a Part, section or Schedule is to a Part or section of, or Schedule to, this Act, unless it is indicated that reference to some other enactment is intended.

(12) In this Act, a reference to a subsection, paragraph, subparagraph, clause or subclause is to the subsection, paragraph, subparagraph, clause or subclause of the provision (including a Schedule) in which the reference occurs, unless it is indicated that reference to some other provision is intended.

SCHEDULE 6
MISCELLANEOUS TECHNICAL AMENDMENTS IN RELATION TO TAX

Notes

Para 2(*a*) and s 138 substituted "subsection (1)(*d*)" for "subsection (1)(*c*)" in CATA 1976 s 6(2) in relation to gifts taken on or after 1 December 1999.
Para 2(*b*) and s 138 substituted "sections 6(1)(*d*) and 12(1)(*c*)" for "sections 6(1)(*c*) and 12(1)(*b*)" in CATA 1976 s 31(6) in relation to gifts or inheritances taken on or after 1 December 1999.

REGULATIONS (CAPITAL ACQUISITIONS TAX)

DEATH DUTIES (PAYMENT IN STOCK) REGULATIONS 1954

(1954 No 15)

1. These Regulations may be cited as the Death Duties (Payment in Stock) Regulations, 1954.

2. Stock of the 5% National Loan, 1962/72 (in these Regulations referred to as the Stock) shall be accepted in payment of any death duty subject to the following conditions:

(*a*)   the Stock shall only be accepted in payment or in part payment (as the case may be) of any death duty on the property passing under the will or intestacy of a deceased person if it is shown to the satisfaction of the Revenue Commissioners that it formed part of such property at his death and that he had been the beneficial owner thereof continuously from the date of the original subscription to the loan up to the date of his death or continuously for a period of not less than three months immediately preceding the date of his death;

(*b*)   the Stock shall only be accepted in payment or in part payment (as the case may be) of any death duty on property passing or deemed to pass on the death of a deceased person under a title other than his will or intestacy if it is shown to the satisfaction of the Revenue Commissioners that such Stock formed part of the property passing or deemed to pass under that title and had formed part thereof continuously from the date of the original subscription to the loan up to the date of his death or continuously for a period of not less than three months immediately preceding his death.

3. In any case in which it is desired to pay any sum on account of any death duty by means of the transfer of the Stock in pursuance of these Regulations, application should be made to the Revenue Commissioners. The application should be addressed to the Secretary, Revenue Commissioners (Estate Duty Branch), Dublin, and should specify the amount of the Stock tendered, whether transferable by deed or not; whether the holding is subject to any lien or charge whatsoever and whether it is under the applicant's control and, if not, under whose control it is.

4. The Revenue Commissioners shall arrange with the applicant the procedure to be followed in each particular case for the transfer of the Stock.

5. The value of the Stock tendered, calculated in accordance with paragraph (*a*) of subsection (12) of section 16 of the Finance Act, 1953, shall not exceed the amount of the duty payable.

6. In all cases, the Stock shall be accepted subject to such verification as may be necessary, and subject to any undertaking to the Revenue Commissioners that all steps necessary to complete the transfer will be taken by or on behalf of the applicant, and the Revenue Commissioners may require such security as they think fit to be given for the completion of the transfer.

7. The Revenue commissioners shall forward to the Bank of Ireland particulars of any holding of the Stock which has been tendered to them under these Regulations, and the Bank of Ireland shall be and is hereby authorised to decline to permit any dealing with, or accept any direction with regard to, such holding except upon the instructions of the Revenue Commissioners.

8. For the purposes of subsection (1) of section 16 of the Finance Act, 1953, the prescribed account of the Minister for Finance shall be the account entitled "Account of the Minister for Finance - Stock accepted in payment of Death Duties".

IRELAND-UNITED KINGDOM (DEATH DUTIES AND GIFT TAX) TREATY

CONVENTION BETWEEN THE GOVERNMENT OF THE UNITED KINGDOM OF GREAT BRITAIN AND NORTHERN IRELAND AND THE GOVERNMENT OF THE REPUBLIC OF IRELAND FOR THE AVOIDANCE OF DOUBLE TAXATION AND THE PREVENTION OF FISCAL EVASION WITH RESPECT TO TAXES ON ESTATES OF DECEASED PERSONS AND INHERITANCES AND ON GIFTS

Date of Conclusion: 7 December 1977.

Entry into Force: In accordance with Article 14, the Convention entered into force on 2 October 1978 upon the exchange of notes confirming that the necessary steps had been taken to give it the force of law in the United kingdom and in Ireland. For the dates on which the Convention shall have effect, see the detailed provisions in Article 14.

The Government of the United Kingdom of Great Britain and Northern Ireland and the Government of the Republic of Ireland;

Desiring to conclude a Convention for the avoidance of double taxation and the prevention of fiscal evasion with respect to taxes on estates of deceased persons and inheritances and on gifts;

Have agreed as follows:

Article 1
Scope

This Convention shall apply to any person who is within the scope of a tax which is the subject of this Convention, and to any property by reference to which there is a charge to such a tax.

Article 2
Taxes covered

(1) The taxes which are the subject of this Convention are:

  (*a*) in the Republic of Ireland:

    (i)   the gift tax, and

    (ii) the inheritance tax;

  (*b*) in the United Kingdom of Great Britain and Northern Ireland, the capital transfer tax.

(2) This Convention shall also apply to any identical or substantially similar taxes which are imposed by either Contracting State after the date of signature of this Convention in addition to, or in place of, the existing taxes.

Article 3
General definitions

(1) In this Convention, unless the context otherwise requires:

(*a*) the term **"nationals"** means:

(i) in relation to the Republic of Ireland, all citizens of Ireland and all legal persons, associations or other entities deriving their status as such from the law in force in the Republic of Ireland;

(ii) in relation to the United Kingdom, citizens of the United Kingdom and Colonies, British subjects under Section 2 of the British Nationality Act 1948 whose notices given under that Section have been acknowledged before the date of signature of this Convention, British subjects by virtue of Section 13(1) or Section 16 of the British Nationality Act 1948 or Section 1 of the British Nationality Act 1965, and British protected persons within the meaning of the British Nationality Act 1948; and all legal persons, associations or other entities deriving their status as such from the law in force in the United Kingdom;

(*b*) the term **"tax"** means the gift tax or inheritance tax imposed in the Republic of Ireland or the capital transfer tax imposed in the United Kingdom, as the context requires;

(*c*) the terms **"a Contracting State"** and **"the other Contracting State"** mean the United Kingdom or the Republic of Ireland, as the context requires;

(*d*) the term **"person"** includes an individual, a company and any other body of persons;

(*e*) the term **"company"** means any body corporate or any entity which is treated as a body corporate for tax purposes;

(*f*) the term **"competent authority"** means, in the case of the United Kingdom, the Commissioners of Inland Revenue or their authorised representative, and in the case of the Republic of Ireland, the Revenue Commissioners or their authorised representative;

(*g*) the term **"event"** includes a death.

(2) As regards the application of this Convention by a Contracting State any term not otherwise defined shall, unless the context otherwise requires, have the meaning which it has under the law of that Contracting State relating to the taxes which are the subject of this Convention.

Article 4
Fiscal domicile

(1) For the purposes of this Convention, the question whether a person is, or was at any material time, domiciled in a Contracting State shall be determined by whether he is, or was at that time, domiciled in that Contracting State in accordance with the law of that Contracting State or is or was treated as so domiciled for the purposes of a tax which is the subject of this Convention.

766

(2) Where by reason of the provisions of paragraph (1) a person is, or was at any material time, domiciled in both Contracting States, then this question shall be determined in accordance with the following rules:

(*a*) he shall be deemed to be domiciled in the Contracting State in which he has, or had at the material time, a permanent home available to him. If he has or had a permanent home available to him in both Contracting States, the domicile shall be deemed to be in the Contracting State with which his personal and economic relations are, or were at the material time, closer (centre of vital interests);

(*b*) if the Contracting State in which he has or had his centre of vital interests cannot be determined, or if he has not or had not a permanent home available to him in either Contracting State, the domicile shall be deemed to be in the Contracting State in which he has, or had at the material time, an habitual abode;

(*c*) if he has or had an habitual abode in both Contracting States or in neither of them, the domicile shall be deemed to be in the Contracting State of which he is, or was at the material time, a national;

(*d*) if he is or was a national of both Contracting States or of neither of them, the competent authorities of the Contracting States shall settle the question by mutual agreement.

Article 5
Taxing rights

(1) Subject to the following provisions of this Convention, each Contracting State shall retain the right to tax which it would have under its own law apart from this Convention.

(2) For the purposes of paragraph (2) of Article 6 and paragraph (2) of Article 8, the Contracting State with subsidiary taxing rights shall be determined as follows:

(*a*) in relation to property other than property comprised in a settlement, where a person's domicile has been determined under paragraph (2) of Article 4, that Contracting State shall be the Contracting State in which the person is or was, by virtue of that paragraph, not domiciled;

(*b*) in relation to property comprised in a settlement:

(i) where the proper law of the settlement as regards that property at the time when the settlement was made was the law of the Republic of Ireland and the settlor's domicile at that time when the settlement was made has been determined under paragraph (1) of Article as being in the United Kingdom, then that Contracting State shall be the United Kingdom;

(ii) where the proper law of the settlement as regards that property at the time when the settlement was made was not the law of the Republic of Ireland and the settlor's domicile at that time has been determined under paragraph (1) of Article 4 as being in the United Kingdom but under its own law the Republic of Ireland would impose tax on property outside its territory because at some time either the proper law of the settlement as regards that property was the law of the Republic of Ireland or the settlor's domicile has been determined under the said paragraph as being in the Republic of Ireland, then that Contracting State shall be the Republic of Ireland;

(iii)   Subject to paragraph (ii) of this sub-paragraph, where the proper law of the settlement as regards that property at the time when the settlement was made was not the law of the Republic of Ireland and the settlor's domicile at that time has been determined under paragraph (2) of Article 4, then that Contracting State shall be the Contracting State in which the settlor was, by virtue of that paragraph, not domiciled at that time.

(3) In sub-paragraph (*a*) of paragraph (2) of this Article, the term **"person"** means, in the Republic of Ireland the disponer, and in the United Kingdom the transferor.

(4) In paragraph (2) of this Article, **"settlement"** has the meaning which it has under the law of the United Kingdom relating to capital transfer tax and for the purposes of that paragraph a settlement is made when property first becomes comprised in it.

Article 6
Situs

(1) For the purposes of this Convention, the situs of any property shall be determined by each Contracting State under its own law, except that, where part of the value by reference to which tax is imposed in the United Kingdom is represented by liability to tax which is satisfied out of property situated outside the United Kingdom, then that part of the value shall be deemed to be attributable to that property.

(2) If the situs of any property as determined by one Contracting State under paragraph (1) of this Article is not the same as that so determined by the other Contracting State, and the credit to be allowed under Article 8 is thereby affected, then the question shall be determined exclusively under the law of the Contracting State which, by virtue of paragraph (2) of Article 5, has subsidiary taxing rights or, if there is no such Contracting State, it shall be determined by mutual agreement.

Article 7
Deduction of debts

In determining the amount on which tax is to computed, permitted deductions shall be allowed under the law in force in the Contracting State in which the tax is imposed.

Article 8
Elimination of double taxation

(1) Where a Contracting State imposes tax on an event by reference to any property which is not situated in that Contracting State but is situated in the other Contracting State, the former Contracting State shall allow against so much of its tax (as otherwise computed) as is attributable to that property a credit (not exceeding the amount of tax so attributable) equal to so much of the tax imposed in the other Contracting State on the same event as is attributable to such property.

(2) Where both Contracting States impose tax on an event by reference to any property which is not situated in either Contracting State but is situated in a third territory, the

Contracting State which, by virtue of paragraph (2) of Article 5, has subsidiary taxing rights shall allow against so much of its tax (as otherwise computed) as is attributable to that property a credit (not exceeding the amount of tax so attributable) equal to so much of the tax imposed in the other Contracting State on the same event as is attributable to such property.

(3) Any credit to be allowed in the Republic of Ireland under this Article in relation to gifts or inheritances shall be allowed only so as to relieve the tax imposed in the Republic of Ireland on the gift or inheritance which is reduced by the payment of the tax in respect of which that credit is to be allowed; and a gift which in the United Kingdom is a chargeable transfer shall be treated as reduced by the amount of tax imposed in the United Kingdom on that gift and borne by the transferor.

(4) For the purposes of this Article:

    (*a*) the tax attributable to any property imposed in a Contracting State is tax as reduced by the amount of any credit allowed by that Contracting State in respect of tax attributable to that property imposed in a territory other than a Contracting State;

    (*b*) tax is imposed in a Contracting State or a territory if it is chargeable under the law of that Contracting State or territory and duly paid; and

    (*c*) property includes property representing property.

Article 9
Time limit

Any claim for a credit or for a repayment of tax founded on the provisions of this Convention shall be made within six years from the date of the event in respect of which the claim is made.

Article 10
Non-discrimination

(1) The nationals of a Contracting State shall not be subjected in the other Contracting State to any taxation or any requirement connected therewith which is other or more burdensome than the taxation and connected requirements to which nationals of that other Contracting State in the same circumstances are or may be subjected.

(2) The taxation on a permanent establishment which an enterprise of a Contracting State has in the other Contracting State shall not be less favourably levied in that other Contracting State than the taxation levied on enterprises of that other Contracting State carrying on the same activities.

(3) Enterprises of a Contracting State, the capital of which is wholly or partly owned or controlled, directly or indirectly, by one or more residents of the other Contracting State, shall not be subjected in the first-mentioned Contracting State to any taxation or any requirement connected therewith which is other or more burdensome than the taxation and connected requirements to which other similar enterprises of the first- mentioned Contracting State are or may be subjected.

(4) Nothing contained in this Article shall be construed as obliging either Contracting State to grant individuals not domiciled in that Contracting State, any of the personal allowances, reliefs, and reductions for tax purposes which are granted to individuals so domiciled.

(5) In this Article the term **"taxation"** means tax covered by this Convention.

Article 11
Mutual agreements procedure

(1) Where a person considers that the actions of one or both of the Contracting States result or will result for him in taxation not in accordance with the provisions of this Convention, he may, irrespective of the remedies provided by the domestic laws of those Contracting States, present his case to the competent authority of either Contracting State.

(2) The competent authority shall endeavour, if the objection appears to it to be justified and if it is not itself able to arrive at a satisfactory solution, to resolve the case by mutual agreement with the competent authority of the other Contracting State with a view to the avoidance of taxation which is not in accordance with the provisions of this Convention.

(3) The competent authorities of the Contracting States shall endeavour to resolve by mutual agreement any difficulties or doubts arising as to the interpretation or application of this Convention.

(4) The competent authorities of the Contracting States may communicate with each other directly for the purpose of reaching an agreement in the sense of the preceding paragraphs.

Article 12
Exchange of information

(1) The competent authorities of the Contracting States shall exchange such information as is necessary for carrying out the provisions of this Convention and the domestic laws of the Contracting States concerning taxes covered by this Convention in so far as the taxation thereunder is in accordance with this Convention. Any information so exchanged shall be treated as secret and shall not be disclosed to any persons other than persons (including a Court or administrative body) concerned with the assessment or collection or, or prosecution in respect of, or the determination of appeals in relation to, the taxes which are the subject of this Convention.

(2) In no case shall the provisions of paragraph (1) be construed so as to impose on the competent authority of either Contracting State the obligation:

- (*a*) to carry out administrative measures at variance with the laws or administrative practice prevailing in either Contracting State;

- (*b*) to supply particulars which are not obtainable under the laws or in the normal course of the administration of that or of the other Contracting State;

- (*c*) to supply information which would disclose any trade, business, industrial, commercial or professional secret or trade process, or information, the disclosure of which would be contrary to public policy.

Article 13
Diplomatic and consular officials

Nothing in this Convention shall affect the fiscal privileges of diplomatic or consular officials under the general rules of international law or under the provisions of special agreements.

Article 14
Entry into force

This convention shall enter into force on the exchange of Notes confirming that the necessary steps have been taken to give it the force of law in the United kingdom and in the Republic of Ireland and shall thereupon have effect:

(*a*)   in the Republic of Ireland:

   (i)   in respect of gift tax, from 28 February 1974;

   (ii)   in respect of inheritance tax, from 1 April 1975;

(*b*)   in the United Kingdom:

   (i)   in respect of capital transfer tax other than capital transfer tax on a death, from 27 March 1974;

   (ii)   in respect of capital transfer tax on a death, from 13 March 1975.

Article 15
Termination

This Convention shall remain in force until terminated by one of the Contracting States. Either Contracting State may terminate the Convention, through the diplomatic channel, by giving notice of termination at least six months before the end of any calendar year after the year 1980. In such event the Convention shall cease to have effect at the end of the calendar year in which the notice is given but shall continue to apply in respect of property by reference to which there was a charge to tax which arose before the end of that calendar year.

CAPITAL ACQUISITIONS TAX (HERITAGE HOUSES AND GARDENS) REGULATIONS 1987

(1987 No 28)

Amendments

Revoked by FA 1997 s 137(2) with effect from 1 January 1997. See now FA 1978 s 39(1A).

TABLE OF CASES (CAPITAL ACQUISITIONS TAX)

TABLE OF STATUTORY REFERENCES
(CAPITAL ACQUISITIONS TAX)

INDEX (CAPITAL ACQUISITIONS TAX)

Books

artistic interest (of), exempt from tax, CATA 1976 s 55(2)

historic interest (of), exempt from tax, CATA 1976 s 55(2)

national interest (of), exempt from tax, CATA 1976 s 55(2)

of public officer to be made accessible to Revenue, CATA 1976 s 35(12)

relating to gift, Revenue may inspect, CATA 1976 s 36(7)(*b*)

scientific interest (of), exempt from tax, CATA 1976 s 55(2)

Brother

class threshold, CATA 1976 Sch 2 para 1

Building society

joint accounts, included under "banker", CATA 1976 s 61(7)

Business relief

business must be carried on in the State, FA 1994 s 127(3)

computation, FA 1994 s 126

discretionary trust tax, does not apply, FA 1994 s 125

farming property, excluded, FA 1994 s 134

holding company shares, may qualify for relief, FA 1994 s 127(5)

instalments, payment by, FA 1995 s 164

investment dealing, excluded activity, FA 1994 s 127(4)

land dealing, excluded activity, FA 1994 s 127(4)

minimum ownership period, FA 1994 s 128

non business property, excluded, FA 1994 s 134

non qualifying subsidiary, assets ignored, FA 1994 s 133

probate tax, does not apply, FA 1994 s 125

qualifying business property, FA 1994 s 127

replaced business assets, minimum ownership period, FA 1994 s 129

sole trader, net asset valuation basis, FA 1994 s 132

withdrawal of relief, FA 1994 s 135

C

Calculation of tax

See COMPUTATION OF TAX

Capital acquisitions tax

charge to, CATA 1976 s 10

Capital gains tax

on the same event,

to be allowed as credit rather than deduction, FA 1985 s 63(1)

apportionment of reliefs or expenditure, FA 1985 s 63(2)

Care and management

of tax, placed with Revenue Commissioners, CATA 1976 s 72

Central Fund

unpaid tax is debt due to, CATA 1976 s 49(1)

Certificate

probate, *See* PROBATE, CERTIFICATE FOR

property, payment of tax on, CATA 1976 s 48

tax paid, Revenue must give, CATA 1976 s 48(2)

Certificate of discharge

fraud or failure to disclose material facts, property not discharged, CATA 1976 s 48(4)

Revenue must give, CATA 1976 s 48(3)

secondarily accountable persons may obtain, CATA 1976 s 48(5)

Cesser

of intervening life interest, CATA 1976 s 3(1)

of liabilities, CATA 1976 s 28

Charge, F(No 2)A 2000, s 5

grant or creation of, may be a disposition, CATA 1976 s 2(1)

on property,

tax due remains, CATA 1976 s 47(1)

tax no longer a charge after twelve years, CATA 1976 s 47(2)

Charities, F(No 2)A 2000 s 11

Gifts taken by,

threshold applicable, CATA 1976 s 54(1)

gifts applied for public or charitable purposes, CATA 1976 s 54(2)

Chattel real property

included under "real property", CATA 1976 s 2(1)

Child

class threshold, CATA 1976 Sch 2 para 1

defined, CATA 1976 s 2(1)

discretionary trust, principal object, FA 1984 s 104

includes adopted child, CATA 1976 s 2(1), (5)

includes illegitimate child, CATA 1976 s 2(5)

issue, case law, CATA 1976 s 2

legal entitlement under Succession Act, may be a disposition, CATA 1976 s 2(1)

maintenance payments, exempt, CATA 1976 s 58(2)

minor, defined, CATA 1976 s 2(1)

of a child, is a "relative", CATA 1976 s 2(4)

of a person, is a "relative", CATA 1976 s 2(4)

of a spouse, father, mother, uncle, or aunt, is a "relative", CATA 1976 s 2(4)

Circuit Court

appeals, personal property,

jurisdiction applicable, CATA 1976 s 52(5)(*c*)

right of appeal to, CATA 1976 s 52(2)

rehearing by, income tax rules apply, CATA 1976 s 52(5)(*a*)

Attorney-General,

may sue for unpaid tax, CATA 1976 s 49(1)

may seek order directing lodgment of return, CATA 1976 s 49(3)

may seek order directing owner of property to pay tax charged, CATA 1976 s 49(4)

Computation of tax (contd)

tax chargeable on, CATA 1976 Sch 2 para 3

rate of tax, CATA 1976 Sch 2 para 2 para 5

gift tax is 75% of inheritance tax, CATA 1976 Sch 2 para 6

gifts and inheritances taken on same day, CATA 1976 Sch 2 para 7

surviving spouse of beneficiary may take his or her place, CATA 1976 Sch 2 para 8

to be made in accordance with CATA 1976 Sch 2, CATA 1976 s 40

Computer records

Revenue power to inspect, FA 1992 s 237

Connected persons

See RELATIVE

retirement payments from,

no exemption, CATA 1976 s 56(2)

appeals, CATA 1976 s 56(3)

Consideration paid

agricultural value, deduction apportionable, CATA 1976 s 19(2)

deduction apportionable, CATA 1976 s 18(6), (10)

deduction in computing taxable value, CATA 1976 s 18(2)

dispositions by or to company,

consideration paid or taken attributable to beneficial owners, CATA 1976 s 34(1)

consideration paid attributable to creator of trust, CATA 1976 s 34(5)

Contingency

benefit taken subject to, recomputation, CATA 1976 s 20

Contingent liability

no deduction in computing taxable value, CATA 1976 s 18(5)(*a*)

Control

private company, defined, CATA 1976 s 16(3)-(4)

Convention

Ireland - USA, confirmation of, FA 1950 s 10

Costs

See LIABILITIES

Court

of competent jurisdiction, unpaid tax may be sued for in, CATA 1976 s 49(1)

officer may not grant probate until Revenue certify, CATA 1976 s 60(4)

rule, form of grant of probate may be prescribed by, CATA 1976 s 60(5)

to provide for payment of tax, CATA 1976 s 62

Covenant

may be a disposition, CATA 1976 s 2(1)

Criminal proceedings

penalty proceedings, not affected by, CATA 1976 s 63(8)

Revenue offences, FA 1983 s 94

Crops

included under "agricultural property", CATA 1976 s 19(1)

D

Dáil Eireann

laying of regulations before, CATA 1976 s 71

Damages

personal injury, exempt, CATA 1976 s 58(1)(*a*)

Date of the disposition

defined, CATA 1976 s 2(1)

Date of the gift

defined, CATA 1976 s 2(1)

Date of the inheritance

defined, CATA 1976 s 2(1)

Death (on a)

defined, CATA 1976 s 3

Death duty

inheritance tax, not a, CATA 1976 s 68

pre 30 April 1991, waiver of interest and penalties, FA 1991 s 122

reference to in deeds and wills, CATA 1976 s 65

references in deeds and wills, etc to, CATA 1976 s 65

Debenture

non-resident, non-domiciled beneficial owner, exempt, CATA 1976 s 57(2)

valuation of private company, regarded as share, CATA 1976 s 16(2)

Debt

creation of, may be a disposition, CATA 1976 s 2(1)

release, forfeiture, surrender or abandonment of, may be a disposition, CATA 1976 s 2(1)

Revenue power to attach debts, FA 1988 s 73

Declaration

return, correctness, CATA 1976 s 37(1)

Deductions

agricultural value, apportionable, CATA 1976 s 19(2)

consideration paid,

deduction for, CATA 1976 s 18(2)

deduction apportionable, CATA 1976 ss 18(6), (10); 19(2)

contingent liability, non deductible cost, CATA 1976 s 18(5)(*a*)

double deduction not allowed, CATA 1976 s 18(7)

exempt property (associated) liability, non deductible cost, CATA 1976 s 18(5)(*e*)

future liability, CATA 1976 s 18(3)

incumbrance-free value, CATA 1976 s 18(1)

liability which deprives beneficiary of use, deduction apportionable, CATA 1976 s 18(8)

limited interest, CATA 1976 s 18(4)

non resident, non deductible cost, CATA 1976 s 18(5)(*f*)

Farm property

See AGRICULTURAL PROPERTY

Farmer

defined, CATA 1976 s 19(1)

Father

of a person, is a "relative", CATA 1976 s 2(4)

Favourite nephew

or niece, relief in computation of tax, CATA 1976 Sch 2 para 9(2)-(3)

discretionary trust, relief does not apply, CATA 1976 Sch 2 para 9(4)

Forestry

included under "agricultural property", CATA 1976 s 19(1)

Fraud

or failure to disclose material facts, certificate of discharge not to apply, CATA 1976 s 48(4), (6)

penalty proceedings,

    incorrect returns, statements etc, CATA 1976 s 63(3), (5)

    failure to rectify within reasonable period, CATA 1976 s 63(4)

    return etc deemed to have been made with person's consent, CATA 1976 s 63(6)

Free loan

deemed gift, CATA 1976 s 31

Free use of property

deemed gift, CATA 1976 s 31

Friendly society

joint accounts, included under "banker", CATA 1976 s 61(7)

Friends of the National Collection of Ireland

objects of artistic, historic, national or scientific interest, sold within six months of valuation date, CATA 1976 s 55(3)

Future interest

disposal before remainderman comes into possession, CATA 1976 s 23

disposal of,

    prior to 1 April 1975, coming into possession thereafter, CATA 1976 s 64

    transferee is primarily accountable for tax, CATA 1976 s 35(1)

    transferee return, CATA 1976 s 36(4)(*d*)

    transferee of future interest, relevant date for self-assessment, CATA 1976 s 36(5)(*b*)

property acquired by discretionary trust,

    future interest not property until it comes into possession, FA 1984 s 106(3)

See INTEREST IN EXPECTANCY

settlement of interest not in possession, CATA 1976 s 25

Future liability

deduction in computing taxable value, CATA 1976 s 18(3)

G

General power of appointment

defined,

disposition involving failure to exercise, or release of, CATA 1976 s 27(1)

exercise of, may be a disposition, CATA 1976 s 2(1)

Gift

aggregable, CATA 1976 s 9

contingencies affecting, CATA 1976 s 29

contingency (taken subject to), recomputation, CATA 1976 s 20

date of the, defined, CATA 1976 s 2(1)

defined, CATA 1976 s 2(1)

future interests, CATA 1976 s 23

gift becoming inheritance,

    gifts after 1 May 1989, disponer primarily accountable, FA 1989 s 81

    set off of tax against inheritance tax, CATA 1976 s 42

    small gifts allowance still applies, CATA 1976 s 53(2)

inheritance if taken within two years prior to disponer's death, CATA 1976 s 3(1)

joint tenants, liability to tax, CATA 1976 s 7

liabilities, cesser of, CATA 1976 s 28

retirement payments, exempt, CATA 1976 s 56(1)

revocation, subject to power of, CATA 1976 s 30

secondarily accountable persons, CATA 1976 s 35(2)

set-off in respect of inheritance, CATA 1976 s 42

shares in private company, FA 1993 s 121

spouses, exemption for, FA 1990 s 127

State, residence of donors to, FA 1977 s 53

statement, Revenue may require, CATA 1976 s 36(7)

subject to power of revocation, CATA 1976 s 30

tax, charge, CATA 1976 s 4

tax-free benefit, no tax on tax, FA 1982 s 97

taxable, defined, CATA 1976 s 6

valuation date, CATA 1976 s 21(1)

value, taxable, CATA 1976 s 18

when taken, CATA 1976 s 5

Gift tax

aggregable gifts, CATA 1976 s 9

appropriate part, defined, CATA 1976 s 5(5)

charge of tax, CATA 1976 s 4

disponer in certain connected dispositions, CATA 1976 s 8

Gift becoming inheritance, set off of tax against inheritance tax, CATA 1976 s 42

gift deemed to be taken, CATA 1976 s 5

joint tenants, gift taken by, CATA 1976 s 7

taxable gift, defined, CATA 1976 s 6(1)

Gilt

See GOVERNMENT SECURITIES

Transferee
future interest, relevant date for self-assessment, CATA 1976 s 36(5)(*b*)

Treaty (Double Taxation)
See DOUBLE TAXATION

Trees
included under "agricultural property", CATA 1976 s 19(1)

Trust
acquisition by, FA 1993 s 110
discretionary,
    defined, CATA 1976 s 2(1)
    See DISCRETIONARY TRUST
disposition by or to a company, consideration paid attributable to creator of trust, CATA 1976 s 34(5)
interest, provisions for, FA 1993 s 117
may be a disposition, CATA 1976 s 2(1)
postponement of tax payment, FA 1993 s 118

Trustee
discretionary trust,
    once-off charge, primarily accountable person, FA 1984 s 107(*c*)
    annual charge, primarily accountable person,, FA 1986 s 106(*c*)
limited interest, Inland Revenue Affidavit, particulars required, CATA 1976 s 38(3)
with care of gift, secondarily accountable person, CATA 1976 s 35(2)
with care of inheritance, secondarily accountable person, CATA 1976 s 35(2)

Trustee Savings Bank
joint accounts, included under "banker", CATA 1976 s 61(7)

Twelve years
purchaser of property, tax due no longer a charge after, CATA 1976 s 47(2)

Twenty years
tax unpaid after, Revenue Commissioners may remit, CATA 1976 s 44(3)

Two years
after valuation date, secondarily accountable person may apply for certificate of discharge, CATA 1976 s 48(5), (7)
prior to death of disponer,
    gift taken becomes inheritance, CATA 1976 s 3(1)
    valuation date, CATA 1976 s 21(3)
    set off of gift tax against inheritance tax, CATA 1976 s 42

U

Uncle
of a person, is a "relative", CATA 1976 s 2(4)

Undertakings for Collective Investment in Transferable Securities (UCITS)
non-domiciled non-resident disponer, transfer of interest exempt, FA 1989 s 85

Underwood
included under "agricultural property", CATA 1976 s 19(1)

Unit trust (units)
non-domiciled non-resident disponer, transfer of interest exempt, FA 1989 s 85
non-resident, non-domiciled beneficial owner, exempt, CATA 1976 s 57(2)

University (in the State)
objects of artistic, historic, national or scientific interest, sold within six months of valuation date, CATA 1976 s 55(3)

Unquoted shares
or securities, market value, CATA 1976 s 15(6)

Use of property
beneficiary deprived of, deduction apportionable in computing taxable value, CATA 1976 s 18(8)

V

Valuation
agricultural property, CATA 1976 s 19
date, for tax purposes, CATA 1976 s 21
inheritance, date of, FA 1993 s 111
property, duty chargeable on, FA 1991 s 105
property, market value, CATA 1976 s 15
shares in private non-trading companies, CATA 1976 s 17
shares in private trading companies, CATA 1976 s 16

Valuation date
appeal against Revenue determination, CATA 1976 s 21(9)
defined, CATA 1976 s 2(1)
discretionary trust,
    once-off charge, FA 1984 s 107(*b*)
    annual charge, FA 1986 s 106(*b*)
gift taken within two years prior to disponer's death,
    becomes inheritance, CATA 1976 s 21(3)
    references to valuation date become references to date of death, CATA 1976 s 41(6)
gift, CATA 1976 s 21(1)
inheritance disposed of etc before valuation date, CATA 1976 s 21(7)
inheritance, CATA 1976 s 21(2), (4)
notice in writing of, CATA 1976 s 21(6)
objects of artistic, historic, national or scientific interest, sold within six months, CATA 1976 s 55(3)
payment of tax,
    gift or inheritance taken before 31 March 1976, CATA 1976 s 41(7)
    limited interest valued as series of absolute interests, CATA 1976 s 41(8)
relevant date for self-assessment, CATA 1976 s 36(5)
Revenue may determine, CATA 1976 s 21(8)
separate dates for separate inheritances, CATA 1976 s 21(5)

LEGISLATION (RESIDENTIAL PROPERTY TAX)

FINANCE ACT 1983

(1983 Number 15)
(Date of passing: 8 June 1983)

ARRANGEMENT OF SECTIONS

PART V
REVENUE OFFENCES

PART VI
RESIDENTIAL PROPERTY TAX

PART VII
MISCELLANEOUS

PART V
REVENUE OFFENCES

94 Revenue offences

Notes

The text of FA 1983 s 94, as amended is contained in the Capital Acquisitions Tax Part of this book.

PART VI
RESIDENTIAL PROPERTY TAX

95 Interpretation (Part VI)

(1) In this Part, save where the context otherwise requires—

"aggregate relevant income" has the meaning assigned to it by section 101(1);

"assessable person" means a person chargeable to tax save that a person shall be an assessable person notwithstanding that he is entitled under section 101 to exemption from tax in respect of the net market value of his relevant residential property on any valuation date;

...¹

"Collector" means the Collector-General appointed under section 162 of the Income Tax Act, 1967;

"the Commissioners" means the Revenue Commissioners;

"income" means total income from all sources as estimated in accordance with the provisions of the Income Tax Acts but without regard to—

   (a) any of the provisions of those Acts (apart from [sections 340, 353, 354 and 463]² of the Income Tax Act, 1967, section 37 of the Finance Act, 1968, [section 18 of the Finance Act, 1970,]³ section 19 of the Finance Act 1973, and section 9 of the Finance Act, 1982) which provide that any income is exempt from income tax or that any income is to be disregarded for the purposes of those Acts or which otherwise provide that any amount of income or any part thereof is not subject to Irish income tax,

   (b) sections 89, 236, 251, 254 and 496 of the Income Tax Act 1967,

   (c) Chapter I of Part IX of the Income Tax Act, 1967,

   (d) Chapter I of Part XIX of the Income Tax Act, 1967,

   (e) section 11 of the Finance Act, 1967,

   [(ee) income arising from savings bonds duly issued under section 54 of the Finance Act, 1970,]⁴

   (f) section 26 of the Finance Act, 1971,

   (g) Chapter II of Part I of the Finance Act, 1972,

   (h) section 14 of the Finance Act, 1977,

   (i) section 25 of the Finance Act, 1978, and

   (j) sections 23 and 24 of the Finance Act, 1981;

"income exemption limit" means the amount ascertained in accordance with section 101;

"the Income Tax Acts" has the same meaning as in section 3 of the Income Tax Act, 1967;

"lease", **"lessee"** and **"rent"** have respectively the meanings assigned to them by section 80 of the Income Tax Act, 1967;

"market value", in relation to any property, means the market value thereof ascertained in accordance with section 98;

"market value exemption limit" has the meaning assigned to it by section 100;

"net market value", in relation to the relevant residential property of a person on a valuation date, means the excess, if any, of the aggregate amount of the market values of all residential properties which in relation to the person are on that date relevant residential properties over the amount of the market value exemption limit applying on that valuation date in the case of the person;

"occupied", in relation to a residential property, means having the use thereof, whether actually used or not, and cognate words shall be construed accordingly;

"personal representatives" has the meaning assigned to it by section 450(2) of the Income Tax Act, 1967;

"relevant person", in relation to an assessable person, means, as respects any valuation date, any person (other than [a person who has attained the age of 65 years and is not an assessable person, or a person who is permanently incapacitated by reason of mental or physical infirmity from maintaining himself and is not an assessable person, or][5] a person who is an employee of the assessable person and whose employment is wholly or mainly connected with the relevant residential property) who in the year ended on that date normally resided at any relevant residential property of the assessable person and who, or whose spouse,—

(*a*) made no payment of rent or other like payment in respect of such residence, or

(*b*) made a payment of rent or other like payment in respect of that residence of such amount that, if it had been paid by a person to whom subsection (2)(*b*)(iv) applies in respect of the relevant residential property under a lease, agreement or licence referred to in subsection (2)(*b*)(iv), that last-mentioned person would, by virtue of subsection (2)(*b*)(iv), be the owner in relation to the relevant residential property;

"relevant residential property", in relation to any person, means any residential property in relation to which he is the owner and which is occupied by him as a dwelling or dwellings;

"residential property" means—

(*a*) a building or part of a building used or suitable for use as a dwelling, and

(*b*) land (other than a garden such as is specified in section 39(1) of the Finance Act, 1978) which the occupier of a building or part of a building used as a dwelling has for his own occupation and enjoyment with the said building or part as its garden or grounds of an ornamental nature,

but does not include an approved building within the meaning of section 19 of the Finance Act, 1982 [,where the Commissioners are satisfied that reasonable access is afforded to the public having regard to subsection (4)(b)(ii) of the said section 19 as amended by the Finance Act, 1994];[5]

"tax" means residential property tax chargeable by virtue of this Part;

"the Tax Acts" has the same meaning as in section 155 of the Corporation Tax Act, 1976;

"valuation date", in relation to any year, means the 5th day of April in that year.

(2) For the purposes of this Part—

(a) notwithstanding that he does not have the use of a residential property as a dwelling on a valuation date, a person shall be treated as having the use of the property as a dwelling on that valuation date if for the greater part of the year ending on that date and the greater part of the year commencing on the day next after that date he has the use of the property as a dwelling;

(b) Subject to paragraph (c) a person is the owner in relation to a residential property if that person beneficially, whether solely, jointly or in common—

(i) holds a freehold estate in the property,

(ii) holds the property under a lease, agreement or licence, the duration of which exceeds 50 years.

(iii) is the owner under a mortgage of the equity of redemption in a freehold estate in the property or of the equity of redemption in an interest in the property under a lease, agreement or licence of the kind mentioned in subparagraph (ii).

(iv) holds the property under a lease, agreement or licence (other than a lease, agreement or licence of the kind referred to in subparagraph (ii)), under or in respect of which no rent or other like payment is made, or—

(I) a rent or other like payment is made of a total amount for the period for which it is agreed upon which, having regard to the values and other circumstances prevailing at the time the amount of the rent or other payment was agreed upon, is less than the total amount of the rent or other payment in respect of such lease, agreement or licence (hereafter referred to as "the arm's length rent") for that period which might be expected to have been agreed upon at that time having regard to those values and other circumstances if the negotiations for such lease, agreement or licence had been conducted in the open market at arm's length and there was no other consideration which the person entitled to the said rent or other payment was entitled to in respect of the lease, agreement or licence, and

(II)   the difference between the total amount aforesaid of the rent or other payment aforesaid and the total amount aforesaid of the arm's length rent aforesaid exceeds **20 per cent** of the latter amount,

or

(v)   holds the property at the will or sufferance of any other person, or under any trust, and in respect thereof—

(I)   pays no rent, or

(II)   pays a rent of such amount that, if it were paid under a lease of a kind mentioned in subparagraph (iv) granted at the time the person commenced to hold the property at the will or sufferance of that other person, or under the trust, the first-mentioned person would, under subparagraph (iv), be the owner in relation to the property;

(c)   a person shall not, by reason of subparagraph (iv) or (v) of paragraph (*b*), be the owner in relation to a residential property if—

(i)   he is chargeable to tax under section 117 of the Income Tax Act, 1967, in respect of the provision of the property, or would be so chargeable but for subsection (2) or (3) of the said section 117,

(ii)   he is chargeable to tax under section 96 of the Corporation Tax Act, 1976, in respect of the provision of the property,

(iii)   the property is comprised in the relevant residential property of the person granting the lease or licence or making the agreement mentioned in the said subparagraph (iv) or is comprised in the relevant residential property of the person at whose will or sufferance the property is held as mentioned in the said subparagraph (v), or

(iv)   he holds the property as a caretaker under an agreement made at arm's length;

(d)   in ascertaining the duration of a lease, agreement or licence, the provisions of section 80(2) of the Income Tax Act 1967, shall, with any necessary modifications, apply in like manner as they apply for the purposes of Chapter VI of Part IV of that Act;

(e)   in ascertaining whether or not any rent or other like payment under or in respect of a lease, agreement or licence is less than the arm's length rent in respect of the property concerned, no regard shall be had to any provision in the lease, agreement or licence concerned or in any agreement relating to such lease, agreement or licence that, in the opinion of the Commissioners, was included for the purpose of concealing or diminishing the amount of the arm's length rent.

Amendments

1   Definition of "child" deleted by FA 1990 s 122.

2   Definition of "income": words substituted by FA 1994 s 115(a)(i), where tax is chargeable on a valuation date, in relation to any year commencing with the year 1994; previously "sections 340, 353 and 354".

3   Definition of "income": words inserted by FA 1994 s 115(a)(ii), where tax is chargeable on a valuation date, in relation to any year commencing with the year 1994.

4   Definition of "income": para (ee) inserted by FA 1994 s 115(a)(iii), where tax is chargeable on a valuation date, in relation to any year commencing with the year 1994.

5   Definition of "relevant person": additional words inserted by FA 1994 s 115(b), where tax is chargeable on a valuation date, in relation to any year commencing with the year 1994.

6   Definition of "residential property": additional words inserted by FA 1994 s 115(c), where tax is chargeable on a valuation date, in relation to any year commencing with the year 1994.

Cross-references

Valuation date, meaning applied: FA 1994 s 114.

Case law

Constitutionality of residential property tax upheld by High Court (20 November 1983) and affirmed by Supreme Court (1984), *Madigan and others v AG* [1986] ILRM 136, III ITR 127.

Definitions

"person": IA 1937 s 11(*c*).

96 Charge of residential property tax

Subject to the provisions of this Part and any regulations thereunder, with effect on and from the 5th day of April, 1983, a tax, to be called residential property tax, shall be charged, levied and paid annually upon the net market value of the relevant residential property on the valuation date in each year of every person [the rate of tax shall be one and one-half per cent. of that net market value].[1]

Amendments

1   Substituted by FA 1995 s 152, as respects any valuation date commencing with the year 1995; previously "the tax chargeable on that net market value shall be computed in accordance with the Seventh Schedule to the Finance Act, 1994" (FA 1994 s 116).

Definitions

"market value": ss 95, 98; "net market value": s 95; "relevant residential property": s 95; "tax": s 95; "valuation date": s 95.

97 Taxable residential property of a person

(1) Subject to the provisions of this Part, the relevant residential property of a person who is domiciled in the State on the valuation date shall comprise all the property, wheresoever situate which is relevant residential property of the person on that date.

(2) Subject to the provisions of this Part, the relevant residential property of a person who is not domiciled in the State on the valuation date shall comprise only the property situate in the State which is relevant residential property of the person on that date.

Definitions

"relevant residential property": s 95; "valuation date": s 95.

98 Market value of property

(1) In this Part, subject to the other provisions thereof and to any regulations thereunder, the market value of any property shall be estimated to be the price which the unencumbered fee simple of such property would fetch if sold for residential use in the open market on the valuation date in such manner and subject to such conditions as might reasonably be calculated to obtain for the vendor the best price for the property.

(2) In estimating the market value of the unencumbered fee simple of any property in accordance with subsection (1) the person in whose relevant residential property the property is comprised shall fix the price of the property according to the price on the relevant valuation date and shall not make any reduction in the estimate on account of the estimate being made on the assumption that the person or any other person may be chargeable to tax.

[(2A)(*a*) Notwithstanding the provisions of subsections (1) and (2), in estimating the market value of any property on the relevant valuation date, a reduction may be made in respect of such value which is attributable on that date to qualifying improvements.

    (*b*) **"Qualifying improvements"** for the purposes of this subsection, means necessary improvements or alterations to the property for the purposes only of accommodating or facilitating a person who is permanently incapacitated by reason of mental or physical infirmity from maintaining himself.

    (*c*) A reduction shall not be available by virtue of this subsection unless the incapacitated person concerned normally resided at the property in the year ended on the relevant valuation date.][1]

(3) If the Commissioners are not satisfied with the market value of any property estimated by any person, or if they consider it necessary to do so, they may, subject to the same conditions and requirements as apply in the case of that person, estimate the market value of that property and, where the market value as so estimated by the Commissioners exceeds the market value estimated by the person, any charge to tax shall be made by reference to the market value estimated by the Commissioners and not by reference to the market value estimated by the person.

(4) The market value of any property for the purposes of subsection (3) or section 104(2) shall be ascertained by the Commissioners in such manner and by such means as they think fit and they may authorise a person suitably qualified for that purpose to inspect any property and report to them the value thereof for the purposes of this Part and the person having the custody or possession of that property shall permit the person so authorised to inspect it at such reasonable times as the Commissioners consider necessary.

(5) Where the Commissioners require a valuation to be made by a person named by them, the costs of such valuation shall be defrayed by them.

Amendments

[1]   Subs (2A) inserted by FA 1994 s 117, where tax is chargeable on a valuation date, in relation to any year commencing with the year 1994.

Definitions

"relevant residential property": s 95; "tax": s 95; "valuation date": s 95.

99 Apportionment of market values

Where as respects any valuation date a residential property is comprised in the relevant residential property of two or more persons, the amount to be taken into account in respect of the market value of that property for the purposes of determining the net market values on that date of the relevant residential property of each of those persons shall be the amount which bears to the market value of the residential property on that date the same proportion as one bears to the number of those persons.

Definitions

"market value": ss 95, 98; "net market value": s 95; "relevant residential property": s 95; "valuation date": s 95.

100 Market value exemption limit

(1) In this section—

["**general exemption limit**" means the general market value exemption limit applying on a valuation date, that is to say, the amount obtained by multiplying [€382,000][1] by the new house price index number relevant to that valuation date and dividing the product by the new house price index number relevant to the valuation date falling on the 5th day of April, [2000][2] [€1,000][3];

Provided that the amount so obtained shall be rounded up to the next [€1,000][3];][4]

"**market value exemption limit**", in relation to an assessable person as respects a valuation date, means the amount of the aggregate of the unit exemption limits attributed to the units of residential property comprised in the relevant residential property of the assessable person on that valuation date;

"**the new house price index number**" means the Trends in Private New House Prices Index Number compiled by the Department of the Environment and the new house price index number relevant to any valuation date means the new house price index number for the three months ended on the [31st day of December next][5] before that valuation date expressed on the basis that the new house price index number for the three months ended on the 31st day of March, [1991],[6] is 100.

"**unit exemption limit**", in relation to a valuation date, means the proportion of the general exemption limit in relation to that valuation date which is attributed to a unit of residential property, and shall be the amount determined by the formula–

$$\frac{A \times G}{B}$$

where—

A   is the market value (ascertained without regard to section 99) on the valuation date of the unit of residential property,

B   is the aggregate of the market values (ascertained without regard to section 99) on the valuation date of all the units comprised in the relevant residential property of the assessable person,

G   is the general exemption limit:

Provided that, in relation to a valuation date, where a unit of residential property is comprised in the relevant residential property of two or more persons, the unit exemption limit in relation to that unit of residential property in the case of the assessable person shall be reduced to the amount which bears to the unit exemption limit calculated without regard to this proviso the same proportion as one bears to the number of those persons.

(2) The amount of the market value exemption limit applying on a valuation date in the case of any person shall not exceed the general exemption limit applying on that date.

Note

1996 Market value exemption limit (valuation date 5 April 1996): £101,000.

Amendments

¹ Substituted by FA 2001 s 240 and Sch 5 Pt 7 with effect from 1 January 2002; previous "£300,000" (FA 2000 s); "£200,000" (FA 1999 s 198), "£94,000" (FA 1995 s 153(a), "£75,000" (FA 1994 s 118), "£90,000" (FA 1992 s 219(*a*)); £96,000 (FA 1991 s 123, as indexed and rounded up by £1,000); £91,000 (1990 as indexed); £82,772 (1989 as indexed); £74,321 (1988 as indexed); £69,971 (1987 as indexed); £68,728 (1986 as indexed); £66,491 (1985 as indexed); £65,622 (1984 as indexed); £65,000 (as enacted).

² Substituted by FA 2000 s 134 in relation to any valuation date (within the meaning of FA 1983 s 95(1)) occuring on or after 5 April 2000; previously "1999" (FA 1999 s 198); "1995", "1994" (FA 1994 s 118), "1992" (FA 1992 s 219(*a*)); "1991" etc.

³ Substituted by FA 2001 s 240 and Sch 5 Pt 7 with effect from 1 January 2002; previously "£1,000".

⁴ Definition of "general exemption limit" substituted by FA 1990 s 123(*a*).

⁵ Substituted by FA 1990 s 123(*b*); previously "31st day of March next".

⁶ Substituted by FA 1995 s 153(*b*); previously "1981" (FA 1992 s 219(*b*)), "1973".

Definitions

"assessable person": s 95; "market value": ss 95, 98; "market value exemption limit": ss 95, 100; "relevant residential property": s 95; "valuation date": s 95.

101 Income exemption limit

(1) Where an assessable person makes a claim in that behalf and proves that the aggregate of his income for the year ending on a valuation date and the income for that year of every person who, as respects that valuation date, is a relevant person in relation to the assessable person (hereafter in this Part referred to as "aggregate relevant income") did not exceed the income exemption limit applying on that valuation date, he shall be entitled to exemption from tax in respect of the net market value on that valuation date of his relevant residential property.

[Provided that the income of a relevant person (other than a person who is an assessable person) shall be disregarded in computing aggregate relevant income—

(*a*) where, in relation to a valuation date, a unit of residential property is comprised in the relevant residential property of one or more persons, and—

(i) any of those persons has attained the age of 65 years, or

(ii) any of those persons is permanently incapacitated by reason of mental or physical infirmity from maintaining himself and the relevant person resides in the unit of residential property as a consequence of that infirmity;

(*b*) where, in relation to a valuation date, the assessable person is a widowed person and the relevant person resides in the relevant residential property as a consequence of the assessable person having a qualifying child [within the meaning of section 102(4)].¹]²

[(2) The income exemption limit applying on a valuation date is the amount obtained by multiplying [£29,500]³ by the consumer price index number relevant to that valuation date and dividing the product by the consumer price index number relevant to the valuation date falling on the 5th day of April, [1995]:⁴

Provided that the amount so obtained shall be rounded up to the next £100.]⁵

(3) In this section "the consumer price index number" means the All Items Consumer Price Index Number compiled by the Central Statistics Office and the consumer price index number relevant to any valuation date means the consumer price index number at the mid-February next before that valuation date expressed on the basis that the consumer price index at mid-November [1989],⁶ is 100.

Note

1996 income exemption limit: £30,100.

Amendments

[1] Inserted by FA 1995 s 154(1)(*a*), where tax is chargeable on a valuation date, in relation to any year commencing with the year 1994.

[2] Subs (1)(proviso) inserted by FA 1994 s 119(*a*), as respects any valuation date in relation to any year commencing with the year 1994.

[3] Substituted by FA 1995 s 154(1)(*b*), where tax is chargeable on a valuation date, in relation to any year commencing with the year 1995; previously "£25,000" (FA 1994 s 119(*b*)), "£27,500" (FA 1992 s 220(*a*)); £28,500 (1991 as indexed and rounded up by £100); £27,800 (FA 1990 s 124 as indexed and rounded up by £100); £26,654 (1989 as indexed); £25,795 (1988 as indexed); £25,307 (1987 as indexed); £24,468 (1986 as indexed); £23,395 (1985 as indexed); £22,030 (1984 as indexed); £20,000 (as enacted).

[4] Substituted by FA 1995 s 154(1)(*b*), where tax is chargeable on a valuation date, in relation to any year commencing with the year 1995; previously "1994" (FA 1992 s 220(*a*)); "1991" etc.

[5] Subs (2) substituted by FA 1990 s 124.

[6] Substituted by FA 1992 s 220(*b*); previously "1982" etc.

Definitions

"aggregate relevant income": ss 95, 101(1); "assessable person": s 95; "income": s 95; "income exemption limit": s 95; "market value": ss 95, 98; "net market value": s 95; "relevant person": s 95; "relevant residential property": s 95; "tax": s 95; "valuation date": s 95.

---

102 Marginal reliefs

(1) Where an assessable person makes a claim in that behalf and proves that his aggregate relevant income as respects any valuation date does not exceed an amount equal to the aggregate of the income exemption limit applying on that valuation date and [£10,000],¹ he shall be entitled to have the tax, if any, payable by him in respect of the net market value of his relevant residential property on that valuation date reduced to an amount equal to the amount determined

by the formula—

$$T \times \frac{A - E}{[10,000]^2}$$

where—

A   is the amount of the aggregate relevant income,

E   is the income exemption limit, and

T   is the tax which, apart from this subsection and subsection (2), would be payable.

[Provided that—

(a) where, in relation to a valuation date, a unit of residential property is comprised in the relevant residential property of one or more persons and any of those persons has attained the age of 65 years, "£15,000" shall be substituted for "£10,000" and "15,000" shall be substituted for "10,000" in the formula, and

(b) where the amount of the aggregate relevant income is not a multiple of £1,000, it shall, for the purposes of relief under this section, be rounded down to the next £1,000.][3]

[(2) Where, for the year of assessment ending on a valuation date, an assessable person was entitled to relief under section 141 of the Income Tax Act, 1967, in respect of any child or children resident with him, he shall be entitled to have the tax payable by him in respect of the net market value of his relevant residential property on that date reduced by the amount determined by the formula—

$$T \times \frac{C}{10}$$

where—

C   is 1 or, if the number of such children is greater than 1, that number (up to a maximum of 10), and

T   is the tax which, apart from this subsection, would be payable:

Provided that no reduction shall be allowed under this subsection for the valuation date in question in respect of a qualifying child—

(a) who is a child to whom section 138A(1)(b)(i)(III)(B) of the Income Tax Act, 1967, relates and who is entitled in his own right to an income exceeding £1,320, or

(b) in any other case, who is entitled in his own right to an income exceeding £720,

in the year or assessment ending on that valuation date.][4]

(3) Any claim under subsection (1) shall be made in writing to the Commissioners not later than two years after the relevant valuation date.

[(4) In this section—

"**child**", in relation to an assessable person, includes—

(a) a stepchild,

[(b) a child—

(i) adopted under the Adoption Acts, 1952 to 1991, or

(ii) adopted under a foreign adoption which by virtue of section 2, 3, 4 or 5 of the Adoption Act, 1991, is deemed to have been effected by a valid adoption order within the meaning of section 1 of that Act,

and]][5]

(*c*) a person who, for the year of assessment ending on the valuation date, is in the custody, and maintained at the expense, of either or both the assessable person and the spouse of that assessable person;

"qualifying child", in relation to an assessable person, means a child referred to in subsections (1)(*b*)(i) or (4)(*a*) of section 138A of the Income Tax Act, 1967, as if the references therein to a child were references to a child within the meaning of this subsection;

"year of assessment" has the meaning assigned to it by section 1 of the Income Tax Act, 1967.][6]

Amendments

[1] Substituted by FA 1994 s 120(*a*), where tax is chargeable on a valuation date, in relation to any year commencing with the year 1994; previously "£5,000".

[2] Substituted by FA 1994 s 120(*a*), where tax is chargeable on a valuation date, in relation to any year commencing with the year 1994; previously "10,000".

[3] Subs (1)(proviso) inserted by FA 1994 s 120(*b*), where tax is chargeable on a valuation date, in relation to any year commencing with the year 1994.

[4] Subs (2) substituted by FA 1990 s 125(*a*).

[5] Subs (4)(*b*) substituted by FA 1992 s 221.

[6] Subs (4) inserted by FA 1990 s 125(*b*).

Definitions

"aggregate relevant income": ss 95, 101(1); "assessable person": s 95; "income": s 95; "income exemption limit": s 95; "net market value": s 95; "relevant residential property": s 95; "tax": s 95; "valuation date": s 95.

---

103 Delivery of returns

(1) An assessable person shall on or before the 1st day of October immediately following each valuation date, deliver to the Commissioners on a form provided by them a return of all property comprised in the relevant residential property of the assessable person on that valuation date stating the market value thereof on that valuation date and shall, if required by notice in writing by the Commissioners, deliver to them within such time, not being less than 30 days, as may be specified in the notice, a statement verifying such particulars, together with such evidence, statements and documents as the Commissioners may require relating to that property or to any property which the Commissioners have reason to believe forms part of the relevant residential property of such assessable person.

(2) A person shall, if he is required by notice in writing by the Commissioners to do so, deliver to the Commissioners, within such time, not being less than 30 days, as may be specified in the notice, on a form provided by them a return of all property comprised in the relevant residential property of that person on the valuation date specified in the notice stating the market value thereof on that valuation date and shall, if he is so required by the Commissioners, deliver to them a statement verifying such particulars, together with such evidence, statements and documents as the Commissioners may require relating to that property.

(3) A return under this section shall be signed by the person by whom it is to be delivered and shall include a declaration by that person that it is, to the best of his knowledge, information and belief, correct and complete.

(4) The Commissioners may require the declaration mentioned in subsection (3) to be made on oath.

Definitions

"assessable person": s 95; "market value": ss 95, 98; "relevant residential property": s 95; "valuation date": s 95.

104 Assessment and payment of tax

(1) Tax in respect of any relevant residential property required to be included in a return under section 103 shall be due on the 1st day of October immediately following the valuation date to which the return relates and tax so due shall be payable by the assessable person without the making of an assessment; but tax which has become due as aforesaid may be assessed on the assessable person (whether or not it has been paid when the assessment is made) if that tax, or any part of it, is not paid on or before the due date.

[(1A)(*a*) Notwithstanding the provisions of subsection (1) and subject to such regulations as the Commissioners may make in accordance with section 115(1A), tax which is due and payable in accordance with this section may, at the option of the person delivering the return, be discharged by making an initial payment of **25 per cent** of the tax due on the 1st day of October immediately following the valuation date to which the return relates and the balance of the tax due, together with an amount equal to **5 per cent** of that balance, shall be paid in ten equal monthly instalments, the first of which shall be due on the 15th day of November immediately following such valuation date and the remaining instalments shall be due on the 15th day of each subsequent month.

   (*b*)   In the event that a person exercising the option under subsection (1A)(*a*) fails to make an initial payment by the due date or any subsequent instalment payment in accordance with such regulations as the Commissioners may make under section 115(1A), the provisions of section 110 of the Finance Act, 1983, as to the recovery of tax shall apply to the outstanding balance of the tax liability as if the said person had not exercised the said option.

   (*c*)   This subsection shall not have effect in respect of any tax or additional tax due under an assessment of tax or an amended assessment of tax made by the Commissioners under subsections (2) or (3).

(1B) Where the Commissioners are satisfied that tax payable in respect of any relevant residential property cannot without excessive hardship be paid in accordance with subsection (1) or (1A), as the case may be, they may allow payment to be postponed for such period, to such extent and on such terms as they think fit.

(1C) Where, in the opinion of the Commissioners, the complication of circumstances affecting any relevant residential property are such as to justify them in doing so, they may compound the tax payable on the relevant residential property upon such terms as they shall think fit.]¹

[(2) In any case in which—

    (*a*)   a return under section 103(1) is not delivered by an assessable person to the Commissioners on or before the 1st day of October immediately following the relevant valuation date, or

    (*b*)   a return under section 103(2) is not delivered by a person within the time specified, or

    (*c*)   the Commissioners are dissatisfied with any return made under section 103(1) or section 103(2),

the Commissioners may make an assessment of tax payable upon the net market value of the relevant residential property, or any part thereof, of the person on the relevant valuation date of such amount or such further amount, as, to the best of their knowledge, information (including information received from a member of the Garda Síochána) and belief, ought to be charged, levied and paid and for this purpose the Commissioners may make such estimate of the market value of any property on that valuation date as they consider necessary:

[Provided that the Commissioners may withdraw an assessment made under this subsection and make an assessment of the amount of tax payable on the basis of a return which, in their opinion, represents reasonable compliance with their requirements and which is delivered to the Commissioners within 30 days after the date of the assessment made by the Commissioners pursuant to this subsection.]²]³

(3) An assessment of tax may be reviewed by the Commissioners at any time and, where any amendment of an assessment is necessary as a result of the review whether in respect of the relevant residential property already assessed to tax or in respect of any additional relevant residential property, the Commissioners may, to the best of their knowledge, information and belief, make an amended assessment of the tax due and payable upon the net market value of the relevant residential property of the assessable person concerned or any part thereof.

(4) The making of an amended assessment shall not prejudice the right of the Commissioners to make further amended assessments of the amount of tax payable or to require delivery from the assessable person concerned of further returns, and the provisions of this section shall apply to such returns.

(5) Any tax or additional tax due under an assessment of tax or an amended assessment of tax made by virtue of this section shall be due and payable on the day next after the day on which the assessment of tax or the amended assessment of tax is made but, for the purposes of section 105, that tax or additional tax shall be treated as having been payable at the time when it would have been payable if it had been payable by virtue of a correct return under section 103(1).

(6) Notwithstanding anything contained in any enactment, but subject to the provisions of this section, an assessment of tax or an amended assessment of tax may be made at any time.

(7) Any amount of tax due or assessed under this section shall be due and payable to the Commissioners.

(8) Section 187 of the Income Tax Act, 1967, shall, with any necessary modifications, apply to an assessment of tax or an amended assessment of tax as it applies in relation to assessments to income tax.

(9) Section 73 of the Finance Act, 1974, shall, subject to any necessary modifications, apply in relation to tax as it applies in relation to income tax chargeable under Schedule D.

[(10) Notwithstanding the provisions of this section, an assessment or an amended assessment of tax may be made by the Commissioners under this section at any time and such assessment or amended assessment shall be made on—

    (a) the assessable person,

    (b) the person whom the Commissioners have reason to believe is an assessable person, or

    (c) the personal representative of the assessable person or of the person whom the Commissioners have reason to believe would, if alive, be an assessable person,

and where the assessment or amended assessment is so made on the personal representative, he shall have the same right of appeal under section 109 as if he were an assessable person.]⁴

Amendments

¹   Subss (1A)-(1C) inserted by FA 1994 s 121, where tax is chargeable on a valuation date, in relation to any year commencing with the year 1994.

²   Subs (2)(proviso) substituted by Criminal Assets Bureau Act 1996 s 24(5).

³   Subs (2) substituted by Disclosure of Certain Information for Taxation and Other Purposes Act 1996 s 9.

⁴   Subs (10) inserted by FA 1991 s 112.

Cross-references

Interest not chargeable (subs (1A)(*a*)): s 105(1A).

Payment of tax by instalments (subs (1)(*a*)) , Revenue may make regulations: s 115(1A).

Definitions

"assessable person": s 95; "income": s 95; "market value": ss 95, 98; "net market value": s 95; "personal representative": s 95, ITA 1967 s 450(2); "relevant residential property": s 95; "tax": s 95; "valuation date": s 95.

---

105 Interest on tax

(1) Simple interest at the rate of [**1 per cent**]¹ per month or part of a month, without any deduction of income tax, shall be payable on tax from the date upon which it becomes due and payable until the date of payment and shall be chargeable and recoverable in the same manner as if it were part of the tax:

Provided that interest shall not be payable unless the total amount thereof exceeds £5.

[(1A) Notwithstanding the provisions of subsection (1), interest shall not be chargeable where tax is paid in accordance with the provisions of section 104(1A)(*a*) and such regulations as the Commissioners may make under section 115(1A).]²

(2) A payment on account of tax shall be applied—

   (*a*)   if there is interest due on tax at the date of the payment, to the discharge, so far as may be, of the interest so due, and

   (*b*)   if there is any balance of that payment remaining, to the discharge of so much tax as is equal to that balance.

(3) Subject to subsections (1) and (2), payments on account of tax due on any date may be made at any time after that date, whereupon interest on so much of the payment on account as is referable to tax shall cease to run.

(4) Interest payable under this section shall not be allowed in computing any income, profits or losses for any of the purposes of the Tax Acts.

(5) Where the Commissioners are dissatisfied with a return under section 103 and an amount or an additional amount of tax is found to be payable by virtue of an assessment of tax made under section 104, no interest shall be payable on that amount of tax or additional amount of tax if—

   (*a*)   the return was made in time, and

   (*b*)   (i)   in the case of an amount of tax where no tax was payable on the basis of the net market value of the relevant residential property included in the return, that amount of tax does not exceed £100, or

          (ii)   in the case of an additional amount of tax—

             (A)   the tax payable on the basis of the net market value of the relevant residential property included in the return was paid on or before the due date, and

             (B)   the additional amount of tax does not exceed **10 per cent** of the aggregate of the additional amount of tax and the tax referred to in clause (A) of this subparagraph, and

   (*c*)   the amount of tax or additional amount of tax is paid not later than one month from—

          (i)   the date of the assessment of tax in which it is contained if there is no appeal under section 108 or 109 against the assessment, or

          (ii)   the date of the determination of an appeal under either of the said sections or, if there is more than one appeal to be determined, the date of the later determination.

Amendments

1   Substituted by FA 1998 s 133(2)(*a*) with effect from 27 March 1998 for any month or part of a month, in respect of an amount paid or remitted or an amount due to be repaid or retained, before on or after that date; previously "1.25 per cent".

2   Subs (1A) inserted by FA 1994 s 122, where tax is chargeable on a valuation date, in relation to any year commencing with the year 1994.

Definitions

"income": s 95; "market value": ss 95, 98; "net market value": s 95; "relevant residential property": s 95; "tax": s 95; "the Tax Acts": s 95, CTA 1976 s 155.

---

106 Payment to the Collector

All sums due under the provisions of this Part shall be paid to the Collector.

Definitions
"Collector": s 95.

107 Overpayment of tax

(1) Where it is proved to the satisfaction of the Commissioners that the amount of tax or interest paid in respect of the relevant residential property of an assessable person on a valuation date exceeds the amount which that person was liable to pay, the excess shall be repaid by the Commissioners to the person who paid the excess, his nominee or personal representative or, at the option of the Commissioners, the excess, or such part of it as is required for that purpose, may be retained by the Commissioners and set off against any liability of the assessable person in respect of tax or interest due and payable by the person who paid the excess at the time the repayment falls to be made, in respect of the relevant residential property of the assessable person on any other valuation date.

(2) Where, under this section, any amount falls to be repaid or retained, there shall be added to such amount simple interest [at the rate of [0.5 per cent][1] or such other rate (if any) as stands prescribed by the Minister for Finance by regulations,][2] of the amount to be repaid or retained for each month or part of a month from the date of the payment of the excess giving rise to the repayment to the date of the repayment or retention as the case may be. Income tax shall not be deductible on payment of interest under this subsection and such interest shall not be reckoned in computing income for the purposes of the Tax Acts.

[(3) Every regulation made under this section shall be laid before Dáil Éireann as soon as may be after it is made and, if a resolution annulling the regulation is passed by Dáil Éireann within the next twenty-one days on which Dáil Éireann has sat after the regulation is laid before it, the regulation shall be annulled accordingly, but without prejudice to the validity of anything previously done thereunder.][3]

Amendments

[1]   Substituted by FA 1998 s 133(2)(*b*) with effect from 27 March 1998 for any month or part of a month, in respect of an amount paid or remitted or an amount due to be repaid or retained, before on or after that date; previously "0.6" (Payment of Interest on Overpaid Tax Regulations 1990 (SI 178/1990)); previously "1 per cent" (FA 1986 s 114(3)); previously "1.25 per cent".

[2]   Substituted by FA 1986 s 114(3)(*a*).

[3]   Subs (3) inserted by FA 1986 s 114(3)(*b*).

Definitions

"assessable person": s 95; "income": s 95; "personal representative": s 95, ITA 1967 s 450(2); "relevant residential property": s 95; "tax": s 95; "the Tax Acts": s 95, CTA 1976 s 155; "valuation date": s 95.

108 Appeals regarding value of residential property

If a person is aggrieved by the decision of the Commissioners as to the market value of any residential property, he may appeal against the decision in the manner prescribed by section 33 of the Finance (1909-10) Act, 1910, and the provisions as to appeals under that section of that Act shall apply accordingly with any necessary modifications.

Note

The procedure involves the reference of the disputed valuation to a panel of referees whose decision (subject to a further appeal to the courts) is final.

Definitions

"market value": ss 95, 98.

109 Appeals in other cases

(1) In this section—

"Appeal Commissioners" has the meaning assigned to it by section 156 of the Income Tax Act, 1967;

"appellant" means a person who appeals to the Appeal Commissioners under this section.

(2) Subject to the provisions of this Part, an assessable person who has been assessed to tax in respect of any relevant residential property and who is aggrieved by the assessment may, in accordance with the provisions of this section, appeal to the Appeal Commissioners against the assessment and the appeal shall be heard and determined by the Appeal Commissioners whose determination shall be final and conclusive unless the appeal is required to be reheard by a judge of the Circuit Court or a case is required to be stated in relation to it for the opinion of the High Court.

(3) An appeal shall not lie under this section in relation to the market value of residential property.

(4) A person who intends to appeal under this section against an assessment shall, within 30 days after the date of the assessment, give notice in writing to the Commissioners of his intention to appeal against the assessment.

(5) An appeal under this section against an assessment shall not be proceeded with or entertained by the Appeal Commissioners unless an amount equal to 75 per cent. of the amount of the assessment is paid to the Collector by or on behalf of the appellant:

Provided that this subsection shall not apply where the appellant is aggrieved by the assessment on the ground that he is entitled to exemption from tax by virtue of section 101 or on the ground that he is not an assessable person.

(6) (a) Subject to the provisions of this section, the provisions of the Income Tax Acts relating to—

   (i) the appointment of times and places for the hearing of appeals;

   (ii) the giving of notice to each person who has given notice of appeal of the time and place appointed for the hearing of his appeal;

   (iii) the determination of an appeal by agreement between the appellant and the Commissioners;

   (iv) the determination of an appeal by the appellant giving notice of his intention not to proceed with the appeal;

(v) the hearing, determination or dismissal of an appeal by the Appeal Commissioners, including the hearing, determination or dismissal of an appeal by one Appeal Commissioner;

(vi) the assessment having the same force and effect as if it were an assessment in respect of which no notice of appeal had been given where the person who has given notice of appeal does not attend before the Appeal Commissioners at the time and place appointed;

(vii) the extension of the time for giving notice of appeal and the readmission of appeals by the Appeal Commissioners and the provisions which apply where action by way of court proceedings has been taken;

(viii) the rehearing of an appeal by a judge of the Circuit Court and the statement of a case for the opinion of the High Court on a point of law;

(ix) the payment of tax in accordance with the determination of the Appeal Commissioners notwithstanding that an appeal is required to be reheard by a judge of the Circuit Court or that a case for the opinion of the High Court on a point of law has been required to be stated or is pending;

(x) the procedures for appeal,

shall, with any necessary modifications, apply to an appeal under this section as if the appeal were an appeal against an assessment to income tax.

(b) The Commissioners shall, subject to their giving notice in writing in that behalf to the appellant within 10 days after the determination of an appeal by the Appeal Commissioners, have the same right as the appellant to have the appeal reheard by a judge of the Circuit Court.

(c) The rehearing of an appeal under this section by a judge of the Circuit Court shall be by a judge of the Circuit Court in whose circuit the appellant resides:

Provided that—

(i) in any case where the appellant is not resident in the State, or

(ii) in any case where there is a doubt or a dispute as to the circuit,

the appeal shall be reheard by a judge of the Circuit Court assigned to the Dublin Circuit.

(7) (a) Any notice or other document which is required or authorised by this section to be served by the Commissioners or by an appellant may be served by post.

(b) Any notice or other document which is required or authorised to be served by the Commissioners on an appellant under this section may be sent to the solicitor, accountant or other agent of the appellant and a notice thus served shall be deemed to have been served on the appellant unless the appellant proves to the satisfaction of the Appeal Commissioners or the Circuit Court, as the case may be, that he had, before the notice or other document was served, withdrawn the authority of such solicitor, accountant or other agent to act on his behalf.

(8) *Prima facie* evidence of any notice given under this section by the Commissioners may be given in any proceedings by production of a document purporting to be a copy of the notice and it shall not be necessary to prove the official position of the person by

whom the notice purports to be given or, if it is signed, the signature, or that the person signing and giving it was authorised so to do.

Definitions

"assessable person": s 95; "Collector": s 95; "income": s 95; "the Income Tax Acts": s 95, ITA 1967 s 3; "market value": ss 95, 98; "relevant residential property": s 95; "tax": s 95.

110 Recovery of tax

(1) All the provisions of the Income Tax Acts relating to the collection and recovery of income tax shall, subject to any necessary modifications, apply in relation to tax as they apply in relation to income tax chargeable under Schedule D.

(2) Without prejudice to subsection (1), every sum due to the Commissioners in respect of tax or interest thereon shall be deemed to be a debt due by an assessable person or his personal representative to the Minister for Finance for the benefit of the Central Fund and shall be payable to the Commissioners and may (without prejudice to any other mode of recovery thereof) be sued for and recovered by action, or other appropriate proceeding, at the suit of the Attorney-General, the Minister for Finance or the Commissioners in any court of competent jurisdiction, notwithstanding anything to the contrary contained in the Inland Revenue Regulation Act, 1890.

Definitions

"assessable person": s 95; "income": s 95; "the Income Tax Acts": s 95, ITA 1967 s 3; "personal representative": s 95, ITA 1967 s 450(2); "tax": s 95.

110A Clearance on sale of certain residential property

[(1) in this section—

"consideration" means the amount of consideration in a sale which is attributable to residential property;

[**"general exemption limit"** has the meaning assigned to it by section 100;][1]

"prior owner", in relation to the sale of an estate or interest in residential property, means a person who, in addition to being the owner of that property, occupied that property immediately prior to the contract for sale;

"the purchaser" has the meaning assigned to it by subsection (2);

"relevant valuation date" means—

    (*a*)   where the date of the contract for sale is the 5th day of April in a year, that date, and

    (*b*)   in any other case, the 5th day of April immediately preceding the date of the contract for sale;

"sale" includes a transaction whereby more than one estate or interest in a unit of residential property is sold to the same purchaser;

"the specified amount", in relation to the consideration in a sale of an estate or interest in residential property, means the amount of the money consideration in the sale, or, if less, the amount determined by the following formula—

B (1.5 per cent x A)

where—

    A   is the difference between the consideration and the general exemption limit on the relevant valuation date, and

    B   is 5 or, where the number of valuation dates concerned is less than 5, the number of valuation dates, after the 4th day of April, 1983, on which such beneficial ownership in possession in that property of which the purchaser would have notice, being notice within the meaning of section 3(1) of the Conveyancing Act, 1882, is wholly or partly the beneficial ownership of a person who the purchaser has reason to believe may be a prior owner;

"tax due and payable" means tax and interest due and payable in respect of every valuation date occurring on or before the date of the contract for sale referred to in subsection (2);

"the vendor" has the meaning assigned to it by subsection (2).

(2) In the event of a sale of an estate or interest in residential property—

    (*a*)   the date of the contract for which is on or after the 1st day of August, 1993, and

    (*b*)   the consideration for which exceeds the general exemption limit applying on the relevant valuation date,

the person by or through whom such consideration falls to be paid (in this section referred to as 'the purchaser') shall, subject to subsection (6), deduct from that consideration an amount equal to the specified amount, and pay it to the Commissioners forthwith, and the person to whom the consideration falls to be paid (in this section referred to as 'the vendor') shall allow such deduction upon receipt of the residue of the consideration, and the purchaser shall, on proof of payment to the Commissioners of the amount so deducted, be acquitted and discharged of so much money as is represented by the deduction as if that sum had been actually paid to the vendor on the day on which payment was made to the Commissioners.

(3) Upon making a deduction under subsection (2), the purchaser shall forthwith deliver to the Commissioners, on a form provided by them, a return of the consideration and of the amount deducted therefrom.

(4) Any deduction to be made by a purchaser under subsection (2) may at any time, so far as it has not been paid to the Commissioners, be collected and recovered from the purchaser by the Commissioners as if it were tax and, accordingly, the provisions of section 110 shall apply to any such deduction.

(5) (*a*)   Where, in the opinion of the Commissioners, the purchaser in a sale referred to in subsection (2) has failed in his obligation to pay in full to the Commissioners the amount to be deducted under that subsection, the Commissioners shall, to the best of their knowledge, information and belief, estimate the amount of the deduction which fell to be made under that subsection, and the amount of that estimate shall, for the purposes of subsection (4), be deemed to be the actual amount of the deduction which fell to be made under subsection (2).

(*b*)   Any purchaser who is aggrieved by an estimate made by the Commissioners under this subsection may appeal to the Appeal Commissioners against that estimate, and the provisions of section 109 shall, with any necessary modifications, apply to an appeal under this subsection as if it were an appeal against an assessment to tax.

(6) (*a*)   Where, before a specified amount falls to be deducted under subsection (2), application to the Commissioners on a form provided by them is made by a vendor, and the Commissioners are satisfied that there is no tax due and payable by that vendor in respect of any property, they shall issue a certificate that the appropriate proportion of the specified amount shall not be deducted under subsection (2), and for this purpose appropriate proportion means the proportion which that vendor's share of the total consideration bears to the total consideration.

(*b*)   Where a certificate has issued in respect of any vendor under paragraph (*a*), no reduction in the interest of that vendor in the consideration shall be made by virtue of any balance of a specified amount falling to be deducted in respect of any other vendor.

(7) An appropriate proportion of any payment made to the Commissioners under subsection (2) shall be regarded as having come out of each appropriate vendor's interest in the total consideration, and where the Commissioners are satisfied in respect of any appropriate vendor that there is no tax due and payable by that vendor in respect of any property, they shall, save to the extent of any relief given under subsection (8)(*b*), repay to that vendor his appropriate proportion of the payment made, and for the purposes of this section an appropriate vendor shall be any vendor in respect of whom a certificate has not issued under subsection (6), and his appropriate proportion of the payment shall be the proportion which his share of the total consideration bears to the aggregate of his share and the shares of all other appropriate vendors (if any) in the total consideration, and the provisions of section 107(2) shall apply, with any necessary modifications, to any repayment which so falls to be made.

(8) Where any estate or interest in residential property, the subject matter of a sale referred to in subsection (2), is held by a vendor—

(*a*)   as trustee for another person absolutely entitled as against the trustee, or for any person who would be so entitled but for being an infant or other person under disability (or for two or more persons who are or would be jointly so entitled), this section shall apply as if the estate or interest were vested in, and the acts of the trustee in relation to the estate or interest were the acts of, the person or persons for whom he is the trustee, or

(*b*)   as trustee for one or more prior owners not absolutely entitled as against the trustee, subsections (6) and (7) shall apply as if the reference to tax due and payable by a vendor were a reference to the tax due and payable by all of those prior owners, and, where a payment has been made to the Commissioners under subsection (2)—

(i)   if the Commissioners are satisfied that there is no tax due and payable by any one or more of those prior owners, they shall, in relation to each prior owner in respect of whom they are so satisfied, give to that vendor, on an application to them in that behalf on a form provided by them, a certificate to that effect,

(ii) that vendor shall be entitled to recover an equal share of his appropriate proportion of the payment from each of those prior owners in respect of whom the Commissioners have refused to issue such a certificate and to so recover in any court of competent jurisdiction as if it were a simple contract debt, and

(iii) appropriate relief shall, on a claim being made in that behalf, be given to any prior owner in respect of whom the vendor has made recovery, or, where the Commissioners are satisfied that the vendor is unable to make full recovery, to that vendor, whether by discharge, or repayment or otherwise.

(9) Where, on or after the date of the passing of the Finance Act, 1993, a person (in this subsection referred to as 'the transferor') transfers to his spouse (in this subsection, and in subsection (10), referred to as the transferee) by sale or other *inter vivos* disposition, an estate or interest in residential property, any tax and interest due and outstanding from the transferor on the date of such transfer shall be and remain for 12 years from that date a first charge on that estate or interest, and such tax and interest shall have priority over all charges and interests created by the transferee or any person claiming in the right or on the behalf of the transferee:

Provided that—

(*a*) where, subsequent to the transfer, there is a *bona fide* sale for full consideration in money or money's worth or a mortgage of the estate or interest transferred, that estate or interest shall not remain charged as against the purchaser or mortgagee unless the amount of the consideration or the amount of the mortgage debt exceeds the general exemption limit applying on the valuation date immediately preceding the date of the agreement for sale or mortgage;

(*b*) tax or interest shall not be a charge on property as against a *bona fide* purchaser or mortgagee for full consideration in money or money's worth without notice, or a person deriving title from or under such a purchaser or mortgagee.

(10) Where the tax and interest charged on property under subsection (9) has been paid, the Commissioners shall, on request, give a certificate to that effect to the transferee or to a person deriving title from him, which shall discharge that property from such tax and interest.

(11) Section 72 of the Registration of Title Act, 1964, shall be construed and have effect as if there were included in subsection (1)(*a*) of that section a reference to residential property tax.

[(12) Subsection (2) of this section shall not apply to the sale of an estate or interest in residential property which has been previously acquired after 5 April 1996 by a bona fide purchaser for full consideration in money or money's worth.][2][3]

Amendments

[1] Definition of "general exemption limit" inserted by FA 1997 s 132 and deemed always to have had effect.

[2] Subs (12) inserted by FA 2000 s 135 in relation to the sale of an estate or interest in residential property (within the meaning of FA 1983 Pt VI) completed after 10 February 2000.

Definitions

"occupied": s 95; "tax": s 95; "valuation date": s 95.

111 Evidence in proceedings for recovery

The provisions of section 39 of the Finance Act, 1926, shall apply in any proceedings in the Circuit Court or the District Court for or in relation to the recovery of tax.

Definitions

"tax": s 95.

112 Penalties

(1) (*a*) A person who contravenes section 103(1) [or section 110A(3)]¹ or fails to comply with a notice under section 103(2) shall be liable to a penalty of [€1,265]².

(*b*) Where the contravention or failure referred to in paragraph (*a*) continues after judgment has been given by the court before which proceedings for the penalty have been commenced, the person concerned shall be liable to a further penalty of [€60]³ for each day on which the contravention or failure so continues.

(2) Where, under or for the purposes of any of the provisions of this Part, a person is authorised to inspect any property for the purpose of reporting to the Commissioners the market value thereof and any person prevents such inspection or obstructs the person so authorised in the performance of his functions in relation to the inspection, that person shall be liable to a penalty of [€1,265]².

(3) Where an assessable person fraudulently or negligently–

(*a*)   delivers any incorrect return or additional return,

(*b*)   makes or furnishes any incorrect statement, declaration evidence or valuation in connection with any property comprised in the relevant residential property of the assessable person,

(*c*)   makes or furnishes any incorrect statement, declaration evidence or valuation in connection with any claim for any allowance, deduction, exemption or relief, or

(*d*)   makes or furnishes any incorrect statement, declaration evidence or valuation in connection with any other matter, whereby the amount of tax payable in respect of the relevant residential property of the assessable person is less than it would have been if that return, statement, declaration, evidence or valuation had been correct, he shall be liable to a penalty of–

(i)   [€2,535]⁴, and

(ii)   the amount, or in the case of fraud, twice the amount of the difference specified in subsection (5).

(4) Where any such return, statement, declaration, evidence or valuation as is mentioned in subsection (3) was delivered, made or furnished neither fraudulently nor negligently by a person and it comes to his notice that it was incorrect, then, unless the error is remedied without unreasonable delay, such matter shall be treated, for the purposes of this section, as having been negligently done by him.

(5) The difference referred to in subsection (3) is the difference between–

(a) the amount of tax payable in respect of the relevant residential property of the assessable person for the valuation date to which the return, additional return, statement, declaration, evidence or valuation relates, and

(b) the amount which would have been the amount so payable if the return, additional return, statement, declaration evidence or valuation as made or submitted by him had been correct.

(6) For the purposes of subsection (3), where anything referred to in that subsection is delivered, made or furnished on behalf of a person, it shall be deemed to have been delivered, made or furnished by that person unless he proves that it was done without his knowledge and consent.

(7) Any person who assists in or induces the delivery, making or furnishing for any purposes of tax of any return, additional return, statement, declaration, evidence or valuation which he knows to be incorrect shall be liable to a penalty of [€2,535][4].

(8) The provisions of this section shall not affect any criminal proceedings.

(9) Subject to the provisions of this section, sections 128(4), 507, 508, 510, 511, 512, 517 and 518 of the Income Tax Act, 1967, shall with any necessary modifications, apply to a penalty under this section as if the penalty were a penalty under the Income Tax Acts.

Amendments

[1]   Inserted by FA 1993 s 108.
[2]   Substituted by FA 2001 s 240 and Sch 5 Pt 7 with effect from 1 January 2002; previously "£1,000".
[3]   Substituted by FA 2001 s 240 and Sch 5 Pt 7 with effect from 1 January 2002; previously "£50".
[4]   Substituted by FA 2001 s 240 and Sch 5 Pt 7 with effect from 1 January 2002; previously "£2,000".

Definitions

"assessable person": s 95; "the Income Tax Acts": s 95, ITA 1967 s 3; "market value": ss 95, 98; "relevant residential property": s 95; "tax": s 95; "valuation date": s 95.

113 Relief from double taxation

(1) If the Government by order declare that arrangements specified in the order have been made with the government of any territory outside the State in relation to affording relief from double taxation in respect of tax payable under the laws of the State and any tax of a similar character imposed under the laws of that territory, and that it is expedient that those arrangements should have the force of law, the arrangements shall, notwithstanding anything in any enactment, have the force of law.

(2) Any arrangements to which the force of law is given under this section may include provision for relief from tax charged before the making of the arrangements and provisions as to property which is not itself subject to double tax, and the provisions of this section shall have effect accordingly.

(3) For the purposes of subsection (1), arrangements made with the head of a foreign state shall be regarded as made with the government thereof.

(4) Where any arrangements have the force of law by virtue of this section, the obligation as to secrecy imposed by any enactment shall not prevent the Commissioners

from disclosing to any authorised officer of the government with which the arrangements are made such information as is required to be disclosed under the arrangements.

(5) (*a*) Any order made under this section may be revoked by a subsequent order and any such revoking order may contain such transitional provisions as appear to the Government to be necessary or expedient.

(*b*) Where an order is proposed to be made under this section, a draft thereof shall be laid before Dáil Éireann and the order shall not be made until a resolution approving of the draft has been passed by Dáil Éireann.

(6) (*a*) Where the Commissioners are satisfied that a tax of a similar character to residential property tax was paid in a territory outside the State in respect of residential property (other than residential property in the State) comprised in the relevant residential property of an assessable person on any valuation date by reference to any date prior to but within twelve months of that valuation date, they may make an allowance by way of credit against the tax due and payable in respect of such residential property for that valuation date for the foreign tax paid in that territory in respect of such residential property and for this purpose the tax due and payable in respect of that residential property for that valuation date shall be the amount which bears to the total tax payable by the assessable person in respect of his relevant residential property on the valuation date the same proportion as the market value of that residential property on that date bears to the aggregate amount of the market values of all residential property comprised in his relevant residential property on that date.

(*b*) This subsection shall have effect in respect of residential property tax due and payable for a valuation date but it shall not have effect in relation to a foreign tax in respect of which there is, for the time being, an order in force under this section providing for double taxation relief.

Definitions

"assessable person": s 95; "market value": ss 95, 98; "relevant residential property": s 95; "tax": s 95; "valuation date": s 95.

---

114 Extension of certain Acts

(1) Section 1 of the Provisional Collection of Taxes Act 1927, is hereby amended by the insertion of "and residential property tax" before "but no other tax or duty".

(2) Section 39 of the Inland Revenue Regulation Act, 1890, is hereby amended by the insertion of "residential property tax," before "stamp duties".

Definitions

"tax": s 95.

---

115 Regulations

(1) The Commissioners may make such regulations as seem to them to be necessary for the purpose of giving effect to this Part and of enabling them to discharge their functions thereunder.

[(1A) Without prejudice to the generality of subsection (1), the Commissioners may make such regulations as seem to them to be necessary for the purpose of giving effect to the payment of tax by instalments under section 104 (1A)(a).][1]

(2) Every regulation made under this section shall be laid before Dáil Éireann as soon as may be after it is made and, if a resolution annulling the regulation is passed by Dáil Éireann within the next twenty-one days on which Dáil Éireann has sat after the regulation is laid before it, the regulation shall be annulled accordingly, but without prejudice to the validity of anything previously done thereunder.

Amendments

[1]   Subs (1A) inserted by FA 1994 s 123, where tax is chargeable on a valuation date, in relation to any year commencing with the year 1994.

Cross-references

Interest on tax: s 105(1A).
Payment of tax: s 104(1A).

Definitions

"Commissioners": s 95(1).

---

116 Authorisation of officers

The Commissioners may authorise any of their officers to perform any act and discharge any function authorised by this Part to be performed or discharged by the Commissioners.

PART VII
MISCELLANEOUS

121 Care and management of taxes and duties

All taxes and duties imposed by this Act (apart from income levy collectible by health boards) are hereby placed under the care and management of the Revenue Commissioners.

122 Short title, construction and commencement

(1) This Act may be cited as the Finance Act, 1983.

...

(8) Any reference in this Act to any other enactment shall, except so far as the context otherwise requires, be construed as a reference to that enactment as amended by or under any other enactment including this Act.

(9) In this Act, a reference to a Part, section or schedule is to a Part or section of, or schedule to, this Act, unless it is indicated that reference to some other enactment is intended.

(10) In this Act, a reference to a subsection, paragraph or subparagraph is to the subsection, paragraph or subparagraph of the provision (including a schedule) in which the reference occurs, unless it is indicated that reference to some other provision is intended.

FINANCE ACT 1990

(1990 Number 10)
(Date of passing: 30 May 1990)

ARRANGEMENT OF SECTIONS

PART V
RESIDENTIAL PROPERTY TAX

Section

PART VII
MISCELLANEOUS

PART V
RESIDENTIAL PROPERTY TAX

121 Application (Part V)

This Part shall apply and have effect where tax is chargeable on a valuation date (as defined by section 95(1) of the Finance Act, 1983) in relation to any year commencing with the year 1990.

122 Amendment of section 95 (interpretation (Part VI) of Finance Act, 1983

Note

This section deleted in FA 1983 s 95 the definition of "child".

123 Amendment of section 100 (market value exemption limit) of Finance Act, 1983

Note

Para (*a*) substituted FA 1983 s 100(1) definition of "general exemption limit"; para (*b*) substituted in FA 1983 s 100 definition of "the new house price index number" the words "31st day of December next" for "31st day of March next".

124 Amendment of section 101 (income exemption limit) of Finance Act, 1983

Note

This section substituted FA 1983 s 101(2).

125 Amendment of section 102 (marginal reliefs) of Finance Act, 1983

Note

This section substituted FA 1983 s 102(2) and inserted FA 1983 s 102(4).

PART VII
MISCELLANEOUS

139 Care and management of taxes and duties

All taxes and duties imposed by this Act are hereby placed under the care and management of the Revenue Commissioners.

140 Short title, construction and commencement

(1) This Act may be cited as the Finance Act, 1990.

...

....

(6) Part V shall be construed together with Part VI of the Finance Act, 1983.

...

...

(10) Any reference in this Act to any other enactment shall, except so far as the context otherwise requires, be construed as a reference to that enactment as amended by or under any other enactment including this Act.

(11) In this Act, a reference to a Part, section or Schedule is to a Part or section of, or Schedule to, this Act, unless it is indicated that reference to some other enactment is intended.

(12) In this Act, a reference to a subsection, paragraph, subparagraph, clause or subclause is to the subsection, paragraph, subparagraph, clause or subclause of the provision (including a Schedule) in which the reference occurs, unless it is indicated that reference to some other provision is intended.

FINANCE ACT 1991

(1991 Number 13)
(Date of passing: 29 May 1991)

ARRANGEMENT OF SECTIONS

PART V
RESIDENTIAL PROPERTY TAX

112 Amendment of section 104 (assessment and payment of tax) of Finance Act, 1983

Note

This section inserted FA 1983 s 104(10).

PART VII
MISCELLANEOUS

125 Repeals

Each enactment specified in column (2) of the Fourth Schedule is hereby repealed to the extent specified in column (3) of that Schedule.

131 Care and management of taxes and duties

All taxes ... imposed by this Act are hereby placed under the care and management of the Revenue Commissioners.

132 Short title, construction and commencement

(1) This Act may be cited as the Finance Act, 1991.

...

(5)...

(6) Part V shall be construed together with Part VI of the Finance Act, 1983, and the enactments amending or extending that Part.

(7) ...

...

(10) Any reference in this Act to any other enactment shall, except so far as the context otherwise requires, be construed as a reference to that enactment as amended by or under any other enactment including this Act.

(11) In this Act, a reference to a Part, section or Schedule is to a Part or section of, or Schedule to, this Act, unless it is indicated that reference to some other enactment is intended.

(12) In this Act, a reference to a subsection, paragraph or subparagraph is to the subsection, paragraph or subparagraph of the provision (including a Schedule) in which the reference occurs, unless it is indicated that reference to some other provision is intended.

FINANCE ACT 1992

(1992 Number 9)
(Date of passing: 28 May 1992)

ARRANGEMENT OF SECTIONS

PART V
RESIDENTIAL PROPERTY TAX

PART VII
ANTI-AVOIDANCE AND ANTI-EVASION

PART VIII
MISCELLANEOUS

PART V
RESIDENTIAL PROPERTY TAX

218 Application (Part V)

This Part shall apply and have effect where tax is chargeable on a valuation date (as defined by section 95(1) of the Finance Act, 1983) in relation to any year commencing with the year 1992.

219 Amendment of section 100 (market value exemption limit) of Finance Act, 1983

Note

This section substituted in FA 1983 s 100(1) the following: para (*a*) in the definition of "general exemption limit" "£90,000" for "£65,000" and "1992" for "1983"; para (*b*) in the definition of "the new house price index number" "1980" for "1973".

---

220 Amendment of section 101 (income exemption limit) of Finance Act, 1983

Note

Para (*a*) substituted in FA 1983 s 101(2) "£27,000" for "£20,000" and "1992" for "1983"; para (*b*) substituted in FA 1983 s 101(3) "1989" for "1982".

221 Amendment of section 102 (marginal reliefs) of Finance Act, 1983

Note

This section substituted FA 1983 s 102(4)(*b*).

PART VII
ANTI-AVOIDANCE AND ANTI-EVASION

232 Inspection of documents and records

Note

This section substituted FA 1976 s 34.

237 Inspection of computer documents and records

(1) In this section—

"the Acts" means—

- (*a*) the Customs Acts,
- (*b*) the statutes relating to the duties of excise and to the management of those duties,
- (*c*) the Tax Acts,
- (*d*) the Capital Gains Tax Acts,
- (*e*) the Value-Added Tax Act, 1972, and the enactments amending or extending that Act,
- (*f*) the Capital Acquisitions Tax Act, 1976, and the enactments amending or extending that Act, and
- (*g*) Part VI of the Finance Act, 1983,

and any instruments made thereunder;

"data" means information in a form in which it can be processed;

"data equipment" means any electronic, photographic, magnetic, optical or other equipment for processing data;

"processing" means performing automatically logical or arithmetical operations on data, or the storing, maintenance, transmission, reproduction or communication of data;

"records" means documents which a person is obliged by any provision of the Acts to keep, to issue or to produce for inspection, and any other written or printed material;

"software" means any sequence of instructions used in conjunction with data equipment for the purpose of processing data or controlling the operation of the data equipment.

(2) Any provision under the Acts which—

    (*a*) requires a person to keep, retain, issue or produce any records or cause any records to be kept, retained, issued or produced, or

    (*b*) permits an officer of the Revenue Commissioners—

        (i) to inspect any records,

        (ii) to enter premises and search for any records, or

        (iii) to take extracts from or copies of or remove any records,

shall, where the records are processed by data equipment, apply to the data equipment together with any associated software, data, apparatus or material as it applies to the records.

(3) An officer of the Revenue Commissioners may, in the exercise or performance of his powers or duties, require—

    (*a*) the person by or on whose behalf the data equipment is or has been used, or

    (*b*) any person having charge of, or otherwise concerned with the operation of, the data equipment or any associated apparatus or material,

to afford him all reasonable assistance in relation thereto.

PART VIII
MISCELLANEOUS

248 Amendment of certain provisions of Tax Acts, etc, relating to penalties

Where, after the passing of this Act (but with respect to any year of assessment, or, as the case may be, accounting period, whether ending before or ending after such passing), an act or omission occurs in respect of which a person would, but for this section, have incurred, the penalty or penalties provided for in any provision of the Tax Acts or Part VI of the Finance Act, 1983, specified in column (2) of the Table to this section at any reference number, the person shall, in lieu of the penalty or penalties so provided for be liable to a penalty specified in column (3) of the said Table at that reference number and that provision shall be construed and have effect accordingly.

TABLE

Reference number	Provision of the Tax Acts, etc	Penalty
(1)	(2)	(3)
		£
1	Section 128(1A) of the Income Tax Act, 1967	750
2	Section 173 (6) of the Income Tax Act, 1967	1,200
3	Section 426(3) of the Income Tax Act, 1967	750

4	Section 500(1) of the Income Tax Act, 1967	750
5	Section 500(2) of the Income Tax Act, 1967	1,200
6	Section 31(5) of the Finance Act, 1979	1,000
7	Section 45(8) of the Finance Act, 1980	1,200
8	Section 112(1)(*a*) of the Finance Act, 1983	1,200
9	Section 112(3) of the Finance Act, 1983	2,500

Definition

"the Tax Acts": CTA 1976 s 155(2).

250 Amendment of Provisional Collection of Taxes Act, 1927

Notes

This section substituted PCTA 1927 s 4A.

253 Care and management of taxes and duties

All taxes and duties (except the excise duties on mechanically propelled vehicles imposed by section 163) imposed by this Act are hereby placed under the care and management of the Revenue Commissioners.

254 Short title, construction and commencement

(1) This Act may be cited as the Finance Act, 1992.

...

(6) Part V shall be construed together with Part VI of the Finance Act, 1983, and the enactments amending or extending that Part.

(7) Part VI shall be construed together with the Capital Acquisitions Tax Act, 1976, and the enactments amending or extending that Act.

...

(12) Any reference in this Act to any other enactment shall, except so far as the context otherwise requires, be construed as a reference to that enactment as amended by or under any other enactment including this Act.

(13) In this Act, a reference to a Part, section or Schedule is to a Part or section of, or Schedule to, this Act, unless it is indicated that reference to some other enactment is intended.

(14) In this Act, a reference to a subsection, paragraph or sub-paragraph is to the subsection, paragraph or subparagraph of the provision (including a Schedule) in which the reference occurs, unless it is indicated that reference to some other provision is intended.

FINANCE ACT 1993

(1993 Number 13)
(Date of passing: 17 June 1993)

ARRANGEMENT OF SECTIONS

PART V
RESIDENTIAL PROPERTY TAX

PART VII
MISCELLANEOUS

PART V
RESIDENTIAL PROPERTY TAX

107 Clearance on sale of certain residential property

Note

This section inserted FA 1983 s 110A.

---

108 Amendment of section 112 (penalties) of Finance Act, 1983

Note

This section inserted in FA 1983 s 112(1)(*a*) the words "or section 110A(3)", after "section 103(1)".

PART VII
MISCELLANEOUS

142 Care and management of taxes and duties

All taxes and duties imposed by this Act are hereby placed under the care and management of the Revenue Commissioners.

143 Short title, construction and commencement

(1) This Act may be cited as the Finance Act, 1993.

...

(6) Part V shall be construed together with Part VI of the Finance Act, 1983, and the enactments amending or extending that Part.

...

(10) Any reference in this Act to any other enactment shall, except so far as the context otherwise requires, be construed as a reference to that enactment as amended by or under any other enactment including this Act.

(11) In this Act, a reference to a Part, section or Schedule is to a Part or section of, or Schedule to, this Act, unless it is indicated that reference to some other enactment is intended.

(12) In this Act, a reference to a subsection, paragraph, subparagraph or clause is to the subsection, paragraph, subparagraph or clause of the provision (including a Schedule) in which the reference occurs, unless it is indicated that reference to some other provision is intended.

FINANCE ACT 1994

(1994 Number 13)
(Date of passing: 23 May 1994)

ARRANGEMENT OF SECTIONS

PART V
RESIDENTIAL PROPERTY TAX

PART VII
MISCELLANEOUS

SEVENTH SCHEDULE
Computation of residential property tax

PART V
RESIDENTIAL PROPERTY TAX

113 Definition (Part V)

In this Part **"the Act of 1983"** means the Finance Act, 1983.

114 Application (Part V)

This Part shall apply and have effect where tax is chargeable on a valuation date (as defined by section 95(1) of the Act of 1983) in relation to any year commencing with the year 1994.

Definitions
"tax": FA 1983 s 95(1); "valuation date": FA 1983 s 95(1); "year": IA 1937 Sch;

115 Amendment of section 95 (interpretation) of Act of 1983

Note
For any valuation date from 5 April 1994:
para (*a*)(i) substituted "sections 340, 353, 354 and 463" for "sections 340, 353 and 354" in the definition of "income" in FA 1983 s 95(1);
para (*a*)(ii) inserted "section 18 of the Finance Act, 1970," in the definition of "income" in FA 1983 s 95(1);
para (*a*)(iii) inserted para (*ee*); in the definition of "income" in FA 1983 s 95(1);

para (*b*) inserted "a person who has attained the age of 65 years and is not an assessable person, or a person who is permanently incapacitated by reason of mental or physical infirmity from maintaining himself and is not an assessable person, or"; in the definition of "relevant person" in FA 1983 s 95(1);

para (*c*) inserted ", where the Commissioners are satisfied that reasonable access is afforded to the public having regard to subsection (4)(*b*)(ii) of the said section 19 as amended by the Finance Act, 1994" in the definition of "residential property" in FA 1983 s 95(1).

Income, for residential property tax purposes does not include income from savings certificates or national instalment saving schemes.

In calculating the income of the householder for residential property tax purposes, income of residents of the house (other than the householder) who are over 65 years of age, or permanently incapacitated, is ignored.

Significant buildings that have been determined (*a*) by the Commissioner of Public Works to be of scientific, historic, architectural or aesthetic interest and (*b*) by the Revenue Commissioners to be accessible to the public, are subject to the new (60 days open per year with 40 days open between 1 May and 30 September) public access rules introduced by FA 1994 s 18. Occupiers of such buildings will not be exempt from residential property tax unless these access requirements are met.

Definitions

"person": IA 1937 s 11(*c*); "residential property": FA 1983 s 95(1);"valuation date": FA 1983 s 95(1);

116 Amendment of section 96 (charge of residential property tax) of Act of 1983

Note

With effect for any valuation date commencing with 1994 this section substituted "the tax chargeable on that net market value shall be computed in accordance with the Seventh Schedule to the Finance Act, 1994" for "the rate of tax shall be one and one-half per cent of that net market value" in FA 1983 s 96.

For valuation dates from 5 April 1994, residential property tax is to be charged at the following rates:

1% on the first £25,000 of net market value (the excess of the property's market value over the exemption threshold),

1.5% on the next £50,000, and

2% on the balance.

117 Amendment of section 98 (market value of property) of Act of 1983

Note

This section inserted FA 1983 s 98(2A) for any valuation date commencing with 1994.

If a property has been adapted to provide for an incapacitated person, then, in computing the property's market value for residential property tax purposes, the value of such improvements may be deducted.

118 Amendment of section 100 (market value exemption limit) of Act of 1983

Note

This section substituted "£75,000" for "£90,000" and "1994" for "1992" in the definition of "general exemption limit" in FA 1983 s 100(1) for any valuation date commencing with 1994.

For valuation dates from 5 April 1994, the property exemption threshold is reduced from £90,000 to £75,000.

119 Amendment of section 101 (income exemption limit) of Act of 1983

Note

For any valuation date commencing with 1994:

para (*a*) inserted FA 1983 s 101(1)(proviso);

para (*b*) substituted "£25,000" for "£27,500 and "1994" for "1992" in FA 1983 s 101(2).

For valuation dates from 5 April 1994:

For residential property tax purposes the income of residents of the house (other than a householder who is over 65 years of age, or permanently incapacitated) is ignored. Similarly, the income of a person who resides with a widowed parent (who has a dependent child) is also ignored in calculating the widowed person's income.

The income exemption threshold is reduced from £27,500 to £25,000 per annum.

120 Amendment of section 102 (marginal reliefs) of Act of 1983

Note

For any valuation date commencing with 1994:
para (*a*) substituted "£10,000" for "£5,000" and "10,000" for "5,000" in FA 1983 s 102)(1);
para (*b*) inserted FA 1983 s 102)(1)(proviso).
For valuation dates from 5 April 1994, persons aged under 65 will obtain marginal relief on £10,000.
Persons aged over 65 will obtain marginal relief on £15,000.
For marginal relief purposes, a household income figure may be rounded down to the nearest £1,000.

121 Amendment of section 104 (assessment and payment of tax) of Act of 1983

Note

This section inserted FA 1983 s 104(1A)-(1C).
Residential property tax may be paid by a 25% down payment on 1 October, with the balance, increased by 5%, being paid by 10 equal instalments over the next 10 months, commencing on 15 November and ending on 15 August.
Persons with tax arrears will not be able to avail of the instalment payment system. If an instalment is not paid on time, the entire outstanding balance becomes due and payable. The Revenue Commissioners are empowered to postpone payment of tax if they are satisfied the payment would cause excessive hardship. The Revenue may also adjust the tax liability where complicated circumstances may justify such adjustment.

122 Amendment of section 105 (interest on tax) of Act of 1983

Note

This section inserted FA 1983 s 105(1A) for any valuation date commencing with 1994.
Interest will not be charged where tax is paid by instalments (see s 121 above).

123 Amendment of section 115 (regulations) of Act of 1983

Note

This section inserted FA 1983 s 115(1A) for any valuation date commencing with 1994.
The Revenue Commissioners are empowered to make regulations setting out the detailed procedures governing the payment of residential property tax by instalments (see s 121 above).

PART VII
MISCELLANEOUS

CHAPTER I
Provisions relating to residence of individuals

Note

These provisions are contained in the Capital Acquisitions Tax Part of this volume in the 1994 section. The new residence determination measures also apply to income tax, corporation tax and capital gains tax.

CHAPTER II
General

165 Care and management of taxes and duties

All taxes and duties imposed by this Act are hereby placed under the care and management of the Revenue Commissioners.

166 Short title, construction and commencement

(1) This Act may be cited as the Finance Act, 1994.

...

(6) Part V shall be construed together with Part VI of the Finance Act, 1983, and the enactments amending or extending that Part.

...

(10) Any reference in this Act to any other enactment shall, except so far as the context otherwise requires, be construed as a reference to that enactment as amended by or under any other enactment including this Act.

(11) In this Act, a reference to a Part, section or Schedule is to a Part or section of, or Schedule to, this Act, unless it is indicated that reference to some other enactment is intended.

(12) In this Act, a reference to a subsection, paragraph, subparagraph, clause or subclause is to the subsection, paragraph, subparagraph, clause or subclause of the provision (including a Schedule) in which the reference occurs, unless it is indicated that reference to some other provision is intended.

SEVENTH SCHEDULE
Computation of residential property tax

Amendments

Repealed by FA 1995 s 155 where tax is chargeable on a valuation date, in relation to any year commencing with the year 1995.

FINANCE ACT 1995

(1995 Number 8)
(Date of passing: 2 June 1995)

ARRANGEMENT OF SECTIONS

PART V
RESIDENTIAL PROPERTY TAX

PART V
RESIDENTIAL PROPERTY TAX

151 Application (Part V)

This Part shall apply and have effect where tax is chargeable on a valuation date (as defined by section 95(1) of the Finance Act, 1983) in relation to any year commencing with the year 1995.

Definitions

"valuation date": FA 1983 s 95(1); "year": IA 1937 Sch.

---

152 Amendment of section 96 (charge of residential property tax) of Finance Act, 1983

Note

This section substituted "the rate of tax shall be one and one-half per cent. of that net market value" for "the tax chargeable on that net market value shall be computed in accordance with the Seventh Schedule to the Finance Act, 1994" in FA 1983 s 96.

For valuation dates on or after 5 April 1995, residential property tax at **1.5%** will apply to the excess of the property value over the market value exemption limit.

153 Amendment of section 100 (market value exemption limit) of Finance Act, 1983

Note

Para (*a*) substituted "£94,000" for "£75,000" and of "1995" for "1994" in FA 1983 s 100(1) definition of "general exemption limit";

para (*b*) substituted "1991" for "1980" in FA 1983 s 100(1) definition of "the new house price index number".

For valuation dates on or after 5 April 1995, residential property tax at 1.5% will apply to the excess of the property value over the market value exemption limit (£94,000) where the annual income of the owner/occupier exceeds £29,500.

154 Amendment of section 101 (income exemption limit) of Finance Act, 1983

...

(2) Notwithstanding the provisions of section 151, subsection (1)(*a*) shall be deemed to have come into operation as respects any valuation date (as defined by section 95(1) of the Finance Act, 1983) in relation to any year commencing with the year 1994.

Note

Subs (1)(*a*) inserted "within the meaning of section 102(4)" after "qualifying child" in FA 1983 s 101(1)(proviso)(*b*);

Subs (1)(*b*) substituted of "£29,500" for "£25,000" and of "1995" for "1994" in FA 1983 s 101(2).

For valuation dates on or after 5 April 1995, residential property tax at 1.5% will apply to the excess of the property value over the market value exemption limit (£94,000) where the annual income of the owner/occupier exceeds £29,500.

155 Repeal (Part V)

Note

This section repealed FA 1994 Sch 7.

PART VII
MISCELLANEOUS

CHAPTER II
General

175 Power to obtain information

(1) For the purposes of the assessment, charge, collection and recovery of any tax or duty placed under their care and management, the Revenue Commissioners may, by notice in writing, request any Minister of the Government to provide them with such information in the possession of the Minister in relation to payments for any purposes made by the Minister, whether on his own behalf or on behalf of any other person, to such persons or classes of persons as the Revenue Commissioners may specify in the notice and a Minister so requested shall provide such information as may be specified.

(2) The Revenue Commissioners may nominate any of their officers to perform any acts and discharge any functions authorised by this section to be performed or discharged by the Revenue Commissioners.

Definitions

"person": IA 1937 s 11(c).

---

178 Care and management of taxes and duties

All taxes and duties (except the excise duties on mechanically propelled vehicles imposed by section 117) imposed by this Act are hereby placed under the care and management of the Revenue Commissioners.

179 Short title, construction and commencement

(1) This Act may be cited as the Finance Act, 1995.

...

(6) Part V shall be construed together with Part VI of the Finance Act, 1983, and the enactments amending or extending that Part.

...

(8) Part VII (so far as relating to income tax) shall be construed together with the Income Tax Acts and (so far as relating to corporation tax) shall be construed together with the Corporation Tax Acts and (so far as relating to capital gains tax) shall be construed together with the Capital Gains Tax Acts and (so far as relating to value-added tax) shall be construed together with the Value-Added Tax Acts, 1972 to 1995, and (so far as relating to stamp duties) shall be construed together with the Stamp Act, 1891, and the enactments amending or extending that Act and (so far as relating to gift tax or inheritance tax) shall be construed together with the Capital Acquisitions Tax Act, 1976, and (so far as relating to residential property tax) shall be construed together with Part VI of the Finance Act, 1983, and (so far as relating to customs) shall be construed together with the Customs Acts and (so far as relating to duties of excise) shall be construed together with the statutes which relate to the duties of excise and to the management of those duties.

...

(11) Any reference in this Act to any other enactment shall, except so far as the context otherwise requires, be construed as a reference to that enactment as amended by or under any other enactment including this Act.

(12) In this Act, a reference to a Part, section or Schedule is to a Part or section of, or Schedule to, this Act, unless it is indicated that reference to some other enactment is intended.

(13) In this Act, a reference to a subsection, paragraph, subparagraph, clause or subclause is to the subsection, paragraph, subparagraph, clause or subclause of the provision (including a Schedule) in which the reference occurs, unless it is indicated that reference to some other provision is intended.

DISCLOSURE OF CERTAIN INFORMATION FOR TAXATION AND OTHER PURPOSES ACT 1996

(1996 Number 25)
(Date of passing: 30 July 1996)

ARRANGEMENT OF SECTIONS

9 Amendment of section 104 (assessment and payment of tax) of Finance Act, 1983

Notes

Section 9 substituted FA 1983 s 104(2).

CRIMINAL ASSETS BUREAU ACT 1996

(1996 Number 31)
(Date of passing: 11 October 1996)

ARRANGEMENT OF SECTIONS

Section

24 Amendment of certain taxation provisions

Notes

Subs (5) substituted the proviso to FA 1983 s 104(2) (inserted by the Disclosure of Certain Information for Taxation and Other Purposes Act 1996).

FINANCE ACT 1997

(1997 Number 22)
(Date of passing: 10 May 1997)

ARRANGEMENT OF SECTIONS

PART V
RESIDENTIAL PROPERTY TAX

131   Abolition of residential property tax

PART VIII
MISCELLANEOUS

165   Care and management of taxes and duties
166   Short title, construction and commencement

PART V
RESIDENTIAL PROPERTY TAX

131 Abolition of residential property tax

Residential property tax shall not be charged, levied or paid under the provisions of section 96 of the Finance Act, 1983, by reference to any valuation date (within the meaning of section 95 (1) of that Act) occurring on or after the 5th day of April, 1997.

Notes

Residential property tax is abolished for valuation dates occurring on or after 5 April 1997.

---

132 Amendment of section 110A (clearance on sale of certain residential property) of Finance Act, 1983

Notes

This section inserted the definition of "general exemption limit" in FA 1983 s 110A. This is a technical amendment.

PART VIII
MISCELLANEOUS

165 Care and management of taxes and duties

All taxes and duties imposed by this Act are hereby placed under the care and management of the Revenue Commissioners.

166 Short title, construction and commencement

(1) This Act may be cited as the Finance Act, 1997.

...

(6) Part V shall be construed together with Part VI of the Finance Act, 1983, and the enactments amending or extending that Part.

...

(8) Part VIII (so far as relating to income tax) shall be construed together with the Income Tax Acts and (so far as relating to corporation tax) shall be construed together with the Corporation Tax Acts and (so far as relating to capital gains tax) shall be construed together with the Capital Gains Tax Acts and (so far as relating to value-added tax) shall be construed together with the Value-Added Tax Acts, 1972 to 1996, and (so far as relating to Residential Property Tax) shall be construed together with Part VI of the Finance Act, 1983, and the enactments amending or extending that Act and (so far as relating to capital acquisitions tax) shall be construed together with the Capital Acquisitions Tax Act, 1976, and the enactments amending or extending that Act.

...

(11) Any reference in this Act to any other enactment shall, except so far as the context otherwise requires, be construed as a reference to that enactment as amended by or under any other enactment including this Act.

(12) In this Act, a reference to a Part, section or Schedule is to a Part or section of, or Schedule to, this Act, unless it is indicated that reference to some other enactment is intended.

(13) In this Act, a reference to a subsection, paragraph, subparagraph, clause or subclause is to the subsection, paragraph, subparagraph, clause or subclause of the provision (including a Schedule) in which the reference occurs, unless it is indicated that reference to some other provision is intended.

TAXES CONSOLIDATION ACT 1997

(1997 Number 39)

ARRANGEMENT OF SECTIONS

INTERPRETATION AND BASIC CHARGING PROVISIONS

PART 1
INTERPRETATION

PART 33
ANTI-AVOIDANCE

CHAPTER 2
Miscellaneous

MANAGEMENT PROVISIONS

PART 37
ADMINISTRATION

PART 38
RETURNS OF INCOME AND GAINS, OTHER OBLIGATIONS AND RETURNS, AND REVENUE POWERS

CHAPTER 3
Other obligations and returns

CHAPTER 4
Revenue powers

INTERPRETATION AND BASIC CHARGING PROVISIONS

PART 1
INTERPRETATION

7 Application to certain taxing statutes of Age of Majority Act, 1985

(1) Notwithstanding subsection (4) of section 2 of the Age of Majority Act, 1985 (in this section referred to as **"the Act of 1985"**), subsections (2) and (3) of that section shall, subject to subsection (2), apply for the purposes of the Income Tax Acts and any other statutory provision (within the meaning of the Act of 1985) dealing with the imposition, repeal, remission, alteration or regulation of any tax or other duty under the care and management of the Revenue Commissioners, and accordingly section 2(4)(*b*)(vii) of the Act of 1985 shall cease to apply.

(2) Nothing in subsection (1) shall affect a claimant's entitlement to [relief][1] under section 462 or 465.

Amendments

¹ Substituted by FA 2000 s 14 and Sch 1 para 2; previously "a deduction".

Cross-references

This section to be construed together with the Customs Acts, in so far as relating to customs, and with the statutes which relate to excise duty, in so far as relating to that duty: s 1104(2).

This section to be construed together with the Value Added Tax Acts 1972-1997, in so far as relating to value added tax: s 1104(3).

This section to be construed together with the Stamp Act 1891 and the enactments amending or extending that Act, in so far as relating to stamp duties: s 1104(4).

This section to be construed together with the Capital Acquisitions Tax Act 1976, and the enactments amending or extending that Act, in so far as relating to capital acquisitions tax: s 1104(5).

This section to be construed together with FA 1983 Pt VI and the enactments amending or extending that Part, in so far as relating to residential property tax: s 1104(6).

Definition

Income Tax Acts: s 1(2).

Former enactment

FA 1986 s 112(1)-(2).

PART 33

ANTI-AVOIDANCE

CHAPTER 2
Miscellaneous

811 Transactions to avoid liability to tax

(1) (*a*) In this section—

"**the Acts**" means—

(i) the Tax Acts,

(ii) the Capital Gains Tax Acts,

(iii) the Value-Added Tax Act, 1972, and the enactments amending or extending that Act,

(iv) the Capital Acquisitions Tax Act, 1976, and the enactments amending or extending that Act,

(v) Part VI of the Finance Act, 1983, and the enactments amending or extending that Part, and

(vi) the statutes relating to stamp duty,

and any instruments made thereunder;

"**business**" means any trade, profession or vocation;

"**notice of opinion**" means a notice given by the Revenue Commissioners under subsection (6);

"**tax**" means any tax, duty, levy or charge which in accordance with the Acts is placed under the care and management of the Revenue Commissioners and any interest, penalty or other amount payable pursuant to the Acts;

"**tax advantage**" means—

(i) a reduction, avoidance or deferral of any charge or assessment to tax, including any potential or prospective charge or assessment, or

(ii) a refund of or a payment of an amount of tax, or an increase in an amount of tax, refundable or otherwise payable to a person, including any potential or prospective amount so refundable or payable,

arising out of or by reason of a transaction, including a transaction where another transaction would not have been undertaken or arranged to achieve the results, or any part of the results, achieved or intended to be achieved by the transaction;

"**tax avoidance transaction**" has the meaning assigned to it by subsection (2);

"**tax consequences**", in relation to a tax avoidance transaction, means such adjustments and acts as may be made and done by the Revenue Commissioners pursuant to subsection (5) in order to withdraw or deny the tax advantage resulting from the tax avoidance transaction;

"**transaction**" means—

(i) any transaction, action, course of action, course of conduct, scheme, plan or proposal,

(ii) any agreement, arrangement, understanding, promise or undertaking, whether express or implied and whether or not enforceable or intended to be enforceable by legal proceedings, and

(iii) any series of or combination of the circumstances referred to in paragraphs (i) and (ii),

whether entered into or arranged by one person or by 2 or more persons—

(I) whether acting in concert or not,

(II) whether or not entered into or arranged wholly or partly outside the State, or

(III) whether or not entered into or arranged as part of a larger transaction or in conjunction with any other transaction or transactions.

(b) In subsections (2) and (3), for the purposes of the hearing or rehearing under subsection (8) of an appeal made under subsection (7) or for the purposes of the determination of a question of law arising on the statement of a case for the opinion of the High Court, the references to the Revenue Commissioners shall, subject to any necessary modifications, be construed as references to the Appeal Commissioners or to a judge of the Circuit Court or, to the extent necessary, to a judge of the High Court, as appropriate.

(2) For the purposes of this section and subject to subsection (3), a transaction shall be a "**tax avoidance transaction**" if having regard to any one or more of the following—

(a) the results of the transaction,

(b) its use as a means of achieving those results, and

(c) any other means by which the results or any part of the results could have been achieved, the Revenue Commissioners form the opinion that—

    (i)   the transaction gives rise to, or but for this section would give rise to, a tax advantage, and

    (ii) the transaction was not undertaken or arranged primarily for purposes other than to give rise to a tax advantage,

and references in this section to the Revenue Commissioners forming an opinion that a transaction is a tax avoidance transaction shall be construed as references to the Revenue Commissioners forming an opinion with regard to the transaction in accordance with this subsection.

(3) (*a*) Without prejudice to the generality of subsection (2), in forming an opinion in accordance with that subsection and subsection (4) as to whether or not a transaction is a tax avoidance transaction, the Revenue Commissioners shall not regard the transaction as being a tax avoidance transaction if they are satisfied that—

    (i)   notwithstanding that the purpose or purposes of the transaction could have been achieved by some other transaction which would have given rise to a greater amount of tax being payable by the person, the transaction—

        (I)   was undertaken or arranged by a person with a view, directly or indirectly, to the realisation of profits in the course of the business activities of a business carried on by the person, and

        (II) was not undertaken or arranged primarily to give rise to a tax advantage,

        or

    (ii) the transaction was undertaken or arranged for the purpose of obtaining the benefit of any relief, allowance or other abatement provided by any provision of the Acts and that the transaction would not result directly or indirectly in a misuse of the provision or an abuse of the provision having regard to the purposes for which it was provided.

(*b*) In forming an opinion referred to in paragraph (*a*) in relation to any transaction, the Revenue Commissioners shall have regard to—

    (i)   the form of that transaction,

    (ii) the substance of that transaction,

    (iii) the substance of any other transaction or transactions which that transaction may reasonably be regarded as being directly or indirectly related to or connected with, and

    (iv) the final outcome and result of that transaction and any combination of those other transactions which are so related or connected.

(4) Subject to this section, the Revenue Commissioners as respects any transaction may at any time—

    (*a*) form the opinion that the transaction is a tax avoidance transaction, (*b*)   calculate the tax advantage which they consider arises, or which but for this section would arise, from the transaction,

(*c*)   determine the tax consequences which they consider would arise in respect of the transaction if their opinion were to become final and conclusive in accordance with subsection (5)(*e*), and

(*d*)   calculate the amount of any relief from double taxation which they would propose to give to any person in accordance with subsection (5)(*c*).

(5) (*a*)   Where the opinion of the Revenue Commissioners that a transaction is a tax avoidance transaction becomes final and conclusive, they may, notwithstanding any other provision of the Acts, make all such adjustments and do all such acts as are just and reasonable (in so far as those adjustments and acts have been specified or described in a notice of opinion given under subsection (6) and subject to the manner in which any appeal made under subsection (7) against any matter specified or described in the notice of opinion has been finally determined, including any adjustments and acts not so specified or described in the notice of opinion but which form part of a final determination of any such appeal) in order that the tax advantage resulting from a tax avoidance transaction shall be withdrawn from or denied to any person concerned.

(*b*)   Subject to but without prejudice to the generality of paragraph (*a*), the Revenue Commissioners may—

   (i)   allow or disallow in whole or in part any deduction or other amount which is relevant in computing tax payable, or any part of such deduction or other amount,

  (ii)   allocate or deny to any person any deduction, loss, abatement, relief, allowance, exemption, income or other amount, or any part thereof, or

 (iii)   recharacterize for tax purposes the nature of any payment or other amount.

(*c*)   Where the Revenue Commissioners make any adjustment or do any act for the purposes of paragraph (*a*), they shall afford relief from any double taxation which they consider would but for this paragraph arise by virtue of any adjustment made or act done by them pursuant to paragraphs (*a*) and (*b*).

(*d*)   Notwithstanding any other provision of the Acts, where—

   (i)   pursuant to subsection (4)(*c*), the Revenue Commissioners determine the tax consequences which they consider would arise in respect of a transaction if their opinion that the transaction is a tax avoidance transaction were to become final and conclusive, and

  (ii)   pursuant to that determination, they specify or describe in a notice of opinion any adjustment or act which they consider would be, or be part of, those tax consequences,

then, in so far as any right of appeal lay under subsection (7) against any such adjustment or act so specified or described, no right or further right of appeal shall lie under the Acts against that adjustment or act when it is made or done in accordance with this subsection, or against any adjustment or act so made or done that is not so specified or described in the notice of opinion but which forms part of the final determination of any appeal made under subsection (7) against any matter specified or described in the notice of opinion.

(e) For the purposes of this subsection, an opinion of the Revenue Commissioners that a transaction is a tax avoidance transaction shall be final and conclusive—

  (i) if within the time limited no appeal is made under subsection (7) against any matter or matters specified or described in a notice or notices of opinion given pursuant to that opinion, or

  (ii) as and when all appeals made under subsection (7) against any such matter or matters have been finally determined and none of the appeals has been so determined by an order directing that the opinion of the Revenue Commissioners to the effect that the transaction is a tax avoidance transaction is void.

(6) (a) Where pursuant to subsections (2) and (4) the Revenue Commissioners form the opinion that a transaction is a tax avoidance transaction, they shall immediately on forming such an opinion give notice in writing of the opinion to any person from whom a tax advantage would be withdrawn or to whom a tax advantage would be denied or to whom relief from double taxation would be given if the opinion became final and conclusive, and the notice shall specify or describe—

  (i) the transaction which in the opinion of the Revenue Commissioners is a tax avoidance transaction,

  (ii) the tax advantage or part of the tax advantage, calculated by the Revenue Commissioners which would be withdrawn from or denied to the person to whom the notice is given,

  (iii) the tax consequences of the transaction determined by the Revenue Commissioners in so far as they would refer to the person, and

  (iv) the amount of any relief from double taxation calculated by the Revenue Commissioners which they would propose to give to the person in accordance with subsection (5)(c).

(b) Section 869 shall, with any necessary modifications, apply for the purposes of a notice given under this subsection or subsection (10) as if it were a notice given under the Income Tax Acts.

(7) Any person aggrieved by an opinion formed or, in so far as it refers to the person, a calculation or determination made by the Revenue Commissioners pursuant to subsection (4) may, by notice in writing given to the Revenue Commissioners within 30 days of the date of the notice of opinion, appeal to the Appeal Commissioners on the grounds and, notwithstanding any other provision of the Acts, only on the grounds that, having regard to all of the circumstances, including any fact or matter which was not known to the Revenue Commissioners when they formed their opinion or made their calculation or determination, and to this section—

(a) the transaction specified or described in the notice of opinion is not a tax avoidance transaction,

(b) the amount of the tax advantage or the part of the tax advantage, specified or described in the notice of opinion which would be withdrawn from or denied to the person is incorrect,

(c) the tax consequences specified or described in the notice of opinion, or such part of those consequences as shall be specified or described by the appellant in the notice of appeal, would not be just and reasonable in order to withdraw or to deny the tax advantage or part of the tax advantage specified or described in the notice of opinion, or

(d) the amount of relief from double taxation which the Revenue Commissioners propose to give to the person is insufficient or incorrect.

(8) The Appeal Commissioners shall hear and determine an appeal made to them under subsection (7) as if it were an appeal against an assessment to income tax and, subject to subsection (9), the provisions of the Income Tax Acts relating to the rehearing of an appeal and to the statement of a case for the opinion of the High Court on a point of law shall apply accordingly with any necessary modifications; but on the hearing or rehearing of the appeal—

(a) it shall not be lawful to enquire into any grounds of appeal other than those specified in subsection (7), and

(b) at the request of the appellants, 2 or more appeals made by 2 or more persons pursuant to the same opinion, calculation or determination formed or made by the Revenue Commissioners pursuant to subsection (4) may be heard or reheard together.

(9) (a) On the hearing of an appeal made under subsection (7), the Appeal Commissioners shall have regard to all matters to which the Revenue Commissioners may or are required to have regard under this section, and—

(i) in relation to an appeal made on the grounds referred to in subsection (7)(a), the Appeal Commissioners shall determine the appeal, in so far as it is made on those grounds, by ordering, if they or a majority of them—

(I) consider that the transaction specified or described in the notice of opinion or any part of that transaction is a tax avoidance transaction, that the opinion or the opinion in so far as it relates to that part is to stand,

(II) consider that, subject to such amendment or addition thereto as the Appeal Commissioners or the majority of them deem necessary and as they shall specify or describe, the transaction, or any part of it, specified or described in the notice of opinion, is a tax avoidance transaction, that the transaction or that part of it be so amended or added to and that, subject to the amendment or addition, the opinion or the opinion in so far as it relates to that part is to stand, or

(III) do not so consider as referred to in clause (I) or (II), that the opinion is void,

(ii) in relation to an appeal made on the grounds referred to in subsection (7)(b), they shall determine the appeal, in so far as it is made on those grounds, by ordering that the amount of the tax advantage or the part of the tax advantage specified or described in the notice of opinion be increased or reduced by such amount as they shall direct or that it shall stand,

(iii) in relation to an appeal made on the grounds referred to in subsection (7)(*c*), they shall determine the appeal, in so far as it is made on those grounds, by ordering that the tax consequences specified or described in the notice of opinion shall be altered or added to in such manner as they shall direct or that they shall stand, or

(iv) in relation to an appeal made on the grounds referred to in subsection (7)(*d*), they shall determine the appeal, in so far as it is made on those grounds, by ordering that the amount of the relief from double taxation specified or described in the notice of opinion shall be increased or reduced by such amount as they shall direct or that it shall stand.

(*b*) This subsection shall, subject to any necessary modifications, apply to the rehearing of an appeal by a judge of the Circuit Court and, to the extent necessary, to the determination by the High Court of any question or questions of law arising on the statement of a case for the opinion of the High Court.

(10) The Revenue Commissioners may at any time amend, add to or withdraw any matter specified or described in a notice of opinion by giving notice (in this subsection referred to as **"the notice of amendment"**) in writing of the amendment, addition or withdrawal to each and every person affected thereby, in so far as the person is so affected, and subsections (1) to (9) shall apply in all respects as if the notice of amendment were a notice of opinion and any matter specified or described in the notice of amendment were specified or described in a notice of opinion; but no such amendment, addition or withdrawal may be made so as to set aside or alter any matter which has become final and conclusive on the determination of an appeal made with regard to that matter under subsection (7).

(11) Where pursuant to subsections (2) and (4) the Revenue Commissioners form the opinion that a transaction is a tax avoidance transaction and pursuant to that opinion notices are to be given under subsection (6) to 2 or more persons, any obligation on the Revenue Commissioners to maintain secrecy or any other restriction on the disclosure of information by the Revenue Commissioners shall not apply with respect to the giving of those notices or to the performance of any acts or the discharge of any functions authorised by this section to be performed or discharged by them or to the performance of any act or the discharge of any functions, including any act or function in relation to an appeal made under subsection (7), which is directly or indirectly related to the acts or functions so authorised.

(12) The Revenue Commissioners may nominate any of their officers to perform any acts and discharge any functions, including the forming of an opinion, authorised by this section to be performed or discharged by the Revenue Commissioners, and references in this section to the Revenue Commissioners shall with any necessary modifications be construed as including references to an officer so nominated.

(13) This section shall apply as respects any transaction where the whole or any part of the transaction is undertaken or arranged on or after the 25th day of January, 1989, and

as respects any transaction undertaken or arranged wholly before that date in so far as it gives rise to, or would but for this section give rise to—

(a) a reduction, avoidance or deferral of any charge or assessment to tax, or part thereof, where the charge or assessment arises by virtue of any other transaction carried out wholly on or after a date, or

(b) a refund or a payment of an amount, or of an increase in an amount, of tax, or part thereof, refundable or otherwise payable to a person where that amount or increase in the amount would otherwise become first so refundable or otherwise payable to the person on a date,

which could not fall earlier than the 25th day of January, 1989.

Cross-references

Meaning of "the Acts" applied: Asset Covered Securities Act 2001 s 81(2).

Shipping tonnage tax, requirement not to enter into tax avoidance arrangements, meaning of "tax advantage" applied: s 697F(2)(a).

This section to be construed together with the Value Added Tax Acts 1972-1997, in so far as relating to value added tax: s 1104(3).

This section to be construed together with the Stamp Act 1891 and the enactments amending or extending that Act, in so far as relating to stamp duties: s 1104(4).

This section to be construed together with the Capital Acquisitions Tax Act 1976, and the enactments amending or extending that Act, in so far as relating to capital acquisitions tax: s 1104(5).

This section to be construed together with FA 1983 Pt VI and the enactments amending or extending that Part, in so far as relating to residential property tax: s 1104(6).

Case law

Bona fide commercial motives: *Marwood Homes Ltd v IRC*, [1996] STI 51.

Expenditure on plant funded by non-recourse borrowings allowable: *Airspace Investments Ltd v Moore*, HC, Lynch J, 15 April 1994. Contrast *Ensign Tankers (Leasing) Ltd v Stokes*, [1992] STC 226.

Meaning of "tax advantage": *IRC v Universities Superannuation Scheme*, [1997] STC 1.

Definitions

Appeal Commissioners: ss 2(1), 5(1); Circuit Court: IA 1937 Sch; High Court: IA 1937 Sch; person: IA 1937 s 11(c); profession: ss 2(1), 5(1); profits: s 4(1); statute: s 2(1), IA 1937 s 3; Tax Acts: s 1(2); trade: s 3(1); writing: IA 1937 Sch.

Former enactments

FA 1989 s 86.

MANAGEMENT PROVISIONS

PART 37
ADMINISTRATION

859 Anonymity of authorised officers in relation to certain matters

(1) In this section—

"authorised officer" means an officer of the Revenue Commissioners nominated by them to be a member of the staff of the body;

"the body" has the meaning assigned to it by section 58;

"proceedings" includes any hearing before the Appeal Commissioners (within the meaning of the Revenue Acts);

"the Revenue Acts" means—

(*a*) the Customs Acts,

(*b*) the statutes relating to the duties of excise and to the management of those duties,

(*c*) the Tax Acts,

(*d*) the Capital Gains Tax Acts,

(*e*) the Value-Added Tax Act, 1972, and the enactments amending or extending that Act,

(*f*) the Capital Acquisitions Tax Act, 1976, and the enactments amending or extending that Act,

(*g*) the statutes relating to stamp duty and the management of that duty,

(*h*) Chapter IV of Part II of the Finance Act, 1992, and

(*i*) Part VI of the Finance Act, 1983,

and any instruments made thereunder or under any other enactment and relating to tax;

"tax" means any tax, duty, levy or charge under the care and management of the Revenue Commissioners.

(2) Notwithstanding any requirement made by or under any enactment or any other requirement in administrative and operational procedures, including internal procedures, all reasonable care shall be taken to ensure that the identity of an authorised officer shall not be revealed.

(3) In particular and without prejudice to the generality of subsection (2):

(*a*) where, for the purposes of exercising or performing his or her powers or duties under the Revenue Acts in pursuance of the functions of the body, an authorised officer may apart from this section be required to produce or show any written authority or warrant of appointment under those Acts or otherwise to identify himself or herself, the authorised officer shall—

(i) not be required to produce or show any such authority or warrant of appointment or to so identify himself or herself, for the purposes of exercising or performing his or her powers or duties under those Acts, and

(ii) be accompanied by a member of the Garda Síochána who shall, on request by a person affected, identify himself or herself as a member of the Garda Síochána and shall state that he or she is accompanied by an authorised officer;

(*b*) where, in pursuance of the functions of the body, an authorised officer exercises or performs in writing any of his or her powers or duties under the Revenue Acts or any provision of any other enactment, whenever passed, which relates to Revenue, such exercise or performance of his or her powers or duties shall be done in the name of the body and not in the name of the individual authorised officer involved, notwithstanding any provision to the contrary in any of those enactments;

(c) in any proceedings arising out of the exercise or performance, in pursuance of the functions of the body, of powers or duties by an authorised officer, any documents relating to such proceedings shall not reveal the identity of any authorised officer, notwithstanding any requirements to the contrary in any provision, and in any proceedings the identity of such officer other than as an authorised officer shall not be revealed other than to the judge or the Appeal Commissioner, as the case may be, hearing the case;

(d) where, in pursuance of the functions of the body, an authorised officer is required, in any proceedings, to give evidence and the judge or the Appeal Commissioner, as the case may be, is satisfied that there are reasonable grounds in the public interest to direct that evidence to be given by such authorised officer should be given in the hearing and not in the sight of any person, he or she may so direct.

Cross-references

This section to be construed together with the Customs Acts, in so far as relating to customs: s 1104(2).

This section to be construed together with the Value Added Tax Acts 1972-1997, in so far as relating to value added tax: s 1104(3).

This section to be construed together with the Stamp Act 1891 and the enactments amending or extending that Act, in so far as relating to stamp duties: s 1104(4).

This section to be construed together with the Capital Acquisitions Tax Act 1976, and the enactments amending or extending that Act, in so far as relating to capital acquisitions tax: s 1104(5).

This section to be construed together with FA 1983 Pt VI and the enactments amending or extending that Part, in so far as relating to residential property tax: s 1104(6).

Former enactment

FA 1993 s 19A; DCITPA 1996 s 12; CABA 1996 s 23.

872 Use of information relating to other taxes and duties

(1) Any information acquired, whether before or after the passing of this Act, in connection with any tax or duty under the care and management of the Revenue Commissioners may be used by them for any purpose connected with any other tax or duty under their care and management.

...

Cross-references

Subs (1) to be construed together with the Customs Acts, in so far as relating to customs: s 1104(2).

Subs (1) to be construed together with the Value Added Tax Acts 1972-1997, in so far as relating to value added tax: s 1104(3).

Subs (1) to be construed together with the Stamp Act 1891 and the enactments amending or extending that Act, in so far as relating to stamp duties: s 1104(4).

Subs (1) to be construed together with the Capital Acquisitions Tax Act 1976, and the enactments amending or extending that Act, in so far as relating to capital acquisitions tax: s 1104(5).

Subs (1) to be construed together with FA 1983 Pt VI and the enactments amending or extending that Part, in so far as relating to residential property tax: s 1104(6).

Former enactment

FA1928 s34(2); FA 1996 s 130.

PART 38

RETURNS OF INCOME AND GAINS, OTHER OBLIGATIONS AND RETURNS, AND REVENUE POWERS

CHAPTER 3
Other obligations and returns

887 Use of electronic data processing

[(1) In this section—

"the Acts" means—

  (a) the Tax Acts,

  (b) the Capital Gains Tax Acts,

  (c) the Value-Added Tax Act, 1972, and the enactments amending or extending that Act,

  (d) the Capital Acquisitions Tax Act, 1976, and the enactments amending or extending that Act, and

  (e) Part VI of the Finance Act, 1983,

and any instrument made under any of these enactments;

"record" means any document which a person is obliged by the Acts to keep, to issue or to produce for inspection, and any other written or printed material.

(2) For the purposes of the Acts, but subject to section 17 of the Value-Added Tax Act, 1972, a record may be stored, maintained, transmitted, reproduced or communicated, as the case may be, by any electronic, photographic or other process that—

  (a) provides a reliable assurance as to the integrity of the record from the time when it was first generated in its final form by such electronic, photographic or other process,

  (b) permits the record to be displayed in intelligible form and produced in an intelligible printed format,

  (c) permits the record to be readily accessible for subsequent reference in accordance with paragraph (b), and

  (d) conforms to the information technology and procedural requirements drawn up and published by the Revenue Commissioners in accordance with subsection (3).

(3) The Revenue Commissioners shall from time to time draw up and publish in Iris Oifigiúil the information technology and procedural requirements to which any electronic, photographic or other process used by a person for the storage, maintenance, transmission, reproduction and communication of any record shall conform.

(4) The authority conferred on the Revenue Commissioners by this section to draw up and publish requirements shall be construed as including the authority exercisable in a like manner to revoke and replace or to amend any such requirements.

(5) (*a*) Every person who preserves records by any electronic, photographic or other process, when required to do so by a notice in writing from the Revenue Commissioners, shall, within such period as is specified in the notice, not being less than 21 days from the date of service of the notice, supply to the Revenue Commissioners full particulars relating to the process used by that person, including full particulars relating to software (within the meaning of section 912).

(*b*) A person who fails or refuses to comply with a notice served on the person under paragraph (*a*) shall be liable to a penalty of £1,000 [€1,265].[1]

(6) (*a*) Subject to paragraph (*b*), where records are kept by a person (being a person who is obliged by the Acts to keep such records) by any electronic, photographic or other process which does not conform with the requirements referred to in paragraphs (*a*) to (*d*) of subsection (2), then the person shall be deemed to have failed to comply with that obligation and that person shall be liable to the same penalties as the person would be liable to if the person had failed to comply with any obligation under the Acts in relation to the keeping of records.

(*b*) Paragraph (*a*) shall not apply where the person referred to in that paragraph complies with any obligation under the Acts in relation to the keeping of records other than in accordance with the provisions of subsection (2).

(7) Where records are preserved by any electronic, photographic or other process, information contained in a document produced by any such process shall, subject to the rules of court, be admissible in evidence in any proceedings, whether civil or criminal, to the same extent as the records themselves.

(8) The Revenue Commissioners may nominate any of their officers to discharge any function authorised by this section to be discharged by the Revenue Commissioners.][2]

Amendments

1   Substituted by FA 2001 s 232(3)(*a*)(i) with effect from 1 January 2002; previously "£1,000".

2   Substituted by FA 2001 s 232(1)(*a*) with effect from 15 February 2001 (as a result of FA 2002 s 138 and Sch 6 paras 5(*f*) and 6(*e*)(i)).

Cross-references

Obligation to keep records, subs (2): s 886(3)(*b*).

Power of inspection, PAYE: s 903(1)("records").

This section to be construed together with the Value Added Tax Acts 1972-1997, in so far as relating to value added tax: s 1104(3).

This section to be construed together with the Capital Acquisitions Tax Act 1976, and the enactments amending or extending that Act, in so far as relating to capital acquisitions tax: s 1104(5).

This section to be construed together with FA 1983 Pt VI and the enactments amending or extending that Part, in so far as relating to residential property tax: s 1104(6).

Tax Briefing

TB46 Dec 2001 pp 24-25 - Electronic Storage - Retention of Tax Records in Electronic Format.

Definitions

Capital Gains Tax Acts: s 1(2); person: IA 1937 s 11(*c*); rules of court: IA 1937 Sch; Tax Acts: s 1(2); writing: IA 1937 Sch.

Former enactments

FA 1986 s 113(1)-(3); FA 1993 s 99.

CHAPTER 4
Revenue powers

905 Inspection of documents and records

(1) In this section—

"authorised officer" means an officer of the Revenue Commissioners authorised by them in writing to exercise the powers conferred by this section;

"property" means any asset relating to a tax liability;

[**"records"** means any document or any other written or printed material in any form, and includes any information stored, maintained or preserved by means of any mechanical or electronic device, whether or not stored, maintained or preserved in a legible form—

   (i)   which relates to a business carried on by a person, or

  (ii) which a person is obliged by any provision relating to tax to keep, retain, issue or produce for inspection or which may be inspected under any provision relating to tax;][1]

"tax" means any tax, duty, levy or charge under the care and management of the Revenue Commissioners;

"tax liability" means any existing liability to tax or further liability to tax which may be established by an authorised officer following the exercise or performance of his or her powers or duties under this section.

(2) (*a*) An authorised officer may at all reasonable times enter any premises or place where the authorised officer has reason to believe that—

     (i)   any trade, profession or other activity, the profits or gains of which are chargeable to tax, is or has been carried on,

    (ii) anything is or has been done in connection with any trade, profession or other activity the profits or gains of which are chargeable to tax,

   (iii) any records relating to—

       (I)   any trade, profession, other source of profits or gains or chargeable gains,

      (II) any tax liability, or

     (III) any repayments of tax in regard to any person,

         are or may be kept, or

    (iv) any property is or has been located,

     and the authorised officer may—

    (A) require any person who is on those premises or in that place, other than a person who is there to purchase goods or to receive a service, to produce any records or property,

    (B) if the authorised officer has reason to believe that any of the records or property which he or she has required to be produced to him or her under this subsection have not been produced, search on those premises or in that place for those records or property,

(C) examine any records or property and take copies of or extracts from any records,

(D) remove any records and retain them for a reasonable time for the purposes of their further examination or for the purposes of any legal proceedings instituted by an officer of the Revenue Commissioners or for the purposes of any criminal proceedings, and

(E) examine property listed in any records.

(b) An authorised officer may in the exercise or performance of his or her powers or duties under this section require any person whom he or she has reason to believe—

(i) is or was carrying on any trade, profession or other activity the profits or gains of which are chargeable to tax,

(ii) is or was liable to any tax, or

(iii) has information relating to any tax liability,

to give the authorised officer all reasonable assistance, including providing information and explanations or furnishing documents and making available for inspection property as required by the authorised officer in relation to any tax liability or any repayment of tax in regard to any person.

(c) Nothing in this subsection shall be construed as requiring any person carrying on a profession, or any person employed by any person carrying on a profession, to produce to an authorised officer any documents relating to a client, other than such documents—

(i) as pertain to the payment of fees to the person carrying on the profession or to other financial transactions of the person carrying on the profession,

(ii) as are otherwise material to the tax liability of the person carrying on the profession, or

(iii) as are already required to be provided following a request issued under [section 128 of the Stamp Duties Consolidation Act, 1999],[2]

and in particular that person shall not be required to disclose any information or professional advice of a confidential nature given to a client.

...[3]

(e) An authorised officer shall not, without the consent of the occupier, enter any premises, or that portion of any premises, which is occupied wholly and exclusively as a private residence, except on production by such officer of a warrant issued by a Judge of the District Court expressly authorising the authorised officer to so enter.

(f) A Judge of the District Court may issue a warrant under paragraph (e) if satisfied by information on oath that it is proper to do so for the purposes of this section.

[(2A)(*a*) In this subsection **"the Acts"** has the meaning assigned to it by section 1078(1).

(*b*)   Without prejudice to any power conferred by subsection (2), if a Judge of the District Court is satisfied by information on oath that there are reasonable grounds for suspecting—

(i)   that a person may have failed or may fail to comply with any provision of the Acts,

(ii)   that any such failure is likely to have led or to lead to serious prejudice to the proper assessment or collection of tax (having regard to the amount of any tax liability that arises or might arise from such failure), and

(iii)   that records, which are material to the proper assessment or collection of tax are likely to be kept or concealed at any premises or place,

the Judge may issue a search warrant.

(*c*)   A search warrant issued under this subsection shall be expressed and shall operate to authorise an authorised officer accompanied by such other named officers of the Revenue Commissioners and such other named persons as the authorised officer considers necessary, at any time or times within one month of the date of issue of the warrant, to enter (if need be by force) the premises or other place named or specified in the warrant, to search such premises or other place, to examine anything found there, to inspect any records found there and, if there are reasonable grounds for suspecting that any records found there are material to the proper assessment or collection of tax, or that the records may be required for the purpose of any legal proceedings instituted by an officer of the Revenue Commissioners or for the purpose of any criminal proceedings, remove such records and retain them for so long as they are reasonably required for the purpose aforesaid.][4]

(3) A person who does not comply with any requirement of an authorised officer in the exercise or performance of the authorised officer's powers or duties under this section shall be liable to a penalty of [€1,265][5].

(4) An authorised officer when exercising or performing his or her powers or duties under this section shall on request show his or her authorisation for the purposes of this section.

Amendments

[1]   Defintion of "records" substituted by FA 2002 s 132(*d*) with effect from 1 January 2002.

[2]   Substituted by SDCA 1999 s 162 and Sch 4 with effect from 15 December 1999; previously "section 16 of the Stamp Act, 1891".

[3]   Subs (2)(*d*) deleted by FA 1999 s 207(*f*)(i) with effect from 25 March 1999.

[4]   Subs (2A) inserted by FA 1999 s 207(*f*)(ii) with effect from 25 March 1999.

[5]   Substituted by FA 2001 s 240(1) and (2)(*k*) and Sch 5 Pt 1 as respects any act or omission which takes place or begins on or after 1 January 2002; previously "£1,000".

Cross-references

Authorised officers and Garda Síochána: s 906.
This section to be construed together with the Customs Acts, in so far as relating to customs: s 1104(2).
This section to be construed together with the Value Added Tax Acts 1972-1997, in so far as relating to value added tax: s 1104(3).

This section to be construed together with the Stamp Act 1891 and the enactments amending or extending that Act, in so far as relating to stamp duties: s 1104(4).

This section to be construed together with the Capital Acquisitions Tax Act 1976, and the enactments amending or extending that Act, in so far as relating to capital acquisitions tax: s 1104(5).

This section to be construed together with FA 1983 Pt VI and the enactments amending or extending that Part, in so far as relating to residential property tax: s 1104(6).

Revenue information

Information leaflet IT32 - Revenue Audit - Guide for Small Businesses

Code of Practice for Revenue Auditors (Nov. 1998)

Statement of practice

Revenue powers: SP GEN/1/94, May 1994.

Case law

Held was a clear implication that the time and place for such inspection set by the taxpayer had to be reasonable: *Johnson v IRC*, [1996] STI 270.

Definition

inspector: ss 2(1), 5(1), 852; person: IA 1937 s 11(*c*); profession: ss 2(1), 5(1); trade: ss 3(1), 4(1), 5(1).

Former enactment

FA 1976 s 34; FA 1992 s 232.

906 Authorised officers and Garda Síochána

Where an authorised officer (within the meaning of section 903, 904 or 905, as the case may be) in accordance with section 903, 904 or 905 enters any premises or place, the authorised officer may be accompanied by a member or members of the Garda Síochána, and any such member may arrest without warrant any person who obstructs or interferes with the authorised officer in the exercise or performance of his or her powers or duties under any of those sections.

Cross-references

This section to be construed together with the Customs Acts, in so far as relating to customs: s 1104(2).

This section to be construed together with the Value Added Tax Acts 1972-1997, in so far as relating to value added tax: s 1104(3).

This section to be construed together with the Stamp Act 1891 and the enactments amending or extending that Act, in so far as relating to stamp duties: s 1104(4).

This section to be construed together with the Capital Acquisitions Tax Act 1976, and the enactments amending or extending that Act, in so far as relating to capital acquisitions tax: s 1104(5).

This section to be construed together with FA 1983 Pt VI and the enactments amending or extending that Part, in so far as relating to residential property tax: s 1104(6).

Former enactment

FA 1992 s 236.

906A Information to be furnished by financial institutions

[(1) In this section and in sections 907 and 908—

"the Acts" has the meaning assigned to it by section 1078(1);

"authorised officer" means an officer of the Revenue Commissioners authorised by them in writing to exercise the powers conferred by this section, or, as the case may be, section 907 or 908;

"books, records or other documents" includes—

- (*a*) any records used in the business of a financial institution, or used in the transfer department of a financial institution acting as registrar of securities, whether—

  - (i) comprised in bound volume, loose-leaf binders or other loose-leaf filing system, loose-leaf ledger sheets, pages, folios or cards, or

  - (ii) kept on microfilm, magnetic tape or in any non-legible form (by the use of electronics or otherwise) which is capable of being reproduced in a legible form,

- (*b*) every electronic or other automatic means, if any, by which any such thing in non-legible form is so capable of being reproduced,

- (*c*) documents in manuscript, documents which are typed, printed, stencilled or created by any other mechanical or partly mechanical process in use from time to time and documents which are produced by any photographic or photostatic process, and

- (*d*) correspondence and records of other communications between a financial institution and its customers;

"connected person" has the same meaning as in section 10; but an individual (other than in the capacity as a trustee of a settlement) shall be connected with another individual only if that other individual is the spouse of or a minor child of the first-mentioned individual;

"deposit" and **"interest"** have, respectively, the meaning assigned to them by section 256(1);

[**"financial institution"** means—

- (*a*) a person who holds or has held a licence under section 9 of the Central Bank Act, 1971,

- (*b*) a person referred to in section 7(4) of the Central Bank Act, 1971, or

- (*c*) a credit institution (within the meaning of the European Communities (Licensing and Supervision of Credit Institutions) Regulations, 1992 (SI No 395 of 1992)) which has been authorised by the Central Bank of Ireland to carry on business of a credit institution in accordance with the provisions of the supervisory enactments (within the meaning of those Regulations);][1]

"liability" in relation to a person means any liability in relation to tax to which the person is or may be, or may have been, subject, or the amount of such liability;

"tax" means any tax, duty, levy or charge under the care and management of the Revenue Commissioners.

(2) Notwithstanding any obligation as to secrecy or other restriction upon disclosure of information imposed by or under statute or otherwise, and subject to this section, an authorised officer may, for the purpose of enquiring into a liability in relation to a person (in this section referred to as the **"taxpayer"**), serve on a financial institution a notice in writing requiring the financial institution, within such period as may be

specified in the notice, not being less than 30 days from the date of the service of the notice, to do either or both of the following, namely—

(*a*)   to make available for inspection by the authorised officer such books, records or other documents as are in the financial institution's power, possession or procurement and as contain, or may (in the authorised officer's opinion formed on reasonable grounds) contain, information relevant to a liability in relation to the taxpayer,

(*b*)   to furnish to the authorised officer, in writing or otherwise, such information, explanations and particulars as the authorised officer may reasonably require, being information, explanations and particulars that are relevant to any such liability,

and which are specified in the notice.

(3) Where, in compliance with the requirements of a notice under subsection (2), a financial institution makes available for inspection by an authorised officer, books, records or other documents, it shall afford the authorised officer reasonable assistance, including information, explanations and particulars, in relation to the use of all the electronic or other automatic means, if any, by which the books, records or other documents, in so far as they are in a non-legible form, are capable of being reproduced in a legible form and any data equipment or any associated apparatus or material.

(4) An authorised officer shall not serve a notice on a financial institution under subsection (2) without the consent in writing of a Revenue Commissioner and without having reasonable grounds to believe that the financial institution is likely to have information relevant to a liability in relation to the taxpayer.

(5) Without prejudice to the generality of subsection (2), the books, records or other documents which a financial institution may be required by notice under that subsection to deliver or to make available and the information, explanations and particulars which it may likewise be required to furnish, may include books, records or other documents and information, explanations and particulars relating to a person who is connected with the taxpayer.

(6) The persons who may be treated as a taxpayer for the purposes of this section include a company which has been dissolved and an individual who has died.

(7) A notice served under subsection (2) shall name the taxpayer in relation to whose liability the authorised officer is enquiring.

(8) Where an authorised officer serves a notice under subsection (2), a copy of such notice shall be given by the authorised officer to the taxpayer concerned.

(9) Where, in compliance with a notice served under subsection (2), a financial institution makes books, records or other documents available for inspection by an authorised officer, the authorised officer may make extracts from or copies of all or any part of the books, records or other documents.

(10) A financial institution which fails or refuses to comply with a notice issued under subsection (2) or which fails or refuses to afford reasonable assistance to an authorised officer as required under subsection (3), shall be liable to a penalty of [€19,045]² and, if

the failure or refusal to comply with such notice continues after the expiry of the period specified in the notice served under subsection (2), a further penalty of [€2,535][3] for each day on which the failure or refusal continues.][4]

Amendments

1   Definition of "financial institution" substituted by FA 2000 s 68(c) with effect from 6 April 2000.
2   Substituted by FA 2001 s 240(1) and (2)(k) and Sch 5 Pt 1 as respects any act or omission which takes place or begins on or after 1 January 2002; previously "£15,000".
3   Substituted by FA 2001 s 240(1) and (2)(k) and Sch 5 Pt 1 as respects any act or omission which takes place or begins on or after 1 January 2002; previously "£2,000".
4   Section 906A inserted by FA 1999 s 207(g) with effect from 25 March 1999.

910 Power to obtain information from Minister of the Government

[(1) For the purposes of the assessment, charge, collection and recovery of any tax or duty placed under their care and management, the Revenue Commissioners may, by notice in writing, request any Minister of the Government or any body established by or under statute to proved them with such information in the possession of that Minister or body in relation to payments for any purposes made by that Minister or by that body, whether on that Minister's or that body's own behalf or on behalf of any other person, to such persons or classes of persons as the Revenue Commissioners may specify in the notice and a Minister of the Government or body of whom or of which such a request is made shall provide such information as may be so specified.][1]

(2) The Revenue Commissioners may nominate any of their officers to perform any acts and discharge any functions authorised by this section to be performed or discharged by the Revenue Commissioners.

Amendments

1   Subs (1) substituted by FA 1999 s 208.

Cross-references

This section to be construed together with the Customs Acts, in so far as relating to customs: s 1104(2).
This section to be construed together with the Value Added Tax Acts 1972-1997, in so far as relating to value added tax: s 1104(3).
This section to be construed together with the Stamp Act 1891 and the enactments amending or extending that Act, in so far as relating to stamp duties: s 1104(4).
This section to be construed together with the Capital Acquisitions Tax Act 1976, and the enactments amending or extending that Act, in so far as relating to capital acquisitions tax: s 1104(5).
This section to be construed together with FA 1983 Pt VI and the enactments amending or extending that Part, in so far as relating to residential property tax: s 1104(6).

Definitions

person: IA 1937 s 11(c); tax: s 3(1).

Former enactment

FA 1995 s 175.

912 Computer documents and records

(1) In this section—

"the Acts" means—

(a)   the Customs Acts,

(b) the statutes relating to the duties of excise and to the management of those duties,

(c) the Tax Acts,

(d) the Capital Gains Tax Acts,

(e) the Value-Added Tax Act, 1972, and the enactments amending or extending that Act,

(f) the Capital Acquisitions Tax Act, 1976, and the enactments amending or extending that Act, and

(g) Part VI of the Finance Act, 1983,

and any instruments made thereunder;

"data" means information in a form in which it can be processed;

"data equipment" means any electronic, photographic, magnetic, optical or other equipment for processing data;

"processing" means performing automatically logical or arithmetical operations on data, or the storing, maintenance, transmission, reproduction or communication of data;

"records" means documents which a person is obliged by any provision of the Acts to keep, issue or produce for inspection, and any other written or printed material;

"software" means any sequence of instructions used in conjunction with data equipment for the purpose of processing data or controlling the operation of the data equipment.

(2) Any provision under the Acts which—

(a) requires a person to keep, retain, issue or produce any records or cause any records to be kept, retained, issued or produced, or

(b) permits an officer of the Revenue Commissioners—

(i) to inspect any records,

(ii) to enter premises and search for any records, or

(iii) to take extracts from or copies of or remove any records,

shall, where the records are processed by data equipment, apply to the data equipment together with any associated software, data, apparatus or material as it applies to the records.

(3) An officer of the Revenue Commissioners may in the exercise or performance of his or her powers or duties require—

(a) the person by or on whose behalf the data equipment is or has been used, or

(b) any person having charge of, or otherwise concerned with the operation of, the data equipment or any associated apparatus or material,

to afford him or her all reasonable assistance in relation to the exercise or performance of those powers or duties.

Cross-references

This section to be construed together with the Customs Acts, in so far as relating to customs: s 1104(2).

This section to be construed together with the Value Added Tax Acts 1972-1997, in so far as relating to value added tax: s 1104(3).

This section to be construed together with the Capital Acquisitions Tax Act 1976, and the enactments amending or extending that Act, in so far as relating to capital acquisitions tax: s 1104(5).

This section to be construed together with FA 1983 Pt VI and the enactments amending or extending that Part, in so far as relating to residential property tax: s 1104(6).

Statement of practice

Revenue powers: SP GEN/1/94, May 1994.

Definition

Tax Acts: s 1(2); person: IA 1937 s 11(*c*).

Former enactment

FA 1992 s 237.

PART 42

COLLECTION AND RECOVERY

CHAPTER 5

Miscellaneous provisions

1006 Poundage and certain other fees due to sheriffs or county registrars

(1) In this section—

"the Acts" means—

    (*a*)   the Tax Acts,

    (*b*)   the Capital Gains Tax Acts,

    (*c*)   the Value-Added Tax Act, 1972, and the enactments amending or extending that Act,

    (*d*)   the Capital Acquisitions Tax Act, 1976, and the enactments amending or extending that Act, and

    (*e*)   Part VI of the Finance Act, 1983, and the enactments amending or extending that Part,

and any instruments made thereunder;

"certificate" means a certificate issued under section 962;

"county registrar" means a person appointed to be a county registrar under section 35 of the Court Officers Act, 1926;

"defaulter" means a person specified or certified in an execution order or certificate on whom a relevant amount specified or certified in the order or certificate is leviable;

"execution order" has the same meaning as in the Enforcement of Court Orders Act, 1926;

"fees" means the fees known as poundage fees payable under section 14(1) of the Enforcement of Court Orders Act, 1926, and orders made under that section for services in or about the execution of an execution order directing or authorising the execution of an order of a court by the seizure and sale of a person's property or, as may be appropriate, the fees corresponding to those fees payable under section 962 for the execution of a certificate;

"interest on unpaid tax" means interest which has accrued under any provision of the Acts providing for the charging of interest in respect of unpaid tax, including interest on an undercharge of tax which is attributable to fraud or neglect;

"relevant amount" means an amount of tax or interest on unpaid tax;

"tax" means any tax, duty, levy or charge which, in accordance with any provision of the Acts, is placed under the care and management of the Revenue Commissioners;

references, as respects an execution order, to a relevant amount include references to any amount of costs specified in the order.

(2) Where—

    (*a*) an execution order or certificate specifying or certifying a defaulter and relating to a relevant amount is lodged with the appropriate sheriff or county registrar for execution,

    (*b*) the sheriff or, as the case may be, the county registrar gives notice to the defaulter of the lodgment or of his or her intention to execute the execution order or certificate by seizure of the property of the defaulter to which it relates, or demands payment by the defaulter of the relevant amount, and

    (*c*) the whole or part of the relevant amount is paid to the sheriff or, as the case may be, the county registrar or to the Collector-General, after the giving of that notice or the making of that demand,

then, for the purpose of the liability of the defaulter for the payment of fees and of the exercise of any rights or powers in relation to the collection of fees for the time being vested by law in sheriffs and county registrars—

    (i) the sheriff or, as the case may be, the county registrar shall be deemed to have entered, in the execution of the execution order or certificate, into possession of the property referred to in paragraph (*b*), and

    (ii) the payment mentioned in paragraph (*c*) shall be deemed to have been levied, in the execution of the execution order or certificate, by the sheriff or, as the case may be, the county registrar,

and fees shall be payable by the defaulter to such sheriff or, as the case may be, country registrar accordingly in respect of the payment mentioned in paragraph (*c*).

Cross-references

This section to be construed together with the Value Added Tax Acts 1972-1997, in so far as relating to value added tax: s 1104(3).

This section to be construed together with the Capital Acquisitions Tax Act 1976, and the enactments amending or extending that Act, in so far as relating to capital acquisitions tax: s 1104(5).

This section to be construed together with FA 1983 Pt VI and the enactments amending or extending that Part, in so far as relating to residential property tax: s 1104(6).

Definition

person: IA 1937 s 11(*c*); Tax Acts: s 1(2).

Former enactment

FA 1988 s 71(1)-(2)(*a*).

1006A Offset between taxes

[(1) In this section—

"Acts" means—

    (*a*) the Tax Acts,

    (*b*) the Capital Gains Tax Acts,

    (*c*) the Value-Added Tax Act, 1972, and the enactments amending or extending that Act,

    (*d*) the statutes relating to the duties of excise and to the management of those duties,

    (*e*) the Capital Acquisitions Tax Act, 1976, and the enactments amending or extending that Act,

    (*f*) the Stamp Duties Consolidation Act, 1999,

    (*g*) Part VI of the Finance Act, 1983, and the enactments amending or extending that Part,

    (*h*) Chapter IV of Part II of the Finance Act, 1992,

and any instrument made thereunder;

["**claim**" means a claim that gives rise to either or both a repayment of tax and a payment of interest payable in respect of such a repayment under any of the Acts and includes part of such a claim;][1]

["**liability**" means any tax due or estimated to be due under the Acts for any period or in respect of any event, as may be appropriate in the circumstances, and includes any interest due under the Acts in respect of that tax;][2]

"**overpayment**" means a payment or remittance under the Acts (including part of such a payment or remittance) which is in excess of the amount of the liability against which it is [credited;][3]

["**tax**" means any tax, duty, levy or other charge under any of the Acts.][4]

[(2) Notwithstanding any other provision of the Acts, where the Revenue Commissioners are satisfied that a person has not complied with the obligations imposed on the person by the Acts, in relation to either or both—

    (*a*) the payment of a liability required to be paid, and

    (*b*) the delivery of returns required to be made,

they may, in a case where a repayment is due to the person in respect of a claim or overpayment—

(i)   where paragraph (*a*) applies, or where paragraphs (*a*) and (*b*) apply, instead of making the repayment set the amount of the claim or overpayment against any liability due under the Acts, and

(ii)   where paragraph (*b*) only applies, withhold making the repayment until such time as the returns required to be delivered have been delivered.

(2A) Where the Revenue Commissioners have set or withheld a repayment by virtue of subsection (2), they shall give notice in writing to that effect to the person concerned and, where subsection (2)(ii) applies, interest shall not be payable under any provision of the Acts from the date of such notice in respect of any repayment so withheld.][5]

(3) The Revenue Commissioners shall make regulations for the purpose of giving effect to this section and, without prejudice to the generality of the foregoing, such regulations shall provide for the order of priority of liabilities due under the Acts against which any claim or overpayment is to be set in accordance with subsection (2).

(4) Every regulation made under this section shall be laid before Dáil Éireann as soon as may be after it is made and, if a resolution annulling the regulation is passed by Dáil Éireann within the next 21 days on which Dáil Éireann has sat after the regulation is laid before it, the regulation shall be annulled accordingly, but without prejudice to the validity of anything previously done thereunder.

[(5) Any act to be performed or function to be discharged (other than the making of regulations) by the Revenue Commissioners which is authorised by this section may be performed or discharged by any of their officers acting under their authority.][6][7]

Amendments

[1]   Definition of "claim" substituted by FA 2002 s 125(*a*)(i)(I) with effect from 25 March 2002.
[2]   Definition of "liability" substituted by FA 2002 s 125(*a*)(i)(II) with effect from 25 March 2002.
[3]   Substituted by FA 2002 s 125(*a*)(i)(III) with effect from 25 March 2002; previously "credited.".
[4]   Definition of "tax" substituted by FA 2002 s 125(*a*)(i)(IV) with effect from 25 March 2002.
[5]   Subs (2) substituted and subs (2A) inserted by FA 2001 s 239(*b*) with effect from 6 April 2001.
[6]   Subs (5) inserted by FA 2002 s 125(*a*)(ii) with effect from 25 March 2002.
[7]   Section 1006A inserted by FA 2000 s 164 with effect from 23 March 2000.

Cross-references

Relief on retirement for certain income of certain sportsperson: s 480A(2).

Regulations

Taxes (Offset of Repayments) Regulations 2001, SI No 399 of 2001.

Tax Briefing

TB45 Oct 2001 pp 10-11 - Offset of Repayment Regulations.

Definitions

Dáil Éireann: IA 1937 Sch; person: IA 1937 s 11(*c*); writing: IA 1937 Sch.

PART 47

PENALTIES, REVENUE OFFENCES, INTEREST ON OVERDUE TAX AND OTHER SANCTIONS

CHAPTER 4
Revenue offences

1078 Revenue offences

(1) In this Part—

"the Acts" means—

    (*a*) the Customs Acts,

    (*b*) the statutes relating to the duties of excise and to the management of those duties,

    (*c*) the Tax Acts,

    (*d*) the Capital Gains Tax Acts,

    (*e*) the Value-Added Tax Act, 1972, and the enactments amending or extending that Act,

    (*f*) the Capital Acquisitions Tax Act, 1976, and the enactments amending or extending that Act,

    (*g*) the statutes relating to stamp duty and to the management of that duty, and

    (*h*) Part VI of the Finance Act, 1983,

and any instruments made thereunder and any instruments made under any other enactment and relating to tax;

"authorised officer" means an officer of the Revenue Commissioners authorised by them in writing to exercise any of the powers conferred by the Acts;

"tax" means any tax, duty, levy or charge under the care and management of the Revenue Commissioners.

(2) A person shall, without prejudice to any other penalty to which the person may be liable, be guilty of an offence under this section if the person—

    (*a*) knowingly or wilfully delivers any incorrect return, statement or accounts or knowingly or wilfully furnishes any incorrect information in connection with any tax,

    (*b*) knowingly aids, abets, assists, incites or induces another person to make or deliver knowingly or wilfully any incorrect return, statement or accounts in connection with any tax,

    (*c*) claims or obtains relief or exemption from, or repayment of, any tax, being a relief, exemption or repayment to which, to the person's knowledge, the person is not entitled,

    (*d*) knowingly or wilfully issues or produces any incorrect invoice, receipt, instrument or other document in connection with any tax,

883

[*(dd)* (i)   fails to make any deduction of dividend withholding tax (within the meaning of Chapter 8A of Part 6) required to be made by the person under section 172B(1),

     (ii)   fails, having made that deduction, to pay the sum deducted to the Collector-General within the time specified in that behalf in section 172K(2),

    (iii)   fails to make any reduction required to be made by the person under section 172B(2),

    (iv)   fails, having made that reduction, to pay to the Collector-General the amount referred to in section 172B(2)(*d*), which amount is treated under that section as if it were a deduction of dividend withholding tax (within the meaning of Chapter 8A of Part 6), within the time specified in that behalf in section 172K(2), or

     (v)   fails to pay to the Collector-General, within the time specified in that behalf in section 172K(2), an amount referred to in section 172B(3)(*a*) which is required to be paid by the person to the Collector-General and which is treated under that section as if it were a deduction of dividend withholding tax (within the meaning of Chapter 8A of Part 6),][1]

 (*e*) (i)   fails to make any deduction required to be made by the person under section 257(1),

     (ii)   fails, having made the deduction, to pay the sum deducted to the Collector-General within the time specified in that behalf in section 258(3), or

    (iii)   fails to pay to the Collector-General an amount on account of appropriate tax (within the meaning of Chapter 4 of Part 8) within the time specified in that behalf in section 258(4),

 (*f*) (i)   fails to make any deduction required to be made by the person under section 734(5), or

     (ii)   fails, having made the deduction, to pay the sum deducted to the Collector-General within the time specified in paragraph 1(3) of Schedule 18,

 (*g*) [fails without reasonable excuse][2] to comply with any provision of the Acts requiring—

     (i)   the furnishing of a return of income, profits or gains, or of sources of income, profits or gains, for the purposes of any tax,

     (ii)   the furnishing of any other return, certificate, notification, particulars, or any statement or evidence, for the purposes of any tax,

    (iii)   the keeping or retention of books, records, accounts or other documents for the purposes of any tax, or

    (iv)   the production of books, records, accounts or other documents, when so requested, for the purposes of any tax,

 (*h*) knowingly or wilfully, and within the time limits specified for their retention, destroys, defaces or conceals from an authorised officer—

     (i)   any documents, or

    (ii) any other written or printed material in any form, including any information stored, maintained or preserved by means of any mechanical or electronic device, whether or not stored, maintained or preserved in a legible form, which a person is obliged by any provision of the Acts to keep, to issue or to produce for inspection,

[(*hh*) knowingly or wilfully falsifies, conceals, destroys or otherwise disposes of, or causes or permits the falsification, concealment, destruction or disposal of, any books, records or other document—

    (i) which the person has been given the opportunity to deliver, or as the case may be, to make available in accordance with section 900(3), or

    (ii) which the person has been required to deliver or, as the case may be, to make available in accordance with a notice served under section 900, 902, 906A or 907, or an order made under section 901, 902A or 908.]³

  (*i*) fails to remit any income tax payable pursuant to Chapter 4 of Part 42, and the regulations under that Chapter, or value-added tax within the time specified in that behalf in relation to income tax or value-added tax, as the case may be, by the Acts, or

  (*j*) obstructs or interferes with any officer of the Revenue Commissioners, or any other person, in the exercise or performance of powers or duties under the Acts for the purposes of any tax.

(3) A person convicted of an offence under this section shall be liable—

  (*a*) on summary conviction to a fine of [€1,900]⁴ which may be mitigated to not less than one fourth part of such fine or, at the discretion of the court, to imprisonment for a term not exceeding 12 months or to both the fine and the imprisonment, or

  (*b*) on conviction on indictment, to a fine not exceeding [€126,970]⁵ or, at the discretion of the court, to imprisonment for a term not exceeding 5 years or to both the fine and the imprisonment.

[(3A) Where a person has been convicted of an offence referred to in subparagraph (i), (ii) or (iv) of subsection (2)(*g*), then, if an application is made, or caused to be made to the court in that regard, the court may make an order requiring the person concerned to comply with any provision of the Acts relating to the requirements specified in the said subparagraph (i), (ii) or (iv), as the case may be.]⁶

[(3B) A person shall, without prejudice to any other penalty to which the person may be liable, be guilty of an offence under this section if the person fails or refuses to comply with an order referred to in subsection (3A).]⁷

(4) Section 13 of the Criminal Procedure Act, 1967, shall apply in relation to an offence under this section as if, in place of the penalties specified in subsection (3) of that section, there were specified in that subsection the penalties provided for by subsection (3)(*a*), and the reference in subsection (2)(*a*) of section 13 of the Criminal Procedure Act, 1967, to the penalties provided for in subsection (3) of that section shall be construed and apply accordingly.

(5) Where an offence under this section is committed by a body corporate and the offence is shown to have been committed with the consent or connivance of any person who, when the offence was committed, was a director, manager, secretary or other officer of the body corporate, or a member of the committee of management or other controlling authority of the body corporate, that person shall also be deemed to be guilty of the offence and may be proceeded against and punished accordingly.

(6) In any proceedings under this section, a return or statement delivered to an inspector or other officer of the Revenue Commissioners under any provision of the Acts and purporting to be signed by any person shall be deemed until the contrary is proved to have been so delivered and to have been signed by that person.

(7) Notwithstanding any other enactment, proceedings in respect of an offence under this section may be instituted within 10 years from the date of the commission of the offence or incurring of the penalty, as the case may be.

(8) Section 1 of the Probation of Offenders Act, 1907, shall not apply in relation to offences under this section.

(9) Sections 987(4) and 1052(4), subsections (3) and (7) of section 1053, and sections 1068 and 1069 and sections 26(6) and 27(7) of the Value-Added Tax Act, 1972, shall, with any necessary modifications, apply for the purposes of this section as they apply for the purposes of those sections, including, in the case of such of those sections as are applied by the Capital Gains Tax Acts, the Corporation Tax Acts, or Part VI of the Finance Act, 1983, the purposes of those sections as so applied.

Amendments

1   Subs (2)(*dd*) inserted by FA 1999 s 27(*b*) with effect from 6 April 1999.
2   Substituted by FA 2002 s 133(*a*) with effect from 25 March 2002; previously "knowingly or wilfully fails".
3   Subs (2)(*hh*) inserted by FA 1999 s 211(*a*) with effect from 25 March 1999.
4   Substituted by FA 2001 s 233(2)(*a*) with effect from 1 January 2002; previously "£1,500".
5   Substituted by FA 2001 s 240(1) and (2)(*k*) and Sch 5 Pt 1 as respects any act or omission which takes place or begins on or after 1 January 2002; previously "£100,000".
6   Subs (3A) inserted by FA 1999 s 211(*c*) with effect from 25 March 1999.
7   Subs (3B) inserted by FA 2002 s 133(*b*) with effect from 25 March 2002.

Cross-references

Application to High Court: information from third party, meaning of "the Acts" applied: s 902A(1).
Company law, subs (1): Companies Act 1990 s 21(1)(*a*)(i)(V).
Deduction from payments due to defaulters: s 1002(5), (9).
Information to be furnished by financial institutions, meaning of "the Acts" applied: s 906A(1).
Information to be furnished by third party: request of an authorised officer: s 902(11).
Inspection of documents and records, meaning of "the Acts" applied: s 905(2A)(*a*).
Penalty for false statement made to obtain allowance, subss (4), (6)-(8): s 1056(4).
Revenue offence: power to obtain information from financial institutions, meaning of "offence" applied: s 908A(1); subs (1): s 908A(1) ("the Acts").
This section to be construed together with the Customs Acts, in so far as relating to customs: s 1104(2).
This section to be construed together with the Value Added Tax Acts 1972-1997, in so far as relating to value added tax: s 1104(3).
This section to be construed together with the Stamp Act 1891 and the enactments amending or extending that Act, in so far as relating to stamp duties: s 1104(4).
This section to be construed together with the Capital Acquisitions Tax Act 1976, and the enactments amending or extending that Act, in so far as relating to capital acquisitions tax: s 1104(5).
This section to be construed together with FA 1983 Pt VI and the enactments amending or extending that Part, in so far as relating to residential property tax: s 1104(6).

Case law

Meaning of "criminal matter": *Director of Public Prosecutions v Seamus Boyle*, ITR Vol IV, p 395.

Subs (2)(*e*): District Justice not entitled to conclude, on basis of Revenue certificate, that taxpayer had "knowingly and wilfully" failed to submit return of income; taxpayer not present at District Court hearing and was entitled to defend himself: *O'Callaghan v Clifford and others*, ITR Vol IV, p 478.

Tax Briefing

TB36 June 1999 pp 3-4 - Revenue's Prosecution Policy.

TB38 Dec 1999 pp 10-11 - Criminal Proceedings.

Definitions

Collector-General: ss 2(1), 851; inspector: ss 2(1), 5(1), 852; month: IA 1937 Sch; person: IA 1937 s 11(*c*); profits: s 4(1); statute: s 2(1), IA 1937 s 3; Tax Acts: s 1(2).

Former enactments

FA 1983 s 94; FA 1986 s 40(2); FA 1989 s 18 and Sch 1 para 3(2); FA 1992 s 243; FA 1996 s 132(1)-(2) and Sch 5 Pt I para 13(2) and Pt II.

CHAPTER 6
Other sanctions

1086 Publication of names of tax defaulters

(1) In this section—

"the Acts" means—

    (*a*)   the Tax Acts,

    (*b*)   the Capital Gains Tax Acts,

    (*c*)   the Value-Added Tax Act, 1972, and the enactments amending or extending that Act,

    (*d*)   the Capital Acquisitions Tax Act, 1976, and the enactments amending or extending that Act,

    [(*e*) the Stamp Duties Consolidation Act, 1999, and the enactments amending or extending that Act][1]

    (*f*)   Part VI of the Finance Act, 1983,

    [(*g*) the Customs Acts,

    (*h*) the statutes relating to the duties of excise and to the management of those duties,][2]

and any instruments made thereunder;

["**tax**" means any tax, duty, levy or charge under the care and management of the Revenue Commissioners.][3]

(2) The Revenue Commissioners shall, as respects each relevant period (being the period beginning on the 1st day of January, 1997, and ending on the 30th day of June, 1997, and each subsequent period of 3 months beginning with the period ending on the 30th day of September, 1997), compile a list of the names and addresses and the occupations or descriptions of every person—

    (*a*)   on whom a fine or other penalty was imposed by a court under any of the Acts during that relevant period,

(b) on whom a fine or other penalty was otherwise imposed by a court during that relevant period in respect of an act or omission by the person in relation to [tax,]⁴

(c) in whose case the Revenue Commissioners, pursuant to an agreement made with the person in that relevant period, refrained from initiating proceedings for the recovery of any fine or penalty of the kind mentioned in paragraphs (a) and (b) and, in place of initiating such proceedings, accepted or undertook to accept a specified sum of money in settlement of any claim by the Revenue Commissioners in respect of any specified liability of the person under any of the Acts for—

   (i) payment of any tax,

  [(ii) except in the case of tax due by virtue of paragraphs (g) and (h) of the definition of "the Acts", payment of interest on that tax, and

  (iii) a fine or other monetary penalty in respect of that tax including penalties in respect of the failure to deliver any return, statement, declaration, list or other document in connection with the tax, or]⁵

[(d) in whose case the Revenue Commissioners, having initiated proceedings for the recovery of any fine or penalty of the kind mentioned in paragraphs (a) and (b), and whether or not a fine or penalty of the kind mentioned in those paragraphs has been imposed by a court, accepted or undertook to accept, in that relevant period, a specified sum of money in settlement of any claim by the Revenue Commissioners in respect of any specified liability of the person under any of the Acts for—

   (i) payment of any tax,

  [(ii) except in the case of tax due by virtue of paragraphs (g) and (h) of the definition of "the Acts", payment of interest on that tax, and

  (iii) a fine or other monetary penalty in respect of that tax including penalties in respect of the failure to deliver any return, statement, declaration, list or other document in connection with the tax.]⁶]⁷

[(2A) For the purposes of subsection (2), the reference to a specified sum in paragraphs (c) and (d) of that subsection includes a reference to a sum which is the full amount of the claim by the Revenue Commissioners in respect of the specified liability referred to in those paragraphs.]⁸

(3) Notwithstanding any obligation as to secrecy imposed on them by the Acts or the Official Secrets Act, 1963—

(a) the Revenue Commissioners shall, before the expiration of 3 months from the end of each relevant period, cause each such list referred to in subsection (2) in relation to that period to be published in Iris Oifigiúil, and

[(b) the Revenue Commissioners may, at any time after each such list referred to in subsection (2) has been published as provided for in paragraph (a), cause any such list to be publicised or reproduced, or both, in whole or in part, in such manner, form or format as they consider appropriate.]⁹

(4) [Paragraph (c) and (d)]¹⁰ of subsection (2) shall not apply in relation to a person in whose case—

(a) the Revenue Commissioners are satisfied that, before any investigation or inquiry had been commenced by them or by any of their officers into any matter occasioning a liability referred to in [those paragraphs]¹¹ of the person, the person had voluntarily furnished to them complete information in relation to and full particulars of that matter,

(b) section 72 of the Finance Act, 1988, or section 3 of the Waiver of Certain Tax, Interest and Penalties Act, 1993, [applied,]¹²

(c) the specified sum referred to in [paragraph (c) or (d), as the case may be,]¹³ of subsection (2) does not exceed [€12,700, or]¹⁴

[(d) the amount of fine or other penalty included in the specified sum referred to in paragraph (c) or (d), as the case may be, of subsection (2) does not exceed 15 per cent of the amount of tax included in that specified sum.]¹⁵

(5) Any list referred to in subsection (2) shall specify in respect of each person named in the list such particulars as the Revenue Commissioners think fit—

(a) of the matter occasioning the fine or penalty of the kind referred to in subsection (2) imposed on the person or, as the case may be, the liability of that kind to which the person was subject, and

(b) of any interest, fine or other monetary penalty, and of any other penalty or sanction, to which that person was liable, or which was imposed on that person by a court, and which was occasioned by the matter referred to in paragraph (a).

[(5A) Without prejudice to the generality of paragraph (a) of subsection (5), such particulars as are referred to in that paragraph may include—

(a) in a case to which paragraph (a) or (b) of subsection (2) applies, a description, in such summary form as the Revenue Commissioners may think fit, of the act, omission or offence (which may also include the circumstances in which the act or omission arose or the offence was committed) in respect of which the fine or penalty referred to in those paragraphs was imposed, and

(b) in a case to which paragraph (c) or (d) of subsection (2) applies, a description, in such summary form as the Revenue Commissioners may think fit, of the matter occasioning the specified liability (which may also include the circumstances in which that liability arose) in respect of which the Revenue Commissioners accepted, or undertook to accept, a settlement, in accordance with those paragraphs.]¹⁶

Amendments

¹   Definition of "the Acts" para (e) substituted by FA 2002 s 126(1)(a)(i)(I) as respects fines or other penalties, as are referred to in s 1086(2)(a) and (b), which are imposed by a court, and as respects specified sums, as are referred to in s 1086(2)(c) and (d), which the Revenue Commissioners accepted, or undertook to accept, in settlement of a specified liability, on or after 25 March 2002.

²   Definition of "the Acts" paras (g) and (h) inserted by FA 2002 s 126(1)(a)(i)(II) as respects fines or other penalties, as are referred to in s 1086(2)(a) and (b), which are imposed by a court, and as respects specified sums, as are referred to in s 1086(2)(c) and (d), which the Revenue Commissioners accepted, or undertook to accept, in settlement of a specified liability, on or after 25 March 2002.

³   Definition of "tax" substituted by FA 2002 s 126(1)(a)(ii) as respects fines or other penalties, as are referred to in s 1086(2)(a) and (b), which are imposed by a court, and as respects specified sums, as are referred to in s 1086(2)(c) and (d), which the Revenue Commissioners accepted, or undertook to accept, in settlement of a specified liability, on or after 25 March 2002.

⁴   Substituted by FA 2000 s 162(1)(*a*)(i) as respects fines or other penalties, as are referred to in s 1086(2)(*a*)-(*b*), which are imposed by a court, and as respects specified sums, as are referred to in s 1086(2)(*c*)-(*d*), which the Revenue Commissioners accepted, or undertook to accept, in settlement of a specified liability, on or after 23 March 2000; previously "tax, or".

⁵   Subs (2)(*c*)(ii)-(iii) substituted by FA 2002 s 126(1)(*b*)(i) as respects fines or other penalties, as are referred to in s 1086(2)(*a*) and (*b*), which are imposed by a court, and as respects specified sums, as are referred to in s 1086(2)(*c*) and (*d*), which the Revenue Commissioners accepted, or undertook to accept, in settlement of a specified liability, on or after 25 March 2002.

⁶   Subs (2)(*d*)(ii)-(iii) substituted by FA 2002 s 126(1)(*b*)(ii) as respects fines or other penalties, as are referred to in s 1086(2)(*a*) and (*b*), which are imposed by a court, and as respects specified sums, as are referred to in s 1086(2)(*c*) and (*d*), which the Revenue Commissioners accepted, or undertook to accept, in settlement of a specified liability, on or after 25 March 2002.

⁷   Subs (2)(*d*) inserted by FA 2000 s 162(1)(*a*)(ii) as respects fines or other penalties, as are referred to in s 1086(2)(*a*)-(*b*), which are imposed by a court, and as respects specified sums, as are referred to in s 1086(2)(*c*)-(*d*), which the Revenue Commissioners accepted, or undertook to accept, in settlement of a specified liability, on or after 23 March 2000.

⁸   Subs (2A) inserted by FA 2000 s 162(1)(*b*) as respects fines or other penalties, as are referred to in s 1086(2)(*a*)-(*b*), which are imposed by a court, and as respects specified sums, as are referred to in s 1086(2)(*c*)-(*d*), which the Revenue Commissioners accepted, or undertook to accept, in settlement of a specified liability, on or after 23 March 2000.

⁹   Subs (3)(*b*) substituted by FA 2002 s 126(1)(*c*) as respects fines or other penalties, as are referred to in s 1086(2)(*a*) and (*b*), which are imposed by a court, and as respects specified sums, as are referred to in s 1086(2)(*c*) and (*d*), which the Revenue Commissioners accepted, or undertook to accept, in settlement of a specified liability, on or after 25 March 2002.

¹⁰   Substituted by FA 2000 s 162(1)(*c*)(i) as respects fines or other penalties, as are referred to in s 1086(2)(*a*)-(*b*), which are imposed by a court, and as respects specified sums, as are referred to in s 1086(2)(*c*)-(*d*), which the Revenue Commissioners accepted, or undertook to accept, in settlement of a specified liability, on or after 23 March 2000; previously "Paragraph (c)".

¹¹   Substituted by FA 2002 s 126(1)(*d*)(i) as respects fines or other penalties, as are referred to in s 1086(2)(*a*) and (*b*), which are imposed by a court, and as respects specified sums, as are referred to in s 1086(2)(*c*) and (*d*), which the Revenue Commissioners accepted, or undertook to accept, in settlement of a specified liability, on or after 25 March 2002; previously "that paragraph".

¹²   Substituted by FA 2002 s 126(1)(*d*)(ii) as respects fines or other penalties, as are referred to in s 1086(2)(*a*) and (*b*), which are imposed by a court, and as respects specified sums, as are referred to in s 1086(2)(*c*) and (*d*), which the Revenue Commissioners accepted, or undertook to accept, in settlement of a specified liability, on or after 25 March 2002; previously "applied, or".

¹³   Substituted by FA 2000 s 162(1)(*c*)(ii) as respects fines or other penalties, as are referred to in s 1086(2)(*a*)-(*b*), which are imposed by a court, and as respects specified sums, as are referred to in s 1086(2)(*c*)-(*d*), which the Revenue Commissioners accepted, or undertook to accept, in settlement of a specified liability, on or after 23 March 2000; previously "paragraph (c)".

¹⁴   Substituted by FA 2002 s 126(1)(*d*)(iii) as respects fines or other penalties, as are referred to in s 1086(2)(*a*) and (*b*), which are imposed by a court, and as respects specified sums, as are referred to in s 1086(2)(*c*) and (*d*), which the Revenue Commissioners accepted, or undertook to accept, in settlement of a specified liability, on or after 25 March 2002; previously "€12,700, or".

¹⁵   Subs (4)(*d*) inserted by FA 2002 s 126(1)(*d*)(iv) as respects fines or other penalties, as are referred to in s 1086(2)(*a*) and (*b*), which are imposed by a court, and as respects specified sums, as are referred to in s 1086(2)(*c*) and (*d*), which the Revenue Commissioners accepted, or undertook to accept, in settlement of a specified liability, on or after 25 March 2002.

¹⁶   Subs (5A) inserted by FA 2000 s 162(1)(*d*) as respects fines or other penalties, as are referred to in s 1086(2)(*a*)-(*b*), which are imposed by a court, and as respects specified sums, as are referred to in s 1086(2)(*c*)-(*d*), which the Revenue Commissioners accepted, or undertook to accept, in settlement of a specified liability, on or after 23 March 2000.

Cross-references

This section to be construed together with the Value Added Tax Acts 1972-1997, in so far as relating to value added tax: s 1104(3).

This section to be construed together with the Stamp Act 1891 and the enactments amending or extending that Act, in so far as relating to stamp duties: s 1104(4).

This section to be construed together with the Capital Acquisitions Tax Act 1976, and the enactments amending or extending that Act, in so far as relating to capital acquisitions tax: s 1104(5).

This section to be construed together with FA 1983 Pt VI and the enactments amending or extending that Part, in so far as relating to residential property tax: s 1104(6).

Definitions

statute: s 2(1), IA 1937 s 3; Tax Acts: s 1(2).

Former enactments

FA 1983 s 23; FA 1992 s 240; WCTIPA 1993 s 3(7); FA 1997 s 158.

PART 48
MISCELLANEOUS AND SUPPLEMENTAL

1093 Disclosure of information to Ombudsman

Any obligation to maintain secrecy or other restriction on the disclosure or production of information (including documents) obtained by or furnished to the Revenue Commissioners, or any person on their behalf, for taxation purposes, shall not apply to the disclosure or production of information (including documents) to the Ombudsman for the purposes of an examination or investigation by the Ombudsman under the Ombudsman Act, 1980, of any action (within the meaning of that Act) taken by or on behalf of the Revenue Commissioners, being such an action taken in the performance of administrative functions in respect of any tax or duty under the care and management of the Revenue Commissioners.

Cross-references

This section to be construed together with the Customs Acts, in so far as relating to customs: s 1104(2).

This section to be construed together with the Value Added Tax Acts 1972-1997, in so far as relating to value added tax: s 1104(3).

This section to be construed together with the Stamp Act 1891 and the enactments amending or extending that Act, in so far as relating to stamp duties: s 1104(4).

This section to be construed together with the Capital Acquisitions Tax Act 1976, and the enactments amending or extending that Act, in so far as relating to capital acquisitions tax: s 1104(5).

This section to be construed together with FA 1983 Pt VI and the enactments amending or extending that Part, in so far as relating to residential property tax: s 1104(6).

Definition

person: IA 1937 s 11(*c*).

Former enactment

FA 1981 s 52.

PART 49
COMMENCEMENT, REPEALS, TRANSITIONAL PROVISIONS, ETC

1104 Short title and construction

(1) This Act may be cited as the Taxes Consolidation Act, 1997.

...

(6) Sections 7, 811, 859, 872(1), 887, 905, 906, 910, 912, 1006, 1078, 1086 and 1093 (in so far as they relate to Part VI of the Finance Act, 1983) shall be construed together with that Part and enactments amending or extending that Part.

FINANCE ACT 1998

(1998 Number 3)
(Date of passing: 27 March 1998)

ARRANGEMENT OF SECTIONS

PART 6
MISCELLANEOUS

Section

AN ACT TO CHARGE AND IMPOSE CERTAIN DUTIES OF CUSTOMS AND INLAND REVENUE (INCLUDING EXCISE), TO AMEND THE LAW RELATING TO CUSTOMS AND INLAND REVENUE (INCLUDING EXCISE) AND TO MAKE FURTHER PROVISIONS IN CONNECTION WITH FINANCE.

BE IT ENACTED BY THE OIREACHTAS AS FOLLOWS:

PART 6
MISCELLANEOUS

133 Interest on unpaid or overpaid taxes

Notes

Subs (2)(*a*) substituted "1 per cent" for "1.25 per cent" in FA 1983 s 105(1) for any month or part of, commencing on or after 27 March 1998 in respect of an amount due to be paid or remitted, or repaid or retained before, on or after that date.

Subs (2)(*b*) substituted "0.5 per cent" for "1.25 per cent" in FA 1983 s 107(2) (notwithstanding Payment of Interest on Overpaid Tax Regulations, 1990 r 3 (SI No 176 of 1990)) for any month or part of, commencing on or after 27 March 1998 in respect of an amount due to be paid or remitted, or repaid or retained before, on or after that date.

137 Care and management of taxes and duties

All taxes and duties imposed by this Act are hereby placed under the care and management of the Revenue Commissioners.

138 Short title, construction and commencement

(1) This Act may be cited as the Finance Act, 1998.

...

(10) Any reference in this Act to any other enactment shall, except so far as the context otherwise requires, be construed as a reference to that enactment as amended by or under any other enactment including this Act.

(11) In this Act, a reference to a Part, section or Schedule is to a Part or section of, or Schedule to, this Act, unless it is indicated that reference to some other enactment is intended.

(12) In this Act, a reference to a subsection, paragraph, subparagraph, clause or subclause is to the subsection, paragraph, subparagraph, clause or subclause of the provision (including a Schedule) in which the reference occurs, unless it is indicated that reference to some other provision is intended.

FINANCE ACT 1999

(1999 Number 2)
(Date of passing: 25 March 1999)

PART 5
RESIDENTIAL PROPERTY TAX

AN ACT TO CHARGE AND IMPOSE CERTAIN DUTIES OF CUSTOMS AND INLAND REVENUE (INCLUDING EXCISE), TO AMEND THE LAW RELATING TO CUSTOMS AND INLAND REVENUE (INCLUDING EXCISE) AND TO MAKE FURTHER PROVISIONS IN CONNECTION WITH FINANCE.

BE IT ENACTED BY THE OIREACHTAS AS FOLLOWS:

PART 5
RESIDENTIAL PROPERTY TAX

198 Amendment of section 100 (market value exemption limit) of Finance Act, 1983

Notes

Subs (1) substituted "£200,000" for "£94,000" in FA 1983 s 100(1) definition of "general exemption limit" in relation to any valuation date occurring on or after 5 April 1999.

PART 7
MISCELLANEOUS

207 Amendment of Chapter 4 (revenue powers) of Part 18 of Taxes Consolidation Act, 1997

Notes

Para (*f*)(i) deleted TCA 1997 s 905(2)(*d*).
Para (*f*)(ii) inserted TCA 1997 s 905(2A).
Para (*g*) inserted TCA 1997 s 906A.

208 Power to obtain information from a Minister of the Government or public body

Notes

Section 208 substituted TCA 1997 s 910(1).

211 Amendment of section 1078 (revenue offences) of Taxes Consolidation Act, 1997

Notes

Para (*a*) inserted TCA 1997 s 1078(2)(*hh*).
Para (*b*) substituted "£10,000" for "£10,000" in TCA 1997 s 1078(3)(*b*).
Para (*c*) inserted TCA 1997 s 1078(3A).

216 Care and management of taxes and duties

All taxes and duties imposed by this Act are hereby placed under the care and management of the Revenue Commissioners.

217 Short title, construction and commencement

(1) This Act may be cited as the Finance Act, 1999.

...

(6) Part 5 shall be construed together with Part VI of the Finance Act, 1983, and the enactments amending or extending that Part.

...

(8) Part 7 (so far as relating to income tax) shall be construed together with the Income Tax Acts and (so far as relating to corporation tax) shall be construed together with the Corporation Tax Acts and (so far as relating to capital gains tax) shall be construed together with the Capital Gains Tax Acts and (so far as relating to customs) shall be construed together with the Custom Acts and (so far as relating to duties of excise) shall be construed together with the statutes which relate to duties of excise and the management of those duties and (so far as relating to value-added tax) shall be construed together with the Value-Added Tax Acts, 1972 to 1999, and (so far as relating to stamp duty) shall be construed together with the Stamp Act, 1891, and the enactments amending or extending that Act and (so far as relating to residential property tax) shall be construed together with Part VI of the Finance Act, 1983, and the enactments amending or extending that Part and (so far as relating to gift tax or inheritance tax) shall be construed together with the Capital Acquisitions Tax Act, 1976, and the enactments amending or extending that Act.

...

(11) Any reference in this Act to any other enactment shall, except so far as the context otherwise requires, be construed as a reference to that enactment as amended by or under any other enactment including this Act.

(12) In this Act, a reference to a Part, section or Schedule is to a Part or section of, or Schedule to, this Act, unless it is indicated that reference to some other enactment is intended.

(13) In this Act, a reference to a subsection, paragraph, subparagraph, clause- or subclause is to the subsection, paragraph, subparagraph, clause or subclause of the provision (including a Schedule) in which the reference occurs, unless it is indicated that reference to some other provision is intended.

FINANCE ACT 2000

(2000 Number 3)

ARRANGEMENT OF SECTIONS

AN ACT TO CHARGE AND IMPOSE CERTAIN DUTIES OF CUSTOMS AND INLAND REVENUE (INCLUDING EXCISE), TO AMEND THE LAW RELATING TO CUSTOMS AND INLAND REVENUE (INCLUDING EXCISE) AND TO MAKE FURTHER PROVISIONS IN CONNECTION WITH FINANCE.
[23rd MARCH 2000]

PART 5
RESIDENTIAL PROPERTY TAX

134 Amendment of section 100 (market value exemption limit) of Finance Act, 1983

Notes

Section 134 substituted "£300,000" for "£200,000" and "2000" for "1999" in FA 1983 s 100(1) (definition of "general exemption limit" in relation to any valuation date (within the meaning of FA 1983 s 95(1)) occurring on or after 5 April 2000.

135 Amendment of section 110A (clearance on sale of certain residential property) of Finance Act, 1983

Notes

Section 135 inserted FA 1983 s 110A(12) in relation to the sale of an estate or interest in residential property (within the meaning of FA 1983 Pt VI) completed after 10 February 2000.

PART 7
MISCELLANEOUS

154 Interpretation (Part 7)

In this Part "Principal Act" means the Taxes Consolidation Act, 1997.

162 Amendment of section 1086 (publication of names of tax defaulters) of Principal Act

164 Amendment of Chapter 5 (miscellaneous provisions) of Part 42 (collection and recovery) of Principal Act

165 Care and management of taxes and duties

All taxes and duties imposed by this Act are by virtue of this section placed under the care and management of the Revenue Commissioners.

166 Short title, construction and commencement

(1) This Act may be cited as the Finance Act, 2000.

...

(6) Part 5 shall be construed together with Part VI of the Finance Act, 1983, and the enactments amending or extending that Part.

...

(11) Any reference in this Act to any other enactment shall, except so far as the context otherwise requires, be construed as a reference to that enactment as amended by or under any other enactment including this Act.

(12) In this Act, a reference to a Part, section or Schedule is to a Part or section of, or Schedule to, this Act, unless it is indicated that reference to some other enactment is intended.

(13) In this Act, a reference to a subsection, paragraph, subparagraph, clause or subclause is to the subsection, paragraph, subparagraph, clause or subclause of the provision (including a Schedule) in which the reference occurs, unless it is indicated that reference to some other provision is intended.

FINANCE ACT 2001

(2001 Number 7)
(Date of passing: 30 March 2001)

ARRANGEMENT OF SECTIONS

AN ACT TO CHARGE AND IMPOSE CERTAIN DUTIES OF CUSTOMS AND INLAND REVENUE (INCLUDING EXCISE), TO AMEND THE LAW RELATING TO CUSTOMS AND INLAND REVENUE (INCLUDING EXCISE) AND TO MAKE FURTHER PROVISIONS IN CONNECTION WITH FINANCE.
[30th MARCH 2001]

PART 8
MISCELLANEOUS

231 Interpretation (Part 8)

In this Part **"Principal Act"** means the Taxes Consolidation Act, 1997.

232 Amendment of Chapter 3 (other obligations and returns) of Part 38 of Principal Act

---

Notes

Subs (1)(*a*) substituted TCA 1997 s 887 [with effect on or after 15 February 2001][1].

Subs (3)(*a*)(i) substituted "€1,265" for "£1,000" in TCA 1997 s 887(5)(*b*) with effect from 1 January 2002.

Amendments

[1] Substituted by subs (2)(*c*) which was substituted by FA 2002 s 138 and Sch 6 para 5(*f*) with effect on and from 30 March 2001; previously "as respects any chargeable period (within the meaning of s 321(2)) commencing on or after 15 February 2001".

---

233 Amendment of section 1078 (revenue offences) of Principal Act

Notes

Subs (1) substituted "£1,500" for "£1,000" in TCA 1997 s 1078(3)(*a*) with effect from 6 April 2001.
Subs (2)(*a*) substituted "€1,900" for "£1,500" in TCA 1997 s 1078(3)(*a*) with effect from 1 January 2002.

238 Amendment of section 1002 (deduction from payments due to defaulters of amounts due in relation to tax) of Principal Act

Notes

This section substituted "14 days" for "one month" in TCA 1997 s 1002(3)(*a*).

239 Amendment of section 1006A (offset between taxes) of Principal Act

Notes

Para (*a*) inserted ", and includes any interest due under the Acts in relation to such tax, duty, levy or other charge" in TCA 1997 s 1006A(1) definition of "liability" with effect from 6 April 2001.
Para (*b*) substituted TCA 1997 s 1006A(2) with effect from 6 April 2001.

240 Amendment of enactments consequent on changeover to Euro

(1) (*a*)   Subject to subsection (2), in each provision specified in column (1) of Schedule 5 for the words or amount set out in column (2) of that Schedule at that entry there shall be substituted the words or amount set out at the corresponding entry in column (3) of that Schedule.

(*b*)   Where words are or an amount is mentioned more than once in a provision specified in column (1) of Schedule 5, then the substitution provided for by paragraph (*a*) shall apply as respects those words or that amount to each mention of those words or that amount in that provision.

(2) Subsection (1) shall apply—

(*a*)   to the extent that the amendments relate to income tax and related matters, other than the amendments relating to such matters referred to in subparagraphs (ii), (iii), (iv), (v) and (vi) of paragraph (*m*), as respects the year of assessment 2002 and subsequent years of assessment,

(*b*)   to the extent that the amendments relate to capital gains tax and related matters, other than the amendments relating to such matters referred to in paragraph (*m*)(vii),as respects the year of assessment 2002 and subsequent years of assessment,

(*c*)   to the extent that the amendments relate to corporation tax and related matters, other than the amendments relating to such matters referred to in subparagraphs (i), (iii) and (iv) of paragraph (*l*), for accounting periods ending on or after 1 January 2002,

...

(*i*)   to the extent that section 1086 of the Taxes Consolidation Act, 1997 is amended, as respects specified sums such as are referred to in paragraphs (*c*) and (*d*) of section 1086(2) of that Act which the Revenue Commissioners accept or undertake to accept on or after 1 January 2002,

(*k*)   to the extent that the enactment amended imposes any fine, forfeiture, penalty or punishment for any act or omission, as respects any act or omission which takes place or begins on or after 1 January 2002,

...

242 Care and management of taxes and duties

All the taxes and duties imposed by this Act are placed under the care and management of the Revenue Commissioners.

243 Short title, construction and commencement

(1) This Act may be cited as the Finance Act, 2001.

...

(8) Part 8 (so far as relating to income tax) shall be construed together with the Income Tax Acts and (so far as relating to corporation tax) shall be construed together with the Corporation Tax Acts and (so far as relating to capital gains tax) shall be construed together with the Capital Gains Tax Acts and (so far as relating to value-added tax) shall be construed together with the Value-Added Tax Acts, 1972 to 2001 and (so far as relating to residential property tax) shall be construed together with Part VI of the Finance Act, 1983, and the enactments amending or extending that Part and (so far as relating to gift tax or inheritance tax) shall be construed together with the Capital Acquisitions Tax Act, 1976, and the enactments amending or extending that Act.

...

(11) Any reference in this Act to any other enactment shall, except so far as the context otherwise requires, be construed as a reference to that enactment as amended by or under any other enactment including this Act.

(12) In this Act, a reference to a Part, section or Schedule is to a Part or section of, or Schedule to, this Act, unless it is indicated that reference to some other enactment is intended.

(13) In this Act, a reference to a subsection, paragraph, subparagraph, clause or subclause is to the subsection, paragraph, subparagraph, clause or subclause of the provision (including a Schedule) in which the reference occurs, unless it is indicated that reference to some other provision is intended.

SCHEDULE 5
Amendment of Enactments Consequent on Changeover to Euro
[Section 240]

PART 7
RESIDENTIAL PROPERTY TAX AND RELATED MATTERS

Notes

Sch 5 Pt 7 amended FA 1983 Pt VI as follows:

s 100(1): "£300,000" substituted by "€382,000"; s 100(1): "£1,000" substituted by "€1,000"; s 112(1)(*a*): "£1,000" substituted by "€1,265"; s 112(1)(*b*): "£50" substituted by "€60"; s 112(2): "£1,000" substituted by "€1,265"; s 112(3)(*d*)(i): "£2,000" substituted by "€2,535"; s 112(7): "£1,000" substituted by "€1,265".

FINANCE ACT 2002

(2002 Number 5)
(Date of passing: 25 March 2002)

ARRANGEMENT OF SECTIONS

PART 6
MISCELLANEOUS

AN ACT TO PROVIDE FOR THE IMPOSITION, REPEAL, REMISSION,
ALTERATION AND REGULATION OF TAXATION OF STAMP DUTIES AND
OF DUTIES RELATING TO EXCISE AND OTHERWISE TO MAKE FURTHER
PROVISION IN CONNECTION WITH FINANCE INCLUDING THE
REGULATION OF CUSTOMS [*25th MARCH 2002*]

PART 6
MISCELLANEOUS

123 Interpretation (Part 6)

In this Part **"Principal Act"** means the Taxes Consolidation Act 1997.

125 Amendment of Chapter 5 (miscellaneous provisions) of Part 42 of Principal Act

---

Notes

Para (*a*)(i)(I) substituted TCA 1997 s 1006A(1) definition of "claim" with effect from 25 March 2002.

Para (*a*)(i)(II) substituted TCA 1997 s 1006A(1) definition of "liability" with effect from 25 March 2002.

Para (*a*)(i)(III) substituted "credited;" for "credited." In TCA 1997 s 1006A(1) definition of "overpayment" with effect from 25 March 2002.

Para (*a*)(i)(IV) inserted TCA 1997 s 1006A(1) definition of "tax" with effect from 25 March 2002.

Para (*a*)(ii) inserted TCA 1997 s 1006A(5) with effect from 25 March 2002.

---

126 Amendment of section 1086 (publication of names of tax defaulters) of Principal Act

---

Notes

Subs (1)(*a*)(i)(I) substituted TCA 1997 s 1086(1) definition of "the Acts" para (*e*) as respects fines or other penalties, as are referred to in TCA 1997 s 1086(2)(*a*)-(*b*), which are imposed by a court, and as respects

specified sums, as are referred to in TCA 1997 s 1086(2)(*c*)-(*d*), which the Revenue Commissioners accepted, or undertook to accept, in settlement of a specified liability, on or after 25 March 2002.

Subs (1)(*a*)(i)(II) inserted TCA 1997 s 1086(1) definition of "the Acts" paras (*g*)-(*h*) as respects fines or other penalties, as are referred to in TCA 1997 s 1086(2)(*a*)-(*b*), which are imposed by a court, and as respects specified sums, as are referred to in TCA 1997 s 1086(2)(*c*)-(*d*), which the Revenue Commissioners accepted, or undertook to accept, in settlement of a specified liability, on or after 25 March 2002.

Subs (1)(*a*)(ii) substituted TCA 1997 s 1086(1) definition of "tax" as respects fines or other penalties, as are referred to in TCA 1997 s 1086(2)(*a*)-(*b*), which are imposed by a court, and as respects specified sums, as are referred to in TCA 1997 s 1086(2)(*c*)-(*d*), which the Revenue Commissioners accepted, or undertook to accept, in settlement of a specified liability, on or after 25 March 2002.

Subs (1)(*b*)(i) substituted TCA 1997 s 1086(2)(*c*)(ii)-(iii) as respects fines or other penalties, as are referred to in TCA 1997 s 1086(2)(*a*)-(*b*), which are imposed by a court, and as respects specified sums, as are referred to in TCA 1997 s 1086(2)(*c*)-(*d*), which the Revenue Commissioners accepted, or undertook to accept, in settlement of a specified liability, on or after 25 March 2002.

Subs (1)(*b*)(ii) substituted TCA 1997 s 1086(2)(*d*)(ii)-(iii) as respects fines or other penalties, as are referred to in TCA 1997 s 1086(2)(*a*)-(*b*), which are imposed by a court, and as respects specified sums, as are referred to in TCA 1997 s 1086(2)(*c*)-(*d*), which the Revenue Commissioners accepted, or undertook to accept, in settlement of a specified liability, on or after 25 March 2002.

Subs (1)(*c*) substituted TCA 1997 s 1086(3)(*b*) as respects fines or other penalties, as are referred to in TCA 1997 s 1086(2)(*a*)-(*b*), which are imposed by a court, and as respects specified sums, as are referred to in TCA 1997 s 1086(2)(*c*)-(*d*), which the Revenue Commissioners accepted, or undertook to accept, in settlement of a specified liability, on or after 25 March 2002.

Subs (1)(*d*)(i) substituted "those paragraphs" for "that paragraph" in TCA 1997 s 1086(4)(*a*) as respects fines or other penalties, as are referred to in TCA 1997 s 1086(2)(*a*)-(*b*), which are imposed by a court, and as respects specified sums, as are referred to in TCA 1997 s 1086(2)(*c*)-(*d*), which the Revenue Commissioners accepted, or undertook to accept, in settlement of a specified liability, on or after 25 March 2002.

Subs (1)(*d*)(ii) substituted "applied," for "applied, or" in TCA 1997 s 1086(4)(*b*) as respects fines or other penalties, as are referred to in TCA 1997 s 1086(2)(*a*)-(*b*), which are imposed by a court, and as respects specified sums, as are referred to in TCA 1997 s 1086(2)(*c*)-(*d*), which the Revenue Commissioners accepted, or undertook to accept, in settlement of a specified liability, on or after 25 March 2002.

Subs (1)(*d*)(iii) substituted "€12,700, or" for "€12,700." in TCA 1997 s 1086(4)(*c*) as respects fines or other penalties, as are referred to in TCA 1997 s 1086(2)(*a*)-(*b*), which are imposed by a court, and as respects specified sums, as are referred to in TCA 1997 s 1086(2)(*c*)-(*d*), which the Revenue Commissioners accepted, or undertook to accept, in settlement of a specified liability, on or after 25 March 2002.

Subs (1)(*d*)(iii) inserted TCA 1997 s 1086(4)(*d*) as respects fines or other penalties, as are referred to in TCA 1997 s 1086(2)(*a*)-(*b*), which are imposed by a court, and as respects specified sums, as are referred to in TCA 1997 s 1086(2)(*c*)-(*d*), which the Revenue Commissioners accepted, or undertook to accept, in settlement of a specified liability, on or after 25 March 2002.

129 Interest on unpaid and overpaid tax

Notes

Subs (4)(*a*)(i) substituted "0.0322 per cent per day or part of a day" for "1 per cent per month or part of a month" in FA 1983 s 105(1) with effect from 1 September 2002 in respect of interest chargeable or payable as regards an amount due to be paid or remitted or to be repaid or retained, whether before, on, or after that date.

Subs (4)(*a*)(ii) deleted FA 1983 s 105(1)(proviso) with effect from 1 September 2002 in respect of interest chargeable or payable as regards an amount due to be paid or remitted or to be repaid or retained, whether before, on, or after that date.

Subs (4)(*b*)(i) substituted "0.0161 per cent, or such other rate (if any) as stands prescribed by the Minister for Finance by regulations, of the amount to be repaid or retained for each day or part of a day" for for "0.5 per cent, or such other rate (if any) as stands prescribed by the Minister for Finance by regulations, of the amount to be repaid or retained for each month or part of a month" in FA 1983 s 107(2) with effect from 1 September 2002 in respect of interest chargeable or payable as regards an amount due to be paid or remitted or to be repaid or retained, whether before, on, or after that date.

132 Amendment of Chapter 4 (revenue powers) of Part 38 of Principal Act

Notes

Para (*d*) inserted TCA 1997 s 905(1) definition of "records" with effect from 25 March 2002.

133 Amendment of section 1078 (revenue offences) of Principal Act

Notes

Para (*a*) substituted "fails without reasonable excuse" for "knowingly or wilfully fails" in TCA 1997 s 1078(2)(*g*) with effect from 25 March 2002.
Para (*b*) inserted TCA 1997 s 1078(3B) with effect from 25 March 2002.

140 Care and management of taxes and duties

All taxes and duties imposed by this Act are placed under the care and management of the Revenue Commissioners.

141 Short title, construction and commencement

(1) This Act may be cited as the Finance Act 2002.

...

(7) Part 6 (so far as relating to income tax) shall be construed together with the Income Tax Acts and (so far as relating to corporation tax) shall be construed together with the Corporation Tax Acts and (so far as relating to capital gains tax) shall be construed together with the Capital Gains Tax Acts and (so far as relating to value-added tax) shall be construed together with the Value-Added Tax Acts 1972 to 2002 and (so far as relating to residential property tax) shall be construed together with Part VI of the Finance Act 1983, and the enactments amending or extending that Part and (so far as relating to gift tax or inheritance tax) shall be construed together with the Capital Acquisitions Tax Act 1976, and the enactments amending or extending that Act.

...

(10) Any reference in this Act to any other enactment shall, except so far as the context otherwise requires, be construed as a reference to that enactment as amended by or under any other enactment including this Act.

(11) In this Act, a reference to a Part, section or Schedule is to a Part or section of, or Schedule to, this Act, unless it is indicated that reference to some other enactment is intended.

(12) In this Act, a reference to a subsection, paragraph, subparagraph, clause or subclause is to the subsection, paragraph, subparagraph, clause or subclause of the provision (including a Schedule) in which the reference occurs, unless it is indicated that reference to some other provision is intended.

TABLE OF CASES (RESIDENTIAL PROPERTY TAX)

TABLE OF STATUTORY REFERENCES
(RESIDENTIAL PROPERTY TAX)

INDEX

LEGISLATION (ANTI SPECULATIVE PROPERTY TAX)

FINANCE (NO 2) ACT 2000

(2000 Number 19)
(Date passed: 5 July 2000)

ARRANGEMENT OF SECTIONS

PART 2
ANTI-SPECULATIVE PROPERTY TAX

PART 3
MISCELLANEOUS

AN ACT TO CHARGE AND IMPOSE CERTAIN DUTIES OF INLAND
REVENUE, TO AMEND THE LAW RELATING TO INLAND REVENUE AND
TO MAKE FURTHER PROVISIONS IN CONNECTION WITH FINANCE

PART 2
ANTI-SPECULATIVE PROPERTY TAX

5 Interpretation (Part 2)

(1) In this Part, save where the context otherwise requires—

"Act of 1976" means the Capital Acquisitions Tax Act, 1976;

"Act of 1997" means the Taxes Consolidation Act, 1997;

"accountable person" means—

(a) if the assessable person is an individual (other than a person to whom paragraph (d) applies), the individual or the individual's personal representative,

(b) if the assessable person is a body corporate, the secretary of the body corporate or the person who performs the duties of secretary,

(c) if the assessable person is a discretionary trust, the trustee of that trust,

(d) if the assessable person is a minor child or is a person of unsound mind having a guardian or a committee, the guardian or committee, as the case may be;

"appropriate part", in relation to property in which a limited interest subsists, means that part of the property which bears the same proportion to the entire property as the gross annual value of the limited interest bears to the gross annual value of the entire property, and where the property concerned comprises more than one unit of residential property the property to which the person concerned is beneficially entitled in possession shall be deemed to include the appropriate part of each and every unit of residential property comprised in the entire property;

"assessable person" means an individual, a body corporate or a discretionary trust;

"Collector" means the Collector-General appointed under section 851 of the Act of 1997;

"the Commissioners" means the Revenue Commissioners;

"date of the disposition" has the meaning assigned to it by section 2 of the Act of 1976;

"discretionary trust" has the meaning assigned to it by section 2 of the Act of 1976;

"disponer" has the meaning assigned to it by section 2 of the Act of 1976;

"disposition" has the meaning assigned to it by section 2 of the Act of 1976;

"donee" has the meaning assigned to it by section 2 of the Act of 1976:

"entitled in possession" has the meaning assigned to it by section 2 of the Act of 1976.

"earned income" has the meaning assigned to it by section 3 of the Act of 1997;

"gift" has the meaning assigned to it by section 2 of the Act of 1976;

"health board" includes the Eastern Regional Health Authority and an Area Health Board established under the Health (Eastern Regional Health Authority) Act, 1999.

"interest in expectancy" has the meaning assigned to it by section 2 of the Act of 1976;

"limited interest" has the meaning assigned to it by section 2 of the Act of 1976;

"market value", in relation to any property, means the market value thereof ascertained in accordance with section 14;

"on a death" has the meaning assigned to it by section 2 of the Act of 1976;

"personal representatives" has the meaning assigned to it by section 799(1) of the Act of 1997;

"relevant residential property" means—

(a) in relation to an assessable person (other than a discretionary trust), all interests in residential property to which that person is beneficially entitled in possession, and

(b) in relation to an assessable person being a discretionary trust, all interests in residential property, other than an interest in expectancy in property to which, for the time being, a person is beneficially entitled in possession, which are comprised in the trust;

"residential property" means—

(a) a building or part of a building situate in the State used or suitable for use as a dwelling, and

(b) land situate in the State which the occupier of a building or part of a building used as a dwelling has for his or her own occupation and enjoyment with the said building or part as its garden or grounds of an ornamental nature,

but does not include—

(i) an approved building within the meaning of section 482 of the Act of 1997,

(ii) a building or part of a building which is a qualifying premises within the meaning of the following sections of the Act of 1997—

(I) sections 325, 326 or 327,

(II) sections 334, 335 or 336,

(III) sections 346, 347 or 348,

(IV) sections 356, 357 or 358,

(V) sections 361, 362 or 363,

(VI) sections 372F, 372G or 372H (inserted by section 76 of the Finance Act, 1998),

(VII) sections 372P, 372Q or 372R (inserted by section 77 of the Finance Act, 1998),

(VIII) sections 380B, 380C or 380D (inserted by section 50 of the Finance Act, 1999),

(IX) section 372X (inserted by section 70(1) of the Finance Act, 1999), or

    (X)   sections 372AE, 372AF or 372AG (inserted by section 89 of the Finance Act, 2000),

and in respect of which a deduction was or is available under any of those sections in computing for the purposes of section 97(1) of the Act of 1997 the amount of a surplus or deficiency in respect of the rent from the qualifying premises,

  (iii) a building or structure which is an industrial building or structure by virtue of being a holiday cottage of the type referred to in section 268(3) of the Act of 1997,

  (iv) a building or structure which is in use as a tourist accommodation facility where the building or structure is—

    (I)   a holiday apartment registered under Part III of the Tourist Traffic Act, 1939, or

    (II) other self-catering accommodation specified in a list published under section 9 of the Tourist Traffic Act, 1957,

   (v) a building let for rent or other valuable consideration, for a period of at least 6 months during the 12 month period immediately prior to the relevant valuation date, in respect of which the lessor is required to comply with and has complied with all the requirements of the following Regulations—

    (I)   the Housing (Standards for Rented Houses) Regulations, 1993 (SI No 147 of 1993),

    (II) the Housing (Rent Books) Regulations, 1993 (SI No 146 of 1993), and

   (III) the Housing (Registration of Rented Houses) Regulations, 1996 (SI No 30 of 1996), as amended by the Housing (Registration of Rented Houses) (Amendment) Regulations, 2000 (SI No 12 of 2000),

  (vi) a building which forms part of the trading stock of a business other than a building from which income is derived being income which is not earned income or which would not be earned income if it were received by an individual,

 (vii) a building which, if it were the subject matter of a conveyance on sale executed on the relevant valuation date, would not be treated as residential property for the purpose of charging stamp duty on that conveyance,

 (viii) a building let by a Minister of the Government, a housing authority (within the meaning of section 23 of the Housing (Miscellaneous Provisions) Act, 1992), a health board or Shannon Free Airport Development Company Limited,

  (ix) a building let by a voluntary body approved by the Minister for the Environment and Local Government under section 6 of the Housing (Miscellaneous Provisions) Act, 1992,

   (x) a building let by a voluntary body standing approved by the Minister for Health and Children, or by a health board, for the purposes of providing accommodation for elderly persons or persons with a mental handicap or psychiatric disorder;

"tax" means anti-speculative property tax chargeable by virtue of this Part;

"trading stock" has the meaning assigned to it by section 89 of the Act of 1997;

"valuation date", in relation to a year, means 6 April in such year.

(2) For the purposes of this Part, where any interest in residential property to which a person is beneficially entitled in possession is a limited interest, the whole or the appropriate part of the property in which the limited interest subsists shall be property to which the person is beneficially entitled in possession.

(3) Where, under or in consequence of any disposition, any person other than the disponer is, on the relevant valuation date, beneficially entitled in possession to a limited interest in residential property, that disponer shall, for the purposes of this Part, be deemed to be the person beneficially entitled in possession to that interest on that date and this Part shall apply accordingly unless—

  (*a*) the date of the disposition is before 15 June 2000, and

  (*b*) some interest in that residential property was already comprised in that disposition, or already in the beneficial ownership of that disponer, before 15 June 2000.

(4) For the purposes of this Part, subsection (2) shall apply with any necessary modifications in relation to property comprised in a discretionary trust which includes an interest which is a limited interest as it applies in relation to property to which a person is beneficially entitled in possession and which includes an interest which is a limited interest.

(5) Where, on the relevant valuation date, an interest in residential property is subject to a compulsory purchase order or to a contract for sale, other than a contract which was evidenced in writing before 15 June 2000, tax shall be payable in respect of that interest on that valuation date in all respects as if that compulsory purchase order or that contract for sale had never come into existence.

(6) For the purposes of this Part, where an individual who occupies residential property as his or her only or main residence acquires another residential property (in this paragraph referred to as the "second property") with a view to the second property becoming his or her only or main residence, neither residential property shall be relevant residential property in relation to the individual in the period of 6 months beginning with the date of acquisition of the second property.

6 Charge of anti-speculative property tax

Amendments

1   Anti-speculative property tax abolished by FA 2001 s 230 with effect from 6 April 2001.

7 Exemption of principal private residence

(1) Subject to subsections (2) and (3), where an individual is beneficially entitled in possession on the relevant valuation date to an interest in residential property and that residential property was—

    (*a*)   on that date and throughout the period of twelve months immediately prior to that date, or

    (*b*)   throughout the period commencing on the date the interest was acquired by that individual and ending on that relevant valuation date,

occupied by that individual as his or her only or main residence, then that residential property shall not be relevant residential property in relation to that individual on that relevant valuation date.

(2) Any period of absence referred to in subsection (5)(*b*) of section 604 of the Act of 1997 which would qualify for relief under section 604 of the Act of 1997 in relation to a notional disposal of residential property on the relevant valuation date by an individual shall, for the purposes of subsection (1), qualify as a period during which that residential property was occupied by that individual as his or her only or main residence.

(3) For the purposes of this section, an individual shall not be treated as having more than one main residence.

8 Exemption for property already owned

(1) Subject to subsection (3), any interest in residential property to which a person was beneficially entitled in possession on 14 June 2000 shall not be relevant residential property of that person on any relevant valuation date.

(2) Subject to subsection (3), any interest in residential property which was comprised in a discretionary trust on 14 June 2000 shall not be relevant residential property of that discretionary trust on any relevant valuation date.

(3) Where a person has entered into a contract before 15 June 2000 to have any interest in residential property transferred to that person or to another in that person's right or on that person's behalf, then for the purposes of subsections (1) and (2), no such person shall be considered to have become beneficially entitled in possession to that interest and, if any such person is a trustee of a discretionary trust, that interest shall not be considered to have become comprised in that trust, until such time as that interest has been transferred to that person or to another in that person's right or on that person's behalf, unless that contract was evidenced in writing before that date.

(4) Residential property built after 14 June 2000 on land to which a person was beneficially entitled in possession on that date or which was comprised in a discretionary trust on that date shall not be relevant residential property of that person or of that discretionary trust on any relevant valuation date.

(5) Where, on any relevant valuation date, an individual is beneficially entitled in possession to an interest in residential property which was acquired by that individual on or after 15 June 2000 and which is not relevant residential property of that individual on that valuation date by virtue of subsection (1) of section 7, then any interest in other

residential property to which that individual is beneficially entitled in possession on that valuation date and which was occupied by that individual as his or her only or main residence on 14 June 2000 shall, notwithstanding subsection (1), be relevant residential property of that individual on that date.

9 Exemption for inheritances

(1) Any interest in residential property to which a person has become beneficially entitled in possession on a death shall not be relevant residential property of that person on any relevant valuation date.

(2) Any interest in residential property which has become comprised in a discretionary trust on a death shall not be relevant residential property of that discretionary trust on any relevant valuation date.

10 Exemption for gifts

(1) Where an interest in residential property has been taken by a donee as a gift from a disponer, then that interest shall not, except to the extent of any money or money's worth paid by that donee for that gift, be relevant residential property of that donee on the relevant valuation date if it would not have been relevant residential property of that disponer, by virtue of section 8(1), had that disponer been still beneficially entitled in possession to that interest on that date.

(2) Where, under or in consequence of any disposition, an interest in residential property has become subject to a discretionary trust, then that interest shall not, except to the extent of any money or money's worth paid by the trustees of that trust for that interest, be relevant residential property of that discretionary trust on the relevant valuation date if it would not have been relevant residential property of the disponer, by virtue of section 8(1), had the disponer been still beneficially entitled in possession to that interest on that date.

11 Exemption for charities

Any interest in residential property that is comprised in a discretionary trust or to which a body corporate is beneficially entitled in possession, being a trust or body corporate that was established or incorporated exclusively for charitable purposes, shall not be relevant residential property of such a trust or of such a body corporate on any relevant valuation date.

12 Exemptions for trusts for permanently incapacitated individuals

(1) Any interest in residential property which, on the relevant valuation date, is comprised in a trust which is a qualifying trust shall not be relevant residential property of any assessable person on that date.

(2) In this section **"qualifying trust"** has the meaning assigned to it by section 189A (inserted by the Finance Act, 1999) of the Taxes Consolidation Act, 1997.

13 Exemption for certain property following upon dissolution of marriage, etc

(1) Any interest in residential property to which an individual is beneficially entitled in possession on the relevant valuation date, and which does not qualify for relief under

subsection (1) of section 7, shall not be relevant residential property of that individual on that date where—

    (*a*)   that individual is or was one of the parties to a marriage,

    (*b*)   that residential property was occupied on that date by the other party to that marriage as his or her only or main residence, and

    (*c*)   a decree of divorce or a decree of judicial separation has been granted on or before that date in respect of that marriage.

(2) In this section—

"decree of divorce" means a decree under section 5 of the Family Law (Divorce) Act, 1996, or any decree to like effect that was granted under the law of a country or jurisdiction other than the State and is recognised in the State;

"decree of judicial separation" means a decree under section 3 of the Judicial Separation and Family Law Reform Act, 1989, or any decree to like effect that was granted under the law of a country or jurisdiction other than the State and is recognised in the State.

14 Market value of property

(1) In this Part, subject to the other provisions thereof, the market value of any property shall be estimated to be the price which the property would fetch if sold in the open market on the valuation date in such manner and subject to such conditions as might reasonably be calculated to obtain for the vendor the best price for the property.

(2) In estimating the market value of any property in accordance with subsection (1) no deduction shall be made from the market value of property for any debts or incumbrances.

(3) Notwithstanding subsections (1) and (2), where as respects the 6 April 2001 valuation date—

    (*a*)   full consideration in money or money's worth has been paid for property by the assessable person concerned or, where the assessable person is a discretionary trust by the trustees of that discretionary trust, or by some other person on behalf of that assessable person, or

    (*b*)   section 10 applies but some consideration in money or money's worth has been paid for the property concerned by the assessable person concerned or, where that assessable person is a discretionary trust by the trustees of that discretionary trust, or by some other person on behalf of that assessable person,

then the market value of that property on that valuation date shall be a sum equal to that consideration.

(4) In estimating the market value of any property in accordance with subsection (1) an accountable person shall fix the price of the property according to the price on the relevant valuation date and shall not make any reduction in the estimate on account of the estimate being made on the assumption that the person or any other person may be chargeable to tax.

(5) If the Commissioners are not satisfied with the market value of any property estimated by any person, or if they consider it is necessary to do so, they may, subject to the same conditions and requirements as apply in the case of that person, estimate the market value of that property and, where the market value as so estimated by the Commissioners exceeds the market value estimated by the person, any charge to tax shall be made by reference to the market value estimated by the Commissioners and not by reference to the market value estimated by the person.

(6) The market value of any property for the purposes of subsection (5) or section 14(2) shall be ascertained by the Commissioners in such manner and by such means as they think fit and they may authorise a person suitably qualified for that purpose to inspect any property and report to them the value thereof for the purposes of this Part and the person having the custody or possession of that property shall permit the person so authorised to inspect it at such reasonable times as the Commissioners consider necessary.

(7) Where the Commissioners require a valuation to be made by a person named by them the costs of such valuation shall be defrayed by them.

15 Delivery of returns

(1) An accountable person shall on or before 1 November immediately following each valuation date, deliver to the Commissioners on a form provided by them a return of all property comprised in the relevant residential property of the assessable person on that valuation date stating the market value thereof on that valuation date and shall, if required by notice in writing by the Commissioners, deliver to them within such time, not being less than 30 days, as may be specified in the notice, a statement verifying such particulars, together with such evidence, statements and documents as the Commissioners may require relating to that property or to any property which the Commissioners have reason to believe forms part of the relevant residential property of such assessable person.

(2) A return under this section shall be signed by the person by whom it is to be delivered and shall include a declaration by that person that it is, to the best of the person's knowledge, information and belief, correct and complete.

(3) The Commissioners may require the declaration mentioned in subsection (2) to be made on oath.

16 Assessment and payment of tax

(1) Tax in respect of any relevant residential property required to be included in a return under section 15 shall be due on 1 November immediately following the valuation date to which the return relates and tax so due shall be payable by the assessable person without the making of an assessment; but tax which has become due as aforesaid may be assessed on the assessable person (whether or not it has been paid when the assessment is made) if that tax, or any part of it, is not paid on or before the due date.

(2) In any case in which—

(*a*) a return under section 15(1) is not delivered by an accountable person to the Commissioners on or before the 1 November immediately following the relevant valuation date, or

(*b*) the Commissioners are dissatisfied with any return made under section 15(1),

the Commissioners may make an assessment of tax payable upon the market value of the relevant residential property, or any part thereof, of the assessable person on the relevant valuation date of such amount or such further amount, as, to the best of their knowledge, information and belief, ought to be charged, levied and paid and for this purpose the Commissioners may make such estimate of the market value of any property on that valuation date as they consider necessary.

(3) The Commissioners may withdraw an assessment made under subsection (2) and make an assessment of the amount of tax payable on the basis of a return which, in their opinion, represents reasonable compliance with their requirements and which is delivered to the Commissioners within 30 days after the date of the assessment made by the Commissioners pursuant to subsection (2).

(4) An assessment of tax may be reviewed by the Commissioners at any time and, where any amendment of an assessment is necessary as a result of the review whether in respect of the relevant residential property already assessed to tax or in respect of any additional relevant residential property, the Commissioners may, to the best of their knowledge, information and belief, make an amended assessment of the tax due and payable upon the market value of the relevant residential property of the assessable person concerned or any part thereof.

(5) The making of an amended assessment shall not prejudice the right of the Commissioners to make further amended assessments of the amount of tax payable or to require delivery from the accountable person concerned of further returns, and this section shall apply to such returns.

(6) Any tax or additional tax due under an assessment of tax or an amended assessment of tax made by virtue of this section shall be due and payable on the day next after the day on which the assessment of tax or the amended assessment of tax is made but, for the purposes of section 18, that tax or additional tax shall be treated as having been payable at the time when it would have been payable if it had been payable by virtue of a correct return under section 15(1).

(7) Notwithstanding anything contained in any enactment, but subject to the provisions of this section, an assessment of tax or an amended assessment of tax may be made at any time.

(8) Any amount of tax due or assessed under this section shall be due and payable to the Commissioners.

(9) Section 928 of the Act of 1997, shall, with any necessary modifications, apply to an assessment of tax or an amended assessment of tax as it applies in relation to assessments to income tax.

(10) Section 898 of the Act of 1997, shall, subject to any necessary modifications, apply in relation to tax as it applies in relation to income tax chargeable under Schedule D.

(11) Notwithstanding the provisions of this section, an assessment or an amended assessment of tax may be made by the Commissioners under this section at any time and such assessment or amended assessment shall be made on—

    (*a*) the accountable person,

    (*b*) the person whom the Commissioners have reason to believe is an accountable person, or

    (*c*) the personal representative of a person whom the Commissioners have reason to believe would, if alive, be an accountable person,

and where the assessment or amended assessment is so made on the personal representative, he or she shall have the same right of appeal under section 21 or as if he or she were an accountable person.

17 Incidence

Any accountable person who is authorised or required to pay tax in respect of any property shall, for the purposes of paying the tax, or raising the amount of the tax when already paid, have power, whether the property is or is not vested in that person, to raise the amount of such tax and any interest and expenses properly paid or incurred by that person in respect thereof by the sale or mortgage of, or a terminable charge on, that property or any part thereof.

18 Interest on tax

(1) Simple interest at the rate of 1 per cent per month or part of a month, without any deduction of income tax, shall be payable on tax from the date upon which it becomes due and payable until the date of payment and shall be chargeable and recoverable in the same manner as if it were part of the tax; but interest shall not be payable unless the total amount thereof exceeds £5.

(2) A payment on account of tax shall be applied—

    (*a*) if there is interest due on tax at the date of the payment, to the discharge, so far as may be, of the interest so due, and

    (*b*) if there is any balance of that payment remaining, to the discharge of so much tax as is equal to that balance.

(3) Subject to subsections (1) and (2), payments on account of tax due on any date may be made at any time after that date, whereupon interest on so much of the payment on account as is referable to tax shall cease to run.

(4) Interest payable under this section shall not be allowed in computing any income, profits or losses for any of the purposes of the Tax Acts.

(5) Where the Commissioners are dissatisfied with a return under section 15 and an additional amount of tax is found to be payable by virtue of an assessment of tax made under section 16, no interest shall be payable on that amount of additional amount of tax if—

    (*a*) the return was made in time, and

(b) the tax payable on the basis of the market value of the relevant residential property included in the return was paid on or before the due date,

(c) the additional amount of tax does not exceed 10 per cent of the aggregate of the additional amount of tax and the tax referred to in paragraph (b), and

(d) the additional amount of tax is paid not later than one month from—

　　(i) the date of the assessment of tax in which it is contained if there is no appeal under section 21 or against the assessment, or

　　(ii) the date of the determination of an appeal under either of the said sections or, if there is more than one appeal to be determined, the date of the later determination.

19 Payment to Collector

All sums due under the provisions of this Part shall be paid to the Collector.

20 Overpayment of tax

(1) Where, on application to the Commissioners for relief under this section, it is proved to their satisfaction that an amount has been paid in excess of the liability for tax or for interest on tax, they shall give relief by way of repayment of the excess or otherwise as is reasonable and just; and any such repayment shall carry simple interest (not exceeding the amount of such excess), at the rate of 0.5 per cent, or such other rate (if any) as stands prescribed by the Minister for Finance by regulations, for each month or part of a month from the date on which the payment was made, and income tax shall not be deductible on payment of interest under this section and such interest shall not be reckoned in computing income for the purposes of the Tax Acts.

(2) Every regulation made under this section shall be laid before Dáil Éireann as soon as may be after it is made and, if a resolution annulling the regulation is passed by Dáil Éireann within the next 21 days on which Dáil Éireann has sat after the regulation is laid before it, the regulation shall be annulled accordingly, but without prejudice to the validity of anything previously done thereunder.

21 Appeals regarding value of residential property

If a person is aggrieved by the decision of the Commissioners as to the market value of any residential property, the person may appeal against the decision in the manner prescribed by section 33 of the Finance (1909-10) Act, 1910, and the provisions as to appeals under that section shall apply accordingly with any necessary modifications.

22 Appeals in other cases

(1) In this section—

"Appeal Commissioners" has the meaning assigned to it by section 850 of the Act of 1997;

"appellant" means a person who appeals to the Appeal Commissioners under this section.

(2) Subject to the provisions of this Part, an accountable person who has been assessed to tax in respect of any relevant residential property and who is aggrieved by the

assessment may, in accordance with this section, appeal to the Appeal Commissioners against the assessment and the appeal shall be heard and determined by the Appeal Commissioners whose determination shall be final and conclusive unless the appeal is required to be reheard by a judge of the Circuit Court or a case is required to be stated in relation to it for the opinion of the High Court.

(3) An appeal shall not lie under this section in relation to the market value of residential property.

(4) A person who intends to appeal under this section against an assessment shall, within 30 days after the date of the assessment, give notice in writing to the Commissioners of his or her intention to appeal against the assessment.

(5) An appeal under this section against an assessment shall not be proceeded with or entertained by the Appeal Commissioners unless an amount equal to 75 per cent of the amount of the assessment is paid to the Collector by or on behalf of the appellant.

(6) (*a*) Subject to this section, the provisions of the Income Tax Acts relating to—

   (i)   the appointment of times and places for the hearing of appeals;

   (ii) the giving of notice to each person who has given notice of appeal of the time and place appointed for the hearing of his or her appeal;

   (iii) the determination of an appeal by agreement between the appellant and the Commissioners;

   (iv) the determination of an appeal by the appellant giving notice of his or her intention not to proceed with the appeal;

   (v)   the hearing, determination or dismissal of an appeal by the Appeal Commissioners, including the hearing, determination or dismissal of an appeal by one Appeal Commissioner;

   (vi) the assessment having the same force and effect as if it were an assessment in respect of which no notice of appeal had been given where the person who has given notice of appeal does not attend before the Appeal Commissioners at the time and place appointed;

   (vii) the extension of the time for giving notice of appeal and the readmission of appeals by the Appeal Commissioners and the provisions which apply where action by way of court proceedings has been taken;

   (viii) the rehearing of an appeal by a judge of the Circuit Court and the statement of a case for the opinion of the High Court on a point of law:

   (ix) the payment of tax in accordance with the determination of the Appeal Commissioners notwithstanding that an appeal is required to be reheard by a judge of the Circuit Court or that a case for the opinion of the High Court on a point of law has been required to be stated or is pending: and

   (x)   the procedures for appeal,

   shall, with any necessary modifications, apply to an appeal under this section as if the appeal were an appeal against an assessment to income tax.

(b) The Commissioners shall, subject to their giving notice in writing in that behalf to the appellant within 10 days after the determination of an appeal by the Appeal Commissioners, have the same right as the appellant to have the appeal reheard by a judge of the Circuit Court.

(c) Subject to paragraph (d), the rehearing of an appeal under this section by a judge of the Circuit Court shall be by a judge of the Circuit Court in whose circuit the appellant resides.

(d) (i) In any case where the appellant is not resident in the State, or

(ii) in any case where there is a doubt or a dispute as to the circuit,

the appeal shall be reheard by a judge of the Circuit Court assigned to the Dublin Circuit.

(7) (a) Any notice or other document which is required or authorised by this section to be served by the Commissioners or by an appellant may be served by post.

(b) Any notice or other document which is required or authorised to be served by the Commissioners on an appellant under this section may be sent to the solicitor, accountant or other agent of the appellant and a notice thus served shall be deemed to have been served on the appellant unless the appellant proves to the satisfaction of the Appeal Commissioners or the Circuit Court, as the case may be, that the appellant had, before the notice or other document was served, withdrawn the authority of such solicitor, accountant or other agent to act on that appellant's behalf.

(8) Prima facie evidence of any notice given under this section by the Commissioners may be given in any proceedings by production of a document purporting to be a copy of the notice and it shall not be necessary to prove the official position of the person by whom the notice purports to be given or, if it is signed, the signature, or that the person signing and giving it was authorised so to do.

23 Recovery of tax

(1) All the provisions of the Income Tax Acts relating to the collection and recovery of income tax shall, subject to any necessary modifications, apply in relation to tax as they apply in relation to income tax chargeable under Schedule D.

(2) Without prejudice to subsection (1), every sum due to the Commissioners in respect of tax or interest thereon shall be deemed to be a debt due by an accountable person or his or her personal representative to the Minister for Finance for the benefit of the Central Fund and shall be payable to the Commissioners and may (without prejudice to any other mode of recovery thereof) be sued for and recovered by action, or other appropriate proceeding, at the suit of the Attorney General, the Minister for Finance or the Commissioners in any court of competent jurisdiction, notwithstanding anything to the contrary contained in the Inland Revenue Regulation Act, 1890.

24 Penalties

(1) (a) A person who contravenes section 15(1) shall be liable to a penalty of £1,000.

(b) Where the contravention or failure referred to in paragraph (a) continues after judgment has been given by the court before which proceedings for the penalty have been commenced, the person concerned shall be liable to a further penalty of £50 for each day on which the contravention or failure so continues.

(2) Where, under or for the purposes of any of the provisions of this Part, a person is authorised to inspect any property for the purpose of reporting to the Commissioners the market value thereof and any person prevents such inspection or obstructs the person so authorised in the performance of his or her functions in relation to the inspection, that person shall be liable to a penalty of £1,000.

(3) Where an accountable person fraudulently or negligently—

    (*a*)   delivers any incorrect return or additional return,

    (*b*)   makes or furnishes any incorrect statement, declaration, evidence or valuation in connection with any property comprised in the relevant residential property of the assessable person,

    (*c*)   makes or furnishes any incorrect statement, declaration, evidence or valuation in connection with any claim for any allowance, deduction, exemption or relief, or

    (*d*)   makes or furnishes any incorrect statement, declaration, evidence or valuation in connection with any other matter, whereby the amount of tax payable in respect of the relevant residential property of the assessable person is less than it would have been if that return, statement, declaration, evidence or valuation had been correct, he or she shall be liable to a penalty of—

        (i)   £2,000, and

        (ii)   the amount, or in the case of fraud twice the amount, of the difference specified in subsection (5).

(4) Where any such return, statement, declaration, evidence or valuation as is mentioned in subsection (3) was delivered, made or furnished neither fraudulently nor negligently by an accountable person and it comes to that person's notice that it was incorrect, then, unless the error is remedied without unreasonable delay, such matter shall be treated, for the purposes of this section, as having been negligently done by that person.

(5) The difference referred to in subsection (3) is the difference between—

    (*a*)   the amount of tax payable in respect of the relevant residential property of the assessable person for the valuation date in accordance with the return, additional return, statement, declaration, evidence or valuation made or submitted, and

    (*b*)   the amount which would have been the amount so payable if the return, additional return, statement, declaration, evidence or valuation as made or submitted by that accountable person had been correct.

(6) For the purposes of subsection (3), where anything referred to in that subsection is delivered, made or furnished on behalf of a person, it shall be deemed to have been delivered, made or furnished by that person unless that person proves that it was done without that person's knowledge and consent.

(7) Any person who assists in or induces the delivery, making or furnishing for any purposes of tax of any return, additional return, statement, declaration, evidence or valuation which that person knows to be incorrect shall be liable to a penalty of £1,000.

(8) The provisions of this section shall not affect any criminal proceedings.

(9) Subject to this section, section 987(4), sections 1061 to 1066 and section 1068 of the Act of 1997 shall with any necessary modifications, apply to a penalty under this section as if the penalty were a penalty under the Income Tax Acts.

25 Extension of certain Acts

(1) Section 1 of the Provisional Collection of Taxes Act 1927, is hereby amended by the insertion of "and anti-speculative property tax" before "and residential property tax".

(2) Section 39 of the Inland Revenue Regulation Act, 1890, is hereby amended by the insertion of "anti-speculative property tax," before "residential property tax".

26 Regulations

(1) The Commissioners may make such regulations in relation to supplementary and ancillary matters as seem to them to be necessary for the purpose of giving effect to this Part and of enabling them to discharge their functions thereunder.

(2) Every regulation made under this section shall be laid before Dáil Éireann as soon as may be after it is made and, if a resolution annulling the regulation is passed by Dáil Éireann within the next 21 days on which Dáil Éireann has sat after the regulation is laid before it, the regulation shall be annulled accordingly, but without prejudice to the validity of anything previously done thereunder.

27 Authorisation of officers

The Commissioners may authorise any of their officers to perform any act and discharge any function authorised by this Part to be performed or discharged by the Commissioners.

PART 3
MISCELLANEOUS

28 Care and management of taxes and duties

All taxes and duties imposed by this Act are by virtue of this section placed under the care and management of the Revenue Commissioners.

29 Short title and construction

(1) This Act may be cited as the Finance (No 2) Act, 2000.

(2) ...

(3) Any reference in this Act to any other enactment shall, except so far as the context otherwise requires, be construed as a reference to that enactment as amended by or under any other enactment including this Act.

(4) In this Act, a reference to a Part, section or Schedule is to a Part or section of, or Schedule to, this Act, unless it is indicated that reference to some other enactment is intended.

(5) In this Act, a reference to a subsection or paragraph is to the subsection or paragraph of the provision in which the reference occurs, unless it is indicated that reference to some other provision is intended.

FINANCE ACT 2001

(No 7 of 2001)

ARRANGEMENT OF SECTIONS

PART 7
ANTI-SPECULATIVE TAX

AN ACT TO PROVIDE FOR THE IMPOSITION, REPEAL, REMISSION, ALTERATION AND REGULATION OF TAXATION, OF STAMP DUTIES AND OF DUTIES RELATING TO EXCISE AND OTHERWISE TO MAKE FURTHER PROVISION IN CONNECTION WITH FINANCE INCLUDING THE REGULATION OF CUSTOMS. [30TH MARCH 2001]

PART 7
ANTI-SPECULATIVE TAX

230 Abolition of anti-speculative property tax

Anti-speculative property tax shall not be charged, levied or paid under section 6 of the Finance (No 2) Act, 2000, by reference to any valuation date (within the meaning of section 5(1) of that Act) occurring on or after 6 April 2001.